July 21-23, 2015
Donostia-San Sebastián, Spain

AF752235

Association for
Computing Machinery

Advancing Computing as a Science & Profession

PODC'15

Proceedings of the 2015 ACM Symposium on

Principles of Distributed Computing

Sponsored by:

ACM SIGACT and ACM SIGOPS

Supported by:

IBM Research, Kutxa Obra Social,
Microsoft Research - Inria Joint Centre, Oracle Labs,
and University of the Basque Country UPV/EHU

Association for
Computing Machinery

Advancing Computing as a Science & Profession

The Association for Computing Machinery
2 Penn Plaza, Suite 701
New York, New York 10121-0701

Copyright © 2015 by the Association for Computing Machinery, Inc. (ACM). Permission to make digital or hard copies of portions of this work for personal or classroom use is granted without fee provided that copies are not made or distributed for profit or commercial advantage and that copies bear this notice and the full citation on the first page. Copyright for components of this work owned by others than ACM must be honored. Abstracting with credit is permitted. To copy otherwise, to republish, to post on servers or to redistribute to lists, requires prior specific permission and/or a fee. Request permission to republish from: permissions@acm.org or Fax +1 (212) 869-0481.

For other copying of articles that carry a code at the bottom of the first or last page, copying is permitted provided that the per-copy fee indicated in the code is paid through www.copyright.com.

Notice to Past Authors of ACM-Published Articles
ACM intends to create a complete electronic archive of all articles and/or other material previously published by ACM. If you have written a work that has been previously published by ACM in any journal or conference proceedings prior to 1978, or any SIG Newsletter at any time, and you do NOT want this work to appear in the ACM Digital Library, please inform permissions@acm.org, stating the title of the work, the author(s), and where and when published.

ISBN: 978-1-4503-3617-8

ACM Order No: 536150

Additional copies may be ordered prepaid from:

ACM Order Department
PO Box 30777
New York, NY 10087-0777, USA

Phone: 1-800-342-6626 (USA and Canada)
+1-212-626-0500 (Global)
Fax: +1-212-944-1318
E-mail: acmhelp@acm.org
Hours of Operation: 8:30 am – 4:30 pm ET

Printed in the USA

PODC 2015 Chairs' Welcome

It is our great pleasure to welcome you to the *2015 ACM Symposium on Principles of Distributed Computing – PODC'15.* This year's symposium continues its tradition of being the premier forum for presentation of research on all aspects of distributed computing, including the theory, design, implementation and application of distributed algorithms, systems and networks. During the years, PODC has been the stage where many landmark results have been presented that have increased our understanding of this exciting and fundamental research endeavor. In the best tradition of theoretical discovery, the insights that have been provided have not only elucidated fundamental conceptual issues but also found their way into the real world of systems and applications.

The call for paper attracted 191 regular submissions and 20 brief announcements. The Program Committee accepted 45 papers and 10 brief announcements that cover a wide variety of topics. Every submitted paper was read and evaluated by at least three reviewers. The final decisions regarding acceptance or rejection of each paper were made through teleconference and electronic Program Committee discussions held during April 2015. Revised and expanded versions of a few selected papers will be considered for publication in a special issue of the journal *Distributed Computing* and in the *Journal of the ACM.*

The Program Committee has selected the paper "Deterministic (Delta+1) Coloring in Sublinear (in Delta) Time, in Static, Dynamic and Faulty Networks" by Leonid Barenboim for this year's Best Paper Award. In addition, the Program Committee selected the paper "Near-Optimal Scheduling of Distributed Algorithms" by Mohsen Ghaffari for the Best Student Paper Award.

Three keynote talks will be given by Christos Papadimitriou, Moti Yung and Friedhelm Meyer auf der Heide.

The 2015 Edsger W. Dijkstra Prize in Distributed Computing is given jointly to the papers "Another Advantage of Free Choice: Completely Asynchronous Agreement Protocols", by Michael Ben-Or, published in *Proceedings of the 2nd ACM Symposium on Principles of Distributed Computing (1983)* and "Randomized Byzantine Generals", by Michael O. Rabin, published in *Proceedings of 24th IEEE Annual Symposium on Foundations of Computer Science (1983).* It will be presented at the International Symposium on Distributed Computing (DISC'15).

The 2015 Principles of Distributed Computing Doctoral Dissertation Award is given to "Efficient Network Utilization in Locality-Sensitive Distributed Algorithms", by Leonid Barenboim, supervised by Professor Michael Elkin at Ben Gurion University. It will be presented here.

Finally, this year we will celebrate the 60th birthday of Alexander A. Shvartsman.

Putting together PODC'15 was a team effort. We first thank the authors for providing the content of the program. We are grateful to the Program Committee and the sub-reviewers, who worked very hard in reviewing papers and providing feedback for authors. The help of the Steering Committee and of the Conference Committee was timely and invaluable. Finally, we thank our sponsors, ACM SIGACT and ACM SIGOPS, and our supporters, IBM Research, Kutxa Obra Social, Microsoft Research – Inria Joint Centre, Oracle Labs, and University of the Basque Country UPV/EHU.

We hope that you will find this program interesting and thought-provoking and that the symposium will provide you with a valuable opportunity to share ideas with other researchers from institutions around the world.

Chryssis Georgiou
PODC'15 General Chair

Paul G. Spirakis
PODC'15 Program Chair

Table of Contents

Session 3

Session Chair: Antonio Fernández Anta *(IMDEA Networks Institute)*

Session 4

Session Chair: Christian Scheideler *(University of Paderborn)*

Session 5

Session Chair: Thomas Erlebach *(University of Leicester)*

Keynote Lecture

Session 6

Session Chair: Nitin Vaidya *(University of Illinois at Urbana-Champaign)*

Session 7

Session Chair: Eric Ruppert *(York University)*

Session 8

Session Chair: Alexander A. Shvartsman *(University of Connecticut)*

Session 9

Session Chair: Moti Yung *(Google Inc. & Columbia University)*

PODC 2015 Symposium Organization

General Chair: Chryssis Georgiou *(University of Cyprus, Cyprus)*

Program Chair: Paul Spirakis *(University of Liverpool, UK & CTI, Greece)*

Organizing Chair: Mikel Larrea *(University of the Basque Country UPV/EHU, Spain)*

Publicity Chair: Mark Tuttle *(Intel, USA)*

Communication Chair: Jukka Suomela *(Aalto University, Finland)*

Workshop Chair: Elad Schiller *(Chalmers University of Technology, Sweden)*

Treasurer: George Giakkoupis *(INRIA, France)*

Steering Committee Chair: Alexander Shvartsman *(University of Connecticut, USA)*

Steering Committee:
Shlomi Dolev *(Ben-Gurion University, Israel)*
Chryssis Georgiou *(University of Cyprus, Cyprus)*
George Giakkoupis *(INRIA, France)*
Paul Spirakis *(University of Liverpool, UK & CTI, Greece)*
Gadi Taubenfeld *(IDC, Israel)*
Nitin Vaidya *(University of Illinois, USA)*

Program Committee:
Hagit Attiya *(Technion, Israel)*
Roberto Baldoni *(Sapienza University of Rome, Italy)*
Keren Censor-Hillel *(Technion, Israel)*
Ioannis Chatzigiannakis *(Sapienza Univ. of Rome, Italy & CTI, Greece)*
Artur Czumaj *(University of Warwick, UK)*
Shlomi Dolev *(Ben-Gurion University, Israel)*
Thomas Erlebach *(University of Leicester, UK)*
Antonio Fernandez Anta *(IMDEA Networks Institute, Spain)*
Leszek Gasieniec *(University of Liverpool, UK)*
Chryssis Georgiou *(University of Cyprus, Cyprus)*
Seth Gilbert *(National University of Singapore, Singapore)*
Seif Haridi *(KTH, Sweden)*
Danny Hendler *(Ben-Gurion University, Israel)*
Ted Herman *(University of Iowa, USA)*
Aggelos Kiayas *(University of Athens, Greece)*
Amos Korman *(CNRS & University of Paris Diderot, France)*
Evangelos Kranakis *(Carleton University, Canada)*
Fabian Kuhn *(University of Freiburg, Germany)*
Mikel Larrea *(University of the Basque Country UPV/EHU, Spain)*
Zvi Lotker *(Ben-Gurion University, Israel)*
Russell Martin *(University of Liverpool, UK)*

Program Committee (continued):

Marios Mavronicolas *(University of Cyprus, Cyprus)*
Friedhelm Meyer auf der Heide *(University of Paderborn, Germany)*
Othon Michail *(CTI, Greece)*
Thomas Moscibroda *(Microsoft Research, China)*
Miguel Mosteiro *(Kean University, USA)*
Giuseppe Persiano *(University of Salerno, Italy)*
Michel Raynal *(IUF and IRISA, University of Rennes, France)*
Luis Rodrigues *(INESC-ID, University of Lisbon, Portugal)*
Adi Rosén *(CNRS & University of Paris Diderot, France)*
Eric Ruppert *(York University, Canada)*
Jared Saia *(University of New Mexico, USA)*
Christian Scheideler *(University of Paderborn, Germany)*
Elad M. Schiller *(Chalmers University of Technology, Sweden)*
Alexander Shvartsman *(University of Connecticut, USA)*
Paul Spirakis, Chair *(University of Liverpool, UK & CTI, Greece)*
Sebastien Tixeuil *(University Pierre and Marie Curie, France)*
Nitin Vaidya *(University of Illinois Urbana-Champaign, USA)*
Jennifer Welch *(Texas A&M University, USA)*
Shmuel Zaks *(Technion, Israel)*

Additional reviewers:

Rachit Agarwal
Chrysovalandis Agathangelou
Eleni C. Akrida
Alex Aravind
Maya Arbel
Sergio Arevalo
Jordi Arjona
John Augustine
Evangelos Bampas
Carlos Baquero
Ohad Ben-Baruch
Petra Berenbrink
Annette Bieniusa
Vincenzo Bonifaci
Silvia Bonomi
Christian Cachin
Stanton Cady
Armando Castaneda
Jeremie Chalopin
Bapi Chatterjee
Luis Nuñez Chiroque
Bogdan Chlebus
Gregory Chockler
Vicent Cholvi
Hyun Chul Chung
Florin Ciucu
Colin Cooper
Lenore Cowen
Hadassa Daltrophe
Shantanu Das
Peter Davies
Seda Davtyan
Gianluca De Marco
Philip Derbeko
Stéphane Devismes
Giuseppe Antonio Di Luna
Nuno Diegues
Benjamin Doerr
Danny Dolev
David Doty
Swan Dubois
Stephane Durocher
Omer Egecioglu
Michael Elkin
Robert Elsässer
Matthias Englert
Irene Finocchi
Dianne Foreback

Additional reviewers (continued):

Pierre Fraigniaud
Tom Friedetzky
Vijay Garg
Cyril Gavoille
Rati Gelashvili
Mohsen Ghaffari
George Giakkoupis
Niv Gilboa
Robert Gmyr
Mika Göös
Christoforos Hadjicostis
Theophanis Hadjistasi
Magnus M. Halldorsson
Sandeep Hans
Ahmed Hassan
David Hay
Xinran He
Maryam Helmi
Maurice Herlihy
Prasad Jayanti
Ernesto Jiménez
Daniel Jung
Tomasz Jurdzinski
Shahin Kamali
Eleni Kanellou
Erez Kantor
Sotirios Kentros
Valerie King
Kishori Konwar
Andreas Koutsopoulos
Lukasz Kowalik
Saptaparni Kumar
Shay Kutten
Christoph Lenzen
Yossi Lev
Ximing Li
Thomas Locher
Víctor M. López Millán
Pedro Lopez-Garcia
Romaric Ludinard
Nuno Machado
Manuel Malatyali
Christine Markarian
Evangelos Markatos
Alain Martin
Toshimitsu Masuzawa
Moti Medina
George Mertzios
Yuri Meshman
Maged Michael
Alessia Milani
Luca Moscardelli
Mahnush Movahedi
Peter Musial
Lars Nagel
Danupon Nanongkai
Mikhail Nesterenko
Thomas Nickson
Nicolas Nicolaou
Ioannis Nikolakopoulos
Alex Olshevsky
Krzysztof Onak
Francesco Orciuoli
Keishla Ortiz-Lopez
Rotem Oshman
Rafail Ostrovksy
Dominik Pajak
Roberto Palmieri
Giorgos Panagiotakos
Panagiota Panagopoulou
Sanat Pandey
Mimmo Parente
Merav Parter
Boaz Patt-Shamir
Ami Paz
Andrzej Pelc
David Peleg
Sebastiano Peluso
Sriram Pemmaraju
Paolo Penna
Fabio Petroni
Pavel Podlipyan
Pascal Poizat
Igor Potapov
Kranti Pothapu
Ravi Prakash
Giuseppe Prencipe
Yuval Rabani
Harald Räcke
Tsvetomira Radeva

Additional reviewers (continued):

Tomasz Radzik
Christoforos Raptopoulos
Srivatsan Ravi
Gregory Reinhold
Sören Riechers
Ben Riva
Liam Roditty
Paolo Romano
Thomas Ropars
Iosif Salem
Katerina Samari
Piotr Sankowski
Srikanth Sastry
Thomas Sauerwald
Valerio Schiavoni
Christian Schindelhauer
Stefan Schmid
Georg Schnitger
Jochen Seidel
Alexander Setzer
Andres Sevilla
Hadas Shachnai
Mordechai Shalom
Shantanu Sharma
Or Sheffet
Alexander Skopalik
Julien Stainer
Thim Strothmann
Adi Suissa-Peleg
He Sun
Jukka Suomela
Edward Talmage
Qiang Tang
Christopher Thraves
Roei Tov
Yiannis Tselekounis
Lewis Tseng
Philippas Tsigas
Shimrit Tzur-David
Florent Urrutia
Przemysław Uznański
Giovanni Viglietta
Xavier Vilaça
Ivan Visconti
Lin Wang
Philipp Woelfel
Prudence W.H. Wong
Thomas Zacharias
Mahdi Zamani
Bingsheng Zhang

PODC 2015 Sponsors & Supporters

Sponsors:

SIGACT

SIGOPS
ACM SIG on Operating Systems

Supporters:

IBM Research

kutxa

Microsoft Research - Inria
JOINT CENTRE

Oracle Labs

eman ta zabal zazu
Universidad del País Vasco
Euskal Herriko Unibertsitatea

The 2015 Edsger W. Dijkstra Prize in Distributed Computing

The E. W. Dijkstra Prize Committee has decided to grant the 2015 Edsger W. Dijkstra Prize in Distributed Computing jointly to the following two papers:

- **Another Advantage of Free Choice: Completely Asynchronous Agreement Protocols**, by **Michael Ben-Or**, published in *Proceedings of the Second ACM Symposium on Principles of Distributed Computing*, pages 27-30, August 1983
- **Randomized Byzantine Generals**, by **Michael O. Rabin**, published in *Proceedings of Twenty-Fourth IEEE Annual Symposium on Foundations of Computer Science*, pages 403-409, November 1983

The Prize is awarded for outstanding papers on the principles of distributed computing, whose significance and impact on the theory and/or practice of distributed computing have been evident for at least a decade.

In these seminal papers, published in close succession in 1983, Michael Ben-Or and Michael O. Rabin started the field of fault-tolerant randomized distributed algorithms.

In 1983, randomized algorithms, still in their infancy, were starting to make headway in sequential algorithms and complexity theory. The role of randomization at that time was to improve the complexity of solving certain problems. It was shown that problems, such as primality testing, that were deterministically solvable with a given time or space complexity, could be solved in less time or space by allowing the algorithm to make random choices.

Ben-Or and Rabin were the first to use randomness to solve the consensus problem in an asynchronous distributed system subject to failures, which had provably no deterministic solution. In other words, they were addressing a computability question and not a complexity one, and the answer was far from obvious.

Underlying both algorithms is the notion of a shared coin, i.e., a mechanism that enables separate processes to make a common random choice. Ben-Or's solution is fully distributed and relies on no assumptions, but requires a potentially exponential series of independent coin tosses to implement a shared coin. Rabin's solution uses cryptographic techniques to implement the shared coin in constant time.

Ben-Or and Rabin's algorithms opened the way to a large body of work on randomized distributed algorithms in asynchronous systems, not only on consensus, but also on both theoretical problems, such as renaming, leader election, and snapshots, as well as applied topics, such as dynamic load balancing, work distribution, contention reduction, and coordination in concurrent data structures.

The E.W. Prize is sponsored jointly by the ACM Symposium on Principles of Distributed Computing (PODC) and the EATCS Symposium on Distributed Computing (DISC). The prize is presented annually, with the presentation taking place alternately at PODC and DISC. This year it will be presented at DISC, to be held at Tokyo, Japan, October 5-9, 2015.

Dijkstra Prize Committee 2015

James Aspnes, *Yale*
Pierre Fraigniaud, *University of Paris Diderot*
Rachid Guerraoui, *EPFL*
Nancy Lynch, *MIT*
Yoram Moses, *Technion*
Paul Spirakis, *University of Liverpool and CTI, Chair*

The 2015 Principles of Distributed Computing Doctoral Dissertation Award

The Doctoral Dissertation Award Committee has awarded the Doctoral Dissertation Award in Distributed Computing 2015 to **Dr. Leonid Barenboim**.

Dr. Barenboim completed his thesis "Efficient Network Utilization in Locality-Sensitive Distributed Algorithms" on December 2013 under the supervision of Professor Michael Elkin at Ben Gurion University.

Leonid's dissertation considers the LOCAL model, a distributed message passing model in which in time t, every node can learn the complete graph topology up to distance t in the network. In this model, the challenge is to compute some global result on a graph in time significantly less than it takes to propagate full information in the graph, that is, in time significantly less than the size or the diameter of the graph. This classical model captures the essence of graph locality issues in distributed network algorithms, and received much attention in the literature.

The dissertation studies several fundamental problems in this setting, including vertex coloring, edge coloring, maximal independent set, and network decomposition. For all of these problems, novel solutions are devised that significantly improve the best previously-known results. In particular, it provides a substantial improvement to the problem of distributed coloring, one of the key problems to study symmetry breaking in networks. The dissertation addresses a c hallenge which has been open over two decades: In particular, it reduces the number of colors achieved in deterministic logarithmic coloring time from quadratic to essentially linear. It also demonstrates the first constant-time locality-sensitive solution for an NP-complete problem. These and other results advance our knowledge in non-trivial ways. The results are deep, technically challenging, and innovative.

The award is sponsored jointly by the ACM Symposium on Principles of Distributed Computing (PODC) and the EATCS Symposium on Distributed Computing (DISC). This award is presented annually, with the presentation taking place alternately at PODC and DISC. This year it will be presented at PODC, to be held at Donostia-San Sebastián, Spain, July 21-23, 2015.

Distributed Computing Doctoral Dissertation Award Committee 2015

Shlomi Dolev, *Ben Gurion University*
Fabian Kuhn, *University of Freiburg*
Dahlia Malkhi, *VMware Research, Chair*
Philipp Woelfel, *University of Calgary*

Cortical Computation

Christos Papadimitriou*
University of California at Berkeley
christos@cs.berkeley.edu

Santosh Vempala†
GeorgiaTech
vempala@cs.gatech.edu

ABSTRACT

A computational theory of cortex necessitates a novel paradigm of exquisitely distributed computation. Here we review recent work on a primitive called *Predictive Join*, or *PJoin*, which is both plausible and useful in regards to cortical computation, and which enables a spontaneous form of unsupervised learning exhibiting many of the characteristics of brain activity. We also outline several immediate goals of a computational research program on the brain.

Categories and Subject Descriptors

F.1.1 [**Computation by Abstract Devices**]: Models of Computation; J.3 [**Life and Medical Sciences**]: Biology

Keywords

Brain; Neuroidal model; PJoin; Synchrony; Control

Introduction

Understanding the brain is the greatest scientific problem of our time — arguably of all times. Despite the current deluge of scientific discoveries regarding the anatomy and function of the brain of all kinds of animals, no overarching theory for the brain's high-level operation and the emergence of the mind appears in the horizon. As the brain is by far the most blatantly computational of all scientific objects, this quest presents a unique opportunity for key research contributions by computer scientists — and in fact, as we shall see, by students of distributed computation. The study of the brain from the computational point of view must deal with the complete disconnect between the remarkable accomplishments of brains on one side, and the triumphs of computers on the other. For example, we are not aware of a single nontrivial computational problem which has been solved in a manner that is neurally plausible, by any stretch. This disjointness suggests that the nature of the computation taking place in the brain must differ dramatically from all extant computational paradigms.

*Research supported by NSF grants CCF-0964033 and CCF-1408635, and by Templeton Foundation grant 3966.

†Research Supported by NSF awards CCF-1217793 and EAGER-1415498.

Permission to make digital or hard copies of part or all of this work for personal or classroom use is granted without fee provided that copies are not made or distributed for profit or commercial advantage, and that copies bear this notice and the full citation on the first page. Copyrights for third-party components of this work must be honored. For all other uses, contact the owner/author(s). Copyright is held by the author/owner(s).
PODC'15, July 21–23, 2015, Donostia-San Sebastián, Spain.
ACM 978-1-4503-3617-8 /15/07.
http://dx.doi.org/10.1145/2767386.2767452.

The Neuroidal Model

The *neuroidal* model was proposed in 1994 by Leslie Valiant as a formal model of low-level cortical computation [2, 3]. Computational nodes called *neuroids* are connected by directed edges called *synapses* in a random directed graph. Each neuroid has a threshold as well as a state, and each synapse has a strength and a state. Communication between neuroids is extremely restricted: a neuroid i can communicate with neuroid j only if (1) there is a synapse ij; (2) i has just *fired* (see below); and (3) the sum of the strength of synapse ij together with all other strengths of synapses kj, such that k too has just fired, happens to exceed j's threshold. If this is the case, then j fires, and this is the only sense in which it can receive a communication from i. In addition, at each step the thresholds, strengths, and states of all neuroids and synapses are updated through a universal update rule, taking into account only local information — for example the new state of synapse ij can depend on the state of neuroid j but not that of i, as it is natural to think that synapse ij lives close to j. By design, the neuroidal model is a deliberately conservative model of what circuits of neurons can accomplish. It can be also seen as an extremely restricted model of distributed computation. Computation in the brain, we believe, must take place within the confines of such a model.

Asynchronous and Spontaneous Computation

How does one evaluate neuroidal algorithms — algorithms programmed in this model? What are the neuroidal analogues of time and space? Parallel time is of course an important criterion here as well; if anything, it is far more stringently crucial: Since neurons take a few milliseconds to fire, and cognitive phenomena happen within roughly a few hundreds of milliseconds, brain algorithms should take only a few dozen steps. The total number of neurons involved should not be excessive. In addition, we propose *synchrony* and *control* as quantitative measures of complexity. Synchrony could be the maximum total number of pairs of neuroids that need to fire in lockstep, while control is the longest chain of synchronized steps required for the algorithm to succeed. These are important resources to be used sparingly, since neurons are independent distant entities, and thus perfect synchrony that is widespread, or total control that goes on for too long, is unrealistic. Furthermore — and importantly — the nature and style of the algorithm must be, in a very specific and subtle sense, appropriate. This is a computational model to be programmed in modesty and restraint, without a trace of extravagance and abuse, and with minimal outside control. Ideally, neuroidal algorithms should be simple and reactive (in the dictionary, not the technical, sense: they should just respond to arising circumstances), essentially self-assembling data structures. Sophistication, cleverness, and shrewd efficiency of the kind admired and lauded in our field are no virtues in this domain.

PJoin

In [1] such a neuroidal algorithm is presented for the task of unsupervised learning. Given a pattern in $\{0,1\}^n$, with each bit represented as a set of neurons, a tree-like structure is spontaneously created which entails a representation of the pattern and includes a special "top element". If — and only if — the same pattern is presented again, the same top element will eventually fire. If another pattern is presented, it will also be learned in the same sense and manner, and with a different top element. Incidentally, all these specifications are met with high probability, not certainty, and the randomness comes from both coin flips by the algorithm and the randomness of the underlying graph. New patterns are learned by appropriately sharing substructures with preexisting ones while also adding their own, thus creating a dag. Importantly, much of the firing by neuroids is transmitted *downwards* — meaning, towards the inputs and away from the top elements. This is in agreement with many experimental findings in neuroscience noting that many more synapses travel downward in the cortical hierarchy — e.g., for vision — than up.

The main idea in this algorithm is a novel operation that we call *PJoin*, or *predictive Join*, the building block of the dag described above, and a primitive which we believe may be a productive paradigm for cortical computation in general. It extends Valiant's Join(A,B) operation [2]. Join(A,B) combines two items A and B — two sets of neurons representing two real-world ideas, such as *almond* and *butter* — to create a new item representing the combined idea. If the two original items A and B happen to fire simultaneously, then Join(A,B) will fire next. In the case of PJoin(A,B), if only one of the constituent items fires — say A fires — then PJoin(A,B) will not quite fire, but will proceed to "predict B." This entails mobilizing B (notice the downward step) which, if it is itself a PJoin of two other items C and D further below, will in turn predict those. Eventually, if an item representing a bit of the pattern being presented is predicted correctly, it will fire. If its prediction of B is eventually verified, PJoin(A,B) will fire, otherwise it will not. We show that PJoin(A,B) can be created by a neuroidal algorithm extending Valiant's algorithm for Join(A,B). We also prove that PJoin enables a very simple and natural algorithm for unsupervised learning with favorable performance, operating as described in the previous paragraph. It is this predictive ability of PJoin that enables the unsupervised learning of patterns; with ordinary Joins, a combinatorial explosion of the data structure would ensue. Furthermore, experiments with the algorithm [1] show that ensembles of patterns of length 100 can be learned almost always within fewer than 80 parallel steps per pattern presentation.

Some Research Questions

Invariants. Can PJoin help make progress on the problem of how the brain learns *invariants?* The brain is capable of a very effective and sophisticated clustering-cum-interpolation operation, whereby several views of the same real-world object — say, the face of a friend — together with the friend's voice or name, are all collected into a single higher-order representation. The mechanism of invariants has been for decades an elusive mystery in brain science.

Prediction. PJoin should be seen not as a concrete scientific prediction of something that actually happens in the brain, but as a possible stance in brain science: is it possible that the brain's success is the result not of elaborate and specialized algorithms, but of very simple and rough primitives available and applied at an astronomical scale, and, through sensors and actuators, reacting to and interacting with an interesting world?

Grunge. Even if primitives like PJoin are a large part of the brain's computational story, they are unlikely to exist as precise and clean as an algorithms designer would have wished them. Can there be an algorithmic theory of amorphous and chaotic computation that will better approximate what happens?

Organic environments. Speaking of which, there is little doubt that human brains would accomplish much less on a boring planet. Animal brains perform as they do by sensing complex environments and affecting them in response. And yet, we evaluate our Learning Theory algorithms on i.i.d. samples, often from uniform distributions. What would a mathematical theory be, of "organic distributions," ones that generate the kind of environments in which brains thrive and evolve?

Language. Among all organic environments, language is unique in that it was created by us less than 100,000 years ago — when our brain was essentially the same as it is now. Presumably, language evolved by exploiting our brain's capabilities, it has adapted so that baby brains can learn it and adult brains can communicate their thoughts effectively through it. What can language teach us about our brains? Incidentally, PJoin, together with another similar "clustering" primitive that could be called PLink, seem apt primitives for learning and representing grammar.

Motor control. The most basic task accomplished by the brian is movement in the physical environment — walking, balancing, self-defense etc. — much of which is learned behavior via complex coordination and continuous feedback from the external world, and with significant variations from one brain to another. What is a plausible mechanism to explain this amazing and ubiquitous ability?

1. REFERENCES

[1] C. H. Papadimitriou and S. S. Vempala. Cortical learning via prediction. In *Proc. of COLT*, 2015.

[2] L. G. Valiant. *Circuits of the mind.* Oxford University Press, 1994.

[3] L. G. Valiant. Memorization and association on a realistic neural model. *Neural Computation*, 17(3):527–555, 2005.

Near-Optimal Scheduling of Distributed Algorithms

Mohsen Ghaffari
MIT
ghaffari@mit.edu

ABSTRACT

This paper studies the question of how to run many distributed algorithms, solving independent problems, together as fast as possible.

Suppose that we want to run distributed algorithms $\mathcal{A}_1, \mathcal{A}_2 \dots, \mathcal{A}_k$ in the $\mathsf{CONGEST}$ model, each taking at most $\mathsf{dilation}$ rounds, and where for each network edge, at most $\mathsf{congestion}$ messages need to go through it, in total over all these algorithms. A celebrated work of Leighton, Maggs, and Rao [22] shows that in the special case where each of these algorithms is simply a *packet routing*—that is, sending a message from a source to a destination along a given path—there is an $O(\mathsf{congestion} + \mathsf{dilation})$ round schedule. Note that this bound is trivially optimal.

Generalizing the framework of LMR [22], we study scheduling general distributed algorithms and present two results: (a) an existential schedule-length lower bound of $\Omega(\mathsf{congestion} + \mathsf{dilation} \cdot \frac{\log n}{\log\log n})$ rounds, (b) a distributed algorithm that produces a near-optimal $O(\mathsf{congestion} + \mathsf{dilation} \cdot \log n)$ round schedule, after $O(\mathsf{dilation} \cdot \log^2 n)$ rounds of pre-computation.

A key challenge in the latter result is to solve the problem with only private randomness, as globally-shared randomness simplifies it significantly. The technique we use for this problem is in fact more general, and it can be used to remove the assumption of having shared randomness from a broad range of distributed algorithms, at the cost of a slow down factor of $O(\log^2 n)$.

Categories and Subject Descriptors

F.2.2 [**Analysis of Algorithms and Problem Complexity**]: Non-numerical Algorithms and Problems—*Computations on Discrete Structures*; G.2.2 [**Discrete Mathematics**]: Graph Theory—*Network Problems*

Permission to make digital or hard copies of all or part of this work for personal or classroom use is granted without fee provided that copies are not made or distributed for profit or commercial advantage and that copies bear this notice and the full citation on the first page. Copyrights for components of this work owned by others than ACM must be honored. Abstracting with credit is permitted. To copy otherwise, or republish, to post on servers or to redistribute to lists, requires prior specific permission and/or a fee. Request permissions from permissions@acm.org.
PODC'15, July 21–23, 2015, Donostia-San Sebastián, Spain.
Copyright is held by the owner/author(s). Publication rights licensed to ACM.
ACM 978-1-4503-3617-8 /15/07 ...$15.00.
http://dx.doi.org/10.1145/2767386.2767417.

Keywords

Distributed Algorithm, Scheduling, Congestion, Dilation, Packet Routing, Shared Randomness

1. INTRODUCTION AND RELATED WORK

Computer networks are constantly running many applications at the same time and because of the bandwidth limitations, each application gets slowed down due to the activities of the others. Despite that, for the vast majority of the distributed algorithms introduced in the area of theoretical distributed computing, the initial design and analysis have been carried out with the assumption that each algorithm uses the network alone. In this paper, we investigate the issue of what happens when many distributed algorithms are to be run together.

Specifically, we study the questions of *how to run these distributed algorithms simultaneously as fast as possible* and *what are the limitations on how fast this can be done.* While being arguably a fundamental issue, to the best of our knowledge, these questions have not been investigated in their full generality. Although, we describe a number of special cases that were studied in the past.

Throughout the paper, we work with the $\mathsf{CONGEST}$ model [29], which is a standard distributed model that takes bandwidth limitations into account. The communication network is represented by an undirected graph $G = (V, E)$ where $|V| = n$. Communications occur in synchronous rounds and in each round each node can send one B-bit message to each of its neighbors, where typically we assume $B = O(\log n)$.

The general scenario we consider is as follows: We want to run independent distributed algorithms $\mathcal{A}_1$, $\mathcal{A}_2$, ..., $\mathcal{A}_k$ together, but we do not know what problem is being solved by each algorithm. Hence, we must run each algorithm essentially in a black-box manner without altering the content of its messages, except for potentially adding a small amount of information to its header. We now mention some special cases of this problem that have been studied in the past:

(I) Broadcasting k messages from different sources, each to the h-hop neighborhood of its source. Note that this can be viewed as running k single-message broadcast algorithms together. Classical analysis [35] shows that the natural algorithm in which at each round each node sends one message that it has not sent before (and has traveled less than h hops so far) solves the problem in $O(k + h)$ rounds. The significant aspect is the additive appearance of k which in a sense implies a perfect pipelining between the k broadcast algorithms.

(II) Running breadth-first search algorithms from different sources. Holzer and Wattenhofer [18] show that one can run n BFSs starting in different nodes all together in $O(n)$ rounds. This is done by delaying BFSs carefully in a way that they do not interfere (once started). More generally, Lenzen and Peleg [24] show that k many h-hop BFSs from different sources can be performed in $O(k + h)$ rounds. This is in a sense a strengthening of the broadcast result of [35], as it shows that in fact each BFS-token (or equivalently, broadcast message) will be delivered to each related destination along a shortest path.

(III) Routing many packets, each from a source to a destination, along a given path. This problem has received the most attention [7, 10, 22, 23, 27, 28, 30, 32, 33, 36] among these special cases. Viewing our distributed algorithm scheduling problem as a generalization of this packet routing problem, we adopt a terminology close to that introduced for packet routing in [22]. We discuss some known results for packet routing after introducing this (generalized) terminology.

Generally, if one of the algorithms $\mathcal{A}_1$, $\mathcal{A}_2$, ..., $\mathcal{A}_k$ that are to be run together takes d rounds, running all of them together will clearly require at least d rounds. We refer to the maximum running time of the algorithms as $\mathsf{dilation}$. Furthermore, there is another simple lower bound due to the bandwidth limitations. Consider a particular edge e of the graph. Let $c_i(e)$ be the number of rounds in which algorithm $\mathcal{A}_i$ sends a message over e. Then, running all the algorithms together will also require at least $\mathsf{congestion} = \max_{e \in E} \mathsf{congestion}(e)$ rounds where $\mathsf{congestion}(e) = \sum_{i=1}^{k} c_i(e)$. Hence, we can conclude that running all algorithms together will need at least $\max\{\mathsf{congestion}, \mathsf{dilation}\} \geq (\mathsf{congestion} + \mathsf{dilation})/2$ rounds. The key question of interest is:

Question: Can we always find a schedule close to the $\Omega(\mathsf{congestion} + \mathsf{dilation})$ round lower bound?

A simple yet powerful technique that proves helpful in this regard is *random delays* [22], which was first introduced in the context of packet routing — the problem we described in item (III) above. In packet routing, $\mathsf{dilation}$ is the length of longest path and $\mathsf{congestion}$ is the maximum number of paths that go through an edge. The random delays method achieves an upper bound within an $O(\log n)$ factor of the lower bound; more precisely, a schedule of size $O(\mathsf{congestion} + \mathsf{dilation} \cdot \log n)$. Improving this simple $O(\log n)$-approximation to an $O(1)$-approximation received quite an extensive amount of attention and by now there are many existence proofs and also algorithmic constructions that give schedules of length $O(\mathsf{congestion} + \mathsf{dilation})$ for packet routing. That is, schedules within an $O(1)$ factor from the trivial lower bound. See e.g. [10, 22, 23, 27, 30, 32, 33, 36]. The classical method [22] is based on $\log^* n$ levels of recursively applying the Lovasz's local lemma[1], each time reducing the parameter $\mathsf{congestion}+\mathsf{dilation}$ of the new problem to a polylogarithmic function of the same parameter in the problem of the previous level.

Going back to the question of scheduling general distributed algorithms, the random delays technique proves useful here as well. If nodes have access to shared randomness, the same simple random delays trick as in [22] provides a schedule for general distributed algorithms that is within an $O(\log n)$ factor of the trivial lower bound. Here the shared randomness is helpful because for each distributed algorithm, there can be many (potentially faraway) nodes that start it and delaying the algorithm by a random delay (with a controlled probability distribution) requires all nodes to do so in a consistent manner.

Theorem 1.1 (Simple extension of [22]). *Given shared randomness, one can distributedly find a schedule that runs all the distributed algorithms in* $O(\mathsf{congestion}+\mathsf{dilation}\cdot\log n)$ *round, with high probability.*

Proof Sketch. Break time into phases, each having $\Theta(\log n)$ rounds. We treat each phase as one round in the sense that the communications of each round of each algorithm will be executed during one phase. We delay the start of each algorithm by a uniform random delay in $[O(\mathsf{congestion}/\log n)]$ phases. Chernoff bound shows that w.h.p., for each edge and each phase, $O(\log n)$ messages are scheduled to traverse this edge in this phase. Hence, all algorithms will run along each other with no interference, and each will be done after at most $O(\mathsf{congestion}/\log n) + \mathsf{dilation}$ phases. □

The above theorem leaves us with two main questions:

Questions:

1. Can one remove the $\log n$ factor in the bound of Theorem 1.1 and get an $O(\mathsf{congestion} + \mathsf{dilation})$ round schedule for general distributed algorithms, perhaps using ideas similar to [10, 22, 23, 27, 30, 32, 33, 36]?
2. What can we do with only private randomness, i.e., without any shared randomness?

Technical Contributions: Regarding the first question, we show that interestingly, unlike in packet routing, when scheduling general distributed algorithms, the lower bound is the one that can be improved to essentially match the simple upper bound. Concretely, using the probabilistic method [6], we construct a hard instance of the scheduling problem which shows that:

Theorem 1.2. *There are instances of distributed algorithm scheduling for which any schedule, even when constructed centralized, requires* $\Omega(\mathsf{congestion}+\mathsf{dilation}\cdot\log n/\log\log n)$ *rounds.*

As for the second question, that is shared randomness, we face two rather orthogonal issues: One is about the amount of randomness to be shared and the other is how (and where) to share even a single bit of randomness. While the first issue is simple, the second requires more work. For the first issue, the saving grace is that for the proof of Theorem 1.1, $\Theta(\log n)$-wise independence between the values of random delays is enough[2] and thus, thanks to the standard

[1] In fact, the packet routing problem and this LLL-baed method of it is now one of the material typically covered in courses on (or around) randomized algorithms for introducing the Lovasz's Local Lemma, see e.g. [1, 2, 4, 5].

[2] See [34, Theorem 5] for a Chernoff bound for k-wise independent random variables.

bounded-independence randomness constructions (e.g., via Reed-Solomon codes), sharing simply $O(\log^2 n)$ bits of randomness is sufficient. As for the second issue, clearly one can elect a leader to pick the required initial "shared" randomness and broadcast it to all nodes. However, this, and moreover any such global sharing procedure, will need at least $\Omega(D)$ rounds, for D being the network diameter, which is not desirable. We explain how to solve the problem with private randomness in a time close to the case with shared randomness.

Theorem 1.3. *For any instance of distributed algorithm scheduling, there is a randomized distributed algorithm using only private randomness that, with high probability, produces a schedule that runs all the algorithms in* $O(\mathsf{congestion} + \mathsf{dilation} \cdot \log n)$ *rounds, after* $O(\mathsf{dilation} \log^2 n)$ *rounds of pre-computation.*

Roughly speaking, the approach is to break each algorithm into sparsely overlapping sub-algorithms that each span only small areas of the network. Particularly, each of these sub-algorithms will span an area of (weak) diameter $O(\mathsf{dilation} \log n)$ hops. Then, we only share randomness inside these smaller areas and show how to run these sub-algorithms in a way that they simulate the main algorithms.

This approach is in fact more general and it can be used to remove the assumption of having shared randomness in a broad family of randomized distributed algorithms, at the cost of an $O(\log^2 n)$ factor increase in their running time. Roughly speaking, the family that this result applies to is those algorithms in which each node outputs one (canonical) output in the majority of the executions of the algorithm (for each given input). That is, algorithms where the randomness does not effect the output (significantly) and is used only to speed up the computation. We note that recently this class was termed *Bellagio algorithms* [15, 17] as a subclass of randomized algorithms with some desirable pseudo-deterministic behavior. Due the space limitations, the explanation of this generalization is deferred to the full version of the paper.

2. PRELIMINARIES

To talk about running many distributed algorithms, we need to be precise about how we view each algorithm. Particularly, the aspect that we will focus on is their *communication pattern* [25, Page 143], that is, in which rounds and over which edges does each algorithm send messages.

Communication Pattern: We define the T-round *time-expanded* graph $G \times [T]$ of a network $G = (V, E)$ as follows: We have $T+1$ copies of V, denoted by $V_0, V_1, \ldots, V_T$, and T copies of E, denoted $E_1, E_2, \ldots, E_T$, where E_i defines the set of edges between V_{i-1} and V_i. For ease of reference, we will refer to the copy of node $v \in V$ that is in V_i as v_i. For each $i \in [1, T]$, $v_i \in V_i$ is connected with a direct edge to $u_{i+1} \in V_{i+1}$, that is $(v_i, u_{i+1}) \in E_{i+1}$, if and only if $(v, u) \in E$. The communications of a T-round algorithm A on network G correspond naturally to a subgraph of $G \times [T]$: For $v \in V_i$ and $u \in V_{i+1}$, we have $(v_i, u_{i+1}) \in A$ if and only if algorithm A sends a message from v to u in round i. We call this subgraph the *communication pattern of A*. Figure 1 shows a simple example. Note that the communication pattern of an algorithm simply captures the footprint of its communications and does not consider the content of the messages sent by the algorithm.

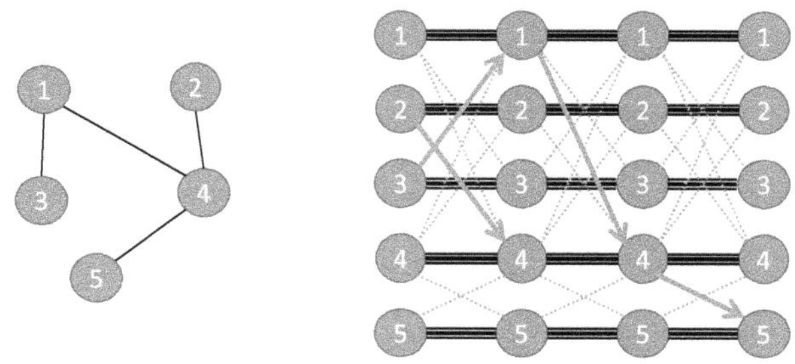

Figure 1: A simple graph, its 3 round time-expanded version, and a communication pattern on it. In round 1, nodes 2 and 3 send messages respectively to nodes 4 and 1; in round 2, node 1 sends a message to node 4; in round 3, node 4 sends a message to node 5.

Generally, the communication pattern of an algorithm is non-deterministic and can depend on the inputs to the nodes and also on their randomness. Hence, it is vital that we do not assume it to be known a priori. Often the communication pattern itself already conveys significant information about the things that the algorithm is supposed to compute, which means that nodes cannot know it in advance, i.e., before running the algorithm. Even throughout the execution, a node v might not know which of its neighbors will send a message to v in the next round. A simple example to stress the vitality of this issue is the case of breadth first search: before running the BFS, node v does not know at which round and from which neighbors it will receive a message[3].

Simulation: Formally, we describe a simulation of a T-round algorithm A in a larger time-span $T' \geq T$ to be a mapping f from A to a sub-graph $B \subseteq G \times [T']$. More precisely, function f maps the edges (v_i, u_{i+1}) of algorithm $A \subseteq G \times [T]$, i.e., its communications, to edges in $G \times [T']$ in a way that preserves the *causal precedence*: that is, if in algorithm A, edge (v_i, u_{i+1}) causally precedes edge (v'_j, u'_{j+1}), then in B, edge $f((v_i, u_{i+1}))$ causally precedes edge $f((v'_{k_\ell}, u'_{j+1}))$. Here, *causal precedence* is formalized as follows: In an algorithm A, we say edge (v_i, u_{i+1}) *causally precedes* (v'_j, u'_{j+1}) if there is chain of edges $e_1 = (v_i, u_{i+1})$, $(u_{k_1}, w_{k_1+1}), \ldots, (w_{k_\ell}, v'_{k_\ell+1})$, (v'_j, u'_{j+1}) that are all in A and we have $i+1 \leq k_1 \leq \cdots \leq k_\ell \leq k_\ell + 1 \leq j$.

The Distributed Algorithm Scheduling (DAS) **Problem**: We are given k algorithms $\mathcal{A}_1$ to $\mathcal{A}_k$, and we should produce an execution so that for each algorithm, each node outputs the same value as if that algorithm was run alone.

Our lower bounds are strong in the sense that they apply to centralized scheduling, which means that everything—particularly the whole network topology and also the communication patterns of all the algorithms—is known to the scheduler, and the lower bound simply says that *there is no "short" schedule*, rather than saying that *a "short" schedule cannot be computed (distributedly)*.

For the purpose of our distributed scheduling algorithm (i.e., upper bound), we assume that the distributed algo-

[3]One can add dummy messages to BFS to fix its communication pattern. However, this will significantly increase the load on edges, i.e., $\mathsf{congestion}$, which is undesirable.

rithms $\mathcal{A}_1$ to $\mathcal{A}_k$ are given in the following format: For each algorithm $\mathcal{A}_i$, when this algorithm is run alone, in each round each node knows what to send in the next round. This clearly depends on the node's input and also what messages the node has received up to, and including, that round. We stress that, we do not assume that the nodes know the correct communication pattern a priori, and in fact, if for some reason the schedule is mixed up and the node does not receive one of the messages that it is supposed to receive in the alone execution of $\mathcal{A}_i$, the node might not notice this and it can proceed with executing the algorithm, although generating a wrong execution. Our algorithms are designed such that they ensure that this does not happen. As for the randomness used by the algorithms $\mathcal{A}_1$ to $\mathcal{A}_k$, we consider it as a part of the input to the node, that is, at the start of the execution, each node samples its bits of randomness, thus fixing them, and it uses these bits throughout the execution, similar to the way it uses its input.

In our algorithms, we will have (a number of) executions of the algorithm $\mathcal{A}_i$ that globally might look different than a simulation of the algorithm $\mathcal{A}_i$, but from the viewpoint of some nodes, they are exactly as if the whole simulation is run. To capture this formally, we define a *partial simulation* of algorithm A for node v to be an execution in which, all the communications that causally influence v are identical to those in a (full) simulation of A.

For our upper bound result, we assume that nodes know constant-factor approximations of congestion and dilation; although both of these assumptions can be removed using standard *doubling* techniques. We defer the explanation of these steps to the full version of this paper.

3. LOWER BOUND

Here we show that the $\log n$ factor in Theorem 1.1 is essentially unavoidable. That is, unlike packet routing [22], general distributed algorithms do not always admit a schedule of length $O(\mathsf{congestion} + \mathsf{dilation})$.

Theorem 3.1. *There is a distributed algorithm scheduling problem instance for which any schedule, even those computed centralized, requires at least* $\Omega(\mathsf{congestion} + \mathsf{dilation} \cdot \log n/\log\log n)$ *rounds.*

Proof. We first explain the general outline of the proof. We use the probabilistic method [6] to show the existence of such a "*hard*" problem instance. Particularly, we present a probability distribution space for distributed algorithm scheduling problems and show that, for a sample instance taken from this distribution, with a nonzero probability (in fact with probability almost 1), no schedule of length $o(\mathsf{congestion} + \mathsf{dilation} \cdot \log n/\log\log n)$ exists.

For that, roughly speaking, we study each fixed schedule of length $o(\mathsf{congestion} + \mathsf{dilation} \cdot \log n/\log\log n)$ against a random sample from the scheduling problem distribution, and we show that this one schedule has an extremely small probability to be good for the sample scheduling problem. This probability will be so small that, even after we take a union bound over all possible schedules, the probability that there exists one of these schedules that is good for the sample scheduling problem is strictly less than 1, and in fact close to 0. Hence, we conclude that there exists one problem instance of distributed algorithm scheduling which does not admit any $o(\mathsf{congestion} + \mathsf{dilation} \cdot \log n/\log\log n)$ round schedule. We next explain how we realize this outline.

We start with describing the probability distribution of the algorithms $\mathcal{A}_1$ to $\mathcal{A}_k$ that are supposed to be scheduled. The network $G = (V, E)$ is as follows: $V = \{v_0, v_1, \ldots, v_L\} \cup U_1 \cup U_2 \cup \cdots \cup U_L$, where $L = n^{0.1}$. Each set U_i contains $\eta = n^{0.9}$ nodes, and each node $u \in U_i$ is connected to v_{i-1} and to v_i. Figure 2 illustrates the structure of this network (and also the edges in the communication pattern of one sample algorithm, which will be discussed soon). The general format of each algorithm $\mathcal{A}_i$ is as follows: in round 1, node v_0 sends a message to a subset $S_1 \subset U_1$, where $|S_1| = \Theta(n^{0.9})$, the choice of S_1 will be described. Then in round 2, these nodes S_1 each send a message to v_1. In round 3, node v_1 sends a message to a subset $S_2 \subset U_2$, and in round 4 these nodes send messages to v_2. The algorithm proceeds similarly over the next blocks, continuing with a speed of one hop progress per round, and containing an arbitrary subset $S_i \subset U_i$ where $|S_i| = \Theta(n^{0.9})$. In a random sample DAS problem from our distribution, for each algorithm $\mathcal{A}_i$, each S_j is determined randomly where each node $u \in U_j$ is added to S_j with probability $n^{-0.1}$, and the choices are independent between different nodes of the same layer, different layers, and different algorithms. Note that if we have $k = n^{0.2}$ algorithms, then $\mathbb{E}[\mathsf{congestion}] = kn^{-0.1} = n^{0.1}$, and thanks to the independence, we know that

$$\Pr[\mathsf{congestion} \geq 2n^{-0.1}] \leq e^{-\Theta(n^{0.1})}.$$

We claim that there is a sample DAS problem in this distribution where $\mathsf{congestion} = O(n^{0.1})$, $\mathsf{dilation} = 2n^{0.1}$, and for which there is no schedule of length at most $\frac{n^{0.1}\log n}{1000\log\log n}$.

To prove this claim, we break the time into $0.1n^{0.1}$ phases of $\frac{\log n}{100\log\log n}$ rounds each. Furthermore, in the schedule, we say algorithm $\mathcal{A}_i$ crosses layer j in a given phase if the message of v_{j-1} is sent in this phase and v_j receives the responses of all the related nodes in U_j during this phase. Even though it is possible that crossing a layer does not fully fall into one phase, it must be true that for at least $\frac{9}{10}$ of the layers, they are each crossed in a phase. This is because otherwise the length of the schedule would be more than $\frac{n^{0.1}}{10} \cdot \frac{\log n}{100\log\log n} = \frac{n^{0.1}\log n}{1000\log\log n}$. For each of the algorithms, we define its *crossing pattering* to be the (partial) assignment of layers to phases which indicates that layer $j \in [n^{0.1}]$ is crossed during phase $t \in [0.1n^{0.1}]$, and at most 0.1 fraction of the layers do not have a phase number assigned to them. For each layer $j \in [n^{0.1}]$ and each phase $t \in [0.1n^{0.1}]$, the load $L(j,t)$ in layer j at phase t is defined to be total number of algorithms that are scheduled to cross layer j during phase t. Since there are $k = n^{0.2}$ algorithms and each of them should cross at least $0.9n^{0.1}$ layers during phases, we have

$$\sum_{j,t} L(j,t) \geq n^{0.2} \cdot 0.9n^{0.1} = 0.9n^{0.3}.$$

Now there are $0.1n^{0.2}$ choices for pair (j,t). Hence, the average load over these pairs is at least $0.9n^{0.1}$, which means that there is at least one pair with such a "semi-large" load of at least $0.9n^{0.1}$. We next focus on this layer-phase pair.

When we are studying this heavily loaded layer-phase in a fixed schedule against the randomly chosen set of algorithms, we get that on average, in this phase, the expected number of messages that have to go through an edge is at least $0.9n^{0.1} \cdot n^{-0.1} = 0.9$. This is because, each algorithm uses each edge with probability $n^{-0.1}$ and by the choice of

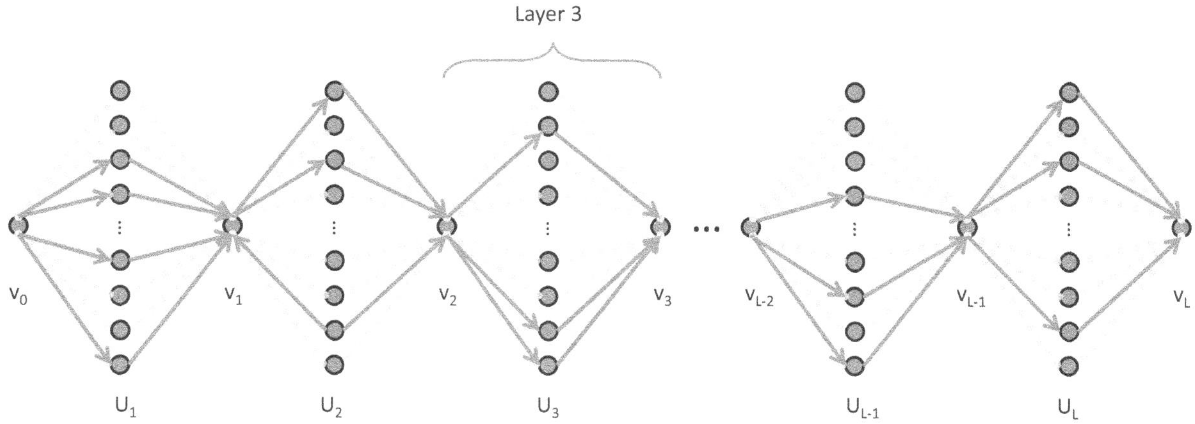

Figure 2: A sample algorithm in the hard distribution. The green links indicate all the edges used by one sampled algorithm (i.e., roughly speaking those in its communication pattern), while the orange dotted lines present all the possible edges that the algorithms in the distribution can use.

this layer-phase, there are $0.9n^{0.1}$ algorithms that cross this layer in this phase. We next use a simple anti-concentration type of argument to say that there is a non-negligible chance that a given edge gets considerably more than this expected load (in this phase). Note that if more than $\frac{\log n}{100 \log\log n}$ algorithms are supposed to cross a single edge during one phase, then the schedule fails simply because the phase has only $\frac{\log n}{100 \log\log n}$ rounds. The probability that the number of algorithms that have to use a given fixed edge is more than $\frac{\log n}{100 \log\log n}$ is at least

$$\sum_{\ell=\frac{\log n}{100 \log\log n}}^{0.9n^{0.1}} \binom{0.9n^{0.1}}{\ell} (n^{-0.1})^{\ell}(1-n^{-0.1})^{0.9n^{0.1}-\ell} \geq n^{-0.2}.$$

Let us now zoom in on one side of the layer, e.g., the side from U_j to node v_j. Note that for each algorithm $\mathcal{A}_i$, the choices of different nodes being in S_j—whether different edges of this side of a layer j are used in $\mathcal{A}_i$—are independent. Thus, the load on different edges of this side of layer j are independent. This means that the probability that there is no such heavily loaded edge is at most $(1-n^{-0.2})^{n^{0.9}} \leq 1-e^{-n^{0.7}}$. That is, the probability that the one fixed crossing pattern we were studying is good for the given random instance of the distributed algorithm scheduling is extremely small, at most $e^{-n^{0.7}}$.

Given that one crossing pattern is very unlikely to succeed, we now explain why none of them is likely to succeed, using a union bound. The number of all possible crossing patterns for all algorithms is at most $e^{\Theta(n^{0.3})}$. This is because, for a single algorithm, to define a possible crossing patterns, we need to specify at most $0.1n^{0.1}$ layers that are not crossed during a phase, and also specify the crossing phase for the rest of the layers. For the layers that are not crossed during a phase, there are $\binom{n^{0.1}}{0.1n^{0.1}} = e^{O(n^{0.1})}$ options. To assign increasing phase numbers in range $[n^{0.1}]$ to the remaining $0.9n^{0.1}$ layers, there are $\binom{1.9n^{0.1}-1}{0.9n^{0.1}} = e^{O(n^{0.1})}$ options[4]. Hence, the total number of possible crossing patterns for a single algorithm is at most $e^{\Theta(n^{0.1})}$, which means that over all the $k = n^{0.2}$ algorithms, the number of all possible crossing patterns is at most $e^{\Theta(n^{0.3})}$.

Now, a union bound over all crossing patterns tells us that the probability that there is one of the crossing patterns that does not fail for the sampled DAS problem is at most $e^{-n^{0.7}} \cdot e^{\Theta(n^{0.3})} \ll 1$. Therefore, there is one DAS problem in the described family for which there is no (short) crossing pattern, and hence, also no schedule of length at most $\frac{n^{0.1} \log n}{1000 \log\log n}$ rounds. □

Remark: We note that the schedule length bound that appears in the proof of the above theorem is indeed tight up to a constant factor for the described setting. This is because, using some small parameter tuning in Theorem 1.1, we can generate a schedule of length $\Omega((\mathsf{congestion}+\mathsf{dilation}) \cdot \log n/\log\log n)$, which matches the bound in the proof as there $\mathsf{congestion} = \Theta(\mathsf{dilation})$. To get this schedule, we use phases of $\Theta(\log n/\log\log n)$ rounds and delay each algorithm by a random number of phases uniformly distributed in $[\Theta(\mathsf{congestion})]$. Thus, the expected number of messages to be sent across an edge per phase is $O(1)$ which means w.h.p., this number will not exceed $O(\log n/\log\log n)$.

4. UPPER BOUND

We start by giving an intuitive explanation of the challenge in scheduling distributed algorithms and a high level description of the ideas we use. We then go on to describe the solution with its details.

In the full version of this paper, we sketch out how to use this approach to remove the assumption of having shared randomness in a broad range of distributed algorithms, at the cost of a slow down factor of $O(\log^2 n)$.

4.1 The Challenge, and the Outline of Our Approach

The key insight in the random delays trick of [22], explained in Section 1, is that this random per-algorithm delay spreads different algorithms over time such that the number of packets scheduled to go through an edge per time goes

[4]Recall that this is essentially a case of the *stars and bars* problem: phases are the stars and layers are the bars, and how many stars there are before a bar indicates the phase in which the related layer is crossed.

down. When working with distributed algorithms, implementing such a random delay (with a controlled probability distribution) might become a non-trivial task. This is mainly because of the local nature of distributed algorithms: typically, while the algorithm is being run over the whole network, each node is influenced only by a small neighborhood around itself, particularly a ball of radius dilation-hops, in our terminology. If we are to keep the running time small, there cannot be any causal dependency between nodes that are far from each other. Hence, particularly, unless we have access to shared randomness, we cannot have a randomly chosen delay for a given algorithm in a way that the delay is "consistent" over the whole network.

The good news however is that we actually do not need such a consistency over the whole network; it is sufficient if we have a consistently delayed execution in each dilation-neighborhood. This is because each node actually sees only a dilation-neighborhood of itself. However, leveraging this positive point is non-trivial, mainly because each edge can be in the dilation-neighborhoods of a large number of nodes, and executing algorithms in each of these neighborhoods separately will need an undesirably large running time.

The solution we use is based on a generic method of *graph partitioning* [9,11,13,21], colloquially referred to as *ball carving*. Particularly, the closest to what we do is the approach Bartal [8] used for probabilistically approximating arbitrary metric spaces with tree-metrics. The end result of the graph partitioning part will be a number of clusters of weak radius $O(\mathsf{dilation} \cdot \log n)$ such that each dilation-neighborhood is covered completely in at least one, and in fact $\Theta(\log n)$, of the clusters and moreover, each edge is in at most $O(\log n)$ clusters. To efficiently implement this idea in the CONGEST, we also use a number of small tricks, which we believe might be useful in other distributed graph partitioning algorithms for the CONGEST model.

Once we have the aforementioned partitioning, we share a sufficient amount of randomness in each of these clusters (efficiently); these randomness are to be fed to a $\Theta(\log n)$-wise independent pseudo-random generator. We then show how to use these locally shared randomness bits to simulate all the distributed algorithms in all the clusters in $O(\mathsf{congestion} + \mathsf{dilation} \cdot \log n)$ rounds, i.e., producing a schedule of length $O(\mathsf{congestion} + \mathsf{dilation} \cdot \log n)$ rounds. We also explain how to let each node pick the right execution for each of the algorithms, from among all the simulations in different clustering layers the node is involved in.

4.2 Scheduling Distributed Algorithms via Locally Sharing Randomness

Here, we describe the algorithm that realizes the above outline and achieves the following result:

Theorem 4.1. *There is a* DAS *algorithm with only private randomness with* $O(\mathsf{dilation} \log^2 n)$ *rounds of pre-computation that simulates all the algorithms in* $O(\mathsf{congestion} + \mathsf{dilation} \cdot \log n)$ *rounds.*

For the graph partitioning mentioned above, which effectively breaks each algorithm into sub-algorithms in local areas, we present the following lemma:

Lemma 4.2. *There is a distributed algorithm that runs in* $O(\mathsf{dilation} \log^2 n)$ *rounds and creates* $\Theta(\log n)$ *layers of clustering of the graph such that: (1) in each layer, the clusters are node-disjoint, (2) each cluster has weak diameter* $O(\mathsf{dilation} \cdot \log n)$*, (3) w.h.p, for each node* v*, there are* $\Theta(\log n)$ *layers such that the* dilation*-neighborhood of* v *is fully contained in one of the clusters of this layer, and (4) in each layer, each node knows what is the maximum radius around it that is fully contained in a cluster.*

Proof. What we do in the $\Theta(\log n)$ layers of clustering is independent repetitions of the following scheme: each node u picks a random radius $r(u)$ distributed according to a truncated exponential distribution, where $\Pr[r(u) = z] = (\frac{n}{n-1})\frac{1}{R}e^{-z/R}$ for $R = \Theta(\mathsf{dilation})$. Node u also picks a random label $\ell(u) \in \{0,1\}^{4\log n}$. Note that w.h.p., for each two nodes $u \neq u$, $\ell(u) \neq \ell(u')$. The radius $r(u)$ defines a ball of radius $r(u)$ centered at u, which we denote $B(u)$. Each node v joins the cluster centered at node w^* where w^* is defined as the node that has the smallest label $\ell(w^*)$ among the labels of nodes w such that $v \in B(w)$. Properties (1) and (2) follow immediately from the definition and the property (3) follows from the analysis of Bartal [8, Section 3] which shows that in each layer, each dilation-neighborhood is fully contained in one of the clusters with constant probability.

What is left to discuss is the distributed implementation and its time complexity, and achieving property (4). We run the layers of clustering separately, each in $O(\mathsf{dilation} \log n)$ rounds, thus all together in $O(\mathsf{dilation} \log^2 n)$ rounds. To save time in the distributed implementation, we will add a small trick. Interestingly, once we move to Lemma 4.3, this simple change will end up saving us two logarithmic factors in the running time. Each node u initiates a message m_u containing its id and label, and an initial hop-count $H - r(u)$, where $H = \Theta(\mathsf{dilation} \log n)$. Note that w.h.p., for each node u, we have $r_u < H$. This (fake) initial hop-count virtually implies that the message m_v is coming from a different node and it has already traveled $H - r(u)$ hops by now and it can only travel $r(u)$ more hops, as we allow each message to travel H hops in total.

Then in each round $i \in [1, H]$, each node v forwards the message with hop-count i that has the smallest label among the messages of hop-count i or smaller that have reached v. Each received message gets its hop-count incremented by 1. Due to the initial hop-counts, the message m_u can reach only nodes that are in $B(u)$. Furthermore, for any node v, if $\ell(u)$ is the smallest label among the labels of balls that contain v, then m_u will indeed reach v. The reason is as follows: if m_u does not reach v, it must be that in a round i, there is a node w on the shortest path from u to v that has received m_u but does not forward m_u because it instead forwards (or has forwarded) $m_{v'}$ for a node v' such that $\ell(v') < \ell(v)$ and at w, the hop count of $m_{v'}$ was less than or equal to that of m_v. But this implies that u is in fact in $B(v')$, which is in contradiction with v having the smallest label among the balls that contain u. Finally, $\ell(u)$ will be the smallest label that v hears, and thus v will join the cluster centered at u.

To achieve property (4), that is each node knowing what radius of it is fully contained in a cluster, we do as follows for each layer: First, each node sends its cluster label to each neighbor. Then, if a node sees a different label in that round, it marks itself as cluster boundary. In the next dilation rounds, each boundary node sends a message declaring it is boundary and for the next $O(\mathsf{dilation} \log n)$ rounds, if a node hears a boundary message, it forwards it to its neighbors (if it has not done so in the past). Hence, if h'

neighborhood of node v is the maximum neighborhood fully contained in a cluster, v will receive the boundary message after h' rounds, thus letting node v learn the value of h'. □

Lemma 4.3. *We can share $\Theta(\log^2 n)$ bits of randomness in each cluster, all together in $O(\mathsf{dilation} \log^2 n)$ rounds. Furthermore, via local computations, this can be turned to poly(n) many $\Theta(\log n)$-bit random values that are $\Theta(\log n)$-wise independent.*

Proof of Lemma 4.3. If we had to share $\Theta(\log n)$ bits of randomness in each cluster, then each cluster center node would simply pick this randomness and append it to its initial message. Sharing the $\Theta(\log^2 n)$ bits requires sending $O(\log n)$ messages from each cluster center. Thus, a naive extension of the approach in Lemma 4.2 would become $O(\mathsf{dilation} \log^2 n)$ rounds per layer, i.e., $O(\mathsf{dilation} \log^3 n)$ in total.

We can do the spreading in each layer in $O(\mathsf{dilation} \log n)$ rounds as follows: make $\Theta(\log n)$ messages from each source v, each containing $\Theta(\log n)$ bits of randomness, all with the same label $\ell(v)$, and an additional smaller label $\ell'(v)$ picked from $\{1, 2, \Theta(\log n)\}$ to distinguish these messages. The initial hop-count is set as in Lemma 4.2 for all these messages. Then, in each round, each node forwards the message with lexicographically smallest (hop-count, $\ell(v), \ell'(v)$) that it has not sent before. The pipelining analysis of Lenzen [24] shows that after $H+\Theta(\log n) = O(\mathsf{dilation} \log n)$ rounds of this protocol, each node v will receive the smallest $\Theta(\log n)$ messages starting in the H neighborhood of v, where smallest is with respect to the lexicographical ordering of $(\ell(v), \ell'(v))$. Because of the initial hop-count settings, this H-neighborhood translates to all centers that could potentially reach v, and particularly means node v will receive all the $\Theta(\log n)$ messages coming from the center u of the cluster that contains v. Repeating this scheme $\Theta(\log n)$ times, once for each clustering layer, solves the local randomness sharing and gets us to $O(\mathsf{dilation} \log^2 n)$ rounds[5].

We now talk about increasing the "size" of randomness as the $O(\log^2 n)$ bits of randomness shared in each cluster is not (directly) sufficient for determining the random delays of all the algorithms. Each node v feeds the $\Theta(\log^2 n)$ bits of shared randomness of each cluster that contains v into the classical k-wise independent pseudo-randomness construction via Reed-Solomon codes, for $k = \Theta(\log n)$, (see e.g., [3, Section 3] and also [6, Theorem 15.2.1][6]). This transforms the randomness to poly(n) many $\Theta(\log n)$-bit random values that are $\Theta(\log n)$-wise independent. These random values will be used to determine the random delays of different algorithms in a way that is consistent in each cluster and for each set of up to $\Theta(\log n)$ algorithms, their random delays are independent. Particularly, we assume each algorithm $\mathcal{A}_i$ has a unique algorithm identifier $\mathsf{AID}(i)$ in a range of $K = \text{poly}(n)$ size, say $[n^{10}]$, and we divide the generated random values into K buckets, each containing poly(n) random values, and the algorithm $\mathcal{A}_i$ will pick its random delays based on the random values in bucket $\mathsf{AID}(i)$. □

We next explain how, given this shared randomness, we derive a schedule of length $O(\mathsf{congestion} + \mathsf{dilation} \cdot \log n)$ rounds that simulates all the algorithms.

Lemma 4.4. *After the local randomness sharing as done in Lemma 4.3, we can run all the distributed algorithms in all the cluster, altogether in $O(\mathsf{congestion} + \mathsf{dilation} \cdot \log n)$ rounds.*

Proof. We first explain a simpler solution that leads to a schedule of length $O(\mathsf{congestion} \cdot \log n + \mathsf{dilation} \cdot \log n)$ and then explain how to improve this to the near-optimal schedule length $O(\mathsf{congestion} + \mathsf{dilation} \cdot \log n)$ using a nonuniform distribution of random delays.

We run a copy of each algorithm in each cluster. Hence, for each edge e, for each algorithm that uses e, there can be up to $\Theta(\log n)$ copies of each of the messages that are to be sent over e, at most one per layer. Thus, we potentially have increased the load on edges to $O(\mathsf{congestion} \cdot \log n)$.

Since we have partitioned algorithms into smaller clusters, we need to be careful that from the viewpoint of the nodes that their dilation-neighborhood is fully contained in a cluster, the behavior of the locally-cut execution of the algorithm stays the same as in the full algorithm. Consider an algorithm $\mathcal{A}_i$ and a clustering layer. If for a node v, only h'-neighborhood of v is fully contained in a cluster of this layer, then v will execute only the first h' rounds of the algorithm and will discard the messages that it would be sending in the later rounds. This change does not effect the execution from the viewpoint of the nodes that their dilation-neighborhood is fully contained in a cluster. This is because, if dilation-neighborhood of node w is fully contained in a cluster, this partial execution will still contain all the messages that can effect w. More concretely, for each node v in the dilation-neighborhood of w, in the algorithm, w causally depends only on the actions of v in the first $h' = \mathsf{dilation} - dist(v, w)$ rounds, and since dilation-neighborhood of w is fully contained in a cluster, so is the h'-neighborhood of v. Moreover, it is easy to see that generally, for any message in the algorithm that it is not discarded, none of the previous messages in the same algorithm that can causally effect it is discarded.

For each cluster, for each algorithm, the start of that algorithm is delayed by a random delay of $\delta \in [\mathsf{congestion}]$ big-rounds, where each big-round is $\Theta(\log n)$ rounds. Then, each algorithm proceeds in a synchronous manner at a rate of one algorithm-round per each big-round. The execution finishes after dilation + congestion big-rounds. W.h.p., the number of the messages scheduled per big-round per edge is $\Theta(\log n)$, thanks to the $\Theta(\log n)$-independence of the random delays. Then, each node v picks its output for each algorithm based on one of the clustering layers that fully contains the dilation-neighborhood of v in a cluster.

We now explain how to improve this schedule length, to the near-optimal bound of $O(\mathsf{congestion} + \mathsf{dilation} \cdot \log n)$ rounds. The key point we leverage is the fact that we only need one copy of each message, instead of all the potentially up to $O(\log n)$ copies (one in each layer). However, the challenge is to keep the executions synchronous (roughly speaking). The main ingredient we use is a nonuniform distribution of the random delays, suited to our setting. We

[5]We note that, it sounds plausible that one might get a bound of $O(\mathsf{dilation} \log n + \log^3 n)$ rounds for this part.

[6]We note that [6, Theorem 15.2.1] only describes the construction on the field GF(2) which yields binary random values that are k-wise independent. But, as also described in [3, Section 3], the construction readily extends to $GF(p)$, for any prime number $p \in \text{poly}(n)$. Furthermore, when desiring random delays in range $[\Theta(R)]$ for a given R, we can pick them from a range $\{1, \ldots, p\}$ for a prime $p \in \Theta(R)$. Note that by Bertrand's postulate, there are many such primes; there is at least one in $[a, 2a]$, for any $a \geq 1$.

next describe this distribution, and then explain how it affects the schedule.

The probability mass function of the random delay is as follows: We have a parameter $L = \Theta(\frac{\mathsf{congestion}}{\log n})$. The support of the distribution is divided to $\beta = \Theta(\log n)$ blocks. The total probability mass given to each block is $1/\beta$. The ith block contains $L\alpha^{i-1}$ points, and the distribution of the probability mass inside the block is uniform, i.e., each point of the ith block has probability $\frac{1/\beta}{L\alpha^{i-1}}$. Here, α is a positive constant slightly less than 1, which we fix later. Note that the total support of the distribution has $\sum_{i=1}^{\Theta(\log n)} L\alpha^{i-1} \leq \frac{L}{1-\alpha} = \Theta(\frac{\mathsf{congestion}}{\log n})$ points.

The above describes the distribution for the initial delay in each algorithm. Once started, the algorithms will again proceed synchronously one algorithm-round per each big-round. However, this time, if there is a message scheduled to be sent over e and a copy of it has been sent before, this message gets dropped. On the other hand, when a node is about to create a message when simulating a round j of algorithm, it takes into account all the messages that it has received in the past about rounds up to $j-1$ of the simulations of the same algorithm.

What is left is to show that with the new distribution of delays, w.h.p., for each big-round, there will be at most $\Theta(\log n)$ messages that actually need to go through an edge e. Note that a message must go through e in a given big-round if no copy of it has done so in the past, i.e., if among the $\Theta(\log n)$ copies of the simulations of the corresponding algorithm, this is the first execution scheduled. For a copy of an algorithm to be the first scheduled, all the $\Theta(\log n)$ copies must be scheduled afterward. We show that for each big-round and each edge, the probability that the first copy of a message is scheduled to go through this edge in that round is at most $\Theta(\frac{\log n}{\mathsf{congestion}})$. This is trivially true for delays in the first block of distribution of the delays as the probability for each of those delays is $\frac{1}{L\beta}$. For the second block, the probability that none of the $\Theta(\log n)$ copies of the algorithm have a delay in the first block is $(1-\frac{1}{\beta})^{\Theta(\log n)}$ which is a constant, say $\gamma < 1$. It is sufficient to pick the constant α equal to this constant γ. Then, the probability that a delay that is in the second block is picked and is the first among the delays is at most $\frac{\gamma/\beta}{L\alpha} \leq \frac{1}{L\beta}$. Generally, for a delay in the ith block, the probability that it is the first of delays is at most $(1-\frac{1}{\beta})^{(i-1)\Theta(\log n)} \leq \gamma^{i-1}$, and hence, the probability that it is picked and is the first among the related delays is at most $\frac{\gamma^{i-1}/\beta}{L\alpha^{i-1}} \leq \frac{1}{L\beta} = \Theta(\frac{\log n}{\mathsf{congestion}})$. Hence, we conclude that the total number of messages to be actually sent over each edge per big-round is at most $\Theta(\log n)$, with high probability. Since each big-round is made of $\Theta(\log n)$ rounds, we can afford to send all these messages across the edge in that big-round. Note that the range of the initial delays is $\Theta(\frac{\mathsf{congestion}}{\log n})$ big-rounds and each algorithm runs for only $\mathsf{dilation}$ big-rounds. Hence, the whole schedule has a length $O(\mathsf{congestion}+\mathsf{dilation}\cdot\log n)$ rounds, thus completing the proof of the lemma. □

5. CONCLUDING REMARKS AND FUTURE WORK

This paper is centered around the issue of running many independent distributed algorithms concurrently. We presented an existential $\Omega(\mathsf{congestion} + \mathsf{dilation} \log n/\log\log n)$ round schedule length lower bound and an algorithm that produces a schedule of length $O(\mathsf{congestion} + \mathsf{dilation} \log n)$ rounds, after $O(\mathsf{dilation} \log^2 n)$ rounds of pre-computation.

We believe that this paper is merely a starting point, as there are many seemingly fundamental aspects that are not addressed here. We next discuss some of these issue, which are conceptually deeper and perhaps somewhat less clear, as well as some other more detailed technical questions.

Broader Questions: Throughout the paper, we worked under the assumption that the algorithms $\mathcal{A}_1$ to $\mathcal{A}_k$ are fixed, and we just want to run them. However, one can imagine a different viewpoint, when considering a higher-level picture: The end goal that we have is to solve the problems that $\mathcal{A}_1$ to $\mathcal{A}_k$ were designed to solve, which means we are allowed to change these algorithms to make them fit with each other better, so long as they solve the same problems. In other words, given k problems, what is the best collection of algorithms $\mathcal{A}_1$ to $\mathcal{A}_k$ solving these problems that can be run together in the shortest possible span of time. This roughly coincides with, what is the collection of algorithms $\mathcal{A}_1$ to $\mathcal{A}_k$ solving these problems that leads to the smallest possible $\mathsf{congestion}$ and $\mathsf{dilation}$. To unify these two measures and make the problem well-defined, one might consider $\mathsf{congestion}+\mathsf{dilation}\cdot\log n$ as the objective that is to be minimized. In fact, once we design a set of algorithms optimizing this measure, then we can use the algorithms presented in this paper to run $\mathcal{A}_1$ to $\mathcal{A}_k$ together essentially optimally, which would be a near-optimal method overall. Hence, one can say that, the algorithmic results in this paper essentially (and approximately) reduce the general question of how to solve k problems together fast to that of designing algorithms that minimize the measure $\mathsf{congestion}+\mathsf{dilation}\cdot\log n$.

Now this latter design question still seems rather broad and it is not clear how to tackle such a question for the general choice of k problems. A clean special case which might provide us with valuable insights is the setting where the k problems are independent instances of the same problem. That is, the setting where we have k independent shots of a single problem, and we want to solve all of them.

We note that this question loosely resembles the well-studied *parallel repetitions* problem (see e.g. [31]) in the complexity theory which, roughly speaking, asks can one solve k independent shots of a given problem using "resources" less than k times that of the single-shot version. However, the author believes that this is rather a superficial similarity and the connection is not strong, mainly because our focus is on the distributed round complexity and we clearly know that pipelining often allows us to solve k shots faster than k times the round complexity of solving a single shot. Although, other less-direct connections between the two areas are plausible. For instance, one can use *direct product* or *direct sum theorems* of communication complexity to derive distributed round complexity lower bounds for k-shot versions of a given distributed problem.

Let us now take a closer look at this distributed k-shot question, by using a classical (single-shot) problem as an example. Consider the k-shot version of the MST problem: For the network graph $G=(V,E)$, we are given k different weight functions w_1 to w_k, each $w_i : E \to \mathbb{R}$, and we want to find the k Minimum Spanning Trees corresponding to these weight functions. It is easy to see that for MST (and in fact for most problems), the naive idea of running k copies of the best single-shot algorithm, even with the best possible pipelining/scheduling, is not optimal. The core of the matter is that, the single-shot algorithm is designed to minimize its running time, i.e., dilation in our terminology, but it typically does not lead to the best congestion.

Let us make the discussion more concrete by considering some examples. For MST, the almost a century-old algorithm of Boruvka [26] from 1926, which has the same outline as the one used by Galleger, Humblet, and Spira [14], has dilation $= \tilde{O}(n)$ rounds and running it once gives a very low congestion of $O(\log n)$. Other algorithms give different values for these two parameters. For instance, an alternative near-linear time algorithm can be achieved by filtering edges—discarding heaviest edge in each cycle—while they are being upcast on a tree towards the root, which leads to dilation and congestion both being $\tilde{O}(n)$. Furthermore, the newer algorithm of Kutten and Peleg [20] has an almost optimal running time of dilation $= \tilde{O}(D + \sqrt{n})$ rounds, but (as is) it has congestion $= \Theta(\sqrt{n})$. This simple example is a witness to the clear fact that the algorithms designed to have optimal dilation do not necessarily have good congestion.

For the case of the MST problem, we can actually understand the tradeoff between congestion and dilation quite well: Using constructs similar to those of Das Sarma et al. [12], one can see that there is indeed an inevitable tradeoff and an MST algorithm that has congestion at most L will require a dilation of at least $\tilde{\Omega}(n/L)$ rounds. Interestingly, using some simple parameter tuning in the algorithm of Kutten and Peleg [20], one can algorithmically match this tradeoff of

$$\text{congestion} = L, \text{dilation} = \tilde{\Theta}(D + n/L).$$

This single-short tradeoff also has direct implications for the k-short version of the problem. For the k-shot version, the aforementioned lower bound can be combined with a *strong direct sum theorem* for communication complexity of k independent shots of two-party set disjointness [19], and some parameter tuning, to show that solving k-shots of MST requires at least $\tilde{\Omega}(D + \sqrt{kn})$ rounds. Again, this can be matched algorithmically: we use the parameter-optimized algorithm of Kutten and Peleg, with the optimal choice $L = \sqrt{n/k}$, as our single-shot algorithm, and we run k copies of it in parallel using (even a simplified version of) our $O(\text{congestion} + \text{dilation} \log n)$ round schedule. As a result, we get an algorithm that solves k independent instances of MST in $\tilde{O}(D + \sqrt{nk})$ rounds, thus essentially matching the aforementioned lower bound.

Perhaps it is simply a lucky coincidence that in the case of MST, we already know how to solve k-shots of it optimally, simply by doing some parameter tuning in the known single-shot algorithms and then running k copies of it in parallel. Can we achieve such a result for a broader family of algorithms (hopefully, ones which have a different "nature" compared to that of MST[7])?

To summarize, we believe that when designing distributed algorithms, it is valuable to keep track of both dilation and congestion, as opposed to merely dilation which is the standard objective in the recent years of theoretical distributed computing. This is because, congestion gives us a sense of what will happen when we run this algorithm along with others. Of course the ideal case would be if one can have an algorithm with a controllable (and efficient) tradeoff between the two parameters, as we saw above for the MST problem. Furthermore, this tradeoff between congestion and dilation deserves a study from a lower bound viewpoint, and even congestion deserves a study of its own. For instance, given a problem, can we solve it with a congestion below the given threshold?

As a side note, we remark that a measure that received more attention in the old days of theoretical distributed computing was *message complexity*. In fact message complexity has some correlation with congestion. However, this correlation is not strong and the message complexity alone does not characterize the related congestion. For instance, an algorithm with message complexity $O(m)$ can have congestion anywhere between $O(1)$ to $O(m)$.

Smaller Technical Questions: We next mention a few smaller questions about the technical results presented in the paper. A particular question is, the lower bound we presented in this paper is merely existential. Is it possible to provide a necessary and sufficient classification of special cases of distributed algorithm scheduling problems which admit $O(\text{congestion} + \text{dilation})$ round schedules? Alternatively, can we get at least a sufficient condition that covers a broad range of problems of interest? If yes, for those, can we also find these schedules distributedly and efficiently?

Another question is regarding Theorem 1.3, which gives a schedule of length $O(\text{congestion} + \text{dilation} \log n)$ but after $O(\text{dilation} \log^2 n)$ rounds of precomputation. Can we improve the latter, hopefully to $O(\text{dilation} \log n)$ rounds?

[7] One can see that for instance, a k-shot version of minimum cut approximation can also be computed in $\Omega(D + \sqrt{kn})$ rounds, by extending [16], and that also is optimal due to essentially the same lower bound constructions. However, this is not really a novel addition but merely an extension of the same tradeoff "nature".

Acknowledgment

The author thanks Nancy Lynch and Fabian Kuhn for valuable conversations about the conceptual point of the paper, i.e., studying the question of running many distributed algorithms together; Badih Ghazi, Bernhard Haeupler, Stephan Holzer, and Christoph Lenzen for discussions about different technical aspects of it; and Tsvetomira Radeva for feedback about the writeup.

This work was supported in part by a Simons award for graduate students in Theoretical Computer Science (number 318723), as well as AFOSR contract number FA9550-13-1-0042, NSF award 0939370-CCF, NSF award CCF-1217506, and NSF award CCF-AF-0937274.

6. REFERENCES

[1] Lecture notes on Algorithmic Power Tools. http://www.ccs.neu.edu/home/rraj/Courses/7880/F09/Lectures/GeneralLLL_Apps.pdf. Accessed: 2015-02.

[2] Lecture notes on Algorithmic Power Tools. http://www.ccs.neu.edu/home/rraj/Courses/7880/F09/Lectures/PacketRouting.pdf. Accessed: 2015-02.

[3] Lecture notes on k-wise uniform (randomness) generators. http://pages.cs.wisc.edu/~dieter/Courses/2013s-CS880/Scribes/PDF/lecture04.pdf. Accessed: 2015-02.

[4] Lecture notes on Randomized Algorithms and Probabilistic Analysis.

http://courses.cs.washington.edu/courses/cse525/13sp/scribe/lec10.pdf. Accessed: 2015-02.

[5] Lecture notes on Randomness and Computation. http://www.cs.berkeley.edu/~sinclair/cs271/n22.pdf. Accessed: 2015-02.

[6] N. Alon and J. H. Spencer. *The probabilistic method.* John Wiley & Sons, 2004.

[7] F. M. Auf der Heide and B. Vöcking. Shortest-path routing in arbitrary networks. *Journal of Algorithms*, 31(1):105–131, 1999.

[8] Y. Bartal. Probabilistic approximation of metric spaces and its algorithmic applications. In *Foundations of Computer Science, 1996. Proceedings., 37th Annual Symposium on*, pages 184–193. IEEE, 1996.

[9] Y. Bartal. Graph decomposition lemmas and their role in metric embedding methods. In *Algorithms–ESA 2004*, pages 89–97. Springer, 2004.

[10] D. Bertsimas and D. Gamarnik. Asymptotically optimal algorithms for job shop scheduling and packet routing. *Journal of Algorithms*, 33(2):296–318, 1999.

[11] G. Calinescu, H. Karloff, and Y. Rabani. Approximation algorithms for the 0-extension problem. *SIAM Journal on Computing*, 34(2):358–372, 2005.

[12] A. Das Sarma, S. Holzer, L. Kor, A. Korman, D. Nanongkai, G. Pandurangan, D. Peleg, and R. Wattenhofer. Distributed verification and hardness of distributed approximation. In *Proc. of the Symp. on Theory of Comp. (STOC)*, pages 363–372, 2011.

[13] J. Fakcharoenphol, S. Rao, and K. Talwar. A tight bound on approximating arbitrary metrics by tree metrics. In *Proceedings of the thirty-fifth annual ACM symposium on Theory of computing*, pages 448–455. ACM, 2003.

[14] R. G. Gallager, P. A. Humblet, and P. M. Spira. A distributed algorithm for minimum-weight spanning trees. *ACM Transactions on Programming Languages and systems (TOPLAS)*, 5(1):66–77, 1983.

[15] E. Gat and S. Goldwasser. Probabilistic search algorithms with unique answers and their cryptographic applications. In *Electronic Colloquium on Computational Complexity (ECCC)*, volume 18, page 136, 2011.

[16] M. Ghaffari and F. Kuhn. Distributed minimum cut approximation. In *Proc. of the Int'l Symp. on Dist. Comp. (DISC)*, pages 1–15, 2013.

[17] S. Goldwasser. Pseudo-deterministic algorithms. In *STACS'12 (29th Symposium on Theoretical Aspects of Computer Science)*, volume 14, pages 29–29. LIPIcs, 2012.

[18] S. Holzer and R. Wattenhofer. Optimal distributed all pairs shortest paths and applications. In *Proceedings of the 2012 ACM symposium on Principles of distributed computing*, pages 355–364. ACM, 2012.

[19] H. Klauck. A strong direct product theorem for disjointness. In *Proceedings of the forty-second ACM symposium on Theory of computing*, pages 77–86. ACM, 2010.

[20] S. Kutten and D. Peleg. Fast distributed construction of k-dominating sets and applications. In *the Proc. of the Int'l Symp. on Princ. of Dist. Comp. (PODC)*, pages 238–251, 1995.

[21] J. R. Lee and A. Naor. Extending lipschitz functions via random metric partitions. *Inventiones mathematicae*, 160(1):59–95, 2005.

[22] F. T. Leighton, B. M. Maggs, and S. B. Rao. Packet routing and job-shop scheduling in O(congestion+ dilation) steps. *Combinatorica*, 14(2):167–186, 1994.

[23] T. Leighton, B. Maggs, and A. W. Richa. Fast algorithms for finding O(congestion+ dilation) packet routing schedules. *Combinatorica*, 19(3):375–401, 1999.

[24] C. Lenzen and D. Peleg. Efficient distributed source detection with limited bandwidth. In *Proceedings of the 2013 ACM symposium on Principles of distributed computing*, pages 375–382. ACM, 2013.

[25] N. A. Lynch. *Distributed algorithms.* Morgan Kaufmann, 1996.

[26] J. Nešetřil, E. Milková, and H. Nešetřilová. Otakar boruvka on minimum spanning tree problem translation of both the 1926 papers, comments, history. *Discrete Mathematics*, 233(1):3–36, 2001.

[27] R. Ostrovsky and Y. Rabani. Universal O(congestion+ dilation+ $\log^{1+\epsilon} n$) local control packet switching algorithms. In *Proceedings of the twenty-ninth annual ACM symposium on Theory of computing*, pages 644–653. ACM, 1997.

[28] B. Peis and A. Wiese. Universal packet routing with arbitrary bandwidths and transit times. In *Integer Programming and Combinatoral Optimization*, pages 362–375. Springer, 2011.

[29] D. Peleg. *Distributed Computing: A Locality-sensitive Approach.* Society for Industrial and Applied Mathematics, Philadelphia, PA, USA, 2000.

[30] Y. Rabani and É. Tardos. Distributed packet switching in arbitrary networks. In *Proceedings of the twenty-eighth annual ACM symposium on Theory of computing*, pages 366–375. ACM, 1996.

[31] R. Raz. A parallel repetition theorem. *SIAM Journal on Computing*, 27(3):763–803, 1998.

[32] T. Rothvoß. A simpler proof for O(congestion + dilation) packet routing. In *Integer Programming and Combinatorial Optimization*, pages 336–348. Springer, 2013.

[33] C. Scheideler. *Universal routing strategies for interconnection networks*, volume 1390. Springer, 1998.

[34] J. P. Schmidt, A. Siegel, and A. Srinivasan. Chernoff-hoeffding bounds for applications with limited independence. *SIAM Journal on Discrete Mathematics*, 8(2):223–250, 1995.

[35] D. M. Topkis. Concurrent broadcast for information dissemination. *Software Engineering, IEEE Transactions on*, (10):1107–1112, 1985.

[36] A. Wiese. *Packet Routing and Scheduling.* Cuvillier, 2011.

Scheduling Loop-free Network Updates: It's Good to Relax!

Arne Ludwig
TU Berlin, Germany
arne@inet.tu-berlin.de

Jan Marcinkowski
University of Wrocław, Poland
jasiekmarc@gmail.com

Stefan Schmid
T-Labs & TU Berlin, Germany
stefan@inet.tu-berlin.de

ABSTRACT

We consider the problem of updating arbitrary routes in a software-defined network in a (transiently) loop-free manner. We are interested in fast network updates, i.e., in schedules which minimize the number of interactions (i.e., rounds) between the controller and the network nodes. We first prove that this problem is difficult in general: The problem of deciding whether a k-round schedule exists is NP-complete already for $k = 3$, and there are problem instances requiring $\Omega(n)$ rounds, where n is the network size. Given these negative results, we introduce an attractive, relaxed notion of loop-freedom. We prove that $O(\log n)$-round relaxed loop-free schedules always exist, and can also be computed efficiently.

Categories and Subject Descriptors

C.2.4 [**Computer-Communication Networks**]: Distributed Systems; G.2.2 [**Graph Theory**]: Network Problems

Keywords

Software-Defined Networking; Graph Algorithms; Scheduling; NP-hardness

1. INTRODUCTION

Computer networks are currently undergoing a phase transition. The paradigm of Software-Defined Networking (SDN) introduces interesting new flexibilities in terms of traffic-engineering and programmatic network control, by outsourcing and consolidating the control over a set of nodes (switches or routers) to a logically centralized (but potentially distributed) software controller. The controller can define and install arbitrary routes (i.e., forwarding rules) which may not necessarily be shortest paths or based on destination IP addresses only.

However, exploiting the benefits of a more dynamic and logically centralized network management is non-trivial. A fundamental problem regards the consistent implementation of *route updates*: In order to update a route r_1 to a route r_2, the controller needs to communicate the new forwarding rules to all nodes. However, as both the transmission as well as the installation of rules take time and are subject to variance [8], inconsistencies can be introduced during the update: For example, the same packet may still be forwarded according to the old rules (of r_1) at some nodes while it is forwarded already according to the new rules (of r_2) at others. The resulting *actual* routes may transiently violate basic consistency properties such as *loop-freedom* [13].

One possible solution is to use a *2-Phase Commit Protocol (2PC)* and *(packet) tagging* [17]: In a first round, the controller communicates the new rules of r_2 to all nodes. However, the rules only apply to packets with a certain tag (say, "*new*"), and hence existing packets without the *new* tag are still forwarded according to r_1. Once all nodes confirmed the successful installation of the new rules, in a second round, the controller instructs the ingress ports of the network to tag all packets with "*new*", forcing the packets to use the new route r_2. The 2PC protocol ensures a strong *per-packet consistency* [17]: each packet will be forwarded according to r_1 *(exclusive-)*or r_2, and loops are avoided. However, the use of tagging is undesirable, as it consumes header space in the packets and requires the installation of additional forwarding rules (matching the tagged packets), wasting precious switch memory; moreover, tagging can be problematic in the presence of middleboxes which change headers. [3]

An alternative approach to ensure loop-free updates, without tagging, is to communicate updates to nodes in a staged manner: The controller first updates only a *safe subset* of nodes $V_1 \subseteq V$. After these nodes asynchronously installed the new rules, they send an acknowledgement to the controller, which then schedules the next subset $V_2 \subseteq V$ of nodes to update, until the final subset V_k completes the route update. This protocol does not require packet tagging, and, as has been argued in [13], also has the advantage that some of the edges of r_2 become available earlier to packets: there is no need to wait for the full installation of r_2.

1.1 Our Contributions

This paper initiates the study of *fast* loop-free network updates, i.e., updates which require a minimal number of controller interactions while providing transient consistency guarantees. We consider a model where network routes can follow arbitrary paths and are not necessarily destination-based (arguably a key benefit of SDN [4]). We ask: *How many communication rounds k are needed to update a network in a (transiently) loop-free manner?*

Permission to make digital or hard copies of all or part of this work for personal or classroom use is granted without fee provided that copies are not made or distributed for profit or commercial advantage and that copies bear this notice and the full citation on the first page. Copyrights for components of this work owned by others than ACM must be honored. Abstracting with credit is permitted. To copy otherwise, or republish, to post on servers or to redistribute to lists, requires prior specific permission and/or a fee. Request permissions from permissions@acm.org.
PODC'15, July 21–23, 2015, Donostia-San Sebastián, Spain.
Copyright is held by the owner/author(s). Publication rights licensed to ACM.
ACM 978-1-4503-3617-8 /15/07 ...$15.00.
http://dx.doi.org/10.1145/2767386.2767412.

We show that answering this question is difficult. In particular, we show that while deciding whether a k-round schedule exists is trivial for $k = 2$, it is already NP-complete for $k = 3$. Moreover, we show that there exist problem instances which require $\Omega(n)$ rounds, where n is the network size. In the Appendix, we will also show that just aiming to "greedily" update a *maximum* number of nodes in each round (as proposed in previous work [13], however, for a different model) may result in $\Omega(n)$-round schedules in instances which actually can be solved in $O(1)$ rounds; even worse, a *single* greedy round may inherently delay the schedule by a factor of $\Omega(n)$ more rounds.

Given these negative results, we propose an attractive alternative to the utterly strict loop-free requirement: *relaxed loop-freedom*. Relaxed loop-freedom is motivated by the observation that loops are only really problematic if they occur on the (changing) path between source and destination: topological loops in other parts of the network will never receive any new packets. We argue that relaxed loop-freedom not only expresses better the actually desired consistency in practice, but we also show that it comes with interesting benefits: We prove that $O(\log n)$-round relaxed loop-free schedules always exist, and can also be computed efficiently, and we present an elegant algorithm accordingly.

1.2 Organization

The remainder of this paper is organized as follows. Section 2 introduces our formal model. Section 3 studies the strong consistency model for transient loop-freedom, and Section 4 studies relaxed loop-freedom. After reviewing related literature in Section 5, we conclude our work in Section 6.

2. MODEL

We are given a network and two routes r_1 (the *old route*) and r_2 (the *new route*). Both r_1 and r_2 are simple directed paths. Initially, packets are forwarded (using the *old rules*, henceforth also called *old edges*) along r_1, and eventually they should be forwarded according to the new rules of r_2. Packets should never be delayed or dropped at a node: whenever a packet arrives at a node, a matching forwarding rule should be present.

Without loss of generality, we assume that r_1 and r_2 lead from a source s to a destination d. Since nodes appearing only in one or none of the two paths are trivially updatable, we focus on the network G induced by the nodes V which are part of *both* routes r_1 *and* r_2, i.e., $V = \{v : v \in r_1 \wedge v \in r_2\}$. Thus, we can represent the routes as $r_1 = (s = v_1, v_2, \ldots, v_\ell = d)$ and $r_2 = (s = v_1, \pi(v_2), \ldots, \pi(v_{\ell-1}), v_\ell = d)$, for some permutation $\pi : V \setminus \{s,d\} \to V \setminus \{s,d\}$ and some number ℓ. In fact, we can represent routes in an even more compact way: we are actually only concerned about the nodes $U \subseteq V$ which need to be updated. Let, for each node $v \in V$, $out_1(v)$ (resp. $in_1(v)$) denote the outgoing (resp. incoming) edge according to route r_1, and $out_2(v)$ (resp. $in_2(v)$) denote the outgoing (resp. incoming) edge according to route r_2. Moreover, let us extend these definitions for entire node sets S, i.e., $out_i(S) = \bigcup_{v \in S} out_i(v)$, for $i \in \{1,2\}$, and analogously, for in_i. We define s to be the first node (say, on r_1) with $out_1(v) \neq out_2(v)$, and d to be the last node with $in_1(v) \neq in_2(v)$. We are interested in the set of to-be-updated nodes $U = \{v \in V : out_1(v) \neq out_2(v)\}$, and define $n = |U|$. Given this reduction, in the following, we will assume that V only consists of interesting nodes ($U = V$).

2.1 Strong Loop-Freedom

We want to find a *schedule* $U_1, U_2, \ldots, U_k$ with minimum k, i.e., a sequence of subsets $U_t \subseteq U$ where the subsets form a partition of U (i.e., $U = U_1 \uplus U_2 \uplus \ldots \uplus U_k$), with the property that for any round t, given that the updates $U_{t'}$ for $t' < t$ have been made, all updates U_t can be performed "asynchronously", that is, in an arbitrary order without violating loop-freedom. That is, consistent paths will be maintained for any subset of updated nodes, independently of how long individual updates may take.

More formally, let $U_{<t} = \bigcup_{i=1,\ldots,t-1} U_i$ denote the set of nodes which have already been updated before round t, and let $U_{\leq t}$, $U_{>t}$ etc. be defined analogously. Since updates during round t occur asynchronously, an arbitrary subset of nodes $X \subseteq U_t$ may already have been updated while the nodes $\overline{X} = U_t \setminus X$ still use the old rules, resulting in a temporary forwarding graph $G_t(U, X, E_t)$ over nodes U, where $E_t = out_1(U_{>t} \cup \overline{X}) \cup out_2(U_{<t} \cup X)$. We require that the update schedule $U_1, U_2, \ldots, U_k$ fulfills the property that for all t and for any $X \subseteq U_t$, $G_t(U, X, E_t)$ is loop-free.

Later in this paper, we will sometimes refer to this definition of loop-freedom as the *Strong Loop-Freedom* (SLF), to distinguish it from *Relaxed Loop-Freedom* (RLF). By default, throughout this paper, the term loop-freedom without additional qualifier will refer to the strong variant.

Example. Fig. 1 illustrates our model: We are given two routes (the old rules of r_1 are *solid*, the new ones of r_2 are *dashed*), see Fig. 1 (*left*). We focus on the updateable nodes which are shared by the two routes. Thus, in our example, the update problem can be reduced to the 5-node chain graph in Fig. 1 (*right*). Throughout this paper, we will stick to this representation, and will indicate the old route r_1 using *solid lines*, and the new route r_2 using *dashed lines*. Moreover, we will depict the initial network configuration (before the update) such that the old route goes from left to right. In the following we will call an edge (u, v) of the new route r_2 *forward*, if v is closer (with respect to r_1) to the destination, resp. *backward*, if u is closer to the destination. It is also convenient to name nodes after their outgoing dashed edges (e.g., *forward* or *backward*); similarly, it is sometimes convenient to say that we *update an edge* when we update the corresponding node. Finally, we will treat the terms *edge* and *rule*, as synonyms in this paper.

2.2 Weak Loop-Freedom

In this paper, we will also propose a weaker notion of loop-freedom: *Relaxed Loop-Freedom* (RLF). Relaxed loop-freedom is motivated by the practical observation that transient loops are not very harmful if they do not occur between the source s and the destination d. If relaxed loop-freedom is preserved, only a constant number of packets can loop: we will never push new packets into a loop "at line rate". In other words, even if switches acknowledge new updates late (or never), new packets will not enter loops. Concretely, and similar to the definition of SLF, we require the update schedule to fulfill the property that for all rounds t and for any subset X, the temporary forwarding graph $G_t(U, X, E'_t)$ is loop-free. The difference is that we only care about the subset E'_t of E_t consisting of edges *reachable from the source* s.

Example. To highlight the difference between SLF and RLF, Fig. 2 presents an example where a relaxed 3-round loop-free update schedule exists: in round 1 all forward edges are updated, in round 2 all backward edges except for the

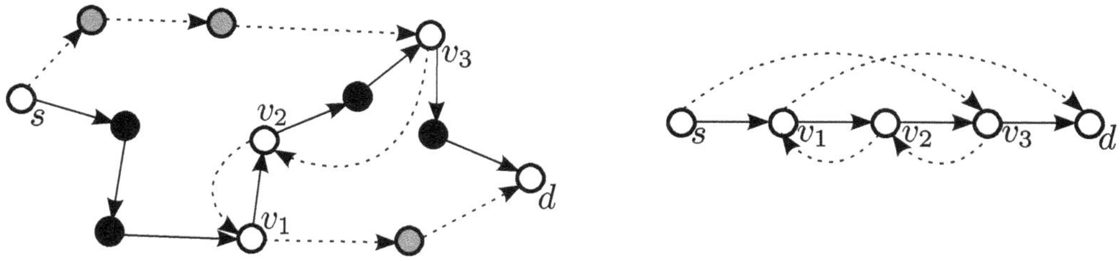

Figure 1: Overview of model and reduction. The network on the *left* is reduced to the line representation on the *right*. The solid lines show the old route r_1 and the dashed lines show the new route r_2. Nodes shown in white are the only ones which are part on both paths, and hence relevant for the problem.

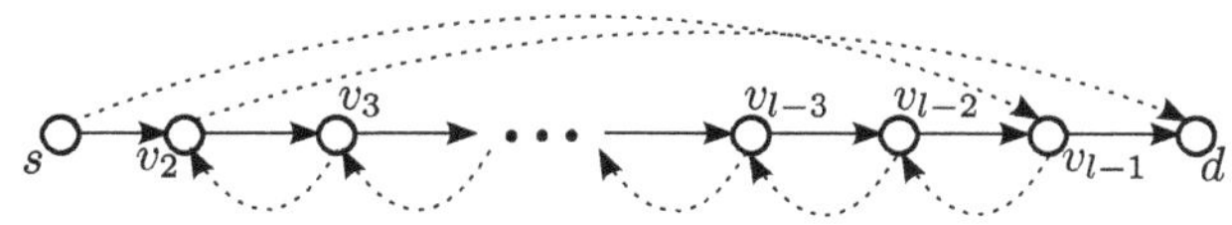

Figure 2: RLF vs SLF: An SLF schedule needs to update backward edges one by one from left to right, requiring $\Omega(n)$ rounds; for RLF, an $O(1)$-round schedule exists.

last one (v_{l-1}, v_{l-2}) are updated, and in round 3, the last backward edge is updated. In contrast, a strong loop-free schedule needs to go through the backward edges one by one, $v_3, v_4, \cdots, v_{l-1}$: updating v_i before v_{i-1} results in a loop. Thus, $n-1$ rounds are required in this case: a factor $\Omega(n)$ more than RLF. This is worst possible.

3. FAST UPDATES ARE DIFFICULT

How many rounds are needed to update a network in a (strongly) loop-free manner? On the one hand, the problem seems difficult: the problem of breaking cycles even in a single round, is related to the well-known NP-hard Feedback Arc Set Problem. On the other hand, our graphs have a very special structure, as they essentially only consist of two simple paths (namely the old and the new route).

In this section, we show that updating networks quickly is difficult, even for such simple graphs: while problem instances allowing for 2-round schedules are trivial (Section 3.1), deciding whether 3-round schedules exist is NP-complete (Section 3.2). Also recall our example from Fig. 2 which shows that there exist problem instances which cannot be updated in less than $\Omega(n)$ rounds. In Appendix A, we will additionally prove that applying a greedy strategy which maximizes the number of node updates *in each round*, can lead—already after one round—to an undesirable configuration from which $\Omega(n)$ rounds are needed to complete the update, although the problem was initially $O(1)$-round solvable.

3.1 2-Round is Easy

Before we show how to find 2-round update schedules efficiently, let us introduce the following edge (resp. node) classification, which will be useful more generally. We already discussed the notion of *forward* and *backward* dashed edges (resp. nodes), indicating whether a dashed edge points in the same direction as the solid edge. This distinction is useful as, for example, it is always safe to update any number of forward-pointing edges: they can never introduce any loops.

However, we can also classify edges from the other side, from the destination and "looking backward in time": as if we were updating edges from the dashed ("new" r_2) rules to the solid ("old" r_1) ones, starting with the last round. Given this backward perspective, we can classify the old (*solid*) rules as *backward* or *forward* relative to the new ones (*dashed*): we just need to draw the new route as a straight path and see, if the old rule points forward or backward.

Based on this classification, we propose two-letter codes to describe the nodes—the first letter will denote, whether the outgoing dashed edge points forward (**F**) or backward (**B**). Similarly, the second letter will describe the solid edge relative to the dashed path. Now, it is easy to see that in the last round, we can update any subset of rules which are either **BF** or **FF**, just like in the first round where we can update any **FB** or **FF**. An example can be seen in Fig. 3 on the left.

Given this intuition, we can determine whether two rounds are sufficient: if there is any **BB** edge, it can neither be updated in the first round, nor in the last, so two rounds are not enough. Otherwise, we update **FB**s in the first round, **BF**s in the second round, and have complete freedom on when to update the **FF** nodes.

3.2 3-Round is Hard

Unfortunately, it is already NP-complete to decide whether a problem instance has a 3-round update schedule.

THEOREM 1. *Deciding whether a $k = 3$-round schedule exists is NP-complete.*

The k-round problem is certainly in NP: the correctness of a schedule can be verified easily. The hardness proof proceeds as follows. First we make a couple of observations which allow us to narrow the ground for choosing 3-round update schedules, reducing the problem to the selection of edge subsets. Second, we will present a slight modification of 3-SAT and—using gadgets—transform it into an instance of the edge selection problem. Finally, the graph built using the gadgets will be patched up to a proper instance of the network update problem (namely, two paths traversing the same set of nodes).

3.2.1 Classifying Nodes

When we aim for three rounds, the **FB** nodes can be updated in the first or second round. As we will observe in the following, it is however never *necessary* to update **FB** nodes in the second round: everything can just as well be done in the first round.

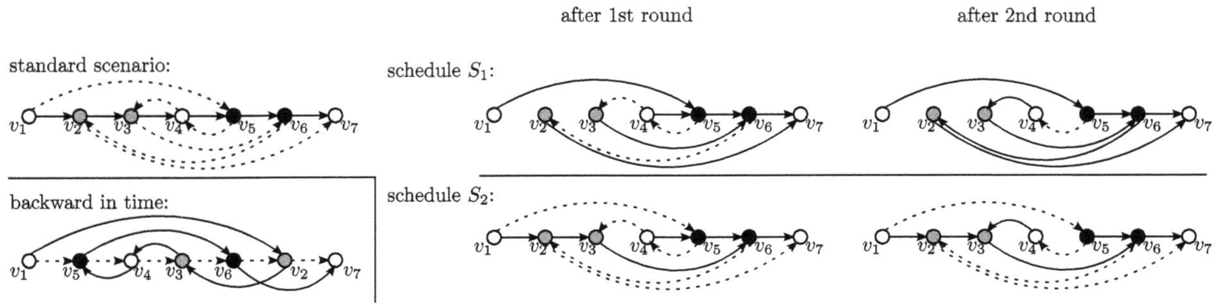

Figure 3: *Left:* "Looking backward in time", an example with reversed update pattern (from *dashed* to *solid* path). We obtain the following classification: v_1 is FF; v_2, v_3 are FB; v_4 is BB and v_5, v_6 are BF. *Right:* Intuition why node updates can be moved from round 2 to round 1 or 3. There are two different valid update schedules for the standard scenario. Schedule S_1 is updating everything as early as possible, e.g., FB node v_2 in round 1 and BF node v_6 in round 2. Schedule S_2 is updating everything as late as possible, e.g., v_2 in round 2 and v_6 in round 3. We depict updated nodes without their outgoing solid edges (no new packets will be sent this way), and dashed edges turn into solid edges.

LEMMA 1. *If there exists a 3-round update schedule* S *which updates any nodes $V' \subseteq V$ of type **FB**, then there is also a 3-round update schedule which updates all nodes of V' in the first round. The same holds true for nodes of type **FF**.*

PROOF. Consider the temporary forwarding graph $G_t(X) = (U, X, E_t)$ during the tth round update of S, for $t \in \{1, 2\}$. Since S is correct, both $G_1(X) = (U, X, E_1)$ and $G_2(X) = (U, X, E_2)$ are loop-free, for any subset $X \subseteq U_t$. By moving updates of forwarding nodes **FB** and **FF** from round 2 to round 1, we will make G_2 only sparser, and will hence not introduce loops. However, also G_1 will remain loop-free, as the forwarding edges **F**· respect the topological order of r_1. □

The same argument also holds in the other direction, using our "backward perspective": We can move **BF** (and **FF**) updates to the last round. Therefore, without loss of generality, we focus our analysis on schedules where all the **BB** nodes are updated in the middle (i.e. second) round, all **FB** nodes in the first round, and all the **BF** nodes in the last round. Thus, the problem boils down to finding a distribution of the **FF** updates to the first and the third round. As we will show in the following, finding such a distribution is NP-hard.

Fig. 3 provides intuition for why **FB** updates can be moved into the first round and **BF** updates in the third round. The right part shows two different 3-round schedules for a given scenario. The **FB** node v_3 needs to be updated in the first round in any valid 3-round schedule, since the only **BB** node v_4 needs to be updated in the second round. Schedule S_2 updates the **FB** node v_2 in round 2 and schedule S_1 shows that it would also be possible to update it in the first round. The **BF** node v_6 is updated in round 2 in S_1 and delayed to round 3 in S_3. According to Lemma 1, there also exists a schedule S_3 updating every **FB** node in the first round and every **BF** node in the third round ($U_1 = \{v_1, v_2, v_3\}, U_2 = \{v_4\}, U_3 = \{v_5, v_6\}$).

In order to be able to update every **BB** node in the second round, one needs to be careful which (of the **FF**) nodes to update in the first and which in the third round. Fig. 4 shows a snippet of a line where the **BB** node v_6 needs to be updated in the second round. An update of **FF** node v_4

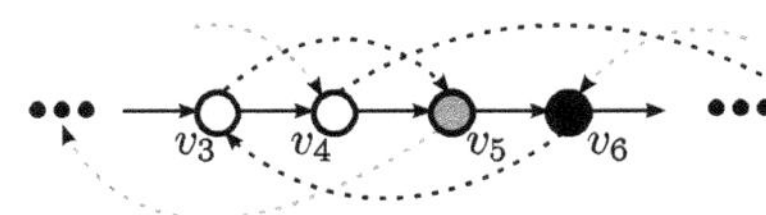

Figure 4: Choosing the right set of FF nodes is important. An update of only v_4 would enable the BB node v_6 to be updated in the second round. An additional update of v_3 would then lead to a loop (note that v_5 will definitely not be updated in the first round).

in the first round would enable this update for the second round, but updating the **FF** node v_3 as well would render an update of v_6 impossible. Node v_5 is **B**· and cannot be updated in the first round, and hence an update of v_6 would result in a loop ($v_3 \to v_5 \to v_6 \to v_3$).

3.2.2 Modifying 3-CNF

For our reduction, we take an instance of the 3-SAT problem, $\mathcal{C}$, which we will eventually transform into an instance of a network update problem that is updatable in 3 rounds, if and only if the formula is satisfiable. However, we will first modify $\mathcal{C}$, using a standard construction, and replace each appearance of a variable in $\mathcal{C}$ using a new variable: concretely, a variable appearing λ times in $\mathcal{C}$ decays into $\lambda + 4$ new variables. By this trick, we will reduce the number of times any (new) variable appears in the (new) formula, allowing us to implement the low in- and out-degree requirements of our network update problem.

We create the following clauses:

1. For every variable x, we create variables

$$x_0, x_1, \dots, x_{p_x}, x_l, \overline{x}_0, \overline{x}_1, \dots, \overline{x}_{n_x}, \overline{x}_l,$$

where p_x is the number of positive appearances of x, and n_x the number of negative appearances. In every clause we replace the literals with the appropriate new variables (from the collections $x_1, \dots, x_{p_x}$ and $\overline{x}_1, \dots, \overline{x}_{n_x}$). Also, for every original variable x we add an "*assignment clause*" $(x_0 \vee \overline{x}_0)$.

2. For every original variable we add "*implication clauses*" $(x_i \to x_{i+1})$ for $i = 0 \dots p_x - 1$ and $(\overline{x}_i \to \overline{x}_{i+1})$ for $i = 0 \dots n_x - 1$; the last implications, for $i = p_x$ resp. $i = n_x$ must lead to x_l and $\overline{x}_l$ respectively ($(x_{p_x} \to x_l)$ and $(\overline{x}_{n_x} \to \overline{x}_l)$).

3. Finally, for every original variable x, we add an "*exclusive clause*" $(\neg x_l \vee \neg \overline{x}_l)$.

For each variable x, with the *assignment clause*, we ensure that at least one literal is true; with the *exclusive clause* we ensure that at most one literal is true; and with the *implication clause*, we ensure that the value is consistently preserved through all clones.

It is straightforward to translate any satisfying assignment of variables of one formula to the other, therefore the satisfiability problem for the new formula is equivalent to the original one. We will refer to the modified formula by $\mathcal{C}'$.

3.2.3 Creating and Connecting the Gadgets

For the reduction, we will create (network) gadgets representing the different clauses. Concretely, first, for every variable x_i in $\mathcal{C}'$, we create a node x_i, which will be of type **FF** (we will refer to the node using the variable's name). The idea is that updating the node in the first round will correspond to the positive valuation of the variable. In general, we will create for each gadget a path of solid edges pointing upward; eventually, we will connect these paths from left to right (using solid edges), to establish route r_1.

Every clause $\mathcal{K}$ is encoded as a gadget in the graph using a separate solid path (drawn as a vertical line pointing upwards) with the variable-related (x_i) **FF** nodes on it. Above those nodes on the path, there is a **BB** node, $v_1^{\mathcal{K}}$, the starting point of a backward, dashed edge that will end just below the variables with a node $v_2^{\mathcal{K}}$ (Fig. 5 *left*). The backward edge and the solid path form a cycle, which needs to be disconnected in the first round. The only way to do this, is by updating at least one of the variable–related edges. Obviously, the dashed, forward edges starting at the **FF** nodes inside the clause must reach outside the clause-related backward edge $(v_1^{\mathcal{K}}, v_2^{\mathcal{K}})$. In fact, they will end just below the nodes representing the variables that are followed in the implications (see Fig. 5 on the *right*), so the dashed edge starting at the node x_i will point to the node x_{i+1} in a gadget representing another clause (actually it points to a special node x_{i+1}^{IN} that serves as a connecting point: we will present the details in the next paragraph; the last x_i will point to x_l situated in the exclusive gadget clause for x, which we describe later). For convenience, we order the clauses from left to right, and name the variables x_i, y_i, and z_i with increasing i from the left to the right according to this order. Thus, every dashed edge connecting two different gadgets points rightwards when it is a forward **F**$\cdot$ edge, and leftwards when it is a backward **B**$\cdot$ edge.

For each implication clause $\mathcal{K} = (x_i \to x_{i+1})$, we already have the nodes representing the two variables x_i and x_{i+1} (lying on two separate solid paths belonging to their respective gadgets) and a dashed edge from the antecedent, x_i, to a new node x_{i+1}^{IN} placed below the consequent one. The gadget (Fig. 5 *right*) assures that if x_i is updated in the first round, then x_{i+1} must be updated as well, or there will be a cycle in the second round $(x_i \to x_{i+1}^{\text{IN}} \to x_{i+1} \to x_{i+1}^{BB} \to x_i^{H} \to x_i^{\text{IN}} \to x_i)$: we draw a new node x_{i+1}^{BB} of type **BB** slightly above x_{i+1} (on its solid path) and a dashed edge pointing from it to

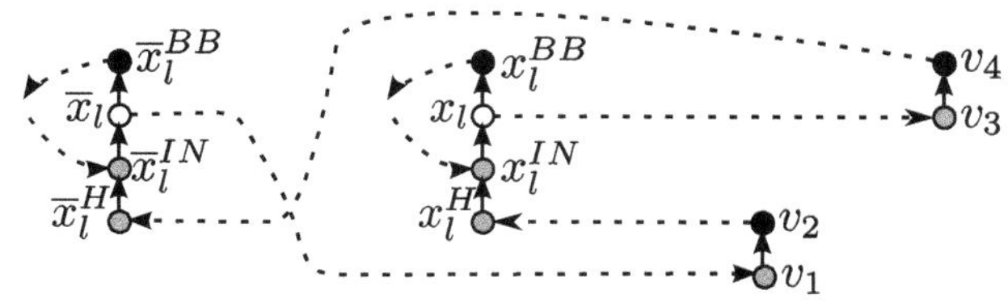

Figure 6: Gadget for exclusive clause. An update of either x_l or $\overline{x}_l$ prevents the other one from being updateable: the BB nodes v_2 and v_4 would form a cycle in the second round.

another new helper node (to meet the in-degree constraint of the network update problem), x_i^H, slightly below x_i (in the figure we draw it below x_i^{IN} as well).

Then for every exclusive clause $\mathcal{K}_x = (\neg x_l \vee \neg \overline{x}_l)$ (shown in Fig. 6), we draw four solid paths. On the first, the **FF** node $\overline{x}_l$ is drawn and a dashed edge pointing from it to another helper node v_1 lying on the third solid path. Similarly, x_l on the second path points, with its forward dashed edge, towards v_3, which we place as the last of the four solid paths. Above v_1 and v_3 we draw another pair of **BB** nodes, v_2 and v_4 respectively. Then v_2 points back to the second solid path with its backward dashed edge, to another new node, x_l^H placed just below x_l on the first path. In the same manner, the backward edge starting at v_4 ends with $\overline{x}_l^H$ below $\overline{x}_l$. This way, updating both x_l and $\overline{x}_l$ in the first round will result in a cycle in the second round, since, as we know, all **BB**s *must* be updated in the second round. The cycle which can exist in the second round includes the following nodes $\overline{x}_l, v_1, v_2, x_l^H, x_l^{\text{IN}}, x_l, v_3, v_4, \overline{x}_l^H, \overline{x}_l^{\text{IN}}, \overline{x}_l$. x_l and $\overline{x}_l$ have been updated in the first round, the nodes v_2 and v_4 have been updated in the second round and the rest of the nodes in the cycle (the grey nodes) have not been updated yet. It will be later assured that they are of type **B**$\cdot$ and therefore cannot be updated in the first round, hence making a scenario possible where they are delayed until the end of the second round. Therefore an update of both x_l and $\overline{x}_l$ is not possible in the first round.

While the composition of gadgets described so far is not yet a proper instance of a network update problem, we can already make some observations about the graph.

THEOREM 2. *If setting $V_{\mathcal{T}} \subset Var(\mathcal{C}')$ to* **true** *satisfies the formula, then there is no cycle ($\Rightarrow$). Moreover, a cycle-free update schedule gives us a satisfying variable assignment ($\Leftarrow$).*

PROOF. We prove the two directions $\Rightarrow$ and $\Leftarrow$ in turn.

$\Rightarrow$: Cycles are composed of: dashed edges starting at $V_{\mathcal{T}}$ nodes, solid edges starting at any other nodes to get somewhere, and any edges starting at **BB** nodes to get back. We will show that by following an arbitrary path consisting only of the listed edge types, we will never return to the starting point of the path. If the path ever chooses to take an **FF** updated dashed edge (starting at x_i), it will need to continue with edges starting at x_{i+1} up to x_l (this is ensured by the implications), and there is no way back from there: it cannot constitute a cycle. Conversely, a path which does not take any **FF** dashed edges would not be able to jump from one of the solid, vertical paths to another one more to the right, so if it returns to the starting point, it must use nodes lying on one of the solid paths. At the same time, a cycle on

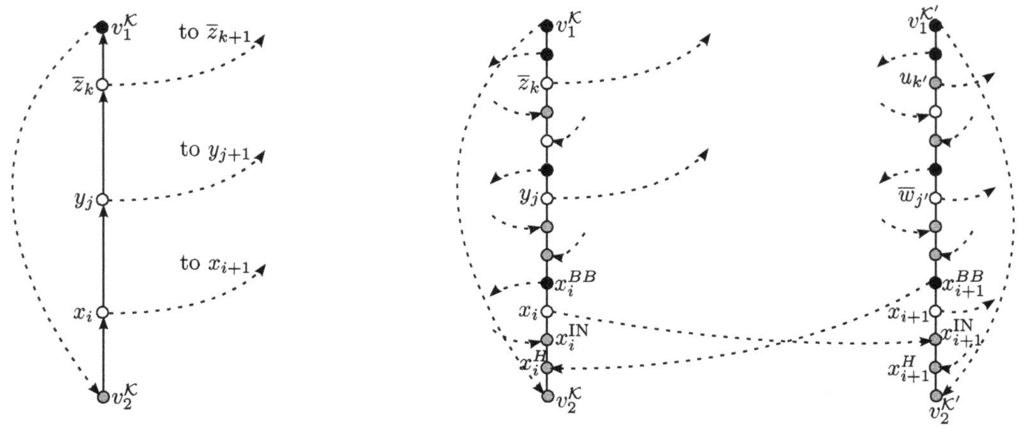

Figure 5: *Left:* Gadget for clause $x_i \vee y_j \vee \overline{z}_k$. At least one node needs to be updated to prevent the loop over $v_1^{\mathcal{K}}$ and $v_2^{\mathcal{K}}$. *Right:* More details about the gadget including also the implication clause $x_i \to x_{i+1}$ representation, and a second clause $x_{i+1} \vee \overline{w}_{j'} \vee u_{k'}$. It is assured that x_{i+1} is updated if x_1 is updated, otherwise the BB edge from x_{i+1}^{BB} would form a cycle. White nodes will eventually be FF, black nodes BB. The grey nodes will later be assured to be of type B·, to guarantee that they cannot be updated in the first round.

one of the solid paths would mean that one of the clauses is not satisfied, which contradicts the definition of $V_{\mathcal{T}}$.

$\Leftarrow$: Clearly, the construction assures that if the formula $\mathcal{C}'$ is not satisfiable, when we have a selection of **FF** nodes which make the situation with *all* **BB** edges (which must be updated) acyclic then each clause must be true: it contains a true variable showing a path out of the cycle. ☐

3.2.4 Connecting the Pieces

The presented gadgets leave us with a number of independent solid paths and many dashed edges starting at nodes of particular types (**FF** or **BB**). In order for the network to represent a valid problem instance, we need to connect the solid paths as well as the dashed paths. Our goal is to connect the solid path from left to right (and vertical lines are from bottom to top). The dashed path will be more complicated.

Let us first focus on connecting the *dashed* edges to a path. From the endpoint of each dashed edge, we will draw a backward dashed edge to a completely new node (one for each) placed far left from our solid paths. Hence, all nodes in R — the set of new nodes — will appear earlier in the concluding solid path: edges pointing to R are backward, edges pointing away from R forward. Then we connect all the resulting 2-length dashed paths (including the previously constructed dashed ones, and the new ones pointing to R), using forward dashed edges starting at the new nodes, as described in the following.

Some of the nodes in our gadgets were of type **BB** while the others were **FF**. Recall, that these type-properties are fairly local: we only need to look at the next node on the solid path and determine if it is preceding on the dashed path. To preserve the types of the nodes, we must therefore connect the 2-length paths in a correct order — first come the **FF** dashed edges, then the clause-related downward-pointing **BB** edges and in the end implication-related horizontal **BB** edges. In each of these groups the edges starting more to the left should precede those more to the right. Also – to ensure, that all the type assignment clause-related edges indeed start with a **BB** node – above each of those nodes $v_1^{\mathcal{C}}$, in their respective gadgets, we draw a new node $v_b^{\mathcal{C}}$. On each of the four solid paths used in the gadgets for the exclusive clauses $\mathcal{K}_x$, we do the same: we create nodes $v_{b\ 1}^{\mathcal{K}_x}, \ldots, v_{b\ 4}^{\mathcal{K}_x}$. Then we connect all the v_b's into a dashed path going from right to left. The path must be connected to the beginning of the dashed path we composed before, which will ensure the **BB** property of the previous nodes: the solid edge now points backwards relative to the dashed path. Each of the new $v_b^{\mathcal{C}}$ nodes will be of type **BF**. The nodes in R are ordered so that the dashed path ends at the leftmost node.

The nodes of R are positioned in a row, followed by our vertical solid paths. We draw a new node above each of them, connect it with a solid edge and connect the new node with what is next in the row, from the top of a vertical path to the bottom of the next one (Fig. 7). This way, we finally have one solid path. The new nodes are connected by a chain of forward dashed edges (so they can all be updated). In the end we add a starting node, which points with the solid edge to the leftmost R node, and with the dashed edge to the beginning of the dashed path which is the beginning of the path we constructed to ensure the **BB** properties (this point is **BF**).

It is important to note that in the last steps we have not jeopardized the reduction by introducing disconnections of the gadget-**BB** edges, nor have we created any loops that cannot be easily broken (by updating all the empty nodes in Fig. 7). Therefore, the possibility of making the second round cycle-free in our instance is still equivalent to the satisfiability of $\mathcal{C}'$, which makes the 3-round network update problem NP-hard.

4. RELAXED LOOP-FREE UPDATES ARE TRACTABLE

Given the potentially large number of rounds required to update a network in a strongly loop-free manner, we now propose to relax loop-freedom to only include *actually used paths*, between source and destination. We believe that this is an attractive alternative: although some unlucky packets currently on transit on an edge may end up in a (temporary)

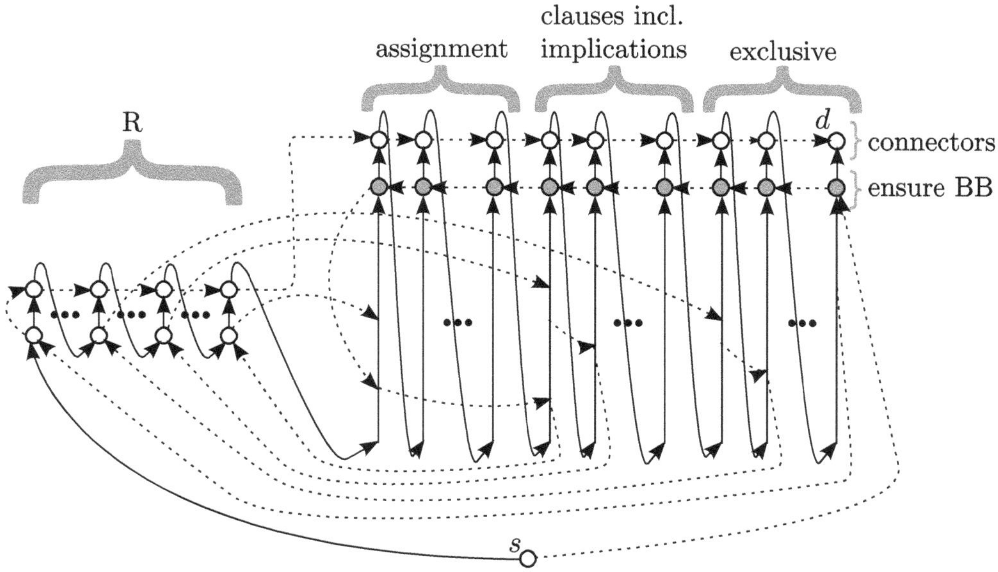

Figure 7: Overview of how the path is connected. The grey nodes are used to connect everything into one solid path. They also join the dashed path at the last nodes. This way, all nodes in R (*white cycles*) are of type FF.

Algorithm 1 *Peacock*

Input: initial network G_0, set of to-be-updated nodes U
Output: (relaxed) loop-free schedule $(U_1, U_2, \ldots, U_k)$

$G \leftarrow G_0$, $t \leftarrow 0$, for all t: $U_t \leftarrow \emptyset$
while (G contains more than one node) **do**
  $t{+}{+}$
  $X \leftarrow U \setminus U_{<t}$
  if (t *odd*) **then**
    sort dashed forward edges in $out_2(X)$
    for $u \in X$, starting with max forward distance **do**
      if $(\nexists v \in U_t$ s.t. $(v < u < out_2(v)) \vee (v < out_2(u) < out_2(v)))$ **then**
        add u to U_t
  else
    add to U_t all nodes not on the path from s to d
return $(U_1, U_2, \ldots, U_t)$

loop, we will never route any packets entering the network at the source into a loop. Moreover, as we will see, relaxing the loop-freedom is also attractive because it enables fast and computationally tractable updates. (Recall also the example in Fig. 2 which permitted a 3-round solution for RLF while SLF required $n-1$ rounds.) In particular, we will present a fast and elegant algorithm which never requires more than $O(\log n)$ rounds: a potentially large gain given the $\Omega(n)$ lower bound for stronger models.

Before presenting the algorithm in detail, let us introduce some concepts. During its execution, our algorithm will repeatedly perform *node merging*: when updating a node v, we will merge it with the node $out_2(v)$ it pointed to with its dashed edge. This can safely be done after each round, due to the irrelevance of already updated nodes (they will simply forward packets to the next node, without influencing the remaining problem at hand). As we will see, while the initial network configuration consists of two paths, in later rounds, the already updated solid edges may no longer form a line from left to right, but rather an arbitrary directed tree, with tree edges directed towards the destination d; due to the node merging, the in-degree (from the solid edges) may also increase, while the out-degree and in-degree from the dashed edges remains one. We will use the terms *forward* and *backward* also in the context of the tree: they are defined with respect to the direction of the tree root. However, there also emerges a third kind of edges: *horizontal edges* in-between two different branches of the tree. Moreover, note that while the destination d will always be the root of the tree, the source s does not necessarily have to be at the leaf all the time (due to merging).

The proposed algorithm *Peacock*[1] is based on repeated node merging, and hence *tree shrinking*: starting from the line, it constructs various trees of decreasing sizes, until only a single node is left. At this point, the update is complete and the algorithm terminates. As we will see, *Peacock* manages to decrease the remaining network size by at least a constant factor, for each *pair of consecutive rounds*, resulting in the $O(\log n)$-round upper bound.

Concretely, *Peacock* toggles between two simple strategies:

1. **Shortcut:** In odd rounds (i.e., in the 1st, 3rd, etc. round), *Peacock* tries to reduce the distance between source s and destination d as much as possible, by updating a disjoint set of "far-reaching" (dashed) forward edges: we define the *distance* of a dashed edge as the number of solid edges it skips on the current path from s to d. The idea is that by updating these far-reaching edges, we obtain a tree with many branches (of which only one contains the s-d path).

2. **Prune (and re-establish line):** In the even rounds (i.e., in the 2nd, 4th, etc. round), *Peacock* updates all

[1] The name of the algorithm is due to its branch resp. "feather" spreading strategy.

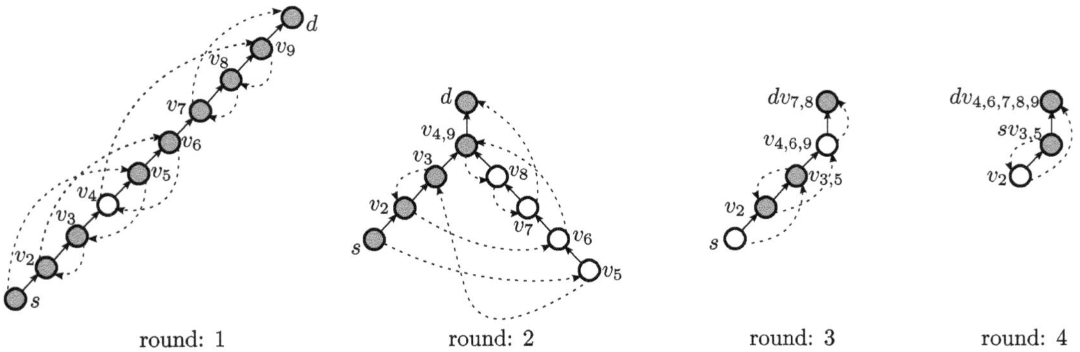

Figure 8: Example execution of *Peacock*. Updated nodes are shown in white. The initial network is a line (on the *left*). An update of the node with the largest distance v_4 and the merging of v_4 and v_9 leads to a tree shown for round 2. Here the nodes $v_5 - v_8$ can be updated since they are not on the $s-d$ path. This results in a line again, shown for round 3. In round 4, v_2 will be updated before the last node, which will be updated in round 5.

nodes which are not on the current path from s to d. Since in the preceding odd round we shortened the length of the path from s to d, we can now update a significant number of nodes (namely a constant fraction of the still to-be-updated ones), and due to the subsequent merging operation, the resulting network size is significantly reduced. Intriguingly, the even round, after pruning and merging nodes, will always result in a simple line network again. Based on this line, we can easily determine the next set of far-reaching updatable edges again, enabling a subsequent "productive" even round.

Algorithm 1 gives the formal listing for *Peacock* and Fig. 8 illustrates an example. In the first round there is only one node (v_4) updated. *Peacock* is in the **Shortcut** phase and updates the "far reaching" edges. Once it adds node v_4 there is no other dashed forward edge remaining which is not interfering with the update of v_4. Hence *Peacock* switches to the **Prune** phase in round 2 and updates every node which is not on the $s-d$ path (v_5, v_6, v_7, v_8). *Peacock* then uses the **Shortcut** strategy again in round 3.

THEOREM 3. Peacock *solves any problem instance in* $O(\log n)$ *rounds.*

PROOF. We will make use of two helper lemmas, one targeting odd rounds (the extent to which the distance from s to d can be shortened) and one targeting even rounds (the number of nodes which can be pruned to produce a smaller resulting tree). We will see that after each pair of a consecutive odd and even round, only a constant fraction of nodes is left due to merging.

LEMMA 2. *In each odd round,* Peacock *reduces the number of nodes on the solid path from s to d by $n_t/3$, where n_t is the number of nodes on the path.*

PROOF. *Peacock* orders the nodes in decreasing order of distance, i.e., the number of solid edges they bridge. Including a node v (and its dashed edge), may block other nodes (resp. their intervals) from being scheduled in this round. However, due to the descending distance order, the set of blocked dashed edges span at most twice the distance from v to $out_2(v)$ on the current path: since we choose a maximal distance edge (say of distance x), edges entering or exiting the corresponding interval may block at most an additional distance of $2x$. Assuming that these distances cannot be covered by any other updates, *Peacock* loses at most twice the distance which it covered. This leaves, in the worst case, at most $2n_t/3$ nodes on the path from s to d. □

LEMMA 3. Peacock *can simultaneously update all nodes which are not on the path from s to d. The subsequent merge operation, re-establishes the line topology. .*

PROOF. First, we observe that by updating these nodes, we cannot introduce any loop, since we do not touch any outgoing dashed edges. Dashed edges, at any time, must form a simple path. Each branch which is currently not on the s-d path will therefore point with at least one new rule to the s-d branch. All nodes of the branch can hence be merged with the respective nodes of the new rules on the s-d branch: a line topology. Also note that the source s does not necessarily have to be at the leaf of a tree. But also in this case, it is possible to update everything on the branch below s. Imagine a node u' which is not on the (solid $s-d$) path. Due to *node merging*, this node will be merged with $out(u')$, which itself is now either part of the $s-d$ path, or will be updated together with another node. Thus, we will successively merge nodes until a node (necessarily) lies on the $s-d$ path and will not be updated. This leads to a line with s as a leaf. □

Lemma 2 shows that *Peacock* reduces the number of nodes on the s-d path by $n_r/3$ if the underlying network is a line. All of these nodes are not part of the s-d path in the next round, and on different branches. This shows that an update of these nodes is possible in even rounds without introducing a (relaxed) loop. Since, according to Lemma 3, an update of every node but those on the s-d path leads to a line again, we have shown that the number of remaining nodes is reduced by a third every second round. The number of rounds is hence logarithmic. □

5. RELATED WORK

Our work is motivated by the SDN paradigm, and especially its traffic engineering flexibilities and its support for a programmatic, dynamic, yet formally verifiable network management. [6] Indeed, a more flexible traffic engineering, that is, selection of forwarding routes, is considered one of the main motivations for SDN, and has been studied intensively over the last years. [4, 7] Our paper is orthogonal to this line of research, in the sense that in our model, the routes are *given* and can be arbitrary.

The problem of updating [1, 8, 11, 12, 13, 17], synthesizing [15] and checking [9] policies [16] as well as routes [2] has also been studied intensively. In their seminal work, Reitblatt et al. [17] initiated the study of network updates providing strong, per-packet consistency guarantees, and the authors also presented a 2-phase commit protocol. This protocol also forms the basis of the distributed control plane implementation in [1].

Mahajan and Wattenhofer [13] started investigating weaker transient consistency properties—in particular also (strong) loop-freedom—for destination-based routing policies. Mahajan and Wattenhofer proposed an algorithm to "greedily" select a maximum number of edges which can be used early during the route installation process. Our work builds upon [13], but focuses on an alternative, round-based model to measure policy installation times, and also shows that a greedy strategy can lead to a large number of communication rounds—an observation which has also been made in [12]. The measurement studies in [8] and [10] provide empirical evidence for the non-negligible time and high variance of switch updates, further motivating our work.

Researchers have also started investigating consistent updates for networks which include (network function virtualized) middleboxes [14]. Ludwig et al. presented update protocols which maintain security critical properties such as waypoint enforcement via a firewall, in a transiently consistent manner; the authors also showed that the loop-freedom and waypoint enforcement properties may even conflict. A different standpoint is promoted by Ghorbani and Godfrey in their work [5]: the authors argue that in the context of network function virtualization, not weaker but rather stronger consistency properties are required.

6. CONCLUSION

We believe that our work opens interesting questions for future research. Most importantly, it would be interesting to derive $\omega(1)$-round lower bounds, or show that $O(1)$-round schedules for relaxed loop-free problems always exist. Our computational experiments (using mixed integer programs) indicate that larger problem instances require more rounds. So far, the worst problem instance (consisting of 1,000 nodes) we found requires 7 rounds.

Acknowledgments

We would like to thank Matthias Rost for conducting computational experiments which provided us with valuable insights into the structure of optimal schedules, and the anonymous reviewers for their detailed feedback which helped us to improve the presentation of this paper. This research was supported by the EU project UNIFY as well as by the German BMBF Software Campus grant 01IS12056.

7. REFERENCES

[1] M. Canini, P. Kuznetsov, D. Levin, and S. Schmid. A distributed and robust sdn control plane for transactional network updates. In *Proc. 34th IEEE Conference on Computer Communications (INFOCOM)*, 2015.

[2] M. Casado, M. J. Freedman, J. Pettit, J. Luo, N. McKeown, and S. Shenker. Ethane: Taking control of the enterprise. In *Proc. ACM SIGCOMM*, 2007.

[3] S. K. Fayazbakhsh, V. Sekar, M. Yu, and J. C. Mogul. Flowtags: Enforcing network-wide policies in the presence of dynamic middlebox actions. In *Proc. ACM SIGCOMM HotSDN*, 2013.

[4] N. Feamster, J. Rexford, and E. Zegura. The road to sdn. *Queue*, 11(12):20:20–20:40, 2013.

[5] S. Ghorbani and B. Godfrey. Towards correct network virtualization. In *Proc. ACM HotSDN*, pages 109–114, 2014.

[6] A. Greenberg, G. Hjalmtysson, D. A. Maltz, A. Myers, J. Rexford, G. Xie, H. Yan, J. Zhan, and H. Zhang. A clean slate 4d approach to network control and management. *SIGCOMM Comput. Commun. Rev.*, 35(5):41–54, 2005.

[7] A. Gupta, L. Vanbever, M. Shahbaz, S. P. Donovan, B. Schlinker, N. Feamster, J. Rexford, S. Shenker, R. Clark, and E. Katz-Bassett. Sdx: A software defined internet exchange. In *Proc. ACM SIGCOMM*, pages 551–562, 2014.

[8] X. Jin, H. Liu, R. Gandhi, S. Kandula, R. Mahajan, J. Rexford, R. Wattenhofer, and M. Zhang. Dionysus: Dynamic Scheduling of Network Updates. In *Annual Conference of the ACM Special Interest Group on Data Communication (SIGCOMM), Chicago, Illinois, USA*, August 2014.

[9] P. Kazemian, M. Chang, H. Zeng, G. Varghese, N. McKeown, and S. Whyte. Real time network policy checking using header space analysis. In *Proc. 10th USENIX Conference on Networked Systems Design and Implementation (NSDI)*, pages 99–112, 2013.

[10] M. Kuzniar, P. Peresini, and D. Kostic. What you need to know about sdn flow tables. In *Proc. Passive and Active Measurements Conference (PAM)*, 2015.

[11] H. H. Liu, X. Wu, M. Zhang, L. Yuan, R. Wattenhofer, and D. A. Maltz. zUpdate: Updating Data Center Networks with Zero Loss. In *Annual Conference of the ACM Special Interest Group on Data Communication (SIGCOMM), Hong Kong*, August 2013.

[12] A. Ludwig, M. Rost, D. Foucard, and S. Schmid. Good network updates for bad packets: Waypoint enforcement beyond destination-based routing policies. In *Proc. ACM Workshop on Hot Topics in Networks (HotNets)*, 2014.

[13] R. Mahajan and R. Wattenhofer. On Consistent Updates in Software Defined Networks. In *Proc. 12th ACM Workshop on Hot Topics in Networks (HotNets)*, 2013.

[14] J. Martins, M. Ahmed, C. Raiciu, V. Olteanu, M. Honda, R. Bifulco, and F. Huici. Clickos and the art of network function virtualization. In *Proc. 11th USENIX Symposium on Networked Systems Design and Implementation (NSDI)*, pages 459–473, 2014.

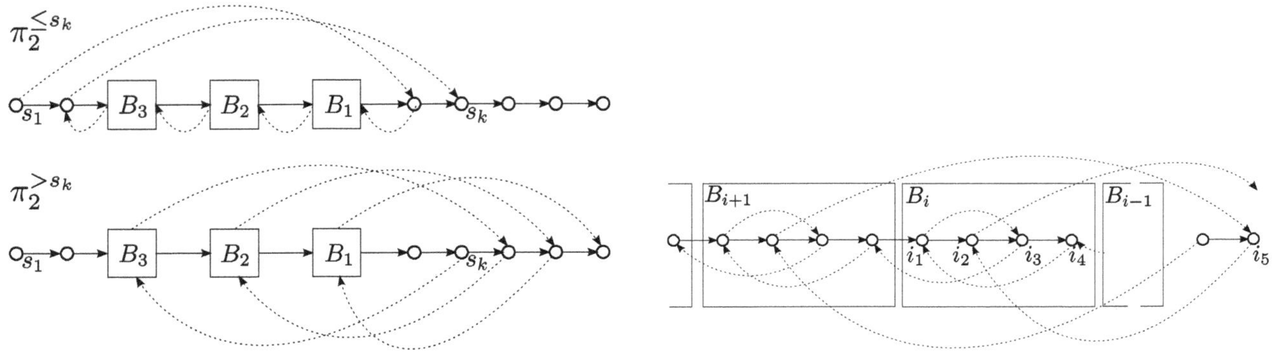

Figure 9: Pattern of a scenario where maximizing the number of updates per round will result in a $\Omega(n)$-round schedule, although a $O(1)$-round schedule would be possible. *Left:* An overview where $\pi_2^{\leq s_k}$ shows the edges of the new route before s_k and $\pi_2^{> s_k}$ those behind s_k. *Right:* A detailed representation of the blocks B_i.

[15] J. McClurg, H. Hojjat, P. Cerny, and N. Foster. Efficient synthesis of network updates. In *Proc. ACM SIGPLAN Conference on Programming Language Design and Implementation (PLDI)*, 2015.

[16] C. Monsanto, J. Reich, N. Foster, J. Rexford, and D. Walker. Composing Software Defined Networks. In *Proc. NSDI*, 2013.

[17] M. Reitblatt, N. Foster, J. Rexford, C. Schlesinger, and D. Walker. Abstractions for network update. In *Proc. ACM SIGCOMM*, pages 323–334, 2012.

APPENDIX

A. IT'S BAD BEING GREEDY

Given the NP-hardness result of Theorem 1, one may wonder whether simple approximation algorithms exist. While we cannot prove the opposite, we conjecture that the problem is generally hard to approximate. To give some intuition, in the following, we show that a "greedy" approach which tries to maximize the number of updatable edges in each round (essentially the model studied in [13]) can fail miserably. In fact, a single greedy round may unrevokably change the required number of rounds from $O(1)$ to $\Omega(n)$.

Fig. 9 shows a scenario where a greedy update takes $\Omega(n)$ rounds even though an $O(1)$ round solution exists. The left side shows the general structure of the scenario which consists of several blocks B_i (more details on the right side). These blocks are connected via backward edges one by one, e.g., see the edge emerging from i_3. If a greedy algorithm picks all forward edges to be updated in a first round, it will include the nodes i_1 and i_2 as well as their representatives in the other blocks. The update of the i_1-type nodes essentially leads to a situation reminiscent of the one shown in Fig. 2, where many backward rules must be updated one after the other. Delaying the i_1-type nodes on the other hand will make it possible to update most of the backward edges in the next round, since the cycle is broken by the edges outgoing from the i_2-type nodes. This allows for an update in 4 rounds, independent of n. In case of the greedy algorithm, each additional block will increase the number of rounds by two. Each block consists of 4 nodes within the block and an additional node for connectivity to the right part of the line, resulting in $2n/5$ rounds: up to $n/10$ additional rounds are required.

New Routing Techniques and their Applications

Liam Roditty
Department of Computer Science
Bar Ilan University
Ramat Gan, Israel
liam.roditty@biu.ac.il

Roei Tov
Department of Computer Science
Bar Ilan University
Ramat Gan, Israel
roei81@gmail.com

ABSTRACT

In this paper we present two new routing techniques that allow us to obtain the following new routing schemes:

- A routing scheme for n-nodes, m-edges unweighted graphs that uses $\tilde{O}(\frac{1}{\varepsilon}n^{2/3})$ space at each vertex and $\tilde{O}(1/\varepsilon)$-bit headers, to route a message between any pair of vertices $u, v \in V$ on a $(2+\varepsilon, 1)$-stretch path, i.e., a path of length at most $(2+\varepsilon)\cdot d+1$, where d is the distance between u and v. This should be compared to the $(2,1)$-stretch and $\tilde{O}(n^{5/3})$ space distance oracle of Pătraşcu and Roditty [FOCS'10 and SIAM J. Comput. 2014] and to the $(2,1)$-stretch routing scheme of Abraham and Gavoille [DISC'11] that uses $\tilde{O}(n^{3/4})$ space at each vertex. It follows from Pătraşcu, Thorup and Roditty [FOCS'12] that a 2-stretch distance oracle with $\tilde{O}(m^{2/3})$ space at each vertex is optimal, assuming a hardness conjecture on set intersection holds.
- A routing scheme for n-nodes weighted graphs with normalized diameter D, that uses $\tilde{O}(\frac{1}{\varepsilon}n^{1/3}\log D)$ space at each vertex and $\tilde{O}(\frac{1}{\varepsilon}\log D)$-bit headers, to route a message between any pair of vertices on a $(5+\varepsilon)$-stretch path. This should be compared to the 5-stretch and $\tilde{O}(n^{4/3})$ space distance oracle of Thorup and Zwick [STOC'01 and J. ACM. 2005] and to the 7-stretch routing scheme of Thorup and Zwick [SPAA'01] that uses $\tilde{O}(n^{1/3})$ space at each vertex. Since a 5-stretch routing scheme must use tables of $\Omega(n^{1/3})$ space our result is almost tight.
- For an integer $\ell > 1$, a routing scheme for n-nodes unweighted graphs that uses $\tilde{O}(\ell\frac{1}{\varepsilon}n^{\ell/(2\ell\pm1)})$ space at each vertex and $\tilde{O}(\frac{1}{\varepsilon})$-bit headers, to route a message between any pair of vertices on a $(3\pm 2/\ell+\varepsilon, 2)$-stretch path. This should be compared to the distance oracles of Pătraşcu, Thorup and Roditty [FOCS'12] for weighted graphs with a stretch of $(3\pm 2/\ell)$ and $\tilde{O}(\ell m^{1+\ell/(2\ell\pm1)})$ total space.
- A routing scheme for n-nodes weighted graphs, that for any integer $k > 2$, uses $\tilde{O}(\frac{1}{\varepsilon}n^{1/k}\log D)$ space at each vertex and $\tilde{O}(\frac{1}{\varepsilon}\log D)$-bit headers, to route a message between any pair of vertices on a $(4k-7+\varepsilon)$-stretch path. This improves the $(4k-5)$-stretch routing scheme of Thorup and Zwick [SPAA'01] and can also be used in the recent $((4-\alpha)k-\beta)$-stretch routing scheme of Chechik [PODC'13] to obtain slightly better values for α and β.

Permission to make digital or hard copies of all or part of this work for personal or classroom use is granted without fee provided that copies are not made or distributed for profit or commercial advantage and that copies bear this notice and the full citation on the first page. Copyrights for components of this work owned by others than ACM must be honored. Abstracting with credit is permitted. To copy otherwise, or republish, to post on servers or to redistribute to lists, requires prior specific permission and/or a fee. Request permissions from permissions@acm.org.
PODC'15, July 21–23, 2015, Donostia-San Sebastián, Spain.
Copyright © 2015 ACM 978-1-4503-3617-8 /15/07 ...$15.00.
DOI: http://dx.doi.org/10.1145/2767386.2767409.

Categories and Subject Descriptors

G.2 [**Discrete Mathematics Graph Theory**]: Network problems; Graph algorithms

Keywords

Compact routing schemes

1. INTRODUCTION

Spanners, *distance oracles* and *compact routing schemes* are fundamental notions in graph theory, data structures and distributed algorithms, respectively, that deal with the natural tradeoff between space and accuracy.

Peleg and Ullman [18] and Peleg and Schäffer [17] introduced the notion of graph spanners. Let $G = (V, E)$ be an n-nodes m-edges undirected graph. For $u, v \in V$, let $d(u, v)$ be the length of a shortest path between u and v. A path between u and v is of (α, β)-stretch if its length is at most $\alpha\cdot d(u, v)+\beta$. For $(\alpha, 0)$-stretch we write α-stretch. A graph $H = (V, E')$, where $E' \subseteq E$, is an (α, β)-stretch spanner of G, if and only if, for every $u, v \in V$ there is an (α, β)-stretch path between u and v in H. It is known how to efficiently construct a $(2k-1)$-spanner of size $\tilde{O}(n^{1+1/k})$ [5, 9], and this size-stretch tradeoff is tight assuming the *girth* conjecture of Erdős [14] holds.

Thorup and Zwick [24] introduced the notion of distance oracles. They showed that it is possible to preprocess a weighted undirected graph in $O(mn^{1/k})$ expected time and create a data structure of size $O(n^{1+1/k})$ that can answer distance queries with a $(2k-1)$-stretch between any two vertices in $O(k)$ time. For $k = 1$ this gives the trivial solution of exact distances with $O(n^2)$ space. For $k = 2$, this gives a 3-stretch distance oracle with $O(n^{3/2})$ space. Pătraşcu and Roditty [20] showed that there is another distance oracle between these two solutions. They presented a $(2, 1)$-stretch distance oracle with $\tilde{O}(n^{5/3})$ space. Pătraşcu, Thorup and Roditty [21] generalized this and showed that for every $\ell \geq 1$, there is a $(3-2/\ell)$-stretch distance oracle with $\tilde{O}(\ell m^{1+\ell/(2\ell-1)})$.

The notion of compact routing schemes was firstly considered in the 80's (e.g. [19, 22]). Awerbuch, Bar-Noy, Linial and Peleg [7] were the first to distinguish between *labeled* routing schemes and *name independent* routing schemes. In compact routing schemes there is a preprocessing phase in which a centralized algorithm computes routing tables. In *labeled* routing schemes a short label is assigned to each vertex. After the preprocessing phase ends, messages with an additional short header can be routed between the vertices of the graph in a distributed manner. More specifically, when a message to destination v reaches a vertex $u \neq v$, the routing scheme algorithm executed at u decides locally, based on the routing table of u, the message header and the label of v on which link to forward the message. For an integer $k > 1$, Thorup and Zwick [23] presented a $(4k-5)$-stretch labeled compact routing scheme with routing tables of size $\tilde{O}(n^{1/k})$-bit at each vertex, $o(k \log^2 n)$-bit labels and $o(\log^2 n)$-bit headers.

In a sense, finding a good spanner is easier than finding a good distance oracle since a distance oracle has to support efficient distance queries between any pair of vertices. Obtaining a routing scheme is, in some sense, harder than obtaining a distance oracle since decisions are made locally at a vertex based on a fraction of the whole information, while in distance oracles the whole information is always available.

Therefore, a general open problem is given a (α, β)-stretch S-space distance oracle can we also obtain a (α, β)-stretch routing scheme with $O(S/n)$-space routing tables? When posing this question for spanners and routing schemes a real gap exists: while there exists, for general graphs, a constant additive-stretch spanner with a size of $O(n^{4/3})$, it is followed from Gavoille and Sommer [16] that a routing scheme that uses a tables of $O(n^{1/3})$ requires an additive-stretch of $\tilde{\Omega}(n^{1/3})$. Both spanners and distance oracles have the same general tradeoff of $(2k-1)$-stretch and $O(n^{1+1/k})$-space which is optimal under the girth conjecture. An important challenge is to obtain also a routing scheme with $(2k-1)$-stretch and $\tilde{O}(n^{1/k})$-space routing tables.

Recently, Chechik [10] made an important breakthrough and improved the stretch of the general routing scheme of Thorup and Zwick [23] from $4k-5$ to $((4-\alpha)k-\beta)$-stretch, for some constants α and β. The routing tables in her scheme are of size $O(n^{1/k} \log D)$, where D is the normalized diameter of the graph.

Routing schemes, and in particular small stretch routing schemes, have been extensively studied over the last three decades. Cowen [11] obtained a 3-stretch labeled routing scheme with routing tables of $\tilde{O}(n^{2/3})$ space. Eilam *et al.* [13] obtained a 5-stretch labeled routing scheme with routing tables of $\tilde{O}(n^{1/2})$ space. Arias *et al.* [6] obtained a 5-stretch name independent routing scheme with routing tables of $\tilde{O}(n^{1/2})$ space. Thorup and Zwick [23] improved the result of Cowen [11] and obtained a 3-stretch labeled routing scheme with routing tables of $\tilde{O}(n^{1/2})$ space. Finally, Abraham *et al.* [3] obtained a 3-stretch name independent routing scheme with routing tables of $\tilde{O}(n^{1/2})$ space.

Remarkably, only these last two routing schemes are optimal routing schemes for general undirected graphs amongst all the possible optimal stretch/space combinations. Even the new routing scheme of Chechik [10] is better than the $(4k-5)$-stretch routing scheme only for $k \geq 4$. In particular, for $k = 4$ the stretch is approximately 10.52 instead of 11 as in the routing scheme of [23]. Therefore, we are evidence to a phenomena in which settling on any stretch factor from the range $(3, 7)$ cannot help in reducing the routing table size below the $\sqrt{n}$ barrier.

In this paper we break this long-standing barrier and show a $(5+\varepsilon)$-stretch routing scheme that uses $\tilde{O}(\frac{1}{\varepsilon} n^{1/3} \log D)$ space at each vertex and $\tilde{O}(\frac{1}{\varepsilon} \log D)$-bit headers. The label of each vertex has a size of $O(\log n)$-bit. This almost matches the optimal stretch/space combination of 5-stretch and $O(n^{1/3})$-space routing tables.

Following the $(2,1)$-stretch distance oracle of [20] for unweighted graphs, Abraham and Gavoille in [1] presented a $(2,1)$-stretch routing scheme with routing tables of size $\tilde{O}(n^{3/4})$ and in general a $(4k-6,1)$-stretch $\tilde{O}(n^{3/(3k-2)})$-space routing tables. In this paper we almost match the $(2,1)$-stretch distance oracle of [20] and present a $(2+\varepsilon, 1)$-stretch routing scheme with routing tables of $\tilde{O}(\frac{1}{\varepsilon} n^{2/3})$ size at each vertex and $\tilde{O}(1/\varepsilon)$-bit headers. In Table 1 we compare our new results for small stretch factors with the previous best bounds.

We obtain our new results by extending a fundamental idea for routing between nearby vertices. In many of the existing routing schemes every vertex $u \in V$ stores the first edge on a shortest path to every vertex in $B(u, \ell)$, the set of ℓ closest vertices of u. A message is routed from u to $v \in B(u, \ell)$ using the edge that u stored for v. It is easy to show that $v \in B(w, \ell)$ for every w that is on a shortest path between u and v. Thus, it is possible to route a message from u to a specific vertex $v \in B(u, \ell)$ on a shortest path by storing at u $O(\log n)$-bits of routing information dedicated for v.

At the heart of our new routing techniques is an extension of this fundamental idea. Roughly speaking, we show that if every $u \in V$ stores the first edge on a shortest path to every $v \in B(u, \ell)$, and an additional routing information on a fixed set of special vertices, it is possible to route a message from u to a specific vertex v that is arbitrarily far away from u on a $(1+\varepsilon)$-stretch path by storing at u $O(\frac{1}{\varepsilon} \log n)$-bits of routing information dedicated for v.

Using this extension we present two new routing techniques. Given a partition $\mathcal{U} = \{U_1, \ldots, U_q\}$ of V into q sets each of size $\tilde{O}(n/q)$, our first technique routes a message between any pair of vertices of $U \in \mathcal{U}$ on a $(1+\varepsilon)$-stretch path with routing tables of size $\tilde{O}(\frac{1}{\varepsilon}(n/q) + q)$. Given a partition $\mathcal{W} = \{W_1, \ldots, W_q\}$ of a set $W \subseteq V$ into q sets each of size $\tilde{O}(|W|/q)$ and assuming that $U \cap B(u, \tilde{O}(q)) \neq \emptyset$, for every $U \in \mathcal{U}$ and $u \in V$, our second technique routes a message, for every $i \in \{1, \ldots, q\}$, from any source in U_i to any destination in W_i on a $(1+\varepsilon)$-stretch path with routing tables of size $\tilde{O}(\frac{1}{\varepsilon}(|W|/q) + q)$.

Our $(5+\varepsilon)$-stretch routing scheme is obtained using our second routing technique together with the routing scheme of Thorup and Zwick [23] and a coloring method used by Abraham *et al.* [3] and Abraham and Gavoille [1]. Our $(2+\varepsilon, 1)$-stretch routing scheme is obtained using our first routing technique together with ideas of Abraham and Gavoille [1] and Pătraşcu and Roditty [20]. Using our first technique it is also possible to obtain a name independent routing scheme with stretch $3+\varepsilon$ and routing tables of $\tilde{O}(\sqrt{n})$ size.

Our second technique is used to obtain also the following two generalizations. The first is a routing scheme for unweighted graphs that for an integer $\ell > 1$ uses $\tilde{O}(\ell \frac{1}{\varepsilon} n^{\ell/(2\ell \pm 1)})$ space at each vertex and $\tilde{O}(\frac{1}{\varepsilon})$-bit headers, to route a message between any pair of vertices on a $(3 \pm 2/\ell + \varepsilon, 2)$-stretch path. This almost matches the distance oracles of Pătraşcu, Thorup and Roditty [21]. The second is a routing scheme that uses $\tilde{O}(\frac{1}{\varepsilon} n^{1/k} \log D)$ space at each vertex and $\tilde{O}(\frac{1}{\varepsilon} \log D)$-bit headers, to route a message between any pair of vertices on a $(4k - 7 + \varepsilon)$-stretch path. The second routing scheme can be used in the $((4-\alpha)k - \beta)$-stretch routing scheme of Chechik [10] instead of the $(4k-5)$-stretch routing scheme of Thorup and Zwick in order to obtain slightly better values for α and β.

The rest of this paper is organized as follows. In the next section we present some preliminaries that are needed throughout the paper. In Section 3 we present our new routing techniques. In Section 4 we present our new routing schemes for small stretch factors. In Section 5 we present our generalized routing schemes.

2. PRELIMINARIES

Let $G = (V, E)$ be an n-vertices m-edges undirected graph. For every $u, v \in V$, let $d(u, v)$ be the length of a shortest path between u and v. Let $D = \frac{\max_{u,v} d(u,v)}{\min_{u \neq v} d(u,v)}$ be the *normalized diameter* of G. Let $B(u, \ell)$ be the ℓ closest vertices of u, breaking ties by lexicographical order of vertex names. Let $r_u(\ell)$ be the largest value for which it holds that every vertex $w \in V$ with $d(u, w) = r_u(\ell)$ is in $B(u, \ell)$. When it will be clear from the context we simply write r_u. Notice that for unweighted graphs it follows from this definition that $d(u, w) \leq r_u(\ell) + 1$ for every $w \in B(u, \ell)$. The following property is a well known property of such vertex vicinities.

Property 1 ([8],[2]). *If $v \in B(u, \ell)$ and w is on a shortest path between u and v then $v \in B(w, \ell)$.*

The next Lemma is a direct result of the above property.

Lemma 2. *Let $G = (V, E)$ be a weighted graph and let $\ell > 0$ be an integer. We can construct a routing scheme that uses routing tables of size $O(\ell)$ in each vertex and $O(\log n)$-bit header, such that a message is routed from u to any $v \in B(u, \ell)$ on a shortest path.*

Proof. Let $u \in V$. For each $v \in B(u, \ell)$ store at u the first edge on a shortest path to v. Assume $v \in B(u, \ell)$ and let (u, w) be the edge saved at u for v. When u receives a message to v, it forwards it to w. From Property 1 it follows that $v \in B(w, \ell)$, therefore, w has the next edge on a shortest path to v and the message is routed from u to v on a shortest path. □

Throughout the paper when we say that u saves $B(u, \ell)$ we mean that u can check membership and to retrieve the saved edge in constant time.

For our routing schemes we assume the standard fixed port model as described by Fraigniaud and Gavoille [15]. We use the following tree routing scheme as a building block in our routing schemes:

Lemma 3 (Tree routing [23, 15]). *Given a weighted tree there is a routing scheme that given the label of a destination vertex in the tree, routes from any source vertex in the tree to the destination on the shortest path in the tree. The storage of a node, its label size and the header size are $O(\log^2 n / \log\log n)$ bits. Each link on the path is obtained in constant time.*

The notions of bunches and clusters were used by Thorup and Zwick in the context of distance oracles [24]. Let $A \subseteq V$. Let $p_A(u) = \arg\min\{d(u, v) \mid v \in A\}$, breaking ties by lexicographical order of vertex names, and $d(u, A) = d(u, p_A(u))$.

The *bunch* of $v \in V$ is $B_A(v) = \{w \in V \mid d(w, v) < d(v, A)\}$. The *cluster* of $w \in V$ is $C_A(w) = \{v \in V \mid d(w, v) < d(v, A)\}$. Notice that $w \in B_A(v)$ if and only if $v \in C_A(w)$.

From the definition of clusters it follows that if $u \in C_A(w)$ and v is on a shortest path between u and w then $v \in C_A(w)$. Thus, there is a shortest path tree $T_{C_A}(w)$ rooted at w that spans the vertices of $C_A(w)$. Let $|A| = s$, the size of each bunch is bounded by $O(n/s)$. Thorup and Zwick [23] showed how to simultaneously bound the size of the bunches and clusters.

Lemma 4 ([23]). *Given an integer parameter $s > 0$, it is possible to construct a set A with expected size of $2s \log n$, such that $|C_A(w)| \leq 4n/s$, for every $w \in V$.*

We will also make use of the following well known Lemma.

Lemma 5 (Hitting set [4, 12]). *Let $1 \leq s \leq n$. Given k sets $S_1, \ldots, S_k$, where $S_i \subseteq V$ and $|S_i| \geq s$, for every $i \in \{1, \ldots, k\}$, we can find a set $H \subseteq V$ of size $\tilde{O}(n/s)$, such that $H \cap S_i \neq \emptyset$.*

Abraham *et al.* [2] introduced a nice coloring technique and used it to obtain a name-independent routing scheme with stretch 3 and routing tables of size $\tilde{O}(\sqrt{n})$. Recently, Abraham and Gavoille [1] used this coloring technique to obtain a labeled routing scheme with stretch $(2, 1)$ and routing tables of size $\tilde{O}(n^{3/4})$. The next Lemma is implicit in [2, 1].

Lemma 6 (Coloring [2, 1]). *Let $0 < q \leq n$ be an integer. Let $S_1, \ldots, S_k$ be vertex sets each of size at least $\alpha q \log n$, where α is a large enough constant. There is a coloring function $c : V \to \{1, \ldots, q\}$ that satisfies the following:*
1. *For each $i \in \{1, \ldots, k\}$ and $j \in \{1, \ldots, q\}$, there exist $w \in S_i$ such that $c(w) = j$.*
2. *For each $j \in \{1, \ldots, q\}$ the number of vertices of color j is $O(n/q)$.*

Abraham *et al.* [2] showed that such a deterministic coloring function can be computed efficiently. Here we show that such a coloring function can be formed, with high probability, from a random uniform coloring of the vertices of the graph. Assume that the number of sets k is polynomial in n. Each vertex is colored by one of the q colors with uniform probability. Let $S \in \{S_1, \ldots, S_k\}$ and $j \in \{1, \ldots, q\}$. Consider the event that there is no vertex in S with color j. The probability for this event to happen is bounded by $(1 - 1/q)^s$ which is at most $(1/n)^\alpha$. From the union bound we get that the first requirement holds with probability $1 - k \cdot q \cdot (1/n)^\alpha$. The expected number of vertices with the same color is n/q, and from Chernoff bound it follows that the second requirement holds with high probability. Using the union bound to bound the probability that one of the requirements does not hold we get that the above function satisfies, whp, both requirements.

To simplify the presentation we define $\tilde{x} = \alpha x \log n$, where $x > 0$ is an integer and α is a large enough constant of our choice.

Reference	Graph	Stretch	Table Size
Abraham and Gavoille [1]	Unweighted	$(2,1)$	$\tilde{O}(n^{3/4})$
Thorup and Zwick [23], Abraham *et al.* [3]	Weighted	3	$\tilde{O}(n^{1/2})$
Thorup and Zwick [23]	Weighted	7	$\tilde{O}(n^{1/3})$
Chechik [10]	Weighted	10.52	$\tilde{O}(n^{1/4}\log D)$
Theorem 10	Unweighted	$(2+\varepsilon,1)$	$\tilde{O}((1/\varepsilon)\cdot n^{2/3})$
Theorem 13	Unweighted	$(2^1/3+\varepsilon,2)$	$\tilde{O}((1/\varepsilon)\cdot n^{3/5})$
Theorem 15	Unweighted	$(4+\varepsilon,2)$	$\tilde{O}((1/\varepsilon)\cdot n^{2/5})$
Theorem 11	Weighted	$5+\varepsilon$	$\tilde{O}((1/\varepsilon)\cdot n^{1/3}\log D)$
Theorem 16	Weighted	$9+\varepsilon$	$\tilde{O}((1/\varepsilon)\cdot n^{1/4}\log D)$

Table 1: Previously available routing schemes and our new routing schemes

3. NEW ROUTING TECHNIQUES

In this section we present two new techniques for routing between predefined vertex sets. We will use these techniques in the next sections to obtain our new routing schemes. The techniques are presented in two lemmas. We first show that for a vertex partition that satisfies certain properties it is possible to route efficiently between vertices of the same set in the partition.

Lemma 7. *Let $G=(V,E,w)$ be a weighted undirected graph, where $w: E \to \mathbb{R}$. Let $\mathcal{U}=\{U_1,\ldots,U_q\}$ be a partition of V into q sets, each of size $\tilde{O}(n/q)$. For every $\varepsilon>0$, there is a routing scheme that uses a header of $O(\frac{1}{\varepsilon}\log n+\log^2 n/\log\log n)$-bit to route a message between any pair of vertices of the same set in partition $\mathcal{U}$, on a $(1+\varepsilon)$-stretch path. The routing table stored at each vertex is of size $\tilde{O}(\frac{1}{\varepsilon}(n/q)+q)$.*

Proof.
Preprocessing: For each $u\in V$, we store $B(u,\tilde{q})$. We compute a hitting set H as in Lemma 5 of size $\tilde{O}(n/q)$ that hits for each $u\in V$ the set $B(u,\tilde{q})$. For each vertex $w\in H$, we compute a shortest path tree $T(w)$ rooted at w that spans V. For each such $T(w)$, we store at each vertex $u\in V$ the tree routing information of $T(w)$ as needed for the tree routing schemes of Lemma 3. Since $|H|=\tilde{O}(n/q)$ and the tree routing information is of poly-logarithmic size, the total storage at each vertex for this purpose is $\tilde{O}(n/q)$.

Let $U\in\mathcal{U}$ and let $u\in U$. For every $v\in U$, we compute a sequence $\langle x_1,\ldots,x_{b'}\rangle$ of vertices. The sequence is computed using the following process:

Let $b=\lceil 2/\varepsilon\rceil$. Set $x_0=u$ and $s=d(u,v)/b$. Let x_i $(i\geq 0)$ be the last vertex added to the sequence so far. If $v\in B(x_i,\tilde{q})$ then set x_{i+1} to v and stop. If $v\notin B(x_i,\tilde{q})$ then let (y_i,z_i) be an edge on a shortest path from x_i to v such that $y_i\in B(x_i,\tilde{q})$ and $z_i\notin B(x_i,\tilde{q})$. Proceed as follows:

- If $z_i=v$ then set $x_{i+1}=y_i$, $x_{i+2}=v$ and stop.
- If $d(x_i,z_i)<s$ then pick $w\in H$ such that $w\in B(x_i,\tilde{q})$, set $x_{i+1}=w$ and stop.
- Otherwise $(d(x_i,z_i)\geq s)$ set $x_{i+1}=y_i$, $x_{i+2}=z_i$ and continue to add vertices to the sequence with x_{i+2} being now the last added vertex.

In this process we add vertices to the sequence as long the progress towards v exceeds the threshold value s. Therefore, the process has at most $d(u,v)/s\leq b$ rounds. Since in each round at most 2 vertices are added to the sequence its total size is at most $2b$. At u we store for v the sequence $\langle x_1,\ldots,x_{b'}\rangle$. In case that $x_{b'}\neq v$ then it must be that $x_{b'}\in H$ and we also store at u the label of v in $T(x_{b'})$. Since $|U|=\tilde{O}(n/q)$, the total storage required at u for this information is $\tilde{O}(b\cdot(n/q))$.

Routing: Given a set $U\in\mathcal{U}$ and a pair of vertices $u,v\in U$ a message is routed from u to v as follows. First, u obtains the sequence $\langle x_1,\ldots,x_{b'}\rangle$ for v from its routing table and adds it to the message header[1]. It also sets x_1 to be a temporary target. Let u' be the current vertex on the routing path and let $x_i\neq u'$ be the temporary target. Assume that we are either in the case that $i<b'$ or in the case that $i=b'$ and $x_{b'}=v$. By the way $\langle x_1,\ldots,x_{b'}\rangle$ was constructed it follows that either $(u',x_i)\in E$ or $x_i\in B(u',\tilde{q})$. In the case that $(u',x_i)\in E$ then we can route from u' to x_i using a direct link[2]. In the case that $x_i\in B(u',\tilde{q})$, it follows from Lemma 2 that we can route to x_i on a shortest path. Each time a temporary target $x_i\neq v$ receives the message, it sets x_{i+1} to be the next temporary target. For the case that $i=b'$ and $x_{b'}\neq v$, it follows from the construction of $\langle x_1,\ldots,x_{b'}\rangle$ that $x_{b'}\in H$. The routing from $x_{b'-1}$ to v is done using the tree $T(x_{b'})$. This routing procedure requires a header of $O(\frac{1}{\varepsilon}\log n+\log^2 n/\log\log n)$-bit.

We now turn to analyze the stretch of the routing path. By the sequence construction, until $x_{b'-1}$, the message is routed on a shortest path. In the case that $x_{b'}=v$ the message is routed from $x_{b'-1}$ to $x_{b'}$ on a shortest path as well. In the case that $x_{b'}\neq v$ the message is routed from $x_{b'-1}$ to v on $T(x_{b'})$, where $x_{b'}\in H\cap B(x_{b'-1},\tilde{q})$. We have added $x_{b'}$ to the sequence because $d(x_{b'-1},z_{b'-1})<d(u,v)/b$. We also know that $z_{b'-1}\notin B(x_{b'-1},\tilde{q})$, thus, $d(x_{b'-1},x_{b'})\leq d(x_{b'-1},z_{b'-1})<d(u,v)/b$. The length of the routing path is bounded by $d(u,x_{b'-1})+d(x_{b'-1},x_{b'})+d(x_{b'},v)$. Using the triangle inequality we bound $d(x_{b'},v)$ with $d(x_{b'-1},x_{b'})+d(x_{b'-1},v)$ and we get $d(u,x_{b'-1})+d(x_{b'-1},x_{b'})+d(x_{b'},v)\leq d(u,x_{b'-1})+2d(x_{b'-1},x_{b'})+d(x_{b'-1},v)$. Since $x_{b'-1}$ is on a shortest path between u and v it follows that $d(u,x_{b'-1})+d(x_{b'-1},v)=d(u,v)$ and we get:

$$d(u,x_{b'-1})+2d(x_{b'-1},x_{b'})+d(x_{b'-1},v)\leq d(u,v)+2d(u,v)/b.$$

[1] In the case that $x_{b'}\neq v$, it adds also the label of v in $T(x_{b'})$ that was stored at u in the preprocessing.

[2] The standard routing scheme model of [19] assumes that at u given a neighbor v it is possible to obtain the link that connects u to v. We can even avoid this assumption by storing in the sequence edges instead of vertices when needed.

Since $b = \lceil 2/\varepsilon \rceil$ we get that the message traverses a $(1+\varepsilon)$-stretch path. □

Next we extend Lemma 7 to the case that the possible destinations are from a subset W of V.

Lemma 8. *Let $G = (V, E, \omega)$ be a weighted undirected graph, where $\omega : E \to \mathbb{R}^+$. Let $\mathcal{W} = \{W_1, \dots, W_q\}$ be a partition of $W \subseteq V$ into q sets, each of size $\tilde{O}(|W|/q)$. Let $\mathcal{U} = \{U_1, \dots, U_q\}$ be a partition of V into q sets, such that $U \cap B(u, \tilde{q}) \neq \emptyset$, for every $U \in \mathcal{U}$ and $u \in V$. For every $\varepsilon > 0$, there is a routing scheme that uses a header size of $O(\frac{1}{\varepsilon}\log(nD))$-bit, and for every $1 \le i \le q$ routes a message from any vertex of U_i to any vertex of W_i on a $(1+\varepsilon)$-stretch path. The routing table stored at each vertex is of size $\tilde{O}(q + \frac{1}{\varepsilon} \cdot \log(D)(|W|/q))$.*

Proof. **Preprocessing:** We first assume that $\omega : E \to [1, M]$. Similarly to Lemma 7, for each vertex $u \in V$ we store $B(u, \tilde{q})$. It requires $\tilde{O}(q)$ space at each vertex.

Let $b = \lceil \frac{2}{\varepsilon} \rceil + 1$. For $1 \le j \le q$, let $U_j \in \mathcal{U}$ and let $W_j \in \mathcal{W}$. Given a vertex $u \in U_j$ and a vertex $w \in W_j$, we store at u a sequence of vertices that will be used to route towards w. Such a sequence has $O(\log(Mn))$ subsequences. A subsequence $\langle x_1, \dots, x_{b'} \rangle$ is computed as follows.

Let x be a start vertex and let s be a threshold value that are given as an input to the computation. Set $x_0 = x$. Let x_i $(i \ge 0)$ be the last vertex added to the subsequence so far. If $w \in B(x_i, \tilde{q})$ then set x_{i+1} to w and stop. If $w \notin B(x_i, \tilde{q})$ then let (y_i, z_i) be an edge on a shortest path from x_i to w such that $y_i \in B(x_i, \tilde{q})$ and $z_i \notin B(x_i, \tilde{q})$. Proceed as follows:

- If $z_i = w$ then set $x_{i+1} = y_i$, $x_{i+2} = w$ and stop.
- If $d(x_i, z_i) < s$ then there is a vertex $z \in B(x_i, \tilde{q}) \cap U_j$, set $x_{i+1} = z$ and stop.
- Otherwise ($d(x_i, z_i) \ge s$) set $x_{i+1} = y_i$, $x_{i+2} = z_i$. If the subsequence is of size $2b$ stop, else continue to add vertices to the subsequence with x_{i+2} being now the last added vertex.

Now, the sequence stored at u for w is computed as follows. Let $P(u, w) = \{u = u_0, u_1, u_2, \dots, u_t = w\}$ be a shortest path between u and w. We start by adding u_1 to the sequence. If $u_1 = w$ we stop, otherwise, we add u_2 to the sequence as well. Next, if $u_2 \neq w$, we start to produce subsequences and add them to the sequence. The first subsequence is produced using $x = u_2$ as the start vertex and $s = 2/b$ as the threshold value. Let s' be the threshold value that was used to produce the last subsequence added so far to the sequence and let w' be its last vertex. If this subsequence has exactly $2b$ vertices and $w' \neq w$ then a new subsequence is produced and added to the sequence using $x = w'$ as the start vertex and $s = 2s'$ as the threshold value.

Each subsequence added to the sequence has at most $2b$ vertices. In every subsequence, beside maybe the last one, all the vertices are on $P(u, w)$. Moreover, if the ith subsequence added to the sequence is not the last subsequence its last vertex is at a distance of at least 2^i from its first vertex. Since the length of every shortest path is less than Mn the total number of subsequences cannot exceed $\log(nM)$ and therefore a sequence can have at most $2b\log(Mn) + 2$ vertices. Each set in $\mathcal{W}$ is of size $|W|/q$, thus, each $u \in U_j$ stores $|W|/q$ sequences which results in a total space of $O(b(\log Mn)|W|/q) = \tilde{O}(\frac{1}{\varepsilon}(\log M)|W|/q)$.

Next, we show that the preprocessing algorithm works also on graphs with non-negative real edge weights. Let $G = (V, E, \omega)$ be a weighted graph with $\omega : E \to \mathbb{R}^+$ and let D be its normalized diameter. Let $E' = \{(u, v) \in E \mid \omega(u, v) = d(u, v)\}$. Let $\omega_{\max} = \max\{\omega(u, v) \mid (u, v) \in E'\}$, and let $\omega_{\min} = \min\{\omega(u, v) \mid (u, v) \in E'\}$. For every $(u, v) \in E'$ let $\omega'(u, v) = \omega(u, v)/\omega_{\min}$. It is easy to see that $\omega' : E' \to [1, M]$, where $M = \frac{\omega_{\max}}{\omega_{\min}}$. Notice that all shortest paths in $G' = (V, E', w')$ are also shortest paths in G. Applying the preprocessing algorithm on G' we get that each $u \in U_j$ stores $|W|/q$ sequences each of size $O(b\log(Mn))$. Since $\omega_{\max} \le \max_{u,v} d(u, v)$ and $\omega_{\min} = \max_{u \neq v} d(u, v)$ it follows that $M = \frac{\omega_{\max}}{\omega_{\min}} \le D$. Therefore, the total space stored at a vertex is $\tilde{O}(\frac{1}{\varepsilon}(\log D)|W|/q)$.

Routing: Given a set $U_j \in \mathcal{U}$ and a set $W_j \in \mathcal{W}$, and a pair of vertices $u \in U_j$ and $w \in W_j$, we show how to route a message from u to w. We route towards the last vertex of the sequence stored at u for w in the same manner as in Lemma 7. It follows from the sequence construction that all its vertices, beside maybe the last, are on a shortest path between u and w. The last vertex is either w or a vertex that belongs to U_j. Let $r_0 = u$. For $i \ge 0$, let r_{i+1} be the last vertex of the sequence stored at r_i for w, and let r'_i be the vertex that precedes r_{i+1} in the sequence. If $r_{i+1} \neq w$ then $r_{i+1} \in U_j$. Let $\alpha_i = d(r_i, r'_i)$.

Claim 9. *For every $i \ge 0$, $d(r_{i+1}, w) < d(r_i, w)$. Moreover, $d(r_{i+1}, w) \le d(r_i, w) - (\alpha_i - \alpha_i/b)$.*

Proof. Let $i \ge 0$. Consider the routing of a message from r_i to r_{i+1}. If $r_{i+1} = w$ then the message is routed on a shortest path, therefore $d(r_{i+1}, w) = d(w, w) < d(r_i, w)$ and also $d(r_{i+1}, w) = 0 \le d(r_i, w) - d(r_i, r'_i) \le d(r_i, w) - (\alpha_i - \alpha_i/b)$. Otherwise, we route from $r_i \in U_j$ to a vertex $r_{i+1} \in U_j$. The sequence stored at $r_i \in U_j$ for $w \in W_j$ contains the first two vertices of a shortest path from r_i to w and then at least one subsequence. Let $k \ge 1$ be the number of subsequences of this sequence. The last vertex of this sequence is r_{i+1}, and r'_i is the vertex that precedes r_{i+1} in the sequence. From the sequence construction it follows that r'_i is on a shortest path between r_i and w. Moreover, r'_i is either the last vertex of the $(k-1)$th subsequence or a vertex of the kth subsequence or the second vertex of the sequence.

The message is routed from r_i to r'_i, and then from r'_i to r_{i+1}. From the way that subsequences are produced it follows that $\alpha_i = d(r_i, r'_i) \ge 2 + (2 + 4 + \ldots + 2^{k-1}) = 1 + (1 + 2 + \ldots + 2^{k-1}) = 2^k$. Moreover, it follows from the threshold used to produce the kth subsequence that $d(r'_i, r_{i+1}) \le 2^k/b \le \alpha_i/b$. Since r'_i is on a shortest path between r_i and w it follows that $d(r'_i, w) = d(r_i, w) - d(r_i, r'_i)$. From the triangle inequality it follows that $d(r_{i+1}, w) \le d(r_{i+1}, r'_i) + d(r'_i, w)$. We get: $d(r_{i+1}, w) \le d(r_{i+1}, r'_i) + d(r'_i, w) = d(r_{i+1}, r'_i) + d(r_i, w) - d(r_i, r'_i) \le d(r_i, w) - (\alpha_i - \alpha_i/b)$. □

Next, we show that the stretch of the routing path is $(1+\varepsilon)$. From Claim 9 it follows that the message eventually reaches a vertex r_t that w is the last vertex in its sequence. For every $0 \le i < t$, the message is routed from r_i to r_{i+1} on a path of length at most $\alpha_i + \alpha_i/b$. For $i = t$ the message is routed on a shortest path between r_t and w. Let $A =$

$\sum_{i=0}^{t-1} \alpha_i$. The message traverses a path of length at most $A(1+1/b)+d(r_t,w)$.

From Claim 9 it follows that $d(r_t,w) \le d(r_{t-1},w) - (\alpha_{t-1} - \alpha_{t-1}/b)$. By applying Claim 9 recursively we get $d(r_t,w) \le d(u,w) - \sum_{i=0}^{t-1}(\alpha_i - \alpha_i/b) = d(u,w) - A(1-1/b)$ which implies that $A(1-1/b) \le d(u,w) - d(r_t,w) \le d(u,w)$ and $A \le \frac{b}{b-1} d(u,w)$. Therefore, we get:

$$\begin{aligned} A(1+1/b) + d(r_t,w) &\le A(1+1/b) + d(u,w) - A(1-1/b) \\ &\le d(u,w) + 2A/b \\ &\le d(u,w) + 2d(u,w)/(b-1) \\ &= (1+\frac{2}{b-1})d(u,w) \le (1+\varepsilon)d(u,w) \end{aligned}$$

□

4. APPLICATIONS FOR SMALL STRETCH ROUTING SCHEMES

In this section we show how to obtain small stretch routing schemes, that almost match the corresponding state-of-the-art distance oracles, using the routing techniques from the previous section. To exemplify the strength of our techniques we first show as a warm-up a new $(3+\varepsilon)$-stretch labeled routing scheme with $\tilde{O}(\frac{1}{\varepsilon})$-bit header size and $\tilde{O}(\frac{1}{\varepsilon}\sqrt{n})$-space routing tables. Using the hash function presented in [2] it is easy to modify this routing scheme to be name-independent. Then we turn to present the main results of this section, our $(2+\varepsilon,1)$-stretch and $(5+\varepsilon)$-stretch routing schemes.

Stretch $3+\varepsilon$. Let $q=\sqrt{n}$. Let c be a coloring function with q colors obtained using Lemma 6 with respect to the sets $B(u,\tilde{q})$, for every $u \in V$. Let $\mathcal{U} = \{U_1,\ldots,U_q\}$ be the color sets induced by c. It follows that $\mathcal{U}$ is a partition and every $U \in \mathcal{U}$ has $\tilde{O}(\sqrt{n})$ vertices. We use Lemma 7 with $\mathcal{U}$. The information stored for this at every vertex is of size $\tilde{O}(\frac{1}{\varepsilon}\sqrt{n})$. Every $u \in V$ stores $B(u,\tilde{q})$. It follows from Lemma 6 that $B(u,\tilde{q})$ contains a vertex of each color. For every $i \in \{1,\ldots,q\}$ we store at u a vertex from $B(u,\tilde{q})$ of color i. For every $v \in V$ the label of v contains v and $c(v)$. A message is routed from u to v as follows. If $v \in B(u,\tilde{q})$ it follows from Lemma 2 that we can route the message from u to v on a shortest path. If $v \notin B(u,\tilde{q})$ then, using the information that is saved at u, we route to $w \in B(u,\tilde{q})$ with color $c(v)$. Again from Lemma 2 it follows that we can route from u to w on a shortest path. We route from w to v using Lemma 7. We now bound the stretch. From Lemma 7 it follows that the message is sent from w to v on a path of length at most $(1+\varepsilon)d(w,v)$. The message traverses a path of length at most $d(u,w)+(1+\varepsilon)d(w,v)$. From the triangle inequality it follows that $d(w,v) \le d(w,u) + d(u,v)$. Also, since $v \notin B(u,\tilde{q})$ and $w \in B(u,\tilde{q})$ it follows that $d(u,w) \le d(u,v)$. Therefore, $d(w,v) \le 2d(u,v)$, and we get that $d(u,w)+(1+\varepsilon)d(w,v) \le (3+2\varepsilon)d(u,v)$.

Stretch $(2+\varepsilon,1)$. We now present a $(2+\varepsilon,1)$-stretch routing scheme with $o(\log^2 n)$-bit labels, $\tilde{O}(1/\varepsilon)$-bit headers and routing tables of $\tilde{O}(\frac{1}{\varepsilon}n^{2/3})$ size. This almost matches the $(2,1)$-stretch distance oracle with $\tilde{O}(n^{5/3})$ total space of [20].

Theorem 10. *There is a routing scheme for unweighted undirected graphs with $o(\log^2 n)$-bit labels, that uses $\tilde{O}(\frac{1}{\varepsilon}n^{2/3})$ space at each vertex and $\tilde{O}(1/\varepsilon)$-bit header size, to route a message between any pair of vertices on a $(2+\varepsilon,1)$-stretch path.*

Proof. Let $q=n^{1/3}$. Every $u \in V$ stores $B(u,\tilde{q})$. We compute using Lemma 4 a set $A \subset V$ of size $\tilde{O}(n^{2/3})$, such that $|C_A(w)| = O(n^{1/3})$ for every $w \in V$. For each $u \in C_A(w)$ we store the routing information for a tree routing scheme of $T_{C_A}(w)$ at u. This information is of poly-logarithmic size. Every vertex u is contained in at most $O(n^{1/3})$ cluster trees as $|B_A(u)| = O(n^{1/3})$. Therefore, the storage required at each vertex u for this is $\tilde{O}(n^{1/3})$.

Let $w \in V$. For each $v \in C_A(w)$ we store at w the label of v in the tree routing scheme of $T_{C_A}(w)$. Since $|C_A(w)| = O(n^{1/3})$ the storage required at w for these labels is $\tilde{O}(n^{1/3})$.

For each $w \in A$ let $T(w)$ be a shortest path tree rooted at w that spans V. For every $v \in V$ we store routing information of a tree routing scheme of $T(w)$. This allows to route from a vertex u to a vertex v on $T(w)$. Since $|A| = \tilde{O}(n^{2/3})$, each vertex stores $\tilde{O}(n^{2/3})$ information for this purpose.

Let $u \in V$. For every $v \in V$, if $B(u,\tilde{q}) \cap B_A(v) \neq \emptyset$ we store in a hash table at u in the entry of v a vertex $w \in \arg\min_{w'}\{d(u,w') + d(w',v) \mid w' \in B(u,\tilde{q}) \cap B_A(v)\}$. There are $\tilde{O}(n^{1/3})$ vertices in $B(u,\tilde{q})$ each with a cluster of $O(n^{1/3})$ vertices. Let $w \in B(u,\tilde{q})$. For every $v \in C_A(w)$ it holds that $B(u,\tilde{q}) \cap B_A(v) \neq \emptyset$ therefore the storage required for this at every vertex is $\tilde{O}(n^{2/3})$.

Let c be a coloring function with q colors obtained using Lemma 6 with respect to the sets $B(u,\tilde{q})$, for every $u \in V$. Let $\mathcal{U} = \{U_1,\ldots,U_q\}$ be the color sets induced by c. It follows that $\mathcal{U}$ is a partition and every $U \in \mathcal{U}$ has $\tilde{O}(n/q) = \tilde{O}(n^{2/3})$ vertices. We use Lemma 7 with the partition $\mathcal{U}$. The information stored at the routing table of every vertex for this is $\tilde{O}(\frac{1}{\varepsilon}n^{2/3})$.

It follows from Lemma 6 that $B(u,\tilde{q})$ contains a vertex of each color. For every $i \in \{1,\ldots,q\}$ we store at u a vertex from $B(u,\tilde{q})$ of color i and its distance from u.

Finally, the label of $v \in V$ contains the following information: v, $c(v)$, $p_A(v)$, $d(v,p_A(v))$ and the label of v in $T(p_A(v))$.

Routing: A message is routed from u to v as follows. At u we check in constant time if $B(u,\tilde{q}) \cap B_A(v) \neq \emptyset$. If this is the case we obtain in constant time the vertex $w \in \arg\min_{w'}\{d(u,w') + d(w',v) \mid w' \in B(u,\tilde{q}) \cap B_A(v)\}$ that was saved at u. From Lemma 2 it follows that we can route the message from u to w on a shortest path. From w to v we can use the tree routing scheme of $T_{C_A}(w)$ as the label of v in the this tree routing scheme is stored at w. Thus, the message is routed on a path of length $d(u,w)+d(w,v)$. Next, we show that $d(u,v) = d(u,w) + d(w,v)$. Assume, towards a contradiction, that w is not on a shortest path between u and v and let P be a shortest path between u and v. There is a vertex $u' \in B(u,\tilde{q}) \cap P$ such that $d(u,u') = r_u$, and there is a vertex $v' \in B_A(v) \cap P$ such that $d(v,v') = d(v,p_A(v)) - 1$ (notice that $B(u,\tilde{q}) \cap B_A(v) \neq \emptyset$ implies that $v \notin A$ and $d(v,p_A(v)) - 1 \ge 0$). Since the intersection is not on a vertex from P it must be that $d(u,v) \ge r_u + d(v,v') + 1$. On the other hand $d(u,w) \le r_u + 1$ and $d(v,w) \le d(v,v')$ and we get that $d(u,w) + d(v,w) \le d(u,v)$, which contradicts the assumption that w is not on a shortest path between u and v.

Consider the case that $B(u,\tilde{q}) \cap B_A(v) = \emptyset$. We obtain $c(v)$, $p_A(v)$ and $d_A(p_A(v))$ from the label of v. A vertex

$w \in B(u, \tilde{q})$ with $c(w) = c(v)$ is stored at u with $d(u,w)$. If $d(v, p_A(v)) \leq d(u,w)$ then the message is routed from u to v on $T(p_A(v))$. If $d(v, p_A(v)) > d(u,w)$, we route on a shortest path from u to w using Lemma 2 and then from w to v on a path of length at most $(1+\varepsilon)d(w,v)$ using Lemma 7.

If $v \in A$, it follows that $d(v, p_A(v)) = 0 \leq d(u,w)$ and the message is routed on a shortest path to v in $T(v) = T(p_A(v))$. Assume $v \notin A$. As $B(u,\tilde{q}) \cap B_A(v) = \emptyset$ it follows that $d(u,v) \geq r_u + (d(v,p_A(v)) - 1) + 1 = r_u + d(v, p_A(v))$. If $d(v,p_A(v)) \leq d(u,w)$ then the message is sent on a path of length $d(u, p_A(v)) + d(p_A(v), v)$. From the triangle inequality it follows that $d(u,p_A(v)) \leq d(u,v) + d(p_A(v), v)$ and thus $d(u,p_A(v)) + d(p_A(v),v) \leq d(u,v) + 2d(p_A(v),v)$. Since $d(u,w) \leq r_u + 1$ we get that $d(v,p_A(v)) - 1 \leq r_u$. Combining this with the fact that $d(u,v) \geq r_u + d(v,p_A(v))$ we get that $d(u,v)+1 \geq 2d(v,p_A(v))$. Therefore, $d(u,v)+2d(p_A(v),v)$ is at most $2d(u,v)+1$. If $d(u,w) < d(v,p_A(v))$ the message is sent on a path of length at most $d(u,w) + (1+\varepsilon)d(w,v)$. From the triangle inequality it follows that $d(w,v) \leq d(u,w) + d(u,v)$ and thus $d(u,w) + (1+\varepsilon)d(w,v) \leq (1+\varepsilon)d(u,v) + (2+\varepsilon)d(u,w)$. We have $d(u,w) \leq d(v,p_A(v)) - 1$. We also have $d(u,w) \leq r_u + 1$. Combining the last two inequalities with $d(u,v) \geq r_u + d(v,p_A(v))$ we get that $2d(u,w) \leq d(u,v)$. Therefore, the message is routed on a path of length at most $(2+2\varepsilon)d(u,v)$. □

Stretch $5+\varepsilon$. We now present a $(5+\varepsilon)$-stretch routing scheme that uses labels of size $(4\log n)$-bit, $\tilde{O}(1/\varepsilon \log D)$-bit headers and routing tables of $\tilde{O}(\frac{1}{\varepsilon} n^{1/3} \log D)$ size. This almost matches the 5-stretch distance oracle with $\tilde{O}(n^{4/3})$ total space of [24]. The current best routing scheme with routing tables of $\tilde{O}(n^{1/3})$ size has a stretch of 7 and $o(\log^2 n)$-bit labels. This routing scheme is obtained by setting $k = 3$ in the $(4k-5)$-stretch routing scheme of Thorup and Zwick [23].

Theorem 11. *Let $G = (V, E, \omega)$ be a weighted undirected graph, where $\omega : E \to \mathbb{R}^+$. There is a routing scheme for G with $O(\log n)$-bit labels that uses $\tilde{O}(\frac{1}{\varepsilon} n^{1/3} \log D)$ space at each vertex and $\tilde{O}(\frac{1}{\varepsilon} \log D)$-bit headers, to route a message between any pair of vertices on a $(5+\varepsilon)$-stretch path.*

Proof.
Preprocessing: Let $q = n^{1/3}$. Every $u \in V$ stores $B(u,\tilde{q})$. We compute using Lemma 4 a set $A \subset V$ of size $\tilde{O}(n^{2/3})$, such that $|C_A(w)| = O(n^{1/3})$ for every $w \in V$. Let $w \in V$, for each $v \in C_A(w)$ we store at w the label of v in the tree routing scheme of $T_{C_A}(w)$. Since $|C_A(w)| = O(n^{1/3})$ the storage required at w is $\tilde{O}(n^{1/3})$. For each $u \in C_A(w)$ we store at u the routing information for a tree routing scheme of $T_{C_A}(w)$. This information is of poly-logarithmic size. Notice that $|B_A(u)| = O(n^{1/3})$, thus u is contained in at most $O(n^{1/3})$ trees and the storage required at u for this is $\tilde{O}(n^{1/3})$.

Let c be a coloring function with q colors obtained using Lemma 6 with respect to the sets $B(u,\tilde{q})$, for every $u \in V$. Let $\mathcal{U} = \{U_1, \ldots, U_q\}$ be the color sets induced by c. Let $\mathcal{W} = \{W_1, \ldots, W_q\}$ be an arbitrary partition of the set A into q sets each with at most $|A|/q$ vertices. For $w \in A$, let $\alpha(w)$ be the index of the set in partition $\mathcal{W}$ that contains w, that is $w \in W_{\alpha(w)}$. We use Lemma 8 with partitions $\mathcal{U}$ and $\mathcal{W}$. The required storage at each vertex is $\tilde{O}(q + \frac{1}{\varepsilon}(\log D)|A|/q) = \tilde{O}(\frac{1}{\varepsilon}(\log D)n^{1/3})$.

It follows from Lemma 6 that $B(u,\tilde{q})$ contains a vertex of each color. For every $i \in \{1,\ldots,q\}$ we store at u a vertex from $B(u,\tilde{q})$ of color i. The storage required for this at u is $\tilde{O}(n^{1/3})$.

Let $v \in V$ and let $(p_A(v), z)$ be the first edge on a shortest path from $p_A(v)$ to v. Notice that $v \in C_A(z)$. The label of v contains the following information: v, $p_A(v)$, $\alpha(p_A(v))$ and $(p_A(v), z)$.

Routing: A message is routed from u to v as follows. At u we check if $v \in B(u,\tilde{q})$. If this is the case then from Lemma 2 it follows that we can route the message from u to v on a shortest path. If not we check if $v \in C_A(u)$. If this is the case then the label of v in the tree routing scheme of $T_{C_A}(u)$ is stored at u. The message is again routed on a shortest path between u and v.

In the case that $v \notin B(u,\tilde{q})$ and $v \notin C_A(u)$ the message is routed on a shortest path to $w \in B(u,\tilde{q})$ that satisfies $c(w) = \alpha(p_A(v))$. The message is routed from w to $p_A(v)$ using Lemma 8. At $p_A(v)$ we obtain $(p_A(v), z)$ from the label of v and forward the message to z. At z we have the label of v in the tree routing scheme of $T_{C_A}(z)$ since $v \in C_A(z)$. Using this label and the tree routing scheme of $T_{C_A}(z)$ the message is routed from z to v. The message is routed on a path of length at most $d(u,w) + (1+\varepsilon)d(w,p_A(v)) + d(p_A(v),v)$. Since $v \notin B(u,\tilde{q})$ it follows that $d(u,w) \leq d(u,v)$. Since $v \notin C_A(u)$ it follows that $d(v,p_A(v)) \leq d(u,v)$. From the triangle inequality it follows that $d(w,p_A(v)) \leq d(u,w) + d(u,v) + d(p_A(v),v) \leq 3d(u,v)$. We get $d(u,w) + (1+\varepsilon)d(w,p_A(v)) + d(p_A(v),v) \leq (5+3\varepsilon)d(u,v)$. □

5. GENERALIZED ROUTING SCHEMES

Stretch $(3 \pm 2/\ell + \varepsilon, 1)$. We now present a $(3 \pm 2/\ell + \varepsilon, 2)$-stretch routing scheme that uses $O(\ell \log n)$-bit labels, $\tilde{O}(1/\varepsilon)$-bit headers and routing tables of $\tilde{O}(\ell \frac{1}{\varepsilon} n^{\ell/(2\ell \pm 1)})$ size. This almost matches the distance oracles presented in [21] for weighted graphs with $(3\pm 2/\ell)$-stretch and $\tilde{O}(\ell m^{1+\ell/(2\ell\pm1)})$ total space.

We start with a simple Lemma given in [21] and repeated here for completeness.

Lemma 12. *Let $\ell > 0$ be an integer. Let $\{x_i\}_{i=0}^{\ell}$ and $\{y_i\}_{i=0}^{\ell}$ be series of real numbers from $[0,1]$, such that $x_0 = y_0 = 0$ and $x_i + y_{\ell-i} \leq 1$, for every $i \in \{0,\ldots,\ell\}$. There exists $i \in \{0,\ldots,\ell-1\}$ that satisfies $x_i + y_{\ell-i-1} \leq 1 - 1/\ell$.*

We now turn to present the $(3-2/\ell+\varepsilon, 2)$-stretch routing scheme.

Theorem 13. *Let $\ell > 1$ be an integer. There is a routing scheme for unweighted undirected graphs that uses $O(\ell \log n)$-bit labels, $\tilde{O}(\ell \frac{1}{\varepsilon} n^{\ell/(2\ell-1)})$ space at each vertex and $\tilde{O}(\frac{1}{\varepsilon})$ header size, to route a message between any pair of vertices on a $(3-2/\ell+\varepsilon, 2)$-stretch path.*

Proof.
Preprocessing: Let $q = n^{1/(2\ell-1)}$ and let $i \in \{0,\ldots,\ell\}$. For every $u \in V$, let $B_i(u) = B(u, \tilde{q}^i)$. Every $u \in V$ stores $B_\ell(u)$. For every $i \in \{0,\ldots,\ell\}$:

- We compute using Lemma 4 a set $L_i \subseteq V$ of size $\tilde{O}(q^{2\ell-i-1})$, such that $|C_{L_i}(w)| = O(n/q^{2\ell-i-1}) = O(q^i)$, for every $w \in V$. For each $u \in C_{L_i}(w)$ we store at u the routing information for a tree routing scheme of $T_{C_{L_i}}(w)$. This information is of poly-logarithmic size. Notice that $|B_{L_i}(u)| = O(q^i)$, thus u is contained in at most $O(q^i)$ trees and the storage required at u for this is $\tilde{O}(q^i)$.

- Let $w \in V$. For each $v \in C_{L_i}(w)$ we store at w the label of v in the tree routing scheme of $T_{C_{L_i}}(w)$. Since $|C_{L_i}(w)| = O(q^i)$ the storage required at w is $\tilde{O}(q^i)$.
- Let $u \in V$. For every $v \in V$, if $B_i(u) \cap B_{L_{\ell-i}}(v) \neq \emptyset$ we store in a hash table i at u in the entry of v a vertex $w \in \arg\min_{w' \in B_i(u) \cap B_{L_{\ell-i}}(v)} \{d(u, w') + d(w', v)\}$. Since $|C_{L_{\ell-i}}(w)| = O(q^{\ell-i})$ and $|B_i(u)| = \tilde{O}(q^i)$, the storage required for this at every vertex is $\tilde{O}(q^\ell)$.

For every $i \in \{0, \ldots, \ell-1\}$:

- Let c_i be a coloring function obtained using Lemma 6 with respect to the sets $B_i(u)$ for every $u \in V$, and let $\mathcal{U}^i = \{U_1^i, \ldots, U_{q^i}^i\}$ be a partition of V into q^i color sets induced by c_i. Let $j = \ell - i - 1$ and let $\mathcal{W}^j = \{W_1^j, \ldots, W_{q^i}^j\}$ be an arbitrary partition of L_j into q^i sets each with at most $|L_j|/q^i = q^{2\ell-(\ell-i-1)-1}/q^i = q^{\ell+i}/q^i = q^\ell$ vertices. For $w \in L_j$, let $\alpha_j(w)$ be the index of the set in $\mathcal{W}^j$ that contains w, that is $w \in W^j_{\alpha_j(w)}$. We use Lemma 8 with the partitions $\mathcal{U}^i$ and $\mathcal{W}^j$. The required storage at each vertex is $\tilde{O}(\frac{1}{\varepsilon}|L_j|/q^i + q^i) = \tilde{O}(\frac{1}{\varepsilon}q^\ell)$.
- At u we store for each $j \in \{1, \ldots, q^i\}$ a vertex $w \in B_i(u)$ with $c_i(w) = j$. By Lemma 6 such a vertex must exist. The storage required for this at u is $\tilde{O}(q^i)$.

In the label of $v \in V$ we store v and $\{p_{L_i}(v), \alpha_i(p_{L_i}(v)), d(v, p_{L_i}(v)), (p_{L_i}(v), v_i')\}_{i=0}^{\ell-1}$, where $(p_{L_i}(v), v_i')$ is the first edge on a shortest path from $p_{L_i}(v)$ to v.

Routing: A message is routed from u to v as follows. At u we check if there exists $i \in \{0, \ldots, \ell\}$ such that $B_i(u) \cap B_{L_{\ell-i}}(v) \neq \emptyset$. If this is the case we can obtain the vertex $w \in B_i(u) \cap B_{L_{\ell-i}}(v)$ that was saved at u. From Lemma 2 it follows that we can route the message from u to w on a shortest path. From w to v we can use the tree routing scheme of $T_{C_{L_{\ell-i}}}(w)$ as the label of v in the this tree routing scheme is stored at w. Thus, the message is routed on a path of length $d(u, w) + d(w, v)$. The vertex w is on a shortest path between u and v. The proof for that is identical to the proof given in Theorem 10 for the case of intersection.

Now consider the case that for every $i \in \{0, \ldots, \ell\}$ we have $B_i(u) \cap B_{L_{\ell-i}}(v) = \emptyset$. Let $a_i = r_u(\tilde{q}^i)$ and let $b_i = d(v, p_{L_i}(v)) - 1$ if $v \notin L_i$ and $b_i = 0$, otherwise. Let $j \in \arg\min_{i \in \{0, \ldots, \ell-1\}} \{a_i + b_{\ell-i-1}\}$. If there is more than one index that achieves the minimum we take the index of the highest value. Let $k = \ell - j - 1$. We obtain $\alpha_k(p_{L_k}(v))$ from the label of v and route on a shortest path to the vertex $w \in B_j(u)$ with $c_j(w) = \alpha_k(p_{L_k}(v))$, that is stored at u. From w the message is routed to $p_{L_k}(v)$ using Lemma 8. From $p_{L_k}(v)$ the message is forwarded to v_k' and then using the tree routing scheme of $T_{C_{L_k}}(v_k')$ it is routed to v. The total length of the path is at most $d(u, w) + (1 + \varepsilon)d(w, p_{L_k}(v)) + d(p_{L_k}(v), v)$. Let $d(u, v) = \Delta$.

We first consider the degenerated case of $\Delta = 1$. Since there is no intersection we have $B_\ell(u) \cap B_{L_0}(v) = \emptyset$, where $B_{L_0}(v) = \{v\}$. Therefore, $a_{\ell-1} \leq a_\ell = 0$ and $b_0 = 0$, and by the selection rule of j it must be that $j = \ell - 1$. The message is routed to $w \in B_{\ell-1}(u)$ and from there to $p_{L_0}(v) = v$. The length of this path is at most $3 + \varepsilon$.

Consider now the case that $\Delta > 1$. From the triangle inequality it follows that $d(w, p_{L_k}(v)) \leq d(u, w) + d(u, v) + d(v, p_{L_k}(v))$. If $j = 0$ then $u = w$, $a_0 = 0$, and we need to bound $(2 + \varepsilon)(b_{\ell-1} + 1) + (1 + \varepsilon)\Delta$. If $j > 0$ then $d(u, w) \leq a_j + 1$, and we need to bound $(2 + \varepsilon)(a_j + b_k + 2) + (1 + \varepsilon)\Delta$.

For every $i \in \{0, \ldots, \ell\}$ we have $B_i(u) \cap B_{L_{\ell-i}}(v) = \emptyset$ thus $a_i + b_{\ell-i} \leq \Delta - 1$. Let $x_0 = a_0/\Delta$ and $x_i = (a_i + 1)/\Delta$, for $i > 0$. Let $y_i = b_i/\Delta$. Since $x_0 = y_0 = 0$ and $x_i + y_{\ell-i} \leq 1$ we can apply Lemma 12 with the series $\{x_i\}_{i=0}^\ell$ and $\{y_i\}_{i=0}^\ell$.

For $j = 0$, we get from Lemma 12 that $a_0 + b_{\ell-1} = b_{\ell-1} \leq (1 - 1/\ell)\Delta$. Therefore,

$$\begin{aligned}
(2+\varepsilon)&(b_{\ell-1}+1) + (1+\varepsilon)\Delta \\
&\leq (2+\varepsilon)((1-1/\ell)\Delta + 1) + (1+\varepsilon)\Delta \\
&= \Delta((1+\varepsilon) + (1-1/\ell)(2+\varepsilon)) + 2 + \varepsilon \\
&= \Delta(3 + 2\varepsilon - (2+\varepsilon)/\ell) + 2 + \varepsilon \\
&\leq \Delta(3 + 3\varepsilon - (2+\varepsilon)/\ell) + 2.
\end{aligned}$$

If $j > 0$, it follows from Lemma 12 that $a_j + 1 + b_{\ell-j-1} = a_j + 1 + b_k \leq (1 - 1/\ell)\Delta$. Therefore,

$$\begin{aligned}
(2+\varepsilon)&(a_j + b_k + 2) + (1+\varepsilon)\Delta \\
&\leq (2+\varepsilon)((1-1/\ell)\Delta + 1) + (1+\varepsilon)\Delta \\
&\leq \Delta(3 + 3\varepsilon - (2+\varepsilon)/\ell) + 2.
\end{aligned}$$

□

The routing scheme of $(3 + 2/\ell + \varepsilon, 2)$-stretch is very similar to the one presented above. For the sake of completeness we provide it here with all the details.

As before we repeat a Lemma that was given in [21].

Lemma 14. *Let $\ell > 0$ be an integer. Let $\{x_i\}_{i=0}^\ell$ and $\{y_i\}_{i=0}^\ell$ be series of real numbers from $[0, 1]$, such that $x_0 = y_0 = 0$ and $x_i + y_{\ell-i} \leq 1$, for every $i \in \{0, \ldots, \ell\}$. There exists $i \in \{0, \ldots, \ell-1\}$ that satisfies $x_{i+1} + y_{\ell-i} \leq 1 + 1/\ell$.*

We now turn to present the $(3 + 2/\ell + \varepsilon, 2)$-stretch routing scheme.

Theorem 15. *Let $\ell > 1$ be an integer. There is a routing scheme for unweighted undirected graphs that uses $O(\ell \log n)$-bit labels, $\tilde{O}(\ell\frac{1}{\varepsilon}n^{\ell/(2\ell+1)})$ space at each vertex and $\tilde{O}(\frac{1}{\varepsilon})$ headers, to route a message between any pair of vertices on a $(3 + 2/\ell + \varepsilon, 2)$-stretch path.*

Proof.

Preprocessing: Let $q = n^{1/(2\ell+1)}$ and let $i \in \{0, \ldots, \ell\}$. For every $u \in V$, let $B_i(u) = B(u, \tilde{q}^i)$. Every $u \in V$ stores $B_\ell(u)$. For every $i \in \{0, \ldots, \ell\}$:

- We compute using Lemma 4 a set $L_i \subseteq V$ of size $\tilde{O}(q^{2\ell-i+1})$, such that $|C_{L_i}(w)| = O(n/q^{2\ell-i+1}) = O(q^i)$, for every $w \in V$. For each $u \in C_{L_i}(w)$ we store at u the routing information for a tree routing scheme of $T_{C_{L_i}}(w)$. This information is of poly-logarithmic size. Notice that $|B_{L_i}(u)| = O(q^i)$, thus u is contained in at most $O(q^i)$ trees and the storage required at u for this is $\tilde{O}(q^i)$.
- Let $w \in V$. For each $v \in C_{L_i}(w)$ we store at w the label of v in the tree routing scheme of $T_{C_{L_i}}(w)$. Since $|C_{L_i}(w)| = O(q^i)$ the storage required at w is $\tilde{O}(q^i)$.

- Let $u \in V$. For every $v \in V$, if $B_i(u) \cap B_{L_{\ell-i}}(v) \neq \emptyset$ we store in a hash table i at u in the entry of v a vertex $w \in \arg\min_{w' \in B_i(u) \cap B_{L_{\ell-i}}(v)} \{d(u,w') + d(w',v)\}$. Since $|C_{L_{\ell-i}}(w)| = O(q^{\ell-i})$ and $|B_i(u)| = \tilde{O}(q^i)$, the storage required for this at every vertex is $\tilde{O}(q^\ell)$.

For every $i \in \{1, \ldots, \ell\}$:

- Let c_i be a coloring function obtained using Lemma 6 with respect to the sets $B_i(u)$ for every $u \in V$, and let $\mathcal{U}^i = \{U_1^i, \ldots, U_{q^i}^i\}$ be a partition of V into q^i color sets induced by c_i. Let $j = \ell - i + 1$ and let $\mathcal{W}^j = \{W_1^j, \ldots, W_{q^i}^j\}$ be an arbitrary partition of L_j into q^i sets each with at most $|L_j|/q^i = q^{2\ell-(\ell-i+1)+1}/q^i = q^{\ell+i}/q^i = q^\ell$ vertices. For $w \in L_j$, let $\alpha_j(w)$ be the index of the set in $\mathcal{W}^j$ that contains w, that is $w \in W^j_{\alpha_j(w)}$. We use Lemma 8 with the partitions $\mathcal{U}^i$ and $\mathcal{W}^j$. The required storage at each vertex is $\tilde{O}(\frac{1}{\varepsilon}|L_j|/q^i + q^i) = \tilde{O}(\frac{1}{\varepsilon}q^\ell)$.

- At u we store for each $j \in \{1, \ldots, q^i\}$ a vertex $w \in B_i(u)$ with $c_i(w) = j$. By Lemma 6 such a vertex must exist. The storage required for this at u is $\tilde{O}(q^i)$.

In the label of $v \in V$ we store v and $\{p_{L_i}(v), \alpha_i(p_{L_i}(v)), d(v, p_{L_i}(v)), (p_{L_i}(v), v_i')\}_{i=1}^{\ell}$, where $(p_{L_i}(v), v_i')$ is the first edge on a shortest path from $p_{L_i}(v)$ to v.

Routing: A message is routed from u to v as follows. As before, at u we check if there exists $i \in \{0, \ldots, \ell\}$ such that $B_i(u) \cap B_{L_{\ell-i}}(v) \neq \emptyset$ and if this is the case we do the same as in Theorem 13.

Now consider the case that for every $i \in \{0, \ldots, \ell\}$ we have $B_i(u) \cap B_{L_{\ell-i}}(v) = \emptyset$. Let $a_i = r_u(\tilde{q}^i)$ and let $b_i = d(v, p_{L_i}(v)) - 1$ if $v \notin L_i$ and $b_i = 0$, otherwise. Let $j \in \arg\min_{i \in \{1,\ldots,\ell\}} \{a_i + b_{\ell-i+1}\}$. If there is more than one index that achieves the minimum we take the index of the highest value. Let $k = \ell - j + 1$. We obtain $\alpha_k(p_k(v))$ from the label of v and route on a shortest path to the vertex $w \in B_j(u)$ with $c_j(w) = \alpha_k(p_{L_k}(v))$, that is stored at u. From w the message is routed to $p_{L_k}(v)$ using Lemma 8. From $p_{L_k}(v)$ the message is forwarded to v_k' and then using the tree routing scheme of $T_{C_{L_k}}(v_k')$ it is routed to v. The total length of the path is at most $d(u,w) + (1+\varepsilon)d(w, p_{L_k}(v)) + d(p_{L_k}(v), v)$. Let $d(u,v) = \Delta$.

We first consider the degenerated case of $\Delta = 1$. Since there is no intersection, we have $B_\ell(u) \cap B_{L_0}(v) = \emptyset$ and thereby $a_\ell = 0$. Also we have that $B_{\ell-1}(u) \cap B_{L_1}(v) = \emptyset$, so it follows that $v \notin C_{L_1}(u)$ and $b_1 = 0$. We get that $a_\ell = b_1 = 0$ and by the selection rule of j it must be that $j = \ell$. The message is routed first to $w \in B_\ell(u)$. From there to $p_{L_1}(v)$ and then to v. The length of this path is at most $5 + \varepsilon$.

Consider now the case that $\Delta > 1$. From the triangle inequality it follows that $d(w, p_{L_k}(v)) \leq d(u,w) + d(u,v) + d(v, p_{L_k}(v))$. Therefore, we need to bound $(2+\varepsilon)(a_j + b_k + 2) + (1+\varepsilon)\Delta$.

For every $i \in \{0, \ldots, \ell\}$ we have $B_i(u) \cap B_{L_{\ell-i}}(v) = \emptyset$ thus $a_i + b_{\ell-i} \leq \Delta - 1$. Let $x_0 = a_0/\Delta$ and $x_i = (a_i+1)/\Delta$, for $i > 0$. Let $y_i = b_i/\Delta$. Since $x_0 = y_0 = 0$ and $x_i + y_{\ell-i} \leq 1$ we can apply Lemma 14 with the series $\{x_i\}_{i=0}^{\ell}$ and $\{y_i\}_{i=0}^{\ell}$ and get $a_j + 1 + b_{\ell-j-1} = a_j + 1 + b_k \leq (1 + 1/\ell)\Delta$. Therefore,

$$\begin{aligned}(2+\varepsilon)(a_j + b_k + 2) + (1+\varepsilon)\Delta \\ &\leq (2+\varepsilon)((1+1/\ell)\Delta + 1) + (1+\varepsilon)\Delta \\ &= \Delta((1+\varepsilon) + (1+1/\ell)(2+\varepsilon)) + 2 + \varepsilon \\ &= \Delta(3 + 2\varepsilon + (2+\varepsilon)/\ell) + 2 + \varepsilon \\ &\leq \Delta(3 + 2/\ell + 4\varepsilon) + 2.\end{aligned}$$

□

Stretch $4k-7+\varepsilon$. We present a $(4k-7+\varepsilon)$-stretch routing scheme that uses $O(k \log^2 n / \log\log n)$-bit labels size, $O(\frac{1}{\varepsilon}\log D + \log^2 n/\log\log n)$-bit headers and routing tables of $\tilde{O}(\frac{1}{\varepsilon}n^{1/k}\log D)$ size, where D is the normalized diameter of the graph. This should be compared with the $(4k-5)$-stretch routing scheme of Thorup and Zwick [23] that has $O(k\log^2 n/\log\log n)$-bit labels, $O(\log^2 n/\log\log n)$-bit headers and routing tables of $\tilde{O}(n^{1/k})$ size.

We start with a short overview of the $(4k-5)$-stretch routing scheme of Thorup and Zwick [23]. Let $k \geq 1$ and let $A_0 \supseteq A_1 \supseteq \ldots \supseteq A_k$ be vertex sets, such that $A_0 = V$, $A_k = \emptyset$ and A_i is formed by picking each vertex of A_{i-1} independently with probability $n^{-1/k}$. The expected size of A_i is $n^{1-i/k}$. For every $u \in V$, let $p_i(u) = p_{A_i}(u)$. The *bunch* of $u \in V$ is

$$B(u) = \cup_{i=0}^{k-1}\{v \in A_i \setminus A_{i+1} \mid d(u,v) < d(u, p_{i+1}(u))\},$$

where $d(u, p_k(u)) = \infty$.

The size of every bunch is $O(kn^{1/k})$ in expectation or $\tilde{O}(kn^{1/k})$ in the worst case. The cluster of $w \in A_i \setminus A_{i+1}$ is $C(w) = \{u \in V \mid d(u,w) < d(u, p_{i+1}(u))\}$.

In the preprocessing we compute $\{A_i\}_{i=0}^{k-1}$. Let $w \in V$ and let $T(w)$ be a shortest path tree rooted at w that spans the vertices of $C(w)$. For every $v \in V$, store $B(v)$ at v and the label of v in the tree routing scheme of $T(w)$ for every $w \in B(v)$. The label of v contains $\{p_i(v)\}_{i=0}^{k-1}$ and the tree labels of v in $\{T(p_i(v))\}_{i=0}^{k-1}$.

A message is routed from u to v as follows. At u we find the smallest i for which $u \in C(p_i(v))$. The message is routed using the tree routing scheme of $T(p_i(v))$ from u to v on a path of length at most $d(u, p_i(v)) + d(p_i(v), v)$. Using the triangle inequality we get $d(u, p_i(v)) + d(p_i(v), v) \leq 2d(p_i(v), v) + d(u,v)$. In [23] they show that for every $j \leq i$ it holds that $d(v, p_j(v)) \leq 2d(u,v) + d(v, p_{j-1}(v))$, and therefore, $d(v, p_j(v)) \leq 2jd(u,v)$. Since $j \leq i \leq k-1$ we get that $2d(p_i(v), v) + d(u,v) \leq 2(2(k-1)d(u,v)) + d(u,v) = (4k-3)d(u,v)$.

In [23] they further reduced the stretch to $4k-5$. Notice that $d(v, p_j(v)) \leq 2(j-1)d(u,v) + d(v, p_1(v))$. Using Lemma 4 they compute a set A_1 such that $|C(u)| = O(n^{1/k})$ for every $u \in A_0 \setminus A_1$. Each such u stores the set $C(u)$ and for every $v \in |C(u)|$ the label of v in the tree routing scheme of $T(u)$. To route a message from $u \in A_0 \setminus A_1$ to v, u checks if $v \in C(u)$ and if it is then the message is routed to v on $T(u)$. If not, then it follows that $d(v, p_1(v)) \leq d(u,v)$ (as opposed to $d(v, p_1(v)) \leq 2d(u,v)$ before) and the stretch is $4k-5$. See [23] for the full description.

We now turn to present our improved routing scheme.

Theorem 16. *Let $G = (V, E, \omega)$ be a weighted undirected graph, where $\omega : E \to \mathbb{R}^+$. For every $\varepsilon > 0$ and any integer $k > 2$, there is a routing scheme for G that uses $o(k\log^2 n)$-bit labels, $\tilde{O}(\frac{1}{\varepsilon}n^{1/k}\log D)$ space at each vertex* *and $\tilde{O}(\frac{1}{\varepsilon}\log D)$-bit header, to route a message between any pair of vertices on a $(4k-7+\varepsilon)$-stretch path.*

Proof.
Preprocessing: We store the same information as in the $(4k-5)$-stretch routing scheme of [23].

Let $q = n^{1/k}$. Additionally, we store $B(u, \tilde{q})$ at u, for every $u \in V$. This requires $\tilde{O}(n^{1/k})$ space at each vertex.

Let c be a coloring function with q colors obtained using Lemma 6 with respect to the sets $B(u, \tilde{q})$, for every $u \in V$. Let $\mathcal{U} = \{U_1, \ldots, U_q\}$ be the color sets induced by c. Let $\mathcal{W} = \{W_1, \ldots, W_q\}$ be an arbitrary partition of A_{k-2} into q sets each with at most $|A_{k-2}|/q = \tilde{O}(n^{2/k}/n^{1/k}) = \tilde{O}(n^{1/k})$ vertices. For $w \in A$, let $\alpha(w)$ be the index of the set in partition $\mathcal{W}$ that contains w, that is $w \in W_{\alpha(w)} \in \mathcal{W}$. We use Lemma 8 with the partitions $\mathcal{U}$ and $\mathcal{W}$. The required storage at each vertex is $\tilde{O}((\frac{1}{\varepsilon}\log D)|A_{k-2}|/q+q) = \tilde{O}(\frac{1}{\varepsilon}n^{1/k}\log D)$.

It follows from Lemma 6 that $B(u, \tilde{q})$ contains a vertex of each color. For every $i \in \{1, \ldots, q\}$ we store at u a vertex from $B(u, \tilde{q})$ of color i. The storage required for this at u is $\tilde{O}(n^{1/k})$.

The label of every $v \in V$ is composed of the label of v in the $(4k-5)$-stretch routing scheme and $\alpha(p_{k-2}(v))$.

Routing: A message is routed from u to v as follows. At u we check if $v \in B(u, \tilde{q})$. If this is the case the message is routed from u to v on a shortest path. If this is not the case we look for the smallest index i for which $u \in C(p_i(v))$. If $i \leq k-2$, the message is routed to v using the tree routing scheme of $T(p_i(v))$ on a path of length at most $d(u, p_i(v)) + d(p_i(v), v)$. It follows from the analysis of [23] that $d(u, p_i(v)) + d(p_i(v), v) \leq (4k-9)d(u, v)$, for $i \leq k-2$. If $i = k-1$ we route the message to a vertex $w \in B(u, \tilde{q})$ for which $c(w) = \alpha(p_{k-2}(v))$. The message is routed from w to $p_{k-2}(v)$ using Lemma 8, and from $p_{k-2}(v)$ to v using the tree routing scheme of $T(p_{k-2}(v))$ (recall that the label of v in the tree routing scheme of $T(p_{k-2}(v))$ is in v's label). The length of the path is at most $d(u, w) + (1+\varepsilon)d(w, p_{k-2}(v)) + d(p_{k-2}(v), v)$. Using the triangle inequality we can bound it with $d(u, v) + (1+\varepsilon)(2d(u, v) + d(p_{k-2}(v), v)) + d(p_{k-2}(v), v)$. From the analysis of [23] it follows that $d(p_{k-2}(v), v) \leq (2(k-3)+1)d(u, v)$ and we get that the stretch is $4k-7+\varepsilon$.

□

6. REFERENCES

[1] I. Abraham and C. Gavoille. On approximate distance labels and routing schemes with affine stretch. In David Peleg, editor, *DISC*, volume 6950 of *Lecture Notes in Computer Science*, pages 404–415. Springer, 2011.

[2] I. Abraham, C. Gavoille, D. Malkhi, N. Nisan, and M. Thorup. Compact name-independent routing with minimum stretch. In Phillip B. Gibbons and Micah Adler, editors, *SPAA*, pages 20–24. ACM, 2004.

[3] I. Abraham, C. Gavoille, D. Malkhi, N. Nisan, and M. Thorup. Compact name-independent routing with minimum stretch. *ACM Transactions on Algorithms*, 4(3), 2008.

[4] D. Aingworth, C. Chekuri, P. Indyk, and R. Motwani. Fast estimation of diameter and shortest paths (without matrix multiplication). *SIAM J. Comput.*, 28(4):1167–1181, 1999.

[5] I. Althöfer, G. Das, D. Dobkin, D. Joseph, and J. Soares. On sparse spanners of weighted graphs. *Discrete & Computational Geometry*, 9:81–100, 1993.

[6] M. Arias, L. Cowen, K. A. Laing, R. Rajaraman, and O. Taka. Compact routing with name independence. *SIAM J. Discrete Math.*, 20(3):705–726, 2006.

[7] B. Awerbuch, A. Bar-Noy, N. Linial, and D. Peleg. Compact distributed data structures for adaptive routing (extended abstract). In *STOC*, pages 479–489, 1989.

[8] B. Awerbuch, A. Bar-Noy, N. Linial, and D. Peleg. Improved routing strategies with succinct tables. *J. Algorithms*, 11(3):307–341, 1990.

[9] S. Baswana and S. Sen. A simple and linear time randomized algorithm for computing sparse spanners in weighted graphs. *Random Struct. Algorithms*, 30(4):532–563, 2007.

[10] S. Chechik. Compact routing schemes with improved stretch. In Panagiota Fatourou and Gadi Taubenfeld, editors, *PODC*, pages 33–41. ACM, 2013.

[11] L. Cowen. Compact routing with minimum stretch. *J. Algorithms*, 38(1):170–183, 2001.

[12] D. Dor, S. Halperin, and U. Zwick. All-pairs almost shortest paths. *SIAM J. Comput.*, 29(5):1740–1759, 2000.

[13] T. Eilam, C. Gavoille, and D. Peleg. Compact routing schemes with low stretch factor. *J. Algorithms*, 46(2):97–114, 2003.

[14] P. Erdős. Extremal problems in graph theory. *Theory of graphs and its applications*, pages 29–36, 1964.

[15] P. Fraigniaud and C. Gavoille. Routing in trees. In *ICALP*, pages 757–772, 2001.

[16] C. Gavoille and C. Sommer. Sparse spanners vs. compact routing. In *SPAA*, pages 225–234, 2011.

[17] D. Peleg and A. A. Schäffer. Graph spanners. *J. Graph Theory*, pages 99–116, 1989.

[18] D. Peleg and J. D. Ullman. An optimal synchronizer for the hypercube. *SIAM J. Computing*, 18(4):740–747, 1989.

[19] D. Peleg and E. Upfal. A trade-off between space and efficiency for routing tables. *J. ACM*, 36(3):510–530, 1989.

[20] M. Pătraşcu and L. Roditty. Distance oracles beyond the Thorup-Zwick bound. *SIAM J. Comput.*, 43(1):300–311, 2014.

[21] M. Pătraşcu, L. Roditty, and M. Thorup. A new infinity of distance oracles for sparse graphs. In *FOCS*, pages 738–747, 2012.

[22] N. Santoro and R. Khatib. Labelling and implicit routing in networks. *Comput. J.*, 28(1):5–8, 1985.

[23] M. Thorup and U. Zwick. Compact routing schemes. In *SPAA*, pages 1–10, 2001.

[24] M. Thorup and U. Zwick. Approximate distance oracles. *J. ACM*, 52(1):1–24, 2005.

Brief Announcement: Routing the Internet with Very Few Entries *

Cyril Gavoille
University of Bordeaux
LaBRI, France
gavoille@labri.fr

Christian Glacet
University of Bordeaux
LaBRI, France
glacet@labri.fr

Nicolas Hanusse
CNRS & Univ. of Bordeaux
LaBRI, France
hanusse@labri.fr

David Ilcinkas
CNRS & Univ. of Bordeaux
LaBRI, France
ilcinkas@labri.fr

ABSTRACT

This paper investigates compact routing schemes that are very efficient with respect to the memory used to store routing tables in internet-like graphs. We propose a new compact name-independent routing scheme whose theoretically proven average memory per node is upper-bounded by n^γ, with constant $\gamma < 1/2$, while the maximum memory of any node is bounded by $\sqrt{n}$ and the maximum stretch of any route is bounded by 5. These bounds are given for the Random Power Low Graphs (RPLG) and hold with high probability. Moreover, we experimentally show that our scheme is very efficient in terms of stretch and memory in internet-like graphs (CAIDA and other maps). We complete this study by comparing our analytic and experimental results to several compact routing schemes. In particular, we show that the average memory requirements is better by at least one order of magnitude than previous schemes for CAIDA maps on 16K nodes.

Keywords

compact routing; routing scheme; power-law graphs

1. INTRODUCTION

To achieve the routing task, a routing protocol typically uses *routing tables* stored at each node in order to find a path in the network. These tables are computed beforehand by what is usually called a *routing scheme*. One of the main goals in the context of routing is to reduce the storage of the routing information at each node (to allow quick routing decisions, fast updates, and scalability), while maintaining routes along paths as short as possible.

*Supported by the ANR project DISPLEXITY (ANR-11-BS02-014).

Permission to make digital or hard copies of part or all of this work for personal or classroom use is granted without fee provided that copies are not made or distributed for profit or commercial advantage and that copies bear this notice and the full citation on the first page. Copyrights for third-party components of this work must be honored. For all other uses, contact the Owner/Author.
Copyright is held by the owner/author(s).

PODC'15, July 21–23, 2015, Donostia-San Sebastián, Spain.
ACM 978-1-4503-3617-8/15/07.
http://dx.doi.org/10.1145/2767386.2767449.

A routing scheme that guarantees a sub-linear[1] routing table size at each node is qualified to be *compact*. There is a trade-off between the route efficiency (measured in terms of *stretch*) and the memory requirements (measured by the size or the number of entries in the routing tables). An extra desirable property of a routing scheme is to use arbitrary routing addresses (say based on processor IDs or MAC addresses) and thus independent of any topological information. Such routing schemes are called *name-independent*, in contrast with *labeled routing schemes* for which nodes are labeled by poly-logarithmic size addresses that do depend on the graph and can be freely designed to help routing decisions. In practical use, a labeled routing scheme has to use a location service that maps local information to labels, which could be a bottle-neck in regards to routing scalability, mobility and multi-homing.

Trade-offs between stretch and memory for routing in arbitrary graphs are well known, and optimal name-independent algorithms exist (see for example [AGM+08]). Nevertheless for some types of routing, like routing in the AS-internet graph, optimizations can be done and trade-offs are still barely known. Indeed, this network, like many others, exhibits several structural properties that can help a lot for routing.

Routing in internet-like graphs has already received some attention in the literature. In particular [CSTW12] and [TZLL13] respectively studied labeled and name-independent compact routing scheme for internet-like graphs. They both proved that the average number of entries in the routing tables for Random Power Low Graphs (RPLG, see Fig. 1) can be significantly lower than for arbitrary graphs, and they both confirmed experimentally their analytic results on large CAIDA and "BC" maps[2].

2. RESULTS

Our contributions are the following. First we present a new stretch-5 name-independent routing scheme, that guar-

[1]W.r.t. the number of nodes in the graph.

[2]The latter maps are the benchmark graphs used in the study of [BC06]. They are based on Power Low Random Graphs (a.k.a. PLRG) a model for internet-like graphs whose analytic study is less convenient than the RPLG model.

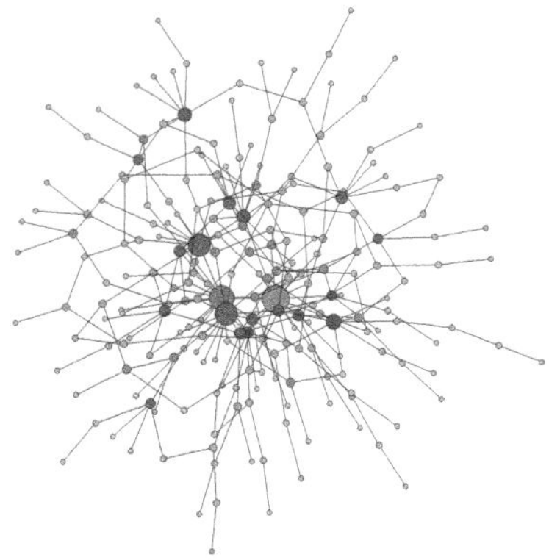

Figure 1: The largest connected component of a graph sampled from RPLG(n,τ) for $n = 300$ and power-law exponent $\tau = 2.9$. This component has 216 nodes (whose size is depicted proportional to their degree), 280 edges, and maximum degree 19.

antees, in internet-like graphs, to produce compact routing tables of very small average size at every node.

THEOREM 1. *For any n-node graph sampled from* RPLG(n,τ) *with power-low exponent* $\tau \in (2,3)$, *within its largest connected component, the name-independent routing scheme* CLUSTER *has w.h.p.*[3] *the following properties:*

1. *the maximal size of the routing tables is* $O(\sqrt{n})$;
2. *the average size of the routing tables is*[4] $\tilde{O}(n^\gamma)$ *with* $\gamma = \frac{1}{2} \cdot \frac{\tau-2}{\tau-1}$ *for* $\tau \le 2.5$, *and* $\gamma = \frac{(\tau-2)^2}{\tau-1}$ *otherwise;*
3. *the stretch factor is at most* 5;
4. *every routing decision takes constant time; and*
5. *headers have poly-logarithmic size.*

Actually, Properties 3,4,5 hold for every connected graph.

Secondly we experimentally compare our scheme to AGMNT [AGM+08], DCR [GGHI13], HDLBR [TZLL13], and TZ$^+$ [CSTW12]. In particular, Table 1 shows that our scheme, CLUSTER, improves significantly the routing table sizes on a CAIDA map (sampled from the AS network [Cai]) and on a BC graph, even though TZ$^+$ (a specialized variant of Thorup-Zwick routing scheme) is a labeled routing scheme. Moreover, TZ$^+$ scheme makes the assumption that τ is known whereas our scheme does not need this parameter. We have provided a fully distributed implementation for the schemes DCR, HDLBR, CLUSTER, and proved that each one generates all the routing tables in $\tilde{O}(n^{3/2})$ messages. No distributed implementation within $o(n^2)$ messages is known for AGMNT.

3. OUR SCHEME

Preliminaries.

Similarly to TZ$^+$ and HDLBR, our algorithm is based on a set of *landmark nodes* positioned in the "center" of the graph. In our case, the k landmarks are composed of the highest degree node ℓ_1 plus its $k-1$ neighbors of highest degree, where $k-1 = \min\{\lceil\sqrt{n}\rceil, \deg(\ell_1)\}$. Moreover, every landmark node ℓ_i, $i \in \{1,\ldots,k\}$, is provided with a distinct color $c(\ell_i) \in \{1,\ldots,k\}$. Landmark nodes also share a balanced (w.h.p.) hash function h, as in [AGM+08], mapping in constant time all node identifiers to the color set $\{1,\ldots,k\}$.

Routing tables.

Any landmark node ℓ_i stores one entry per node v whose hash value is equal to the color of ℓ_i, namely $c(\ell_i)$. This entry corresponds to the path from ℓ_i to v in some fixed shortest-path spanning tree T rooted at ℓ_1. Each path of T can be compressed into a poly-logarithmic size entry, e.g. by using the classical labeled compact routing scheme for trees from [FG01]. This adds one entry to every node. Every landmark also stores one entry for each color c. This entry corresponds to the next-hop from ℓ_i to the landmark with color c along a shortest path in the subgraph induced by the landmarks, a diameter two subgraph. As the hash function is balanced, the number of entries for landmark routing tables is at most $k + n/k + O(1)$.

For every non-landmark node u, we define its *vicinity ball* $\mathcal{B}_u$ as the set of all nodes that are strictly closer to u than ℓ_u, where ℓ_u is a landmark closest to u. For every node v in $\mathcal{B}_u \cup N(u) \cup \{\ell_u\}$, node u stores the next-hop on a shortest path to v, where $N(u)$ denotes the neighbors of u. Thus, the number of entries for the routing table of u is at most $|\mathcal{B}_u| + \deg(u) + O(1)$. However, for each node u with no landmark neighbors, $N(u) \subseteq \mathcal{B}_u$.

Routing from u to v.

If u has an entry for v, then u can route directly to v. Otherwise u forwards the packet to ℓ_u, its closest landmark. At this point, ℓ_u computes the hash value $h(v)$ of node v and forwards the packet to the landmark ℓ_h of color $h(v)$. Finally, the information stored in the entry corresponding to v in the routing table of ℓ_h is used to route the packet to its final destination v via the tree T.

4. SKETCH OF THE PROOF

The proof of our main theorem is based on topological observations done on RPLG(n,τ) graphs [CL03]. Those graphs are defined as follows. With each node v_i, $i \in \{1,\ldots,n\}$, we assign a weight $w_i = (n/i)^{1/(\tau-1)}$. There is an edge between node v_i and v_j with probability $\min\{1, w_i w_j/\sigma\}$, where $\sigma = \sum_i w_i$.

Memory size analysis.

The first step is to show that, w.h.p., $k = \lceil\sqrt{n}\rceil$, i.e., the highest degree node ℓ_1 is larger than $\sqrt{n}$. This implies that landmark routing tables have at most $2\sqrt{n}$ entries, and contributes to at most $k \cdot 2\sqrt{n} = 2n$ to the total number of entries. The degree of every non-landmark u is also lower than $\sqrt{n}$. So, the maximum number of entries in a routing table is dominated by $\max_u |\mathcal{B}_u| + \sqrt{n}$. And, the average number of entries is bounded by $\frac{1}{n}\sum_u |\mathcal{B}_u| + O(1)$ since the average degree is $O(\sigma/n) = O(1)$, the main component has $\Omega(n)$ nodes, and the landmark routing tables contribute to only $2n/\Omega(n) = O(1)$ entries on the average.

Next we show that the sum of the weights, called the *volume*, of the set of nodes inside the cluster is polynomial, depends on $\tau \in (2,3)$, but is always much larger than $\sqrt{n}$. Then, we use one lemma from [CL03] which states that (w.h.p.) two sets of nodes with high volumes are adjacent

[3] I.e., with probabilty at least $1 - 1/n$.

[4] The notation $\tilde{O}(f(n))$ stands for $O(f(n) \cdot \text{polylog} f(n))$.

Name-indep.	RPLG(n,τ) for $\tau = 2.1$			AS graph ($n = 16\,301$)			BC graph (n = 10K, $\tau = 2.1$)		
	Stretch$_{\max}$	Mem$_{\text{avg}}$	Mem$_{\max}$	Stretch$_{\text{avg}}$	Mem$_{\text{avg}}$	Mem$_{\max}$	Stretch$_{\text{avg}}$	Mem$_{\text{avg}}$	Mem$_{\max}$
AGMNT	3	$\tilde{O}(\sqrt{n})$	$\tilde{O}(\sqrt{n})$	??	465	1 261	1.56	396	1 143
DCR	7	$\tilde{O}(\sqrt{n})$	$\tilde{O}(\sqrt{n})$	1.74	465	1 261	1.63	396	1 143
HDLBR	$\geq$6	$O(\sqrt{n})$	$\Omega(n^{1/2+\varepsilon})$	1.52	106	2 324	1.24	404	1 877
CLUSTER	5	$\tilde{O}(n^{1/22})$	$O(\sqrt{n})$	1.59	4.05	415	1.75	6.47	228
Labeled									
TZ$^+$	5	$O(n^{1/12})$	$O(n^{1/12})$	??	??	??	1.30	55.2	??

Table 1: According to [VPSV02] the AS power-law exponent τ can be estimated to 2.1. The main component of the BC graph has 7873 nodes, whereas the AS graph is connected. It is proved in [TZLL13] that the route length for HDLBR is at most $2d + 2\delta(\tau)$ where d is the source-destination distance and $\delta(\tau)$ the inter-landmark distance. We note that, w.h.p., $\delta(2.1) > 1$, and from this observation one can derive that the maximum stretch is at least 6. We ran our own (distributed) version of HDLBR since results for AS and BC maps were not available. TZ$^+$ is not a name-independent routing scheme, and we have not implemented it. Thus, we have some unknown experimental values for this algorithm.

or intersect. This implies that the volume of every vicinity ball is upper bounded by a small polynomial. The last part consists in exhibiting a strong relationship between the volume and the number of nodes in the vicinity balls. We use the facts, shown in [CSTW12], that the volume of a set of nodes is likely to be equal to the sum of their degrees, and that two balls of radius r and $r+1$ do not differ too much in terms of their number of nodes.

Stretch analysis.

From the routing algorithm from u to v taken from the main connected component of G, we derive that the route length is either the distance $d = d_G(u,v)$ if $v \in \mathcal{B}_u$, or bounded by $d_G(u,\ell_u)+d_G(\ell_u,\ell_h)+d_T(\ell_h,v)$ otherwise. (Recall that the route goes first from u to ℓ_u along a shortest path in G, then to ℓ_h using the landmark subgraph, and then to v using T.) If w denotes the closest ancestor of v in T in the cluster, then the length of the route from ℓ_h to v can be bounded by $d_T(\ell_h,v) \leq d_T(\ell_h,w)+d_T(w,v) \leq d_G(\ell_v,v)+2$ by definition of ℓ_v and T. Since $d_G(\ell_u,\ell_h) \leq 2$, the route length is at most $d_G(u,\ell_u) + d_G(v,\ell_v) + 4$. Note also that $d_G(v,\ell_v) \leq d_G(v,u)+d_G(u,\ell_u) = d+d_G(u,\ell_u)$ since otherwise ℓ_u would be a closer landmark for v than ℓ_v. Assuming that $v \notin \mathcal{B}_u$ (otherwise the stretch is 1), it turns out also that $d_G(u,\ell_u) \leq d$. Overall, combining these inequalities, the route length is at most $3d+4$. However, if u is a landmark, the route length is at most $d_G(u,\ell_u)+d_G(v,\ell_v)+4 \leq d_G(u,\ell_u) + [d + d_G(u,\ell_u)] + 4 = d+4$ since in this case $\ell_u = u$.

To summarize, either u is a landmark and the stretch is at most $(d+4)/d = 1+4/d \leq 5$, or u is not a landmark and the stretch is at most $(3d+4)/d = 3+4/d$. This is at most 5 if $d \geq 2$. On the other hand, if $d=1$ then the stretch is only 1 since each non-landmark node u has the entries for $N(u)$. Thus, the stretch factor of our scheme is at most 5 for all connected graphs.

Optimization.

For our experimentations, we proceed to several optimizations for the CLUSTER scheme. In particular, for every non-landmark node u, we remove every entry for $w \in \mathcal{B}_u$ such that the shortest-path routing from u to w can actually be achieved by routing from u to its landmark ℓ_u. In other words, we can clean $\mathcal{B}_u$ by removing every node w such that $d_G(u,w) = 1 + d_G(u',w)$ where u' is the next-hop to reach ℓ_u from u. Another optimization addresses the landmark routing tables. For a landmark ℓ_i, the set of entries to each node v with $h(v) = c(\ell_i)$ is partionned into: 1) the entries for nodes at distance at most $r = \lceil \log n/\log\log n \rceil$ from ℓ_i; and 2) the remaining entries (for further nodes). For these latter entries we store a routing label of $\log^2 n/\log\log n = r\log n$ bits used for the routing in T as described in [FG01]. And, for the former entries we use a different routing label, still of $r\log n$ bits, composed of the first r next-hops on a shortest path from ℓ_i to v. Overall, this improves the average route length without extra cost on the number of entries or their size.

5. REFERENCES

[AGM+08] I. Abraham, C. Gavoille, D. Malkhi, N. Nisan, and M. Thorup. Compact name-independent routing with minimum stretch. *ACM Transactions on Algorithms*, 4(3):37, 2008.

[BC06] A. Brady and L. J. Cowen. Compact routing on power law graphs with additive stretch. In *8th ALENEX*, pp. 119–128, 2006.

[Cai] The CAIDA AS Relationships Dataset, www.caida.org/data/active/as-relationships.

[CL03] F. Chung and L. Lu. The Average Distance in a Random Graph with Given Expected Degrees. *Internet Mathematics*, 1(1):91–113, 2003.

[CSTW12] W. Chen, C. Sommer, S.-H. Teng, and Y. Wang. A compact routing scheme and approximate distance oracle for power-law graphs. *ACM Transactions on Algorithms*, 9(1):A4, 2012.

[FG01] P. Fraigniaud and C. Gavoille. Routing in trees. *28th ICALP*, vol. 2076 of LNCS, pp. 757–772, 2001.

[GGHI13] C. Gavoille, C. Glacet, N. Hanusse, and D. Ilcinkas. On the communication complexity of distributed name-independent routing schemes. In *27th DISC*, vol. 8205 of LNCS, pp. 418–432, 2013.

[TZLL13] M. Tang, G. Zhang, T. Lin, and J. Liu. HDLBR: A name-independent compact routing scheme for power-law networks. *Computer Communications*, 36(3):351–359, 2013.

[VPSV02] A. Vázquez, R. Pastor-Satorras, and A. Vespignani. Internet topology at the router and autonomous system level. *ArXiv preprint [cond-mat/0206084]*, 2002.

Terminating Distributed Construction of Shapes and Patterns in a Fair Solution of Automata*

Othon Michail
Computer Technology Institute & Press "Diophantus" (CTI)
Patras, Greece
michailo@cti.gr

ABSTRACT

In this work, we consider a *solution of automata* similar to *Population Protocols* and *Network Constructors*. The automata, also called *nodes*, move passively in a well-mixed solution and can *cooperate* by interacting in pairs. During every such interaction, the nodes, apart from updating their states, may also choose to connect to each other in order to start forming some required structure. The model introduced here is a more applied version of Network Constructors, imposing *geometrical constraints* on the permissible connections. Each node can connect to other nodes only via a very limited number of *local ports*, which implies that at any given time it has only a *bounded number of neighbors*. Connections are always made at *unit distance* and are *perpendicular to connections of neighboring ports*. Though this variation can no longer form abstract networks, it is still capable of forming very practical *2D or 3D shapes*. We develop *new techniques* for determining the computational and constructive capabilities of our model. One of the main novelties, concerns our attempt to overcome the inherent inability of such systems to terminate. In particular, exploiting the assumptions that the system is well-mixed and has a unique leader, we *give terminating protocols that are correct with high probability* (w.h.p.). This allows us to develop terminating subroutines that can be *sequentially composed* to form larger *modular protocols*. One of our main results is a *terminating protocol counting the size n of the system* w.h.p.. We then use this protocol as a subroutine in order to develop our *universal constructors*, establishing that *it is possible for the nodes to self-organize w.h.p. into arbitrarily complex shapes and additionally always terminate.*

Categories and Subject Descriptors:
C.2.4 [Computer-communication Networks]: Distributed Systems; C.2.1 [Computer-communication Networks]: Network Architecture and Design—*distributed networks, network communications, network topology*; F.1.1 [Computation By Abstract Devices]: Models of Computation—*automata, computability theory, unbounded-action devices*; F.1.2 [Computation By Abstract Devices]: Modes of Computation—*parallelism and concurrency, probabilistic computation*; J.2 [Computer Applications]: Physical Sciences and Engineering—*Chemistry, Physics*

Keywords: network construction; programmable matter; shape formation; population; distributed protocol; interacting automata; fairness; random schedule; self-organization

1. INTRODUCTION

Recent research in distributed computing theory and practice is taking its first timid steps on the pioneering endeavor of investigating the possible *relationships of distributed computing systems to physical and biological systems.* The first main motivation for this is the fact that a wide range of physical and biological systems are governed by underlying laws that are essentially *algorithmic.* The second is that the higher-level physical or behavioral properties of such systems are usually the outcome of the coexistence and constant interaction, which may include both cooperation and competition, of *very large numbers of relatively simple distributed entities* respecting such laws. This effort, to the extent that its perspective allows, is expected to promote our understanding of the algorithmic aspects of our (distributed) natural world and to develop innovative artificial systems inspired by these aspects.

Ulam's and von Neuman's Cellular Automata (cf. e.g. [16]), essentially a distributed grid network of automata, have been used as models for self-replication, for modeling several physical systems (e.g. neural activity, bacterial growth, pattern formation in nature), and for understanding emergence, complexity, and self-organization issues. Population Protocols of Angluin *et al.* [1] were originally motivated by highly dynamic networks of simple sensor nodes that cannot control their mobility. Recently, Doty [4] demonstrated their formal equivalence to *chemical reaction networks* (CRNs), which model chemistry in a *well-mixed solution.* Moreover, the *Network Constructors* extension of population protocols [12], showed that a population of finite-automata that interact randomly like molecules in a well-mixed solution and that can establish bonds with each other according to the rules of a common small protocol, can construct arbitrarily complex stable networks. In the young area of DNA self-assembly it has been already demonstrated that it is possible to fold long, single-stranded

*Supported in part by the project FOCUS, implemented under the "ARISTEIA" Action of the OP EdLL co-funded by the EU (ESF) and Greek National Resources.
Full version: http://arxiv.org/abs/1503.01913

Permission to make digital or hard copies of all or part of this work for personal or classroom use is granted without fee provided that copies are not made or distributed for profit or commercial advantage and that copies bear this notice and the full citation on the first page. Copyrights for components of this work owned by others than the author(s) must be honored. Abstracting with credit is permitted. To copy otherwise, or republish, to post on servers or to redistribute to lists, requires prior specific permission and/or a fee. Request permissions from permissions@acm.org.
PODC'15, July 21–23, 2015, Donostia-San Sebastián, Spain.
Copyright is held by the owner/author(s). Publication rights licensed to ACM.
ACM 978-1-4503-3617-8/15/07 ...$15.00.
http://dx.doi.org/10.1145/2767386.2767402.

DNA molecules into arbitrary nanoscale two-dimensional shapes and patterns [14]. Recently, an interesting theoretical model was proposed, the *Nubot* model, for studying the complexity of self-assembled structures with active molecular components [17]. Finally a system, called the *Kilobot*, was reported recently [15], that demonstrates programmable self-assembly of complex two-dimensional shapes by a swarm consisting of *a thousand* small, cheap, and simple autonomous robots designed to operate in large groups and to cooperate through local interactions.

The established and ongoing research seems to have opened the road towards a vision that will further reshape society to an unprecedented degree. This vision concerns our ability to *manipulate matter* via information-theoretic and computing mechanisms and principles. It will be the jump from amorphous information to the *incorporation of information to the physical world*. Information will not only be part of the physical environment: it will constantly interact with the surrounding environment and will have the ability to reshape it. *Matter will become programmable* [7] which is a plausible future outcome of progress in high-volume nanoscale assembly that makes it feasible to inexpensively produce millimeter-scale units that integrate computing, sensing, actuation, and locomotion mechanisms. This will enable the astonishing possibility of transferring the discrete dynamics from the computer memory black-box to the real world and to achieve a *physical realization of any computer-generated object*. It will have profound implications for how we think about chemistry and materials. Materials will become user-programmed and smart, adapting to changing conditions in order to maintain, optimize or even create a whole new functionality using means that are intrinsic to the material itself. It will even change the way we think about engineering and manufacturing. We will for the first time be capable of building smart machines that adapt to their surroundings, such as an airplane wing that adjusts its surface properties in reaction to environmental variables [18], or even further realize machines that can self-built autonomously.

1.1 Our Approach-Contribution

We imagine here a "solution" of automata (also called *nodes* or *processes* throughout the paper), a setting similar to that of Population Protocols and Network Constructors. Due to its highly restricted computational nature and its very local perspective, each individual automaton can practically achieve nothing on its own. However, when many of them cooperate, each contributing its meager computational capabilities, impressive global outcomes become feasible. This is also, for example, the case in the Kilobot system, where each individual robot is a remarkably simple artifact that can perform only primitive locomotion via a simple vibration mechanism. Still, when a thousand of them work together, their global dynamics and outcome resemble the complex functions of living organisms. From our perspective, cooperation involves the capability of the nodes to communicate by interacting in pairs and to bind to each other in an algorithmically controlled way. In particular, during an interaction, the nodes can update their local states according to a small common program that is stored in their memories and may also choose to connect to each other in order to start forming some required structure. Later on, if needed, they may choose to drop their connection, e.g. for rearrangement purposes. We may think of such nodes as the smallest possible programmable pieces of matter. For example, they could be tiny nanorobots or programmable molecules (e.g. DNA strands). Naturally, such elementary entities are not (yet) expected to be equipped with some internal mobility mechanism. Still, it is reasonable to expect that they could be part of some dynamic environment, like a boiling liquid or the human circulatory system, providing an external (to the nodes) interaction mechanism. This, together with the fact that the dynamics of such models have been recently shown to be equivalent to those of CRNs, motivate the idea of regarding such systems as *a solution of programmable entities*. We model such an environment by imagining an *adversary scheduler* operating in discrete steps and selecting in every step a pair of nodes to interact with each other.

Our main focus in this work, building upon the findings of [12], is to further investigate the cooperative structure formation capabilities of such systems. Our first main goal is to introduce a more realistic and more applicable version of network constructors by adjusting some of the abstract parameters of the model of [12]. In particular, we introduce some physical (or geometrical) constraints on the connections that the processes are allowed to form. In the network constructors model of [12], there were no such imposed restrictions, in the sense that, at any given step, any two processes were candidates for an interaction, independently of their relative positioning in the existing structure/network. This was very convenient for studying the capability of such systems to self-organize into abstract networks and it helped show that arbitrarily complex networks are in principle constructible. On the other hand, this is not expected to be the actual mechanism of at least the first potential implementations. First implementations will most probably be characterized by physical and geometrical constraints. To capture this in our model, we assume that each device can connect to other devices only via a very limited number of ports, usually four or six, which implies that, at any given time, a device has only a bounded number of neighbors. Moreover, we further restrict the connections to be always made at unit distance and to be perpendicular to connections of neighboring ports. Though such a model can no longer form abstract networks, it may still be capable of forming very practical 2D or 3D shapes. This is also in agreement with natural systems, where the complexity and physical properties of a system are rarely the result of an unrestricted interconnection between entities.

It can be immediately observed that the universal constructors of [12] do not apply in this case. In particular, those constructors cannot be adopted in order to characterize the constructive power of the model considered here. The reason is that they work by arranging the nodes in a long line and then exploiting the fact that connections are "elastic" and allow any pair of nodes of the line to interact independently of the distance between them. In contrast, no elasticity is allowed in the more local model considered here, where a long line can still be formed but only adjacent nodes of the line are allowed to interact with each other. As a result, we have to develop new techniques for determining the computational and constructive capabilities of our model. The other main novelty of our approach, concerns our attempt to overcome the inability of such systems to detect termination due to their limited global knowledge and their limited computational resources. For example, it can be easily shown that deterministic termination of population protocols can fail even in determining whether there is a single a in an input assignment, mainly because the nodes do not know and cannot store in their memories neither the size of the network nor some upper bound on the time it takes to meet (or to influence or to be influenced by) every other node. To overcome the storage issue, we exploit the ability of nodes to self-assemble into larger structures that can then be used as distributed memories of any desired length. Moreover, we exploit the common (and natural in several cases) assumption that the system is *well-mixed*, meaning that, at any given time, all permissible pairs of node-ports have an equal probability to interact, in order to give *terminating protocols that are correct with high probability*. This is crucial not only because it allows to improve eventual stabilization to eventual termination but, most importantly, because it allows to develop terminating subroutines that can be sequentially composed to form larger modular protocols. Such protocols are more efficient, more natural, and more amenable to clear proofs of correctness, compared to existing protocols that are based on composing all subroutines in parallel and "sequentializing" them eventually by perpetual reinitializations. To the best of our knowledge, [13] is the only work that has considered this issue but with totally different and more deterministic assumptions. Several other papers [1, 2, 12] have already exploited a uniform random interaction model, but in all cases for analyzing the expected time to convergence of stabilizing protocols and not for maximizing the correctness probability of terminating protocols, as we do here.

Our model for shape construction is strongly inspired by the Population Protocol model [1] and the Mediated Population Protocol model [10]. For introductory texts on population protocols see [3, 11]. For further literature related to the present work, consult the full paper and [12].

Section 2 formally defines the model under consideration and brings together all definitions and basic facts that are used throughout the paper. Section 3 introduces our technique for counting the size n of the system with high probability. The main result of that section (i.e. Theorem 1) is of particular importance as it underlies all sequential composition arguments that follow in the paper. In particular, the protocol of Section 3.1 is used as a subroutine in our *universal constructors*, establishing that *it is possible to construct with high probability arbitrarily complex shapes (and patterns) by terminating protocols*. These *universality* results are discussed in Section 4. Finally, in Section 5 we conclude and give further research directions that are opened by our work. In the full paper we also provide direct constructors for some basic shape construction problems and study the problem of shape self-replication.

2. THE MODEL

The system consists of a population V of n distributed *processes* (finite-state machines), called *nodes* throughout. Every node has a bounded number of ports which it uses to interact with other nodes. In the 2-dimensional (2D) case, there are four ports p_y, p_x, p_{-y}, and p_{-x}, which for notational convenience are usually denoted u, r, d, and l, respectively (for *up*, *right*, *down*, and *left*, respectively). Neighboring ports are perpendicular to each other, forming local axes; that is $u \perp r$, $r \perp d$, $d \perp l$, and $l \perp u$. Similar assumptions hold for the 3D case. An important remark is that the above coordinates are only for local purposes and do not necessarily represent the actual orientation of a node in the system. Nodes may interact in pairs, whenever a port of one node w is at unit distance and in straight line (w.r.t. to the local axes) from a port of another node v.

DEFINITION 1. *A 2D protocol is defined by a 4-tuple* $(Q, q_0, Q_{out}, \delta)$, *where* Q *is a finite set of* node-states, $q_0 \in Q$ *is the* initial node-state, $Q_{out} \subseteq Q$ *is the set of* output node-states, *and* $\delta : (Q \times P) \times (Q \times P) \times \{0,1\} \to Q \times Q \times \{0,1\}$ *is the* transition function, *where* $P = \{u, r, d, l\}$ *is the set of* ports. *When required, also a special* initial leader-state $L_0 \in Q$ *may be defined.*

If $\delta((a,p_1),(b,p_2),c) = (a',b',c')$, we call $(a,p_1),(b,p_2), c \to (a',b',c')$ a *transition* (or *rule*). A transition $(a,p_1),(b, p_2), c \to (a',b',c')$ is called *effective* if $x \neq x'$ for at least one $x \in \{a,b,c\}$ and *ineffective* otherwise.

Let $E = \{(v_1,p_1)(v_2,p_2) : v_1 \neq v_2 \in V \text{ and } p_1,p_2 \in P\}$ be the set of all unordered pairs of node-ports (cf. [12] for more details on unordered interactions). A *configuration* C is a pair (C_V, C_E), where $C_V : V \to Q$ specifies the state of each node and $C_E : E \to \{0,1\}$ specifies the state of every possible pair of node-ports (or edge). In particular, an edge in state 0 is called *inactive* and an edge in state 1 is called *active*. The initial configuration is always the one in which all nodes are in state q_0 (apart possibly from a unique leader in state L_0) and all edges are *inactive*. Execution of the protocol proceeds in discrete steps. In every step, a pair of node-ports $(v_1,p_1)(v_2,p_2)$ is selected by an *adversary scheduler* and these nodes interact via the corresponding ports and update their states and the state of the edge joining them according to the transition function δ.

Every configuration C defines a *set of shapes* $G[A(C)]$, where $A(C) = C_E^{-1}[1]$; i.e. the network induced by the active edges of C. Observe that not all possible $A(C)$ are valid given our geometrical restrictions, that connections are made at unit distance and are perpendicular whenever they correspond to consecutive ports of a node. For example, if $(v_1,r)(v_2,l) \in A(C)$ then $(v_1,l)(v_2,r) \notin A(C)$. In general, $A(C)$ is *valid* if any connected component defined by it (when arranged according to the geometrical constraints) is a subnetwork of the *2D grid network with unit distances*. A valid $A(C_{t-1})$ also restricts the possible selections of the scheduler at step $t \geq 1$. In particular, $(v_1,p_1)(v_2,p_2) \in E$ can be selected for interaction (or *is permitted*) at step t iff $A(C_{t-1}) \cup \{(v_1,p_1)(v_2,p_2)\}$ is valid. Observe that any edge that is active before step t is trivially permitted at step t. From now on, we call a 2D (3D) *shape* any connected subnetwork of the 2D (3D) grid network with unit distances.

Throughout the paper we restrict attention to configurations C in which $A(C)$ is valid. We write $C \to C'$ if C' *is reachable in one step from* C (meaning via a single interaction that is permitted on C). We say that C' is *reachable* from C and write $C \rightsquigarrow C'$, if there is a sequence of configurations $C = C_0, C_1, \ldots, C_t = C'$, such that $C_i \to C_{i+1}$ for all i, $0 \leq i < t$. An *execution* is a finite or infinite sequence of configurations $C_0, C_1, C_2, \ldots$, where C_0 is the initial configuration and $C_i \to C_{i+1}$, for all $i \geq 0$. We only consider *fair* executions, so we require that for every pair of configurations C and C' such that $C \to C'$, if C occurs infinitely often in the execution then so does C'. In most cases, we assume that interactions are chosen by a *uniform random scheduler* which in every step selects independently and uniformly at random one of the permitted interactions. The uniform random scheduler is fair with probability 1. In this work, with high probability (abbreviated w.h.p.) means with probability at least $1 - 1/n^c$ for some constant $c \geq 1$.

We define the *output of a configuration* C as the set of shapes $G_{out}(C) = (V_s, E_s)$ where $V_s = \{u \in V : C_V(u) \in Q_{out}\}$ and $E_s = A(C) \cap \{(v_1, p_1)(v_2, p_2) : v_1 \neq v_2 \in V_s$ and $p_1, p_2 \in P\}$. In words, the output shapes of a configuration consist of those nodes that are in output states and those edges between them that are active. Throughout this work, we are interested in obtaining a single shape as the final output of the protocol. As already mentioned, our main focus will be on terminating protocols. In this case, we assume that $Q_{out} \subseteq Q_{halt} \subseteq Q$, where, for all $q_{halt} \in Q_{halt}$, every rule containing q_{halt} is ineffective.

DEFINITION 2. *We say that an execution of a protocol on* n *processes* constructs (stably constructs) a shape G, *if it terminates (stabilizes, resp.) with output* G.

Every 2D shape G has a unique minimum 2D rectangle R_G enclosing it. R_G is a shape with its nodes labeled from $\{0, 1\}$. The nodes of G are labeled 1, the nodes in $V(R_G) \backslash V(G)$ are labeled 0, and all edges are active. It is like filling G with additional nodes and edges to make it a rectangle. In fact, R_G can also be constructed by a protocol, given G (see the full paper). The dimensions of R_G are defined by h_G, which is the horizontal distance between a leftmost node and a rightmost node of the shape (x-dimension), and v_G, which is the vertical distance between a highest and a lowest node of the shape (y-dimension). Let also $max\_dim_G := \max\{h_G, v_G\}$ and $min\_dim_G := \min\{h_G, v_G\}$. Then R_G can be extended by $max\_dim_G - min\_dim_G$ extra rows or columns, depending on which of its dimensions is smaller, to yield a $max\_dim_G \times max\_dim_G$ square S_G enclosing G (we mean here a $\{0, 1\}$-node-labeled square, as above, in which G can be identified). Observe, that such a square is not unique. For example, if G is a horizontal line of length d (i.e. $h_G = d$ and $v_G = 1$) then it is already equal to R_G and has to be extended by $d - 1$ rows to become S_G. These rows can be placed in d distinct ways relative to G, but all these squares have the same size $max\_dim_G \times max\_dim_G$ denoted by $|S_G|$.

A 2D (3D) *shape language* $\mathcal{L}$ is a subset of the set of all possible 2D (3D) shapes. We restrict our attention here to shape languages that contain a unique shape for each possible maximum dimension of the shape. In this case, it is equivalent, and more convenient, to translate $\mathcal{L}$ to a language of labeled squares. In particular, we define in this work a *shape language* $\mathcal{L}$ by providing for every $d \geq 1$ a single $d \times d$ square with its nodes labeled from $\{0, 1\}$. Such a square may also be defined by a d^2-sequence $S_d = (s_0, s_1, \ldots, s_{d^2-1})$ of bits or *pixels*, where $s_j \in \{0, 1\}$ corresponds to the jth node as follows: We assume that the pixels are indexed in a "zig-zag" fashion, beginning from the bottom left corner of the square, moving to the right until the bottom right corner is encountered, then one step up, then to the left until the node above the bottom left corner is encountered, then one step up again, then right, and so on. The shape G_d defined by S_d, called *the shape of* S_d, is the one induced by the nodes of the square that are labeled 1 and throughout this work we assume that $max\_dim_{G_d} = d$.

For simulation purposes, we also need to introduce appropriate shape-constructing Turing Machines (TMs). We now describe such a TM M: M's goal is to construct a shape on the pixels of a $\sqrt{n} \times \sqrt{n}$ square, which are indexed in the zig-zag way described above. M takes as input an integer $i \in \{0, 1, \ldots, n-1\}$ and the size n or the dimension $\sqrt{n}$ of the square (all in binary) and decides whether pixel i should belong or not to the final shape, i.e. if it should be *on* or *off*, respectively. [1] Moreover, in accordance to our definition of a shape, the construction of the TM, consisting of the pixels that M accepts (as *on*) and the active connections between them, should be *connected* (i.e. it should be a single shape).

DEFINITION 3. *We say that a shape language* $\mathcal{L} = (S_1, S_2, S_3, \ldots)$ *is* TM-computable *(or* TM-constructible*) in space* $f(d)$, *if there exists a TM* M *(as defined above) such that, for every* $d \geq 1$, *when* M *is executed on the pixels of a* $d \times d$ *square results in* S_d *(in particular, on input* (i, d), *where* $0 \leq i \leq d^2 - 1$, M *gives output* $S_d[i]$*), by using space* $O(f(d))$ *in every execution.*

DEFINITION 4. *We say that a protocol* $\mathcal{A}$ constructs *a shape language* $\mathcal{L}$ *with useful space* $g(n) \leq n$, *if* $g(n)$ *is the greatest function for which: (i) for all* n, *every execution of* $\mathcal{A}$ *on* n *processes constructs a shape* $G \in \mathcal{L}$ [2] *of order at least* $g(n)$ *(provided that such a* G *exists) and, additionally, (ii) for all* $G \in \mathcal{L}$ *there is an execution of* $\mathcal{A}$ *on* n *processes, for some* n *satisfying* $|V(G)| \geq g(n)$, *that constructs* G. *Equivalently, we say that* $\mathcal{A}$ constructs $\mathcal{L}$ *with* waste $n - g(n)$.

We now give as an illustrating example, a stabilizing protocol for the problem of constructing a spanning square. More protocols are given in the full paper. We assume, for simplicity, that $\sqrt{n}$ is integer and that there is a preelected unique leader in state L_u and all other nodes are initially in state q_0. The effective rules are $(L_u, u), (q_0, d), 0 \to (q_1, L_r, 1)$, $(L_r, r), (q_0, l), 0 \to (q_1, L_d, 1)$, $(L_d, d), (q_0, u), 0 \to (q_1, L_l, 1)$, $(L_l, l), (q_0, r), 0 \to (q_1, L_u, 1)$, $(L_u, u), (q_1, d), 0 \to (L_l, q_1, 1)$, $(L_r, r), (q_1, l), 0 \to (L_u, q_1, 1)$, $(L_d, d), (q_1, u), 0 \to (L_r, q_1, 1)$, and $(L_l, l), (q_1, r), 0 \to (L_d, q_1, 1)$.

The protocol first constructs a 2×2 square. When it is done, the leader is at the bottom-right corner and is in state L_d. In general, whenever the leader is at the left (the up, right, and down cases are symmetric) of the already constructed square it tries to move right in order to walk above the square. If it does not succeed, it is because it has not yet passed over the upper boundary, so it activates the edge to the right, takes another step up and then tries again to move right. In this way, the leader always grows the square perimetrically and clockwise.

3. PROBABILISTIC COUNTING

In this section, we consider the problem of counting n. In particular, we assume a uniform random scheduler and we want to give protocols that always terminate but still w.h.p. count n correctly (or a satisfactory upper bound on n). The importance of such protocols is further supported by the fact that we cannot guarantee anything much better than this. In particular, if we require a population protocol

[1]Note that if the TM is not provided with the square size together with the pixel, then it can only compute uniform/symmetric shapes that are independent of n.

[2]G is the shape of a labeled square $S \in \mathcal{L}$ in case $\mathcal{L}$ is defined in terms of such squares.

to always terminate and additionally to always be correct, then we immediately obtain an impossibility result.

In Section 3.1, we present a protocol with a unique leader that solves w.h.p. the counting problem and always terminates. To the best of our knowledge, this is the first protocol of this sort in the relevant literature. Additionally, this protocol is crucial because all of our generic constructors, that are developed in Section 4, are terminating by assuming knowledge of n (stored distributedly on a line of length $\log n$). They obtain access to this knowledge w.h.p. by executing the counting protocol as a subroutine. Finally, knowing n w.h.p. allows to develop protocols that exploit sequential composition of (terminating) subroutines, which makes them much more natural and easy to describe than the protocols in which all subroutines are executed in parallel and perpetual reinitializations is the only means of guaranteeing eventual correctness (the latter is the case e.g. in [8, 10, 12], but not in [13] which was the first extension to allow for sequential composition based on some non-probabilistic assumptions). In Section 3.2 we establish that if the nodes have unique ids (UIDs) then it is possible to solve the problem without a unique leader.

3.1 Fast Probabilistic Counting With a Leader

Keep in mind that in order to simplify the discussion, a sort of population protocol is presented here. So, there are no ports, no geometry, and no activations/deactivations of connections. In every step, a uniform random scheduler selects equiprobably one of the $n(n-1)/2$ possible node pairs, and the selected nodes interact and update their states according to the transition function. The only difference from the classical population protocols is that a distinguished leader node has unbounded local memory (of the order of n). Later, in Section 4.1, we will adjust the protocol to make it work in our model (thus also dropping this unbounded local memory assumption).

Counting-Upper-Bound Protocol: There is initially a unique leader l and all other nodes are in state q_0. Assume that l has two n-counters in its memory, initially both set to 0. So, the state of l is denoted as $l(r_0, r_1)$, where r_0 is the value of the first counter and r_1 the value of the second counter, $0 \leq r_0, r_1 \leq n$. The rules of the protocol are $(l(r_0, r_1), q_0) \rightarrow (l(r_0+1, r_1), q_1)$, $(l(r_0, r_1), q_1) \rightarrow (l(r_0, r_1+1), q_2)$, and $(l(r_0, r_1), \cdot) \rightarrow (halt, \cdot)$ if $r_0 = r_1$.

Observe that r_0 counts the number of q_0s in the population while r_1 counts the number of q_1s. Initially, there are $n-1$ q_0s and no q_1s. Whenever l interacts with a q_0, r_0 increases by 1 and the q_0 is converted to q_1. Whenever l interacts with a q_1, r_1 increases by 1 and the q_1 is converted to q_2. The process terminates when $r_0 = r_1$ for the first time. We also give to r_0 an initial head start of b, where b can be any desired constant. So, initially we have $r_0 = b$, $r_1 = 0$ and $i = \#q_0 = n-b-1$, $j = \#q_1 = b$ (this can be easily achieved by the protocol). So, we have two competing processes, one counting q_0s and the other counting q_1s, the first one begins with an initial head start of b and the game ends when the second catches up the first. We now prove that when this occurs the leader will almost surely have already counted at least half of the nodes.

THEOREM 1. *The above protocol halts in every execution. Moreover, if the scheduler is a uniform random one, when this occurs, w.h.p. it holds that* $r_0 \geq n/2$.

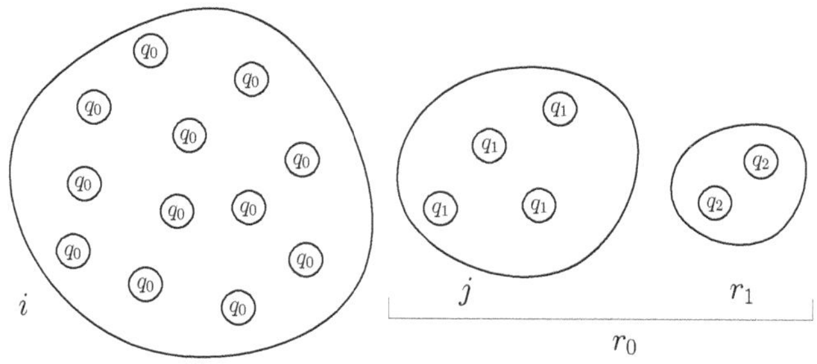

Figure 1: A configuration of the system (excluding the leader).

PROOF. The random variable i denotes the number of q_0s and j denotes the number of q_1s in the configuration, where initially $i = n-b-1$ and $j = b$. Observe also that all the following hold: $j = r_0 - r_1$, $r_0 \geq r_1$, $r_1 = (n-1) - (i+j)$, and $r_0 + r_1$ is equal to the number of effective interactions (see Figure 1).

Given that we have an effective interaction, the probability that it is an (l, q_0) is $p_{ij} = i/(i+j)$ and the probability that it is an (l, q_1) is $q_{ij} = 1 - p_{ij} = j/(i+j)$. This random process may be viewed as a random walk (r.w.) on a line with $n+1$ positions $0, 1, \ldots, n$ where a particle begins from position b and there is an absorbing barrier at 0 and a reflecting barrier at n. The position of the particle corresponds to the difference $r_0 - r_1$ of the two counters which is equal to j. Observe now that if $j \geq n/2$ then $r_0 - r_1 \geq n/2 \Rightarrow r_0 \geq n/2$, so it suffices to consider a second absorbing barrier at $n/2$. The particle moves forward (i.e. to the right) with probability p_{ij} and backward with probability q_{ij}. This is a "difficult" r.w. because the transition probabilities not only depend on the position j but also on the sum $i+j$ which decreases in time. In particular, the sum decreases whenever an (l, q_1) interaction occurs, in which case a q_1 becomes q_2. Observe also that, in our case, the duration of the r.w. can be at most $n-b$, in the sense that if the particle has not been absorbed after $n-b$ steps then we have success. The reason for this is that $n-b$ effective interactions imply that $r_0 + r_1 = n$, but as $r_0 \geq r_1$, we have $r_0 \geq n/2$. In fact, $r_0 \geq n/2 \Leftrightarrow j + r_1 \geq n/2$. We are interested in upper bounding P[failure] = P[reach 0 before $r_0 \geq n/2$ holds], which is in turn upper bounded by the probability of reaching 0 before reaching $n/2$ and before $n-b$ effective interactions have occurred (this is true because, in the latter event, we have disregarded some winning conditions). It suffices to bound the probability of reaching 0 before n effective interactions have occurred. Thus, we have $r_0 + r_1 \leq n$ but $r_1 \leq r_0 \Rightarrow 2r_1 \leq r_0 + r_1$, thus $2r_1 \leq n \Rightarrow r_1 \leq n/2 \Rightarrow (n-1) - (i+j) \leq n/2 \Rightarrow i+j \geq (n/2) - 1 = n'$. And if we set $n' = (n/2) - 1$ we have $i + j \geq n'$. Moreover, observe that when $r_0 + r_1 = n+1$ we have $n+1 = r_0 + r_1 \leq 2r_0 \Rightarrow r_0 \geq n/2$. In summary, during the first n effective interactions, it holds that $i + j \geq n' = (n/2) - 1$ and when interaction $n+1$ occurs it holds that $r_0 \geq n/2$, that is, if the process is still alive after time n, then r_0 has managed to count up to $n/2$ and the protocol has succeeded.

Now, $i+j \geq n'$ implies that $p_j \geq (n'-j)/n'$ and $q_j \leq j/n'$ so that now the probabilities only depend on the position j. This is the well-studied Ehrenfest r.w. coming from the theory of brownian motion [5, 9]. We will reduce this walk

to one in which the probabilities do not depend on j by restricting it to the prefix $[0, b]$ of the line. In this part, it holds that $j \leq b$ which implies that $p \geq (n' - b)/n'$ and $q \leq b/n'$. Now we set $p = (n' - b)/n'$ and $q = b/n'$. Observe that this may only increase the probability of failure. Recall that initially the particle is on position b. Imagine now an absorbing barrier at 0 and another one at b. Whenever the r.w. is on $b-1$ it will either return to b before reaching 0 or it will reach 0 (and fail) before returning to b. Due to symmetry it is equivalent to assume that the particle begins from position 1, moves forward with probability $p' = q$, backward with probability $q' = p$, and it fails at b. Thus, it is equivalent to bound P[reach b before 0 (when beginning from 1)], i.e. the probability of winning in the classical ruin problem analyzed e.g. in [6] page 345. If we set $x = q'/p' = p/q = (n' - b)/b$ we have that: P[reach b before 0] $= 1 - \frac{x^b - x}{x^b - 1} = \frac{x-1}{x^b-1} \leq \frac{x}{x^b-1} \approx \frac{1}{x^{b-1}} \approx \frac{1}{n^{b-1}}$. Thus, whenever the original walk is on $b-1$, the probability of reaching 0 before reaching b again, is at most $1/n^{b-1}$. Now assume that we repeat the above walk n times, i.e. we place the particle on $b-1$, play the game, then if it returns to b we put again the particle on $b-1$ and play the game again, and so on. From Boole-Bonferroni inequality, we have that:
P[fail at least once] $\leq \sum_{m=1}^{n}$ P[fail at repetition m] $\leq \sum_{m=1}^{n} \frac{1}{n^{b-1}} = \frac{n}{n^{b-1}} = \frac{1}{n^{b-2}}$. □

REMARK 1. *For the Counting-Upper-Bound protocol to terminate, it suffices for the leader to meet every other node twice. This takes twice the expected time of a* meet everybody *(cf. [12]), thus the expected running time of Counting-Upper-Bound is $O(n^2 \log n)$ (interactions).*

REMARK 2. *When the Counting-Upper-Bound protocol terminates, w.h.p. the leader knows an r_0 which is between $n/2$ and n. So any subsequent routine can use directly this estimation and pay in an* a priori *waste which is at most half of the population. In practice, this estimation is expected to be much closer to n than to $n/2$ (in all of our experiments for up to 1000 nodes, the estimation was always close to $(9/10)n$ and usually higher). On the other hand, if we want to determine the exact value of n and to have no* a priori *waste, then we can have the leader wait an additional large polynomial (in r_0) number of steps, to ensure that the leader has met every other node w.h.p..*

In the full paper, we also give some evidence that the unique leader assumption *is probably necessary*, but leave it as an interesting open question. In contrast, we show in the next section that it can be dropped if UIDs are available.

3.2 Counting Without a Leader but With UIDs

Now nodes have unique ids from a universe $\mathcal{U}$. Nodes initially do not know the ids of other nodes nor n. The goal is again to count n w.h.p.. All nodes execute the same program and no node can initially act as unique leader, because nodes do not know which ids from $\mathcal{U}$ are actually present in the system. Nodes have unbounded memory but we try to minimize it, e.g. if possible store only up to a constant number of other nodes' ids. We show that under these assumptions, the counting problem can be solved without the necessity of a unique leader.

The idea of the protocol is to have the node with the maximum id in the system to perform the same process as the unique leader in the protocol with no ids of Theorem 1. Of course, initially all nodes have to behave as if they were the maximum (as they do not know in advance who the maximum is) and we must also guarantee that no other node ever terminates (with sufficiently large probability) early, giving as output a wrong count.

Informal description: Every node u has a unique id id_u and tries to simulate the behavior of the unique leader of the protocol of Theorem 1. In particular, whenever it meets another node for the first time it wants to mark it once and the second time it meets that node it wants to mark it twice, recording the number of first-meetings and second-meetings in two local counters. The problem is that now many nodes may want to mark the same node. One idea, of course, could be to have a node remember all the nodes that have marked it so far but we want to avoid this because it requires a lot of memory and communication. Instead, we allow a node to only remember a single other node's id at a time. Every node tries initially to increase its first-meetings counter to b so that it creates an initial b head start of this counter w.r.t. the other. Every node that succeeds, starts executing its main process. The main idea is that whenever a node u interacts with another node that either has or has been marked by an id greater than id_u, u becomes sleeping and stops counting. This guarantees that only u_{max} will forever remain awake. Moreover, every node u always remembers the maximum id that has marked it so far, so that the probabilistic counting process of a node u can only be affected by nodes with id greater than id_u and, as a result, no one can affect the counting process of u_{max}. The formal protocol and the proof that it correctly simulates the counting process of Theorem 1, thus providing w.h.p. an upper bound on n, can be found in the full paper.

4. GENERIC CONSTRUCTORS

In this section, we give a characterization for the class of constructible 2D shape languages. In particular, we establish that shape constructing TMs (defined in Section 2), can be simulated by our model and therefore we can realize their output-shape in the actual distributed system. To this end, we begin in Section 4.1 by adapting the Counting-Upper-Bound protocol of Section 3.1 to work in our model. The result is w.h.p. a line of length $\Theta(\log n)$, containing n in binary, and having a unique leader. Then, in Section 4.2 the leader exploits the knowledge of n to construct a $\sqrt{n} \times \sqrt{n}$ square. In the sequel (Section 4.3), it simulates the TM on the square n distinct times, one for each pixel of the square. Each time, the input provided to the TM is the index of the pixel and $\sqrt{n}$, both in binary. Each simulation decides whether the corresponding pixel should be *on* or *off*. When all simulations have completed, the leader releases in the solution the connected shape consisting of the *on* pixels and the active edges between them. The connections of all other (*off*) pixels become deactivated and the corresponding nodes become free (isolated) nodes in the solution.

4.1 Storing the Count on a Line

We begin by adapting the Counting-Upper-Bound protocol of Theorem 1 so that when the protocol terminates the final correct count is stored distributedly in binary on an active line of length $\log n$.

Counting-on-a-Line Protocol: The probabilistic process that is being executed is essentially the same as that of the Counting-Upper-Bound protocol. Again the protocol assumes a unique leader that forever controls the process. A difference now is that every node has four ports (in the 2D case). The leader operates as a TM that stores the r_0 and r_1 counters in its tape in binary. The ith cell of the tape has two components, one storing the ith bit of r_0 and the other storing the ith bit of r_1. We say that the tape is *full*, if the bits of all r_0 components of the tape are set to 1. The tape of the TM is the active line that the leader has formed so far, each node in the line implementing one cell of the tape. Initially the tape consists of a single cell, stored in the memory of the unique leader node. As in Counting-Upper-Bound, the leader first tries to obtain an initial advantage of b for the r_0 counter. To achieve the advantage, the leader does not count the q_1s that it interacts with until it holds that $r_0 \geq b$. Observe that the initial length of the tape is not sufficient for storing the binary representation of b (of course b is constant so, in principle, it could be stored on a single node, however we prefer to keep the description as uniform as possible). In order to resolve this, the leader does the following. Whenever it meets the left port of a q_0 from its right port, if its tape is not full yet, it switches the q_0 to q_1, leaving it free to move in the solution, and increases the r_0 counter by one. To increase the counter, it freezes the probabilistic process (that is, during freezing it ignores all interactions with free nodes), and starts moving on its tape, which is a distributed line attached to its left port. After incrementing the counter, the leader keeps track of whether the tape is now full and then it moves back to the right endpoint of the line to unfreeze and continue the probabilistic process. On the other hand, if the tape is full, it binds the encountered q_0 to its right by activating the connection between them (thus increasing the length of the tape by one), then it reorganizes the tape, it again increases r_0 by one, and finally moves back to the right endpoint to continue the probabilistic process. This time, the leader also records that it has bound a q_0 that should have been converted to q_1. This *debt* is also stored on the tape in another counter r_2. Whenever the leader meets a q_2, if $r_2 \geq 1$, it converts q_2 to q_1 and decreases r_2 by one. So, q_2s may be viewed as a *deposit* that is used to pay back the debt. In this manner, the q_0s that are used to form the tape of the leader are not immediately converted to q_1 when first counted. Instead, the missing q_1s are introduced at a later time, one after every interaction of the leader with a q_2, and all of them will be introduced eventually, when a sufficient number of q_2s will become available. Finally, whenever the leader interacts with the left port of a q_1 from its right port, it freezes, increases the r_1 counter by one (observe that $r_0 \geq r_1$ always holds, so the length of the tape is always sufficient for r_1 increments), and checks whether $r_0 = r_1$. If equality holds, the leader terminates, otherwise it moves back to the right endpoint and continues the process. Correctness is captured by the following lemma.

LEMMA 1. *Counting-on-a-Line protocol terminates in every execution. Moreover, when the leader terminates, w.h.p. it has formed an active line of length* $\log n$ *containing* n *in binary in the* r_0 *components of the nodes of the line (each node storing one bit).*

PROOF. We begin by showing that the probabilistic process of the Counting-Upper-Bound protocol is not negatively affected in the Counting-on-a-Line protocol. This implies that the high probability argument of Theorem 1 holds also for Counting-on-a-Line. First, observe that the four ports of the nodes introduce more choices for the scheduler in every step. However, these new choices, if treated uniformly, result in the same multiplicative factor for both the "positive" (an (l, q_0) interaction) and the "negative" (an (l, q_1) interaction) events, so the probabilities of the process are not affected at all by this. Moreover, neither the debt affects the process. The reason is that the only essential difference w.r.t. to the process is that the conversion of some counted q_0s to the corresponding q_1s is delayed. But this only decreases the probability of early termination and thus of failure. It remains to show that not even a single q_1 remains forever as debt, because, otherwise, some executions of the protocol would not terminate. The reason is that the protocol cannot terminate before converting all the q_1s plus the debt to q_2. To this end, observe that the line of the leader has always length $\lfloor \lg r_0 \rfloor + 1$, thus $r_2 \leq \lfloor \lg r_0 \rfloor$, because the debt is always at most the length of the line excluding the initial leader. So, at least $r_0 - \lfloor \lg r_0 \rfloor$ nodes have been successfully converted from q_0 to q_1 which implies that there is an eventual deposit of at least $r_0 - \lfloor \lg r_0 \rfloor$ nodes in state q_2. These q_2s are not immediately available, but they will become available in the future, because every interaction of the leader with a q_1 results in a q_2. Finally, observe that $r_0 - \lfloor \lg r_0 \rfloor \geq \lfloor \lg r_0 \rfloor$ holds for all $r_0 \geq 1$. Thus, $r_0 - \lfloor \lg r_0 \rfloor \geq r_2$, which means that the eventual deposit is not smaller than the debt, so the protocol eventually pays back its debt and terminates. □

4.2 Constructing a $\sqrt{n} \times \sqrt{n}$ Square

We now show how to organize the nodes into a spanning square, i.e. a $\sqrt{n} \times \sqrt{n}$ one. As before, we assume that $\sqrt{n}$ is integer and that the leader has n stored in its line (w.h.p.) after executing the Counting-on-a-Line subroutine. Observe that knowledge of n allows the protocol to terminate after constructing the square and to know that the square has been successfully constructed.

Square-Knowing-n Protocol: The initial leader L first computes $\sqrt{n}$ on its line by any plausible algorithm and then expands its line to the right by attaching free nodes to make its length $\sqrt{n}$. Then it exploits the down ports to create a replica of its line. The replica has also length $\sqrt{n}$ and has its own leader but in a distinguished state L_s. This new line plays the role of a *seed* that starts creating other self-replicating lines of length $\sqrt{n}$. In particular, the seed attaches free nodes to its down ports, until all positions below the line are filled by nodes and additionally all horizontal connections between those nodes are activated. Then it introduces a leader L_r to one endpoint of the replica and starts deactivating the vertical connections to release the new line of length $\sqrt{n}$. These lines with L_r leaders are *totally self-replicating*, meaning that their children also begin in state L_r. The initial leader L waits until the up ports of a non-seed replica r become totally aligned with the down ports of the square segment that has been constructed so far. So, initially it waits until a replica becomes attached to the lower side of its own line. When this occurs, it activates all intermediate vertical connections to make the construction rigid, increments a row-counter by one (initially 0), and moves to the new lowest row. If at the time of attachment r was in the middle of an incomplete replication, then there

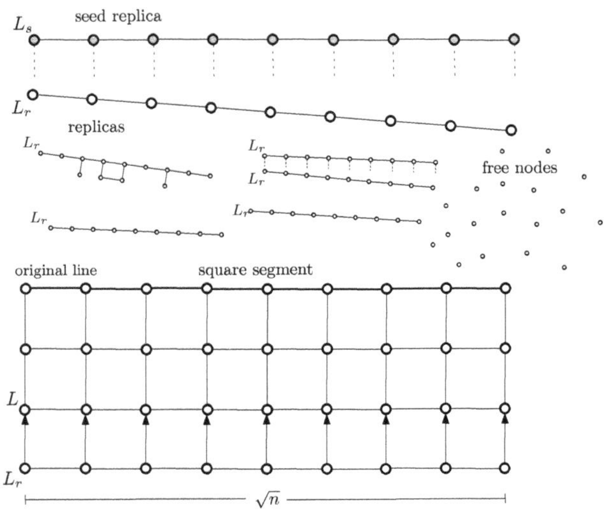

Figure 2: The seed at the top has created another replica which has just been released in the solution. At the bottom appears the square segment that has been constructed so far. A replica has just arrived (from below) and will be attached to the segment.

will be nodes attached to the down ports of r. L releases all these nodes, by deactivating the active connections of r to them, and then waits for another non-seed replica to arrive. When the row-counter becomes equal to $\sqrt{n}-1$, the leader for the first time accepts the attachment of the seed to its construction and when the seed is successfully attached the leader terminates. This completes the construction of the $\sqrt{n}\times\sqrt{n}$ square. See Figure 2 for an illustration.

The reason for attaching the seed last, and in particular when no further free nodes have remained, is that otherwise self-replication could possibly cease in some executions. Observe also that we have allowed the L-leader to accept the attachment of a replica to the square segment even though the replica may be in the middle of an incomplete replication. This is important in order to avoid reaching a point at which some free lines are in the middle of incomplete replications but there are no further free nodes for any of them to complete. For a simple example, consider the seed and a replica r and $\sqrt{n}$ free nodes (all other nodes have been attached to the square segment). It is possible that $\sqrt{n}-1$ of the free nodes become attached to the seed and the last free node becomes attached to r. We have overcome this deadlock by allowing L to accept the attachment of r to the square segment. When this occurs, the free node will be released and eventually it will be attached to the last free position below the seed.

We now give, in Protocol 1, one of the possible codes for replicating the lines. We present a version that does not use the line's leader in order to successfully self-replicate. A direct replication controlled by the leader is simpler to conceive but its code is lengthy (it can be found in the full paper). Without loss of generality, we assume that one line has e on both of its endpoints and i on the internal nodes, and every (free) node is in state q_0. The protocol works as follows. Free nodes are attached below the nodes of the original line. When a node is attached below an internal node i, both become i_1 and when a node is attached below an endpoint e, both become e_1. Moreover, adjacent nodes of the replica connect to each other and every such connection increases their index, so that their index counts their degree. An internal node of the replica can detach from the original line only when it has degree 3, that is when, apart from its vertical connection, it has also already become connected to both a left and a right neighbor on the replica. On the other hand, an endpoint detaches when it has a single internal neighbor. It follows that the replica can only detach when its length (counted in number of horizontal active connections) is equal to that of the original line. To see this, assume that a shorter line detaches at some point. Clearly, such a line must have at least one endpoint that corresponds to an internal node i_j of the replica. But this node is an endpoint of the shorter line, so its degree is less than 3, i.e. $j<3$, and we conclude that it cannot have detached. To make the protocol also replicate the leader-state simply replace one e with L, L_s, or L_r and map it to L_s, L_r, L_r, resp., in the replica, when detaching.

Protocol 1 *No-Leader-Line-Replication*

$Q=\{q_0,e,e_1,i,i_1,i_2,i_3\}$
δ:

$$(i,d),(q_0,u),0\rightarrow(i_1,i_1,1)$$
$$(e,d),(q_0,u),0\rightarrow(e_1,e_1,1)$$
$$(i_j,r),(i_k,l),0\rightarrow(i_{j+1},i_{k+1},1)\text{ for all } j,k\in\{1,2\}$$
$$(i_1,r),(e_1,l),0\rightarrow(i_2,e_2,1)$$
$$(i_2,r),(e_1,l),0\rightarrow(i_3,e_2,1)$$
$$(e_1,r),(i_1,l),0\rightarrow(e_2,i_2,1)$$
$$(e_1,r),(i_2,l),0\rightarrow(e_2,i_3,1)$$
$$(i_3,u),(i_1,d),1\rightarrow(i,i,0)$$
$$(e_2,u),(e_1,d),1\rightarrow(e,e,0)$$

Lemma 2. *There is a protocol (described above) that when executed on n nodes (for all n with integer $\sqrt{n}$) w.h.p. constructs a $\sqrt{n}\times\sqrt{n}$ square and terminates.*

4.3 Simulating a TM

We now assume as given (from the discussion of the previous section) a $\sqrt{n}\times\sqrt{n}$ square with a unique leader L at the bottom left corner. However, keep in mind that, in principle, the simulation described here can begin before the construction of the $\sqrt{n}\times\sqrt{n}$ square is complete. The only difference in this case, is that the two processes are executed in parallel and if at some point the TM needs more space, it has to wait until it becomes available. The square may be viewed as a TM-tape of length n traversed by the leader in a "zig-zag" fashion, first moving to the right until the bottom right corner is encountered, then one step up, then to the left until the node above the bottom left corner is encountered, then one step up again, then right, and so on. To simplify this process, we may assume that a preprocessing has marked appropriately the turning points. The tape will be used to simulate a TM M of the form described in the Section 2. The n pixels of the square are numbered according to the above zig-zag process beginning from the bottom left node, each node corresponding to one pixel. The space available to the TM is exponential in the binary representation of the input (i,n) (or $(i,\sqrt{n})$), because

$i \leq n-1$ and therefore the length of its binary representation $|i| = O(\log n)$, thus $|(i,n)| = O(\log n)$, but the available space is $\Theta(n) = \Theta(2^{\log n}) = \Omega(2^{|(i,n)|})$ (still it is linear in the size of the whole shape to be constructed).

The protocol invokes n distinct simulations of M, one for each of the pixels $i \in \{0, 1, \ldots, n-1\}$, beginning from $i = 0$ and every time incrementing i by one. The leader maintains the current value of i in binary, in a pixel-counter *pixel* stored in the $O(\log n)$ leftmost cells of the tape. Recall that the leader knows n from the procedures of the previous sections. So, we may assume that the tape also holds in advance n and $\sqrt{n}$ in binary (again in the leftmost cells). Initially $pixel = 0$ and the leader marks the 0th node, that is the bottom left corner of the square. Then it simulates M on input $(pixel, \sqrt{n})$. When M decides, if its decision is *accept*, the leader marks the node corresponding to *pixel* as *on*, otherwise it marks it as *off*. Then the leader increments *pixel* by one, marks the node corresponding to the new value of *pixel* (which is the next node on the tape), clears the tape from residues of the previous simulation, invokes another simulation of M on the new value of *pixel*, and marks the corresponding node as *on* or *off* according to M's decision. The process stops when $pixel = n$, in which case no further simulation is executed. When this occurs, the leader starts walking the tape in the opposite direction until it reaches the bottom left corner. In the way, it deactivates all connections involving at least one *off* node, leaving active only the connected 2D shape consisting of the *on* nodes.

The following theorem states the lower bound implied by the construction described in this section.

THEOREM 2. *Let $\mathcal{L} = (S_1, S_2, \ldots)$ be a connected 2D shape language, such that $\mathcal{L}$ is TM-computable in space d^2. Then there is a protocol (described above) that w.h.p. constructs $\mathcal{L}$. In particular, for all $d \geq 1$, whenever the protocol is executed on a population of size $n = d^2$, w.h.p. it constructs S_d and terminates. In the worst case, when G_d (that is, the shape of S_d) is a line of length d, the waste is $(d-1)d = O(d^2) = O(n)$.*

REMARK 3. *If the system designer knew n in advance, then he/she could preprogram the nodes to simulate a TM that constructs a specific shape of size n, e.g. the TM corresponding to the Kolmogorov complexity of the shape. In this work,* n is not known in advance, *so we had to preprogram the nodes with a TM that can work for all n.*

REMARK 4. *The above results can be immediately modified to construct* patterns *instead of shapes. The idea is to keep the same constructor as above and simulate TMs that for every pixel output a color from a set of colors $\mathcal{C}$.*

REMARK 5. *In all the above constructions the unique leader assumption can be dropped in the price of sacrificing termination. In this case, the constructions become stabilizing by the reinitialization technique, as e.g. in [12], but should be carefully rewritten.*

4.4 Parallelizing the Simulations

We now present an approach for parallelizing the simulations. Assume that there is a TM M deciding each pixel in space k, that k and d are computable in space $O(n)$, and that $n = k \cdot d^2$.

The leader, instead of constructing a square, constructs now a spanning line of length d^2, say in the x dimension, corresponding to a linear expansion of the pixels of a $d \times d$ square. Moreover, the leader creates a seed of length $k-1$ and uses it to partition the rest of the nodes into lines of length $k-1$ in the y dimension. Each such line will be attached below one of the nodes of the x-line. When all y-lines have been attached, the leader, for all $0 \leq i \leq d^2 - 1$, initializes the memory of the line attached below pixel i with (i, d). Then all simulations of M are executed in parallel and eventually each one of them sets its x-pixel to either *on* or *off*. When all simulations have ended, the leader releases the y-lines and then partitions the x-line into consecutive segments of length d (see Figure 3(a)). Each segment corresponds to a row of the $d \times d$ square to be constructed. In particular, segment $i \geq 1$ (counting from left) corresponds to row i (bottom-up). Moreover, if i is even (odd), segment i should match with its upper (lower) side to the upper (lower) side of segment $i-1$. The leader marks appropriately the nodes of each segment to make them aware of the orientation that they should have in the square. Moreover, it assigns a unique key-marking to each segment so that segment i can easily and locally detect segment $i-1$. In particular, if i is odd (even), it marks nodes i and $i-1$ of the segment counting from left to right (right to left); see Figure 3(b). Then the leader releases, one after the other, all segments. The segments are free to move in the solution until they meet and recognize their counterpart, and when this occurs the two segments bind together. Eventually, the $d \times d$ square is constructed and every pixel is in the correct position. The leader can detect this and release the constructed shape consisting of the *on* pixels.

5. CONCLUSION AND OPEN PROBLEMS

There are several interesting open problems related to the findings of this work. A very intriguing problem is to give a proof, or strong experimental evidence (we have already some preliminary such evidence), that there is no analogue of Theorem 1 if all processes are identical (i.e. no unique leader). A possibility left open then would be to achieve high probability counting with $f(n)$ leaders. There is also work to be done w.r.t. analyzing the running times of our protocols and our generic constructors and proposing more efficient solutions. Also it is not yet clear whether the protocol of Section 3.1 is the fastest possible nor that its success probability or the upper bound on n that it guarantees cannot be improved; a proof would be useful. Moreover, it is not obvious what is the class of shapes and patterns that the TMs considered here compute. Of course, it was sufficient as a first step to draw the analogy to such TMs because it helped us establish that our model is quite powerful. However, still we would like to have a characterization that gives some more insight to the actual shapes and patterns that the model can construct.

A possible refinement of the model could be a distinction between the *speed of the scheduler* and the *internal operation speed of a component.* Such a distinction is very natural, because a connected component should operate at a different speed than it takes for the scheduler to bring two nodes into contact. It would also be interesting to consider for the first time a *hybrid model* combining active mobility controlled by the protocol and passive mobility controlled by the environment.

There is also work to be done towards the development of even more applied models (e.g. variations of the one pro-

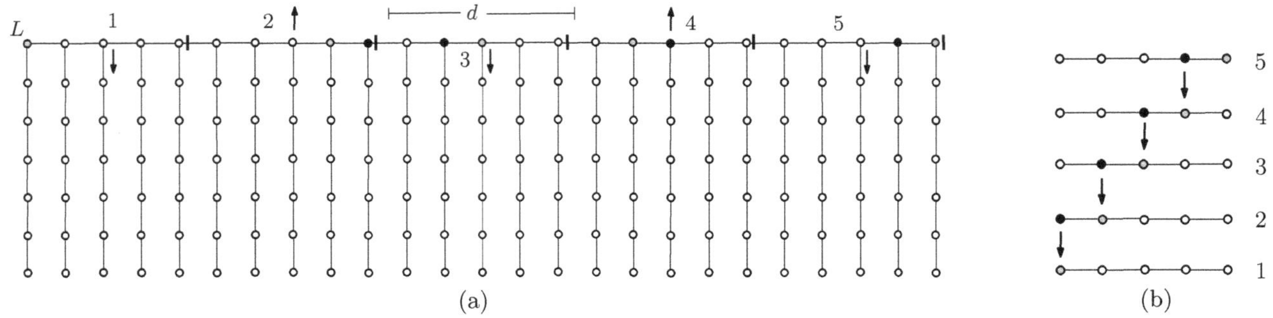

Figure 3: (a) d^2 lines of length $k-1$ each, are pendent below the d^2 pixels. The pixels are arranged linearly in dimension x and have been partitioned into equal segments of length d each (see the black delimiters). (b) The segments have been released in the solution, and now they have to gather together and form the square.

posed here) that take other real physical considerations into account. In this work, we have restricted attention on some geometrical constraints. Other properties of interest could be weight, mass, strength of bonds, rigid and elastic structure, collisions, and the interplay of these with the interaction pattern and the protocol. Moreover, in real applications mere shape construction will not be sufficient. Typically, we will desire to output a shape/structure that *optimizes some global property*, like energy and strength, or that achieves a *desired behavior in the given physical environment.*

Finally, it would be interesting to develop routines that can rapidly reconstruct broken parts. For example, imagine that a shape has stabilized but a part of it detaches, all the connections of the part become deactivated, and all its nodes become free. Can we detect and reconstruct the broken part efficiently (and without resetting the whole population and repeating the construction from scratch)? What knowledge about the whole shape should the nodes have in order to be able to reconstruct missing parts of it?

Acknowledgments: The author would like to thank D. Amaxilatis and M. Logaras for implementing (in Java) the counting protocol of Section 3.1 and experimentally verifying its correctness and also D. Doty for a few fruitful discussions on the same protocol at the very early stages of this work.

6. REFERENCES

[1] D. Angluin, J. Aspnes, Z. Diamadi, M. J. Fischer, and R. Peralta. Computation in networks of passively mobile finite-state sensors. *Distributed Computing*, pages 235–253, March 2006.

[2] D. Angluin, J. Aspnes, and D. Eisenstat. Fast computation by population protocols with a leader. *Distributed Computing*, 21(3):183–199, September 2008.

[3] J. Aspnes and E. Ruppert. An introduction to population protocols. *Bulletin of the European Association for Theoretical Computer Science*, 93:98–117, October 2007.

[4] D. Doty. Timing in chemical reaction networks. In *Proc. of the 25th Annual ACM-SIAM Symp. on Discrete Algorithms (SODA)*, pages 772–784, 2014.

[5] P. Ehrenfest and T. Ehrenfest-Afanassjewa. Über zwei bekannte einwände gegen das boltzmannsche h-theorem. *Phys.Zeit.*, 8:311–314, 1907.

[6] W. Feller. *An Introduction to Probability Theory and Its Applications, Vol. 1, 3rd Edition, Revised Printing.* Wiley, 1968.

[7] S. C. Goldstein, J. D. Campbell, and T. C. Mowry. Programmable matter. *Computer*, 38(6):99–101, 2005.

[8] R. Guerraoui and E. Ruppert. Names trump malice: Tiny mobile agents can tolerate byzantine failures. In *36th International Colloquium on Automata, Languages and Programming (ICALP)*, volume 5556 of *LNCS*, pages 484–495. Springer-Verlag, 2009.

[9] M. Kac. Random walk and the theory of brownian motion. *American Mathematical Monthly*, pages 369–391, 1947.

[10] O. Michail, I. Chatzigiannakis, and P. G. Spirakis. Mediated population protocols. *Theoretical Computer Science*, 412(22):2434–2450, May 2011.

[11] O. Michail, I. Chatzigiannakis, and P. G. Spirakis. *New Models for Population Protocols.* N. A. Lynch (Ed), Synthesis Lectures on Distributed Computing Theory. Morgan & Claypool, 2011.

[12] O. Michail and P. G. Spirakis. Simple and efficient local codes for distributed stable network construction. In *Proceedings of the 33rd ACM Symposium on Principles of Distributed Computing (PODC)*, pages 76–85. ACM, 2014.

[13] O. Michail and P. G. Spirakis. Terminating population protocols via some minimal global knowledge assumptions. *Journal of Parallel and Distributed Computing (JPDC)*, 81:1–10, 2015.

[14] P. W. Rothemund. Folding dna to create nanoscale shapes and patterns. *Nature*, 440(7082):297–302, 2006.

[15] M. Rubenstein, A. Cornejo, and R. Nagpal. Programmable self-assembly in a thousand-robot swarm. *Science*, 345(6198):795–799, 2014.

[16] J. L. Schiff. *Cellular automata: a discrete view of the world*, volume 45. Wiley-Interscience, 2011.

[17] D. Woods, H.-L. Chen, S. Goodfriend, N. Dabby, E. Winfree, and P. Yin. Active self-assembly of algorithmic shapes and patterns in polylogarithmic time. In *Proceedings of the 4th conference on Innovations in Theoretical Computer Science*, pages 353–354. ACM, 2013.

[18] M. Zakin. The next revolution in materials. *DARPA's 25th Systems and Technology Symposium (DARPATech)*, 2007.

Fast and Exact Majority in Population Protocols

Dan Alistarh
Microsoft Research
daalista@microsoft.com

Rati Gelashvili*
MIT
gelash@mit.edu

Milan Vojnović
Microsoft Research
milanv@microsoft.com

ABSTRACT

Population protocols, roughly defined as systems consisting of large numbers of simple identical agents, interacting at random and updating their state following simple rules, are an important research topic at the intersection of distributed computing and biology. One of the fundamental tasks that a population protocol may solve is *majority*: each node starts in one of two states; the goal is for all nodes to reach a correct consensus on which of the two states was initially the majority. Despite considerable research effort, known protocols for this problem are either exact but slow (taking linear parallel time to converge), or fast but approximate (with non-zero probability of error).

In this paper, we show that this trade-off between precision and speed is not inherent. We present a new protocol called *Average and Conquer (AVC)* that solves majority *exactly* in expected parallel convergence time $O(\log n/(s\epsilon) + \log n \log s)$, where n is the number of nodes, ϵn is the initial node advantage of the majority state, and $s = \Omega(\log n \log\log n)$ is the number of states the protocol employs. This shows that the majority problem can be solved exactly in time poly-logarithmic in n, provided that the memory per node is $s = \Omega(1/\epsilon + \log n \log 1/\epsilon)$. On the negative side, we establish a lower bound of $\Omega(1/\epsilon)$ on the expected parallel convergence time for the case of four memory states per node, and a lower bound of $\Omega(\log n)$ parallel time for protocols using any number of memory states per node.

Categories and Subject Descriptors

F.1.1 [**Computation by Abstract Devices**]: Models of Computation; F.1.1 [**Computation by Abstract Devices**]: --*Parallelism and concurrency*

Keywords

Population protocols, majority computation, randomized algorithms

*Work performed in part while an intern with Microsoft Research.

Permission to make digital or hard copies of all or part of this work for personal or classroom use is granted without fee provided that copies are not made or distributed for profit or commercial advantage and that copies bear this notice and the full citation on the first page. Copyrights for components of this work owned by others than ACM must be honored. Abstracting with credit is permitted. To copy otherwise, or republish, to post on servers or to redistribute to lists, requires prior specific permission and/or a fee. Request permissions from permissions@acm.org.
PODC'15, July 21–23, 2015, Donostia-San Sebastián, Spain.
Copyright © 2015 ACM 978-1-4503-3617-8 /15/07 ...$15.00.
DOI: http://dx.doi.org/10.1145/2767386.2767429..

1. INTRODUCTION

Population protocols [AAD+06], roughly defined as systems consisting of large numbers of randomly interacting identical agents, which update their state using simple rules, have recently become an important topic of research in distributed computing. In particular, considerable research effort has gone into determining the set of tasks solvable by population protocols, e.g., [AAD+06, AAER07], and into understanding the convergence bounds achievable by these algorithms in the case of fundamental tasks, e.g., [AAE08, PVV09, DV12, MNRS14]. Recently, research in biology and nanotechnology has shown that such algorithms can in fact be implemented at the level of molecules [CDS+13], and that there are non-trivial connections between population protocols and the computational tasks which biological cells must solve in order to function correctly [CCN12].

One fundamental task in the context of population protocols is *majority computation*: given a set of n nodes, starting in one of two distinct states (A or B), the task requires the nodes to reach consensus on a value associated to one of the two initial states. Crucially, the final value the nodes converge on should be associated to the *majority initial state*.

Evidence suggests that the cell cycle switch in eukaryotic cells solves an approximate version of majority [CCN12]; a three-state population protocol for approximate majority was empirically studied as a model of epigenetic cell memory by nucleosome modification [DMST07]; also, this task is a key component when simulating register machines via population protocols [AAE08]. The majority task has been studied by different research communities by considering population protocols in computation models defined in discrete and continuous time. In the discrete model, e.g., [AAE08], in each *round*, a pair of nodes is drawn at random to interact. Alternatively, other sources, e.g., [PVV09, DV12] assume that pairs of nodes interact at instances of a Poisson process in continuous time. The two models are essentially equivalent. Possible interactions are usually specified as a graph on n nodes, where the complete graph is an interesting special case, especially in the context of biological computations. In both models, we are interested in the amount of time until the algorithm converges to the correct state. In the discrete-time model, the metric of interest is *parallel time*, defined as number of rounds to convergence divided by the number of nodes n, which corresponds to "real-time" until convergence in the continuous-time model.

The complexity landscape of the majority task is quite intriguing. Assuming a system of n nodes, where one of the initial states (say, A) has an initial relative advantage over the other state (B) of ϵn nodes, there exists an elegant four-state protocol that can solve the problem in expected $O(\log n/\epsilon)$ parallel time [DV12, MNRS14]. This algorithm solves *exact* majority, i.e. has 0 probability of error; however, its running time is polynomial in n for small initial discrepancy between the two states, e.g., $\epsilon n = \Theta(n^\alpha)$, for $\alpha < 1$. At the same time, there exists an even simpler *three-state* protocol which can compute *approximate majority* in $O(\log n)$ parallel time, with high probability in n, assuming that the initial relative advantage is $\epsilon n = \omega(\sqrt{n}\log n)$ [AAE08, PVV09]. For small ϵ, this can be exponentially faster than the four-state protocol, but the price of fast convergence is *approximation*: the failure probability of the three-state protocol is $\exp(-c\epsilon^2 n)$ for constant $c > 0$ and small ϵ [PVV09], which becomes constant for small ϵ. Furthermore, it has recently been shown that it is impossible to solve majority *exactly* if each node only has three memory states [MNRS14].

Given this apparent trade-off between correctness and performance, it is natural to ask: is there a population protocol for majority which is both *fast* (converging in logarithmic or poly-logarithmic time for any ϵ), and *exact* (with 0 probability of error)?

In this paper, we answer this question in the affirmative. We present a new protocol, called AVC (for *Average-and-Conquer*), which solves *exact* majority in expected parallel time $O(\log n/(m\epsilon) + \log n \log m)$, for any parameter $m \leq n$ where n is the number of nodes, ϵ is the margin, and $s = \Theta(m + \log n \log m)$ is the number of *states* employed by the protocol. Specifically, for number of states $s = \Omega(1/\epsilon + \log n \log 1/\epsilon)$, the expected convergence time of the protocol is always poly-logarithmic in n. (Similar bounds hold with high probability in n.) In other words, AVC uses $O(\log(1/\epsilon) + \log\log n)$ local bits to solve exact majority in poly-logarithmic time. Our protocol exhibits a new trade-off between the algorithm's error probability and convergence time, versus the number of states s employed by each node, and the discrepancy ϵ.

The AVC protocol roughly works as follows. Let $m \geq 1$ be an odd integer parameter. Each state in the protocol will correspond to an integer value between $-m$ and m, which will be either odd, or 0. The *sign* of the value corresponds to the node's current opinion (by convention, + corresponds to initial majority A), and its absolute value corresponds will be the *weight* of this opinion. Therefore, in the following, we will use the terms *state* and *value* interchangeably. Initially, nodes with initial state A start with initial value $+m$, and nodes with initial value B start with initial value $-m$.

At a high level, the protocol combines two components: an *averaging* reaction, by which nodes with values > 1 average their initial values whenever interacting, and a *neutralization* reaction, by which nodes with absolute value 1 and opposite signs become neutralized and stop influencing the decision value. More precisely, whenever a node with weight > 1 interacts with a node with weight > 0, their updated states will correspond the *average* of their initial values, rounded to odd integers. (For example, input states 5 and -1 will yield output states 1 and 3.) Nodes with the same weight but different signs do not average directly to 0 states, but to intermediate states corresponding to values $+1$ and -1, respectively. States corresponding to value 0 (with positive or negative sign) are created by a *neutralization* reaction, when nodes in states $+1$ and -1 interact. Zero states are *weak*, in that they will not influence the *weight* of their interaction partner, and automatically adopt its *opinion*. (For example, input states 3 and -0 will yield output states 3 and 0.)

While the protocol is relatively simple, its analysis is non-trivial. To illustrate, take $m = 1$, and notice that in this special case the protocol would be identical to the four-state algorithm of [DV12, MNRS14]: nodes start in states $+1$ or -1; whenever two such nodes meet, they are downgraded to weak states $+0$ and -0, respectively. Weak 0 nodes shift their opinion whenever meeting a node with weight > 0, and preserve their weight. The process dynamics on a clique are relatively simple: given an initial state with discrepancy ϵ in favor of state A $(+1)$, the minority state B (-1) will eventually be depleted (downgraded to state -0) in expected $O(\log n/\epsilon)$ parallel time [DV12]. At this point, there still exist ϵn nodes in state $+1$, and it will take additional $O(\log n/\epsilon)$ expected parallel time to shift all the -0 states to the correct opinion $+0$.

Our algorithm leverages additional states to speed up *both* components of this dynamics, and overcome the linear dependence on $1/\epsilon$. This works for two main reasons: first, initial states, corresponding to large initial weight $\pm m$, will always be depleted fast, since reactions of the type $+m$ meets $-m$ are frequent at first, while, as the algorithm progresses, high values will start interacting often with small values of the opposite sign, again decreasing their weight.

Further, our algorithm is designed to keep the *total sum of values in the system invariant.* This is initially ϵmn (assuming that A is the initial majority by a margin of ϵn nodes). In particular, as the absolute values of states in the majority decrease, their *number* must increase to maintain the invariant. Our analysis formalizes this augmentation in the number of majority nodes to prove the expected convergence time bounds. The protocol's correctness follows by a variation on the total sum invariant.

It is interesting to contrast AVC with a trivial algorithm in which each node maintains an array of n initial values, one for each other possible interaction partner, and nodes merge their arrays on each interaction, deciding when they have all input values. Such an algorithm would converge in $O(\log n)$ parallel time, by standard gossip analysis. However, there are two issues: first, nodes would need *distinct identifiers* for this to work, which is not standard in population protocols. Moreover, even with identifiers, the trivial protocol would require an exponential number of states per process, to cover all possible input combinations.

We complement our upper bound by two lower bounds showing that the trade-off between the number of states and convergence time is tight within a log factor at its two extremes. The first lower bound uses a complex case analysis to prove that any dynamics based on agents with four states must have parallel convergence time $\Omega(1/\epsilon)$. At the other extreme, we leverage an information-propagation argument to prove that any population protocol solving exact majority converges in $\Omega(\log n)$ parallel time, irrespective of the number of states it employs.

Finally, we provide an implementation of the AVC protocol, and compare its empirical performance both with the four-state protocol of [DV12, MNRS14], and with the three-state algorithm of [AAE08, PVV09]. The simulation results confirm the tightness of our theoretical analysis, and show that AVC provides significant speedup over the four-state protocol by increasing the number of memory states per node, with the convergence time being competitive to that of the three-state protocol for large enough number of memory states per node.

Related Work: The framework of population protocols was first formally introduced by [AAD+06]. A two-state population protocol was studied by [HP99] in a discrete-time model such that in each round every node picks a neighbor node with probability of selection allowed to be specific to this pair of nodes, and adopts the observed opinion of the selected neighbor. For the complete-graph pairwise interactions and continuous-time model where each node picks a neighbor at instances of a Poisson process, this corresponds to *the voter model* studied in the context of interacting particle systems, see e.g. Chapter 5 in [Lig85]. In particular, a subset of the results in [HP99] show that, for the case of complete graph pairwise interactions, the error probability of the two-state protocol is equal to the portion of nodes in the initial minority state $(1-\epsilon)/2$, and that the expected parallel convergence time is $\Omega(n)$.

Reference [AAE08] studied a three-state population protocol for computing approximate majority in a discrete-time computation model. They established the parallel time convergence bound $O(\log n)$ with high probability given that the initial margin is $\epsilon n = \omega(\sqrt{n \log n})$. The same three-state protocol was empirically studied as a model of epigenetic cell memory by nucleosome modification [DMST07]. Independently, the same three-state population protocol for approximate majority was studied by [PVV09] in a continuous-time computation model. They established a tight bound on the probability of error for convergence to the correct terminal state $\exp(-D((1+\epsilon)/2||1/2)n)$ where $D(p||q)$ is the Kullback-Leibler divergence between two Bernoulli distributions with parameters p and q. This implies the asymptotic bound on the error probability $\exp(-c\epsilon^2 n)$ for constant $c > 0$ and small ϵ. Moreover, they established a parallel convergence time bound $O(\log(1/\epsilon) + \log n)$ for the limit system dynamics described by a system of ordinary differential equations as the number of nodes n grows large. [CCN12] showed that the dynamics of this three-state population protocol is under certain initial conditions equivalent of the cell cycle switch and other dynamics.

[DV12] first proposed a four-state protocol for exact majority computation and studied it for the case of arbitrary rates of pairwise interactions, which are such that the underlying graph G of pairwise interactions is connected. They showed an expected parallel time convergence bound of $(\log n + 1)/\delta(G, \epsilon)$ where $\delta(G, \epsilon) > 0$ is the smallest eigenvalue gap for a family of pairwise interaction rate matrices. For the case of a complete graph, this yields the expected parallel time bound of $O(\log n/\epsilon)$. A similar four-state protocol was also studied by [MNRS14] in a discrete-time computation model, who established that four memory states are necessary for exact majority computation.

A random process similar to the averaging stage of our algorithm was studied by Sauerwald and Sun [SS12], for arbitrary graphs. Their goal is to bound the necessary time for every node's value to converge within a constant, whereas we are interested in the time it takes for all minority values to reach absolute value ≤ 1, after which we bound the remaining time until all nodes with a minority opinion are eliminated. Another similar process, where nodes store values and update according to a dynamics that resembles averaging, is studied in [KDG03].

Related Work: The framework of population protocols was first formally introduced by [AAD+06]. A two-state population protocol was studied by [HP99] in a discrete-time model such that in each round every node picks a neighbor node with probability of selection allowed to be specific to this pair of nodes, and adopts the observed opinion of the selected neighbor. For the complete-graph pairwise interactions and continuous-time model where each node picks a neighbor at instances of a Poisson process, this corresponds to *the voter model* studied in the context of interacting particle systems, see e.g. Chapter 5 in [Lig85]. In particular, for the complete graph pairwise interactions, [HP99] showed that the error probability of the two-state protocol is equal to the portion of nodes in the initial minority state $(1-\epsilon)/2$, and that the expected parallel convergence time is $\Omega(n)$.

[AAER07] studied a three-state population protocol for computing approximate majority in a discrete-time computation model. They established the parallel time convergence bound $O(\log n)$ with high probability given that the initial margin is $\epsilon n = \omega(\sqrt{n \log n})$. The same three-state protocol was empirically studied as a model of epigenetic cell memory by nucleosome modification [DMST07]. Independently, the same three-state population protocol for approximate majority was studied by [PVV09] in a continuous-time computation model. They established a tight bound on the probability of error for convergence to the correct terminal state $\exp(-D((1+\epsilon)/2||1/2)n)$ where $D(p||q)$ is the Kullback-Leibler divergence between two Bernoulli distributions with parameters p and q. This implies the asymptotic bound on the error probability $\exp(-c\epsilon^2 n)$ for constant $c > 0$ and small ϵ. Moreover, they established a parallel convergence time bound $O(\log(1/\epsilon) + \log n)$ for the limit system dynamics described by a system of ordinary differential equations as the number of nodes n grows large. [CCN12] showed that the dynamics of this three-state population protocol is under certain initial conditions equivalent of the cell cycle switch and other dynamics. [FHK14] have provided an algorithm in a push gossip model with one-bit messages that can be flipped with small probability. Similar to the three-state algorithm, for a sufficiently large margin, this algorithm also converges to the correct majority w.h.p. within time logarithmic in n. The main difference besided model is resiliency against message corruptions.

[DV12] first proposed a four-state protocol for exact majority computation and studied it for the case of arbitrary rates of pairwise interactions, which are such that the underlying graph G of pairwise interactions is connected. They showed an expected parallel time convergence bound of $(\log n + 1)/\delta(G, \epsilon)$ where $\delta(G, \epsilon) > 0$ is the smallest eigenvalue gap for a family of pairwise interaction rate matrices. For the case of a clique, this yields the expected parallel time convergence bound $O(\log n/\epsilon)$. A similar four-state protocol was also studied by [MNRS14] in a discrete-time computation model, who established that four memory states are necessary for exact majority computation.

In population protocols, it is known that increasing the number of states can lead to faster algorithms. For example, with constant states, leader election has been shown to require at least linear time [DS15]. However there is an algorithm using polylogarithmic number of states that converges in polylogarithmic time [AG15].

A random process similar to the averaging stage of our algorithm was studied by Sauerwald and Sun [SS12], for arbitrary graphs. Their goal is to bound the necessary time for every node's value to converge within a constant, whereas we are interested in the time it takes for all minority values to reach absolute value ≤ 1, after which we bound the remaining time until all nodes with a minority opinion are eliminated. Another process where nodes store values and update according to a dynamics that resembles averaging is studied in [KDG03], and its analysis also critically relies on the sum being invariant. However, the values can be arbitrary requiring an infinite state space in our model.

2. PRELIMINARIES

Population Protocols: We assume a population consisting of n agents, or cells, each executing as a deterministic state machine with states from a finite set Q, with a finite set of input symbols $X \subseteq Q$, a finite set of output symbols Y, a transition function $\delta : Q \times Q \to Q \times Q$, and an output function $\gamma : Q \to Y$. Initially, each agent starts with an input from the set X, and proceeds to update its state following interactions with other agents, according to the transition function δ. For simplicity of exposition, we assume that agents have identifiers from the set $V = \{1, 2, \ldots, n\}$, although these identifiers are not known to agents, and not used by the protocol.

The agents' interactions proceed according to a directed *interaction graph* G without self-loops, whose edges indicate possible agent interactions. Usually, the graph G is considered to be the complete graph on n vertices, a convention we also adopt in this work.

The execution proceeds in *steps*, where in each step a new edge (u, w) is chosen uniformly at random from the set of edges of G. Each of the two chosen agents updates its state according to the function δ.

We say that a population protocol computes a function $g : X^V \to Y$ within ℓ steps with probability $1 - \phi$ if for all $x \in g^{-1}(Y)$, the configuration $c : V \to Q$ reached by the protocol after ℓ steps satisfies the following two properties with probability $1 - \phi$:

1. For all $v \in V$, $g(x) = \gamma(c(v))$. Specifically, all agents have the correct output in c.

2. For every configuration c' reachable from c, and for all $v \in V$, $g(x) = \gamma(c'(v))$.

Parallel Time: The above setup considers sequential interactions; however, in general, interactions between pairs of distinct agents are independent, and are usually considered as occurring in parallel. In particular, it is customary to define one unit of *parallel time* as n consecutive steps of the protocol.

The Majority Problem: In the *majority problem*, agents start with arbitrary initial states in the input set $X = \{A, B\}$. Let a be the number of agents starting in state A, and b be the number of agents starting in state B, and let $\epsilon = |a - b|/n$ denote the relative advantage of an initial state. The output set is $Y = \{0, 1\}$.

A population protocol solves the majority problem within ℓ steps with probability $1 - \phi$, if, for any configuration $c : V \to Q$ reachable by the protocol after $\geq \ell$ steps, it holds with probability $1 - \phi$ that (1) If $a > b$ for the given input, then for any agent i, $\gamma(c(i)) = 1$, and, conversely, (2) If $b > a$ for the given input, then for any agent i, $\gamma(c(i)) = 0$.

3. THE AVC ALGORITHM

In this section, we describe the *Average and Conquer* (AVC) algorithm, which solves the majority problem in population protocols *exactly*, using s states. Throughout the rest of the exposition, we fix an odd integer parameter $m \geq 1$, which will determine the number of states of the protocol and its running time.

Overview: The intuition behind the protocol is as follows. Each node state is associated with a *sign* (+ or −) and a *weight* (an non-negative odd integer between 0 and m), whose product determines the *value* corresponding to each state. Throughout the exposition, we will identify the node *state* with corresponding *integer value*, making the distinction where appropriate. (The formal mapping is given for each state in lines 1–3 of the pseudocode in Figure 2.)

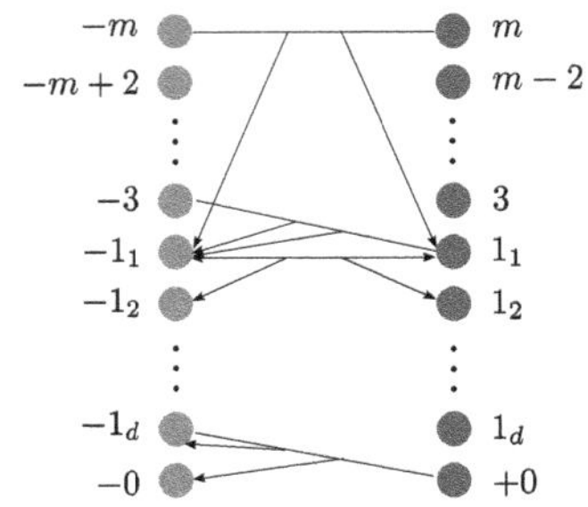

Figure 1: Structure of the states, and some reaction examples. Initially, nodes are in state $-m$ or $+m$. Each line corresponds to a reaction between two states; the two arrows point to the resulting states. For example, states m and $-m$ react to produce states -1_1 and 1_1.

Nodes start in one of two distinguished states. By convention, nodes starting in state A have initial value (state) $+m$, while nodes starting in state B have initial value (state) $-m$. The protocol is based on the following idea: whenever two nodes holding non-zero values interact, they *average* their current values. (Since states only represent odd values, the algorithm rounds the average if needed.) States $+0$ and -0 are *weak*: a node in this state does not influence other values in interactions, and will change its state's sign to match the that of the interaction partner. Also, for technical reasons, value 1 corresponds to d distinct *intermediate states*, which we denote by $1_1, 1_2, \ldots, 1_d$ (and, symmetrically, states $-1_1, -1_2, \ldots, -1_d$ for value -1). A node in such a state must interact several times with other nodes of opposite sign and intermediate value in order to eventually downgrade to 0.

Nodes continue to interact according to these simple rules. We prove that all nodes will converge to values of the same sign as the initial majority, and that convergence is fast with high probability. This solves the majority problem since we can define γ as mapping each state to the output based on its sign. We present the algorithm in detail below.

State Parameters: Each state in the protocol corresponds to an integer value, composed by a *sign* (+ or −) and a and a *weight*, which is either 0, or an odd positive integer between 1 and m. Intuitively, a node's sign gives its tentative output, whereas its *weight* gives the "confidence" in that specific output. *Strong* states (with weight ≥ 3) can drive weaker states, of lower absolute value, to change sign. *Weak* states (absolute value 0) will not influence other states' sign. States with weight 1 (denoted by $\pm 1_j$, where j is a positive integer denoting the state's level) are *intermediate*, and are interpreted as having weight 1, and sign ± 1. (Intuitively, the reason why we grade values of 1 is to prevent nodes from becoming weak too quickly.) The total number of states in the protocol is $s = m + 2d + 1$.

Nodes start in one of two initial states: state A, which we identify as having *sign* $= +1$ and *weight* $= m$, and state B, which corresponds to *sign* $= -1$ and *weight* $= m$. The algorithm, specified in Figure 2, consists of a set of simple deterministic update rules for the node state, depending on the *sign* and *weight* of the interacting node, and will ensure that, after some time, all nodes converge to the correct (majority) opinion. In the pseudocode, the node states before an interaction are denoted by x and y, while their new states are given by x' and y'. The algorithm is entirely symmetric, requiring no order on the agents in the interaction.

Parameters:
m, an odd integer > 0, and d, integer > 0
State Space:
$StrongStates = \{-m, -m+2, \ldots, -3, 3, 5, \ldots, m-2, m\}$,
$IntermediateStates = \{-1_1, -1_2, \ldots, -1_d, 1_d, 1_{d-1}, \ldots, 1_1\}$,
$WeakStates = \{-0, +0\}$
Input: States of two nodes, x and y
Output: Updated states x' and y'
Auxiliary Procedures:
/* Functions mapping states to integers */

1 $weight(x) = \begin{cases} |x| & \text{if } x \in StrongStates \text{ or } x \in WeakStates; \\ 1 & \text{if } x \in IntermediateStates. \end{cases}$

2 $sgn(x) = \begin{cases} 1 & \text{if } x \in \{+0, 1_d, \ldots, 1_1, 3, 5, \ldots, m\}; \\ -1 & \text{otherwise.} \end{cases}$

3 $value(x) = sgn(x) \cdot weight(x)$

/* Functions for rounding state interactions */

4 $\phi(x) = -1_1$ if $x = -1$; 1_1 if $x = 1$; x, otherwise

5 $R_\downarrow(k) = \phi(k$ if k odd integer, $k-1$ if k even)

6 $R_\uparrow(k) = \phi(k$ if k odd integer, $k+1$ if k even)

7 $Shift\text{-}to\text{-}Zero(x) = \begin{cases} -1_{j+1} & \text{if } x = -1_j \text{ for some index } j < d \\ 1_{j+1} & \text{if } x = 1_j \text{ for some index } j < d \\ x & \text{otherwise.} \end{cases}$

8 $Sign\text{-}to\text{-}Zero(x) = \begin{cases} +0 & \text{if } sgn(x) > 0 \\ -0 & \text{oherwise.} \end{cases}$

9 **procedure** update$\langle x, y \rangle$
10   **if** $(weight(x) > 0$ *and* $weight(y) > 1)$ *or* $(weight(y) > 0$ *and* $weight(x) > 1)$ **then**
11     $x' \leftarrow R_\downarrow\left(\frac{value(x)+value(y)}{2}\right)$ and $y' \leftarrow R_\uparrow\left(\frac{value(x)+value(y)}{2}\right)$
12   **else if** $weight(x) \cdot weight(y) = 0$ *and* $value(x) + value(y) > 0$ **then**
13   **if** $weight(x) \neq 0$ **then** $x' \leftarrow Shift\text{-}to\text{-}Zero(x)$ and $y' \leftarrow Sign\text{-}to\text{-}Zero(x)$
14   **else** $y' \leftarrow Shift\text{-}to\text{-}Zero(y)$ and $x' \leftarrow Sign\text{-}to\text{-}Zero(y)$
15   **else if** $(x \in \{-1_d, +1_d\}$ *and* $weight(y) = 1$ *and* $sgn(x) \neq sgn(y))$ *or*
16       $(y \in \{-1_d, +1_d\}$ *and* $weight(x) = 1$ *and* $sgn(y) \neq sgn(x))$ **then**
17     $x' \leftarrow -0$ and $y' \leftarrow +0$
18   **else**
19     $x' \leftarrow Shift\text{-}to\text{-}Zero(x)$ and $y' \leftarrow Shift\text{-}to\text{-}Zero(y)$

Figure 2: The state update rules for the majority computation.

Interactions: The core of the update rule is the *averaging* of nodes' values after each interaction, where for each state x, $value(x) = sgn(x) \cdot weight(x)$, where states $\pm 1_j$ have weight 1. Intuitively, the values of the two participants after an interaction will equal the average of their previous values, where we round values up and down to the closest odd numbers. Note that this rule always preserves the total sum of values in the system. Values 0 and 1 are special, and therefore we consider them separately in the update rules. We have three cases for the update rules: *strong meets non-zero* (line 11), *zero meets non-zero* (lines 12—14), and *intermediate meets intermediate* (lines 15—19), with a special case if one of the nodes is 1_d (lines 15—17). (The *zero meets zero* reaction does not change the participants' states.) Figure 1 gives examples of reactions.

If a node in a strong state (with weight > 1) meets a node in strong or intermediate state (with weight > 0), their new values will correspond to the average of their initial value (line 11). Specifically, if the average of the two node values is even, the updated states will encode values *average* $- 1$ and *average* $+ 1$. If the average is odd, then both states encode *average*. When a node reaches value 1 or -1, its state becomes either 1_1 or -1_1. This rounding is performed through the functions $R_\uparrow$ and $R_\downarrow$.

Second, if a node with 0 weight meets a node with non-zero weight, then it will adopt the sign of the interaction partner via the *Sign-to-Zero* function, whose weight remains unchanged (lines 12—14). Nodes $\pm 1_j$ with $j < d$ are a slight exception, as they become downgraded to $\pm 1_{j+1}$. Thus, the ordering of states corresponding to value 1 is such that 1_d is the weakest / closest to value 0.

Third, if the participants have different signs, weight 1, and one of them is in state 1_d or -1_d, then both are downgraded to value 0, albeit with different signs (lines 15—17).

In the last case unless both values are zero (and nothing changes) both participants have weight 1 but none of them is in state 1_d or -1_d. Then, both keep weight 1, but are downgraded to the next level of state 1 via the *Shift-to-Zero* function. For example, a node in a state 1_j with $j < d$ now moves to state 1_{j+1}.

4. ANALYSIS OF THE AVC ALGORITHM

In this section, we provide a complete analysis of the AVC algorithm. We first prove correctness, showing that the algorithm always converges to a correct answer, and also characterize the distribution of its convergence time.

Notation: Throughout this proof, we denote the set of nodes executing the protocol by V. We measure execution time in discrete steps (rounds), where each step corresponds to an interaction. The *configuration* at a given time t is a function $c : V \to Q$, where $c(v)$ is the state of the node v at time t. (We omit the explicit time t when clear from the context.) We use the quantities $sgn(c(v))$, $weight(c(v))$ and $value(c(v))$ associated with the state $c(v)$ of the node

v in configuration c, as defined on Figure 2 lines 1-3. We will refer to them as the sign, weight and value of the node, respectively.

Analysis Overview: The analysis first considers correctness, and then speed of convergence. For correctness, we prove that nodes never converge to the sign of the initial minority (safety), and that they eventually converge to the sign of the initial majority (termination). The first statement follows since the algorithm is designed to keep the total sum of values in the system *invariant*: for instance, if the initial sum is positive, then positive values must always exist in the system. Further, we prove that, eventually, all minority values are eliminated, implying termination.

The convergence bound is more involved. We first focus on the *extremal* weights in the system, showing that, roughly, either their weight is halved every $\log n$ parallel time steps, or the number of nodes in strong states is depleted for one of the signs. Further, this halving process, which takes expected $O(\log n \log m)$ parallel time, still preserves the initial system sum: therefore, instead of having a few deciding nodes with high values, after the halving completes, we will have many deciding nodes of small value. We then show that these nodes sway the remaining minority states to the correct decision within expected $O(\log n/(\epsilon m))$ parallel time, completing the bound. Our main result is the following theorem.

THEOREM 1. *The* AVC *algorithm solves majority problem with probability* 1. *There is a setting of parameters, such that it uses* $s = m + O(\log n \log m)$ *states for parameter* $m \leq n$ *and has parallel convergence time* $O(\log n/(m\epsilon) + \log n \log m)$ *in expectation and* $O(\log^2 n/(m\epsilon) + \log^2 n)$ *with high probability.*

An interesting setting $m = 1/\epsilon$ gives the following.

COROLLARY 1. *There is a setting of parameters, such that the* AVC *algorithm uses* $s = 1/\epsilon + O(\log n \log 1/\epsilon)$ *states, and has parallel convergence time* $O(\log n \log 1/\epsilon)$ *in expectation and* $O(\log^2 n)$ *with high probability.*

Correctness: We observe that, given the interaction rules of the algorithm, the sum of the encoded values stays constant as the algorithm progresses. The proof follows by the structure of the algorithm. In particular, the averaging reaction is designed to maintain the sum. Same holds for all other types of interactions.

INVARIANT 2. *The sum* $\sum_{v \in V} value(c(v))$ *never changes, for all reachable configurations* c *of the protocol.*

This invariant implies that the algorithm may never converge to a wrong decision value, as at least a node with the sign of the initial majority must exist in the system. We therefore only need to show that the algorithm converges to a state where all nodes have the same sign, which we do via a rough convergence bound, assuming an arbitrary starting configuration.

LEMMA 1. *Let* c *be an arbitrary starting configuration for the the* AVC *algorithm and define* $S := \sum_{v \in V} value(c(v)) \neq 0$. *With probability* 1, *the algorithm will reach a configuration* f *such that* $sgn(f(v)) = \text{sgn}(S)$ *for all nodes* $v \in V$. *Moreover, in all later configurations* e *reachable from* f, *no node can ever have a different sign, i.e.* $\forall v \in V : sgn(e(v)) = sgn(f(v))$. *The convergence time to* f *is at most* $n^3(m + d + 1)$ *expected communication rounds, i.e. parallel time* $n^2(m + d + 1)$.

PROOF. Assume without loss of generality that the sum S is positive. At any time, given the current configuration is r, let us define $P := \sum_{v \in V \mid sgn(r(v))>0} weight(r(v))$ and $N := \sum_{v \in V \mid sgn(r(v))<0} weight(r(v))$. Then, by Invariant 2, $P - N = S > 0$ holds throughout the execution. Also, $N \leq nm$, as each of the at most n contributing weights to the sum is at most m.

We estimate the expected convergence time by splitting the execution into three phases. The first phase starts at the beginning of the execution, and lasts until either i) N becomes 0, *or* ii) until all nodes are in states that encode values in $\{-1, 0, 1\}$. Therefore, throughout this phase, there are always nodes that encode non-zero values with different signs and at least one node in a strong state (with weight > 1).

Consequently, in any communication round in the first phase, with at least $1/n^2$ probability this node of large weight interacts with a node with opposite sign and non-zero value, and therefore N (and P) both decrease by at least 1. At the same time, because of the update rules of the algorithm, N can never increase. In expected n^2 rounds, N will decrease by at least 1. By $N < nm$ and the linearity of expectation, expected number of rounds until N becomes 0, or until no nodes remain in a strong state (maximum weight of nodes ≤ 1), is at most $n^3 m$. This upper bounds the expected number of rounds in the first phase.

The second phase starts immediately after the first, and ends when N becomes 0. Note that if the first phase ended because of $N = 0$, the second phase is trivially empty. Now consider the case when all nodes are in states with values -1, 0 and 1 at the beginning of the second phase. There are clearly N nodes with value -1, P nodes with value 1 ($N < P < n$) and the remaining nodes must be in weak states (weight 0).

Under these circumstances, because of the update rules, no node will ever be in a strong state (weight > 1) again in any future configuration. Also, the number of nodes in intermediate states (weight 1) can only decrease. In each round, with probability at least $1/n^2$, two nodes with weights 1_i and 1_j and opposite signs meet. Either $\max(i, j) = d$ and both new values become zero, meaning N (and P) decreases by 1, or the weights become 1_{i+1} and 1_{j+1} without affecting the signs. But this can only happen nd times, since there can be at most n nodes encoding value -1, and each becomes 0 after at most d meetings with a nodes of opposite sign. Therefore, the expected number of rounds in the second phase is at most $n^3 d$.

After the second phase, $P = S$ holds and all nodes with negative sign ought to have weight 0. From this time, all rounds belong to the final, third phase, throughout which N clearly remains equal to zero. The third phase lasts until the system converges, that is, until all nodes with weight 0 get a positive sign. Since $S \geq 1$ there is at least one node with a positive sign and non-zero weight, and there are at most $n - 1$ *conflicting* nodes with a negative sign, all with value zero as $N = 0$. Thus, independently in each round, with probability at least $1/n^2$, a conflicting node meets a node with strictly positive value and the number of conflicting nodes decreases by one. The number of conflicting nodes never increases because of the update rules and when it becomes zero, the system has converged to the desired configuration f. Therefore, the expected number of rounds in the third phase is at most n^3.

Combining the results, the total expected number of rounds is at most $n^3(m+d+1)$. The expectation being finite implies that the algorithm converges with probability 1. Finally, when two nodes with positive sign meet, they both remain positive, so any configuration e reachable from f also contains every node with the correct sign. □

Convergence Time Bounds: We now focus on bounding the time until all nodes converge to the correct sign. We begin by establishing some notation. We call a round a *negative-round* if, in the configuration c at the beginning of the round, at least a *third* of the nodes encode a strictly negative value, i.e. $|\{v \in V : value(c(v)) < 0\}| \geq |V|/3$. Analogously, we call a round a *positive-round* if a third of the nodes encode a strictly positive value. A round can be simultaneously negative *and* positive. Our first claim bounds the speed at which the maximum weight present in the system decreases. The proof follows by bounding the probability that a node with the maximum weight meets a node with non-zero value and opposite sign in a round. This decreases the weight of the node, and we use Chernoff and Union Bounds to bound the probability that the node avoids such a meeting for logarithmic parallel time.

CLAIM 1. *Let $w > 1$ be the maximum weight among the nodes with a negative (resp., positive) sign. For constant $\beta \geq 54$, after $\beta n \log n$ positive-rounds (resp., negative-rounds) the maximum weight among the nodes with a negative (resp., positive) sign will be at most $\lfloor w/2 \rfloor$ with probability at least $1 - \log n / n^{\beta/54}$.*

PROOF. We will prove the claim for nodes with strictly negative values. (The converse claim follows analogously.) Fix a round r, and recall that w is the maximum weight of a node with a negative value at the beginning of the round. Let U be the set of nodes encoding negative values between $-\lceil w/2 \rceil$ and $-w$, with $w > 1$, at the beginning of the round, and let $u = |U|$. We call these nodes *target nodes*.

By the structure of the AVC algorithm, the number of target nodes never increases, and decreases by one in every *eliminating* round where a target node meets a node with a strictly positive value. Consider a set of αn consecutive positive-rounds after r, for $\alpha \geq 18$. In each round, if there are still at least $\lceil u/2 \rceil$ target nodes, then the probability of this round being eliminating is at least $\lceil u/2 \rceil / 3n$ (recall that by definition of a positive round at least third of the nodes have strictly positive value). Let us describe the process by considering a random variable $X \sim \text{Bin}(\alpha n, \frac{\lceil u/2 \rceil}{3n})$, where each success event corresponds to an eliminating round. By a Chernoff Bound, the probability of having αn iterations ($\alpha \geq 18$) with at most $\lceil u/2 \rceil$ eliminations is at most:

$$\begin{aligned}\mathbf{Pr}\left[X \leq \lceil u/2 \rceil\right] = \quad & \mathbf{Pr}\left[X \leq \frac{\alpha \lceil u/2 \rceil}{3}\left(1 - \frac{\alpha - 3}{\alpha}\right)\right] \\ \leq \quad & \exp\left(-\frac{\alpha \lceil u/2 \rceil (\alpha - 3)^2}{6\alpha^2}\right) \leq 2^{-\frac{u\alpha}{18}}.\end{aligned}$$

For $u \geq \log n$, the probability of this event is at most $\frac{1}{n^{\alpha/18}}$ for αn positive-rounds. Applying the same rationale iteratively as long as $u \geq \log n$, we obtain by using a Union Bound that the number of target nodes will become less than $\log n$ within $\alpha n(\log n - \log\log n)$ positive-rounds, with probability at least $1 - (\log n - \log\log n)/n^{\alpha/18}$.

Finally, we wish to upper bound the remaining number of positive-rounds until no target node remains. When $u < \log n$, we get from the same argument as above that the number of target nodes is reduced to $\lfloor u/2 \rfloor$ within $\frac{\alpha n \log n}{u}$ consecutive positive-rounds with probability $1/n^{\alpha/18}$. So we consider increasing numbers of consecutive positive-rounds, and obtain that no target nodes will be left after at most $\alpha n + 2\alpha n + \ldots + \alpha n \log n \leq 2\alpha n \log n$ positive-rounds, with probability at least $1 - \log\log n / n^{\alpha/18}$, where we have taken the union bound over $\log\log n$ events. The original claim follows by setting $\beta = 3\alpha$, and taking the Union Bound over the above two events ($u \geq \log n$ and $u < \log n$). □

In the following, we consider the AVC algorithm with parameters $\log n \log\log n \leq m \leq n$ and $d = 1000 \log m \log n$, for the total of $s = m + O(\log m \log n)$ states. We first prove that in this setting, no node will reach value 0 within the first $432n \log m \log n$ rounds, w.h.p. The proof follows from Chernoff Bound by showing that the probability that a node gets selected at least d times (necessary for it to downgrade to 0) during this interval is extremely low.

CLAIM 2. *The probability that any node gets weight 0 during the first $432n \log m \log n$ rounds is $\leq 1/n^4$.*

PROOF. In each round, the probability that a particular node is selected is $2/n$. Let us describe the number of times a given node is selected in $432n \log m \log n$ rounds by considering a random variable $Z \sim \text{Bin}(432n \log m \log n, 2/n)$. Given that $d = 1000 \log m \log n$, by the Chernoff Bound, the probability that the node gets selected more than d times in these rounds is at most:

$$\begin{aligned}\mathbf{Pr}\left[Z \geq d\right] &= \mathbf{Pr}\left[Z \geq (864 \log m \log n) \cdot \left(1 + \frac{136}{864}\right)\right] \\ &\leq \exp\left(-\frac{864 \cdot 136^2}{3 \cdot 864^2} \log m \log n\right) \leq \frac{1}{(mn)^5}.\end{aligned}$$

A node cannot get weight 0 during the first $432n \log m \log n$ rounds unless it is selected for interactions at least d times in total. Thus, the probability that a given node gets value zero is at most $1/(mn)^5$. Applying the Union Bound over all nodes, we conclude that no node gets *weight* $= 0$ during the first $432n \log m \log n$ rounds, with probability at least $1 - 1/(m^5 n^4) \geq 1 - 1/n^4$. □

Claim 1 gave a condition for halving the maximum positive and the minimum negative values in the system with high probability. The initial maximum weight in the system is m, which can only be halved $\log m$ times for each sign. This motivates the following claim:

CLAIM 3. *During the first $432n \log m \log n$ rounds, if no node gets value 0, then with probability at least $1 - (2 \log n \log m)/n^4$, one of the following three events occurs at some point during these rounds:*

1. *Nodes only have values in $\{-1, 1\}$;*
2. *There are less than $n/3$ nodes with negative values, all with value -1,*
3. *There are less than $n/3$ nodes with positive values, all with value 1.*

PROOF. Since no node gets value 0 during the first $432n \log m \log n$ rounds, each round during this interval is either a negative-round, a positive-round, or both. Unless the maximum positive value in the system is 1, by Claim 1, a stretch of $216n \log n$ negative-rounds halves the maximum positive value available, with probability at least $1 - \log n/n^4$. The same occurs for stretches of $216n \log n$ positive-rounds and the minimum negative value.

Assume that none of the three events hold at any time during the first $432n \log m \log n$ rounds. In that case, each round can be classified as either a negative round where the maximum positive value is strictly larger than 1, or a positive round where the minimum negative value is strictly smaller than -1. Thus, each round contributes to at least one of the stretches of $216n \log n$ rounds that halve the maximum positive of minimum negative value, w.h.p. However, this may happen at most $2 \log m$ times. By applying Claim 1 $2 \log m$ times (using $\beta = 216$) and the Union Bound we get that after the first $432n \log m \log n$ rounds, with probability at least $1 - 2 \log n \log m / n^4$ only values -1 and 1 will remain.

However, this is the same as the first event above. Thus, the probability that none of these events happen is at most $2 \log n \log m / n^4$. □

Returning to the proof, recall that we assumed without loss of generality that the initial majority of nodes was in A (positive) state, i.e. $a > b$. The following claim provides the last piece of the puzzle.

CLAIM 4. *Consider a configuration after the first* $432n \log m \log n + 4dn$ *rounds. With probability at least* $1 - (2 \log n \log m + 2)/n^4$, *all nodes with a strictly negative value will be in state* -1_d *while at least* $n \cdot \min(1/3, \epsilon m)$ *more nodes will encode a strictly positive value than the nodes in state* -1_d.

PROOF. By our assumption about the initial majority and Invariant 2, $\sum_{v \in V} value(c(v)) = \epsilon n m$ holds in every reachable configuration c. Let us focus on the high probability events in Claim 2 and Claim 3: no node gets a value 0 within the first $432n \log m \log n$ rounds, and during these rounds the execution reaches a configuration where one of the three events from Claim 3 holds. Consider this point T in the execution.

Since no node has value 0, the third event is impossible, because the total sum would be negative. Second event implies that there are at least $n/3$ more strictly positive values than strictly negative values. In the first event, the total sum is $\geq \epsilon n m$ and values are all -1 and 1, so there must be at least $\epsilon m n$ more strictly positive than negative values. Hence, at point T during the first $432n \log n \log m$ rounds there are at least $n \cdot \min(1/3, \epsilon m)$ more strictly positive than strictly negative values.

In both cases, -1's are the only strictly negative values of the nodes at point T, and this will be the case for the rest of the execution because of the update rules. Also, for any level $i < d$, every time one of the nodes in state -1_i interacts with another node with value not equal to -1 (has to be value ≥ 0), either both nodes get values ≥ 0, or the node moves to state -1_{i+1} via the *Shift-to-Zero* function.

In each round, the probability that a given node with value -1 interacts with a node with value ≥ 0 is at least $\min(2/3, (1 + \epsilon m)/2)/n \geq 1/(2n)$. Let us describe the number of times the given node is selected in for such an interaction during the at least $4dn$ rounds after T by a random variable $Y \sim \text{Bin}(4dn, 1/2n)$. Then, by Chernoff Bound, the probability that the node is selected less than d times is at most:

$$\mathbf{Pr}[Y \leq d] = \mathbf{Pr}\left[Y \leq 2d\left(1 - \frac{1}{2}\right)\right] \leq$$
$$\exp\left(-\frac{2d}{2 \cdot 2^2}\right) \leq 2^{-d/4} < \frac{1}{n^5},$$

where we have used that d is set to $1000 \log m \log n$. Union Bound over all the $\leq n$ nodes that had value -1 at point T, we get that after $4dn$ more rounds, with probability $1 - 1/n^4$, all these nodes interacted at least d times with nodes with non-negative values. Hence, they either have value ≥ 0 or are in state -1_d.

After T, the number of nodes with strictly positive values only decreases in an interaction with a node in state -1_i, in which case the number of nodes with strictly negative values also decreases by one. Hence there must still be at least $n \cdot \min(1/3, \epsilon m)$ more nodes with strictly positive that strictly negative values.

A Union Bound over Claim 2, Claim 3 and the above argument completes the proof. □

By Claim 4, with high probability after $432n \log m \log n + 4dn$ rounds we reach a configuration, from which the convergence bares many similarities to the four state protocol of [DV12] and can be analyzed similarly. We describe its convergence below.

CLAIM 5. *Consider a configuration where all nodes with strictly negative values are in state* -1_d, *while at least* $n\delta$ *more nodes encode a strictly positive value than the nodes in state* -1_d. *The number of rounds until convergence is* $O(\frac{n \log n}{\delta})$ *in expectation and* $O(\frac{n \log^2 n}{\delta})$ *w.h.p.*

PROOF. In any configuration, let us call *conflicting* any node that is in state -1_d, and *target* node any node that has a strictly positive value. Because of the structure of the algorithm, and that in configuration c the only nodes with negative sign are in states -1_d or -0, in all configurations reachable from c nodes with negative values will also only be in states -1_d or -0. Moreover, the number of conflicting nodes can never increase after an interaction. As in Claim 4, observe that the number of target nodes can only decrease after an interaction where a node with value 1 meets a node in state -1_d, in which case the number of conflicting nodes also decreases by one. There are $n\delta$ more target nodes than conflicting nodes in c, therefore, in every later configuration, there must always be at least $n\delta$ target nodes.

Every time a conflicting node meets a target node, both nodes get value ≥ 0, so the number of conflicting nodes decreases by one. Let us estimate the number of rounds until each conflicting node has interacted with a target node, at which point no more conflicting nodes may exist. Let us say there were x conflicting nodes in configuration c. The expected number of rounds until the first conflicting node meets a target node is at most $\frac{n}{x\delta}$, since the probability of such an interaction happening in each round is at least $\frac{x}{n} \cdot \frac{n\delta}{n}$. The expected number of rounds for the second node is then $\frac{n}{(x-1)\delta}$, and so on. By linearity of expectation, the expected number of rounds until all conflicting nodes are eliminated is $O(\frac{n \log x}{\delta}) \leq O(\frac{n \log n}{\delta})$.

At this point, all nodes that have a negative sign must be in state -0. If we redefine *conflicting* to describe these nodes, it is still true that an interaction of a conflicting node with a target node brings the conflicting node to state $+0$, thus decreasing the number of conflicting nodes. As we discussed at least $n\delta$ target nodes are still permanently present in the system. By the structure of the algorithm no interaction can increase the number of nodes with negative sign, the system will converge when all conflicting nodes are eliminated. But this takes expected $O(\frac{n \log n}{\delta})$ rounds by exactly the same argument as above.

To get the high probability claim, simply observe that when there are x conflicting nodes in the system, a conflicting node will interact with a target node within $\frac{nO(\log n)}{x\delta}$ rounds, with high probability. The same applies for the next conflicting node, etc. Taking Union Bound over these events gives the desired result. □

Thus, after the first $432n \log m \log n + 4dn$ rounds, in the high probability case, plugging $\delta = \min(1/3, \epsilon m)$ in Claim 5, we get that the remaining number of rounds is at most $O(n \log n + (n \log n)/(m\epsilon))$ in expectation and $O(n \log^2 n + (n \log^2 n)(m\epsilon))$ w.h.p. The high probability statement immediately follows by the Union Bound.

We only have to bound expectation in the remaining low probability event. With probability at most $(2 \log n \log m + 2)/n^4$, the expected remaining number of rounds is at most $O(n^3(m+d))$ by Lemma 1 and since in our parameter setting $m+d = O(n)$, it is negligible compared to the previous case.

5. LOWER BOUNDS

5.1 Convergence Time with Four States

We prove an $\Omega(1/\epsilon)$ lower bound on the convergence time of any four-state protocol for exact majority. The proof extends the approach introduced by [MNRS14] to show impossibility of exact three-state majority protocols, in that it explores all possible state transitions and output mappings. However, there are considerably more possibilities to consider, among which, unlike the three-state case, some yield correct four-state protocols. We combine indistinguishability arguments to demonstrate that certain algorithms could converge to the incorrect output, with potential-based arguments to show that certain algorithms may never converge, and with convergence analysis of the correct algorithms. Due to space limitations, the proof is deferred to the full version of this paper [AGV15].

We slightly alter notation in this section. We call the initial states S_1 (corresponding to A) and S_0 (corresponding to B). The output (formally defined by the mapping γ) should be $i \in \{0, 1\}$ if a majority of the nodes start in state S_i. We define C_i as a set of all *absorbing* configurations c for output i: for all configurations c_i reachable from $c \in C_i$, we must have $\forall v \in V : \gamma(c_i(v)) = i$.

THEOREM 3. *Consider any majority algorithm using four states, providing the following correctness properties for any* $|V| = n \geq 1$:

- *For each possible outcome $i \in \{0, 1\}$, the set C_i of absorbing configurations is non-empty.*
- *The system never converges to the wrong decision: if in the initial configuration the majority of nodes are in S_i for $i \in \{0, 1\}$, it must be impossible to reach any configuration $c \in C_{1-i}$ under* any *schedule of interactions.*
- *It is always possible to converge to the correct solution: if a majority of nodes start in S_i for $i \in \{0, 1\}$, from every reachable configuration there is a sequence (schedule) of interactions leading to a configuration $c \in C_i$.*

Then, if in the initial configuration ϵn more nodes start in state S_i than in S_{1-i} for $i \in \{0, 1\}$, the expected parallel convergence time to reach some configuration $c \in C_i$ is $\Omega(1/\epsilon)$.

5.2 Arbitrary Number of States

We now prove that any algorithm solving exact majority must take expected $\Omega(\log n)$ parallel time until convergence on a worst-case input, irrespective of the number of states it uses. The structure is as follows: we start from an input state where the outcome is decided by a *constant* number of nodes (the initial states of other nodes are balanced). We then bound expected parallel time for the initial states of these nodes to propagate to every node by $\Omega(\log n)$ by a standard information-based argument, e.g. [CDR86, Jay98].

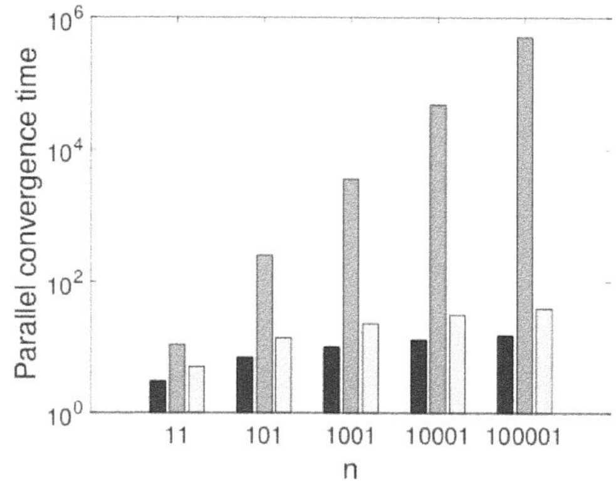

Figure 3: Comparison of performance of different protocols (left bar) 3-state protocol, (middle bar) 4-state protocol, and (right bar) n-state protocol.

We then argue that any node that does not have this decisive information may only have converged with *constant probability*, completing the proof. Due to space limitations, we defer the proof to the full version of our paper.

THEOREM 4. *Any algorithm $\mathcal{A}$ for exact majority takes expected $\Omega(\log n)$ parallel time until convergence under a worst-case input.*

6. DISCUSSION

We have tested the performance of our protocol through implementation, and compared it with the three-state protocol of [AAE08, PVV09], which has non-zero probability of error, and with the exact four-state protocol of [DV12, MNRS14].

For $\epsilon = 1/n$, the n-state version of AVC is orders of magnitude faster than the four-state protocol, and has comparable running time with the three-state protocol, noting that the latter has constant failure probability in this case (see Figure 3). Experiments varying parameters s and ϵ support the claim that the running time of the protocol is linear in these parameters, and that the constant factors are small (see Figure 4).

We have given the first sub-linear time population protocol solving exact majority, which highlights a new trade-off between the number of memory states of the algorithm (alternatively, number of local bits), the convergence time, and the error probability of the protocol. We have also shown that this trade-off is tight up to logarithmic factors when considered at its extremal points in s.

The above experiments were performed setting $d = 1$, i.e., with a single version of the 1 states. This suggests that this variant is also correct and efficient. The multiple levels of 1 and -1 are necessary in the analysis; however, setting $d > 1$ does not significantly affect the running time of the protocol in the experiments. It is therefore an interesting question whether the protocol can be further simplified.

The main open question left by our work is that of matching lower bounds. It would also be interesting to explore whether the average-and-conquer technique would also be useful in the context of other problems in population protocols. Further, we highlight the question of obtaining a fast *approximate* majority protocol which is correct with high probability for all possible values of the discrepancy ϵ.

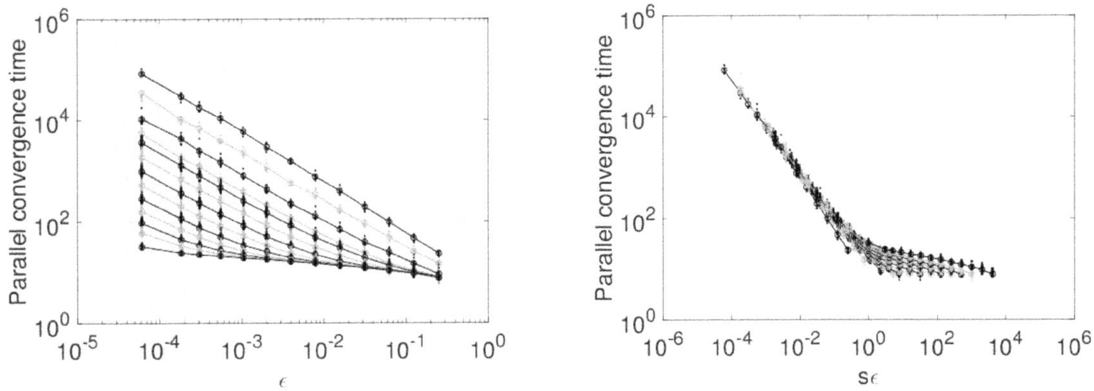

Figure 4: (left) Convergence time vs. parameter ϵ for for the number of states per node $s = 4, 6, 12, 24, 34, 66, 130, 258, 514, 1026, 2050, 4098, 16340$ for the respective curves in the graph from the top to bottom. (right) Convergence time vs. the product $s\epsilon$.

7. REFERENCES

[AAD+06] Dana Angluin, James Aspnes, Zoë Diamadi, Michael J Fischer, and René Peralta. Computation in networks of passively mobile finite-state sensors. *Distributed computing*, 18(4):235–253, 2006.

[AAE08] Dana Angluin, James Aspnes, and David Eisenstat. A simple population protocol for fast robust approximate majority. *Distributed Computing*, 21(2):87–102, July 2008.

[AAER07] Dana Angluin, James Aspnes, David Eisenstat, and Eric Ruppert. The computational power of population protocols. *Distributed Computing*, 20(4):279–304, November 2007.

[AG15] Dan Alistarh and Rati Gelashvili. Polylogarithmic-time leader election in population protocols. In *Proceedings of ICALP 2015*, 2015.

[AGV15] Dan Alistarh, Rati Gelashvili, and Milan Vojnovic. Fast and exact majority in population protocols. Technical Report MSR-TR-2015-13, February 2015.

[CCN12] Luca Cardelli and Attila Csikasz-Nagy. The cell cycle switch computes approximate majority. *Nature Scientific Reports*, 2:656, 2012.

[CDR86] Stephen Cook, Cynthia Dwork, and Ruediger Reischuk. Upper and lower time bounds for parallel random access machines without simultaneous writes. *SIAM J. Comput.*, 15(1):87–97, February 1986.

[CDS+13] Yuan-Jyue Chen, Neil Dalchau, Niranjan Srnivas, Andrew Phillips, Luca Cardelli, David Soloveichik, and Georg Seelig. Programmable chemical controllers made from dna. *Nature Nanotechnology*, 8(10):755–762, 2013.

[DMST07] Ian B. Dodd, A. M. Micheelsen, Kim Sneppen, and Geneviéve Thon. Theoretical analysis of epigenetic cell memory by nucleosome modification. *Cell*, 129(4):813–822, 2007.

[DS15] David Doty and David Soloveichik. Stable leader election in population protocols requires linear time. ArXiv preprint. http://arxiv.org/abs/1502.04246, 2015.

[DV12] Moez Draief and Milan Vojnovic. Convergence speed of binary interval consensus. *SIAM Journal on Control and Optimization*, 50(3):1087–1109, 2012.

[FHK14] Ofer Feinerman, Bernhard Haeupler, and Amos Korman. Breathe before speaking: efficient information dissemination despite noisy, limited and anonymous communication. In *Proceedings of PODC 2014*, pages 114–123. ACM, 2014.

[HP99] Yehuda Hassin and David Peleg. Distributed probabilistic polling and applications to proportionate agreement. In *Proceedings of ICALP 1999*, pages 402–411, London, UK, UK, 1999. Springer-Verlag.

[Jay98] Prasad Jayanti. A time complexity lower bound for randomized implementations of some shared objects. In *Proceedings of the Seventeenth Annual ACM Symposium on Principles of Distributed Computing*, PODC '98, pages 201–210, New York, NY, USA, 1998. ACM.

[KDG03] David Kempe, Alin Dobra, and Johannes Gehrke. Gossip-based computation of aggregate information. In *Foundations of Computer Science, 2003. Proceedings. 44th Annual IEEE Symposium on*, pages 482–491. IEEE, 2003.

[Lig85] Thomas M. Liggett. *Interacting Particle Systems*. Springer, 1985.

[MNRS14] George B. Mertzios, Sotiris E. Nikoletseas, Christoforos Raptopoulos, and Paul G. Spirakis. Determining majority in networks with local interactions and very small local memory. In *Proceedings of ICALP 2014*, pages 871–882, 2014.

[PVV09] Etienne Perron, Dinkar Vasudevan, and Milan Vojnovic. Using three states for binary consensus on complete graphs. In *INFOCOM 2009, IEEE*, pages 2527–2535. IEEE, 2009.

[SS12] Thomas Sauerwald and He Sun. Tight bounds for randomized load balancing on arbitrary network topologies. In *Proceedings of FOCS 2012*, pages 341–350, 2012.

Distributed House-Hunting in Ant Colonies*

Mohsen Ghaffari
MIT
Cambridge, MA, USA
ghaffari@csail.mit.edu

Cameron Musco
MIT
Cambridge, MA, USA
cnmusco@csail.mit.edu

Tsvetomira Radeva
MIT
Cambridge, MA, USA
radeva@csail.mit.edu

Nancy Lynch
MIT
Cambridge, MA, USA
lynch@csail.mit.edu

ABSTRACT

We introduce the study of the *ant colony house-hunting* problem from a distributed computing perspective. When an ant colony's nest becomes unsuitable due to size constraints or damage, the colony relocates to a new nest. The task of identifying and evaluating the quality of potential new nests is distributed among all ants. They must additionally reach consensus on a final nest choice and transport the full colony to this single new nest. Our goal is to use tools and techniques from distributed computing theory in order to gain insight into the house-hunting process.

We develop a formal model for the house-hunting problem inspired by the behavior of the *Temnothorax* genus of ants. We then show a $\Omega(\log n)$ lower bound on the time for all n ants to agree on one of k candidate nests. We also present two algorithms that solve the house-hunting problem in our model. The first algorithm solves the problem in optimal $\mathcal{O}(\log n)$ time but exhibits some features not characteristic of natural ant behavior. The second algorithm runs in $\mathcal{O}(k \log n)$ time and uses an extremely simple and natural rule for each ant to decide on the new nest.

Categories and Subject Descriptors

F.2.m [**Analysis of Algorithms and Problem Complexity**]: Miscellaneous; G.3 [**Mathematics of Computing**]: Probability and Statistics—*Probabilistic Algorithms*

Keywords

distributed algorithms; randomized algorithms; social insect colonies; biology-inspired algorithms; house-hunting; *Temnothorax* ants

*This work is sponsored in part by AFOSR contract number FA9550-13-1-0042 and NSF award numbers 0939370-CCF and CCF-AF-0937274.

Permission to make digital or hard copies of all or part of this work for personal or classroom use is granted without fee provided that copies are not made or distributed for profit or commercial advantage and that copies bear this notice and the full citation on the first page. Copyrights for components of this work owned by others than ACM must be honored. Abstracting with credit is permitted. To copy otherwise, or republish, to post on servers or to redistribute to lists, requires prior specific permission and/or a fee. Request permissions from permissions@acm.org.
PODC'15, July 21–23, 2015, Donostia-San Sebastián, Spain.
Copyright is held by the owner/author(s). Publication rights licensed to ACM.
ACM 978-1-4503-3617-8 /15/07 ...$15.00.
DOI: http://dx.doi.org/10.1145/2767386.2767426.

1. INTRODUCTION

Some recent work in distributed computing theory has focused on biological problems inspired by algorithmic tasks carried out by ant colonies; for example, [7, 9, 11, 19] study collaborative food foraging and [3] models and proposes algorithms for task allocation within a colony. Often computer scientists study biologically-inspired algorithms with the aim of engineering better computing systems. An alternative line of work uses tools developed to analyze and design distributed computer systems to better understand the behavior of biological systems [10]. In this paper, we follow the second approach in an attempt to better understand the house-hunting behavior of the *Temnothorax* ant. The essence of this process is a collaborative search, consensus decision, and relocation of the entire ant colony to a new home, with an emphasis on the decision making component.

We first model the ant colony and its computational constraints, and formally define an algorithmic problem that it solves. The challenge is to develop a model that is simultaneously tractable to theoretical analysis and close enough to reality to give meaningful insights into ant behavior. For example: Is ant behavior in some sense optimal given ants' biological constraints? One hypothesis may be that behavior has been optimized through evolution. Lower bounds matching the performance of algorithms seen in nature can provide mathematical support for this hypothesis. Alternatively, results may show that behavior is far from optimal, suggesting the existence of hidden constraints or goals yet to be fully understood. Can we identify why certain behavioral patterns have developed and what environmental and biological constraints they are adaptations to?

One motivation for studying the house-hunting process of *Temnothorax* ants is that it has received significant attention from biologists. Researchers have studied ants' preferences and capabilities [16, 27], the general structure of the algorithms used by the ants [20, 23], variations due to colony size [13], and trade-offs between the speed and accuracy of the process [25]. This work forms a wide basis of scientifically tested hypotheses that we can use for the foundation of our model and inspiration for our algorithms.

From a distributed computing perspective, house-hunting is closely related to the fundamental problem of consensus [12, 18]. This makes the problem conceptually different from other ant colony inspired problems studied by computer scientists. Task allocation and foraging are both intrinsically related to parallel optimization. The main goal is to divide work optimally amongst a large number of ants in a process similar to load balancing. This is commonly achieved using random allocation or *negative feedback* [1] against work that has already been completed. In contrast, the house-hunting problem is a decision problem in which all ants must converge to the same choice. Both in nature and in our proposed algorithms, this is achieved through *positive feedback* [1], by reinforcing viable nest candidates until a single choice remains. At a high level, our work is related to previous work on rumor spreading in biological populations [8].

1.1 The House-Hunting Process

Temnothorax ants live in fragile rock crevices that are frequently destroyed. It is crucial for colony survival to quickly find and move to a new nest after their home is compromised. This process is highly distributed and involves several stages of searching for nests, assessing nest candidates, recruiting other ants to do the same, and finally, transporting the full colony to the new home.

In the search phase, some ants begin searching their surroundings for possible new nests. Experimentally, this phase has not been studied much; it has been assumed that ants encounter candidate nests fairly quickly through random walking. In the assessment phase, each ant that arrives at a new nest evaluates it based on various criteria, e.g., whether the nest interior is dark and therefore likely free of holes, and whether the entrance to the nest is small enough to be easily defended. These criteria may have different priorities [16, 27] and, in general, it is assumed that nest assessments by an individual ant are not always precise or rational [26]. After some time spent assessing different nests, going back to the old nest and searching for new nests, an ant becomes sufficiently satisfied with a nest and proceeds to the recruitment phase, which consists of *tandem runs* – one ant leading another ant from the old to a new nest. The recruited ant learns the new nest location and can assess the nest itself and begin performing tandem runs if the nest is acceptable.

At this point many nest sites may have ants recruiting to them, so a decision has to be made in favor of one nest. The ants must solve the classic distributed computing problem of consensus. One strategy that ants are believed to use is a *quorum threshold* [24, 23] – a threshold of the number of ants in a candidate nest, that, when exceeded, indicates that the nest should be chosen as the new home. Each time an ant returns to the new nest, it evaluates (not necessarily accurately) whether a quorum has been reached. If so, it begins the transport phase – picking up and carrying other ants from the old to the new nest. These transports are generally faster than tandem runs and conclude the house-hunting process by bringing the full colony to the new nest.

1.2 Main Results and Organization

Our main results are a mathematical model of the house-hunting process, a lower bound on the number of rounds required by any algorithm solving the house-hunting problem in the given model, and two house-hunting algorithms.

Our model (Section 2) is based on a synchronous model of execution with n probabilistic ants and communication limited to one ant leading another ant (tandem run or transport), chosen randomly from the ants at the home nest, to a candidate nest. Ants can also search for new nests by choosing randomly among all k candidate nests. We do not model the time for an ant to find a nest or to lead a tandem run; each of these actions are assumed to take one round.

Our lower bound (Section 3) states that, under this model, no algorithm can solve the house-hunting problem in time sub-logarithmic in the number of ants. The main proof idea is that, in any step of an algorithm's execution, with constant probability, an ant that does not know of the location of the eventually-chosen nest remains uninformed. Therefore, with high probability, $\Omega(\log n)$ rounds are required to inform all n ants. This technique closely resembles lower bounds for rumor spreading in a complete graph, where the rumor is the location of the chosen nest [17].

Our first algorithm (Section 4) solves the house-hunting problem in asymptotically optimal time. The main idea is a typical example of positive feedback: each ant leads tandem runs to some suitable nest as long as the population of ants at that nest keeps increasing; once the ants at a candidate nest notice a decrease in the population, they give up and wait to be recruited to another nest. With high probability, within $\mathcal{O}(\log n)$ rounds, this process converges to all n ants committing to a single winning nest. Unfortunately, this algorithm relies heavily on a synchronous execution and on the ability to precisely count nest populations, suggesting that the algorithm is susceptible to perturbations of our model and most likely does not match real ant behavior.

The goal of our second algorithm (Section 5) is to be more natural and resilient to perturbations of the environmental parameters and ant capabilities. The algorithm uses a simple positive-feedback mechanism: in each round, an ant that has located a candidate nest recruits other ants to the nest with probability proportional to its current population. We show that, with high probability, this process converges to all n ants being committed to one of the k candidate nests within $\mathcal{O}(k \log n)$ rounds. While this algorithm is not optimal, except when k is assumed to be constant, it exhibits a much more natural process of converging to a single nest. In Section 6, we discuss in more detail possible modifications to the algorithm and various perturbations and faults to which it is resilient. Such robustness criteria are necessary in nature and generally desirable for distributed algorithms.

2. MODEL

We present a simple model of *Temnothorax* ants behavior that is tractable to rigorous analysis, yet rich enough to provide a starting point for understanding real ant behavior.

The environment consists of a home nest, denoted n_0, along with k candidate nests, denoted n_i for $i \in \{1, ..., k\}$. Each nest n_i is assigned a quality $q(i) \in Q$, for some set Q. Throughout this paper we let $Q = \{0, 1\}$, where quality 0 indicates an unsuitable nest, and 1 a suitable one. We assume that there is always at least one nest with $q(i) = 1$.

The colony consists of n identical probabilistic finite state machines, representing the ants. We assume n is significantly larger than k, with $k = O(n/\log n)$. Additionally, ants know the value of n but not k, so the state machines may be parameterized by n but must be uniform for all k. This assumption is based on evidence that real *Temnothorax* ants and other species are able to estimate colony size and change their behavior in response [4, 6].

The general behavior of the state machines is unrestricted but their interactions with the environment and other ants are limited to the functions **search**(), **go**(), and **recruit**(), defined below. Ants execute synchronously in numbered rounds starting with round 1. In each round, each ant may perform unlimited local computation (transition through an arbitrary sequence of states), along with exactly one call to one of the functions: **search**(), **go**(), or **recruit**().

At the end of each round r, each ant a is located at a nest, denoted $\ell(a,r) \in \{0,1,...,k\}$; before round 1, all ants are located at the home nest. The value of $\ell(a,r)$ is set by the calls to **search**(), **go**(), or **recruit**() made in round r. Let $A(i,r) = \{a \mid \ell(a,r) = i\}$ denote the set of all ants located at nest n_i at the end of round r and let $c(i,r) = |A(i,r)|$.

In each round, each ant a performs exactly one call to the following functions:

search(): Returns a triple $< i, q(i), c(i,r) >$ where i is chosen uniformly at random from $\{1,\cdots,k\}$. Sets $\ell(a,r) := i$. This function represents ant a searching randomly for a nest; the return value of the function includes the nest index, the nest's quality and the number of ants at the nest.

go(i): Takes input $i \in \{1,\cdots,k\}$ such that there exists a round $r' < r$ in which $\ell(a,r') = i$. Returns $c(i,r)$. Sets $\ell(a,r) := i$. The function represents ant a revisiting a candidate nest n_i; the function returns the number of ants at nest n_i at the end of round r.

recruit(b, i): Takes input $b \in \{0,1\}$ and $i \in \{1,\cdots,k\}$ such that there exists a round $r' < r$ in which $\ell(a,r') = i$. Returns a pair $< j, c(0,r) >$ where $j \in \{1,\cdots,k\}$. Sets $\ell(a,r) := 0$. The return value j is determined as follows. Let R be the set of all ants that call *recruit*$(\cdot,\cdot)$, and let P be a uniform random permutation of all ants in R. Let $S \subseteq R$ be the set of ants that call *recruit*$(1,\cdot)$.

Return value j of **recruit**$(\cdot,\cdot)$ for all ants $a \in R$

M: a set of pairs (a,a') of ants, initially $\emptyset$
for $i = 1$ *to* $|R|$ **do**
  if $a_{P(i)} \in S$ *and* $(\cdot, a_{P(i)}) \notin M$ **then**
    $a' :=$ uniform random ant from R
    if $(a',\cdot) \notin M$ *and* $(\cdot,a') \notin M$ **then**
      $M := M \cup (a_{P(i)}, a')$
for $i = 1$ *to* $|R|$ **do**
  if $(a^*, a_{P(i)}) \in M$ **then**
    return j *to ant* $a_{P(i)}$ *where* j *is input to* *recruit*$(1,j)$ *called by* a^*
  else return j *to ant* $a_{P(i)}$ *where* j *is input to* *recruit*$(\cdot,j)$ *called by* $a_{P(i)}$

In short, all actively recruiting ants in S randomly choose an ant to recruit. P simply serves as tie breaker to avoid conflicts between recruitments. It is important to note that this process is not a distributed algorithm executed by the ants, but just a modeling tool to formalize the idea of ants recruiting other ants randomly without introducing dependency chains between the ordered pairs of recruiting and recruited ants. The algorithm can be thought of as a centralized process run by the environment of the home nest in order to pair ants appropriately. We believe our results also hold under other natural models for randomly pairing ants.

An ant *recruits successfully* if it is the first element of a pair in M. If an ant recruits successfully or is not recruited, **recruit**() just returns the input nest id i. Otherwise, it returns the id of the nest that the ant is recruited to.

We intentionally define **recruit**() to locate ants back to the home nest, where recruitment happens. Additionally, **go(i)** is only applicable to a candidate nest n_i for $i \neq 0$, so calling **recruit**() is the only way to return to the home nest. Since ants are required to call one of the three functions in each round, if an ant does not search (call **search**()) or go to a nest (call **go**()), it is required to stay at the home nest. In this way, all ants located in the home nest participate in recruitment in each round, either actively recruiting ($b = 1$) or waiting to be recruited ($b = 0$).

Recruitment encompasses both the tandem runs and direct transport behavior observed in *Temnothorax* ants. Since direct transport is only about three times faster than tandem walking [22], and since we focus on asymptotic behavior, we do not model this action separately.

Next, we prove a general statement about the probability that a recruiting ant is successful.

LEMMA 2.1. *Let a be any ant that executes recruit$(1,\cdot)$ in some round r, and assume* $c(0,r) \geq 2$. *Then, with probability at least* $1/16$, $(a,\cdot) \in M$.

PROOF. With probability $1/2$ ant a is located in the first half of the random permutation. Conditioning on this, the probability that a is not recruited by some ant with higher precedence in round r is at least: $\left(1 - \frac{1}{c(0,r)}\right)^{c(0,r)/2} \geq 1/2$, where $c(0,r) \geq 2$ is the number of ants at the home nest. Further, with probability $1/2$, ant a chooses to recruit an ant a' located in the second half of the permutation, and with probability $\geq \left(1 - \frac{1}{c(0,r)}\right)^{c(0,r)/2} \geq 1/2$, a' is not recruited by any ant with higher precedence than a. So, in total a recruits successfully with probability at least $1/16$. □

Problem Statement: An algorithm $\mathcal{A}$ solves HOUSE-HUNTING with k nests in $T \in \mathbb{N}$ rounds with probability $1-\delta$, for $0 \leq \delta \leq 1$, if with probability $1-\delta$, taken over all executions of $\mathcal{A}$, there exists a nest $i \in \{1,\cdots,k\}$ with $q(i) = 1$ and $\ell(a,r) = i$ for all ants a and all rounds $r \geq T$.

3. LOWER BOUND

In this section, we present a lower bound on the number of rounds required for an algorithm to solve the house-hunting problem. The key idea is similar to lower bounds on spreading a rumor in a complete graph [17] where neighbors contact each other randomly. Assuming a house-hunting process with a single good nest, its location represents the rumor to be spread among all ants, and communication between random neighbors is analogous to the recruiting process.

Assume that only a single nest n_w has quality 1, and so it is the only option for the ants to relocate to. Additionally, assume that each ant is able to recognize nest n_w once it knows its id. These assumptions only restrict the environment and add to the ants' power, so a lower bound under these assumptions is sufficient. Note that each ant has only two ways of reaching a nest: (1) by searching, or (2) by getting recruited to it. Throughout this section, an ant is considered to be *informed* if it knows the id of the winning nest n_w; otherwise, an ant is considered to be *ignorant*.

LEMMA 3.1. *With probability at least $1/4$ an ant that is ignorant at the beginning of round r remains ignorant at the end of round r.*

PROOF. In round r, ant a may either (1) not participate in recruitment or search (2) participate in recruitment at the home nest or (3) search. In the first case, ant a is guaranteed to remain ignorant. In the second case, ant a calls **recruit**(). Let $X_r \leq c(0,r)$ be the number of informed ants at the beginning of round r that are recruiting at the home nest to the winning nest; these ants are calling **recruit(1, w)**. The probability that ant a is ignorant after round r is at least $\left(1-\frac{1}{c(0,r)}\right)^{c(0,r)} \geq \frac{1}{4}$ when $c(0,r) \geq 2$. If $c(0,r) < 2$, ant a is forced to recruit itself, so it remains ignorant. In the third case, for $k \geq 2$, the probability that ant a remains ignorant after searching is $(k-1)/k \geq 1/2$.

Therefore, the overall probability that an ignorant ant remains ignorant in round r, after either searching or participating in recruitment, is at least 1/4 (since $1/2 > 1/4$). □

Let random variable $\bar{X}_r$ denote the number of ignorant ants at the beginning of round r. In order for the algorithm to solve the house hunting problem, it is necessary that $\bar{X}_r = 0$ for some round r. Otherwise, at least one ant is ignorant.

THEOREM 3.2. *For any constant $c > 0$, and any algorithm $\mathcal{A}$ that solves* HOUSEHUNTING *with $k \geq 2$ nests in T rounds with probability at least $1/n^c$, $T = \Omega(\log n)$.*

PROOF. By Lemma 3.1, with probability at least 1/4 an ant that is ignorant at the beginning of round r remains ignorant at the end of round r. The probability that an ignorant ant remains ignorant for $r = (\log_4 n)/2 - \log_4(12c)$ consecutive rounds is at least $(1/4)^r \geq 12c/\sqrt{n}$. So the expected number of ignorant ants at the beginning of round $r = (\log_4 n)/2 - \log_4(12c)$ is $\mathbb{E}[\bar{X}_r] \geq (12c/\sqrt{n})(n) = 12c\sqrt{n}$.

Note that the random variable $\bar{X}_r$ can be expressed as a sum of indicator random variables $\bar{X}_r^a$, where for each ant a, $\bar{X}_r^a$ is 1 if ant a is ignorant, and 0 if it is informed, at the beginning of round r. These indicator random variables are not independent, so we cannot directly apply a Chernoff bound. We instead show that their sum is bounded by defining random variables that dominate the $\bar{X}_r^a$ variables.

Let Y_r^a be a random variable such that $P[Y_r^a = 1] = (1/4)^r$ for each a and each r. Let Y_r be the sum of these independent random variables for all ants a. Note that $\mathbb{E}[Y_r] = n(1/4)^r$, so for $r = (\log_4 n)/2 - \log_4(12c)$, $\mathbb{E}[Y_r] = 12c\sqrt{n}$. Therefore, by a Chernoff bound $\Pr[Y_r < 6c\sqrt{n}] \leq 1/n^c$.

By Lemma 3.1, the probability that an uninformed ant remains uninformed is at least 1/4, regardless of the other ants' actions in round r. Therefore,

$$\Pr[\bar{X}_r^a = 1 | \text{all } \bar{X}_r^{a'} \text{ for } a' \text{ before } a \text{ in } P] \geq (1/4)^r,$$

where P is the random permutation used to model the recruitment process. So, by the definition of Y_r^a:

$$\Pr[\bar{X}_r^a = 1 | \bar{X}_r^{a'} \text{ for all } a' \text{ before } a \text{ in } P] \geq \frac{1}{4^r} = \Pr[Y_r^a = 1].$$

By Lemma 1.18 in [5][Chapter 1], $\Pr[\bar{X}_r < x] \leq \Pr[Y_r < x]$ for any $x \leq n$. In particular, for $r = (\log_4 n)/2 - \log_4(12c)$, it follows that $\Pr[\bar{X}_r < 6c\sqrt{n}] \leq \Pr[Y_r < 6c\sqrt{n}] \leq \frac{1}{n^c}$.

Therefore, with probability at least $1 - 1/n^c$, at least $6c\sqrt{n}$ ants are ignorant at the end of round $r = (\log_4 n)/2 - \log_4(12c)$. These ants are not informed of the id of the winning nest, and so cannot be located at this nest.

Since algorithm $\mathcal{A}$ solves the HOUSEHUNTING problem with probability at least $1/n^c$ in T rounds, then, with probability at least $1/n^c$, after T rounds, all ants are informed of the winning nest. We showed that with probability at least $1-1/n^c$, at least $6c\sqrt{n}$ ants are ignorant at the end of round $r = (\log_4 n)/2 - \log_4(12c)$. Therefore, $T \geq r = \Omega(\log n)$. □

4. OPTIMAL ALGORITHM

We present an algorithm that solves the HOUSEHUNTING problem and is asymptotically optimal. In the key step of the algorithm, each ant tries to recruit other ants to the nest it found after searching; after each round of recruiting, each ant checks if the number of ants at its nest has increased or decreased. Nests with a non-decreasing population continue competing while nests with a decreasing population drop out. In each round, the population of at least one nest is non-decreasing, so at least one nest remains in the competition. Additionally, other nests drop out at a constant rate, meaning a single winning nest will be identified quickly.

This algorithm relies heavily on the synchrony in the execution and the precise counting of the number of ants in a nest, which makes it sensitive to perturbations of these values, and therefore, not a natural algorithm that resembles ant behavior. However, the algorithm demonstrates that HOUSEHUNTING is solvable in optimal time in our model.

4.1 Algorithm Pseudocode and Description

The pseudocode of the algorithm is presented in Algorithm 1. Each call to the functions from Section 2 (in bold) takes exactly one round. The remaining lines of the algorithm are considered to be local computation and are executed in the same round as the preceding function call.

Each ant is in one of four states: *search*, *active*, *passive*, or *final*, initially *search*. Based on the state of the ant, it executes the corresponding case block from the pseudocode.

The *search* subroutine is executed only once, during the first round, and the *final* subroutine is used by active ants at the end of the execution to recruit all ants to the winning nest. The other two subroutines, *active* and *passive*, represent the actions of active (recruiting) ants, and ants from bad/dropped-out nests, respectively. Each of these subroutines takes exactly four rounds, labeled as R1, R2, R3, or R4 in the pseudocode. The subroutines are carefully scheduled such that these two types of ants do not meet until the end of the competition process when a single winning nest remains; otherwise, the competition between ants from competing nests would be slowed down by ants from dropped-out nests. The *active* and *passive* subroutines are padded with *recruit*$(0,\cdot)$ and *go*(*nest*) calls to achieve such interleaving (lines 12, 17–18, 32–33, 39 are such padding rounds).

Search (lines 6–11): In the first round, each ant searches for a nest. If the nest has quality 0, the ant moves to the *passive* state; otherwise, it moves to the *active* state.

Passive (lines 12–19): An ant is passive if it either found a bad nest or its nest has dropped-out. The ant spends a round at its (non-competing) nest, then it goes home to be recruited. This call to *recruit*(0, *nest*) never coincides with a *recruit*(1, *nest*) of an active ant, so a passive ant can only be recruited by an ant in the *final* state. Once recruited, the passive ant moves to the *final* state.

Final (lines 20–21): An ant in the final state is aware that a single winning nest remains, so it recruits to it in each round. This call to *recruit*(1, *nest*) coincides with the call to *recruit*(0, *nest*) of passive ants, so once a single nest remains, passive ants are recruited to it in every fourth round.

Active (lines 22–42): An active ant tries to recruit to its nest by executing *recruit*(1, *nest*). It then goes to the resulting nest to assess its population. Based on the nest ($nest_t$) and population ($count_t$), we consider three cases:

Algorithm 1: Optimal HOUSEHUNTING Algorithm

```
1  state : {search, active, passive, final}, initially search
2  nest : nest index i ∈ {0, ··· , k}, initially 0
3  count : an integer in {0, ··· , n}, initially 0
4  quality : a boolean in {0, 1}, initially 0
5  case state = search
6  |  < nest, count, quality >:= search()
7  |  if quality = 0 then
8  |  |  state := passive
9  |  else
10 |  |  state := active
11 case state = passive
12 |  go(nest) (R1)
13 |  < nest_t, · >:= recruit(0, nest) (R2)
14 |  if nest_t ≠ nest then
15 |  |  nest := nest_t
16 |  |  state := final
17 |  go(nest) (R3)
18 |  go(nest) (R4)
19 case state = final
20 |  < nest, · >:= recruit(1, nest) (R1, R2, R3, R4)
21 case state = active
22 |  < nest_t, · >:= recruit(1, nest) (R1)
23 |  count_t := go(nest_t) (R2)
24 |  if (nest_t = nest) and (count_t ≥ count) then
25 |  |  count := count_t
26 |  |  go(nest) (R3)
27 |  |  < ·, count_h >:= recruit(0, nest) (R4)
28 |  |  if count_h = count then
29 |  |  |  state := final
30 |  else if (nest_t = nest) and (count_t < count) then
31 |  |  state := passive
32 |  |  recruit(0, nest) (R3)
33 |  |  go(nest) (R4)
34 |  else
35 |  |  nest := nest_t
36 |  |  count_n := go(nest) (R3)
37 |  |  if count_n < count_t then
38 |  |  |  state := passive
39 |  |  go(nest) (R4)
```

Case 1 (lines 25–31): $nest_t = nest$ and the number of ants in *nest* has not decreased, so the nest remains competing. The ant updates the new count and spends an extra round at the nest that has a special purpose with respect to Cases 2 and 3 below. Finally, if the number of ants at the home nest is equal to the number of ants at the competing nest, all ants have been recruited to a single winning nest and the ant switches to the *final* state.

Case 2 (lines 32–36): $nest_t = nest$ but the population has decreased so the nest drops out. The ant becomes passive and spends a round at the home nest, which coincides with the round active ants spend at competing nests in Case 1.

Case 3 (lines 37–42): $nest_t \neq nest$, so the ant got recruited to another nest. Although it already knows the population ($count_t$) of the new nest, the ant updates that value ($count_n$) to determine if this new nest is about to compete or drop out. If $count_t = count_n$, the nest is competing because the active ants in Case 1 are spending the same round at the nest; if $count_t > count_n$, the nest is dropping out because the ants in Case 2 already determined a decrease in population and are spending this round at the home nest.

4.2 Correctness Proof and Time Bound

As written, Algorithm 1 never terminates; after all ants are in the *final* state, they continuously recruit each other. This issue can easily be handled if ants check whether the number of ants at the home nest is the same as the number of ants at the candidate nest. For simplicity we just assume the algorithm terminates once all ants are in the *final* state.

Proof Overview: The proof of correctness and time bound analysis of Algorithm 1 are structured as follows. In Lemma 4.1, we show that a competing nest is equally likely to continue competing and to drop out. Consequently, as we show in Lemma 4.2, each competing nest has a constant probability of dropping out. We put these lemmas together in Theorem 4.3 to show that, with high probability, Algorithm 1 solves the HOUSEHUNTING problem in $\mathcal{O}(\log n)$ rounds: $\mathcal{O}(\log k)$ rounds to converge to a single nest and $\mathcal{O}(\log n)$ rounds until all passive ants are recruited to it.

Let R_1 be the set of round numbers r such that $r \in R_1$ iff $(r-1) \mod 4 = 1$; these rounds, labeled $R1$ in the pseudocode, are exactly the rounds in which only ants from active nests are located at the home nest and recruiting each other. Let $C(i, r)$ for each $r \in R_1$ and each nest n_i denote the set of active ants for which $nest = n_i$. This implies that $|\cup_{i \in [1,k]} C(i, r)| = c(0, r)$ for $r \in R_1$.

Let random variable X_r^a, for each ant a and round $r \in R_1$, take on values in $\{-1, 0, 1\}$. If ant a gets recruited by another ant in round r, then $X_r^a = -1$; if ant a successfully recruits another ant, then $X_r^a = 1$; otherwise, $X_r^a = 0$. Let $\mathbf{o}_r$ be a vector of length $c(0, r)$, where $\mathbf{o}_r(a) = X_r^a$. Let random variable Y_r^i denote the change in the number of ants at nest n_i after round r, where $r \in R_1$. $Y_r^i = \sum_{a \in C(i,r)} X_r^a$.

Informally, the change in population of nest n_i is simply the sum of identically distributed $\{-1, 0, 1\}$ random variables with mean 0 that are non-zero with constant probability. Therefore, the sum of these variables is negative with constant probability. Proving this fact requires a more rigorous argument because the X_r^a variables are not independent.

Recall that, as specified by the recruitment model, Y_r^i is the result of a random recruitment process in which all ants are ordered by a random permutation. Then, in order of the permutation, ants choose uniformly at random other ants at the home nest to recruit. The random variables involved in this process are the random permutation P as well as the set of random choices of ants.

LEMMA 4.1. *Let nest n_i be a competing nest in round $r \in R_1$. Then,* $\Pr[Y_r^i < 0] = \Pr[Y_r^i > 0]$.

PROOF. Random variable Y_r^i is simply the sum of values of $\mathbf{o}_r(a)$ corresponding to ants $a \in C(i, r)$. Since $\mathbf{o}_r$ has exactly the same number of -1s and 1s, it is possible to choose some (non-random) permutation P' that swaps the locations of the -1s and 1s in $\mathbf{o}_r$. Choosing a random permutation P in the recruitment process and then applying the swapping permutation P' negates the value of Y_r^i. Moreover, choosing a uniform random permutation P and then applying this swapping permutation P' still yields a uniform random permutation. So, $-Y_r^i$ is distributed according to the exact same distribution as Y_r^i. Therefore, Y_r^i is symmetric around 0 and $\Pr[Y_r^i < 0] = \Pr[Y_r^i > 0]$. □

LEMMA 4.2. *Let nest n_i be a competing nest in round $r \in R_1$. If $|C(i,r)| < c(0,r)$, then $\Pr[Y_r^i < 0] \geq 1/66$.*

PROOF. Let P_1 be the uniform random permutation in in the recruitment process that determines Y_r^i. Let permutation P_2 swap the position of a fixed ant a^* such that $a^* \notin C(i,r)$ with the position of an ant a chosen uniformly from $C(i,r)$. The existence of such an ant is guaranteed by the assumption that $|C(i,r)| < c(0,r)$.

By Lemma 2.1, $\Pr[X_r^{a^*} = 1] \geq 1/16$. Conditioning on $Y_r^i = 0$, at most $1/2$ the ants $a \in C(i,r)$ have $X_r^a = 1$. Therefore, with probability at least $1/2$, the ant a chosen uniformly at random by permutation P_2 has $X_r^a < 1$. Conditioning on $X_r^{a^*} = 1$ can only increase this probability. So with probability at least $(1/2)(1/16)$, applying the composition of P_1 and P_2 to compute Y_r^i increases its value by at least 1. Since the composition of P_1 and P_2 is also a uniform random permutation, the distribution of Y_r^i remains exactly the same as the case when only P_1 is applied. Therefore,

$$\Pr[Y_r^i = 0] \quad \leq 1 - \tfrac{1}{32}\Pr[Y_r^i = 0] \text{ so } \Pr[Y_r^i = 0] \leq \tfrac{32}{33}.$$

By Lemma 4.1, $\Pr[Y_r^i < 0] = \Pr[Y_r^i > 0]$. Therefore, $\Pr[Y_r^i < 0] \geq 1/66$. □

THEOREM 4.3. *For any constant $c > 0$, with probability at least $1 - 1/n^c$, Algorithm 1 solves the* HOUSEHUNTING *problem in $\mathcal{O}(\log n)$ rounds.*

PROOF. In the first round, all ants search for nests, so the expected number of ants located at each good nest is n/k. Assuming $k \leq n/(12(c+1)\log n) = \mathcal{O}(n/\log n)$, by a Chernoff bound, with probability at least $1 - 1/n^{c+1}$, at least $n/(2k) = \Omega(\log n)$ ants visits each good nest.

Let k_r be a random variable denoting the number of competing nests in round $r \in R_1$. Suppose $k_r > 1$, and so $|C(i,r)| < c(0,r)$. By Lemma 4.2, $\Pr[Y_r^i < 0] \geq 1/66$ for each nest n_i among the k_r competing nests. Therefore, $\mathbb{E}[k_{r+4}] \leq (65/66)k_r$. Also, note that for any round r, $k_r \leq k$. For $r = \log_{66/65} k + (c+1)\log_{66/65} n = \mathcal{O}(\log n)$, it follows that $\mathbb{E}[k_r] = 1/n^{c+1}$. By a Markov bound, $\Pr[k_r \geq 1] \leq 1/n^{c+1}$, so with probability at least $1 - 1/n^{c+1}$, $k_r \leq 1$. It is never possible for all nests to decrease in population, so for each round r, $k_r \geq 1$. So, overall, after $\mathcal{O}(\log n)$ rounds, with probability $1 - 1/n^{c+1}$, there is exactly one competing nest.

Once there is only one competing nest in some round $r \in R_1$, all ants from that nest switch to the *final* state and start recruiting the passive ants every fourth round. The recruited ants transition to the final state, and in at most $\mathcal{O}(\log n)$ rounds all ants are recruited to the winning nest.

Therefore, in total, with probability at least $1 - 1/n^c$, each nest is discovered by at least one ant and all ants are located at a single good nest in $\mathcal{O}(\log n)$ rounds. □

5. SIMPLE ALGORITHM

In this section, we present a simple algorithm that solves the HOUSEHUNTING problem in $\mathcal{O}(k \log n)$ rounds with high probability. The main idea of the algorithm is that all ants initially search for nests and those that find good nests simply continuously recruit to their nests with probability proportional to nest population in each round. Ants in larger nests recruit at higher rates, and eventually their populations swamp the populations of smaller nests. This process is similar to the well-known *Polya's urn* model [2].

Algorithm 2: Simple House-Hunting

```
state : {active, passive}, initially active
< nest, count, quality > := search()
if quality = 0 then
 |  state := passive
case state = active
 |  b := 1 with probability count/n, 0 otherwise
 |  nest := recruit(b, nest)
 |  count := go(nest)
case state = passive
 |  nest_t := recruit(0, nest)
 |  if nest_t ≠ nest then
 |   |  state := active
 |   |  nest := nest_t
 |   |  count := go(nest)
```

5.1 Algorithm Description and Pseudocode

In each round of Algorithm 2, each ant can be in one of two states: *active* or *passve*, initially starting in the *active* state. In the first round of the algorithm, all ants search for nests; the ants that find good nests remain in the *active* state, and the ants that find bad nests switch to the *passive* state. Then, the algorithm proceeds in alternating rounds of recruitment by all ants at the home nest (either active **recruit**$(\mathbf{1},\cdot)$ or passive **recruit**$(\mathbf{0},\cdot)$), and population assessment at candidate nests. In each round of population assessment, each ant chooses to recruit actively in the next round with probability *count*$/n$, where *count* is the assessed population at the candidate nest, and n is the total number of ants. When a passive ant gets recruited to a nest, it becomes active again. When an active ant gets recruited to a different nest, it starts recruiting to that new nest.

5.2 Correctness Proof and Time Bound

For each nest n_i and each round r let random variable $p(i,r) = c(i,r)/n$ denote the proportion of ants at nest n_i in round r. By the pseudocode, ants located at nest n_i in round r will recruit with probability $p(i,r)$ in round $r+1$. Define $\Sigma^2(r) = \sum_{i=1}^{k} p(i,r)^2$, the expected proportion of ants that will recruit in total, in round r. Since $\sum_{i=1}^{k} p(i,r) = 1$, by the ℓ_1 versus ℓ_2 norm bound $\Sigma^2(r) \geq 1/k$.

Proof Overview: The proof of correctness and runtime analysis of the algorithm are structured as follows. In Lemmas 5.1, 5.2, and 5.3, we show some basic bounds on the expected number of ants recruited and the change of the value of $p(i,r)$ for a single nest in each round. Then, in Lemmas 5.5, 5.6, and 5.7, we use a Taylor series expansion of the ratio between the populations of two nests to show that in expectation this ratio increases multiplicatively by $(1 + \Omega(1/k))$ in each round of recruiting, provided that both nests have a $\Omega(1/k)$ fraction of the total population. On the other hand, if a nest has less than a $\Omega(1/k)$ fraction of the total population, in Lemmas 5.8 and 5.9, we show that the ants in such a nest recruit so slowly that the nest completely drops out within $\mathcal{O}(k \log n)$ rounds with high probability. Finally, in Theorem 5.11, we consider all $\binom{k}{2}$ pairs of nests to show that the widening population gaps lead to only a single nest remaining in each pair within $\mathcal{O}(k \log n)$ rounds, ensuring, by a union bound, that a single nest remains overall.

Throughout this section, let $c > 0$ be an arbitrary constant and let d be an arbitrary constant such that $d \geq 64$. In the analysis, we assume that $k \leq \sqrt{n/(8d^2(c+6)\log n)} =$

$\mathcal{O}(\sqrt{n/\log n})$. While we feel that this assumption is reasonable, we are also hopeful that it is not necessary.

Let R_1 be the set of all odd rounds, excluding round 1; by the pseudocode, in these rounds, ants are located at the candidate nests. So, for each $r \in R_1$ and each ant a, $\ell(a,r) = i \neq 0$; for each round $r' \notin R_1$ and for each ant a, $\ell(a,r') = 0$.

5.2.1 *Change in Population of a Nest in One Round*

We first study how the population of a single nest changes in a round. Intuitively, we expect a $p(i,r)$ proportion of the ants in n_i to recruit, and a $\Sigma^2(r)$ proportion to be recruited. So we expect a total change of $p(i,r)(p(i,r)-\Sigma^2(r))$. Qualitatively, we show this in Lemma 5.3, up to constant factors; the main difficulty is handling dependencies in the recruiting process. Before proving Lemma 5.3, we give two lemmas that state the expected outcome of a single ant recruiting.

As before, define random variable X_r^a to take on value -1 if ant a is recruited away from its current nest in round r, 1 if it successfully recruits another ant, and 0 otherwise.

The following lemma applies to an ant a recruiting with any probability p in a given round r. It is clear that whenever an ant recruits, it is always with probability $p(i,r)$, so the majority of the time we will apply the lemma for $p = p(i,r)$; however, the general statement of the lemma helps reason about the expected value of X_r^a for ants from different nests in Lemma 5.2.

LEMMA 5.1. *Let n_i be any nest and let ant a be located in nest n_i in some round $r \in R_1$. Also, suppose ant a recruits with probability p in round r. Then, there exist functions ξ_1 and ξ_2 such that $\mathbb{E}[X_r^a] = p\xi_1(i,r) - \xi_2(i,r)$ and $\xi_1(i,r) \geq \xi$ for a fixed constant $\xi > 0$.*

PROOF. Let A_r^a be a random variable indicating whether some ant a chooses to recruit (executes **recruit(1,·)**) in round $r+1$. By assumption, $\Pr[A_r^a = 1] = p$. Whether ant a is actually successful in recruiting another ant depends on: (1) the order of the random recruiting permutation P, (2) the choices of other ants to recruit or not, and (3) the choices by recruiting ants of whom to recruit. Let B be a random variable encompassing all these random variables that affect X_r^a, excluding A_r^a. Therefore, B is a triple $(P, \{A_r^{a'} | a' \neq a\}, \{1, \cdots, n\}^n)$ and it takes on values from the set $\mathcal{B}$ of all such triples. The expected value of X_r^a is:

$$\mathbb{E}[X_r^a] = \sum_{b\in\mathcal{B}} \Pr[B=b]\, p\mathbb{E}[X_r^a | B=b, A_r^a = 1] + \sum_{b\in\mathcal{B}} \Pr[B=b]\,(1-p)\mathbb{E}[X_r^a | B=b, A_r^a=0].$$

Fix some value $B = b$. We consider several cases based on all the possible ways the value of A_r^a can affect X_r^a. We can immediately eliminate some of these cases. If $A_r^a = 0$ (the ant chooses not to recruit), it is not possible that $X_r^a = 1$ (the ant succeeds in recruiting). Also, since $B = b$ is already fixed, ant a is either chosen by another ant or not, regardless of the value of A_r^a. This fact rules out two more cases: (1) the case where $X_r^a = 0$ if $A_r^a = 0$, and $X_r^a = -1$ if $A_r^a = 1$, and (2) the case where $X_r^a = -1$ if $A_r^a = 0$, and $X_r^a = 0$ if $A_r^a = 1$. In (1), since the choices of the other ants are already fixed and included in $B = b$, it is not possible that ant a gets recruited if it chooses to recruit but it does not get recruited otherwise. Similarly, in (2), it is not possible that ant a gets recruited when it chooses not to recruit but does not get recruited when it fails to recruit. All remaining cases are listed below:

Case 1: $X_r^a = -1$ for both $A_r^a = 0$ and $A_r^a = 1$. That is, the ant is recruited by another ant no matter its decision.

Case 2: $X_r^a = -1$ if $A_r^a = 0$, and $X_r^a = 1$ if $A_r^a = 1$. That is, if the ant chooses to recruit it succeeds, and if not, it is recruited by another ant.

Case 3: $X_r^a = 0$ for both $A_r^a = 0$ and $A_r^a = 1$. That is, whether the ant chooses to recruit or not, it will not be part of a successful recruitment.

Case 4: $X_r^a = 0$ if $A_r^a = 0$, and $X_r^a = 1$ if $A_r^a = 1$. That is, if the ant chooses to recruit it succeeds, but if not, it is not recruited by another ant.

Let p_x^b be the probability of case x occurring given $B = b$. The expected value of X_r^a is:

$$\sum_{b\in\mathcal{B}} \Pr[B=b]\cdot\left(p\left(p_2^b + p_4^b - p_1^b\right) + (1-p)\left(-p_1^b - p_2^b\right)\right)$$
$$= \sum_{b\in\mathcal{B}} \Pr[B=b]\left(p\left(2p_2^b + p_4^b\right) - \left(p_1^b + p_2^b\right)\right)$$
$$= p\mathbb{E}_B\left[2p_2^b + p_4^b\right] - \mathbb{E}_B\left[p_1^b + p_3^b\right].$$

Now, we need to show that $\mathbb{E}_B[2p_2^b + p_4^b] \geq \xi$ for some fixed constant $\xi > 0$. By Lemma 2.1, each recruiting ant succeeds with constant probability. A recruiting ant only succeeds in cases 2 and 4 so we have $\mathbb{E}_B[p_2^b + p_4^b] \geq \xi$ for some constant $\xi > 0$. Therefore, $\mathbb{E}_B[2p_2^b + p_4^b] \geq \mathbb{E}_B[p_2^b + p_4^b] \geq \xi$.

Overall, $\mathbb{E}[X_r^a] = p\xi_1(i,r) - \xi_2(i,r)$, for constants $\xi_1(i,r) = \mathbb{E}_B[2p_2^b + p_4^b] \geq \xi > 0$ and $\xi_2(i,r) = \mathbb{E}_B[p_1^b + p_2^b]$. □

Note that the values of $\xi_1(i,r)$ and $\xi_2(i,r)$ are slightly different for different nests. For example, the different probabilities corresponding to the cases in Lemma 5.1 vary based on the population of a given nest in a given round and the populations of the remaining nests in that round. In our full version [14], we prove a bound on the $\xi_1(i,r)$ and $\xi_2(i,r)$ values of two different nests that will be useful in later proofs.

LEMMA 5.2. *Let n_i and n_j be two nests with $p(i,r) \leq p(j,r)$ in some round $r \in R_1$. Then, $\xi_1(i,r)\cdot p(i,r) - \xi_2(i,r) \leq \xi_1(j,r)\cdot p(i,r) - \xi_2(j,r)$.*

It is simple to use Lemma 5.1 to calculate the expected change in $p(i,r)$. The calculation is given in [14].

LEMMA 5.3. *For each nest n_i and each round $r \in R_1$, $\mathbb{E}[p(i,r+2)] = p(i,r)\cdot[1 + \xi_1(i,r)\cdot p(i,r) - \xi_2(i,r)]$.*

Lemma 5.3 shows that the population change of a nest depends *quadratically* on $p(i,r)$ so larger nests will 'swamp' smaller nests, causing their populations to drop to 0.

5.2.2 *Relative Changes in the Populations of Two Nests in One Round*

We first define a measure of the population gap between two nests.

DEFINITION 1. *For any nests n_i and n_j, let $n_H(i,j,r) \in \{i,j\}$ be the id of the nest with the higher population in round r. Let $n_L(i,j,r)$ be the nest with the lower population. Define:*

$$\epsilon(i,j,r) = \frac{p(n_H(i,j,r),r)}{p(n_L(i,j,r),r))} - 1.$$

$\epsilon(i,j,r)$ is the relative population gap between the larger and smaller of nests n_i and n_j in round r. In [14] we show:

LEMMA 5.4. *For any two nests n_i and n_j, $\mathbb{E}[\epsilon(i,j,1)] \geq 1/(3(n-1))$.*

Since $\epsilon(i,j,r)$ is a ratio of two populations, it is not immediately clear how to compute its expected change between rounds. However, using a Taylor series expansion we bound this ratio by a linear function, and use Lemma 5.3 to compute its expected change. We first show how to use the Taylor series expansion in our setting. In [14] we compute:

LEMMA 5.5. *For positive numbers x_0, x_1, y_0, and y_1 let $\Delta x = x_1 - x_0$, $\Delta y = y_1 - y_0$, and $\Delta\left(\frac{x}{y}\right) = \frac{x_1}{y_1} - \frac{x_0}{y_0}$. Then:*

$$\Delta\left(\frac{x}{y}\right) = \left[\frac{\Delta x}{y_0} - \frac{x_0 \Delta y}{y_0^2}\right] \cdot \sum_{i=0}^{\infty} \left(\frac{-\Delta y}{y_0}\right)^i$$

For simplicity of notation, write $p_H = p(n_H(i,j,r),r)$, $p_L = p(n_L(i,j,r),r)$. Also, $\Delta p_H = p(n_H(i,j,r),r+2) - p(n_H(i,j,r),r)$, $\Delta p_L = p(n_L(i,j,r),r+2) - p(n_L(i,j,r),r)$ and $\Delta\left(\frac{p_H}{p_L}\right) = \frac{p(n_H(i,j,r),r+2)}{p(n_L(i,j,r),r+2)} - \frac{p(n_H(i,j,r),r)}{p(n_L(i,j,r),r)}$. We can now apply Lemma 5.5 to show:

LEMMA 5.6. *Let n_i and n_j be two nests with $\Delta p_L < p_L$ in some round $r \in R_1$. Then, $\Delta\left(\frac{p_H}{p_L}\right) \geq \frac{1}{2}\left(\frac{\Delta p_H}{p_L} - \frac{p_H \Delta p_L}{p_L^2}\right)$.*

PROOF. Note that we are not considering expectations for now, just the actual values. Applying Lemma 5.5, we can write $\Delta\left(\frac{p_H}{p_L}\right)$ in terms of Δp_H and Δp_L. We have:

$$\Delta\left(\frac{p_H}{p_L}\right) = \left(\frac{\Delta p_H}{p_L} - \frac{p_H \Delta p_L}{p_L^2}\right) \sum_{i=0}^{\infty} \left(-\frac{\Delta p_L}{p_L}\right)^i.$$

The value $\frac{\Delta p_L}{p_L}$ is strictly less than 1 by the assumption that $\Delta p_L < p_L$, so the infinite sum above converges to $\frac{1}{1+\Delta p_L/p_L} \geq 1/2$. □

We now use $\Delta(p_H/p_L)$ to calculate the expected change in $\epsilon(i,j,r)$ for two nests after one recruitment round.

LEMMA 5.7. *Let n_i and n_j be two nests with $\Delta p_L < p_L$, $p(i,r) \geq 1/(dk)$ and $p(j,r) \geq 1/(dk)$ for some round $r \in R_1$. Then, $\mathbb{E}\left[\epsilon(i,j,r+2)\right] \geq (1+\xi/(2dk))\,\mathbb{E}\left[\epsilon(i,j,r)\right]$ for fixed constant $\xi > 0$.*

PROOF. First we show that:

$$\epsilon(i,j,r+2) \geq \frac{p(n_H(i,j,r),r+2)}{p(n_L(i,j,r),r+2)} - 1.$$

This is because, if the larger of the two nests in round r remains larger in round $r+2$, then $n_H(i,j,r) = n_H(i,j,r+2)$ and $n_L(i,j,r) = n_L(i,j,r+2)$, so, by the definition of ϵ, $\epsilon(i,j,r+2) = \frac{p(n_H(i,j,r),r+2)}{p(n_L(i,j,r),r+2)} - 1$. Alternatively, if the two nests flip positions, then $\frac{p(n_H(i,j,r),r+2)}{p(n_L(i,j,r),r+2)} - 1$ must be smaller than $\epsilon(i,j,r+2)$ since it contains the population of the larger nest in the denominator. Fixing $p(i,r)$ and $p(j,r)$, we have:

$$\mathbb{E}[\epsilon(i,j,r+2)] \geq \mathbb{E}\left[\frac{p(n_H(i,j,r),r+2)}{p(n_L(i,j,r),r+2)} - 1\right]$$
$$= \epsilon(i,j,r) + \mathbb{E}\left[\frac{p(n_H(i,j,r),r+2)}{p(n_L(i,j,r),r+2)} - \frac{p(n_H(i,j,r),r)}{p(n_L(i,j,r),r)}\right]$$

So we have reduced our question of how we expect the *absolute difference* between the nests to change to the question of how we expect the population ratio to change. By Lemma 5.6, it follows that:

$$\mathbb{E}[\epsilon(i,j,r+2)] \geq \epsilon(i,j,r) + \frac{1}{2}\left(\frac{p_L\mathbb{E}[\Delta p_H] - p_H\mathbb{E}[\Delta p_L]}{p_L^2}\right).$$

By Lemma 5.3 we have:

$$\begin{aligned} p_L\mathbb{E}[\Delta p_H] - p_H\mathbb{E}[\Delta p_L] &= p_L p_H^2 \xi_1(n_H,r) - p_L p_H \xi_2(n_H,r) \\ &\quad - p_H p_L^2 \xi_1(n_L,r) + p_L p_H \xi_2(n_L,r) \\ &\geq \xi p_L p_H (p_H - p_L), \end{aligned}$$

where the inequality follows from the guarantee of Lemma 5.2 that $p_L\xi_1(n_L,r) - \xi_2(n_L,r) \leq p_L\xi_1(n_H,r) - \xi_2(n_H,r)$. Noting that $\epsilon(i,j,r) = \frac{p_H - p_L}{p_L}$ we have:

$$\begin{aligned} \mathbb{E}[\epsilon(i,j,r+2)] &\geq \epsilon(i,j,r) + \frac{\xi p_L p_H (p_H - p_L)}{2p_L^2} \\ &\geq \epsilon(i,j,r)\left(1 + \frac{\xi p_H}{2}\right) \geq \epsilon(i,j,r)\left(1 + \frac{\xi}{2dk}\right). \quad \square \end{aligned}$$

5.2.3 Changes in Populations of Multiple Nests over O(k log n) Rounds

We now show that once the population of a nest is very small, it will quickly drop to zero. We first give a lemma, proven in [14], that once the population of a nest drops below a certain threshold, ants will recruit at a slow enough rate that the population will remain small for a number of rounds. We then show that over these rounds, the population will in fact drop to 0 with high probability.

LEMMA 5.8. *Let n_i be any nest with $p(i,r) \leq 1/(dk)$ in some round $r \in R_1$. Then, with probability at least $1 - 1/n^{c+4}$, $p(i,r') \leq 1/(dk)$ for all rounds $r' \in [r, r + 64(c+4)k\log n)]$.*

LEMMA 5.9. *Let n_i be a nest with $p(i,r) \leq 1/(dk)$ in some round $r \in R_1$. Then, with probability at least $1 - 1/n^{c+3}$, $c(i,r') = 0$ for $r' = 64(c+4)k\log n$.*

PROOF. We calculate the expected change in the number of ants in nest n_i by first calculating $\mathbb{E}[X_r^a]$ for some ant a in nest n_i and some round $r \in R_1$ such that $p(i,r) \leq 1/(dk)$.

Suppose ant a does not recruit. Let random variable $Y_r^{a'}$ have value 1 if ant a' successfully recruits ant a, and value 0 otherwise. By Lemma 2.1, it follows that $\mathbb{E}[Y_r^{a'}] \geq p(i',r)/(16n)$ where $i' = \ell(a',r)$. Therefore:

$$\begin{aligned} \mathbb{E}\left[\sum_{a' \neq a} Y_r^{a'}\right] &= \sum_{a' \neq a} \mathbb{E}[Y_r^{a'}] \geq \frac{1}{16n}\sum_{j=1}^{k} \sum_{\substack{a' \neq a \\ a' \in A(j,r)}} p(j,r) \\ &\geq \frac{1}{16n}\left(\sum_{j=1}^{k} \sum_{a' \in A(j,r)} p(j,r)\right) - \frac{1}{dk} \\ &\geq \frac{1}{16n}\left(\sum_{j=1}^{k} np(j,r)^2\right) - \frac{1}{dk} \geq \frac{\Sigma^2(r)}{16} - \frac{1}{dk}. \end{aligned}$$

Therefore, the expected value of X_r^a is:

$$\mathbb{E}[X_r^a] \leq \frac{1}{dk} - \left(1 - \frac{1}{dk}\right) \mathbb{E}\left[\sum_{a' \notin A(j,r)} Y_r^{a'}\right]$$
$$= \frac{1}{dk} - \left(1 - \frac{1}{dk}\right)\left(\frac{\Sigma^2(r)}{16} - \frac{1}{dk}\right) \leq -\frac{1}{64k},$$

where the bound follows from the assumption $d \geq 64$. So $\mathbb{E}[p(i, r+2)] = p(i,r)(1 + \mathbb{E}[X_r^a]) \leq p(i,r)\,(1 - 1/64k)$.

By Lemma 5.8, $p(i, r') \leq 1/(dk)$ for all $r' \in [r, r + 64(c+4)k \log n]$. Therefore, for $r' = 64(c+4)k\log n$, it is true that $\mathbb{E}[p(i,r')] \leq 1/n^{c+3}$ and, by a Markov bound, nest n_i has at least one ant with probability at most $1/n^{c+3}$. Therefore, with probability at least $1 - 1/n^{c+3}$, $c(i, r') = 0$. □

Next, for any pair of nests, both with population proportions $\geq 1/(dk)$, we can use Lemma 5.7 to argue that the populations of these nests diverge quickly. As soon as a nest drops below the $1/(dk)$ threshold we can use Lemma 5.9 to show that it will not be the winning nest.

LEMMA 5.10. *Let n_i and n_j be two nests with $q(i) = q(j) = 1$ and $\xi > 0$ be a fixed constant. For $r' = (6d/\xi + 64(c+6))k \log n$, with probability at least $1 - 1/n^{c+2}$, at least one of the following is true: $c(i, r') = 0$ or $c(j, r') = 0$.*

PROOF. Note that if at any point a nest has no ants in it, it remains having no ants thereafter. We consider two possible cases based on how many ants are in each nest in each round $r \in [1, 6dk \log n/\xi)]$:

Case 1: In some round $r \in [1, 6dk \log n/\xi)]$ either n_i of n_j has fewer than $n/(dk)$ ants. Then, by Lemma 5.9, with probability at least $1 - 1/n^{c+3}$, this nest has no ants after $64(c+4)k \log n$ rounds.

Case 2: In every round $r \in [1, 6dk \log n/\xi)]$ both n_i and n_j have at least $n/(dk)$ ants. We will show that, with probability at least $1 - 1/n^{c+3}$ this case does not happen. First, we show that $\Delta p_L < p_L$ in all rounds with high probability, so that we can apply Lemma 5.7. Since both nests have at least $n/(dk)$ ants, $p_L \geq 1/(dk)$, so the expected number of ants recruiting for that nest is at least $n/(d^2k^2) = \Omega(\log n)$, by our assumption $k \leq \sqrt{n/(8d^2(c+6)\log n)} = \mathcal{O}(\sqrt{n/\log n})$. By a Chernoff bound, with probability at least $1 - 1/n^{c+3}$, the number of recruiting ants is at most $2n/(d^2k^2)$. With probability at least $1 - 1/n^{c+3}$, not all ants from the nest with lower population recruit so $\Delta p_L < p_L$. By Lemma 5.7,

$$\mathbb{E}[\epsilon(i,j,6dk\log n/\xi)] \geq [1 + \xi/(2dk)]^{6dk \log n/\xi}\, \mathbb{E}[\epsilon(i,j,1)]$$
$$\geq n^3 \cdot \mathbb{E}[\epsilon(i,j,1)].$$

By Lemma 5.4, $\mathbb{E}[\epsilon(i,j,1)] \geq 1/(3(n-1))$. So, we have $\mathbb{E}[\epsilon(i,j,6dk\log n/\xi)] \geq n$. However, this is a contradiction to the fact that $\epsilon(i,j,6dk\log n/\xi) \leq n-1$, by definition, and consequently $\mathbb{E}[\epsilon(i,j,6dk\log n/\xi)] \leq n-1$.

Each case holds with probability at least $1 - 1/n^{c+3}$, so union bounding them, we get that, with probability at least $1 - 1/n^{c+2}$, either $c(i,r') = 0$ or $c(j,r') = 0$. □

THEOREM 5.11. *With probability at least $1 - 1/n^c$, Algorithm 2 solves* HOUSEHUNTING *in $\mathcal{O}(k \log n)$ rounds.*

PROOF. By our bound on k ($k \leq \sqrt{n/(8d^2(c+6)\log n)} = \mathcal{O}(\sqrt{n/\log n})$), with probability at least $1 - 1/n^{c+1}$, in the first round of the algorithm (a round of searching), at least some ant will arrive at a nest with quality 1. So, with high probability, since only ants at nests with quality 1 recruit, there is always at least one ant recruiting to a good nest.

By Lemma 5.10, with probability at least $1 - 1/n^{c+2}$, for each pair of nests n_i and n_j, at least one nest contains no ants by the end of $\mathcal{O}(k \log n)$ rounds. Union bounding over all, at most $\binom{k}{2} < k^2 < n$ (by the bound on k), pairs of good nests, we conclude that, with probability at least $1 - 1/n^{c+1}$, after $\mathcal{O}(k\log n)$ rounds, each pair contains at least one nest with no ants. This can only be true if all nests have no ants (not possible) or if all ants are located at one good nest.

Union bounding over the initial search phase and subsequent competition between nests, with probability at least $1 - 1/n^c$, HOUSEHUNTING is solved in $\mathcal{O}(k \log n)$ rounds. □

6. DISCUSSION AND FUTURE WORK

Extensions to the Model: For the analysis, we make many simplifying assumptions about the house-hunting process. We are confident that some of these assumptions can be weakened. Possible changes include assuming only approximate knowledge of n, allowing arbitrary values of k, and allowing non-binary nest qualities along with some measure of performance based on the chosen nest quality. Distinguishing between direct transport and tandem runs may also be interesting, paired with more fine-grained runtime analysis.

Additionally, real ants can only assess nest quality and population approximately. For example, they may estimate nest area by random walking inside the nest and counting how often they cross their own path [21]. They seem to estimate nest population by tracking encounter rates with other ants, with more encounters indicating higher population [15, 22]. Adding noisy measurements to our model and designing algorithms that handle this noise would be very interesting. It may even be possible to explicitly model low level behavior and implement modular algorithms for nest assessment, population measurement, recruitment, and search that give various runtime and error guarantees.

Extensions to the Algorithms: We believe that Algorithm 2 may be a good starting point for work on more realistic house-hunting models. Below we discuss some possible extensions to the algorithm. Some seem to simply require a more sophisticated analysis, while others require trade-offs in the algorithm's running time and its level of simplicity.

Improved running time: The $\mathcal{O}(k \log n)$ runtime of Algorithm 2 is required because, on average each nest initially contains n/k ants, so ants only recruit with probability $1/k$. $\mathcal{O}(k)$ time is required to amplify population gaps by a constant factor. Ideally, ants would all recruit with a probability lower bounded by a constant, but still linearly dependent on the nest populations, allowing convergence in $\mathcal{O}(\log n)$ rounds. If ants keep track of the round number, they can map this to an estimate $\tilde{k}(r)$ of how many competing nests remain, allowing them to recruit at rate $\mathcal{O}(c(i,r)/n \cdot \tilde{k}(r))$. We believe that such a strategy should yield a relatively natural algorithm converging in $\mathcal{O}(\text{polylog}\, n)$ rounds.

Non-binary nest qualities: Assuming a real-valued nest quality in the range $(0,1)$ affects Algorithm 2 because ants no longer have the notion of a good nest. However, it should be possible to incorporate nest quality into the recruitment probability in order to make the algorithm converge to a high-quality nest, without significantly affecting runtime.

Approximate counting, nest assessment, and knowledge of n: The analysis of Algorithm 2 does not require each ant to recruit with a specific probability, but just that the total number of ants recruiting to a nest is proportional to its population. So, it should be resilient to noisy quality and population measurements. If ants have unbiased estimators of these values, we believe the algorithm should remain correct, with some runtime dependence on estimator variance.

Fault tolerance: Similarly, Algorithm 2 should be fault tolerant. A small number of ants suffering from crash-faults or even malicious faults, should not affect the overall populations of recruiting ants and the algorithm's performance.

Asynchrony: Finally, Algorithm 2 currently works in synchronous rounds and relies on this assumption to get the correct number of ants at a given nest. However, we believe that, as long as the distribution of ants in candidate nests over time stays close to the distribution in the synchronous model, Algorithm 2 can be extended to work in a partially-synchronous model, potentially at some runtime cost.

7. REFERENCES

[1] Karl Johan Aström and Richard M Murray. *Feedback systems: an introduction for scientists and engineers.* Princeton University Press, 2010.

[2] Fan Chung, Shirin Handjani, and Doug Jungreis. Generalizations of Polya's urn problem. *Annals of Combinatorics*, 7(2):141–153, 2003.

[3] Alejandro Cornejo, Anna Dornhaus, Nancy Lynch, and Radhika Nagpal. Task allocation in ant colonies. In *Distributed Computing*, pages 46–60. Springer, 2014.

[4] Adam L Cronin. Synergy between pheromone trails and quorum thresholds underlies consensus decisions in the ant myrmecina nipponica. *Behavioral Ecology and Sociobiology*, 67(10):1643–1651, 2013.

[5] Benjamin Doerr and Anne Auger. *Theory of Randomized Search Heuristics.* World Scientific, 2011.

[6] A Dornhaus and NR Franks. Colony size affects collective decision-making in the ant temnothorax albipennis. *Insectes sociaux*, 53(4):420–427, 2006.

[7] Yuval Emek, Tobias Langner, Jara Uitto, and Roger Wattenhofer. Solving the ANTS problem with asynchronous finite state machines. In *Proceedings of the 41st International Colloquium on Automata, Languages, and Programming*, 2014.

[8] Ofer Feinerman, Bernhard Haeupler, and Amos Korman. Breathe before speaking: efficient information dissemination despite noisy, limited and anonymous communication. In *Proceedings of the ACM Symposium on Principles of Distributed Computing*, pages 114–123, 2014.

[9] Ofer Feinerman and Amos Korman. Memory lower bounds for randomized collaborative search and implications for biology. In *Distributed Computing*, pages 61–75. Springer, 2012.

[10] Ofer Feinerman and Amos Korman. Theoretical distributed computing meets biology: A review. In *Distributed Computing and Internet Technology*, pages 1–18. Springer, 2013.

[11] Ofer Feinerman, Amos Korman, Zvi Lotker, and Jean-Sébastien Sereni. Collaborative search on the plane without communication. In *Proceedings of the ACM Symposium on Principles of Distributed Computing*, 2012.

[12] Michael Fischer, Nancy Lynch, and Michael Paterson. Impossibility of distributed consensus with one faulty process. *Journal of the ACM*, 32(2):374–382, 1985.

[13] Nigel R. Franks, Anna Dornhaus, Charlotte S. Best, and Elizabeth L. Jones. Decision making by small and large house-hunting ant colonies: one size fits all. *Animal Behaviour*, 72(3):611–616, 2006.

[14] Mohsen Ghaffari, Cameron Musco, Tsvetomira Radeva, and Nancy Lynch. Distributed house-hunting in ant colonies. *Preprint. arXiv:1505.03799*, 2015.

[15] Deborah M Gordon. *Ant encounters: interaction networks and colony behavior.* Princeton University Press, 2010.

[16] Christiane Healey and Stephen Pratt. The effect of prior experience on nest site evaluation by the ant Temnothorax curvispinosus. *Animal Behaviour*, 76(3):893–899, 2008.

[17] Richard Karp, Christian Schindelhauer, Scott Shenker, and Berthold Vocking. Randomized rumor spreading. In *Proceedings of the 41st Annual Symposium on Foundations of Computer Science*, 2000.

[18] Leslie Lamport. The part-time parliament. *ACM Transactions on Computer Systems*, 1998.

[19] Christoph Lenzen, Nancy Lynch, Calvin Newport, and Tsvetomira Radeva. Trade-offs between selection complexity and performance when searching the plane without communication. In *Proceedings of the ACM Symposium on Principles of Distributed Computing*, 2014.

[20] E Mallon, S Pratt, and N Franks. Individual and collective decision-making during nest site selection by the ant Leptothorax albipennis. *Behavioral Ecology and Sociobiology*, 50(4):352–359, 2001.

[21] Eamonn B Mallon and Nigel R Franks. Ants estimate area using Buffon's needle. *Proceedings of the Royal Society of London. Series B: Biological Sciences*, 267(1445):765–770, 2000.

[22] S.C. Pratt. Nest site choice in social insects. In Michael D. Breed and Janice Moore, editors, *Encyclopedia of Animal Behavior*, pages 534–540. Academic Press, Oxford, 2010.

[23] S.C. Pratt, Eamonn B Mallon, David J Sumpter, and Nigel R Franks. Quorum sensing, recruitment, and collective decision-making during colony emigration by the ant Leptothorax albipennis. *Behavioral Ecology and Sociobiology*, 52(2):117–127, 2002.

[24] Stephen C Pratt. Quorum sensing by encounter rates in the ant Temnothorax albipennis. *Behavioral Ecology*, 16(2):488–496, 2005.

[25] Stephen C Pratt and David JT Sumpter. A tunable algorithm for collective decision-making. *Proceedings of the National Academy of Sciences*, 103(43):15906–15910, 2006.

[26] Takao Sasaki and Stephen C Pratt. Emergence of group rationality from irrational individuals. *Behavioral Ecology*, 22(2):276–281, 2011.

[27] Takao Sasaki and Stephen C Pratt. Ants learn to rely on more informative attributes during decision-making. *Biology letters*, 9(6), 2013.

Brief Announcement: On the Feasibility of Leader Election and Shape Formation with Self-Organizing Programmable Matter*

Zahra Derakhshandeh†
Arizona State University, USA
zderakhs@asu.edu

Robert Gmyr‡
University of Paderborn, Germany
gmyr@mail.upb.de

Thim Strothmann‡
University of Paderborn, Germany
thim@mail.upb.de

Rida Bazzi
Arizona State University, USA
bazzi@asu.edu

Andréa W. Richa†
Arizona State University, USA
aricha@asu.edu

Christian Scheideler‡
University of Paderborn, Germany
scheideler@.upb.de

ABSTRACT

Imagine that we had a piece of matter that can change its physical properties like shape, density, conductivity, or color in a programmable fashion based on either user input or autonomous sensing. This is the vision behind what is commonly known as *programmable matter*. Many proposals have already been made for realizing programmable matter, ranging from DNA tiles, shape-changing molecules, and cells created via synthetic biology to reconfigurable modular robotics. We are particularly interested in programmable matter consisting of simple elements called *particles* that can compute, bond, and move, and the feasibility of solving fundamental problems relevant for programmable matter with these particles. As a model for that programmable matter, we will use a general form of the amoebot model first proposed in SPAA 2014, and as examples of fundamental problems we will focus on leader election and shape formation. For shape formation, we investigate the line formation problem, i.e. we are searching for a local-control protocol so that for any connected structure of particles, the particles will eventually form a line.

Prior results on leader election imply that in the general amoebot model there are instances in which leader election cannot be solved by local-control protocols. Additionally, we can show that if there is a local-control protocol that solves the line formation problem, then there is also a protocol that solves the leader election problem, which implies that in the general amoebot model also the line formation problem cannot be solved by a local-control protocol.

We also consider a geometric variant of the amoebot model by restricting the particle structures to form a connected subset on a triangular grid. For these structures we can show that there are local-control protocols for the leader election problem and the line formation problem. The protocols can also be adapted to other regular geometric structures demonstrating that it is advisable to restrict particle structures to such structures.

*A full paper presenting the results outlined in this brief announcement will appear at the 21st International Conference on DNA Computing and Molecular Programming (DNA21).

†This work was supported in part by the NSF under Awards CCF-1353089 and CCF-1422603.

‡Supported in part by DFG grant SCHE 1592/3-1

Permission to make digital or hard copies of part or all of this work for personal or classroom use is granted without fee provided that copies are not made or distributed for profit or commercial advantage, and that copies bear this notice and the full citation on the first page. Copyrights for third-party components of this work must be honored. For all other uses, contact the owner/author(s). Copyright is held by the author/owner(s).

PODC'15, July 21–23, 2015, Donostia-San Sebastián, Spain.

Copyright © 2015 ACM 978-1-4503-3617-8 /15/07.

http://dx.doi.org/10.1145/2767386.2767451.

Categories and Subject Descriptors

C.2.4 [**Computer-Communication Networks**]: Distributed Systems; F.2.0 [**Analysis of Algorithms and Problem Complexity**]: General

1. INTRODUCTION

There have been many conceptions of programmable matter, and thus many avenues of research using that name, each pursuing solutions for specific application scenarios with their own, special capabilities and constraints. However, most of the research in this area has been done by scientists from the natural sciences and the robotics area and not so much from theoretical computer science, so not much is known yet about which assumptions or primitives allow the development of distributed algorithms that can solve relevant problems for programmable matter in a self-organizing way. Notable exceptions are DNA tile assembly and population protocols. However, most of these approaches are passive in one or more aspects or require powerful entities while we are interested in studying the feasibility of solving problems with simple entities that can not just compute but also control their movements. For that we use a general form of the amoebot model first proposed in [2].

1.1 The general amoebot model

In the general amoebot model, programmable matter consists of a set of simple uniform computational units called particles that can move and bond to other particles and use these bonds to exchange information. The particles have very limited memory, act asynchronously, and they achieve locomotion by expanding and contracting, which resembles the behavior of amoeba.

As a base for our amoebot model, we assume that we have a set of particles that aim at maintaining a connected structure at all times. This is needed to prevent the particles from drifting apart in an uncontrolled manner like in fluids and because in our case particles communicate only via bonds. The shape and positions of the bonds of the particles mandate that they can only assume discrete positions in the particle structure. This justifies the use of a possibly infinite, undirected graph $G = (V, E)$, where V represents all possible positions of a particle (relative to the other particles in their structure) and E equals all possible transitions between positions.

Each particle occupies either a single node or a pair of adjacent nodes in G, and every node can be occupied by at most one particle. Two particles occupying adjacent nodes are *connected*, and we refer to such particles as *neighbors*. Particles are *anonymous* but the bonds of each particle have unique labels, which implies that a particle can uniquely identify each of its outgoing edges. Each particle has a local memory in which it can store some bounded amount of information, and any pair of connected particles has a bounded shared memory that can be read and written by both of them and that can be accessed using the edge label associated with that connection.

Particles move through *expansions* and *contractions*: If a particle occupies one node (i.e., it is *contracted*), it can expand to an unoccupied adjacent node to occupy two nodes. If a particle occupies two nodes (i.e., it is *expanded*), it can contract to one of these nodes to occupy only a single node. Performing movements via expansions and contractions has various advantages. For example, it would easily allow a particle to abort a movement if its movement is in conflict with other movements. A particle always knows whether it is contracted or expanded — in the latter case, it also knows along which edge it is expanded — and this information will be available to neighboring particles. In a *handover*, two scenarios are possible: a) a contracted particle p can "push" a neighboring expanded particle q and expand into the neighboring node previously occupied by q, forcing q to contract, or b) an expanded particle p can "pull" a neighboring contracted particle q to a cell occupied by it thereby expanding that particle to that cell, which allows p to contract to its other cell. The ability to use a handover allows the system to stay connected while particles move (e.g., for particles moving in a worm-like fashion). Note that while expansions and contractions may represent the way particles physically move in space (resembling loosely the movement of amoeba), they can also be interpreted as a particle "looking ahead" and establishing new connections (by expanding) before it fully moves to a new position and severs the old connections it had (by contracting). In Figure 1, we illustrate a set of particles (some contracted, some expanded) using the infinite regular triangular grid graph G_{eqt} as the underlying graph G.

Figure 1: The left part shows an example of a particle structure in G_{eqt}. A contracted particle is depicted as a black dot, and an expanded particle is depicted as two black dots connected by an edge. The right part shows a particle structure with 3 borders. The outer border is solid and the two inner borders are dashed.

We assume the standard asynchronous computation model, i.e., only one particle can be active at a time. Whenever a particle is active, it can perform an arbitrary bounded amount of computation (involving its local memory as well as the shared memories with its neighboring particles) followed by no or a single movement. A *round* is over once every particle has been activated at least once.

2. LEADER ELECTION AND LINE FORMATION IN THE GENERAL AMOEBOT MODEL

Here we focus on the feasibility of leader election and shape formation for particles with constant memory. For the shape formation, we just focus on forming a line of particles, that is, we are searching for a local-control algorithm such that for any initial set $A \subseteq V$ of positions occupied by particles where $G|_A$ (i.e., the subgraph of G induced by A) is connected, the particles will eventually rearrange themselves into a line without losing connectivity. Given that we do not assume any underlying geometric information regarding G, by forming a line, we mean that for the final set of occupied positions A', $G|_{A'}$ forms an arbitrary simple path.

Suppose that there is a protocol for the line formation problem in the general amoebot model. Then it is easy to extend it to a leader election protocol: once the line has been formed, its two endpoints contend for leadership using tokens with random bits sent back and forth. On the other hand, one can deduce from [3] that in the general amoebot model there is no local-control protocol for leader election. Hence, also line formation cannot be solved. So additional assumptions are needed to solve these.

3. LEADER ELECTION IN THE GEOMETRIC AMOEBOT MODEL

In this section we assume that G is equal to G_{eqt} (see Figure 1) and that the edges are labeled in a consecutive way in clockwise direction so that every particle has the same sense of clockwise direction, but the labelings do not have to be consistent. So the particles may not have a common sense of orientation. However, our model allows a particle to maintain a fixed orientation as it moves because in an expanded state it knows along which edge it expands from both sides.

Let $A \subseteq V$ be any initial distribution of contracted particles such that $G_{\text{eqt}}|_A$ is connected. Consider the graph $G_{\text{eqt}}|_{V \setminus A}$ induced by the unoccupied nodes in G_{eqt}. We call a connected component of $G_{\text{eqt}}|_{V \setminus A}$ an *empty region*. Let $N(R)$ be the neighborhood of an empty region R in G_{eqt}. Then all nodes in $N(R)$ are occupied and we call the graph $G_{\text{eqt}}|_{N(R)}$ a *border*. Since $G_{\text{eqt}}|_A$ is a connected finite graph, exactly one empty region has infinite size while the remaining empty regions have finite size. We define the border corresponding to the infinite empty region to be the unique *outer border* and refer to a border that corresponds to a finite empty region as an *inner border*, see Figure 1. The common sense of clockwise rotation can be used to give each border a unique orientation.

The leader election algorithm operates independently on each border. Due to the nature of G_{eqt} a particle can be adjacent to at most three different empty regions for each region a particle simulates one agent. For simplicity and ease of presentation we assume for now that agents have a global view of the border they are part of and that agents act synchronously. At any given time, some subset of agents on a border will consider themselves *candidates*, i.e. potential leaders of the system. Initially, every agent considers itself a candidate. Between any two candidates on a border there is a (possibly empty) sequence of non-candidate agents. We call such a sequence a *segment* and specifically refer to the segment coming after (before) a candidate c in the direction of the border as the *front segment* (*back segment*) of c. We denote the lengths of those segments as $|fs(c)|$ and $|bs(c)|$. We use *front candidate* ($fc(c)$) and *back candidate* ($bc(c)$) to denote the candidates at the end of these segments. We drop the c in parentheses if it is clear from the context. We define the distance $d(c_1, c_2)$ between candidates c_1 and

c_2 as the number of agents between c_1 and c_2 when going from c_1 to c_2 in the direction of the border. We say a candidate c_1 *covers* a candidate c_2 (or c_2 *is covered by* c_1) if $|fs(c_1)| > d(c_2, c_1)$. The leader election progresses in *phases*. In each phase, each candidate executes Algorithm 1. A phase consists of three synchronized *subphases*, i.e., agents can only progress to the next subphase once all agents have finished the current subphase.

Algorithm 1 Leader Election in the Geometric Amoebot Model

Subphase 1:
$pos \leftarrow$ position of fc
if covered by any candidate or $|fs| < |bs|$ **then**
    return not leader

Subphase 2:
if coin flip results in heads **then**
    transfer candidacy to agent at pos

Subphase 3:
if only candidate on border **then**
    if outside border **then**
        return leader
    else
        return not leader

In the first subphase candidates are eliminated deterministically. In the second subphase candidates that survived the first subphase are eliminated in a randomized fashion by transferring candidacy to another agent. This transferral of candidacy means that c withdraws its own candidacy but at the same time promotes the agent at position pos (i.e., the front candidate of c in subphase 1) to be a candidate. Subphase 1 and 2 make sure that eventually there is only one leader on each border. Since we assume that each particle has a global view, it can detect whether it is on the outer or an inner border. Hence, the algorithm will elect a unique leader.

Algorithm 1 can be implemented entirely as a local-control protocol. This implementation heavily relies on token passing. Since a detailed description of the protocol cannot be presented in this brief announcement, we focus on the local-control protocol for one part of the algorithm: the test whether the last remaining candidate of a border is on the outer border or an inner border. We can achieve this as follows. The candidate sends a token along its border that keeps track of the sum of angles the path takes with respect to the orientation of the candidate. Once the token manages to return to its origin (the candidate itself), the sum of angles stored in the token is inspected. It turns out that it is always $360°$ for the outer border and $-360°$ for an inner border. Since we work on G_{eqt}, we just need to count integer multiples of $60°$ so that instead of the actual angle we can simply store an integer k in the token such that the angle is $k \cdot 60°$. Note that the range of k during the traversal of the path is unbounded. However, since we are only interested in whether the value of k is 6 or -6 once the token returns to its origin, we can use a counter modulo 5 so that for the outer border we get $k = 1$ and for an inner border $k = 4$. This way, the token only needs 3 bits of memory independently of the shape of the border.

4. LINE FORMATION IN THE GEOMETRIC AMOEBOT MODEL

Our line formation algorithm is based on the leader election strategy above. Once a leader has been determined, the leader is used as a seed to arrange the particles in a straight line starting from that leader. Every time the line can be extended by a particle, that particle simply joins the line. Whenever the line cannot be extended any more because of an empty spot, particles are drawn to that spot using the following idea:

All particles connected to the line that are not yet part of it, and have an empty spot in the direction in which the line needs to grow, form the root of a tree of particles so that all particles belong to one of these trees. Every root tries to travel along the line in the direction in which it is grown. If this is not possible any more because the next spot is already occupied by an particle, it joins the tree of that particle. Otherwise, it moves forward on top of the line and drags the particles of its tree with it in a worm-like fashion (which can be realized with the handover operation). This guarantees that eventually all particles end up being part of the line.

5. SELF-STABILIZING ALGORITHMS

The leader election algorithm for G_{eqt} can be extended to a self-stabilizing leader election algorithm with $O(\log^* n)$ memory using the results of [1, 4] (i.e., we use their self-stabilizing reset algorithm on every border in order to recover from failure states). However, it is not possible to design a self-stabilizing algorithm for the line formation problem. The reason for this is that even a much simpler problem we call the *movement problem* cannot be solved in a self-stabilizing manner.

In the movement problem we are given an initial distribution A of particles that can be in a contracted as well as expanded state, and the goal is to change the set of nodes occupied by the particles without causing disconnectivity. For the ring of expanded particles it holds that for any protocol P there is an initial state so that P does not solve the movement problem. To show this we essentially consider two cases: suppose that there is any state s for some particle in the ring that would cause that particle to contract. In this case set two particles on opposite sides of the ring to that state, and the ring will break due to their contractions. Otherwise, P would not move any particle of the ring, so also in this case it would not solve the movement problem. It is easy to see that if the movement problem cannot be solved in a self-stabilizing manner, then also the line formation problem cannot be solved in a self-stabilizing manner. Hence, while self-stabilizing leader election is possible, self-stabilizing line formation is not possible, which also implies that it is not possible for the particles to *decide* in this setting when a leader has been successfully chosen.

6. REFERENCES

[1] Baruch Awerbuch and Rafail Ostrovsky. Memory-efficient and self-stabilizing network RESET (extended abstract). In *13th Annual ACM Symposium on Principles of Distributed Computing, Los Angeles, California, USA, August 14-17, 1994*, pages 254–263, 1994.

[2] Zahra Derakhshandeh, Shlomi Dolev, Robert Gmyr, Andréa W. Richa, Christian Scheideler, and Thim Strothmann. Brief announcement: amoebot - a new model for programmable matter. In *26th ACM Symposium on Parallelism in Algorithms and Architectures, Prague, Czech Republic - June 23 - 25, 2014*, pages 220–222, 2014.

[3] Alon Itai and Michael Rodeh. Symmetry breaking in distributive networks. In *22nd Annual Symposium on Foundations of Computer Science, Nashville, Tennessee, USA, 28-30 October 1981*, pages 150–158, 1981.

[4] Gene Itkis and Leonid A. Levin. Fast and lean self-stabilizing asynchronous protocols. In *35th Annual Symposium on Foundations of Computer Science, Santa Fe, New Mexico, USA, 20-22 November 1994*, pages 226–239, 1994.

Construction and Impromptu Repair of an MST in a Distributed Network with o(m) Communication

Valerie King*
Computer Science
University of Victoria
Victoria, Canada
val@uvic.ca

Shay Kutten†
Faculty of IE&M, Technion,
Haifa 32000.
kutten@ie.technion.ac.il

Mikkel Thorup‡
University of Copenhagen,
Denmark.
mikkel2thorup@gmail.com.

ABSTRACT

In the CONGEST model, a communications network is an undirected graph whose n nodes are processors and whose m edges are the communications links between processors. At any given time step, a message of size $O(\log n)$ may be sent by each node to each of its neighbours. We show for the synchronous model: If all nodes start in the same round, and each node knows its ID and the ID's of its neighbors, or in the case of MST, the distinct weights of its incident edges and knows n, then there are Monte Carlo algorithms which succeed w.h.p. to determine a minimum spanning forest (MST) and a spanning forest (ST) using $O(n \log^2 n/ \log\log n)$ messages for MST and $O(n \log n)$ messages for ST, resp. These results contradict the "folk theorem" noted in Awerbuch, et.al., JACM 1990 that the distributed construction of a broadcast tree requires $\Omega(m)$ messages. This lower bound has been shown there and in other papers for some CONGEST models; our protocol demonstrates the limits of these models.

A dynamic distributed network is one which undergoes online edge insertions or deletions. We also show how to repair an MST or ST in a dynamic network with asynchronous communication. An edge deletion can be processed in $O(n \log n/ \log\log n)$ expected messages in the MST, and $O(n)$ expected messages for the ST problem, while an edge insertion uses $O(n)$ messages in the worst case. We call this "impromptu" updating as we assume that between processing of edge updates there is no preprocessing or storage of additional information. Previous algorithms for this problem that use an amortized $o(m)$ messages per update require substantial preprocessing and additional local storage between updates.

*Research supported by Simons Institute for the Theory of Computing, Berkeley; Institute for Advanced Study, Princeton; ENS Paris; NSERC; and a Google Faculty Research Award

†Research supported in parts by the Israel Science Foundation, by the Israeli Ministry of Science, and by the Technion TASP center.

‡Research is partly supported by Advanced Grant DFF-0602-02499B from the Danish Council for Independent Research under the Sapere Aude research career programme.

Permission to make digital or hard copies of all or part of this work for personal or classroom use is granted without fee provided that copies are not made or distributed for profit or commercial advantage and that copies bear this notice and the full citation on the first page. Copyrights for components of this work owned by others than ACM must be honored. Abstracting with credit is permitted. To copy otherwise, or republish, to post on servers or to redistribute to lists, requires prior specific permission and/or a fee. Request permissions from permissions@acm.org.
PODC'15, July 21–23, 2015, Donostia-San Sebastián, Spain.
Copyright © 2015 ACM 978-1-4503-3617-8 /15/07..$15.00
DOI http://dx.doi.org/10.1145/2767386.2767405.

1. INTRODUCTION

The problem of finding a minimum spanning tree (MST) or computing a spanning tree (ST) in a communications network is one of the most fundamental and heavily studied problems in distributed computing. This problem is important for facilitating broadcast and coordination in a message-efficient manner. With such a tree, messages may be broadcast from one node to all others or values from all nodes can be combined from the leaves up to one node in time proportional to the diameter of the tree, with a number of messages which is proportional to the size of the tree, rather than all edges in the network, as when communication is by flooding. For this reason, a tree is useful for tasks such as leader election, mutual exclusion, and reset (adaptation of any static algorithm to changes in the network topology). Below, we consider a network to be a graph with n nodes and m edges.

In 1983, Gallager, Humlet and Spira gave a now classic algorithm for finding a MST in a distributed asynchronous communications network with message complexity $O(m + n \log n)$ for a network with n nodes and m edges. The asymptotic message complexity for this problem has not been improved until now, even for the easier context we consider here For the unweighted problem of ST, a single node starting a flooding algorithm can construct a broadcast tree with $O(m)$ messages in time equal to the diameter of the network (see, e.g. [32]).

That $\Omega(m)$ messages are required for broadcast (and the construction of an ST) is mentioned as "folklore" by Awerbuch, Goldreich, Peleg and Vainish (1990) [4]. They prove this lower bound in what is referred to as the "standard" KT_1 model, where each node knows (its own identity) and the identity of its neighbors. The $\Omega(m)$ lower bound holds for randomized (Monte Carlo) comparison protocols, where the basic computation step is to compare two processors' identities, and for general algorithms where the set of ID's is very large and grows independently with respect to message size, time and randomness. In 2013 Kutten, Pandurangan, Peleg, Robinson, and Trehan showed an $\Omega(m)$ lower bound for randomized general algorithms in the KT_0 model, where each node does not know the identities of its neighbors [19]. All these lower bounds hold when the size of the network is known to all the nodes, the network is synchronous, and all the nodes start simultaneously. Our MST and ST algorithms avoid both lower bounds by assuming KT_1 and an exponential bound on the size of the identity space.

Communication networks are inherently dynamic, in that a link may be either deleted or inserted over time. This paper also presents algorithms to repair an MST or ST in an asynchronous network upon an edge insertion or deletion. These algorithms have the new property (for an efficient dynamic graph algorithm) of being "impromptu", that is, they require no preprocessing or storage of auxiliary information except during the processing of the current updates. Between updates, a node knows only the names and weights of its incident edges and whether these edges are in the currently maintained MST or ST. While there are previously known algorithms for updating MST and ST with $O(n)$ messages, these have significant memory requirements and require the communication costs to be amortized over a sequence of sufficiently long updates. For example, the 2008 algorithm of Awerbuch et. al. [5] to maintain an MST uses $O(n)$ amortized messages per update (somewhat better then our second algorithm), but stores $\Theta(\Delta_v n \log n)$ bits at each node v, where Δ_v is the number of node v's neighbors [1].

A communications network is a graph. We assume that every node knows the same upper bound n on the actual number of nodes. An interesting case is when the known upper bound on the size of the network is very tight (e.g the actual size multiplied by some small positive integer constant). In this case, all our asymptotic results are in terms of the actual network size. Hence for simplicity, we refer below to n as the network size (rather than an upper bound). The communication links are undirected edges and each node has a unique ID $\in \{1, 2, .., n^d\}$. In fact, with Karp-Rabin [16] fingerprinting, w.h.p., distinct ID's $\in \{1, 2, ..., 2^n\}$ can be locally mapped to distinct ID's $\in \{1, 2, ..., n^d\}$ with no increase in the asymptotic message complexity. For the MST problem, each edge has a weight $\in \{1, 2, ..., u\}$ for any positive integer u. Each node knows its own ID, the weight of each incident edge, the ID of its other endpoint, and n. No other information about the graph is known to any node at the start of any of our algorithms. A message is a communication of $O(\log(n + u))$ bits which is passed along a single edge.

A network is *properly marked* if every edge is marked by both or neither of its endpoints. *A tree T is maintained by a network* if the network is properly marked and T is a maximal tree in the subgraph of marked edges. For a node x, let T_x denote the tree maintained by the network and containing node x. We call an (unmarked) edge with exactly one endpoint in T an edge *leaving* T or *outgoing*. A tree construction problem assumes that initially all edges are unmarked and every node knows to begin construction. At the end of the algorithm the network should maintain the MST (or ST). We use the usual definitions of synchrony and asynchrony: A *synchronized* network assumes a global clock, and messages are received in one time step. An *asynchronous* network assumes that messages are eventually received. Each node's action is triggered by the receiving of a message or other change to its state. We say an event occurs "w.h.p." (with high probability) if for any constant c (which is given as a parameter of the algorithm), the probability of the event is at least $1 - n^{-c}$. We show:

[1] According to [5], "keeping track of history enables significant improvements in the communication complexity of dynamic networks protocols." Atop its abstract, this was also stated in a more lyrical way: "Those who cannot remember the past are condemned to repeat it (George Santayana)." A part of the message of the current paper may be adding "unless they flip coins..." Here we show that history can be replaced by random coin tosses.

THEOREM 1.1. *There are algorithms to construct a minimum spanning tree or forest (MST) and spanning tree or forest (ST) succeeding w.h.p. in a synchronous networks of n nodes using time and messages $O(n \log^2 n / \log\log n)$ for MST and $O(n \log n)$ for ST, and $O(\log(n+u))$ local memory per node. This assumes that each node is initialized to start the algorithm and its only initial knowledge of the graph is its ID, its neighbors' ID's, the weight of each of its incident edge, and n.*

THEOREM 1.2. *Upon deletion or increase in weight of an edge, there are algorithms FindAny and FindMin to repair an ST and an MST, respectively, which find a replacement edge if there is any, in an asynchronous distributed network using expeced time and messages $O(n)$ for the ST, and $O(n \log n / \log\log n)$ for the MST, and $O(\log(n + u))$ local memory per node. Upon insertion or decrease in weight of an edge, a deterministic algorithm with $O(n)$ time and messages suffices to repair the tree. All repairs are impromptu, i.e, no preprocessing or extra storage is needed between updates. This assumes each node knows its ID and the ID's of their neighbors and the weight of each incident edge. To achieve success with probability $1-n^{-c}$, each node must know an upper bound on n which is within a polynomial of n.*

Modified versions $FindAny-C$ and $FindMin-C$ are also presented. Their worst case cost matches the expected cost of $FindAny$ and $FindMin$. When there is a replacement for a deleted tree edge, w.h.p., they return either a correct replacement edge or $\emptyset$, and with constant probability, they return the former.

Our algorithms are based on the following new procedures which may be useful in other contexts. Below, node x initiates the procedure and receives the output, and $j, k \in \{1, .., u\}$:

- TestOut(x, j, k): Returns true with constant probability if there is an edge leaving T_x with edge weight in the interval $[j, k]$; false otherwise. Always correct if true is returned.
- HP-TestOut(x, j, k): The same as $TestOut$ but w.h.p.

A basic communication step in our network is a simple distributed routine *broadcast-and-echo* [13]. It is initiated by the broadcast of a message by a node x which becomes the "root" of a tree. When a node v receives a broadcast message from its neighbor y, it designates y as its "parent" (for the sake of the current communication step) and sends a broadcast message to each of its other neighbors in T, its "children". When a leaf node in T receives a broadcast message, it sends a message ("echo") to its parent, possibly carrying some value. When a non-leaf message has received an echo message from every child, it sends an echo message to its parent, possibly aggregating its value with the values sent by its children. When the root has received echo messages from all its children, the broadcast-and-echo is done. We show:

LEMMA 1. *TestOut and $HP - TestOut$ can be performed with one broadcast-and-echo with message size $O(\log(n+u))$. The echo of TestOut requires only a message of only one bit.*

Other previous work

Techniques: *TestOut* uses the principle that each edge with two endpoints in a tree contributes 0 to the parity of the sum of the degrees of the nodes in a tree, while each edge which leaves a tree contributes 1. Therefore, in a randomly sampled graph, there is a 1/2 chance that if there are one or more edges leaving a tree, the parity of the sum of the degrees is odd. This observation is used in a paper on graph sketching [6] and a paper on sequential dynamic graph connectivity data structures [15]. It is not clear how to adapt the techniques of [6] to the distributed setting. Those of [15] were adapted to a distributed setting [26], however, the algorithms there required supplemental storage between updates, did not address weighted graph problems, and were more complicated.

MST and ST construction: The complexity of the first distributed MST construction algorithm was not analyzed [8]. Following the seminal paper of [13] mentioned above, Awerbuch improved the time complexity to $O(n)$ [2], retaining the same message complexity of $O(m+n\log n)$. Distributed algorithms that are faster (when the diameter of the network or the diameter of the MST are smaller) do exist [20, 14, 11]. However, their message and memory space complexities are much higher.

Simultaneous edge changes: As opposed to the previous $o(m)$ (but non impromptu) repair algorithms [5, 21], ours has not been extended to deal with multiple updates at a time, though we believe it can be. [2]

Definitions and Organization

Definitions: An edge $\{u,v\}$'s *edge number* is the concatenation of the unique ID's of the edge's endpoints, smallest first. We create unique weights (as in [13]) by concatenating the weight to the front of its edge number. For any tree, *maxID(T)*, *maxEdgeNum(T)*, and *maxWt(T)* denote the maximum ID of any node in T, the maximum edge number, and maximum weight edge, resp. of any node in T. T is omitted where it is understood from context. Let $[j,k]$ denote the set of integers $\{j, j+1, ..., , k\}$ and $\lg n$ denote $\log_2 n$.

Organization: The functions *TestOut* and $HP - TestOut$ are described in Section 2. Section 3 describes *FindMin*, an algorithm for dynamic MST and an algorithm for constructing an MST 3.3. Section 4.1 describes *FindAny* and reduces the complexity for construction and repair for ST. The Appendix contains an extension to the case where edge weights may be superpolynomial in n.

2. TestOut

In this section, we describe *TestOut* and $HP - TestOut$.

2.1 Random odd hash functions and TestOut

As a method to sample edges, we use the concept of an *odd* hash functions: We say that a random hash function $h : [1,m] \to \{0,1\}$ is ε*-odd*, if for any given non-empty set $S \subseteq [1,m]$, there are an odd number of elements in S which hash to 1 with probability ε, that is,

$$\Pr_h\left[\sum_{x\in S} h(x) = 1 \mod 2\right] \geq \varepsilon. \qquad (1)$$

An odd hash function is a type of "distinguisher" described in [33]; we use their construction here[3]. Let $m \leq 2^w$. We pick uniformly at random an odd multiplier a from $[1, 2^w]$ and a threshold $t \in [1, 2^w]$. From these two components, we define $h : [1, 2^w] \to \{0,1\}$ as

$$\begin{aligned} h(x) &= 1 \text{ if } (ax \bmod 2^w) \leq t \\ &= 0 \text{ otherwise.} \end{aligned}$$

The above is particularly efficient if $w \in \{8, 32, 64\}$ in a programming language like C, for there the mod-operation comes for free as part of an integer multiplication which automatically discards overflow beyond the w bits. From [33] we see that h is an (1/8)-odd hash function.

Let $h : [1, maxEdgeNum] \to \{0,1\}$ be an odd hash function. We show how to compute *TestOut*. Let $E(v)$ denote the edge numbers of edges incident to node v. Let $Cut(T, V\setminus T)$ denote the set of edges with exactly one endpoint in T. To test with constant probability whether there exists any edge leaving a tree T, each node $v \in T_x$ with $E(v) \neq \emptyset$ computes

$$\sum_{e\in E(v)} h(e) \mod 2$$

locally. If $E(v) = \emptyset$, then 0 is returned. These values are aggregated over the nodes in T to compute

$$\sum_{v\in V(T)}\sum_{e\in E(v)} h(e) \mod 2 = \sum_{e\in Cut(T,V\setminus T)} h(e) \mod 2$$

TestOut(x) can be done with one broadcast of h from node x and one 1-bit echo. First x broadcasts h in one message. The leaves return the parity of their sum to their parent; the parent passes to its own parent the parity of the sums of nodes in its subtree including its own sum.

TestOut(x,j,k) checks if there is any edge leaving T_x whose weight is in a given interval $[j,k]$. To do so, in each local computation at node v, the definitions above for *TestOut*(x) are changed so that

$$\sum_{e\in E(v)} h(e) \mod 2 \to \sum_{e\in E(v)\wedge weight(e)\in[j,k])} h(e) \mod 2$$

2.2 High probability TestOut

TestOut achieves a constant probability of correctness if the set is non-empty and is always correct if it is empty. The probability can be amplified to high probability by $O(\log n)$ independent parallel repetitions. However this would require $O(\log^2 n)$ bits. Alternatively, deterministic amplification methods can bring down the randomness to $O(\log n)$. However, this is not simple and would require each node to construct a portion of an averaging sampler.

---

[2]The idea behind such an extension would be, essentially, to use the algorithm of Awerbuch et. al of 2008, but replace their method of finding replacement edges with the method used here.

[3][33] was originally inspired by the developments in the current paper.

Instead, we take advantage of the type of set we are looking at and introduce a high probability version of $TestOut$. W.h.p., $HP - TestOut(x)$ outputs 1 if the tree T_x has any leaving edge. If there is no such edge, it always returns 0.

For a vertex u, let $E^{\uparrow}(u) = \{(u,v) \in E\}$ and $E^{\downarrow}(u) = \{(v,u) \in E\}$. For the tree T, $E^{\uparrow}(T) = \bigcup_{u \in T} E^{\uparrow}(u)$ and $E^{\downarrow}(T) = \bigcup_{u \in T} E^{\downarrow}(u)$.

Observation 1. *There is an edge $\{u,v\} \in E$ with only one endpoint in T if and only if $E^{\uparrow}(T) \neq E^{\downarrow}(T)$.*

Thus, to implement $HP - TestOut$, we need only test if $E^{\uparrow}(T) \neq E^{\downarrow}(T)$. To test set equality efficiently, we use a method from [7] based on the Schwartz-Zippel [30] polynomial identity testing. Let B be the number of edges incident to nodes in T. To achieve probability of error $\epsilon(n)$, it suffices to use any prime $p > \max\{maxEdgeNum(T), B/\epsilon(n)\}$, with $|p| \leq w$, the maximum message size [4]. For p and an edge set D, we define a polynomial over $\mathbb{Z}_p$ by $\mathcal{P}(D)(z) = \prod_{e \in D}(z - edge\_number(e)) \mod p$. If $E^{\uparrow}(T) \neq E^{\downarrow}(T)$ then $Pr_{\alpha \in \mathbb{Z}_p}[\mathcal{P}(E^{\uparrow}(T))(\alpha) = \mathcal{P}(E^{\downarrow}(T))(\alpha)] < \epsilon(n)$.

$HP - TestOut(x)$:{assumes x knows $\epsilon(n)$}

1) x initiates a $Broadcast - and - echo$ in which a randomly selected $\alpha \in \mathbb{Z}_p$ (and p if necessary) is passed to all nodes in the tree in the broadcast phase. Each node y locally computes $Local^{\uparrow}(y) = \mathcal{P}(E^{\uparrow}(y))(\alpha)$ and $Local^{\downarrow}(y) = \mathcal{P}(E^{\downarrow}(y))(\alpha)$. Upon receiving $\mathcal{P}(E^{\uparrow}(T_z))(\alpha)$ and $\mathcal{P}(E^{\downarrow}(T_z))(\alpha)$ from each of its children z, each node computes and sends to its parent:

$$\mathcal{P}(E^{\uparrow}(T(y))(\alpha) = Local^{\uparrow}(y) * \prod_{z \text{ child of } y} \mathcal{P}(E^{\uparrow}(T_z))(\alpha) \text{ and}$$

$$\mathcal{P}(E^{\downarrow}(T(y))(\alpha) = Local^{\downarrow}(y) * \prod_{z \text{ child of } y} \mathcal{P}(E^{\downarrow}(T_z))(\alpha)$$

3) x determines there is an edge leaving T iff $\mathcal{P}(E^{\uparrow}(T))(\alpha) \neq \mathcal{P}(E^{\downarrow}(T))(\alpha)$.

Lemma 2. *$HP - TestOut(x)$ returns a 0 if there is no edge leaving T_x and, if there is an edge leaving T_x, then for any constant c, with probability $1 - 1/n^c$, $HP - TestOut(x)$ returns a 1. The time and message complexity is $O(|T_x|)$.*

Proof. Let $\epsilon(n) = 1/n^c$ and pick a prime $p > \max\{maxEdgeNum(T), B/\epsilon(n)\} \geq n^{2d+c+2}$ with $|p| = O(\log n)$ bits. (By the Prime Number Theorem, there is such a prime p.) As all computations are over $\mathbb{Z}_p$, the number of messages sent is $\leq 4|T_x|$ with each containing $O(\log n)$ bits. □

As noted above,

$HP - TestOut(x, j, k)$ checks if there is any edge leaving T_x whose weight is in a given interval $[j, k]$. To do so, in each local computation at node v, the definitions above for $HP - TestOut(x)$ are changed so that $E^{\uparrow}(u) = \{(u,v) \in E\}$ and $E^{\downarrow}(u) = \{(v,u) \in E\}$ are replaced by $E^{\uparrow}(u) = \{(u,v) \in E \wedge weight(u,v) \in [j,k]\}$ and $E^{\downarrow}(u) = \{(v,u) \in E \wedge weight(v,u) \in [j,k]\}$.

[4] If p is not known by all nodes, then x initiates a $Broadcast - and - echo$ to find $maxEdgeNum$ and B to determine p.

3. MST BUILD AND REPAIR

We present a simple method to find the lightest leaving edge using a w-wise search on the edge weights. This yields a method using $O(\log n/\log\log n)$ broadcast-and-echoes with $w = O(\log n)$ bit messages when the weight of every edge is polynomial. In the appendix, we give a more complicated method which uses $O(\log n/\log\log n)$ for superpolynomial edge weights of size u which assumes wordsize $O(\log(n+u))$.

3.1 Integer edge weights of polynomial size

Since $TestOut$ uses a single bit "echo", a single $broadcast-and-echo$ can test $w = O(\log n)$ subranges concurrently, as the same hash function can be used for each of the parallel $TestOut$'s, while the single bit responses for each subrange $TestOut$'s are returned concurrently in one word. The smallest subrange testing positive becomes the next range of edge weights to be tested. Before narrowing the range, the result is verified w.h.p. using $HP - TestOut$.

Below we describe $FindMin$ and $FindMin$-C. $FindMin$-C is like $FindMin$ except that the number of repetitions of the loop in the algorithm is limited to double the expected number, $O(\log n/\log\log n)$, rather than $O(\log n)$ in the worst case. Let q be the probability that $TestOut$ succeeds. We assume for any constant c, x knows a polynomial bound on the network size n in order to set an error parameter for $HP - TestOut$, $\epsilon(n) \leq n^{-c-1}$ such that $\epsilon(n)^{-1}$ is polynomial in n and a bound for $Count$ for $FindMin$ which exceeds $(c/q)\lg n$ and is $O(\log n)$.

$FindMin(x)$ $[FindMin - C]$ *{finds minimum cost edge in $(T_x, V \setminus T_x)$}*

1. $Count \leftarrow 0$.
2. x determines $maxWt(T_x)$ and $maxEdgeNum(T_x)$ through one broadcast-and-echo and computes $\epsilon(n)$.
3. x sets $j \leftarrow 1$; $k \leftarrow maxWt(T_x)$
4. x broadcasts an odd hash function $f : [1, maxEdgeNum(T_x$ $\{0, 1\}$ and also j and k.
5. In parallel for $i = 0, 1, 2, ..., w - 1$:
   Set $j_i \leftarrow j + i\lceil(k - j + 1)/w\rceil$; $k_i \leftarrow j + (i+1)\lceil k - j + 1)/w\rceil$- 1, and return word in which i^{th} bit is the "echo" of $TestOut(x, j_i, k_i)$
6. Upon receiving the echo, x determines the index $min = \min\{i \mid TestOut(x, j_i, k_i) = 1)$ and initiates $TestLow = HP - TestOut(x, 0, j_{min} - 1)$ and $TestHigh = HP - TestOut(x, j_{min}, k_{min})$.
7. Upon receiving results,
   (a) if $TestLow = 0$ and $TestHigh = 1$ and if $j_{min} < k_{min}$ then x sets $j = j_{min}$ and $k = k_{min}$; else if $j_{min} = k_{min}$ then x broadcasts "stop" and returns j_{min}.
   (b) else if both return 0, x broadcasts "stop" and returns $\emptyset$.
8. For $FindMin$ [resp., $FindMin - C$]:
   If $Count < (c/q)\lg n + (c/q)(\lg maxWt(T_x)/\lg(w - 1)$, [resp., $Count < (2c/q)\lg maxWt(T_x)/\lg(w - 1)$], increment Count and repeat from Step 4. Else return $\emptyset$.

Proof of correctness

LEMMA 3. *Let c be any constant s.t. $c \geq 1$. With probability $1 - n^{-c}$, using asynchronous communication, $FindMin(x)$ returns the lightest edge leaving a tree T_x in expected time and messages $O(|T_x| \log n / \log \log n)$ (and worst case $O(\log n)$ time and messages. With probability $1 - o(1) - 1/n^c$, $FindMin - C(x)$ returns the lightest edge and with probability $1 - n^{-c}$ it returns the lightest edge or $\emptyset$, using worst case $O(|T_x| \log n / \log \log n)$ messages and time. If there is no edge leaving the tree, both procedures always return $\emptyset$. This assumes x knows an upper bound on the size n of the network which is polynomial in n.*

PROOF. *FindMin* is analyzed first. We observe that if $HP - TestOut$ is always successfully, then *FindMin* will terminate successfully after no more than $\lg maxWt / \lg(w-1)$ successful executions of *TestOut*: Let $I = (j_i, k_i)$ be the first interval containing an edge leaving T_x. *TestOut* always returns a 0 for earlier intervals, and returns a 1 with constant probability $q = 1/8$ when I is tested. If *TestOut* fails to return a 1 for interval I, then *TestLow* will detect a 1 and the loop is repeated; otherwise the range is successfully narrowed. The range is narrowed no more than $\lg maxWt / \lg(w-1)$ times. Each successful narrowing requires an expected $1/q$ repetitions and overall, in expectation $(1/q) \lg maxWt / \lg(w-1) = O(\log n / \log n \log n)$ iterations of Steps 4-8 suffice to return the lightest edge leaving T (if such exists).

We bound the probability that *TestOut* fails K times before succeeding $\lg maxWt / \lg(w-1) = O(\log n / \log \log n)$ times, where $K = (c/q) \lg n$: This is given by a tail bound on a random variable with a binomial distribution with $K + \lg maxWt / \lg(w-1)$ trials and constant probability q of heads (success). Using Chernoff bounds, the probability of this type of failure is $< 1/(2n^c)$ for sufficiently large n.

We now bound the probability that $HP - TestOut$ fails at least once after any of these calls to *TestOut*: With an error parameter of $\leq n^{-c-1}$ for $HP - TestOut$, the probability of the latter over $2K = 2(c/q) \lg n$ trials is less than $1/(2n^c)$ by a union bound.

We conclude that the probability of either event occurring is less than $1/n^c$, again by a union bound. Hence, w.h.p., the range is successfully narrowed to the minimum weight edge after $2(c/q) \log n$ iterations of Steps 4-8 or, if there is no edge leaving T, then Step 7(b) is executed and $\emptyset$ is returned.

For $FindMin - C$, there are no more than $K' = (2c/q) \lg maxWt / \lg(w-1)$ parallel calls to *TestOut*. For $FindMin - C$ to return the lightest edge, (1) *TestOut* must achieve $\lg maxWt / \lg(w-1) = qK'/(2c) \leq qK'/2$ successes, and we require that (2) $HP - TestOut$ cannot fail once any of its $2K'$ calls. To bound the probability that (1) does not occur, we can again use Chernoff bounds as above to get a $o(1)$ probability of error, since here the expected number of successes is $\mu = qK' = \Theta(\log n / \log \log n)$. We next bound the probability that $HP - TestOut$ fails during any one of its $2K'$ calls, as before, by a union bound to get a probability of error less than $1/n^c$. For $HP - TestOut$ to return an incorrect lightest edge, $HP - TestOut$ must fail at least once. Hence, if there is an edge leaving then with probability $1 - o(1) - 1/n^c$, $TestOut - C$ returns the correct edge, with probability $1 - 1/n^c$ it returns $\emptyset$ or the correct edge, and with probability $< 1/n^c$ it returns an edge leaving the tree which is not the lightest edge.

□

3.2 Impromptu repairs of MST

We now apply *FindMin* to the problem of repairing an MST. Assume that the updates are well-separated in the sense that we can complete the processing of an edge update before the next one arrives. Before any update, assume the network maintains a minimum spanning tree, and each node knows some polynomial (in n) upper bound on the size n[5].

Delete(u, v).
When an edge $\{u, v\}$ is deleted, if $u < v$, then if $\{u, v\}$ was in the MST, then u initiates *FindMin* in the marked subtree containing u, T_u. If *FindMin* returns $\emptyset$, it means that $\{u, v\}$ was a bridge, and we are done. Otherwise *FindMin* returns an edge $\{u', v'\}$. Then u broadcasts that $\{u', v'\}$ should be added to the minimum spanning forest, and u' forwards this message to v'. Both u' and v' mark the edge $\{u', v'\}$. The bottleneck of the complexity is the call $FindMin(u)$ which uses $O(n_u \log n)$ messages for $n_u \leq n$ nodes in T_u.

Insert(u, v).
When an edge $\{u, v\}$ is inserted, and $u < v$, u determines if its tree T_u contains v and if so, it determines the heaviest edge e on the path from u to v. This is easily done by a broadcast-and-echo from u. If e is heavier than $\{u, v\}$, $\{u, v\}$ is included in the minimum spanning forest, and u broadcasts that e should be removed from the MST. A constant number of broadcast-and-echoes are used, for a total number of messages which is proportional to the size of T_u.

The analysis of these operations follow from Lemma 3. With the extension of *FindMin* to superpolynomial edge weights given in the Appendix, the proof of Theorem 1.2 follows.

3.3 Building an MST

In a synchronous network, building an MST from scratch is a straightforward application of *FindMin*. Recall (the Introduction) that we assume that every node knows n[6] and the list of the edge weights of its incident edges and that the edge weights of all edges are distinct.

The goal is for each node to mark a subset of its neighbors so that the resulting marked edges form an MST. The algorithm is an implementation of Borůvka's parallel algorithm for constructing an MST. During the execution, the nodes are partitioned into disjoint trees, each a connected component of the final MST. (Initially, each node is a singleton tree). At each phase in parallel, a search for a minimum weight edge incident to each tree is started by the *tree leader*.

Electing a tree leader in a synchronous network is straightforward and is similar to a broadcast-and-echo and ideas in [18]. We omit this here.

Let $maxTimeMST(n)$ be the maximum amount of time needed to carry out Steps (a)–(c) below in a tree of size n. In our model it is easy to implement a global clock with value *time*. Let C be the (constant) probability that $FindMin - C$ returns the minimum edge incident to a tree, if there is one. Let c in the algorithm below be the desired (constant) parameter, such that the probability of success of the Build

[5]This is only required to compute with probability of error a function of n

[6]up to some constant factor.

MST algorithm should be $1-n^{-c}$. Let $a = \lceil \log_{4/(4-C)} n \rceil$, $\alpha = (1-C)/(1-C/2)$, and $M = \max\{2a/\alpha, 8c\ln n/\alpha\}$.

Build MST {*executed by every node x*}

1. $time \leftarrow 0$
2. For $i = 1$ to M
   (a) Elect a leader in T_x
   (b) If $x = leader$ then x initiates $FindMin - C$; else x participates in $FindMin - C$.
   (c) If x is an endpoint of the edge $\{x, y\}$ which has been returned by $FindMin{-}C$, x sends Add_Edge message to y across $\{x, y\}$.
   (d) While $time < i * maxTimeMST(n)$ wait; while waiting, if any Add_Edge message is received over an edge, mark that edge.

LEMMA 4. *Let c be any constant, $c \geq 1$. With probability $1-n^{-c}$, Build_MST constructs an MST in time and message complexity $O(n \log^2 n/\log\log n)$.*

PROOF. We call each for-loop a *phase* . At the start of each phase, there is a forest of trees consisting of all marked tree edges. If there is an edge leaving the tree (in the the graph of all edges), it is a *fragment*. The variable $maxTime(n)$ is set so that every node enters phase i at the same time, after completing phases $j < i$. We first show:

Claim 1: Let F be the number of fragments at the start of a phase. At the end of the phase, there are no more than $(1-C/4)F$ fragments with probability at least $\alpha = (1-C)/(1-C/2)$.

Proof of Claim 1: The expected number of fragments which fail to find a tree edge is $\mu = (1-C)F$ since each has probability C of finding a tree edge. By Markov's Inequality, the probability that $(1-C/2)F$ fail to find a tree edge is no more than $\mu/(1-C/2)F$. If at least $(C/2)F$ trees find edges leaving, then in the worst case, each new tree edge is found by pairs of trees and the number of fragments is reduced by at least $(C/4)F$, proving the claim.

Claim 2: For any c, after $O(\log n)$ phases, there are no fragments, with probability $1 - 1/n^c$.

Proof of Claim 2: We call a phase starting with F fragments successful if the number of fragments is reduced by at least $(C/4)F$. Let $X_i = 1$ if phase i is successful and 0 otherwise. By Claim 1, $Pr(X_i = 1) \geq \alpha$. Let $a = \lceil \log_{4/(4-C)} n \rceil$. Then a successful phases suffice to bring the number of fragments to 0, as there can't be 1. If we flip $\max\{2a/\alpha, 8c\ln n/\alpha\}$ coins with probability of heads α, the expected number of heads is $\mu = \max\{2a, 8c\ln n\}$. The probability that the number of heads is less than $a \leq (1-\delta)\mu$ for $\delta \geq 1/2$ is is less than $e^{-\delta^2\mu/2} = e^{-((1/2)^2(8c\ln n)/2)} = 1/n^c$, using a Chernoff bound.

We conclude by noting that each phase of executing $FindMin - C$ on disjoint trees requires $O(n \log n/\log\log n)$ messages and $O(\log n/\log\log n)$ time. Since there are $O(\log n)$ phases, the bounds follow. □

4. UNWEIGHTED EDGES

We now present analogous results for unweighted graphs using less costly, somewhat different techniques.

4.1 Find any edge leaving a tree

$FindAny$, presented below, uses an expected constant number of broadcast-and-echoes, to find some edge leaving T_x. Thus in expectation, we save a factor $\log n/\log\log n$ in the asymptotic cost of $FindMin$.

The procedure starts with $HP - TestOut$ to determine if there is an edge in the cut w.h.p. If $HP - TestOut$ returns 1, a routine to find such an edge with a constant probability of success is run repeatedly until such an edge is found, yielding a constant expected time and message procedure. To achieve a probability of error n^{-c} in the running times claimed, we assume x knows an $\epsilon(n) < 1/(2n^c)$ where $\epsilon^{-1}(n)$ is polynomial in n. T below is T_x. We let $[r]$ denote the set $\{1, ..., r\}$.

$FindAny(x)$

1. $Count \leftarrow 0$.
2. x initiates $HP - TestOut$ in T with error parameter $\epsilon(n)$. If $\neg(HP - TestOut)$ then return $\emptyset$.
3. Determine the identity of an edge as follows:

   a) x broadcasts a random pairwise independent hash function $h : [1, maxEdgeNum(T)] \to [r]$ where r is a power of 2 > sum of degrees of nodes in T.

   b) Each node y hashes the edge numbers of its incident edges using h, and computes the vector $\vec{h}(y)$ s.t. $h_i(y)$ is the parity of the set of its incident edges whose edge numbers hash to values in $[2^i]$ for $i = 1, ..., \lg r$. If y has no incident edges then $\vec{h}(y) = \vec{0}$.

   c) The vector $h(\vec{T}) = \bigoplus_{y \in T} \vec{h}(y)$ is computed up the tree, in the broadcast-and-echo return to x. Then x broadcasts $min = \min\{i \mid h_i(T) = 1\}$.

   d) Let $E(x)$ be the set of edge numbers of edges incident to x. Each node x computes $w(x) = \bigoplus\{e \mid \{e \in E(x) \wedge h(e) < 2^{min}\}$ and $w(T) = \bigoplus_{x \in T} w(x)$ is computed up the tree in the broadcast echo and returned to x.
   {*If there is exactly one edge leaving T with $h(e) < 2^{min}$, then $w(T)$ is its edge number.*}

4. Test: x broadcasts $w(T)$ to obtain Sum = the number of endpoints in T incident to the edge given by $w(T)$. Test succeeds iff $Sum = 1$.
5. If Test succeeds, return $w(T)$ else
   for $TestOut - C$, return $\emptyset$;
   for $TestOut$, if $Count \geq 16\ln(\epsilon^{-1}(n))$ then return $\emptyset$; else increment $Count$ and repeat steps 3-5.

Proof of correctness

Let h be a 2-wise independent function from a universe U into $[2^\ell]$ for some $\ell \geq 2$. Let $W \subseteq U$ s.t. $0 < |W| < 2^{\ell-1}$. For k a positive integer.

LEMMA 5. *With probability 1/16, there is an integer j such that exactly one $w \in W$ hashes to a value in $[2^j]$.*

PROOF. We prove the statement of the lemma for $j = \ell - \lceil \lg |W| \rceil - 1$. Then $1/(4|W|) < 2^j/2^\ell < 1/|W|$. Now,

$$\Pr_h[\exists! w \in W : h(w) \in [2^j]]$$

$$= \sum_{w \in W} \Pr_h[h(w) \in [2^j] \wedge \forall w' \in W \setminus \{w\} : h(w') \notin [2^j]]$$

Let $A(w)$ denote $\Pr_h[h(w) \in [2^j]]$:

$$= \sum_{w \in W} A(w) \Pr_h[\forall w' \in W \setminus \{w\} : h(w') \notin [2^j] \mid h(w) \in [2^j]]$$

$$\geq \sum_{w \in W} A(w)(1 - \sum_{w' \in W \setminus \{w\}} \Pr_h[h(w') \in [2^j] \mid h(w) \in [2^j]])$$

By 2-wise independence:

$$= \sum_{w \in W} A(w)(1 - \sum_{w' \in W \setminus \{x\}} \Pr_h[h(w') \in [2^j]])$$

$$= |W|(2^j/2^\ell \cdot (1 - (|W|-1)2^j/2^\ell))$$

$$> |W|/(4|W|)(1 - |W|/(2|W|)) = 1/16.$$

□

LEMMA 6. *If there is no edge leaving T_x, then $FindAny(x)$ and $FindAny - C(x)$ return $\emptyset$. Otherwise,*

- *$FindAny(x)$ returns an edge leaving T_x w.h.p. It uses expected time and messages $O(n)$; and*
- *$FindAny - C(x)$ returns an edge leaving T_x with probability at least $1/16$, else it returns $\emptyset$. It uses worst case time and messages $O(n)$.*

PROOF. Let W be the set of edge numbers of edges leaving T. If $|W| = 0$, then $HP - TestOut$ returns $\emptyset$ and x returns $\emptyset$. If $|W| > 0$ then with probability $\geq 1 - 1/(2n)^c$ $HP - TestOut$ succeeds and x continues to Step 3. Given x goes on to Step 3, by Lemma 5, with probability at least $1/16$, there is a j such that exactly one edge with distinct edge number e in W hashes to a value in $[2^j]$ ("Event A"). Because all edges incident to T which are not leaving T have both endpoints in T, their edge numbers $\bigoplus$ to $\vec{0}$, when summed over T. Hence, when Event A occurs, $\bigoplus_{y \in T} h_j(y) = \bigoplus_{e' \in W} h_j(e') = h_j(e) = 1$, so $min \leq j$. However, $\bigoplus_{y \in T} h_{min}(y) = 1$ implies that there is at least one edge number in W which hashes to $[2^{min}] \subseteq [2^j]$, so we conclude that there is exactly one such edge number $e \in W$ hashing to $[2^{min}]$.

When Event A occurs, in Step 4, $w(T) = e$, Test succeeds, and an edge leaving T is given by $w(T)$ in Step 5. Thus the probability of success of $FindAny - C$ is the probability that $HP - TestOut$ succeeds, followed by Event A which is $\geq 1/16 - 1/(2n^c)$. In $FindAny$, if $HP - TestOut$ succeeds, then Steps 3-5 are repeated up to $16\ln(\epsilon^{-1}(n)) = 16\ln(2n^c)$ times until they succeed. The probability of failure of all these repetitions is $\leq (1 - 1/16)^{16\ln(2n^c)} < 1/(2n^c)$. The total probability of failure is therefore no more than this probability plus the probability of failure of $HP - TestOut$ for a total probability of failure $\leq 1/n^c$. The expected number of repetitions of Steps 3-5 until success is 16 (and the worst case is $O(\log n)$).

Since a single run of Steps 1-5 requires $O(n)$ time and messages, the lemma follows.

□

4.2 Building an ST

This algorithm is obtained by modifying the algorithm for building the MST. Two modifications are necessary. The first is the substituting of $FindAny - C$ for $FindMin - C$ in each. The replacement of $FindMin - C$ by $FindAny - C$ reduces the asymptotic costs by a factor of $\log n / \log\log n$.

The second modification is more subtle. In $FindMin$, when fragments find minimum weight edges leaving them, all of them are MST edges. This is because when the weights of the edges are distinct, there is only one minimum weight edge leaving any fragment, and such an edge must be in the MST. When fragments of the unweighted graph find edges leaving them which cause them to form a connected component, if these edges are distinct, then there is a cycle formed by possibly some marked edges from before the phase and also two or more newly marked edges.

To preserve the property that the marked edges form a tree, one or more edges in the cycle are unmarked to "break" the cycle before the next phase begins. The following routines are performed at the end of each phase of *BuildST*:

1. *Cycle detection:* Each leaf sends a message to its neighbor; each node after receiving a message from all but one of its neighbors, sends a message to the neighbor not yet heard from. After time sufficient to hear from all but one neighbor in a worst case tree, if a node has not heard from two neighboring nodes then it has detected that it lies on a cycle and edges to those neighbors are edges on the cycle.

2. *Cycle breaking:* If a node is on a cycle and one or two of its neighboring edges on the cycle are newly marked, for each such edge, it sends a fair coin flip to the other endpoint of the edge. If both endpoints of the edge toss heads, then the edge is unmarked.

3. *Check and fix if necessary:* The cycle detection algorithm is again run to test if there is a cycle. If there still is a cycle, all the newly marked edges in the cycle are unmarked and not included as tree edges in the next phase.

LEMMA 7. *Let c be any constant, $c \geq 1$. With probability $1 - n^{-c}$, there is an algorithm which constructs an ST in time and message complexity $O(n \log n)$.*

PROOF. We analyze Build ST by modifying the analysis of Build MST. We replace Claim 1 from Lemma 3 by the following:

Claim 1-unweighted: Let F be the number of fragments at the start of a phase. Let C be the probability that $FindAny - C$ returns an edge. At the end of the phase there are no more than $(1 - C/8)F$ fragments with probability at least $\alpha = (1 - C/4)/(1 - C/8)$.

Proof of Claim 1-unweighted: Any edge returned by $FindAny - C$ which is not in a cycle formed by edges chosen in a phase by $FindAny - C$, reduces the number of fragments by 1. Any such edge in a cycle reduces the number of fragments by 1 if its cycle is broken and it is not unmarked by both its endpoints. The probability that a newly marked edge e is unmarked by both its endpoints is $1/4$. Every cycle that is formed must have at least two newly marked edges, thus the probability that the cycle containing e is not broken is no greater than $1/2$. The probability that e is unmarked because of either of these events is thus no greater than $3/4$, by a union bound. It follows that the probability that a fragment finds an edge leaving using $FindAny - C$ and that edge reduces the number of fragments by 1 at least $C/4$. Let F' be the number of fragments at the end of the phase. Then $E[F'] \leq (1-C/4)F$. By Markov's Inequality, $Pr[F' > (1 - C/8)F] \leq E[F']/(1 - C/8)F \leq (1 - C/4)/(1 - C/8)$.

Claim 2-unweighted is the same as Claim 2, and its proof is very similar.

We conclude by noting that each phase of executing $FindAny - C$ on disjoint trees requires $O(n)$ messages and $O(\log n/\log\log n)$ time. Since there are $O(\log n)$ phases, the bounds follows.

□

4.3 Repairing an ST

This is a straightforward adaptation of the methods used for repairing an MST, except that $FindAny$ is used in place of $FindMin$ and a factor of $\log n/\log\log n$ is saved from the asymptotic cost.

5. OPEN PROBLEMS AND CONCLUSIONS

We have adapted a technique from streaming and dynamic sequential graphs to find a surprising result, that the problem of constructing a broadcast tree can be done with $O(n \log n)$ messages (and time) in the CONGEST model w.h.p., a problem believed to have a lower bound of $\Omega(m)$ on the number of message for 25 years or more. (In a model allowing much longer messages, it was known how to avoid sending messages over some edges [17]; intuitively, [4] showed that for each such avoided edge, the identity of one of its endpoints needs to be delivered uncompressed to the other endpoint; we have shown that those identities could be compressed significantly if the ID space is of a reasonable size, up to even exponential in n). We also have shown a very simple way to repair ST's and MST's in $O(n)$ and $O(n \log n/\log\log n)$ expected time and messages; previously it was suggested that reducing the message complexity to $o(m)$, requires auxiliary information to be stored between updates. By avoiding the need to (store and) distribute auxiliary information, we also manage to make the $o(m)$ message complexity worst case rather than just amortized as in previous papers. Can these yield practical methods for real dynamic networks?

A number of interesting theoretic problems remain. For ST and MST construction, Can ST be constructed by a deterministic or Las Vegas algorithm in $o(m)$ messages in the K_1 model? What kind of bounds need the nodes know of n? Can these results be made to work in the asynchronous model of communication? Is it possible to form an ST in time less than $O(n \log n)$ with $o(m)$ messages? Finally, are $O(n \log n/\log\log n)$ messages required for $FindMin$ or can this be pushed closer to the cost of $FindAny$?

Acknowledgment: We would like to thank Moni Naor, Gopal Pandurangan, and Ely Porat for useful comments.

6. REFERENCES

[1] Afek, Yehuda, Baruch Awerbuch, and Eli Gafni. Applying static network protocols to dynamic networks. Foundations of Computer Science, 1987., 28th Annual Symposium on. IEEE, 1987.

[2] Awerbuch, B. Optimal distributed algorithms for minimum weight spanning tree, counting, leader election, and related problems. In Proceedings of the nineteenth annual ACM symposium on Theory of computing (pp. 230-240), January 1987.

[3] Baruch Awerbuch, I. Cidon, and S. Kutten. Communication-optimal maintenance of replicated information. In *Foundations of Computer Science, 1990. Proceedings., 31st Annual Symposium on*, pages 492–502 vol.2, 1990.

[4] Baruch Awerbuch, Oded Goldreich, David Peleg, and Ronen Vainish. A Trade-Off between Information and Communication in Broadcast Protocols. J. ACM 37(2): 238-256 (1990)

[5] Baruch Awerbuch, Israel Cidon, and Shay Kutten. Optimal maintenance of a spanning tree. J. ACM 55(4) (2008).

[6] Kook Jin Ahn, Sudipto Guha, and Andrew McGregor. Analyzing graph structure via linear measurements. In *Proceedings of the Twenty-Third Annual ACM-SIAM Symposium on Discrete Algorithms, SODA 2012, Kyoto, Japan, January 17-19, 2012*, pages 459–467, 2012.

[7] M. Blum and S. Kannan. Designing Programs That Check Their Work. STOC 1989: 86–97.

[8] Y. K. Dalal. A distributed algorithm for constructing minimal spanning trees. *IEEE Transactions on Software Engineering*, 13(3), 398–405 (1987).

[9] M. Dietzfelbinger. Universal hashing and k-wise independent random variables via integer arithmetic without primes. In *Proc. 13th STACS, LNCS 1046*, pages 569–580, 1996.

[10] Dijkstra, Edsger W. Self-stabilizing systems in spite of distributed control. Communications of the ACM 17.11 (1974): 643-644.

[11] Elkin, Michael. A faster distributed protocol for constructing a minimum spanning tree. Journal of Computer and System Sciences 72.8 (2006): 1282-1308.

[12] Frederickson, G. N. and Lynch, N. A. (1987). Electing a leader in a synchronous ring. Journal of the ACM (JACM), 34(1), 98-115.âĂŔ

[13] Gallager, R. G., Humblet, P. A., and Spira, P. M. (1983). A distributed algorithm for minimum-weight spanning trees. ACM Transactions on Programming Languages and systems (TOPLAS), 5(1), 66-77.

[14] J. Garay, S. Kutten, and D. Peleg. A sub-linear time distributed algorithm for minimum-weight spanning trees. *FOCS*, 659–668 (1993).

[15] Bruce M. Kapron, Valerie King, and Ben Mountjoy. Dynamic graph connectivity in polylogarithmic worst case time. In *SODA*, pages 1131–1142, 2013.

[16] R.M. Karp and M.O. Rabin. Efficient randomized pattern-matching algorithms. IBM Journal of Research and Development 31 (2): 249–260, 1987.

[17] Ephraim Korach, Shay Kutten, Shlomo Moran. A Modular Technique for the Design of Efficient Distributed Leader Finding Algorithms. ACM Trans. Program. Lang. Syst. 12(1): 84-101 (1990).

[18] Ephraim Korach, Doron Rotem and Nicola Santoro.

Distributed Algorithms for Finding Centers and Medians in Networks, ACM Trans. Program. Lang. Syst., vol. 6, num. 3, pages 380–401, 1984.

[19] Shay Kutten, Gopal Pandurangan, David Peleg, Peter Robinson, and Amitabh Trehan. On the complexity of universal leader election. JACM 62(1): 7:1–27 (2015).

[20] S. Kutten and D. Peleg. Fast distributed construction of k-dominating sets and applications. *PODC*, 238–249 (1995).

[21] Kutten, Shay, and Avner Porat. Maintenance of a spanning tree in dynamic networks. Distributed Computing. Springer Berlin Heidelberg, 1999. 342-355.

[22] Nati Linial. personal communication.

[23] Maroti, M., Kusy, B., Simon, G., and Ledeczi, A. The flooding time synchronization protocol. The 2nd ACM international conference on Embedded networked sensor systems (pp. 39-49), November 2004.

[24] Lamport, Leslie. Paxos made simple. ACM Sigact News 32.4 (2001): 18-25.

[25] Le Lann, Gerard. Distributed Systems-Towards a Formal Approach. IFIP Congress. Vol. 7. 1977.

[26] Ben Mountjoy. Applications of a Novel Sampling Technique to Fully Dynamic Graph Algorithms. (unpublished Masters Thesis supervised by Valerie King, University of Victoria, 2013).

[27] Erik Nygren, Ramesh K. Sitaraman, and Jennifer Sun. The akamai network: a platform for high-performance internet applications. SIGOPS Oper. Syst. Rev., 44(3):2?19, August 2010.

[28] D. Peleg. Distributed Computing: A Locality-Sensitive Approach. SIAM, Philadelphia, PA, 2000.

[29] Perlman, Radia. An algorithm for distributed computation of a spanningtree in an extended LAN. ACM SIGCOMM Computer Communication Review. Vol. 15. No. 4. ACM, 1985.

[30] Schwartz, Jack (October 1980). "Fast probabilistic algorithms for verification of polynomial identities" (pdf). Journal of the ACM 27: 701âĂŞ717.

[31] Shenker, Scott. The future of networking, and the past of protocols. Open Networking Summit (2011).

[32] Adrian Segall. Distributed network protocols. IEEE Transactions on Information Theory, vol. 2, number 1, pages 23–34, 1983.

[33] M. Thorup. `Sample(x)=(a*x<=t)` is a distinguisher with probability 1/8. arXiv:1411.4982v2, 2014.

[34] M. Wegman and J. Carter. New hash functions and their use in authentication and set equality. *J. Comp. Syst. Sci.*, 22:265–279, 1981.

[35] Wieselthier, J. E., Nguyen, G. D., and Ephremides, A. On the construction of energy-efficient broadcast and multicast trees in wireless networks. In INFOCOM 2000. Nineteenth Annual Joint Conference of the IEEE Computer and Communications Societies. Proceedings. IEEE (Vol. 2, pp. 585-594), 2000.

[36] David Zuckerman. Randomness-optimal oblivious sampling. *Random Struct. Algorithms*, 11(4):345–367, 1997.

APPENDIX

A. ACCOMMODATING SUPERPOLYNOMIAL SIZED EDGE WEIGHTS

Suppose the maximum edge weight has w bits where w is the message size. We show that $O(\log n/\log\log n)$ broadcast-and-echoes suffice. In the *FindMin* shown previously, once the range of weights to be searched is set, the range is partitioned into subranges of equal value. Here, we partition the range into subranges based on the weights of randomly chosen edges. We assume w.l.o.g. that edge weights are distinct and an edge is identified by its weight. The string $x \cdot y$ denotes the concatenation of x followed by y. Let $r = \sqrt{\log n/\log\log n}$.

We first introduce the subroutine for sampling non-tree edges incident to nodes in a tree. If we are sampling from a tree T, let S_T (or S if T is understood from the context) be an ordered multiset of non-tree edges, which appear once or twice depending on whether one or two of its endpoints are in T.

Sample(p, j, k): Assumes p is a prefix of j and k. For the r edges drawn uniformly at random from S whose weights are in the range $[j, k]$, returns substrings $v_1, v_2, ..., v_r$, each of length w/r such that $p \cdot v_i$ is a prefix of the selected edge and $v_i \leq v_{i+1}$.

Each node y in a tree T numbers its children $1, ..., last_y$. Let S_i denote the sub-multiset of S_y of edges incident to the subtree rooted at the ith child, and S_{last_y+1} denote the sub-multiset of edges rooted at y itself. Let $z \in \{1, ..., |S_y|\}$; we say z *falls into the range* of a child i's subtree or the parent node (where $i = last_y + 1$) if $\sum_{j<i} |S_j| < z \leq \sum_{j \leq i} |S_j|$.

To implement *Sample*(p, j, k), broadcast-and-echo is done to enable each node y in the tree to determine $|S_i|$ for each of its children. The leader randomly picks r integers between 1 and $|S|$. Let r_i denote the number of integers which falls into the range of S_i. It randomly selects r_{last_y+1} edges from S_{last_y+1}. Otherwise, it sends r_i to child i. Each child i repeats this procedure to select r_i random edges from S_i.

When an edge is chosen for the sample, only the substring v in its weight, $|v| = w/r$ which follows the prefix p is returned. One echo returns these substrings for all r samples in parallel as each node affixes these bits. No more than r substrings are sent to the root in total, of size w/r so that they all fit in one message. We observe that each non-tree edge with prefix p incident to T is picked with probability $1/|S|$ or $2/|S|$.

FindMin for superpolynomial sized weights is like *FindMin* (Section 3.1) for polynomial weights except that the pivots are provided by the weights of the sampled edges rather than being at regular intervals and at each iteration, more of the prefix of the string describing the minimal weight is learned or the size of S which contains the minimal weight edge is reduced by a factor of $r/2$. Below, let $z \cdot \bar{0}$ (resp., $z \cdot \bar{1}$) denote the weight with prefix z followed by all 0's (resp., all 1's).

The following changes to *FindMin* are made:

Insert new line at start:

p is initialized to the empty string.

Step 5:
In parallel for $i = 0, 1, 2, ..., w - 1$:
$j_i \leftarrow j + i\lceil(k - j + 1)/w\rceil$; $k_i \leftarrow j + (i+1)\lceil k - j + 1)/w\rceil - 1$,
and return word in which i^{th} bit is the "echo" of $TestOut(x, j_i, k_i)$

is replaced by:

In parallel for $i = 1, 2, ..., r$:
Set $j_i = p \cdot v_i \cdot \bar{0}$, $k_i = (p \cdot v_{i+1} \cdot \bar{0}) - 1$ and $j_0 = j$, $v_{r+1} = k$
where $Sample(p, j, k)$ returns $v_1, ..., v_r$.
Return word in which i^{th} bit is the "echo" of $TestOut(x, j_i, k_i)$

And Step 7(a):

if $TestLow = 0$ and $TestHigh = 1$
and if $j_{min} < k_{min}$ then x sets $j = j_{min}$ and $k = k_{min}$;
else if $j_{min} = k_{min}$ then x broadcasts "stop" and returns j_{min}.

is replaced by

if $TestLow = 0$ and $TestHigh = 1$
and if $j_{min} < j_{min+1}$, $j \leftarrow j_{min}$ and $k \leftarrow k_{min}$;
else $\{j_{min} = j_{min+1}\}$ $p \leftarrow p \cdot v_{min}$ and if $|p| = |w|$, return p;
else $j \leftarrow p \cdot \{0\}^{w/r}$ and $k \leftarrow p \cdot \{1\}^{w/r}$.

LEMMA 8. *W.h.p., the lightest edge is in the weight interval $[j, k]$, where p is a prefix of j and k, or there is no such edge and the algorithm returns $\emptyset$.*

PROOF. The proof is nearly the same as the proof in the case of polynomial sized weights, except: if j_{min} and j_{min+1} agree then $p \cdot v_{min}$ must be the prefix of the lightest edge weight, w.h.p. If they don't agree, then, as in the original algorithm, w.h.p., the range of the next search is the lowest weight interval which contains an edge leaving the tree, w.h.p. □

LEMMA 9. *In a tree whose nontree edge weights are of length w bits, there is an asynchronous algorithm to find the lightest edge leaving the tree in $O(\log n / \log\log n)$ expected broadcast-and-echoes with message size w.*

PROOF. Correctness follows from the lemma. Let e be the lightest edge leaving the tree. Consider the edges (and possible duplicates) in S ordered by weight. We say a $Sample(p, j, k)$ is successful if it produces two samples s_1, s_2 such that $s_1 \leq e \leq s_2$ and $s_2 - s_1 \leq 2|S|/r$; alternatively (informally, if e is near j then) $s_1 = j$ and $Sample(p, j, k)$ produces such an s_2, or similarly, $s_2 = k$ and it produces such an s_1. It is not hard to see that there is a constant probability of success. Hence if $j_{min} \neq j_{min+1}$, if $Sample$ is successful, $|S|$ in the next round is reduced by a factor of $r/2$. The number of these "successful" samplings needed to shrink the number of such edges to less than r is $O(\log_r |S|)$. Let m be the total number of edges. The expected number of samplings to achieve this many successful rounds is $O(log_r m) \leq \log(n^2)/\log r = O(\log n / \log\log n)$.

On the other hand, if $j_{min} = j_{min+1}$, the lightest edge leaving the tree must have prefix $p \cdot v_{min}$, then we extend the prefix another w/r bits. The maximum number of these samplings is $w/(w/r) = r = \sqrt{\log n / \log\log n}$.

□

Near-Optimal Distributed Maximum Flow

Extended Abstract

Mohsen Ghaffari
Massachusetts Institute of Technology
02139 Cambridge, USA
ghaffari@csail.mit.edu

Andreas Karrenbauer*
MPI for Informatics
66123 Saarbrücken, Germany
karrenba@mpi-inf.mpg.de

Fabian Kuhn
University of Freiburg
79110 Freiburg, Germany
kuhn@cs.uni-freiburg.de

Christoph Lenzen
MPI for Informatics
66123 Saarbrücken, Germany
clenzen@mpi-inf.mpg.de

Boaz Patt-Shamir†
Tel Aviv University
Tel Aviv 6997801, Israel
boaz@tau.ac.il

ABSTRACT

We present a near-optimal distributed algorithm for $(1+o(1))$-approximation of single-commodity maximum flow in undirected weighted networks that runs in $(D+\sqrt{n})\cdot n^{o(1)}$ communication rounds in the CONGEST model. Here, n and D denote the number of nodes and the network diameter, respectively. This is the first improvement over the trivial $O(m)$ time bound, and it nearly matches the $\tilde{\Omega}(D+\sqrt{n})$ round complexity lower bound.

The algorithm contains two sub-algorithms of independent interest, both with running time $(D+\sqrt{n})\cdot n^{o(1)}$:

- Distributed construction of a spanning tree of average stretch $n^{o(1)}$.
- Distributed construction of an $n^{o(1)}$-congestion approximator consisting of the cuts induced by $O(\log n)$ virtual trees. The distributed representation of the cut approximator allows for evaluation in $(D+\sqrt{n})\cdot n^{o(1)}$ rounds.

All our algorithms make use of randomization and succeed with high probability.

Categories and Subject Descriptors

G.2.2 [**Discrete Mathematics**]: Graph Theory—*Network Problems*; F.2.2 [**Analysis of Algorithms and Problem Complexity**]: Non-numerical Algorithms and Problems—*Computations on Discrete Structures*

*Supported by the Max Planck Center for Visual Computing and Communication (www.mpc-vcc.org).

†Supported in part by the Israel Science Foundation (grant no. 1444/14) and by a grant from the Israel Ministry of Science, Technology and Space.

Permission to make digital or hard copies of all or part of this work for personal or classroom use is granted without fee provided that copies are not made or distributed for profit or commercial advantage and that copies bear this notice and the full citation on the first page. Copyrights for components of this work owned by others than the author(s) must be honored. Abstracting with credit is permitted. To copy otherwise, or republish, to post on servers or to redistribute to lists, requires prior specific permission and/or a fee. Request permissions from Permissions@acm.org.
PODC'15, July 21–23, 2015, Donostia-San Sebastián, Spain.
Copyright is held by the owner/author(s). Publication rights licensed to ACM.
ACM 978-1-4503-3617-8 /15/07 ...$15.00.
http://dx.doi.org/10.1145/2767386.2767440.

1. INTRODUCTION

Computing a maximum flow is a fundamental task in network optimization. While the problem has a decades-old history rich with developments and improvements in the sequential setting, little is known in the distributed setting. In fact, prior to this work, the best known distributed time complexity in the standard CONGEST model remained at the trivial bound of $O(m)$, i.e., the time to collect the entire topology and solve locally. In this paper we improve this unsatisfying state of affairs to near-optimality:

THEOREM 1.1. *On undirected weighted graphs, a $(1+\varepsilon)$-approximation of a maximum s-t flow can be computed in $(D+\sqrt{n})\cdot n^{o(1)}\varepsilon^{-3}$ rounds of the CONGEST model with high probability.*

This round complexity almost matches the $\tilde{\Omega}(D+\sqrt{n})$ lower bound of Das Sarma et al. [11], which holds for any non-trivial approximation.

1.1 Related Work

Network flow, being one of the canonical and most useful optimization problems, has been the target of innumerable research efforts since the 1930s [22] (see, e.g., the classic book [2] and the recent survey [12]). However, to the dismay of many, and despite the fact that the word "network" even appears in the problem's name, only little progress was made over the years from the standpoint of distributed algorithms. For example, Goldberg and Tarjan's push-relabel algorithm, which is very local and simple to implement in the CONGEST model, requires $\Omega(n^2)$ rounds to converge, where n is the number of nodes. This is very disappointing, because in the CONGEST model, any problem whose input and output can be encoded with $O(\log n)$ bits per edge, can be trivially solved in $O(m)$ rounds, where m is the number of edges, by collecting all input at a single node, solving it there, and distributing the results back.

Early attempts focused, as customary in those days, on reducing the number of messages in asynchronous executions. For example, Segall [23] gives an $O(nm^2)$-messages, $O(n^2m)$-time algorithm for exact max flow, and Gafni and Marberg [16] give an an algorithm whose message and time complexities are $O(n^2m^{1/2})$. Awerbuch has attacked the problem repeatedly with the following results. In an early work [5] he adapts Dinic's centralized algorithm using a synchronizer, giving rise to an algorithm whose time and message complexities are $O(n^3)$. With Leighton, in [8] they give an algorithm for solving multicommodity flow approximately in $O(\ell m \log m)$ rounds, where $\ell < n$ is the length of the longest flow path. Later he considers the model where each flow path (variable) has an "agent" which can find the congestion of all links on its path in *constant time*. In this model, he shows with Khandekar [6] how to approximate any positive LP (max flow with given routes included) to within $(1-\epsilon)$ in time polynomial in $\log(mnA_{\max}/\epsilon)$ (here n is the number of variables, which is at least the number of paths considered). The same model is used with Khandekar and Rao in [7], where they show how to approximate multicommodity flow to within $(1-\epsilon)$ in $O(\ell \log n)$ rounds. Using a straightforward implementation of this algorithm in the CONGEST model results in running time $\tilde{O}(n^2)$.

Thus, up to the current paper, there was no distributed implementation of a max-flow algorithm which always requires subquadratic number of rounds. Even an $O(n)$-time algorithm would have been considered a significant improvement, even for the 0/1 capacity case.

1.2 The Model

We use the standard CONGEST model of synchronous computation [19]. We are given a connected, weighted graph $G=(V,E,\text{cap})$, where $\text{cap}: E \to \mathbb{N}$, $\text{cap}(e) \in \text{poly}\, n$, are the edge capacities.[1] By D, we denote the (hop) diameter of G. Each of the $n := |V|$ nodes hosts a processor with a unique identifier of $O(\log n)$ bits, and over each of the $m := |E|$ edges $O(\log n)$ bits can be sent in each synchronous round of communication. We assume that nodes have access to infinite strings of independent unbiased random bits. We say that an event occurs *with high probability* (w.h.p.), if it happens with probability $1-n^{-c}$ for any desired constant $c>0$ specified upfront.[2] Initially, each node only knows its identifier, its incident edges, and their capacities.

1.3 The Problem

We fix an arbitrary orientation of the edges. In the following, we write $(u,v) \in E$ if $\{u,v\} \in E$ is directed from u to v. An instance of the (single-commodity) *max flow* problem is specified by a graph G, and by two designated nodes: a *source* denoted s and a *sink* denoted t . A (feasible) *flow of value* $F \in \mathbb{R}$ is a vector $\boldsymbol{f} \in \mathbb{R}^E$ satisfying:

1. capacity constraints (edges): $\forall e \in E: \ |f_e| \le \text{cap}(e)$;
2. conservation constraints (nodes):

$$\forall v \in V \setminus \{s,t\}: \sum_{(u,v)\in E} f_e - \sum_{(v,u)\in E} f_e = 0; \text{ and}$$

3. value constraints (at source and sink):

$$\sum_{(s,u)\in E} f_e - \sum_{(u,s)\in E} f_e = \sum_{(u,t)\in E} f_e - \sum_{(t,u)\in E} f_e = F.$$

A *max flow* is a flow of maximum value. For $\varepsilon > 0$, a $(1+\varepsilon)$-*approximate max flow* is a flow whose value is at most factor $1+\varepsilon$ smaller than that of a max flow. In this work, we focus on solving the problem of finding a $(1+\varepsilon)$-approximate max flow in the above model, where it suffices that each node u learns f_e for each of its incident edges $e=\{u,v\} \in E$.

1.4 Organization of this Article

Our result builds heavily on a few major breakthroughs in the understanding of max flow in the centralized setting, most notably [24], as well as a few other contributions. Due to lack of space, in this paper we focus on the presentation of the key concepts relevant to our results (along with credit).

We start by carefully revisiting Sherman's approach [24] and the main building blocks he relies on in Section 2. This sets the stage for shedding light on the challenges that must be overcome for its distributed implementation and presentation of our results in Section 3. There, we also provide a top-level view of the components of the algorithm; for lack of space, complete proofs are deferred to the full version of the paper. Finally, in Section 4, we outline the distributed construction of an $n^{o(1)}$-*congestion approximator*, which is our key technical contribution; the role of a congestion approximator is to estimate the congestion induced by optimally routing an arbitrary demand vector very quickly, which lies at the heart of the algorithm.

2. OVERVIEW OF THE CENTRALIZED FRAMEWORK

Sherman's approach [24] is based on *gradient descent* (see, e.g., [17]) for *congestion minimization* with a clever dualization of the flow conservation constraints. The flow problem is re-formulated as a *demand vector* $\boldsymbol{b} \in \mathbb{R}^n$ such that $\sum_{i\in V} b_i = 0$. In the case of the s-t flow problem, we have a negative b_s and positive b_t with the same absolute value and the demand is zero everywhere else. The objective is to find a flow $\boldsymbol{f}^*$ that meets the given demand vector, i.e., the total excess flow in node i is equal to b_i, and minimizes the maximum *edge congestion*, which is the ratio of the flow over an edge to its capacity. Formally:

$$\text{minimize } \left\|C^{-1}\boldsymbol{f}\right\|_\infty \text{ subject to } B\boldsymbol{f} = \boldsymbol{b}, \qquad (1)$$

where $C = (C_{ee'})_{e,e'\in E}$ is an $m \times m$ diagonal matrix with

$$C_{ee'} = \begin{cases} \text{cap}(e) & \text{if } e = e' \\ 0 & \text{else}, \end{cases}$$

and $B = (B_{ve})_{v\in V, e\in E}$ is an $n \times m$ matrix with

$$B_{ve} = \begin{cases} 1 & \text{if } e = (u,v) \text{ for some } u \in V \\ -1 & \text{if } e = (v,u) \text{ for some } u \in V \\ 0 & \text{else}. \end{cases}$$

Note that given a general (i.e., unconstrained) flow vector $\boldsymbol{f} \in \mathbb{R}^m$, $(B\boldsymbol{f})_v$ is exactly the excess flow at node v. Hence, by the max-flow min-cut theorem, if we can solve problem (1), a simple binary search will find an approximate max flow.

Instead of directly solving this constrained system, Sherman allows for general vectors and adds a penalty term for any violation of flow constraints, i.e.,

$$\text{minimize } \left\|C^{-1}\boldsymbol{f}\right\|_\infty + 2\alpha \left\|R(\boldsymbol{b} - B\boldsymbol{f})\right\|_\infty,$$

where $\alpha \ge 1$ and the matrix R are chosen so that the optimum of this unconstrained optimization problem does not

[1] As merely an approximate flow is required, we can reduce the general case to this setting in $\tilde{O}((\sqrt{n}+D)\log C)$ rounds, where C is an upper bound on the ratio between the largest and smallest capacity.

[2] Taking the union bound over polynomially many events does not affect this property. We use this fact frequently and implicitly throughout the paper.

violate the flow constraints. As we are interested in an approximate max flow, we can compute an approximate solution and argue that the violation of the flow constraints will be small, too. Then one simply re-routes the remaining flow in a trivial manner, e.g., on a spanning tree, to obtain a near-optimal solution. Finally, to ensure that the objective function is differentiable (i.e., a gradient descent is actually possible), $\|\cdot\|_\infty$ is replaced by the so-called soft-max.

2.1 The Congestion Approximator R

The *congestion* of an edge e (for a given flow $\boldsymbol{f}$) is defined as the ratio $|f_e|/\text{cap}(e)$. When referring to the congestion of a cut in a given flow, we mean the ratio between the net flow crossing the cut to the total capacity of the cut. Suppose for a moment that $\alpha = 1$ and R contains one row for each cut of the graph, chosen such that each entry of the vector $RB\boldsymbol{f}$ equals the congestion of the corresponding cut. In particular, R would correctly reproduce the congestion of min cuts (which give rise to maximal congestion). Moreover, the vector $R\boldsymbol{b}$ describes the inevitable congestion of the cuts for any feasible flow. Thus, the components of $R(\boldsymbol{b} - B\boldsymbol{f})$ are the residual congestions to be dealt with to make $\boldsymbol{f}$ feasible (neglecting possible cancellations). The max-flow min-cut theorem and the factor of 2 in the second term of the objective function imply that it always improves the value of the objective function to route the demands arising from a violation of flow constraints optimally. Moreover, the gradient descent concentrates on the most congested edges and those that are contained in cuts with the top residual congestion. In particular, flow is pushed over the edges into the cut with the highest residual congestion to satisfy its demand until other cuts become more important in the second part of the objective. The first part of the objective impedes flow on edges the more they are congested (on an absolute scale and relative to others). Thus, approximately minimizing the objective function is equivalent to simultaneously approximating the minimum congestion and having small violation of flow constraints; solving up to polynomially small error and naively resolving the remaining violations then yields sufficiently accurate results.

Unfortunately, trying to make R capture congestion *exactly* is far too inefficient. Instead, one uses an α-*congestion approximator*, that is a matrix R such that for any demand vector $\boldsymbol{b}$, it holds that

$$\|R\boldsymbol{b}\|_\infty \leq \text{opt}(\boldsymbol{b}) \leq \alpha \|R\boldsymbol{b}\|_\infty ,$$

where $\text{opt}(\boldsymbol{b})$ is the maximum congestion caused on any cut by optimally routing $\boldsymbol{b}$. Since the second term in the objective function is scaled up by factor α, we are still guaranteed that optimally routing any unsatisfied demands improves the objective function. However, this implies that the second term of the objective function may dominate its gradient and thus emphasis is shifted rather to feasiblity than optimality. Sherman proves that this slows down the gradient descent by at most a factor of α^2, i.e., if $\alpha \in n^{o(1)}$, so is the number of iterations of the gradient descent algorithm that need to be performed.

2.2 Congestion Approximators: Räcke's Construction

For any spanning tree T of G, deleting an edge partitions the nodes into two connected components and thus induces an (edge) cut of G. Note that on T, this cut contains only the single deleted edge, and in terms of congestion any cut of T is dominated by such an edge-induced cut: For any cut, the maximum congestion of an edge is at least the average congestion of the cut, and in T, there is a cut containing only this edge.

These basic properties motivate the question of how well the cut structure of an arbitrary graph can be approximated by trees. Intuitively, the goal is to find a tree T (not necessarily a subgraph) spanning all nodes with edge weights such that routing *any* demand vector in G and in T results in roughly the same maximal congestion. Because routing flows on trees is trivial, such a tree T would give rise to an efficient congestion approximator R: R would consist of one row for each cut induced by an edge (u, v) of T with capacity C, where the matrix entry corresponding to node w is $1/C$ if w is on u's "side" of the cut and 0 otherwise; multiplying a demand vector with the row then yields the flow that needs to pass through (u, v) divided by the capacity of the cut.

In a surprising result [21], Räcke showed that, using multiplicative weight updates (see e.g. [4, 20, 25]), one can construct a distribution of $\tilde{O}(m)$ trees so that (i) in each tree of the distribution, each cut has at least the same capacity as in G and (ii) given any cut of G of total capacity C, sampling from the distribution results in a tree T where this cut has *expected* capacity $O(\alpha C)$; here α is the approximation ratio of a *low average stretch spanning tree* algorithm Räcke's construction uses as subroutine. Note that this bound on the expectation implies that for any cut of capacity C, there must be a tree in the distribution for which the cut has capacity $O(\alpha C)$. Hence, the cuts given by *all* trees in the distribution give rise to an $O(\alpha)$-congestion approximator R with $\tilde{O}(mn)$ rows.

2.3 Low Average Stretch Spanning Trees

In order to perform Räcke's construction, one requires an efficient algorithm for computing low average stretch spanning trees. More precisely, given a graph $G = (V, E, \ell)$ with polynomially bounded lengths $\ell : E \to \mathbb{N}$, the goal is to construct a spanning tree T of G so that

$$\sum_{\{u,v\}\in E} d_T(u, v) \leq \alpha \sum_{\{u,v\}\in E} \ell(\{u, v\}) ,$$

where $d_T(u, v)$ is the sum of the lengths of the unique path from u to v in T and α is the *stretch* factor.

Sherman's algorithm builds on a sophisticated low average stretch spanning tree algorithm that achieves $\alpha \in O(\log n \log^2 \log n)$ within $\tilde{O}(m)$ centralized steps [1]. We use a simpler approach providing $\alpha \in 2^{O(\sqrt{\log n \log\log n})}$ [3] that has been shown to parallelize well, i.e., has an efficient implementation in the PRAM model [10].

2.4 Congestion Approximators: Madry's Construction

Räcke's construction has the drawback that one needs to sequentially compute a linear number of trees, which is prohibitively expensive from our point of view as well as Sherman's. Madry generalized Räcke's approach to a construction resulting in a distribution over $\tilde{O}(m/j)$ so-called j-*trees* [15], where j is a parameter. A j-tree consists of a *forest* of j connected components (trees) and a *core graph*, which is an arbitrary connected graph with j nodes: one from each tree (see Fig. 1).

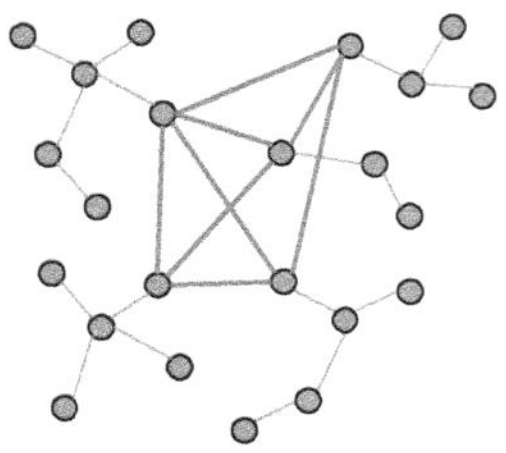

Figure 1: A 5-tree with core links depicted in brown.

The properties of the distribution are the same as for Räcke's: sampling from the distribution preserves cut capacities up to an expected $O(\alpha)$-factor, where α is the stretch of the utilized spanning tree algorithm. Likewise, using all (dominant) cuts of all j-trees in the distribution to construct R yields an $O(\alpha)$-congestion approximator. Note that any cut in a j-tree is *dominated* by either a cut induced by an edge of the forest, or by a cut of the core, in the following sense: Consider any demand vector and any "mixed" cut. If there is an edge in the forest crossing the cut that has at least the same congestion as the whole cut, then the cut induced by the forest edge dominates the mixed cut. Otherwise, we can remove all forest edges from the mixed cut without reducing its congestion. As routing demands in the forest part of the graph is trivial, Madry's construction can be seen as an efficient reduction of the problem size.

2.5 Congestion Approximators: Combining Cut Sparsifiers and Madry's Construction

Using j-trees, Sherman derives a suitable congestion approxmiator, i.e., one with $\alpha \in n^{o(1)}$ that can be constructed and evaluated in $\tilde{O}(m + n^{1+o(1)})$ rounds, as follows. First, a *cut sparsifier* is applied to G. A $(1+\varepsilon)$-sparsifier computes a subgraph of G with modified edge weights so that the capacities of all cuts are preserved up to factor $1+\varepsilon$. It is known how to compute a $(1+o(1))$-sparsifier with $\tilde{O}(n)$ edges in $\tilde{O}(m)$ steps [9]. As the goal is merely to compute a congestion approximator with $\alpha \in n^{o(1)}$, the multiplicative $1+o(1)$ approximation error is negligible. Hence, this essentially breaks the problem of computing a congestion approximator down to the same problem on sparse graphs.

Next, Sherman applies Madry's construction with $j = n/\beta$, where $\beta = 2^{\sqrt{\log n}}$. This yields a distribution of $\tilde{O}(\beta)$ many n/β-trees. The issue is now that the cores are arbitrary graphs, implying that it may be difficult to evaluate congestion for cuts in the cores. However, the number of nodes in the core is $n' = n/\beta$. Thus, recursion does the trick: apply the cut sparsifier to the core, use Madry's construction on the resulting graph (with $j' = n'/\beta = n/\beta^2$), rinse and repeat. In total, there are $\log_\beta n = \sqrt{\log n}$ levels of recursion until the core becomes trivial, i.e., we arrive at a tree. For each level of Sherman's recursion, the approximation ratio deteriorates by a multiplicative $\alpha \in \operatorname{polylog} n$, where α is the stretch factor of the low-stretch spanning tree algorithm, and a multiplicative $1+o(1)$, for applying the cut sparsifier. This yields an α'-congestion approximator with

$$\alpha' \in ((1+o(1))\alpha)^{\sqrt{\log n}} \subset 2^{O(\sqrt{\log n}\log\log n)} \subset n^{o(1)}.$$

While the total number of constructed trees is $\tilde{O}(\beta^{\log_\beta n}) = \tilde{O}(n)$, the number of nodes in a graph (i.e., a core from the previous level) on the ith level of recursion is only n/β^{i-1}. The cut sparsifier ensures that the number of edges in this graph is reduced to $\tilde{O}(n/\beta^{i-1})$ *before* recursing. Since the number of edges in the core is (trivially) bounded by the number of edges of the graph in Madry's construction, the total number of sequential computation steps for computing the distribution is thus bounded by

$$\tilde{O}(m) + \sum_{i=1}^{\log_\beta n} \tilde{O}(\beta^i \cdot n/\beta^{i-1}) \subset \tilde{O}(m + n^{1+o(1)}).$$

2.6 Step Complexity of the Flow Algorithm

The above recursive structure can also be exploited to *evaluate* the α'-congestion approximator Sherman uses in $n^{1+o(1)}$ steps. The cuts of a j-tree are dominated by those induced by edges of the forest and those which are crossed by core edges only (cf. Fig. 1). In the forest component, routing demands is unique, takes linear time in the number of nodes (simply start at the leaves), and results in a modified demand vector at the core on which we recurse.

Sherman proves that his algorithm obtains a $(1+\varepsilon)$-approximate flow in $O(\varepsilon^{-3}\alpha^2\log^2 n)$ gradient descent steps, provided R is an α-congestion approximator.[3] It is straightforward to see (cf. Section 5.1) that each of these steps requires $O(m)$ computational steps besides doing two matrix-vector multiplications with R and $R^\top$, respectively. Using the above observation and plugging in the time to construct the (implicit) representation of R, one arrives at a total step complexity of $\tilde{O}(mn^{o(1)})$.

3. DISTRIBUTED ALGORITHM: CONTRIBUTION AND KEY IDEAS

For a distributed implementation of Sherman's approach, many subproblems need to be solved (sufficiently fast) in the CONGEST model. We summarize them in the following list, where stars indicate that these components are readily available from prior work.

* Decomposing trees into $O(\sqrt{n})$ components of strong diameter $O(\sqrt{n})$, within $\tilde{O}(\sqrt{n}+D)$ rounds. This can, e.g., be done by techniques pioneered by Kutten and Peleg for the purpose of minimum-weight spanning tree construction [14].
* Constructing cut sparsifiers. Koutis [13] provides a solution that completes in polylog n rounds of the CONGEST model. We prove a simulation result for use in the recursive construction.

1. Constructing low average stretch spanning trees on multigraphs.
2. Applying the construction of Madry in the CONGEST model, even when recursing in the context of Sherman's framework.
3. Sampling from the recursively constructed distribution.
4. Avoiding the use of the entire distribution for constructing the congestion approximator (see below).
5. Performing a gradient descent step. This involves, e.g., matrix-vector multiplications with R, $R^\top$ and C^{-1}, evaluation of the soft-max, etc.

[3] Sherman mentions that Nesterov's accelerated gradient descent method [18] could reduce this to $O(\varepsilon^{-2}\alpha\log^2 n)$ steps.

3.1 Low Average Stretch Spanning Trees

THEOREM 3.1. *Suppose H is a multigraph obtained from G by assigning arbitrary edge lengths in $\left[2^{n^{o(1)}}\right]$ to the edges of G and performing an arbitrary sequence of contractions. Then we can compute a spanning tree of H of expected stretch $2^{O(\sqrt{\log n \log\log n})}$ within $(\sqrt{n}+D)n^{o(1)}$ rounds.*

To obtain this theorem, we translate a PRAM algorithm by Blelloch et al. [10] to the CONGEST model. The main issue when transitioning from the PRAM to the CONGEST model is that in the PRAM model, information about distant parts of the graph may be readily accessed. In the CONGEST model, we handle this by pipelining long-distance communication over a global BFS tree of G; communication over $O(\sqrt{n})$ hops is handled using the edges that have already been selected for inclusion into the spanning tree and spanning trees of the contracted regions of G.

3.2 Implementing Madry's Scheme

This is technically the most challenging part. Also here, we have to overcome the difficulty of potentially needing to communicate a large amount of information over many hops; doing this naively results in too much contention and thus slow algorithms. We approach this by modifying Madry's construction so that:

- Instead of "aggregating" edges so that the core becomes a graph, we admit a multigraph as core.
- We do not explicitly construct the core. Instead, we simulate both the sparsifier and the low average stretch spanning tree algorithm using the abstraction of *cluster graphs.*
- In doing so, we maintain that every core edge is also a graph edge. This enables to handle all communication over this edge by using the corresponding graph edge.
- The cluster hierarchy that is established during the construction permits a straightforward recursive evaluation of the corresponding congestion approximator.

3.3 Sampling from the Distribution

This is now straightforward, because for each sample, on each level of the recursion we need to construct only $n^{o(1)}$ different j-trees for some j.

THEOREM 3.2 (INFORMAL). *Within $\tilde{O}((\sqrt{n}+D)\cdot\beta)$ rounds of the CONGEST model, we can sample a virtual tree from the distribution used in Sherman's framework, where $\tilde{O}(\beta)$ is the number of j-trees in the distribution constructed when recursing on a core. The distributed representation allows to evaluate the dominant cuts of the tree when using it in a congestion approximator within $\tilde{O}(\sqrt{n}+D)$ rounds.*

3.4 Avoiding the Use of the entire Distribution for the Congestion Approximator

While Sherman can afford to use all trees in the (recursively constructed) distribution, the above theorem is not strong enough to allow for fast evaluation of all $\tilde{\Theta}(n)$ trees. As Madry points out [15], it suffices to sample and use $O(\log n)$ j-trees from the distribution he constructs to speed up any β-approximation algorithm for an "undirected cut-based minimization problem", at the expense of an increased approximation ratio of $2\alpha\beta$, where α is the approximation ratio of the congestion approximator corresponding to the distribution of j-trees. The reasoning is as follows:

- The number of cuts that need to be considered for such a problem is polynomially bounded.
- The expected approximation ratio for any fixed cut when sampling from the distribution is α. By Markov's bound, with probability at least $1/2$ it is at most 2α.
- For $O(\log n)$ samples, the union bound shows that w.h.p. *all* relevant cuts are 2α-approximated.
- Applying a β-approximation algorithm relying on the samples only, which can be evaluated much faster, results in a $2\alpha\beta$-approximation w.h.p.

Recall that the problem of approximating a max flow was translated to minimizing congestion for demands $-F$ and F at s and t and performing binary search over F. The max-flow min-cut theorem implies the respective congestion to be the function of a single cut, which can be used to verify that the problem falls under Madry's definition.

Unfortunately, applying the sampling strategy as indicated by Madry is infeasible in Sherman's framework. As the goal is a $(1+\varepsilon)$-approximation, applying it to the above problem directly will yield a too inaccurate approximation. Alternatively, we can apply it in the construction of a congestion approximator. However, a congestion approximator must return a good approximation for *any* demand vector. There are exponentially many such vectors even if we restrict $\boldsymbol{b}\in\{-1,0,1\}^n$, and we are not aware of any result showing that the number of min-cuts corresponding to the respective optimal flows is polynomially bounded.

We resolve this issue with the following simple, but essential insight, at the expense of squaring the approximation ratio of the resulting congestion approximator.

LEMMA 3.3. *Suppose we are given a distribution of poly n trees so that given any cut of G of capacity C, sampling from the distribution results in a tree whose corresponding cut has at least capacity C and at most capacity αC in expectation. Then sampling $O(\log n)$ such trees and constructing a congestion approximator from their single-edge induced cuts results in a $2\alpha^2$-congestion approximator of G w.h.p.*

PROOF. Recall that cut approximators estimate the maximum congestion when optimally routing an arbitrary demand. Consider any demand vector and denote by C the capacity of the corresponding cut that is most congested when routing the demand. As sampling from the distribution yields approximation factor α in expectation, there must be *some* tree T in the distribution whose corresponding cut has capacity at most αC. However, this means that when routing the demand via T, there is some edge in T that experiences at least $1/\alpha$ times the maximum congestion when routing the demand optimally in G. As the capacity of the edge is at least that of the corresponding cut in G, it follows that the corresponding cut of G has congestion at least $1/\alpha$ of that of the min-cut when routing the demand.

As there are poly n trees, each of which has $n-1$ edges, this shows that for any demand vector there is one of polynomially many cuts of G that experience at least $1/\alpha$ times the maximum congestion when optimally routing the demand vector. By Markov's bound and the union bound, w.h.p. the congestion on each of these cuts will be approximated up to another factor of 2α when using $O(\log n)$ samples. □

3.5 Performing a Gradient Descent Step

Most of the high-level operations required for executing a gradient descent algorithm are straightforward to implement using direct communication between neighbors or broadcast and convergecast operations on a BFS tree. The most involved part is multiplying the (implicitly constructed) congestion approximator R with an arbitrary demand vector $\boldsymbol{b}$, and multiplying the transposed of the approximator matrix, $R^\top$, with a given vector that specifies a *cost* for each edge of the trees.

Multiplying by R is done by exploiting that routing on trees is trivial and using standard techniques: during the construction, we already decomposed each tree into $O(\sqrt{n})$ components of strong diameter $O(\sqrt{n})$, which can be used to solve partially by contracting components, make the resulting tree of $O(\sqrt{n})$ nodes globally known, then determine modified demand vectors for the components out of the now locally computable partial solution, and finally resolve these remaining demands within each component. Multiplication with $R^\top$ is implemented using similar ideas. We refer to Section 5 for a detailed discussion of these procedures. Plugging the building blocks outlined in this section into this machinery, we obtain our main result Theorem 1.1.

4. THE DISTRIBUTED CONGESTION APPROXIMATOR CONSTRUCTION

In this section, we outline how to adapt Madry's construction to its recursive application in the distributed setting. We formally prove that we achieve the same guarantees as Madry's distribution [15] in each recursive step and that our distributed implementation is fast. Here, we focus on presenting the main ideas of the required modifications to Madry's scheme and its distributed implementation; to this end, it suffices to consider a single step of the recursion.

4.1 Centralized Algorithm

As a starting point, let us summarize the main steps of one iteration of the centralized construction. We state a slightly simplified variant of Madry's construction, which offers the same worst-case performance and is a better starting point for what follows. From the previous step of constructing the distribution, an edge length function ℓ_e is known (in the distributed setting, this knowledge will be local). Given $j \leq n-1$, the following construction yields a $\Theta(j)$-tree.

1. Compute a spanning tree $\mathcal{T}$ of G of stretch α.
2. For each edge $e = \{v, w\} \in E$ of the graph G, route $\mathrm{cap}(e)$ units of a commodity com_e from v to w on (the unique path from v to w in) $\mathcal{T}$.[4] Denote by $\boldsymbol{f}$ the vector of the sum of absolute flows passing through the edges of $\mathcal{T}$. Recall that $\max_{e\in E}\{\mathrm{cap}(e)\} \in \mathrm{poly}\, n$ and thus $\|\boldsymbol{f}\|_\infty \in \mathrm{poly}(n)$.
3. For $e \in \mathcal{T}$, define the *relative load* of e as $\mathrm{rload}(e) := |f_e|/\mathrm{cap}(e) \in \mathrm{poly}\, n$. We decompose the edge set of $\mathcal{T}$ into $O(\log n)$ subsets $\mathcal{F}_i$, $i \in \{1, \ldots, \lceil \log(\|\boldsymbol{f}\|_\infty + 1)\rceil\}$, where $e \in \mathcal{T}$ is in $\mathcal{F}_i$ if $\mathrm{rload}(e) \in (R/2^i, R/2^{i-1}]$ for $R := \max_{e\in\mathcal{T}}\{\mathrm{rload}(e)\}$. As $\mathcal{T}$ has $n-1 \geq j$ edges, there must be some $\mathcal{F}_i$ with $\Omega(j/\log n)$ edges; let i_0 be minimal with this property. Define $\mathcal{F} := \{e \in \mathcal{T} \mid \mathrm{rload}(e) > 2^{i_0-1}\}$. Note that $|\mathcal{F}| \leq j$.
4. $\mathcal{T} \setminus \mathcal{F}$ is a spanning forest of at most $j+1$ components. Define H as the graph on node set V whose edge set is the union of $\mathcal{T} \setminus \mathcal{F}$ and all edges of G between different components of $(V, \mathcal{T} \setminus \mathcal{F})$.
5. For components C and C' of $(V, \mathcal{T}\setminus\mathcal{F})$, pick arbitrary $v \in C$ and $w \in C'$ and denote by $p(C, C') \in C$ the last node from C on the v-w path in $\mathcal{T}$; note that $p(C, C')$ does not depend on the choice of v and w. Denote by P the set of such *portals*. Replace all edges between different components C, C' of $(V, \mathcal{T} \setminus \mathcal{F})$ by parallel edges $\{p(C, C'), p(C', C)\}$ (of the same capacity).
6. In the resulting multigraph, iteratively delete nodes from $V \setminus P$ of degree 1 until no such node remains. Note that the leaves of the induced subtree of $\mathcal{T}$ must be in P, showing that the number of remaining nodes in $V \setminus P$ of degree larger than 2 is bounded by $|P| - 1 < 2j$. Add all such nodes to P.
7. For each path with endpoints in P and no inner nodes in P, delete an edge of minimum capacity and replace it by an edge of the same capacity between its endpoints.
8. Re-add the nodes and edges of $\mathcal{T} \setminus \mathcal{F}$ that have been deleted in Step 6.
9. For any $p, q \in P$, merge all parallel edges $\{p, q\}$ into a single one whose capacity is the sum of the individual capacities. The result is a j'-tree for $j' = |P| < 4j$.

In his paper, Madry provides a scheme for updating the edge lengths between iterations so that this construction results in a distribution on $\tilde{O}(m/j)$ $\Theta(j)$-trees that approximate cuts up to an expected $O(\alpha)$-factor, where α is the stretch of the spanning tree construction. Updating the edge length function poses no challenges, so we will focus on the distributed implementation of the above steps in this section.

4.2 Modifications to the Centralized Algorithm

Before we come to the distributed algorithm, let us first discuss a few changes we make to the algorithm in centralized terms. These do not affect the reasoning underlying the scheme, but greatly simplify its distributed implementation.

- We will omit the last step of the algorithm and instead operate on cores that are multigraphs. This changes the computed distribution, as we formally use a different graph as input to the recursion. However, Räcke's arguments (and Madry's generalization) work equally well on multigraphs, as one can see by replacing each edge of the multigraph by a path of length 2, where both edges have the same capacity as the original edge. This recovers a graph of $2m$ edges from a multigraph of m edges without affecting the cut structure, and the resulting trees can be interpreted as trees on the multigraph by contraction of the previously expanded edges. Similarly, both the low average stretch spanning tree construction and the cut sparsifier work on multigraphs without modification.
- After computing the spanning tree, we will immediately delete a subset of $\tilde{O}(\sqrt{n})$ edges to ensure that the new clusters will have low-depth spanning trees. The deleted edges are replaced by all edges of G crossing the corresponding cuts and will end up in the core. The same procedure is, in fact, applied to all edges selected into $\mathcal{F}$ in Step 3 of the centralized routine; Madry's arguments show that removing *any* subset of edges of $\mathcal{T}$ and replacing it this way can only improve the quality of cut approximation. The main point of his analysis is that choosing $\mathcal{F}$ in the way he does guar-

[4]The difference to a single commodity is simply that flows in opposing directions do not cancel out. This means that *any* given feasible (i.e., congestion-1) flow in G can be routed on T with at most the congestion of this multi-commodity flow.

antees that, in terms of constructing the final distribution of j-trees, progress proportional to the number of edges in $\mathcal{R}_{i_0}$ is made. We will apply the construction to cores of size $n' \gg \tilde{O}(\sqrt{n})$, which implies that removing the additional edges has asymptotically no effect on the progress guarantee.
- In the counterpart to Step 6 in Madry's routine, also nodes from P may be removed if their degree becomes 1. Also here, there is no asymptotic difference in the worst-case performance of our routine from Madry's.

To simplify the presentation, in this section we will assume that all trees involved in the construction have depth $\tilde{O}(\sqrt{n})$. This means that we can omit the deletion of $\tilde{O}(\sqrt{n})$ additional edges and further related technicalities. The general case is handled by standard techniques for decomposing trees into $O(\sqrt{n})$ components of depth $\tilde{O}(\sqrt{n})$ and relying on a BFS tree to communicate "summaries" of the components to all nodes in the graph within $\tilde{O}(\sqrt{n}+D)$ rounds. This approach was first used for MST construction [14]; we use a simpler randomized variant.

4.3 Cluster Graphs

Recall that we will recursively call (a variant of) the above centralized procedure on the core. We need to simulate the algorithm on the core by communicating on G. To this end, we will use *cluster graphs*, in which G is decomposed into components that play the role of core nodes We maintain the following invariants during the recursion:

1. There is a one-to-one correspondence between nodes of the core and *clusters*.
2. Each cluster c has a rooted spanning tree of depth $\tilde{O}(\sqrt{n})$.
3. No other edges exist inside clusters. Contracting clusters yields the multigraph resulting from the above construction without Step 9. From now on, we will refer to this multigraph as the core.
4. All edges in the (non-contracted) graph are also edges of G, and their endpoints know their lengths from the previous iteration of the recursion.

4.4 Overview of the Distributed Routine

We follow the same strategy as the centralized algorithm, with the modifications discussed above. This implies that the core edges for the next recursive call will simply be the graph edges between the newly constructed clusters. The following sketches the main steps of the distributed implementation of our overall approach.

1. Compute a spanning tree $\mathcal{T}$ of stretch α of the core. This is done by the spanning tree algorithm of Theorem 3.1, which can operate on the cluster graph.
2. For each edge $e \in \mathcal{T}$, determine its absolute flow $|f_e|$ (and thus $\text{rload}(e) = |f_e|/\text{cap}(e)$) as follows (cf. Fig. 2).
   (*) For each cluster c, consider the cut induced by the edge to its parent. For each "side" of the cut, we want to determine the total capacity of all edges incident to nodes of c that connect to the respective side of the cut. Denote by c_+ the total "outgoing" capacity of cluster c towards the root's side and by c_- the "incoming" capacity.
   (a) Each cluster c learns its ancestor clusters in the spanning tree of C.
   (b) Observe that for a cluster c, an edge does contribute to c_- if and only if it connects to a node within its subtree $\mathcal{T}_c$. From the previous step, this information is known to one of the endpoints of the edge. We communicate this and determine in each cluster c the values c_+ and c_- by aggregation on its spanning tree.
   (c) Suppose $e \in \mathcal{T}$ is the edge from cluster c to its parent. Using aggregation on the spanning tree of C, we compute $|f_e| = \sum_{c' \in \mathcal{T}_c} c'_+ - c'_-$.
3. Determine the index i_0 (as in Step 3 of the centralized routine). Given that $\text{rload}(e)$ for each $e \in \mathcal{T}$ is locally known, this is done in $\tilde{O}(D)$ rounds using binary search in combination with converge- and broadcasts on a BFS tree. We set $\mathcal{F} := \{e \in \mathcal{T} \mid \text{rload}(e) > 2^{i_0-1}\}$.
4. Define P as the set of clusters incident to edges in $\mathcal{F}$. A simple broadcast on the cluster spanning trees makes membership known to all nodes of each cluster $c \in P$.
5. Iteratively mark clusters $c \notin P$ with at most one unmarked neighboring cluster, until this process stops. Add all unmarked clusters that retain more than 2 unmarked neighboring clusters to P.
6. For each path with endpoints in P whose inner nodes are unmarked clusters not in P, find the edge $e \in \mathcal{T} \setminus \mathcal{F}$ of minimal capacity and add it to $\mathcal{F}$. This disconnects any two clusters $c, c' \in P$, $c \neq c'$, in $\mathcal{T} \setminus \mathcal{F}$.
7. Each component of $\mathcal{T} \setminus \mathcal{F}$ and the spanning trees of clusters induce a spanning tree of the corresponding component of G. Each such component is a new cluster. Make the identifier of the unique $c \in P$ of each cluster known to its nodes and delete all edges between nodes in the cluster not being part of its spanning tree.

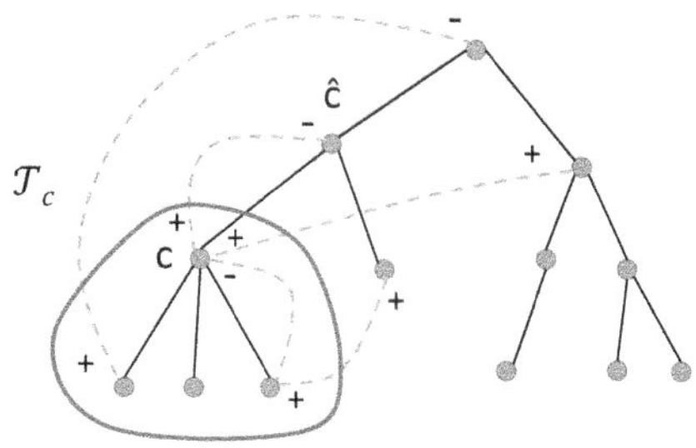

Figure 2: Illustration of the underlying idea of the aggregation scheme for the cut capacities. The cut corresponding to edge $(c, \hat{c})$ of the tree has a total capacity given by all graph edges leaving the subtree $\mathcal{T}_c$. By labeling the endpoint of graph edge by "+" if it leaves the subtree and by "−" if it connects to a descendant, the cut capacity is thus the sum of all capacities of edges labeled "+" minus all those of edges labeled "−" within $\mathcal{T}_c$.

If all trees have depth $\tilde{O}(\sqrt{n})$, all the above steps can be completed in $\tilde{O}(\sqrt{n}+D)$ rounds. Clearly, the first three stated invariants are satisfied by the given construction. As mentioned earlier, it is also straightforward to update the edge lengths, i.e., establish the fourth invariant. Once the distribution on the current level of recursion is computed, one can hence sample and then move on to the next level.

5. THE HIGH-LEVEL ALGORITHM

The algorithm is a distributed implementation of Sherman's algorithm [24]. It consists of a logarithmic number of calls to algorithm AlmostRoute and one computation of a maximum-weight spanning tree and routing the left-over demand through this tree. Most of this section is dedicated to explaining how to implement the AlmostRoute algorithm.

Let us first quickly outline how we implement the final steps using standard techniques.

LEMMA 5.1. *Routing the leftover demands over an MST can be implemented in the* CONGEST *model in* $\tilde{O}(D + \sqrt{n})$ *rounds w.h.p.*

PROOF SKETCH. A maximum weight spanning tree T can be computed in $\tilde{O}(D + \sqrt{n})$ rounds using the minimum weight spanning tree algorithm of Kutten and Peleg [14]. To compute the flow, we use the following observation: if T was rooted at one of its nodes, then to route the demand over T, it would suffice for each node v to learn the total demand d_v in the subtree rooted at v. Then, v assigns d_v units of flow to the edge leading from v to its parent.

We now show how to root the tree and find the total demand in each subtree in $\tilde{O}(D + \sqrt{n})$ rounds. The algorithm is as follows. Remove each edge of the tree independently with probability $1/\sqrt{n}$. W.h.p.,

(i) each connected component induced by the remaining edges contains has strong diameter $\tilde{O}(\sqrt{n})$,
(ii) $O(\sqrt{n})$ edges are removed, and hence
(iii) the number of components is $O(\sqrt{n})$.

Within each component, all demands are summed up, and this sum is made known to all nodes. The summation takes $\tilde{O}(\sqrt{n})$ rounds due to (i), and we can pipeline the announcement over a BFS tree in $\tilde{O}(\sqrt{n} + D)$ rounds due to (iii).

Moreover, in this time we can also assign unique identifiers to the components (e.g., the minimum identifier) and make the tree resulting from contracting components globally known. Using local computation only, nodes then can root this tree (e.g. at the cluster of minimum identifier) and determine the sum the demands of the clusters that are fully contained in their subtree. Using a simple broadcast, the orientation of edges within components is determined, and using a convergecast on the components, each node can determine the sum of demands in its subtree. These steps take another $\tilde{O}(\sqrt{n})$ rounds. □

5.1 Algorithm AlmostRoute: the Gradient Descent

We now explain how to implement Algorithm AlmostRoute in a distributed setting. The idea is to use gradient descent with the potential function

$$\phi(\boldsymbol{f}) = \operatorname{smax}(C^{-1}\boldsymbol{f}) + \operatorname{smax}(2\alpha R(\boldsymbol{b} - B\boldsymbol{f})) \ ,$$

where the "soft-max" function, defined by

$$\operatorname{smax}(\boldsymbol{y}) = \log\left(\sum_{i=1}^{k} e^{y_i} + e^{-y_i}\right) \quad \text{for all } \boldsymbol{y} \in \mathbb{R}^k \ ,$$

is used as a differentiable approximation to the max-norm.

AlmostRoute performs $O(\alpha^2\varepsilon^{-3}\log n)$ iterations to compute a flow $\boldsymbol{f}$ optimizing the potential up to factor $(1+\varepsilon)$. Pseudocode for this algorithm is given in Algorithm 1.

To implement this algorithm in a distributed setting, we need to compute R, and multiply by R or its transpose $R^\top$. These multiplications are required for computing $\phi(\boldsymbol{f})$ and and its partial derivatives. We remark that R and $R^\top$ are not constructed explicitly, as we need to ensure a small time complexity for each iteration. Assuming that we can perform these operations, each step of AlmostRoute can be completed in $\tilde{O}(D)$ additional rounds.

Algorithm 1 AlmostRoute$(\boldsymbol{b}, \varepsilon)$

1: $k_b \leftarrow 2\alpha \|R\boldsymbol{b}\|_\infty \varepsilon/(16\log n)$; $\boldsymbol{b} \leftarrow k_b\boldsymbol{b}$.
2: **repeat**
3: $\quad k_f \leftarrow 1$
4: $\quad$ **while** $\phi(\boldsymbol{f}) < 16\varepsilon^{-1}\log n$ **do**
5: $\quad\quad \boldsymbol{f} \leftarrow \boldsymbol{f}\cdot(17/16)$; $\boldsymbol{b} \leftarrow \boldsymbol{b}\cdot(17/16)$; $k_f \leftarrow k_f\cdot(17/16)$
6: $\quad \delta \leftarrow \sum_{e\in E} |\operatorname{cap}(e)\frac{\partial\phi}{\partial f_e}|$
7: $\quad$ **if** $\delta \geq \varepsilon/4$ **then**
8: $\quad\quad f_e \leftarrow f_e - \operatorname{sgn}\left(\frac{\partial\phi}{\partial f_e}\right)\cdot \operatorname{cap}(e)\frac{\delta}{1+4\alpha^2}$
9: $\quad$ **else**
10: $\quad\quad f_e \leftarrow f_e/k_f$ for all edges $e \in E$.
11: $\quad\quad b_v \leftarrow b_v/(k_b k_f)$ for all nodes $v \in V$
12: $\quad\quad$ **return**
13: **until** done

We maintain the invariant that at the beginning of each iteration of the **repeat** loop, each node v knows the current flow over each of the links v is incident to, and the current demand at v (i.e., $(\boldsymbol{b} - B\boldsymbol{f})_v$). Let us break the potential function ϕ in two, i.e.,

$$\phi(\boldsymbol{f}) = \phi_1(\boldsymbol{f}) + \phi_2(\boldsymbol{f}) \ , \text{ where}$$

$$\phi_1(\boldsymbol{f}) = \operatorname{smax}(C^{-1}\boldsymbol{f}) \ \text{ and } \ \phi_2(\boldsymbol{f}) = \operatorname{smax}(2\alpha R(\boldsymbol{b} - B\boldsymbol{f})).$$

We proceed as follows. First, we compute $\phi_1(\boldsymbol{f})$: to find $\operatorname{smax}(C^{-1}\boldsymbol{f})$, it suffices to sum both $\exp(f_e/\operatorname{cap}(e))$ and $\exp(-f_e/\operatorname{cap}(e))$ over all edges e, which can be done in $O(D)$ rounds. As Sherman points out, $\phi(\boldsymbol{f}) = \Theta(\varepsilon^{-1}\log n)$ due to the scaling, and thus, encoding $\exp(\phi(\boldsymbol{f}))$ with sufficient accuracy requires $O(\varepsilon^{-1}\log n)$ bits, which is thereby also a bound on the encoding length of all individual terms in the sums for ϕ_1 and ϕ_2. The error introduced by rounding theses values to integers is small enough to not affect the asymptotics of the running time.

For determining $\phi_2(\boldsymbol{f})$, we first compute the vector $\boldsymbol{y} := 2\alpha R(\boldsymbol{b} - B\boldsymbol{f})$ and then do an aggregation on a BFS tree as for $\phi_1(\boldsymbol{f})$. Since $B\boldsymbol{f}$ can be computed instantly ($(B\boldsymbol{f})_v$ is exactly the net flow into v), this boils down to multiplying a locally known vector with R. Before we discuss how implement this operation, let us explain more about the structure of R and how we determine $\frac{\partial\phi}{\partial f_e}$, which is required in Lines 6 and 8.

The linear operator R is induced by graph cuts. More precisely, in the matrix representation of R, there is one row for each cut our congestion approximator (explicitly) considers. We will clarify the structure of R shortly; for now, denote by I the set of row indices of R. Observe that

$$\frac{\partial\phi}{\partial f_e} = \frac{\exp(f_e/\operatorname{cap}(e)) - \exp(-f_e/\operatorname{cap}(e))}{\operatorname{cap}(e)\exp(\phi_1)} + \frac{\partial\phi_2}{\partial f_e} \qquad (2)$$

and hence, given that ϕ_1 is known, the first term is locally computable. The second term expands to

$$\frac{\partial\phi_2}{\partial f_e} = \sum_{i\in I}\frac{\partial\phi_2}{\partial y_i}\cdot\frac{\partial y_i}{\partial f_e} = \sum_{i\in I}\frac{\exp(y_i) - \exp(-y_i)}{\exp(\phi_2)}\cdot\frac{2\alpha B_{i,e}}{\operatorname{cap}(i)},$$

where $\operatorname{cap}(i)$ is the capacity of cut i in the congestion approximator and $B_{i,e} \in \{-1, 0, 1\}$ denotes whether e is outgoing (-1), ingoing (1), or not crossing cut i.[5]

The cuts $i \in I$ are induced by the edges of a collection of (rooted, virtual, capacitated) spanning trees $\mathbb{T}$, where for

[5]Technically, $B_{i,e} = \sum_{v\in S_i} B_{ve}$ where S_i is the set of nodes defining cut i.

$\mathcal{T} \in \mathbb{T}$ we write $(v, \hat{v}) \in \mathcal{T}$ if $\hat{v}$ is the parent of v and denote by $\mathcal{T}_v$ the subtree rooted at v. For each $\mathcal{T} \in \mathbb{T}$, each edge $(v, \hat{v}) \in \mathcal{T}$ now induces a (directed) cut $(\mathcal{T}_v; \overline{\mathcal{T}_v})$ with index $i(\mathcal{T}, (v, \hat{v}))$. We denote the set of edges crossing this cut by by $\delta(\mathcal{T}_v)$. Let us also define

$$p(\mathcal{T}, v) = \frac{\exp(y_{i(\mathcal{T},(v,\hat{v}))}) - \exp(-y_{i(\mathcal{T},(v,\hat{v}))})}{\exp(\phi_2)} \cdot \frac{2\alpha}{\mathrm{cap}_{\mathcal{T}}((v, \hat{v}))} .$$

With this notation, we have that

$$\frac{\partial \phi_2}{\partial f_e} = \sum_{\mathcal{T} \in \mathbb{T}} \sum_{\substack{(v,\hat{v}) \in \mathcal{T} \\ e \in \delta(\mathcal{T}_v)}} p(\mathcal{T}, v) \cdot B_{i(\mathcal{T},(v,\hat{v})),e} .$$

We call $p(\mathcal{T}, (v, \hat{v}))$ the *price* of the (virtual) edge $(v, \hat{v}) \in \mathcal{T}$. Let $\mathcal{P}_{v,\mathcal{T}}$ denote the unique path in $\mathcal{T}$ from v to the root of $\mathcal{T}$. We define a *node potential* for each node v by

$$\pi_v := \sum_{\mathcal{T} \in \mathbb{T}} \sum_{(w,\hat{w}) \in \mathcal{P}_{v,\mathcal{T}}} p(\mathcal{T}, (w, \hat{w})) .$$

For any $e = (u, v)$, the cuts induced by edges in $\mathcal{T} \in \mathbb{T}$ that e crosses correspond to the edges on the unique path from u to v in $\mathcal{T}$. For all edges $(w, \hat{w}) \in \mathcal{T}$ on the path from u to the least common ancestor of u and v in $\mathcal{T}$, $B_{i(\mathcal{T},(w,\hat{w})),e} = -1$, while $B_{i(\mathcal{T},(w,\hat{w})),e} = +1$ for the edges on the path between v and this least common ancestor. Thus,

$$\frac{\partial \phi_2}{\partial f_e} = \pi_v - \pi_u , \qquad (3)$$

and our task boils down to determining the value of the potential π_v at each node $v \in V$. For that, we use two subroutines to compute distributedly the following quantities:

(1) y_i for each cut i. Note that $\boldsymbol{b} - B\boldsymbol{f}$ is known distributedly, i.e., each node knows its own coordinate of this vector. For each tree in $\mathcal{T} \in \mathbb{T}$, we need to aggregate this information from the leaves to the root, i.e., simulate a convergecast on the virtual tree $\mathcal{T}$.

(2) π_v for each node v. Provided that each (virtual) tree edge knows its y-value and ϕ_2, the prices can be computed locally. Then the contribution of each tree to the node potentials can be computed by a downcast from the corresponding root to its leaves.

With these routines, one iteration of the **repeat** loop is now executed as follows:

1. Compute ϕ_1, $\boldsymbol{y}$ (local knowledge), and ϕ_2 (aggregation on BFS tree once $\boldsymbol{y}$ is known).
2. Check the condition in Line 4. If it holds, locally update $\boldsymbol{b}$, $\boldsymbol{f}$, and k_f, and go to the previous step.
3. Compute the potential $\boldsymbol{\pi}$ (local knowledge).
4. For each $e \in E$, its incident nodes determine $\frac{\partial \phi}{\partial f_e}$ (based on Equations 2 and 3, it suffices to exchange π_u and π_v over e).
5. Compute δ (aggregation on BFS tree).
6. Locally update f_e and b_v for all $e \in E$ and $v \in V$.

Note that all of the individual operations except for computation of $\boldsymbol{y}$ and $\boldsymbol{\pi}$ can be completed in $O(D)$ rounds. Sherman proved [24] that AlmostRoute terminates after $\tilde{O}(\varepsilon^{-3}\alpha^2)$ iterations. As it is only called $O(\log n)$ times by the max-flow algorithm, Theorem 1.1 follows if we can compute $\boldsymbol{y}$ and $\boldsymbol{\pi}$ in $(\sqrt{n}+D)n^{o(1)}$ rounds for an α-congestion approximator with $\alpha = n^{o(1)}$; this is subject of the next subsection.

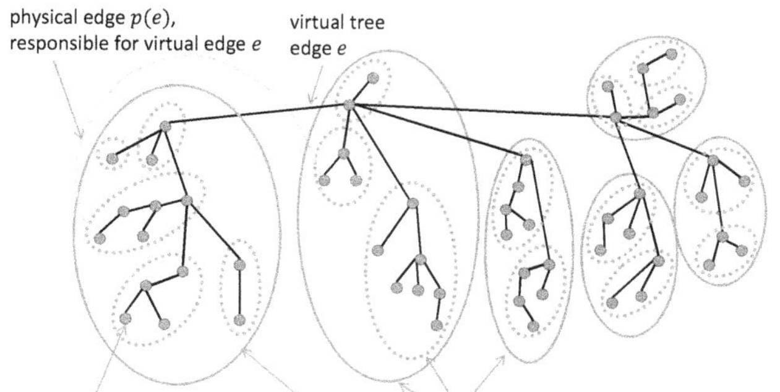

Figure 3: Hiearchical cluster decomposition of a virtual tree $\mathcal{T} \in \mathbb{T}$. Black edges are virtual tree edges represented by a physical edge connecting the top-level clusters they connect (the orange dotted edge $p(e)$ corresponds to the edge labeled e). Each cluster is spanned by a tree in G of depth $\tilde{O}(\sqrt{n})$, which is not shown.

5.2 Congestion Approximation

Our congestion approximator R is defined by the edge-induced cuts of a sample $\mathbb{T}$ of virtual trees $\mathcal{T}$ from a recursively constructed distribution. The trees are represented distributedly by a hierarchy of *cluster graphs* (see Fig. 3 for an illustration). Intuitively, a cluster graph partitions the nodes into clusters, each of which has a spanning tree rooted at a leader, and a collection of edges between clusters that are represented by corresponding graph edges between some nodes of the clusters they connect.

THEOREM 5.2. *W.h.p., within $(\sqrt{n} + D)n^{o(1)}$ rounds of the CONGEST model, we can sample a tree $\mathcal{T}$ from a distribution of $n^{1+o(1)}$ (virtual) rooted spanning trees on G with the following properties.*

- *For any cut of G of capacity C, the capacity of the cut in $\mathcal{T}$ is at least C.*
- *For any cut of G of capacity C, the expected capacity of the cut in $\mathcal{T}$ is at most αC, where $\alpha \in n^{o(1)}$.*
- *The distributed representation of $\mathcal{T}$ is given by a hierarchy of cluster graphs $\mathcal{G}_i$ on cluster sets $\mathcal{V}_i$ (their "nodes"), $i \in \{0, \dots, i_0\}$, $i_0 \in o(\log n)$, on network graph G, with the following properties.*
  - *Spanning trees of clusters of $\mathcal{G}_i$ have depth $\tilde{O}(\sqrt{n})$.*
  - $|\mathcal{V}_{i_0}| = n^{1/2+o(1)}$.
  - *$\mathcal{G}_i$ (as graph on node set $\mathcal{V}_i$) is the (rooted) tree resulting from $\mathcal{T}$ by contracting the clusters of $\mathcal{G}_i$.*
  - *For $i > 0$, $\mathcal{G}_i$ is also a cluster graph on network graph $\mathcal{G}_{i-1}$.*
  - *For $i > 0$, each cluster $c_i \in \mathcal{V}_i$ of $\mathcal{G}_i$, interpreted as cluster graph on $\mathcal{G}_{i-1}$, contains a unique* portal cluster *$p(c_i) \in \mathcal{V}_{i-1}$ of $\mathcal{G}_{i-1}$ that is incident to all edges of $\mathcal{G}_i$ containing c_i. That is, $\mathcal{G}_{i-1}$ is a $|\mathcal{V}_i|$-tree with core $p(\mathcal{V}_i)$.*

The first two properties of each $\mathcal{T}$ stated in the theorem imply that we can use them to construct a good congestion approximator R. More precisely, Lemma 3.3 implies:

COROLLARY 5.3. *Sampling a collection $\mathbb{T}$ of $O(\log n)$ virtual trees given by Theorem 3.2 and using them as congestion approximator R in the way specified in Section 5.1 implies that the total number of iterations of Algorithm 1 is $n^{o(1)}$.*

All that remains now is to show that the distributed representation of each sampled $\mathcal{T} \in \mathbb{T}$ allows to simulate a convergecast and a downcast on $\mathcal{T}$ in $(\sqrt{n}+D)n^{o(1)}$ rounds: then we can implement the key subroutines (1) and (2) (i.e., compute $\boldsymbol{y}$ and $\boldsymbol{\pi}$) outlined in Section 5.1 with this time complexity, and by Corollary 5.3 the total number of rounds of the computation is bounded by $(\sqrt{n}+D)n^{o(1)}$.

Fortunately, the recursive structure of the decomposition is very specific. The cluster graphs of the different levels of recursion are nested, i.e., the clusters of the $(i-1)^{th}$ level of recursion are subdivisions of the clusters of the ith level. What is more, each cluster is a subtree of the virtual tree and is spanned by a tree of depth $\tilde{O}(\sqrt{n})$ in G (cf. Fig. 3) Hence, while the physical graph edges representing the virtual tree edges are between arbitrary nodes within the clusters they connect, we can (i) identify each cluster on each hierarchy level with the root of the subtree induced by its nodes, (ii) handle such subtrees recursively (both for convergecasts and downcasts), (iii) on each level of recursion but the last, perform the relevant communication by broadcasting or upcasting on the underlying cluster spanning trees in G of depth $\tilde{O}(\sqrt{n})$, and (iv) communicate over a BFS tree of G on the final level of recursion, where merely $n^{1/2+o(1)}$ clusters/nodes of the virtual tree remain.

COROLLARY 5.4. *On each virtual tree $\mathcal{T} \in \mathbb{T}$, we can simulate convergecast and upcast in $\tilde{O}(\sqrt{n}+D)$ rounds.*

Theorem 1.1 now follows from Sherman's results on the number of iterations of the gradient descent algorithm [24], the discussion in Section 5.1, and Corollaries 5.3 and 5.4.

6. REFERENCES

[1] I. Abraham, Y. Bartal, and O. Neiman. Nearly tight low stretch spanning trees. In *Proc. of the Symp. on Found. of Comp. Sci. (FOCS)*, pages 781–790. IEEE, 2008.

[2] R. K. Ahuja, T. L. Magnanti, and J. B. Orlin. *Network Flows*. Prentice-Hall, Engelwood Cliffs, New Jersey, 1993.

[3] N. Alon, R. M. Karp, D. Peleg, and D. West. A graph-theoretic game and its application to the k-server problem. *SIAM Journal on Computing*, 24(1):78–100, 1995.

[4] S. Arora, E. Hazan, and S. Kale. The multiplicative weights update method: a meta-algorithm and applications. *Theory of Computing*, 8(1):121–164, 2012.

[5] B. Awerbuch. Reducing complexities of the distributed max-flow and breadth-first-search algorithms by means of network synchronization. *Networks*, 15(4):425–437, Winter 1985.

[6] B. Awerbuch and R. Khandekar. Stateless distributed gradient descent for positive linear programs. *SIAM Journal on Computing*, 38(6):2468–2486, 2009.

[7] B. Awerbuch, R. Khandekar, and S. Rao. Distributed algorithms for multicommodity flow problems via approximate steepest descent framework. *ACM Transactions on Algorithms*, 9(1):3, 2012.

[8] B. Awerbuch and T. Leighton. Improved approximation algorithms for the multi-commodity flow problem and local competitive routing for dynamic networks. In *Proc. 26th Ann. ACM Symp. on Theory of Computing*, pages 487–496, 1994.

[9] A. A. Benczúr and D. R. Karger. Randomized approximation schemes for cuts and flows in capacitated graphs. *CoRR*, cs.DS/0207078, 2002.

[10] G. E. Blelloch, A. Gupta, I. Koutis, G. L. Miller, R. Peng, and K. Tangwongsan. Nearly-linear work parallel SDD solvers, low-diameter decomposition, and low-stretch subgraphs. *Theory Comput. Syst.*, 55(3):521–554, 2014.

[11] A. Das Sarma, S. Holzer, L. Kor, A. Korman, D. Nanongkai, G. Pandurangan, D. Peleg, and R. Wattenhofer. Distributed verification and hardness of distributed approximation. In *Proc. of the Symp. on Theory of Comp. (STOC)*, pages 363–372, 2011.

[12] A. V. Goldberg and R. E. Tarjan. Efficient maximum flow algorithms. *Commun. ACM*, 57(8):82–89, August 2014.

[13] I. Koutis. Simple parallel and distributed algorithms for spectral graph sparsification. In *the Proceedings of the Symposium on Parallel Algorithms and Architectures*, pages 61–66, 2014.

[14] S. Kutten and D. Peleg. Fast distributed construction of k-dominating sets and applications. In *the Proc. of the Int'l Symp. on Princ. of Dist. Comp. (PODC)*, pages 238–251, 1995.

[15] A. Madry. Fast approximation algorithms for cut-based problems in undirected graphs. In *Proc. of the Symp. on Found. of Comp. Sci. (FOCS)*, pages 245–254, 2010.

[16] J. M. Marberg and E. Gafni. An $O(n^2m^{1/2})$ distributed max-flow algorithm. In *Int. Conf. on Parallel Processing, (ICPP'87)*, pages 213–216, 1987.

[17] Y. Nesterov. *Introductory lectures on convex optimization*, volume 87. Springer Science & Business Media, 2004.

[18] Y. Nesterov. Smooth minimization of non-smooth functions. *Mathematical programming*, 103(1):127–152, 2005.

[19] D. Peleg. *Distributed Computing: A Locality-Sensitive Approach*. Society for Industrial and Applied Mathematics, Philadelphia, PA, USA, 2000.

[20] S. A. Plotkin, D. B. Shmoys, and É. Tardos. Fast approximation algorithms for fractional packing and covering problems. *Mathematics of Operations Research*, 20(2):257–301, 1995.

[21] H. Räcke. Optimal hierarchical decompositions for congestion minimization in networks. In *Proc. of the Symp. on Theory of Comp. (STOC)*, pages 255–264, 2008.

[22] A. Schrijver. On the history of the transportation and maximum flow problems. *Mathematical Programming*, 91(3):437–445, 2002.

[23] A. Segall. Decentralized maximum-flow protocols. *Networks*, 12(3):213–230, Fall 1982.

[24] J. Sherman. Nearly maximum flows in nearly linear time. In *Proc. of the Symp. on Found. of Comp. Sci. (FOCS)*, pages 263–269, 2013.

[25] N. E. Young. Sequential and parallel algorithms for mixed packing and covering. In *Proc. of the Symp. on Found. of Comp. Sci. (FOCS)*, pages 538–546. IEEE, 2001.

Toward Optimal Bounds in the Congested Clique: Graph Connectivity and MST

James W. Hegeman[†]
The University of Iowa
Iowa City, IA 52242, USA
james-hegeman@uiowa.edu

Gopal Pandurangan[*]
University of Houston
Houston, TX 77204, USA
gopalpandurangan@gmail.com

Sriram V. Pemmaraju[†]
The University of Iowa
Iowa City, IA 52242, USA
sriram-pemmaraju@uiowa.edu

Vivek B. Sardeshmukh[†]
The University of Iowa
Iowa City, IA 52242, USA
vivek-sardeshmukh@uiowa.edu

Michele Scquizzato[*]
University of Houston
Houston, TX 77204, USA
michele@cs.uh.edu

ABSTRACT

We study two fundamental graph problems, Graph Connectivity (GC) and Minimum Spanning Tree (MST), in the well-studied *Congested Clique* model, and present several new bounds on the time and message complexities of randomized algorithms for these problems. No non-trivial (i.e., super-constant) time lower bounds are known for either of the aforementioned problems; in particular, an important open question is whether or not constant-round algorithms exist for these problems. We make progress toward answering this question by presenting randomized Monte Carlo algorithms for both problems that run in $O(\log\log\log n)$ rounds (where n is the size of the clique). Our results improve by an exponential factor on the long-standing (deterministic) time bound of $O(\log\log n)$ rounds for these problems due to Lotker et al. (SICOMP 2005). Our algorithms make use of several algorithmic tools including graph sketching, random sampling, and fast sorting.

The second contribution of this paper is to present several almost-tight bounds on the *message* complexity of these problems. Specifically, we show that $\Omega(n^2)$ messages are needed by any algorithm (including randomized Monte Carlo algorithms, and regardless of the number of rounds) that solves the GC (and hence also the MST) problem if each machine in the Congested Clique has initial knowledge only of itself (the so-called *KT0* model). In contrast, if the machines have initial knowledge of their neighbors' IDs (the so-called *KT1* model), we present a randomized Monte Carlo algorithm for MST that uses $O(n \operatorname{polylog} n)$ messages and runs in $O(\operatorname{polylog} n)$ rounds. To complement this, we also present a lower bound in the *KT1* model that shows that $\Omega(n)$ messages are required by any algorithm that solves GC, regardless of the number of rounds used. Our results are a step toward understanding the power of randomization in the Congested Clique with respect to both time and message complexity.

[*]Supported, in part, by US-Israel Binational Science Foundation grant 2008348.

[†]Supported, in part, by National Science Foundation grant CCF-1318166.

Permission to make digital or hard copies of all or part of this work for personal or classroom use is granted without fee provided that copies are not made or distributed for profit or commercial advantage and that copies bear this notice and the full citation on the first page. Copyrights for components of this work owned by others than ACM must be honored. Abstracting with credit is permitted. To copy otherwise, or republish, to post on servers or to redistribute to lists, requires prior specific permission and/or a fee. Request permissions from permissions@acm.org.
PODC'15, July 21–23, 2015, Donostia-San Sebastián, Spain.
Copyright © 2015 ACM 978-1-4503-3617-8 /15/07 ...$15.00.
DOI: http://dx.doi.org/10.1145/2767386.2767434.

Categories and Subject Descriptors

F.2.0 [**Analysis of Algorithms and Problem Complexity**]: General; C.2.4 [**Computer-Communication Networks**]: Distributed Systems

General Terms

Algorithms, Theory

Keywords

Congested Clique; Graph connectivity; Minimum spanning tree; Graph sketches; Message complexity; Randomization

1. INTRODUCTION

The *Congested Clique* model consists of n machines that can communicate with each other via an underlying complete network. A key feature of the model is the *bandwidth restriction* on the communication links, i.e., only a limited number of bits (typically $O(\log n)$ bits, as assumed here) can be sent along each link in each round. In the Congested Clique, since the diameter of the communication network is just one, every machine is within one hop of every other machine and thus all information is quite local. The main algorithmic issue lies then in dealing with the potential congestion caused by the bandwidth restrictions. Indeed, there has been a lot of recent work in studying various fundamental problems in the Congested Clique model, including facility location [12, 6], minimum spanning tree (MST) [22, 14], shortest paths and distances [7, 15, 25], triangle finding [10, 9], subgraph detection [10], ruling sets [6, 14], sorting [28, 21], and routing [21]. The modelling assumption in solving these problems is that the input graph $G = (V, E)$ is "embedded" in the Congested Clique, that is, each node of G is uniquely mapped to a machine and the edges of G are naturally mapped to the links between the corresponding machines (cf. Section 1.2).

Research on the Congested Clique has focused mostly on the *time complexity* (i.e., the number of synchronous *rounds*) of these problems. The complete network allows $\Theta(n^2)$ (different) messages (each message is of size $O(\log n)$ bits) to be exchanged in each round, and many of the time-efficient algorithms for various problems have exploited this vast parallel communication ability to give "super-fast" algorithms that run in a sub-logarithmic (in n) number of rounds. An important early result is the work of Lotker et al. [22], which presented an $O(\log \log n)$-round deterministic algorithm for the MST problem. This was a significant improvement at the time (only an $O(\log n)$-round algorithm was known [29]). Lotker et al. left open the question of whether or not an even faster algorithm was possible—in particular, whether a *constant-round* algorithm could be possible for MST or for the (simpler) problem of graph connectivity (GC). Regarding lower bounds, almost nothing non-trivial is known.[1] In particular, for the GC and MST problems, no *super-constant* time lower bounds are known.[2] The situation is not promising from the lower bounds side: the recent results of [11] have proved that showing substantially super-constant lower bounds on time in the Congested Clique is as hard as proving long-open lower bounds in circuit complexity. However, this leaves open the important question of whether or not constant-time algorithms are possible for GC as well as the MST problem.

Thus far there has been little work on understanding the *message complexity* of problems in the Congested Clique. Message complexity refers to the number of messages (typically of polylogarithmic size) sent and received by all machines over the course of an algorithm; in many applications, this is the dominant cost as it plays a major role in determining the running time and auxiliary resources (e.g., energy) consumed by the algorithm. For example, communication cost is one of the dominant costs in distributed computation on large-scale data in modern data centers [19]. In the particular context of the Congested Clique, optimizing messages as well as time has direct applications to the performance of distributed algorithms in other models such as the Big Data (k-machine) model [19], which was recently introduced to study distributed computation on large-scale graphs. The above work shows how to "convert" algorithms (cf. Conversion theorem of [19]) designed in the Congested Clique model to the Big Data model; the running time in the Big Data model depends on *both* the time *and* the message complexities of the corresponding algorithm in the Congested Clique model. Another related motivation comes from the connection between the Congested Clique model and the MapReduce model. In [13] it is shown that if a Congested Clique algorithm runs in T rounds and, in addition, has moderate message complexity, then it can be simulated in the MapReduce model in $O(T)$ rounds.

1.1 Our Contributions

In this paper we focus on two fundamental graph problems in the Congested Clique, namely graph connectivity (GC) and minimum spanning tree (MST), and present several new results that make progress toward understanding the time and message complexities of randomized algorithms for these problems.

Faster Algorithms for GC and MST. Our first contribution consists of randomized (Monte Carlo) algorithms, running in $O(\log \log \log n)$ rounds and succeeding with high probability (w.h.p.), for both GC and MST (cf. Section 2.3).[3] Our results improve by an exponential factor on the long-standing time upper bound of $O(\log \log n)$ rounds for MST due to Lotker et al. [22]. It is worth mentioning that the Lotker et al. MST algorithm is deterministic, in contrast to ours, which uses randomness in a crucial way. Our algorithms make use of several tools including sketching, random sampling, and fast sorting. We first show how to solve GC in $O(\log \log \log n)$ rounds. We do this by making use of *linear sketches* [3, 2, 23] in addition to Lotker et al.'s algorithm. The latter is used as a "pre-processing" step to first decrease the size of the graph with which we must work. Specifically, we run the algorithm of Lotker et al. for $O(\log \log \log n)$ rounds and this yields enough MST edges so that the number of connected components induced by these edges shrinks to $O(n/\operatorname{polylog} n)$. This in turn lends itself to an application of sketching. Linear sketching [3, 2, 23] is a powerful technique which is helpful in efficiently determining an outgoing edge of a component. A *sketch* of a vertex (or a component) is a short $O(\operatorname{polylog} n)$-bit vector that efficiently encodes the neighborhood of the vertex. Sampling from this sketch gives a random (outgoing) edge of this vertex (component). A critically useful property arises from the linearity of the sketches: adding the sketches of a set of vertices gives the sketch of the component induced by vertex set; the edges between the nodes within a component (i.e., the intra-component edges) are automatically "cancelled", leaving only a sketch of the outgoing edges. After reducing the size of the graph to $O(n/\operatorname{polylog} n)$, it is possible to check connectivity locally by simply sending the sketches to a single node in the clique. We use our connectivity algorithm as a key ingredient in our MST algorithm. MST is a more-challenging problem, and (likely) cannot be solved using sketches alone or by simply collecting information at a single node. However, by leveraging the fact that our connectivity algorithm (except the Lotker et al. part) uses only $O(n)$ messages, we can run several GC subroutines in parallel. In our MST algorithm, edges are partitioned into $O(\sqrt{n})$ groups by weight and each group of edges is processed by a separate GC subroutine; therefore, up to $\Theta(\sqrt{n})$ GC subroutines could be running in parallel. We note that the runtimes of our algorithms are dominated by the pre-processing step that employs the subroutine of Lotker et al. (which takes $O(\log \log \log n)$ rounds); all other parts require only constant time.

It is worth emphasizing that if we allow $O(\operatorname{polylog} n)$ bits per message, instead of $O(\log n)$ bits per message (which is the standard bound for the Congested Clique model), then our algorithm solves MST in $O(1)$ rounds. In other words, enlarging the per-link bandwidth to $O(\operatorname{polylog} n)$ obviates the need for using the Lotker et al. MST algorithm as a pre-processing step. Lotker et al. point out that their algorithm also extends to a larger bandwidth setting; specifically, running in $O(\log 1/\epsilon)$ rounds if each message is n^ϵ bits long. For example, this implies that the Lotker et al. algorithm would run in $O(1)$ rounds if each message was allowed to contain $\Theta(\sqrt{n})$ bits. This need for poly-sized messages should be contrasted with our MST algorithm which is capable of running in $O(1)$ rounds using only $O(\operatorname{polylog} n)$-sized messages.

Message Complexity Bounds. Our second contribution is a collection of almost-tight lower bounds on the *message complexity* of GC and MST. Unlike time complexity, when we talk about message complexity there are subtle distinctions that must be made relating to the models. In particular, the distinction between having and not having initial knowledge of neighbors' IDs is relevant. Our $O(\log \log \log n)$-round randomized MST algorithm has a message

[1]This is the case with respect to the standard *unicast/multicast* version of the Congested Clique—the model assumed in this paper—where each node can send a *different* message (or no message at all) along each of its incident links in each round. Recently, time lower bounds have been shown in the weaker *broadcast* version of the Congested Clique—where machines can send only the *same* message across its incident links in a round—for some problems such as shortest paths [15] and the subgraph detection problem [10].

[2]This is true even in the broadcast version of the model.

[3]Throughout this paper, by "w.h.p." we mean with probability at least $1 - 1/n^{\Omega(1)}$.

complexity of $\Theta(n^2)$ (as does the algorithm of Lotker et al. [22]). As we improved on the time complexity using randomization, a natural question is whether we can improve the message complexity as well. It turns out that the answer depends on the distinction relating to initial knowledge, mentioned above. Specifically, in Section 3 we show that $\Omega(n^2)$ messages are needed by any (randomized) algorithm (regardless of the number of rounds) to solve the GC (and hence the MST) problem if each machine in the clique has (initial) knowledge of only itself (the so-called *KT0* model, cf. Section 1.2). This result improves on the $\Omega(n^2)$ MST lower bound of Korach et al. [20], which applies only to deterministic algorithms. On the other hand, if machines begin with knowledge of their neighbors' IDs (the so-called *KT1* model, cf. Section 1.2), it turns out that by exploiting the synchronous nature of the model one can solve *any* problem fairly trivially with an algorithm that communicates only $O(n)$ bits. We show that this is optimal in the *KT1* model by showing that $\Omega(n)$ messages are needed by any algorithm, regardless of the running time of the algorithm. These two results hold for all algorithms, including randomized Monte Carlo algorithms, thus extending previously known lower bounds. The $O(n)$ bits message complexity upper bound mentioned above is not particularly satisfying because the algorithm it depends on uses super-polynomially many rounds. This naturally leads to the question of whether MST (or GC) can be solved fast and using only a small number of messages. We provide a partial answer to this question by presenting an MST algorithm in the *KT1* model that requires only $O(n \operatorname{polylog} n)$ messages and $O(\operatorname{polylog} n)$ rounds. This result is obtained by adapting to the Congested Clique model the algorithm in [2] that combines the use of linear sketches with a standard Borůvka-type MST algorithm.

1.2 The Model

The *Congested Clique* is a set of n computing entities connected through a complete network. Specifically, the model consists of a point-to-point network described by a graph $N = (V, E)$ where the vertices V represent independent computing entities pairwise connected through a complete network of $|E| = \binom{n}{2}$ bidirectional communication channels, represented by the edges E of N.

Each vertex $v \in V$ of the network has a distinct identifier of $O(\log n)$ bits. At the beginning of the computation, each vertex knows its own identity, the number n, and the part of the input it gets assigned. There are then two possible variants of the model based on the amount of knowledge available at the vertices regarding the network. In the first one, each computing entity initially knows, in addition to its own identity, the identity of its $n-1$ neighbors, while in the second one a computing entity initially does not know the identities of its $n-1$ neighbors. Following, e.g., [5], we denote these two variants as *KT1* and *KT0*, respectively. Thus, in the *KT0* model, each node can send and receive messages along $n-1$ communication links (without loss of generality, numbered $1, 2, \ldots, n-1$), without being aware of the identity of nodes at the other end of the communication links.

The computation proceeds in synchronous rounds. In each round each node can perform some local computation and send a (possibly different) message of $O(\log n)$ bits to each of its $n-1$ neighbors. It is assumed that both the computing entities and the communication links are fault-free. The Congested Clique model is therefore specifically geared toward understanding the role of the limited bandwidth as a fundamental obstacle in distributed computing, in contrast to other classical models for distributed computing that instead focus, e.g., on the effects of latency (the LOCAL model) or on the effects of both latency and limited bandwidth (the CONGEST model). It is assumed that both the computing entities and the communication links are fault-free.

In distributed computing two complexity measures are usually relevant: the *time complexity* of a computation is the total number of rounds to complete the computation, while the *message complexity* of a computation is the total number of messages exchanged to complete the computation. In this paper, we consider both complexity measures.

Graph problems in the Congested Clique. In the Congested Clique, the input graph of a graph problem is assumed to be a spanning subgraph of the underlying machine network. Specifically, the input is a spanning subgraph $G = (V, E')$, $E' \subseteq E$, of the underlying clique communication network $N = (V, E)$. The input to each node $v \in V$ consists of an $(n-1)$-bit vector where the i-th bit is associated with the i-th channel of v, and indicates whether or not in E' there is an edge between node v and the endpoint of its i-th channel; when the *KT1* variant of the model is assumed, then the i-th bit indicates whether or not edge $(v, \mathrm{ID}(i)) \in E'$, where $\mathrm{ID}(i)$ is the identifier of the node at the other end of v's i-th channel. Recall that in the *KT1* model v knows the IDs of all its neighbors and can associate these with its communication channels. This definition can be easily generalized to deal with directed and/or weighted input graphs (in the latter case we shall also assume that edge weights are integers that can be represented with $O(\log n)$ bits).

For the MST problem, we require that when the algorithm ends each machine knows which of its incident edges belong to the output MST; for verification problems such as GC, we require that when the algorithm ends at least one machine knows the output value.

Input distribution. Notice that in the Congested Clique model the input graph G is tightly coupled with the communication network N and the graph is distributed among the machines via a vertex partition. This is not the case in other related models for distributed graph processing, such as [1, 30, 19]. In these papers the input graph can be much larger than the machine network and the distribution of the graph among machines is via an edge partition. In [19] this edge partition is assumed to be random (initially), in [30] the edge partition can be worst case, whereas in [1] the edge partition is worst case, but with the requirement that each processor has the same number of edges. It is worth noting that [30] does prove message complexity lower bound for problems such as GC, but these lower bounds make crucial use of the worst case distribution of edges and do not apply in our model. Similarly, the lower bounds in the setting of [1] do not seem to directly apply in the Congested Clique model.

2. MST CONSTRUCTION IN $O(\log \log \log n)$ ROUNDS

In this section we present a randomized algorithm in the Congested Clique model that computes an MST in $O(\log \log \log n)$ rounds, w.h.p. As a first step toward this algorithm, we present a randomized algorithm that solves GC w.h.p. in $O(\log \log \log n)$ rounds. Both algorithms use $\Theta(n^2)$ messages. Given this message complexity, the *KT0* and *KT1* model are equivalent since a *KT0* algorithm can start with each node broadcasting its ID to all $n-1$ other nodes. Therefore, for convenience we describe our algorithms in the *KT1* model. Our GC algorithm constructs a *maximal spanning forest* of the input graph (i.e., a spanning forest with as many trees as the number of components in the input graph), and at the end of the algorithm every node will know such a spanning forest.

2.1 Linear Sketches of a Graph

A key tool used by our algorithm is *linear sketches* [2, 3, 23]. An important aspect of using sketches for connectivity is working with an appropriate graph representation. As described in [23], we use the following graph representation. For each node $v \in V$, we define the incidence vector $\mathbf{a}_v \in \{-1, 0, 1\}^{\binom{n}{2}}$ which describes the edges incident on node v as follows:

$$\mathbf{a}_v((x,y)) = \begin{cases} 0 & \text{if } \{x,y\} \notin E \\ 1 & \text{if } \{x,y\} \in E \text{ and } v = x < y \\ -1 & \text{if } \{x,y\} \in E \text{ and } x < y = v. \end{cases}$$

With this representation it is easy to see the following property of these vectors: for any subset of nodes S, the non-zero entries of $\sum_{v \in S} \mathbf{a}_v$ corresponds exactly to the edges in the cut $(S, V \setminus S)$.

Once we have this representation, the next step is to project these vectors into lower dimensional space, i.e., *sketch space*. Specifically, for each vector $\mathbf{a}_v$, we compute a random $O(\text{poly} \log n)$–dimensional sketch $\mathbf{s}_v$, such that two properties are satisfied: (i) sampling from the sketch $\mathbf{s}_v$ returns a non-zero entry of $\mathbf{a}_v$ with uniform probability (over all non-zero entries in $\mathbf{a}_v$) and (ii) when nodes in a connected component are merged, the sketch of the new "super node" is obtained by coordination-wise addition of the sketches of the nodes in the component. The first property is referred as ℓ_0-sampling in the streaming literature [8, 23, 16] and the second property is referred as linearity (hence, the name linear sketches). The graph sketches used in [2, 3, 23] rely on the ℓ_0-sampling algorithm by Jowhari et al. [16]. Sketches constructed using the Jowhari et al. [16] approach are small, using only $\Theta(\log^2 n)$ bits per sketch and are obtained by using a (random) linear projection. Specifically, the approach of Jowhari et al. [16] requires the construction of a random $O(\log^2 n) \times \binom{n}{2}$ matrix L, such that $\mathbf{s}_v = L \cdot \mathbf{a}_v$. Note that this implies that the sketch of the component obtained by merging neighboring nodes u and v is simply the sum of the sketches $\mathbf{s}_u$ and $\mathbf{s}_v$:

$$s_{u+v} = L \cdot (\mathbf{a}_u + \mathbf{a}_v) = L \cdot \mathbf{a}_u + L \cdot \mathbf{a}_v = \mathbf{s}_u + \mathbf{s}_v.$$

To ensure this linearity property all nodes need to compute the same matrix L and thus need access to shared randomness, i.e., polynomially many mutually independent random bits. Sharing this volume of information is not feasible, given how fast we require our algorithms to be. So instead, we appeal to the ℓ_0-sampling algorithm of Cormode and Firmani [8] which requires, for the construction of the matrix L, a family of $\Theta(\log n)$-wise independent hash functions. As we make precise below, avoiding the requirement of full independence reduces the volume of information that needs to be shared considerably.

To be more precise, let $\mathcal{H}_k$ denote a family of k-wise independent hash functions. For positive real x, let $[x]$ denote the set $\{1, 2, \ldots, \lceil x \rceil\}$. Let $h : [N] \to [N^3]$ be a randomly selected hash function from $\mathcal{H}_k$, where $N = \binom{n}{2}$. For each $r \in [c \log N]$ for constant $c > 1$, let $g_r : [N] \to [2 \log N]$, be randomly selected from $\mathcal{H}_2$. Given $\mathcal{H}_k$, $k = \Theta(\log n)$ and $\mathcal{H}_2$, Cormode and Firmani show that one can construct a $O(\log^4 N) = O(\log^4 n)$-bits linear sketch $\mathbf{s}_v$ of $\mathbf{a}_v$ such that their ℓ_0-sampler succeeds with probability at least $1 - \frac{1}{N^c}$ and, conditioned on this, outputs a non-zero entry of $\mathbf{a}_v$ with probability $\frac{1}{N'} + N^{-c}$, where N' is the number of non-zero elements in $\mathbf{a}_v$. For the linearity property to hold, the same hash functions h and $\{g_r\}_r$ need to be used by all nodes v. For our purpose what this means is that the $\Theta(\log n)$-wise independent hash function h and the $O(\log n)$, pair-wise independent hash functions $\{g_r\}_r$ need to be shared among all nodes in the network. A k-wise independent hash function whose range is polynomial in n can be constructed using $\Theta(k \log n)$ mutually independent random bits [4]. Therefore, this implies that $\Theta(\log^2 n)$ mutually independent random bits are sufficient to generate h and the $\Theta(\log n)$ g_r's. Thus $\Theta(\log^2 n)$ mutually independent random bits need to be shared among all nodes in the network and this will allows every node v to construct a sketch $\mathbf{s}_v$ of size $O(\log^4 n)$. This sharing of $O(\log^2 n)$ bits can be achieved in the following simple way. Designate $\Theta(\log n)$ nodes for generating $\lceil \log n \rceil$ random bits each. Each of these designated node then sends these $\lceil \log n \rceil$ bits (using a constant number of messages each) to all other nodes. In the applications of linear sketches to GC and MST, we need every node v to compute $t = \Theta(\log n)$ independent sketches $\mathbf{s}_v^1, \mathbf{s}_v^2, \ldots, \mathbf{s}_v^t$, such that each family $\{\mathbf{s}_v^j\}_v$, $1 \leq j \leq t$ has the linearity property. Using the simple approach describe above, $\Theta(\log^2 n)$ nodes to could designated to generate and share in $O(1)$ rounds all the mutually independent random bits needed for generating all the sketches. We summarize this in the following theorem.

THEOREM 1. *Given a graph $G = (V, E)$, $n = |V|$, there is a Congested Clique algorithm running in $O(1)$ rounds, at the end of which every node $v \in V$ has computed an independent collection of $t = \Theta(\log n)$ sketches, $\mathbf{s}_v^1, \mathbf{s}_v^2, \ldots, \mathbf{s}_v^t$, such that each family $\{\mathbf{s}_v^j\}_v$, $1 \leq j \leq t$ has the linearity property. The size of each computed sketch is $O(\log^4 n)$ bits. The ℓ_0-sampling algorithm on each sketch $\mathbf{s}_v^j$ returns an edge in $\mathbf{a}_v$ with probability $1/(\text{non-zero entries in } \mathbf{a_v}) + n^{-2}$.*

2.2 Using Linear Sketches to Solve GC

In this section we describe how to utilize *linear sketches* to solve GC w.h.p. on a Congested Clique in $O(\log \log \log n)$ rounds. Our algorithm runs in two phases. Initially, the input graph can be viewed as having n components, one for each vertex. In the first phase, we reduce the number of components to $O(n/\log^4 n)$ by running the deterministic MST algorithm of Lotker et al. [22] for $O(\log \log \log n)$ rounds. Phase 2 operates on the resulting *component graph*. This is the graph whose vertices are the components computed in Phase 1 and whose edges represent adjacencies between components. Each component leader (e.g., node with minimum ID in the component) computes $\Theta(\log n)$ independent linear sketches of its neighborhood *in the component graph*. Since this graph has $O\left(n/\log^4 n\right)$ vertices and each linear sketch has size $O(\log^4 n)$ bits, the entire volume of all linear sketches at all nodes has size $O(n \log n)$ bits. Thus, if we want to send all linear sketches to a single (global) leader machine, we would have to solve a routing problem in which each sender has $O(\log^4 n)$ messages (of size $O(\log n)$ each) and the receiver (leader) is required to receive $O(n)$ messages. This problem can be solved using, for example, Lenzen's routing algorithm [21], in $O(1)$ rounds. The rest of the algorithm is simply local computation by the leader followed by the leader communicating the output, which is of size $O(n)$, to all nodes in an additional $O(1)$ rounds. We now provide the most important details.

The Lotker et al. MST algorithm takes an edge-weighted clique as input. The algorithm runs in phases, taking constant number of communication rounds per phase. At the end of phase $k \geq 0$, the algorithm has computed a partition $\mathcal{F}^k = \{F_1{}^k, F_2{}^k, \ldots, F_m{}^k\}$ of the nodes of G into *clusters*, where each cluster is a connected component of the graph induced by the edges selected thus far. Furthermore, for each cluster $F \in \mathcal{F}^k$, the algorithm has computed a minimum spanning tree $T(F)$. It is worth noting that at the end of Phase k every node in the network knows the partition $\mathcal{F}^k$ and the collection $\{T(F) \mid F \in \mathcal{F}^k\}$ of trees. It is shown that at the end of phase k the size of the smallest cluster is at least $2^{2^{k-1}}$ and hence

$|\mathcal{F}^k| \leq n/2^{2^{k-1}}$. In the following, we refer to the Lotker et al. algorithm as the CC-MST algorithm. Let CC-MST(G, k) denote the execution of CC-MST on an edge-weighted clique graph G for k phases.

THEOREM 2 (LOTKER ET AL. [22]). *CC-MST computes an MST of an n-node edge-weighted clique in $O(\log \log n)$ rounds. At the end of phase k, CC-MST has computed a vertex-partition $\mathcal{F}^k$ and a collection of trees $\mathcal{T}^k = \{T(F) \mid F \in \mathcal{F}^k\}$ with the following properties: (i) $|F| \geq 2^{2^{k-1}}$ for all $F \in \mathcal{F}^k$, (ii) every node knows $\mathcal{F}^k$ and $\mathcal{T}^k$, and (iii) if the largest weight of an edge in $T(F)$, for cluster $F \in \mathcal{F}^k$ is w, then there is no edge with weight $w' < w$ connecting F to a different cluster $F' \in \mathcal{F}^k$.*

Algorithm REDUCECOMPONENTS describes Phase 1 of our GC algorithm. The input to this algorithm is an arbitrary graph G (not a clique and not edge-weighted) and the algorithm returns a forest $\mathcal{T}_1$ and a component graph G_1 induced by the edges in this forest. After Steps 2-3 of the algorithm, each node in the network knows the forest $\mathcal{T}_1$, by Theorem 2. In Step 4, the subroutine BUILDCOMPONENTGRAPH computes the component graph G_1 of the forest $\mathcal{T}_1$ using one round of communication, as follows. Each node u examines each incident edge $\{u, v\}$ and if v belongs to a different connected component, then u send a message to the component leader of v's component. (Note that if u has two neighbors v_1 and v_2 that belong to the same connected component, distinct from u's connected component, then u only sends one message to the component leader of the component containing v_1 and v_2.) Each component leader v, processes each of the messages it has received in the previous step, and if it has received a message from a node u, then it marks the leader of u's component as a neighbor in the component graph. Thus, at the end of BUILDCOMPONENTGRAPH, every component leader knows all neighboring component leaders in the component graph.

A tree T in forest $\mathcal{T}_1$ is called *finished* if it is a spanning tree of a connected component of G; otherwise we call T *unfinished*. Finished trees correspond to isolated nodes in the component graph and play no further role in the algorithm. (In fact, if we only wanted to verify connectivity, as opposed to computing a maximal spanning forest, we could have the algorithm stop and report "disconnected" as soon as a finished tree, not spanning the entire graph, is detected.) Unfinished trees (represented by their component leaders) can be viewed as vertices of the graph that will processed in Phase 2. Note that at the end of Algorithm REDUCECOMPONENTS, it is guaranteed that every node knows the ID of the leader of the component it belongs to and every component leader knows *incident* inter-component edges. Now we prove the following lemma that bounds the number of vertices in the graph that will be processed in Phase 2 of the GC algorithm.

LEMMA 3. *The number of unfinished trees in $\mathcal{T}_1$ are $O\left(\frac{n}{\log^4 n}\right)$.*

PROOF. In Step 1, we build a weighted clique from the input graph G by assigning to every edge in G, the weight 1; non-adjacent pairs of vertices are assigned weight ∞. Step 2 simply executes CC-MST on this weighted clique for $\log \log \log n + 3$ iterations, which returns a set of clusters $\mathcal{F}$ and a forest $\mathcal{T}_\infty$ of trees, one spanning tree per cluster. By Theorem 2(i), every cluster in $\mathcal{F}$ has size at least $\log^4 n$. Now note that some edges of weight ∞ might have been selected by CC-MST to be part of $\mathcal{T}_\infty$; and in Step 3 we discard these edges. By Theorem 2(iii), if a tree $T \in \mathcal{T}_\infty$ contains an edge of weight ∞, it is finished because all edges incident on T and connecting to a different tree in $\mathcal{T}_\infty$ have weight ∞ (i.e., they are non-edges in G). Thus no unfinished tree in $\mathcal{T}_\infty$ contains an edge of weight ∞. This implies that no unfinished tree is fragmented in Step 3 of Algorithm REDUCECOMPONENTS and thus each unfinished tree has size at least $\log^4 n$. Therefore, there can be at most $O(n/\log^4 n)$ unfinished trees. □

Algorithm 1 Phase 1: REDUCECOMPONENTS

Input: A graph $G = (V, E)$.

Output: $\mathcal{T}_1$, a spanning forest of G with at most $O(n/\log^3 n)$ unfinished trees and G_1, the component graph induced by the edges of $\mathcal{T}_1$.

1. Assign unit weights to edges in G to obtain a weighted graph G_w; make G_w a clique by adding edges not in G and assign weight ∞ to these newly added edges.
2. $(\mathcal{F}, \mathcal{T}_\infty) \leftarrow$ CC-MST$(G_w, \lceil \log \log \log n + 3 \rceil)$
3. $\mathcal{T}_1 \leftarrow \mathcal{T}_\infty \setminus \{\{u, v\} \in E(\mathcal{T}_\infty) \mid wt(u, v) = \infty\}$
4. $G_1 \leftarrow$ BUILDCOMPONENTGRAPH$(G, \mathcal{T}_1)$
5. **return** $(\mathcal{T}_1, G_1)$

Phase 2 runs on the component graph G_1 returned by Phase 1. Note that G_1 has $O(n/\log^4 n)$ non-isolated nodes and the $\Theta(\log n)$, $O(\log^4 n)$-bit-sized linear sketches computed for each non-isolated node would result in a total volume of $O(n \log n)$ bits of information, which can be sent to a single node in $O(1)$ rounds using Lenzen's routing algorithm. At a high level, this is what happens in Phase 2 followed by local computation of the maximal spanning forest. Phase 2 is described in more detail in Algorithm SKETCHANDSPAN below. Let v^* denote the vertex in V with minimum ID.

Algorithm 2 Phase 2: SKETCHANDSPAN

Input: $G_1 = (V_1, E_1)$, $V_1 \subseteq V$.

Output: $\mathcal{T}_2$, a maximal spanning forest of G_1

1. Each vertex $v \in V_1$ that is not isolated computes sketches $s_v{}^i$ for $i = 1, 2, \ldots, c \log n$ of its neighborhood.
2. Each vertex $v \in V_1$ sends these $c \log n$ sketches to v^*.
3. v^* uses these sketches to locally sample edges betwee connected components to compute a maximal spanning forest $\mathcal{T}_2$ of G_1.
4. v^* assigns each edge in $\mathcal{T}_2$ to a node in V such that each node is assigned a single edge. v^* then sends each edge to its assigned node. Each node in V then broadcast the edge it received from v^* so that all nodes now know $\mathcal{T}_2$.
5. **return** $\mathcal{T}_2$

Our final GC algorithm executes Phase 1 (Algorithm REDUCECOMPONENTS) followed by Phase 2 (Algorithm SKETCHANDSPAN). Edges in $\mathcal{T}_2$ are inter-component edges and each such edge needs to be mapped to a real edge in input graph G. For each edge $\{C_1, C_2\}$ in $\mathcal{T}_2$ the leaders of components C_1 and C_2 know edges in G that have induced edge $\{C_1, C_2\}$. One of the leaders, say the one with smaller ID, picks an edge in G corresponding to $\{C_1, C_2\}$. Leaders send all their picked edges to v^*. Denote by $\mathcal{T}_2'$ the set of the all picked edges. Since $\mathcal{T}_2$ is a forest, v^* is the target of fewer than n edges and this communication takes $O(1)$ rounds.

THEOREM 4 (GC ALGORITHM). *The GC problem can be solved in $O(\log \log \log n)$ rounds w.h.p. in the Congested Clique model. Furthermore, if the bandwidth of each communication link was $O(\log^5 n)$ bits, instead of $O(\log n)$ bits, then GC could be solved in $O(1)$ rounds.*

REMARK 5. *It is worth noting that this approach of reducing number of components and then using linear-sketch-based algorithm to solve the GC problem can be used to solve the* bipartiteness *problem in* $O(\log\log\log n)$ *rounds w.h.p. and also the* k-edge-connectivity *problem in* $O(k \log\log\log n)$ *rounds w.h.p. using the approach of Ahn et al. [2].*

2.3 Using Linear Sketches to Solve MST

In this section we show how to obtain an exact solution to the MST problem on a Congested Clique. The algorithm starts (in Step 1) with a pre-processing phase in which:

(i) the number of components is reduced from n to $O(n/\log^4 n)$ using the Lotker et al. MST algorithm, similar to Phase 1 of our GC algorithm and

(ii) the number of edges is reduced to $O(n^{3/2})$ by using the classical sampling result of Karger, Klein, and Tarjan (KKT sampling) [18].

Part (ii) of the pre-processing phase runs in $O(1)$ rounds and thus the running time of this phase is dominated by Part (i), in which $O(\log\log\log n)$ rounds of the Lotker et al. MST algorithm are executed. The use of KKT sampling yields two MST subproblems, each with $O(n^{3/2})$ edges and $O(n/\log^4 n)$ vertices. Following the pre-processing phase, in the main phase of our algorithm, we solve each of the two above-mentioned MST problems in $O(1)$ rounds. At a high level, this MST algorithm partitions by edge-weight the $O(n^{3/2})$ edges in the graph into $O(\sqrt{n})$ groups of size n each. We then solve $O(\sqrt{n})$ instances of the GC problem in parallel. We now provide details of this algorithm.

2.3.1 *Pre-Processing: Reducing Number of Components and Edges*

We first reduce the number of components to at most $O(n/\log^4 n)$ components by executing CC-MST for $\lceil \log\log\log n + 3 \rceil$ phases, similar to Phase 1 our GC algorithm. Let $\mathcal{T}_1$ be the spanning forest and G_1 be the component graph obtained by executing the above step. Here, we think of the component graph G_1 as being edge-weighted, with the weight of an edge connecting components C and C' set to the minimum weight of an edge between a node in C and a node in C'. By Theorem 2, $\mathcal{T}_1$ is a subset of a MST of G. Our goal now is to complete this MST by determining which edges in G_1 are in the MST.

Karger, Klein, and Tarjan [18] present a randomized linear-time algorithm to find a MST in an edge-weighted graph in a sequential setting (RAM model). A key component of their algorithm is a random edge sampling step to discard edges that cannot be in the MST. For completeness we state their sampling result and the necessary terminology.

DEFINITION 1 (F-LIGHT EDGE [18]). *Let F be a forest in a graph G and let $F(u, v)$ denote the path (if any) connecting u and v in F. Let $wt_F(u, v)$ denote the maximum weight of an edge on $F(u, v)$ (if there is no path then $wt_F(u, v) = \infty$). We call an edge $\{u, v\}$ F*-heavy *if $wt(u, v) > wt_F(u, v)$, and F*-light *otherwise.*

LEMMA 6 (KKT SAMPLING LEMMA [18]). *Let H be a subgraph obtained from G by including each edge independently with probability p, and let F be the minimum spanning forest of H. The number of F-light edges in G is at most n/p, w.h.p.*

The implication of the above lemma is that if we set $p = 1/\sqrt{n}$ then the number of sampled edges in H and the number of F-light edges in G both are $O(n^{3/2})$ w.h.p. Crucially, none of the F-heavy edges can be in an MST of G. Therefore if we compute a minimum spanning forest F of H, then we can discard all F-heavy edges and compute a minimum spanning forest of the graph induced by the remaining F-light edges in G. We have thus reduced the problem into two MST problems: (i) compute a minimum spanning forest F of H where the number of edges in H is $O(n^{3/2})$ w.h.p. and (ii) compute a minimum spanning forest of the graph induced by F-light edges in G. Note that these two problems cannot be solved in parallel since the latter problem depends on the output of the first problem. Specifically, after problem (i) has been solved we need to identify all F-light edges; these will serve as input to problem (ii). Identifying F-light edges is easy because after problem (i) has been solved every node knows F and can therefore determine which incident edges are F-light.

Algorithm 3 summarizes our approach. In the beginning of Algorithm EXACT-MST every node knows weights of incident edges and at the end of the execution every node knows all the edges that are in the MST computed by the algorithm. The subroutine BUILDCOMPONENTGRAPH invoked in Step 2 now builds an *edge-weighted* component graph. Like the unweighted version of BUILDCOMPONENTGRAPH, this subroutine also runs in $O(1)$ rounds. The only difference is that each node u (in a component C) considers all edges to a component C' ($\neq C$) and informs the leader of C' about the edge between u and C' of smallest weight. After this round of communication, component leaders have enough information to determine the smallest weight edge to every other component. The subroutine SQ-MST is called twice (in Steps 4 and 6), to compute a minimum spanning forest of a graph with $O(n/\log^4 n)$ vertices and $O(n^{3/2})$ edges. We describe SQ-MST in detail in the next subsection and show that it runs in $O(1)$ rounds w.h.p. Algorithmn SQ-MST comes with the guarantee that at the end of its execution, all nodes know the MST computed by it.

Algorithm 3 EXACT-MST

Input: An edge-weighted clique $G(V, E)$
Output: An MST of G
1. $(\mathcal{F}, \mathcal{T}_1) \leftarrow$CC-MST$(G, \lceil \log\log\log n + 3 \rceil)$
2. $G_1 \leftarrow$ BUILDCOMPONENTGRAPH$(G, \mathcal{T}_1)$
3. $H \leftarrow$ a subgraph of G_1 obtained by sampling each edge in G_1 independently with probability $\frac{1}{\sqrt{n}}$
4. $F \leftarrow$ SQ-MST(H)
5. $E_\ell \leftarrow \{\{u, v\} \in E(G_1) \mid \{u, v\}$ is F-light$\}$
6. $\mathcal{T}_2 \leftarrow$ SQ-MST(E_ℓ)
7. **return** $\mathcal{T}_1 \cup \mathcal{T}_2$

2.3.2 *Computing MST of $O(n^{3/2})$-size Graph*

We now describe Algorithm SQ-MST, which computes in $O(1)$ rounds an MST of a subgraph $G' = (V', E')$ of G with $O(n^{3/2})$ edges and $O(n/\log^4 n)$ vertices. (Pseudocode appears in Algorithm 4.) The bounds on number of vertices and number of edges are critical to ensuring that our MST algorithm runs in $O(1)$ rounds. The algorithm starts with edges in E' being sorted, i.e., each node computes the *rank* $r(e)$ of each incident edge e in a sorted (by edge-weights) sequence of all edges in E'. This sorting problem can be solved in $O(1)$ rounds on the Congested Clique by using Lenzen's distributed sorting algorithm [21]. Then each node partitions (in Step 2) the incident edges based on their ranks. Thus we partition E' into $O(\sqrt{n})$ sets $E_1, E_2, \ldots, E_p$ ($p = O(\sqrt{n})$) each containing n edges (E_p might have less than n edges) such that E_1 contains all the edges whose ranks are in the range 1 to n, E_2 contains the edges with ranks between $n + 1$ and $2n$, and so on. Since nodes know ranks of incident edges, each node can identify, for each incident edge e, an index $i \in [p]$ such that $e \in E_i$.

Algorithm 4 SQ-MST

Input: A weighted subgraph $G'(V', E', wt)$ with $O\left(\frac{n}{\log^4 n}\right)$ vertices and $O(n^{3/2})$ edges
Output: An MST of G'

1. $r(E) \leftarrow$ DISTRIBUTEDSORT(E); each edge $e \in E'$ is assigned a rank $r(e)$, in non-decreasing order of edge-weights.
2. Partition edges in E based on their ranks $r(e)$ into p partitions $E_1, E_2, \ldots E_p$ ($p = O(\sqrt{n})$), each partition having n edges (E_p might have less than n edges) such that E_1 contains edges with ranks $1, 2, \ldots, n$; E_2 contains edges with ranks $n+1, n+2, \ldots, 2n$; and so on.
3. Let $g(i)$ be the node in G with ID i. Assign $g(i)$ as the "guardian" of part E_i. Nodes send edges in E_i to $g(i)$.
4. **for** $i = 1$ **to** $i = p$ **in parallel do**
5. Let $G_i = (V', \cup_{j=1}^{i-1} E_j)$. Each vertex $v \in V'$ constructs $t = \Theta(\log n)$ sketches $\mathbf{s}_v^{i,1}, \mathbf{s}_v^{i,2}, \ldots, \mathbf{s}_v^{i,t}$. of its neighborhood with respect to G_i.
6. Each node $v \in V'$ sends the sketch collection $\{\mathbf{s}_v^{i,j}\}_{j=1}^{t}$ to $g(i)$.
7. $g(i)$ executes locally:
   (a) $\mathcal{T}_i \leftarrow$ SPANNINGFOREST(G_i) (based on linear sketches received)
   (b) $g(i)$ processes edges in E_i in rank-based order.
   for each edge $e_j = \{u, v\}$ in $e_1, e_2, \ldots$:
   if there is a path between u and v in $\mathcal{T}_i \cup \{e_\ell \mid \ell < j\}$ then discard e_j
   else add e_j to $\mathcal{M}_i$.
8. **return** $\cup_{i=1}^{p} \mathcal{M}_i$

In the next step (Step 3) we gather each set E_i at a *guardian* node $g(i)$. This can be done in $O(1)$ rounds as well, using Lenzen's routing algorithm, because (i) the number of edges incident on a node is less than n and therefore each node is the sender of less than n edges, and (ii) $|E_i| \leq n$ and therefore each node is the receiver of at most n edges. The role of a guardian node $g(i)$ is to determine which of the edges in E_i are a part of the MST. Specifically, $g(i)$ wants to know for each edge $e = \{u, v\} \in E_i$ whether there is a path between u and v in the graph induced by edges with ranks less than $r(e)$. (Note that these are edges of weight no greater than e). That is, for each edge $e \in E_i$, $g(i)$ needs to determine whether there is a path between u and v in the graph induced by edges $\cup_{k=0}^{i-1} E_k \cup \{e_\ell \in E_i \mid r(e_\ell) < r(e)\}$. Let G_i be the subgraph of G' induced by the edge set $\cup_{k=0}^{i-1} E_k$. One way to solve this problem would be for $g(i)$ to compute a maximal spanning forest $\mathcal{T}_i$ of G_i. Then $g(i)$ could locally check uv-connectivity in the graph $\mathcal{T}_i \cup \{e_\ell \in E_i \mid r(e_\ell) < r(e)\}$. Thus each $g(i)$ needs to have available a solution to GC on the graph G_i. There are $O(\sqrt{n})$ such guardians — one for each part E_i and hence the challenge is executing $O(\sqrt{n})$ instances of GC computations in parallel in the Congested Clique network.

What provides crucial help in permitting these $p = O(\sqrt{n})$ GC instances to run in parallel is that G' has $O(n/\log^4 n)$ nodes and $O(n^{3/2})$ edges. Note that since G' has $O(n/\log^4 n)$ nodes, Phase 1 of GC is not required and only Phase 2 of GC needs to be executed in parallel on $O(\sqrt{n})$ instances. The main communication step in Phase 2 of the GC algorithm is nodes sending their $\Theta(\log n)$ linear sketches to single node for local computation. Each node $v \in V'$ has a set of incident edges belonging to each graph G_i, $1 \leq i \leq p$. Thus v computes $\Theta(p \log n) = \Theta(\sqrt{n} \log n)$ different linear sketches, each of size $\Theta(\log^4 n)$ bits. Therefore, in total each node v has $O(\sqrt{n} \cdot \log^4 n)$ different $O(\log n)$-sized messages to send. On the receiver's side, a guardian $g(i)$ is the target of $O(n)$ messages of size $O(\log n)$ bits. This communication can be completed in $O(1)$ using Lenzen's routing algorithm, and thus we obtain the following theorem.

THEOREM 7. *Algorithm* EXACT-MST *computes an MST of an n-node edge-weighted clique in $O(\log \log \log n)$ rounds w.h.p. on the Congested Clique. Furthermore, if the bandwidth of each communication link is $O(\log^5 n)$ bits, then MST can be computed in $O(1)$ rounds.*

3. MESSAGE LOWER BOUNDS IN THE *KT0* MODEL

In this section we show that, at least in the *KT0* model, it is impossible to avoid the $\Omega(n^2)$ message complexity of the algorithms of the previous section. We show that any algorithm that solves GC, even a randomized Monte Carlo algorithm, needs to send $\Omega(n^2)$ messages. In the following, we use GC(m) to denote the problem of determining, in the *KT0* model, whether or not an input graph with m edges is connected.

3.1 Construction

To show a lower bound on the message complexity of Monte Carlo algorithms, we construct a hard distribution H on the inputs and use Yao's Minimax Principle (Prop. 2.6 in [24]).

We assume without (much) loss of generality that n is even. Consider any $m, n \leq m \leq \frac{n}{2} \cdot (\frac{n}{2} - 1)$. Then, for a given n, partition the n nodes into two subsets U and V of size $n/2$. Next, we construct biconnected (2-connected) graphs G_U and G_V on U and V, respectively. Assume w.l.o.g. that the nodes of U are $u_0, u_1, \ldots, u_{n/2-1}$ and the nodes of V are $v_0, v_1, \ldots, v_{n/2-1}$. We next use m edges to construct our graph $G = G_U \cup G_V$.

Since m should be at least as large as n, with the first n edges of G we connect u_j to u_{j+1} and v_j to v_{j+1} for each j (where indices are interpreted mod $n/2$). If $m \geq 2n$, we connect u_j to u_{j+2} and v_j to v_{j+2} for each j; and in general, if $m \geq k \cdot n$ we connect u_j to u_{j+k} and v_j to v_{j+k} for each j. This procedure is performed for each $k = 1, 2, \ldots$ until $k = k'$ such that $m < k' \cdot n$. With the final $m - (k'-1) \cdot n$ "leftover" edges, we connect u_0 to $u_{k'}$, u_1 to $u_{1+k'}$, u_2 to $u_{2+k'}$, etc. in that order until we run out of edges to add to the graph. Let G_U be the graph on the nodes U and G_V be the graph on the nodes V constructed in this manner. Then $G = G_U \cup G_V$ is a nearly-regular disconnected graph composed of two biconnected components G_U and G_V. Assuming n is even, every vertex has degree $\lfloor \frac{2m}{n} \rfloor$ or $\lceil \frac{2m}{n} \rceil$.

We next construct the input distribution H. One-half of the probability mass of H will be placed on the (disconnected) graph $G = G_U \cup G_V$. The other 1/2 of the probability mass will be distributed uniformly among the members of the following set S_G. An element of S_G is formed by choosing two edges of G – one from G_U and one from G_V – and "swapping" the endpoints. That is, suppose $e_1 = (u_1, u_2) \in G_U$ and $e_2 = (v_1, v_2) \in G_V$ are chosen in G. For each such pair e_1, e_2, add the following graphs to S_G: $G - e_1 - e_2 + (u_1, v_1) + (u_2, v_2)$ and $G - e_1 - e_2 + (u_1, v_2) + (u_2, v_1)$. Since G_U and G_V are biconnected, each member of S_G is connected (in contrast to $G = G_U \cup G_V$, which is disconnected). The half of the probability mass of H assigned to S_G is distributed uniformly over the elements of S_G.

3.2 Lower Bounds

We first show how to extend the lower bound argument of Korach et al. [20] for deterministic MST algorithms in *KT0* to GC.

THEOREM 8. *Let $\mathcal{A}_D$ be a deterministic algorithm solving* GC(m) *in the KT0 model, where $n \leq m \leq \frac{n}{2} \cdot (\frac{n}{2} - 1)$. Then the worst-case number of messages sent during the execution of $\mathcal{A}_D$ is $\Omega(m)$.*

PROOF. As in [20], consider the execution of $\mathcal{A}_D$ on G, and suppose that there exists a "square" u_1, v_1, v_2, u_2, with (u_1, u_2) an edge in G_U and (v_1, v_2) an edge in G_V, such that during the execution of $\mathcal{A}_D$, no messages are sent along the communication links (u_1, u_2), (u_1, v_1), (v_1, v_2), or (u_2, v_2). As Korach et al. do in [20], we claim that if this is the case, then the execution of $\mathcal{A}_D$ proceeds *identically* on the input $G' = G - (u_1, u_2) - (v_1, v_2) + (u_1, v_1) + (u_2, v_2)$ (which is an element of S_G). To see this point, note that in the *KT0* model, no node (including u_1) can distinguish between the situation where an edge leaving u_1 at a certain "port" goes to v_1 and the situation where the edge leaving that "port" goes to u_2. This is true for the other edges and nodes involved in the "square." Therefore, since the output of $\mathcal{A}_D$ must be different on G (disconnected) and G' (connected), it cannot be the case that there exists such a "square" in the execution of $\mathcal{A}_D$ on G. To complete the proof, as in [20], one can show that there exists a set of at least $\Omega(m)$ edge-disjoint "squares" and hence there is no set of edges of size less than $\Omega(m)$ that can intersect all such G_U-G_V squares. In summary, then, in order to be correct on G and all members of S_G, $\mathcal{A}_D$ must use a set of links, during its execution on G, of size $\Omega(m)$, and hence must have worst-case message complexity $\Omega(m)$. □

We now combine the above argument with the hard distribution H (defined in previous subsection) to obtain a lower bound on deterministic algorithms that err with (at most) a certain constant probability. Then, by applying Yao's Minimax Principle we obtain a lower bound on the message complexity of Monte Carlo randomized algorithms.

THEOREM 9. *Let $\mathcal{A}_{MC}$ be a Monte Carlo algorithm solving* GC(m) *with probability at least $4/5$ in the KT0 model, where $n \leq m \leq \frac{n}{2} \cdot (\frac{n}{2} - 1)$. Then the expected number of messages sent during the execution of $\mathcal{A}_{MC}$ (on a worst-case input) is $\Omega(m)$.*

PROOF. To show a lower bound on the (expected) message complexity of $\mathcal{A}_{MC}$, by Yao's Minimax Principle (Prop. 2.6 in [24]), it suffices to consider deterministic algorithms that err with probability at most $2/5$ (i.e., twice the error probability of $\mathcal{A}_{MC}$) on the hard distribution on the input. Consider any such deterministic algorithm $\mathcal{A}_D$. Since $\mathcal{A}_D$ is correct with probability at least $3/5$, we conclude that (i) $\mathcal{A}_D$ is correct on at least one-tenth of the mass assigned to G (implying $\mathcal{A}_D$ is correct on G, since $\mathcal{A}_D$ is deterministic); and (ii) $\mathcal{A}_D$ is correct on at least one-tenth of the input instances in S_G.

The correctness of $\mathcal{A}_D$ on G together with at least one-tenth of the instances of S_G allows a re-use of the analysis for deterministic case (see proof of Theorem 8). The result follows. □

4. MESSAGE COMPLEXITY IN THE *KT1* MODEL

We start with the simple, but important observation that n bits of communication suffice to solve MST (or any problem, for that matter) in the *KT1* model. The idea is that each node u can view the initial information it possesses as number r_u and simply send a bit to a "leader" (e.g., node with smallest ID) in round r_u. The leader can solve the problem locally and communicate the solution back in a similar manner using an additional n bits. Hence, all the information is encoded using the synchronized clock. This sets up a significant contrast with the *KT0* model, where we have shown an $\Omega(n^2)$ lower bound on the number of messages needed to solve GC, even assuming a synchronous setting. We now show an unconditional, matching lower bound in the *KT1* model, namely that any algorithm (even randomized Monte Carlo) for solving GC (and hence MST) needs to communicate $\Omega(n)$ bits of information. In fact, what we show is stronger: we show that at least $\Omega(n)$ distinct messages are sent, in the worst case, during the course any algorithm that solves GC.

4.1 Message Lower Bounds in the *KT1* Model

Definitions. We define the $GC(x, y)$ problem, in the *KT1* variant of the Congested Clique model, to be the problem of determining the connectivity of an input graph (with the usual assumption that nodes have initial knowledge of their incident edges and neighbors in the input graph—as GC has been posed previously), with the extra condition that, during the last round of any algorithm solving $GC(x, y)$, node x must send a message to node y containing the final output ("connected" or "disconnected", as 1 or 0). The identities of x and y are known to all nodes as part of the input to $GC(x, y)$.

We now define a set of forests, $\{G_{i,j}\}$, for $i \geq 1$ and $0 \leq j \leq i+1$. In $G_{i,j}$, there are $n = 2i+2$ nodes $\{u_0, u_1, \ldots, u_i, v_0, v_1, \ldots, v_i\}$. The edges of $G_{i,0}$ are as follows: u_0 is connected to v_0, and v_0 is connected to u_k for each $k \in \{1, \ldots, i\}$. Then, for each $k \in \{1, \ldots, i\}$, u_k is connected to v_k. See Figure 1.

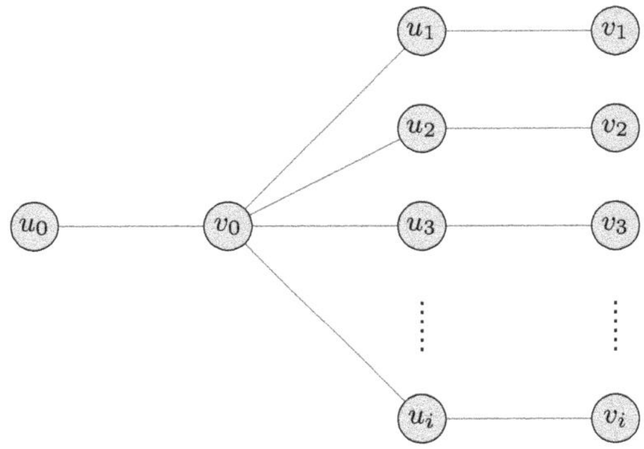

Figure 1: The graph $G_{i,0}$.

Next, for $j \in \{1, \ldots, i\}$, $G_{i,j}$ is constructed from $G_{i,0}$ by deleting edge (u_j, v_j). (Thus each such $G_{i,j}$ has two components.) Lastly, let $G_{i,i+1}$ be the intersection $\bigcap_{j=1}^{i} G_{i,j}$, which is the graph formed from $G_{i,0}$ in which *all* of the edges $\{(u_j, v_j)\}_{j=1}^{i}$ have been deleted (and thus $G_{i,i+1}$ has $i+1$ components).

THEOREM 10. *Let A_{i,u_0,v_0} be a deterministic algorithm, running in the KT1 variant, that solves $GC(u_0, v_0)$ on the family of graphs $\{G_{i,j}\}_j$ for $j \in \{0, 1, \ldots, i, i+1\}$. Then the worst-case message-complexity of A_{i,u_0,v_0} is $\Omega(n)$. In particular, there exists a $j \in \{0, i+1\}$ such that A_{i,j_0,v_0} uses (sends) $\Omega(i) = \Omega(n)$ messages during its execution on $G_{i,j}$.*

PROOF. We partition the $n = 2i + 2$ nodes of each $G_{i,\cdot}$ as follows: For each $j \in \{1, \ldots, i\}$, let $P_{i,j}^{(1)}$ be the set of nodes $\{u_j, v_j\}$; let $P_{i,j}^{(2)} = \overline{P_{i,j}^{(1)}}$ be the complement of $P_{i,j}^{(1)}$. We say that partition $P_{i,j} = \{P_{i,j}^{(1)}, P_{i,j}^{(2)}\}$ is *crossed* during the running of an algorithm (on some $G_{i,\cdot}$) if a message is sent (i) from a node in $P_{i,j}^{(1)}$ to a node in $P_{i,j}^{(2)}$; or (ii) from a node in $P_{i,j}^{(2)}$ to a node in $P_{i,j}^{(1)}$.

We claim that each partition $P_{i,j}$ is crossed *either* during the running of A_{i,u_0,v_0} on $G_{i,0}$ *or* during the running of A_{i,u_0,v_0} on $G_{i,i+1}$. Indeed, suppose not, and let j' be one such j. Since the inputs to the $GC(u_0, v_0)$ problem for graphs $G_{i,0}$ and $G_{i,j'}$ are the same for each node of $P^{(2)}_{i,j'}$, we can first conclude that $P_{i,j'}$ is crossed during the running of A_{i,u_0,v_0} on $G_{i,j'}$. If not, then the operation of A_{i,u_0,v_0} would be identical on the nodes of $P^{(2)}_{i,j'}$ for both of the graphs $G_{i,0}$ and $G_{i,j'}$, which is impossible since u_0 must eventually decide the connectivity of the graph and send the result to v_0—and unlike $G_{i,0}$, $G_{i,j'}$ is disconnected. So a message is sent across $P_{i,j'}$ on the input graph $G_{i,j'}$. Furthermore, we can also conclude that, during the first round r' in which a message is sent across $P_{i,j'}$ (on input $G_{i,j'}$), a message is sent from a node in $P^{(1)}_{i,j'}$ to a node in $P^{(2)}_{i,j'}$. The reason for this is precisely that it is the only possibility—during round r', no node in $P^{(2)}_{i,j'}$ can send a message across $P_{i,j'}$, for otherwise that same message would be sent during the running of A_{i,u_0,v_0} on input $G_{i,0}$ (because the decision to send such a message is made prior to the receipt of any messages from $P^{(1)}_{i,j'}$).

Therefore, we conclude that during the (again, deterministic) running of A_{i,u_0,v_0} on $G_{i,j'}$, one of the nodes of $P^{(1)}_{i,j'}$ (either $u_{j'}$ or $v_{j'}$) makes the decision to send a message across $P_{i,j'}$ prior to the receipt of any messages from $P^{(2)}_{i,j'}$. The consequence of this conclusion, however, is that exactly the same behavior must occur during the running of A_{i,u_0,v_0} on $G_{i,i+1}$, because the information at $u_{j'}$ and $v_{j'}$ is identical for both of the inputs $G_{i,j'}$ and $G_{i,i+1}$. Thus a message must be sent from $P^{(1)}_{i,j'}$ to $P^{(2)}_{i,j'}$ during the running of A_{i,u_0,v_0} on $G_{i,i+1}$, which is a contradiction.

Any single message sent between two of the n nodes can cross only two of the partitions $P_{i,j}$ (because the sets $P^{(1)}_{i,j}$ are pairwise disjoint), so, in total, at least $i = \frac{n-2}{2}$ messages are sent during the runnings of A_{i,u_0,v_0} on both $G_{i,0}$ and $G_{i,i+1}$. Therefore the number of messages sent by A_{i,u_0,v_0} is at least $\frac{i}{2} = \frac{n-2}{4} = \Omega(n)$ on at least one of $G_{i,0}$, $G_{i,i+1}$. □

COROLLARY 11. *Let A_n be a deterministic algorithm, running in the KT1 variant of the Congested Clique model, that solves GC on inputs having n nodes. Then the worst-case message-complexity of A_n is $\Omega(n)$.*

PROOF. It is straightforward to reduce $GC(u, v)$, on an input graph G', to GC using two additional messages: (i) Run A_n on G'; (ii) At the conclusion of A_n, whichever node knows the result sends that result to u (note that *each* node of the input graph is assumed to be provided the identities of u and v as part of the input); and (iii) u sends the result to v. It follows that no deterministic algorithm for GC in the *KT1* Congested Clique model can have a worst-case message-complexity less than the smallest worst-case message-complexity for an algorithm solving a problem $GC(u, v)$ (in *KT1*) minus 2. The result follows. □

4.1.1 *Lower Bound for Monte Carlo Algorithms*

The above lower bound can be extended to randomized Monte Carlo algorithms via a straightforward application of Yao's Minimax Principle (Prop. 2.6 in [24]). (A lower bound of the same form for Monte Carlo algorithms has recently been derived using a different technique [27].)

COROLLARY 12. *Let A_n be a randomized algorithm for solving GC on n-node graphs, running in the KT1 variant of the Congested Clique model with error probability of at most 1/10. Then the worst-case message-complexity of A_n is $\Omega(n)$.*

PROOF. Consider the family of graphs $\{G_{i,j}\}_j$, for $0 \leq j \leq i+1$, and a "hard distribution" on this family that assigns probability 1/4 to $G_{i,0}$, 1/4 to $G_{i,i+1}$ and distributes the remaining 1/2 uniformly to the graphs $G_{i,j}$, $j = 1, 2, \ldots, i$. Consider any deterministic algorithm solving $GC(u_0, v_0)$, that errs with probability at most 1/5 over this distribution. Such an algorithm would have to be correct on $G_{i,0}$ and $G_{i,i+1}$ and correct on at least $3i/10$ of the instances $G_{i,j}$. The argument in the proof of Theorem 10 can be then repeated for $G_{i,0}$, $G_{i,i+1}$, and the $\Omega(i)$ instances $G_{i,j}$ for which the algorithm is correct. As in the deterministic case, this yields the result that at least one of the executions, on $G_{i,0}$ or $G_{i,i+1}$ uses at least $3i/40$ messages for $GC(u_0, v_0)$. This leads to an $\Omega(n)$ lower bound on message complexity of any Monte Carlo algorithm solving $GC(u_0, v_0)$ that errs with probability at most 1/10. The reduction in the proof of Corollary 11 then leads to the result for GC. □

4.2 MST in $O(\text{polylog}\, n)$ Rounds and $O(n\, \text{polylog}\, n)$ Messages

In this subsection we show that if we allow the use of $O(\text{polylog}\, n)$ rounds, then we can obtain an algorithm that solves MST using only $O(n\, \text{polylog}\, n)$ messages in the *KT1* Congested Clique model. This should be contrasted with our $O(\log \log \log n)$-round algorithm, which uses $\Theta(n^2)$ messages. This algorithm is an adaption of the sketch-based algorithm in [26, 2, 17].

THEOREM 13. *An MST can be computed in the KT1 Congested Clique model in $O(\log^5 n)$ rounds using $O(n \log^5 n)$ messages (of size $O(\log n)$-bits each).*

PROOF. The algorithm proceeds in $O(\log n)$ *phases*, where in each phase a minimum-weight outgoing edge (MWOE) incident on each node is selected (w.h.p.) and the resulting connected components are merged together to form a new node. Components are indicated by their component label; all nodes in a component hold the ID of the leader of that component. Initially, each node is in a component on its own.

Consider an arbitrary phase of the algorithm. Each component leader generates $O(\log^2 n)$ mutually independent random bits and sends these to each node in its component. (Recall from the description of linear sketches in Section 2.1 that the Cormode-Firmani [8] construction of linear sketches requires $O(\log^2 n)$ mutually independent random bits.) This communication can be done naively, taking $O(\log n)$ rounds and using a total of $O(n \log n)$ messages. Each node in the graph uses the received random bits to compute an $O(\log^4 n)$-bit linear sketch of its neighborhood with respect to the original graph. Each node in the graph then sends its sketch to its component leader, simply using $O(\log^3 n)$ rounds. Each component leader computes the sum of the received linear sketches and then samples an outgoing edge, w.h.p. Suppose that a component leader v has obtained an outgoing edge with weight w_v. Node v sends w_v to all its followers who then delete all incident edges of weight more than w_v and obtain new, possibly smaller, neighborhoods. The entire process is repeated $O(\log n)$ times, at which point v has found a MWOE, w.h.p. Each MWOE is then sent to the node v^* with minimum ID, which then merges components, updates labels, and then informs nodes of their component labels. This completes the current phase and yields the theorem. □

5. CONCLUSIONS

Our work makes progress in understanding both the time and message complexity of two important graph problems, graph connectivity and minimum spanning tree, in the Congested Clique. We improve the upper bound on the round complexity of MST in the Congested Clique model significantly, presenting an $O(\log\log\log n)$-round algorithm, and this makes the question of whether there is an $O(1)$-round MST algorithm in the Congested Clique model even more tantalizing. Our work also suggests new questions, that simultaneously focus on both round and message complexity. For example, is it possible to design sub-logarithmic GC or MST algorithms that use $O(n \operatorname{polylog} n)$ messages?

6. REFERENCES

[1] M. Adler, W. Dittrich, B. H. H. Juurlink, M. Kutylowski, and I. Rieping. Communication-optimal parallel minimum spanning tree algorithms. In *Proceedings of the 10th Annual ACM Symposium on Parallel Algorithms and Architectures (SPAA)*, pages 27–36, 1998.

[2] K. J. Ahn, S. Guha, and A. McGregor. Analyzing graph structure via linear measurements. In *Proceedings of the 23rd annual ACM-SIAM Symposium on Discrete Algorithms (SODA)*, pages 459–467, 2012.

[3] K. J. Ahn, S. Guha, and A. McGregor. Graph sketches: sparsification, spanners, and subgraphs. In *Proceedings of the 31st Symposium on Principles of Database Systems (PODS)*, pages 5–14, 2012.

[4] N. Alon, R. Rubinfeld, S. Vardi, and N. Xie. Space-efficient local computation algorithms. In *Proceedings of the twenty-third annual ACM-SIAM symposium on Discrete Algorithms*, pages 1132–1139. SIAM, 2012.

[5] B. Awerbuch, O. Goldreich, R. Vainish, and D. Peleg. A trade-off between information and communication in broadcast protocols. *J. ACM*, 37(2):238–256, 1990.

[6] A. Berns, J. Hegeman, and S. V. Pemmaraju. Super-fast distributed algorithms for metric facility location. In *Proccedings of the 39th International Colloquium on Automata, Languages, and Programming (ICALP)*, pages 428–439, 2012.

[7] K. Censor-Hillel, P. Kaski, J. H. Korhonen, C. Lenzen, A. Paz, and J. Suomela. Algebraic methods in the congested clique. *arXiv preprint, arXiv:1503.04963*, 2015.

[8] G. Cormode and D. Firmani. A unifying framework for ℓ_0-sampling algorithms. *Distributed and Parallel Databases*, 32(3):315–335, 2014.

[9] D. Dolev, C. Lenzen, and S. Peled. "Tri, tri again": Finding triangles and small subgraphs in a distributed setting. In *Proceedings of the 26th International Symposium on Distributed Computing (DISC)*, pages 195–209, 2012.

[10] A. Drucker, F. Kuhn, and R. Oshman. The communication complexity of distributed task allocation. In *Proceedings of the 30st ACM Symposium on Principles of Distributed Computing (PODC)*, pages 67–76, 2012.

[11] A. Drucker, F. Kuhn, and R. Oshman. On the power of the congested clique model. In *Proceedings of the 32nd ACM Symposium on Principles of Distributed Computing (PODC)*, pages 367–376, 2014.

[12] J. Gehweiler, C. Lammersen, and C. Sohler. A distributed $O(1)$-approximation algorithm for the uniform facility location problem. In *Proceedings of the 18th Annual ACM Symposium on Parallelism in Algorithms and Architectures (SPAA)*, pages 237–243, 2006.

[13] J. W. Hegeman and S. V. Pemmaraju. Lessons from the congested clique applied to MapReduce. In *Proceedings of the 21th International Colloquium on Structural Information and Communication Complexity (SIROCCO)*, pages 149–164, 2014.

[14] J. W. Hegeman, S. V. Pemmaraju, and V. B. Sardeshmukh. Near-constant-time distributed algorithms on a congested clique. In *Proceedings of the 28th International Symposium on Distributed Computing (DISC)*, pages 514–530, 2014.

[15] S. Holzer and N. Pinsker. Approximation of Distances and Shortest Paths in the Broadcast Congest Clique. *arXiv preprint, arXiv:1412.3445*, 2014.

[16] H. Jowhari, M. Sağlam, and G. Tardos. Tight bounds for L_p samplers, finding duplicates in streams, and related problems. In *Proceedings of the thirtieth ACM SIGMOD-SIGACT-SIGART Symposium on Principles of Database Systems (PODS)*, pages 49–58, 2011.

[17] B. M. Kapron, V. King, and B. Mountjoy. Dynamic graph connectivity in polylogarithmic worst case time. In *Proceedings of the 24th Annual ACM-SIAM Symposium on Discrete Algorithms (SODA)*, pages 1131–1142, 2013.

[18] D. R. Karger, P. N. Klein, and R. E. Tarjan. A randomized linear-time algorithm to find minimum spanning trees. *J. ACM*, 42(2):321–328, Mar. 1995.

[19] H. Klauck, D. Nanongkai, G. Pandurangan, and P. Robinson. Distributed computation of large-scale graph problems. In *Proceedings of the 26th Annual ACM-SIAM Symposium on Discrete Algorithms (SODA)*, pages 391–410, 2015.

[20] E. Korach, S. Moran, and S. Zaks. The optimality of distributive constructions of minimum weight and degree restricted spanning trees in a complete network of processors. *SIAM J. Comput.*, 16(2):231–236, 1987.

[21] C. Lenzen. Optimal Deterministic Routing and Sorting on the Congested Clique. In *Proceedings of the 31st ACM Symposium on Principles of Distributed Computing (PODC)*, pages 42–50, 2013.

[22] Z. Lotker, B. Patt-Shamir, E. Pavlov, and D. Peleg. Minimum-weight spanning tree construction in $O(\log\log n)$ communication rounds. *SIAM Journal on Computing*, 35(1):120–131, 2005.

[23] A. McGregor. Graph stream algorithms: A survey. *ACM SIGMOD Record*, 43(1):9–20, 2014.

[24] R. Motwani and P. Raghavan. *Randomized Algorithms*. Cambridge University Press, New York, NY, USA, 1995.

[25] D. Nanongkai. Distributed approximation algorithms for weighted shortest paths. In *Proceedings of the 46th ACM Symposium on Theory of Computing (STOC)*, pages 565–573, 2014.

[26] G. Pandurangan, P. Robinson, and M. Scquizzato. Almost optimal distributed algorithms for large-scale graph problems. *arXiv preprint, arXiv:1503.02353*, 2015.

[27] G. Pandurangan and M. Scquizzato. Message lower bounds in synchronous distributed models via communication complexity. *Manuscript*, 2015.

[28] B. Patt-Shamir and M. Teplitsky. The round complexity of distributed sorting. In *Proceedings of the 30th Annual ACM Symposium on Principles of Distributed Computing (PODC)*, pages 249–256, 2011.

[29] D. Peleg. *Distributed Computing: A Locality-Sensitive Approach*. Society for Industrial Mathematics, 2000.

[30] D. P. Woodruff and Q. Zhang. When distributed computation is communication expensive. *Distrib. Comput.*, to appear.

Fast Distributed Almost Stable Matchings

Rafail Ostrovsky
University of California, Los Angeles
Departments of Computer Science and Mathematics
4732 Boelter Hall
Los Angeles, CA 90095
rafail@cs.ucla.edu

Will Rosenbaum
University of California, Los Angeles
Department of Mathematics
520 Portola Plaza
Los Angeles, CA 90095-1555
wrosenbaum@math.ucla.edu

ABSTRACT

In their seminal work on the Stable Marriage Problem, Gale and Shapley [4] describe an algorithm which finds a stable matching in $O(n^2)$ communication rounds. Their algorithm has a natural interpretation as a distributed algorithm where each player is represented by a single processor. In this distributed model, Floréen, Kaski, Polishchuk, and Suomela [3] recently showed that for bounded preference lists, terminating the Gale-Shapley algorithm after a constant number of rounds results in an *almost* stable matching. In this paper, we describe a new deterministic distributed algorithm which finds an almost stable matching in $O(\log^5 n)$ communication rounds for *arbitrary* preferences. We also present a faster randomized variant which requires $O(\log^2 n)$ rounds. This run-time can be improved to $O(1)$ rounds for "almost regular" (and in particular complete) preferences. To our knowledge, these are the first sub-polynomial round distributed algorithms for any variant of the stable marriage problem with unbounded preferences.

Categories and Subject Descriptors

C.2.4 [**Computer-Communication Networks**]: Distributed Systems—*Distributed applications*; F.2.2 [**Analysis of Algorithms and Problem Complexity**]: Nonnumercal Algorithms and Problems—*Computations on discrete structures*; G.2.1 [**Discrete Mathematics**]: Combinatorics—*Combinatorial algorithms*; J.4 [**Social and Behavioral Sciences**]: Economics

Keywords

stable marriage problem; stable matchings; distributed algorithms; approximation algorithms

Permission to make digital or hard copies of all or part of this work for personal or classroom use is granted without fee provided that copies are not made or distributed for profit or commercial advantage and that copies bear this notice and the full citation on the first page. Copyrights for components of this work owned by others than ACM must be honored. Abstracting with credit is permitted. To copy otherwise, or republish, to post on servers or to redistribute to lists, requires prior specific permission and/or a fee. Request permissions from permissions@acm.org.
PODC'15, July 21–23, 2015, Donostia-San Sebastián, Spain.
Copyright is held by the owner/author(s). Publication rights licensed to ACM.
ACM 978-1-4503-3617-8 /15/07 ...$15.00.
http://dx.doi.org/10.1145/2767386.2767424.

1. INTRODUCTION

1.1 Historical Background

In their seminal work, Gale and Shapley [4] consider the following problem. Members of disjoint sets of n ***men*** and n ***women*** each rank all members of the opposite sex. The men and women (which we collectively call ***players***) wish to form a ***matching***—a one-to-one correspondence between the men and women—which is ***stable*** in the sense that it contains no ***blocking pairs***: pairs of players who mutually prefer each other to their assigned partners in the matching. Gale and Shapley showed that a stable matching always exists by giving an explicit algorithm for finding one. The centralized Gale-Shapley algorithm runs in time $\tilde{O}(n^2)$, and this run-time is asymptotically optimal for centralized algorithms [5]. The Gale-Shapley algorithm easily generalizes to the case of ***incomplete preferences*** where each player ranks only a subset of the members of the opposite sex [5].

The Gale-Shapley algorithm has a natural interpretation as a distributed algorithm, where each player is represented by a separate processor which privately holds that player's preferences. The communication links between players are formed by pairs of players who appear on each other's preference lists. This model is natural in, for example, social networks where players may be constrained to be matched with acquaintances and do not communicate with strangers. In this model, the input to each processor has size $\tilde{O}(n)$, yet there is still no known distributed algorithm which improves upon the Gale-Shapley algorithm's $\tilde{O}(n^2)$ run-time for arbitrary preferences.[1]

Recently, there has been interest in approximate versions of the stable marriage problem [1, 2, 3, 7, 9], where the goal is to find a matching which is "almost stable." There is no consensus in the literature on precisely how to measure almost stability, but typically almost stability requires that a matching induces relatively few blocking pairs. Eriksson and Häggström [2] argue that, "the proportion of blocking pairs among all possible pairs is usually the best measure of instability." Using a finer notion of almost stability, Floréen, Kaski, Polishchuk, and Suomela show [3] that for *bounded* preference lists, truncating the Gale-Shapley algorithm after

[1] In the distributed computational model with complete preferences, each player can broadcast their preferences to all other players in $O(n)$ rounds, after which each player runs a centralized version of the Gale-Shapley algorithm. While this process requires only $O(n)$ communication *rounds*, the synchronous distributed run-*time* is still $\tilde{\Theta}(n^2)$ in the worst case.

boundedly many communication rounds yields a matching that induces at most $\varepsilon |M|$ blocking pairs. Here $|M|$ is the size of the matching produced. More recently, Hassidim, Mansour and Vardi [7] show a similar result in a more restrictive "local" computational model, so long as the men's preferences are chosen uniformly at random.

Kipnis and Patt-Shamir [9] give an algorithm which finds an almost stable matching using $O(n)$ communication rounds in the worst case, using a finer notion of approximate stability than we consider. Specifically, in their notion of almost-stability, a matching is almost stable if no pair of players can both improve their match by more than an ε-fraction of their preference list by deviating from their assigned partners. They also prove an $\Omega(\sqrt{n}/\log n)$ communication round lower bound for finding an almost stable matching for this notion of approximation.

1.2 Overview of Results

We consider an approximate version of the stable marriage problem where an almost stable matching is allowed to have $\varepsilon |E|$ blocking pairs. Here E is the set of pairs of men and women who rank one another (that is, the set of edges in the communication graph). Our notion of approximation, which generalizes almost stability as described in [2], is strictly coarser than those used in [3] and [9]. However, for bounded preferences (the context of [3]), our notion of instability agrees with that of [3] up to a constant factor.

Using the notion of almost stability given above, we describe a deterministic distributed algorithm, **ASM**, which produces an almost stable matching in $O(\log^5(n))$ rounds. We note that in order to obtain this sub-polynomial runtime, we cannot use a finer notion of approximation than [9], who prove an $\Omega(\sqrt{n}/\log n)$ round lower bound for their model. We remark that after removing an arbitrarily small fraction of "bad" players, the output of **ASM** is almost stable in the sense of [9] as well. We further describe a faster randomized variant of **ASM** which runs in $O(\log^2(n))$ rounds. For preferences which are "almost regular," (and in particular for complete or bounded preferences) this run-time can be improved to $O(1)$.

THEOREM 1. *There exists a deterministic distributed algorithm **ASM** which produces a $(1-\varepsilon)$-stable matching in $O(\log^5(n))$ communication rounds. A randomized variant of the algorithm, **RandASM** runs in $O(\log^2(n))$ rounds for general preferences, and can be improved to $O(1)$ rounds for almost regular (and in particular complete or bounded) preferences.*

ASM can be viewed as a generalization of the classical Gale-Shapley algorithm [4] which allows for multiple simultaneous proposals by the men and acceptances by the women. In **ASM**, the players quantize their preferences into $O(\varepsilon^{-1})$ quantiles of equal size. In each step of the algorithm, the men propose to all women in their best nonempty quantile. Each woman accepts proposals only from her best quantile receiving proposals. A maximal matching is then found among the accepted proposals, and matched women reject men they do not prefer to their matches. This procedure is iterated until a large fraction of men are either matched or have been rejected by all women.

The analysis of our algorithm follows in two steps. We first show that by quantizing preferences, the matching found by **ASM** cannot contain a large fraction of blocking pairs among the matched (or rejected) players. We bound the number of blocking pairs from the remaining "bad" players by showing there are few such players, and that only a small fraction can participate in many blocking pairs.

The remainder of the paper is organized as follows. In Section 2 we formalize our notion of almost stable matchings and our computational model. We also overview methods of computing maximal matchings which our algorithm will require as subroutines. Section 3 describes **ASM** and its subroutines in detail and states basic guarantees for the subroutines. Section 4 proves the performance guarantees for **ASM**. Finally, in Section 5 we describe the randomized variants of **ASM**.

2. PRELIMINARIES

2.1 Stable and almost stable matchings

We consider the stable marriage problem as originally described by Gale and Shapley [4] with incomplete preferences or, equivalently, unacceptable partners (cf. [5, 10]). Let X and Y be sets of women and men, respectively. For simplicity, we assume $|X| = |Y| = n$. Each player $v \in X \cup Y$ holds a ***preference list*** or ***ranking*** P^v—a linear order on a subset of the members of the opposite sex. We denote the set of all player's preferences by $\mathcal{P} = \{P^v | v \in X \cup Y\}$. We refer to the players u that appear on v's preference list P^v as v's ***acceptable partners***. We call $\mathcal{P}$ ***complete*** if each player ranks all players of the opposite sex. If a man m precedes m' on woman w's preference list, we write $m \succ_w m'$, and we say that w ***prefers*** m to m'. For simplicity, we assume that preferences are symmetric in the sense that if m appears in P^w, then w appears in P^m. Given players v and u of opposite genders, we let $P^v(u)$ denote v's ***rank*** of u. For example, $P^v(u) = 1$ means that u is v's most favored partner, et cetera.

We define the ***communication graph*** $G = (V, E)$ for a set of preferences $\mathcal{P}$ to be

$$V = Y \times X, \qquad E = \{(m, w) | m \in P^w,\ w \in P^m\}.$$

For a communication graph $G = (V, E)$, we denote the degree of $v \in V$ by $\deg v$, which is the number of players that appear on v's preference list.

A ***matching*** $M \subseteq E$ is a set of edges in E such that no two edges share a vertex. Given a matching M and $(m, w) \in M$, we call m and w ***partners*** and write $p(w) = m$ and $p(m) = w$. Given preferences and a matching M, we say that an edge $(m, w) \in E$ is a ***blocking pair*** if $(m, w) \notin M$, but m and w mutually prefer each other to their partners in M; that is,

$$m \succ_w p(w) \quad \text{and} \quad w \succ_m p(m).$$

By convention, we assume each unmatched player ($p(v) = \varnothing$) prefers all acceptable partners to being without a partner. A ***stable matching*** is a matching which contains no blocking pairs.

We are primarily concerned with finding matchings which are "almost stable" in the sense that they induce relatively few blocking pairs. We use a definition of almost stability given by Eriksson and Häggström [2], modified to allow for incomplete preference lists.

Definition 1. Given $\varepsilon \geq 0$ and preferences $\mathcal{P}$, we say that a matching M is $(1-\varepsilon)$***-stable*** with respect to $\mathcal{P}$ if M induces at most $\varepsilon |E|$ blocking pairs with respect to $\mathcal{P}$.

We refer to the problem of finding a matching which is $(1-\varepsilon)$-stable for fixed $\varepsilon > 0$ as the ***almost stable matching problem***. Note that a 1-stable matching corresponds precisely to the classical stable matching definition.

Remark 1. We reiterate that there is no consensus in the literature on the precise definition of almost stability. For example, the authors of [3] compare the number of blocking pairs to $|M|$, the size of the matching rather than $|E|$, as we do. Since in [3], they only consider bounded preference lists, their notion of almost stability agrees with Definition 1 up to a constant factor.

The following definition is due to Kipnis and Patt-Shamir [9].

Definition 2. Given $\varepsilon \geq 0$, preferences $\mathcal{P}$, and a matching M we call an edge $(m, w) \in E$ ***ε-blocking*** if m and w appear an ε-fraction higher on each other's preferences than their assigned partners. Specifically, (m, w) is ε-blocking if

$$P^m(p(m)) - P^m(w) \geq \varepsilon \deg m$$

and

$$P^w(p(w)) - P^w(m) \geq \varepsilon \deg w.$$

We say that M is ***ε-blocking-stable*** if it contains no ε-blocking pairs.

Remark 2. Kipnis and Patt-Shamir [9] prove an $\Omega(\sqrt{n}/\log n)$ round lower bound for finding an ε-blocking-stable matching. That we are able to achieve a polylogarithmic round algorithm for the almost stable matching problem using Definition 1 bolsters the use of Definition 1 for almost stability, at least for practical applications. Further, **ASM** produces a matching which is nearly ε-blocking-stable in the sense that after the removal of an arbitrarily small fraction of "bad" men, the resulting matching is ε-blocking-stable with respect to the remaining players.

2.2 Computational model

We describe **ASM** in terms of the CONGEST model formalized by Peleg [11]. In this distributed computational model, each player $v \in X \cup Y$ represents a processor. Given preferences $\mathcal{P}$, the communication links between the players are given by the set of edges E in the communication graph G. Communication is performed in synchronous rounds. Each communication round occurs in three stages: first, each processor receives messages (if any) sent from its neighbors in G during the previous round. Next, each processor performs local calculations based on its internal state and any received messages. We make no restrictions on the complexity of local computations. Finally, each processor sends short ($O(\log n)$ bit) messages to its neighbors in G—the processor may send distinct messages to distinct neighbors. In the CONGEST model, complexity is measured by the number of communication rounds needed to solve a problem.

Remark 3. Although the CONGEST model allows for unbounded local computation during each round, the computations required by **ASM** can be implemented in linear or near-linear time in each processor's input.

2.3 Maximal matchings

As a subroutine, **ASM** requires a method for computing maximal matchings in a graph.

Definition 3. A matching M is a ***maximal matching*** if it is not properly contained in any larger matching. Equivalently, M is maximal if and only if every $v \in V$ satisfies precisely one of the following conditions:

1. there exists a unique $u \in V$ with $(v, u) \in M$;
2. for all $u \in N(v)$ there exists $v' \in V$ with $v' \neq v$ such that $(v', u) \in M$.

For the deterministic version of our algorithm, we invoke the work of Hańćkowiak, Karoński, and Panconesi [6] who give a deterministic distributed algorithm which finds a maximal matching in a polylogarithmic number of rounds.

THEOREM 2 (HAŃĆKOWIAK, ET AL.[6]). *There exists a deterministic distributed algorithm, **MaximalMatching**, which finds a maximal matching in a communication graph $G = (V, E)$ in $O(\log^4(n))$ rounds, where $n = |V|$.*

We remark that while the authors of [6] do not explicitly use the CONGEST model of computation, their algorithm can easily be implemented in this model.

The randomized variants of **ASM** require faster (randomized) subroutines for computing maximal and "almost maximal" matchings in a communication graph. In Appendix A, we describe how to modify an algorithm of Israeli and Itai [8] to give the necessary results.

3. DETERMINISTIC ALGORITHM DESCRIPTION

In this section, we describe in detail the almost stable matching algorithm, **ASM**. The main algorithm invokes the subroutine **QuantileMatch** which in turn calls **ProposalRound**. In Section 3.1 we introduce notation, and describe the internal state of each processor during the execution of **ASM**. Section 3.2 contains a description of the **ProposalRound** subroutine, while Section 3.3 describes the **QuantileMatch** subroutine. Finally, Section 3.4 describes **ASM**.

3.1 The state of a processor

In our algorithm, we assume that each player is represented by an independent processor. Each processor has a unique id and a gender (male or female) both of which are known to that processor. The only global information known to each processor is (an upper bound on) n, the total number of processors. At each step of the algorithm, we specify the state of each processor as well as any messages the processor might send or receive. Throughout, k is a parameter (the number of quantiles) to be chosen later. The state of a player v consists of:

- Quantized preferences $Q_1, Q_2, \ldots, Q_k$ where we denote $Q = \bigcup Q_i$. For each u in v's preference list, denote $q(u) = \lceil P(u)/k \rceil$. Initially we set $Q_i = \{u | q(u) = i\}$, so that Q_1 is the set of v's $\deg(v)/k$ favorite partners, Q_2 is her next favorite $\deg(v)/k$, and so on. We call Q_i v's ***ith quantile***. If we wish to make explicit the player to whom the preferences belong, we may adorn these symbols with a superscript. For example, Q_i^v is v's ith quantile. Throughout the execution of the algorithm, elements may be removed from Q and the Q_is, but elements will never be added to any of these sets.

- A partner p (possibly empty). The partner p is v's current partner in the matching M our algorithm constructs. To emphasize that p is player v's partner, we will write $p(v)$. The (partial) matching M produced by the algorithm at any step is given by $M = \{(p(w), w) | w \in X, p(w) \neq \varnothing\}$.

Additionally, subroutines of our algorithm will require each processor to store the following variables:

- A set G_0 of "neighbors" of the opposite sex which correspond to accepted proposals.
- A partner p_0 in a matching found in the graph determined by G_0.

Thus each player knows their preferences, partners (if any) as well as any of their accepted proposals from the current round (stored in G_0). The men $m \in Y$ hold the following additional information:

- A set A of "active" potential mates, initially set to Q_1.

3.2 The ProposalRound subroutine

At the heart of our algorithm is the **ProposalRound** subroutine (Algorithm 1). **ProposalRound** works in 5 steps which are described in Algorithm 1.

Algorithm 1 ProposalRound(Q, k, A)

Step 1: Each man m proposes to all women in A^m by sending each $w \in A$ the message PROPOSE.

Step 2: Each woman w receiving proposals responds with the message ACCEPT to all proposals from her most preferred quantile Q_i^w from which at least one man proposed in Step 1.

Step 3: Let G_0 denote the bipartite graph G_0 of accepted proposals from Step 2. The players compute a maximal matching M_0 in G_0, using **MaximalMatching**(G_0), storing their match in G_0 as p_0.

Step 4: Each woman w matched in M_0 sends REJECT to all men $m \in Q^w$ in a lesser or equal quantile to her partner $p_0(w)$ in M_0 other than $p_0(w)$. She then removes all of these men from Q^w and the corresponding Q_i^w. The matched women then set $p \leftarrow p_0$, so the partial matching M now contains the edge $(p_0(w), w)$. Any man m matched in M_0 sets $p \leftarrow p_0$ and sets $A \leftarrow \varnothing$.

Step 5: The men remove all w from whom they received the message REJECT from their preferences Q, the various Q_i, and A. If a man m receives a rejection from his match $p(m)$ from a previous round, he sets $p \leftarrow \varnothing$.

We observe that if each player v takes $k = \deg v$, then **ProposalRound** mimics the classical (extended) Gale-Shapley algorithm [4, 5]. In this case, each man proposes to his most favored woman that has not yet rejected him, and each woman rejects all but her most favored suitor. Computing a maximal matching is trivial, as the accepted proposals already form a matching. The general case has one crucial feature in common with the Gale-Shapley algorithm, which follows immediately from the description of **ProposalRound**.

LEMMA 1 (MONOTONICITY). *Once a woman w has $p(w) \neq \varnothing$ in some execution of **ProposalRound**, she is guaranteed to always have $p(w) \neq \varnothing$ after each subsequent execution of **ProposalRound**. Further, once matched, she will only accept proposals from men in a strictly higher quantile than $p(w)$.*

3.3 The QuantileMatch subroutine

Here we describe the **QuantileMatch** subroutine (Algorithm 2), which simply iterates **ProposalRound** until each man m has either been rejected by all women in A^m or is matched with some woman in A^m. In either case, $A^m = \varnothing$ when **QuantileMatch** terminates. We will argue that k (the number of quantiles) iterations suffice.

Algorithm 2 QuantileMatch(Q, k)

```
i ← min {i|Q_i ≠ ∅} ∪ {k} (male only)
if p = ∅ then
  A ← Q_i (male only)
end if
for i ← 1 to k do
  ProposalRound(Q, k, A)
end for
```

LEMMA 2 (**QuantileMatch** GUARANTEE). *At the termination of **QuantileMatch**(Q, k) every man m satisfies $A^m = \varnothing$. In particular, each man who had $A^m \neq \varnothing$ before the first iteration of the loop in **QuantileMatch** has either been rejected by all women in A^m or is matched with some woman in A^m.*

PROOF. Suppose a woman w receives proposals in the first iteration of the loop in **QuantileMatch**. If she is matched with one of these suitors when **ProposalRound** terminates, she rejects all other men and receives no further proposals during the current **QuantileMatch**. On the other hand, if she is not matched with one of these suitors after the first round, then by the maximality of the matching found in Step 3 of **ProposalRound**, all of the suitors in her best quantile receiving proposals are matched with other women. Thus, in the next iteration, she only receives proposals from men in strictly worse quantiles than she accepted in the first. Similarly, in each iteration of the loop, her best quantile receiving proposals (if any) is strictly worse than the previous iteration. Therefore, after k iterations, no woman will receive proposals, hence each man m must have $A^m = \varnothing$. □

3.4 The ASM algorithm

In this section, we describe the main algorithm **ASM** (Algorithm 3). The idea of **ASM** is to iterate **QuantileMatch** until a large fraction men with high degree are either matched or have been rejected by all acceptable partners. We call such men ***good***. By iterating **QuantileMatch** a constant number of times, we can ensure that the fraction of good men is close to 1. In order to bound the number of blocking pairs from men which are ***bad*** (not good), we must ensure that bad men comprise only a small fraction of players with relatively high degree. To this end, we only allow men who are potentially involved in many blocking pairs (that is, with $|Q|$ relatively large) to participate in later calls to **QuantileMatch**.

Algorithm 3 **ASM**(P, ε, n)

```
k ← ⌈8ε^{-1}⌉, δ ← ε/8
for all i ≤ k do
  Q_i ← {v|q(v) = i}
end for
Q ← ∪_i Q_i, p ← ∅
for i ← 0 to log n do
  if |Q| ≥ 2^i then
    for j ← 1 to 2δ^{-1}k do
      QuantileMatch(Q, k)
    end for
  end if
end for
```

4. PERFORMANCE GUARANTEES

Here we analyze the performance of **ASM** and its subroutines. The run-time guarantee (Theorem 4) is a simple consequence of the description of **ASM** and its subroutines. To prove the approximation guarantee (Theorem 3), we consider blocking edges from two sets of men separately. We call a man m ***good*** if when **ASM** terminates, he is either matched or has been rejected by all of his acceptable partners. A man who is not good is ***bad***. We denote the sets of good and bad men by G and B, respectively.

THEOREM 3 (APPROXIMATION GUARANTEE). *The matching M output by **ASM** induces at most $\varepsilon|E|$ blocking pairs with respect to $\mathcal{P}$. Thus M is $(1-\varepsilon)$-stable.*

4.1 Bounding blocking pairs from good players

We bound the number of blocking pairs from good men in two steps. First we show that the good men are not involved in any $(2/k)$-blocking pairs (see Definition 2). Next, we show that as a result, the good men can only be incident with a small fraction of blocking pairs.

LEMMA 3 ($(2/k)$-BLOCKING-STABILITY OF GOOD MEN). *Let $m \in G$ be good. Then m is not incident with any $(2/k)$-blocking pairs.*

PROOF. Suppose $m \in G$ and that (m, w) is $(2/k)$-blocking. First consider the case where m is matched, $p(m) \neq \varnothing$. Since m's preferences are divided into k quantiles, w must be in a strictly better quantile than $p(m)$. Thus, m must have proposed to w in a strictly earlier call to **QuantileMatch** than the call in which he was matched with $p(m)$. Thus, by Lemma 2, m must have been rejected by w, implying that w was matched with a man m' in the same or better quantile than m in this round. By Lemma 1, w's partner when **ASM** terminates is at least as desirable as m'. This contradicts that (m, w) is ε-blocking.

On the other hand, if $p(m) = \varnothing$, then since m is good, he must have been rejected by all of his acceptable partners, and in particular, by w. Thus, as in the previous paragraph, w must be matched with a man in the same or better quantile than m. □

LEMMA 4 (FEW NON-$(2/k)$-BLOCKING PAIRS). *There are at most $4|E|/k$ blocking pairs which are not $(2/k)$-blocking.*

PROOF. Suppose (m, w) is a blocking pair which is not $(2/k)$-blocking. Thus, at least one of the following holds:

$$P^m(w) - P^m(p(m)) \leq 2\deg(m)/k \quad (1)$$
$$P^w(m) - P^w(p(w)) \leq 2\deg(w)/k, \quad (2)$$

where by convention we take $P^m(\varnothing) = \deg(m) + 1$. Let E_N denote the set of blocking pairs which are not $(2/k)$-blocking. For each m, the number of edges satisfying (1) is at most $2\deg(m)/k$, and similarly for the women. Thus

$$|E_N| \leq \sum_{m \in Y} 2\deg(m)/k + \sum_{w \in X} 2\deg(w)/k = 4|E|/k,$$

as desired. □

Lemma 3 shows that no good player is involved in any $(2/k)$-blocking pairs. Combining Lemmas 3 and 4, we can bound the number of blocking pairs incident with good men. All that remains is to bound the number of $(2/k)$-blocking pairs incident with bad men. In the next section, we show that the proportion of bad men is small (at most δn), and bound the number of $(2/k)$-blocking pairs they contribute. We remark that by Lemma 4 and the lower bound of Kipnis and Patt-Shamir [9], we cannot hope to have all men be good in $o(\sqrt{n}/\log n)$ rounds.

4.2 Bounding blocking pairs from bad players

In this section, we prove the following bound on the number of blocking pairs contributed by the bad men at the termination of **ASM**. Throughout the section, for simplicity of notation, we assume that $\log n$ is an integer.

LEMMA 5 (BAD MEN GUARANTEE). *At the termination of **ASM**, for any $\delta \leq \frac{1}{2}$ the bad men contribute at most $4\delta|E|$ $(2/k)$-blocking pairs.*

The proof of Lemma 5 is in two parts corresponding to guarantees for each of the two nested loops in **ASM**. We refer to men m with $|Q^m| \geq 2^i$ as ***active in the ith iteration*** of the outer loop; the remaining men are ***inactive*** in the ith iteration.

LEMMA 6 (FEW BAD MEN). *When the inner loop in **ASM** terminates, at most a δ-fraction of active men are bad.*

PROOF. Let $\mathcal{A}$ denote the set of active men before executing the inner loop in **ASM**. Suppose that after ℓ iterations of the inner loop, there are b bad men in $\mathcal{A}$. We claim that there must have been at least b bad players in every iteration of the inner loop. To see this, first note that by Lemma 1, the number of matched players (and hence matched men) can only increase with each call to **ProposalRound**. Second, if a man is rejected by all women on his preference list, he will never become bad. Therefore, the number of good players can only increase with each iteration of the inner loop. Thus there must have been at least b bad men after each of the ℓ iterations of the inner loop.

Suppose m was bad before some call to **QuantileMatch**, so that $A^m \neq \varnothing$. By Lemma 2, after **QuantileMatch** m is either matched, or has been rejected by all women $w \in A^m$. In the former case, $p(m)$ rejected all men in her quantile containing m. In either case, m witnessed the rejection of a quantile of men—either by precipitating the rejection of $p(m)$'s quantile, or by being rejected by all women in A. Notice that the number of women who are matched with new partners during an iteration of the outer loop cannot exceed $|\mathcal{A}|$, as if $|\mathcal{A}|$ women did receive new partners, all active men would be matched. Therefore, the women can send at most $k|\mathcal{A}|$ quantile rejections (after which all active men will be rejected by all women). Similarly, the men can receive at most $k|\mathcal{A}|$ quantile rejections. Thus, in total the active men can witness at most $2k|\mathcal{A}|$ quantile rejections. Therefore, if there are b bad men after ℓ calls to **QuantileMatch**, we must have $b\ell \le 2k|\mathcal{A}|$. Choosing $\ell = 2\delta^{-1}k$ gives the desired result. □

We say that a man m is ***bad in the ith iteration*** of the outer loop in **ASM** if m became bad during the ith iteration and $|Q^m| < 2^i$. We denote the set bad men in the i iteration by B_i, so that $B = B_1 \cup B_2 \cup \cdots \cup B_{\log n}$. Thus, $m \in B_i$ is bad and will not participate in any further calls to **QuantileMatch**, so he will be bad when **ASM** terminates.

LEMMA 7 (FEW $(2/k)$-BLOCKING PAIRS). *Each $m \in B_i$ participates in fewer than 2^i $(2/k)$-blocking pairs at the termination of **ASM**.*

PROOF. We will show that each bad $m \in B$ participates in at most $|Q^m|$ $(2/k)$-blocking pairs, whence the lemma follows. To this end, notice that if $w \notin Q^m$, then w must have rejected m in some call to **QuantileMatch**. Therefore, w must have been matched with some m' that is in the same or better quantile as m. By Lemma 1, when **ASM** terminates, w is still matched with someone in at least as desirable quantile as m, implying that (m, w) is not $(2/k)$-blocking. Thus, every $(2/k)$-blocking pair (m, w) must have $w \in Q^m$. □

PROOF PROOF OF LEMMA 5. Let $G_i \subseteq G$ be the set of men which are good at the termination of **ASM** and active after the ith iteration of the outer loop in **ASM**. Then we have $G = G_1 \cup G_2 \cup \cdots \cup G_{\log n}$. Since the number of bad men cannot increase after a call to **QuantileMatch**. By Lemma 6, if there were b men which became bad in some iteration of the outer loop of **ASM**, there were $\frac{1-\delta}{\delta}b$ good men still active during the ith iteration. Since the number of good men can only increase in subsequent iterations, we have

$$\begin{aligned}|B_i \cup B_{i+1} \cup \cdots \cup B_{\log n}| &\le b \\ &\le \frac{\delta}{1-\delta}|G_i \cup G_{i+1} \cup \cdots \cup G_{\log n}|.\end{aligned} \quad (3)$$

Applying (3), we can greedily form disjoint sets

$$H_{\log n} \subseteq G_{\log n},\ H_{\log n-1} \subseteq G_{\log_n -1} \cup G_{\log n}, \ldots, H_1 \subseteq G$$

such that for all i, H_i is active in the ith iteration and $|H_i| = \frac{1-\delta}{\delta}|B_i|$. Then we compute

$$\begin{aligned}\sum_{m\in B}|Q^m| &= \sum_{i=1}^{\log n}\sum_{m\in B_i}|Q^m| \\ &\le \sum_{i=1}^{\log n}|B_i|\,2^i \\ &\le \sum_{i=1}^{\log n}\frac{2\delta}{1-\delta}|H_i|\,2^i \\ &\le \frac{2\delta}{1-\delta}\sum_{m\in G}|Q^m| \\ &\le \frac{2\delta}{1-\delta}|E|.\end{aligned}$$

The first inequality holds by Lemma 7, while the second holds by the choice of the H_i and the definition of the G_i. □

4.3 Approximation guarantee

PROOF PROOF OF THEOREM 3. By Lemma 4, there are at most $4|E|/k$ blocking pairs which are not $(2/k)$-blocking. By Lemma 3, all $(2/k)$-blocking pairs are incident with B. Finally, by Lemma 5, the bad men contribute at most $4\delta|E|$ blocking pairs for $\delta \le 1/2$. Therefore, the total number of blocking pairs is at most $4(\delta + 1/k)|E|$. Choosing $\delta = \varepsilon/8$ and $k = \lceil 8/\varepsilon \rceil$ gives the desired result. □

4.4 Run-time Guarantee

THEOREM 4. ***ASM**(P, ε, n) runs in $O(\varepsilon^{-3}\log^5(n))$ communication rounds.*

PROOF. Notice that the only communication between processors occurs in **ProposalRound**. **ASM**(P, ε, n) iterates **QuantileMatch**(P, k) a total of $O(\varepsilon^{-2}\log n)$ times, while quantile match invokes **ProposalRound**(Q, k, A) $O(\varepsilon^{-1})$ times. Finally, each step of **ProposalRound** can be performed in $O(1)$ communication rounds, except for Step 3, which calls **MaximalMatching**. By [6], **MaximalMatching** runs in $O(\log^4 n)$ communication rounds. Thus, **ASM** requires $O(\varepsilon^{-3}\log^5(n))$ communication rounds, as claimed. □

Remark 4. While the CONGEST model allows for unbounded local computation in each round, the local computations required by **ASM** are quite simple. In fact, each communication round can easily be implemented in nearly-linear time in n. Thus the synchronous run-time of **ASM** is $\tilde{O}(n)$. To our knowledge, this gives the first distributed algorithm whose synchronous run-time is sub-quadratic in n, even for unbounded preferences.

5. RANDOMIZED ALGORITHMS

The main source of complexity in **ASM** comes from finding a maximal matching. While Hańćkowiak, Karoński, and Panconesi's algorithm [6] is the most efficient known deterministic algorithm, faster randomized algorithms are known. Specifically, we consider the algorithm of Israeli and Itai [8]. They describe a simple randomized distributed algorithm which finds a maximal matching in expected $O(\log n)$ rounds. By simply replacing **MaximalMatching** with a truncated version Israeli and Itai's algorithm, we obtain a faster randomized algorithm for finding almost stable matchings. We refer the reader to Appendix A for details on the guarantees for Israeli and Itai's algorithm.

5.1 General preferences

THEOREM 5. *There exists a randomized distributed algorithm, **RandASM**$(P, \varepsilon, n, \delta)$, which for any $\delta, \varepsilon > 0$ finds a $(1-\varepsilon)$-stable matching with probability at least $1-\delta$ in $O(\varepsilon^{-3}\log^2(n/\delta\varepsilon^3))$ rounds.*

PROOF SKETCH. We take **RandASM** to be exactly the same as **ASM**, except that we use Israeli and Itai's algorithm [8] for the **MaximalMatching** subroutine. Specifically, for **MaximalMatching**, we iterate **MatchingRound** (see Appendix A) $O(\log(n/\delta\varepsilon^3))$ times. By Corollary 1, each call to **MaximalMatching** will succeed in finding a maximal matching with probability at least $1 - O(\delta\varepsilon^3/\log n)$. Since **RandASM** calls **MaximalMatching** $O(\varepsilon^{-3}/\log n)$ times, by the union bound, every call to **MaximalMatching** succeeds with probability at least $1-\delta$. The remaining analysis of **RandASM** is identical to that of **ASM**. □

5.2 Almost-regular preferences

For $\alpha \geq 1$, we call preferences $\mathcal{P}$ ***α-almost-regular*** if $\max_{m\in Y} \deg m \leq \alpha \min_{m\in Y} \deg m$. For example, complete preferences (where all men rank all women) are 1-almost-regular, while uniformly bounded preferences are α-almost-regular for $\alpha = \max_{m\in Y} \deg m$. From an algorithmic standpoint, α-almost-regular preferences are advantageous because in order to bound the proportion of blocking edges from bad men, it suffices only to bound the number of bad men. By Lemma 6, to obtain such a guarantee, one need only iterate **QuantileMatch** $O(1)$ rounds (instead of $O(\log n)$ times as required by **ASM**).

Further, for α-almost-regular preferences, we can relax our requirement that **MaximalMatching** actually find a maximal matching. We say that a player v is ***unmatched*** in G_0 if v does not satisfy property 1 or 2 in Definition 3. We call a subroutine **AMM**(η, δ) which finds a matching in which only an η-fraction of players are left unmatched with probability at least $1-\delta$ (see Appendix A for details). These unmatched players are immediately removed from play. With these simplifications, we obtain the following result.

THEOREM 6. *There exists a randomized distributed algorithm **AlmostRegularASM**$(P, \varepsilon, \delta, \alpha)$ which for α-almost-regular preferences P finds a $(1-\varepsilon)$-stable matching with probability at least $1-\delta$. The run-time of **AlmostRegularASM**$(P, \varepsilon, \delta, \alpha)$ is $O(\alpha\varepsilon^3 \log(\alpha/\delta\varepsilon))$ rounds.*

PROOF SKETCH. **AlmostRegularASM**$(P, \varepsilon, \delta, \alpha)$ works by iterating **QuantileMatch** $O(\alpha\varepsilon^{-2})$ times, which by Lemma 6 implies that only $\varepsilon/4\alpha$ fraction of men are bad.

We modify **ProposalRound** to call **AMM**(η, δ') instead of **MaximalMatching**. **AMM** runs in $O(\log((\eta\delta')^{-1}))$ and finds a $(1-\eta)$-maximal matching with probability $(1-\delta')$. Since **AMM** is called $O(\alpha\varepsilon^{-3})$ times, choosing $\eta = O(\varepsilon^4/\alpha)$ and $\delta' = O(\delta\varepsilon^3/\alpha)$, **AMM** will leave at most an $\varepsilon/4\alpha$ fraction of men unmatched in any call **AMM** with probability at least $1-\delta$, by the union bound. Such unmatched men are immediately removed from play.

By the preceding two paragraphs, **AlmostRegularASM** produces a matching in which at most an $\varepsilon/2\alpha$ fraction of men are either bad or unmatched. By α-almost-regularity, these men can contribute at most $\frac{\varepsilon}{2}|E|$ blocking pairs. The remaining men are good, and therefore by Lemmas 3 and 4[2] contribute at most $\frac{\varepsilon}{2}|E|$ blocking pairs. □

6. ACKNOWLEDGMENTS

The first author is supported in part by NSF grants 09165174, 1065276, 1118126 and 1136174, US-Israel BSF grant 2008411, OKAWA Foundation Research Award, IBM Faculty Research Award, Xerox Faculty Research Award, B. John Garrick Foundation Award, Teradata Research Award, and Lockheed-Martin Corporation Research Award. This material is based upon work supported by the Defense Advanced Research Projects Agency through the U.S. Office of Naval Research under Contract N00014-11-1-0392. The views expressed are those of the author and do not reflect the official policy or position of the Department of Defense or the U.S. Government.

The second author thanks the anonymous referees for their helpful comments.

7. REFERENCES

[1] David J Abraham, Péter Biró, and David F Manlove. Almost stable matchings in the roommates problem. In *Approximation and online algorithms*, pages 1–14. Springer, 2006.

[2] Kimmo Eriksson and Olle Häggström. Instability of matchings in decentralized markets with various preference structures. *International Journal of Game Theory*, 36(3):409–420, March 2008.

[3] Patrik Floréen, Petteri Kaski, Valentin Polishchuk, and Jukka Suomela. Almost Stable Matchings by Truncating the Gale–Shapley Algorithm. *Algorithmica*, 58(1):102–118, 2010.

[4] D Gale and L S Shapley. College Admissions and the Stability of Marriage. *The American Mathematical Monthly*, 69(1):pp. 9–15, 1962.

[5] Dan Gusfield and Robert W Irving. *The stable marriage problem: structure and algorithms*, volume 54. MIT press Cambridge, 1989.

[6] Michal Hańćkowiak, Michal Karoński, and Alessandro Panconesi. On the distributed complexity of computing maximal matchings. *SIAM Journal on Discrete Mathematics*, 15(1):41–57, 2001.

[7] Avinatan Hassidim, Yishay Mansour, and Shai Vardi. Local computation mechanism design. In *Proceedings of the fifteenth ACM conference on Economics and computation*, pages 601–616. ACM, 2014.

[8] Amos Israeli and Alon Itai. A fast and simple randomized parallel algorithm for maximal matching. *Information Processing Letters*, 22(2):77–80, 1986.

[9] Alex Kipnis and Boaz Patt-Shamir. A note on distributed stable matching. In *Proceedings of the 28th ACM symposium on Principles of distributed computing*, pages 282–283, New York, NY, USA, 2009. ACM.

[10] David Manlove. *Algorithmics of matching under preferences*. World Scientific Publishing, 2013.

[2]Although these lemmas were proven assuming that **MaximalMatching** found a maximal matching (not an almost maximal matching) the proofs remain valid as long as the small fraction of unmatched players immediately remove themselves from play.

[11] David Peleg. *Distributed Computing: A Locality-Sensitive Approach.* Society for Industrial and Applied Mathematics, 2000.

APPENDIX

A. RANDOMIZED MAXIMAL AND ALMOST MAXIMAL MATCHINGS

Israeli and Itai's [8] algorithm for finding a maximal matching works by identifying a sparse subgraph of G, then finding a large matching M_1 in the sparse subgraph. The edges and incident vertices of M_1, as well as remaining isolated vertices, are removed from G resulting in a subgraph G_1. The process is iterated, giving a sequence of subgraphs $G_1, G_2, \ldots$ and matchings $M_1, M_2, \ldots$, until $G_k = \varnothing$. At this point, $M = \bigcup_{i=1}^{k} M_i$ is a maximal matching. We give pseudocode for Israeli and Itai's main subroutine, which we call **MatchingRound**, in Algorithm 4. In [8], Israeli and Itai prove the following performance guarantee for **MatchingRound**.

Algorithm 4 MatchingRound(G): Finds a large matching in a graph

1: Each $v \in V$ picks a neighbor w uniformly at random, forms oriented edge (v, w).
2: Each $v \in V$ with $\deg_{in}(v) > 0$ picks one in-coming edge (w, v) uniformly at random, deletes remaining in-edges. Let G' be the (undirected) graph formed by the chosen edges with orientation ignored.
3: Each $v \in V$ with $\deg_{G'}(v) > 0$ chooses one incident edge (v, w) uniformly at random.
4: The matching M_1 consists of edges $(v, w) \in G'$ which were chosen by both v and w in the previous round. $G_1 = (V_1, E_1)$ is the induced subgraph of G formed by removing all vertices contained in M_1 and any remaining isolated vertices from G.
5: Output (G_1, M_1).

LEMMA 8. *(Israeli and Itai [8]) There exists an absolute constant $c < 1$ such that on input $G = G_0 = (V_0, E_0)$, the resulting graph $G_1 = (V_1, E_1)$ found by **MatchingRound** satisfies $\mathbf{E}(|V_1|) \leq c\,|V_0|$.*

As a consequence of Lemma 8, we obtain the following useful result.

COROLLARY 1. *Let $\eta > 0$ be a parameter. Then $s = O(\log(n/\eta))$ iterations of **MatchingRound** suffice to produce a maximal matching in G with probability at least $1-\eta$.*

PROOF. By Lemma 8, we have $\mathbf{E}(|V_s|) \leq c^s n$. Therefore, applying Markov's inequality gives

$$\Pr(|V_s| \geq 1) \leq \frac{\mathbf{E}(|V_s|)}{1} \leq c^s n.$$

The result follows by taking $s \geq \log(n/\eta)/\log(c^{-1})$. □

The almost regular variant of **ASM** only requires a subroutine that we finds matchings which are almost maximal.

Definition 4. Let $G = (V, E)$ be a communication graph and $M \subset E$ a matching in G. For $0 < \eta \leq 1$, we say that M is $(1-\eta)$-***maximal*** if the set V' of vertices not satisfying conditions 1 or 2 in Definition 3 satisfies $|V'| \leq \eta\,|V|$.

We can apply Lemma 8 to give a constant round algorithm which finds almost maximal matchings.

COROLLARY 2. *There exists a randomized distributed algorithm **AMM**(G, η, δ) which finds a $(1-\eta)$-maximal matching with probability at least $(1-\delta)$. **AMM**(G, η, δ) runs in $O(\log(\eta^{-1}\delta^{-1}))$ rounds.*

PROOF. Consider the algorithm which iterates **MatchingRound** s times. We apply Lemma 8 and Markov's inequality to obtain

$$\Pr(|V_s| \geq \eta n) \leq \frac{c^s n}{\eta n} = \eta^{-1} c^s.$$

Choosing $s = O(\log(\delta^{-1}\eta^{-1}))$, we have $\eta^{-1}c^s \leq \delta$, which gives the desired result. □

A (Truly) Local Broadcast Layer for Unreliable Radio Networks

Nancy Lynch
MIT CSAIL
Cambridge, MA
lynch@csail.mit.edu

Calvin Newport
Georgetown University
Washington, DC
cnewport@cs.georgetown.edu

ABSTRACT

In this paper, we implement an efficient *local broadcast* service for the dual graph model, which describes communication in a radio network with both reliable and unreliable links. Our local broadcast service offers probabilistic latency guarantees for: (1) message delivery to all reliable neighbors (i.e., neighbors connected by reliable links), and (2) receiving *some* message when one or more reliable neighbors are broadcasting. This service significantly simplifies the design and analysis of algorithms for the otherwise challenging dual graph model. To this end, we also note that our solution can be interpreted as an implementation of the *abstract MAC layer* specification—therefore translating the growing corpus of algorithmic results studied on top of this layer to the dual graph model. At the core of our service is a *seed agreement* routine which enables nodes in the network to achieve "good enough" coordination to overcome the difficulties of unpredictable link behavior. Because this routine has potential application to other problems in this setting, we capture it with a formal specification—simplifying its reuse in other algorithms. Finally, we note that in a break from much work on distributed radio network algorithms, our problem definitions (including error bounds), implementation, and analysis do not depend on global network parameters such as the network size, a goal which required new analysis techniques. We argue that breaking the dependence of these algorithms on global parameters makes more sense and aligns better with the rise of ubiquitous computing, where devices will be increasingly working locally in an otherwise massive network. Our push for locality, in other words, is a contribution independent of the specific radio network model and problem studied here.

Categories and Subject Descriptors

C.2.1 [**Network Architecture and Design**]: Wireless Communication; G.2.2 [**Discrete Mathematics**]: Graph Theory—*network problems*

Permission to make digital or hard copies of all or part of this work for personal or classroom use is granted without fee provided that copies are not made or distributed for profit or commercial advantage and that copies bear this notice and the full citation on the first page. Copyrights for components of this work owned by others than ACM must be honored. Abstracting with credit is permitted. To copy otherwise, or republish, to post on servers or to redistribute to lists, requires prior specific permission and/or a fee. Request permissions from permissions@acm.org.
PODC'15, July 21–23, 2015, Donostia-San Sebastián, Spain.
Copyright © 2015 ACM 978-1-4503-3617-8 /15/07 ...$15.00.
DOI: http://dx.doi.org/10.1145/2767386.2767411.

Keywords

radio network; local broadcast; abstract MAC layer; dual graph; unreliability

1. INTRODUCTION

In this paper, we implement an efficient *local broadcast* service in the dual graph radio network model [14, 16, 3, 7, 10, 8], which captures wireless communication over both reliable and unreliable links. In more detail, the dual graph model describes a network with two graphs, one for each type of link. In each round, the network topology used for node communication is a combination of the edges from reliable link graph and some subset of the edges from the unreliable link graph, the latter chosen adversarially. As argued in our earlier studies of this setting, the inclusion of unpredictable links in formal models of radio communication is motivated by the ubiquity of such behavior in real networks (e.g., [23]).

Our local broadcast algorithm yields two types of probabilistic latency guarantees: a fast *progress bound*, which bounds the time for a node to receive *something* when one or more of its reliable neighbors (i.e., neighbors connected by reliable links) are transmitting, and a slower but still reasonable *acknowledgment bound*, which bounds the time for a sender to finish delivering a broadcast message to all of its reliable neighbors. The service we implement operates in an ongoing manner, which makes it suitable for use as an abstraction layer for developing higher-level distributed algorithms for unreliable radio networks. To this end, we note that our algorithm can be interpreted as an implementation of the *Abstract MAC Layer* specification [13, 15]. It follows that the growing corpus of results designed to run on top of this abstraction (e.g., [9, 20, 6, 12, 11, 5]) can be composed with our implementation, automatically porting these existing solutions to the dual graph model for the first time.

More generally speaking, we note that since 2009 [14] we have waged (algorithmic) battle with the complexities introduced by the presence of unpredictable link behavior in the dual graph model—describing upper and lower bounds for a variety of problems [14, 16, 3, 7, 10, 8]. This paper can be seen as the culmination of this half-decade of effort, in which we integrate what we have learned into a powerful abstraction that renders this realistic but difficult setting tractable to a wider community of algorithm designers.

True Locality. Before proceeding to the details or our results, we must first emphasize an important property of our service: its implementation is "truly local," by which we mean that its specification, time complexity, and error bounds are expressed independent of global parameters such as network size. To make this work: we define our correctness and performance properties locally, in terms of individual nodes, rather than globally, in terms of all the nodes; we express our time complexity bounds with respect to local properties, such as bounds on local neighborhood size, not the full network size, n; and we capture our error probabilities as generic ϵ parameters, rather than the common approach of bounding the error in terms of $(1/n^c)$, for some constant $c \geq 1$. Though locality of this type has been well-studied in other network models (e.g., [19, 17]), it is less understood in the wireless setting—a deficiency we believe must be addressed. There are two justifications for this belief.

First, the common practice of seeking "high probability" (i.e., an error probability bound of the form n^{-c}) seems unnatural for most deployment scenarios—why should you have to grow your network size to decrease your error probability?[1] Of course, by instead introducing a generic error parameter, ϵ, as we do in this paper, we are *not* eliminating the possibility of high probability error bounds when useful, as you can simply set $\epsilon = (1/n^c)$ if needed. But we believe that one should try to postpone considering such dependence until it is really necessary. Second, as we see an increasing emphasis on an *Internet of Things* style ubiquity in the wireless setting [1], global properties such as network size can grow to a massive scale. In studying local algorithms for such scenarios, it is important that we separate time complexity and error guarantees from global parameters and instead reorient them toward the relevant local conditions. This paper provides an example of what is required for a reorientation of this type.

Results. Our local broadcast service is parametrized by two time bounds, t_{ack} and t_{prog}, and an error bound, ϵ. It assumes a dual graph model with an oblivious link scheduler (i.e., decisions about which unreliable links to include in the topology in each round are made at the beginning of the execution), and a natural geographic constraint that requires all nodes within distance 1 be connected by a reliable edge, and no nodes at distance more than $r \geq 1$ be connected by an unreliable edge. (We typically assume r is constant and therefore omit it in our result summary below. For the sake of completeness, however, we keep r as a parameter in our analysis during all steps leading to these results.) Our service guarantees: (1) for each broadcast of a message m by a node u, with probability at least $1 - \epsilon$, every reliable neighbor of u will receive m within t_{ack} rounds; and (2) for a given receiver v and span of t_{prog} rounds, such that at least one reliable neighbor of v is broadcasting throughout the entire span, the probability that v *fails* to receive at least one message during these rounds is no more than ϵ. We present an algorithm that takes ϵ as a parameter and implements this service for values of t_{ack} and t_{prog} bounded as follows:

- $t_{prog} = O\left(\log \Delta \log \left(\frac{\log^4 \Delta}{\epsilon}\right)\right)$
- $t_{ack} = O\big(\Delta \log (\Delta/\epsilon) \log \Delta \log \left(\frac{\log^4 \Delta}{\epsilon}\right)\left(\frac{1}{1-\epsilon}\right)\big)$

where Δ is an upper bound on node degree. We emphasize that that these results are near optimal, as even in the absence of unreliable links: (1) any progress bound (which reduces to symmetry breaking among an unknown set of nodes) requires logarithmic rounds (e.g., [21]); and (2) any acknowledgement bound requires at least Δ rounds in the worst case (imagine a receiver u neighboring Δ broadcasters: u can only receive one message per round, delaying one of these broadcasters by at least Δ rounds).

Discussion. A core difficulty in solving local broadcast in the dual graph model is the presence of the unreliable links, which are included or excluded in the network topology according to an arbitrary link schedule (see the model section below for details). To understand this difficulty, recall that the standard strategy for broadcast in a radio network is to cycle through a fixed schedule of geometrically decreasing broadcast probabilities [2]. The intuition for this fixed schedule approach is that for each receiver, one of these probabilities will be well-suited for the local contention among its nearby broadcasters. In the dual graph model, however, there is no fixed amount of local contention: the link schedule can effectively change this amount at each receiver at each round by changing the edges included in the network topology. It is possible, for example, that the link schedule was constructed with the intent of thwarting this fixed schedule strategy by including many links (i.e., increasing contention) when the schedule selects high probabilities, and excluding many links (i.e., decreasing contention) when the schedule selects low probabilities.

To overcome this difficulty, we use as a starting point the general strategy we originally identified in [10]: permute the broadcast probability schedule *after* the execution begins (and therefore, *after* the link schedule has already been generated) to regain independence from the topology. The challenge in permuting a broadcast probability schedule, however, is coordinating the nodes sufficiently that they can apply the same permutation. This creates a chicken and egg problem: to share information among processes requires that we solve broadcast, but we are sharing this information to help solve broadcast. Our solution is to instead solve a form of loose coordination we call *seed agreement*. This problem assumes each participant generates a *seed* (for our purposes, this seed will be random bits for use in generating a probability permutation), and then attempts to convince nearby nodes to *commit* to its seed. A solution to this problem must guarantee that every node commits to some nearby seed (perhaps its own), and, crucially, that there are not too many unique seeds committed in any node's neighborhood (in this paper, we achieve a bound on the order of $\log(1/\epsilon)$, for error probability ϵ). If nodes subsequently use these seeds to permute their broadcast probability schedules (thereby gaining independence from the link schedule), we are assured that there are not *too many* different schedules in a given neighborhood. An extra conflict resolution mechanism is then introduced to our broadcast strategy to help resolve contention among these competing schedules.

We note that the seed agreement subroutine provides a general strategy for taming adversarial link scheduling, and is therefore of independent interest. Accordingly, in this

[1]The most likely answer for why these high probability bounds persist is that they make life easier for the algorithm designer. In particular, if a property holds with high probability in n, a basic union bound provides that the property holds for all nodes in a network for all rounds of any reasonable length execution, which greatly simplifies subsequent analysis. We believe, however, that the algorithm designer should do more work to make the treatment of error probability more natural to the practitioner using the algorithms.

paper we provide a standalone formal specification for the problem that is satisfied by our algorithm. This simplifies the process of subsequently integrating our seed agreement solution into other algorithms.

Finally, we note that to solve these problems in the absence of global parameters such as n requires the introduction of new and non-trivial proof techniques, also of independent interest for the general pursuit of true locality in radio network algorithms. For example, in analyzing our seed agreement subroutine, we could not simply assume that certain key parameters involving local contention hold for the whole network, as this would require a dependence on n. We instead established a *region of goodness* surrounding the target node in our analysis. Using a careful induction on algorithm steps, we showed that although the guaranteed radius of this region must contract as time advances (due to the influence of nodes outside the region for whom we make no assumptions), this contraction is slow enough that our target node safely completes its computation in time. Similarly, in analyzing the local broadcast routines that leverage the seed agreement bits, we had to leverage a new notion of "high probability" that is defined with respect to node degree, not network size (this is the source of the $\log(\Delta/\epsilon)$ factors in the t_{ack} bound described above).

Related Work. The dual graph model of unreliable radio communication was introduced by Clementi et al. [4], and subsequently given the name "dual graph" by Kuhn et al. [14]. It has since been well-studied [14, 16, 3, 7, 10, 22]. Under the pessimistic assumption of an adaptive adversary (as oppose to the oblivious adversary considered in this paper), we previously explored bounds for global broadcast [14, 16], local broadcast [7], and graph structuring algorithms [3, 22]. In [10], we studied the impact of different link scheduler models by proving that some of the more pessimistic bounds from our previous work depended on the assumption that the link schedule was constructed by an adaptive adversary. Of particular relevance to this paper, we proved in [10] that local broadcast with efficient progress is impossible with an adaptive link scheduler of this type, but is feasible with an oblivious link schedule. To establish this latter point, we designed and analyzed a one-shot local broadcast algorithm that offers a progress guarantee (i.e., every node that neighbors a broadcaster will get *some* message quickly) but no reliability guarantees (i.e., no particular message is guaranteed to be delivered). The algorithm in [10] introduced the basic ideas that we developed into the seed agreement specification and *SeedAlg* algorithm presented in this paper. We also note that all results [10] depend on global parameters, whereas here we invest significant effort in gaining true locality.

The abstract MAC layer [13, 15] is an approach to designing wireless network algorithms that defines an abstraction that captures the main guarantees of most wireless link layers, and then divides the task of algorithm design into two efforts: (1) describing and analyzing algorithms that run on top of the abstraction, and (2) implementing the abstraction in specific low-level wireless models. Our local broadcast problem was defined with the standard parameters of a (probabilistic) abstract MAC layer in mind. Our algorithm, therefore, can be interpreted as a strategy for implementing this layer in the dual graph radio network model, and therefore providing a way to translate to the dual graph low level model the growing corpus of algorithms designed and analyzed onto of the abstract MAC layer [9, 20, 6, 12, 11, 5]. We note, however, that the translation from our algorithm to an abstract MAC layer implementation is not immediate, as some (presumably straightforward) work will be required to mediate between our definition, expressed in terms of low-level details like rounds and receiving messages, and the higher level specification of the abstract MAC layer, which is usually expressed only in terms of the ordering and timing of input and output events.

2. THE DUAL GRAPH MODEL

We use a radio network model based on dual graphs, which describes randomized algorithms executing in a synchronous multihop radio network with both reliable and unreliable links. The model describes the network topology with a dual graph (G, G'), where $G = (V, E)$, $G' = (V, E')$, and $E \subseteq E'$, where E describes reliable links and $E' \setminus E$ describes unreliable links. We use n to denote $|V|$, the number of vertices in the graphs. For $u \in V$, we write $N_G(u)$ ($N_{G'}(u)$) to denote u's immediate neighbors in G (G'), not including u itself. We assume two degree bounds: Δ, an upper bound on $|N_G(u) \cup \{u\}|$, and Δ', an upper bound on $|N_{G'}(u) \cup \{u\}|$, defined over every u.

An *embedding* of a (finite) set V of graph vertices in the Euclidean plane is simply a mapping $emb : V \to \mathbb{R}^2$; this provides a pair of (x, y) coordinates for each vertex V. If emb is an embedding of the vertices V of a dual graph (G, G') and r is a real number, $r \geq 1$, then we say that (G, G') is *r-geographic* with respect to emb provided that, for every $u, v \in V, u \neq v$, the following conditions hold (where d represents Euclidean distance):

1. If $d(emb(u), emb(v))) \leq 1$ then $\{u, v\} \in E$.
2. If $d(emb(u), emb(v)) > r$, then $\{u, v\} \notin E'$.

In other words, nearby vertices must be neighbors in G, and distant vertices cannot even be neighbors in G', but vertices in the grey zone represented by the intermediate distances in $(1, r]$ might or might not be neighbors in G or G'. We say that (G, G') is *r-geographic* provided that there exists an embedding emb of the vertex set V such that (G, G') is r-geographic with respect to emb. We sometimes also say that (G, G') is *geographic* provided that there exists a real $r \geq 1$ such that (G, G') is r-geographic.

The dual graphs we consider in this paper are assumed r-geographic, for some particular r, which we fix for the rest of the paper. Moving forward, fix an space I. An *algorithm* is an injective mapping $proc()$ from I to some set of *processes*, which are some type of probabilistic timed automata that model wireless devices. Thus, $proc(i)$ denotes the process with id i. We assume that each process knows (e.g., has in a special component of its initial state) its own id, and also knows the quantities Δ, and Δ'. Notice, we do not assume processes know n (as is typical in such models) as we seek problem definitions and solutions that operate independently of the network size. A *process assignment* for a dual graph (G, G') and id space I is an injective mapping $id()$ from V to I, that assigns a different id to each graph vertex. The two mappings, $proc$ and id, together serve to assign a distinct process to each graph vertex. That is, $proc(id(u))$ is the process assigned to graph vertex u. To simplify terminology, we often write *node* u to indicate $proc(id(u))$ or *process i* to indicate *proc(i)*. We assume that processes do not know the *id*() mapping in advance.

An execution of an algorithm in a given dual graph network topology (G, G') proceeds in synchronous rounds $1, 2, \ldots$. In each round t, each node decides whether to transmit a message or receive, based on its process definition; this might involve a random choice. The communication topology in round t consists of the edges in E plus an arbitrary subset of the edges in $E' \setminus E$. This subset, which can change from round to round, is determined by an adversary that we call a *link scheduler* (see below). Once the topology is fixed for a given round, we use the following standard collision rules to determine communication: node u receives a message m from node v in round t, if and only if: (1) u is receiving; (2) v is transmitting m; and (3) v is the only node transmitting among the neighbors of u in the communication topology chosen by the link scheduler for round t. If node u does not receive a message, then we assume that it receives a special "null" indicator $\perp$: that is, we assume no collision detection.

We now formalize the notion of a *link scheduler*: the entity responsible for resolving the non-determinism concerning which edges from $E' \setminus E$ are added to the topology in each round. Formally, we define a link scheduler to be a sequence $\mathbb{G} = G_1, G_2, G_3, \ldots$, where each G_t (also denoted $\mathbb{G}[t]$) is the graph used for the communication topology in round t. We assume each G_t is allowable given our above model definition.[2] We assume the link scheduler for a given execution is specified at the beginning of the execution. Notice, this definition implies oblivious behavior concerning the network dynamism, as all decisions on the topology are made at the beginning of an execution.

The other relevant source of non-determinism in our model is the *environment* which we use to provide inputs and receive outputs as required by a specific problem (when relevant). For example, in solving local broadcast, an environment provides the messages to broadcast, whereas for a problem like consensus, it provides the initial values. The details of what defines a *well-formed* environment is specified on a problem-by-problem basis. As with the scheduler, when analyzing an execution we first fix the environment for the execution. Though it is possible to conceive of an environment as a probabilistic entity, for the sake of simplicity, the environments we consider in this paper are all deterministic (i.e., once you fix an environment for an execution, all non-determinism regarding inputs is resolved). To formally model the interaction with an environment, we break down the synchronous steps each process takes within a round as follows: first all processes receive inputs (if any) from the environment, next all processes that decide to transmit do so, they then all receive, and finally, they generate outputs (if any) which are processed by the environment to end the round.

We call the combination of a dual graph, process assignment, link scheduler, and environment a *configuration*. Notice, a configuration resolves all relevant model and problem nondeterminism. It follows that a configuration combined with a probabilistic algorithm defines a distribution over possible executions (which we sometimes call the execution tree). When we say an algorithm satisfies a certain property with a given probability, we mean that for all allowable configurations, in the execution tree that results from combining the algorithm with the configuration, the property is satisfied with that probability.

[2]That is, it is a graph that includes all the nodes and edges of G with (perhaps) some edges from $E' \setminus E$ also included.

3. SEED AGREEMENT

The *seed agreement* problem provides a loose form of coordination: each participating node u generates a *seed* s from some known seed domain S, and then eventually commits to a seed generated by a node in its neighborhood (perhaps its own). The safety goal is to bound the number of unique seeds committed in any given neighborhood by a sufficiently small factor δ, while the liveness goal is to do so in a minimum of rounds. In this section, we provide a dual graph algorithm that yields a bound δ that is roughly $O(\log(\frac{1}{\epsilon}))$, and that operates within time that is polynomial in $\log(\Delta)$ and $\log(\frac{1}{\epsilon})$, with (provided) error probability ϵ.

In Section 4, we use seed agreement as a crucial subroutine in our local broadcast service implementation. It is potentially useful, however, to any number of problems in the dual graph model (and elsewhere), so we take our time here to first provide a careful formal specification, which we then satisfy with a new dual graph algorithm. The analysis of our algorithm was rendered particularly tricky by our goal of avoiding dependence on global parameters such as n, and provides some of the main technical contributions of this paper. Due the long length of this analysis, we defer the details to the full version of this paper [18]. The strategy deployed in this section is to bound the rate at which a region of "goodness" (i.e., sufficiently bounded contention) surrounding our target node contracts as the node races toward termination.

3.1 The Seed Agreement Problem

Fix a finite *seed domain* S. We specify the problem as $Seed(\delta, \epsilon)$, where δ is a positive integer representing the seed partition bound, and ϵ is a small nonnegative real representing an error probability. This specification describes correctness for a system based on some arbitrary system configuration, running according to our execution definition. The specification has no inputs. Its outputs are of the form $decide(j, s)_u$, where $j \in I$, $s \in S$, and $u \in V$. This represents a decision by the node at graph vertex i to commit to the seed s proposed by the node with id j (in the following, we call j the *owner* of seed s). We begin with two basic non-probabilistic conditions on the outputs; these must hold in every execution:

1. *Well-formedness:* In every execution, for each vertex u, exactly one $decide(*, *)_u$ occurs.

2. *Consistency:* In every execution, for each pair of vertices u_1, u_2, if $decide(j, s_1)_{u_1}$ and $decide(j, s_2)_{u_2}$ both occur, then $s_1 = s_2$.

That is, if outputs contain the same owners then they also contain the same seeds. The two remaining conditions are probabilistic. To talk about probabilities of events, we must first specify the probability distribution. As noted in Section 2, the combination of the system configuration fixed above and a given seed agreement algorithm defines a distribution on executions. We state our remaining properties in terms of this distribution. In more detail, we start by considering an agreement property. Let $B_{u,\delta}$ be the event (in the probability space of executions) that at most δ distinct ids appear as seed-owners in *decide* outputs at nodes in $N_{G'}(u) \cup \{u\}$.

3. *Agreement:* For each vertex u, $Pr(B_{u,\delta}) \geq 1 - \epsilon$.

Note that we state Condition 3 for each vertex u separately, rather than in terms of all vertices, as in [10]. This change is needed for expressing costs in terms of local parameters.

We now express independence of the choices of seed values corresponding to different owners. An *owner mapping* M_o is a mapping from V to I, that is, an assignment of an (owner) id to each vertex. A *seed mapping* M_s is a mapping from V to S, that is, an assignment of a seed to each vertex. We say that a seed mapping M_s is *consistent* with an owner mapping M_o provided that, if two vertices have the same owner, then also have the same seed. That is, if $M_o(u) = M_o(v)$ then $M_s(u) = M_s(v)$. Let Own_{M_o} be the event in the probabilistic execution that M_o is the owner mapping.

4. *Independence:* Suppose that M_o is an owner mapping and M_s is a seed mapping, where M_s is consistent with M_o. Suppose that $\Pr(Own_{M_o}) > 0$. Then, conditioned on Own_{M_o}, the probability that M_s is the seed mapping that appears in the execution is exactly $(\frac{1}{|S|})^{|range(M_o)|}$.

Condition 4 says that the probability of each consistent seed mapping is just what it would be if the seed mapping were determined in the following way: All processes first choose a seed from S, uniformly at random. Then after every process chooses a seed owner, it also adopts the associated seed value.

3.2 A Seed Agreement Algorithm

We now describe our seed agreement algorithm, *SeedAlg*, which takes as its sole parameter, an error bound, ϵ_1. We will show, in Theorem 3.1, that this algorithm implements $Seed(\delta, \epsilon)$ for values of δ and ϵ that depend on ϵ_1. Its main strategy is to hold aggressive local leader elections that yield bounded safety violations (i.e., multiple nearby leaders). In the following description, we assume for simplicity that Δ is a power of 2. We also use a "sufficiently large" constant c_4 for the phase length.

Algorithm $SeedAlg(\epsilon_1)$, for process i at graph vertex u, where $0 < \epsilon_1 \leq \frac{1}{4}$:

The algorithm uses $\log \Delta$ *phases*, each consisting of $c_4 \log^2(\frac{1}{\epsilon_1})$ rounds.
Process i maintains a local variable containing its "initial seed" in S, which it chooses uniformly at random from the seed domain S. It also keeps track of its *status* $\in$ {"*active*", "*leader*", "*inactive*"}, and the current phase number and round number.

Now we describe process i's behavior in any particular phase $h \in \{1, \dots, \log \Delta\}$. If *status* = *active* at the beginning of phase h, then process i becomes a leader; i.e., sets *status* to *leader*, with probability $2^{-(\log \Delta - h + 1)}$. Thus, it uses probabilities: $\frac{1}{\Delta}, \frac{2}{\Delta}, \dots, \frac{1}{4}, \frac{1}{2}$, as it progresses through the phases.

If process i becomes a leader at the start of phase h, it immediately outputs $decide(i, s)$, where s is its initial seed. Then, during the remaining rounds of the phase, process i broadcasts (i, s) with probability $\frac{1}{\log(\frac{1}{\epsilon_1})}$ in each round. At the end of the phase, it becomes inactive.

If process i is active but does not become a leader at the start of phase h, then it just listens for the entire phase. If it receives a message containing a pair (j, s), then it immediately outputs $decide(j, s)$ and becomes inactive. If it receives no messages during this phase, then it remains active.

If process i completes all phases and is still active, then it outputs $decide(i, s)$, where s is its initial seed.

3.3 Correctness of *SeedAlg*

The analysis of *SeedAlg* contained in the full version [18] culminates with the main theorem below. For the following, recall that r is the value used in defining the r-geographic property assumed of our dual graph (Section 2), and Δ is the maximum node degree in G.

THEOREM 3.1. *$SeedAlg(\epsilon_1)$ satisfies the $Seed(\delta, \epsilon)$ specification, where:*

- $\delta = O(r^2 \log(\frac{1}{\epsilon_1}))$, *and*
- $\epsilon = O(r^4 \log^4(\Delta)(\epsilon_1)^{c^{r^2}})$, *for a constant c,* $0 < c < 1$.

The algorithm takes $O((\log \Delta) \log^2(\frac{1}{\epsilon_1}))$ rounds.

4. LOCAL BROADCAST

We now define our local broadcast service, then describe and analyze an efficient solution which uses the *SeedAlg* algorithm from Section 3 as a key subroutine.

4.1 The Local Broadcast Problem

The local broadcast problem described here requires nodes to implement an ongoing probabilistic local communication service with timing and reliability guarantees. In more detail, we call the problem $LB(t_{ack}, t_{prog}, \epsilon)$, where $t_{ack} \geq t_{prog} \geq 1$ are integer round bounds, and ϵ is a small real representing an upper bound on the error probability. To define the problem, we must first fix the underlying dual graph network in which it is being solved: $(G = (V, E), G' = (V, E'))$. We then define a set $\mathcal{M}_u$ of possible messages for each $u \in V$. For simplicity, we assume these sets are pairwise disjoint. Let $\mathcal{M} = \bigcup_u \mathcal{M}_u$ be the set of all possible messages. Every node $u \in V$ has a $bcast(m)_u$ input and $ack(m)_u$ output, for each $m \in \mathcal{M}_u$. Node u also has a $recv(m')_u$ output for each $m' \in \mathcal{M}$.

We now restrict the behavior of the environments we consider for this problem. In more detail, we assume that (1) the environment generates each input at a given node u at most once per execution (i.e., each message it passes a node to broadcast is unique), and (2) if the environment generates a $bcast(m)_u$ input at u at some round r, it must then wait until u subsequently generates a $ack(m)_u$ output (if ever) before it can generate another *bcast* input at u. To simplify analysis, we restrict our attention to deterministic environments. Therefore, we can assume the environment is modeled as synchronous deterministic automaton that receives the nodes' *ack* outputs as input, and generates their *bcast* inputs as its output.

In the following, we say a node u is *actively broadcasting m in round r*, if node u received a $bcast(m)_u$ input in some round $r' \leq r$, and through round r, node u has not yet generated a subsequent $ack(m)_u$ output. Similarly, we say u is *active* in a given round if there is some message that u is actively broadcasting during this round. The problem places deterministic and probabilistic constraints on the nodes' output behavior. We begin with the deterministic constraints.

In every execution, the following must always hold:

1. *Timely Acknowledgement.* If node u receives a $bcast(m)_u$ input in round r, it will generate a single corresponding $ack(m)_u$ output in the interval r to $r+t_{ack}$. These are the only *ack* outputs that u generates.

2. *Validity.* If node u performs a $recv(m)_u$ output in some round r, then there exists some $v \in N_{G'}(u)$ such that v is actively broadcasting m in round r.

Recall that if we fix some configuration and an algorithm, the combination yields a well-defined probability distribution (equiv., execution tree) over executions of the algorithm in this configuration. To aid our probabilistic constraint definitions, we first introduce some notation for discussing an execution tree determined by a configuration. When considering any execution from such a tree, we can partition time into *phases* of length t_{prog} starting in the first round. We number these $1, 2, \ldots$. We use the terminology *phase i prefix* to describe a finite execution prefix that includes every round up to the beginning of phase i (i.e., it does not include the first round of phase i but does include the last round—if any—before phase i begins). For a given execution tree, phase i prefix α in this tree, and node u, let A^u_α describe the set of t_{prog}-round extensions of α in which there is a G-neighbor of u that is active throughout every round of phase i, and let B^u_α describe the set of t_{prog}-round extensions where u receives at least one message $m_v \in M_v$ from a node v in a round r such that v is actively broadcasting m_v in r.

We now define two probabilistic constraints that must hold for every configuration:

1. *Reliability.* For every configuration, node u, and r-round execution prefix such that u receives a $bcast(m)_u$ input at the beginning of round r: the probability that every $v \in N_G(u)$ generates a $recv(m)_u$ output before u's corresponding $ack(m)_u$ output, is at least $1 - \epsilon$.

   (Notice: this property leverages the *timely acknowledgment* property which tells us that in every extension of this prefix, u generates an $ack(m)_u$ output wihin t_{ack} rounds.)

2. *Progress.* For every configuration, node u, phase i, and phase i prefix α in the resulting execution tree: $\Pr(B^u_\alpha \mid A^u_\alpha) \geq 1 - \epsilon$.

4.2 Constants

Below is a summary of the constants used in the algorithm description and analysis that follow. In the following, we assume Δ is a power of two.

- ϵ_1 is the notation used in the below algorithm description to describe the desired error probability.

- ϵ' is the maximum error probability bound that guarantees, given the constraints of Theorem 3.1, that the $SeedAlg(\epsilon')$ algorithm satisfies the $Seed(\delta, \epsilon)$ spec for an $\epsilon \leq \epsilon_1/2$.

  Note: given the relationship between *SeedAlg* and *Seed*'s error bounds, as established in Theorem 3.1, $\epsilon' = \Theta((\frac{\epsilon_1}{r^4 \log^4 \Delta})^{(1/(cr^2))})$, where c, $0 < c < 1$, is the constant provided by Theorem 3.1. Because $c < 1$, we can rewrite the bound as $\Theta((\frac{\epsilon_1}{r^4 \log^4 \Delta})^{(\gamma/r^2)})$, for some constant $\gamma > 1$.

- $\epsilon_2 = \min\{\epsilon', \epsilon_1\}$.[3]

- c_2 is a constant used in our analysis of successful receptions of messages.

- c_1 is a constant we use in defining the length of a phase in the algorithm (see T_{prog} below).

- $T_{prog} = \lceil c_1 \cdot r^2 \cdot \log(\frac{1}{\epsilon_1}) \cdot \log(\frac{1}{\epsilon_2}) \cdot \log \Delta \rceil = O(r^2 \log(\frac{1}{\epsilon_1}) \log(\frac{1}{\epsilon_2}) \log \Delta)$ is the number of rounds required by our algorithm to ensure progress.

- $\kappa = T_{prog} \cdot \lceil \log(r^2 \log(\frac{1}{\epsilon_2})) \rceil \cdot \log\log \Delta$: the maximum number of bits consumed from a seed agreement seed in a single *phase* of length T_{prog} worth of broadcasting.

- $T_{ack} = \frac{r^2 12 \log(1/\epsilon_2) \log \Delta \ln(\frac{2\Delta}{\epsilon_1})\Delta'}{c_2 T_{prog}(1-\epsilon_1/2)} = \frac{12 \ln(\frac{2\Delta}{\epsilon_1})\Delta'}{c_2 c_1 \log(1/\epsilon_1)(1-\epsilon_1/2)} = O(\frac{\Delta \log(\Delta/\epsilon_1)}{(1-\epsilon_1)})$ is the number of phases a node will spend attempting to send a message that arrives as a *bcast* input.

- Let $T_s = O(\log \Delta \log^2(\frac{1}{\epsilon_2}))$ be the number of rounds required for the seed agreement algorithm $SeedAlg(\epsilon_2)$ (as provided by Theorem 3.1).

4.3 A Local Broadcast Algorithm

We now describe *LBAlg*: our solution to the local broadcast problem. This description makes use of several constants described in the previous section.

Algorithm $LBAlg(\epsilon_1)$, for process i at vertex u for some real $\epsilon_1, 0 < \epsilon_1 \leq \frac{1}{2}$.

Node u partitions rounds into *phases* of length $T_s + T_{prog}$ rounds. We label these phases $1, 2, 3, \ldots$. During each phase, u can be in one of two states:

[3] *Note:* For asymptotic concision, we want to ensure that the error probability we use for *SeedAlg* is no more than ϵ_1. We cannot simply claim that ϵ', as defined above, satisfies this constraint because given its relationship to to ϵ_1 from above, it is possible that if γ is sufficiently small compared to r^2, and ϵ_1 is sufficiently small compared to r and $\log \Delta$, that this exponent will be a sufficiently small fraction to increase $(\frac{\epsilon_1}{r^4 \log^4 \Delta})$ to something larger than ϵ_1. This min statement handles this possibility.

receiving or *sending*. Node u begins the execution in the receiving state. After receiving a $bcast(m)_u$ input, u will spend the next T_{ack} full phases in the sending state (if it receives the *bcast* input in the middle of a phase, it waits until the beginning of the next phase to switch to the sending state). At the end of the last round of the last of these T_{ack} phases, node u generates an $ack(m)_u$ output, and then returns to the receiving state.

We now define what happens during these phases. At the beginning of each phase, regardless of u's state, it executes $SeedAlg(\epsilon_2)$ as a subroutine, using the seed set $S_\kappa = \{0,1\}^\kappa$; i.e., the set describing every bit sequence of length κ. Let $s_u^{(j)}$ be the seed that node u commits in the beginning of phase j. We call the rounds spent at the beginning of a phase running *SeedAlg* the *preamble* of the phase, and the remaining rounds the *body* of the phase.

Node u's behavior during the body of a given phase j depends on its state. If it is in the receiving state, it simply receives during each of these rounds. If during one of these rounds, node u receives a message m' that it has not yet previously received, it generates a $recv(m')_u$ output.

On the other hand, if u is in the sending state for this phase, during each of the body rounds, it does the following:

1. Node u consumes $\lceil \log (r^2 \log (\frac{1}{\epsilon_2})) \rceil$ new bits from its seed $s_u^{(j)}$. If all of these bits are 0 (which occurs with probability $a \cdot \frac{1}{r^2 \log(\frac{1}{\epsilon_2})}$, for some $a \in [1,2)$) it sets its status to *participant*, otherwise it sets its status to *non-participant*.
2. If u is a non-participant, it receives.
3. If u is a participant, it next consumes $\log\log\Delta$ new bits from $s_u^{(j)}$. Let b be the value in $[\log \Delta]$ specified by these bits. The node then uses an independent (with respect to the other processes) local source of randomness (i.e., *not* bits from $s_u^{(j)}$), to generate b bits with uniform randomness. If all b bits are 0 (which occurs with probability 2^{-b}), u broadcasts its message.

As with the receiving state, if during any of these body rounds, node u receives a message m' that it has not yet previously received, it generates a $recv(m')_u$ output.

The above algorithm divides rounds into phases and then runs a seed agreement algorithm at the beginning of each phase to synchronize shared random bits for the remainder of the phase. Notice that there is nothing fundamental about this frequency of seed agreements. In some settings, it might make sense to run the agreement protocol less frequently, and generate seeds of sufficient length to satisfy the demands of multiple phases. Such modifications do not change our worst-case time bounds but might improve an average case cost or practical performance.

4.4 Correctness of *LBAlg*

Our goal here is to analyze *LBAlg* to prove the following theorem:

THEOREM 4.1. *$LBAlg(\epsilon_1)$ solves the $LB(t_{ack}, t_{prog}, \epsilon_1)$ problem for parameters:*

- $t_{prog} = T_s + T_{prog} = O\left(r^2 \log\Delta \log(\frac{r^4 \log^4 \Delta}{\epsilon_1})\right)$
- $t_{ack} = (T_{ack}+1)(T_s + T_{prog}) = O\left(r^2 \Delta \log(\Delta/\epsilon_1) \log\Delta \log(\frac{r^4 \log^4\Delta}{\epsilon_1})(\frac{1}{1-\epsilon_1})\right)$

Below is the core lemma on which we build our proof of Theorem 4.1. This lemma bounds the behavior of *LBAlg* within the scope of a single phase. To do so, we first introduce some useful notation. For a given phase i of an execution, let B_i be the set of nodes that are in sending status during phase i, and $R_i = N_G(B_i)$ be the set of nodes that neighbor B_i in G. Notice, because sending status is fixed for the duration of a given phase, both B_i and R_i are determined at the beginning of phase i and cannot change during the phase. Also recall from the model definitions that Δ' bounds the maximum degree in G'. Using this notation, we specify and prove the following key probabilistic behavior:

LEMMA 4.2. *Fix some phase i and an execution prefix through the $(j-1)^{th}$ body round of this phase, for some $j \in \{2, ..., T_{prog}\}$. Fix nodes u and v, where $u \in R_i$ and $v \in N_G(u) \cap B_i$. Assume the call to SeedAlg at the beginning of phase i in this prefix satisfies $B_{u,\delta}$. Let p_u be the probability that u receives some message in the jth round, and let $p_{u,v}$ be the probability that u receives a message* from *v in this round. It follows that:*

- $p_u \geq \frac{c_2}{r^2 \log(\frac{1}{\epsilon_2}) \log\Delta}$
- $p_{u,v} \geq p_u/\Delta'$

PROOF. Fix some u, v, t and a prefix, as specified by the lemma statement. (Notice, we know that a node v satisfying the constraints of the statement exists due to the assumption that $u \in R_i$, which implies that $|N_G(u) \cap B_i| > 0$.) Let $\mathcal{S} = \{S_1, S_2, ..., S_k\}$ be a minimum-sized partition of the nodes in $N_{G'}(u) \cap B_i$ such that all nodes in S_j committed to the same seed in the beginning of this phase. Given the lemma assumption that the preamble of this phase satisfies $B_{u,\delta}$, it follows: $k \leq \delta$. Finally, let S_{i_v} be the set from $\mathcal{S}$ that contains v.

We now analyze the next broadcast round. In this round, nodes in B_i use their seeds to decide whether or not to become a participant. In particular, they become a participant with probability $\frac{1}{r^2 \log(\frac{1}{\epsilon_2})} = c/\delta$, for some constant $c > 0$, using bits from their seeds to resolve the random choice. For each $S_j \in \mathcal{S}$, all nodes in S_j make the same decision in each round because they are using bits from the same seed. Let p_{i_v} be the probability that set S_{i_v} decides to be a participant, and *all other* sets in $\mathcal{S}$ decide to be non-participants. To bound p_{i_v}, we apply Lemmata B.17 and B.18 from the analysis of seed agreement in the full version of this paper [18] to obtain the uniformity and independence properties needed to prove the following:

$$
\begin{aligned}
p_{i_v} &= (c/\delta)(1-(c/\delta))^{k-1} \\
&> (c/\delta)(1/4)^{\frac{c(k-1)}{\delta}} \\
&\overset{(k\leq\delta)}{>} (c/\delta)(1/4)^{c} \\
&= \Theta(1/\delta)
\end{aligned}
$$

Assume this event—that only S_{i_v} decides to participate from among the sets in $\mathcal{S}$—occurs. It follows that only nodes in S_{i_v} can potentially broadcast in this round. Let ℓ be the number of links from nodes in S_{i_v} to u included in the network topology for the round by the link scheduler included in our configuration definition. Because S_{i_v} contains the G-neighbor v (by definition), we know that v is connected to u and that therefore $\ell > 0$.

The next thing that happens in this round is that the nodes in S_{i_v} use more random bits from their shared seed to choose a value uniformly from $[\log\Delta]$. If $\ell = 1$, we define the *correct* choice of value from $[\log\Delta]$ to be 1. If $\ell > 1$, we define the *correct* choice to be $\lceil \log \ell \rceil$. By Lemma B.17 (from [18]), we know the nodes in S_{i_v} will choose a value from this set with uniform probability. The probability they choose a correct value with respect to ℓ is therefore at least $1/\log\Delta$.

Assume that this event also occurs. At this point, by assumption, only nodes in S_{i_v} are potential broadcasters. Each such node decides to broadcast with the correct probability, p_c, which, as defined above, is within a factor of 2 of $1/\ell$. Let us consider the possibilities. We first note that with probability at least $1/2$, u will decide to receive in this round (broadcast probability $1/2$, which corresponds to choosing the value 1 from $[\log\Delta]$, is the largest possible broadcast probability).

Assume this event occurs. The probability that *exactly one* neighbor among the ℓ neighbors connected to u subsequently decides to broadcast is constant (as there are ℓ neighbors, each deciding to broadcast with probability $p_c = \Theta(1/\ell)$). To calculate p_u we must now combine all three independent probabilities: the $\Theta(1/\delta)$ probability that S_{i_v} is the only set in $\mathcal{S}$ to participate, the $1/\log\Delta$ probability that S_{i_v} nodes choose the correct value, and the $\Theta(1)$ probability that u decides to receive and exactly one neighbor of u in the topology for the round broadcasts. We combine the constants in these asymptotic expression to define a lower bound on the constant c_2 used in our definition of p_u from the lemma statement.

Now we step back to consider $p_{u,v}$. Whereas we just calculated that there is a constant probability that exactly one node from among ℓ nodes decides to broadcast using broadcast probability p_c, we must now ask the probability that a specific node—i.e., v—is this broadcaster. We can bound this probability as:

$$
p_c(1-p_c)^{\ell-1} = \frac{c'}{\ell}(1-\frac{c'}{\ell})^{\ell-1} \geq \frac{c'}{\ell}(\frac{1}{4})^{c'} \geq \frac{1}{4\Delta'},
$$

where c' is a constant of size at least 1 used in the definition of p_c. By replacing the constant probability for this final step used in the derivation of p_u above with this new $\approx 1/\Delta'$ probability, we get the $p_{u,v}$ bound required by the lemma statement. (As a slight technicality, we omit the $1/4$ in the $\frac{1}{4\Delta'}$ calculation above in this final $p_{u,v}$ bound, as this can be captured by adjusting the constant c_2 calculated for p_u by a factor of 4 to include this extra amount.) □

We can now draw on Lemma 4.2 to prove the progress and reliability properties required by the *LB* specification. We begin with progress:

LEMMA 4.3. *$LBAlg(\epsilon_1)$ solves the $LB(t_{ack}, t_{prog}, \epsilon_1)$ problem for: $t_{prog} = T_s + T_{prog}$.*

PROOF. Notice that this definition of t_{prog} is the same as the length used by the phases in our algorithm. It follows that the boundaries of the phases in the progress property align with the phase boundaries used by *LBAlg*, so we can refer to both types of phases interchangeably. To prove progress, therefore, it is sufficient to show that for any node u and phase i such that u has an active G neighbor, the probability that u receives at least one broadcast message in this phase is at least $1-\epsilon_1$.

To do so, fix some node u, phase i, and phase i prefix α such that A^u_α is non-empty; i.e., there is at least one G neighbor of u that is active throughout phase i. Let α' be the extension of α through the call to *SeedAlg* at the beginning of phase i. By Theorem 4.16, and the definition of the ϵ_2 error parameter passed to *SeedAlg*, this call to *SeedAlg* in this α' extension satisfies $B_{u,\delta}$ with probability at least $1-(\epsilon_1/2)$.

Assume our above assumptions (including the assumption that $B_{u,\delta}$ is satisfied) hold. It follows that Lemma 4.2 applies with respect to u for all T_{prog} of the subsequent body rounds in phase i Let $p_u^{(j)}$ be the (independent) probability that u receives a message in body round j of the phase. Notice, that Lemma 4.2 tells us that $p_u^{(j)} \geq p_u \geq \frac{c_2}{r^2 \log(\frac{1}{\epsilon_2})\log\Delta}$ for each such round. We can now bound the probability that u *fails* to receive a message in all T_{prog} body rounds as:

$$
p_{fail} = \prod_{j=1}^{T_{prog}} (1-p_u^{(j)}) \leq \prod_{j=1}^{T_{prog}} (1-p_u) <
$$

$$
(1/e)^{T_{prog}p_u} = (1/e)^{c_1 c_2 \cdot \log(1/\epsilon_1)}.
$$

It is straightforward to show that for sufficiently large values of constants c_1 and c_2, we get $p_{fail} \leq \epsilon_1/2$. To conclude the proof, we use a union bound to show that the probability that $B_{u,\delta}$ does not hold and/or the probability that u fails to receive a message when this property does hold, is less than ϵ_1: providing the needed $1-\epsilon_1$ probability for u receiving a least one message in phase i. □

We now turn our attention to the reliability property of our local broadcast problem:

LEMMA 4.4. *$LBAlg(\epsilon_1)$ solves the $LB(t_{ack}, t_{prog}, \epsilon_1)$ problem for: $t_{ack} = (T_{ack}+1)(T_{prog}+T_s)$.*

PROOF. Fix some nodes u and v that are neighbors in G. Let $k = \ln(\frac{2\Delta}{\epsilon_1})/p$, for $p = \frac{c_2}{r^2 \log(\frac{1}{\epsilon_2})\log\Delta}$ (i.e., p is the lower bound for $p_{u,v}$ from the statement of Lemma 4.2). In the following, we define a body round to be *useful* with respect to u, if it occurs in a phase such that $B_{u,\delta}$ holds for the preceding *SeedAlg* preamble. Let p_1 be the probability that u fails to receive a message m from v during k useful rounds in which v is active with m. Applying Lemma 4.2 to lower bound the receive probability in each of these rounds, it follows:

$$p_1 \leq (1-p)^k < (1/e)^{pk} = \frac{\epsilon_1}{2\Delta}.$$

We now investigate the number of phases necessary to ensure that v experiences at least k useful rounds with a sufficiently high probability. To do so, we first fix $q = \lceil \frac{12k}{T_{prog}(1-\epsilon_1/2)} \rceil$. Consider an experiment where we run q consecutive phases. Let X_i, for $i \in [q]$, be a random variable that describes the number of useful rounds in phase i of the experiment. Notice, X_i either takes on the value T_{prog} (with probability at least $1 - \epsilon_1/2$) or 0 (else). Let $Y = X_1 + X_2 + ... + X_q$ be the total number of useful rounds generated by the experiment. It follows:

$$\mathbb{E}[Y] = q \cdot T_{prog} \cdot (1 - \epsilon_1/2) = 12k.$$

We now apply a Chernoff Bound, to bound the probability that Y is more than a factor of 2 smaller than its expectation $\mu = \mathbb{E}[Y]$:

$$\Pr(Y < (1/2)\mu = 6k) < e^{-\frac{\mu}{12}} = e^{-k} \leq e^{-\ln(\frac{2\Delta}{\epsilon_1})} = \epsilon_1/(2\Delta).$$

(Notice, in the above we can bound $e^{-k} \leq e^{-\ln(\frac{2\Delta}{\epsilon_1})}$ because $k \geq \ln(\frac{2\Delta}{\epsilon_1})$.)

We have now established that with probability at least $1 - \epsilon_1/(2\Delta)$, u will experience at least $6k > k$ useful rounds in q phases. We earlier established that if u experiences at least k useful rounds during which v is broadcasting m, then u receives m from v with probability at least $1 - \epsilon_1/(2\Delta)$. Assume u broadcasts m for at least q consecutive phases. By a union bound, the probability that both events occur with respect to these phases, and u therefore receives v's message m, is greater than $1 - \epsilon_1/\Delta$.

To conclude, we want to calculate, under the assumption that v broadcasts m for at least q phases, that *every* G neighbor of v succeeds in receiving m. Because there are at most Δ such neighbors, and each succeeds with probability at least $1 - \epsilon_1/\Delta$, a union bound says that every neighbor succeeds with probability at least $1 - \epsilon_1$, as required by the reliability property.

To satisfy reliability, therefore, it is sufficient for any node v receiving a $bcast(m)_u$ input to spend at least q full phases with sending status. Notice, this is exactly what $LBAlg$ requires, as by definition it has v spend the next $T_{ack} = q$ full phases after a $bcast(m)_v$ input in sending status. The t_{ack} in the lemmas statement is defined to be long enough for v to wait up to a full phase length until the next phase boundary, plus the rounds required for an additional q phases. □

We now pull together the pieces to prove Theorem 4.1:

PROOF PROOF (OF THEOREM 4.1). The definition of the local broadcast problem had four conditions, two deterministic and two probabilistic. We consider each in turn and argue that $LBAlg$ satisfies the conditions for the parameter values specified in the theorem statement.

We first note that *timely acknowledgment* holds because $LBAlg$, by definition, has each node generate an *ack* in response to a *bcast* within a fixed number of rounds that is strictly less than the t_{ack} factor from the theorem statement. Similarly, the *validity* condition holds as $LBAlg$, by definition, only has nodes broadcast messages they received in a *bcast* input, and nodes only *recv* messages that they actually received from another node. Moving on to the probabilistic properties, Lemma 4.3 tells us that $t_{prog} = T_s + T_{prog}$ rounds, and that $t_{ack} = (T_{ack}+1)t_{prog}$ rounds. Notice, T_{ack} shows up in t_{ack} unchanged from its definition. The definition of t_{prog}, however, shows up in a form that is simplified as compared to the definition provided for T_s and T_{prog} (which contain both ϵ_1 and ϵ_2 facotrs). To match the bounds in the Theorem statement, therefore, it is sufficient to show that $T_s + T_{prog} = O\big(\log\Delta \log^2(\frac{1}{\epsilon_2}) + r^2 \log\Delta \log(\frac{1}{\epsilon_2}) \log(\frac{1}{\epsilon_1})\big)$ can be upper bounded by $O\left(r^2 \log\Delta \log(\frac{r^4 \log^4 \Delta}{\epsilon_1})\right)$. We dedicate the remainder of this proof to this effort.

By definition, $\epsilon_2 \leq \epsilon_1$. We can, therefore, substitute the former for the latter in our sum, yielding:

$$T_s + T_{prog} = O\big(r^2 \log\Delta \log^2(\frac{1}{\epsilon_2})\big).$$

We need a bound, however, that is expressed with respect the problem parameter ϵ_1. This requires us to dive deeper into the relationship between ϵ_2 and ϵ_1. There are two cases to consider given our definition above that $\epsilon_2 = \min\{\epsilon', \epsilon_1\}$. The first case is that $\epsilon_2 = \epsilon_1$. If this is true, we can simply replace ϵ_2 with ϵ_1 in our above equation, and the result is clearly upper bounded by $O\left(r^2 \log\Delta \log(\frac{r^4 \log^4 \Delta}{\epsilon_1})\right)$ (which strictly increases the log factor by adding the $r^4 \log^{\Delta}$ term).

The second case is that $\epsilon_2 = \epsilon' < \epsilon_1$. By definition of ϵ', it would then follow that $\epsilon_2 = \Theta\big((\frac{\epsilon_1}{r^4 \log^4 \Delta})^{(\gamma/r^2)}\big)$, for some constant $\gamma > 1$. The properties of γ allows us to simplify (asymptotically) the $\log^2(\frac{1}{\epsilon_2})$ term in our above equation as follows:

$$\log^2(\frac{1}{\epsilon_2}) = \big[\log(\frac{(r^4 \log^4 \Delta)^{(\gamma/r^2)}}{(\epsilon_1)^{(\gamma/r^2)}})\big]^2 =$$

$$\big[(\gamma/r^2)\log(\frac{(r^4 \log^4 \Delta)}{(\epsilon_1)})\big]^2 = O\big(\log^2(\frac{r^4 \log^4 \Delta}{\epsilon_1})\big).$$

Notice in the above we simply drop the $(1/r^2)$, as it too is bounded to be at least 1, so dropping it simply increases the value of the upper bound. Now to conclude our argument, we simply substitute this upper bound for $\log^2(\frac{1}{\epsilon_2})$ in our above sum to get the desired equation. □

5. CONCLUSION

In this paper, we described and analyzed an ongoing local broadcast service for the dual graph model. This service hides the complexities introduced by unpredictable link behaviors and therefore has the potential to significantly simplify the development of distributed algorithms for this challenging setting. As noted in the introduction,

Our solution can also be adapted to implement the abstract MAC layer specification [13, 15], allowing existing results for this abstraction to translate to the dual graph model (e.g., [9, 20, 6, 12, 11, 5]). Though we leave the details of this adaptation to future work, we note that it would likely be straightforward, with the main effort focused on aligning our local broadcast problem definition—which depends on low level model details, such as rounds and receiving messages—with the higher level of the abstract MAC layer, which is specified in terms of the timing and ordering of input and output events.

Finally, we emphasize that our commitment to *truly local* algorithms, which required us to avoid global parameters in problem definitions, algorithm strategies, and analysis, is of standalone interest to those studying radio network algorithms. As we argued at this paper's opening, a local perspective provides more flexibility to practitioners, and will become increasingly necessary as network sizes grows.

6. ACKNOWLEDGMENTS

This research is supported in part by: Ford Motor Company University Research Program, NSF Award CCF-1320279, NSF Award CCF-0937274, NSF Award CCF-1217506, NSF CCF-0939370, and AFOSR Award Number FA9550-13-1-0042.

7. REFERENCES

[1] Luigi Atzori, Antonio Iera, and Giacomo Morabito. The Internet of Things: A Survey. *Computer Networks*, 54(15):2787–2805, 2010.

[2] Reuven Bar-Yehuda, Oded Goldreigch, and Alon Itai. On the Time-Complexity of Broadcast in Multi-Hop Radio Networks: An Exponential Gap between Determinism and Randomization. *Journal of Computer and System Sciences*, 45(1):104–126, 1992.

[3] Keren Censor-Hillel, Seth Gilbert, Fabian Kuhn, Nancy Lynch, and Calvin Newport. Structuring unreliable radio networks. *Distributed Computing*, 27(1):1–19, 2014.

[4] A. E. F. Clementi, A. Monti, and R. Silvestri. Round Robin is Optimal for Fault-Tolerant Broadcasting on Wireless Networks. *Journal of Parallel and Distributed Computing*, 64(1):89–96, 2004.

[5] Alejandro Cornejo, Nancy Lynch, Saira Viqar, and Jennifer L Welch. Neighbor Discovery in Mobile Ad Hoc Networks Using an Abstract MAC Layer. In *Annual Allerton Conference on Communication, Control, and Computing*, 2009.

[6] Alejandro Cornejo, Saira Viqar, and Jennifer L Welch. Reliable Neighbor Discovery for Mobile Ad Hoc Networks. In *Proceedings of the International Workshop on Foundations of Mobile Computing*, 2010.

[7] Mohsen Ghaffari, Bernhard Haeupler, Nancy Lynch, and Calvin Newport. Bounds on contention management in radio networks. In *The International Symposium on Distributed Computing (DISC)*, 2012.

[8] Mohsen Ghaffari, Erez Kantor, Nancy Lynch, and Calvin Newport. Multi-message broadcast with Abstract MAC layers and unreliable links. In *Proceedings of the ACM Symposium on Principles of Distributed Computing (PODC)*, 2014.

[9] Mohsen Ghaffari, Erez Kantor, Nancy Lynch, and Calvin Newport. Multi-message broadcast with abstract mac layers and unreliable links. In *Proceedings of the ACM Symposium on Principles of Distributed Computing (PODC)*, 2014.

[10] Mohsen Ghaffari, Nancy Lynch, and Calvin Newport. The cost of radio network broadcast for different models of unreliable links. In *Proceedings of the ACM Symposium on Principles of Distributed Computing (PODC)*, 2013.

[11] Majid Khabbazian, Fabian Kuhn, Dariusz Kowalski, and Nancy Lynch. Decomposing Broadcast Algorithms Using Abstract MAC Layers. In *Proceedings of the International Workshop on Foundations of Mobile Computing*, 2010.

[12] Majid Khabbazian, Fabian Kuhn, Nancy Lynch, Muriel Medard, and Ali ParandehGheibi. MAC Design for Analog Network Coding. In *Proceedings of the International Workshop on Foundations of Mobile Computing*, 2011.

[13] Fabian Kuhn, Nancy Lynch, and Calvin Newport. The Abstract MAC layer. In *Proceedings of the International Symposium on Distributed Computing (DISC)*, 2009.

[14] Fabian Kuhn, Nancy Lynch, and Calvin Newport. Brief announcement: Hardness of broadcasting in wireless networks with unreliable communication. In *Proceedings of the ACM Symposium on the Principles of Distributed Computing (PODC)*, 2009.

[15] Fabian Kuhn, Nancy Lynch, and Calvin Newport. The Abstract MAC layer. *Distributed Computing*, 24(3-4):187–206, November 2011. Special Issue for *DISC 2009: 23rd International Symposium on Distributed Computing*.

[16] Fabian Kuhn, Nancy Lynch, Calvin Newport, Rotem Oshman, and Andrea Richa. Broadcasting in unreliable radio networks. In *Proceedings of the ACM Symposium on Principles of Distributed Computing (PODC)*, 2010.

[17] Fabian Kuhn, Thomas Moscibroda, and Rogert Wattenhofer. What cannot be computed locally! In *Proceedings of the ACM Symposium on Principles of Distributed Computing (PODC)*, 2004.

[18] Nancy Lynch and Calvin Newport. A (truly) local broadcast layer for unreliable radio networks. Technical Report MIT-CSAIL-TR-2015-016, MIT Computer Science and Artificial Intelligence Laboratory, Cambridge, MA, May 2015.

[19] Moni Naor and Larry Stockmeyer. What can be computed locally? *SIAM Journal on Computing*, 24(6):1259–1277, 1995.

[20] Calvin Newport. Consensus with an abstract mac layer. In *Proceedings of the ACM Symposium on Principles of Distributed Computing (PODC)*, 2014.

[21] Calvin Newport. Lower bounds for radio networks made easy. In *Proceedings of the International Symposium on Distributed Computing (DISC)*, 2014.

[22] Calvin Newport. Lower bounds for structuring unreliable radio networks. In *Proceedings of the International Symposium on Distributed Computing (DISC)*, 2014.

[23] Calvin Newport, David Kotz, Yougu Yuan, Robert S Gray, Jason Liu, and Chip Elliott. Experimental Evaluation of Wireless Simulation Assumptions. *Simulation*, 83(9):643–661, 2007.

Efficient Communication in Cognitive Radio Networks*

Seth Gilbert
Natl. University of Singapore
Dept. of Computer Science
Singapore, 117417
gilbert@comp.nus.edu.sg

Fabian Kuhn
University of Freiburg
Dept. of Computer Science
Freiburg, Germany, 79110
kuhn@cs.uni-freiburg.de

Calvin Newport
Georgetown University
Dept. of Computer Science
Washington D.C., U.S., 20057
cnewport@cs.georgetown.edu

Chaodong Zheng
Natl. University of Singapore
Dept. of Computer Science
Singapore, 117417
chaodong@comp.nus.edu.sg

ABSTRACT

Devices in a cognitive radio network use advanced radios to identify pockets of usable spectrum in a crowded band and make them available to higher layers of the network stack. A core challenge in designing algorithms for this model is that different devices might have different views of the network. In this paper, we study two problems for this setting that are well-motivated but not yet well-understood: local broadcast and data aggregation.

We consider a single hop cognitive radio network with n nodes that each has access to c channels. We assume each pair of nodes overlaps on at least $1 \leq k \leq c$ channels.

We first describe and analyze COGCAST, a randomized algorithm that solves local broadcast in $O((c/k) \cdot \max\{1, c/n\} \cdot \lg n)$ time, with high probability, by spreading information in an epidemic manner through the network.

We then propose COGCOMP, a randomized algorithm that solves data aggregation in $O((c/k) \cdot \max\{1, c/n\} \cdot \lg n + n)$ time, with high probability. The COGCOMP algorithm uses COGCAST as a key primitive to establish a spanning tree among the nodes, so that data can be aggregated from leaves to root.

We conclude with a collection of lower bounds that show COGCAST is near optimal (in particular, within a $\lg n$ factor) in many cases. These bounds introduce new techniques of potential standalone interest for those concerned with proving fundamental limits in the cognitive radio network setting.

Categories and Subject Descriptors

C.2.1 [**Computer Communications Networks**]: Network Architecture and Design—*Wireless communication*

Keywords

Cognitive radio networks; local broadcast; data aggregation

1. INTRODUCTION

In a traditional wireless network, devices are assigned with one (or a set of) dedicated channel(s) for their network communication. In a *cognitive radio network*, by contrast, each device is equipped with an advanced radio (called a *cognitive radio*) that surveys a crowded spectrum band to identify available fragments. These fragments are partitioned into appropriately sized frequency bands, and are then presented to the higher layers of the stack as a set of abstract communication channels. Cognitive radio networks are increasingly relevant due to two scenarios: allowing secondary users (e.g., mobile wireless devices) to use leftover spectrum in licensed bands assigned to primary users (e.g., television broadcasters) [10, 21, 22], and improving the number of networks that can practically coexist in an unlicensed band.

A core challenge of cognitive radio networks is that network conditions can vary between devices. A pair of devices, therefore, might end up with two different channel sets that overlap in only a limited number of unknown positions. This challenge is bad news for network practitioners, as it complicates their efforts to provide reliable services, but it is good news for distributed algorithm designers, as it generates many practically-motivated, interesting, and tractable theory problems well-suited to our analytical strengths.

Rendezvous and Beyond

The majority of algorithmic results for cognitive radio network models focus on the problem of *deterministic rendezvous*. In its basic form, this problem assumes two devices (called "nodes" below), u and v, have access to channel sets C_u and C_v, respectively. Both sets are of size c and $|C_u \cap C_v| \geq k$, for some $1 \leq k \leq c$. Executions proceed in rounds. In each round, each node can participate only on a single channel in its set. Nodes do not know each other's channel set in advance. The rendezvous problem is solved in the first round that u and v choose some common channel in $C_u \cap C_v$.

Many papers have focused on creating deterministic channel selection schedules that guarantee a rendezvous in bounded time [6, 11, 12, 15, 16, 19]. The best solutions achieve an $O(c^2)$ bound [6, 11]. It is straightforward to show that basic uniform randomized

*Research supported by Singapore NUS FRC T1 251RES1404, Ford Motor Company University Research Program, NSF Award CCF-1320279, and ERC Grant No. 336495 (ACDC).

Permission to make digital or hard copies of all or part of this work for personal or classroom use is granted without fee provided that copies are not made or distributed for profit or commercial advantage and that copies bear this notice and the full citation on the first page. Copyrights for components of this work owned by others than ACM must be honored. Abstracting with credit is permitted. To copy otherwise, or republish, to post on servers or to redistribute to lists, requires prior specific permission and/or a fee. Request permissions from permissions@acm.org.
PODC'15, July 21–23, 2015, Donostia-San Sebastián, Spain.
© 2015 ACM. ISBN 978-1-4503-3617-8 /15/07...$15.00.
DOI: http://dx.doi.org/10.1145/2767386.2767422 .

channel hopping would improve this bound to $O(c^2/k)$ (which is better for non-constant k).[1]

In this paper, we turn our attention to two related problems in a generalization of this model with n nodes where every pair of nodes maintains a channel overlap of size at least k. These problems are equally as useful as rendezvous but much less well-understood. In both cases, we deploy randomization to achieve high efficiency and simple algorithms. We present our results below.

Result #1: Local Broadcast

We begin by studying *local broadcast*: a designated *source* node must disseminate a message to all other $n-1$ nodes in the network. This problem is a key primitive in cognitive radio networks because it allows a source to synchronize the remaining nodes in the network (e.g., perhaps disseminating shared random bits or network configuration parameters). A simple strategy to solve local broadcast is for all nodes to run (randomized) rendezvous with the source transmitting its message in each slot. Given the rendezvous bound from above, this would solve the problem in $O(c^2/k)$ slots (with perhaps an extra $\lg n$ factor if high probability with respect to n is required).

In this paper, we describe and analyze a broadcast algorithm CogCast that solves the problem in $O((c/k)\cdot\max\{1, c/n\}\cdot\lg n)$ slots, with high probability. For $n \geq c$, this time bound reduces to $O((c/k)\cdot\lg n)$ slots, which is a factor of c faster than the straightforward solution.

The CogCast algorithm itself is simple: in each time slot, each node randomly chooses a channel among its channel set, all nodes that know the message broadcast, and all other nodes listen.[2] This algorithm gains its complexity advantage by embracing, like a biological virus, an epidemic spread of information through the network: the more nodes that know the message, the faster it disseminates. The advantage of our algorithm's simplicity is that it is robust: because nodes do the same thing in every slot, it can gracefully handle changes to the network conditions, temporary faults, and so on—suitable properties for such a basic primitive.

Result #2: Data Aggregation

We next turn our attention to a more general problem: *data aggregation*. In this case, each node in the network has some data (e.g., a sensor reading), and a designated source node wants to compute a function based on these data. A solution to this problem can be used to solve many theoretical tasks (e.g., reaching consensus to maintain consistency) as well as practical tasks (e.g., analyzing network condition snapshots to calculate a quality of service metric), and is therefore widely useful.

As before, a straightforward solution would be for each node to once again run basic (randomized) rendezvous. In this case, the source node should listen while the non-source nodes transmit their data. As noted, each non-source node will rendezvous with the source within $O(c^2/k)$ slots. However, if multiple nodes share the same channel during the rendezvous, only one can succeed in its transmission. As n grows, this crowding will also grow. Assuming that the contention resolution is fair, the obvious upper bound for this straightforward strategy is $O(c^2 n/k)$.

In this paper, we describe and analyze a new data aggregation algorithm CogComp that instead solves the problem in $O((c/k)\cdot\max\{1, c/n\}\cdot\lg n + n)$ slots, with high probability. For $n \geq c$, this reduces to $O(n\lg n/k + n)$, which can be significantly faster than the straightforward solution.

The CogComp algorithm operates in multiple phases and uses CogCast as a key subroutine. In more detail, the source begins by broadcasting an initiation message using CogCast. This execution of CogCast constructs a spanning tree among the n nodes, with the source node being the root. The phases that follow coordinate nodes sufficiently so that they can use this tree to aggregate data to the root (i.e., the source node) efficiently. This process is complicated by the lack of a common control channel and the corresponding inability for the aggregation to proceed in a well-synchronized manner: the structure of the tree depends on which processes overlap on which channels.

Result #3: Lower Bounds

A natural follow-up question given our local broadcast solution is whether more complex algorithms could beat CogCast's performance. We answer this question in the negative by proving two lower bounds. First, we prove that $\Omega((c/k)\cdot\max\{1, c/n\})$ slots are necessary to solve local broadcast with constant probability, matching our upper bound within an $O(\lg n)$ factor. This bound, however, requires the assumption that local channel labels are arbitrary (e.g., if u and v share channel q, they might each have a different local label for this channel)—an assumption for which CogCast works. Under the assumption of global channel labels, our third lower bound proves the necessity of $\Omega(c/k)$ slots, (nearly) matching our upper bound in the $c \leq n$ case. The first lower bound leverages arguments based on the properties of randomized matchings generated in bipartite graphs, while the second leverages a careful treatment of expectations. We note that lower bounds are relatively rare to date in the related cognitive radio network literature, especially for randomized algorithms.

2. MODEL

We consider a single-hop cognitive radio network containing n nodes (each with a unique identity) and C channels. We divide time into synchronous *slots* and assume all nodes are activated simultaneously. We assume each node has access to c of the C channels, for some $1 \leq c \leq C$, and that each pair of nodes overlap on at least k channels, for some $1 \leq k \leq c$. Each node knows the value of k and its own set of available channels. However, nodes do not know anything about the channels assigned to other nodes. We assume that this channel assignment is static. (Nevertheless, as we shall later see in the discussion section, CogCast can also tolerate changing (dynamic) channel assignments and provide similar guarantees.)

We assume nodes assign *local labels* to their c channels. These labels are assigned arbitrarily and are not necessarily uniform among nodes: i.e., for a given channel q, it might be labeled as i at node u, and as $j \neq i$ at node v. This assumption highlights the reality that nodes in cognitive radio networks are not dealing with a uniform view of the network or pre-assigned channels (e.g., as discussed in [11]). This assumption strengthens our upper bounds but potentially weakens our lower bounds. (With this in mind, we explicitly address the channel label assumption when presenting our lower

[1] The preference for determinism in this literature is common but should not be seen as a necessity. A main justification in these papers is that determinism guarantees success, whereas randomized solutions have a failure probability. While true in many cases (see discussion section for more details), we argue that these error bounds can be easily tuned in practice to be negligible. Another justification for determinism is that once a pair of nodes swap information, they can calculate each other's schedule going forward, simplifying subsequent rendezvous. The same result can be achieved with randomization; e.g., nodes can swap the seed for a pseudorandom number generator.

[2] A detail we are skipping here but is addressed in the model section is contention. In particular, we assume that if multiple nodes transmit on the same channel simultaneously, *one* message succeeds.

bounds and prove results for both local channel label and global channel label assumptions.)

In each time slot, each node can operate (i.e., broadcast or listen) on one of its c available channels. If only one node broadcasts on a channel, then all nodes listening on that channel will receive the message. For the case of multiple broadcasts, we use a collision model that abstracts away a standard backoff procedure: if multiple nodes send messages concurrently on one channel, then one of these messages—chosen uniformly at random—is received by all nodes that are listening on the channel. Each broadcaster gets feedback as to whether it has succeeded or failed, and failed ones receive the message that was sent.[3] This behavior can be implemented via standard backoff protocols, with poly-logarithmic cost (with respect to n), in almost all reasonable radio network models.[4] Interested readers can refer to the full version of this paper for more implementation details.

3. RELATED WORK

Cognitive radio networks is an area under active research. From our point of view, in this domain, researchers usually focus on two sub-areas. In the first sub-area, the goal is to build cognitive radios, with an emphasis on physical layer issues such as detecting spectrum use. (E.g., see [4, 8], also see survey papers from Akyildiz et al. [2], and Yucek et al. [23].) In the second sub-area, researchers assume there exists a low-level cognitive radio providing a simple model in which each node has access to a subset of all channels; the question at hand is to develop algorithms to solve various problems (typically, rendezvous). This paper belongs to the second sub-area, where we focus on solving broadcast and aggregation. We will provide a short review of related work below, along with a discussion of rendezvous in cognitive radio networks.

Broadcast

Broadcasting is a fundamental problem in computer networking. Although it has been extensively studied in the context of traditional wireless networks, there has been limited research addressing it in the cognitive radio network setting.

For example, in a system paper [14], the authors consider a multi-hop cognitive radio network. They construct a "minimal neighbor graph" for each node—which contains the minimum set of channels through which the node can reach all its neighbors—so broadcast can be efficiently conducted. More recently, in a paper by Song et al. [20], by carefully constructing channel hopping sequences, the authors were also able to accomplish broadcast in multi-hop cognitive radio networks. Both of these papers focus on simulations to show the effectiveness of their protocols. In this paper, we focus on an algorithmic approach, guaranteeing successful local broadcast with high probability and analyzing our algorithms for worst-case performance.

Another approach for tackling the broadcast problem is to assume that all necessary information is known in advance (e.g., sets channels that are available to nodes in each slot, sets of overlapping channels that are available to pairs of nodes in each slot), and then focus on developing efficient algorithms which can find good schedules to solve the broadcast problem. Both [17] and [13] belong to this category. In this paper, we focus on assuming minimal a priori environmental knowledge.

Rendezvous

Rendezvous is perhaps the most studied problem today in cognitive radio networks (e.g., see [16] for a short survey). The basic requirement is that each pair of nodes in the network must meet every so often. The performance of rendezvous protocols is usually measured in terms of the time it takes for two nodes to meet. Rendezvous can be used to solve local broadcast: once the source node has met all its neighbors, broadcast is completed.

There are several important earlier papers on rendezvous worth mentioning, including [19] by Shin et al., [15] by Lin et al., and [12] by Gu et al. These algorithms typically have time complexity that is polynomial of the total number of channels.

A more recent paper from Gu et al. [11] presents an algorithm that can guarantee rendezvous between two users in $O(\max\{c_u, c_v\}^2)$ time, where c_u and c_v are the number of channels available to the two users, respectively. The key novelty of this work is that the proposed algorithm only relies on local information. Another recent paper from Chen et al. [6] guarantees rendezvous between any two users in $O(c_u \cdot c_v \cdot \lg\lg C)$ time, where C is the total number of channels. Although authors of [6, 11] have shown that their algorithms are (near) optimal when solving rendezvous, CogCast proves that more efficient algorithms exist when solving local broadcast, as the time complexity of CogCast is only $O((c/k) \cdot \max\{1, c/n\} \cdot \lg n)$.

Data Aggregation

Data aggregation provides a powerful tool for performing generic computation. Although there exist numerous works on aggregation in traditional wireless networks (e.g., see [7] for a survey), we are only able to identify one paper [5] that explicitly targets aggregation in cognitive radio networks. However, the models and approaches employed by [5] are very different from the ones considered in this paper. Lastly, we note here that although rendezvous algorithms can potentially be used to solve data aggregation, CogComp is more efficient in many (if not all) cases.

4. THE COGCAST PROTOCOL

In this section, we will describe the CogCast protocol and prove its correctness. Pseudocode and omitted proofs can be found in the full version of the paper.

Protocol Description

CogCast takes a classic epidemic approach: each node that has previously received the message simply chooses a random channel on which to broadcast the message. (We say that a node is *informed* if it has previously received the message; otherwise it is *uninformed*.) More specifically, each node repeats the following for $\Theta((c/k) \cdot \max\{1, c/n\} \cdot \lg n)$ slots: it chooses a channel uniformly at random from its set of c available channels; if it is uninformed, then it listens; otherwise, it broadcasts.

Analysis

We now show that, after $\Theta((c/k) \cdot \max\{1, c/n\} \cdot \lg n)$ slots, every node is informed. The proof divides into two cases, depending on the relationship between n and c. Here we focus on the $c \leq n$ case (as the analysis for the $c \geq n$ case is similar); the complete proof is in the full version of this paper.

[3] In the cognitive radio network community, the collision model is usually stronger: even if multiple nodes are sending messages concurrently on one channel, *all* of these messages will be received by all nodes that are listening on this channel (e.g., [6, 11]).

[4] For example, broadcasting with exponentially decreasing probabilities (e.g., [1, 3]), will ensure a message succeeds with high probability within $O(\log^2 n)$ rounds. Whenever a message succeeds, everyone else receives it and aborts. The only node that does not abort is the node that succeeded, and hence it knows that it succeeded.

The high-level strategy is similar to traditional epidemic analysis: we divide the protocol execution into two stages, and show that by the end of each stage, the set of informed nodes will reach certain size. However, the unknown underlying channel overlapping pattern complicates detailed analysis. For example, if all the nodes share the same k channels, then finding one overlapping channel is hard, yet each overlapping channel is likely to have many nodes. On the other hand, if every pair of nodes share a distinct set of channels, then finding one overlapping channel is easy, yet each overlapping channel is likely to have only a few nodes. As a result, a key challenge in the analysis is to correctly bound the various probabilities so that they hold despite the underlying pattern of overlap.

We now focus on stage one, which is defined to last as long as there are at most $c/2$ informed nodes. In this stage, the message spreads fast: since the number of informed nodes is low, in each slot, each informed node is likely to meet some uninformed node, yielding a typical exponential doubling process. One potential issue, however, is that two broadcasters may choose the same channel and attempt to inform the same uniformed node. We have to be careful to give "credit" to only one of them. We say that a node u *independently informs* v in a slot if, in that slot: u is informed, v is uniformed, u and v both choose the same channel, and no other informed node chooses the same channel.

We now describe the analysis for stage one in more detail.

Assume there are at most $c/2$ informed nodes. Fix an informed node u and a time slot. For channel i, define z_i to be the random variable for the number of uniformed nodes that share channel i with u in this slot. We claim:

CLAIM 1. *When $c \leq n$, if there are at most $c/2$ informed nodes in some fixed time slot, then for an informed node u, the probability that u independently informs an uninformed node is at least $\Theta(1/c^2) \cdot \sum_{i=1}^{C} \min\{z_i, c\}$.*

PROOF. Assume there are $n - c/2 \leq x \leq n-1$ uninformed nodes, and $1 \leq n - x \leq c/2$ informed nodes.

Fix a time slot. For a given informed node u, assume it overlaps the x uninformed nodes on y different channels in total. (Recall that it overlaps each of the uninformed nodes on at least k channels.) Moreover, assume for the ith overlapping channel, there are z_i uninformed nodes that overlap with u on this channel. On the other hand, assume for the ith overlapping channel, there z'_i other informed nodes that overlap with u on this channel. Since there are at most $c/2$ informed nodes, we know $z'_i \leq c/2$.

Based on the above definition, we know in a slot, the probability that u informs at least one uninformed node and no other informed nodes have picked the same channel, is:

$$\begin{aligned}
& \Sigma_{i=1}^{y}(1/c) \cdot (1-(1-1/c)^{z_i}) \cdot (1-1/c)^{z'_i} \\
\geq\ & \Sigma_{i=1}^{y}(1/c) \cdot (1-(1-1/c)^{z_i}) \cdot (1-1/c)^{c/2} \\
\geq\ & \Sigma_{i=1}^{y}(1/c) \cdot (1-(1-1/c)^{z_i}) \cdot (e^{-1}) \\
=\ & \Theta(1/c) \cdot \Sigma_{i=1}^{y}(1-(1-1/c)^{z_i}) \\
\geq\ & \Theta(1/c) \cdot \Sigma_{i=1}^{y}\left(1-(1-1/c)^{\min\{z_i,c\}}\right) \\
\geq\ & \Theta(1/c) \cdot \Sigma_{i=1}^{y}\min\{z_i/c, 1-e^{-1}\} \\
=\ & \Theta(1/c^2) \cdot \Sigma_{i=1}^{y}\min\{z_i, c\}
\end{aligned}$$

This immediately leads to the claim. □

Notice that the summation here depends on the pattern of overlap, i.e., whether the set of shared channels is highly congested or widely distributed. At this point, there are two cases, depending on whether many channels have $\min\{z_i, c\} = z_i$ or $\min\{z_i, c\} = c$. For both cases, we show that:

CLAIM 2. *When $c \leq n$, during the execution of* COGCAST, *if there are at most $c/2$ informed nodes, then for an informed node u, in a slot, $\sum_{i=1}^{C} \min\{z_i, c\} = \Omega(kc)$.*

PROOF. Assume there are $n - c/2 \leq x \leq n-1$ uninformed nodes, and $1 \leq n - x \leq c/2$ informed nodes.

Fix a time slot. For a given informed node u, assume it overlaps with the x uninformed nodes on y different channels. Moreover, assume for the ith overlapping channel, there are z_i uninformed nodes that overlap with u on this channel. Based on this definition, we know $\sum_{i=1}^{y} z_i \geq kx$, as we have assumed each pair of nodes overlap on at least k channels.

To calculate $\sum_{i=1}^{y} \min\{z_i, c\}$, consider two cases: (a) for at most $y - k/2 - 1$ different i, $\min\{z_i, c\} = z_i$; or (b) for at least $y - k/2$ different i, $\min\{z_i, c\} = z_i$. In the first case, we know for at least $k/2 + 1$ different i, $\min\{z_i, c\} = c$. Hence, $\sum_{i=1}^{y} \min\{z_i, c\} \geq (k/2+1) \cdot c = \Theta(kc)$. In the second case, we claim $\sum_{i=1}^{y} \min\{z_i, c\}$ is at least $kx/2 \geq k(n-c/2)/2 \geq kc/4 = \Theta(kc)$. This is because, for each channel that u overlaps with some uninformed nodes, u will overlap with at most x uninformed nodes on that channel. I.e., for any i, we have $z_i \leq x$. Hence, for any $k/2$ overlapping channels, the sum of z_i on those channels is at most $kx/2$. As a result, for the remaining $y - k/2$ overlapping channels, the sum of z_i on those channels is at least $kx - kx/2 = kx/2$. (Recall the sum of all z_i is at least kx.) □

Hence we conclude that during stage one, in a slot, with probability at least $\Omega(k/c)$ an uniformed node u will independently inform an uninformed node. From this we can prove (via a Chernoff bound) that with high probability, within $O((c/k) \cdot \lg n)$ slots, at least $c/2$ nodes will be informed.

From this point onwards, the epidemic doubling process slows down since the number of channels limits the number of new nodes that can be uniquely informed in each slot. As a result, we enter stage two, in which we focus on the uninformed nodes. In particular, assume there are at least $c/2$ informed nodes. Fix an uninformed node u and a time slot. For channel i, define z_i to denote the number of informed nodes that share channel i with u in this slot. With a similar calculation as in Claim 1, we show:

CLAIM 3. *When $c \leq n$, during the execution of* COGCAST, *if there are at least $c/2$ informed nodes, then for an uninformed node u, in a slot, the probability that u becomes informed is at least $\Theta(1/c^2) \cdot \sum_{i=1}^{C} \min\{z_i, c\} = \Omega(k/c)$.*

As before, the key part here is bounding the summation of the channel distributions. Via a union bound, we see that in $O((c/k) \cdot \lg n)$ slots everyone is informed.

The case where $n \leq c$ proceeds similarly, where stage one continues until $n/2$ nodes are informed. In this case, during stage one, in each time slot, each informed node uniquely informs some other nodes with probability $\Omega(kn/c^2)$; in stage two, in each time slot, each uninformed node is informed with probability $\Omega(kn/c^2)$.

Combining the the analysis from both cases, we conclude that:

THEOREM 4. *After executing* COGCAST, *which takes $\Theta((c/k) \cdot \max\{1, c/n\} \cdot \lg n)$ time slots, all nodes will be informed, w.h.p.*

Other Notes

Notice, due to the simple randomized structure of the algorithm, there is no need to assume a static fixed channel assignment. As long as each pair of nodes, in each slot, share at least k common channels, the process completes in the same manner. Similarly, the algorithm itself does not depend explicitly on n or k *except* to determine the running time. In a long-lived system where there is no need to terminate, the algorithm has no dependence on any non-observable system parameters.

5. THE COGCOMP PROTOCOL

In this section, we will describe and analyze the CogComp protocol, which solves the data aggregation problem in $O((c/k) \cdot \max\{1, c/n\} \cdot \lg n + n)$ slots. CogComp contains four phases. We will first give an overview of the protocol, and then explain each phase in more detail.

Protocol Overview

Executing CogCast (described in Section 4) constructs an implicit spanning tree among the n nodes, with the source node being the root: each node designates as its parent the first node from which it was informed. (In fact, each node is informed only once, because after that it broadcasts in each slot.) We call this tree the *distribution tree*. The goal of CogComp is to aggregate values from the leaves of the tree to the root: each child will pass the aggregated information from its subtree to its parent.

Even after the tree is built (via CogCast), there are several challenges in aggregating data. First, nodes do not know their positions in the distribution tree: each node initially knows only its parent. Thus, after building the tree in the first phase, we proceed in the second and third phases to exchange "local" information on a node's neighborhood in the tree. By the end of these two phases, each node will know how many direct children it has. The second problem has to do with contention during the aggregation process. Each channel can be used by only one node at a time, but many parent-child pairs may be sharing that same channel. If this contention is not handled carefully, one might imagine being delayed by $\Theta(n/c)$ time (for example) at each level of the distribution tree. Hence, in the fourth phase where we carry out aggregation, we use a coordination mechanism to limit contention.

We now describe and analyze each phase in more detail.

Phase One

In phase one, each node executes the CogCast protocol. The source node broadcasts a fixed message called Init. Each node records all its actions in phase one. I.e., for each node, for each slot, a node records whether it broadcasts or listens; if it listens in that slot, it records whether it receives Init; if it broadcasts in that slot, it records whether its message is successfully transmitted. This yields the following lemma:

Lemma 5. *After phase one of* CogComp, *a distribution tree is constructed among nodes, with the source node as the root, w.h.p.*

Phase Two

We first introduce the notion of an (r, c)-cluster.

Definition 6. *An (r, c)-cluster is the set of nodes that were first informed in slot r on channel c during phase one.*[5]

Each node, except the source, belongs to one (r, c)-cluster. The (r, c) tuple will help nodes to recognize their parent, children, and siblings.

[5]Since nodes may have different labels for same channel, the channel label inside an (r, c) tuple can be considered as the label from a global oracle's perspective.

In phase two, each node will determine the size of its cluster. Another goal in phase two is to elect a *mediator* for each channel on which some nodes were informed during phase one. As we shall see in phase four, mediators will help avoid contention among nodes so that the aggregation process can quickly make progress.

We now describe phase two in more detail. Phase two contains n slots. Assume that u is a non-source node that was first informed in slot r on channel c during phase one. In each slot during phase two, u goes to channel c and broadcasts the tuple $\langle u, r \rangle$. Notice, either u's broadcast succeeds, or some other node succeeds (as per the assumption that collisions are resolved at a lower layer of the protocol stack). If u fails, then it checks the information within the succeeded message. In particular, if the sender and u are in same cluster, u will add one to a counter that is initially set to one. Otherwise, if u succeeds, then it remains silent and only listens for the rest of the phase, keeps counting number of nodes in its cluster. By the end of the phase, each node has a count of the number of nodes in the cluster in which it itself was informed.

Recall we also elect mediators in phase two. In particular, for a channel c on which some nodes were informed during phase one, let r be the last round in which any node was informed on channel c; the mediator is the node with the smallest identifier in this (r, c)-cluster (i.e., the nodes informed in round r on channel c). Each mediator will record the size and slot number (i.e., the r within an (r, c) tuple) of each cluster that was informed (during phase one) on its channel.

The following lemma summarizes the properties of phase two:

Lemma 7. *After phase two of* CogComp, *the following guarantees hold, w.h.p.: (a) for each (r, c)-cluster, each node within the cluster knows the size of the cluster; and (b) for each channel on which some nodes were informed during phase one, one unique mediator is elected for that channel, and this mediator knows the size and slot number of each (r, c)-cluster that were informed (during phase one) on this channel.*

Phase Three

We now introduce the notion of an (r, c)-informer:

Definition 8. *(r, c)-informer is the node which informed the nodes in the (r, c)-cluster during phase one.*

Obviously, for each node that is not the source node, it has only one informer: the informer of its cluster (i.e., its parent in the distribution tree). A node may, however, be the informer for multiple different clusters, as it may have informed different sets of nodes in different slots. The purpose of phase three is to let each node know the size of the clusters for which it is the informer.

Phase three is implemented as the reverse of phase one, i.e., it is a "rewind" of phase one. More specifically, assume phase one took l slots. Then in slot i of phase three, for a node u, it will go to the channel that it used in slot $l - i + 1$ during phase one. Moreover, if u broadcast in slot $l - i + 1$ during phase one and succeeded, then it will listen in this slot and record the information it has heard. Otherwise, if u listened in slot $l - i + 1$ during phase one and was informed (for the first time), then it will broadcast the size of its cluster.

Notice, not every broadcast will succeed, as a cluster may contain multiple nodes. At least one succeeds, however, as is guaranteed by our collision model, and is sufficient to yield the following:

Lemma 9. *After phase three of* CogComp, *for each (r, c)-cluster, the corresponding informer will know that it is the informer of this cluster, and the size of this cluster, w.h.p.*

Phase Four

In phase four, nodes' values are propagated to the source node: each node will first collect values from its children (in the distribution tree), and then pass them along with its own value to its parent.

Phase four contains multiple *steps*, each of which contains three slots. For a node u, it will stay on the same channel within a step. In a step, a node's role is either a *sender* or a *receiver*: if u is still trying to collect values from its children, then it is a receiver in this step; otherwise, if u is trying to pass values to its parent, then it is a sender in this step. In the following description, if u is a receiver in the current step, then we assume it is the informer of cluster (r, c). Otherwise, if u is a sender, then we assume it is in cluster (r, c).

During phase four, a sender can also be a *mediator*. In particular, if a node u was chosen to be the mediator for a channel during phase two, it runs phase four as a non-mediator until it starts sending values to its parent. From that point on, its mediator duties start. Notice, unlike a normal sender—which can terminate after its values have been sent to the corresponding parent, a mediator needs to continue execution until all nodes that were informed on its channel during phase one have passed their values to their parents.

We now describe each step in more detail.

Slot 1. In the first slot within a step, if u is a receiver or a non-mediator sender, it will listen on channel c in this slot. Otherwise, if u is a mediator, it will broadcast a slot number r' on channel c, indicating nodes in cluster (r', c) should send values to their parent in the following slot. (It chooses r' from the list of (r, c)-clusters for which it is the mediator, in descending order of r.)

Slot 2. In the second slot within a step, if u is a receiver, it will listen. Otherwise, if u is a sender and has heard r' in the previous first slot (or knows r', if u is the mediator) such that $r = r'$, it will broadcast the values it has collected from its children along with its own value, and its identity.

Slot 3. In the last slot within a step, if u is a receiver that is the informer of cluster (r, c), and has heard a message from some node v in cluster (r, c) in the previous second slot, it will broadcast v's identity. If this message is the last message it needs to collect from cluster (r, c), then after this step, it will start collecting values from the next cluster, in descending order of slot number, or start sending values to its parent if there are no more clusters from which it needs to collect values, or terminate if the node itself is the source node and there are no more clusters from which it needs to collect values.

On the other hand, if u is a non-mediator sender, then it will listen in slot three. If it has heard its own identity, then it will terminate as it knows its message has been delivered to its parent.

Finally, if u is a mediator, then it will also listen in slot three. If it has heard an identity which is the last identity that needs to send values in cluster (r', c), then after this step, it will let next cluster (in slot number's descending order) start aggregation, or terminate if there are no more clusters need aggregation on this channel.

In the following theorem, we argue that phase four will finish within $O(n)$ slots (and correctly aggregate all data to the source node), which implies the total time of CogComp is $O((c/k) \cdot \max\{1, c/n\} \cdot \lg n + n)$. The high-level strategy we employ in the proof is as follows: Assume the length of phase one is l slots. During phase four, let r_i be the first step after which the values of nodes that were informed in slot $l - i + 1$ during phase one have been aggregated. We prove that $r_i = r_{i-1} + O(k_i)$, where k_i is the size of the largest cluster that was informed in slot $l - i + 1$ during phase one. Hence, we know the total time consumption of phase four is $O(\sum_{i=1}^{l} k_i) \leq O(n)$.

THEOREM 10. CogComp *aggregates data to the root within* $O((c/k) \cdot \max\{1, c/n\} \cdot \lg n + n)$ *slots, w.h.p.*

PROOF. To prove this theorem, we need only to show that since the start of phase four, every node will terminate within $O(n)$ steps (as each step contains $\Theta(1)$ slots); and when the source node terminates, it knows the values of all other nodes.

In the reminder of this proof, for the ease of presentation, we use r_i to denote the first step (during phase four) after which the values of nodes that were informed in slot $l - i + 1$ during phase one have been aggregated (i.e., the values of these nodes' descendants, along with their own values, have been passed to their parents). Here, l is length of phase one. Notice, for $1 \leq i \leq l$, r_i is well defined. For $i = 0$, we define $r_0 = 1$: at the first step of phase four, nodes that were informed in the last slot of phase one are ready to pass their values to their parents. We further define the term *section* i to refer to the steps (during phase four) in which nodes that were informed in slot $l - i + 1$ during phase one are aggregating. I.e., section i refers to the steps between step r_{i-1} and step r_i. Here, $1 \leq i \leq l$.

Key Claim. We first show a key claim regarding phase four which bounds the time it takes to aggregate: for any $1 \leq i \leq l$, $r_i = r_{i-1} + O(k_i)$, where k_i is the size of the largest cluster that were informed in slot $l - i + 1$ during phase one.

We prove the above claim by induction.

We first consider the base case, where $i = 1$. If at the beginning of step one, the aggregation for section one is already done, then $r_1 = r_0 = 1$, and we have our base case.

Thus let us assume that at the beginning of step one, the aggregation for section one is *not* yet completed. In particular, consider a channel c on which a node u needs to pass values to its parent v. We know u must be in cluster (l, c). According to Lemma 7, assume w is the mediator for channel c.

First, notice u must be on channel c. This is because it was informed in the last slot during phase one, hence it must not have informed anyone else in phase one. Therefore, from the beginning of phase four, it must be on channel c trying to pass its value to v.

Similarly, we know v must be on channel c as well. This is because, by Lemma 9, v knows it needs to collect values from u (more precisely, from cluster (l, c)), and cluster (l, c) has the largest slot number among all clusters it needs to collect values from. Hence, from the beginning of phase four, it must be on channel c trying to collect values from nodes in cluster (l, c).

Lastly, w must be on channel c too. This is because, slot l is the last slot in phase one, and the existence of cluster (l, c) implies the mediator for channel c must be in cluster (l, c). The fact that slot l is the last slot in phase one also implies w will not need to collect values from other nodes. Hence, from the beginning of phase four, w must be on channel c playing the role of mediator.

Now, according to our protocol, from the beginning of phase four, in slot one of each step, w announces that cluster (l, c) is currently being aggregated. (There cannot exist cluster (l', c) such that $l' > l$. Similarly, for any cluster (l', c) where $l' < l$, it will not be processed until cluster (l, c) is done.) Moreover, after each step, on channel c, one node in cluster (l, c) will pass its value to its parent. Since the size of cluster (l, c) is at most k_1, we know that by the end of step $r_0 + k_1 - 1$ nodes in cluster (l, c) must have passed their values to their parent. This completes the proof for the base case.

We now consider the inductive step. Assume for all $j \leq i - 1$, we have $r_j = r_{j-1} + O(k_j)$. Consider $j = i$. If at the beginning of step r_{i-1}, the aggregation for section i is already done, then $r_i = r_{i-1}$, and we have our inductive step. Assume, then, that at the beginning of step r_{i-1}, the aggregation for section i is *not* done yet. In particular, consider a channel c on which a node u needs to pass values to its parent v. We know u must be in cluster

$(l - i + 1, c)$. According to Lemma 7, assume w is the mediator for channel c.

Firstly, notice u must be on channel c. This is because, by the above assumption, at the beginning of step r_{i-1}, u must have already collected all values from its descendants, and is ready to pass these values (along with its own value) to v. Similarly, we know v must be on channel c as well. This is because, by Lemma 9, v knows it needs to collect values from u (more precisely, from cluster $(l - i + 1, c)$), and by the inductive hypothesis, at the beginning of step r_{i-1}, it must have finished collecting values from any cluster (l', c') where $l' > l - i + 1$. Hence, at the beginning of step r_{i-1}, it must be on channel c trying to collect values from nodes in cluster $(l - i + 1, c)$.

Lastly, w must be on channel c too. This is because, by the inductive hypothesis, at the beginning of step r_{i-1}, for any cluster (l', c') where $l' > l - i + 1$, its aggregation process must have already completed. Hence, at the beginning of step r_{i-1}, if w is the informer for any cluster (l', c') where $l' > l - i + 1$, it must have already finished collecting values from these clusters. On the other hand, the existence of cluster $(l - i + 1, c)$ implies the mediator for channel c must be in cluster $(\hat{l}, c)$ such that $\hat{l} \geq l - i + 1$. Thus, w will not be a receiver during the aggregation process of cluster $(l - i + 1, c)$. As a result, we know at the beginning of step r_{i-1}, w must be on channel c playing the role of mediator.

Now, according to our protocol, from the beginning of step r_{i-1}, in slot one of each step, w announces that cluster $(l - i + 1, c)$ is currently being aggregated. (As, by the inductive hypothesis, for any cluster (l', c) where $l' > l - i + 1$, its aggregation process is already completed. Similarly, for any cluster (l', c) where $l' < l - i + 1$, it will not be processed until cluster $(l - i + 1, c)$ is completed.) Moreover, after each step, on channel c, one node in cluster $(l - i + 1, c)$ will pass its value to its parent. Since the size of cluster $(l - i + 1, c)$ is at most k_i, we know that by the end of step $r_{i-1} + k_i - 1$ nodes in cluster $(l - i + 1, c)$ must have passed their descendants' values, along with their own values, to their parent. This completes the proof for the inductive step.

Termination. For a non-source node that is not a mediator, assume it was informed in slot r during phase one. Then according to our protocol and the above analysis, by the beginning of step r_{l-r+1}, it must have terminated. For a non-source node that is a mediator. Assume it is the mediator for channel c, further assume during phase one, slot r was the first slot in which some node were informed on channel c. Then according to our protocol and above analysis, by the beginning of step r_{l-r+1}, it must have terminated. Lastly, for the source node, according to our protocol and above analysis, by the beginning of step r_l, it must have terminated.

Time consumption. According to our above analysis, it is easy to see the time consumption of phase four is bounded by $O(r_l) = O(\sum_{i=1}^{l} k_i)$. Notice, for any node, it will only be counted once in one unique k_i, as, for each non-source node, it belongs to one unique (r, c)-cluster. Therefore, we know $\sum_{i=1}^{l} k_i \leq n$. Hence, the time consumption of phase four is at most $O(n)$ slots. □

Other Notes

Before proceeding to the next section, we would like to highlight an advantage of CogComp: small message overhead. In particular, if the nodes' values are used to compute a function that is *associative* (e.g., `min`/`max`, `count`), then each node in the tree can locally compute this function based on the values it has already known (i.e., values from its children and itself), and only pass the outcome (instead of all values) to its parent. This still guarantees the source node will eventually get the correct result, yet the message size can be restricted to $O(\texttt{polylog}(n))$.

Another point to note is that there is a simple $\Omega(n/k)$ lower bound for aggregation: if all the nodes share the same k channels, and each channel can only be used by one node at a time, then it takes $\Omega(n/k)$ slots for every node to reports its data. Thus, our aggregation protocol is near optimal for small values of k (i.e., $O(1)$) when $c \leq n$; and there is room for improvement for larger k.

6. LOWER BOUNDS

In this section, we will derive two lower bounds for the local broadcast problem, considering both local and global channel labels. These lower bounds show that the time complexity of CogCast is near optimal in many cases.

The Local Channel Label Case

In this section, we consider the local channel label model, i.e., each node may assign a different name to each channel. To prove the $\Omega((c/k) \cdot \max\{1, c/n\})$ bound, our strategy is to first identify a simple game that captures the core difficulty of the problem. The structure of the game will allow us to generate a strong lower bound. We then connect the game to the local broadcast problem by a reduction argument. To obtain the needed bound, the game we consider is slightly different when $k \leq c/2$ and $c/2 < k \leq c$. We will first focus on the $k \leq c/2$ scenario.

The $k \leq c/2$ Scenario

In this setting, we consider a game called the (c, k)-*bipartite hitting game*. In this game, we fix $\beta \geq 2$ as a global constant. The input is two integers c, k such that $1 \leq k \leq c/\beta$. Consider two sets of nodes each of size c: $A = \{a_1, a_2, \cdots, a_c\}$ and $B = \{b_1, b_2, \cdots, b_c\}$. Let G be a complete bipartite graph on bipartition (A, B). The game is played between a *player* and a *referee*. At the beginning of the game the referee privately selects a matching M of size k from G. The game then proceeds in rounds. In each round, the player *proposes* an edge e in G. If $e \in M$, the player *wins*. Otherwise, the game moves on to the next round. We allow the player to be an arbitrary probabilistic automaton. (We place no restrictions on how it uses probabilistic behavior to generate its proposals).

In the lemma below, we show a lower bound for winning the (c, k)-bipartite hitting game. In particular, we first calculate the player's losing probability. Then, through a series of inequalities, we show that for $\Theta(c^2/k)$ rounds, the player's losing probability is larger than $1/2$.

Lemma 11. *Let $\mathcal{P}$ be a player that wins the (c, k)-bipartite hitting game in $f(c, k)$ rounds with probability at least $1/2$, for $1 \leq k \leq c/\beta$ where $\beta \geq 2$ is a constant. It follows that $f(c, k) \geq c^2/(\alpha k) = \Theta(c^2/k)$, where $2 < \alpha = 2(\beta/(\beta - 1))^2 \leq 8$.*

Proof. We consider $\mathcal{P}$'s performance against a referee which chooses each of the k edges in its matching M with uniform and independent randomness, that is, it chooses the first edge randomly, removes those endpoints from consideration, then chooses a second edge, and so on. Assume $\mathcal{P}$ runs for $l = c^2/(\alpha k)$ rounds, where $\alpha = 2(\beta/(\beta - 1))^2$. This generates a sequence $P = \{e_1, e_2, \cdots, e_l\}$ of l edge proposals. Notice, for the ease of presentation, we assume the referee makes its choice of edges after the player has generated the l proposals (but the referee is oblivious to the player's proposals). This is possible as the referee makes its choices independent of the player's behavior.

Define L to be the event that the referee's k edge selections are *not* included in these l proposals. We consider the probability that L happens. To calculate this probability, define $n_i = (c - i +$

$1)^2$ to be the number of edges that is available for the referee to select when it is choosing the ith edge for M. The probability that the referee's i^{th} selection is in P is therefore less than or equal to l/n_i. (Notice, this probability is not necessarily equal to l/n_i as the number of edges in P that is eligible for the referee to select might be less than l.) Hence, it follows that the probability that the player does not win with its ith proposal is as least $1 - l/n_i$. Therefore, we have $\mathbb{P}(L) \geq \Pi_{i=1}^{k}(1 - l/n_i)$.

We now lower bound this probability:

$$
\begin{aligned}
\mathbb{P}(L) &\geq \Pi_{i=1}^{k}(1 - l/n_i) \\
&\geq \Pi_{i=1}^{k}(1/4)^{l/n_i} \\
&\geq \Pi_{i=1}^{k}(1/4)^{l/n_k} \geq (1/4)^{k \cdot \frac{c^2}{\alpha k} \cdot \frac{1}{(c-k+1)^2}} \\
&> (1/4)^{\frac{c^2}{\alpha(c-k)^2}} = (1/4)^{\frac{1}{\alpha} \cdot \frac{1}{(1-k/c)^2}} \\
&\geq (1/4)^{\frac{1}{\alpha} \cdot \frac{1}{(1-1/\beta)^2}} = (1/4)^{\frac{1}{\alpha} \cdot \left(\frac{\beta}{\beta-1}\right)^2} \\
&= (1/4)^{1/2} = 1/2
\end{aligned}
$$

Before proceeding, we will provide some explanations for the second inequality in the above derivation. Firstly, notice that $l/n_i \leq 1/2$ as $l/n_i = \frac{c^2}{kn_i} \cdot \frac{1}{\alpha} = \frac{c^2}{kn_i} \cdot \frac{1}{2} \cdot \left(\frac{\beta-1}{\beta}\right)^2 = \frac{c^2}{2kn_i} \cdot (1 - 1/\beta)^2 \leq \frac{c^2}{2kn_i} \cdot (1 - k/c)^2 = \frac{c^2}{2kn_i} \cdot \left(\frac{c-k}{c}\right)^2 \leq \frac{c^2}{2k \cdot (c-k+1)} \cdot \left(\frac{c-k}{c}\right)^2 < 1/2k \leq 1/2$. Secondly, notice that it is easy to verify the inequality that for any probability $p \leq 1/2$, we have $1 - p \geq (1/4)^p$. With these two observations, we can obtain the second inequality.

The above result implies: within the first l rounds, the probability that the player wins is $1 - \mathbb{P}(L) < 1/2$. □

We then reduce (c, k)-bipartite hitting to local broadcast by demonstrating a strategy for using a fast broadcast algorithm to create a fast solution to the (c, k)-bipartite hitting game—a relationship that allows our above lower bound to transfer over. Notice, the following lemma does not restrict $k \leq c/2$.

LEMMA 12. *Let $\mathcal{A}$ be an algorithm that solves local broadcast with local channel labels in $g(c, k, n)$ slots in a cognitive radio network, with probability at least $1/2$. Then, one can use $\mathcal{A}$ to construct a player $\mathcal{P}_{\mathcal{A}}$ that wins the (c, k)-bipartite hitting game in $\min\{c, n\} \cdot g(c, k, n)$ rounds, for any $1 \leq k \leq c$, with probability at least $1/2$.*

PROOF. We construct our player $\mathcal{P}_{\mathcal{A}}$ to simulate the n nodes in a network where the $n - 1$ initially uninformed nodes share the same channel set which overlaps with the source node's channel set in exactly k locations. Let $A = \{a_1, a_2, \cdots, a_c\}$ be the source node's channel set and $B = \{b_1, b_2, \cdots, b_c\}$ be the channels shared by the remaining $n - 1$ nodes. Since we consider local channel label model, we assume the source node sees each a_i labeled as i, and the other $n - 1$ nodes see each b_i labeled as i.

The first key observation for our simulation is that a k-matching M over the complete bipartite graph with bipartition (A, B) also describes a valid overlap of k channels between the source node and the remaining $n - 1$ nodes (i.e., each $(a_i, b_j) \in M$ corresponds to the source node's local channel i being the same as other nodes' local channel j). The second key observation for our simulation is that in order for $\mathcal{A}$ to solve local broadcast in such a network, there must exist a round in which the source node lands on a shared channel with at least one other node (until this happens, the message starting at the source node makes no progress). When the overlaps are viewed as a matching, this is the same as saying that there must exist a round in which the source node chooses some a_i and some other nodes choose b_j such that $(a_i, b_j) \in M$.

Pulling together these pieces we are ready to describe our simulation and establish its correctness. The player $\mathcal{P}_{\mathcal{A}}$ simulates the source node running with channel set A, the other $n - 1$ nodes running with channel set B, and the (unknown to the player) matching M chosen by the referee for this execution defining the k overlapping channels. In each simulated round r, for each simulated non-source node u, $\mathcal{P}_{\mathcal{A}}$ guesses (a_r, b_r^u) if it has not tried this proposal before, where a_r is the channel selected by the source node in this round, and b_r^u is the channel selected by node u in this round. Notice, this implies player $\mathcal{P}_{\mathcal{A}}$ can get at most $\min\{c, n\}$ unique guesses in each simulated round: when $c \leq n$, every channel in B may be picked by some non-source nodes, giving at most c unique guesses; and when $c \geq n$, every non-source node may be able to pick a different channel in B, giving at most n unique guesses.

If none of these guesses win the game, it follows that the source node has failed to land on a shared channel with some other nodes, so $\mathcal{P}_{\mathcal{A}}$ can correctly complete the simulated round by simulating no communication between the source node and other nodes. (If some non-source nodes share a channel, $\mathcal{P}_{\mathcal{A}}$, of course, will simulate their communication correctly.)

As noted, to complete local broadcast, their must be a round in which the source node shares a channel with some other nodes. During that round, $\mathcal{P}_{\mathcal{A}}$'s guesses will win the bipartite hitting game. Because $\mathcal{P}_{\mathcal{A}}$ gets up to $\min\{c, n\}$ unique guesses per simulated round, its time complexity is at most a factor of $\min\{c, n\}$ slower than the time complexity of $\mathcal{A}$. □

Lastly, by combining Lemma 11 and Lemma 12, we immediately have the following result.

LEMMA 13. *For any algorithm, when $1 \leq k \leq c/2$, to solve local broadcast under the local channel label model with probability at least $1/2$, the time consumption is at least $\Omega((c/k) \cdot \max\{1, c/n\})$.*

The $k > c/2$ Scenario

In this setting, we use a similar strategy as the $k \leq c/2$ scenario, but focusing on a different hitting game. In particular, we consider a game called the *c-complete bipartite hitting game*. The input to this game is an integer $c \geq 1$. Consider two sets of nodes $A = \{a_1, a_2, \cdots, a_c\}$ and $B = \{b_1, b_2, \cdots, b_c\}$. Let G be a complete bipartite graph on bipartition (A, B). The game is played between a *player* and a *referee*. At the beginning of the game the referee privately selects a *maximum* matching M in G (M can be interpreted as a bijection from from A to B). The game then proceeds in rounds. In each round, the player *proposes* an edge e in G. If $e \in M$ the player *wins*. Otherwise, it moves on to the next round. We allow the player to be an arbitrary probabilistic automaton.

Again, we can show a lower bound for the c-complete bipartite hitting game:

LEMMA 14. *Let $\mathcal{P}$ be a player that wins the c-complete bipartite hitting game in $f(c)$ rounds with probability at least $1/2$, for some positive constant c. It follows that $f(c) \geq c/3$.*

Now, notice Lemma 12 is also applicable to the $k > c/2$ scenario (as the (c, k)-bipartite hitting game becomes the c-complete bipartite hitting game when $k = c$). This implies there exists a strategy for using a fast broadcast algorithm to solve c-complete bipartite hitting fast. Therefore, by combining Lemma 12, 13, and 14, we conclude with the following theorem, which proves that under the local channel label model, COGCAST is near optimal (within a multiplicative $O(\lg n)$ factor).

THEOREM 15. *For any algorithm, to solve the local broadcast problem under the local channel label model with probability at least* $1/2$*, the time consumption is at least* $\Omega((c/k)\cdot\max\{1, c/n\})$.

The Global Channel Label Case

In this subsection, we will turn our attention to the global channel label model, in which all nodes assign the same label to a given channel. Notice, COGCAST and COGCOMP work in this setting without any modification, as the global channel label model is just a special case of the local channel label model.

In the following theorem, we show a lower bound for solving local broadcast in the global channel label model. It is derived from calculating the time it will take for the source node to find a channel (among the set of channels that is available to it) on which it overlaps with at least one uninformed node.

THEOREM 16. *For any algorithm, the expected time consumption to solve the local broadcast problem under the global channel label model is at least* $\Omega(c/k)$.

PROOF. Consider the following setup: there are $C = k+n(c-k)$ channels in total. Among these C channels, k channels are chosen uniformly at random, and all nodes have access to these channels. For the remaining $n(c-k)$ channels, they are partitioned into n disjoint parts (each of which contains $c-k$ channels) uniformly at random. Each node has access to the channels in one part; and different nodes have access to different parts. In this setup, we ensure each node has access to c channels, and each pair of nodes overlap on at least k channels. Therefore, this setup is legitimate.

With the above setup, we begin to prove the lower bound. Notice, for any algorithm $\mathcal{A}$, to accomplish local broadcast, a necessary (but not sufficient) condition is that the source node chooses an overlapping channel in one slot. Therefore, the expected number of slots for $\mathcal{A}$ to accomplish local broadcast is at least the expected number of slots until the source node lands on an overlapping channel (for the first time).

Let X_i be an indicator random variable which takes value one if the source node chooses the ith non-overlapping channel before it chooses any overlapping channel, where $1 \le i \le c-k$. We know $\mathbb{P}(X_i = 1) = 1/(k+1)$, in spite of the strategy employed by $\mathcal{A}$. (Notice, the randomness comes from the unknown network setup, and the algorithm $\mathcal{A}$ itself if it is randomized.) On the other hand, we know the expected number of slots until the source node lands on an overlapping channel (for the first time) is at least $\mathbb{E}(\sum_{i=1}^{c-k} X_i)+1 = \sum_{i=1}^{c-k}\mathbb{E}(X_i)+1 = \sum_{i=1}^{c-k}\mathbb{P}(X_i = 1)+1 = \sum_{i=1}^{c-k} 1/(k+1)+1 = (c+1)/(k+1) = \Theta(c/k)$. Hence, the expected number of slots for $\mathcal{A}$ to accomplish local broadcast is at least $\Omega(c/k)$, which proves the lemma. □

As can be seen, for the $c \le n$ case, COGCAST is only off from optimal by an $O(\lg n)$ factor. For the $c \ge n$ case, unfortunately, the gap is larger.

In fact, as one would expect, when $c \gg n$, we can confirm there exist other algorithms that can out-perform COGCAST in some cases. For example, consider the following network setup: there are $C = k+n(c-k)$ channels in total, and all pairs of nodes overlap on the same k channels which are chose uniformly at random. Imagine an algorithm in which all nodes hop among these channels using the same predefined hopping sequence (e.g., a sequential scan). Under such scenario, in expectation, within $O(C/k)$ slots, all nodes will hop to one of the k overlapping channels and hence complete the broadcast process. Now, if we assume $c = n^2$ and $c = k+1$, then the simple hopping-together algorithm can solve broadcast in $O(C/k) = O((k+n)/k) = O(1)$ slots (in expectation), whereas COGCAST will need $O((c^2/nk)\cdot\lg n) = O(n\lg n)$ slots. By contrast, notice, in the local channel label model, such hopping-together algorithm is not possible.

Intuitively, the above result is not surprising: when most of the channels are overlapping channels and all nodes are hopping together, nodes can quickly find one overlapping channel and hence become informed. On the other hand, in COGCAST, each node is independently and randomly hopping among the channels that are available to it. As a result, when $c \gg n$, a lot of time will be consumed before uninformed nodes and informed nodes can land on some common channel, even if the overlap itself is large.

7. DISCUSSION

In this paper, we have developed a simple yet efficient local broadcast algorithm for cognitive radio networks. Building on the broadcast algorithm, we then describe an algorithm for data aggregation. We have also derived two lower bounds, which prove our broadcast algorithm is near optimal in many cases. We believe the techniques used in this paper can be helpful when designing or analyzing other algorithms in cognitive radio networks.

One point worth discussing is the correctness guarantee provided by COGCAST. As we have mentioned earlier, in the cognitive radio network community, there is a tendency of favoring determinism over randomization, as deterministic algorithms can guarantee correctness *all the time*.

Consider, however, a setting where the available channels are not completely stable, e.g., a *dynamic* setting in which the sets of channels that are available to nodes and the sets of channels on which pairs of nodes overlap can change over time. In such setting, COGCAST works as stated and provides the same guarantees without any modification. (In particular, the proof of Theorem 4 is still valid.) Nevertheless, under such model, when $k < c$, it is easy to see that no algorithm exists that can *guarantee* a solution to the local broadcast problem within a finite time period, as (even for a randomized algorithm) there is always some possibility that the channel availability will conspire to prevent communication:

THEOREM 17. *Under the dynamic model, when* $k < c$*, no algorithm exists that can guarantee a solution to the local broadcast problem within a finite time period.*

Another interesting point worth discussing is the potential close connection between broadcast in cognitive radio networks and *n-uniform jamming resistant broadcast in multi-channel wireless networks.*[6] In the current literature, there only exists limited research (e.g., [9, 18]) which attempts to achieve communication in the presence of an n-uniform jamming adversary. Moreover, these few algorithms all focus on single-channel wireless networks. Understanding the relationship between these two not well understood problems may allow researchers to find more solutions and insights.

According to our preliminary analysis, we observe that if an algorithm is able to solve local broadcast in *dynamic* cognitive radio networks with only local channel labels, then it is also able to solve n-uniform jamming resistant broadcast in multi-channel wireless networks. More specifically:

[6]An x-uniform jamming adversary is capable of partitioning n nodes into x disjoint groups, and make jamming decision for each group individually. For example, a 3-uniform jamming adversary may jam channel one for group one, jam channel one and six for group two, and do nothing for group three. Thus, an n-uniform jamming adversary can make jamming decision for each node individually.

THEOREM 18. *Assume $\mathcal{N}'$ is a multi-channel wireless network which contains n nodes and c channels. Assume there is an n-uniform jamming adversary Eve in $\mathcal{N}'$ that can jam at most $0 < k < c/2$ channels in each time slot. Assume $\mathcal{N}$ is a dynamic cognitive radio network in which nodes have only local channel labels. Assume there are n nodes in $\mathcal{N}$, each of which has access to c channels, and each pair of nodes overlap on at least $0 < c - 2k < c$ channels. If an algorithm $\mathcal{A}$ exists that can solve local broadcast in $\mathcal{N}$ in $T(n, c, k)$ time with probability p, then there must exist another algorithm $\mathcal{A}'$ that can solve local broadcast in $\mathcal{N}'$ in $T(n, c, k)$ time with probability p.*

This result implies COGCAST can also be used to solve local broadcast in traditional multi-channel wireless networks, even if an n-uniform jamming adversary is present.

References

[1] N. Abramson. The Aloha system: Another alternative for computer communications. In *Proc. of the November 17–19, 1970, Fall Joint Computer Conf.*, AFIPS 70 (Fall), pages 281–285, 1970.

[2] I. Akyildiz, W.-Y. Lee, M. C. Vuran, and S. Mohanty. A survey on spectrum management in cognitive radio networks. *IEEE Communications Magazine*, 46(4):40–48, 2008.

[3] V. Bharghavan, A. Demers, S. Shenker, and L. Zhang. Macaw: A media access protocol for wireless LAN's. *SIGCOMM Comput. Commun. Rev.*, 24(4):212–225, 1994.

[4] D. Cabric, S. Mishra, and R. Brodersen. Implementation issues in spectrum sensing for cognitive radios. In *Conf. Record of the 38th Asilomar Conf. on Signals, Systems and Computers*, volume 1, pages 772–776, 2004.

[5] Z. Cai, S. Ji, J. He, L. Wei, and A. Bourgeois. Distributed and asynchronous data collection in cognitive radio networks with fairness consideration, 2014.

[6] S. Chen, A. Russell, A. Samanta, and R. Sundaram. Deterministic blind rendezvous in cognitive radio networks. In *Proc. 34th Int. Conf. on Distributed Computing Systems (ICDCS)*, pages 358–367, 2014.

[7] E. Fasolo, M. Rossi, J. Widmer, and M. Zorzi. In-network aggregation techniques for wireless sensor networks: a survey. *IEEE Wireless Communications*, 14(2):70–87, 2007.

[8] A. Ghasemi and E. Sousa. Spectrum sensing in cognitive radio networks: requirements, challenges and design trade-offs. *IEEE Communications Magazine*, 46(4):32–39, 2008.

[9] S. Gilbert and M. Young. Making evildoers pay: Resource-competitive broadcast in sensor networks. In *Proc. 31st Symp. on Principles of Distributed Computing (PODC)*, pages 145–154. ACM, 2012.

[10] R. Goodwins. Next-generation wireless networks: from gigabit WiFi to white space, 2013.

[11] Z. Gu, Q.-S. Hua, and W. Dai. Fully distributed algorithms for blind rendezvous in cognitive radio networks. In *Proc. 15th ACM Int. Symp. on Mobile Ad Hoc Networking and Computing (MOBIHOC)*, pages 155–164, 2014.

[12] Z. Gu, Q.-S. Hua, Y. Wang, and F. Lau. Nearly optimal asynchronous blind rendezvous algorithm for cognitive radio networks. In *Proc. 10th IEEE Communications Society Conf. on Sensor, Mesh and Ad Hoc Communications and Networks*, pages 371–379, 2013.

[13] S. Ji, R. Beyah, and Z. Cai. Minimum-latency broadcast scheduling for cognitive radio networks. In *Proc. 10th IEEE Communications Society Conference on Sensor, Mesh and Ad Hoc Communications and Networks (SECON)*, pages 389–397, 2013.

[14] Y. Kondareddy and P. Agrawal. Selective broadcasting in multi-hop cognitive radio networks. In *Proc. IEEE Sarnoff Symposium*, pages 1–5, 2008.

[15] Z. Lin, H. Liu, X. Chu, and Y.-W. Leung. Jump-stay based channel-hopping algorithm with guaranteed rendezvous for cognitive radio networks. In *Proc. 30th Int. Conf. on Computer Communications (INFOCOM)*, pages 2444–2452, 2011.

[16] H. Liu, Z. Lin, X. Chu, and Y.-W. Leung. Taxonomy and challenges of rendezvous algorithms in cognitive radio networks. In *Proc. Int. Conf. on Computing, Networking and Communications (ICNC)*, pages 645–649, 2012.

[17] C. J. Liyana Arachchige, S. Venkatesan, R. Chandrasekaran, and N. Mittal. Minimal time broadcasting in cognitive radio networks. In *Proc. 12th Int. Conf. on Distributed Computing and Networking (ICDCN)*, pages 364–375. 2011.

[18] A. Richa, C. Scheideler, S. Schmid, and J. Zhang. A jamming-resistant mac protocol for multi-hop wireless networks. In *Proc. 24th Int. Symp. on Distributed Computing (DISC)*, pages 179–193. 2010.

[19] J. Shin, D. Yang, and C. Kim. A channel rendezvous scheme for cognitive radio networks. *IEEE Communications Letters*, 14:954–956, 2010.

[20] Y. Song and J. Xie. A distributed broadcast protocol in multi-hop cognitive radio ad hoc networks without a common control channel. In *Proc. 31st Int. Conf. on Computer Communications (INFOCOM)*, pages 2273–2281, March 2012.

[21] The WhiteSpace Alliance. `http://www.whitespacealliance.org/InTheNews.html`, 2015.

[22] WG802.22 - Wireless Regional Area Networks Working Group. 802.22-2011 - IEEE standard for information technology–local and metropolitan area networks–specific requirements–part 22: Cognitive wireless ran medium access control (MAC) and physical layer (PHY) specifications: Policies and procedures for operation in the TV bands, 2011.

[23] T. Yucek and H. Arslan. A survey of spectrum sensing algorithms for cognitive radio applications. *IEEE Communications Surveys Tutorials*, 11(1):116–130, 2009.

A Local Broadcast Layer for the SINR Network Model*

Magnús M. Halldórsson†
Reykjavik University
Reykjavik, Iceland
mmh@ru.is

Stephan Holzer‡§
Massachusetts Institute of Technology (MIT)
Cambridge, MA, USA
holzer@csail.mit.edu

Nancy Lynch‡
Massachusetts Institute of Technology (MIT)
Cambridge, MA, USA
lynch@csail.mit.edu

ABSTRACT

We present the first algorithm that implements an *abstract MAC (absMAC)* layer in the *Signal-to-Interference-plus-Noise-Ratio (SINR)* wireless network model. We first prove that efficient SINR implementations are not possible for the standard absMAC specification. We modify that specification to an "approximate" version that better suits the SINR model. We give an efficient algorithm to implement the modified specification, and use it to derive efficient algorithms for higher-level problems of global broadcast and consensus.

In particular, we show that the absMAC *progress* property has no efficient implementation in terms of the SINR strong connectivity graph $G_{1-\varepsilon}$, which contains edges between nodes of distance at most $(1-\varepsilon)$ times the transmission range, where $\varepsilon > 0$ is a small constant that can be chosen by the user. This progress property bounds the time until a node is guaranteed to receive *some* message when at least one of its neighbors is transmitting. To overcome this limitation, we introduce the slightly weaker notion of *approximate progress* into the absMAC specification. We provide a fast implementation of the modified specification, based on decomposing the algorithm of [10] into local and global parts. We analyze our algorithm in terms of local parameters such as node degrees, rather than global parameters such as the overall number of nodes. A key contribution is our demonstration that such a local analysis is possible even in the presence of global interference.

Our absMAC algorithm leads to several new, efficient algorithms for solving higher-level problems in the SINR model. Namely, by combining our algorithm with high-level algorithms from [26], we obtain an improved (compared to [10]) algorithm for global single-message broadcast in the SINR model, and the first efficient algorithm for multi-message broadcast in that model. We also derive the first efficient algorithm for network-wide consensus, using a result of [32]. This work demonstrates that one can develop efficient algorithms for solving high-level problems in the SINR model, using graph-based algorithms over a local broadcast abstraction layer that hides the technicalities of the SINR platform such as global interference. Our algorithms do not require bounds on the network size, nor the ability to measure signal strength, nor carrier sensing, nor synchronous wakeup.

Categories and Subject Descriptors

C.2.1 [**COMPUTER-COMMUNICATION NETWORKS**]: Network Architecture and Design—*Distributed networks; Wireless communication*; F.2.2 [**ANALYSIS OF ALGORITHMS AND PROBLEM COMPLEXITY**]: Nonnumerical Algorithms and Problems— *Computations on discrete structures*

General Terms

Wireless Networks; Theory; Algorithms

Keywords

SINR Model; Abstract MAC Layer; Global Broadcast; Global Consensus; Lower Bounds; Approximation

1. INTRODUCTION

Two active areas in Distributed Computing Theory are the attempts to understand wireless network algorithms in the *Signal-to-Interference-plus-Noise-Ratio (SINR) model* and *abstract Medium Access Control layers (absMAC)*.

- The SINR model captures wireless networks in a more precise way than traditional graph-based models, taking into account the fact that signal strength decays according to geometric rules and interference and does not simply stop at a certain border.
- Abstract MAC layers (a.k.a Local Broadcast Layers), express guarantees for local broadcast while hiding the complexities of managing message contention. These guarantees include message delivery latency bounds: an *acknowledgment bound* on the time for a sender's message to be received by all neighbors, and a *progress bound* on the time for a receiver to receive some message when at least one neighbor is sending.

†Supported by Icelandic Research Fund grants 120032011 and 152679-051.
‡Supported by the following grants: AFOSR Contract Number FA9550-13-1-0042, NSF Award 0939370-CCF, NSF Award CCF-1217506, NSF Award CCF-AF-0937274.
§Contact author.
*Full version [17] available at arxiv.org.

Permission to make digital or hard copies of all or part of this work for personal or classroom use is granted without fee provided that copies are not made or distributed for profit or commercial advantage and that copies bear this notice and the full citation on the first page. Copyrights for components of this work owned by others than ACM must be honored. Abstracting with credit is permitted. To copy otherwise, or republish, to post on servers or to redistribute to lists, requires prior specific permission and/or a fee. Request permissions from permissions@acm.org.
PODC'15, July 21–23, 2015, Donostia-San Sebastián, Spain.
Copyright is held by the owner/author(s). Publication rights licensed to ACM.
ACM 978-1-4503-3617-8 /15/07 ...$15.00.
DOI: http://dx.doi.org/10.1145/2767386.2767432.

In this paper we combine the strengths of both models by abstracting and modularizing broadcast with respect to global interference and decay via the SINR formula. This marks the start of a systematic study that simplifies the development of algorithms for the SINR model. At the same time we provide an example that modularizing and abstracting broadcast using MAC layers is beneficial and does not necessarily result in worse time-bounds than those of the broadcast algorithm being decomposed.

Traditionally, SINR platforms are quite complicated (compared to graph-based platforms), and consequently are very difficult to use directly for designing and analyzing algorithms for higher-level problems[1]. We show how absMACs can help to mask their complexity and make algorithms easier to design. This demonstrates the potential power of absMACs with respect to algorithm design for the SINR model. During this process we point out and overcome inherent difficulties that at first glance seem to separate the MAC layers from the SINR model and other physical models. These difficulties arise because absMACs are graph-based interference models, while physical models capture (global) interference by specific signal-propagation formulas. Overcoming this mismatch is a key difficulty addressed in this work.

We tackle this mismatch by introducing the concept of *approximate progress* into the absMAC specification and analysis. The definition of approximate progress enables us to obtain a good implementation of an absMAC, which enables anyone to immediately transform generic algorithms designed for an absMAC into algorithms for the SINR model. The main observation that inspired the definition of approximate progress is a proof, that no SINR absMAC implementation is able to guarantee fast progress in an SINR-induced graph G, while fast progress can be guaranteed with respect to an approximation $\tilde{G}$ of G. Roughly speaking, as SINR-induced strong connectivity graphs are defined based on discs representing transmission ranges, we choose $\tilde{G} := G_{1-2\varepsilon}$ to approximate $G := G_{1-\varepsilon}$ by making the disc a tiny bit smaller than in G.

This abstraction makes it easier to design algorithms for higher-level problems in the SINR model and has further benefits. One of the most intriguing properties of abstract MAC layers is their separation of global from local computation. This is beneficial in two ways. On the one hand this separation allows us to expose useful SINR techniques in the simple setting of local broadcast. On the other hand this separation provides the basic structure to perform an analysis based on local parameters, such as the number of nodes in transmission/communication range and the distance-ratios between them, which is beneficial as pointed out in the full version of this paper [17]. Due to this, and the plug-and-play nature of the absMAC theory, we obtain a faster algorithms for global single-message broadcast than [10] and fast algorithms for global multi-message broadcast and consensus in the SINR model. To achieve these results, we simply plug our absMAC implementation and bounds into the results of [26] and [32].

[1]We refer by *higher-level problems* to e.g. network-wide broadcast, consensus, or computing fast relaying-routes, max-flow and other problems whose solution requires a good understanding of lower-level problems. Here, we refer by *lower-level problems* to e.g. achieving connectivity, minimizing schedules and capacity maximization, which are better understood by now.

Future Benefits of Abstract MAC Layers in the SINR Model.
Many higher-level problems such as global broadcast, routing and reaching consensus are not yet well understood in the SINR model and recently gained more attention [10, 12, 19, 20, 22, 35, 36]. Many of these problems in the algorithmic SINR can be attacked in a structured way by using and implementing absMACs that hide all complications arising from the SINR model and global interference. Using MAC layers, graph-based algorithms can be analyzed in the SINR model even without knowledge of the SINR model and might still lead to almost optimal algorithms as we demonstrate here.

2. CONTRIBUTIONS AND RELATED WORK

We devote large parts of this article to prove theorems on implementing an absMAC in the SINR model and how to modify the absMAC specification to get better results. Based on these theorems we derive results on higher-level problems in the SINR model. We provide more details on contributions in the full version of this paper [17]. Our model assumptions in the SINR model and absMAC are listed in Section 3 and are adapted from [10] and [21]. Table 1 summarizes our algorithmic contributions.

Efficient implementation of acknowledgments. Theorem 4.1 transfers Algorithm 1 of [18] and its analysis to implement fast acknowledgments of the absMAC and modifies it to use local parameters. The full version of this paper [17] provides a close lower bound.

Proof of impossibility of efficient progress. Theorem 4.2 shows that one cannot expect an efficient implementation of progress using the standard definition of absMAC. In particular one cannot implement an absMAC in the SINR model that achieves progress much faster than acknowledgments.

The notion of approximate progress. Achieving progress faster than acknowledgment is key to several algorithms designed for absMACs. Motivated by the above lower bound, we relax the notion of progress in the specification of an absMAC to *approximate progress.* Definition 5.1 introduces approximate progress with respect to an approximation (or some subgraph) of the graph in which local broadcast is performed. Although this new notion of approximate progress is weaker than the usual (single-graph) notion of progress, bounds on approximate progress turn out to be strong enough to yield, e.g., good bounds for global broadcast as long as G is, e.g., connected—see Theorem 7.2. The introduction of approximate progress is the main conceptual contribution of this article.

Efficient implementation of approximate progress. We modify the global single-message broadcast algorithm of [10] to guarantee approximate progress in an absMAC (a local multi-message environment). Our modifications make this algorithm suitable for a localized analysis, which bounds the runtime in terms of local parameters and the desired success probability, see Theorem 6.1. This analysis, which removes the parameter n from the runtime is the main technical contribution of this article and leads to the improved global broadcast algorithms mentioned below.

Task/Bound	Lower bound	Upper bound presented here
f_{ack}	$\Delta_{G_{1-\varepsilon}}{}^{(+)}$	$\mathcal{O}\left(\Delta_{G_{1-\varepsilon}} \cdot \log\left(\frac{\Lambda}{\varepsilon_{ack}}\right) + \log(\Lambda)\log\left(\frac{\Lambda}{\varepsilon_{ack}}\right)\right)$
f_{prog}	$\Delta^{(*)}_{G_{1-\varepsilon}}$	$\mathcal{O}\left(\Delta_{G_{1-\varepsilon}} \cdot \log\left(\frac{\Lambda}{\varepsilon_{ack}}\right) + \log(\Lambda)\log\left(\frac{\Lambda}{\varepsilon_{ack}}\right)\right)$
f_{approg}	–	$\mathcal{O}\left(\left(\log^{\alpha}(\Lambda) + \log^{*}\left(\frac{1}{\varepsilon_{approg}}\right)\right)\log(\Lambda)\log\left(\frac{1}{\varepsilon_{approg}}\right)\right)$
global SMB	$\Omega\left(D_{G_{1-\varepsilon}}\log\left(\frac{n}{D_{G_{1-\varepsilon}}}\right) + \log^2(n)\right)^{(\ddagger)}$	$\mathcal{O}\left(\left(D_{G_{1-2\varepsilon}} + \log\left(\frac{n}{\varepsilon_{SMB}}\right)\right)\log^{\alpha+1}(\Lambda)\right)^{(\dagger)}$
global MMB	$\Omega\left(D_{G_{1-\varepsilon}}\log\left(\frac{n}{D_{G_{1-\varepsilon}}}\right) + k\log(n) + \log^2(n)\right)^{(\ddagger)}$	$\mathcal{O}\left(D_{G_{1-2\varepsilon}}\log^{\alpha+1}(\Lambda) + k\Delta_{G_{1-\varepsilon}}\log\left(\frac{nk}{\varepsilon_{MMB}}\right) + \text{polylog}\left(\frac{nk\Lambda}{\varepsilon_{MMB}}\right)\right)^{(\dagger)}$
global CONS	–	$\mathcal{O}\left(D_{G_{1-\varepsilon}}(\Delta_{G_{1-\varepsilon}} + \log(\Lambda))\log\left(\frac{n\Lambda}{\varepsilon_{CONS}}\right)\right)^{(\dagger)}$

Table 1: Summary of algorithmic results, see Section 3 for details on notation. The table compares our new upper bounds to (known and new) lower bounds. Known lower bounds are graph-based and transfer to our setting, as we use weaker assumptions. To compare graph-based lower bounds with our upper bounds, one might choose $\Lambda = n$ to account for possible high degree and choose $\varepsilon_{SMB} = \varepsilon_{MMB} = n^{-c}$ to achieve w.h.p. correctness. (*) Lower bound proven in this paper using absMAC assumptions of [26]. (†) Lower bounds require runtimes of global broadcast to depend on n even though we perform a local analysis. (‡) Combinations of lower bounds of [1, 13, 30] for graph based models. (+) Trivial lower bound (the full version of this paper [17] provides more details.)

Global consensus, single-message and multi-message broadcast in the SINR model. We immediately derive an algorithm for global consensus (CONS) in Corollary 4.3 by combining our acknowledgment-bound with a result of [32]. Section 7 combines our absMAC implementation with results of [26] in a straightforward way to derive algorithms for global single-message broadcast (SMB) and global multi-message broadcast (MMB).

2.1 Comparison of Algorithmic Results with Previous Work

Global single-message broadcast. Table 2 compares the runtime of our algorithm for global *SMB* with previous work. Currently [10] and [21] provide the best implementations of global SMB in the SINR model (see the runtimes in Table 2). The result of [10] is as good or better than [21] in case $\log^{\alpha+1}(\Lambda) \leq \log(n)$ and vice versa. To make it possible to compare our result to theirs, we need to choose $\varepsilon_{SMB} = 1/n^c$ such that global SMB is correct w.h.p.. Furthermore, we execute our algorithm with $\varepsilon' := \varepsilon/2$ instead of ε, while algorithms in previous work are executed without changing ε. This ensures that our bounds are stated in terms of the same parameter $D_{G_{1-\varepsilon}}$ rather than the possibly larger parameter $D_{G_{1-2\varepsilon}}$. At the same time the choice of ε' affects the runtime only by a constant factor. This results in a runtime of our algorithm of $\mathcal{O}\left((D_{G_{1-\varepsilon}} + \log(n))\log^{\alpha+1}(\Lambda)\right)$ in the strong connectivity graph $G_{1-\varepsilon}$. This improves over the algorithm presented in [10] in the full range of all parameters, and improves in case of $\log^{\alpha+1}(\Lambda) \leq \min(D_{G_{1-\varepsilon}}\log(n), \log^2(n))$ over the algorithm of [21]. Note that compared to [21] we (and [10]) assume knowledge of a bound on Λ. The key-ingredient of this improvement is our localized analysis in combination with [26].

Global multi-message broadcast. The algorithm for global MMB derived from [18] runs in $\mathcal{O}((D_{G_{1-\varepsilon}} + k)(\Delta_{G_{1-\varepsilon}} \cdot \log n + \log^2 n))$ time. Roughly speaking, our algorithm replaces the dependency on the potentially large multiplicative term $D_{G_{1-\varepsilon}}\Delta_{G_{1-\varepsilon}}$ by $D_{G_{1-\varepsilon}}$ up to polylog factors. Section 2.2 summarizes global MMB in related models.

2.2 Related Work

We provide more details on related work in the full version of this paper [17].

Graph Based Wireless Networks (Chlamtac et al. [6]). Upper bounds for global SMB [9, 28] in networks of unknown topology are tight due to a lower bound of $\Omega(D\log(n/D) + \log^2 n)$ by Alon et al. [1, 30]. The sequence of work [4, 14, 25] considered global MMB. Ghaffari et al. [13] presented a lower bound of $\Omega(k\log n)$ for global broadcast of k messsages. These lower bounds can be transferred to the SINR-model using SINR-induced graphs.

Abstract MAC layer (Kuhn et al. [29]). The probabilistic absMAC we consider was defined by Khabbazian et al. [26]. AbsMAC implementations were provided in [26, 27] and applications were provided in [7, 8, 15, 26, 29, 32]. We use optimal algorithms for global SMB and MMB in the probabilistic absMAC due to [26] and results on CONS by Newport [32].

SINR model (e.g. Moscibroda and Wattenhofer [31]). Local broadcast was studied in various models, e.g in [16, 18, 34]. We modify the analysis of [18] to use purely local parameters. Global MMB algorithms can be implied once local broadcast is available. Yu et al. [35, 36] obtained almost optimal bounds using arbitrary power control. Arbitrary power control used in [36] can yield arbitrary speed ups compared to our model [23, 31] and we get close to their runtime. Global SMB was studied in the sequence of papers [10, 20, 21, 22] using various model assumptions. Daum et al. [10] proposed a model that uses weak model assumptions, which we use as well. Thanks to a completely new approach they show how to perform global broadcast

Article	Runtime bound for global SMB	We improve this runtime in case of
this	$\mathcal{O}\left(\left(D_{G_{1-\varepsilon}} + \log(n)\right)\log^{\alpha+1}(\Lambda)\right)$	
[10]	$\mathcal{O}\left(D_{G_{1-\varepsilon}} \log^{\alpha+1}(\Lambda)\log(n)\right)$	all parameters and ranges
[21]	$\mathcal{O}\left(D_{G_{1-\varepsilon}} \log^{2}(n)\right)$	$\log^{\alpha+1}(\Lambda) \leq \min(D_{G_{1-\varepsilon}}\log(n)\ ,\ \log^2(n))$

Table 2: Comparison of the runtime of our global SMB protocol with previous results.

in $G_{1-\varepsilon}$ within $\mathcal{O}(D\log^{\alpha+1}(\Lambda)\log(n))$ rounds w.h.p.. We transfer and modify this algorithm to implement approximate progress in a probabilistic absMAC and provide a significantly extended analysis. Shortly after [10], Jurdzinski et al. [21] came up with a $\mathcal{O}(D\log^2 n)$ algorithm that improves over the one of [10] for a range of parameters. Table 2 compares these results to ours. Power control was also used in [5] to achieve connectivity and aggregation, which in turn can be used for broadcast as well.

3. MODEL AND DEFINITIONS

Graphs and their properties.

Let $G = (V, E)$ be a graph over n nodes V and edges E. We denote by $d_G(v, w)$ the hop-distance between w and v (the number of edges on a shortest (u, v)-path), and by $D_G := \max_{u,v\in V} d_G(u, v)$ the *diameter* of graph G. All neighbors of v in G are called *G-neighbors* of v. We define v's neighborhood to be $N_G(v) := \{u|(v, u) \in E\}$ and extend this to $N_{G,r}(v) := \{u|d_G(v, u) \leq r\}$ for the r-neighborhood, $r \in \mathbb{N}$. For any set $W \subseteq V$ we generalize this to $N_{G,r}(W) := \bigcup_{w\in W} N_{G,r}(w)$. $\delta_G(v) := |N_G(v) \setminus \{v\}|$ denotes the degree of v and $\Delta_G := \max_{v\in V} \delta_G(v)$ the degree of G. Let $S \subseteq V$ be a subset of G's vertices, then $G|_S = (S, E|_S)$ denotes the subgraph of G induced by nodes S, where $E|_S := \{(u, v) \in E|u, v \in S\}$. A set $S \subseteq S' \subseteq V$ is called a *maximal independent set (MIS)* of S' in G if 1) any two nodes $u, v \in S$ are independent, that is $(u, v) \notin E$, and 2) any node $v \in S'$ is covered by some neighbor in S, that is $N_G(v) \cap S \neq \emptyset$. A graph $G = (V, E)$ is *(polynomial) growth-bounded* if there is a polynomial bounding function $f(r)$ such that for each node $v \in V$, the number of nodes in the neighborhood $N_{G,r}(v)$ that are in any independent set of G is at most $f(r)$ for all $r \geq 0$. This allows us to bound the size of neighborhoods depending on the maximal degree of the network. When performing a localized analysis this yields union-bounds depending on the maximal degree, rather than the size of the network.

Lemma 3.1. *Let G be polynomially growth-bounded by function f, then it holds that $|N_{G,r}(v)| \leq \Delta f(r)$ for all $v \in V$ and $r \in \mathbb{N}$.*

Proof. The proof appears in the full version of this paper [17]. □

The SINR model.

Nodes are located in a plane and we write $d(v, w)$ for the Euclidean distance between points v, w (often corresponding to node's positions). It is clear from the context when d refers to hop-distance or Euclidean distance. When a node v (of a wireless network) sends a message, it transmits with (uniform) power $P > 0$. A transmission of v is received successfully at a node u, if and only if $SINR_u(v) := \frac{P/d(v,u)^\alpha}{\sum_{w\in S\setminus\{u,v\}} P/d(w,u)^\alpha + N} \geq \beta$, where N is a universal constant denoting the ambient noise. The parameter $\beta > 1$ denotes the minimum SINR (signal-to-interference-noise-ratio) required for a message to be successfully received, α is the so-called path-loss constant. Typically it is assumed that $\alpha \in (2, 6]$, see [16]. Here, S is the subset of nodes in V that are sending. By $R := (P/\beta N)^{1/\alpha}$ we denote the transmission range, i.e. the maximum distance at which two nodes can communicate assuming no other nodes are sending at the same time. For $a \in \mathbb{R}^+$, we define $R_a := a \cdot R$. If $d(v, u) \leq R_a$ and $a < 1$, we say u and v are connected by a *a-strong* link. Like previous literature [2, 10, 11, 16, 24] we consider a link to be strong if it is $(1 - \varepsilon)$-strong for constant $\varepsilon > 0$. If $R_a < d(u, v) \leq R_1$, we say u and v are connected by an *a-weak* link. A $(1-\varepsilon)$-weak link is just called weak link. We consider the strong connectivity graph $G_{1-\varepsilon} = (V, E_{1-\varepsilon})$, where $(u, v) \in E_{1-\varepsilon}$, if $u, v \in V$ are connected by a strong link. Given a graph G, we denote by Λ_G the ratio between the maximum and minimum Euclidean length of an edge in E. In case that G is $G_{1-\varepsilon}$, we simply write Λ instead of $\Lambda_{G_{1-\varepsilon}}$.

Abstract MAC layers.

We use the definitions of Ghaffari et al. [15] adapted to the probabilistic setting of [26]. To initiate a broadcast in a graph G, the MAC layer provides an interface to higher layers via input *bcast*$(m)_i$ for any node $i \in V$ and message $m \in M$. To simplify the definition of this primitive, assume w.l.o.g. that all local broadcast messages are unique. When a node $u \in V$ broadcasts a message m, the model delivers the message to all neighbors in E. It then returns an acknowledgment of m to u indicating the broadcast is complete, denoted by *ack*$(m)_u$. In between it returns a *rcv*$(m)_v$ event for each node v that received message m. This model provides two timing bounds . The first is the acknowledgment bound, which guarantees that each broadcast will complete and be acknowledged within f_{ack} time. The second is the progress bound, which guarantees : fix some $(u, v) \in E$ and interval of length f_{prog} throughout which u is broadcasting a message m; during this interval v must receive some message (though not necessarily m, but a message that some location is currently working on, not just some ancient message from the distant past). The progress bound, in other words, bounds the time for a node to receive some message when at least one of its neighbors is broadcasting. In both theory and practice f_{prog} is typically much smaller than f_{ack} [26]. Further motivation and power of these delay bounds is demonstrated e.g. in [15, 26, 29]. We emphasize that in abstract MAC layer models the order of receive events is determined non-deterministically by an arbitrary message scheduler. The timing of these events is also determined nondeterministically by the scheduler, constrained only by the above time bounds.

The Standard Abstract MAC Layer. Nodes are modeled as event-driven automata. While [15] assumes that an environment abstraction fires a wake-up event at each node at the beginning of each execution, we assume conditional wake-up to be consistent with the model of [10], see Definition 3.2. This is a weaker wake-up assumption with respect to upper bounds when compared to synchronous wake-up [15]. This strengthens our algorithmic results. In contrast to this our lower bounds assume synchronized wake-up, which is in turn the weaker assumption with respect to lower bounds. The environment is also responsible for any events specific to the problem being solved. In multi-message broadcast, for example, the environment provides the broadcast messages to nodes at the beginning.

Definition 3.2 (Conditional (a.k.a non-spontaneous) wake-up of [10] adapted to absMACs). *Once a node receives an input from the MAC-environment (above the MAC layer) or a transmission from the network below the MAC layer, the node wakes up and participates in the algorithm.*

The enhanced abstract MAC layer. The enhanced abstract MAC layer model differs from the standard model in two ways. First, it allows nodes access to time (formally, they can set timers that trigger events when they expire), and assumes nodes know f_{ack} and f_{prog}. Second, the model also provides nodes an abort interface that allows them to abort a broadcast in progress.

The probabilistic abstract MAC layer. We use parameters ε_{prog} and ε_{ack} to indicate the error probabilities for satisfying the delay bounds f_{prog} and f_{ack}. Roughly speaking this means that the MAC layer guarantees that progress is made with probability $1-\varepsilon_{prog}$ within f_{prog} time. With probability $1-\varepsilon_{ack}$ the MAC layer correctly outputs an acknowledgment within f_{ack} time steps. More details can be found in Section 4.2 of [26].

Problems.

We derive algorithms in the SINR-model that perform the tasks listed below correctly with probability $1-\varepsilon_{task}$. When choosing $\varepsilon_{task} \leq n^{-c}$ we say that an algorithm performs a task with high probability (w.h.p.). Here, $c > 0$ is an arbitrary constant provided to the algorithm as an input-parameter. We use the notation w.h.p. only to compare our results with previous work.

Multi-message broadcast (MMB) problem [26]. This problem inputs $k \geq 1$ messages into the network at the beginning of an execution, perhaps providing multiple messages to the same node. We assume k is not known in advance. The problem is solved once every message m, starting at some node u, reaches every node in G. Note that we assume G is connected to be consistent with previous work in the SINR model, while in [15] this is not assumed. We treat messages as black boxes that cannot be combined.

Single-message broadcast (SMB) problem [26]. The SMB problem is the special case of MMB with $k = 1$. The single node at which the message is input is denoted by i_0.

Consensus problem (CONS) problem [32]. In this problem each node begins an execution with an initial value from $\{0,1\}$. Every node has the ability to perform a single irrevocable *decide* action for a value in $\{0,1\}$. To solve consensus, an algorithm must guarantee the following three properties: 1) *agreement*: no two nodes decide different values; 2) *validity*: if a node decides value v, then some node had v as its initial value; and 3) *termination*: every non-faulty process eventually decides.

General model assumptions.

As in [10] wake up of nodes is conditional, see Definition 3.2. Nodes are located in the Euclidean plane[2] and locations are unknown. Nodes send with uniform power, where the fixed power level P is not known to the nodes. We use the common assumption that $\alpha > 2$, see [16]. No collision detection mechanism is provided. As previous work we assume $G_{1-\varepsilon}$ is connected. MAC-layer based work [26] requires us to assume that nodes can detect if a received message originates from a neighbor in a graph G–in our setting this is $G_{1-\varepsilon}$–(only one graph G is used in [26], while messages from any sender in the network might arrive but do not cause rcv-events). We remark that the assumption that nodes can detect if a received message originated in the $G_{1-\varepsilon}$-neighborhood is not used by any of the algorithms presented in this paper. Therefore this assumption could be dropped if one is not interested in implementing an absMAC that performs local broadcast exactly in $G_{1-\varepsilon}$. In particular, our absMAC implementation outputs *rcv* events for all *bcast*-messages received, which can be modified if required by other higher-level algorithms designed for absMACs and when the $G_{1-\varepsilon}$-neighborhood is known. The reader might consider the full version of this paper [17] for further details.

4. EFFICIENT ACKNOWLEDGMENTS AND IMPOSSIBILITY OF FAST PROGRESS

Theorem 4.1. *In the SINR model using the assumptions of Section 3, acknowledgments of an absMAC can be implemented w.r.t. graph $G_{1-\varepsilon}$ with probability guarantee $1-\varepsilon_{ack}$ in time*

$$f_{ack} = \mathcal{O}\left(\Delta_{G_{1-\varepsilon}} \log\left(\frac{\Lambda}{\varepsilon_{ack}}\right) + \log(\Lambda)\log\left(\frac{\Lambda}{\varepsilon_{ack}}\right)\right).$$

The proof of Theorem 4.1 is a straightforward modification of [18] to local parameters.

Many algorithms that are implemented in an absMAC benefit from the fact that typically f_{prog} is much smaller than f_{ack}. Often it is the case that $f_{prog} = \mathcal{O}(\text{polylog}(f_{ack}))$. We show that for any implementation of the absMAC [26] for $G_{1-\varepsilon}$ in the SINR model such a difference of the runtime is impossible. As the bound on f_{ack} in Theorem 4.1 is close to our lower bound on f_{prog}, we conclude that this algorithm is an almost optimal implementation of absMAC in the SINR-model with respect to both f_{ack} and f_{prog}.

Theorem 4.2. *For worst-case locations of points there is no implementation of the absMAC in the SINR model that provides local broadcast in $G_{1-\varepsilon}$ and achieves fast progress. In particular it holds that $f_{prog} \geq \Delta_{G_{1-\varepsilon}}$. This is true even for an optimal schedule computed by an (even central) entity that has unbounded computational power, has full knowledge as well as control of the network and can choose an arbitrary power assignment.*

[2] Our results can be generalized to any growth-bounded metric space when revising the assumption on α.

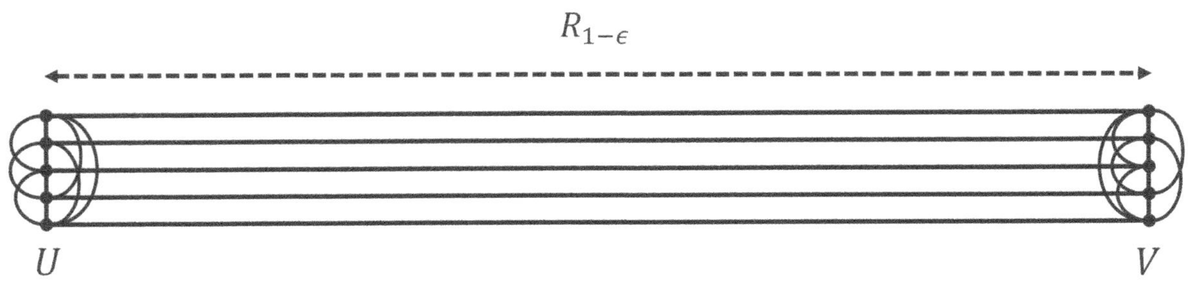

Figure 1: Graph $G_{1-\varepsilon}$ based on the construction used in the proof of Theorem 4.2. Here we choose $\Delta = 5$.

We defer the full proof to the full paper [17]. The key idea is to have two sets U and V of nodes, each set of nodes on a line with unit distance between nodes. These two lines are located at distance $R_{1-\varepsilon} := 10\Delta$ to each other such that at most one node in set V can receive a message from U at a time. Note that this is independent of ε.

Despite this lower bound we can already provide a first application of designing an absMAC for the SINR. Corollary 4.3 is an application of Theorem 4.1 to [32], see the full version of this paper [17].

Corollary 4.3 (Theorem 4.2. of [32] transferred to our setting). *In the SINR model using the assumptions of Section 3, network-wide consensus can be solved with probability $1 - \varepsilon_{CONS}$ in time*

$$f_{CONS} = \mathcal{O}\left(D_{G_{1-\varepsilon}}(\Delta_{G_{1-\varepsilon}} + \log(\Lambda)) \log\left(\frac{n\Lambda}{\varepsilon_{CONS}}\right)\right).$$

5. APPROXIMATE PROGRESS

Motivated by the lower bound of the previous section we modify the absMAC specification. An easy way would be to relax the progress bound and output a rcv-event not only for messages sent by $G_{1-\varepsilon}$-neighbors, but for all message received (i.e. sent by any G_1 neighbor). This is problematic when considering randomized algorithms. In particular when computing e.g. overlay networks. It might happen that only $G_1 \setminus G_{1-\varepsilon}$-neighbors of a node v are chosen for the overlay due to the random event of low interference. This could of course be avoided by directly implementing the absMAC with respect to G_1 rather than $G_{1-\varepsilon}$, which in turn results in a $\Omega(n)$ lower bound for f_{prog} and f_{ack} (e.g. when all nodes are located at distance at least R_1 such that messages can only be received when exactly one node is sending). Later these overlay nodes might not be able to serve v. To avoid such a setting, we introduce an *approximate* progress bound into the absMAC specification, where we use a graph G and an *approximation* (or any subgraph) $\tilde{G}$ of G in which progress is measured.

In the next sections we show that this generalization of progress has three desirable properties, it 1) captures SINR behavior in the sense that we present an absMAC implementation in the SINR model that provides fast (approximate) progress, and 2) replaces (with minor assumptions and effects) the progress bound in the runtime-analysis of e.g. global single-message and multi-message broadcast in the MAC layer [26], and 3) does not affect the correctness of these algorithms. Therefore we consider this notion of approximate progress to be a good modification of the specification of abstract MAC layers with respect to the SINR model.

Definition 5.1 (Approximate progress). *Let there be (reliable[3]) broadcast implemented with respect to a graph G and let $\tilde{G} := (V, \tilde{E})$ be a subgraph[4] of G. Consider a node i and assume that a $\tilde{G}$-neighbor of i is broadcasting a message. The approximate progress bound guarantees that a rcv event with a message originating in a G-neighbor occurs at node i within time f_{approg} with probability $1 - \varepsilon_{approg}$. We say that approximate progress is implemented with respect to graphs G and (its approximation) $\tilde{G}$.*

We formalize this using the notation of [26]: Let β be a closed execution that ends at time t. Let I be the set of $\tilde{G}$-neighbors of j that have active bcasts at the end of β, where $bcast(m_i)_i$ is the bcast at i. Suppose that I is nonempty. Let I' be the set of G-neighbors of j that have active bcasts at the end of β. Suppose that no $rcv(m_i)_j$ event occurs in β, for any $i \in I'$. Define the following sets A and B of time-unbounded executions that extend β. Set A contains all executions in which no $abort(m_i)_i$ occurs for any $i \in I$. Set B contains all executions in which, by time $t + f_{approg}$, at least one of the following occurs: 1) an $ack(m_i)_i$ for every $i \in I$, 2) a $rcv(m_i)_j$ for some $i \in I'$, or 3) A rcv_j for some message whose bcast occurs after β. If $\mathbb{P}_\beta[A] > 0$, then $\mathbb{P}_\beta[B|A] \geq 1 - \varepsilon_{approg}$.

This notation is useful, as there are settings where it is not crucial that progress is made with respect to exactly G. Already progress in subgraph $\tilde{G}$ might yield good overall bounds for solving a problem on G especially when e.g. (depending on the problem at hand) $D_{\tilde{G}} \approx D_G$ or $\tilde{G}^2$. As we show in Theorem 7.1, in the global SMB and MMB algorithms of [26] local broadcast does not need to be precise such that under some conditions progress can be replaced by approximate progress. In the SINR model one might choose, e.g., $G := G_{1-\varepsilon} \supseteq G_{1-2\varepsilon} =: \tilde{G}$, as we do. This choice captures that any $G_{1-\varepsilon}$-neighbor is almost a $G_{1-2\varepsilon}$-neighbor. In addition its signal has a similar strength when it arrives at the receiver and in reality might even be the same, as signal strengths can vary slightly. We discuss differences to

[3]The notation of approximate progress might later be extended to unreliable broadcast [15].

[4]Graph $\tilde{G}$ can be any subgraph of G but will typically be an approximation of G, which results in the name approximate progress. Later we consider graph $\tilde{G} := G_{1-2\varepsilon}$, which approximates $G := G_{1-\varepsilon}$ with respect to the SINR formula and Euclidean distances in the sense that it contains all, but the longest edges of G.

the dual-graph model for unreliable communication of [15] in the full version of this paper [17].

5.1 Decay Fails to yield a Fast Implementation of Approximate Progress

Inspired by a proof of [10], we transfer this result into our setting. We show that using a (standard) DECAY method, one cannot achieve fast approximate progress in the SINR model.

Theorem 5.2. *When using the* DECAY *method of [3] to implement local broadcast of a MAC layer in the SINR model, it holds that* $f_{approg} = \Omega(\Delta_{G_{1-\varepsilon}} \log(1/\varepsilon_{approg}))$.

Proof. We provide a proof in the full version of this paper [17]. □

6. IMPLEMENTATION OF FAST APPROXIMATE PROGRESS

We implement approximate progress with respect to $G := G_{1-\varepsilon}$ and $\tilde{G} := G_{1-2\varepsilon}$. In the full version of this paper [17] we show that the DECAY method cannot achieve fast approximate progress in the SINR model. Therefore we describe a method different from DECAY and obtain:

Theorem 6.1. *In the SINR model using the assumptions of Section 3, we implement approximate progress of an absMAC with respect to graphs* $G_{1-\varepsilon}$ *and its approximation* $G_{1-2\varepsilon}$ *with probability at least* $1-\varepsilon_{approg}$ *in time approximate progress of an absMAC with respect to graphs* $G_{1-\varepsilon}$ *and its approximation* $G_{1-2\varepsilon}$ *with probability at least* $1-\varepsilon_{approg}$ *in time*

$$f_{approg} = \mathcal{O}\left(\left(\log^{\alpha}(\Lambda) + \log^{*}\left(\frac{1}{\varepsilon_{approg}}\right)\right) \cdot \log(\Lambda)\log\left(\frac{1}{\varepsilon_{approg}}\right)\right).$$

6.1 Algorithm

The algorithm presented by [10] achieves w.h.p. global SMB in $G_{1-\varepsilon}$. We review this algorithm and show how to modify it to guarantee fast (probabilistic) approximate progress with respect to $G_{1-2\varepsilon}$. In the following, set S_1 contains all nodes with an ongoing broadcast. Set S_1 changes after each epoch depending on the algorithm using the absMAC.

High-level description of Algorithm 1 of [10] and the intuition behind it.

This algorithm performs $D_{G_{1-\varepsilon}}$ many epochs. For $\Phi = \Theta(\log \Lambda)$, each epoch of the algorithm computes approximations $\tilde{H}_1, \tilde{H}_2, \ldots, \tilde{H}_\Phi$ of a sequence of constant degree graphs $H_1, H_2, \ldots, H_\Phi$. Each H_ϕ is defined based on nodes S_ϕ, s.t. when each node in S_ϕ transmits with probability $p \in (0, 1/2]$, the transmission corresponding to an edge of H_ϕ is successful with probability $\mu \in (0, p)$. Sets S_ϕ, $\phi \in [2, \Phi]$, are maximal independent sets in $\tilde{H}_{\phi-1}$ and the algorithm of [33] is simulated to compute such MIS (and uses a node's unique ID $\in$ poly n as an input). Each transmission during the computations of S_ϕ and $\tilde{H}_\phi$ is repeated $T := \Theta(\log n)$ to ensure w.h.p. correctness. Finally for each ϕ, all nodes S_ϕ transmit their bcast-message $\Theta(\log^{\alpha}(\Lambda)\log(n))$ times. Intuitively S_ϕ is a sparser version of $S_{\phi-1}$ and [10] shows that S_Φ contains only nodes that cannot communicate with each other. Using this and further insights they argue that for any node in $N_{G_{1-\varepsilon}}(S_1)$ there is a $\phi \in [1, \Phi]$ such that 1) there is a node $u \in S_\phi$ at distance at most $R_{1-\varepsilon}$, and 2) the density of S_ϕ is so low that interference from other nodes allows u_ϕ's message to reaches u w.h.p. (when the transmission is repeated sufficiently often). This shows that in each epoch all nodes in $N_{G_{1-\varepsilon}}(S_1)$ receive the (single!) bcast-message[5] w.h.p.. We provide more details in the full version of this paper [17].

Our modifications and motivation behind these changes.

(I) We replace the inputs for the MIS algorithm. Instead of unique ID $\in$ poly n we use temporary labels $l_{i,\phi} \in [1, (\text{poly } \Lambda)/\varepsilon_{approg}]$. (II) We replace $T = \Theta(\log n)$ by $\Theta(\log(\Lambda/\varepsilon_{approg}))$ and reduce the number of repeated transmissions of bcast-messages from $\mathcal{O}(\log^{\alpha}(\Lambda)\log(n))$ to $\mathcal{O}(\log^{\alpha}(\Lambda)\log(1/\varepsilon_{approg}))$. (III) We rename the computed graphs from $\tilde{H}_\phi$ to $\tilde{\tilde{H}}_\phi$. (IV) We execute the algorithm with respect to $G_{1-2\varepsilon}$ instead of $G_{1-\varepsilon}$. If $\varepsilon_{approg} > n^{-c}$, these modifications reduce the runtime of an epoch, but also lower the probability of correctness. Therefore computed graphs are very unlikely to be global approximations of H_ϕ (and we change their name to $\tilde{\tilde{H}}_\phi$). Still, the parameters are chosen such that we can show that the probability of approximate progress is at least $1 - \varepsilon_{approg}$ as outlined in Section 6.2.

6.2 Outline of the Analysis

We analyze the effect of the two main modifications of the algorithm of [10] with respect to their analysis and put it into the context of approximate progress. More details of this careful analysis are provided in the full version of this paper [17].

First modification: non-unique labels in the MIS computation.

We argue in the model of [33] the sets S_ϕ computed by our modified MIS-algorithm are independent sets in $\tilde{\tilde{H}}_{\phi-1}$. Furthermore, for any given node v, with probability $1 - \varepsilon_{approg}/3$, this set is maximal in a neighborhood around v "large enough" to ensure that this part of computations involved in approximate progress at node v is correct.

Second modification: fewer repetitions of transmissions.

In the algorithm of [10] each node sends every bcast-message $\mathcal{O}(\log^{\alpha}(\Lambda)\log n)$ times, while we repeat transmissions only $\mathcal{O}(\log^{\alpha}(\Lambda)\log(1/\varepsilon_{approg}))$ times. This implies that [10] can assume that all communication is successful at any point w.h.p.. For large ε_{approg} we only have weak probability guarantees for success of communication. One side-effect is that with very high probability the computed graphs $\tilde{\tilde{H}}_\phi$ are not the desired global approximations of graphs H_ϕ. This in turn affects correctness of approximate progress and we need to analyze local and global implications caused by reducing the number of repeated transmissions.

[5]We denote by *bcast-message* any messages that contains information to be broadcast due to a bcast-event. By *messages*, we refer to messages sent for coordination among the nodes.

1. **Global implications of unsuccessful transmissions:** Global interference might increase in the long term and we need to bound this. Unsuccessful transmissions during the computation of $\tilde{H}_\phi$ might remain undetected and cause that edges are missing in $\tilde{\tilde{H}}_\phi$. This event influences future computations of nearby nodes until the current epoch ends. Influenced nodes might cause additional global interference. In the full version of this paper [17] we bound the expected additional interference from these nodes. It turns out that T is chosen such that this interference can be tolerated in other parts of our proof and when transferring the analysis of [10]. After $\tilde{\tilde{H}}_\phi$ is computed, all transmissions are successful. They use the same schedule used to compute $\tilde{\tilde{H}}_\phi$.
2. **Local implications of unsuccessful transmissions:** Transmissions of messages need to be successful in all "large enough" neighborhoods of v in graphs $\tilde{\tilde{H}}_\phi$ to guarantee approximate progress at point v. These unsuccessful transmissions can only appear during the computation of $\tilde{\tilde{H}}^\mu_p[S_\phi]$ and while transmitting the bcast-message. Only if communication is locally successful, it is guaranteed that graph $\tilde{\tilde{H}}_\phi$ is an approximation of H_ϕ w.r.t. the above mentioned neighborhood of v, which is necessary in order to transfer the analysis of [10]. We analyze the probability that $\tilde{\tilde{H}}_\phi$ is locally an approximation in the full version of this paper [17]. Finally, approximate progress is made only if communication of bcast-messages succeeds locally.

6.3 Key Lemmas of the Analysis

Full proofs of the following lemmas appear in the full version of this paper [17]. We start by analyzing the effect of using (potentially) non-unique labels chosen uniformly at random $\in \left[1, \frac{\text{poly } \Lambda}{\varepsilon_{approg}}\right]$ in the modified MIS computation, which is the first difference to [10], as pointed out in Section 6.2.

Lemma 6.2. *Let $H = (V, E)$ be a constant degree growth-bounded graph and let $U \subseteq V$ be a set of nodes of size at most $\mathcal{O}(\Lambda^2)$. Consider an execution of our modification of the MIS-algorithm of [33] on H in the CONGEST model using random labels $\in \left[1, \frac{\text{poly } \Lambda}{\varepsilon_{approg}}\right]$. Then the set of nodes in state dominator is 1) an independent set, and 2) with probability at least $1 - \frac{\varepsilon_{approg}}{3\Phi}$ this set is maximal with respect to $N_{H, c\cdot 4^\Phi \cdot \log^*(\Lambda/\varepsilon_{approg})}(U)$, the $c \cdot 4^\Phi \cdot \log^*(\Lambda/\varepsilon_{approg})$-neighborhood of U in H.*

We analyze Case 1 pointed out in Section 6.2, i.e. we bound the global interference from nodes with undetectable unsuccessful transmissions.

Definition 6.3 (Set W of nodes with wrong neighborhoods (due to unsuccessful transmissions)). *Denote by $W \subseteq S_1$ the set of all those nodes v such that for at least one $\phi \in \{1, \cdots, \Phi\}$ it is not the case that $N_{H^\mu_p[S_\phi]}(v) \subseteq N_{\tilde{\tilde{H}}^\mu_p[S_\phi]}(v) \subseteq N_{H^{\mu(1-\gamma)}_p[S_\phi]}(v)$, i.e. v's direct neighborhood does not $(1-\gamma)$-approximate $N_{H^\mu_p[S_\phi]}(v)$.*

Lemma 6.4. *Given point i in space, the expected total additional interference $I_W(i)$ that point i receives from all nodes in W at any given time is less than $\left(\frac{\varepsilon_{approg}}{\Lambda}\right)^{\Theta(1)}$.*

Definition 6.5 (Local success of an epoch). *An epoch is successful at point i if*

1. *the computations of each graph $\tilde{\tilde{H}}^\mu_p[S_1], \ldots, \tilde{\tilde{H}}^\mu_p[S_\Phi]$ are successful at point i, and*
2. *the computations of each set $S_2, \ldots, S_\Phi$ are successful at point i, and*
3. *there is a $\phi \in \{1, \ldots, \Phi\}$, such that i receives the bcast-message m transmitted by some node $u_\phi \in U_{\phi,i}$ of phase ϕ.*

The full paper [17] defines in a formal way what it means that a computation is successful at a given point i. In summary, given point i, a computation of a graph $\tilde{\tilde{H}}^\mu_p[S_\phi]$ and set S_ϕ is successful at point i, if they are computed correctly within a certain area around i. We show that

Note that in the proofs of the Lemmas in this Section we never assume that we know the location of i nor that we know u_ϕ or u_ϕ's location/distance to i.

Lemma 6.6. *Given set S_1 and a node i and let there be a $G_{1-2\varepsilon}$-neighbor of i with an ongoing broadcast event $bcast(m)_j$. Assume Properties 1 and 2 of the definition [17] of a successful epoch at point i are satisfied. Then there is a phase $\phi' \in \{1, \ldots, \Phi\}$ such that in phase ϕ node i receives a bcast-message from a $G_{1-\varepsilon}$-neighbor of i with probability $1 - \varepsilon_{approg}/3$.*

These are the key lemmas that are used together with the following bound on the runtime of an epoch to derive Theorem 6.1.

Lemma 6.7. *The runtime of an epoch is*

$$\mathcal{O}\Bigg(\log^{\alpha+1}(\Lambda) \cdot \log\left(\frac{1}{\varepsilon_{approg}}\right) + \log(\Lambda) \cdot \log\left(\frac{1}{\varepsilon_{approg}}\right) \cdot \log^*\left(\frac{1}{\varepsilon_{approg}}\right)\Bigg).$$

7. APPLICATION: IMPROVED NETWORK-WIDE BROADCAST

In the full version of this paper [17] we implement the probabilistic absMAC of [26] in a formal way using Theorems 4.1 and 6.1 and the corresponding algorithms. We combine this absMAC implementation with algorithms from [26] for global broadcast in this absMAC. In Theorem 7.1 we argue that we can replace f_{prog} and ε_{prog} in the relevant Theorems of [26] by f_{approg} and ε_{approg} under certain conditions and state the effect that this replacement has on other parameters of the runtime.

Theorem 7.1. *Let G be a graph in which local broadcast is available via the probabilistic absMAC of [26]. Let $\tilde{G}$ be the graph in which approximate progress is measured and let the vertex sets of the connected components of $\tilde{G}$ and G be the same. Then one can replace $f_{prog}, \varepsilon_{prog}$ and D_G in Theorems 7.7 and 8.20 of [26] concerning their global SMB and MMB algorithms by $f_{approg}, \varepsilon_{approg}$ and $D_{\tilde{G}}$.*

In the algorithms of [26], once a node i receives a message, node i broadcasts the message if it did not broadcast it before. The result of global broadcast is independent of whether a message was received due to transmission from a $\tilde{G}$-neighbor or a G-neighbor as long as the components of $\tilde{G}$ and G are the same. Only the runtime changes. In time f_{prog} with probability $1 - \varepsilon_{prog}$ a message is received by a node v when a $G_{1-\varepsilon}$-neighbor of v is sending. Therefore the runtime presented in [26] depends on $D_{G_{1-\varepsilon}}$. Compared to this, with probability $1 - \varepsilon_{approg}$ in time f_{approg} a message arrives when a $G_{1-2\varepsilon}$-neighbor is sending. Therefore $D_{G_{1-\varepsilon}}$ needs to be replaced by $D_{G_{1-2\varepsilon}}$, see the full version of this paper [17] for details.

Theorem 7.2. *Consider the SINR model using the model assumptions stated in Section 3. We present an algorithm that performs global SMB in graph $G_{1-\varepsilon}$ with probability at least $1 - \varepsilon_{SMB}$ in time*

$$\mathcal{O}\left(\left(D_{G_{1-2\varepsilon}} + \log\left(\frac{n}{\varepsilon_{SMB}}\right)\right) \cdot \log^{\alpha+1}(\Lambda)\right).$$

The second algorithm presented in the proof performs global MMB in graph $G_{1-\varepsilon}$ with probability at least $1 - \varepsilon_{MMB}$ in time

$$\mathcal{O}\Bigg(D_{G_{1-2\varepsilon}} \log^{\alpha+1}(\Lambda) + k'\left(\Delta_{G_{1-\varepsilon}} + polylog\left(\frac{nk\Lambda}{\varepsilon_{MMB}}\right)\right)\log\left(\frac{nk}{\varepsilon_{MMB}}\right)\Bigg).$$

The proof applies our Theorems 4.1, 6.1 and 7.1 to Theorems 7.7 and 8.20 of [26], see the full version of this paper [17] for details.

Acknowledgments.
We thank Sebastian Daum, Mohsen Ghaffari, Fabian Kuhn and Calvin Newport for answering questions concerning their earlier work and helpful discussions. In particular we thank Erez Kantor for many helpful discussions—especially in the early stages of this work.

8. REFERENCES

[1] A. Alon, A. Bar-Noy, N. Linial, and D. Peleg. A lower bound for radio broadcast. *J. Compt. Syst. Science*, 43:290–298, 1991.

[2] M. Andrews and M. Dinitz. Maximizing capacity in arbitrary wireless networks in the SINR model: Complexity and game theory. In *Proc. of the 28th International Conference on Computer Communications, INFOCOM, Rio de Janeiro*, pages 1332–1340. IEEE, 2009.

[3] R. Bar-Yehuda, O. Goldreich, and A. Itai. On the time-complexity of broadcast in multi-hop radio networks: An exponential gap between determinism and randomization. *Journal of Computer and System Sciences*, 45(1):104–126, 1992.

[4] R. Bar-Yehuda, A. Israeli, and A. Itai. Multiple communication in multihop radio networks. *SIAM J. Comput.*, 22(4):875–887, 1993.

[5] M. H. L. Bodlaender, M. M. Halldórsson, and P. Mitra. Connectivity and aggregation in multihop wireless networks. In *ACM Symposium on Principles of Distributed Computing, PODC '13, Montreal, QC, Canada, July 22-24, 2013*, pages 355–364, 2013.

[6] I. Chlamtac and S. Kutten. On broadcasting in radio networks–problem analysis and protocol design. *IEEE Transactions on Communications*, 33(12):1240–1246, 1985.

[7] A. Cornejo, N. Lynch, S. Viqar, and J. L. Welch. Neighbor discovery in mobile ad hoc networks using an abstract mac layer. In *Communication, Control, and Computing, 2009. Allerton 2009. 47th Annual Allerton Conference on*, pages 1460–1467. IEEE, 2009.

[8] A. Cornejo, S. Viqar, and J. L. Welch. Reliable neighbor discovery for mobile ad hoc networks. *Ad Hoc Networks*, 12:259–277, 2014.

[9] A. Czumaj and W. Rytter. Broadcasting algorithms in radio networks with unknown topology. *J. Algorithms*, 60(2):115–143, 2006.

[10] S. Daum, S. Gilbert, F. Kuhn, and C. C. Newport. Broadcast in the ad hoc SINR model. In *Distributed Computing - 27th International Symposium, DISC 2013, Jerusalem, Israel, October 14-18, 2013. Proceedings*, pages 358–372, 2013.

[11] M. Dinitz. Distributed algorithms for approximating wireless network capacity. In *INFOCOM 2010. 29th IEEE International Conference on Computer Communications, Joint Conference of the IEEE Computer and Communications Societies, 15-19 March 2010, San Diego, CA, USA*, pages 1397–1405, 2010.

[12] G. Even, Y. Matsri, and M. Medina. Multi-hop routing and scheduling in wireless networks in the SINR model. In *Algorithms for Sensor Systems - 7th International Symposium on Algorithms for Sensor Systems, Wireless Ad Hoc Networks and Autonomous Mobile Entities, ALGOSENSORS 2011, Saarbrücken, Germany, September 8-9, 2011, Revised Selected Papers*, pages 202–214, 2011.

[13] M. Ghaffari, B. Haeupler, and M. Khabbazian. A bound on the throughput of radio networks. *CoRR*, abs/1302.0264, 2013.

[14] M. Ghaffari, B. Haeupler, and M. Khabbazian. Randomized broadcast in radio networks with collision detection. In *ACM Symposium on Principles of Distributed Computing, PODC '13, Montreal, QC, Canada, July 22-24, 2013*, pages 325–334, 2013.

[15] M. Ghaffari, E. Kantor, N. Lynch, and C. Newport. Multi-message broadcast with abstract MAC layers and unreliable links. In *Proceedings of the 33rd Annual ACM Symposium on Principles of Distributed Computing, PODC 2014, Paris, France, July 15-18, 2014*, pages 56–65, extended version available at http://arxiv.org/abs/1405.1671, 2014.

[16] O. Goussevskaia, T. Moscibroda, and R. Wattenhofer. Local broadcasting in the physical interference model. In *DIALM-POMC*, pages 35–44, 2008.

[17] M. M. Halldorsson, S. Holzer, and N. Lynch. A local broadcast layer for the sinr network model. *arXiv preprint arXiv:1505.04514*, 2015.

[18] M. M. Halldórsson and P. Mitra. Towards tight bounds for local broadcasting. In *FOMC'12, The Eighth ACM International Workshop on Foundations of Mobile Computing (part of PODC 2012), Funchal, Portugal, July 19, 2012, Proceedings*, page 2, 2012.

[19] N. Hobbs, Y. Wang, Q.-S. Hua, D. Yu, and F. C. M. Lau. Deterministic distributed data aggregation under the SINR model. In M. Agrawal, S. B. Cooper, and A. Li, editors, *TAMC*, volume 7287 of *Lecture Notes in*

Computer Science, pages 385–399. Springer, Heidelberg, 2012.

[20] T. Jurdzinski, D. R. Kowalski, M. Rozanski, and G. Stachowiak. Distributed randomized broadcasting in wireless networks under the SINR model. In *Distributed Computing*, pages 373–387. 2013.

[21] T. Jurdzinski, D. R. Kowalski, M. Rozanski, and G. Stachowiak. On the impact of geometry on ad hoc communication in wireless networks. In M. M. Halldórsson and S. Dolev, editors, *Proceedings of the Thirty-Third Annual ACM Symposium on Principles of Distributed Computing, PODC '14, Paris, France, July 15-18, 2014*, pages 357–366, 2014.

[22] T. Jurdzinski, D. R. Kowalski, and G. Stachowiak. Distributed deterministic broadcasting in wireless networks of weak devices. In *Automata, Languages, and Programming - 40th International Colloquium, ICALP 2013, Riga, Latvia, July 8-12, 2013, Proceedings, Part II*, pages 632–644, 2013.

[23] T. Kesselheim. A constant-factor approximation for wireless capacity maximization with power control in the SINR model. In D. Randall, editor, *Proceedings of the Twenty-Second Annual ACM-SIAM Symposium on Discrete Algorithms, SODA 2011, San Francisco, California, USA, January 23-25, 2011*, pages 1549–1559, 2011.

[24] T. Kesselheim and B. Vöcking. Distributed contention resolution in wireless networks. In N. A. Lynch and A. A. Shvartsman, editors, *Distributed Computing (proceedings of DISC)*, volume 6343 of *Lecture Notes in Computer Science*, pages 163–178. Springer, Heidelberg, 2010.

[25] M. Khabbazian and D. R. Kowalski. Time-efficient randomized multiple-message broadcast in radio networks. In C. Gavoille and P. Fraigniaud, editors, *Proceedings of the 30th Annual ACM Symposium on Principles of Distributed Computing, PODC 2011, San Jose, CA, USA, June 6-8, 2011*, pages 373–380, 2011.

[26] M. Khabbazian, D. R. Kowalski, F. Kuhn, and N. A. Lynch. Decomposing broadcast algorithms using abstract MAC layers. *Ad Hoc Networks*, 12:219–242, 2014.

[27] M. Khabbazian, F. Kuhn, N. A. Lynch, M. Médard, and A. ParandehGheibi. MAC design for analog network coding. In A. Chaintreau and D. R. Kowalski, editors, *FOMC'11, The Seventh ACM SIGACT/SIGMOBILE International Workshop on Foundations of Mobile Computing (part of FCRC 2011), San Jose, CA, USA, June 9, 2011, Proceedings*, pages 42–51, 2011.

[28] D. R. Kowalski and A. Pelc. Broadcasting in undirected ad hoc radio networks. *Distributed Computing*, 18(1):43–57, 2005.

[29] F. Kuhn, N. A. Lynch, and C. C. Newport. The abstract MAC layer. *Distributed Computing*, 24(3-4):187–206, 2011.

[30] E. Kushilevitz and Y. Mansour. An $\Omega(D \log(N/D))$ lower bound for broadcast in radio networks. *SIAM J. on Computing*, 27:702–712, 1998.

[31] T. Moscibroda and R. Wattenhofer. The Complexity of Connectivity in Wireless Networks. In *Proceedings of the 25th annual IEEE International Conference on Computer Communications, Joint Conference of the IEEE Computer and Communications Societies, INFOCOM 2006, Barcelona, Catalunya, Spain, 23-29 April 2006*, pages 1–13, 2006.

[32] C. C. Newport. Consensus with an abstract MAC layer. In M. M. Halldórsson and S. Dolev, editors, *ACM Symposium on Principles of Distributed Computing, PODC '14, Paris, France, July 15-18, 2014*, pages 66–75, 2014.

[33] J. Schneider and R. Wattenhofer. A log-star distributed maximal independent set algorithm for growth-bounded graphs. In R. A. Bazzi and B. Patt-Shamir, editors, *Proceedings of the Twenty-Seventh Annual ACM Symposium on Principles of Distributed Computing, PODC 2008, Toronto, Canada, August 18-21, 2008*, pages 35–44, 2008.

[34] D. Yu, Q. Hua, Y. Wang, and F. C. M. Lau. An o(log n) distributed approximation algorithm for local broadcasting in unstructured wireless networks. In *IEEE 8th International Conference on Distributed Computing in Sensor Systems, DCOSS 2012, Hangzhou, China, 16-18 May, 2012*, pages 132–139, 2012.

[35] D. Yu, Q.-S. Hua, Y. Wang, H. Tan, and F. C. M. Lau. Distributed multiple-message broadcast in wireless ad-hoc networks under the SINR model. In G. Even and M. M. Halldórsson, editors, *Structural Information and Communication Complexity - 19th International Colloquium, SIROCCO 2012, Reykjavik, Iceland, June 30-July 2, 2012, Revised Selected Papers*, volume 7355 of *Lecture Notes in Computer Science*, pages 111–122. Springer, Heidelberg, 2012.

[36] D. Yu, Q.-S. Hua, Y. Wang, J. Yu, and F. C. M. Lau. Efficient distributed multiple-message broadcasting in unstructured wireless networks. In *Proceedings of the IEEE INFOCOM 2013, Turin, Italy, April 14-19, 2013*, pages 2427–2435, 2013.

Brief Announcement: Fast and Simple Node Coloring in the SINR Model

Fabian Fuchs
Institute of Theoretical Informatics, KIT
Karlsruhe, Germany
fabian.fuchs@kit.edu

ABSTRACT

We present two distributed node coloring algorithms operating in the Signal-to-interference-and-noise-ratio (SINR) model. The first algorithm is very simple and achieves a (4Δ)-coloring in $\mathcal{O}(\Delta \log n)$ time slots. The results of our experimental evaluation show that the algorithm is extremely fast. Combined with a new color reduction scheme, the algorithm computes a $(\Delta+1)$-coloring in $\mathcal{O}(\Delta \log n)$ time. This improves on current distributed coloring algorithms for the SINR model either in terms of the number of colors or runtime, and matches the asymptotical runtime of one round of local broadcasting, which can be seen as a lower bound.

Categories and Subject Descriptors

F.2.m [**Analysis of Algorithms**]: Miscellaneous; C.2.1 [**Computer-Communication Networks**]: Network Architecture and Design—*distributed networks*; G.2.2 [**Discrete Mathematics**]: Graph Theory—*graph algorithms*

Keywords

Algorithms; Distributed Node Coloring; SINR Model; Wireless Ad Hoc Networks; Experiments

1. INTRODUCTION

Distributed node coloring algorithms can be used to make communication in wireless (ad-hoc) networks more efficient by establishing coordinated medium access, for example by using Time Division Multiple Access (TDMA). We use the geometric Signal-to-interference-and-noise-ratio (SINR) model of interference, which is widely considered to be realistic. Thus, many algorithmic works considered this model in the last decade. Communication of distributed algorithms in the SINR model is often based on probabilistic medium access. This yields the best solutions to the local broadcasting problem (see [1] and the references in [2]), in which all nodes in the network must transmit one message to all their neighbors. In distributed node coloring algorithms, one aims for $\Delta+1$ colors, as this can be achieved for any communication graph, and minimizing the number of colors beyond this level is hard even for the centralized case. There are currently two algorithms on a pareto front: The Yu *et al.* algorithm [3] computes a $(\Delta+1)$-coloring in $\mathcal{O}(\Delta \log n + \log^2 n)$ time slots, while the MW-coloring algorithm [4, 5] executed in the SINR model establishes an $\mathcal{O}(\Delta)$-coloring in $\mathcal{O}(\Delta \log n)$ time slots.

In this announcement, we briefly state recent results regarding more efficient distributed node coloring algorithms in the SINR model by Fuchs and Prutkin [6,7]. They adapted simple and well-known coloring algorithms from the message-passing model to the SINR model. The first algorithm runs in $\mathcal{O}(\Delta \log n)$ time slots and computes a valid (4Δ)-coloring. The results on an experimental evaluation show that the algorithm is fast, even compared to a local broadcast. Additionally, it can be combined with a new color reduction scheme, which reduces a given d-coloring in $\mathcal{O}(d \log n)$ time slots to a $(\Delta+1)$-coloring, yielding a $(\Delta+1)$-coloring that can be computed in $\mathcal{O}(\Delta \log n)$ time. This outperforms MW-coloring (under the same assumptions) by using less colors, and the Yu *et al.* algorithm by requiring less time slots. Also, this essentially closes the field—unless faster local broadcast algorithms emerge—as the goal of $\Delta+1$ colors is achieved in a runtime that matches current local broadcasting algorithm.

1.1 Preliminaries

We consider a network of n nodes, and use the SINR model to decide whether a transmission from a node v can be decoded at a node u. The transmission is *feasible* at u iff $\frac{P/\operatorname{dist}(v,u)^\alpha}{\sum_{w\in I} P/\operatorname{dist}(w,u)^\alpha + N} > \beta$, where P is the transmission power, $\operatorname{dist}(u,v)$ is the Euclidean distance from u to v, I the set of nodes transmitting simultaneously to v, α the attenuation coefficient depending on the environment, β a hardware-dependent threshold, and N the environmental noise. We define the broadcasting range of each node based on these constants, which induces a communication graph $G=(V,E)$, and more specifically a set of neighbors N_v for each node v. The maximum number of neighbors (max. degree) is denoted by Δ. Two nodes are called *independent*, if they are not neighbors. A set of nodes is independent if no two nodes are neighbors. The network is *colored* with d colors if the nodes are partitioned in d sets. The coloring is *valid*, if each set is independent. We say that a transmission of v is *successful*, if it can be received by all neighbors of v. Apart from classical local broadcasting, which achieves successful transmission with high probability (w.h.p.–with probability

Permission to make digital or hard copies of part or all of this work for personal or classroom use is granted without fee provided that copies are not made or distributed for profit or commercial advantage, and that copies bear this notice and the full citation on the first page. Copyrights for third-party components of this work must be honored. For all other uses, contact the owner/author(s). Copyright is held by the author/owner(s).
PODC'15, July 21–23, 2015, Donostia-San Sebastián, Spain.
ACM 978-1-4503-3617-8 /15/07.
http://dx.doi.org/10.1145/2767386.2767445.

at least $1-\frac{1}{n}$) in $\mathcal{O}(\Delta \log n)$ time using a transmission probability $p_1 = \frac{1}{\mathcal{O}(\Delta)}$, we use two straight-forward extensions to this result in our coloring algorithms. The extensions are stated as lemmas 1 and 2. Our assumptions match those of local broadcasting with known Δ, i.e. we assume Δ, α, β, N, and a polynomial estimate of n to be given.

LEMMA 1. *Let all nodes transmit with transmission probability $p_1 = \frac{1}{\mathcal{O}(\Delta)}$, then a transmission from a node v is successful within $\mathcal{O}(\Delta)$ time slots with probability at least $\frac{3}{4}$.*

LEMMA 2. *Let $\mathcal{I}$ be a set of independent nodes transmitting with probability $p_2 = \frac{1}{\mathcal{O}(1)}$ and the remaining nodes with probability p_1. A transmission from node $v \in \mathcal{I}$ is successful within $\mathcal{O}(\log n)$ time slots w.h.p.*

Both, local broadcasting and our extensions, guarantee that the transmission can successfully be decoded by nodes in the broadcasting range. However, the transmission might also be received by nodes in the transmission range, which is larger than the broadcasting range to enable spacial reuse. Thus, to guarantee a $(\Delta+1)$-coloring, we increase Δ by a constant factor or assume that the nodes discard transmissions from outside the broadcasting range (e.g. based on the received signal strength). Note that the maximum degree Δ is defined as in previous $\Delta+1$ coloring algorithms [3].

2. RESULTS

Let us first consider RAND4ΔCOLORING (Algorithm 1), which is based on a folklore algorithm for the message-passing model: Each node repeatedly transmits its color and selects a new color once a conflict is detected. Our main idea is to speed up the algorithm by restricting the algorithm to transmissions that are successful with constant probability, which requires only $\mathcal{O}(\Delta)$ time, cf. Lemma 1, instead of with high probability, which would require $\mathcal{O}(\Delta \log n)$ time. This allows to run the algorithm in $\mathcal{O}(\Delta \log n)$ time in the SINR model instead of $\mathcal{O}(\Delta \log^2 n)$ time slots for a simple simulation of the algorithm. However, the improved runtime comes at the price that the introduced uncertainty must be handled in the analysis.

Algorithm 1: RAND4ΔCOLORING for node v

1 **for** $t \leftarrow 0; t \le \mathcal{O}(\ln n); t \leftarrow t+1$ **do** // each: one phase
2   Transmit c_v^t with prob. p for $\mathcal{O}(\Delta)$ time slots;
3   **foreach** *received color c_w^t from neighbor $w \in N_v$* **do**
4     $F_v \leftarrow F_v \backslash \{c_w^t\}$
5   **if** $c_v^t \notin F_v$ **then** $c_v^{t+1} \leftarrow [4\Delta]$.rand(); // conflict
6   **else** $c_v^{t+1} \leftarrow c_v^t$; // otherwise, keep color
7   $F_v \leftarrow [4\Delta]$;

The algorithm itself is divided in several phases. During each phase, the considered node v transmits its current color and receives colors of some neighbors. By removing those colors from the set of free colors F_v, they are marked as taken. At the end of each phase, v evaluates whether it detected a conflict with a neighbor (Line 5), and resets the color if so. Otherwise it keeps the color and the set of free colors is reset for the next phase. We can show that

THEOREM 3. *Algorithm 1 computes a valid (4Δ)-coloring in $\mathcal{O}(\Delta \log n)$ time w.h.p.*

This holds for the synchronous case without restriction, however, for the asynchronous case we need to account for conflicts introduced by nodes waking-up late. Thus, the result holds for nodes with a stable $\log n$ neighborhood, while the bound cannot be guaranteed if nodes in the $\log n$ neighborhood wake-up in the meantime. Once the nodes in the $\log n$ neighborhood are awake, the bound holds.

2.1 Color Reduction

The COLORREDUCTION algorithm is based on the simple observation that an independent set of nodes (or even a constant number of independent sets) can transmit with increased probability, allowing a local broadcast of these independent sets in $\mathcal{O}(\log n)$ time w.h.p., as stated in Lemma 2. Thus, once we have computed a valid coloring, this can be used to increase the communication efficiency. As the asynchronous case requires considerably more synchronization effort, let us first describe the case of a synchronous, simultaneous start (see Algorithm 2; for pseudocode of the asynchronous version cf. [6]).

Given a valid d-coloring of the network and assume each color is an integer from the set $[d]$. Divide the time in epochs of length $\mathcal{O}(\log n)$ and let the nodes of color i transmit in epoch i. This ensures that during an epoch nodes of only one color transmit, hence those nodes can select a free color from $[\Delta]$ and inform their neighbors about their selection. This does not lead to a conflict w.h.p., as nodes from previous epochs informed their neighbors, and no two neighbors are active at the same time due to the valid coloring. Thus, after d epochs the networks is colored with $\Delta+1$ colors w.h.p.

Algorithm 2: COLORREDUCTION for v; color c_v

$F_v \leftarrow [\Delta]$;
for $i \leftarrow 0; i \le d; i \leftarrow i+1$ **do** // each: one epoch
  if $c_v = i$ **then** transmit $c_v \leftarrow F_v$.rand() with ;
  probability p_2 for $\mathcal{O}(\log n)$ time slots;
  else // wait
    listen for $\mathcal{O}(\log n)$ time slots;
    foreach *received color c_w* **do** $F_v \leftarrow F_v \backslash \{c_w\}$;

Let us now briefly consider the asynchronous case. In this case, nodes cannot implicitly decide on a common start of the schedule as done in the synchronous case. Thus, without global synchronization we cannot guarantee that only the nodes of a constant number of colors transmit. However, it is sufficient if this property holds locally - thus in each neighborhood only the nodes of a constant number of colors are allowed to transmit. We can achieve this by computing two layers of maximal independent sets (MIS). Nodes of the first layer MIS act as leaders and decide on a schedule. All other nodes select a leader in their neighborhood and follow its schedule. If all nodes follow their leaders schedule, it holds for each node that at most a constant number of neighbors may be active at the same time. This is sufficient to apply a variant of Lemma 2, as the active nodes can be grouped to a constant number of independent sets. Executing an MIS algorithm amongst the active nodes reduces the set to an actual MIS, which allows the nodes in the MIS to select a color from $[\Delta]$ and communicate the selected color to its neighbors successfully without a conflict. Let us consider the runtime: The first layer of MIS runs in $\mathcal{O}(\Delta \log n)$ time slots, for example by using a known MIS algorithm [5]. Selecting a leader and communicating the schedule requires the same asymptotic time. By reducing the number of active nodes to a constant, we can modify the MIS algorithm to run in $\mathcal{O}(\log n)$ time slots. Using an epoch of length $\mathcal{O}(\log n)$ suffices to ensure that each active node is in the MIS once after a constant number of MIS executions, as there are a constant number of active nodes in each epoch. As we assume a valid d-coloring to be given, d epochs, and thus $\mathcal{O}(d \log n)$ time slots are sufficient to validly color the network with $\Delta + 1$ colors.

2.2 Experiments

We use the Sinalgo simulator for our experiments (cf. [7] for more details). The nodes are deployed uniformly at random on an area of 1000×1000 meters. We use a uniform transmission power of 1 and SINR constants $\alpha = 4$, $\beta = 10$, $N = 1^{-9}$, resulting in a broadcasting range of 84 meters. Algorithm 1 uses a phase length equivalent to 10 time slots, the nodes start asynchronous but within the first phase. Our results are robust regarding those parameters, and are obtained using 100 runs each. Figure 1 shows that it takes significantly less time to compute a valid (4Δ)-coloring for the network than for each node to transmit a message to its neighbors (i.e. finish one round of local broadcasting).

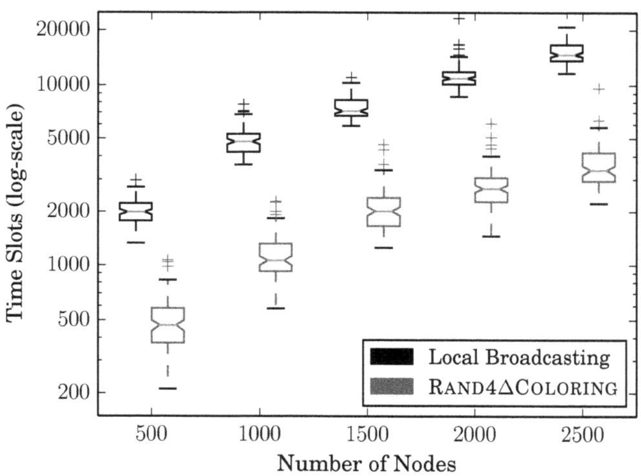

Figure 1: Required time to finish one round of local broadcasting, and computing a valid (4Δ)-coloring using Algorithm 1. Note the log-scaled y-axis.

We consider mobility of the nodes according to the random direction mobility model with variable node speed in Fig. 2. Note that in such a network some conflicts are inevitable due to the movement of nodes. As mobility in only available for synchronous execution, this simulation uses synchronous rounds[1]. We observe that RAND4ΔCOLORING is relatively robust. Even under moderate mobility values of 1 meter per time slot, more than 90% of the nodes have a valid color. We note that other current distributed node coloring algorithms for the SINR model are not viable in the mobile setting, as they do not resolve conflicts, which inevitably emerge using mobile nodes.

[1]The synchronized variant without mobility finishes within 600 slots in Fig. 2 compared to about 1000 slots for the asynchronous setting in Fig. 1. This exposes the gap between slotted vs. unslotted transmissions, see e.g. [1].

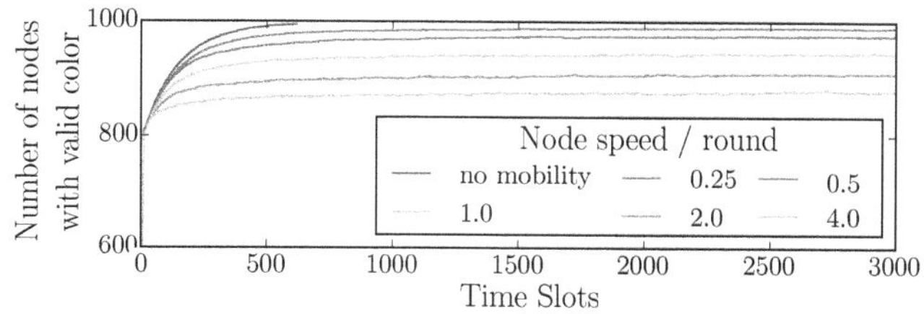

Figure 2: Consider a network of 1000 mobile nodes. We measure the number of nodes that have a valid color in each time step. The performance decreases with increasing mobility.

3. CONCLUSSION

We proposed two very simple node coloring algorithms for the SINR model, which are based on well-known message-passing algorithms. The first algorithm is very simple and computes a (4Δ)-coloring in $\mathcal{O}(\Delta \log n)$ time slots. Our experiments validated that RAND4ΔCOLORING is extremely fast, even compared to a simple local broadcast. Our second algorithm is based on a color reduction scheme, which has an almost trivial synchronous implementation in the SINR model. For the asynchronous case, the algorithm is based on two layers of MIS, which allow the nodes to compute a $(\Delta+1)$-coloring in $\mathcal{O}(\Delta \log n)$ time slots based on an $\mathcal{O}(\Delta)$-coloring. This results in an $(\Delta + 1)$-coloring algorithm in $\mathcal{O}(\Delta \log n)$ time slots, which is essentially optimal.

4. ACKNOWLEDGEMENTS:

We thank Magnús M. Halldórsson for helpful discussions on an early stage of this work, and the German Research Foundation (DFG), which supported this work within the Research Training Group GRK 1194 "Self-organizing Sensor-Actuator Networks".

5. REFERENCES

[1] O. Goussevskaia, T. Moscibroda, and R. Wattenhofer, "Local Broadcasting in the Physical Interference Model," in *Proc. 5th DialM-POMC*. ACM Press, 2008, pp. 35–44.

[2] M. M. Halldórsson and P. Mitra, "Towards tight bounds for local broadcasting," in *Proc. 8th FOMC*. ACM Press, July 2012.

[3] D. Yu, Y. Wang, Q.-S. Hua, and F. C. M. Lau, "Distributed $(\Delta + 1)$ Coloring in the Physical Model," in *ALGOSENSORS*, ser. LNCS, vol. 7111. Springer, 2011, pp. 145–160.

[4] T. Moscibroda and M. Wattenhofer, "Coloring unstructured radio networks," *J. Distr. Comp.*, vol. 21, no. 4, pp. 271–284, 2008.

[5] B. Derbel and E.-G. Talbi, "Distributed Node Coloring in the SINR Model," in *ICDCS*. IEEE, 2010, pp. 708–717.

[6] F. Fuchs and R. Prutkin, "Simple distributed $\Delta + 1$ coloring in the SINR model," 2015. [Online]. Available: http://arxiv.org/abs/1502.02426

[7] F. Fuchs, "On asynchronous node coloring in the SINR model," 2015, manuscript. [Online]. Available: http://i11www.iti.kit.edu/f-oancs-15.pdf

Algebraic Methods in the Congested Clique*

Keren Censor-Hillel†
Technion
ckeren@cs.technion.ac.il

Petteri Kaski‡
Helsinki Institute for Information Technology & Aalto University
petteri.kaski@aalto.fi

Janne H. Korhonen
Helsinki Institute for Information Technology & University of Helsinki
janne.h.korhonen@helsinki.fi

Christoph Lenzen
MPI for Informatics
clenzen@mpi-inf.mpg.de

Ami Paz
Technion
amipaz@cs.technion.ac.il

Jukka Suomela
Helsinki Institute for Information Technology & Aalto University
jukka.suomela@aalto.fi

ABSTRACT

In this work, we use algebraic methods for studying distance computation and subgraph detection tasks in the *congested clique* model. Specifically, we adapt parallel matrix multiplication implementations to the congested clique, obtaining an $O(n^{1-2/\omega})$ round matrix multiplication algorithm, where $\omega < 2.3728639$ is the exponent of matrix multiplication. In conjunction with known techniques from centralised algorithmics, this gives significant improvements over previous best upper bounds in the congested clique model. The highlight results include:

- triangle and 4-cycle counting in $O(n^{0.158})$ rounds, improving upon the $O(n^{1/3})$ triangle counting algorithm of Dolev et al. [DISC 2012],
- a $(1 + o(1))$-approximation of all-pairs shortest paths in $O(n^{0.158})$ rounds, improving upon the $\tilde{O}(n^{1/2})$-round $(2+o(1))$-approximation algorithm of Nanongkai [STOC 2014], and
- computing the girth in $O(n^{0.158})$ rounds, which is the first non-trivial solution in this model.

In addition, we present a novel constant-round combinatorial algorithm for detecting 4-cycles.

Categories and Subject Descriptors

F.1.1 [**Computation by Abstract Devices**]: Models of Computation; F.2.0 [**Analysis of Algorithms and Problem Complexity**]: General; G.2.2 [**Mathematics of Computing**]: Discrete Mathematics—*Graph Theory*

Keywords

Distributed computing; congested clique model; lower bounds; matrix multiplication; subgraph detection; distance computation

*A full version of this paper is available at [18].

†Supported by ISF Individual Research Grant 1696/14

‡Supported by the European Research Council under the European Union's Seventh Framework programme (FP/2007–2013) / ERC Grant Agreement n. 338077.

Permission to make digital or hard copies of all or part of this work for personal or classroom use is granted without fee provided that copies are not made or distributed for profit or commercial advantage and that copies bear this notice and the full citation on the first page. Copyrights for components of this work owned by others than ACM must be honored. Abstracting with credit is permitted. To copy otherwise, or republish, to post on servers or to redistribute to lists, requires prior specific permission and/or a fee. Request permissions from permissions@acm.org.
PODC'15, July 21–23, 2015, Donostia-San Sebastián, Spain.
Copyright © 2015 ACM 978-1-4503-3617-8 /15/07 ...$15.00.
DOI: http://dx.doi.org/10.1145/2767386.2767414 .

1. INTRODUCTION

Algebraic methods have become a recurrent tool in centralised algorithmics, employing a wide range of techniques (e.g., [10–16, 21–23, 27, 29, 30, 44, 45, 51, 59, 72, 73]). In this paper, we bring techniques from the algebraic toolbox to the aid of distributed computing, by leveraging fast matrix multiplication in the *congested clique* model.

In the congested clique model, the n nodes of a graph G communicate by exchanging messages of $O(\log n)$ size in

Problem	Running time: This work	Running time: Prior work	
mat. mult. (semiring)	$O(n^{1/3})$	—	
mat. mult. (ring)	$O(n^{0.158})$	$O(n^{0.373})$	[26]
triangle counting	$O(n^{0.158})$	$O(n^{1/3}/\log n)$	[25]
4-cycle detection	$O(1)$	$O(n^{1/2}/\log n)$	[25]
4-cycle counting	$O(n^{0.158})$	$O(n^{1/2}/\log n)$	[25]
k-cycle detection	$2^{O(k)}n^{0.158}$	$O(n^{1-2/k}/\log n)$	[25]
girth	$O(n^{0.158})$	—	
APSP:			
weighted, directed	$O(n^{1/3}\log n)$	—	
· weighted diameter U	$O(Un^{0.158})$	—	
· $(1+o(1))$-approx.	$O(n^{0.158})$	—	
· $(2+o(1))$-approx.		$\tilde{O}(n^{1/2})$	[58]
APSP:			
unweighted, undirected	$O(n^{0.158})$	—	
· $(2+o(1))$-approx.		$\tilde{O}(n^{1/2})$	[58]

Table 1: Our results versus prior work, using $\omega < 2.3729$ [34]; $\tilde{O}$ hides polylogarithmic factors.

a *fully-connected* synchronous network; initially, each node is aware of its neighbours in G. In comparison with the traditional CONGEST model [61], the key difference is that a pair of nodes can communicate directly even if they are not adjacent in graph G. The congested clique model masks away the effect of *distances* on the computation and focuses on the limited *bandwidth*. As such, it has been recently gaining increasing attention [25, 26, 37, 38, 47, 50, 52, 58, 60, 64], in an attempt to understand the relative computational power of distributed computing models.

The key insight of this paper is that matrix multiplication algorithms from parallel computing can be adapted to obtain an $O(n^{1-2/\omega})$ round matrix multiplication algorithm in the congested clique, where $\omega < 2.3728639$ is the matrix multiplication exponent [34]. Combining this with well-known centralised techniques allows us to use fast matrix multiplication to solve various combinatorial problems, immediately giving $O(n^{0.158})$-time algorithms in the congested clique for many classical graph problems. Indeed, while most of the techniques we use in this work are known beforehand, their combination gives significant improvements over the best previously known upper bounds. Table 1 contains a summary of our results, which we overview in more details in what follows.

1.1 Matrix Multiplication in the Congested Clique

As a basic primitive, we consider the computation of the product $P = ST$ of two $n \times n$ matrices S and T on a congested clique of n nodes. We will tacitly assume that the matrices are initially distributed so that node v has row v of both S and T, and it will receive row v of P in the end. Recall that the matrix multiplication exponent ω is defined as the infimum over σ such that the product of two $n \times n$ matrices can be computed with $O(n^{\sigma})$ arithmetic operations; it is known that $2 \leq \omega < 2.3728639$ [34], and it is conjectured, though not unanimously, that $\omega = 2$.

THEOREM 1. *The product of two $n \times n$ matrices can be computed in a congested clique of n nodes in $O(n^{1/3})$ rounds over semirings. Over rings, $O(n^{1-2/\omega+\varepsilon})$ rounds suffice (for any constant $\varepsilon > 0$).*

Theorem 1 follows by adapting known parallel matrix multiplication algorithms for semirings [1, 55] and rings [7, 53, 56, 71] to the clique model, via the routing technique of Lenzen [47]. In fact, with little extra work one can show that the resulting algorithm is also *oblivious*, that is, the communication pattern is predefined and does not depend on the input matrices. Hence, the oblivious routing technique of Dolev et al. [25] suffices for implementing these algorithms.

The above addresses matrices whose entries can be encoded with $O(\log n)$ bits, which is sufficient for dealing with integers of absolute value at most $n^{O(1)}$. In general, if b bits are sufficient to encode matrix entries, the bounds above hold with a multiplicative factor of $b/\log n$; for example, working with integers with absolute value at most $2^{n^{\varepsilon}}$ merely incurs a factor n^{ε} overhead in running times.

Distributed matrix multiplication exponent. Analogously to the matrix multiplication exponent, we denote by ρ the exponent of matrix multiplication in the congested clique model, that is, the infimum over all values σ such that there exists a matrix multiplication algorithm in the congested clique running in $O(n^{\sigma})$ rounds. In this notation, Theorem 1 gives us

$$\rho \leq 1 - 2/\omega < 0.15715\,;$$

prior to this work, it was known that $\rho \leq \omega - 2$ [26].

For the rest of this paper, we will – as is convention for centralised algorithmics – slightly abuse notation by writing n^{ρ} for the complexity of matrix multiplication in the congested clique. This hides factors of $O(n^{\varepsilon})$ resulting from the fact that ρ is defined as infimum of an infinite set. We also use $\tilde{O}$ and $\tilde{\Omega}$ notation to hide polylogarithmic factors.

Lower bounds for matrix multiplication. Our results are optimal in the sense that for any sequential matrix multiplication implementation, no scheme simulating it on the congested clique can give a faster algorithm than the construction underlying Theorem 1; this follows from known results for parallel matrix multiplication [2, 8, 42, 70]. Moreover, we note that for the *broadcast congested clique model*, where each node is required to send the same message to all nodes in any given round, recent lower bounds [39] imply that matrix multiplication requires $\tilde{\Omega}(n)$ rounds.

1.2 Applications in Cycle Detection and Counting

Our first application of fast matrix multiplication is to the problems of triangle counting [43] and 4-cycle counting.

COROLLARY 2. *On directed and undirected graphs, counting triangles and 4-cycles takes $O(n^{\rho})$ rounds.*

For $\rho \leq 1-2/\omega$, this is an improvement upon the previously best known $O(n^{1/3})$-round triangle detection algorithm of Dolev et al. [25]. In particular, we disprove the conjecture of Dolev et al. [25] that any deterministic oblivious algorithm for detecting triangles requires $\tilde{\Omega}(n^{1/3})$ rounds.

When only detection of cycles is required, we observe that combining fast distributed matrix multiplication with the well-known technique of *colour-coding* [5] allows to detect k-cycles in $\tilde{O}(n^{\rho})$ rounds for any constant k. This improves upon the subgraph detection algorithm of Dolev et al. [25], which requires $\tilde{O}(n^{1-2/k})$ rounds for detecting (arbitrary) subgraphs of k nodes.

COROLLARY 3. *For any graph, the existence of k-cycles can be detected in $2^{O(k)}n^{\rho}\log n$ rounds.*

For the specific case of $k = 4$, we provide a novel algorithm that does not use matrix multiplication and detects 4-cycles in only $O(1)$ rounds.

THEOREM 4. *On undirected graphs, the existence of 4-cycles can be detected in $O(1)$ rounds. If such a cycle exists, one such cycle can also be reported in $O(1)$ rounds.*

1.3 Applications in Girth Computation

We compute the girth of a graph by leveraging a known trade-off between the girth and the number of edges of the graph [54]. Roughly, we detect short cycles fast, and if they do not exist then the graph must have sufficiently few edges to be learned by all nodes. As far as we are aware, this is the first algorithm to compute the girth in this setting.

THEOREM 5. *For undirected graphs, the girth can be computed in $\tilde{O}(n^\rho + n^{o(1)})$ rounds.*

A similar result on directed girth follows by adapting an algorithm by Itai and Rodeh [43].

COROLLARY 6. *For directed graphs, the girth can be computed in $\tilde{O}(n^\rho)$ rounds.*

1.4 Applications in Distance Computation

The *all-pairs shortest paths* problem (APSP) likewise admits algorithms based on matrix multiplication. The basic idea is to compute the nth power of the input graph's weight matrix over the min-plus semiring, by iteratively computing squares of the matrix [28, 33, 57].

COROLLARY 7. *For directed graphs with integer weights in $\{-M, -M+1, \dots, M\}$, APSP can be computed in $O(n^{1/3}$ $(\log n + \log M))$ rounds.*

We can leverage fast ring matrix multiplication to improve upon the above result; however, the use of ring matrix multiplication necessitates some trade-offs or extra assumptions. For example, for unweighted and undirected graphs, it is possible to recover the exact shortest paths from powers of the adjacency matrix over the Boolean semiring [66].

COROLLARY 8. *For undirected, unweighted graphs, APSP can be computed in $\tilde{O}(n^\rho)$ rounds.*

For small integer weights, we use the well-known idea of embedding a min-plus semiring matrix product into a matrix product over a ring; this gives a multiplicative factor to the running time proportional to the length of the longest path.

COROLLARY 9. *For directed graphs with positive integer weights and weighted diameter U, APSP can be computed in $\tilde{O}(Un^\rho)$ rounds.*

While this is relevant only for graphs of a small weighted diameter, the idea can be combined with weight rounding [58, 65, 76] to obtain a fast approximate APSP algorithm without such limitations.

COROLLARY 10. *For directed graphs with integer weights in $\{0, 1, \dots, 2^{n^{o(1)}}\}$, APSP can be approximated within a factor of $1 + o(1)$ in $O(n^{\rho+o(1)})$ rounds.*

This improves on a $(2 + o(1))$-approximation algorithm in $\tilde{O}(n^{1/2})$ rounds by Nanongkai [58].

1.5 Additional Related Work

Computing distances in graphs, such as the diameter, all-pairs shortest paths (APSP), and single-source shortest paths (SSSP) are fundamental problems in most computing settings. The reason for this lies in the abundance of applications of such computations, evident also by the huge amount of research dedicated to it [19, 20, 31, 35, 36, 68, 69, 74–77].

In particular, computing graph distances is vital for many distributed applications and, as such, has been widely studied in the CONGEST model of computation [61], where n processors located in n distinct nodes of a graph G communicate over the graph edges using $O(\log n)$-bit messages. Specifically, many algorithms and lower bounds were given for computing and approximating graph distances in this setting [24, 32, 40, 41, 46, 48, 49, 58, 62, 63]. Some lower bounds apply even for graphs of small diameter; however, these results boil down to graphs with *bottleneck* edges limiting the amount of information that can be exchanged between different parts of the graph quickly.

The intuition that the congested clique model would abstract away distances and bottlenecks and bring to light only the congestion challenge has proven inaccurate. Indeed, a number of tasks have been shown to admit sub-logarithmic or even constant-round solutions, exceeding by far what is possible in the CONGEST model with only low diameter. The pioneering work of Lotker et al. [52] shows that a minimum spanning tree (MST) can be computed in $O(\log \log n)$ rounds; this result was later improved by Pemmaraju and Sardeshmukh [64], showing that MST can be constructed in $O(\log \log \log n)$ rounds. Hegeman et al. [38] show how to construct a 3-ruling set, with applications to maximal independent set and an approximation of the MST in certain families of graphs; sorting and routing have been recently addressed by various authors [47, 50, 60]. A connection between the congested clique model and the MapReduce model is discussed by Hegeman and Pemmaraju [37], where algorithms are given for colouring problems. On top of these positive results, Drucker et al. [26] recently proved that essentially *any* non-trivial unconditional lower bound on the congested clique would imply novel circuit complexity lower bounds.

The same work also points out the connection between fast matrix multiplication algorithms and triangle detection in the congested clique. Their construction yields an $O(n^{\omega-2+\varepsilon})$-round algorithm for matrix multiplication over rings in the congested clique model, giving also the same running bound for triangle detection; if $\omega = 2$, this gives $\rho = 0$, matching our result. However, with the currently best known centralised matrix multiplication algorithm, the running time of the resulting triangle detection algorithm is $O(n^{0.3729})$ rounds, still slower than the combinatorial triangle detection of Dolev et al. [25], and if $\omega > 2$, the solution presented in this paper is faster.

2. MATRIX MULTIPLICATION ALGORITHMS

In the congested clique matrix multiplication, we want to compute the product $P = ST$ of two $n \times n$ matrices $S = (S_{ij})$ and $T = (T_{ij})$ on a congested clique with n nodes; the local input for each node $v \in V$ is the row v of both S and T, and the at the end of the computation each node $v \in V$ will output the row v of P.

THEOREM 1. *The product of two $n \times n$ matrices can be computed in a congested clique of n nodes in $O(n^{1/3})$ rounds over semirings. Over rings, $O(n^{1-2/\omega+\varepsilon})$ rounds suffice (for any constant $\varepsilon > 0$).*

Theorem 1 follows by simulating known parallel matrix multiplication algorithms in the congested clique model using the routing schemes of Dolev et al. [25] or Lenzen [47]. Roughly speaking, the idea in both of these algorithms is to reduce the $n \times n$ matrix product into n products of smaller matrices, where each product is handled locally by a single node.

The first part of the theorem follows from the so-called parallel 3D matrix multiplication algorithm [1, 55], essentially a parallel implementation of the school-book solution, which splits the multiplied matrices into $n^{1/3} \cdot n^{1/3} = n^{2/3}$ blocks of size $n^{2/3} \times n^{2/3}$. Since each block needs to be multiplied by $n^{1/3}$ other blocks, we need $n^{1/3}$ nodes to hold a copy of each block. This allows us to distribute the multiplications such that each node locally multiplies a single pair of blocks. Communicating the input blocks and collecting the entries of the output matrix takes $O(n^{1/3})$ rounds, as each node needs to collect and send information about $n^{4/3}$ entries.

For the second part of the theorem, we use a known result [17] that says that any $O(n^\sigma)$ matrix multiplication algorithm can be converted into a *bilinear* matrix multiplication algorithm with running time of $O(n^{\sigma+\varepsilon})$, for any $\varepsilon > 0$. In a bilinear matrix multiplication algorithm, such as the algorithm of Strassen [67], the matrix product is computed by first computing $m < n^3$ linear combinations of entries of both matrices, then performing m multiplications of pairs of linear combinations, and finally computing the output matrix entries as linear combinations of the multiplication outputs. This can be computed over a ring, and can be obtained by recursively performing the above on a partition of the matrix into blocks, giving the speed-up in running time.

We then use a scheme that allows to adapt any bilinear matrix multiplication algorithm into a fast parallel matrix multiplication algorithm [7, 53, 56, 71]. Hence, with some additional details, the result is obtained by using an $O(n^\sigma)$ centralised bilinear matrix multiplication algorithm to reduce the $n \times n$ product to n products of $n^{1-1/\sigma} \times n^{1-1/\sigma}$ matrices. Communicating these smaller matrices of $n^{2-2/\sigma}$ entries between the nodes takes only $O(n^{1-2/\sigma})$ rounds using Dolev et al. [25] or Lenzen [47].

We refer the reader to the full version of the paper [18] for additional details.

3. UPPER BOUNDS

3.1 Subgraph Detection and Counting

The subgraph detection and counting algorithms we present are mainly based on applying the fast matrix multiplication to the *adjacency matrix* A of a graph $G = (V, E)$, defined as

$$A_{uv} = \begin{cases} 1 & \text{if } (u,v) \in E\,, \\ 0 & \text{if } (u,v) \notin E\,, \end{cases}$$

where we assume that for undirected graphs edges $\{u, v\} \in E$ are oriented both ways.

Counting triangles and 4-cycles. For counting triangles, that is, 3-cycles, we use a technique first observed by Itai and Rodeh [43]. That is, in an undirected graph with adjacency matrix A, the number of triangles is known to be $\frac{1}{6}\operatorname{tr}(A^3)$, where the *trace* $\operatorname{tr}(S)$ of a matrix S is the sum of its diagonal entries S_{uu}. Similarly, for directed graphs, the number of triangles is $\frac{1}{3}\operatorname{tr}(A^3)$.

Alon et al. [6] generalise the above formula to counting undirected and directed k-cycles for small k. For example, the number of 4-cycles in an undirected graph is given by

$$\frac{1}{8}\Big[\operatorname{tr}(A^4) - \sum_{v\in V}\Big(2(\deg(v))^2 - \deg(v)\Big)\Big]\,.$$

Likewise, if G is a loopless directed graph and we denote for $v \in V$ by $\delta(v)$ the number of nodes $u \in V$ such that $\{(u,v),(v,u)\} \subseteq E$, then the number of directed 4-cycles in G is

$$\frac{1}{4}\Big[\operatorname{tr}(A^4) - \sum_{v\in V}\Big(2(\delta(v))^2 - \delta(v)\Big)\Big]\,.$$

Combining these observations with Theorem 1, we immediately obtain Corollary 2:

COROLLARY 2. *On directed and undirected graphs, counting triangles and 4-cycles takes $O(n^\rho)$ rounds.*

We note that similar trace formulas exists for counting k-cycles for $k \in \{5, 6, 7\}$, requiring only computation of small powers of A and local information. We omit the detailed discussion of these in the context of the congested clique; see Alon et al. [6] for details.

Detecting k-cycles. For detection of k-cycles we leverage the *colour-coding* techniques of Alon et al. [5] in addition to the matrix multiplication. Again, the distributed algorithm is a straightforward adaptation of a centralised one.

Fix a constant $k \in \mathbb{N}$. Let $c\colon V \to [k]$ be a labelling (or colouring) of the nodes by k colours, such that node v knows its colour $c(v)$; it should be stressed here that the colouring need not to be a proper colouring in the sense of the graph colouring problem. As a first step, we consider the problem of finding a *colourful k-cycle*, that is, a k-cycle such that each colour occurs exactly once on the cycle. We present the details assuming that the graph G is directed, but the technique works in an identical way for undirected graphs.

LEMMA 11. *Given a graph $G = (V, E)$ and a colouring $c\colon V \to [k]$, a colourful k-cycle can be detected in $O(3^k n^\rho)$ rounds.*

PROOF. For each subset of colours $X \subseteq [k]$, let $C^{(X)}$ be a Boolean matrix such that $C^{(X)}_{uv} = 1$ if there is a path of length $|X| - 1$ from u to v containing exactly one node of each colour from X, and $C^{(X)}_{uv} = 0$ otherwise. For a singleton set $\{i\} \subseteq [k]$, the matrix $C^{(\{i\})}$ contains 1 only on the main diagonal, and only for nodes v with $c(v) = i$; hence, node v can locally compute the row v of the matrix from its colour. For a non-singleton colour set X, we have that

$$C^{(X)} = \bigvee_{\substack{Y\subseteq X\\ |Y|=\lceil|X|/2\rceil}} C^{(Y)} A C^{(X\setminus Y)}\,, \qquad (1)$$

where the products are computed over the Boolean semiring and $\vee$ denotes element-wise logical or. Thus, we can compute $C^{(X)}$ for all $X \subseteq [k]$ by applying (1) recursively; there is a colourful k-cycle in G if and only if there is a pair of nodes $u, v \in V$ such that $C^{([k])}_{uv} = 1$ and $(v, u) \in E$.

To leverage fast matrix multiplication, we simply perform the operations stated in (1) over the ring $\mathbb{Z}$ and observe that an entry of the resulting matrix is non-zero if and only if the corresponding entry of $C^{(X)}$ is non-zero. The application of (1) needs two matrix multiplications for each pair (Y, X) with $Y \subseteq [k]$ and $|Y| = \lceil |X|/2 \rceil = \lceil k/2 \rceil$. The number of such pairs is bounded by 3^k; to see this, note that the set $\{(Y,X)\colon Y \subseteq X \subseteq [k]\}$ can be identified with the set $\{0,1,2\}^k$ of trinary strings of length k via the bijection $w_1 w_2 \dots w_k \mapsto (\{i\colon w_i = 0\}, \{i\colon w_i \le 1\})$, and the set $\{0,1,2\}^k$ has size exactly 3^k. Thus, the total number of matrix multiplications used is at most $O(3^k)$. □

We can now use Lemma 11 to prove Theorem 3; while we cannot directly construct a suitable colouring from scratch for an uncoloured graph, we can try an exponential in k number of colourings to find a suitable one.

COROLLARY 3. *For any graph, the existence of k-cycles can be detected in $2^{O(k)} n^{\rho} \log n$ rounds.*

PROOF. To apply Lemma 11, we first have to obtain a colouring $c\colon V \to [k]$ that assigns each colour once to at least one k-cycle in G, assuming that one exists. If we pick a colour $c(v) \in [k]$ for each node uniformly at random, then for any k-cycle C in G, the probability that C is colourful in the colouring c is $k!/k^k > e^{-k}$. Thus, by picking $e^k \log n$ uniformly random colourings and applying Lemma 11 to each of them, we find a k-cycle with high probability if one exists.

This algorithm can also be derandomised using standard techniques. A *k-perfect family of hash functions $\mathcal{H}$* is a collection of functions $h\colon V \to [k]$ such that for each $U \subseteq V$ with $|U| = k$, there is at least one $h \in \mathcal{H}$ such that h assigns a distinct colour to each node in U. There are known constructions that give such families $\mathcal{H}$ with $|\mathcal{H}| = 2^{O(k)} \log n$ and these can be efficiently constructed [5]; thus, it suffices to take such an $\mathcal{H}$ and apply Lemma 11 for each colouring $h \in \mathcal{H}$. □

3.2 Detecting 4-Cycles

We have seen how to *count* 4-cycles with the help of matrix multiplication in $O(n^{\rho})$ rounds. We now show how to *detect* 4-cycles in $O(1)$ rounds. The algorithm does not make direct use of matrix multiplication algorithms. However, the key part of the algorithm can be interpreted as an efficient routine for sparse matrix multiplication, under a specific definition of sparseness.

Let

$$P(X,Y,Z) = \{(x,y,z) \in X \times Y \times Z : \{x,y\} \in E, \{y,z\} \in E\}$$

consist of all distinct 2-walks (paths of length 2) from X through Y to Z. We use the shorthand notation v for $\{v\}$ and $*$ for V; for example, $P(x,*,*)$ consists of all walks of length 2 from node x. There exists a 4-cycle if and only if $|P(x,*,z)| \geq 2$ for some $x \neq z$.

On a high level, the algorithm proceeds as follows.

1. Each node x computes $|P(x,*,*)|$. If $|P(x,*,*)| \geq 2n-1$, then there exists some $z \neq x$ such that $|P(x,*,z)| \geq 2$, thus a 4-cycle exists and the algorithm stops.
2. Otherwise, each node x finds $P(x,*,*)$ and checks if there exists some $z \neq x$ satisfying $|P(x,*,z)| \geq 2$.

The first phase is easy to implement in $O(1)$ rounds. The key idea is that if the algorithm does not stop in the first phase, then the total volume of $P(*,*,*)$ is sufficiently small and we can afford to gather $P(x,*,*)$ for each node x in $O(1)$ rounds.

We now present the algorithm in more detail. We write $N(x)$ for the neighbours of node x. To implement the first phase, each node y broadcasts $\deg(y) = |N(y)|$ to all other nodes; we have

$$|P(x,*,*)| = \sum_{y \in N(x)} \deg(y).$$

To find a 4-cycle, each node x broadcasts a single bit indicating whether $|P(x,*,*)| \geq 2n-1$; let x be a specific node fulfilling the inequality, e.g. the one with the smallest identifier. Each node y broadcast a bit indicating if it is a neighbor of x, and now a node z with two common neighbors with x, y and y', can find a cycle (x,y,z,y',x).

Now let us explain the second phase. Each node y is already aware of $N(y)$ and hence it can construct $P(*,y,*) = N(y) \times \{y\} \times N(y)$. Our goal is to distribute the set of all 2-walks

$$\bigcup_y P(*,y,*) = P(*,*,*) = \bigcup_x P(x,*,*)$$

so that each node x will know $P(x,*,*)$. Due to the first phase, we have

$$\sum_y \deg(y)^2 = \sum_y |P(*,y,*)| = \sum_x |P(x,*,*)| < 2n^2.$$

Using this bound, we obtain the following lemma.

LEMMA 12. *It is possible to find sets $A(y)$ and $B(y)$ for each $y \in V$ such that the following holds:*

- *$A(y) \subseteq V$, $B(y) \subseteq V$, and $|A(y)| = |B(y)| \geq \deg(y)/8$,*
- *the tiles $A(y) \times B(y)$ are disjoint subsets of the square $V \times V$.*

Moreover, this can be done in $O(1)$ rounds in the congested clique.

PROOF. Let $f(y)$ be $\deg(y)/4$ rounded down to the nearest power of 2, and let k be n rounded down to the nearest power of 2. We have $\sum_y f(y)^2 \leq \sum \deg(y)^2/16 < n^2/8 < k^2$. Now it is easy to place the tiles of dimensions $f(y) \times f(y)$ inside a square of dimensions $k \times k$ without any overlap with the following iterative procedure:

- Before step $i = 1, 2, \dots$, we have partitioned the square into sub-squares of dimensions $k/2^{i-1} \times k/2^{i-1}$, and each sub-square is either completely full or completely empty.
- During step i, we divide each sub-square in 4 parts, and fill empty squares with tiles of dimensions $f(y) = k/2^i$.
- After step i, we have partitioned the square in sub-squares of dimensions $k/2^i \times k/2^i$, and each sub-square is either completely full or completely empty.

This way we have allocated disjoint tiles $A(y) \times B(y) \subseteq [k] \times [k] \subseteq V \times V$ for each y, with $|A(y)| = |B(y)| = f(y) \geq \deg(y)/8$.

To implement this in the congested clique model, it is sufficient that each y broadcasts $\deg(y)$ to all other nodes, and then all nodes follow the above procedure to compute $A(y)$ and $B(y)$ locally. □

Now, we use the tiles $A(y) \times B(y)$ to implement the second phase of 4-cycle detection. For convenience, we use the following notation for each $y \in Y$:

- The sets $N_A(y,a)$ for $a \in A(y)$ form a partition of $N(y)$ such that $|N_A(y,a)| \leq 8$.
- The sets $N_B(y,b)$ for $b \in B(y)$ form a partition of $N(y)$ such that $|N_B(y,b)| \leq 8$.

Note that we can assume that $A(y)$ and $B(y)$ are globally known by Lemma 12. Hence a node can compute $N_A(y,a)$ and $N_B(y,b)$ if it knows $N(y)$.

With this notation, the algorithm proceeds as follows (see Figure 1):

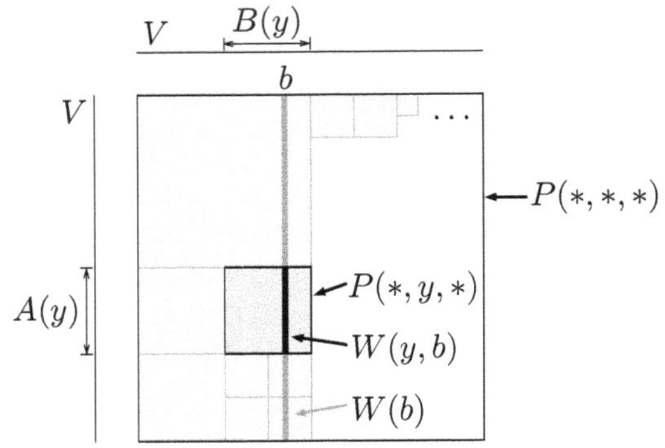

Figure 1: 4-cycle detection: how $P(*,*,*)$ is partitioned among the nodes.

1. For all $y \in V$ and $a \in A(y)$, node y sends $N_A(y,a)$ to a. This step can be implemented in $O(1)$ rounds.
2. For each y and each pair $(a,b) \in A(y) \times B(y)$, node a sends $N_A(y,a)$ to b. Note that for each (a,b) there is at most one y such that $(a,b) \in A(y) \times B(y)$; hence over each edge we send only $O(1)$ messages. Therefore this step can be implemented in $O(1)$ rounds.
3. At this point, each $b \in V$ has received a copy of $N(y)$ for all y with $b \in B(y)$. Node b computes
$$W(y,b) = N(y) \times \{y\} \times N_B(y,b);$$
$$W(b) = \bigcup_{y:\, b \in B(y)} W(y,b).$$
This is local computation; it takes no communication rounds.

We now give a lemma that captures the key properties of the algorithm.

LEMMA 13. *The sets $W(b)$ form a partition of $P(*,*,*)$. For each b we have $|W(b)| = O(n)$.*

PROOF. For the first claim, observe that the sets $P(*,y,*)$ for $y \in V$ form a partition of $P(*,*,*)$, the sets $W(y,b)$ for $b \in B(y)$ form a partition of $P(*,y,*)$, and each set $W(y,b)$ is part of exactly one $W(b)$.

For the second claim, let Y consist of all $y \in V$ with $b \in B(y)$. As the tiles $A(y) \times B(y)$ are disjoint for all $y \in Y$, and all $y \in Y$ have the common value $b \in B(y)$, it has to hold that the sets $A(y)$ are disjoint subsets of V for all $y \in Y$. Therefore
$$\sum_{y \in Y} |N(y)| = \sum_{y \in Y} \deg(y) \leq \sum_{y \in Y} 8|A(y)| \leq 8|V| = 8n.$$
With $|N_B(y)| \leq 8$ we get
$$|W(b)| = \sum_{y \in Y} |W(y,b)| \leq 8 \sum_{y \in Y} |N(y)| \leq 64n,$$
which completes the proof. □

Now we are almost done: we have distributed $P(*,*,*)$ evenly among V so that each node only holds $O(n)$ elements. Finally, we use the dynamic routing scheme [47] to gather $P(x,*,*)$ at each node $x \in V$; each node needs to send and receive $O(n)$ words, and therefore $O(1)$ rounds suffice. If a 4-cycle exists, any node x in it can now detect it from $P(x,*,*)$.

THEOREM 4. *On undirected graphs, the existence of 4-cycles can be detected in $O(1)$ rounds. If such a cycle exists, one such cycle can also be reported in $O(1)$ rounds.*

3.3 Girth

Recall that the *girth* g of a graph $G = (V,E)$ is the length of the shortest cycle in G. For *undirected* girth, we leverage the fast cycle detection algorithm and the following lemma giving a trade-off between the girth and the number of edges. A similar approach of bounding from above the number of edges of a graph that contains no copies of some given subgraph was taken by Drucker et al. [26].

LEMMA 14 ([54, PP. 362–363]). *A graph with girth g has at most $n^{1+1/\lfloor (g-1)/2 \rfloor} + n$ edges.*

If the graph is dense, then by the above lemma it must have small girth and we can use fast cycle detection to compute it; otherwise, the graph is sparse and we can learn the complete topology.

THEOREM 5. *For undirected graphs, the girth can be computed in $\tilde{O}(n^\rho + n^{o(1)})$ rounds.*

PROOF. Assume for now that $\rho > 0$, and fix $\ell = \lceil 2 + 2/\rho \rceil$. Each node collects all graph degrees and computes the total number of edges. If there are at most $n^{1+1/\lfloor \ell/2 \rfloor} + n = O(n^{1+\rho})$ edges, we can collect full information about the graph structure to all nodes in $O(n^\rho)$ rounds using an algorithm of Dolev et al. [25], and each node can then compute the girth locally. Otherwise, by Lemma 14, the graph has girth at most ℓ. Thus, for $k = 3, 4, \dots, \ell$, we try to find a k-cycle using Corollary 3, in $\ell \cdot 2^{O(\ell)} n^\rho \log n = \tilde{O}(n^\rho)$ rounds. When such a cycle is found for some k, we stop and return k as the girth. Finally, if $\rho = 0$, we pick $\ell = \log \log n$, and both cases take $n^{o(1)}$ rounds. □

For a directed graph, the girth is defined as the length of the shortest directed cycle; the main difference comparing to the undirected case is that directed girth can be 1 or 2. While the trade-off of Lemma 14 cannot be used for directed graphs, we can use a simpler technique of Itai and Rodeh [43].

Let $G = (V,E)$ be a directed graph; we can assume that there are no self-loops in G, as otherwise girth is 1 and we can detect this with local computation. Let $B^{(i)}$ be a Boolean matrix defined as
$$B^{(i)}_{uv} = \begin{cases} 1 & \text{if there is a path from } u \text{ to } v \text{ of length} \leq i, \\ 0 & \text{otherwise.} \end{cases}$$
Clearly, we have that $B^{(1)} = A$. Moreover, if $i = j + k$, we have
$$B^{(i)} = \left(B^{(j)} B^{(k)}\right) \vee A, \tag{2}$$
where the matrix product is over the Boolean semiring and $\vee$ denotes element-wise logical or.

COROLLARY 15. *For directed graphs, the girth can be computed in $\tilde{O}(n^\rho)$ rounds.*

PROOF. It suffices to find the smallest ℓ such that there is $v \in V$ with $B^{(\ell)}_{vv} = 1$; clearly ℓ is then the girth of graph G. We first compute $B^{(1)} = A, B^{(2)}, B^{(4)}, B^{(8)}, \dots$ using (2) with $j = k = i/2$ until we find i such that $B^{(i)}_{vv} = 1$ for some

$v \in V$. We then know that the girth is between i and $i/2$; we can perform binary search on this interval to find the girth, using (2) to evaluate the intermediate matrices. This requires $O(\log n)$ calls to the matrix multiplication algorithm. $\square$

3.4 All-pairs Shortest Paths from Matrix Multiplication

Matrix multiplication can be used to compute the shortest path distances via *iterated squaring* of the weight matrix W – entry W_{uv} is the weight of the edge (u, v) or ∞ if the edge does not exist – over the min-plus semiring [28, 33, 57]. That is, the matrix product is the *distance product*, also known as the *min-plus product* or *tropical product*, defined as

$$(S \star T)_{uv} = \min_{w}(S_{uw} + T_{wv}) .$$

Given a graph $G = (V, E)$ with weight matrix W, the nth distance product power W^n gives the actual distances in G as $d(v, u) = W^n_{vu}$. Computing W^n can be done with $\lceil \log n \rceil$ distance products by iteratively squaring W, that is, we compute $W^{2i} = W^i \star W^i$, for values of i that are powers of 2. Using this basic idea, we can compute all-pairs shortest path distances in various settings:

- For general weights, we compute the distance product using semiring matrix multiplication (Corollary 7).
- For unweighted and undirected graphs, we use a slightly different recursive technique of Seidel [66], which allows deducing distances in G based on those of the *square graph* G^2 (Corollary 8).
- If the weights are bounded by a small integer M, we can compute the distance product in $O(Mn^\rho)$ rounds by embedding the min-plus semiring into a suitable ring (Corollary 9).
- For approximate APSP, we adapt a lemma of Zwick [76] to show that we can compute a $(1 + \delta)$-approximate distance product in $O(n^\rho/\delta)$ rounds for any $\delta > 0$ (Corollary 10).

These algorithms can also be extended to compute full shortest path information by modifying the distance product algorithms so that they provide *witnesses*; an index w is a witness for uv if $(S \star T)_{uv} = S_{uw} + T_{wv}$. The semiring matrix multiplication can be directly modified to provide witnesses, and for distance product algorithms based on fast matrix multiplication known techniques from the centralised setting can be applied [4, 66, 76]

For more details on the APSP algorithms, see the full version of this paper [18].

4. LOWER BOUNDS

Lower bounds for matrix multiplication implementations. While proving unconditional lower bounds for matrix multiplication in the congested clique model seems to be beyond the reach of current techniques, as discussed in Section 1.5, it can be shown that the results given in Theorem 1 are essentially optimal distributed implementations of the corresponding centralised algorithms. To be more formal, let C be an arithmetic circuit for matrix multiplication; we say that an *implementation* of C in the congested clique model is a mapping of the gates of C to the nodes of the congested clique. This naturally defines a congested clique algorithm for matrix multiplication, with communication cost given by the wires in C between gates assigned to different nodes.

Various authors, considering different parallel models, have shown that in any implementation of the trivial $\Theta(n^3)$ matrix multiplication on a parallel machine with P processors there is at least one processor that has to send or receive $\Omega(n^2/P^{2/3})$ matrix entries [2, 42, 70]. As these models can simulate the congested clique, a similar lower bound holds for congested clique implementations of the trivial $O(n^3)$ matrix multiplication. In the congested clique, each processor sends and receives $\tilde{\Theta}(n)$ messages per round and $P = n$, yielding a lower bound of $\tilde{\Omega}(n^{1/3})$ rounds.

The trivial $\Theta(n^3)$ algorithm is optimal for circuits using only semiring addition and multiplication. The task of $n \times n$ matrix multiplication over the min-plus semiring can be reduced to APSP with a constant blowup [3, pp. 202–205], hence the above bound applies also to any APSP algorithm that only uses minimum and addition operations. Thus, current techniques for similar problems, like the one used in the fast MST algorithm of Lotker et al. [52], cannot be extended to solve APSP.

COROLLARY 16. *Any implementation of the trivial $\Theta(n^3)$ matrix multiplication and any APSP algorithm which only sums weights and takes the minimum of such sums require $\tilde{\Omega}(n^{1/3})$ communication rounds in the congested clique model.*

However, known results on centralised APSP and distance product computation give reasons to suspect that this bound can be broken if we allow subtraction; in particular, translating the recent result of Williams [74] might allow for running time of order $n^{1/3}/2^{\Omega(\sqrt{\log n})}$ for APSP in the congested clique.

Concerning fast matrix multiplication algorithms, Ballard et al. [8] have proven lower bounds for parallel implementations of *Strassen-like* algorithms. Their seminal work is based on building a DAG representing the linear combinations of the inputs before the block multiplications, and the linear combinations of the results of the multiplications ("decoding") as the output matrix. The parallel computation induces an assignment of the graph vertices to the processes, and the edges crossing the partition represent the communication. Using an expansion argument, Ballard et al. show that in any partition a graph representing an $\Omega(n^\sigma)$ algorithm there is a process communicating $\Omega(n^{2-2/\sigma})$ values. See also [9] for a concise account of the technique.

The lower bound holds for Strassen's algorithm, and for a family of similar algorithms, but not for any matrix multiplication algorithm [8, §5.1.1]. A matrix multiplication algorithm is said to be *Strassen-like* if it is recursive, its decoding graph discussed above is connected, and it computes no scalar multiplication twice. As each process communicates at most $O(n)$ values in a round, the implementation of an $\Omega(n^\sigma)$ strassen-like algorithm must take $\Omega(n^{1-2/\sigma})$ rounds.

COROLLARY 17. *Any implementation of a Strassen-like matrix multiplication algorithm using $\Omega(n^\sigma)$ element multiplications requires $\tilde{\Omega}(n^{1-2/\sigma})$ communication rounds in the congested clique model.*

Lower bound for broadcast congested clique. Recall that the broadcast congested clique is a version of the congested clique model with the additional constraint that all $n-1$ messages sent by a node in a round must be identical.

Holzer and Pinsker [39] show that computing any approximation better than factor 2 to all-pairs shortest paths in weighted graphs takes $\tilde{\Omega}(n)$ rounds in the congested clique. As discussed in Section 3.4, $\tilde{o}(n)$-round matrix multiplication algorithms imply $\tilde{o}(n)$-round algorithms for $(1+o(1))$-approximate weighted APSP.

COROLLARY 18. *In the broadcast congested clique model, matrix multiplication over the Boolean semiring and APSP algorithms require* $\tilde{\Omega}(n)$ *communication rounds.*

We remark that the restriction "over the Boolean semiring" refers to the issue that, in principle, it is possible that matrix multiplication exponents may be different for different underlying semirings. However, at the very least the lower bound also applies to matrix multiplication over integers and rationals, as well as the min-plus semiring, as in all cases a Boolean matrix multiplication algorithm trivially follows. We stress that this bound holds without any assumptions on the algorithm itself.

5. CONCLUSIONS

In this work, we demonstrate that algebraic methods – especially fast matrix multiplication – can be used to design efficient algorithms in the congested clique model, resulting in solutions that outperform all previous combinatorial algorithms. Moreover, we have certainly not exhausted the known centralised literature of algorithms based on matrix multiplication, so similar techniques should also give improvements for other problems. It remains open whether corresponding unconditional lower bounds exist; however, suspicion grows that these would imply strong lower bounds for centralised algorithms, and will thus be highly challenging to prove.

While the present work focuses on a fully connected communication topology (clique), we expect that the same techniques can be applied more generally in the usual CONGEST model. For example, fast triangle detection in the CONGEST model is trivial in those areas of the network that are sparse. Only dense areas of the network are non-trivial, and in those areas we may have enough overall bandwidth for fast matrix multiplication algorithms. On the other hand, there are non-trivial lower bounds for distance computation problems in the CONGEST model [24], though significant gaps still remain [58].

Acknowledgements

We thank Morteza Zadimoghaddam for pointing out that our 4-cycle detection algorithm can also be used to report a cycle, and we thank Keijo Heljanko, Juho Hirvonen, Fabian Kuhn, Tuomo Lempiäinen, and Joel Rybicki for discussions.

References

[1] Ramesh C. Agarwal, Susanne M. Balle, Fred G. Gustavson, Mahesh V. Joshi, and Prasad V. Palkar. A three-dimensional approach to parallel matrix multiplication. *IBM Journal of Research and Development*, 39(5):575–582, 1995.

[2] Alok Aggarwal, Ashok K. Chandra, and Marc Snir. Communication complexity of PRAMs. *Theoretical Computer Science*, 71(1):3–28, 1990.

[3] Alfred V. Aho, John E. Hopcroft, and Jeffrey D. Ullman. *The Design and Analysis of Computer Algorithms*. Addison-Wesley, 1974.

[4] Noga Alon and Moni Naor. Derandomization, witnesses for Boolean matrix multiplication and construction of perfect hash functions. *Algorithmica*, 16(4–5):434–449, 1996.

[5] Noga Alon, Raphael Yuster, and Uri Zwick. Color-coding. *Journal of the ACM*, 42(4):844–856, 1995.

[6] Noga Alon, Raphael Yuster, and Uri Zwick. Finding and counting given length cycles. *Algorithmica*, 17(3): 209–223, 1997.

[7] Grey Ballard, James Demmel, Olga Holtz, Benjamin Lipshitz, and Oded Schwartz. Communication-optimal parallel algorithm for Strassen's matrix multiplication. In *Proc. 24th ACM Symposium on Parallelism in Algorithms and Architectures (SPAA 2012)*, pages 193–204, 2012.

[8] Grey Ballard, James Demmel, Olga Holtz, and Oded Schwartz. Graph expansion and communication costs of fast matrix multiplication. *Journal of the ACM*, 59 (6):32, 2012.

[9] Grey Ballard, James Demmel, Olga Holtz, and Oded Schwartz. Communication costs of strassen's matrix multiplication. *Commun. ACM*, 57(2):107–114, 2014.

[10] Andreas Björklund. Determinant sums for undirected hamiltonicity. *SIAM Journal on Computing*, 43(1): 280–299, 2014.

[11] Andreas Björklund and Thore Husfeldt. Shortest two disjoint paths in polynomial time. In *Proc. 41st International Colloquium on Automata, Languages, and Programming (ICALP 2014)*, pages 211–222, 2014.

[12] Andreas Björklund, Thore Husfeldt, Petteri Kaski, and Mikko Koivisto. Fourier meets Möbius: fast subset convolution. In *Proc. 39th Annual ACM Symposium on Theory of Computing (STOC 2007)*, pages 67–74, 2007.

[13] Andreas Björklund, Thore Husfeldt, and Mikko Koivisto. Set partitioning via inclusion-exclusion. *SIAM Journal on Computing*, 39(2):546–563, 2009.

[14] Andreas Björklund, Petteri Kaski, and Łukasz Kowalik. Probably optimal graph motifs. In *Proc. 30th International Symposium on Theoretical Aspects of Computer Science (STACS 2013)*, pages 20–31, 2013.

[15] Andreas Björklund, Petteri Kaski, and Łukasz Kowalik. Counting thin subgraphs via packings faster than meet-in-the-middle time. In *Proc. 25th Annual ACM-SIAM Symposium on Discrete Algorithms (SODA 2014)*, pages 594–603, 2014.

[16] Hans L. Bodlaender, Marek Cygan, Stefan Kratsch, and Jesper Nederlof. Deterministic single exponential time algorithms for connectivity problems parameterized by treewidth. In *Proc. 40th International Colloquium on Automata, Languages, and Programming (ICALP 2013)*, pages 196–207, 2013.

[17] Peter Bürgisser, Michael Clausen, and M. Amin Shokrollahi. *Algebraic Complexity Theory*. Springer, 1997.

[18] Keren Censor-Hillel, Petteri Kaski, Janne H. Korhonen, Christoph Lenzen, Ami Paz, and Jukka Suomela.

Algebraic methods in the congested clique, 2015. arXiv:1503.04963 [cs.DC].

[19] Timothy M. Chan. All-pairs shortest paths with real weights in $O(n^3/\log n)$ time. *Algorithmica*, 50(2): 236–243, 2008.

[20] Timothy M. Chan. More algorithms for all-pairs shortest paths in weighted graphs. *SIAM Journal on Computing*, 39(5):2075–2089, 2010.

[21] Marek Cygan, Jesper Nederlof, Marcin Pilipczuk, Michal Pilipczuk, Johan M. M. van Rooij, and Jakub Onufry Wojtaszczyk. Solving connectivity problems parameterized by treewidth in single exponential time. In *Proc. 52nd Annual Symposium on Foundations of Computer Science (FOCS 2011)*, pages 150–159, 2011.

[22] Marek Cygan, Stefan Kratsch, and Jesper Nederlof. Fast Hamiltonicity checking via bases of perfect matchings. In *Proc. 45th ACM Symposium on Theory of Computing (STOC 2013)*, pages 301–310, 2013.

[23] Artur Czumaj and Andrzej Lingas. Finding a heaviest triangle is not harder than matrix multiplication. In *Proc. 18th Annual ACM-SIAM Symposium on Discrete Algorithms (SODA 2007)*, pages 986–994, 2007.

[24] Atish Das Sarma, Stephan Holzer, Liah Kor, Amos Korman, Danupon Nanongkai, Gopal Pandurangan, David Peleg, and Roger Wattenhofer. Distributed verification and hardness of distributed approximation. In *Proc. 43th ACM Symposium on Theory of Computing (STOC 2011)*, pages 363–372, 2011.

[25] Danny Dolev, Christoph Lenzen, and Shir Peled. "Tri, tri again": Finding triangles and small subgraphs in a distributed setting. In *Proc. 26th International Symposium on Distributed Computing (DISC 2012)*, pages 195–209, 2012.

[26] Andrew Drucker, Fabian Kuhn, and Rotem Oshman. On the power of the congested clique model. In *Proc. 33rd ACM Symposium on Principles of Distributed Computing (PODC 2014)*, pages 367–376, 2014.

[27] Friedrich Eisenbrand and Fabrizio Grandoni. On the complexity of fixed parameter clique and dominating set. *Theoretical Computer Science*, 326(1–3):57–67, 2004.

[28] M. J. Fischer and A. R. Meyer. Boolean matrix multiplication and transitive closure. In *Proc. 12th Symposium on Switching and Automata Theory (FOCS 1971)*, pages 129–131, 1971.

[29] Fedor V. Fomin, Daniel Lokshtanov, Venkatesh Raman, Saket Saurabh, and B. V. Raghavendra Rao. Faster algorithms for finding and counting subgraphs. *Journal of Computer and System Sciences*, 78(3):698–706, 2012.

[30] Fedor V. Fomin, Daniel Lokshtanov, and Saket Saurabh. Efficient computation of representative sets with applications in parameterized and exact algorithms. In *Proc. 25th Annual ACM-SIAM Symposium on Discrete Algorithms (SODA 2014)*, pages 142–151, 2014.

[31] Michael L. Fredman. New bounds on the complexity of the shortest path problem. *SIAM Journal on Computing*, 5(1):83–89, 1976.

[32] Silvio Frischknecht, Stephan Holzer, and Roger Wattenhofer. Networks cannot compute their diameter in sublinear time. In *Proc. 23rd Annual ACM-SIAM Symposium on Discrete Algorithms (SODA 2012)*, pages 1150–1162, 2012.

[33] M. E. Furman. Application of a method of fast multiplication of matrices to problem of finding graph transitive closure. *Doklady Akademii Nauk SSSR*, 194 (3):524, 1970.

[34] François Le Gall. Powers of tensors and fast matrix multiplication. In *Proc. 39th Symposium on Symbolic and Algebraic Computation (ISSAC 2014)*, pages 296–303, 2014.

[35] Yijie Han. An $O(n^3(\log\log n/\log n)^{5/4})$ time algorithm for all pairs shortest path. *Algorithmica*, 51 (4):428–434, 2008.

[36] Yijie Han and Tadao Takaoka. An $O(n^3 \log\log n/\log^2 n)$ time algorithm for all pairs shortest paths. In *Proc. 13th Scandinavian Symposium on Algorithm Theory (SWAT 2012)*, pages 131–141, 2012.

[37] James W. Hegeman and Sriram V. Pemmaraju. Lessons from the congested clique applied to mapreduce. In *Proc. 21st Colloquium on Structural Information and Communication Complexity (SIROCCO 2014)*, pages 149–164, 2014.

[38] James W. Hegeman, Sriram V. Pemmaraju, and Vivek B. Sardeshmukh. Near-constant-time distributed algorithms on a congested clique. In *Proc. 28th International Symposium on Distributed Computing (DISC 2014)*, pages 514–530, 2014.

[39] Stephan Holzer and N. Pinsker. Approximation of distances and shortest paths in the broadcast congest clique, 2014. arXiv:1412.3445 [cs.DC].

[40] Stephan Holzer and Roger Wattenhofer. Optimal distributed all pairs shortest paths and applications. In *Proc. 31st ACM Symposium on Principles of Distributed Computing (PODC 2012)*, pages 355–364, 2012.

[41] Stephan Holzer, David Peleg, Liam Roditty, and Roger Wattenhofer. Brief announcement: Distributed 3/2-approximation of the diameter. In *Proc. 28th International Symposium on Distributed Computing (DISC 2014)*, pages 562–564, 2014.

[42] Dror Irony, Sivan Toledo, and Alexandre Tiskin. Communication lower bounds for distributed-memory matrix multiplication. *Journal of Parallel and Distributed Computing*, 64(9):1017–1026, 2004.

[43] Alon Itai and Michael Rodeh. Finding a minimum circuit in a graph. *SIAM Journal on Computing*, 7(4): 413–423, 1978.

[44] Ioannis Koutis. Faster algebraic algorithms for path and packing problems. In *Proc. 35th International Colloquium on Automata, Languages and Programming (ICALP 2008)*, pages 575–586, 2008.

[45] Miroslaw Kowaluk, Andrzej Lingas, and Eva-Marta Lundell. Counting and detecting small subgraphs via equations and matrix multiplication. In *Proc. 22nd Annual ACM-SIAM Symposium on Discrete Algorithms (SODA 2011)*, pages 1468–1476, 2011.

[46] Shay Kutten and David Peleg. Fast distributed construction of small k-dominating sets and applications. *Journal of Algorithms*, 28(1):40–66, 1998.

[47] Christoph Lenzen. Optimal deterministic routing and sorting on the congested clique. In *Proc. 32nd ACM Symposium on Principles of Distributed Computing (PODC 2013)*, pages 42–50, 2013.

[48] Christoph Lenzen and Boaz Patt-Shamir. Fast routing table construction using small messages. In *Proc. 45rd ACM Symposium on Theory of Computing (STOC 2013)*, pages 381–390, 2013.

[49] Christoph Lenzen and David Peleg. Efficient distributed source detection with limited bandwidth. In *Proc. 32nd ACM Symposium on Principles of Distributed Computing (PODC 2013)*, pages 375–382, 2013.

[50] Christoph Lenzen and Roger Wattenhofer. Tight bounds for parallel randomized load balancing. In *Proc. 43rd ACM Symposium on Theory of Computing (STOC 2011)*, pages 11–20, 2011.

[51] Daniel Lokshtanov and Jesper Nederlof. Saving space by algebraization. In *Proc. 42nd ACM Symposium on Theory of Computing (STOC 2010)*, 2010.

[52] Zvi Lotker, Boaz Patt-Shamir, Elan Pavlov, and David Peleg. Minimum-Weight Spanning Tree Construction in $O(\log \log n)$ Communication Rounds. *SIAM Journal on Computing*, 35(1):120–131, 2005.

[53] Qingshan Luo and John B. Drake. A scalable parallel Strassen's matrix multiplication algorithm for distributed-memory computers. In *Symposium on Applied Computing (SAC)*, pages 221–226, 1995.

[54] Jirí Matoušek. *Lectures on Discrete Geometry*. Graduate Texts in Mathematics. Springer, 2002.

[55] William F. McColl. Scalable computing. In *Computer Science Today*, pages 46–61. Springer, 1995.

[56] William F. McColl. A BSP realisation of Strassen's algorithm. In *Abstract Machine Models for Parallel and Distributed Computing*, volume 48 of *Concurrent Systems Engineering*, pages 43–46. IOS Press, 1996.

[57] Ian Munro. Efficient determination of the transitive closure of a directed graph. *Information Processing Letters*, 1(2):56–58, 1971.

[58] Danupon Nanongkai. Distributed approximation algorithms for weighted shortest paths. In *Proc. 46th ACM Symposium on Theory of Computing (STOC 2014)*, pages 565–573, 2014.

[59] Jaroslav Nešetřil and Svatopluk Poljak. On the complexity of the subgraph problem. *Commentationes Mathematicae Universitatis Carolinae*, 26(2):415–419, 1985.

[60] Boaz Patt-Shamir and Marat Teplitsky. The round complexity of distributed sorting. In *Proc. 30th ACM Symposium on Principles of Distributed Computing (PODC 2011)*, pages 249–256, 2011.

[61] David Peleg. *Distributed Computing: A Locality-Sensitive Approach.* Society for Industrial and Applied Mathematics, 2000.

[62] David Peleg and Vitaly Rubinovich. Near-tight lower bound on the time complexity of distributed MST construction. *SIAM Journal on Computing*, 30(5): 1427–1442, 2000.

[63] David Peleg, Liam Roditty, and Elad Tal. Distributed algorithms for network diameter and girth. In *Proc. 39th International Colloquium on Automata, Languages and Programming (ICALP 2012)*, pages 660–672, 2012.

[64] Sriram V. Pemmaraju and Vivek B. Sardeshmukh. Minimum-weight Spanning Tree Construction in $O(\log \log \log n)$ Rounds on the Congested Clique, 2014. arXiv:1412.2333 [cs.DC].

[65] P Raghavan and C D Thompson. Provably Good Routing in Graphs: Regular Arrays. In *Proc. 7th ACM Symposium on Theory of Computing (STOC 1985)*, pages 79–87, 1985.

[66] Raimund Seidel. On the all-pairs-shortest-path problem in unweighted undirected graphs. *Journal of Computer and System Sciences*, 51(3):400–403, 1995.

[67] Volker Strassen. Gaussian elimination is not optimal. *Numerische Mathematik*, 13(4):354–356, 1969.

[68] Tadao Takaoka. A faster algorithm for the all-pairs shortest path problem and its application. In *Proc. 10th International Conference on Computing and Combinatorics (COCOON 2004)*, pages 278–289, 2004.

[69] Tadao Takaoka. An $O(n^3 \log \log n / \log n)$ time algorithm for the all-pairs shortest path problem. *Information Processing Letters*, 96(5):155–161, 2005.

[70] Alexandre Tiskin. Bulk-synchronous parallel multiplication of boolean matrices. In *Proc. 25th Colloquium on Automata, Languages and Programming (ICALP 1998)*, pages 494–506. Springer Berlin Heidelberg, 1998.

[71] Alexandre Tiskin. *The Design and Analysis of Bulk-Synchronous Parallel Algorithms.* PhD thesis, University of Oxford, 1999.

[72] Virginia Vassilevska Williams and Ryan Williams. Finding, minimizing, and counting weighted subgraphs. *SIAM Journal of Computing*, 42(3):831–854, 2013.

[73] Ryan Williams. Finding paths of length k in $O^*(2^k)$ time. *Information Processing Letters*, 109(6):315–318, 2009.

[74] Ryan Williams. Faster all-pairs shortest paths via circuit complexity. In *Proc. 46th ACM Symposium on Theory of Computing (STOC 2014)*, pages 664–673. ACM, 2014.

[75] Uri Zwick. Exact and approximate distances in graphs – A survey. In *Proc. 9th European Symposium on Algorithms (ESA 2001)*, pages 33–48, 2001.

[76] Uri Zwick. All pairs shortest paths using bridging sets and rectangular matrix multiplication. *Journal of the ACM*, 49(3):289–317, 2002.

[77] Uri Zwick. A slightly improved sub-cubic algorithm for the all pairs shortest paths problem with real edge lengths. *Algorithmica*, 46(2):181–192, 2006.

Fast Partial Distance Estimation and Applications

Christoph Lenzen
MPI for Informatics
Saarbrücken, Germany
clenzen@mpi-inf.mpg.de

Boaz Patt-Shamir*
Tel Aviv University
Tel Aviv, Israel
boaz@tau.ac.il

ABSTRACT

We study approximate distributed solutions to the weighted *all-pairs-shortest-paths* (APSP) problem in the CONGEST model. We obtain the following results.

• A deterministic $(1+\varepsilon)$-approximation to APSP with running time $\mathcal{O}(\varepsilon^{-2} n \log n)$ rounds. The best previously known algorithm was randomized and slower by a $\Theta(\log n)$ factor.

In many cases, routing schemes involve relabeling, i.e., assigning new names to nodes and that are used in distance and routing queries. It is known that relabeling is necessary to achieve running times of $o(n/\log n)$. In the relabeling model, we obtain the following results.

• A randomized $\mathcal{O}(k)$-approximation to APSP, for any integer $k > 1$, running in $\tilde{\mathcal{O}}(n^{1/2+1/k} + D)$ rounds, where D is the hop diameter of the network. This algorithm simplifies the best previously known result and reduces its approximation ratio from $\mathcal{O}(k \log k)$ to $\mathcal{O}(k)$. Also, the new algorithm uses $\mathcal{O}(\log n)$-bit labels, which is asymptotically optimal.

• A randomized $\mathcal{O}(k)$-approximation to APSP, for any integer $k > 1$, running in time $\tilde{\mathcal{O}}((nD)^{1/2} \cdot n^{1/k} + D)$ and producing *compact routing tables* of size $\tilde{\mathcal{O}}(n^{1/k})$. The node labels consist of $\mathcal{O}(k \log n)$ bits. This improves on the approximation ratio of $\Theta(k^2)$ for tables of that size achieved by the best previously known algorithm, which terminates faster, in $\tilde{\mathcal{O}}(n^{1/2+1/k} + D)$ rounds.

In addition, we improve on the time complexity of the best known deterministic algorithm for distributed approximate Steiner forest.

Categories and Subject Descriptors

F.2.2 [**Analysis of Algorithms and Problem Complexity**]: Nonnumerical Algorithms and Problems

*Supported in part by the Israel Science Foundation (grant No. 1444/14) and by a grant from Israel Ministry of Science and Technology.

Permission to make digital or hard copies of all or part of this work for personal or classroom use is granted without fee provided that copies are not made or distributed for profit or commercial advantage and that copies bear this notice and the full citation on the first page. Copyrights for components of this work owned by others than ACM must be honored. Abstracting with credit is permitted. To copy otherwise, or republish, to post on servers or to redistribute to lists, requires prior specific permission and/or a fee. Request permissions from permissions@acm.org.
PODC'15, July 21–23, 2015, Donostia-San Sebastián, Spain.
Copyright © 2015 ACM 978-1-4503-3617-8 /15/07 ...$15.00.
DOI: http://dx.doi.org/10.1145/2767386.2767398 .

Keywords

CONGEST model, weighted all-pairs shortest paths, routing table construction, Steiner forests, source detection

1. INTRODUCTION

To allow a network to be useful, it must facilitate routing messages between nodes. By the very nature of networks, this computation must be distributed, i.e., there must be a distributed algorithm that computes the local data structures that support routing at network junctions (i.e., routing tables at nodes). A trivial distributed algorithm for this purpose is to collect the entire topology at a single location, apply a centralized algorithm, and distribute the result via the network. This simplistic approach is costly, in particular if the available bandwidth is limited. To study the distributed time complexity of routing table computation, we use the CONGEST model, i.e., we assume that in an n-node network, each link can carry only $\mathcal{O}(\log n)$ bits in each time unit.

In this work, we consider networks modeled by weighted undirected graphs, where the edge weights represent some abstract link cost, e.g., latency. As to the task routing, we note that it is a generic problem with many variants. The specific problems we focus on are the following.

• *Distance Estimation*: How fast can each node obtain an estimate of its distance to each other node, and how good is that estimate?

• *All-Pairs Shortest Paths:* How fast can we construct local data structures so that when given a destination node identifier, the node can locally determine the next hop on a path to the destination, and what is the *stretch* of the resulting route w.r.t. the shortest path?

In modern routing systems, it is common practice to assign to nodes labels (identifiers) that contain some routing information. IP addresses, for example, contain a "network" and a "host" parts which allow for hierarchical routing. Thus, the following questions are also of interest to us.

• *Routing Table Construction:* What are the answers to the above questions if we permit *relabeling*, i.e., allow the algorithm to choose (small) *labels* as node identifiers, and require that distance and routing queries refer to nodes using these labels?

• *Compact Routing:* What are the answers to the above questions when the storage space at the nodes (i.e., routing table size) is small?

Some history. Shortest paths are a central object of study since the dawn of the computer era. The Bellman-Ford algorithm [4, 8], although originally developed for centralized optimization, is one of the very few fundamental distributed algorithms. Implemented as RIP, the algorithm was used in the early days of the Internet (when it was still called ARPANET) [19]. Measured in terms of the CONGEST model, a Bellman-Ford all-pairs shortest paths computation in weighted graphs takes $\Theta(n^2)$ time in the worst case, and requires $\Theta(n \log n)$ bits of storage at each node. Another simple solution to the problem is to collect the complete topology at each node (by flooding) and then apply a local single-source shortest paths algorithm, such as Dijkstra's. This solution has time complexity $\Theta(m)$ and storage complexity $\tilde{\Theta}(n)$, where m denotes the number of links in the network.[1] Since it also enjoys improved stability and flexibility, it became the Internet's routing algorithm in its later stages of evolution (see [18]). Standardized as OSPF [20], it also contains provisions for hierarchical routing.

State of the art: Lower bounds. Recently there has been a flurry of new results about routing in the CONGEST model. Below we review some known lower bounds to help placing our results in the context of what is possible. We use D to denote the *hop diameter*, i.e., the diameter of the network when ignoring weights.

- Without relabeling, any polylog-ratio approximation to APSP requires $\tilde{\Omega}(n)$ rounds [21, 22]. This holds also if tables must only enable either distance estimates or routing.
- With node relabeling, any non-trivial approximation to APSP requires $\tilde{\Omega}(\sqrt{n} + D)$ rounds [7]. The bound holds for both routing and distance queries, and even for $D \in \mathcal{O}(\log n)$. (However, if routing may be *stateful*, i.e., routing decisions may depend on the tables of previously visited nodes, no non-trivial lower bound is known; all our routing algorithms are stateless.)
- If the routing table size is $\tilde{\mathcal{O}}(n^{1/k})$, then the approximation ratio of the induced routes is at least $2k - 1$ [1, 25]. (This result does not hold for stateful routing.) For distance approximation, the same bound has been established for the special cases of $k \in \{1, 2, 3, 5\}$, and is conjectured to hold for any k (see [29]).
- Any randomized $(2 - o(1))$-approximation of APSP, and any $(2 - o(1))$-approximation of the weighted diameter requires $\tilde{\Omega}(n)$ time in the worst case [12]. In the *unweighted* case, $\tilde{\Omega}(n)$ time is required to f-approximate the diameter for $f < 3/2$ [9].

Upper bounds: Our results vs. previous work. We now list our new results (which are all upper bounds), and compare them to the best previously known bounds.

- For any $\varepsilon > 0$, we give a *deterministic* $(1 + \varepsilon)$-approximation to APSP that runs in $\mathcal{O}(\varepsilon^{-2} n \log n)$ rounds. The best known previous result, due to Nanongkai [21], achieves the same approximation ratio within $\mathcal{O}(\varepsilon^{-2} n \log^2 n)$ rounds with high probability—Nanongkai's algorithm is randomized. We note that independently and concurrently to our work, Holzer and Pinsker [12] derived the same algorithm and result for the Broadcast Congested Clique model, in which in each round, each node posts a single $\mathcal{O}(\log n)$-bit message which is delivered to all other nodes.
- Given $k \in \mathbb{N}$, we can compute a randomized $(6k - 1 + o(1))$-approximation to APSP in time $\tilde{\mathcal{O}}(n^{1/2+1/(4k)} + D)$. The algorithm succeeds with high probability (cf. Section 2), as do all our randomized algorithms. This simplifies our previous work [22] and reduces the approximation ratio from $\mathcal{O}(k \log k)$ to $\mathcal{O}(k)$. Also, the new algorithm relabels nodes with labels of $\mathcal{O}(\log n)$ bits, whereas the previous one required $\mathcal{O}(\log n \log k)$-bit labels.
- For any $k \in \mathbb{N}$, we can compute a randomized $(4k - 3 + o(1))$-approximation to APSP running in $\tilde{\mathcal{O}}(\min\{(nD)^{1/2} \cdot n^{1/k}, n^{2/3+2/(3k)}\} + D)$ rounds with tables of size $\tilde{\mathcal{O}}(n^{1/k})$. This improves over the stretch of $\mathcal{O}(k^2)$ in [22], at the cost of increasing the running time (from $\tilde{\mathcal{O}}(n^{1/2+1/k} + D)$). We point out, however, that the proposed algorithm is the first to achieve an asymptotically optimal trade-off between table size and stretch in time $\tilde{o}(n)$ for all $k > 2$ and graphs of diameter $D \in \tilde{o}(n)$.
- Using partial distance estimation, we also improve on the running time of the best known algorithm for distributed Steiner forest construction. A precise statement is provided in Section 4.3; let us just say here that in the worst case, the previous algorithm may give rise to a trivial $\tilde{\mathcal{O}}(n^2)$ time complexity, while the running time of the new algorithm is always bounded by $\tilde{\mathcal{O}}(n^{3/2})$.

Technical Summary. Our key algorithmic tool is a generalization of the (S, h, σ)-detection problem, defined as follows [16].[2] Given a graph with a distinguished set of *source nodes* S, the task is for each node to find the distances to its closest $\sigma \in \mathbb{N}$ sources within $h \in \mathbb{N}$ hops (cf. Definition 2.1). In [16] it is shown that this task can be solved in $h + \sigma$ rounds on *unweighted* graphs. The main new ingredient in all our results is an algorithm that, within a comparable running time, produces an *approximate* solution to (S, h, σ)-detection in *weighted* graphs. We call this version *partial distance estimation*, abbreviated PDE.[3]

Weighted graphs present significant difficulty, because the number of hops in a shortest (by weight) path between two nodes may be a factor of $\Theta(n)$ larger than the minimal number of hops on any path connecting the same two nodes (a weighted clique may demonstrate this phenomenon). Therefore, naïvely finding the absolute closest σ sources (w.r.t. weighted distance) within h hops may require $\Omega(n)$ rounds in the worst case, for any h and σ. One may circumvent this difficulty by replacing the underlying graph metric by *h-hop distances*, which for $v, w \in V$ is defined as the minimum weight of all v-w paths that consist of at most h hops. The collection of h-hop distances does not constitute a metric, but one can solve the (S, h, σ)-detection problem under h-hop distances in time σh using techniques similar to those used in the unweighted case [22].

Unfortunately, as illustrated in Figure 1, this time complexity is optimal in the worst case. To avoid this bottleneck, Nanongkai [21] uses a rounding technique that had previously been employed in the centralized setting [30], solving the problem to within a $(1 + \varepsilon)$-factor by essentially reducing the weighted instance to $\mathcal{O}(\log n/\varepsilon)$ unweighted instances and solving each instance using breadth-first-search. To avoid collisions, independent random delays are applied in [21] to the starting times of these instances. The result is, w.h.p., $(1 + \varepsilon)$-approximate distances to all sources in $\mathcal{O}(\varepsilon^{-2}(h + |S|) \log^2 n)$ rounds. We replace this part of

[1]Throughout this paper, we use $\tilde{\mathcal{O}}$-notation, which hides poly-logarithmic factors. See Section 2.

[2]In [16], the third parameter is called k. We use σ because here, k denotes the parameter controlling the trade-off between approximation ratio and table size.

[3]We note that Henziger et al. already employed our PDE algorithm for deterministic $(1+o(1))$-approximation of single-source shortest paths in almost optimal time [11].

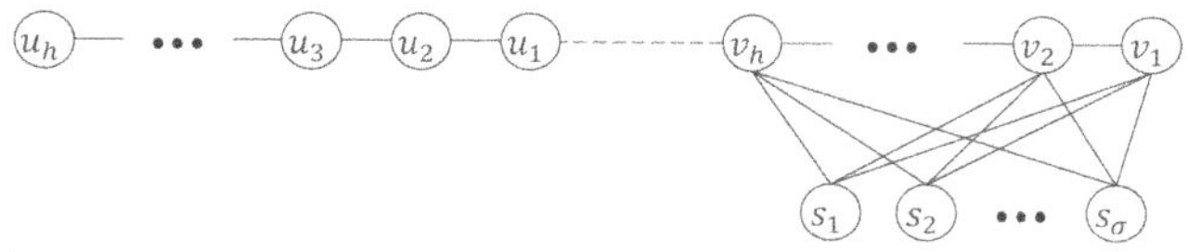

Figure 1: *A graph where $(S, h+1, \sigma)$-detection cannot be solved in $o(h\sigma)$ rounds. Edge weights are $4ih$ for edges $\{v_i, s_{i,j}\}$ for all $i \in \{1, \ldots, h\}$ and $j \in \{1, \ldots, \sigma\}$, and 1 (i.e., negligible) for all other edges. Node u_i, $i \in \{1, \ldots, h\}$, needs to learn about all nodes $s_{i,j}$ and distances $\mathrm{wd}_{h+1}(u_i, s_{i,j})$, where $j \in \{1, \ldots, \sigma\}$. Hence all this information must traverse the dashed edge $\{u_1, v_h\}$. The example can be modified to attach the same source set to each v_h. Varying distances, then still $\sigma h = |S|h$ values must be communicated over the dashed edge. Hence, the special case $|S| = \sigma$ is not easier.*

the algorithm with the deterministic source detection algorithm from [16], obtaining a deterministic algorithm that runs in $\mathcal{O}(\varepsilon^{-2}(h+|S|)\log n)$ rounds. This, using $S = V$ and $h = \sigma = n$, yields the immediate corollary of a deterministic $(1+o(1))$-approximation to APSP.

For our other results, we abandon the special case of $S = V$ and define (see Definition 2.2) a $(1+\varepsilon)$-approximate version of the (S, h, σ)-detection problem which we call *partial distance estimation (PDE)*. The crucial insight is that by combining Nanongkai's and Zwick's rounding scheme with the algorithm from [16], PDE can be solved within $\mathcal{O}((h+\sigma)\log n/\varepsilon^2)$ rounds, so that no node sends more than $\mathcal{O}(\sigma^2)$ messages. Exploiting these properties carefully, we obtain our other results.

Further ingredients. Our compact routing schemes can be viewed as distributed constructions of the routing hierarchies of Thorup and Zwick [28]. These make use of efficient tree labeling schemes presented in the same paper, which allow for a distributed implementation in time $\tilde{\mathcal{O}}(h)$ in trees of depth h if relabeling is permitted. For compact routing table construction, we continue the Thorup-Zwick construction by simulating the partial distance estimation algorithm on the *skeleton graph* [22], broadcasting all messages via a BFS tree. This avoids the quadratic stretch incurred by the approach in [22] due to approximating distances in the skeleton graph using a *spanner* [24], which is constructed by simulating the Baswana-Sen algorithm [3]. If compact tables are not required, the partial distance estimation algorithm enables to collapse the Thorup-Zwick hierarchy of the lower levels into a single step, giving constant approximation ratio. This shaves off an $\mathcal{O}(\log k)$-factor from [22].

Paper organization. In Section 2 we define the model and problems. In Section 3 we give an algorithm for partial distance estimation. In Section 4 we present applications to the tasks of APSP, compact routing table construction, and Steiner forest construction. Due to lack of space, many details are omitted from this extended abstract; we refer to the full paper for further details [14].

2. MODEL AND PROBLEMS

Computational Model. We follow the CONGEST model as described by [23]. The distributed system is represented by a simple, connected weighted graph $G = (V, E, W)$, where V is the set of nodes, E is the set of edges, and $W : E \to \mathbb{N}$ is the edge weight function. As a convention, we use n to denote the number of nodes. We assume that all edge weights are bounded by some polynomial in n, and that each node $v \in V$ has a unique identifier of $\mathcal{O}(\log n)$ bits (we use v to denote both the node and its identifier).

Initially, nodes are aware only of their neighbors; input values (if any) are assumed to be fed by the environment before the first round. Throughout this paper, we assume that node v is given the weight of each edge $\{v, w\} \in E$ as input. Output values, which are computed at the end of the final round, are placed in special output-registers. In each round, each edge can carry a message of B bits for some given parameter B of the model; we assume that $B \in \Theta(\log n)$ throughout this paper.

Graph-Theoretic Concepts. Fix a weighted undirected graph $G = (V, E, W)$. A *path* p connecting $v, w \in V$ is a sequence of nodes $\langle v = v_0, \ldots, v_k = w\rangle$ such that for all $0 \le i < k$, $\{v_i, v_{i+1}\}$ is an edge in G. Let paths(v, w) denote the set of all paths connecting nodes v and w. We use the following unweighted concepts.

- The *hop-length* of a path p, denoted $\ell(p)$, is the number of edges in it.
- A path p_0 between v and w is a *shortest unweighted path* if its hop-length $\ell(p_0)$ is minimum among all $p \in \mathrm{paths}(v, w)$.
- The *hop distance* $\mathrm{hd} : V \times V \to \mathbb{N}_0$ is defined as the hop-length of a shortest unweighted path, $\mathrm{hd}(v, w) \stackrel{\text{def}}{=} \min\{\ell(p) \mid p \in \mathrm{paths}(v, w)\}$.
- The *hop-diameter* of G is $D \stackrel{\text{def}}{=} \max_{v,w \in V}\{\mathrm{hd}(v, w)\}$.

We use the following weighted concepts.

- The *weight* of a path p, denoted $W(p)$, is its total edge weight, i.e., $W(p) \stackrel{\text{def}}{=} \sum_{i=1}^{\ell(p)} W(v_{i-1}, v_i)$.
- A path p_0 between v and u is a *shortest weighted path* if $W(p_0) = \min\{W(p) \mid p \in \mathrm{paths}(v, w)\}$.
- The *weighted distance* $\mathrm{wd} : V \times V \to \mathbb{N}$ is $\mathrm{wd}(v, u) \stackrel{\text{def}}{=} \min\{W(p) \mid p \in \mathrm{paths}(v, u)\}$.
- The *weighted diameter* of G is $\mathrm{WD} \stackrel{\text{def}}{=} \max\{\mathrm{wd}(v, u) \mid v, u \in V\}$.

Finally, we define the notion of the *shortest paths distance.*

- If $p_0 \in \mathrm{paths}(v, w)$ is a shortest weighted path and $\ell(p_0) = \min\{\ell(p) \mid W(p) = \mathrm{wd}(v, w)\}$, then p_0 is a *min-hop shortest path*. The *shortest path distance* of v and w in this case is $h_{v,w} \stackrel{\text{def}}{=} \ell(p_0)$.
- $\mathrm{SPD} \stackrel{\text{def}}{=} \max\{h_{v,w} \mid v, w \in V\}$ is the *shortest path diameter* of G.

Routing. In the *routing table construction* problem (abbreviated RTC), the output at each node v consists of (i) a unique *label* $\lambda(v)$ and (ii) a function "next_v," that takes a destination label λ and produces a neighbor of v, such that given the label $\lambda(w)$ of any node w, and starting from any node, following the "next" pointers leads to w. Formally, the requirement is as follows. Given a start node v and a destination label $\lambda(w)$, let $v_0 = v$ and define $v_{i+1} = \mathrm{next}_{v_i}(\lambda(w))$ for $i \ge 0$. Then $v_i = w$ for some i.

The performance of a solution is measured by its *stretch.* A route has stretch $\rho \ge 1$ if its total weight is at most ρ times the weighted distance between its endpoints, and a solution to RTC has stretch ρ if all its induced routes have stretch at most ρ.

Distance Approximation. The *distance approximation* problem is closely related to the routing problem. Again, each node v outputs a label $\lambda(v)$, but now, v needs to construct a function $\text{dist}_v : \lambda(V) \to \mathbb{R}^+$ (the table) such that for all $w \in V$ it holds that $\text{dist}_v(\lambda(w)) \geq \text{wd}(v,w)$. The stretch between v and w is $\text{dist}_v(\lambda(w))/\text{wd}(v,w)$, and the solution has stretch $\rho \geq 1$ if $\max_{v,w\in V}\{\text{dist}_v(\lambda(w))/\text{wd}(v,w)\} = \rho$.

Partial Distance Estimation. The basic problem we attack in this paper is partial distance estimation, which generalizes the source detection problem. Let us start by defining the simpler variant.

Given a set of nodes $S \subseteq V$ and a parameter $h \in \mathbb{N}$, $L_v^{(h)}$ denotes the list obtained by ordering $\{(\text{wd}(v,w),w) \mid w \in S \wedge h_{v,w} \leq h\}$ lexicographically in ascending order. Formally, we say that $(\text{wd}(v,w),w) < (\text{wd}(v,u),u)$ if either $\text{wd}(v,w) < \text{wd}(v,u)$ or $(\text{wd}(v,w){=}\text{wd}(v,u) \wedge w{<}u)$.

Definition 2.1 ((S,h,σ)-detection). *The input consists of a set of* sources $S \subseteq V$ *and parameters* $h,\sigma \in \mathbb{N}$. *Each node is assumed to know h, σ, and whether it is in S or not. The goal is to compute at each node $v \in V$ the list L_v of the top σ entries in $L_v^{(h)}$, or the complete $L_v^{(h)}$ if $|L_v^{(h)}| \leq \sigma$.*

Relaxing this by allowing approximation to within $(1{+}\varepsilon)$, we arrive at the following definition.

Definition 2.2 (Partial Distance Estimation). *Given $S \subseteq V$, $h,\sigma \in \mathbb{N}$, and $\varepsilon > 0$, $(1+\varepsilon)$-approximate (S,h,σ)-estimation is defined as follows. Determine a* distance function $\text{wd}' : V \times S \to \mathbb{N} \cup \{\infty\}$ *satisfying*

- $\forall v \in V, s \in S : \text{wd}'(v,s) \geq \text{wd}(v,s)$ *and*
- *if* $h_{v,s} \leq h$, *then* $\text{wd}'(v,s) \leq (1+\varepsilon)\,\text{wd}(v,s)$.

For each $v \in V$, sort the set $\{(\text{wd}'(v,s),s) \mid s \in S\}$ in ascending lexicographical order. The output L_v at each node v are the (at most) top σ elements with $\text{wd}'(v,s) < \infty$.

Note that setting $\varepsilon = 0$ and choosing wd' as h-hop distances results in an exact weighted version of the source detection problem. Specializing further to unweighted graphs, h-hop distances just become hop distances to nodes within h hops.

General Concepts. We extensively use "soft" asymptotic notation that ignores polylogarithmic factors. Formally, we say that $g(n) \in \tilde{\mathcal{O}}(f(n))$ if and only if there exists a constant $c \in \mathbb{R}_0^+$ such that $f(n) \leq g(n)\log^c n$ for all but finitely many values of $n \in \mathbb{N}$. We define $\tilde{o}(\cdot)$, $\tilde{\Omega}(\cdot)$ and $\tilde{\Theta}(\cdot)$ similarly.

When we say that a certain event occurs "with high probability" (abbreviated "w.h.p."), we mean that the probability of the event not occurring can be set to be less than $1/n^c$ for any desired constant c. Using the union bound, this definition implies that any polynomial number of events that occur w.h.p. also jointly occur w.h.p. We make frequent use of this fact throughout the paper.

3. FROM WEIGHTED TO UNWEIGHTED

Fix $0 < \varepsilon \in \mathcal{O}(1)$. Following Nanongkai [21] and others [5, 13, 17, 26], we reduce PDE to $\mathcal{O}(\log_{1+\varepsilon}\text{WD})$ instances of the unweighted problem as follows. Let $i_{\max} = \lceil \log_{1+\varepsilon} w_{\max}\rceil$, where $w_{\max}$ is the largest edge weight in G. Note that by assumption that edge weights are polynomial in n, $i_{\max} \in \mathcal{O}(\varepsilon^{-1}\log n)$. Clearly $i_{\max}$ can be determined in $\mathcal{O}(D)$ rounds.

For $i \in \{0,\ldots,i_{\max}\}$, let $b(i) = (1+\varepsilon)^i$, and define $W_i : E \to b(i)\cdot\mathbb{N}$ by $W_i(e) \overset{\text{def}}{=} b(i)\lceil W(e)/b(i)\rceil$, i.e., by rounding up edge weights to integer multiples of $(1+\varepsilon)^i$. Denote by wd_i the resulting distance function, i.e., the distance function of the graph (V,E,W_i). Clearly $\text{wd}_i(v,w) \geq \text{wd}(v,w)$ for any $v,w \in V$. Regarding an upper bound, we have the following property.

Lemma 3.1 (adapted from [21]). *For all $v,w \in V$ let* $i_{v,w} \overset{\text{def}}{=} \max\left\{0, \left\lfloor \log_{1+\varepsilon}\left(\varepsilon\frac{\text{wd}(v,w)}{h_{v,w}}\right)\right\rfloor\right\}$. *Then*

$$\text{wd}_{i_{v,w}}(v,w) < (1+\varepsilon)\,\text{wd}(v,w) \in \mathcal{O}\left(\varepsilon^{-1}b(i_{v,w})h_{v,w}\right).$$

Proof. If $i_{v,w} = 0$, then $b_0 = 1$, $\text{wd}_0 = \text{wd}$ and the claim is clear. Assume now that $i_{v,w} > 0$. By definition of $i_{v,w}$, $\varepsilon\frac{\text{wd}(v,w)}{(1+\varepsilon)h_{v,w}} < b_{i_{vw}} \leq \frac{\varepsilon\,\text{wd}(v,w)}{h_{v,w}}$ and hence

$$\text{wd}_{i_{v,w}}(v,w) < \text{wd}(v,w) + b(i_{v,w})h_{v,w} \leq (1+\varepsilon)\,\text{wd}(v,w).$$

To see the second bound, note that by definition of $i_{v,w}$ and $b(i_{v,w})$, $\text{wd}(v,w) \leq \varepsilon^{-1}(1+\varepsilon)b(i_{v,w})h_{v,w}$. Due to the previous inequality and the constraint that $\varepsilon \in \mathcal{O}(1)$, the claim follows. □

Next, let G_i be the *unweighted* graph obtained by replacing each edge e in (V,E,W_i) by a path of $W_i(e)/b(i)$ unweighted edges. Let $\text{hd}_i(v,w)$ denote the distance (minimal number of hops) between v and w in G_i. The previous lemma implies that in $G_{i_{v,w}}$, the resulting hop distance between v and w is not too large.

Corollary 3.2. $\forall v,w \in V$, $\text{hd}_{i_{v,w}}(v,w) \in \mathcal{O}(h_{v,w}/\varepsilon)$.

Therefore, an efficient algorithm for unweighted source detection can be used to solve partial distance estimation at the cost of a small increase in running time.

Theorem 3.3. *Given a deterministic algorithm $\mathcal{A}$ for unweighted (S,h,σ)-detection that runs in $R(h,\sigma)$ rounds, $(1{+}\varepsilon)$-approximate (S,h,σ)-estimation can be solved within $\mathcal{O}(\log_{1+\varepsilon} n \cdot R(h',\sigma) + D)$ rounds, for some $h' \in \mathcal{O}(h/\varepsilon)$.*

Proof Sketch. Consider the following algorithm for PDE.

1. Let h' be an upper bound on $\text{hd}_{i_{v,s}}(v,s)$ for all $v \in V$ and $s \in S$ with $h_{v,s} \leq h$. By Corollary 3.2, $h' \in \mathcal{O}(h/\varepsilon)$.
2. For all $i \in \{0,\ldots,i_{\max}\}$, solve (S,h',σ)-detection on G_i by $\mathcal{A}$. Communication over an edge e in G simulates communication over a path in G_i by introducing a delay of $\text{wd}_i(e)$ steps. Denote by $L_{v,i}$ the computed list.
3. For $s \in S$, define

$$\tilde{\text{wd}}(v,s) \overset{\text{def}}{=} \inf\{\text{hd}_i(v,s)b(i) \mid (\text{hd}_i(v,s),s) \in L_{v,i}\}.$$

Each node v outputs the list L_v consisting of the (up to) first σ elements of the set $\{(\tilde{\text{wd}}(v,s),s) \mid \tilde{\text{wd}}(v,s) < \infty\}$, with respect to ascending lexicographical order. This concludes the description of the algorithm.

Clearly, the resulting running time is as stated. The approximation guarantee follows from Lemma 3.1. □

Applying Theorem 3.3 with the source detection algorithm from [16], we obtain the following.

Corollary 3.4. *For $0 < \varepsilon \in \mathcal{O}(1)$, $(1+\varepsilon)$-approximate (S,h,σ)-estimation can be solved in $\mathcal{O}((h+\sigma)\varepsilon^{-2}\log n + D)$ rounds. Tables of size $\mathcal{O}(\sigma\log n)$ for routing with stretch $1+\varepsilon$ from each $v \in V$ to the (up to) σ detected nodes can be constructed in the same time. Moreover, nodes only broadcast (i.e., send the same message to all neighbors), and each node broadcasts in at most $\mathcal{O}(\sigma^2\varepsilon^{-1}\log n)$ rounds.*

4. APPLICATIONS

We now apply Corollary 3.4 to a few distributed tasks. We improve on (i) the best known results for the running time required to compute small-stretch routes with and without node relabeling, (ii) the stretch we can achieve within a given running time bound, (iii) routing table size, and (iv) the time required for Steiner forest construction.

4.1 Almost Exact APSP With and Without Node Relabeling

First we state our results for distributed computation of all-pairs $(1+\varepsilon)$-approximate shortest paths. The result follows simply by applying Corollary 3.4 with all nodes as sources and $h = \sigma = n$. As $h_{v,w} < n$ for all $v, w \in V$, $\mathrm{wd}'(v,w) \leq (1+\varepsilon)\,\mathrm{wd}(v,w) < \infty$ (cf. Definition 2.2). The returned lists thus contain entries for all $n = \sigma$ nodes.

THEOREM 4.1. *$(1+\varepsilon)$-approximate APSP can be solved deterministically in $\mathcal{O}(\varepsilon^{-2} n \log n)$ rounds.*

We note that Theorem 4.1 improves on the best known result for computing approximate shortest paths in the CONGEST model [21] in two ways: first, it is deterministic, and second, the running time is reduced by a logarithmic factor.

When computing routing tables, node relabeling is usually allowed. In the remainder of this subsection we use Corollary 3.4 to improve upon the best known previous result to compute routing tables when node relabeling is allowed [22]. Specifically, we prove the following result.

THEOREM 4.2. *For any $k \in \mathbb{N}$, routing table construction with stretch $6k - 1 + o(1)$ and labels of size $\mathcal{O}(\log n)$ can be solved in $\tilde{\mathcal{O}}(n^{1/2+1/(4k)} + D)$ rounds.*

The idea is to modify the algorithm of [22]. In [22], for any given integer $0 < k \leq \log n$, the algorithm computes (w.h.p.) in $\tilde{\mathcal{O}}(n^{1/2\cdot(1+1/k)} + D)$ rounds node labels of size $\mathcal{O}(\log n \log k)$ and routes with stretch $\mathcal{O}(k \log k)$. We reduce both the stretch and node label size by a $\log k$ factor without changing the running time. We start with a brief review of the algorithm from [22].

1: Skeleton. Sample nodes independently with probability $\tilde{\Theta}(1/\sqrt{n})$, forming the *skeleton set* S.

2: Skeleton Spanner. Construct and make known to all nodes an α-spanner of the *skeleton graph* (S, E_S, W_S). Here, $\{s,t\} \in E_S$ if $\mathrm{hd}(s,t) \leq h$ for a certain $h \in \tilde{\Theta}(\sqrt{n})$, and $W_S(\{s,t\})$ is the minimum weight of an s-t path of at most h hops. It is shown that w.h.p., distances in the skeleton graph are identical to distances in the original graph.

3: Short Range. For each $v \in V$, let s_v be the skeleton node closest to v. For each node v, compute distance and routing tables with stretch β to all nodes $w \in V$ with $(\mathrm{wd}(v,w), w) \leq (\mathrm{wd}(v,s_v), s_v)$ and from s_v to v (we use the tree routing scheme of [28]).

4: Long Range. If $(\mathrm{wd}(v,w), w) > (\mathrm{wd}(v,s_v), s_v)$, then the v-w route is obtained by concatenating the short-range route from v to s_v, the route from s_v to s_w in the skeleton spanner (whose edges represent paths of the same weight in G), and the short-range route from s_w to w.

The induced routes have stretch $\mathcal{O}(\alpha\beta)$. The same holds for distance estimation.

To facilitate routing, the label of each node v contains the following components: for the long range, the identity of the closest skeleton node s_v, its distance $\mathrm{wd}(v,s_v)$, and v's tree routing label for the tree rooted at s_v;[4] and, of course, whatever is needed for the short-range scheme.

Spanner construction can be employed as black box, giving stretch $\alpha \in \Theta(k)$ within $\tilde{\mathcal{O}}(n^{1/2+1/k} + D)$ time. Also, it is known how to construct labels for tree routing of size $(1+o(1))\log n$ in time $\tilde{\mathcal{O}}(h)$ in trees of depth h [27, 28].

We follow the general structure of [22] by implementing the short range part so that $\beta \in \mathcal{O}(1)$ and the shortest-paths trees are not too deep. To this end, we apply Corollary 3.4 with $h = \sigma \in \tilde{\Theta}(\sqrt{n})$ and source set V. Note that the error due to approximation is not limited to inaccurate distance estimations: we may also consider nodes to fall under the long-range scheme that should be treated by the short-range scheme and vice versa. However, we can bound the effect of such errors on the approximation ratio as follows.

LEMMA 4.3. *Sample each node into S with independent probability p and solve $(1+\varepsilon)$-approximate (V,h,σ)-estimation with $\min\{h,\sigma\} \geq c\log n/p$, where c is a sufficiently large constant. Then w.h.p., the following holds for all $v, w \in V$, where $s'_v = \operatorname{argmin}\{(\mathrm{wd}'(v,s), s) \mid s \in S\}$.*

(1) $(\mathrm{wd}'(v,w), w) \leq (\mathrm{wd}'(v,s'_v), s'_v)$
$\Rightarrow [\mathrm{wd}'(v,w) \leq (1+\varepsilon)\,\mathrm{wd}(v,w)] \wedge [(\mathrm{wd}'(v,w), w) \in L_v]$

(2) $(\mathrm{wd}(v,w), w) \leq (\mathrm{wd}(v,s_v), s_v)$
$\Rightarrow \mathrm{wd}'(v,w) \leq (1+\varepsilon)\,\mathrm{wd}(v,w)$

(3) $(\mathrm{wd}(v,w), w) > (\mathrm{wd}(v,s_v), s_v)$
$\Rightarrow \mathrm{wd}'(v,s_v) \leq (1+\varepsilon)\,\mathrm{wd}(v,w)$

(4) $(\mathrm{wd}'(v,w), w) > (\mathrm{wd}'(v,s'_v), s'_v)$
$\Rightarrow \mathrm{wd}'(v,s'_v) \leq (1+\varepsilon)\,\mathrm{wd}(v,w)$

PROOF. Fix $v \in V$ and order $\{(\mathrm{wd}'(v,w), w) \mid w \in V\}$ in ascending lexicographic order. Suppose $s'_v \in S$ is the ith element of the resulting list. Then, since s'_v minimizes $(\mathrm{wd}'(v,s), s)$ among nodes $s \in S$,

$$\Pr[i \geq \min\{h,\sigma\}] \leq (1-p)^{\min\{h,\sigma\}} \in e^{-\Theta(c\log n)} = n^{-\Theta(c)}.$$

When c is a sufficiently large constant, this implies that $i < h$ w.h.p., and thus $h_{v,w} < i < \min\{h,\sigma\}$ for all w with $(\mathrm{wd}'(v,w), w) \leq (\mathrm{wd}'(v,s'_v), s'_v)$. By the properties of (V,h,σ)-estimation, it follows that, w.h.p., $\mathrm{wd}'(v,w) \leq (1+\varepsilon)\,\mathrm{wd}(v,w)$ and $(\mathrm{wd}'(v,w), w) \in L_v$ for all such w.

To show (2), we perform the same calculation for the list $\{(\mathrm{wd}(v,w), w) \mid w \in V\}$; the element from S minimizing $(\mathrm{wd}(v,s), s)$ is s_v. For (3), we apply the (2) to s_v, deducing that w.h.p.,

$$\mathrm{wd}'(v,s_v) \leq (1+\varepsilon)\,\mathrm{wd}(v,s_v) \leq (1+\varepsilon)\,\mathrm{wd}(v,w)$$

For (4), note that if $\mathrm{wd}'(v,w) \leq (1+\varepsilon)\,\mathrm{wd}(v,w)$ then

$$\mathrm{wd}'(v,s'_v) \leq \mathrm{wd}'(v,w) \leq (1+\varepsilon)\,\mathrm{wd}(v,w)\ .$$

Otherwise, (2) shows that $\mathrm{wd}(v,w) \geq \mathrm{wd}(v,s_v)$ w.h.p., implying that

$$\begin{aligned}\mathrm{wd}'(v,s'_v) \leq \mathrm{wd}'(v,s_v) &\leq (1+\varepsilon)\,\mathrm{wd}(v,s_v)\\ &\leq (1+\varepsilon)\,\mathrm{wd}(v,w).\end{aligned}$$ □

We use s'_v where s_v was used in the original scheme. By Lemma 4.3 and Corollary 3.4, this achieves $\beta \in 1 + o(1)$ stretch within the desired time bound for $p \approx 1/\sqrt{n}$. However, since possibly $s'_v \neq s_v$, we must show that the resulting approximation ratio is still $\mathcal{O}(\alpha)$; another problem is that the $|S|$ trees induced by the *approximately* shortest paths

[4]We ignore the low-probability event that $S = \emptyset$.

from each v to s'_v might overlap. The following two lemmas address these issues, as well as the depth of the trees.

LEMMA 4.4. *Sample each node into S with independent probability p and solve $(1+\varepsilon)$-approximate (S,h,σ)-estimation with $h = c\log n/p$, where c is a sufficiently large constant. Denote by wd'_S the associated distance function, and by wd' and L_v the distance function and output of $v \in V$, respectively, of a solution to $(1+\varepsilon)$-approximate (V,h,h)-estimation. If for $v,w \in V$ it holds that $(\mathrm{wd}'(v,w),w) \notin L_v$, then w.h.p. there exist $s_0,\dots,s_{j_0} = s'_w \in S$ such that*

- *$\mathrm{wd}'(w,s'_w) \in (2+\mathcal{O}(\varepsilon))\,\mathrm{wd}_S(v,w)$, and*
- *$\mathrm{wd}'_S(v,s_0)+\sum_{j=1}^{j_0}\mathrm{wd}'_S(s_{j-1},s_j) \in (3+\mathcal{O}(\varepsilon))\,\mathrm{wd}(v,w)$.*

PROOF. By (1) and (4) of Lemma 4.3, $(\mathrm{wd}'(v,w),w) \notin L_v$ implies that $\mathrm{wd}'(v,s'_v) \le (1+\varepsilon)\,\mathrm{wd}(v,w)$ w.h.p. Hence,

$$\mathrm{wd}(v,s_v) \le \mathrm{wd}(v,s'_v) \le \mathrm{wd}'(v,s'_v) \le (1+\varepsilon)\,\mathrm{wd}(v,w)\ .$$

By the triangle inequality, it follows that w.h.p.,

$$\begin{aligned}\mathrm{wd}(w,s_w) \le \mathrm{wd}(w,s_v) &\le \mathrm{wd}(v,w)+\mathrm{wd}(v,s_v)\\ &\le (2+\varepsilon)\,\mathrm{wd}(v,w)\end{aligned}$$

Applying (2) of Lemma 4.3 to w and s_w, we obtain

$$\begin{aligned}\mathrm{wd}(w,s'_w) \le \mathrm{wd}'(w,s'_w) \le \mathrm{wd}'(w,s_w) &\le (1+\varepsilon)\,\mathrm{wd}(w,s_w)\\ &\le 2(1+\varepsilon)^2\,\mathrm{wd}(v,w)\,,\end{aligned}$$

and, from (1) of Lemma 4.3

$$\mathrm{wd}'(w,s'_w) \le (1+\varepsilon)\,\mathrm{wd}(w,s'_w) \le 2(1+\varepsilon)^3\,\mathrm{wd}(v,w)\ ,$$

and the first part of the lemma follows (recall that $\varepsilon \in \mathcal{O}(1)$). Moreover, we have that

$$\mathrm{wd}(v,s'_w) \le \mathrm{wd}(v,w)+\mathrm{wd}(w,s'_w) \le 3(1+\varepsilon)^2\,\mathrm{wd}(v,w)\ .$$

Consider a shortest path from v to s'_w, and denote the sampled nodes that are encountered when traversing it from v to s'_w by $s_0,\dots,s_{j_0} \in S$; in particular, $s_{j_0} = s'_w$. By the same calculation as for Lemma 4.3, w.h.p. any two consecutive sampled nodes are no more than h hops apart. As the path is a shortest path from v to s'_w, the subpaths from s_{j-1} to s_j, $j \in \{1,\dots,j_0\}$, and from v to s_0 are also shortest paths. Therefore, $h_{v,s_0} \le h$ and, for each j, $h_{s_{j-1},s_j} \le h$. We conclude that

$$\begin{aligned}&\mathrm{wd}'_S(v,s_0)+\sum_{j=1}^{j_0}\mathrm{wd}'_S(s_{j-1},s_j)\\ &\le (1+\varepsilon)\left(\mathrm{wd}(v,s_0)+\sum_{j=1}^{j_0}\mathrm{wd}(s_{j-1},s_j)\right)\\ &= (1+\varepsilon)\,\mathrm{wd}(v,s'_v)\ \le\ 3(1+\varepsilon)^3\,\mathrm{wd}(v,w)\ ,\end{aligned}$$

and the second part of the lemma follows. □

LEMMA 4.5. *Sample each node into S with independent probability p and solve $(1+\varepsilon)$-approximate (V,h,σ)-estimation with $h = c\log n/p$, where c is a sufficiently large constant. For $s \in S$, denote by T_s the tree induced by the routing paths from v to s for all $v \in V$ with $s'_v = s$. The depth of T_s is bounded by $\mathcal{O}(h\log n/\varepsilon^2)$, and each node participates in at most $\mathcal{O}(\log n/\varepsilon)$ different trees.*

PROOF. Recall that routing from v to s'_v is based on the routing tables $L_{v,i}$ determined by the unweighted source detection instances on G_i, $i \in \{0,\dots,i_{\max}\}$. The induced shortest-paths trees in G_i have depth at most $h' \in \mathcal{O}(h/\varepsilon)$, and they cannot overlap. By construction, the respective paths in G cannot have more hops. However, it is possible that when routing from v to s'_v, some node on the way knows of a shorter path to s'_v due to a source detection instance on G_j, $j \neq i$, and therefore "switches" to the shortest-path tree in G_j. Because $\mathrm{wd}_j(v,w) \ge \mathrm{wd}_i(v,w)$ for all $v,w \in V$ and $j \ge i$, we may however w.l.o.g. assume that the index i such that routing decisions are made according to $L_{v,i}$ is decreasing on each routing path from some node v to s'_v. Thus, the total hop count of the path is bounded by $\mathcal{O}(i_{\max}h') \subseteq \mathcal{O}(h\log n/\varepsilon^2)$. Consequently, the depth of each T_s is bounded by this value.

Concerning the number of trees, observe that if some node v decides that the next routing hop to s'_v is its neighbor u, it does so because s'_v minimizes the hop distance from v to s'_v in G_i, according to its list $L_{v,i}$. As there are $i_{\max}+1 \in \mathcal{O}(\log n/\varepsilon)$ different lists $L_{v,i}$, this is also a bound on the number of different trees v may participate in. □

We can now prove Theorem 4.2.

PROOF OF THEOREM 4.2. Construct S by sampling nodes independently with probability $p := n^{-1/2-1/(4k)}$. W.h.p., $|S| \in \Theta(n^{1/2-1/(4k)})$. Using Corollary 3.4, we solve $(1+\varepsilon)$-approximate (V,h,σ)-estimation with $h = \sigma = c\log n/p$, for $c \in \mathcal{O}(1)$ sufficiently large, and, say, $\varepsilon = 1/\log n$. This takes $\tilde{\mathcal{O}}(1/p) = \tilde{\mathcal{O}}(n^{-1/2-1/(4k)})$ rounds and enables each node $v \in V$ to route to all nodes $w \in V$ with $(\mathrm{wd}'(v,w),w) \in L_v$ along a path of weight at most $\mathrm{wd}'(v,w)$. By Lemma 4.3, this enables each $v,w \in V$ with $(\mathrm{wd}'(v,w),w) \le (\mathrm{wd}'(v,s'_v),s'_v)$ to determine that this condition is satisfied and route from v to w with stretch $(1+\varepsilon)$.

In case that $(\mathrm{wd}'(v,w),w) \notin L_v$, we invoke Corollary 3.4 once more. This time we solve $(1+\varepsilon)$-approximate $(S,h,|S|)$-detection. W.h.p., $\tilde{\mathcal{O}}(n^{-1/2-1/(4k)})$ rounds suffice. Let wd'_S denote the corresponding distance function. Lemma 4.4 shows that there are $s_0,\dots,s_{j_0} = s'_w \in S$ so that $\mathrm{wd}'(s'_w,w) \in (2+\mathcal{O}(\varepsilon))\,\mathrm{wd}(v,w)$ and $\mathrm{wd}'_S(v,s_0)+\sum_{j=1}^{j_0}\mathrm{wd}'_S(s_{j-1},s_j) \in (3+\mathcal{O}(\varepsilon))\,\mathrm{wd}(v,w)$. If we can route from v to s'_w incurring an additional stretch factor of $2k-1$ and from s'_w to w over a path of weight $\mathrm{wd}'(s'_w,w)$, the total stretch will be

$$(2+\mathcal{O}(\varepsilon))+(2k-1)(3+\mathcal{O}(\varepsilon)) \in 6k-1+\mathcal{O}(\varepsilon) \subset 6k-1+o(1),$$

i.e., the routing scheme satisfies the claimed stretch bound.

Concerning routing from s'_w to w, we employ the algorithm from [28] that terminates in $\tilde{\mathcal{O}}(h)$ rounds in trees of depth h. By Lemma 4.5, this can be done in $\tilde{\mathcal{O}}(h) = \tilde{\mathcal{O}}(n^{-1/2-1/(4k)})$ rounds: since each node is a member in $\mathcal{O}(\log n)$ trees, by time-multiplexing we can simulate a round for all trees in $\mathcal{O}(\log n)$ rounds. We add the computed $(1+o(1))\log n$-bit label to the label of w, inducing an s'_w-w route of weight at most $\mathrm{wd}'(w,s'_w)$.

To route from v to s'_w, consider the graph on node set S with edge set $\{\{s,t\} \mid \mathrm{wd}'_S(s,t) < \infty\}$, where the edge weights are given by wd'_S. For this graph, each node $s \in S$ knows its incident edges and their weights. Using the simulation of the Baswana-Sen algorithm [3] given in [22], we can construct and make known to all nodes a $2k-1$ spanner[5] of this graph in $\tilde{\mathcal{O}}\left(|S|^{1+1/k}+D\right) \subset \tilde{\mathcal{O}}\left(n^{1/2+1/(4k)}+D\right)$

[5] I.e., a subgraph in which distances increase by at most a factor $2k-1$.

rounds. Using this knowledge, the fact that v is aware of $\mathrm{wd}'_S(v, s_0)$, and the routing tables from the second application of Corollary 3.4, w.h.p. we can route with the desired stretch from v to s'_w based on the identifier of s'_w, which we add to the label of v. This completes the proof of the stretch bound. Checking the individual bounds we picked up along the way, we see that the label size is $\mathcal{O}(\log n)$ and the running time is $\tilde{\mathcal{O}}(n^{1/2+1/(4k)} + D)$ w.h.p. $\square$

4.2 Compact Routing on Graphs of Small Diameter

We now show how to reduce routing tables size when computing routing tables distributedly. The idea in the algorithm is to construct an (approximate) Thorup-Zwick routing hierarchy [28]. Our approach is efficient if D is small.

Using exact distances, the construction would look as follows. Let $K_0 \stackrel{\text{def}}{=} \{0, \dots, k-1\}$.

1. For each node $v \in V$, choose its *level* independently by a geometric distribution, i.e., the probability to have level at least $l \in K_0$ is $p_l = n^{-l/k}$. Denote the set of nodes of level at least l by S_l; trivially $S_0 = V$.

2. For each node v and level $l \in K_0 \setminus \{0\}$, determine the node $s_l(v) \in S_l$ closest to v and the set $S_{l-1}(v) \subseteq S_{l-1}$ of nodes closer to v than $s_l(v)$ (ties broken by node identifiers); for convenience, let $s_0(v) \stackrel{\text{def}}{=} v$ and $S_{k-1}(v) \stackrel{\text{def}}{=} S_{k-1}$.

3. Determine tables and labels for routing and distance approximation (i) from v to all nodes in $S_l(v)$ for all $l \in K_0$, and (ii) from $s_l(v)$ to v, where $l \in K_0 \setminus \{0\}$. The final label of v is obtained by concatenating its individual labels and the labels for routing from $s_l(v)$, $l \in K_0 \setminus \{0\}$.

In our implementation, we replace exact distances by $(1+\varepsilon)$-approximate distances for sufficiently small ε. Henceforth, we assume that the sets $S'_l(v)$ and nodes $s'_l(v)$ are defined as above, but with respect to wd'_l, the distance function corresponding to the instance of partial distance estimation we solve for level $l \in K_0$. First we bound the effect of the approximate distances on stretch. This is done by a repeated application of the argument of Lemma 4.4.

LEMMA 4.6. *For $l \in K_0 \setminus \{0\}$, denote by wd'_l the distance function corresponding to a $(1+\varepsilon)$-approximate solution to (S_l, h_l, σ_l)-estimation, where $h_l = \sigma_l = c \log n / p_l$ for a sufficiently large constant c. Suppose $v, w \in V$ and $\ell \in K_0 \setminus \{0\}$ is minimal so that $s'_\ell(w) \in S'_\ell(v)$. Then w.h.p.,*

$$\mathrm{wd}(v, s'_\ell(w)) + \mathrm{wd}(s'_\ell(w), w) \leq (1+\varepsilon)^{4\ell}(4\ell+1)\,\mathrm{wd}(v, w).$$

Lemma 4.6 shows that for $\varepsilon \in o(1/k)$, routing from v to w via $s'_\ell(w) \in S'_\ell(v)$ for minimal ℓ achieves stretch $4k-3+o(1)$. It remains to construct the hierarchy efficiently. We start with a general algorithm.

LEMMA 4.7. *For each level $l \in K_0$, we can determine w.h.p. for all nodes v the set $S'_l(v)$ and the respective distance and routing information in $\tilde{\mathcal{O}}(\varepsilon^{-2} n^{(l+1)/k})$ rounds, where tables have $\mathcal{O}(n^{1/k} \log^2 n/\varepsilon)$ bits. Within this time, we can also determine labels of $(1+o(1))\log n$ bits and tables of $\mathcal{O}(\log^2 n/\varepsilon)$ bits at each node for routing from $s'_l(v)$ to v.*

PROOF. For a sufficiently large constant c, we perform $(1+\varepsilon)$-approximate (S_l, h_{l+1}, σ)-estimation with parameters $h_{l+1} = cn^{(l+1)/k} \log n$ and $\sigma = cn^{1/k} \log n$. For $l < k-1$, the probability that $(\mathrm{wd}'(v, s'_{l+1}(v)), s'_{l+1}(v))$ has index $i \geq \sigma$ if we sort $\{(\mathrm{wd}'(v, s), s) \mid s \in S_l\}$ in increasing order is $(1 - p_l/p_{l+1})^\sigma \in n^{-\Omega(c)}$. The probability that $(\mathrm{wd}'(v, s'_{l+1}(v)), s'_{l+1}(v))$ has index $j \geq h_{l+1}$ if we order $\{(\mathrm{wd}'(v, w), w) \mid w \in V\}$ ascendingly is $(1 - 1/p_{l+1})^{h_{l+1}} \in n^{-\Omega(c)}$. By appending a bit to messages indicating whether $s \in S_l$ is also in S_{l+1}, we can thus use Corollary 3.4 to show that, w.h.p., we obtain suitable tables for routing from $v \in V$ to $S_l(v)$ and $s_{l+1}(v)$ within the stated time bound. If $l = k-1$, we have that $h_{l+1} > n$ and $|S_l| = |S_{k-1}| \leq \sigma$ w.h.p.; in this case, Corollary 3.4 shows that the construction can be performed as well.

Regarding the second part of the statement, observe that analogously to Lemma 4.5, the routing trees rooted at each node $s_{l+1} \in S_{l+1}$ have depth $\mathcal{O}(h_{l+1} \log n/\varepsilon^2)$ and each node participates in at most $\mathcal{O}(\log n/\varepsilon)$ of them. Thus, we can apply the construction from [28] to obtain labels (and tables) of size $(1+o(1))\log n$ for tree routing on each of the trees in $\tilde{\mathcal{O}}(h_{l+1}/\varepsilon^2) \subseteq \tilde{\mathcal{O}}(\varepsilon^{-2} n^{(l+1)/k})$ rounds. As each node participates in $\mathcal{O}(\log n/\varepsilon)$ trees, the table size for this routing information is $\mathcal{O}(\log^2 n/\varepsilon)$. $\square$

We can now state a useful result for small SPD.

THEOREM 4.8. *In the CONGEST model, a routing scheme guaranteeing stretch $4k-3+o(1)$ using tables of size $\tilde{\mathcal{O}}(n^{1/k})$ and node labels of size $\tilde{\mathcal{O}}(1)$ can be computed in $\tilde{\mathcal{O}}(SPD + n^{1/k})$ rounds for any $k \geq 1$.*

Unfortunately, the strategy of Theorem 4.8 can be applied only if an upper bound on SPD is known (and the running time depends on that bound), unlike the algorithm of running time $\tilde{\mathcal{O}}(\mathrm{SPD} \cdot n^{1/k})$ from [6].[6] On the other hand, applying Lemma 4.7 to all levels (without modifying h) results in running time $\tilde{\mathcal{O}}(n)$. In the remainder of this subsection, we explain how to improve on Theorem 4.8 by "short-circuiting" the higher levels of the hierarchy. This approach yields better results when the hop diameter is small.

The construction is as follows. Let $l_0 < k-1$ be some level to be determined later. We truncate the hierarchy at level l_0 by constructing a skeleton graph as follows.

DEFINITION 4.9 (l_0 SKELETON). *Let $h_{l_0} \stackrel{\text{def}}{=} cn^{l_0/k} \log n$ for some sufficiently large constant c. The* skeleton graph *on level l_0 is $G(l_0) = (S_{l_0}, E_{l_0}, \mathrm{wd})$, where $\{s, t\} \in E_{l_0}$ if and only if $h_{s,t} \leq h_{l_0}$.*

The l_0 skeleton graph preserves the original skeleton distances, as the following lemma states.

LEMMA 4.10. *For any $\varepsilon > 0$, $h, \sigma \in \mathbb{N}$, and $S \subseteq S_{l_0}$, denote by $\mathrm{wd}_{S_{l_0}}$ the distance function resulting from solving $(1+\varepsilon)$-approximate $(S_{l_0}, h_{l_0}, |S_{l_0}|)$-estimation and by wd_S the distance function resulting from solving $(1+\varepsilon)$-approximate $(S, ch\log n, \sigma)$-estimation on $G(l_0)$, where c is a sufficiently large constant. Then w.h.p.,*

$$\mathrm{wd}'(v, s) \stackrel{\text{def}}{=} \min\{\mathrm{wd}'_{S_{l_0}}(v, t) + \mathrm{wd}'_S(t, s) \mid t \in S_{l_0}\}$$

is a suitable distance function for $(1+\varepsilon)$-approximate $(S, h \cdot h_{l_0}, \sigma)$-estimation on G.

[6] In [6], the algorithm only handles distance queries and assumes that also the table of the destination can be accessed (i.e., the labels are identical to the tables). Both assumptions can be removed to achieve the same properties as our solution within $\tilde{\mathcal{O}}(\mathrm{SPD} \cdot n^{1/k})$ rounds.

PROOF. By the triangle inequality, for any $v \in V$, $t \in S_{l_0}$, and $s \in S$,

$$\mathrm{wd}(v,s) \leq \mathrm{wd}(v,t) + \mathrm{wd}(t,s) \leq \mathrm{wd}'_{S_{l_0}}(v,t) + \mathrm{wd}'_S(t,s).$$

Suppose $h_{v,s} \leq h \cdot h_{l_0}$ for some $v \in V$ and $s \in S$. The expected number of nodes in S_{l_0} on a shortest path from v to s of $h_{v,s}$ hops is $p_{l_0} h_{v,s} \in \mathcal{O}(h \log n)$. By Chernoff's bound, this number is smaller than $ch \log n$ w.h.p., as c is sufficiently large. Another application of Chernoff's bound shows that the maximum hop distance between nodes from S_{l_0} on the path is bounded by h_{l_0} w.h.p.

Denoting by $t_{v,s} \in S_{l_0}$ the first sampled node on the path, the above shows that the following properties hold w.h.p.

- $\mathrm{wd}(v,s) = \mathrm{wd}(v,t_{v,s}) + \mathrm{wd}(t_{v,s},s)$,
- $\mathrm{wd}_{G(l_0)}(t_{v,s},s) = \mathrm{wd}(t_{v,s},s)$, where $\mathrm{wd}_{G(l_0)}$ denotes the weighted distance in $G(l_0)$,
- $\mathrm{wd}'_{S_{l_0}}(v,t_{v,s}) \leq (1+\varepsilon)\,\mathrm{wd}(v,t_{v,s})$, and
- $\mathrm{wd}'_S(t_{v,s},s) \leq (1+\varepsilon)\,\mathrm{wd}_{G(l_0)}(t_{v,s},s)$.

Overall, this yields

$$\begin{aligned}\mathrm{wd}'(v,s) &= \min_{t \in S_{l_0}} \{\mathrm{wd}'_{S_{l_0}}(v,t) + \mathrm{wd}'_S(t,s)\}\\ &\leq \mathrm{wd}'_{S_{l_0}}(v,t_{v,s}) + \mathrm{wd}'_S(t_{v,s},s)\\ &\leq (1+\varepsilon)(\mathrm{wd}(v,t_{v,s}) + \mathrm{wd}_{G(l_0)}(t_{v,s},s))\\ &= (1+\varepsilon)(\mathrm{wd}(v,t_{v,s}) + \mathrm{wd}(t_{v,s},s))\\ &= (1+\varepsilon)\,\mathrm{wd}(v,s).\end{aligned}$$

□

COROLLARY 4.11. *If in the construction of Lemma 4.10 we replace $G(l_0)$ by the graph $\tilde{G}(l_0)$ constructed by solving $(1+\varepsilon)$-approximate $(S_{l_0}, h_{l_0}, |S_{l_0}|)$-estimation and assigning weight $\mathrm{wd}'_{S_{l_0}}(s,t)$ to edge $\{s,t\}$, the resulting function wd' is a suitable distance function for $(1+\varepsilon)^2$-approximate $(S, h \cdot h_{l_0}, \sigma)$-estimation.*

Next, we address the "truncated" levels. The general idea is to simulate the construction on the (approximate) skeleton graph given by Corollary 4.11, where communication is pipelined over a global BFS tree. Since nodes broadcast only $\tilde{\mathcal{O}}(\sigma^2)$ times in a call to our PDE algorithm (by Corollary 3.4), the total amount of communication does not become too large. However, each simulated round of the algorithm may incur an additive delay of $\mathcal{O}(D)$ (the depth of the BFS tree), which is reflected in the running time bound.

LEMMA 4.12. *For any integer $l_0 \geq k/2+1$, we can construct level $l \geq l_0$ of the routing hierarchy in $\tilde{\mathcal{O}}(\varepsilon^{-2}(n^{l_0/k} + n^{(k-l_0)/k}D))$ rounds w.h.p., where the tables and labels are of size $\tilde{\mathcal{O}}(n^{1/k}/\varepsilon)$ and $\tilde{\mathcal{O}}(\varepsilon^{-1})$, respectively.*

PROOF. Recall that $\varepsilon \in \mathcal{O}(1)$. We choose $\varepsilon' \in \Theta(\varepsilon)$ such that $(1+\varepsilon')^2 = (1+\varepsilon)$. We solve $(1+\varepsilon')$-approximate $(S_{l_0}, h_{l_0}, |S_{l_0}|)$-estimation using Corollary 3.4, w.h.p. in time

$$\begin{aligned}\tilde{\mathcal{O}}(\varepsilon^{-2}(h_{l_0} + |S_{l_0}|) + D) &= \tilde{\mathcal{O}}\left(\varepsilon^{-2}\left(n^{l_0/k} + n^{(k-l_0)/k}\right) + D\right)\\ &\subseteq \tilde{\mathcal{O}}\left(\varepsilon^{-2} n^{l_0/k} + D\right).\end{aligned}$$

To apply Corollary 4.11, we simulate, for $h = h_{l+1}/h_{l_0}$ and a sufficiently large constant c, $(1+\varepsilon')$-approximate estimation on $\tilde{G}(l_0)$ with parameters $(S_l, ch\log n, cn^{1/k}\log n)$, in a way such that *all* nodes will learn the output of *all* nodes in S_{l_0}. As in Lemma 4.7, a bit indicating whether a source is in S_{l+1} is added to messages if $l < k-1$.

Before we explain how to do this, let us show how this allows the construction of level l of the routing hierarchy. From the collected information, w.h.p. nodes can locally compute the distance function wd' from Corollary 4.11 for the σ closest nodes in S_l w.r.t. wd' and, as in Lemma 4.7, derive their table for routing from v to S'_l and $s'_l(v)$.

To enable tree routing from $s'_l(v)$ to v, split the tree rooted at $s'_l(v)$ into the unique maximal subtrees rooted at $s \in S_{l_0}$ that contain no internal nodes from S_{l_0} (i.e., all such nodes are either the root or leaves). By Lemma 4.5, these subtrees have depth at most $\tilde{\mathcal{O}}(h_{l_0}/\varepsilon^2)$. We use separate labeling schemes for the (globally known) tree on $\tilde{G}(l_0)$ that describes the connections between nodes in S_{l_0} in the routing tree rooted at $s'_l(v)$ and the subtrees rooted at each $s \in S_{l_0}$. The former can be computed locally. The latter can be labeled in time $\tilde{\mathcal{O}}(\varepsilon^{-3}h_{l_0})$, provided that each node participates in $\tilde{\mathcal{O}}(\varepsilon^{-1})$ different trees only. Analogously to Lemma 4.5, this holds true because each routing decision must correspond to one of the $\mathcal{O}(\log n/\varepsilon)$ top entries of the routing tables (either for routing in G to some node in S_{l_0} or in $\tilde{G}(l_0)$). This approach requires each node in the tree to store two labels of size $(1+o(1))\log n$. Routing can now be executed by determining the next node from S_{l_0} to visit on the path from $s'_l(v)$ to v (if there still is one) and then use the label for the current subtree to find the next routing hop.

It remains to discuss how to solve $(1+\varepsilon')$-approximate $(S_l, h, cn^{1/k}\log n)$-estimation on $\tilde{G}(l_0)$ quickly. Recall that each node in S_{l_0} knows its neighbors and the weights of incident edges from the solution of $(1+\varepsilon')$-approximate $(S_{l_0}, h_{l_0}, |S_{l_0}|)$-estimation computed earlier. We simulate the algorithm given by Corollary 3.4, exploiting the fact that each node broadcasts in only $\tilde{\mathcal{O}}(n^{2/k})$ rounds in total. For each simulated round $i \in \{1,\ldots,h'+\sigma\}$ and all of the $\mathcal{O}(\log n/\varepsilon)$ instances of the unweighted algorithm, we pipeline the communication over a BFS tree, which takes $\mathcal{O}(M_i + D)$ rounds in G, where M_i is the number of messages broadcasted by nodes in $\tilde{G}(l_0)$ in simulated round i; this time bound includes $\mathcal{O}(D)$ rounds for global synchronization of when the next simulated round starts. Therefore, the total number of communication rounds in G is

$$\begin{aligned}\sum_{i=1}^{h'+\sigma} \mathcal{O}(M_i + D) &\subseteq \tilde{\mathcal{O}}(\varepsilon^{-1}(\sigma^2|S_{l_0}| + (h'+\sigma)D))\\ &\subseteq \tilde{\mathcal{O}}(\varepsilon^{-2}(n^{2/k}\cdot n^{(k-l_0)/k} + n^{(l-l_0+1)/k}D))\\ &\subseteq \tilde{\mathcal{O}}(\varepsilon^{-2}(n^{l_0/k} + n^{(k-l_0)/k}D))\end{aligned}$$

w.h.p., as $|S_{l_0}| \in \tilde{\mathcal{O}}(n^{(k-l_0)/k})$ w.h.p. The bounds on table and label size follow from Lemma 4.7 and the above discussion of the tree labeling scheme. □

We can now put all the pieces together to obtain the following result.

THEOREM 4.13. *Suppose we are given $k \in \mathbb{N}$ and some integer $k/2+1 \leq l_0 \leq k$. Then tables of size $\tilde{\mathcal{O}}(n^{1/k})$ and labels of size $\mathcal{O}(k\log n)$ facilitating routing and distance approximation with stretch $4k-3+o(1)$ can be constructed in $\tilde{\mathcal{O}}(n^{l_0/k} + n^{(k-l_0)/k}D)$ rounds w.h.p.*

We can pick an appropriate value for l_0 depending on D. If the running time is worse than about $n^{2/3}$, we handle the higher levels simply by making $\tilde{G}(l_0)$ known to all nodes and solving locally.

COROLLARY 4.14. *In the* CONGEST *model, $\tilde{O}(n^{1/k})$-bit tables and $\tilde{O}(1)$-bit labels for routing with stretch $4k-3+o(1)$ can be computed in $\tilde{O}\left(D+\min\left\{(Dn)^{\frac{1}{2}}n^{\frac{1}{k}}, n^{\frac{2}{3}+\frac{2}{3k}}\right\}\right)$ rounds, for any $k \in \mathbb{N}$.*

4.3 A Faster $(2+\varepsilon)$-approximation of Steiner Forests

The distributed Steiner forest problem (abbreviated SF henceforth) is defined as follows.

DEFINITION 4.15 (DISTRIBUTED STEINER FOREST).
Input: *At each node v, $\lambda(v) \in \Lambda \cup \{\bot\}$, where Λ is the set of* component identifiers *s.t.* $\bot \notin \Lambda$.
Output: *An edge set $F \subseteq E$ such that $\forall u, v \in V$, if $\lambda(u) = \lambda(v) \neq \bot$ then u and v are connected by F.*
Goal: *Minimize $W(F) = \sum_{e \in F} W(e)$.*

The set of nodes v with $\lambda(v) \neq \bot$ is called *terminals* and is denoted by T. As customary, we denote $t \stackrel{\text{def}}{=} |T|$ and $k \stackrel{\text{def}}{=} |\Lambda|$. For $\lambda \in \Lambda$, define *input component* $C_\lambda \subseteq T$ to be the set of all terminals v with $\lambda(v) = \lambda$. The problem specializes to minimum spanning tree (MST) by letting all nodes be terminals in a single input component, and to shortest s-t path by letting s and t be the only terminals, in the same input component. However, general SF is NP-hard [10].

In the CONGEST model, any randomized approximation algorithm for SF requires $\tilde{\Omega}(k + \min\{\sqrt{n}, \text{SPD}\} + D)$ rounds, and it is known how to get a randomized $\mathcal{O}(\log n)$-approximation within that time (up to a polylog n factor) [15]. The best known deterministic algorithm finds a $(2+\varepsilon)$-approximation in $\tilde{O}(\text{SPD}\,k + \sqrt{\min\{\text{SPD}\,t, n\}})$ rounds, for any $\varepsilon \in 1/\operatorname{polylog} n$. Note the large gap between the lower and upper bounds on deterministic construction. In this paper, using our improved PDE result, we reduce this gap as stated in the following theorem.

THEOREM 4.16. *If SPD is known, a $(2+o(1))$-approximate Steiner forest can be deterministically constructed in $\tilde{O}(\sqrt{\min\{D,k\}}(D+k) + SPD + \sqrt{\min\{SPD\,t, n\}})$ rounds.*

While the time bound of the algorithm in [15] may be as high as $\tilde{O}(n^2)$ if both SPD and k are $\tilde{\Theta}(n)$, the time complexity in Theorem 4.16 is never more than $\tilde{O}(n^{3/2})$ (even if we use n as an upper bound on SPD).

The algorithm suggested in Theorem 4.16 builds on the algorithm of [15], which is already quite involved. We only give a very high level overview of the new ideas we use here. More details can be found in the full version of the paper [14].

Approximate Distances. The deterministic algorithm in [15] (which follows the approach of [2]) works in any metric space. In particular, distorting distances in the input graph G by a factor of $1+\varepsilon'$ degrades the approximation ratio by at most a factor of $1+\varepsilon'$. In total, our algorithm computes approximate distances $\mathcal{O}(\log n)$ times, so choosing $\varepsilon' \in 1/\operatorname{polylog} n$ sufficiently small, we can guarantee that the approximation ratio grows only by a multiplicative $1+o(1)$ factor. Note that with this choice of ε', the running time of PDE (cf. Corollary 3.4) is $\tilde{O}(h+\sigma+D)$, and each node broadcasts in no more than $\tilde{O}(\sigma^2)$ rounds of the algorithm.

Fast Deterministic Algorithm. The main idea of the algorithm is to let *moats*, rooted at terminals, grow in uniform speed until they touch each other, at which point they merge. A moat becomes inactive and stops growing when it contains only whole input components, at which point the whole moat is logically contracted into a single node (by assigning zero weight to all its edges). To construct the required forest, the sequence of merges is traced back, and edges along the paths connecting the moat centers are added if they don't close cycles. The problem boils down to determining the order of merges. We do that using a graph defined as follows.

1. For each inactive moat M, identify all its nodes with a single source s_M.
2. Identify each terminal in an active moat with a single source s.
3. Compute for each node $(1+\varepsilon')$-approximate distances wd' to all sources.

There are at most k sources: up to $k-1$ sources for inactive moats and s. Thus, applying Corollary 3.4 with $h = \text{SPD}$ and $\sigma = k$, we can complete this computation in $\tilde{O}(\text{SPD}+k)$ rounds. Using these distances we define a multigraph H_{moat} with nodes $s \cup \{s_M \mid M \text{ is an inactive moat}\}$ and there is an edge $\{s_1, s_2\}$ of weight w if there is a node v associated with s_1 with $\text{wd}'(v, s_2) = w$. An inactive moat M becomes active after time equal to the distance between s and s_M in this graph—provided that no moats become inactive in the meantime. This can be computed at a single node, and the results distributed back, in $\mathcal{O}(Dk)$ time. In fact, we can do better by simulating the PDE algorithm on H_{moat}. The resulting running time depends on $\text{SPD}(H_{\text{moat}})$, and is better than $\mathcal{O}(Dk)$ if $\text{SPD}(H_{\text{moat}}) \ll k$.

COROLLARY 4.17. *For any $0 < \delta \in 1/\operatorname{polylog} n$, we can solve $(1+\delta)$-approximate single-source shortest paths with source s on H within $\tilde{O}(D \cdot SPD(H_{moat}) + k)$ communication rounds of G. This requires knowledge of $SPD(H_{moat})$.*

Using the shortcut technique of [21], $\text{SPD}(H_{\text{moat}})$ can be reduced to at most $k/\sqrt{kD/(D+k)}$ before applying Corollary 4.17, yielding the following result.

COROLLARY 4.18. *For any $0 < \delta \in 1/\operatorname{polylog} n$, we can solve $(1+\delta)$-approximate single-source shortest paths with source s on H in $\tilde{O}(\sqrt{\min\{D,k\}}(D+k))$ communication rounds of G.*

Thus we can reduce the leading term in the complexity of the algorithm from $\text{SPD} \cdot k$ to $\sqrt{\min\{D,k\}}(D+k)$ and arrive at Theorem 4.16.

Leveraging Randomization. Alternatively, we observe that we can "reduce" SPD by sampling nodes with independent probability $1/\sqrt{n}$ and making them into "dummy" terminals, each of them with their unique input component label. We obtain the following result.

COROLLARY 4.19. *A $(2+o(1))$-approximate Steiner forest can be computed in $\tilde{O}(\sqrt{\min\{D,k\}}(D+k) + \sqrt{n})$ rounds w.h.p.*

Acknowledgements. The authors thank Stephan Holzer for providing us with a preprint of [12] and Danupon Nanongkai for useful comments.

5. REFERENCES

[1] I. Abraham, C. Gavoille, D. Malkhi, N. Nisan, and M. Thorup. Compact name-independent routing with minimum stretch. *ACM Trans. Algorithms*, 4(3):37:1–37:12, 2008.

[2] A. Agrawal, P. Klein, and R. Ravi. When trees collide: An approximation algorithm for the generalized Steiner tree problem on networks. *SIAM Journal of Computing*, 24:440–456, 1995.

[3] S. Baswana and S. Sen. A simple and linear time randomized algorithm for computing sparse spanners in weighted graphs. *Random Structures and Algorithms*, 30(4):532–563, 2007.

[4] R. E. Bellman. On a routing problem. *Quart. Appl. Math.*, 16:87–90, 1958.

[5] A. Bernstein. Maintaining shortest paths under deletions in weighted directed graphs: [extended abstract]. In *Symp. Theory of Computing Conference, STOC'13, Palo Alto, CA, USA, June 1-4, 2013*, pages 725–734, 2013.

[6] A. Das Sarma, M. Dinitz, and G. Pandurangan. Efficient computation of distance sketches in distributed networks. In *Proc. 24th ACM Symp. on Parallelism in Algorithms and Architectures*, 2012.

[7] A. Das Sarma, S. Holzer, L. Kor, A. Korman, D. Nanongkai, G. Pandurangan, D. Peleg, and R. Wattenhofer. Distributed Verification and Hardness of Distributed Approximation. *SIAM Journal on Computing*, 41(5):1235–1265, 2012.

[8] L. R. Ford. Network flow theory. Technical Report P-923, The Rand Corp., 1956.

[9] S. Frischknecht, S. Holzer, and R. Wattenhofer. Networks cannot compute their diameter in sublinear time. In *Proc. 23rd ACM-SIAM Symp. on Discrete Algorithms*, pages 1150–1162, 2012.

[10] M. R. Garey and D. S. Johnson. *Computers and Intractability: A Guide to the Theory of NP -Completeness.* W.H. Freeman and Company, San Francisco, 1979.

[11] M. Henzinger, S. Krinninger, and D. Nanongkai. An Almost-Tight Distributed Algorithm for Computing Single-Source Shortest Paths. *CoRR*, abs/1504.07056, 2015.

[12] S. Holzer and N. Pinsker. Approximation of Distances and Shortest Paths in the Broadcast Congest Clique. *CoRR*, abs/1412.3445, 2014.

[13] P. N. Klein and S. Subramanian. A fully dynamic approximation scheme for shortest paths in planar graphs. *Algorithmica*, 22:235–249, 1998.

[14] C. Lenzen and B. Patt-Shamir. Fast Partial Distance Estimation and Applications. *CoRR*, abs/1412.7922, 2014.

[15] C. Lenzen and B. Patt-Shamir. Improved distributed steiner forest construction. In *Proc. 32nd ACM Symp. on Principles of Distributed Computing*, pages 262–271, 2014.

[16] C. Lenzen and D. Peleg. Efficient distributed source detection with limited bandwidth. In *Proc. 32nd ACM Symp. on Principles of Distributed Computing*, 2013.

[17] A. Madry. Faster approximation schemes for fractional multicommodity flow problems via dynamic graph algorithms. In *Proc. 42nd ACM Symp. on Theory of Computing, STOC 2010, Cambridge, Massachusetts, USA, 5-8 June 2010*, pages 121–130, 2010.

[18] J. McQuillan, I. Richer, and E. Rosen. The new routing algorithm for the ARPANET. *IEEE Trans. Communication*, 28(5):711–719, May 1980.

[19] J. M. McQuillan and D. C. Walden. The ARPANET design decisions. *Networks*, 1, 1977.

[20] J. Moy. OSPF ver. 2, April 1998. Internet RFC 2328.

[21] D. Nanongkai. Distributed Approximation Algorithms for Weighted Shortest Paths. In *Proc. 46th Symp. on Theory of Computing (STOC)*, pages 565–573, 2014.

[22] B. Patt-Shamir and C. Lenzen. Fast Routing Table Construction Using Small Messages [Extended Abstract]. In *Proc. 45th Symposium on the Theory of Computing (STOC)*, 2013. Full version at `http://arxiv.org/abs/1210.5774`.

[23] D. Peleg. *Distributed Computing: A Locality-Sensitive Approach.* SIAM, Philadelphia, PA, 2000.

[24] D. Peleg and A. A. Schäffer. Graph spanners. *J. Graph Theory*, 13(1):99–116, 1989.

[25] D. Peleg and E. Upfal. A trade-off between space and efficiency for routing tables. *Journal of the ACM*, 36(3):510–530, 1989.

[26] P. Raghavan and C. D. Thompson. Provably good routing in graphs: Regular arrays. In *Proc. 17th Ann. ACM Symp. on Theory of Computing*, STOC '85, pages 79–87, New York, NY, USA, 1985. ACM.

[27] N. Santoro and R. Khatib. Labelling and Implicit Routing in Networks. *Computer J.*, 28:5–8, 1985.

[28] M. Thorup and U. Zwick. Compact routing schemes. In *Proc. 13th ACM Symp. on Parallel Algorithms and Architectures*, 2001.

[29] U. Zwick. Exact and approximate distances in graphs – a survey. In *Proc. 9th European Symp. on Algorithms*, pages 33–48, 2001.

[30] U. Zwick. All pairs shortest paths using bridging sets and rectangular matrix multiplication. *Journal of the ACM*, 49(3):289–317, 2002.

Brief Announcement: Distributed Single-Source Reachability

Mohsen Ghaffari
MIT
ghaffari@mit.edu

Rajan Udwani
MIT
rudwani@mit.edu

ABSTRACT

In the *directed single-source reachability* problem, input is a directed graph $G = (V, E)$ and a source $s \in V$, and the objective is to identify nodes t for which there is a directed path in G from s to t. Recently Nanongkai [2] presented a distributed algorithm that solves this problem in $\tilde{O}(D + \sqrt{n}D^{1/2})$ rounds, where D and n respectively denote the network diameter and the number of nodes.

This note presents an algorithm that improves the round complexity to $\tilde{O}(D + \sqrt{n}D^{1/4})$, thus getting closer to the $\tilde{\Omega}(D + \sqrt{n})$ lower bound of Das Sarma et al. [1].

Categories and Subject Descriptors

F.2.2 [**Analysis of Algorithms and Problem Complexity**]: Non-numerical Algorithms and Problems—*Computations on Discrete Structures*; G.2.2 [**Discrete Mathematics**]: Graph Theory—*Network Problems*

Keywords

Distributed Algorithm, Reachability, Directed Graphs

1. PROBLEM

Directed graphs typically pose challenges that are fundamentally different than those of undirected graphs. Due to this, for a vast majority of the graph problems, the known distributed algorithms for directed graphs are considerably weaker than their counterparts in undirected graphs. This makes directed graph problems an interesting subarea of distributed graph algorithms which deserves more attention. In this note, we take a look at one of the basic problems of directed graphs, the *single-source reachability problem.*

Given a directed graph $G = (V, E)$ and a source node s, we want a distributed algorithm that identifies nodes t for which there is a directed path from s to t. We use n and D to denote, respectively, the number of nodes and the *undirected* hop-diameter of G.

Permission to make digital or hard copies of part or all of this work for personal or classroom use is granted without fee provided that copies are not made or distributed for profit or commercial advantage and that copies bear this notice and the full citation on the first page. Copyrights for third-party components of this work must be honored. For all other uses, contact the Owner/Author.
Copyright is held by the owner/author(s).
PODC'15, July 21–23, 2015, Donostia-San Sebastián, Spain.
ACM 978-1-4503-3617-8 /15/07
http://dx.doi.org/10.1145/2767386.2767444.

The communication model we use is the standard CONGEST model [3], where communications occur in synchronous rounds and per round, $O(\log n)$ bits can be sent over each edge. Moreover, following Nanongkai [2], we assume that the communication network itself is undirected.

Next, we review Nanongkai's reachability algorithm which has round complexity of $\tilde{O}(D + \min\{n^{2/3}, \sqrt{n}D^{1/2}\})$, and then we explain an algorithm that slightly improves this bound to $\tilde{O}(D + \min\{n^{2/3}, \sqrt{n}D^{1/4}\})$ rounds.

2. NANONGKAI'S REACHABILITY ALGORITHM

Nanongkai [2] gives a distributed algorithm for $1 + o(1)$ approximation of undirected weighted Single-Source Shortest Path (SSSP) problem, in $\tilde{O}(D + \min\{n^{2/3}, \sqrt{n}D^{1/4}\})$ rounds. He then notes that some of the components in his algorithm can be used for the single-source reachability problem, yielding a $\tilde{O}(D + \min\{n^{2/3}, \sqrt{nD}\})$ round algorithm. This reachability algorithm is roughly as follows:

1. **Sampling:** Every node v *samples* itself w.p. α/n where $\alpha = \max\{n^{1/3}, \sqrt{n/D}\}$. Let S be the set of sampled nodes and also add source s to S. We know $|S| = \tilde{O}(\alpha)$, w.h.p.

2. **h-hop Distances and Skeleton:** Every S-node runs an h-hop outgoing BFS, where we have $h = \Theta(\frac{n \log n}{\alpha})$ $= \tilde{\Theta}(\min\{n^{2/3}, \sqrt{nD}\})$. These BFSs are performed all (essentially) in parallel, in $\tilde{O}(h + n/h)$ rounds, using the standard *random delays* technique to control the congestion on edges. Given the range of h, this is equal to $\tilde{O}(h)$ rounds. At the end of the process, every node u knows for each sampled node $v \in S$ whether there is directed path with at most h-hops from v to u or not. Construct a (virtual) *skeleton graph* $G' = (S, E_S)$ where for each two nodes $v, u \in S$, node v puts a directed edge from u to v if there is a directed path with at most h-hops from u to v. Using a similar method but with running the BFSs in the reverse direction, node u will also know if it has a directed path to v with at most h-hops. Thus, each node in S knows its incoming and outgoing G' neighbors.

3. **Total Broadcast, or BFS on Skeleton:** If $\alpha = n^{1/3}$, broadcast all the skeleton edges, in $\tilde{O}(D + \alpha^2)$ rounds. From these, each node t can locally figure out whether it is reachable from s. If $\alpha = \sqrt{n/D}$, simulate α rounds of directed outgoing BFS from s on the skeleton G', in $O(D\alpha)$ rounds. Then broadcast

the names of all sampled nodes reachable from s, in at most $\tilde{O}(D+\alpha)$ rounds.

All in all, the algorithm works in $\tilde{O}(\min\{n^{1/3}+n^{2/3}+D, \sqrt{nD}+D\sqrt{n/\alpha}+D\}) = D+\min\{n^{2/3}, \sqrt{n/D}\}$ rounds. We note that the technique of shortening diameter of the skeleton graph G', which has node set consisting of s,t and all sampled nodes and edges between any two that are within h hop of each other in G, breaks down for the directed case. We use a different procedure which introduces shortcuts dynamically meanwhile building a BFS to reduce the runtime to $\tilde{O}(D+\sqrt{n}D^{1/4})$.

3. THE ALGORITHM

In this section, we explain our algorithm which leads to the following result:

Theorem 3.1. *There is a randomized distributed algorithm that solves the single-source reachability problem in $\tilde{O}(D+\min\{n^{2/3}, \sqrt{n}D^{1/4},\})$ rounds of the* CONGEST *model, with high probability.*

We only describe the algorithm with round complexity $\tilde{O}(D+\sqrt{n}D^{1/4})$. Interleaving it with Nanongkai's $\tilde{O}(D+n^{2/3})$ algorithm, one can easily achieve the best of the two. We do steps 1 and 2 as above with $\alpha=\sqrt{n}/D^{1/4}$. Then, instead of running the full BFS on the skeleton graph G', which takes $O(D\alpha)$ rounds to simulate, we will perform a BFS-like procedure with *active short-cutting*.

In the algorithm, we only talk about the sampled nodes S, and transmissions over the skeleton graph G' will be broadcast to all nodes. We call a node *active* if it knows a path from s to itself, in G'. Initially, only s is active. The algorithm proceeds in *phases* and in each phase, a few more nodes become active. At the end, all S-nodes reachable from source s will be active and their ids will be publicly known. Hence, each node of the graph G can determine if it's reachable from s. The algorithm works as follows:

Reachability Algorithm on G', to be simulated via broadcasts on G:

1. Activate node s.
2. Repeat phases, where in each phase, the following steps occur in sequence:
   (a) *Announcing Newly Activated Nodes:* All nodes activated in the previous phase broadcast their ids. In the first phase, announce the id of s. If no id is announced, terminate.
   (b) *Shortcutting:* Every node with at most $\sqrt{D}$ inactive outgoing neighbors broadcasts the corresponding ($\leq\sqrt{D}$) outgoing edges.
   (c) *New Activations:* Each inactive node u that discovers that it is reachable from s becomes active. This happens if the union of the set of G'-edges broadcasted so far with the incoming edges of u, known to u itself, include a path from an active node to u.

Notice that the length of a phase, and even the length of each of the steps, is not fixed and it depends on the number of messages broadcast in the phase. However, simply by adding a step-start and step-end broadcast from s, which can be done in $O(D)$, we can keep all nodes consistently aware of which step is happening. Furthermore, the only steps that use communication are steps $2(a)$ and $2(b)$. Using standard broadcast routines, each of these steps can be implemented in $O(D+k)$ rounds, where k is the number of messages to be broadcast in that step.

Lemma 3.2. *Once the algorithm terminates, a node is active if and only if it is reachable from s.*

Proof. A node becomes active only if it discovers that there is a path from s to it, or from a node activated in an earlier phase. Hence, activated nodes are reachable from s. On the other hand, so long as there is a node u that is reachable from s but it has not become active, in each phase, at least one more node along the path from s to u becomes active in step $2(c)$. This means that the algorithm will not terminate at least until the node u has been activated as well. That is, all reachable nodes will be activated. □

Lemma 3.3. *The algorithm terminates after at most $\tilde{O}(D+\sqrt{n}D^{1/4})$ rounds.*

Proof. Clearly the ith phase takes $O(D+b_i)$ rounds where b_i is the total number of messages broadcast in steps $2(b)$ and $2(c)$. That is, the number of nodes activated in phase $i-1$ plus the number of edges reported from nodes that have less than $\sqrt{D}$ inactive neighbors. Hence, the summation of the running time of all phases has an $O(D)$ term for each phase, plus each node can contribute at most $\sqrt{D}+1$ to the summation of b_i values over all phases. Thus, the total running time is at most

$$p\cdot O(D)+\tilde{O}(\sqrt{n}/D^{1/4})\cdot(\sqrt{D}+1) = p\cdot O(D)+\tilde{O}(\sqrt{n}D^{1/4}),$$

where p is the total number of phases. Therefore, to complete the proof, it suffices to show that $p=\tilde{O}(\sqrt{n}/D^{3/4})$.

We prove this by roughly speaking showing that in each phase the size of the set of active nodes grows by at least $\sqrt{D}$, amortized. Hence, the total number of phases p is at most $\tilde{O}(\sqrt{n}/D^{1/4})/\sqrt{D}=\tilde{O}(\sqrt{n}/D^{3/4})$.

Consider an outgoing BFS in G' rooted in s and let us call the set of nodes at a given depth i of this BFS—i.e., distance i from s—its ith layer and use L_i to denote this set. Define the first block to be the set of nodes in layers 0 to B_1, where B_1 is the layer number such that $\sum_{i=0}^{B_1}|L_i|\leq\sqrt{D}$ and $\sum_{i=0}^{B_1+1}|L_i|>\sqrt{D}$. Then, notice that in the first phase, all nodes of layers 0 to B_1-1 will announce all their outgoing edges (if $B_1\geq 1$). This is simply because, these nodes cannot have any outgoing edge to layers above B_1. Therefore, at the end of phase one, all nodes of the first block are active, which means that at the end of phase 2, all nodes in blocks 0 to B_1+1 are active. That is, after 2 phases, at least $\sqrt{D}$ nodes became active. We can now repeat a similar argument for the next phases. Particularly, define B_j to be such that $\sum_{i=0}^{B_j}|L_i|\leq j\sqrt{D}$ and $\sum_{i=0}^{B_j+1}|L_i|>j\sqrt{D}$. Now that we know that by the end of phase 2, all nodes in layers 0 to B_1+1 are active, using a similar argument as above, we can conclude that by the end of phase 3, all nodes in layers 0 to B_2 are active, which means at the end of phase 4, all nodes in layers 0 to B_2+1 are active. Repeating this argument, we know all nodes in layers 0 to B_j are active by the end of phase $2j-1$. Since there are only $\tilde{O}(\sqrt{n}/D^{1/4})$ nodes, there are only $\tilde{O}(\sqrt{n}/D^{3/4})$ blocks, which means by the end of phase $\tilde{O}(\sqrt{n}/D^{3/4})$, all reachable nodes are active. □

4. DISCUSSION

A natural generalization of the question studied in this paper is to find shortest paths from a given source s in a *weighted* directed graph G. This directly corresponds to the question of whether the above algorithm can be modified to find the shortest paths from s on a *weighted* directed skeleton graph G' (ideally with similar runtime).

An intermediate step would be to extend the algorithm to find shortest paths on G' when all its edges have the same weight (uniform G'-weights), in which case the problem becomes finding the shortest path in terms of the number of hops. As described above, the algorithm does not necessarily find paths from s with minimum hops. In fact the very process of active shortcutting, which helps cut down the runtime, hampers this by possibly reaching nodes, that are otherwise a few hops away from s, through a longer path which was broadcast/revealed sooner due to shortcutting. We claim without proof that with a minor change, our algorithm can address this G'-uniform case with the same runtime guarantee. The idea is essentially to not activate nodes until we are sure that the shortest path has been found, which would behave like a BFS for the skeleton graph.

We however note that the case of uniform G' weights, on its own, does not give a significant and meaningful end-result in terms of graph G. This is because even a uniformly weighted G might lead to a nonuniform skeleton G'.

The primary obstacle in generalizing the idea further to skeleton graphs G' with non-uniform weights is that our runtime analysis relies on the number of nodes in graph G' and this seems to obstruct us (or at least complicate) using ideas such as the *rounding technique* in [2, Algorithm 3.2], which effectively (and roughly speaking) turn general weighted cases to polylogarithmic iterations of uniform ones.

5. REFERENCES

[1] A. Das Sarma, S. Holzer, L. Kor, A. Korman, D. Nanongkai, G. Pandurangan, D. Peleg, and R. Wattenhofer. Distributed verification and hardness of distributed approximation. In *Proc. of the Symp. on Theory of Comp. (STOC)*, pages 363–372, 2011.

[2] D. Nanongkai. Distributed approximation algorithms for weighted shortest paths. In *Proc. of the Symp. on Theory of Comp. (STOC)*, pages 565–573. ACM, 2014.

[3] D. Peleg. *Distributed Computing: A Locality-sensitive Approach.* Society for Industrial and Applied Mathematics, Philadelphia, PA, USA, 2000.

Brief Announcement: A Hierarchy of Congested Clique Models, from Broadcast to Unicast*

Florent Becker
Université d'Orléans
Orléans, France
florent.becker@univ-orleans.fr

Antonio Fernández Anta
IMDEA Networks Institute
Madrid, Spain
antonio.fernandez@imdea.org

Ivan Rapaport
DIM-CMM (UMI 2807 CNRS)
Universidad de Chile
Santiago, Chile
rapaport@dim.uchile.cl

Eric Rémila
Université de Lyon - GATE
LSE (UMR 5824 - CNRS)
St-Etienne, France
eric.remila@univ-st-etienne.fr

ABSTRACT

The $\mathcal{CONGEST}$ model is a synchronous, message-passing model of distributed computation in which each node can send (possibly different) messages of $\mathcal{O}(\log n)$ bits along each of its incident communication links in each round, where n is the number of computing nodes in the system. In the particular case where the communication network is a complete graph, we have the unicast *congested clique model*. On the other end is the broadcast version of the congested clique model, in which each node can only broadcast a single message over all its links in each round. In this paper we explore the space, in terms of round complexity, that lies between these two congested clique models. Hence, we parametrize the congested clique model with the *range* r, the maximum number of different messages a node can send over its incident links in one round. Additionally, we study the effect of the *bandwidth* b, the maximum size in bits of these messages.

We show that the space between the unicast and broadcast congested clique models is very rich and interesting. For instance, we show that a problem (especially designed for this work) takes $\Omega(n/\log n)$ rounds in the broadcast model ($r = 1$), while it can be solved in two rounds if two messages can be sent ($r = 2$). Other gaps are found in other parts of the spectrum of values of r. We do this by providing techniques to simulate protocols with different parameters. Therefore, we conclude that, with respect to their power to solve certain problems, there is a strict hierarchy of congested clique models.

*Partially supported by CONICYT via Basal in Applied Mathematics (I.R.), Núcleo Milenio Información y Coordinación en Redes ICM/FIC RC130003 (I.R.), Fondecyt 1130061 (I.R.), Regional Government of Madrid (CM) grant Cloud4BigData (S2013/ICE-2894, cofunded by FSE & FEDER, and grant ANR Quasicool (ANR-12-JS02-011-01).

Permission to make digital or hard copies of part or all of this work for personal or classroom use is granted without fee provided that copies are not made or distributed for profit or commercial advantage, and that copies bear this notice and the full citation on the first page. Copyrights for third-party components of this work must be honored. For all other uses, contact the owner/author(s). Copyright is held by the owner/author(s).
PODC'15, July 21–23, 2015, Donostia-San Sebastián, Spain.
ACM 978-1-4503-3617-8 /15/07.
http://dx.doi.org/10.1145/2767386.2767447..

Categories and Subject Descriptors

D.1.3 [**Software**]: Programming Techniques—*Concurrent programming*; F.1.1 [**Theory of Computation**]: Computation by Abstract Devices—*Models of computation*

General Terms

Theory; Algorithms

Keywords

$\mathcal{CONGEST}$ model; congested clique model; message passing; distributed computation

1. INTRODUCTION

The $\mathcal{CONGEST}$ model is a synchronous, message-passing model of distributed computation in which each node can send (possibly different) messages of $\mathcal{O}(\log n)$ bits along each of its incident communication links in each round [12], where n is the number of computing nodes in the system. In the particular case where the communication network is a complete graph, all the information distributed in the nodes becomes local and therefore the only obstacle to perform any task is due to congestion. In fact, the main theoretical purpose of this model, known as congested clique [6, 7, 8, 9, 10, 11], is to serve as a basic model for understanding the role played by congestion in distributed computation.

In the much more restricted broadcast version of the congested clique model, each node can only broadcast a single $\mathcal{O}(\log n)$-bit message over all its links in each round [7]. This setting is equivalent to the multi-party, number-in-hand computation model, where communication takes place in a shared whiteboard [1, 2, 3, 4, 5, 7]: writing a message $\mathcal{M}$ on the whiteboard is equivalent to broadcasting $\mathcal{M}$.

In this paper we explore the space, in terms of round complexity, that lies between the model in which a different message can be sent over each link, and the model in which all the links of the node carry the same message. Hence, we parametrize the congested clique model with the *range* r, the maximum number of different messages a node can send over its outgoing links in one round. Additionally, we study the effect of the *bandwidth* b, the maximum size in bits of these messages.

The congested clique model with n nodes, and parameters r and b, will be denoted by $\mathrm{RCAST}_n(r \times b)$. Observe that the two extreme cases $r = 1$ and $r = n-1$, which correspond to the broadcast and the unicast communication modes, are the cases already considered in the literature [7]. More precisely, $\mathrm{RCAST}_n((n-1) \times b) = \text{CLIQUE-UCAST}_{n,b}$, and $\mathrm{RCAST}_n(1 \times b) = \text{CLIQUE-BCAST}_{n,b}$.

One important type of problem solved in these models has to do with computing some function or identifying some property of an input graph. In this case, the joint input to the n nodes in the congested clique model is an undirected weighted graph $G = (V, E, \omega)$. The only information each node u initially has is its own ID (the ID of each node is a unique number between 0 and $n-1$), the network size n, the list of IDs of its neighbors v in G, and the weights $\omega(uv)$ of its incident edges. At the end of the protocol every node must know the solution to some particular problem (for instance, a minimum spanning tree of G [10]).

Related Work.

Broadcast. In [4] it was proved that, if the degeneracy m of the input graph G is bounded and known in advance, then it is possible to reconstruct G with a one-round protocol of $\mathcal{O}(\log n)$ message size. Drucker, Kuhn and Oshman [7] gave an upper bound to the round complexity of the subgraph detection problem. They made the following remark: the degeneracy of H-free graphs can be upper bounded in terms of the Turán number $ex(n, H)$, which is the maximal number of edges of an n-node graph which does not contain a subgraph isomorphic to H. Plugging this into the reconstruction protocol introduced by Becker *et al.* [4], they designed a randomized protocol that solves the H detection problem in $\mathcal{O}(ex(n,H)\log^2 n/(nb) + \log^3 n/b)$ rounds with high probability (where b is the number of bits each player can broadcast in each round). Ahn, Guha and McGregor [1, 2] introduced a powerful technique that allows to decide in one round whether G is connected using messages of size $\mathcal{O}(\log^3 n)$, with high probability.

Some negative results have also been obtained. For instance, deciding deterministically in one round whether a graph has a triangle requires messages of size $\Theta(n)$ [4]. On the other hand, if instead of bounding the number of rounds we bound the message size b, then the best known result is the following: detecting deterministically a triangle requires $\Omega(n/(e^{\mathcal{O}(\sqrt{\log n})}b))$ rounds [7].

In [5], the authors consider three variants of the broadcast congested clique model: randomized protocols with public coins, randomized protocols with private coins and deterministic protocols. They showed that this choice affects the message size complexity of some problems. More precisely, they introduced a problem called TRANSLATED-TWINS. They proved that if only one round is allowed, then the message size complexity is $\Theta(n)$ in the deterministic case and $\mathcal{O}(\log n)$ in the randomized, public coin case. For the private coins setting, the message size complexity is lower bounded by $\Omega(\sqrt{n})$ and upper bounded by $\mathcal{O}(\sqrt{n}\log n)$.

Unicast. No lower bounds are known for the general, unicast congested clique model, where nodes may send different messages to each of its neighbors. Drucker, Kuhn and Oshman gave in [7] a possible explanation for the difficulty of finding such bounds. In fact, they proved that in this model it is possible to simulate powerful classes of bounded-depth circuits (and therefore lower bounds in the congested clique would yield lower bounds in circuit complexity).

The intrinsic power of the model has allowed some authors to provide extremely fast protocols for some natural problems: $\mathcal{O}(1)$-round protocols for routing and sorting [9, 11], a $\mathcal{O}(n^{(d-2)/d}/\log n)$- round protocol for finding a particular d-vertex subgraph [6], and a $\mathcal{O}(\log\log\log n)$-round protocol (in expectation) for finding a 3-ruling set [8]. Finally, Dolev, Lenzen, and Peled describe in [6] a protocol for reconstructing deterministically any graph in $\mathcal{O}(|E|/n)$ rounds, which is efficient for sparse graphs.

2. OUR RESULTS

We first prove that there exists a clear round complexity difference between the broadcast model and the model where two different messages are possible. To prove these results, we introduce a useful problem, called edge translation problem and denoted EDGE-TRANS$_k$.

DEFINITION 1. *Assume that n is even and that $n = 2n'$. Let k be a positive integer, and let the input graph $G = (V, E, \omega)$ be a clique such that $\omega(e) \in \{0,1\}^k$ for each $e \in E$. (The nodes have IDs in $\{0, \ldots, n-1\}$). The problem* EDGE-TRANS$_k$ *consists in deciding whether for all $0 \le i, j < n'$, $\omega(\{i,j\}) = \omega(\{i+n', j+n'\})$.*

As mentioned, we use the number of rounds as the complexity measure of a problem.

DEFINITION 2. *Let* PROBLEM *be a problem defined on undirected, simple, weighted graphs. The* round complexity, *denoted $ROUND^n_{r\times b}$(*PROBLEM*), is the minimal number of rounds for solving* PROBLEM *on any n-node graph with a protocol in $RCAST_n(r \times b)$.*

Round Complexity of Broadcast versus Two Messages.

The first question we would like to answer is how much can be gained if, instead of broadcasting, we have the possibility of sending two different messages in each round? This seems like a simple but fundamental question in order to evaluate the power of the different congested clique models we have defined. To answer this question, at least partially, we first show that, in the model $\mathrm{RCAST}_n(2 \times 1)$, the problem EDGE-TRANS$_1$ can be solved with a two-round protocol.

THEOREM 1. *$ROUND^n_{2\times 1}$(*EDGE-TRANS$_1$*) ≤ 2.*

PROOF. Let $K_n = (V, E)$ be the n-node clique and let $\omega : E \to \{0, 1\}$. The protocol is as follows.

`Round 1`. Each node i, with $0 \le i < n'$ sends to each node j, with $n' \le j < 2n'$, the bit $\omega(\{i, j-n'\})$, and, say, 0 to the other nodes.

`Round 2`. Each node i, with $0 \le i < n'$, broadcasts the bit 1. Each node j, with $n' \le j < 2n'$, broadcasts also only one bit, as follows.

- 1 if j received $\omega(\{i, j-n'\}) = \omega(\{i+n', j\}))$ from all $0 \le i < n'$,

- 0 otherwise.

Clearly, EDGE-TRANS$_1$ is satisfied if and only if no 0 is broadcasted by any node in the second round. Therefore, every node will know the answer after the second round. □

On the other hand, we show that any protocol that solves EDGE-TRANS$_1$ in the model RCAST$_n(1 \times b)$ needs $\Omega(n/b)$ rounds. In other words, in order to solve EDGE-TRANS$_1$ in the broadcast model in a constant number of rounds, the bandwidth b needs to be linear in the number of nodes n. Hence, there is in fact a gain by having the possibility of sending two different packets instead of one.

A Hierarchy of Congested Clique Models.

We continue our study of the power of the congested clique models with various values of range and bandwidth. First, we give a universal bound on the number of rounds to solve EDGE-TRANS$_k$, for any integer $k > 0$, in the model RCAST$_n(r \times b)$ where $r = 2^k$ and $b = \log n$.

THEOREM 2. *For any integer $k > 0$, $r = 2^k \leq n-1$, $b = \log n \geq k$, $ROUND^n_{r\times b}$(EDGE-TRANS$_k$) ≤ 2.*

Then, we give a lower bound on the number of rounds to solve the same problem EDGE-TRANS$_k$ in RCAST$_n(r \times b)$ when $r = k$ and $b = \log n$.

THEOREM 3. *For any integer $k > 0$, $r = k \leq n-1$, $k > 2$, $b = \log n$, $ROUND^n_{r\times b}$(EDGE-TRANS$_k$) $\geq \frac{(n-2)k}{4k \log n + 2\lceil \log k \rceil n} = \Omega\left(\frac{k}{\log k}\right)$.*

These two bounds combined show the existence of a hierarchy among the classical congested clique models (those with $b = \log n$), since the complexity in number of rounds to solve the same problem can vary significantly as a function of the range r. In particular, we have the following result.

COROLLARY 1. *For every integer $k = \omega(1)$ such that $2^k \leq n-1$, there is a gap of $\Omega\left(\frac{k}{\log k}\right) = \omega(1)$ on the round complexity of problem EDGE-TRANS$_k$ between the congested clique models $RCAST_n(2^k \times \log n)$ and $RCAST_n(k \times \log n)$.*

This corollary shows that there is a non-constant gap of complexity $\omega(1)$ in the number of rounds required by the model RCAST$_n(k \times \log n)$ with respect to the model RCAST$_n(2^k \times \log n)$ to solve the same problem EDGE-TRANS$_k$, as long as $k = \omega(1)$.

Simulation between Congested Clique Models.

Finally, we give techniques to simulate protocols designed for a model RCAST$_n(r' \times b')$ in another model RCAST$_n(r \times b)$, where $2 \leq r \leq r' < n$. These techniques yield upper bounds on the complexity gap between two models for any problem. In particular, our results show that this gap between models RCAST$_n(r' \times b')$ and RCAST$_n(r \times b)$ with $2 \leq r \leq r' < n$ is upper bounded by $\min\left(\left\lceil \frac{b'}{\lfloor \log r \rfloor} \right\rceil, \left\lceil \frac{r'}{r-1} \right\rceil \left\lceil \frac{b'}{b} \right\rceil\right)$. This bound becomes $\left\lceil \frac{b'}{b} \right\rceil$ for the special case in which $r = 2^b$ and $r = r'$.

3. REFERENCES

[1] K. J. Ahn, S. Guha, and A. McGregor. Analyzing graph structure via linear measurements. In *Proceedings of the 23rd Annual ACM-SIAM Symposium on Discrete Algorithms (SODA 2012)*, pages 459–467, 2012.

[2] K. J. Ahn, S. Guha, and A. McGregor. Graph sketches: Sparsification, spanners, and subgraphs. In *Proceedings of 31st Symposium on Principles of Database Systems (PODS 2012)*, pages 5–14, 2012.

[3] F. Becker, A. Kosowski, N. Nisse, I. Rapaport, and K. Suchan. Allowing each node to communicate only once in a distributed system: shared whiteboard models. In *Proceedings of the 24th ACM Symposium on Parallelism in Algorithms and Architecture (SPAA 2012)*, pages 11–17, 2012.

[4] F. Becker, M. Matamala, N. Nisse, I. Rapaport, K. Suchan, and I. Todinca. Adding a referee to an interconnection network: What can (not) be computed in one round. In *Proceedings of the 25th IEEE International Parallel and Distributed Processing Symposium (IPDPS 2011)*, pages 508–514, 2011.

[5] F. Becker, I. Rapaport, P. Montealegre, and I. Todinca. The simultaneous number-in-hand communication model for networks: private coins, public coins and determinism. In *Proceedings of the 21st International Colloquium on Structural Information and Communication Complexity (SIROCCO 2014)*, pages 83–95, 2014.

[6] D. Dolev, C. Lenzen, and S. Peled. Tri, tri again: Finding triangles and small subgraphs in a distributed setting. In *Proceedings of the 25th Symposium on Distributed Computing (DISC 2012)*, pages 195–209, 2012.

[7] A. Drucker, F. Kuhn, and R. Oshman. On the power of the congested clique model. In *Proceedings of the 33rd ACM Symposium on Principles of Distributed Computing (PODC 2014)*, pages 367–376, 2014.

[8] J. W. Hegeman, S. V. Pemmaraju, and V. B. Sardeshmukh. Near-constant-time distributed algorithms on a congested clique. In *Proceedings of the 27tth Symposium on Distributed Computing (DISC 2014)*, pages 514–530, 2014.

[9] C. Lenzen. Optimal deterministic routing and sorting on the congested clique. In *Proceedings of the 33rd ACM Symposium on Principles of Distributed Computing (PODC 2013)*, pages 42–50, 2013.

[10] Z. Lotker and E. Pavlov. MST construction in $O(\log \log n)$ communication rounds. In *Proceedings of the 15th ACM Symposium on Parallelism in Algorithms and Architecture (SPAA 2003)*, pages 94–100, 2003.

[11] B. Patt-Shamir and M. Teplitsky. The round complexity of distributed sorting. In *Proceedings of the 30th ACM Symposium on Principles of Distributed Computing (PODC 2011)*, pages 249–256, 2011.

[12] D. Peleg. *Distributed computing: a locality-sensitive approach.* Society for Industrial and Applied Mathematics, Philadelphia, PA, USA, 2000.

The "Mobile Adversary" Paradigm in Distributed Computation and Systems

Moti Yung
Google Inc.
and Columbia University, New York, NY
moti@cs.columbia.edu

ABSTRACT

The notion of *mobile adversary*, where the opponent can capture parties in a multi-party protocol dynamically, as long as at any given point in time its capturing capability is limited by a bound on number of parties (processors) it can control, has been suggested as an extensions of the traditionally static adversary. The motivation for this adversary was a result of a few issues: First, it was originated in systems corruption phenomena like virus injection into a computer network (such as the Internet), where viruses are spread but also detected and eliminated at network computers. Secondly, it is natural to assume that for managed networks, there will be efforts to recover failed processors, so the adversary control may cease to exist in a node locally while its control of other nodes continues. Thirdly, the notion of self-stabilization implies that a system tries to get rid of failures and the notion represents a strong fault-tolerance aspect, and should be extended (i.e., augmented by assuming bound on faults and extending initial benign fault to adversarial perpetual ones). As a result, the mobile adversary notion and a methodology for coping with it (proactive fault-tolerance, or proactive security in security oriented protocols) and its perpetual self-healing character, have been suggested. This work will review the development and influence of this notion on fault-tolerant secure distributed computing.

General Terms

Distributed Computing; Theory; Information Security; Computer Networks; Cryptography; Fault Tolerance.

Keywords

Distributed Systems; Multi-party Secure Computation; Mobile Adversary; Dynamic Adversary; Proactive Security; Self Healing; Self-Recovery.

Permission to make digital or hard copies of part or all of this work for personal or classroom use is granted without fee provided that copies are not made or distributed for profit or commercial advantage, and that copies bear this notice and the full citation on the first page. Copyrights for third-party components of this work must be honored. For all other uses, contact the owner/author(s). Copyright is held by the author/owner(s).
PODC'15, July 21–23, 2015, Donostia-San Sebastián, Spain.
ACM 978-1-4503-3617-8 /15/07.
http://dx.doi.org/10.1145/2767386.2767453.

The Mobile Adversary and Proactive Protocols

A central issue in computing is the notion of fault tolerance. The notion has appeared in early computational circuit designs and architectures, and is specifically a major issue in distributed computing and in networking, since in these systems redundancy is natural and, at times, a major reason for employing a distributed multi processor or multi computer setting is the need to increase computing power combined with the notion of tolerating faults (i.e., avoiding the case of a few failures breaking the system). Benign faults are typical in systems where technical failures occur, while more malicious intentional failures are expected in systems where the opponent is a human motivated and orchestrated one (e.g., in security system an organization may be willing to target system for failures so they leak secrets and are disrupted).

Traditional failures in distributed computing are typically static (i.e., once the failure is at a party it stays) and this has been the case with cryptographic and security protocols as well. The major problem in this area is known as "Byzantine Agreement" (by Lamport, Shostak, and Pease) and the required quorum typically assures its correct termination (as there are various variants to the problem). Quorum requirement, namely system redundancy, typically involves conditions like 'honest (non faulty) majority,' or 'over 2/3 of processors are non-faulty' which is the most typical requirement without cryptographic support (e.g., signatures). The same failure structure was extended to general multi-party secure computation (by Goldreich, Micali, and Wigderson), where a set of processors with private inputs attempt to jointly compute a function while keeping the inputs secret, where correctness, termination, and security against the adversary controlling the faulty processors is assured. These set of results from the 80's are by now classical and they are part of the foundations of safe, correct, and secure distributed computing.

Another set of faults that have been considered are transient benign faults that may be part of a system (e.g., a circuit that may have some noise in its initial state). The classical notion of "self stabilizing" protocols (by Dijkstra) assumes processors with correct control (program) but which are put at an arbitrary transient memory state (initial faulty stage). The protocol, in turn, is designed to achieve liveness and recover from any arbitrary state to a (legal) safe state, eventually, which is a very significant protocol program property from fault tolerance point of view.

The model of **mobile adversary** was considered by Ostrovsky and Yung [1] It was motivated by the phenomena of virus spread and virus elimination, and as a method to enhance self-stabilization protocol, with the power of assured quorum, namely redundancy, and as a result get a new system where it can withstand malicious faults, where faults can be introduced perpetually (rather than being transient), and where faults should not be limited to memory state, but can also be present at the control level (the program itself) where all that is needed is a minimal working platform (hardware and basic firmware). This results in a system where given a bound on number of faulty parties which holds at each time unit (period), but at each time unit the faulty parties' identities can change. This means that at each time unit there are newly faulty parties, and newly recovered parties which need to rejoin the computation so as to allow for the quorum of non-faulty condition to hold. To support such a system, it is mandatory that the system, by itself, supports (1) healing of newly recovered parties' state, which is done via secure multi-party computation itself (demonstrating how it can be used not only for computing but for system maintenance tasks); (2) advancing the state of the computation which includes (k-wise) re-randomizing the storage elements held by the system so that any up to the quorum of faulty parties (k) elements obtained earlier are random with respect to the new distributed representation of values, and includes step of the secure distributed computations over the values; (3) doing all, so that the adversary does not learn any secret; and moreover (4) the adversary does not stop the system from reaching its task (task being an output computation, or being a dynamic method for system computation and storage maintenance without output. In some configurations, we can have, in addition, (5) agreeing on what software at what state to run next (this applies when we allow the adversary to manipulate control); this is done via majority agreement, where the community serves as the trusted computing platform.

The original work dealt with the notion of maintaining systems securely and dynamically, assuring the system is correct and safe at any point, and performing multi-party secure computation against the mobile adversary. This type of protection was then called "proactive security" since healing and randomizing distributed values is performed in a proactive fashion and without requiring the processors to be aware of attacks. Note that the notion captures, both, the mobile adversary behavior as well as the protocol style of self-recovery (of parties), self-healing (of the system), as well as self-re-randomization (of distributed memory). In general, one can view traditional fault tolerance, in some analogy to noisy channels and error-correcting codes, as allowing redundancy by enlarging the space of the system compared to the space allowed to be occupied by the adversary. The mobile adversary paradigm, allows the system to consider the *space* and *time* dimensions, as combined limitations on the capabilities of the adversary.

The notion was further implemented and improved, and it was applied to agreement and replication under dynamic mobile faults and in the asynchronous model as well (see [2,3,4,5,6]). Further, since malicious mobile attempts may typify adversary trying to break security, many distributed cryptographic services have been developed in the proactive security model: decryption, signing, and so on (see, e.g., [7,8,9]). Numerous related theoretical and applied notions were suggested that re-randomize keys, states, and contribute to active defense and self-maintenance of systems, or deal with variants of mobile adversaries (e.g., [10,11,12]). Since dynamic randomization and mobile faults are present in current systems the employment of the paradigm in the future is expected to continue.

Acknowledgment: Part of this work was done while visiting the Simons Institute for Theory of Computing, U.C. Berkeley.

1. REFERENCES

[1] Rafail Ostrovsky, Moti Yung. How to withstand mobile virus attacks. PODC 1991: 51-59.

[2] Juan A. Garay. Reaching (and Maintaining) Agreement in the Presence of Mobile Faults (Extended Abstract). WDAG 1994: 253-264.

[3] Miguel Castro, Barbara Liskov. Practical byzantine fault tolerance and proactive recovery. ACM Trans. Comput. Syst. 20(4): 398-461 (2002).

[4] Christian Cachin, Klaus Kursawe, Anna Lysyanskaya, Reto Strobl. Asynchronous verifiable secret sharing and proactive cryptosystems. ACM Conference on Computer and Communications Security 2002: 88-97

[5] Lidong Zhou, Fred B. Schneider, Robbert van Renesse. APSS: proactive secret sharing in asynchronous systems. ACM Trans. Inf. Syst. Secur. (TISSEC) 8(3):259-286 (2005)

[6] Joshua Baron, Karim El Defrawy, Joshua Lampkins, Rafail Ostrovsky. How to withstand mobile virus attacks, revisited. PODC 2014: 293-302

[7] Ran Canetti, Amir Herzberg. Maintaining Security in the Presence of Transient Faults. CRYPTO 1994: 425-438

[8] Amir Herzberg, Stanislaw Jarecki, Hugo Krawczyk, Moti Yung. Proactive Secret Sharing Or: How to Cope With Perpetual Leakage. CRYPTO 1995: 339-352

[9] Yair Frankel, Peter Gemmell, Philip D. MacKenzie, Moti Yung. Optimal Resilience Proactive Public-Key Cryptosystems. FOCS 1997: 384-393

[10] Matthew K. Franklin, Zvi Galil, Moti Yung. Eavesdropping Games: A Graph-Theoretic Approach to Privacy in Distributed Systems . FOCS 1993: 670-679

[11] Paul G. Spirakis, Basil Tampakas, Hera Antonopoulou. Distributed Protocols Against Mobile Eavesdroppers. WDAG 1995: 160-167

[12] Tom Roeder, Fred B. Schneider. Proactive obfuscation. ACM Trans. Comput. Syst. 28(2) (2010)

Trading Fences with RMRs and Separating Memory Models* (Extended Abstract)

Hagit Attiya
Dept. of Computer Science
Technion
hagit@cs.technion.ac.il

Danny Hendler
Dept. of Computer Science
Ben-Gurion University
hendlerd@cs.bgu.ac.il

Philipp Woelfel
Dept. of Computer Science
University of Calgary
woelfel@cpsc.ucalgary.ca

ABSTRACT

Out-of-order execution of instructions is a common optimization technique for multicores and multiprocessors, which is governed by the *memory model* of the architecture. Relatively strong memory models, like TSO (supported by x86 and AMD), only allow reads to bypass earlier writes, while other models, like RMO (supported by ARM, POWER and Alpha) and PSO (supported by older SPARC), also allow the *reordering of writes to different locations*. These reorderings can be prevented by the use of costly *fence* instructions.

In this paper we prove that when writes can be reordered (e.g, in RMO or even PSO), there is a tradeoff between the number of fences, f, and the number of *remote memory references* (*RMR*s), r, for a large class of objects, including locks, counters and queues:

$$f(\log \frac{r}{f} + 1) \in \Omega(\log n) \ .$$

For example, when one of these objects is implemented using a constant number of fences (e.g., in the Bakery lock), the tradeoff implies that a linear number of RMRs is required (as indeed is the case with the Bakery lock). This gives a complexity separation between the memory models that allow write reordering and those that prohibit it, since a recent paper shows that a lock can be implemented in the stronger TSO memory model, with a small, constant number of fences, and a logarithmic number of RMRs.

The lower bound uses an information theoretic argument, relating the *encoding* of $n!$ distinguishable executions to the number of fences and RMRs performed in the course of these executions.

We also present a family of algorithms matching the lower bound, which explicitly enforce the required ordering, and hence, are correct even with weak memory models. This shows that the tradeoff is tight, and indicates that for many important objects, fences are mostly needed for avoiding reordering of writes.

*The first author is supported by a grant from Yad-Hanadiv Foundation; the first and second authors are supported by the Israel Science Foundation (grants 1227/10 and 1749/14); the third author is partially supported by the Canada Research Chairs program, as well as the Discover Grants and Discovery Accelerator Supplements programs of the Natural Sciences and Engineering Research Council of Canada (NSERC).

Permission to make digital or hard copies of all or part of this work for personal or classroom use is granted without fee provided that copies are not made or distributed for profit or commercial advantage and that copies bear this notice and the full citation on the first page. Copyrights for components of this work owned by others than the author(s) must be honored. Abstracting with credit is permitted. To copy otherwise, or republish, to post on servers or to redistribute to lists, requires prior specific permission and/or a fee. Request permissions from Permissions@acm.org.
PODC'15, July 21–23, 2015, Donostia-San Sebastián, Spain.
Copyright is held by the owner/author(s). Publication rights licensed to ACM.
ACM 978-1-4503-3617-8 /15/07 ...$15.00.
http://dx.doi.org/10.1145/2767386.2767427.

Categories and Subject Descriptors

D.1.3 [**Programming Techniques**]: Concurrent Programming—*Concurrent programming*; F.1.2 [**Computation By Abstract Devices**]: Modes of Computation—*Parallelism and concurrency*

General Terms

Algorithms, Architecture

Keywords

Shared memory; fences; total store ordering

1. INTRODUCTION

Modern multicores and multiprocessors optimize code so as to execute certain instructions out of program order. The memory model supported by the architecture dictates which operation pairs can be reordered; for example, the *total store order* (*TSO*) model [13, 18] permits to perform a read from address a before an earlier write to address $b \neq a$. This reordering is also allowed in the weaker *partial store ordering* (*PSO*) model [18], which permits writes to be reordered. An even weaker model, called *relaxed memory ordering* (*RMO*) [18], allows to reorder any pair of instructions. (See Table 1 in [1] and [19, 20].)

To ensure the correctness of a concurrent algorithm, it is possible to prohibit the reordering of memory instructions, by inserting a *fence* instruction (also called a *barrier*) between them. A fence incurs significant overhead, but there are cases when it is unavoidable since it has been shown [7] that many concurrent objects, including locks (mutual exclusion), counters and queues, must ensure that there is *a read after a write to a different location*, unless strong atomic operations such as, e.g., *compare-and-swap* (CAS) are used (and these also incur significant overhead).

It is possible to acquire a lock using a constant number of fences. For example, in Lamport's well-known Bakery algorithm [17] (Algorithm 1), the acquisition of the lock (as well as its release) requires only a constant number of fences. However, acquiring the Bakery lock also requires reading a linear number of different memory locations, even when the process runs alone without interruption from other processes. Even worse, these reads are classified as *remote*, since they cannot be served from the process' local cache or memory segment. Counting the *remote memory references* (RMRs), namely, reads and writes that cannot be served from the local cache or memory segment of the process, is considered a good way to compare local-spin concurrent algorithms (see e.g., [2–5, 10, 14–16, 23]).

In this paper we prove that when writes may be reordered, a *linear* number of RMRs is needed when the number of fences is constant, showing that the Bakery lock is asymptotically optimal.

Algorithm 1: n-process Bakery lock for process $i, 0 \leq i < n$

```
shared C[0, ..., n − 1]: array of bits
shared T[0, ..., n − 1]: array of integers
Procedure Acquire(){
write(C[i],1) ; fence()
tmp := 1 + max{T[0, ..., n − 1]}
write(C[i],0) ; fence()
write(T[i],tmp) ; fence()
foreach j = 0, ..., n − 1, j ≠ i do
    wait until C[j] == 0
    wait until T[j] == 0 or (T[i], i) < (T[j], j)
end
}
Procedure Release(){
write(T[i],0) ; fence() }
```

That is, one cannot win on both the fence and RMR complexities of read/write algorithms for many fundamental objects, including locks, counters and queues. This is a special case of a general result we prove: if f and r denote the numbers of fences respectively RMRs performed per passage (one acquisition and release of the lock), then in the worst-case

$$f \cdot \left(1 + \log \frac{r}{f}\right) \in \Omega(\log n) \tag{1}$$

Hence, to get an optimal, logarithmic number of RMRs per passage the number of fences per passage must also be logarithmic, matching the complexity of the tournament-tree lock [23].

When writes are performed in program order, there is a lock in which each passage incurs a *constant* number of fences and a *logarithmic* number of RMRs [8] (which is optimal [9]). This gives an exponential separation between models without reordering of writes (like TSO) and weaker models in which write reordering is allowed (like PSO, Power and RMO).

Our lower bound holds for the two standard theoretical models for measuring RMR complexity: the *Distributed Shared Memory* (DSM) and the *Cache Coherent* (CC) model. In the DSM model, shared memory is partitioned into segments, and each segment is local to one process. Only accesses to non-local memory segments incur RMRs. In the CC model, processes are equipped with caches, and RMRs correspond to cache-misses. Contrary to, e.g., the tight RMR lower bound in [9], our lower bound proof is for a shared memory model combining the power of the DSM and the CC models. Specifically, processes are equipped with caches, and an access of a memory location by a process incurs an RMR only if the location is not local to that process *and* it is a cache miss. Thus, our tradeoff holds for modern NUMA architectures with caches.

The tradeoff is tight and we present a family of algorithms that trade the number of fences with the number of RMRs: for every f, $1 \leq f \leq \log n$, a passage incurs $O(f)$ fences and $O(fn^{1/f})$ RMRs. These algorithms are correct in any memory model, since they explicitly order reads and writes with fences.

To prove the tradeoff, we construct an execution E_π for each permutation π of $[n] := \{0, \ldots, n-1\}$, and we encode these executions so that *the code length of an execution is a function of both the number of fences and the number of RMRs* incurred in it.

In every execution E_π, processes access the shared object once (for example, to increment a counter or acquire the lock) according to their order in π. Each execution E_π is encoded by a sequence of *commands*, some of which receive integer parameters, so that, roughly, the number of commands in the encoding is linear in the total number of fences performed in the execution, denoted $\beta(E_\pi)$, while the total sum of parameter values is linear in the number of RMRs, denoted $\rho(E_\pi)$. As we show, the length of the encoding is bounded from above by $\beta(E_\pi)(\log \frac{\rho(E_\pi)}{\beta(E_\pi)} + 1)$.

In E_π, processes are unaware of processes that appear after them in the permutation π. As we prove, this ensures that π can be reconstructed from E_π. Since an execution code uniquely determines an execution (and therefore a permutation over $[n]$), there are $n!$ different execution codes. Therefore, $\beta(E)(\log \frac{\rho(E)}{\beta(E)} + 1)$, for at least one of these executions, is asymptotically at least logarithmic in $n!$, that is, in $\Omega(n \log n)$.

Our proof significantly extends the technique used to prove the $\Omega(n \log n)$ lower bound on the RMR complexity of mutual exclusion [9, 11]. That proof also goes by encoding executions corresponding to different permutations in a way that allows to uniquely reconstruct them, but is only able to capture the RMR complexity. In contrast, the codes constructed by our proof capture both fence and RMR complexities: A sequence of w write operations issued by a process p may be delayed by the system and committed to memory only when a fence is performed. When writes can be reordered, these writes can be committed *in any order*, and our encoding technique exploits this freedom to encode a *batch of writes* in its entirety by using a constant number of commands, instead of encoding each write separately. These commands encode the exact manner in which the writes in a batch should be interleaved within the steps of preceding processes. Some of these commands receive a parameter that represents the number of write steps to which they apply. Thus, the values of these parameters may be encoded by using $O(\log w)$ bits. Each fence, on the other hand, is encoded using a constant number of bits.

Very informally, we capture the tradeoff between fences and RMRs as follows. The number of code-bits representing fences changes linearly with the number of fences ($\beta(E_\pi)$). However, as the number of fences decreases, the average size of write batches $\left(\frac{\rho(E_\pi)}{\beta(E_\pi)}\right)$ increases. If the number of code bits has to remain in $\Theta(n \log n)$, a linear decrease in the number of fences implies a linear increase in $\log \frac{\rho(E_\pi)}{\beta(E_\pi)}$, which is an exponential increase in the number of RMRs.

2. MODEL

We consider an asynchronous shared memory system where n processes with IDs $0, \ldots, n-1$ communicate by accessing shared registers from a totally ordered set $\mathcal{R}$ with values from a domain $\mathcal{D} \supseteq \{\sqcup\}$. For simplicity but without loss of generality let $\mathcal{R} = \mathcal{D} - \{\sqcup\} = \mathbb{N}$. Initially, each register has value $\sqcup$.

Each process p is equipped with a *write-buffer* [21] that stores an (initially empty) unordered set $WB_p \subseteq \mathcal{R} \times \mathcal{D}$ (without duplicates). Processes execute an algorithm A in which they perform the operations `read(R)`, `write(R,x)` or `fence()`, where $(R, x) \in \mathcal{R} \times \mathcal{D}$. A `write(R,x)` operation by process p writes (R, x) to p's write-buffer, replacing WB_p with $(WB_p - \{(R, x') \mid x' \in \mathcal{D}\}) \cup \{(R, x)\}$. If p executes `read(R)` at a time when there is a write (R, x) in WB_p, then the read is *served from the write-buffer* and the value x is returned; if no such pair is in WB_p, then the value of register R is returned, and thus the read is *served from shared memory*. At any point in time, if WB_p contains some write (R, x), then that write may be *committed to shared memory* (by the system), meaning that (R, x) is removed from WB_p, and the value of R changes to x. A `fence()` operation does not affect the shared memory or write-buffers directly; it only guarantees that the system does not allow the calling process to take any further steps before its write-buffer is empty.

To facilitate our proofs, we assume w.l.o.g. that there is a special `return()` operation that takes one *return* value, a non-negative integer. Each process has to execute `return()` exactly once, and after executing `return(x)` the process enters a *final state with value x*.

An *execution* is a (possibly infinite) sequence of *steps* executed by processes. Each step is either a *read, write, fence, or return step* that happens when the process executes a `read()`, `write()`, `fence()`, or `return()` operation, respectively; or it is a *commit* of a write from p's write-buffer (to shared memory). Unlike other step types, commit steps are not instructions in a process' program and their position in the execution is controlled by the system; for notational convenience, we regard them as process steps.

A process p *participates* in an execution E, if E contains at least one step by p. If only processes $p_1, \ldots, p_k$ participate in execution E, then we say E is an execution *by* $p_1, \ldots, p_k$. An execution is *complete*, if it contains a return step by each participating process. For any execution E and any set $P \subseteq [n]$ of processes, $E|_P$ denotes the execution obtained from E by removing all steps by processes in $[n] - P$.

A *system configuration* is the state of the entire system, i.e., it comprises the state of each process, each register, and each write-buffer. The *initial* system configuration is denoted C_{init}. For system configuration C, $next_p(C)$ denotes the operation that process $p \in [n]$ is poised to execute; we write $next_p(C) = \emptyset$, if in C process p is in a final state. Process p's write-buffer in system configuration C is denoted $WB_p(C)$, and the value stored in register $R \in \mathcal{R}$ is denoted $R(C)$. An execution E is *permissible by algorithm A starting from system configuration C* if E may result as processes execute algorithm A starting from C. If E is permissible by A starting from the initial system configuration, C_{init}, then we say it is *A-permissible*. A system configuration C is *reachable*, if there exists an A-permissible execution E, such that C is reached from C_{init} by executing E.

A *schedule* is a (possibly infinite) sequence $\sigma = (\sigma_1, \sigma_2, \ldots)$, where each element σ_i in the schedule is a pair in $[n] \times (\mathcal{R} \cup \{\bot\})$. A schedule σ, together with an algorithm A and a system configuration C, uniquely determines an execution $Exec_A(C;\sigma)$ as follows: If σ is the empty schedule, then $Exec_A(C;\sigma)$ is the empty execution. Now suppose σ contains exactly one element $(p, R) \in [n] \times (\mathcal{R} \cup \{\bot\})$. If p is in a final state in C, i.e., $next_p(C) = \emptyset$, then again, $Exec_A\big(C; (p, R)\big)$ is the empty execution. Now suppose $next_p(C) \neq \emptyset$. Then $Exec_A\big(C; (p, R)\big)$ consists of a single step s determined as follows:

- If there is a value $x \in \mathcal{D}$ such that $(R, x) \in WB_p(C)$, then s is the step that commits (R, x) (clearly this is only possible if $R \neq \bot$).
- Otherwise, if $next_p(C)$ is a `fence()` operation and $WB_p(C) \neq \emptyset$, then s is a commit step in which write $(R, x) \in WB_p(C)$ gets committed, where R is the register with the smallest identifier for which there is a write in $WB_p(C)$. (Recall that $\mathcal{R}$ is totally ordered.)
- In all other cases, s is a step that corresponds to operation $next_p(C)$, i.e., s is a read, write, fence, or return step, but not a commit step.

Each step in an execution E will be defined as either *local* or *remote*. Our definition is such that every remote step in E corresponds to an RMR in both the DSM and the CC models (although not necessarily vice versa). Therefore, our lower bound applies for both the CC and DSM models. The set $\mathcal{R}$ of all registers is partitioned into n *memory segments*, $\mathcal{R}_0, \ldots, \mathcal{R}_{n-1}$, each of infinite size. In the following we assume (w.l.o.g.) for presentation simplicity that in any execution, all arguments of `write()` operations are distinct. A `read(R)` step by process p is local, if either $R \in \mathcal{R}_p$, or the read operation returns value x and p has previously executed `write(R, x)` or read the value x from R; all other `read()` steps are remote. All `write()` and `fence()` steps are local. A commit of a write (R, x) is local, if either $R \in \mathcal{R}_p$, or p previously committed a write $(\cdot, R)$ to shared memory, and since then no other process committed a write $(\cdot, R)$; all other commits are remote. A process p *accesses* process q's local memory, if p reads a register $R \in \mathcal{R}_q$, and that read is served from shared memory, or when it commits a write to $R \in \mathcal{R}_q$.

Algorithm A satisfies *weak obstruction-freedom* (see [9]), if for every process p and every reachable configuration C such that every process other than p is either in its initial or in its final state in C, p enters a final state in $Exec_A(C, \sigma)$, for every infinite $\{p\}$-only schedule σ (which contains only pairs (p, R)). Note that deadlock freedom implies weak obstruction-freedom.

3. ALGORITHMS

A *lock* supports two methods: *Acquire*, which allows a process to grab the lock, and *Release*, which is invoked after using the lock. Any lock satisfies the following requirements: (1) at most a single process has the lock in any given time (*mutual exclusion*), (2) if some process invokes *Acquire* then, eventually, some process gets the lock (*deadlock freedom*), and (3) a process completes the *Release* method in a finite number of steps (*finite exit*).

The well-known Bakery [17] and tournament-tree [22,23] locks realize the two extreme cases of the tradeoff between the numbers of RMRs and fences. Even in an uncontended situation, Acquiring the Bakery lock (Algorithm 1) requires three writes, each followed by a fence to ensure it is visible in the shared memory, and reading the values written by all other processes, each requiring an RMR since these locations are read for the first time. Releasing the lock requires a single write (followed by a fence). (This algorithm also works under the RMO model.) Therefore, a passage through the Bakery lock requires only a constant number of fences but a linear number of RMRs. Thus, $f \log(r/f + 1) \in \Theta(\log n)$. On the other hand, a passage through a tournament-tree lock incurs $O(\log n)$ fences and $O(\log n)$ RMRs, hence, $f \log(r/f + 1) \in \Theta(\log n)$.

To obtain intermediate points on the spectrum of the tradeoff, when the number of fences f is between a constant and $\log n$, note that Equation (1) is asymptotically matched when

$$r \in O(f \cdot n^{1/f}) . \tag{2}$$

Viewing the bound in this manner immediately inspires a generalized tournament Algorithm GT_f, $1 \leq f \leq \log n$, which uses a tree of height f and branching factor $n^{1/f}$. The tree has n leaves, each one statically assigned to a single process. To win the lock in GT_f, a process has to win the locks in all the f internal nodes along the path from its leaf to the root. In each node, there are (at most) $n^{1/f}$ processes, which compete using a Bakery lock for $n^{1/f}$ processes. Clearly, GT_1 is the Bakery algorithm and $GT_{\log n}$ is essentially the binary tournament-tree algorithm. (See Figure 1.)

The resulting number of fences per passage is therefore linear in f and the resulting number of RMRs per passage is $O(f \cdot n^{1/f})$. Thus, the numbers of fences and RMRs satisfy Equation (2), showing that the bound of Equation (1) is tight.

4. ORDERING ALGORITHMS AND OVERVIEW OF THE MAIN RESULT

The lower bound holds for a general class of objects, for which all algorithms must order processes in specific, clean executions. Informally, an algorithm is *ordering* if for any permutation $\pi = (p_0, \ldots, p_{n-1})$ over $[n]$ and execution E by $\{p_0, \ldots, p_m\}$, $0 \leq$

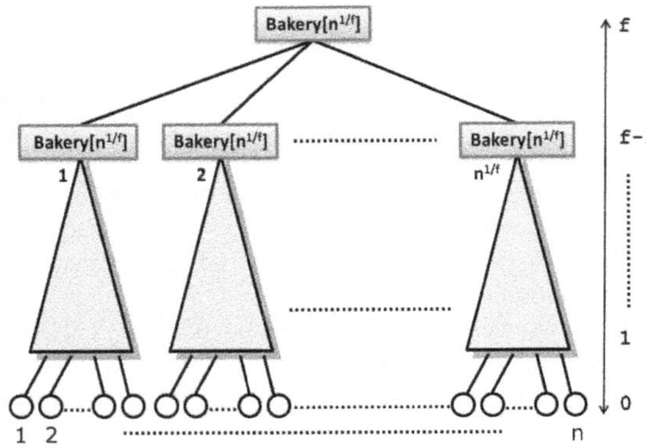

Figure 1: Schematic view of algorithm GT_f; Bakery[$n^{1/f}$] denotes the Bakery lock for $n^{1/f}$ processes.

$m < n$, if processes $\{p_0, \ldots, p_{m-1}\}$ are unaware of p_m in E,[1] and each process p_i returns i, $0 \le i < m$, then p_m returns m in E. In particular, we can prove by induction that if the execution is *sequential*, namely, each process p_{i-1}, $0 < i \le m$, returns before p_i starts, then each process p_i returns i.

For a permutation $\pi = (p_0, \ldots, p_{n-1})$ over $[n]$, let $[\pi]_k$ denote the sequence $(p_0, \ldots, p_{k-1})$ of length k.

DEFINITION 4.1. *Algorithm A is* ordering, *if for any permutation $\pi = (p_0, \ldots, p_{n-1})$ over $[n]$, any $k \in [n]$, and any complete A-permissible execution E by $\{p_0, \ldots, p_k\}$: if $E|_{\{p_0,\ldots,p_{k-1}\}}$ is A-permissible and each process p_i, $i \in [k]$ returns value i in E, then p_k returns value k in E.*

The following algorithm, `Count`, is a simple ordering algorithm that uses a single lock: Upon entering the critical section, each process reads a shared register C (initialized to 0), adds one to it, and writes back the result, followed by a fence; the process then exits the critical section and returns the value read from C. The sequence of values returned by processes (and the associated sequence of process identifiers) is a permutation, and it is not hard to see that `Count` is ordering. Clearly, the numbers of fences and RMRs in `Count` are asymptotically the same as those of a single passage through the lock it uses. More details appear in the full version of the paper, which also shows that other objects—queue, counter and fetch-and-increment—may be similarly used for constructing ordering algorithms. Thus, our tradeoff holds for implementations of these objects.

We capture the tradeoff between the *total* number of fences and RMRs in an execution, in which each process accesses the object exactly once (e.g., each process acquires and releases the lock once). Recall that $\rho(E)$, $\beta(E)$, respectively, denote the total number of RMRs and fences performed by the processes in such an execution E. The next theorem states our main result.

THEOREM 4.2. *If A is an ordering algorithm, then it has an execution E, in which every process executes the algorithm once, and $\beta(E)(\log(\rho(E)/\beta(E)) + 1) \in \Omega(n \log n)$.*

Dividing by n implies that at least for one process in E, the tradeoff between the number of fences, f, and number of RMRs, r, satisfies $f\big(\log(r/f) + 1\big) \in \Omega(\log n)$.

[1] Formally, this means that the execution E projected on $\{p_0, \ldots, p_{k-1}\}$ is also an execution of the algorithm.

command	meaning
proceed	take steps until there is a fence with non-empty write buffer
commit	commit all write steps
wait-hidden-commit(k)	wait until k write steps are hidden by earlier processes
wait-read-finish(k)	wait for k early processes that read a write to complete
wait-local-finish(k)	wait for k early processes that access local memory to complete

Table 1: Commands used in the encoding and their meaning.

Recall that we prove the tradeoff by constructing an execution E_π, for each permutation π of $[n] := \{0, \ldots, n-1\}$, and encoding these executions so that the code length of an execution is a function of the number of fences and the number of RMRs incurred in it.

We start with an informal description of how, given a permutation $\pi = (p_0, p_1, \ldots, p_{n-1})$, we construct and encode a unique execution. Our construction ensures that no process is aware of the participation of later processes (that follow it in π) in the execution, that is, it maintains the property that process p_i is unaware whether a later process in the permutation, p_j, $j > i$, participates in E_π. Since the algorithm is ordering, this allows to prove that each process p_i returns the value i in E_π. It follows that the sequence of values returned in E_π and $E_{\pi'}$ are different for $\pi \ne \pi'$, implying that π can be uniquely determined from E_π.

Each execution E_π is encoded by a sequence of *commands*, with possible parameters. Roughly speaking, the number of commands in the encoding is in $O(\beta(E_\pi))$, while the total sum of parameter values is in $O(\rho(E_\pi))$. We prove that E_π is uniquely encoded using $B(E_\pi) = O\Big(\beta(E_\pi)\big(\log(\rho(E_\pi)/\beta(E_\pi)) + 1\big)\Big)$ bits. Since the $n!$ different executions must have $n!$ different codes, the function $B(E_\pi)$ in at least one of these executions is asymptotically at least $\log n!$, that is, in $\Omega(n \log n)$.

Executions are constructed and *encoded* iteratively (see Section 5.2). In the first iteration, the steps of process p_0 (as it runs solo) are determined and encoded. Since p_0 is unaware of other processes, it does not have to wait for any other process. Then, the steps of process p_1 are determined and encoded. These steps are interleaved within the steps of p_0, so process p_1 may have to wait for process p_0 (we soon explain when). We proceed in this manner, until the steps of all processes have been incorporated into execution E_π, and we have created *command stacks* $St_0, \ldots, St_{n-1}$, where, for $j \in [n]$, St_j encodes the steps of process p_j and, collectively, $St_0, \ldots, St_{n-1}$ encode the manner in which steps by different processes should be interleaved.

Assume we have constructed execution E^i_π of processes $p_0, \ldots, p_i$. Roughly, as long as p_{i+1} does not issue a fence step when its write-buffer is non-empty, it may continue taking steps. The resulting sequence of steps is encoded by a single *proceed* command. When p_{i+1} issues a fence step and its write-buffer is non-empty, then the batch of writes to be committed to shared-memory is encoded by three commands, at most. The *wait-hidden-commit*(k) command means that k write-steps by p_{i+1} should be *hidden* (i.e., overwritten before being read) before other write-steps may be committed; the *wait-read-finish*(k) command means that there are k early processes that must complete their execution before p_{i+1} is allowed to commit writes to registers read by these processes; finally, the *commit* command means that p_{i+1} can commit the rest of the writes in its buffer (if any) and proceed with its execution. (Table 1 summarizes the commands.)

In more detail, this is how we interleave the steps of process p_{i+1} into execution E^i_π and construct E^{i+1}_π.

- Before process p_{i+1} is allowed to take its first step, it has to wait for all earlier processes that access its local memory segment in E^i_π to terminate. This is encoded by the *wait-local-finish* command, whose parameter is the number of processes for whose completion p_{i+1} must wait.
- As long as process p_{i+1} performs read, write, or fence instructions that have no impact (i.e., fences issued when the write-buffer of p_{i+1} is empty), then p_{i+1} may proceed taking steps. This is encoded by the parameterless *proceed* command. (To avoid infinite executions, a process is not scheduled to take such steps if it is in a state where it would not enter a final state when running by itself.)
- Otherwise, p_{i+1}'s next step is a fence instruction and its write-buffer is not empty. This is the only case in which writes by p_{i+1} are committed to shared memory. In this case, the batch of write steps taken by p_{i+1} since its preceding fence (or since it began its execution) is collectively encoded by using a constant number of commands according to the following principles:
  – Whenever possible, writes about to be committed by p_{i+1} are scheduled so they will be hidden by writes committed in E^i_π by earlier processes before they are read. Upon encoding a batch of writes to be committed by p_{i+1}, the number of writes that may be overwritten is encoded as a parameter of the *wait-hidden-commit* command. These writes will be committed before any other writes in p_{i+1}'s write-buffer and will be interleaved in the execution so that they are hidden.
  – If there are no writes that may be hidden in p_{i+1}'s write-buffer, but there are writes to registers from which an earlier process reads in E^i_π, then the number of such early processes is a parameter of the *wait-read-finish* command. Process p_{i+1} will commit these writes only after these early processes terminate their execution.
  – Otherwise, if p_{i+1}'s write-buffer is not empty, then the writes in it should be committed. This is encoded by the parameterless *commit* command.
  – Otherwise, p_{i+1} can take its next step. This is encoded by the parameterless *proceed* command.

5. PROOF OF THE LOWER BOUND

Fix an ordering algorithm A and assume w.l.o.g. that every process executes a `fence()` operation just before it enters a final state, i.e., before its `return()` operation. (Since the proof fixes algorithm A, in the following we write permissible instead of permissible by A, and omit A from the notation defined earlier.)

Somewhat counter-intuitively, we first describe the decoding of executions (Section 5.1). The reason is that the encoding, which is done inductively (in Section 5.2), relies on interpreting the decoding of earlier parts of the encoding.

5.1 Codes: Commands and Their Decoding

We now describe codes and how they are *decoded*, that is, how they are used to construct an execution. The codes use the following *commands*: *commit*, *proceed*, *wait-hidden-commit*(k), *wait-local-finish*(k, S), and *wait-read-finish*(k, S), where $k \in \mathbb{N}$ and $S \subseteq [n]$ are parameters.

Each process p has a *command stack* St_p, which stores a sequence of commands. Let $top(St_p)$ denote the element on top of stack St_p. An *extended configuration* is an $(n+1)$-tuple $\Gamma = (C; St_0, \ldots, St_{n-1})$, where C is a system configuration and $St_0, \ldots, St_{n-1}$ are command stacks. If $\vec{S} = (St_1, \ldots, St_n)$ is a command stack sequence and $q \in [n]$, then $\vec{S}|_q$ is process q's stack St_q.

We now show how an extended configuration $\Gamma = (C; St_0, \ldots, St_{n-1})$ uniquely determines an execution $E(\Gamma)$, which is permissible starting from system configuration C. From Γ, we determine a zero- or one-step schedule, σ, and a new sequence $(St'_0, \ldots, St'_{n-1})$ of command stacks. $E(\Gamma)$ is defined recursively. If σ is a zero-element schedule, then $E(\Gamma)$ is the empty execution. Otherwise, σ is a one-element schedule (representing a step by some process i); let C' be the system configuration reached at the end of execution $Exec(C; \sigma)$, then:

$$E(\Gamma) = Exec(C; \sigma) \circ E(C'; St'_0, \ldots, St'_{n-1}),$$

where St'_i, $i \in [n]$, is a new command stack obtained by popping elements from and/or pushing elements to St_i. Our recursive definition does not guarantee that $E(\Gamma)$ is finite for every Γ, i.e, the recursion may not terminate; however, the codes Γ we will construct later will only yield finite executions $E(\Gamma)$. To completely define $E(\Gamma)$, it suffices to state for each extended configurations Γ whether $E(\Gamma)$ is the empty execution, and otherwise to define σ and $St'_0, \ldots, St'_{n-1}$ as a function of Γ.

We partition the set of processes into sets of *finished*, *commit enabled*, *non-commit enabled*, and *waiting* processes, defined as follows. Process p is *finished* in configuration C, if it is in a final state in C; $NbFinal(C)$ denotes the number of processes that are finished in system configuration C. Process p is *commit enabled* in $(C; St_0, \ldots, St_{n-1})$, if

$$top(St_p) = commit \wedge next_p(C) = \texttt{fence()} \wedge WB_p(C) \neq \emptyset.$$

Process p is *non-commit enabled* if $top(St_p) = proceed$, p enters a final state in every p-only execution from C, and one of the following holds:

- $next_p(C)$ is a `read()` or `write()` operation;
- $next_p(C)$ is `return(r)`, where $r = NbFinal(C)$; or
- $next_p(C)$ is `fence()` and $WB_p(C) = \emptyset$.

Process p is *waiting* in all other cases (it is not finished, commit enabled, or non-commit enabled).

Decoding Rule (D1): Commit Step. Suppose in configuration C with command stacks $St_0, \ldots, St_{n-1}$ there is at least one commit enabled process. Let p be the one with the smallest ID. Let R be the smallest register such that (R, x) is in $WB_p(C)$. If there are processes q' such that $top(St_{q'}) = wait\text{-}hidden\text{-}commit(k)$, $k > 0$, and $WB_{q'}(C)$ contains a write to R, then let q be the one with the smallest ID and let $p^* = q$. Otherwise, let $p^* = p$. Then we define $\sigma = (p^*, R)$. I.e., in $Exec(C; \sigma)$, p^* commits its write to R.

A commit step is *hidden* if executed by a waiting process p^*; otherwise, the commit step is *visible*.

The command stacks St'_i, $i \in [n]$ are determined as follows.

(D1a) For $i = p^*$, if $top(St_{p^*}) = commit$ (i.e., $p^* = p$) and $|WB_p(C)| = 1$, then we obtain St'_{p^*} from St_{p^*} by simply popping the top element from the stack.
(Informally: a commit of a batch of writes from the write-buffer of p was now completed.)

(D1b) For $i = p^*$, if $top(St_{p^*}) = wait\text{-}hidden\text{-}commit(k)$ (i.e., $p^* = q$), then we pop that element from the stack, and if $k - 1 > 0$, we push $wait\text{-}hidden\text{-}commit(k-1)$ back on the stack.
(Informally: another write commit by q is about to be hidden - by p. If additional write commits must be hidden, then push wait-hidden-commit$(k-1)$ back to q's stack, other-

wise no more of q's commits in the current batch should be hidden.)

(D1c) For $i \neq p^*$, if $R \in \mathcal{R}_i$, $i \in [n]$, and $top(St_i) = \mathit{wait\text{-}local\text{-}finish}(\ell, S)$, then we obtain St'_i from St_i by replacing that top element with $\mathit{wait\text{-}local\text{-}finish}(\ell, S \cup \{p^*\})$.
(Informally: if there is a process $i \neq p^*$ that is waiting for earlier processes who access its local segment to terminate, then i should wait for the termination of p^*.)

(D1d) All other command stacks remain unchanged.

Decoding Rule (D2): Read, Write, Return, or Fence Step. Now suppose there is no commit enabled process, but there is at least one non-commit enabled one. Let p be the non-commit enabled process with smallest ID. Then σ is $(p, \bot)$, i.e., $Exec(C; \sigma)$ is the permissible one-step execution in which p executes its read, write, return, or fence step. We now show how to determine St'_i for all $i \in [n]$. Recall that C' is the system configuration reached at the end of $E(C; \sigma)$. First, we consider process p.

(D2a) If $next_p(C') \in \{\texttt{fence()}, \texttt{return()}, \emptyset\}$, then we obtain St'_p from St_p by popping the *proceed* command from the top of St_p. Otherwise, $St'_p = St_p$.
(Informally: if the next step of p is read or write, then the top of p's stack remains proceed. Otherwise, the next command (if any) reaches the top of p's stack.)

For each other process $q \in [n] - \{p\}$, the command stack St'_q is obtained from St_q as follows.

(D2b) If $Exec(C; \sigma)$ is a return step and $top(St_q)$ is $\mathit{wait\text{-}read\text{-}finish}(k, S)$ or $\mathit{wait\text{-}local\text{-}finish}(k, S)$, where S contains p, then we pop the top element from the stack, and if $k-1 > 0$ we push $\mathit{wait\text{-}read\text{-}finish}(k-1, S)$ (respectively $\mathit{wait\text{-}local\text{-}finish}(k-1, S)$) back on the stack.
(Informally: if p's execution terminated, then every process q that waits for p to terminate no longer needs to wait for it. If q needs to wait for the termination of additional processes, then parameter k is updated to $k-1$, otherwise the next command in q's stack becomes effective.)

(D2c) If $top(St_q)$ is $\mathit{wait\text{-}read\text{-}finish}(k, S)$ and $Exec(C; \sigma)$ is a read step in which process p reads register R from shared memory (not the write buffer), where $R \in WB_q(C)$, then we replace the top element of St_q with $\mathit{wait\text{-}read\text{-}finish}(k, S \cup \{p\})$.
(Informally: if there are processes $q \neq p$ that are about to commit a write to R and are waiting for the termination of earlier processes who read a register they are about to write to, then each such process should wait for the termination of p.)

(D2d) If $top(St_q)$ is $\mathit{wait\text{-}local\text{-}finish}(k, S)$ and in $Exec(C; \sigma)$ process p reads a register from $\mathcal{R}_q$, then we replace the top stack element with $\mathit{wait\text{-}local\text{-}finish}(k, S \cup \{p\})$.
(Informally: if there is a process q that is waiting for earlier processes who access its local segment to terminate, then q should wait for the termination of p.)

(D2e) In all other cases, q's command stack remains unchanged, i.e., $St'_q = St_q$.

Decoding Rule (D3): End of Execution. If all processes are waiting or finished, $E(\Gamma)$ is the empty execution.

5.2 Encoding an Execution

Recall that C_{init} is the initial system configuration, and fix a permutation $\pi = (p_0, \ldots, p_{n-1})$ over $[n]$. We construct inductively command stack sequences $\vec{S}_0, \vec{S}_1, \vec{S}_2, \ldots$, where the base case is $\vec{S}_0 = (\emptyset, \ldots, \emptyset)$.

For the inductive step, suppose we have constructed $\vec{S}_i$ for some integer $i \geq 0$. Let C_i be the system configuration reached at the end of $E_i = E(C_{init}; \vec{S}_i)$. In other words, C_i is the configuration reached after the execution determined by $(C_{init}; \vec{S}_i)$ is constructed (decoded) according to the decoding rules specified in Section 5.1. If in configuration C_i process p_{n-1} is in a final state, the inductive construction ends. Otherwise, let τ_i be the largest index in $[n]$ such that $\vec{S}_i|_{p_{\tau_i}} \neq \emptyset$, and $\tau_i = -1$ if no such index exists. We let

$$\ell = \begin{cases} \tau_i + 1 & \text{if } \tau_i = -1 \text{ or if } p_{\tau_i} \text{ is in a final state in } C_i\text{; and} \\ \tau_i & \text{otherwise.} \end{cases} \tag{3}$$

We obtain $\vec{S}_{i+1}$ from $\vec{S}_i$ by adding exactly one command cmd_{i+1} to the *bottom* of process p_ℓ's command stack; all other command stacks remain unchanged. I.e., $\vec{S}_{i+1}|_{p_\ell}$ is $\vec{S}_i|_{p_\ell}$ with cmd_{i+1} added at the bottom, and for all $k \in [n] - \{\ell\}$, $\vec{S}_{i+1}|_{p_k} = \vec{S}_i|_{p_k}$. There are several cases to determine cmd_{i+1}:

Case (E1): $\vec{S}_i|_{p_\ell} = \emptyset$ and there are $\lambda > 0$ distinct processes different from p_ℓ that access registers in $\mathcal{R}_{p_\ell}$ during E_i. Then $cmd_{i+1} = \mathit{wait\text{-}local\text{-}finish}(\lambda, \emptyset)$.

Case (E2): Either $\vec{S}_i|_{p_\ell} \neq \emptyset$ or no process different from p_ℓ accesses a register in $\mathcal{R}_{p_\ell}$ during E_i. We distinguish between two sub-cases.

Case (E2a): $next_{p_\ell}(C_i) \neq \texttt{fence()}$ or $WB_{p_\ell}(C_i) = \emptyset$. Then $cmd_{i+1} = \mathit{proceed}$.

Case (E2b): $next_{p_\ell}(C_i) = \texttt{fence()}$ and $WB_{p_\ell}(C_i) \neq \emptyset$. Let E_i^* be the prefix of E_i that ends when p_ℓ's command stack is empty for the first time, and E_i^{**} the postfix of $E(C_{init}; \vec{S}_i)$ such that $E_i = E(C_{init}; \vec{S}_i) = E^* \circ E^{**}$. (Lemma 5.1 (I6) below implies that E_i^* always exists.) Let γ be the number of distinct registers appearing in $WB_{p_\ell}(C_i)$, to which at least one process commits a write during E^{**}. Let ζ be the number of distinct processes that read during E^{**} at least one register that appears in $WB_{p_\ell}(C_i)$. Then

$$cmd_{i+1} = \begin{cases} \mathit{wait\text{-}hidden\text{-}commit}(\gamma) & \text{if } \gamma > 0; \\ \mathit{wait\text{-}read\text{-}finish}(\zeta, \emptyset) & \text{if } \gamma = 0 \text{ and } \zeta > 0\text{; and} \\ \mathit{commit} & \text{if } \gamma = \zeta = 0. \end{cases}$$

The next lemma summarizes several important structural properties of the stack sequences $\vec{S}_i$ and the corresponding executions E_i. Its proof, by induction, is omitted due to space restrictions.

LEMMA 5.1. *The following properties hold:*

(I1) For all $k \in [n]$, $\vec{S}_i|_{p_k} = \emptyset$ if and only if $k > \tau_i$.

(I2) For all $k \in [n]$, in system configuration C_i process p_k is in a final state if $k < \tau_i$, it is in its initial state if $k > \tau_i$, and if p_k is in a final state, then the value of that state is k.

(I3) $E(C_{init}; \vec{S}_i)|_{[n]-\{p_{\tau_i}\}} = E(C_{init}; \vec{S}_{i-1})|_{[n]-\{p_{\tau_i}\}}$, if $i \geq 1$.

(I4) For all $r \in [n]$, each stack $\vec{S}_i|_{p_r}$ contains at most one $\mathit{wait\text{-}local\text{-}finish}()$ command, and only at the top of the stack.

(I5) Suppose $\vec{S}_i|_{p_r} \neq \emptyset$, $r \in [n]$. Then $\vec{S}_i|_{p_r}$ contains a $\mathit{wait\text{-}local\text{-}finish}(\lambda)$ command if and only if there are exactly

λ *processes in* $\{p_1, \ldots, p_{r-1}\}$, *that access registers in* $\mathcal{R}_{p_r}$ *during* $E(C_i; \vec{S}_i)$.

(I6) *Execution* $E(C_{init}; \vec{S}_i)$ *is finite and when it ends,* p_{τ_i}*'s command stack is empty.*

(I7) *For each* $k \in [n]$, $E_i|_{\{p_0,\ldots,p_k\}} = E(C_{init}; \vec{S}_i^{(k)})$, *where* $\vec{S}_i^{(k)} = (\vec{S}_i|_{p_0}, \ldots, \vec{S}_i|_{p_k}, \emptyset, \ldots, \emptyset)$. *In particular,* $E_i|_{\{p_0,\ldots,p_k\}}$ *is permissible starting from* C_{init}.

(I8) *If the bottom element of* $\vec{S}_i|_{p_{\tau_i}}$ *is* $\textit{wait-read-finish}(\zeta, \emptyset)$ *for some* $\zeta \in \mathbb{N}$, *and* $(C_i^{\emptyset}; \vec{S}_i^{\emptyset})$ *is the extended configuration reached, when* p_{τ_i}*'s stack is empty for the first time during* $E(C_{init}; \vec{S}_i)$, *then* $next_{p_{\tau_i}}(C_i^{\emptyset}) = \texttt{fence()}$, $WB_{p_{\tau_i}}(C_i^{\emptyset}) \neq \emptyset$, *and throughout* $E(C_i^{\emptyset}; \vec{S}_i^{\emptyset})$ *no process other than* p_{τ_i} *accesses a register that appears in* $WB_{p_{\tau_i}}(C_i^{\emptyset})$.

(I9) *If the bottom element of* $\vec{S}_i|_{p_{\tau_i}}$ *is* $\textit{wait-hidden-commit}(\gamma)$, $\gamma \in \mathbb{N}$, *and* $(C_i^{\emptyset}; \vec{S}_i^{\emptyset})$ *is the extended configuration reached, when* p_{τ_i}*'s stack is empty for the first time during* $E(C_{init}; \vec{S}_i)$, *then* $next_{p_{\tau_i}}(C_i^{\emptyset}) = \texttt{fence()}$ *and throughout* $E(C_i^{\emptyset}; \vec{S}_i^{\emptyset})$ *no process other than* p_{τ_i} *commits a write to a register that appears in* $WB_{p_{\tau_i}}(C_i^{\emptyset})$.

(I10) *If stack* $\vec{S}_i$ *contains a command cmd right below a* *wait-read-finish*() *command, then cmd = commit; if cmd is right below a wait-hidden-commit() command, then cmd is either a wait-read-finish(), proceed, or commit command; and if cmd is right below a commit command, then cmd is a proceed command.*

Property (I7) implies that in execution E_i processes $p_0, \ldots, p_k$ are not influenced by the steps made by processes $p_{k+1}, \ldots, p_{n-1}$. This is central for establishing all other properties. Properties (I4) and (I10) imply that the number of *proceed* commands on p's stack is proportional to the number of fence steps p executes.

We conclude this section with a simple claim that will be useful for the proof of our main theorem, in Section 5.3. The proof of the claim is omitted due to space restrictions.

CLAIM 5.2. *In configuration* C_i *all processes* $p_0, \ldots, p_{\ell-1}$ *are in a final state, process* p_ℓ *is not in a final state, and* $p_{\ell+1}, \ldots, p_{n-1}$ *are in their initial states. In particular,* $WB_{p_k}(C_i) = \emptyset$ *for all* $k \in [n] - \{\ell\}$.

5.3 Proof of Theorem 4.2

In this section, we prove the lower bound stated in Theorem 4.2. For the ease of notation, whenever we refer to one of the statements (I1)-(I10), we mean the corresponding statement of Lemma 5.1.

We will show that for each permutation $\pi = (p_0, \ldots, p_{n-1})$ the inductive construction of stacks $\vec{S}_0^\pi, \vec{S}_1^\pi, \ldots$ ends eventually, i.e., there exists an $m_\pi \in \mathbb{N}$ such that in $E(C_{init}; \vec{S}_{m_\pi}^\pi)$ all processes enter a final state. From (I2), in that execution each process p_k, $k \in [n]$, enters a final state with value k. Hence, $\vec{S}_{m_\pi}^\pi$ uniquely encodes permutation π, and thus there exists a permutation π so that we need at least $\Omega(n \log n)$ bits to encode all stacks of $\vec{S}_{m_\pi}^\pi$. In this section, we show how the number of commands of $\vec{S}_{m_\pi}^\pi$ and the sum of their parameter values, and thus the shortest encoding of $\vec{S}_{m_\pi}^\pi$, yields a lower bound for the total number of remote and fence steps executed during $E(C_{init}; \vec{S}_{m_\pi}^\pi)$.

For a stack S, let $|S|$ denote the number of elements in S. For now, we consider only an arbitrary fixed permutation $\pi = (p_0, \ldots, p_{n-1})$ over $[n]$. For $i = 0, 1, \ldots$ let $\vec{S}_i$ be the stack sequence constructed as described at the beginning of Section 5.2 for this permutation. Further, as before let $E_i = E(C_{init}; \vec{S}_i)$.

Consider a non-empty command stack $\vec{S}_i|_p$, and let cmd be a command on the stack. Note that if cmd is a $\textit{wait-local-finish}(k, Q)$ or $\textit{wait-read-finish}(k, Q)$ command, then $Q = \emptyset$ (see cases (E1) and (E2b) in the construction).

We assign each command cmd on $\vec{S}_i|_p$ a *value* val(cmd). Each of the commands *proceed* and *commit* have value 1. For $k \in \mathbb{N}$, each of the commands $\textit{wait-hidden-commit}(k)$, $\textit{wait-local-finish}(k, \emptyset)$, and $\textit{wait-read-finish}(k, \emptyset)$ has value k. The value of command stack $\vec{S}_i|_p$, val($\vec{S}_i|_p$), is the sum of values of its commands.

In the following sections, we relate the values of commands on the stacks of $\vec{S}_i$, as well as the sizes of the stacks, to the number of remote steps executed during E_i. In Section 5.3.1, we show that the sum of values of *wait-read-finish*() commands on $\vec{S}_i$ is bounded asymptotically by the number of remote steps in E_i. In Section 5.3.2, we show the same for the sum of values of *wait-hidden-commit*() and *wait-local-finish*() commands. Thus, by averaging over these three types of commands, we obtain that the sum of values of commands is bounded within a constant factor of the number of remote steps. In Section 5.3.3, we show that the sum of stack sizes, and thus the total number of commands, is bounded asymptotically by the number of `fence` steps. These results yield Theorem 4.2, as we discuss in Section 5.3.4.

5.3.1 Analysis of Wait-Read-Finish() Commands

The aim of this section is to bound from below the number of remote steps of the final execution E_{m_π} constructed for permutation π by the sum of values of *wait-read-finish*() commands on the stacks of $\vec{S}_{m_\pi}^\pi$. The following lemma summarizes this bound.

LEMMA 5.3. *Suppose in* $E_j = E(C_{init}; \vec{S}_j)$ *all participating processes enter a final state. Let* V *be the sum of values of* *wait-read-finish*() *commands on stacks of* $\vec{S}_j$. *Then* E_j *contains at least* $\lceil V/2 \rceil$ *remote steps.*

To prove this lemma, we use an amortized analysis, in which we charge remote read steps of some processes to other processes. The rest of this section is devoted to the proof of this lemma. We first start with a simple observation, which follows immediately from (I4) and (I5) and the fact that p_ℓ must execute a write step to add some element to its write-buffer.

OBSERVATION 5.4. *During any execution* $E(C_{init}; \vec{S}_i)$, *after process* p_ℓ *has executed its first step, no process* p_b, $b < \ell$, *accesses any register in* $\mathcal{R}_{p_\ell}$. *In particular no process* p_b, $b < \ell$, *accesses a register* $R \in \mathcal{R}_{p_\ell}$ *after* p_ℓ *has added* R *to its write-buffer for the first time.*

In the following, let τ_j be defined as in Section 5.2, i.e., it is the largest index in $[n]$ such that $\vec{S}_j|_{p_{\tau_j}} \neq \emptyset$, and $\tau_j = -1$ if no such index exists.

CLAIM 5.5. *If during* $E(C_{init}; \vec{S}_j)$ *an extended configuration* $(C; \vec{S})$ *is reached, such that as a result of the last step leading to* $(C; \vec{S})$ *a* $\textit{wait-read-finish}(\zeta, \emptyset)$ *command cmd appears on top of* p_{τ_j}*'s stack, then for all* $b < \tau_j$ *and all* $R \in WB_{p_{\tau_j}}(C)$,

(a) *process* p_b *commits no write to* R *during* $E(C; \vec{S})$*; and*

(b) *process* p_b *does not read* R *during* $E(C; \vec{S})$ *after the point in which cmd was popped from the top of* p_{τ_j}*'s stack without being pushed back to it.*

PROOF. Let $i < j$ be the index such that $\vec{S}_{i+1}$ is constructed from $\vec{S}_i$ by adding the command $cmd_{i+1} = \mathit{wait\text{-}read\text{-}finish}(\zeta, \emptyset)$ to the bottom of $\vec{S}_i|_{p_\ell}$. Let $\ell = \tau_i$ and note that $\ell = \tau_j$. Since cmd_{i+1} is a $\mathit{wait\text{-}read\text{-}finish}()$ command, Encoding Rule (E2b) was applied to construct $\vec{S}_{i+1}$ (with $\gamma = 0$). In particular, if $(X; \vec{T})$ is the extended configuration reached during $E(C_{init}; \vec{S}_i)$, when p_ℓ's stack is empty for the first time, then

$$\text{throughout } E(X;\vec{T}) \text{ no process } p_b, b < \ell \text{ commits a write to a register that appears in } WB_{p_\ell}(X). \quad (4)$$

Since $S_j|_{p_\ell}$ is equal to S_i but with additional commands added on the bottom of the stack (i.e., below cmd_i), and all other stacks are identical in S_j and S_i, executions $E(C_{init}; \vec{S}_j)$ and $E(C_{init}; \vec{S}_i)$ are identical up to the point when p_ℓ's stack becomes empty in $E(C_{init}; \vec{S}_i)$, which is the point in $E(C_{init}; \vec{S}_j)$ when cmd_{i+1} becomes the top element of p_ℓ's stack. Thus, both executions have a common prefix D, such that $E(C_{init}; \vec{S}_j) = D \circ E(C; \vec{S})$ and $E(C_{init}; \vec{S}_i) = D \circ E(X; \vec{T})$. In particular, $X = C$, and thus $WB_{p_\ell}(C) = WB_{p_\ell}(X)$. Moreover, by (I3) $E(C; \vec{S})|_{[n]-\{p_\ell\}} = E(X; \vec{T})|_{[n]-\{p_\ell\}}$, so Part (a) of the claim follows from (4)

For Part (b) note that with the same arguments as above, $E(C_{init}; \vec{S}_{i+1})$ and $E(C_{init}; \vec{S}_j)$ have a common prefix D' such that $E(C_{init}; \vec{S}_{i+1}) = D' \circ E(C^{\emptyset}_{i+1}; \vec{S}^{\emptyset}_{i+1})$, where $(C^{\emptyset}_{i+1}; \vec{S}^{\emptyset}_{i+1})$ is the extended configuration reached when p_ℓ's stack is empty for the first time. Then D is a prefix of D' that ends when system configuration X is reached. By the decoding rules, p_ℓ takes no steps while a $\mathit{wait\text{-}read\text{-}finish}()$ command is on top of its stack, and $\mathit{wait\text{-}read\text{-}finish}()$ commands can only be replaced by other $\mathit{wait\text{-}read\text{-}finish}()$ commands or removed. Hence, in $E(C_{init}; \vec{S}_{i+1})$, p_ℓ takes no steps between the point when configuration X and when configuartion $C^{\emptyset}_{i+1}$ is reached, and so in both system configurations p_ℓ's state is the same. In particular $WB_{p_\ell}(C^{\emptyset}_{i+1}) = WB_{p_\ell}(X) = WB_{p_\ell}(C)$. By (I8), process p_b, $b < \ell$, does not access a register $R \in WB_{p_\ell}(C)$ throughout $E(C_{init}; \vec{S}_{i+1})$ after the prefix D', and by (I7) the same is true in $E(C_{init}; \vec{S}_j)$. □

To prove Lemma 5.3, we charge read steps of some processes to the processes whose stacks contain $\mathit{wait\text{-}read\text{-}finish}()$ commands.

Let Γ be some extended configuration. We say that the pair $(p_b, R) \in [n] \times \mathcal{R}$ is *charged to* process p_ℓ in $E(\Gamma)$, if $R \notin \mathcal{R}_{p_b}$, p_b reads register R during $E(\Gamma)$ at some point t, it does not read it again after point t, and $\ell > b$ is the smallest index such that at point t R appears in p_ℓ's write buffer. Clearly, every pair (p_b, R) can only be charged to one process.

For any execution E, let $\mathit{Write}_p(E)$ denote the set of registers on which p executes write steps during E, i.e., registers that p adds to its write-buffer at some point during E.

CLAIM 5.6. *Suppose* $\vec{S}_j|_{p_\ell}$, $\ell \in [n]$, *contains* K $\mathit{wait\text{-}read\text{-}finish}()$ *commands* $\omega_1, \ldots, \omega_K$. *Then in* $E_j = E(C_{init}; \vec{S}_j)$ *there are at least*

$$\mathrm{val}(\omega_1) + \cdots + \mathrm{val}(\omega_K) - |\mathit{Write}_{p_\ell}(E_j) - \mathcal{R}_{p_\ell}|$$

distinct process/register pairs charged to process p_ℓ.

PROOF. If $\vec{S}_j|_{p_\ell} = \emptyset$, then the claim is trivially true. Hence, assume that $\vec{S}_j|_{p_\ell} \neq \emptyset$.

Recall that $\vec{S}_{i+1}$ is obtained from $\vec{S}_i$ by adding an element to the bottom of the stack of process p_{τ_i}, and τ_i is non-decreasing. Let $j' \leq j$ be the largest index such that $\vec{S}_{j'}$ is obtained from $\vec{S}_{j'-1}$ by adding a command to (the bottom of) p_ℓ's stack. Then $\ell = \tau_{j'}$. Moreover, $\vec{S}_{j'}|_{p_s} = \vec{S}_j|_{p_s}$ for $s \leq \ell$ and by (I1) $\vec{S}_{j'}|_{p_s} = \emptyset$ for $s > \ell$. Hence, $\vec{S}_{j'}|_{p_\ell}$ contains also exactly the $\mathit{wait\text{-}read\text{-}finish}()$ commands $\omega_1, \ldots, \omega_K$, and since by (I7) (applied to $\vec{S}_j$), $E(C; \vec{S}_{j'})|_{\{p_1,\ldots,p_\ell\}} = E(C; \vec{S}_j)|_{\{p_1,\ldots,p_\ell\}}$, it suffices to prove the claim for $\vec{S}_{j'}$. For the ease of notation assume w.l.o.g. $j = j'$, i.e., $\ell = \tau_j$.

Assume w.l.o.g. that $\omega_1, \ldots, \omega_K$ appear in this order (from top to bottom) on $\vec{S}_j|_{p_\ell}$. Let t_k be the point in time during $E(C_{init}; \vec{S}_j)$ when ω_k, $k \in \{1, \ldots, K\}$, is on top of the stack for the first time, and let $(X_k; \vec{T}_k)$ be the extended configuration reached at that point. By (I6), at the end of $E(C_{init}; \vec{S}_j)$, p_ℓ's stack is empty, so at some point $t'_k > t_k$ the command that is initially below ω_k moves to the top or the stack becomes empty. (By Decoding Rule (D2d) in each step in which p_ℓ's stack has a $\mathit{wait\text{-}read\text{-}finish}()$ command on top, either the stack doesn't change, or the top command gets replaced by a different $\mathit{wait\text{-}read\text{-}finish}()$ command or is removed.) Note that by the deocoding rules process p_ℓ cannot execute any step as long as a $\mathit{wait\text{-}read\text{-}finish}()$ command is on top of its stack, so its write buffer remains $WB_{p_\ell}(X_k)$ throughout $[t_k, t'_k]$. Let W_k denote the set of registers appearing in $WB_{p_\ell}(X_k)$ throughout $[t_k, t'_k]$. Then

$$\bigcup_{1 \leq k \leq K} W_k \subseteq \mathit{Write}_{p_\ell}(E_j). \quad (5)$$

Recall that ω_k is a $\mathit{wait\text{-}read\text{-}finish}(\mathrm{val}(\omega_k), \emptyset)$ command. Let Q_k be the set of pairs $(q_a, R) \in [n] \times \mathcal{R}$, $a \neq \ell$, such that during $[t_k, t'_k]$ process q_a reads register R and R appears in $WB_{p_\ell}(X_k)$. Let $\mathit{Reg}(Q_k)$ denote the set of registers such that a pair $(\cdot, R)$ appears in Q_k. In the full version of the paper, we show that there are exactly $\mathrm{val}(\omega_k)$ processes, such that during $[t_k, t'_k]$ each of them reads a register in W_k and enters a final state during $[t_k, t'_k]$. Hence, $|Q_k| \geq \mathrm{val}(\omega_k)$.

For every register R there can be at most one pair $(q, R) \in Q_k$ such that $R \in \mathcal{R}_q$. Moreover, from Observation 5.4, we conclude that $R \notin \mathcal{R}_{p_\ell}$. Hence, we have

$$\left|\{(q_a, R) \in Q_k \mid R \notin \mathcal{R}_q\}\right| + |(W_k \cap \mathit{Reg}(Q_k)) - \mathcal{R}_{p_\ell}| \geq |Q_k| \geq \mathrm{val}(\omega_k). \quad (6)$$

Now note that if $R \in \mathit{Reg}(Q_k)$, then according to Claim 5.5 (b), no process p_b, $b < \ell$, accesses register R after t'_k . Hence, since time interval $[t_{k+1}, t'_{k+1}]$ starts only after $[t_k, t'_k]$ is finished $R \notin \mathit{Reg}(Q_{k'})$ for any $k' > k$. I.e., $\mathit{Reg}(Q_{k'}) \cap \mathit{Reg}(Q_k) = \emptyset$ for all $1 \leq k < k' \leq K$, and thus

$$\sum_{1 \leq k \leq K} |(W_k \cap \mathit{Reg}(Q_k)) - \mathcal{R}_{p_\ell}| = \left|\bigcup_{1 \leq k \leq K} ((W_k \cap \mathit{Reg}(Q_k)) - \mathcal{R}_{p_\ell})\right| \leq \left|\Big(\bigcup_{1 \leq k \leq K} W_k\Big) - \mathcal{R}_{p_\ell}\right| \leq |\mathit{Write}_{p_\ell}(E_j) - \mathcal{R}_{p_\ell}|.$$

Thus, (6) implies $\sum_{1 \leq k \leq K} \mathrm{val}(\omega_k) \leq |\mathit{Write}_{p_\ell}(E_j) - \mathcal{R}_{p_\ell}| + \sum_{1 \leq k \leq K} \left|\{(q_a, R) \in Q_k \mid R \notin \mathcal{R}_q\}\right|$.

Therefore, to complete the proof of the lemma, it suffices to show that every pair $(q_a, R) \in Q_k$, $R \notin \mathcal{R}_{q_a}$, is charged to p_ℓ. Since $(p_a, R) \in Q_k$, p_a reads a register $R \in W_k = WB_{p_\ell}(X_k)$ at some point in $[t_k, t'_k]$ during $E_j = E(C_{init}; \vec{S}_j)$. Let t be the last point in $[t_k, t'_k]$ at which p_a reads register R. Then at that point R is in p_ℓ's write-buffer. By Claim 5.5 (b) p_a does not read R after t'_k, so t is the last point at which p_a reads R throughout the entire execution E_j . Since the stacks of processes $p_{\ell+1}, \ldots, p_{n-1}$ are empty, none of them takes a step in this interval (as is the case for p_ℓ), and so $a < \ell$. Thus, if (p_a, R) is not charged to p_ℓ, then it must be charged to a different process p_b, where $a < b < \ell$. I.e., at point t during $E(C_{init}; \vec{S}_j)$ R is also in p_b's write-buffer. By Claim 5.2, p_b's write-buffer is empty in configuration C_j, which is reached at the end of execution $E(C_{init}; \vec{S}_j)$, so at some point $t' > t > t_k$ p_b commits a write to R. But since at point t_k register R appears in p_ℓ's write-buffer and ω_k is on top of its stack, this contradicts Claim 5.5 (a). □

We are now ready to prove Lemma 5.3.

PROOF OF LEMMA 5.3. Let Z_q denote the number of pairs (q, R) that are charged to processes, and let $Z = Z_0 + \cdots + Z_{n-1}$. Recall that if (q, R) is charged to some process, then by definition $R \notin \mathcal{R}_q$, and q reads register R at least once during E_j. Since the first (read or commit) access by q of a register in $\mathcal{R} - \mathcal{R}_q$ must be a remote step, q executes at least Z_q remote steps during E_j. Hence, Z is a lower bound for the total number of remote steps executed during E_j.

Let $W_q = |Write_q(E_j) - \mathcal{R}_q|$ and $W = W_0 + \cdots + W_{n-1}$. Recall that just before a process executes a return step, it must execute a final fence step. Hence, since q enters a final state during E_j, all its writes get committed during E_j. Since for every register $R \in \mathcal{R} - \mathcal{R}_q$ the first commit by q to R must be a remote commit, the total number of remote commit steps q executes during E_j is at least W_q, and so W is also a lower bound for the total number of remote steps executed during E_j.

By definition, every pair (q, R) can only be charged to one process, so by Claim 5.6 we have $Z + W \geq V$, and thus either $Z \geq \lceil V/2 \rceil$ or $W \geq \lceil V/2 \rceil$. □

5.3.2 *Analysis of Wait-Hidden-Commit() and Wait-Local-Finish() Commands*

We now show that the number of remote steps in execution E_j is bounded asymptotically from below by sum of values of *wait-hidden-commit*() and of *wait-local-finish*() commands used to encode E_j.

LEMMA 5.7. *Let $\vec{S}_j$ be a command stack sequence and let V_1 denote the sum of values of wait-hidden-commit() commands and V_2 the sum of values of wait-local-finish() commands. Then $E_j = E(C_{init}; \vec{S}_j)$ contains at least $\max\{V_1/2, V_2\}$ remote steps.*

To prove the lemma, we first consider commit steps executed by waiting processes and relate them to the sum of values of *wait-hidden-commit*() commands.

CLAIM 5.8. *Let Γ be an extended configuration, and suppose in some step s of $E(\Gamma)$ a waiting process p commits a write to some register R. Then after step s process p does not commit to R again, and no non-commit step gets executed until in some step a commit enabled process $q \neq p$ has committed a write to R.*

PROOF. Let $(C; \vec{S})$ be the extended configuration reached during $E(\Gamma)$ such that s is the first step of $E(C; \vec{S})$. Since p is waiting in $(C; \vec{S})$, by Decoding Rule (D1), there must be some other process $q \neq p$, that is commit enabled in $(C; \vec{S})$, and it contains a write to R in its write-buffer $WB_q(C)$. From the decoding rules it also follows that a commit enabled process will remain commit enabled until it committed all the writes in its write-buffer. By Decoding Rule (D1), as long as there is at least one commit enabled process in an extended configuration, the first step will always be a commit step. In particular, in $E(C; \vec{S})$ no process can execute any non-commit step before q has committed all its writes in $WB_q(C)$. It follows that all read, fence, write, or return steps of $E(C; \vec{S})$ must occur after q has committed to R. Moreover, since at any time p's write-buffer can contain only one write to each register, after executing step s p cannot commit to R again until it has added a new write $(R, \cdot)$ to its write-buffer in a write step, which, as argued above, cannot happen until q has committed its write to R. □

Let Γ be an extended configuration. Recall that a commit step s during $E(\Gamma)$ is *hidden* if s is executed by a waiting process. Every other commit step is called *visible*. Note that a commit step by p is hidden, if and only if the command cmd that is on top of p's stack when s gets executed is a *wait-hidden-commit*() command, and it is visible if and only if $cmd = commit$.

CLAIM 5.9. *Let p be a process and $R \in \mathcal{R} - \mathcal{R}_p$. In execution $E(C_{init}; \vec{S}_j)$ process p executes at least as many remote steps on R as it executes hidden commits on R.*

PROOF. Let $s_1, s_2, \ldots, s_k$ be the hidden commit steps on R that process p executes (in this order) during $E(C_{init}; \vec{S}_j)$. By Claim 5.8, any two hidden commit steps s_t, s_{t+1}, by p are separated by some visible commit step s^* of a process $q \neq p$. Hence, if s_{t+1} is not a remote commit by p, then p must have executed a remote commit to R after q's commit step s^* and before its own commit step s_{t+1}. Since in addition, the very first commit by p to R is remote, p executes at least k remote commit steps. □

CLAIM 5.10. *Let R be some register, and let h_R be the number of hidden commit steps on R executed during some execution $E(C_{init}; \vec{S}_j)$. Then the number of remote steps executed on R during that execution is at least $h_R/2$.*

PROOF. Let $h_{R,p}$ denote the number of hidden commits executed by process p on register R, and z the process for which $R \in \mathcal{R}_z$. By Claim 5.9, for each process $p \in [n] - \{z\}$ all $h_{R,p}$ hidden commits by p are remote steps.

By Claim 5.8, any hidden commit step by z on R is followed by a visible commit by a process $q \neq z$, which gets executed before z can execute any other hidden commit. Thus, each hidden commit by z is followed by a remote step on R. Hence, the execution contains at least $h_{R,z}$ remote steps on R.

Using the bound above for processes $p \neq z$, we obtain that the number of remote steps on R is at least $\max\left\{h_{R,z}, \sum_{p\in[n]-\{p\}} h_{R,p}\right\} \geq h_R/2$. □

PROOF OF LEMMA 5.7. By (I6), at the end of $E(C_{init}; \vec{S}_j)$ all command stacks are empty. Hence, it follows immediately from Decoding Rule (D1b) that the total number of hidden commit steps executed during that execution is at least V_1. Then by Claim 5.10, E_j contains at least $V_1/2$ hidden commit commands.

By (I4), each stack of $\vec{S}_j$ contains at most one *wait-local-finish*() command. If $\vec{S}_j|_p$ contains a *wait-local-finish*(γ_p) command, then by (I5) there are at least γ_p processes in $[n] - \{p\}$ that access registers in $\mathcal{R}_p$ during E_j. Since for each such process the first access of a register in $\mathcal{R}_p$ is a remote step, it follows that there are at last γ_p remote steps on registers in $\mathcal{R}_p$. Hence, by summing over all processes p, we obtain that E_j contains at least V_2 remote steps. □

5.3.3 *Fence Steps vs. Stack Size*

The following lemma states that the number of fence steps executed in an execution E_j is asymptotically at least as large as the number of elements on all stacks used to encode E_j.

LEMMA 5.11. *In execution $E(C_{init}; \vec{S}_j)$ process p_ℓ executes at least $\lceil(|S| - 1)/4\rceil - 3$ fence steps, where $S = \vec{S}_j|_{p_\ell}$.*

PROOF. By (I4) S contains at most one *wait-local-finish*() command. By (I10), below a *wait-read-finish*() command there can only be a *commit* command and below a *wait-hidden-commit*() command there can only be a *wait-read-finish*(), *proceed*, or *commit* command. Finally, also by (I10), below a *commit* command there can only be a *proceed* command. Hence, if we remove the single *wait-local-finish*() command, then among the remaining commands at least every fourth one must be *proceed*. I.e., S contains at least $\lceil(|S|-1)/4\rceil$ *proceed* commands. By (D2a), a *proceed* command on p_ℓ's stack can only be removed due to a step in which p_ℓ becomes poised to execute a `fence()` or `return()` operation, or in which it enters a final state. Clearly, throughout $E(C_{init}; \vec{S}_j)$ a *proceed* command can be removed at most once for the reason that p_ℓ becomes poised to execute a `return()` operation, and at most once for the reason that p_ℓ enters a final state. Hence, the claim follows from the fact that by (I6) p_ℓ's stack is empty at the end of $E(C_{init}; \vec{S}_j)$. □

5.3.4 Putting Things Together

Consider a permutation π and the command stack sequences $\vec{S}_0^\pi, \vec{S}_1^\pi, \ldots$, constructed in Section 5.2, for this permutation. Since $\vec{S}_0^\pi$ consists only of empty stacks, and in each step of the construction exactly one command is added to some stack, the stacks of $\vec{S}_i^\pi$ contain in total i commands. The iterative construction ends only when a command stack sequence $\vec{S}_{m_\pi}^\pi$ has been constructed such that during $E_{m_\pi}^\pi = E(C_{init}; \vec{S}_{m_\pi}^\pi)$, all processes enter a final state. If then construction does not end at all, then by Lemma 5.11 the execution has an unbounded number of fence steps. Hence, assume that the iterative construction ends with a command stack sequence $\vec{S}_{m_\pi}^\pi$, for every permutation π.

Let $v_1^\pi, v_2^\pi, \ldots, v_{m_\pi}^\pi$ be the values of the m_π commands on the n stacks of $\vec{S}_{m_\pi}^\pi$, and $v_\pi = v_1^\pi + \cdots + v_{m_\pi}^\pi$. Then we can encode $\vec{S}_{m_\pi}$ using at most

$$\log(v_1^\pi) + \cdots + \log(v_{m_\pi}^\pi) + O(m_\pi + n) \leq m_\pi \cdot \log(v_\pi/m_\pi) + O(m_\pi + n) \text{ bits.} \quad (7)$$

By (I2), if $\pi = (p_0, \ldots, p_{n-1})$, then during $E_m^\pi = E(C_{init}; \vec{S}_{m_\pi}^\pi)$ each process p_k, $k \in [n]$, enters a final state with value k. Therefore, the stack sequence $\vec{S}_{m_\pi}^\pi$ uniquely identifies permutation π. Since there are $n!$ permutations, we need on average $\Omega(n \log n)$ bits to encode each permutation. Hence, for at least one permutation π, we obtain from (7)

$$m_\pi \cdot \big(\log(v_\pi/m_\pi) + 1\big) = \Omega(n \log n).$$

Since there are in total m_π commands on all stacks of $\vec{S}_{m_\pi}$, we have from Lemma 5.11 that E_π contains $\Omega(m_\pi)$ fence steps. From Lemmas 5.3 and 5.7, and by averaging the sum of values of *wait-read-finish*(), *wait-hidden-commit*(), and *wait-local-finish*() commands, it follows that $\Omega(v_\pi)$ steps of E_π are remote steps. This completes the proof of Theorem 4.2.

6. SUMMARY

We proved an inherent tradeoff between the number of fences and the number of remote accesses that must be incurred in implementations of certain concurrent operations, e.g., on locks, counters and queues. The proof assumes a model in which each process has both a local segment of shared memory and a cache. Thus, Theorem 4.2 holds for both *cache-coherent* and *distributed shared-memory* architectures [6]. Following [9, 12], our lower bound applies also to algorithms that may use *comparison* primitives, such as CAS, in addition to reads and writes.

7. REFERENCES

[1] S. V. Adve and K. Gharachorloo. Shared memory consistency models: A tutorial. *IEEE Computer*, 29(12):66–76, 1996.

[2] D. Alistarh, J. Aspnes, S. Gilbert, and R. Guerraoui. The complexity of renaming. In *FOCS*, pages 718–727, 2011.

[3] J. Anderson and Y.-J. Kim. An improved lower bound for the time complexity of mutual exclusion. *Dist. Comp.*, 15(4):221–253, 2002.

[4] J. H. Anderson and Y.-J. Kim. Adaptive mutual exclusion with local spinning. In *DISC*, pages 29–43, 2000.

[5] J. H. Anderson and Y.-J. Kim. Nonatomic mutual exclusion with local spinning. In *PODC*, pages 3–12, 2002.

[6] J. H. Anderson, Y.-J. Kim, and T. Herman. Shared-memory mutual exclusion: major research trends since 1986. *Dist. Comp.*, 16(2-3):75–110, 2003.

[7] H. Attiya, R. Guerraoui, D. Hendler, P. Kuznetsov, M. M. Michael, and M. T. Vechev. Laws of order: expensive synchronization in concurrent algorithms cannot be eliminated. In *POPL*, pages 487–498, 2011.

[8] H. Attiya, D. Hendler, and S. Levy. An $O(1)$-barriers optimal RMRs mutual exclusion algorithm. In *PODC*, pages 220–229, 2013.

[9] H. Attiya, D. Hendler, and P. Woelfel. Tight RMR lower bounds for mutual exclusion and other problems. In *STOC*, pages 217–226, 2008.

[10] R. Danek and W. M. Golab. Closing the complexity gap between FCFS mutual exclusion and mutual exclusion. In *DISC*, pages 93–108, 2008.

[11] R. Fan and N. Lynch. An $\Omega(n \log n)$ lower bound on the cost of mutual exclusion. In *PODC*, pages 275–284, 2006.

[12] W. M. Golab, V. Hadzilacos, D. Hendler, and P. Woelfel. RMR-efficient implementations of comparison primitives using read and write operations. *Dist. Comp.*, 25(2):109–162, 2012.

[13] Intel Corporation. *Intel® 64 and IA-32 Architectures Software Developer's Manual.* Number 253669-033US. December 2009.

[14] P. Jayanti. Adaptive and efficient abortable mutual exclusion. In *PODC*, pages 295–304, 2003.

[15] P. Jayanti, S. Petrovic, and N. Narula. Read/write based fast-path transformation for FCFS mutual exclusion. In *SOFSEM*, pages 209–218, 2005.

[16] Y.-J. Kim and J. Anderson. A time complexity bound for adaptive mutual exclusion. In *DISC*, pages 1–15, 2001.

[17] L. Lamport. A new solution of Dijkstra's concurrent programming problem. *Comm. ACM*, 17(8):453–455, 1974.

[18] D. L.Weaver and T. Germond, editors. *The SPARC Architecture Manual.* Prentice Hall, 1994.

[19] P. E. McKenney. Memory ordering in modern microprocessors, part I. *Linux Journal*, 2005(136):2, 2005.

[20] P. E. McKenney. Memory barriers: a hardware view for software hackers. *Linux Tech. Center, IBM Beaverton*, 2010.

[21] S. Park and D. L. Dill. An executable specification and verifier for relaxed memory order. *IEEE Transactions on Computers*, 48(2):227 –235, 1999.

[22] G. L. Peterson and M. J. Fischer. Economical solutions for the critical section problem in a distributed system. In *STOC*, pages 91–97, 1977.

[23] J.-H. Yang and J. Anderson. A fast, scalable mutual exclusion algorithm. *Dist. Comp.*, 9(1):51–60, 1995.

The Price of being Adaptive*

[Extended Abstract]

Ohad Ben-Baruch
Department of Computer-Science
Ben-Gurion University of the Negev
Be'er Sheva, Israel
bbohad@gmail.com

Danny Hendler
Department of Computer-Science
Ben-Gurion University of the Negev
Be'er Sheva, Israel
hendlerd@cs.bgu.ac.il

ABSTRACT

Mutual exclusion is a fundamental distributed coordination problem. Shared-memory mutual exclusion research focuses on *local-spin* algorithms and uses the *remote memory references* (RMRs) metric. To ensure the correctness of concurrent algorithms in general, and mutual exclusion algorithms in particular, it is often required to prohibit certain re-orderings of memory instructions that may compromise correctness, by inserting *memory fence* (a.k.a. *memory barrier*) instructions. Memory fences incur non-negligible overhead and may significantly increase time complexity.

A mutual exclusion algorithm is *adaptive to total contention* (or simply adaptive), if the time complexity of every passage (an entry to the critical section and the corresponding exit) is a function of *total contention*, that is, the number of processes, k, that participate in the execution in which that passage is performed. We say that an algorithm A is *f-adaptive* (and that f is an *adaptivity function* of A), if the time complexity of every passage in A is $O(f(k))$. Adaptive implementations are desirable when contention is much smaller than the total number of processes, n, sharing the implementation.

Recent work [5] presented the first read/write mutual exclusion algorithm with asymptotically optimal complexity under both the RMRs and fences metrics: each passage through the critical section incurs O(log n) RMRs and a constant number of fences. The algorithm works in the popular Total Store Ordering (TSO) model. The algorithm of [5] is non-adaptive, however, and they posed the question of whether there exists an adaptive mutual exclusion algorithm with the same complexities.

We provide a negative answer to this question, thus capturing an inherent cost of adaptivity. In fact, we prove a stronger result: adaptive read/write mutual exclusion algorithms with constant fence complexity do not exist, regardless of their RMR complexity. This result follows from a general tradeoff that we establish for such algorithms, between the fence complexity and the growth rate of adaptivity functions. Specifically, we prove that the fence complexity of any such algorithm with a linear (or sub-linear) adaptivity function is $\Omega(\log\log n)$. The tradeoff holds for implementations that may use compare-and-swap operations, in addition to reads and writes.

We show that our results apply also to obstruction-free implementations of well-known objects, such as counters, stacks and queues.

Categories and Subject Descriptors

D.1.3 [**Programming Techniques**]: Concurrent Programming—*Parallel programming*; D.2.8 [**Analysis of Algorithms and Problem Complexity**]: Tradeoffs between Complexity Measures; F.1.3 [**Complexity Measures and Classes**]: Relations among complexity measures

General Terms

Theory, Performance

Keywords

Mutual exclusion; shared-memory; lower bounds; total store ordering; time complexity; remote memory reference (RMR)

1. INTRODUCTION

In the *mutual exclusion* problem, a set of processes must coordinate their accesses to a *critical section* (CS) so that, at any point in time, at most a single process is inside the CS. Introduced by Dijkstra in 1965 [9], the mutual exclusion problem is a fundamental Distributed Computing problem and is still the focus of intense research [2, 23].

For more than 20 years, shared-memory mutual exclusion research has investigated the *remote memory references* (RMR) complexity of local-spin mutual exclusion algorithms; much of this work focuses on (deterministic) read/write mutual exclusion (e.g. [8, 14, 15, 17, 25]). Anderson and Yang were the first to present an n-process mutual exclusion algorithm, where every *passage* (an entry to the critical section and the corresponding exit) incurs $O(\log n)$ RMRs. This is optimal [7].

A mutual exclusion algorithm A is adaptive, if its RMR complexity is a function of the number of active processes.

*Partially supported by the Israel Science Foundation (grants 1227/10, 1749/14) and by the Lynne and William Frankel Center for Computing Science at Ben-Gurion University.

Permission to make digital or hard copies of all or part of this work for personal or classroom use is granted without fee provided that copies are not made or distributed for profit or commercial advantage and that copies bear this notice and the full citation on the first page. Copyrights for components of this work owned by others than ACM must be honored. Abstracting with credit is permitted. To copy otherwise, or republish, to post on servers or to redistribute to lists, requires prior specific permission and/or a fee. Request permissions from permissions@acm.org.
PODC'15, July 21–23, 2015, Donostia-San Sebastián, Spain.
Copyright is held by the owner/author(s). Publication rights licensed to ACM.
ACM 978-1-4503-3617-8 /15/07 ...$15.00.
DOI: http://dx.doi.org/10.1145/2767386.2767428.

More formally, an algorithm is *f-adaptive to total contention* (henceforth simply *adaptive*), if the RMR complexity of every passage is $O(f(k))$, where k denotes *total contention*, that is, the number of processes that participate in the execution. It is *f-adaptive to interval contention* (respectively, *point contention*) if the RMR complexity of every passage $\mathcal{P}$ is $O(f(k))$, where k is the number of processes that are active during $\mathcal{P}$ (respectively, the maximum number of processes that are concurrently active at some point in time during $\mathcal{P}$). We call f the *adaptivity function* of A. Adaptive algorithms are desirable when the number of active processes is often significantly smaller than n, the total number of processes.

Mutual exclusion algorithms are almost always designed under the assumption that memory accesses are atomic, i.e. linearizable [12], or at least sequentially consistent [18]. In practice, however, modern compilers optimize code so as to issue certain instructions out of order, based on the memory model supported by the architecture.

The memory model dictates which operation pairs can be reordered [1, Figure 8]. For example, the widely-supported *total store ordering* (*TSO*) model [19] ensures that writes are not reordered, but it is possible to perform a read from address a before a write to address $b \neq a$ that is earlier in program order is performed.

The TSO model is supported by several common architectures, including SPARC [19] and x86 [13].[1] It is weaker than sequential consistency, and hence, also weaker than linearizability.

To ensure the correctness of a concurrent algorithm, it is possible to prohibit the reordering of memory instructions, by inserting a *fence* (also called a *barrier*) instruction between them. The use of fences was shown to be unavoidable for read/write mutual exclusion algorithms [3].

Since memory fences incur significant overhead, the number of fence instructions incurred by each passage of an algorithm (henceforth called its *fence complexity*) is a significant contributor to its time complexity, alongside the algorithm's RMR complexity.

Recent work by Attiya, Hendler and Levy [5] presented the first TSO mutual exclusion algorithm that is optimal in terms of both its RMR and fence complexities: each passage incurs a logarithmic number of RMRs and a constant number of fences. Their algorithm is not adaptive, however, and they posed the question of whether an adaptive TSO mutual exclusion algorithm with the same RMR and fence complexities exists. This is the question that we address in this work.

Our Contributions

We provide a negative answer to the question posed by [5]. In fact, we prove a stronger result: read/write mutual exclusion algorithms with constant fence complexity cannot be adaptive to total (hence also to interval- or point-) contention. This impossibility result holds regardless of the RMR complexity of the algorithm.

Our result follows from a general tradeoff that we establish between the fence complexity and the growth rate of adaptivity functions. Specifically, we prove that the fence complexity of any read/write algorithm with a linear (or sub-linear) adaptivity function is $\Omega(\log \log n)$. Our results apply for both the cache-coherent (CC) and the distributed shared-memory (DSM) models.

Following [5, 10], our tradeoff applies also to algorithms that may use *comparison* primitives, such as *compare-and-swap* (CAS), in addition to reads and writes. We show that our results also hold for obstruction-free [11] implementations of well-known objects, such as counters, stacks and queues.

Our results establish a time complexity separation between adaptive and non-adaptive implementations, thus capturing an inherent cost incurred by adaptive algorithms in the TSO model.

The rest of this paper is organized as follows. The model we use and required definitions are provided in Section 2. An overview of our proofs is presented in Section 3. The paper is concluded with a short discussion in Section 4.

2. MODEL AND DEFINITIONS

We assume the standard asynchronous shared memory model [12], in which a set of processes P communicate by applying operations to a set of shared variables V, each of which is assigned an initial value. We consider both the *cache-coherent* (CC) and the *distributed shared-memory* (DSM) computation models [2].

In the DSM model, each processor owns a segment of shared memory that can be locally accessed without traversing the processor-to-memory interconnect. Thus, every variable is permanently *local* to a single processor and *remote* to all others.[2] An access of a remote variable is an RMR.

In the CC model, all variables are remote to all processes. Each processor maintains copies of shared variables inside its private cache, whose consistency is ensured by a coherence protocol. Our results apply to both the *write-through* and *write-back* [22] CC coherence protocols. An access made by a process in a CC system is an RMR, if the corresponding cache does not contain an up-to-date copy of the variable.

Our model assumes that each variable is permanently local to *at most* a single process (and remote to all others) and thus applies to both DSM and CC systems. For variable v, we denote by $owner(v)$ the process to which v is local. We write $owner(v) = \perp$ if v is remote to all processes.

A primitive *operation* α is a read or write by some $p \in P$ issued to a variable $v \in V$. The operation α includes the value read or written. We write $\alpha = read(v)$ ($write(v)$) if α is a read (write) operation issued to variable v. Following [17], we define an *event* e as a sequence of primitive operations by some process p, such that *at most one operation is issued to a remote variable of* p. The remote variable accessed in e (if any) and the type of operation applied to it (read/write) is determined before any shared variable is accessed by e, that is, it depends only on p's internal state when e starts. We denote by $op(e) = read(v)$ ($write(v)$) the operation to the remote variable issued in e; we write $op(e) = \perp$ if there is no such operation in e. We say that e is a *read (write) event* if $op(e) = read(v)$ ($write(v)$) for some variable v. Later we extend the definition of an event by defining new types of special events.

An *execution fragment* is a (finite or infinite) sequence of events. An *execution* is an execution fragment that starts

[1] Owens, Sarkar and Sewell [20] prove Intel x86 is equivalent to Sparc TSO.

[2] For simplicity and without loss of generality, we assume that each of the processes participating in the algorithms we consider runs on a unique processor.

from the initial configuration, resulting when processes apply operations to the implemented object as they execute their algorithm. If a process has not completed its operation, it has exactly one enabled event, which is the next event it will execute, as specified by the algorithm it is using. We consider finite execution fragments, unless otherwise specified. For execution fragments E and F, the execution fragment EF denotes the concatenation of E and F. For execution E, we say that F is an *extension* of E if EF is an execution.

TOTAL STORE ORDERING (TSO)

We now present an operational model for the behavior of a shared-memory system with relaxed memory ordering, which is a simplified version of the model used by Park and Dill [21].

A set of n processes, $p_1, \ldots, p_n$, each with its own abstract *write buffer*, execute read and write memory operations in the order specified by their algorithm, called *program order*. Write operations may be delayed and executed after read operations following them in program order. This is modeled by having write operations go to the write buffer rather than directly to shared memory.

A *configuration* describes the state of a system: It contains the local state of each process, including its location in its algorithm and the contents of its write buffer. It also contains the value of each shared variable. In the *initial configuration*, all processes are in their initial state and their write buffers are empty; all shared variables hold their initial values.

In each step, a scheduling adversary picks a process and then decides whether to let it execute another event according to its algorithm or to *commit* the first write operation in its write buffer (if any). In the latter case, the write is committed by changing the value of the respective shared variable to the parameter of the write and the write *becomes visible*. The write operation is *committed* at this step.

What happens when a process p issues an event depends on the type of the event. A *fence* event e forces the adversary to commit all the writes in p's write buffer (if any) in the order they were issued. That is, whenever the adversary schedules p, it commits the next write from p's write buffer, as long as the buffer is not empty. We say that process p *completes fence e in execution E* if all the writes that were in p's write buffer when e was issued by p were committed in E.

Otherwise, event e is a sequence of operations. An operation is executed according to its type:

1. A write operation is placed at the write buffer. If there is already a write operation to this variable in p's write buffer, then the older write in the write buffer is replaced with the new one; otherwise, the write is placed at the end of the write buffer. The write operation is *issued* at this event.

2. A read operation returns the value of the variable, and the process changes its local state accordingly. If there is a write to this variable in the write buffer, the value is read from that write; otherwise, the value of the variable is read from shared memory. The read operation is *issued* at this event.

Let E be an execution fragment. For a set of processes Y, we denote by E^{-Y} the execution fragment obtained from E by removing all the events issued by processes in Y, and we say that the processes of Y are *erased* from E. We write $p = writer(v, E)$, and say that p is *visible* on v after E, if p is the last process to commit a write to v in E, and $writer(v, E) = \perp$ if there exists no such p. We say that an event $e \in E$ *accesses* a variable v if e is an event by process p that either commits a write to v or issues a read to v, and there is no copy of v in p's write buffer when e is executed (hence e accesses shared memory). We say that process p *accesses* variable v in E if there is an event by p in E that accesses v. We denote by $Accessed(v, E)$ the set of processes that accessed v in E. For event $e \in E$, e is a *remote event* in E if e accesses a remote variable, and a *local event* otherwise. Notice that whether an event e is considered remote depends on the execution containing the event.

We now capture the extent by which processes are aware of the participation of other processes in an execution. We do so by adapting a definition used for this purpose by [4].

DEFINITION 1. *We say that p is* aware *of q after E if either $p = q$ or if there is an event $e \in E$ by p that reads a shared memory variable v such that one of the following holds:*

1. *the last process to commit write to v before e is q;*

2. *the last process to commit write to v before e is r, and r is aware of q at the time it issued that write.*

The awareness-set *of p after E, denoted by $AW(p, E)$, is the set of processes that p is aware of after E.*

Intuitively, a process p is aware of the participation of another process q in an execution if there is (either direct or indirect) information flow from q to p in that execution via shared memory. For simplicity and without loss of generality, we assume that different write events write different values.

Mutual Exclusion Systems

Each process p has a private variable $section_p$ that represents which section in the mutual exclusion algorithm p is currently in. $section_p$ is initially ncs, indicating that p is in the non-critical section. Each process p has three special events which only p may execute, called transition events:

1. $Enter_p$ causes p to transit from its non-critical section to its entry section and sets $section_p = entry$. This event is enabled if and only if $section_p = ncs$.

2. CS_p causes p to transit from its entry section to its exit section and updates $section_p = exit$. (For notational simplicity and WLOG we assume that the execution of the critical section is instantaneous.) This event is enabled only if $section_p = entry$.

3. $Exit_p$ causes p to transit from its exit section to its non-critical section and updates $section_p = ncs$. This event is enabled only if $section_p = exit$.

For execution E and process p, we let $status(p, E)$ denote the value of $section_p$ after E. A mutual exclusion system is required to satisfy the following properties:

Exclusion For any execution E, if both CS_p and CS_q are extensions of E, then $p = q$.

Progress Given an execution E, let $X = \{q \in P | status(q, E) \neq ncs\}$. If $X = \{p\}$, then there exists a solo extension F by p such that $EFExit_p$ is an execution.

The exclusion property prevents multiple critical-section events from being simultaneously enabled. If two events CS_p and CS_q are simultaneously enabled after an execution E, then mutual exclusion may be violated. The exclusion property states that such a situation does not arise. The progress property we use was defined in [7] and is called *weak obstruction-freedom.* It is implied by deadlock-freedom and obstruction-freedom [11], although it is strictly weaker than both. In particular, it permits livelock. This weaker progress condition is sufficient for our purposes.

Next, we define the notion of a *critical event* and explain the relationship between a critical event and an RMR in different cache-coherence protocols.

Definition 2. *Let $E = E_1 e E_2$ be an execution fragment, where e is an event by process p. We say that e is a* critical event *in E if one of the following holds:*

critical read: *e is a remote read of v and this is the first remote read of v by p (i.e., E_1 does not contains a remote read to v by p).*

critical write: *e is a remote write to v such that $writer(v, E_1) \neq p$ (i.e., e is the first remote write of v by p in E, or e overwrites a value written to v by another process).*

In the DSM model, each critical event accesses a remote variable, thus generating an RMR. In the CC model with a write-through protocol, writes always generate an RMR. In the CC model with a write-back protocol, if $writer(v, E_1) = q \neq p$ then v is stored in the local cache of q, thus p must invalidate or update the cached copy of v, generating an RMR. It follows that in both the write-through and write-back protocols, a critical write and a critical read that is the first access of v by p are both RMRs.

A first write followed by a first read are two critical events, but the read does not necessarily generate a cache miss. Nevertheless, since the first write is always an RMR, at least half of all critical events are RMRs. Consequently, if A is f-adaptive then each process may encounter at most $2f(k)$ critical events during a single passage, where k is total contention. We may therefore assume for simplicity that $f(k)$ bounds the number of critical events incurred by a process during a single passage.

3. PROOF OVERVIEW

Here we provide a detailed overview of our proofs. Complete proofs are provided in the full paper.

We fix an N-process f-adaptive mutual exclusion system $\mathcal{A}$. Our goal is to construct an execution in which there is a process that executes "many" fences while attempting to gain access to the critical section. The number of fences will be a function of f. We first present the definition of an *invisible-set*, a key notion in the constructing of this execution.

Given an execution E, we define two sets of processes. *Active processes*, denoted by $Act(E)$, is the set of processes that start a passage in E and are yet to complete it. Informally, an active process is a process in its entry section, trying to enter its critical section. *Finished processes*, denoted by $Fin(E)$, is the set of processes that completed a passage in E.

Definition 3. *Let E be an execution and INV be a set of processes such that $INV \subseteq Act(E)$. We say that INV is an* invisible set *(IN-set), and we call a process in INV an invisible process, if the following conditions hold:*

IN1: $\forall p \in P: \quad AW(p, E) \cap INV \subseteq \{p\}$
Informally, no process is aware of any invisible process other than itself.

IN2: $\forall p \in INV: \quad status(p, E) = entry.$
informally, all invisible processes are in the entry section.

IN3: *$\forall Y \subseteq INV$, and for any $e \in E^{-Y}$: e is a critical event in E^{-Y} if and only if e is a critical event in E. Informally, erasing invisible processes does not affect the criticality of remaining events.*

IN4: *For event $e \in E$ by process $p \in INV$, if p accesses a remote variable v in e then $owner(v) \notin Act(E)$. Informally, if a process p accesses a remote variable v local to some process q, then q is not an active process.*

IN5: *$\forall v \in V$: If $|Accessed(v, E) \cap Act(E)| > 1$ then $writer(v, E) \notin INV$. Informally, if variable v has been accessed by more than a single active process, then v was not last written by an invisible process.*

IN1 ensures that no process is aware of any invisible process (other than itself). This property allows us to erase from the execution we construct any invisible process, that is, to remove its events from the execution.

IN2 ensures that all invisible processes are in their entry section, trying to gain access to the critical section.

IN3 ensures that erasing invisible processes does not affect the number of critical events executed so far by processes that remain active.

IN4 ensures that no process can become aware of an invisible process by reading a variable local to it.

Let p be an invisible process that is visible on some variable v. IN5 ensures that if we need to erase p from the execution, no other invisible process becomes visible on v. Note that any subset of an IN-set is itself an IN-set.

In Section 3.1, we describe in detail the execution we construct. Before that, we present a few technical lemmas that are required for arguing about its properties.

Lemma 1. *Let E be an execution and let $p \in P$ be a process such that $p \notin AW(q, E)$ for any $q \neq p$. Then E^{-p} is an execution.*

IN1 ensures that no process is aware of any invisible process. Hence, if E is an execution and p is an invisible process, Lemma 1 ensures us that when we erase the events of p from E we obtain a legal execution.

The following lemma considers executions obtained by erasing the events of a set of invisible processes. It establishes that processes whose events are not erased remain in the invisible set.

Lemma 2. *Let E be an execution, $INV \subseteq P$ be an IN-set of E, and $Y \subseteq INV$. Then the following hold:*

- *E^{-Y} is an execution.*

- *Each $p \in Act(E^{-Y})$ executes the same critical events in E^{-Y} and in E.*
- *$INV \setminus Y$ is an IN-set of E^{-Y}.*

PROOF. We prove the lemma for the case $Y = \{p\}$, a singleton. The general case is easily proven by induction. From Lemma 1, E^{-p} is an execution, establishing the first property. By IN3, an event in E^{-p} is critical if and only if it is critical in E. Since each $q \in Act(E^{-p})$ executes the same events in E and in E^{-p}, it executes the same critical events in both executions, and the second property follows. We now prove that $INV \setminus \{p\}$ is an IN-set of E^{-p}:

IN1: IN1 clearly holds for p, as it does not participate in E^{-p}. Consider $q \neq p$. Since q executes the same events in E and in E^{-p}, we have $AW(q, E) = AW(q, E^{-p})$. By IN1, $AW(q, E) \cap INV \subseteq \{q\}$ and, in particular, $AW(q, E^{-p}) \cap (INV \setminus \{p\}) \subseteq \{q\}$, implying that IN1 holds for q in E^{-p}.

IN2: Every $q \in INV \setminus \{p\}$ executes the same events in E and E^{-p}, thus $status(q, E^{-p}) = status(q, E) = entry$.

IN3: Consider $Z \subseteq INV \setminus \{p\}$ and $e \in (E^{-p})^{-Z} = E^{-Z \cup \{p\}}$. Note that e is an event also in E and in E^{-p}. $Z, \{p\} \subseteq INV$ and INV is an IN-set of E. Therefore, it follows from IN3 applied to E that e is a critical event in $E^{-Z \cup \{p\}}$ if and only if e is a critical event in E. This proves IN3, since e is a critical event in E if and only if it is a critical event in E^{-p}.

IN4: Consider an event $e \in E^{-p}$ by a process q accessing a remote variable v. By IN4, $owner(v) \notin Act(E)$, hence $owner(v) \notin Act(E^{-p}) \subseteq Act(E)$.

IN5: Assume $|Accessed(v, E^{-p}) \cap Act(E^{-p})| > 1$ for some v. Since $Act(E^{-p}) \subseteq Act(E)$, we get $|Accessed(v, E) \cap Act(E)| > 1$ and, by IN5 applied to E, $writer(v, E) \notin INV$. The only events removed are by $p \in INV$, thus $writer(v, E^{-p}) = writer(v, E) \notin INV$ and, in particular, $writer(v, E^{-p}) \notin INV \setminus \{p\}$. □

Our proof constructs executions in which all active processes are in the invisible set. A useful property of invisible sets is the ability to extend an execution with non-critical events without affecting the set. Consider a process p in the invisible set of an execution E and consider any variable v. If v is local to p, IN4 ensures that no other process accessed v in E. If v is remote to p, IN5 ensure that if p already accessed v, then either p is the only active process that has accessed it, or that the last process to commit a write to v is not in the set. In any of these cases, accessing v does not cause any information flow that may violate any of the conditions IN1-IN5. This property is established by the following lemma.

LEMMA 3. *Let E be an execution and let $INV \subseteq P$ be an IN-set of E. Also, let F be an extension of E such that F contains no critical or transition events in EF. Then INV is an IN-set of EF.*

PROOF. We prove the claim for the case $F = f$, a singleton. The general case is easily proven by induction.

Let $p \in Act(E)$ be the process that executes f. Note that $Act(Ef) = Act(E)$, as f is not a transition event. If f is a fence or local event, then f does not access any remote variable and no process changes its state. By IN4, no process except p accesses any of p's local variables in E. Thus, as f does not access any remote variable, none of conditions IN1-IN5 is violated and INV is an IN-set of Ef as well.

Assume, then, that f is a remote event and let v be the remote variable accessed in f. As f is not critical in Ef, f is not the first event by p to access v, that is, p accesses v in E.

IN1: For any $p' \neq p$ we have $AW(p', Ef) = AW(p', E)$, thus IN1 holds for p' in Ef as well. Let $q = writer(v, E)$. If $q \in INV$ then, by IN5, $p = q$, otherwise both p and q access v in E, thus $writer(v, E) \notin INV$, in contradiction. Since $p = writer(v, E)$, accessing v does not change p's awareness-set.

If $q \notin INV$ then, by IN1, $AW(q, E) \cap INV = \emptyset$, thus p cannot become aware of any invisible process by accessing v. Altogether, p cannot become aware of any invisible process when executing e, that is, $AW(p, Ef) \cap INV \subseteq \{p\}$ and IN1 holds for p in Ef.

IN2: Since f is not a transition event, we have $\forall q \in INV$: $status(q, Ef) = status(q, E) = entry$.

IN3: Consider $Y \subseteq INV$. As IN3 holds for E, it is sufficient to prove that it also holds for f. Assume $f \in (Ef)^{-Y}$, implying that $p \notin Y$. In this case, p executes the same events in Ef and in $(Ef)^{-Y}$.

If f is a remote read, then f is not the first remote read by p to v in Ef and thus also not in $(Ef)^{-Y}$. Hence, f is non-critical in both.

If f commits a write to v, then $writer(v, E) = p$. It follows that $writer(v, E^{-Y}) = writer(v, E) = p$ and f is non-critical in both Ef and $(Ef)^{-Y}$.

IN4: IN4 holds in E and $Act(E) = Act(Ef)$, thus it holds for any variable $u \neq v$ in F. The only remote variable accessed in f is v. Since p accessed v in E, we get from IN4 applied to E: $owner(v) \notin Act(E) = Act(Ef)$.

IN5: IN5 holds in E, thus it holds for any variable not accessed in f. By IN4, no invisible process other than p accesses p's local variables in Ef, thus IN5 holds for p's local variables as well.

If f is a remote read of v, then $writer(v, Ef) = writer(v, E)$ and IN5 holds for v in Ef as well.

Otherwise, f commits a non-critical write to v, hence $writer(v, Ef) = writer(v, E) = p$. We have $writer(v, Ef) = writer(v, E)$ and $Accessed(v, Ef) = Accessed(v, E)$, since p accesses v in E. Since IN5 holds for v in E, IN5 holds for v in Ef as well. □

The following theorem, due to Turán [24], is required for proving the properties of our construction.

THEOREM 1 (TURÁN). *Let $\mathcal{G} = (V, E)$ be an undirected graph, with vertex set V and edge set E. If the average degree of $\mathcal{G}$ is d, then an independent set exists with at least $\lceil |V|/(d+1) \rceil$ vertices.*

3.1 Execution Construction

Our construction starts with an execution H_0 where every process p executes the $Enter_p$ event only. We then inductively construct longer and longer executions. In execution H_i, exactly i processes have completed a passage through the CS and all active processes have completed exactly i fences and issued exactly l_i critical steps, for some $l_i \leq f(i)$. Our goal is to extend the execution so that as many processes as possible perform an additional fence.

The TSO model allows to delay issuing writes until a fence is performed. These writes may be preceded by reads that follow them in program order. This makes it possible to construct executions in which reads always precede writes in-between fences. In turn, this execution structure allows us to restrict the knowledge gained by processes in-between fences and to retain a sufficiently large IN-set. Technically, the inductive construction of execution H_{i+1} from H_i is composed of a *read phase*, a *write phase*, and a *regularization phase* (see Figure 1).

We say that an execution is "regular", if all its active processes are invisible. All the executions H_i that we construct are regular. However, as we soon explain, regularity may be violated in the course of the write phase and only a weaker condition of *semi-regularity* is guaranteed to be satisfied during this phase. The write phase is followed by a regularization phase that restores the stronger condition. These notions are formalized by the following definition.

DEFINITION 4. *An execution E is* regular *if $Act(E)$ is an IN-set of E. If $Act(E)$ satisfies properties IN1-IN4 in E, we say that E is a* semi-regular *execution.*

Read phase:

In the read phase, we iteratively extend the execution by allowing active processes to preform additional critical reads. Starting with regular execution $G_0 = H_i$, we construct executions $G_1, G_2, \ldots, G_s$. We prove that executions G_k, for $k \in \{0, \ldots s\}$, satisfy the following conditions:

(1) G_k is a regular execution;

(2) Each $p \in Act(G_k)$ executes $l_i + k$ critical events in G_k.

(3) Each $p \in Act(G_k)$ completes i fences and does not yet issue its $(i+1)$'th fence event in G_k.

(4) $Fin(G_k) = Fin(H_i)$.

(5) $|Act(G_k)| \geq (|Act(G_{k-1})| - 1)/10$.

For $k > 0$, G_k is an extension of G_{k-1} in which all active processes (except for, possibly, a single process that may finish its entry section) run until they are about to execute either a fence or a critical read. In order to obtain such extension, we let each active process, in turn, run until it is about to execute its next critical or fence event. Lemma 3 ensures that the resulting execution is a regular execution.

If at least half of the active processes are about to execute a fence, then we erase the rest of the active processes. We then obtain an execution J_0 by letting each of the remaining active processes execute its fence instruction. In this case, the read phase ends and a write phase begins.

Otherwise, we consider the set of active processes that are about to execute a critical read. In order to eliminate information flow, we may need to erase a constant fraction of the active processes so that regularity is maintained. We do so by constructing a conflict graph.

The vertices of the conflict graph are the active processes. An active process p that executes a critical read may become aware of another active process q by either reading one of q's local variables (thus violating IN4) or by reading a variable last written by q (thus violating IN1). In both cases, we add an edge $\{p, q\}$ to the conflict graph. Thus, each process may introduce at most two new edges to the graph, hence the average degree of the graph is at most 4.

By Theorem 1, we can find an independent set of size at least $INV/5$. We construct G_k by erasing all the active processes except those in the independent set and then allowing the remaining processes to execute their reads (interleaved in an arbitrary order).

A key point in arguing about the properties of our construction is to bound from above the number of iterations, s, required before all remaining active processes are about to issue their next fence event.

Informally, this is done by using the following argument. Active processes are unaware of each other and may only become aware of finished processes. Consequently, the number of critical reads each of them may execute is bounded from above by a function of $i = |Fin(G_k)| = |Fin(H_i)|$. This follows from the fact that processes are allowed at most $f(i)$ critical events, since the algorithm is f-adaptive.

Therefore, if a sufficient number of processes start the read phase, eventually a large subset of processes cannot execute additional reads and must commit their writes by executing a fence. The following claim states the exact bound.

CLAIM 1. *The number of executions constructed during the read phase, s, is bounded from above by $f(i+1) - \ell_i$.*

Proof sketch: Assume towards a contradiction that the construction proceeds for k iterations, where $\ell_i + k > f(i+1)$. Erasing all the active processes from G_k except for a single process, p, yields an execution G in which at most $i+1$ processes (those in $Fin(G_k) \cup p$) participate, and in which p executes $\ell_i + k > f(i+1)$ critical events in the course of a single passage. This is a contradiction.

Write phase:

The write phase determines the order in which writes, issued by active processes since their previous fence was completed (or since they began their execution), are committed. We iteratively extend the execution by allowing active processes to preform additional critical writes.

Starting with J_0, we iteratively construct executions $J_1, J_2, \ldots, J_t$. We prove that each of the executions $J_0, \ldots, J_t$ satisfies the following conditions:

(1) J_k is a semi-regular execution, in which multiple writes by active processes to the same variable (if any) are scheduled in increasing order of process ID.

(2) Each $p \in Act(J_k)$ executes $l_i + s + k$ critical events in J_k.

(3) Each $p \in Act(J_k)$ completes i fences and does not yet complete its $(i+1)$'th fence in J_k.

(4) $Fin(J_k) = Fin(H_i)$.

(5) $|Act(J_k)| \geq \sqrt{|Act(J_{k-1})|}/4(l_i + s + k)$.

For $k > 0$, J_k is an extension of J_{k-1} in which we let each process run until it either completes its fence or it is about to perform another critical write.

If at least half of the processes complete their fence, we erase the rest of the active processes, constructing an execution L_0 in which all active processes have completed $i+1$ fences. In this case, the write phase ends and a regularization phase begins.

Otherwise, we consider the set of active processes that are about to perform another critical write. We proceed in one of two ways, according to where processes are about to write to.

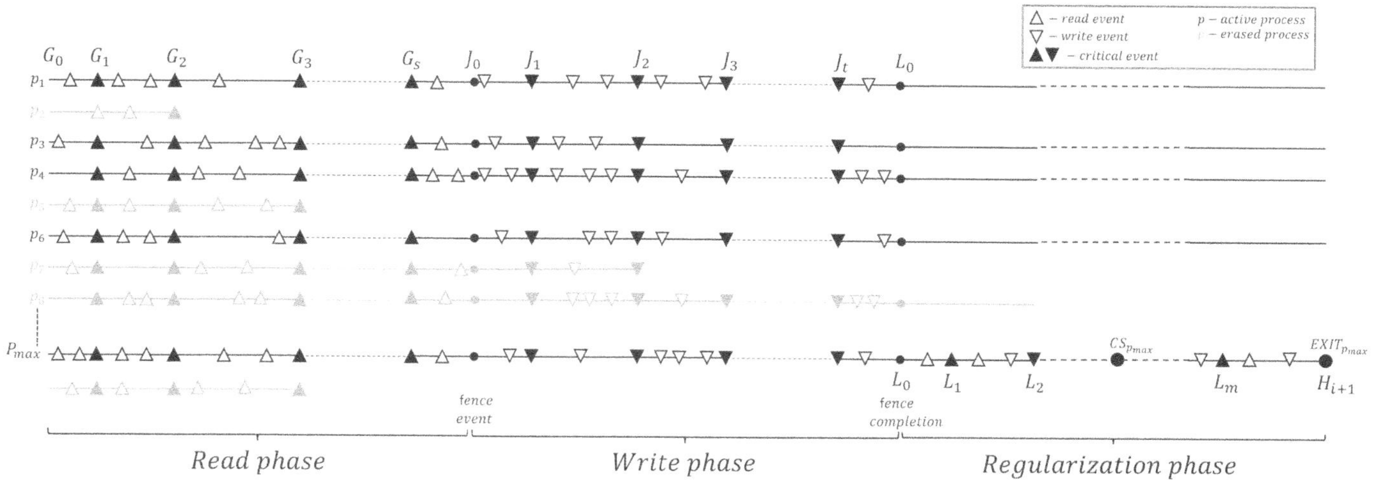

Figure 1: Structure of inductive construction. Gray-colored lines show events executed by erased processes.

In the *low-contention case*, at least $\sqrt{|Act(J_{k-1})|/2}$ of the processes are about to commit writes to different variables. In this case, we retain a single process per each such variable v and erase all other processes accessing v.

We also eliminate future information flow by erasing a fraction of the retained processes. The size of this fraction is a function of the number of critical events each process executed so far. Using the same technique as in the read phase, we build a conflict graph. Its vertices are the active processes. Note that processes do not gain new information in the course of a write phase, since they only commit writes (thus no violation of IN1 can occur).

An active processes p may conflict with another active process q if either p writes to one of q's local variables (violating IN4), or if p writes to a variable that has been accessed by q (violating IN5). In any of these cases, we add an edge $\{p, q\}$ to the conflict graph.

Each process accesses at most $\ell_i+s+k-1$ different remote variables in the course of J_{k-1}, thus each process presents at most ℓ_i+s+k new edges to the conflict graph. Consequently, the average degree of the graph is bounded from above by $2(\ell_i + s + k)$.

From Theorem 1, there exists an independent set of size at least $\sqrt{|Act(J_{k-1})|/2}/\left(2(\ell_i+s+k)+1\right)$. We obtain execution J_k by erasing all the active processes except for those in the independent set and by then allowing remaining processes to execute their critical writes (in an arbitrary order).

In the *high-contention case*, there is a variable v such that at least $\sqrt{|Act(J_{k-1})|/2}$ processes are about to commit their writes to v. In this case, we construct J_k by erasing the rest of the processes and by then allowing the remaining processes to commit their writes to v in an increasing order of their IDs. The process with the highest ID is visible on v in J_k.

Our construction of write phases is similar to a construction by Kim and Anderson [17], but unlike it, we consider fence complexity in addition to RMR complexity. Moreover, in our construction unlike in [17], writes committed during the same write phase are scheduled such that the process with the highest ID is visible on *all* high-contention variables, if any; this is guaranteed by the second part of Condition (1) above and is essential for obtaining our tradeoff.

Technically, this implies that some intermediate executions constructed during the write phase are allowed to be semi-regular but not regular: they violate invariant IN5 of Definition 3, since the last writer of high-contention variables is only allowed to finish its passage at the end of the phase. Ensuring the regularity of these intermediate executions would have required a large subset of processes to finish their passage (one per every high-contention write), which would weaken our complexity tradeoff.

Using the same argumentation as for the read phase, if a sufficient number of active processes start the phase, eventually a sufficiently large subset of these processes complete another fence and the write phase terminates.

Claim 2. *The number of executions constructed during the read and write phases is bounded from above by $f(i+1) - \ell_i$. In other words: $\ell_i + s + t \leq f(i+1)$.*

Regularization phase:

The regularization phase transforms the semi-regular (and possibly not regular) execution constructed by the write phase, L_0, into a regular execution. This is done by letting the active process with the largest ID, denoted p_{max}, finish its passage. Since p_{max} is visible on all the high-contention variables of the write-phase (if any), $Act(J_t) \setminus p_{max}$ is an IN-set.

Starting with L_0, we construct executions $L_1, L_2, \ldots, L_m$, H_{i+1}. We prove that each of the executions $L_0, \ldots, L_m$ satisfies the following conditions:

(1) $Act(L_k)$ can be written as $W_k \cup \{p_{max}\}$ ($p_{max} \notin W_k$).

(2) W_k is an IN-set of L_k.

(3) p_{max} executes $l_i + s + t + k$ critical events in L_k.

(4) Each $p \in W_k$ executes $l_i + s + t$ critical events in L_k.

(5) Each $p \in W_k$ completes $i + 1$ fences in L_k and does not yet issue its $(i + 2)$'nd fence event.

(6) $Fin(L_k) = Fin(H_i)$.

(7) $|Act(L_k)| \geq |Act(L_{k-1})| - 1$.

For $k \in \{1, \ldots, m\}$, we construct L_k from L_{k-1} by letting p_{max} run until it either terminates or until it is about to execute a critical event e. By Lemma 3, W_{k-1} is an IN-set of the resulting execution. In the latter case, in order to prevent information flow, we may need to erase the active process that owns the remote variable accessed by e or the process that is the last to have committed a write to it (there is at most a single such process).

All the active processes except p_{max} form an IN-set of the resulting execution, thus p_{max} is not aware of any other active process in executions L_k, for $0 \leq k \leq m$. Consequently, the number of critical events p_{max} may execute is a function of i, thus the number of intermediate executions constructed in the course of the regularization phase, m, is bounded from above, and eventually p_{max} finishes its passage. The resulting execution, denoted H_{i+1}, is regular, and each active process finishes $i+1$ fences in it. This completes the inductive step of our construction.

CLAIM 3. *The number of executions constructed during the regularization phase is bounded from above by $f(i+1)$. In other words, $m < f(i+1)$.*

Proof sketch: The proof is similar to the proof of Claim 1. We assume for contradiction that the construction can proceed for $k \geq f(i+1)$ iterations, producing execution L_k. By erasing all the active processes but p_{max} we get an execution in which at most $i+1$ processes take steps, in which p_{max} executes $\ell_i + s + t + k > f(i+1)$ critical events. This is a contradiction.

We now prove a lower bound on the size of the active processes set for the executions in our construction. As long as the lower bound guarantees that the active set is non-empty, the construction may proceed.

THEOREM 2. *Let $i \in \mathbb{N}$ be such that $f(i) \leq \frac{N^{2^{-f(i)}}}{f(i)! \cdot 4^{f(i)+2i}}$. Then the following lower bound holds:*

$$|Act(H_i)| \geq \frac{N^{2^{-\ell_i}}}{\ell_i! \cdot 4^{\ell_i+2i}}$$

Proof sketch: The theorem is proved by induction on i. The base case $i = 0$ is trivial, as $|Act(H_0)| = N$. From induction hypothesis, we have:

$$|Act(H_i)| = |Act(G_0)| \geq \frac{N^{2^{-\ell_i}}}{\ell_i! \cdot 4^{\ell_i+2i}}$$

We now prove the claim for $i+1$. The induction step follows the phases of the construction. Note that we retain at least half of the processes when constructing J_0 from G_s, and L_0 from J_t. By the inequalities of condition (5) of the read and write phases construction:

$$|Act(G_k)| \geq \frac{|Act(G_{k-1})| - 1}{10}, \quad |Act(J_k)| \geq \frac{\sqrt{|Act(J_{k-1})|}}{4(\ell_i + s + k)}$$

The following lower bound is easy to derive using the above two inequalities inductively:

$$|Act(L_0)| \geq \frac{N^{2^{-(\ell_i+s+t)}}}{(\ell_i + s + t)! \cdot 4^{(\ell_i+s+t)+2i+1}}$$

Let $\ell_{i+1} = \ell_i + s + t$. Using the inequality $|Act(L_k)| \geq |Act(L_{k-1})| - 1$ inductively, and since $|Act(H_{i+1})| = |Act(L_m)| - 1$, we get:

$$|Act(H_{i+1})| \geq \frac{N^{2^{-\ell_{i+1}}}}{\ell_{i+1}! \cdot 4^{\ell_{i+1}+2i+1}} - (m+1). \quad (1)$$

From Claim 3 and from our assumption: $m + 1 \leq f(i+1) \leq \frac{N^{2^{-f(i+1)}}}{f(i+1)! \cdot 4^{f(i+1)+2(i+1)}}$. By Claim 2, $\ell_{i+1} \leq f(i+1)$, thus we may replace $f(i+1)$ with ℓ_{i+1} to get:

$$m + 1 \leq \frac{1}{4} \cdot \frac{N^{2^{-\ell_{i+1}}}}{\ell_{i+1}! \cdot 4^{\ell_{i+1}+2i+1}}. \quad (2)$$

Using Inequalities 1-2, we obtain the required result:

$$|Act(H_{i+1})| \geq \frac{N^{2^{-\ell_{i+1}}}}{\ell_{i+1}! \cdot 4^{\ell_{i+1}+2(i+1)}}.$$

In the appendix, we show that a weak obstruction-free mutual exclusion lock can be easily implemented from a weak obstruction-free implementation of either one of the following objects: counter, stack, or queue. Moreover, the implementation is such that any passage through the CS invokes a single operation on the respective object (*fetch&increment*, *dequeue*, or *pop*) and has the same asymptotic RMR and fence complexities. We get:

THEOREM 3. *Let $\mathcal{A}$ be an N-process weak obstruction-free f-adaptive implementation of a mutual-exclusion lock, counter, stack or queue, and let $i \in \mathbb{N}$ be such that $f(i) \leq \frac{N^{2^{-f(i)}}}{f(i)! \cdot 4^{f(i)+2i}}$. Then there exists an execution H with total contention $i+1$ and a process p such that p executes i fences in H during a single passage of its CS (respectively, in the course of performing a fetch&increment, dequeue, or pop operation).*

Theorem 1 follows from Theorem 2, as under the conditions specified by the theorem the construction can proceed for i steps, yielding an execution H_i such that $Act(H_i) \geq 1$. Therefore there is an active process p after H_i, and from the properties of H_i, p is in a middle of a passage in H_i in which it completed i fences.

Moreover, by erasing all active processes but p from H_i we obtain an execution H in which p executes i fences in the course of a single passage, and the total contention of H is $i+1$, that is the number of fences p executes is linear in the total contention of the execution.

COROLLARY 1. *There exists no weak obstruction-free implementation of an adaptive mutual exclusion lock, counter, stack or queue with $O(1)$ fence complexity.*

PROOF. Assume towards a contradiction that there exists such an f-adaptive algorithm $\mathcal{A}$, for some function f, such that no process executes c or more fences during a single passage/operation, for some constant c. We choose large enough N such that $f(c) \leq \frac{N^{2^{-f(c)}}}{f(c)! \cdot 4^{f(c)+2c}}$. By Theorem 3, there exists an execution H and a process p such that p executes c fences in H during a single passage/operation, contradicting our assumption. □

Kim and Anderson prove that a sub-linear adaptivity function is impossible [17]. We now present a lower bound on the fence complexity of the family of algorithms whose adaptivity function is linear.

COROLLARY 2. *Let $\mathcal{A}$ be an N-process f-adaptive implementation of a mutual-exclusion lock, counter, stack or queue, such that f is a linear function, that is $f(i) = c \cdot i$ for some constant c. Then the fence complexity of $\mathcal{A}$ is $\Omega(\log\log N)$.*

PROOF. By Theorem 3, it suffices to prove that, for $i = \Omega(\log\log N)$, the inequality $f(i) \leq \frac{N^{2^{-f(i)}}}{f(i)! \cdot 4^{f(i)+2i}}$ holds, thus there exists an execution E and a process p that executes $i = \Omega(\log\log N)$ fences during a single passage/operation in E.

$$\begin{aligned} c\cdot i\cdot(c\cdot i)!\cdot 4^{c\cdot i+2i} &\leq N^{2^{-c\cdot i}} \\ \log(c\cdot i\cdot(c\cdot i)!\cdot 4^{c\cdot i+2i}) &\leq 2^{-c\cdot i}\cdot\log N \\ \log\log(c\cdot i\cdot(c\cdot i)!\cdot 4^{c\cdot i+2i}) &\leq -c\cdot i+\log\log N \\ \log\log(c\cdot i\cdot(c\cdot i)!\cdot 4^{c\cdot i+2i})+c\cdot i &\leq \log\log N. \end{aligned}$$

$\Rightarrow \log\log(c\cdot i\cdot(c\cdot i)!\cdot 4^{c\cdot i+2i})+c\cdot i \leq \log\log((c\cdot i)^{2\cdot c\cdot i})+c\cdot i = \log(2\cdot c\cdot i)+\log\log(c\cdot i)+c\cdot i \leq 3\cdot c\cdot i$. It follows that the inequality holds for $i = \frac{1}{3c}\log\log N = \Omega(\log\log N)$ and the claim follows. □

The following corollary can be proven in a similar manner.

COROLLARY 3. *Let $\mathcal{A}$ be an N-process f-adaptive implementation of a mutual-exclusion lock, counter, stack or queue, such that f is an exponential function, that is $f(i) = 2^{c\cdot i}$ for some constant c. Then the fence complexity of $\mathcal{A}$ is $\Omega(\log\log\log N)$.*

4. DISCUSSION

We establish a time complexity separation between adaptive and non-adaptive implementations of mutual-exclusion locks, counters, stacks and queues, thus capturing an inherent cost incurred by adaptive algorithms in the TSO model.

This separation follows from a tradeoff that we prove between fence complexity and the growth rate of adaptivity functions. Specifically, we prove that the fence complexity of any read/write n-process algorithm with a linear (or sub-linear) adaptivity function is $\Omega(\log\log n)$. Our results apply for both the cache-coherent (CC) and the distributed shared-memory (DSM) models.

A corollary of our tradeoff is that constant fence-complexity adaptive implementations for these objects do not exist. Moreover, the impossibility result holds regardless of the RMR complexity of the algorithm. Following [5, 10], our tradeoff applies also to algorithms that may use comparison primitives, such as *compare-and-swap* (CAS), in addition to reads and writes.

Kim and Anderson presented an adaptive mutual exclusion algorithm whose RMR complexity is $O(min(k,\log n))$, where k is point contention [16], hence it is f-adaptive for a linear f. The fence complexity of their algorithm is logarithmic. However, our tradeoff only implies $\log\log n$ fence complexity (see Corollary 2). Finding the tight tradeoff between fence complexity and the adaptivity function growth rate is an interesting research direction.

The memory model considered by this work is TSO. We remind the reader that TSO ensures that writes are not reordered, but it is possible to perform a read from address a before a write to address $b \neq a$ that is earlier in program order is performed. The *partial store ordering* (PSO) model, supported by older SPARC, is weaker than TSO, as it also allows the reordering of writes to different locations.

Recent work by Attiya, Hendler and Woelfel [6] showed that one cannot win on both the fence and RMR complexities of read/write PSO algorithms for many fundamental objects, including locks, counters and queues. They proved the following lower bound: let f and r respectively denote the numbers of fences and RMRs performed in an operation on such an object, then

$$f \cdot \log\frac{r}{f} + 1 \in \Omega(\log n). \tag{3}$$

They also showed that the bound is tight.

Attiya et al. [5] presented a TSO read/write mutual exclusion algorithm where each passage incurs a logarithmic number of RMRs and a constant number of fences. Inequality 3 establishes a complexity separation between the TSO and PSO models, since it follows from it that no such algorithm exists for the PSO model. Another interesting research direction is to find a tight tradeoff between the RMR-complexity and fence-complexity of adaptive PSO algorithms.

5. REFERENCES

[1] S. V. Adve and K. Gharachorloo. Shared memory consistency models: A tutorial. *computer*, 29(12):66–76, 1996.

[2] J. H. Anderson, Y. Kim, and T. Herman. Shared-memory mutual exclusion: major research trends since 1986. *Distributed Computing*, 16(2-3):75–110, 2003.

[3] H. Attiya, R. Guerraoui, D. Hendler, P. Kuznetsov, M. M. Michael, and M. T. Vechev. Laws of order: expensive synchronization in concurrent algorithms cannot be eliminated. In *POPL*, pages 487–498, 2011.

[4] H. Attiya and D. Hendler. Time and space lower bounds for implementations using -cas. In *In DISC*, pages 169–183, 2005.

[5] H. Attiya, D. Hendler, and S. Levy. An o(1)-barriers optimal rmrs mutual exclusion algorithm: extended abstract. In *ACM Symposium on Principles of Distributed Computing, PODC '13, Montreal, QC, Canada, July 22-24, 2013*, pages 220–229, 2013.

[6] H. Attiya, D. Hendler, and P. Woelfel. *To appear in ACM Symposium on Principles of Distributed Computing, PODC*.

[7] H. Attiya, D. Hendler, and P. Woelfel. Tight RMR lower bounds for mutual exclusion and other problems. In *STOC*, pages 217–226, 2008.

[8] R. Danek and W. M. Golab. Closing the complexity gap between FCFS mutual exclusion and mutual exclusion. In *DISC*, pages 93–108, 2008.

[9] E. W. Dijkstra. Solution of a problem in concurrent programming control. *Communications of the ACM*, 8(9):569, September 1965.

[10] W. M. Golab, V. Hadzilacos, D. Hendler, and P. Woelfel. Rmr-efficient implementations of comparison primitives using read and write operations. *Distributed Computing*, 25(2):109–162, 2012.

[11] M. Herlihy, V. Luchangco, and M. Moir. Obstruction-free synchronization: Double-ended queues as an example. In *Proceedings of the 23rd IEEE International Conference on Distributed Computing Systems (ICDCS'03)*, pages 522–529, 2003.

[12] M. Herlihy and J. M. Wing. Linearizability: a correctness condition for concurrent objects. *ACM Trans. Prog. Lang. Syst.*, 12(3):463–492, June 1990.

[13] Intel Corporation. *Intel® 64 and IA-32 Architectures Software Developer's Manual.* December 2009.

[14] P. Jayanti. Adaptive and efficient abortable mutual exclusion. In *PODC*, pages 295–304, New York, NY, USA, 2003. ACM Press.

[15] P. Jayanti, S. Petrovic, and N. Narula. Read/write based fast-path transformation for FCFS mutual exclusion. In *SOFSEM*, pages 209–218, 2005.

[16] Y. Kim and J. H. Anderson. Adaptive mutual exclusion with local spinning. *Distributed Computing*, 19(3):197–236, 2007.

[17] Y. Kim and J. H. Anderson. A time complexity lower bound for adaptive mutual exclusion. *Distributed Computing*, 24(6):271–297, 2012.

[18] L. Lamport. How to make a correct multiprocess program execute correctly on a multiprocessor. *IEEE Trans. Computers*, 46(7):779–782, 1997.

[19] D. L.Weaver and T. Germond. *The SPARC Architecture Manual.* Prentice Hall, 1994.

[20] S. Owens, S. Sarkar, and P. Sewell. A better x86 memory model: x86-tso. In *Theorem Proving in Higher Order Logics, 22nd International Conference, TPHOLs 2009, Munich, Germany, August 17-20, 2009. Proceedings*, pages 391–407, 2009.

[21] S. Park and D. L. Dill. An executable specification and verifier for relaxed memory order. *IEEE Trans. Computers*, 48(2):227–235, 1999.

[22] D. A. Patterson and J. L. Hennessy. *Computer Organization & Design: The Hardware/Software Interface.* Morgan Kaufmann, 1994.

[23] G. Taubenfeld. *Synchronization Algorithms and Concurrent Programming.* Prentice Hall, 2006.

[24] P. Turán. On an extremal problem in graph theory (in hungarian). *Mat. Fiz. Lapok*, 48:436–452, 1941.

[25] J.-H. Yang and J. Anderson. A fast, scalable mutual exclusion algorithm. *Distributed Computing*, 9(1):51–60, 1995.

APPENDIX

A. ADDITIONAL OBJECTS

A *one-time* mutual exclusion algorithm is a ME algorithm in which each process completes at most a single passage. Since our proofs consider executions in which each process is allowed to complete a passage at most once, our results apply to one-time mutual exclusion algorithms.

LEMMA 4. *Let $\mathcal{C}$ be an object of one of the following types: counter, stack or queue. Then for any $N \in \mathbb{N}$, there exists an N-process one-time mutual exclusion algorithm $\mathcal{A}$ using $\mathcal{C}$ (and read/write variables), such that each passage through the CS invokes a single operation Op on $\mathcal{C}$ (fetch&increment, dequeue, or pop respectively), and has the same RMR and fence complexities as those of Op, up to a constant additive factor, in both the DSM and CC models.*

PROOF. We first prove the lemma for counter, by presenting Algorithm 1 for an N-process one-time mutual exclusion.

Algorithm 1 One-time mutual exclusion

Shared Data: $release[N]$: initially $[1, 0, \cdots, 0]$.
$waiting[N]$: initially $[\bot, \bot, \cdots, \bot]$.
$spin[N]$: initially $[0, 0, \cdots, 0]$.
$\mathcal{C}$: a counter, initially 0.

program for process p:

```
1: v ← C.fetch&increment();
2: waiting[v] ← p;
3: if release[v] = 0 then
4:     await (spin[p] = 1)
   CS
5: release[v + 1] ← 1;
6: q ← waiting[v + 1];
7: if q ≠⊥ then
8:     spin[q] ← 1;
```

The correctness of the algorithm follows easily from the properties of the counter object.

We assume that each write in Algorithm 1 (lines 2-8 only) is followed by a fence instruction, and omit these fences from the code for presentation simplicity. Consequently, the fence complexity of Algorithm 1 is the same as that of the *fetch&increment* operation, up to a constant additive factor.

In the DSM model, variable $spin[p]$ resides in the local memory segment of process p. Note p busy-waits only when it waits for $spin[p]$ to be set. In the CC model (with either write-back or write-through), since once $spin[p]$ is set its value does not change, p may encounter at most 2 RMRs during the wait in line 4. Therefore, under both models, the ME algorithm has the same RMR complexity as of the *fetch&increment* operation, up to a constant additive factor.

It is easy to see that $\mathcal{C}$'s value never exceeds N in the course of executing Algorithm 1. It follows that $\mathcal{C}$ can be implemented using a single queue or stack in the following manner:

Queue: initialize $Q = \langle 0; 1; \cdots; N \rangle$. The *fetch&increment* operation is simply invoking $Q.dequeue()$.

Stack: initialize $S = \langle N; \cdots; 1; 0 \rangle$. The *fetch&increment* operation is simply invoking $S.pop()$.

Using Algorithm 1 with any of these implementations yields the required result. □

On the Time and Space Complexity of ABA Prevention and Detection*

Zahra Aghazadeh
Dept. of Computer Science
University of Calgary
zaghazad@ucalgary.ca

Philipp Woelfel
Dept. of Computer Science
University of Calgary
woelfel@ucalgary.ca

ABSTRACT

We investigate the time and space complexity of detecting and preventing ABAs in shared memory algorithms for systems with n processes and bounded base objects. To that end, we define ABA-detecting registers, which are similar to normal read/write registers, except that they allow a process q to detect with a read operation, whether some process wrote the register since q's last read. ABA-detecting registers can be implemented trivially from a single unbounded register, but we show that they have a high complexity if base objects are bounded: An obstruction-free implementation of an ABA-detecting single bit register cannot be implemented from fewer than $n-1$ bounded registers. Moreover, bounded CAS objects (or more generally, conditional read-modify-write primitives) offer little help to implement ABA-detecting single bit registers: We prove a linear time-space tradeoff for such implementations. We show that the same time-space tradeoff holds for implementations of single bit LL/SC primitives from bounded writable CAS objects. This proves that the implementations of LL/SC/VL by Anderson and Moir [2] as well as Jayanti and Petrovic [15] are optimal.

We complement our lower bounds with tight upper bounds: We give an implementation of ABA-detecting registers from $n+1$ bounded registers, which has step complexity $O(1)$. We also show that (bounded) LL/SC/VL can be implemented from a single bounded CAS object and with $O(n)$ step complexity. Both upper bounds are asymptotically optimal with respect to their time-space product.

These results give formal evidence that the ABA problem is inherently difficult, that even writable CAS objects do not provide significant benefits over registers for dealing with the ABA problem itself, and that there is no hope of finding a more efficient implementation of LL/SC/VL from bounded CAS objects and registers than the ones from [2, 15].

*This research was undertaken, in part, thanks to funding from the Canada Research Chairs program and from the Discovery Grants program of the Natural Sciences and Engineering Research Council of Canada (NSERC).

Permission to make digital or hard copies of all or part of this work for personal or classroom use is granted without fee provided that copies are not made or distributed for profit or commercial advantage and that copies bear this notice and the full citation on the first page. Copyrights for components of this work owned by others than ACM must be honored. Abstracting with credit is permitted. To copy otherwise, or republish, to post on servers or to redistribute to lists, requires prior specific permission and/or a fee. Request permissions from permissions@acm.org.
PODC'15, July 21–23, 2015, Donostia-San Sebastián, Spain.
Copyright is held by the owner/author(s). Publication rights licensed to ACM.
ACM 978-1-4503-3617-8 /15/07 ...$15.00.
DOI: http://dx.doi.org/10.1145/2767386.2767403.

Categories and Subject Descriptors

E.1 [**Data Structures**]: Distributed data structures; F.2.2 [**Analysis of Algorithms and Problem Complexity**]: Nonnumerical Algorithms and Problems; D.1.3 [**Programming Techniques**]: Concurrent Programming

Keywords

Shared memory; ABA problem; Load-link/store-conditional

1. INTRODUCTION

Since the beginning of shared memory computing, programmers and researchers have had to deal with the ABA problem: Even though a process retrieves the same value twice in a row from a shared memory object, it is still possible that the value of the object has changed multiple times.

Especially algorithms using the standard Compare-and-Swap (CAS) primitive seem to be susceptible. A CAS object provides two operations: `Read()` returns the value of the object, and `CAS(`x,y`)` changes the value of the object to y provided that its value v prior to the operation equals x, and it returns v. (According to some specifications a `CAS(`x,y`)` returns a Boolean, which is `True` if and only if the `CAS()` succeeded, i.e., it wrote y.) Often, `CAS()` objects are used in the following way: First, a process p reads the value x stored in the CAS object, then it performs some computation, and finally it tries to propagate the result of the computation by performing a `CAS(`x,y`)`. The idea is that if another process has already updated the data structure, p's `CAS()` should fail, and so inconsistencies are avoided. However, if multiple successful `CAS()` operations have occurred and the value of the object has changed back to x, p's `CAS()` might still succeed, possibly yielding inconsistencies.

ABAs are also a problem for algorithms using other strong primitives, or even only registers. For example, in mutual exclusion algorithms often processes busy-wait for certain events to happen, by repeatedly reading the same register. In systems with caches, the cost of waiting is small, because as long as no process changes the register value, all reads are cache hits. The event is signaled by other processes through a change in the register value. But it may also be desirable to eventually reset the register to its state, before the event was signaled, in order to be able to reuse it. But this may result in the ABA problem, and as a consequence waiting processes may miss events. Therefore, algorithm designers have to devise more complicated code in order to avoid unnoticed cache misses, or even lack of progress.

Many shared memory algorithms and data structures have to deal with the ABA problem. Often this is done in an ad-hoc, application specific way [31], or solutions are based on tagging [10, 19, 23–25, 27–29] (see below). Other papers combine tagging and memory management techniques, or suggest both as alternatives [10, 18].

Tagging, introduced by IBM [14], requires augmenting an object with a tag (which is sometimes called sequence number) that gets changed with every write operation. This technique avoids the ABA problem only, if tags never repeat. Therefore, theoretically, an infinite number of tags and thus base objects of unbounded size are required. One may argue that, in practice, for reasonably large base objects, a system will never run out of tags. However, this is unrealistic in cases where the tag has to be stored together with other information in the same object. In some cases, it is possible to store the tag in a separate object (e.g., [15]), but this requires technically difficult algorithms and tedious correctness proofs. Some architectures like the IBM System/370 [14] introduced a double-width CAS primitive, which allows one of two (32-bit) words to be used for storing tags. While using bounded tags does not completely avoid the ABA problem (because tag values may wrap around), it has been argued [24, 25, 28, 29] that an erroneous algorithm execution due to an unexpected ABA becomes very unlikely. From a theoretical perspective this is unsatisfactory. Moreover, for practical applications, it is often necessary to use the entire object space (today usually comprising 64 bits) for data, so the tagging technique requires double-width atomic instructions. Those are not supported by most mainstream architectures [20].

ABAs cause problems in algorithms that use some form of memory management, where a pointer to some memory space may change its value in an ABA fashion. In this context, memory reclamation techniques based on reference counting [32], Hazard pointers [20, 21], the repeat-offender problem technique [12], or the memory reclamation technique introduced in [1] deal with the ABA problem. But those techniques are application specific.

A more methodological approach has been followed by research that showed how a load-linked store-conditional (LL/SC) object can be implemented from CAS objects and registers. Such an object provides two operations, `LL()` and `SC()`, where `LL()` returns the current value of the object. `SC(`x`)` may either fail and not change anything, or succeed and write the value x to the object. Specifically, an `SC(`x`)` operation by process p succeeds if and only if no other `SC()` operation succeeded since p's last `LL()`. A Boolean return value of an `SC()` operation indicates its success (`True`) or failure (`False`). An extended specification also allows for a `VL()` (verify-link) operation, which does not change the state of the object, but it returns `False` if a successful `SC()` has been performed since the calling process' last `LL()`, and `True` otherwise. LL/SC (or LL/SC/VL) objects can in almost all cases replace CAS objects in algorithms, and are an effective way of avoiding the ABA problem. Unfortunately, existing multiprocessor systems only provide weak versions of LL/SC that restrict programmers severely in how they can use the objects [26], and hence they "offer little or no help with preventing the ABA problem" [22].

For that reason, a line of research has been dedicated to finding time and space efficient LL/SC implementations from CAS objects and registers [2, 5, 15, 16, 20, 22, 26]. While many of those solutions are wait-free and often even guarantee constant time execution of each `LL()` and `SC()` operation, they still have drawbacks: Existing implementations either require unbounded tags (e.g., [26]) and thus use unbounded CAS objects or registers, or they need at least linear space. Jayanti and Petrovic [15] and Anderson and Moir [2] presented the most space efficient implementations of an LL/SC object from bounded CAS and registers, which achieves constant step-complexity: it uses only one CAS object but requires $\Theta(n)$ registers. This raises the question, whether time efficient implementations of LL/SC from a smaller number of bounded CAS objects and registers may exist. More generally, in order to understand the power and limits of shared memory primitives, it seems important to learn how much time and space is required to avoid or detect ABAs, and not to restrict this question to the implementation of LL/SC objects from CAS objects and registers.

CAS and LL/SC objects have a consensus number of infinity [11], while registers have a consensus number of one. Therefore, it is impossible to implement wait-free LL/SC from registers or other objects with a bounded consensus number. Time and space lower bounds for implementations of LL/SC objects may not necessarily imply that it is the ABA problem that is hard to solve, but such lower bounds may follow inherently from other properties of the LL/SC specification.

Results.

To investigate the complexity of detecting or preventing ABAs, we define a natural object, the *ABA-detecting register*. It supports two operations, `DRead()` and `DWrite()`. Operation `DWrite(`x`)` writes value x to the register, and returns nothing. Operation `DRead()` by process p returns, in addition to the value of the register, a Boolean flag, which is `True` if and only if some process executed a `DWrite()` since p's last `DRead()` operation. We distinguish between *single-writer* ABA-detecting registers, where only one dedicated process is allowed to call `DWrite()`, and *multi-writer* ones that don't have this restriction.

A wait-free ABA-detecting register can be implemented from registers, and thus has consensus number 1. (Therefore, they are weaker with respect to wait-freedom than CAS or LL/SC.) Using a single unbounded register with an unbounded tag that gets changed whenever some process writes to it, it is trivial to obtain an ABA-detecting register with constant time complexity. But if base objects have only bounded size, the situation is completely different: For implementations of ABA-detecting registers in a system with n processes and bounded registers, we obtain a linear (in n) space lower bound, even if the implementation satisfies only nondeterministic solo-termination (the non-deterministic variant of obstruction-freedom), which is a progress condition strictly weaker than wait-freedom. The availability of CAS seems to be of little help: For wait-free implementations from CAS objects and registers we obtain a time-space tradeoff that is linear in n. The same asymptotic time-space tradeoff is obtained if the base objects support arbitrary conditional read-modify-write operations [7]. Each conditional operation can be simulated by a single operation on a *writable* CAS objects, i.e., an object that supports a

`Write()` operation in addition to `Read()` and `CAS()`. For that reason we state the lower bound for implementations from conditional read-modify-write operations in terms of writable CAS base objects.

THEOREM 1. *Any linearizable implementation of a single-writer 1-bit ABA-detecting register from m bounded base objects satisfies:*

(a) $m \geq n-1$ if the base objects are bounded registers, and the implementation satisfies nondeterministic solo-termination;

(b) $m \geq (n-1)/t$, if the the base objects are bounded CAS objects and registers, and the implementation is deterministic and wait-free with worst-case step-complexity at most t; and

(c) $m \geq (n-1)/(2t)$, if the base objects are bounded writeable CAS objects, and the implementation is deterministic and wait-free with worst-case step-complexity at most t.

The requirement that base objects are bounded is necessary for this lower bound, because, as mentioned earlier, an ABA-detecting register can be trivially obtained by augmenting a normal register with an unbounded tag.

There is a simple implementation of a (bounded) ABA-detecting registers with constant step-complexity from a single (bounded) LL/SC/VL object of the same size: Each process uses a local variable *old*. To `DWrite(`x`)`, the process executes a `LL()` operation followed by a `SC(`x`)`. To `DRead()`, the process first executes a `VL()`. If `VL()` returns `True`, the process returns (*old*, `False`); otherwise, it reads the value of the LL/SC/VL object into *old* (by executing `LL()`), and then returns (*old*, `True`). It is not hard to see that this implementation is linearizable. Thus, by reduction we obtain the same lower bound as the one stated in Theorem 1 for implementations of single bit LL/SC/VL. Unfortunately, for that reduction the `VL()` operation is needed, and at least we do not know how to obtain a similarly efficient ABA-detecting register from an LL/SC object that does not support `VL()`. However, the proofs of Theorem 1 can be easily modified to accommodate LL/SC objects:

COROLLARY 1. *Any linearizable implementation of a single bit LL/SC object from m bounded base objects satisfies*

(a) $m \geq (n-1)/t$, if the the base objects are bounded CAS objects and registers, and the implementation is deterministic and wait-free with worst-case step-complexity at most t; and

(b) $m \geq (n-1)/(2t)$, if the base objects are bounded writeable CAS objects, and the implementation is deterministic and wait-free with worst-case step-complexity at most t.

A linear space lower bound (corresponding to Part (a) of Theorem 1) for nondeterministic solo-terminating implementations of LL/SC from (even unbounded) registers follows from the fact that LL/SC objects are *perturbable* [17].

As in Theorem 1, the assumption that base objects are bounded is necessary, because there is an implementation of an LL/SC/VL object from a single unbounded CAS object with constant step complexity by Moir [26]. Our time-space tradeoff is asymptotically tight for implementations with constant step-complexity, as it matches known upper bounds [2,15]. We show that it also asymptotically tight for implementations using a single CAS object:

THEOREM 2. *A single bounded CAS object suffices to implement a bounded LL/SC/VL object or a bounded multi-writer ABA-detecting register with $O(n)$ step-complexity.*

These results raise the question, whether bounded CAS objects are helpful for ABA detection. We determine that for this problem bounded CAS objects do not provide additional benefits over bounded registers:

THEOREM 3. *There is a linearizable wait-free implementation of a multi-writer b-bit ABA-detecting register from $n+1$ $(b+2logn+O(1))$-bit registers with constant step complexity.*

Not only do our lower bounds show that Anderson's and Moir's [2] as well as Jayanti's and Petrovic's [15] implementations of LL/SC from CAS objects and registers are optimal with respect to their time- and space-product, but they also clearly indicate that ABA detection is inherently difficult, even if bounded conditional read-modify-write primitives such as (writable) CAS objects are available. Therefore, other primitives that provide a solution to the ABA problem would most likely be as difficult to obtain as LL/SC. Our upper bounds demonstrate that bounded CAS objects (and in fact any conditional read-modify-write operations) are not more helpful than bounded registers with respect to ABA detection. On the other hand, ABA detection is difficult only if base objects are bounded, but for our lower bounds it does not matter how large that bound on the size of the base object is, as long as it is finite.

Other Related Work.

Our lower bounds use covering arguments. Covering arguments were first used by Burns and Lynch [4] to prove a space lower bound for mutual exclusion, and essentially all space lower bounds are based on this technique. Examples are space lower bounds for one-time test-and-set objects [30], consensus [8], timestamps [6,9], and the general class of perturbable objects [17] (which includes LL/SC among others). These lower bounds have in common that they do not apply if CAS objects are available as base objects. (They allow for registers, swap objects, and, in case of [17], resettable consensus.) An overview of covering arguments can be found in Attiya's and Ellen's recent textbook [3].

In our time-space tradeoffs we construct executions, where a sequence of operations by a process p is interleaved with successful `CAS()` and `Write()` operations of other processes, so that p's steps remain "hidden". Such a technique has been also used by Ellen, Hendler, and Shavit [7] to prove linear space lower bounds for wait-free implementations of *visible* objects implemented from conditional read-modify-write (i.e., writable CAS) objects. Visible objects include counters, queues, stacks, or snapshots. Neither ABA-detecting registers nor LL/SC objects are visible, because they can be implemented from a single unbounded CAS object. In fact, we are not aware of any other non-trivial lower bounds that, like ours, separate bounded from unbounded base objects.

Preliminaries.

We consider a system with n processes with unique IDs in $\mathcal{P} = \{0, \ldots, n-1\}$. Processes communicate through shared memory operations, called steps, that are executed on atomic base objects provided by the system. Each process executes a possibly nondeterministic program. If processes are deterministic, a *schedule* is a sequence of process

IDs, that determines the order in which processes execute their steps. If processes are nondeterministic, a *schedule* is a sequence of process IDs together with coin-flips, and it describes the order in which processes take steps together with the nondeterministic decisions they make. The sequence of shared memory steps taken by processes is called *execution*. A *history* on some implemented object is the sequence of method call invocations and responses that occur in an execution on that object. A *configuration* describes the state of the system, i.e., of all processes and all base objects.

Our implementations are deterministic and *wait-free*, which means that every method call terminates within a finite number of the calling process' steps, in any execution. The step-complexity of a deterministic wait-free method is the maximum number of steps a process needs to terminate the method call in any execution. Our lower bounds hold for implementations that satisfy a progress condition which is strictly weaker than wait-freedom: A nondeterministic method m satisfies *nondeterministic solo-termination*, if for every process p and every configuration C in which a call of method m by p is pending, there is a p-only execution that starts in C and during which p finishes method m. For deterministic algorithms, nondeterministic solo-termination is the same as *obstruction-freedom*. Our algorithms are *linearizable* [13], but our lower bounds work for much weaker correctness conditions.

2. LOWER BOUNDS

For a configuration C and a schedule σ, let $\text{Exec}(C, \sigma)$ denote the execution arising from processes taking steps, starting in configuration C, in the order defined by σ, and using the nondeterministic decisions defined by σ, if the algorithm is nondeterministic. Let $\text{Conf}(C, \sigma)$ denote the configuration resulting from execution $\text{Exec}(C, \sigma)$ started in C. For two configurations C and D and a schedule α, we write $C \overset{\alpha}{\rightsquigarrow} D$ to indicate that $\text{Conf}(C, \alpha) = D$. Let C_{init} denote the initial configuration. If there exists a schedule α such that $C \overset{\alpha}{\rightsquigarrow} D$, then we say D is reachable from C, and if D is reachable from C_{init}, we simply say D is reachable.

An execution E or a schedule α is P-only for a set $P \subseteq \{0, \ldots, n-1\}$ of processes, if only processes in P take steps during E respectively α. If $P = \{p\}$ is the set of a single process, then we sometimes write p-only instead of $\{p\}$-only.

For an execution E, let $\prec_E$ denote the happens-before order on operations in E, i.e., if operation *op* responds in E before *op'* gets invoked, then and only then $op \prec_E op'$ (*op* happens before *op'*). We write simply $\prec$ instead of $\prec_E$, if is clear from the context which execution E the relation refers to. For a schedule α, an execution E and a process p, $E|p$ and $\alpha|p$ denote the sub-sequences of steps by p in E and in α, respectively.

Two configurations C and D are *indistinguishable* to process p, if every register has the same value in C as in D, and p is in the same state in both configurations. We write $C \sim_p D$ to denote that C and D are indistinguishable to p. We write $C \sim_S D$ for a set S of processes to denote that $C \sim_p D$ for every process $p \in S$. We say process p is *idle* in configuration C, if it has no pending method call, and if all processes are idle, then the configuration is *quiescent*. A process *completes* a method call in an execution E, if that method terminates in E.

For our lower bounds, we do not require that the implementation of the ABA-detecting registers is linearizable. Instead, we consider methods `WeakRead()` and `WeakWrite()` that take no arguments, and where `WeakRead()` returns a Boolean value, and `WeakWrite()` returns nothing. A correct concurrent implementation of these methods must guarantee for every execution, that a `WeakRead()` operation r by process p returns `True` if and only if there exists a `WeakWrite()` operation w such that w happens before r and every other `WeakRead()` operation by p happens before w.

Linearizability of an ABA-detecting register R guarantees that the operations R.`DRead()` (in place of `WeakRead()`) and R.`DWrite()` (in place of `WeakWrite()`) satisfy the correctness properties above. Therefore, every lower bound on the time and/or space complexity for correct implementations of those methods implies the same lower bound for linearizable ABA-detecting registers.

Let p be some process and C a configuration. We say C is *p-clean*, if there exists a schedule α, $C_{init} \overset{\alpha}{\rightsquigarrow} C$, such that $\text{Exec}(C_{init}, \alpha)$ contains a complete `WeakRead()` operation r^* by p, and every `WeakWrite()` happens before r^*. Configuration C is *p-dirty*, if there exists a schedule α, $C_{init} \overset{\alpha}{\rightsquigarrow} C$, and $\text{Exec}(C_{init}, \alpha)$ contains a complete `WeakWrite()` operation w^* such that no `WeakRead()` by p is pending at any point after w^* has been invoked. Note that some configurations are neither p-dirty nor p-clean.

Throughout this section we assume that each process executes an infinite program, in which it repeatedly calls `WeakRead()` and `WeakWrite()` methods. More specifically, process 0 repeatedly executes `WeakWrite()`, while every process in $\{1, \ldots, n-1\}$ repeatedly calls `WeakRead()`.

Then in a p-only execution starting from a configuration C, the first `WeakRead()` operation by p returns `False` if C is p-clean and `True` if C is p-dirty. Therefore, each process must be able to distinguish p-clean configurations from p-dirty ones:

OBSERVATION 1. *Suppose the* `WeakRead()` *method satisfies nondeterministic solo-termination. For any process* $p \in \{1, \ldots, n-1\}$ *and any two reachable configurations* C_1, C_2, *if* C_1 *is p-clean and* C_2 *is p-dirty, then* $C_1 \not\sim_p C_2$.

2.1 A Space Lower Bound for Implementations from Bounded Registers

Let $\mathcal{R}$ be a set of k registers and P a set of processes. We say the processes in P *cover* $\mathcal{R}$ in configuration C, if for each register $R \in \mathcal{R}$ there is a process in P that is poised to write to R. A *block-write* to $\mathcal{R}$ is an execution in which k processes participate, and each of them takes exactly one step in which it writes to a distinct register in $\mathcal{R}$. (The only block-write to $\emptyset$ is the empty execution.)

In the following we assume an implementation of methods `WeakRead()` and `WeakWrite()` from m bounded registers. The *register configuration* of a configuration C is an m-tuple, $\text{reg}(C) = (v_1, \ldots, v_m)$, where v_i is the value of the i-th register.

LEMMA 1. *Suppose methods* `WeakRead()` *and* `WeakWrite()` *satisfy nondeterministic solo-termination. For any quiescent configuration* Q *and any set* $P_k = \{p_1, \ldots, p_k\} \subseteq \mathcal{P} \setminus \{0\}$, *where* $k \in \{0, \ldots, n-1\}$, *there exists a* $(P_k \cup \{0\})$*-only schedule* α *such that in* $\text{Conf}(Q, \alpha)$ *process 0 is idle and* k *distinct registers are covered by* $p_1, \ldots, p_k$.

Lemma 1 immediately implies Theorem 1 (a).

PROOF OF LEMMA 1. The proof is by induction on k. If $k = 0$, we let α be the empty schedule, and the lemma is immediate because $Conf(Q, \alpha) = Q$ is a quiescent configuration (so 0 is idle).

Now suppose we have proved the inductive hypothesis for some integer $k < n - 1$. Let $\beta = (p_1, \ldots, p_k)$ be the schedule in which each of $p_1, \ldots, p_k$ takes exactly one step. Let $Q_0 = Q$. By the inductive hypothesis there is a schedule α_1 such that in $C_1 := \text{Conf}(Q_0, \alpha_1)$ a set $\mathcal{R}_1$ of exactly k registers is covered, and process 0 is idle. Hence, $\text{Exec}(C_1, \beta)$ is a block-write to $\mathcal{R}_1$ yielding a configuration $D_1 = \text{Conf}(C_1, \beta)$. We let γ_1 be the schedule such that in $\text{Exec}(D_1, \gamma_1)$ first each process in $\{p_1, \ldots, p_k\}$ takes enough unobstructed steps to finish its `WeakRead()` method call, and after that process 0 takes enough unobstructed steps to complete exactly one `WeakWrite()` method. Then $Q_1 = \text{Conf}(D_1, \gamma_1)$ is quiescent, and during $\text{Exec}(D_1, \gamma_1)$ exactly one complete `WeakWrite()` gets executed. Repeating this construction (using the inductive hypothesis repeatedly) we obtain a schedule $\alpha_1\beta\gamma_1\alpha_2\beta\gamma_2\alpha_3\ldots$ and configurations $Q_0, C_1, D_1, Q_1, C_2, D_2, Q_2, \ldots$ and sets of k registers $\mathcal{R}_1, \mathcal{R}_2, \ldots$, such that for any $i \geq 1$:

- $Q_{i-1} \overset{\alpha_i}{\rightsquigarrow} C_i \overset{\beta}{\rightsquigarrow} D_i \overset{\gamma_i}{\rightsquigarrow} Q_i$;
- Q_i is quiescent;
- during $\text{Exec}(D_i, \gamma_i)$ process 0 executes a complete `WeakWrite()` operation; and
- in C_i process 0 is idle and $\mathcal{R}_i$ is covered by P_k (and thus $\text{Exec}(C_i, \beta)$ is a block-write to $\mathcal{R}_i$).

Since the number or registers is finite, and all registers are bounded, there exist indices $1 \leq i < j$ such that $\text{reg}(D_i) = \text{reg}(D_j)$. Let $\sigma = \gamma_i\alpha_{i+1}\beta\gamma_{i+1}\alpha_{i+2}\ldots\alpha_j\beta$, i.e.,

$$C_i \overset{\beta}{\rightsquigarrow} D_i \overset{\sigma}{\rightsquigarrow} D_j. \tag{1}$$

Now let λ' be a p_{k+1}-only schedule such that in $\text{Exec}(C_i, \lambda')$ process p_{k+1} completes exactly one `WeakRead()` method call. By the nondeterministic solo-termination property, such a schedule λ' exists. Let λ be the prefix of λ', such that $\text{Exec}(C_i, \lambda)$ ends when p_{k+1} is poised to write to a register $R \notin \mathcal{R}_i$ for the first time, or $\lambda = \lambda'$ if p_{k+1} finishes its `WeakRead()` method call without writing to a register outside of $\mathcal{R}_i$.

First assume $\lambda \neq \lambda'$, i.e., in $\text{Exec}(C_i, \lambda)$ process p_{k+1} does not finish its `WeakRead()` method call, but instead the execution ends when p_{k+1} covers a register $R \notin \mathcal{R}_i$. Since in C_i process 0 is idle and $\mathcal{R}_i$ is covered by P_k, and since λ is p_{k+1}-only, in configuration $\text{Conf}(C_i, \lambda) = \text{Conf}(Q, \alpha_1\beta\gamma_1\ldots\alpha_i\lambda)$ processes $p_1, \ldots, p_{k+1}$ cover $k+1$ registers, and process 0 is still idle. This completes the proof of the inductive step for $\alpha = \alpha_1\beta\gamma_1\ldots\alpha_i\lambda$.

Now we consider the case $\lambda = \lambda'$, i.e., during $\text{Exec}(C_i, \lambda)$ process p_{k+1} finishes its `WeakRead()` method call without writing to a register outside of $\mathcal{R}_i$. To complete the proof of the lemma, it suffices to show that this case cannot occur.

Since in C_i the processes in P_k cover $\mathcal{R}_i$, and p_{k+1} only writes to registers in $\mathcal{R}_i$ during $\text{Exec}(C_i, \lambda)$, it follows that $\text{Exec}(C_i, \lambda\beta)$ ends with a block-write by P_k in which all writes by p_{k+1} get obliterated. In particular, for $D'_i := \text{Conf}(C_i, \lambda\beta)$ we have

$$D'_i \underset{\mathcal{P}\setminus\{p_{k+1}\}}{\sim} D_i \tag{2}$$

Hence, since schedule σ is $(P_k \cup \{0\})$-only, i.e., p_{k+1} does not participate, we obtain $\text{Exec}(D'_i, \sigma) = \text{Exec}(D_i, \sigma)$, and in particular using Eq. (1)

$$C_i \overset{\lambda\beta}{\rightsquigarrow} D'_i \overset{\sigma}{\rightsquigarrow} D'_j, \quad \text{where} \quad D_j \underset{\mathcal{P}\setminus\{p_{k+1}\}}{\sim} D'_j. \tag{3}$$

Now recall that we chose i and j in such a way that $\text{reg}(D_i) = \text{reg}(D_j)$. Thus, from Eq. (2) and (3) we get $\text{reg}(D'_i) = \text{reg}(D_i) = \text{reg}(D_j) = \text{reg}(D'_j)$. Because $D'_i \overset{\sigma}{\rightsquigarrow} D'_j$ (Eq. (3)), and since by construction only processes $\{0, p_1, \ldots, p_k\}$ appear in σ, p_{k+1} is in D'_i in exactly the same state as in D'_j. Hence,

$$D'_i \underset{p_{k+1}}{\sim} D'_j. \tag{4}$$

Now recall that $C_i \overset{\lambda\beta}{\rightsquigarrow} D'_i$, and in the corresponding execution process p_{k+1} executes a complete `WeakRead()` method, while process 0 takes no steps, and p_{k+1} is idle in D'_i. Hence, D'_i is p_{k+1}-clean. On the other hand, $\text{Exec}(D'_i, \sigma) = \text{Exec}(D_i, \sigma)$ starts with a complete `WeakWrite()` operation (during the prefix $\text{Exec}(D'_i, \gamma_i)$) by process 0, while process p_{k+1} takes no steps, and thus remains idle. It follows that the configuration resulting from that execution, D'_j, is p_{k+1}-dirty. Summarizing, we have two reachable configurations, D'_i and D'_j, where one of them is p_{k+1}-clean and the other one is p_{k+1}-dirty, and both are indistinguishable to p_{k+1}, according to Eq. (4). This contradicts Observation 1. □

2.2 A Time-Space Tradeoff for Implementations from CAS Objects

We now consider deterministic wait-free implementations of `WeakRead()` and `WeakWrite()` from m writable bounded CAS objects. We assume without loss of generality that every `CAS(`x`,`y`)` operation satisfies $x \neq y$. (A `CAS(`x`,`x`)` operation can be replaced by a `Read()`).

For any configuration C and any shared CAS object R let $\text{CCov}(C, R)$ and $\text{WCov}(C, R)$ denote the sets of processes that are poised in C to execute a `CAS()` respectively `Write()` operation on R. Let P be a set of processes and C a configuration. A schedule β is called *P-successful* for C, if it contains every process in P exactly once, and every step of $\text{Exec}(C, \beta)$ is either a `Write()` or a successful `CAS()`. If a configuration C has a P-successful schedule β, then we also say execution $\text{Exec}(C, \beta)$ is P-successful.

As before, we assume that all processes run an infinite loop, where process 0 repeatedly calls `WeakWrite()` while all other processes repeatedly call `WeakRead()`.

LEMMA 2. *Let $P \subsetneq \mathcal{P} \setminus \{0\}$, $q \in \mathcal{P} \setminus P$, $q \neq 0$. Let C be a configuration, in which either q is idle, or in no execution starting from C process q executes more than t shared memory steps before finishing a pending* `WeakRead()` *call. If β is a P-successful schedule for C, then there is a schedule σ such that*

$$\text{Conf}(C, \beta) \underset{\mathcal{P}\setminus\{q\}}{\sim} \text{Conf}(C, \sigma), \tag{5}$$

and at least one of the following is the case:

(a) In $\text{Conf}(C, \sigma)$ process q is idle;

(b) in $\text{Conf}(C, \sigma)$ process q is poised to write to some object R and $|\text{WCov}(C, R) \cap P| < t$; or

(c) in $\text{Conf}(C, \sigma)$ process q is poised to execute a `CAS(`x`,`y`)` *operation on some object R, where x is the value of R*

in configuration $\mathrm{Conf}(C,\sigma)$, *and* $|\mathrm{WCov}(C,R)\cap P| + |\mathrm{CCov}(C,R)\cap P| < t$.

PROOF. We prove the lemma by induction on t. If $t=0$, then q is idle in C. Hence, for $\sigma=\beta$ we obtain Eq. (5) and Case (a).

Let op_q be the step q is poised to execute in C, and let V be the object affected by op_q. Further, let $\mathrm{val}_C(V)$ denote the value of V in configuration C.

Case 1: First, assume that op_q is a `Read()` or a `CAS()` operation. Let z be the first process in P that executes a step in $\mathrm{Exec}(C,\beta)|V$, and let op_z be that step. We construct a two-step schedule λ that contains q and z, such that

$$C' := \mathrm{Conf}(C,\lambda) \underset{\mathcal{P}\setminus\{q\}}{\sim} \mathrm{Conf}(C,z). \tag{6}$$

First suppose op_z is a `CAS`(a,b) operation and op_q a `CAS`(x,y) operation that would succeed in C (i.e., $x = \mathrm{val}_C(V)$). Then we define $\lambda=(z,q)$. Since β is P-successful, the `CAS`(a,b) by z in configuration C succeeds and changes the value of V from a to b. In this case, $x=a$, so in the execution $\mathrm{Exec}(C,\lambda)$ the `CAS`(x,y) by q fails. Eq. (6) follows.

In all other cases (i.e., if op_z is a `Write()` operation or op_q is a `Read()` or a `CAS()` that fails in C), then we let $\lambda=(q,z)$. Then in $\mathrm{Exec}(C,\lambda)$ either operation op_q does not change the value of object V, or op_z executes a `Write()` and overwrites any changes that may have resulted from op_q. It follows that Eq. (6) is true.

Now let $\beta' = \beta|(P\setminus\{z\})$, and recall that $C'=\mathrm{Conf}(C,\lambda)$. Since β is P-successful and in $\mathrm{Exec}(C,\beta)$ process z executes the first step on V, it follows that β' is P-successful in C'.

Hence, we can apply the inductive hypothesis for configuration C', process set $P' = P\setminus\{z\}$, and schedule β', to obtain a schedule σ' that satisfies one of the Cases (a)-(c). Let $\sigma=\lambda\circ\sigma'$. Then by construction, $\mathrm{Conf}(C,\sigma) = \mathrm{Conf}(C',\sigma') \sim_{P\setminus\{q,z\}} \mathrm{Conf}(C',\beta') = \mathrm{Conf}(C,\beta)$. Because of Eq. (6), process z can also not distinguish between $\mathrm{Conf}(C,\sigma)$ and $\mathrm{Conf}(C,\beta)$, so we obtain Eq. (5). If (a) of the inductive hypothesis applies for C' and σ', then the same also applies for C and σ, because $\mathrm{Conf}(C,\sigma)=\mathrm{Conf}(C',\sigma')$. Now suppose that Case (b) applies for C' and σ'. Let R be the object on which process q is poised to execute a `Write()` in $\mathrm{Conf}(C',\sigma')=\mathrm{Conf}(C,\sigma)$. Starting from configuration C', process q must finish its `WeakRead()` method within $t'=t-1$ steps. Hence, $|\mathrm{WCov}(C',R)\cap P'| \le t'$. Since all processes other than z are poised to execute the same step in C as in C', we have $|\mathrm{WCov}(C,R)\cap P| \le |\mathrm{WCov}(C',R)\cap P'|+1 \le t'+1 = t$. Hence, Case (b) follows for C, σ and P. With exactly the same argument, if Case (c) applies for C', σ', and P', then it also applies for C, σ, and P.

Case 2: We now assume that in C process q is poised to execute a `Write()` operation op_q on object V. If $|\mathrm{WCov}(C,V)\cap P| < t$, we let $\sigma=\beta$. Then Eq. (5) and Case (b) (for $R=V$) of the lemma are trivially satisfied.

Hence, assume that $|\mathrm{WCov}(C,V)\cap P| \ge t$. Then $\mathrm{Exec}(C,\beta)$ contains at least t writes to V. Let $z_1,\dots,z_{\ell-1}$ be the processes accessing V in this order in $\mathrm{Exec}(C,\beta)|V$ before the first write to V occurs, and let z_ℓ be the first process writing to V. Let $Z=\{z_1,\dots,z_\ell\}$, $\lambda = (z_1,\dots,z_{\ell-1},q,z_\ell)$, $\gamma=\beta|Z=(z_1,\dots,z_\ell)$ and $\beta'=\beta|(P\setminus Z)$. Then in $\mathrm{Exec}(C,\gamma\circ\beta')$ all processes in P execute exactly one step, as they do in $\mathrm{Exec}(C,\beta)$, and for each object U the steps executed on U occur in the same order in both executions. Hence, processes cannot distinguish these executions from each other, and in particular

$$\mathrm{Conf}(C,\gamma\circ\beta') = \mathrm{Conf}(C,\beta). \tag{7}$$

In $\mathrm{Exec}(C,\lambda)$, first processes $z_1,\dots,z_{\ell-1}$ execute successful `CAS` operations on V, then q writes to V, and finally, z_ℓ overwrites what q has written. It follows that

$$C' := \mathrm{Conf}(C,\lambda) \underset{\mathcal{P}\setminus\{q\}}{\sim} \mathrm{Conf}(C,\gamma). \tag{8}$$

Combining this with Eq. (7) we obtain that β' is P'-successful in C'. Moreover, since q executed one step in the execution leading from C to C', in any execution starting from C' it finishes its `WeakRead()` method after at most $t'=t-1$ steps. Thus, we can apply the inductive hypothesis to obtain a schedule σ' such that $\mathrm{Conf}(C',\beta') \sim_{\mathcal{P}\setminus\{q\}} \mathrm{Conf}(C',\sigma')$, and one of Cases (a)-(c) holds. Let $\sigma=\lambda\circ\sigma'$. Then $\mathrm{Conf}(C,\sigma) = \mathrm{Conf}(C',\sigma') \sim_{\mathcal{P}\setminus\{q\}} \mathrm{Conf}(C',\beta') \sim_{\mathcal{P}\setminus\{q\}} \mathrm{Conf}(C,\beta)$, where the last relation follows from Eq. (7) and (8). This proves Eq. (5).

If Case (a) of the inductive hypothesis holds for C' and σ', then it is also true for C and σ because $\mathrm{Conf}(C,\sigma) = \mathrm{Conf}(C',\sigma')$. Now suppose either Case (b) or (c) applies to C' and σ'. Let R be the object process q is poised to access in $\mathrm{Conf}(C,\sigma)=\mathrm{Conf}(C',\sigma')$. If $R\ne V$, then by construction we have $|\mathrm{WCov}(C,R)\cap P| = |\mathrm{WCov}(C',R)\cap P'|$ and $|\mathrm{CCov}(C,R)\cap P| = |\mathrm{CCov}(C',R)\cap P'|$. Hence, Case (b) or (c) for C', σ', and P' immediately implies the same case for C, σ, an P. Finally, suppose Case (b) or (c) occurs for $R=V$. By construction in $\mathrm{Exec}(C,\lambda)$ only one process among all processes in $\mathrm{WCov}(C,V)$ writes to V, namely process z_ℓ. Hence, in the configuration C' reached by $\mathrm{Exec}(C,\lambda)$ all other processes in $\mathrm{WCov}(C,V)$ are still poised to write to V. Thus, for $R=V$ we obtain $|\mathrm{WCov}(C',R)\cap P'| = |\mathrm{WCov}(C,R)\cap P| - 1 \ge t-1 = t'$, so neither Case (b) nor Case (c) can apply to C', σ', and P'—contradiction. □

LEMMA 3. *Suppose* `WeakRead()` *and* `WeakWrite()` *have step complexity at most* t. *For any reachable quiescent configuration* Q *and any set* $P_k=\{p_1,\dots,p_k\}\subseteq\mathcal{P}\setminus\{0\}$, *where* $k\in\{0,\dots,n-1\}$, *there exists a* $(P_k\cup\{0\})$*-only schedule* α *such that* $C:=\mathrm{Conf}(Q,\alpha)$ *satisfies all of the following:*

(i) all processes in $\mathcal{P}\setminus P_k$ *are idle in* C;

(ii) there is a P_k*-successful schedule for* C; *and*

(iii) $|\mathrm{WCov}(C,R)\cap P_k|\le t$ *and* $|\mathrm{CCov}(C,R)\cap P_k|\le t$ *for all objects* R.

PROOF. Throughout this proof let P_k^0 denote the set $P_k\cup\{0\}$. We prove the lemma by induction on k. For $k=0$, we let α be the empty schedule, so $C=\mathrm{Conf}(Q,\alpha)=Q$. Then C is quiescent and (i) is true. Statements (ii)–(iii) follow immediately from $P_k=\emptyset$.

Now suppose the inductive hypothesis is true for some value of $k\in\{0,\dots,n-2\}$. We let $Q_0=Q$ and $P_{k+1} = P_k\cup\{p_{k+1}\}$ for an arbitrary process $p_{k+1}\in\mathcal{P}\setminus P_k^0$. Then, for $i=1,2,\dots$ we iteratively construct executions $\alpha_i,\beta_i,\gamma_i$ and configurations Q_i,C_i,D_i, where $Q_{i-1}\overset{\alpha_i}{\rightsquigarrow} C_i \overset{\beta_i}{\rightsquigarrow} D_i \overset{\gamma_i}{\rightsquigarrow} Q_i$, and $\alpha_i,\beta_i,\gamma_i$ are determined as follows: α_i is a P_k^0-only schedule that guarantees properties (i)-(iii) from the inductive hypothesis for configuration Q_{i-1}; β_i is a P_k-successful schedule for C_i; and γ_i is an arbitrary P_k-only schedule followed by a 0-only schedule such that Q_i is quiescent,

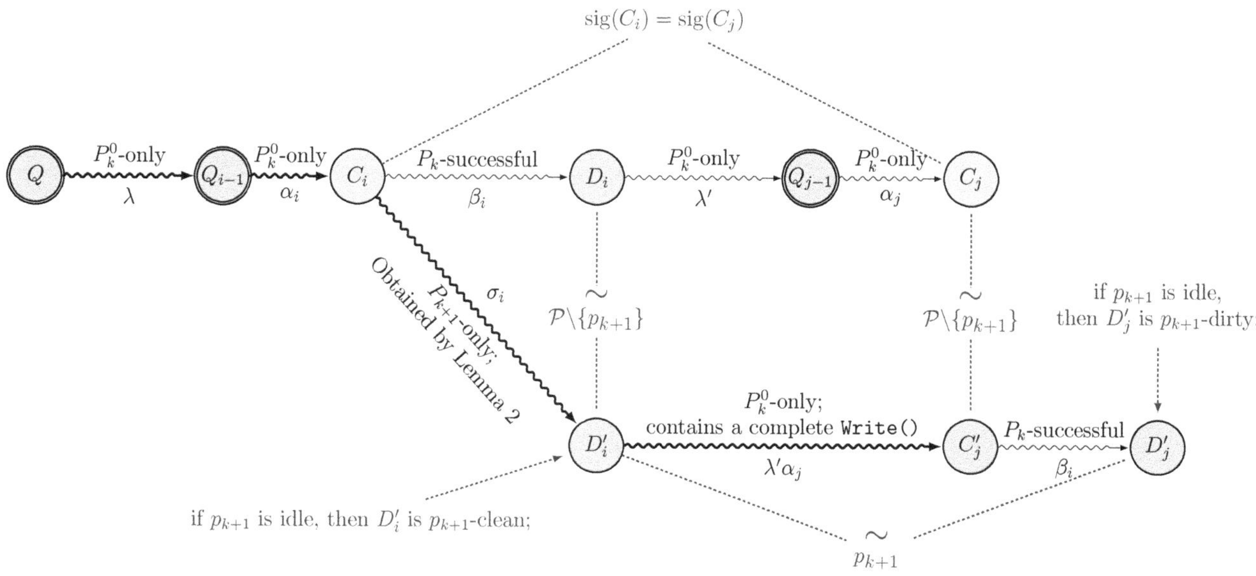

Figure 1: Proof of Lemma 3. Double circles denote quiescent configurations.

and where Exec(D_i, γ_i) contains exactly one complete `WeakWrite()` operation by process 0. By the assumption that `WeakRead()` and `WeakWrite()` are wait-free, γ_i exists.

We define for each configuration C_i a signature, sig(C_i), which encodes for every process p the exact shared memory operation p is poised to execute next (including its parameters), and for every base object R its value.

Since there is only a finite number of bounded base objects in the system, there is a finite number of signatures, and thus there exist $1 \le i < j$ such that C_i and C_j have the same signature. We let $\lambda = \alpha_1\beta_1\gamma_1\alpha_2 \dots \alpha_{i-1}\beta_{i-1}\gamma_{i-1}$, and $\lambda' = \gamma_i\alpha_{i+1}\beta_{i+1}\gamma_{i+1}\alpha_{i+1} \dots \alpha_{j-1}\beta_{j-1}\gamma_{j-1}$. From the construction above we have $Q \overset{\lambda}{\rightsquigarrow} Q_{i-1} \overset{\alpha_i}{\rightsquigarrow} C_i \overset{\beta_i}{\rightsquigarrow} D_i \overset{\lambda'}{\rightsquigarrow} Q_{j-1} \overset{\alpha_j}{\rightsquigarrow} C_j$, where Q_{i-1} and Q_{j-1} are quiescent, C_i satisfies (i)-(iii) from the inductive hypothesis, and sig(C_i) = sig(C_j). This situation, as well as the following construction is depicted in Figure 1.

Now we apply Lemma 2 to configuration C_i. For the purpose of applying this lemma, we may assume that in C_i process p_{k+1} has just invoked a `WeakRead()` operation but not yet executed its first shared memory step during that operation. Hence, in all executions starting from C_i, p_{k+1} will finish that pending `WeakRead()` operation in at most t steps. Then Lemma 2 yields a P_{k+1}-only schedule σ_i such that for $D'_i = \text{Conf}(C_i, \sigma_i)$

$$D_i \underset{\mathcal{P}\setminus\{p_{k+1}\}}{\sim} D'_i, \tag{9}$$

and one of the Cases (a)-(c) of Lemma 2 hold. Let $C'_j = \text{Conf}(D'_i, \lambda'\alpha_j)$, and $D'_j = \text{Conf}(C'_j, \beta_i)$. (The use of β_i instead of β_j is intentional.) Then $Q_{i-1} \overset{\alpha_i}{\rightsquigarrow} C_i \overset{\sigma_i}{\rightsquigarrow} D'_i \overset{\lambda'\alpha_j}{\rightsquigarrow} C'_j \overset{\beta_i}{\rightsquigarrow} D'_j$. Since $\lambda'\alpha_j$ does not contain p_{k+1}, which is the only process that, according to Eq. (9), may be able to distinguish D_i from D'_i, we obtain

$$C'_j \underset{\mathcal{P}\setminus\{p_{k+1}\}}{\sim} C_j. \tag{10}$$

Configurations C_i and C_j have the same signature. Therefore, every process is poised to execute the same step in C_i as in C_j, and all objects have the same values in both configurations. This, together with the fact that β_i is P_k-only and every process appears at most once in β_i implies

$$\text{Exec}(C_i, \beta_i) = \text{Exec}(C_j, \beta_i) \overset{(10)}{=} \text{Exec}(C'_j, \beta_i). \tag{11}$$

Hence, all objects have the same value in $D_i = \text{Conf}(C_i, \beta_i)$ as in $D'_j = \text{Conf}(C'_j, \beta_i)$, and thus from Eq. (9), all objects have the same value in D'_i as in D'_j. Since p_{k+1} does not appear in $\lambda'\alpha_j\beta_i$, and thus takes no step in the execution leading from D'_i to D'_j, we conclude

$$D'_i \underset{p_{k+1}}{\sim} D'_j. \tag{12}$$

Now recall that σ_i is the schedule σ guaranteed by Lemma 2 (applied with $C = C_i$ and $q = p_{k+1}$), and the claim guarantees one of three Cases (a)-(c). First, assume Case (a) occurs, i.e., p_{k+1}. Then it completes a `WeakRead()` method call in Exec(C_i, σ_i) (recall that in C_i it had just invoked that method call) and is idle in $D'_i = \text{Conf}(C_i, \sigma_i)$. Since process 0 takes no steps in Exec(C_i, σ_i) it follows that D'_i is p_{k+1}-clean. On the other hand, Exec($D'_i, \lambda'\alpha_j\beta_i$) contains no steps by p_{k+1}, but instead a complete `WeakWrite()` by process 0. Hence, $D'_j = \text{Conf}(D'_i, \lambda'\alpha_j\beta_j)$, is p_{k+1}-dirty. But this contradicts Observation 1, because according to Eq. (12) process p_{k+1} cannot distinguish D'_i from D'_j. Hence, we know that Case (a) from Lemma 2 cannot apply.

Now, suppose that instead Case (b) or (c) applies. We show that statments (i)–(iii) of the lemma are true for $\alpha = \lambda\alpha_i\sigma_i\lambda'\alpha_j$ and $C = \text{Conf}(Q, \alpha) = C'_j$. By the inductive hypothesis (i), in C_j all processes in $\mathcal{P} \setminus P_k$ are idle, so from Eq. (10) it follows that in C'_j all processes in $\mathcal{P} \setminus P_{k+1}$ are idle. This proves (i).

According to Cases (b) and (c) of Lemma 2, in configuration D'_i (and thus also in C'_j and D'_j) process p_{k+1} is poised to execute an operation *op* that is either a `Write()` or a `CAS(`x,y`)` on some object R^*. Moroever, in case that

```
shared
Register X = (⊥,⊥,⊥)
Register A[0...n−1] = ((⊥,⊥),...,(⊥,⊥))

Method DWrite_p(x)
 1 s ← GetSeq()
 2 X.Write(x,p,s)

Method GetSeq_p()
 3 (r, s_r) ← A[c].Read()
 4 if r = p then
 5 |  na ← (na \ {(c,i) | i ∈ ℕ}) ∪ (c, s_r)
 6 else
 7 |_ na ← na \ {(c,i) | i ∈ ℕ}
 8 c ← (c+1) mod n
 9 choose arbitrary s ∈ {0,...,2n+1} \ ({i | (j,i) ∈ na} ∪ usedQ)
10 usedQ.enq(s)
11 usedQ.deq()
12 return s
```

```
local (to each process)
Boolean b = False
Queue usedQ[n+1] = (⊥,...,⊥)
Set na = {}
int c = 0

Method DRead_q()
13 (x,p,s) ← X.Read()
14 (r,s_r) ← A[q].Read()
15 A[q].Write(p,s)
16 (x',p',s') ← X.Read()
17 if (p,s) = (r,s_r) then
18 |  ret ← (x,b)
19 else
20 |_ ret ← (x,True)
21 if (x,p,s) = (x',p',s') then
22 |  b ← False
23 else
24 |_ b ← True
25 return ret
```

Figure 2: An ABA-detecting register implemented from bounded registers.

op is a CAS(x,y), in configuration D'_i object R^* has value x. Then Eq. (12) implies that the value of R^* is also x in configuration D'_j, and in partiular, if p_{k+1} executes CAS(x,y) in that configuration, that CAS() succeeds. We conclude that in the execution $\text{Exec}(C'_j, \beta_i \circ p_{k+1})$ process p_{k+1} takes exactly one step, which is either a Write() or a successful CAS(x,y). By construction, $\text{Exec}(C_i, \beta_i)$ is P_k-successful, and so Eq. (11) implies that $\text{Exec}(C'_j, \beta_i)$ is also P_k-successful. It follows that $\text{Exec}(C'_j, \beta_i \circ p_{k+1})$ is P_{k+1}-successful. Hence, $\text{Exec}(C'_j, \beta_i \circ p_{k+1})$ is P_{k+1}-successful, which proves statement (ii).

Finally, since in C'_j process p_{k+1} is poised to execute operation *op* on R^*, and all other processes are poised to execute exactly the same step as in C_i, we have: In case *op* is a Write(), $\text{WCov}(C'_j, R^*) = \text{WCov}(C_i, R^*) \cup \{p_{k+1}\}$, and in case *op* is a CAS(), $\text{CCov}(C'_j, R^*) = \text{CCov}(C_i, R^*) \cup \{p_{k+1}\}$. All other sets $\text{WCov}(\cdot,\cdot)$ and $\text{CCov}(\cdot,\cdot)$ are the same for C_i as for C'_j. Therefore, Cases (b) and (c) of Lemma 2 together with the inductive hypothesis (iii) immediately imply $|\text{WCov}(C'_j, R) \cap P_{k+1}| \le t$ and $|\text{CCov}(C'_j, R) \cap P_{k+1}| \le t$ for all objects R. This proves (iii) and completes the inductive step. □

Parts (b) and (c) of Theorem 1 follow immediately from this lemma. Replacing each WeakWrite() with a LL()/SC() pair by process 0, and accommodating the definition of p-clean and p-dirty configurations, we obtain Corollary 1.

3. UPPER BOUNDS

3.1 Constant-Time ABA-Detecting Registers from Registers

Figure 2 depicts an optimal linearizable implementation of an ABA-detecting register from $n+1$ bounded registers with constant step-complexity. We use two more registers than needed according to the lower bound in Theorem 1 (a). The main idea of the algorithm is similar to one used in the multi-layered construction of LL/SC/VL from CAS by Jayanti and Petrovic [15], which itself is a modified version of the implementation by Anderson and Moir [2].

Here, we briefly discuss the implementation. The correctness proof is omitted due to space restrictions. We use a shared bounded register X that stores a triple (x, p, s), where $x \in D$, $p \in \mathcal{P}$ is a process ID, and $s \in \{0, \dots, 2n+1\}$ is a sequence number. We also use a shared *announce array* $A[0 \cdots n-1]$, where only process q can write to $A[q]$. Each array entry $A[q]$ stores a pair (p, s), where $p \in \{0, \dots, n-1\}$ is a process ID and $s \in \{0, \dots, 2n+1\}$ is a sequence number. Register X is initialized to $(\bot, \bot, \bot)$ and all entries of A are initialized to $(\bot, \bot)$.

In a DWrite(x) operation, the calling process q first determines a suitable sequence number, s, using the helper method GetSeq(), and writes the pair (x, p, s) to X (lines 1–2). Method GetSeq() ensures that the sequence number s it returns satisfies the following: If there is any point at which $X = (\cdot, p, s)$ and $A[q] = (p, s)$ for some process q, then p will not use sequence number s again in any following DWrite() call, until $A[q] \neq (p, s)$. To achieve that, in a sequence of n consecutive GetSeq() calls process p scans through the entire announce array, reading one array entry with each GetSeq() call. It then returns a sequence number that p has not used in its preceding n DWrite() method calls, and which it has not found in any array entry of $A[]$, when it read that entry last.

For its DRead() operation each process q uses a local variable, b, that indicates whether a DWrite() operation linearized already during q's previous DRead() operation after that operation's linearization point. Our algorithms ensure that if b = True at the beginning of a DRead() operation, then such a DWrite() has happened. In a DRead() operation, a process reads X twice to obtain the triples (x, p, s) in line 13, and (x', p', s') in line 16. Between those two reads q first reads the old value of $A[q]$ into (r, s_r) (line 14), and then it *announces* the pair (p, s) by writing it to $A[q]$ (line 15). Now (r, s_r) stores the "old" announcement from q's preceding DRead() operation, and $A[q]$ stores the current one. In

```
Method SC_p(x)
26 if b then return False
27 for i ← 1 to n do
28     (y, a) ← X.Read()
29     if ⌊a/2^p⌋ is odd then /* if p's bit is 1 */
30         return False
31     if X.CAS((y, a), (x, 2^n − 1)) then
32         return True
33 return False
```

```
Method VL_p()
34 (x, a) ← X.Read()
35 if (⌊a/2^p⌋ is even ∧ b = False) then /* if p's
       bit is 0 and b = False */
36     return True
37 else
38     return False
```

```
shared: CAS X
local: Boolean b
```

```
Method LL_p()
39 (x, a) ← X.Read()
40 if ⌊a/2^p⌋ is even then            /* if p's bit is 0 */
41     b ← False
42     return x
43 else
44     for i ← 1 to n do
45         (x', a') ← X.Read()
46         if X.CAS((x', a'), (x', a' − 2^p)) then    /* try
               to reset p's bit */
47             b ← False
48             return x'
49     b ← True
50     return x
```

Figure 3: An LL/SC/VL implementation from bounded CAS.

lines 17–20, q now decides the return value: If $b =$ `True` or if $(p, s) \neq (r, s_r)$, then q returns $(x,$ `True`$)$, and otherwise $(x,$ `False`$)$. Moreover, in preparation for the next `DRead()`, if $(x, p, s) = (x', p', s')$, q sets b to `False`, and otherwise it sets it to `True`.

First suppose q reads two different triples from X in line 13 and line 16, i.e., $(x, p, s) \neq (x', p', x')$. Then the `DRead()` operation will linearize with the first read of X (line 13). We now know that the value of X has changed between the linearization point and the response of q's `DRead()`. Hence, q sets flag b to indicate that its next `DRead()` should return a pair $(\cdot,$ `True`$)$. If $(x, p, s) = (x', p', s')$, then, on the other hand, it is ensured that $A[q] = (p, s)$ at the point when q read (x, p, s) from X in line 16. As explained above, in this case the pair (p, s) will not be used again in any following `DWrite()` operation, until q has replaced its announcement (p, s) with a new one. Hence, q resets b because in the following `DRead()` operation, q will be able to detect any `DWrite()` that has happened inbetween by comparing $A[q]$ with the corresponding pair stored in X.

3.2 LL/SC/VL from a Single Bounded CAS

We now briefly sketch our wait-free implementation of LL/SC/VL from a single bounded CAS object. The implementation has $O(n)$ step complexity, and thus, by Corollary 1, is optimal. The pseudo-code is presented in Figure 3. The correctness proof is omitted due to space restrictions.

In a CAS object X, we store a pair (x, a), where x represents the value of the implemented LL/SC/VL object, and a is an n-bit string. The p-th bit of a is used to indicate whether an `SC()` operation linearized since p's last `LL()` (the bit is usually set in this case). As in the previous algorithm, we use a local variable b for each process p. In an `LL()` call, a process p tries to reset *its* bit (the p-th bit of the second component) of X. As we explain below, this may fail, but only if an `SC()` *sc* linearizes during p's attempts to reset that bit. If that happens, p sets the flag b and its `LL()` linearizes before *sc*. Thus, in a subsequent `SC()` or `VL()`, p determines from the set flag b that it does not have a valid link, and that `SC()` or `VL()` can fail, even though p's bit in X is not set.

More precisely, in a `LL()` method call, process p reads the pair (x, a) from X (line 39) and checks whether its bit in a is set. If not, in lines 41–42 it simply resets b (because in subsequent `SC()` or `VL()` calls p's bit in X will indicate whether p has a valid link or not) and returns x. That `LL()` operation linearizes with the `Read()` of X in line 39. Now suppose p's bit in X is set. Then p tries to reset that bit, using a `CAS()` operation on X. However, that `CAS()` may fail because of some other process' successful `CAS()` during a `LL()` or `SC()` call. Therefore, p repeatedly reads X followed by a `CAS()` to set its bit in the second component of X, until its `CAS()` operation succeeds, or until it has failed n times (lines 45–46). If a `CAS()` succeeds, p resets b and returns the first component of X that it read just before its last, successful `CAS()` attempt (lines 47–48); the `LL()` linearizes with that `CAS()`, and since p's bit in X is now reset, in the next `DRead()` operation p can use its bit in X to determine whether an `SC()` linearized since the linearization point of the current `DRead()`. If p's `CAS()` fails n times, then X must have changed n times since p's first `Read()` of X. We argue that then at least one such change must be due to a `CAS()` operation during some process' `SC()`: Suppose not. Then X must have changed at least n times, and every time it must have changed because of a `CAS()` executed in a `LL()` operation. But this is not possible, because each time such a `CAS()` succeeds, one of the bits in the second part of X changes from 1 to 0, and p's bit does not change at all. We conclude that at least once, while p has been trying to reset its bit in X, a successful `CAS()` on X must have occurred during an `SC()` operation. As we discuss below, this means that a successful `SC()` linearized. Hence, in this case p can set its bit to `True` (line 49), which guarantees that p's next `SC()` or `VL()` will fail, and return in line 50 the value x it read at the very beginning from X. The linearization point of that `LL()` is the `Read()` of X in line 39.

In an `SC(`y`)` operation a process p first checks flag b, and if it is set, p immediately returns `False`—this indicates that an `SC()` linearized during p's last `LL()` but after the linearization point of that `LL()`. If b is not set, then p reads X to determine whether its bit in X is set, and if yes, it can also return `False` (lines 28–30), because this indicates that some other `SC()` has linearized since p's last `LL()`. If p's bit in X is not set, then p tries to write $(y, 2^n - 1)$ into X using a `CAS()` operation (line 31). If that `CAS()` succeeds, as a result the value of the LL/SC/VL object change to y, and the bits of all processes are now set in X. Hence, p's `SC(`y`)` linearizes with that successful `CAS()`, and p returns `True` (line 32). If the `CAS()` fails, then p repeats up to n times, until either it finds that its bit in X is set (and thus some other process' `SC()` succeeded), or its own `CAS()` succeeds. If p's `CAS()` fails n times, then for the same reasons as explained earlier, we know that some process' `SC()` must have linearized during p's ongoing `SC(`y`)` operation, and thus p can return `False` (the unsuccessful `SC()` linearizes with its response).

Operation `VL()` is very simple: A process simply checks whether flag b or its bit in X is set, and if yes, it returns `False`, otherwise it returns `True`.

4. REFERENCES

[1] Z. Aghazadeh, W. Golab, and P. Woelfel. Making objects writable. In *Proc. of 33rd PODC*, pages 385–395, 2014.

[2] J. H. Anderson and M. Moir. Universal constructions for multi-object operations. In *Proc. of 14th PODC*, pages 184–193, 1995.

[3] H. Attiya and F. Ellen. *Impossibility Results for Distributed Computing*. Synthesis Lectures on Distributed Computing Theory. Morgan & Claypool Publishers, 2014.

[4] J. Burns and N. Lynch. Bounds on shared memory for mutual exclusion. *Information and Computation*, 107(2):171–184, 1993.

[5] S. Doherty, M. Herlihy, V. Luchangco, and M. Moir. Bringing practical lock-free synchronization to 64-bit applications. In *Proc. of 23rd PODC*, pages 31–39, 2004.

[6] F. Ellen, P. Fatourou, and E. Ruppert. The space complexity of unbounded timestamps. *Distr. Comp.*, 21(2):103–115, 2008.

[7] F. E. Fich, D. Hendler, and N. Shavit. On the inherent weakness of conditional primitives. *Distr. Comp.*, 18(4):267–277, 2006.

[8] F. E. Fich, M. Herlihy, and N. Shavit. On the space complexity of randomized synchronization. *J. of the ACM*, 45(5):843–862, 1998.

[9] M. Helmi, L. Higham, E. Pacheco, and P. Woelfel. The space complexity of long-lived and one-shot timestamp implementations. *J. of the ACM*, 61(1):7, 2014.

[10] D. Hendler, N. Shavit, and L. Yerushalmi. A scalable lock-free stack algorithm. *J. Parallel Distrib. Comp.*, 70(1):1–12, 2010.

[11] M. Herlihy. Wait-free synchronization. *ACM Trans. Program. Lang. Syst.*, 13(1):124–149, 1991.

[12] M. Herlihy, V. Luchangco, and M. Moir. The repeat offender problem: A mechanism for supporting dynamic-sized, lock-free data structures. In *Proc. of 16th DISC*, pages 339–353, 2002.

[13] M. Herlihy and J. M. Wing. Linearizability: A correctness condition for concurrent objects. *ACM Trans. Program. Lang. Syst.*, 12(3), 1990.

[14] IBM. IBM system/370 extended architecture, principles of operation. Technical report, 1983. Publication No. SA22-7085.

[15] P. Jayanti and S. Petrovic. Efficient and practical constructions of LL/SC variables. In *Proc. of 22nd PODC*, pages 285–294, 2003.

[16] P. Jayanti and S. Petrovic. Efficiently implementing a large number of LL/SC objects. In *Proc. of 9th OPODIS*, pages 17–31, 2005.

[17] P. Jayanti, K. Tan, and S. Toueg. Time and space lower bounds for nonblocking implementations. *SIAM J. on Comp.*, 30(2):438–456, 2000.

[18] E. Ladan-Mozes and N. Shavit. An optimistic approach to lock-free FIFO queues. *Distr. Comp.*, 20(5):323–341, 2008.

[19] M. Michael. High performance dynamic lock-free hash tables and list-based sets. In *Proc. of 14th SPAA*, pages 73–82, 2002.

[20] M. Michael. ABA prevention using single-word instructions. Technical report, IBM T. J. Watson Research Center, 2004.

[21] M. Michael. Hazard pointers: Safe memory reclamation for lock-free objects. *IEEE Trans. Parallel Distrib. Syst.*, 15(6):491–504, 2004.

[22] M. Michael. Practical lock-free and wait-free LL/SC/VL implementations using 64-bit CAS. In *Proc. of 18th DISC*, pages 144–158, 2004.

[23] M. Michael. Scalable lock-free dynamic memory allocation. In *Proc. of PLDI*, pages 35–46, 2004.

[24] M. Michael and M. L. Scott. Simple, fast, and practical non-blocking and blocking concurrent queue algorithms. In *Proc. of 15th PODC*, pages 267–275, 1996.

[25] M. Michael and M. L. Scott. Nonblocking algorithms and preemption-safe locking on multiprogrammed shared memory multiprocessors. *J. Parallel Distrib. Comp.*, 51(1):1–26, 1998.

[26] M. Moir. Practical implementations of non-blocking synchronization primitives. In *Proc. of 16th PODC*, pages 219–228, 1997.

[27] S. Prakash, Y. Lee, and T. Johnson. A non-blocking algorithm for shared queues using compare-and-swap. In *Proc. of ICPP*, pages 68–75, 1991.

[28] C. Shann, T. Huang, and C. Chen. A practical nonblocking queue algorithm using compare-and-swap. In *Proc. of 7th ICPADS*, pages 470–475, 2000.

[29] J. M. Stone. A simple and correct shared-queue algorithm using compare-and-swap. In J. L. Martin, D. V. Pryor, and G. Montry, editors, *Proceedings Supercomputing*, pages 495–504. IEEE Computer Society / ACM, 1990.

[30] E. Styer and G. Peterson. Tight bounds for shared memory symmetric mutual exclusion problems. In *Proc. of 8th PODC*, pages 177–191, 1989.

[31] P. Tsigas and Y. Zhang. A simple, fast and scalable non-blocking concurrent FIFO queue for shared memory multiprocessor systems. In *Proc. of 13th SPAA*, pages 134–143, 2001.

[32] J. D. Valois. Lock-free linked lists using compare-and-swap. In *Proc. of 14th PODC*, pages 214–222, 1995.

Brief Announcement: Fault-tolerant Broadcast in Anonymous Distributed Systems with Fair Lossy Communication Channels *

Jian Tang
Distributed Systems Laboratory (LSD)
Technical University of Madrid
28031 Madrid, Spain
tjapply@gmail.com

Mikel Larrea
University of Basque Country UPV/EHU
20018 San Sebastián, Spain
mikel.larrea@ehu.eus

Sergio Arévalo
Technical University of Madrid
28031 Madrid, Spain
sergio.arevalo@eui.upm.es

Ernesto Jiménez
Technical University of Madrid
28031 Madrid, Spain
Prometeo Researcher
Escuela Politécnica Nacional
170515 Quito, Ecuador
ernes@eui.upm.es

ABSTRACT

Fault-tolerant broadcast is a fundamental service in distributed systems, by which processes can communicate with each other consistently and reliably. It has two main forms: Reliable Broadcast (RB) and Uniform Reliable Broadcast (URB). This service has been extensively investigated in non-anonymous distributed systems where processes have unique identifiers, usually assume the communication channels are reliable, which is not always the case in real systems. In this paper, the fault-tolerant broadcast service is studied in an anonymous asynchronous message passing distributed system model with fair lossy communication channels. Firstly, two simple and non-quiescent algorithms implementing RB and URB are given. Secondly, two new classes of failure detectors $A\Theta$ and AP^* are proposed. Finally, with the information provided by $A\Theta$ and AP^*, quiescent algorithms for both RB and URB are given.

Categories and Subject Descriptors

H.3.4 [**System and Software**]: Distributed Systems

General Terms

Algorithms, Design, Theory

Keywords

Anonymous, reliable broadcast, failure detector, quiescent.

*The full version of this work can be found in [6].

Permission to make digital or hard copies of part or all of this work for personal or classroom use is granted without fee provided that copies are not made or distributed for profit or commercial advantage and that copies bear this notice and the full citation on the first page. Copyrights for third-party components of this work must be honored. For all other uses, contact the Owner/Author. Copyright is held by the owner/author(s).
PODC'15, July 21–23, 2015, Donostia-San Sebastián, Spain.
ACM 978-1-4503-3617-8 /15/07.
http://dx.doi.org/10.1145/2767386.2767443.

1. INTRODUCTION

Fault-tolerant broadcast is a fundamental service in distributed systems, which is helpful to build dependable applications. This service is used to disseminate messages among a set of processes, and has two forms according to its guarantee of delivery [1]. The weakest form is *Reliable Broadcast* (RB), with *RB-broadcast()* and *RB-deliver()* operations, introduced in [2]. In short, RB is a broadcast service requiring all correct processes to deliver the same set of messages, and this set must include all messages broadcast by correct processes. However, this broadcast form can cause some inconsistencies when a process fails after delivering a message. Hence, a stronger broadcast form called *Uniform Reliable Broadcast* (URB) has been proposed [3], with *URB-broadcast()* and *URB-deliver()* operations, guaranteeing that if a process (no matter correct or incorrect) delivers a message m, then all correct processes must deliver m too.

In this paper, the fault-tolerant broadcast service is studied in the anonymous asynchronous message passing distributed system model with fair lossy communication channels.

2. SYSTEM MODEL AND DEFINITIONS

We consider an anonymous asynchronous message passing distributed system in which processes have no identifiers and communicate with each other via a completely connected network of fair lossy channels. The system is composed of n processes, and denoted by $\Pi = \{p_i\}(i = 1, ..., n)$ (i is the index of each process in the system. This index is just used as a notation to simplify the description of the model and the algorithms, and it is not known by any process).

Processes can fail by crashing. A process that does not crash in a run is *correct* in that run, otherwise it is *faulty*. A process executes its algorithm correctly until it crashes. A crashed process can neither execute any more statements nor recover. There is a global clock whose values are positive natural numbers, which is also used for notation purposes.

Processes communicate with each other by sending and receiving messages through fair lossy communication channels. Formally, a channel between two processes p and q is fair lossy if it satisfies the following properties [4]: If p sends a message m to q an infinite number of times and q is correct, then q eventually receives m from p (Fairness); If q receives a message m from p, then p previously sent m to q; and if q receives m infinitely often from p, then p sends m infinitely often to q (Uniform Integrity). Two basic primitives are used in the system to send and receive messages: *broadcast(m)* and *receive(m)*. We say that a process p_i broadcasts a message m when it invokes $broadcast_i(m)$. Similarly, a process p_i receives a message m when it invokes $receive_i(m)$. Note that in anonymous distributed systems, when a process receives a message m it cannot determine who is the sender of m.

The system model is denoted by either $AAS\_F_{n,t}[\emptyset]$ or $AAS\_F_{n,t}[D]$. AAS_F is an acronym for anonymous asynchronous message passing distributed system with fair lossy communication channels; $\emptyset$ means that there is no additional assumption, while D means that the system is enriched with a failure detector of class D. The variable n represents the total number of processes in the system, and t represents the maximum number of processes that can fail.

Reliable Broadcast (RB) is a broadcast form that satisfies the following three properties:

- *Validity*: If a correct process broadcasts a message m, then it eventually delivers m.
- *Agreement*: If a correct process delivers a message m, then all correct processes eventually deliver m.
- *Uniform Integrity*: For any message m, every process delivers m at most once, and only if m was previously broadcast by a process.

Note that Validity and Agreement imply that all correct processes deliver all the messages broadcast by correct processes. Uniform Reliable Broadcast (URB) is a broadcast form stronger than RB, satisfying Validity and Uniform Integrity (as RB), and *Uniform* Agreement, defined as follows:

- *Uniform Agreement*: If some process (correct or not) delivers a message m, then all correct processes eventually deliver m.

3. IMPLEMENTATION OF FAULT TOLERANT BROADCAST IN AAS_F

A key point to implement the fault-tolerant broadcast service in AAS_F is how to distinguish a process or a message from others. In this paper, we solve this by making each message to be unique. This idea is easily implemented in non-anonymous systems, usually by using the identifier of the sender process and a sequence number. However, in anonymous systems this method cannot be used due to the fact that processes do not have identifiers. Hence, we propose to use a random function, assigning a different random number to each message as its unique label or *tag*. We assume that each number generated randomly is unique in the system. Note that assigning a label to a message is better than to a process, because there is no way to deduce the messages sent from a given process. Indeed, all processes still maintain their anonymity in the system.

With the idea mentioned above and a simple flooding transmission technique, an implementation algorithm of RB in $AAS\_F[\emptyset]$ and another algorithm implementing URB in $AAS\_F[t<n/2]$ are proposed in our full paper [6]. Both algorithms are non-quiescent, i.e., delivered messages need to be re-broadcast periodically in order to cope with fair lossy communication. Additionally, we show that it is impossible to implement URB without a majority of correct processes. Hence, in the next section we enrich the anonymous system model with two failure detectors in order to implement RB and URB quiescently and with any number of correct processes.

4. TWO CLASSES OF ANONYMOUS FAILURE DETECTORS

The failure detector abstraction was proposed Chandra and Toueg [5], which defined them in terms of completeness and accuracy properties. A failure detector can be seen as a module that gives (possibly unreliable) failure information of processes. Usually, this failure information is composed of the identifiers of processes in non-anonymous distributed systems. However, in anonymous distributed systems processes have no identifier. So, the key point to define and implement a failure detector in an anonymous distributed system is how to identify a process without breaking the anonymity of the system. We were inspired by the definition of the failure detector class $A\Sigma$, which was introduced by Bonnet and Raynal [7], that assigns a random *label* to each process as a temporal identifier. This assignment does not break the anonymity of the system, because this *label* is given in the failure detector layer, and no process knows the mapping relationship between labels and processes.

4.1 Failure Detector $A\Theta$

$A\Theta$ provides each process p_i with a read-only local variable a_theta_i that contains several pairs of (*label*, *number*), in which each *label* represents a temporary identifier of one process and *number* represents the number of correct processes who have known this *label*. For example, process p_j's local variable at time τ $a\_theta_j^{\tau} = \{(label_1, number_1), \ldots, (label_i, number_i), \ldots, (label_n, number_n)\}$ if p_j has known the *label* of n processes of the system. As we said previously, labels are assigned randomly to each process without breaking the anonymity of the system.

The definition of $A\Theta$ is given as follows:

- *$A\Theta$-completeness*: There is a time after which variables *a_theta* only contain pairs of (*label*, *number*) associated to correct processes.
- *$A\Theta$-accuracy*: If there is a correct process, then at every time, all pairs of (*label*, *number*) output by failure detector $A\Theta$ hold that every subset T of size *number* of processes that know *label* contains at least one correct process (i.e., for each *label*, there always exists one correct process in any set of *number* processes that know this label).

Let us define $A\Theta$ more formally:

$S(label)=\{i \mid \exists\, \tau \in \mathbb{N}\colon (label, -) \in a\_theta_i^{\tau}\}$. $S(label)$ is the set of all processes that know *label* at time τ.

- *$A\Theta$-completeness*: $\exists\, \tau \in \mathbb{N}$, $\forall\, i \in Correct$, $\forall\, \tau' \geq \tau$, $\forall\, (label, number) \in a\_theta_i^{\tau'}$: $|S(label) \cap Correct| = number$.

- *AΘ-accuracy*: $Correct \neq \emptyset \implies \forall\ \tau \in \mathbb{N}, \forall\ i \in \Pi, \forall\ (label, number) \in a\_theta_i^{\tau}: \forall\ T \subseteq S(label), |T| = number: T \cap Correct \neq \emptyset$.

4.2 Failure Detector AP^*

The anonymous perfect failure detector AP^* provides each process p_i with a read-only local variable $a\_p_i^*$ that contains several pairs of (*label*, *number*), similar to failure detector $A\Theta$. The definition of AP^* is as follows:

- *AP^*-completeness*: There is a time after which variables a_p^* only contain pairs of (*label*, *number*) associated to correct processes.
- *AP^*-accuracy*: If a process crashes, the *label* of this process and the corresponding *number* to the *label* will be permanently removed from variables a_p^*.

It is assumed that the *number* of each *label* is monotonically non-increasing. Eventually the number of pairs of (*label*, *number*) is equal to the number of correct processes.

Let us define AP^* more formally:

$S(label)=\{i \mid \exists\ \tau \in \mathbb{N}: (label, -) \in a\_p{^*}_i^{\tau}\}$. $S(label)$ is the set of all processes that know *label* at time τ.

- *AP^*-completeness*: $\exists\ \tau \in \mathbb{N}, \forall\ i \in Correct, \forall\ \tau' \geq \tau, \forall\ (label, number) \in a\_p{^*}_i^{\tau'}: |S(label) \cap Correct| = number$.
- *AP^*-accuracy*: $\forall\ i, j \in \Pi, i \in Correct, j \in Faulty, \exists\ \tau, \forall\ \tau' \geq \tau: (label_j, number_j) \notin a\_p{^*}_i^{\tau'}$.

5. QUIESCENT FAULT TOLERANT BROADCAST IN $AAS\_F[A\Theta, AP^*]$

Before solving the quiescence problem, the impossibility result of implementing URB without a majority of correct processes is circumvented firstly with $A\Theta$. To do so, in our algorithm an adequate use of $A\Theta$ ensures that the acknowledge of a message m has been received by at least one correct process before delivering m.

The reason why both the RB and URB algorithms of Section 3 are non-quiescent is that each correct process has to broadcast periodically the messages it has delivered in order to overcome message losses caused by the fair lossy communication channels. Therefore, the intuitive idea to make them to be quiescent is to stop the periodical broadcast when a message has been delivered by all correct processes. The following question arises: how can we confirm that a message has been delivered by all correct processes in an anonymous system? In order to answer this question, we propose to combine two mechanisms: (1) each process broadcasts an acknowledgment message after it has delivered a message m, and waits for the acknowledgment messages of m from all processes (including itself); (2) the failure detector AP^* is used to provide the information of all correct processes. With these two mechanisms, a process p_i can stop the periodical broadcast of message m when it has received the acknowledgment of m from all correct processes. Note that these two mechanisms do not break the anonymity of the system.

Following this approach, a quiescent RB algorithm implemented in $AAS\_F[AP^*]$ and a quiescent URB algorithm in $AAS\_F[A\Theta, AP^*]$ are given in our full paper [6].

6. CONCLUSION

In this paper, the fault-tolerant broadcast service has been studied in anonymous asynchronous message passing distributed systems with fair lossy communication channels. Initially, two non-quiescent algorithms have been proposed: the non-quiescent reliable broadcast (RB) algorithm can be implemented under the assumption of anynumber of correct processes, while the non-quiescent uniform reliable broadcast (URB) algorithm requires either a majority of correct processes or a failure detector of class $A\Theta$. In order to implement the fault-tolerant broadcast service quiescently, a new anonymous perfect failure detector AP^* is proposed. Finally, two quiescent algorithms using AP^* and implementing RB and URB respectively are proposed.

Acknowledgment

We would like to thank the anonymous reviewers. This research is partially supported by the Community of Madrid under grant S2013/ICE-2894, the Spanish Research Council under grants TIN2013-41123-P and TIN2013-46883-P, the Basque Government under grant IT395-10, the University of the Basque Country (UPV/EHU) under grant UFI11/45, and the scholarship of Chinese Scholarship Council.

7. REFERENCES

[1] C. Cachin, R. Guerraoui, and L. Rodrigues. Reliable and secure distributed programming. Springer (second edition), 2011.

[2] F. Schneider, D. Gries, and R. Schlichting. Fault-tolerant broadcast. Science of Computer Programming 4(1), pp. 1–15, 1984.

[3] V. Hadzilacos and S. Toueg. Fault tolerant broadcasts and related problems. S.J. Mullender (Ed.), Distributed Systems. New York: ACM Press & Addison-Wesley, 1993.

[4] M. Aguilera, S. Toueg, and B. Deianov. Revisiting the weakest failure detector for uniform reliable broadcast. Proceedings of the 13th International Symposium on Distributed Computing (DISC 1999), pp. 19–33, Bratislava, Slovak Republic, September 1999.

[5] T. Chandra and S. Toueg. Unreliable failure detectors for reliable distributed systems. Journal of the ACM, 43(2), pp. 225–267, March 1996.

[6] J. Tang, M. Larrea, S. Arévalo, and E. Jiménez. Fault-tolerant broadcast in anonymous distributed systems with fair lossy channels. Technical Report EHU-KAT-IK-06-14 of the University of the Basque Country UPV/EHU, December 2014, http://www.sc.ehu.es/acwlaalm/research/EHU-KAT-IK-06-14.pdf.

[7] F. Bonnet and M. Raynal. Anonymous asynchronous systems: the case of failure detectors. Proceedings of the 24th International Symposium on Distributed Computing (DISC 2010), pp. 206–220, Cambridge, MA, USA, September 2010.

Impossibility Results for Distributed Transactional Memory

Costas Busch
Louisiana State University
Baton Rouge, LA
busch@csc.lsu.edu

Maurice Herlihy
Brown University
Providence, RI
herlihy@cs.brown.edu

Miroslav Popovic
University of Novi Sad
Novi Sad, Serbia
Miroslav.Popovic@rt-rk.com

Gokarna Sharma
Louisiana State University
Baton Rouge, LA
gokarna@csc.lsu.edu

ABSTRACT

We consider scheduling problems in the data flow model of distributed transactional memory. Objects shared by transactions move from one network node to another by following network paths. We examine how the objects' transfer in the network affects the completion time of all transactions and the total communication cost. We show that there are problem instances for which there is no scheduling algorithm that can simultaneously minimize the completion time and communication cost. These instances reveal a trade-off, minimizing execution time implies high communication cost and vice versa. On the positive side, we provide scheduling algorithms which are independently communication cost near-optimal or execution time efficient.

Categories and Subject Descriptors

C.2.1 [**COMPUTER-COMMUNICATION NETWORKS**]: Network Architecture and Design—*Distributed networks*; F.2.0 [**Theory of Computation**]: Analysis of Algorithms and Problem Complexity—*General*

General Terms

Algorithms; Theory

Keywords

Transactional memory; distributed systems; impossibility results; communication cost; execution time

1. INTRODUCTION

Transactional memory (TM) [15, 37] provides an alternative synchronization mechanism to traditional lock-based synchronization that is non-blocking, composable, and easier to write than lock-based code. TM has fundamentally changed the way programming is done in multi-core computers both from theoretical and practical aspect, and it is an immense area of research interest in both academia and industry [1]. TM-based synchronization has recently been included in IBM's Blue Gene/Q [13, 38] and Intel's Haswell processors [19]. TM is predicted to be widely used in future processors, possibly even GPUs, clusters, and distributed networked systems [7, 9, 10, 24, 25].

We study here TM implementations in distributed networked systems. Distributed networked systems are widely available in recent days and there is a growing interest in implementing TM in them [32, 29, 26, 5, 16, 36, 40, 41, 14, 9, 7, 25, 24]. In distributed TM, there is an underlying network modeled as a weighted graph G. Each transaction resides at a node of G and requires one or more shared objects for read or write. TM implementations in distributed networked systems are divided into three categories: *data-flow*, *control-flow*, and *hybrid-flow* based implementations. In the data-flow approach [5, 16, 36, 35, 40, 41], objects are mobile and move from one node to another by traversing the network. This movement is dictated by the object requests from the transactions executing at different network nodes. In the control-flow approach [32, 26], objects are immobile and transactions move to the network nodes where the required objects reside. More precisely, when a transaction performs an operation on an object stored on a remote node, the operation is invoked as a remote procedure call on that node. The hybrid-flow [29, 26] is a combination of the data-flow and control-flow approaches so that sometimes the objects move and other times the control moves.

Besides these categories, there is a line of work to implement TMs in distributed systems through replication and multi-versioning [14, 29, 28, 26, 30, 17, 22, 25]. In replicated TMs, there are multiple copies available in the system for each shared object [26], whereas in multi-versioning TMs, multiple versions of each object are available [25, 21]. Recently, the speculative execution of transactions is also studied [30, 27].

In this paper, we consider scheduling problems in the data-flow based implementation of TM in distributed networked systems and provide impossibility results and upper bounds. Scheduling[1] is an important aspect of any TM implementa-

[1]Scheduling in TM is also called *contention management* as it is related to handling transaction conflicts appropriately to optimize performance metrics of interest.

Permission to make digital or hard copies of all or part of this work for personal or classroom use is granted without fee provided that copies are not made or distributed for profit or commercial advantage and that copies bear this notice and the full citation on the first page. Copyrights for components of this work owned by others than ACM must be honored. Abstracting with credit is permitted. To copy otherwise, or republish, to post on servers or to redistribute to lists, requires prior specific permission and/or a fee. Request permissions from permissions@acm.org.
PODC'15, July 21–23, 2015, Donostia-San Sebastián, Spain.
Copyright © 2015 ACM 978-1-4503-3617-8 /15/07 ...$15.00.
DOI: http://dx.doi.org/10.1145/2767386.2767433.

tion in any system since its performance directly depends on it. Most of the existing theoretical results for scheduling on distributed TM are given for the data-flow model. It is shown that the data-flow model exploits object locality very well and the communication costs for objects can be controlled. On the other hand, in a control-flow based implementation through Remote Procedure Calls (RPCs), an object's home might become a bottleneck in a hot spot situation and it might be difficult to control communication costs [16]. We focus on impossibility results as such results accurately identify the power of a TM implementation in any system and its ramifications. Although several impossibility results of different kind are known for TM implementations in (tightly-coupled) multi-core systems [3, 4, 33, 34], to the best of our knowledge, no such results are known for TM implementations in distributed systems.

For the system model, we assume bidirectional edges in G which allow objects to traverse each edge concurrently in either direction. An object takes time equal to the weight of the edge to traverse it. An execution schedule specifies which transactions execute at any moment of time and, in a distributed setting, it also determines the network paths that the objects follow while moving from one transaction to another. Given a set of transactions in G, we evaluate an execution schedule with two typical performance metrics:

- *communication cost*, which is the total distance traversed by all the objects in G, and
- *execution time*, which is the total time to execute all the transactions.

In order to guarantee *consistency* in a data-flow based implementation, an object can have only one write-able copy at any moment of time. When a transaction starts execution at a node, it requests shared objects for read or write. When the requested object is in the local memory of a node then a transaction at that node can use the object. If the object is not available in the local memory it sends an appropriate read/write request to the node where the object currently resides. The object request is sent by invoking a *cache-coherence* protocol (e.g. [5, 36, 16]) to locate the object in the network. A transaction completes its execution after it receives all requested objects. Once a transaction finishes execution it releases the writable objects to other transactions that need them. For simplicity in the analysis, we assume that once a transaction has obtained all requested objects its actual computation time is instantaneous, which implies that the execution time for a set of transactions depends only on the edge traversal times of the objects.

Previous works on theoretical analysis of transaction scheduling in data-flow distributed TMs focused on minimizing either the communication cost or the execution time. The communication cost minimization is considered in several papers [16, 36, 40, 5, 23] for problem instances with only one shared object. Kim and Ravindran [23] provided improved communication bounds for special workloads and problem instances with multiple shared objects. Recently, the execution time minimization is considered for the very first time by Zhang *et al.* [41] where they use traveling salesman problem (TSP) tours for object paths. An open problem is to provide general algorithms that provide small communication cost and small execution time for scheduling transactions that work on multiple objects. The aforementioned algorithms [16, 36, 40, 5] can replicate the data structure book-keeping information for each object to handle multiple objects. The performance bounds (i.e. communication cost) of these algorithms typically scale linearly with the number of objects and a natural question is whether there are more efficient approaches.

1.1 Contributions

We assume batch problems where all transactions and their requested objects are known before execution starts. This setting is helpful in obtaining impossibility results that can also apply to dynamic scenarios. We give trade-offs between communication cost and execution time that show that these metrics cannot be minimized simultaneously. On the positive side, we give algorithms that have near optimal communication cost and separately efficient execution time. Our detailed contributions are as follows.

Impossibility Results.

We give a scheduling problem instance on a grid graph G with n nodes such that there is one transaction per node requesting three shared objects. We show that in this instance it is impossible to simultaneously optimize execution time and communication cost. In particular, if the execution time is within a factor $O(k)$ from optimal, then the communication cost is a factor $\Omega(n^{1/4}/k)$ suboptimal, where $1 \leq k \leq n^{1/4}/16$. We also obtain a symmetric result such that if the communication cost is within a factor $O(k)$ from optimal then the execution time is a factor $\Omega(n^{1/4}/k)$ suboptimal. We provide two separate schedules that achieve the optimal communication cost and optimal execution time, respectively, and we show that both of these schedules achieve the best possible execution time and communication cost, respectively, given the trade-off result above.

These impossibility results imply that we cannot have a single scheduling algorithm that simultaneously minimizes both execution time and communication cost, and therefore, these two metrics have to be optimized independently by different algorithms.

Positive Results.

We give algorithms which minimize independently the communication cost or execution time in an arbitrary graph G. We first observe that the problem of minimizing the communication cost is NP-hard with a reduction from the graph TSP problem. In order to obtain an upper bound we use a *universal TSP tour* [20] that defines a traversal order of the nodes in G so that any subsequence of nodes in the tour is also an approximate TSP tour. Transactions execute in an order determined by the approximate TSP tours of the objects within the universal TSP. The overall schedule has communication cost within $O(\log^4 n/\log\log n)$ factor from optimal, where n is the number of nodes. We obtain better bounds for planar graphs and low doubling metrics.

We then study algorithms for efficient execution time. We observe that the problem of optimizing the execution time is also NP-hard and moreover hard to approximate within any factor smaller than the number of transactions (reduction from vertex-coloring). We give an $O(\Delta)$ approximation algorithm for the execution time, where Δ is the maximum number of conflicts between transactions. This bound is obtained with a greedy coloring of a weighted conflict graph of transactions.

Even though our impossibility results and bounds are derived on a data-flow based implementation in mind, they can also apply to restricted versions of other implementations such as replicated and multiversioning TMs. This is because there is only one copy (a version) for each object in the data-flow implementation compared to multiple copies (versions) in replicated (multiversioning) TMs. Deriving similar results in a control-flow based implementation is intriguing as locality can not be exploited as in the data-flow model.

1.2 Related Work

Busch *et al.* [8] give a preliminary brief announcement with earlier results of this work. Scheduling (or contention management) problems are widely studied in (tightly-coupled) multi-core systems and several scheduling algorithms with provable upper and lower bounds, and impossibility results are given [4, 6, 11, 33, 34, 35], besides other scheduling algorithms which are evaluated only experimentally [2, 39, 18]. These multi-core scheduling algorithms are not suitable for transaction scheduling in distributed systems as they do not typically deal with the latency (communication cost) in accessing shared resources.

Several researchers [7, 9, 24, 25, 31] present techniques to implement TM in distributed networked systems. However, they either use global lock, serialization lease, or commit-time broadcasting technique in their algorithms which may not scale well with the size of the network [5]. Moreover, they do not provide formal analysis of neither the execution time nor the communication cost. The most closely related works to ours are [16, 36, 40, 5, 23, 41], which most of them considered the data-flow model with only one shared object in the system. Herlihy and Sun [16] provided the first formal bounds for a distributed TM scheduling algorithm. The algorithm is based on a *hierarchical directory* which is built upon a multi-level distance clustering of the nodes around independent sets. The transaction execution schedule is implemented with appropriate book-keeping along a path from the directory root towards the current object owner node. For low doubling dimension networks and for a sequential access pattern of the object, they prove that the communication cost is within a $\log D$ factor from optimal, where D is the diameter of the network. Sharma *et al.* [36] generalized this approach for general network topologies, using sparse covers (a form of distance-based hierarchical clustering), where they give a poly-log approximation on the communication cost for a sequential access scenario of the single object and also for a batch concurrent access scenario.

An alternative approach to schedule transactions is using spanning trees. Zhang and Ravindran [40] proposed a scheduling algorithm that runs on a pre-selected *spanning tree* of the network graph. Attiya *et al.* [5] proposed a scheduling algorithm that runs on an *overlay tree*. The approximation of spanning and overlay trees can be as much as the diameter of the network. Kim and Ravindran [23] improved the tree bounds for special workloads and also give bounds for problem instances with multiple shared objects.

The execution time is ignored in these aforementioned papers [16, 36, 40, 5, 23]. The only work that considered execution time is Zhang *et al.* [41]. They showed that an online, *work-conserving*[2] deterministic scheduling algorithm provides an $\Omega(\max[s, \frac{s^2}{\overline{D}}])$ competitive ratio for s shared objects in a network G with normalized diameter $\overline{D}$. They also designed a randomized scheduling algorithm CUTTING which achieves the average case competitive ratio of $O(s \cdot \phi_A \cdot \log^2 m \cdot \log^2 n)$ for n transactions invoked by m nodes, where ϕ_A is the approximation ratio of a TSP algorithm. They further showed for the case of $s = 1$ that finding the optimal execution time schedule is NP-hard because it is equivalent to finding the TSP path in G. However, this work ignores the communication cost. In this paper we study the interplay between two different performance metrics studied separately in the aforementioned papers under the data-flow model which is crucial in efficiently executing transactions in distributed systems.

Several other works on distributed TMs considered different models. A control-flow based (where transactions can migrate) distributed TM scheduling algorithm is studied by Saad and Ravindran [32]. Kim and Ravindran [22] studied transaction scheduling in replicated distributed TMs. Hendler *et al.* [14] studied a lease based hybrid distributed TM scheduling mechanism which dynamically determines whether to migrate transactions to the nodes that own the leases, or to demand the acquisition of these leases by the node that originated the transaction. A comparative study of which implementation to use, data-flow or control-flow, is performed by Palmieri *et al.* [26] for distributed TMs in partially replicated environments. Furthermore, the speculative execution of transactions under the framework of replicated distributed TMs [27, 30], and the replicated and multiversioning distributed TMs with consistent snapshots of objects [29, 28, 26, 30, 17, 25, 22] are also studied to minimize the total execution time of transactions. However, all these works ignore the total communication cost of objects and no formal theoretical bounds are given.

1.3 Roadmap

The rest of the paper is organized as follows. In Section 2 we provide the detailed specifications for the data-flow distributed TM model. Impossibility results with execution time and communication trade-offs for scheduling in this model are presented in Section 3. In Section 4 we give hardness results and upper bounds for the communication cost and execution time. We conclude with a short discussion in Section 5.

2. MODEL

We model a distributed network as a weighted graph $G = (V, E, \mathfrak{w})$, with n nodes (representing network machines) $V = \{v_1, v_2, \ldots, v_n\}$, where $|V| = n$, edges (representing interconnection links between machines) $E \subseteq V \times V$, and edge weight function $\mathfrak{w} : E \to \mathbb{Z}^+$. A path p in G is a sequence of nodes (with respective edges between adjacent nodes) with $\text{length}(p) = \sum_{e \in p} \mathfrak{w}(e)$. For simplicity assume that G is connected, that is, there is a path in G between any pair of nodes. Let $\text{dist}(u, v)$ denote the shortest path length (distance) between nodes u and v.

We assume the synchronous communication model such that at each time step a node receives messages, performs a local computation, and then transmits messages to adjacent nodes. If the communication delay varies among nodes (i.e., the system is not completely synchronous), then our bounds are affected only by the synchronicity factor (maximum delay divided by minimum delay). For an edge $e = (u, v) \in E$

[2] A scheduling algorithm is work conserving if it always runs a maximal set of non-conflicting transactions.

it takes $\mathfrak{w}(e)$ time steps to transfer a message m between u and v; the *communication cost* contributed by m is equal to $\mathfrak{w}(e)$. We assume that the message size is sufficient to convey the information about an object over the network. We will assume bidirectional links, where at each moment of time messages can transmit in either direction of e. We do not impose a limit on the number of messages that may traverse concurrently an edge, since congestion does not affect the impossibility analysis.

Let $R = \{r_1, \ldots, r_l\}$ denote l shared memory objects. Each object has some value which can be read or modified (written). The shared objects reside at nodes and are mobile, that is, an object can move from node to node by being piggy-packed in a message. A transaction T_i is an atomic code executed at some node v_i which requires a set of objects $R(T_i) \subseteq R$. Transaction T_i can finish execution and commit only after all its required objects are gathered at v_i. We assume that the transaction computation time is instantaneous once it possesses the required objects. A transaction T_i may modify some objects while others may remain unchanged. To simplify the analysis, we assume that each object has a single copy (for both read or write) and an object resides at one node at any moment of time (initially, an object is at some arbitrary node of G). Recall that in the data-flow model, there is only a single write copy and possibly many read copies of each object. Our results and bounds still hold even if we allow multiple read copies for each object.

We assume that each network node runs only a single thread.[3] A node's thread issues transactions sequentially, i.e., a node can issue a new transaction only after its previous transaction has finished execution. Consider now a set of m transactions $\mathcal{T}$, where $m \leq n$, such that there is at most one transaction per node. This is the batch problem setting that we use for proving the results which is similar to the batch setting considered in scheduling in multi-core systems [34, 4, 6]. The transactions are distributed to network nodes and at most n transactions execute concurrently. Conflicts among transactions in accessing shared objects are defined in the usual way where an aborted transaction restarts immediately from its beginning. A *scheduling algorithm* A determines the time steps that objects move from one node to another and the time steps that transactions execute. Note that an object may have to traverse multiple node hops while moving from one transaction to the next, and part of the scheduling algorithm is to determine the paths that the objects follow (e.g. shortest paths). Let $\mathcal{E}$ be an execution schedule based on scheduling algorithm A.

DEFINITION 1 (COMMUNICATION COST). *For a set of transactions $\mathcal{T}$ in graph G, the communication cost of an execution $\mathcal{E}$ is the sum of the traversed path lengths of all messages sent during $\mathcal{E}$. The communication cost of scheduling algorithm A is the maximum communication cost over all possible executions for $\mathcal{T}$.*

DEFINITION 2 (EXECUTION TIME). *For a set of transactions $\mathcal{T}$ in graph G, the time of an execution $\mathcal{E}$ is the time elapsed until the last transaction finishes its execution in $\mathcal{E}$. The execution time of scheduling algorithm A is the maximum time over all possible executions for $\mathcal{T}$.*

[3]When a node is assumed to execute multiple threads then scheduling techniques widely studied for (tightly-coupled) multi-core systems can be used in each node to improve scheduling performance and the trade-off results are obtained only considering the transactions executing in different nodes.

3. IMPOSSIBILITY RESULTS

In this section we prove that it is impossible to have a single algorithm that simultaneously minimizes the execution time and the communication cost. To prove the result we construct a transaction scheduling problem on the grid, such that any schedule that minimizes execution time has suboptimal communication cost, and vice versa. We continue with describing the specific problem instance, and then we give individual execution schedules that minimize independently the communication cost and execution time. Then, we give the trade-off bounds for the two metrics followed by the statements of our main results.

3.1 A Problem Instance on the Grid

For proving this result, we consider a grid graph $G = (V, E, \mathfrak{w})$ with $n = a \times b$ nodes that consists of a rows and b columns of nodes (Fig. 1), and $\mathfrak{w}(e) = 1$ for each edge $e \in E$. A node in the xth row and yth column has coordinate (x, y). The top-left node has coordinate $(1, 1)$ while the bottom right node has coordinate (a, b). Each node in G connects with an edge to four neighbors (up, down, left, right), except for the nodes at corners or borders which have two or three neighbors, respectively. Graph G is divided into consecutive disjoint blocks each of size $a \times c$, that we denote $B_1, B_2, \ldots, B_\gamma$, where $\gamma = b/c$ (assume b is a multiple of c), such that block B_i occupies columns $(i-1)c+1$ to ic. In a similar way, each block B_i is further divided into consecutive sub-blocks of size $a \times d$ that we denote as $B_{i,1}, \ldots, B_{i,\delta}$, where $\delta = c/d$ (assume c is a multiple of d, and that d is even).

In each node of G there is exactly one transaction. There is a set of a *global* shared objects $o_1, \ldots, o_a$, used by the transactions across all blocks in G for write, such that o_i is requested by every transaction in the ith row. Fig. 1 highlights the set of transactions in the 5th row (from the top) that use global object o_5. Within each block B_i there is a respective *internal* shared object p_i which is requested by every transaction in B_i for write. In B_i there is also an additional set of d *internal* objects $q_{i,1}, \ldots, q_{i,d}$, such that object $q_{i,k}$ is requested by all transactions in the kth column of every sub-block of B_i for write. Fig. 1 highlights the sets of transactions to use $q_{1,2}$ in block B_1 Therefore, each transaction requests in total three shared objects, one global and two internal. The initial positions of the objects in the grid are not critical for the analysis. For simplicity, we assume that the global objects are initially positioned in the leftmost column of G in their respective rows, and the internal objects are initially positioned in the top left corner of their respective block.

3.2 A Communication Cost Efficient Schedule

We give here a transaction execution schedule which achieves optimal communication cost but suboptimal time. In this schedule the transactions in G execute sequentially, one after another, in a column by column way starting from the leftmost column of G up to the rightmost column. All transactions in column j finish execution before the transactions in column $j+1$ start execution. The total communica-

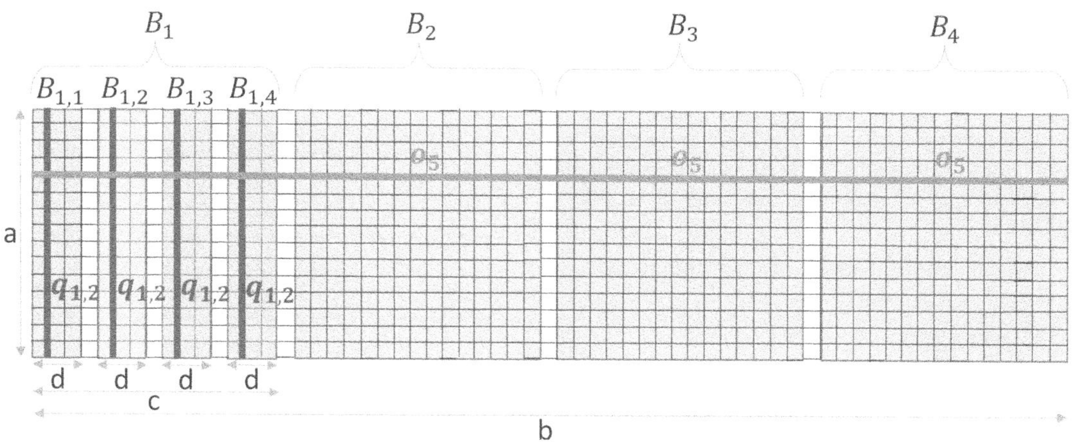

Figure 1: The graph G for the time-communication impossibility result, with $a = c = 16$, $b = 64$, $d = 4$, and $\gamma = \delta = 4$.

tion cost can be estimated as the sum of the communication costs of the objects within the blocks, plus the cost to transfer the global objects from one block to the next.

Within a block B_i, each global object incurs communication cost at most c, since it traverses at most c edges on its own row, counting also the edge to move to the next block. Thus, the cost from the a global objects is at most ac. In B_i the cost of the internal object p_i that is used at every node is also at most ac, since there are c columns, and it traverses at most $a - 1$ edges within each column, and then it can traverse one more edge to transfer to the next column, giving a cost of a per column. To minimize the communication cost due to the transfer of object p_i from column to column, we can execute the transactions in the columns alternatively from top to bottom and bottom to top as p_i moves from one column to the next.

Consider now the internal objects $Q_i = \{q_{i,1}, \ldots, q_{i,d}\}$ in B_i. The communication cost due to the transfer of an internal object $q_{i,j}$ within B_i is at most $2a\delta + c$, since it takes a time steps to transfer the object within the a nodes of the jth column in each of the δ sub-blocks, and it takes additional $a\delta + c$ total steps to transfer the object between the sub-blocks of B_i. Since $|Q_i| = d$ and $\delta = c/d$, the total cost due to these internal objects in B_i is at most $2ad\delta + cd = O(ac + cd)$.

Adding all the above costs we have $O(ac + cd)$ total cost per block, and since there are $\gamma = b/c$ blocks, the total communication cost is bounded by $O(\gamma(ac + cd)) = O(ab + bd) = O(n + bd)$. This bound is optimal within a constant factor, since the combined path of each object is optimal within a constant factor.

Lemma 3.1. *The sequential schedule achieves asymptotically optimal communication cost* $\Theta(n + bd)$.

Due to the sequential nature of the schedule, the total time to execute the transactions is proportional to total number of transactions $ab = n$, which is also the number of nodes in G.

Lemma 3.2. *The sequential schedule executes the transactions within time* $\Theta(n)$.

3.3 An Execution Time Efficient Schedule

Here we give a schedule with optimal execution time and suboptimal communication cost. In this schedule, we pipeline the requests of the global objects in each block. Time is divided into periods of length $2c$ such that at each period each global object is in a different block. Global object o_1 starts at block B_1 at the first period where all transactions in the first row of that block execute. Then at the second period, object o_1 continues to block B_2 and visits all the transactions of the first row in that block. This repeats until global object o_1 reaches in the γth period block B_γ. Object o_2 starts in B_1 in the second period where all transactions in the second row execute, and then in the third period o_2 moves in B_2 for execution of the second row transactions, and so on until the $(\gamma+1)$th period where it executes in B_γ. A similar schedule repeats for the remaining global objects, such that object o_i starts in the ith period at B_1 and at the $(i + \gamma - 1)$th period at block B_γ, executing the transactions in the ith row in each block.

The time length $2c$ of a period is long enough to guarantee that within each block there is enough time for the internal objects to reposition for the next global object that will enter in the next period in the immediately next row (at most c steps are needed to move objects from the end of the current row to the beginning of the next row). The total time that is required for the schedule is the total number of periods until object o_a reaches block B_γ, which is $a + \gamma - 1$ periods, or equivalently $(a + \gamma - 1)2c = O(ac + b)$ time steps.

Note that ac is a lower bound for the execution time, since within each block B_i (of size $a \times c$) the internal object p_i requires time at least ac steps to traverse all the transactions. Further, b is also a lower bound for the execution time, since the path of each global object consists of b transactions in its respective row in G. Thus, a lower bound for execution time is $\Omega(ac + b)$. Consequently, we have the following result:

Lemma 3.3. *The pipelined schedule has asymptotically optimal execution time* $\Theta(ac + b)$.

For the communication cost, each global object follows an optimal path with b nodes and therefore incurs communication cost $\Theta(b)$, and therefore the a global objects contribute cost $\Theta(ab)$. Each internal object p_i incurs communication cost $\Theta(ac)$, since it has to traverse each node within its block B_i, giving total cost $\Theta(ac\gamma) = \Theta(ab)$ considering all $\gamma = b/c$ blocks. Each internal object $q_{i,j}$ incurs cost $\Theta(ad\delta) = \Theta(ac)$, since in each period it has to visit $\delta = c/d$ columns spaced d nodes apart within a block, and has to repeat the process in all periods for the a rows. Since there are d internal objects of type $q_{i,j}$ within a block, and there are γ total blocks, the total cost from the internal objects is $\Theta(acd\gamma) = \Theta(abd) = \Theta(nd)$. Combining the costs from all the objects, we obtain:

LEMMA 3.4. *The pipelined schedule has communication cost $\Theta(nd)$.*

3.4 Trade-off Analysis

Divide time into time periods $T_1, T_2, \ldots$ each of duration c time steps. We will focus on the execution of the transactions in *odd blocks* $B_1, B_3, \ldots$ (the results are symmetric for even blocks). Note that it is impossible for any global object to be at two different odd blocks at the same time period, since the distance between nodes within any two odd blocks is at least c.

LEMMA 3.5. *If in a period T_l a global object o_k is requested by transactions within the same block B_i at least λd times, where $\lambda \geq 1$, then the total communication cost contributed during T_l due to executions of transactions in block B_i is at least $(\lambda - 1)d^2$.*

PROOF. In the best case scenario the global object o_k is requested by transactions in the kth row in λ consecutive sub-blocks of B_i, which is a scenario that minimizes the movement of the internal objects in B_i. The respective d internal objects in B_i, of type $q_{i,j}$, have to move each $\lambda - 1$ times from one sub-block to the next requiring total communication cost at least $(\lambda - 1)d^2$. □

LEMMA 3.6. *If a global object o_j is requested by transactions in a block B_i in at most $x \leq \delta/4$ distinct time periods then, the total communication cost due to the internal objects in B_i is at least $cd/8$.*

PROOF. We can write $x = \delta/(4\xi)$, for some $\xi \geq 1$. Consider the time periods (among the x) which contribute at most $2d\xi - 1$ object o_j requests from transactions in block B_i. The total number of requests for o_j in those periods is at most:

$$\begin{aligned} x(2d\xi - 1) &= \frac{\delta}{4\xi} \cdot (2d\xi - 1) \\ &\leq \frac{\delta}{4} \cdot \left(2d - \frac{1}{\xi}\right) \\ &= \frac{c}{4d} \cdot \left(2d - \frac{1}{\xi}\right) \\ &\leq \frac{c}{2}. \end{aligned}$$

Since object o_j has exactly c requests in total in B_i, at least $c/2$ of these requests must occur in periods with at least $2d\xi$ requests for o_j. Let ζ_y denote the number of periods with requests in range $[2^y\xi d, 2^{y+1}\xi d)$. Note that $\sum_{y\geq 1} \zeta_y 2^y \xi d \geq c/4$, since the total sum for object o_j requests from the ranges is at least $c/2$ and we get a factor 2 approximation for each range. From Lemma 3.5, we have that the total communication cost is at least:

$$\sum_{y\geq 1} \zeta_y (2^y\xi - 1)d^2 \geq d \sum_{y\geq 1} \zeta_y 2^{y-1}\xi d \geq \frac{cd}{8}.$$

□

LEMMA 3.7. *If an execution has duration at most kb time steps, for some $k \geq 1$, then each global object is requested in at least $\gamma/4$ distinct blocks for at most $4k$ periods in each block.*

PROOF. Note that the total number of odd blocks is $\gamma/2$. Let x (and y) be the number of blocks that require the global object for at most $4k$ periods each (and $4k + 1$ periods or more). We have that $x+y = \gamma/2$. We want to prove that $x \geq \gamma/4$. Suppose for the sake of contradiction $x < \gamma/4$. Then we have $y > \gamma/4$. Therefore, the total time that the global object spends in the respective transactions that request it in all the y blocks is at least $(4k + 1)\gamma/4$ periods, which is at least $(4k + 1)b/(4c) > kb$ time steps, a contradiction. □

THEOREM 3.8. *If in G an execution schedule has duration at most kb, where $k \leq \delta/16$, then the total communication cost is $\Omega(nd/k)$.*

PROOF. We can write $4k = \delta/(4\xi)$ for some $\xi \geq 1$. From Lemma 3.7, each global object o_j is requested by transactions in at least $\gamma/4$ of the blocks for at most $x = 4k \leq \delta/4$ periods in each block. Thus, from Lemma 3.6, the communication cost due to object o_j in all these blocks is at least $(\gamma/4)(cd/8) = bd/32$, since $\gamma = b/c$. From the proof of Lemma 3.6, for the communication cost of o_j we only consider the blocks and periods which issue at least $2d\xi$ requests for o_j. In any such period and block B_i, we can only have at most $c/(2d\xi) = \delta/(2\xi) = 8k$ total number of global objects executing concurrently with o_j, since otherwise the internal object p_i would have been used by two different transactions at the same time step within the same block. Consequently, the total communication cost considering the requests of all a global objects is at least $a(bd/32)/(8k) = \Omega(abd/k) = \Omega(nd/k)$. □

3.5 Implications

Here we state specific instance trade-off bounds implied from Theorem 3.8. We have that in G the optimal communication cost is $\Theta(n+bd)$ (achieved by the sequential schedule) and the optimal execution time is $\Theta(ac+b)$ (achieved by the pipelined schedule). Consider the case where $bd = \Theta(n)$ and $ac = \Theta(b)$. This can be achieved with the following parameter choices: $a = n^{1/4}$, $b = n^{3/4}$, $c = n^{2/4}$, and $d = n^{1/4}$. Then, $\gamma = b/c = n^{1/4}$ and $\delta = c/d = n^{1/4}$. In this case the optimal communication cost is $\Theta(n)$ and the optimal execution time is $\Theta(b) = \Theta(n^{3/4})$. Suppose that the execution time is kb, where $1 \leq k \leq \delta/16$. From Theorem 3.8, the communication cost is $\Omega(nd/k)$. Since $\delta = d = n^{1/4}$, we obtain the following result:

COROLLARY 3.9. *There is a problem instance such that for any scheduling algorithm, if the execution time is within a factor $O(k)$ from optimal, then the communication cost is a factor $\Omega(n^{1/4}/k)$ suboptimal, where $1 \leq k \leq n^{1/4}/16$.*

This can also translate to a symmetric result:

COROLLARY 3.10. *There is a problem instance such that for any scheduling algorithm, if the communication cost is within a factor $O(k)$ from optimal, then the execution time is a factor $\Omega(n^{1/4}/k)$ suboptimal, where $1 \leq k \leq n^{1/4}/16$.*

For these parameter choices, the sequential schedule has optimal communication cost $\Theta(n)$, and execution time $\Theta(n)$

which is suboptimal by a factor $k = \Theta(n^{1/4})$. However, from Corollary 3.10 this execution time is the best possible given the communication cost. Symmetrically, the pipelined schedule has optimal execution time $\Theta(n^{3/4})$ and communication cost $\Theta(nd) = \Theta(n^{5/4})$ which is suboptimal by a factor $k = \Theta(n^{1/4})$. However, from Corollary 3.9 this communication cost is the best possible given the execution time bound.

4. POSITIVE RESULTS

4.1 Algorithms for Small Communication Cost

The problem of minimizing the communication cost is NP-hard, by a reduction from graph TSP. Any graph TSP instance can be directly converted to a transactional scheduling problem instance on the same graph such that each node has a transaction and there is a single object shared by all transactions. The transactional memory schedule has optimal communication cost if and only if the respective TSP tour cost is optimal.[4]

Given a graph G, we can approximate the optimal communication cost using a *universal TSP tour*. Jia *et al.* [20] prove that there exists a universal TSP tour Q that traverses all the nodes in G so that for any subset of nodes S the induced sub-tour in Q approximates the optimal tour for S within a factor of $O(\log^4 n/\log\log n)$.

We can use the universal tour Q to construct a schedule for transactions and the object moves as follows. We execute the transactions in sequence according to the order that they appear in Q. Once a transaction finishes execution, it passes each object along any of the shortest path to the next transaction that requires the object according to the order in Q. When an object is requested for the first time it moves along a shortest path from its initial position to the first transaction that requests it. We refer to this as the *universal TSP schedule*. We can prove the following result.

THEOREM 4.1. *The universal TSP schedule guarantees communication cost within $O(\log^4 n/\log\log n)$ factor from optimal.*

PROOF. Let $\mathcal{T}_{r_i} \subseteq \mathcal{T}$ denote the set of transactions that request object $r_i \in R$. Let V_{r_i} denote the respective nodes where the transactions in $\mathcal{T}_{r_i}$ reside. Let u_{r_i} denote the node that initially contains r_i. Let C_{r_i} denote the total distance traversed by object r_i for visiting the nodes in $\{u_{r_i}\} \cup V_{r_i}$ when following the universal TSP schedule. We can write $C_{r_i} = \text{dist}(u_{r_i}, v'_{r_i}) + \overline{C}_{r_i}$, where v'_{r_i} is the first transaction in V_{r_i} with respect to the universal TSP schedule that requested r_i, and $\overline{C}_{r_i}$ is the remaining distance in the schedule.

Let $\lambda = O(\log^4 n/\log\log n)$ be the approximation from the universal TSP tour for any object's optimal tour length. Let $\overline{C}^*_{r_i}$ denote the optimal cost for traversing the all the nodes in V_{r_i} once (starting from some node in V_{r_i}). The universal TSP schedule guarantees that $\overline{C}_{r_i}/\overline{C}^*_{r_i} \le 2\lambda$, since the optimal TSP tour length for V_{r_i} is no more than twice the shortest total distance to traverse each of the nodes in V_{r_i} once.

Let $C^*_{r_i}$ denote the optimal cost for traversing the nodes in $\{u_{r_i}\} \cup V_{r_i}$. We have that $C^*_{r_i} \ge \text{dist}(u_{r_i}, v'_{r_i})$ and also $C^*_{r_i} \ge \overline{C}^*_{r_i}$. Consequently,

$$\begin{aligned}
\frac{C_{r_i}}{C^*_{r_i}} &= \frac{\text{dist}(u_{r_i}, v'_{r_i}) + \overline{C}_{r_i}}{C^*_{r_i}} \\
&\le \frac{\text{dist}(u_{r_i}, v'_{r_i}) + \overline{C}_{r_i}}{\max(\text{dist}(u_{r_i}, v'_{r_i}), \overline{C}^*_{r_i})} \\
&\le \frac{\overline{C}_{r_i}}{\overline{C}^*_{r_i}} + 1 \\
&\le 2\lambda + 1.
\end{aligned}$$

The total communication cost C is equal to the sum of the individual costs for the objects, that is, $C = \sum_{i=1}^{k} C_{r_i}$. The optimal cost is $C^* = \sum_{i=1}^{k} C^*_{r_i}$, since objects do not combine and their individuals costs need to be added to obtain the optimal cost C^*. Therefore,

$$\begin{aligned}
C &= \sum_{i=1}^{k} C_{r_i} \\
&\le \sum_{i=1}^{k} (2\lambda + 1) C^*_{r_i} \\
&= (2\lambda + 1) \sum_{i=1}^{k} C^*_{r_i} \\
&= (2\lambda + 1) C^*,
\end{aligned}$$

which implies that $C/C^* = O(\log^4 n/\log\log n)$, as needed. □

We can obtain improved communication cost bounds for planar and minor-free metrics using the universal TSP results from [12], and for doubling metrics using the universal TSP results from [20].

THEOREM 4.2. *In arbitrary weighted planar graph metrics and H-minor-free metrics, the universal TSP schedule guarantees communication cost within $O(\log^2 n)$ factor from optimal. In doubling metrics, which includes both constant-dimensional Euclidean and growth-restricted metrics, the universal TSP schedule guarantees communication cost within $O(\log n)$ factor from optimal.*

4.2 Algorithms for Small Execution Time

We show here that the problem of minimizing the execution time is NP-hard, and then we give an approximation algorithm. We will reduce the vertex coloring problem to this problem. The coloring problem aims at finding the chromatic number $\chi(H)$ of a graph H, and it is an NP-hard problem.

We can transform in polynomial time any vertex coloring problem instance in an arbitrary graph H to a transaction scheduling problem in a graph G. We construct G to be isomorphic with H such that each edge in G has weight 1. Each node in G holds a transaction. For each edge $e = (u, v)$ in H we create a new object in G to be used only by the respective transactions in the adjacent nodes in G. Objects can be initially placed in any of the nodes with transactions that request them. Given a transaction execution schedule

[4]A similar observation for NP-hardness was made in [41] in the context of execution time with transactions that use only one shared object in which case the execution time and communication cost optimality coincide.

in G, we can find a valid vertex coloring in H by simply converting the time step that each transaction executes to a color. Therefore, an execution schedule in G has duration χ time steps if and only if H has a valid coloring with χ colors. Since, for all $\epsilon > 0$, approximating the chromatic number within a factor $n^{1-\epsilon}$ is NP-hard [42], approximating the optimal execution time within a factor $n^{1-\epsilon}$ is NP-hard too.

We now give an approximation algorithm for the optimal time schedule. Consider a transaction scheduling problem instance in a graph G. Let Z denote the transaction conflict graph, such that each node in Z is a transaction and each edge represents a conflict between the adjacent transactions, that is, the transactions sharing one or more objects. The graph Z is weighted so that the weight on an edge is the distance between the respective transactions in G.

A valid coloring of Z with non-negative integer colors guarantees that any two adjacent transactions will receive colors that differ at least as much as the weight of the edge connecting them. The *weighted-degree* of a trancaction T_i is the sum of the weights of the edges adjacent to T_i in Z. Let Γ denote the maximum weighted-degree in Z over all transactions. We can color the conflict graph with a simple *greedy* algorithm, by assigning the first available color to each node, and we can obtain a coloring with $\Gamma + 1$ colors. We refer to the respective schedule as the *greedy schedule*.

Let Δ denote the maximum (unweighted) node degree in Z. Note that Δ denotes the maximum number of transactions that any transaction can conflict with. The maximum edge weight, denoted $w_{\max}$, in Z is a lower bound for the schedule time, since it takes at least so much time to transfer a shared object in G from one transaction to another transaction that it conflicts with. Since $\Gamma \leq w_{\max}\Delta$, the algorithm above provides a $\Delta + 1$ approximation for the optimal execution time. When we consider the initial positions of the object, the approximation becomes $\Delta + 2$, since the first move distance of an object is also a lower bound.

THEOREM 4.3. *The greedy schedule provides a $O(\Delta)$ approximation to the optimal time schedule.*

5. CONCLUSIONS

We presented a set of comprehensive impossibility results and upper bounds for scheduling multiple objects in distributed transactional memory. We have demonstrated that it is impossible to optimize both execution time and communication cost simultaneously. This justifies the reason why we studied the communication cost and execution time independently in Section 4.

We provided a near optimal algorithm for the communication cost based on a universal TSP tour. We also provided an approximation algorithm for the execution time. Note that a hardness result for execution time follows also from the hardness of the communication cost when using a single object for all transactions, since the optimal TSP tour for an object provides the best time bound for scheduling the object in its transactions. However, this reduction does not prove that the execution time is hard to approximate. A reduction from vertex coloring that uses multiple objects helps to obtain the approximation hardness of the execution time.

Our study does not take into account the congestion (or load) caused by the messages spread in the network over time. Congestion is an important performance metric besides communication cost and execution time, because unbalanced load can affect the overall performance of the system and sometimes it is a major bottleneck. Moreover, our study does not consider response time which is related to execution time metric and the study of response time alongside execution time will be very interesting. We leave the interplay of these aspects for scheduling problems in distributed TMs for future work.

Acknowledgments

This work is supported by the National Science Foundation grants 1320835 and 1420673, and partly supported by the Serbian Ministry of Education & Science, through grants No. III 44009, and TR 32031.

6. REFERENCES

[1] Marcos K. Aguilera, Dahlia Malkhi, Keith Marzullo, Alessandro Panconesi, Andrzej Pelc, and Roger Wattenhofer. Announcing the 2012 edsger w. dijkstra prize in distributed computing. *SIGARCH Computer Architecture News*, 40(4):1–2, 2012.

[2] Mohammad Ansari, Mikel Luján, Christos Kotselidis, Kim Jarvis, Chris C. Kirkham, and Ian Watson. Steal-on-abort: Improving transactional memory performance through dynamic transaction reordering. In *HiPEAC*, pages 4–18, 2009.

[3] Hagit Attiya. Lower bounds and impossibility results for transactional memory computing. *Bulletin of the EATCS*, 112, 2014.

[4] Hagit Attiya, Leah Epstein, Hadas Shachnai, and Tami Tamir. Transactional contention management as a non-clairvoyant scheduling problem. *Algorithmica*, 57(1):44–61, 2010.

[5] Hagit Attiya, Vincent Gramoli, and Alessia Milani. Directory protocols for distributed transactional memory. In Rachid Guerraoui and Paolo Romano, editors, *Transactional Memory*, volume 8913 of *Lecture Notes in Computer Science*, pages 367–391. Springer International Publishing, 2015.

[6] Hagit Attiya and Alessia Milani. Transactional scheduling for read-dominated workloads. *J. Parallel Distrib. Comput.*, 72(10):1386–1396, 2012.

[7] Robert L. Bocchino, Vikram S. Adve, and Bradford L. Chamberlain. Software transactional memory for large scale clusters. In *PPoPP*, pages 247–258, 2008.

[8] Costas Busch, Maurice Herlihy, Miroslav Popovic, and Gokarna Sharma. Brief announcement: Scheduling multiple objects in distributed transactional memory. In *DISC*, pages 538–539, 2014.

[9] Maria Couceiro, Paolo Romano, Nuno Carvalho, and Luís Rodrigues. D2stm: Dependable distributed software transactional memory. In *PRDC*, pages 307–313, 2009.

[10] Wilson W. L. Fung, Inderpreet Singh, Andrew Brownsword, and Tor M. Aamodt. Hardware transactional memory for gpu architectures. In *MICRO*, pages 296–307, 2011.

[11] Rachid Guerraoui, Maurice Herlihy, and Bastian Pochon. Toward a theory of transactional contention managers. In *PODC*, pages 258–264, 2005.

[12] Mohammad T. Hajiaghayi, Robert Kleinberg, and Tom Leighton. Improved lower and upper bounds for universal tsp in planar metrics. In *SODA*, pages 649–658, 2006.

[13] Ruud Haring, Martin Ohmacht, Thomas Fox, Michael Gschwind, David Satterfield, Krishnan Sugavanam, Paul Coteus, Philip Heidelberger, Matthias Blumrich, Robert Wisniewski, Alan Gara, George Chiu, Peter Boyle, Norman Chist, and Changhoan Kim. The ibm blue gene/q compute chip. *IEEE Micro*, 32(2):48–60, 2012.

[14] Danny Hendler, Alex Naiman, Sebastiano Peluso, Francesco Quaglia, Paolo Romano, and Adi Suissa. Exploiting locality in lease-based replicated transactional memory via task migration. In *DISC*, pages 121–133, 2013.

[15] Maurice Herlihy and J. Eliot B. Moss. Transactional memory: Architectural support for lock-free data structures. In *ISCA*, pages 289–300, 1993.

[16] Maurice Herlihy and Ye Sun. Distributed transactional memory for metric-space networks. *Distributed Computing*, 20(3):195–208, 2007.

[17] Sachin Hirve, Roberto Palmieri, and Binoy Ravindran. Archie: a speculative replicated transactional system. In *Middleware*, pages 265–276, 2014.

[18] William N. Scherer III and Michael L. Scott. Advanced contention management for dynamic software transactional memory. In *PODC*, pages 240–248, 2005.

[19] Intel. http://software.intel.com/en-us/blogs/2012/02/07/transactional-synchronization-in-haswell.

[20] Lujun Jia, Guolong Lin, Guevara Noubir, Rajmohan Rajaraman, and Ravi Sundaram. Universal approximations for tsp, steiner tree, and set cover. In *STOC*, pages 386–395, 2005.

[21] Idit Keidar and Dmitri Perelman. Multi-versioning in transactional memory. In Rachid Guerraoui and Paolo Romano, editors, *Transactional Memory*, volume 8913 of *Lecture Notes in Computer Science*, pages 150–165. Springer International Publishing, 2015.

[22] Junwhan Kim and B. Ravindran. Scheduling transactions in replicated distributed software transactional memory. In *CCGrid*, pages 227–234, 2013.

[23] Junwhan Kim and Binoy Ravindran. On transactional scheduling in distributed transactional memory systems. In *SSS*, pages 347–361, 2010.

[24] Christos Kotselidis, Mohammad Ansari, Kim Jarvis, Mikel Luján, Chris Kirkham, and Ian Watson. Distm: A software transactional memory framework for clusters. In *ICPP*, pages 51–58, 2008.

[25] Kaloian Manassiev, Madalin Mihailescu, and Cristiana Amza. Exploiting distributed version concurrency in a transactional memory cluster. In *PPoPP*, pages 198–208, 2006.

[26] Roberto Palmieri, Sebastiano Peluso, and Binoy Ravindran. Transaction execution models in partially replicated transactional memory: The case for data-flow and control-flow. In Rachid Guerraoui and Paolo Romano, editors, *Transactional Memory*, volume 8913 of *Lecture Notes in Computer Science*, pages 341–366. Springer International Publishing, 2015.

[27] Roberto Palmieri, Francesco Quaglia, and Paolo Romano. Asap: An aggressive speculative protocol for actively replicated transactional systems. In *NCA*, pages 203–211, 2012.

[28] Sebastiano Peluso, Paolo Romano, and Francesco Quaglia. Score: A scalable one-copy serializable partial replication protocol. In *Middleware*, pages 456–475, 2012.

[29] Sebastiano Peluso, Pedro Ruivo, Paolo Romano, Francesco Quaglia, and Luís Rodrigues. When scalability meets consistency: Genuine multiversion update-serializable partial data replication. In *ICDCS*, pages 455–465, 2012.

[30] Paolo Romano, Roberto Palmieri, Francesco Quaglia, Nuno Carvalho, and Luís Rodrigues. On speculative replication of transactional systems. *J. Comput. Syst. Sci.*, 80(1):257–276, 2014.

[31] Paolo Romano, Luis Rodrigues, Nuno Carvalho, and João Cachopo. Cloud-tm: harnessing the cloud with distributed transactional memories. *SIGOPS Oper. Syst. Rev.*, 44(2):1–6, 2010.

[32] Mohamed M. Saad and Binoy Ravindran. Snake: Control flow distributed software transactional memory. In *SSS*, pages 238–252, 2011.

[33] Johannes Schneider and Roger Wattenhofer. Bounds on contention management algorithms. *Theor. Comput. Sci.*, 412(32):4151–4160, 2011.

[34] Gokarna Sharma and Costas Busch. A competitive analysis for balanced transactional memory workloads. *Algorithmica*, 63(1-2):296–322, 2012.

[35] Gokarna Sharma and Costas Busch. Window-based greedy contention management for transactional memory: Theory and practice. *Distrib. Comput.*, 25(3):225–248, 2012.

[36] Gokarna Sharma and Costas Busch. Distributed transactional memory for general networks. *Distrib. Comput.*, 27(5):329–362, 2014.

[37] Nir Shavit and Dan Touitou. Software transactional memory. *Distrib. Comput.*, 10(2):99–116, 1997.

[38] Amy Wang, Matthew Gaudet, Peng Wu, José Nelson Amaral, Martin Ohmacht, Christopher Barton, Raul Silvera, and Maged Michael. Evaluation of blue gene/q hardware support for transactional memories. In *PACT*, pages 127–136, 2012.

[39] Richard M. Yoo and Hsien-Hsin S. Lee. Adaptive transaction scheduling for transactional memory systems. In *SPAA*, pages 169–178, 2008.

[40] Bo Zhang and Binoy Ravindran. Relay: A cache-coherence protocol for distributed transactional memory. In *OPODIS*, pages 48–53, 2009.

[41] Bo Zhang, Binoy Ravindran, and Roberto Palmieri. Distributed transactional contention management as the traveling salesman problem. In *SIROCCO*, pages 54–67, 2014.

[42] David Zuckerman. Linear degree extractors and the inapproximability of max clique and chromatic number. *Theory of Computing*, 3(1):103–128, 2007.

Disjoint-Access Parallelism: Impossibility, Possibility, and Cost of Transactional Memory Implementations

Sebastiano Peluso
ECE Department
Virginia Tech
Blacksburg VA, USA
peluso@vt.edu

Roberto Palmieri
ECE Department
Virginia Tech
Blacksburg VA, USA
robertop@vt.edu

Paolo Romano
IST & INESC-ID
Universidade de Lisboa
Lisbon, Portugal
romano@inesc-id.pt

Binoy Ravindran
ECE Department
Virginia Tech
Blacksburg VA, USA
binoy@vt.edu

Francesco Quaglia
DIAG
Sapienza University of Rome
Rome, Italy
quaglia@dis.uniroma1.it

ABSTRACT

Disjoint-Access Parallelism (DAP) is considered one of the most desirable properties to maximize the scalability of Transactional Memory (TM). This paper investigates the possibility and inherent cost of implementing a DAP TM that ensures two properties that are regarded as important to maximize efficiency in read-dominated workloads, namely having invisible and wait-free read-only transactions. We first prove that relaxing Real-Time Order (RTO) is necessary to implement such a TM. This result motivates us to introduce *Witnessable Real-Time Order* (WRTO), a weaker variant of RTO that demands enforcing RTO only between directly conflicting transactions. Then we show that adopting WRTO makes it possible to design a strictly DAP TM with invisible and wait-free read-only transactions, while preserving strong progressiveness for write transactions and an isolation level known in literature as Extended Update Serializability. Finally, we shed light on the inherent inefficiency of DAP TM implementations that have invisible and wait-free read-only transactions, by establishing lower bounds on the time and space complexity of such TMs.

Categories and Subject Descriptors

D.1.3 [**Programming Techniques**]: Concurrent Programming—*distributed programming, parallel programming*; D.4.1 [**Operating Systems**]: Process Management—*concurrency, synchronization*; F.1.2 [**Computation by Abstract Devices**]: Modes of Computation—*parallelism and concurrency*

General Terms

Algorithms, Theory

Permission to make digital or hard copies of all or part of this work for personal or classroom use is granted without fee provided that copies are not made or distributed for profit or commercial advantage and that copies bear this notice and the full citation on the first page. Copyrights for components of this work owned by others than ACM must be honored. Abstracting with credit is permitted. To copy otherwise, or republish, to post on servers or to redistribute to lists, requires prior specific permission and/or a fee. Request permissions from permissions@acm.org.
PODC'15, July 21–23, 2015, Donostia-San Sebastián, Spain.
Copyright © 2015 ACM 978-1-4503-3617-8 /15/07 ...$15.00.
http://dx.doi.org/10.1145/2767386.2767438.

Keywords

Disjoint-access parallelism; Wait-freedom; Real-time order; Transactional memory; Invisible reads; Impossibility results

1. INTRODUCTION

Over the last decade, Transactional Memory (TM) [30] has emerged as an attractive paradigm for simplifying parallel programming. Further, the recent integration of TM support in hardware by major chip vendors (e.g., Intel, IBM), along with the development of dedicated GCC extensions for TM (i.e., GCC-4.7), have significantly increased TM's traction, paving the way for its mainstream adoption.

Disjoint-access parallelism (or DAP) [22] is a long studied property that assesses the ability of a TM implementation to avoid any contention on shared objects (also called *base objects*), between transactions that access disjoint data sets. Roughly speaking, DAP prescribes that non-conflicting transactions should not contend on the same memory locations, thus minimizing expensive inter-processor coordination and enhancing scalability [5, 11]. Several consistency criteria have been proposed for TM, such as *opacity* [16], *virtual world consistency* [21], and *TMS1* [13], which are widely adopted because they all prevent erroneous computations that can occur as a consequence of observing arbitrarily stale snapshots during the transaction execution.

All the above correctness criteria require serializability of committed transactions[1], but the existing TM literature has established that having DAP and serializable committed transactions in the same TM implementation is impossible under certain conditions for read-only transactions or different progress guarantees [4, 28, 15, 14, 8]. In particular, Attiya et al. [4] proved that a TM cannot be weak DAP (a weaker version of the original DAP [22]), while ensuring minimal progressiveness [18] for write transactions (a progress condition weaker than obstruction-freedom [20]), and providing invisible and wait-free read-only transactions if the correctness guarantee is (Strict) Serializability [7] or Snapshot Isolation [6] (and hence opacity, virtual world consistency, or TMS1). More recently, Bushkov et al. [8] proved

[1]Opacity also requires serializability of all (including pending and aborted) transactions.

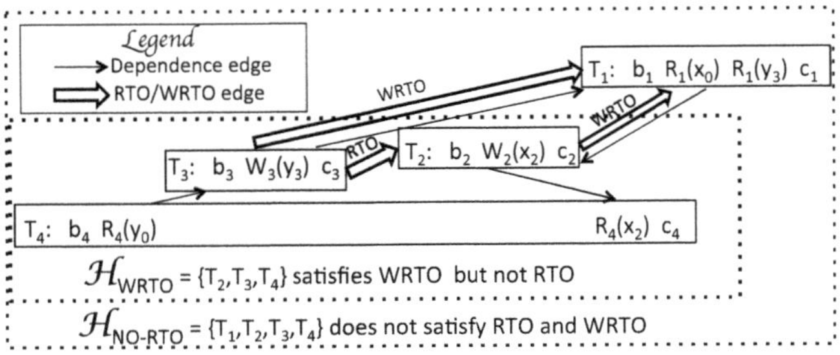

Figure 1: Histories accepted or rejected by WRTO.

the impossibility of implementing a strict DAP [15] (a stronger version of the original DAP [22]) TM that guarantees obstruction-freedom and Weak Adaptive Consistency, which is weaker than opacity, virtual world consistency, and TMS1.

However, the invisibility of read-only transactions as well as their ability to always commit in a finite number of steps (wait-freedom), are desirable requirements for enhancing the performance of TM in case of read-dominated workloads.

For this reason, in this paper we seek an answer to the following questions: *what are the correctness and progress guarantees that a DAP TM algorithm can ensure while having invisible and wait-free read-only transactions?* And for those guarantees, *which are the unavoidable costs to consider in terms of both time and space complexity?*

Along the path that will lead us to answer the above questions, we present two impossibility results and lower bounds that should be taken into account while designing a DAP TM. Specifically, in Section 3 we show that if one defines as target correctness criterion *any* criterion that includes Real-Time Order (RTO) then, independently of the particular isolation level ensured among concurrent transactions, it is impossible to ensure wait-free read-only transactions, obstruction-free write transactions, and the weakest form of DAP. We also show that, even when assuming weakly progressive write transactions [17] we still have an impossibility result if we enforce read-only transactions to be invisible.

These results highlight the need for relaxing RTO to implement a DAP TM that guarantees wait-free and invisible read-only transactions. Such an observation leads us to introduce a weaker variant of RTO, namely *Witnessable Real-Time Order* (WRTO), which demands that the RTO relation between two transactions is enforced only if they exhibit a direct conflict or they are executed by the same process. WRTO preserves some desirable properties of the classic RTO, including that if a transaction T running solo issues a read on a transactional object x, T is guaranteed to return the version of x produced by the last transaction that committed before T's beginning and updated x. On the other hand, WRTO admits schedules in which a set of sequential transactions (e.g., T_2, T_3 in Figure 1) accessing disjoint data sets can be observed in an arbitrary order by a concurrent transaction T_4 (as in the history $\mathcal{H}_{WRTO}$ of Figure 1), which possibly contradicts their RTO relations.

The WRTO property is indeed designed to cope with DAP TM implementations, as it demands that RTO is enforced only among conflicting (and hence non-disjoint) transactions, or trivially among transactions executed by the same process. In fact, these transactions can use shared base-objects involved in a conflict and thread-local base objects as witnesses to truck RTO relations.

In Section 4 we show that, by adopting WRTO and by restricting serializability to committed write transactions, it is indeed possible to design a TM with wait-free and invisible read-only transactions, which guarantees the strongest variant of DAP, strong progressiveness for write transactions, and a consistency criterion strictly weaker than opacity, i.e., Extended Update Serializability [1] (EUS). Informally, EUS guarantees serializability of committed write transactions, and it ensures that each transaction observes a state produced by a serializable schedule. Despite the theoretical relevance of this algorithm, we note that it comes with overheads, which can hinder its practical relevance. This observation motivates us to investigate whether such costs could be avoided, or are inherently implied by any DAP design. In Section 5 we prove that these costs are actually necessary, by deriving two lower bounds on the space and time complexity of any DAP TM that guarantees wait-free and invisible read-only transactions, WRTO, and obstruction-freedom or weak progressiveness for write transactions, when considering a consistency criterion strictly weaker than EUS, i.e., Consistent View [1]. Informally, Consistent View allows a specific type of non-serializable schedules, but it ensures that transactions read from a causally consistent snapshot, and prevents observing the effects of aborted transactions. In particular, such a TM has: *i)* a read-only time complexity equal to $\Omega(k \cdot N_o)$, where k is the number of versions a transactional object can have, and N_o is the total number of transactional objects; and *ii)* a space complexity equal to $\Omega(min(N_o, N_p))$ for the meta data associated with each transactional object version, where N_p is the maximum number of concurrent processes executing.

These lower bounds have implications of both theoretical and practical nature. From a theoretical perspective, they prove the optimality of the space and time complexity of the algorithm that we present. From a practical perspective, they provide useful guidelines to aim future research in the area by suggesting that, in order to allow the implementation of efficient DAP TM, lowering the correctness property is not enough (although remaining as strong as Consistent View), rather either WFRO or IRO should be sacrificed.

2. FORMALISM AND ASSUMPTIONS

System and Transaction Execution Model. We consider an asynchronous shared memory system composed of N_p processes $p_1, \ldots, p_{N_p}$ that communicate by executing transactions on N_o shared objects, which we call transactional objects, and may be faulty by crashing (i.e., slow down or block indefinitely). We use the term transactional objects to distinguish them from base objects, which are used to encapsulate any information (data and meta data) associated with a transactional object, and are manipulated via primitive operations (*primitives*, hereafter). We say that a primitive is non-trivial if it may change the value of a base object (e.g., *Compare-And-Swap* or *Store*), otherwise it is trivial (e.g., *Load*). Also primitives are atomic and wait-free.

A transaction starts with a *begin* operation, and can be followed by a sequence of *read* and *write* operations on transactional objects not known a priori, and finally completed by either a *commit* or an *abort* operation. A transaction only performing read operations is named read-only; otherwise it is called write. We denote with x_i the version of the transactional object x committed by transaction T_i, where i is an index that univocally identifies a transaction. We denote by op_i an operation issued by T_i, and by OP_i the set of operations issued by T_i, which is assumed to be totally ordered. We denote a write operation of T_i on a transactional object x as $W_i(x_i)$; and we use the notation $R_i(x_j)$ to indicate that a transaction T_i has read a version x_j of x written by transaction T_j. We say that two operations op_i and op_j are *conflicting* if they access a common transactional object x and at least one of them is a write.

History and DSG. A history $\mathcal{H}$ over a set of transactions $\{T_1, \ldots, T_n\}$ is a partial order $\prec_{\mathcal{H}}$ defined over the set of operations $OP_{\mathcal{H}} = \bigcup_{i=1}^{n} OP_i$ such that $\prec_{\mathcal{H}}$ preserves the ordering of the operations of each transaction T_i ($\prec_{\mathcal{H}} \supseteq \bigcup_{i=1}^{n} OP_i$); and for any two conflicting operations op_i, $op_j \in \mathcal{H}$, either $op_i \prec_{\mathcal{H}} op_j$ or $op_j \prec_{\mathcal{H}} op_i$. $\mathcal{H}$ implicitly induces a total order $\ll$ on the committed versions of a given transactional object [1]. Specifically, the order of the versions associated with that object follows the order of the write operations successfully executed on it.

We define the Direct Serialization Graph $DSG(\mathcal{H})$ on a history $\mathcal{H}$ (as in [1, 7]) as a direct graph with a vertex for each transaction T_i in $\mathcal{H}$ and a directed edge from T_i to T_j, with $i \neq j$, if there exist two operations op_i, $op_j \in OP_{\mathcal{H}}$ such that $op_i \prec_{\mathcal{H}} op_j$ or $op_j \prec_{\mathcal{H}} op_i$. We distinguish three types of edges depending on the type of conflicts between T_i and T_j: *i) Direct read-dependence edge*, if there exists a transactional object x such that both $W_i(x_i)$ and $R_j(x_i)$ are in $\mathcal{H}$. We say that T_j directly read-depends on T_i and we use the notation $T_i \xrightarrow{wr} T_j$. *ii) Direct write-dependence edge*, if there exists a transactional object x such that both $W_i(x_i)$ and $W_j(x_j)$ are in $\mathcal{H}$ and x_j immediately follows x_i in the total order defined by $\ll$ on x. We say that T_j *directly write-depends* on T_i and we use the notation $T_i \xrightarrow{ww} T_j$. *iii) Direct anti-dependence edge*, if there exists a transactional object x and a committed transaction T_k in $\mathcal{H}$, with $k \neq i$ and $k \neq j$, such that both $R_i(x_k)$ and $W_j(x_j)$ are in $\mathcal{H}$ and x_j immediately follows x_k in the total order defined by $\ll$ on x. We say that T_j *directly anti-depends* on T_i and we use the notation $T_i \overset{rw}{\dashrightarrow} T_j$.

Configurations, Events and Executions. A *configuration* is a tuple characterizing the status of each process, and of the base objects at some point in time. On the other hand, an *event* is a step performed by a process in a configuration, which encompasses the execution of a local computation, the application of a primitive on a base object, and a change to the status of the process. An event is generated by an operation of a transaction and in general an operation of a transaction can generate one or more events. An *execution interval* is a sequence $\Psi_i \cdot \phi_i \cdot \Psi_{i+1} \cdot \phi_{i+1} \cdot \Psi_{i+2} \cdot \phi_{i+2} \cdot \ldots$ that alternates configurations Ψ_k and events ϕ_k, and where the sequence $\Psi_k \cdot \phi_k$ generates the configuration Ψ_{k+1}. An event ϕ_k is said to be pending when configuration Ψ_{k+1} has not been generated yet. We also refer an *execution* E to as an execution interval starting from an initial configuration Ψ_0, and we say that two executions are *indistinguishable* to a process p_i if p_i observes the same sequence of configurations and steps in both the executions.

Since an execution E is actually a low-level history of configurations and events that are generated by operations of transactions in a history $\mathcal{H}$, we may also want to derive a history $\mathcal{H}$ from one of the possible executions, say E. In particular, given an execution E, we define $E|\mathcal{H}$ as the history derived from E by removing all the events and configurations, and where each sequence of events (which may possibly contain one event) is replaced by the corresponding operation that generated it.

Two events contend on a base object o if they both access o, and at least one of them applies a non-trivial primitive to o. Two processes concurrently contend on a base object o if they have pending events at the same configuration, which contend on o.

DAP and Invisible Reads. We consider two versions of *disjoint-access parallelism* (DAP), namely *strict disjoint-access parallelism* [15] (SDAP), and *weak disjoint-access parallelism* [4] (WDAP). A TM ensures SDAP if two transactions contend on a common base object only if they access some common transactional object; while a TM ensures WDAP if two concurrent transactions concurrently contend on a common base object only if they are not *disjoint-access*. Two transactions are not *disjoint-access*, according to the definition provided in [4], if there is a path that connects the two transactions in the undirected version of the DSG. A read operation R_i performed by T_i is called *invisible* if it does not apply any non-trivial primitive on any base object. Otherwise it is called *visible*. A read-only transaction performing only invisible reads is also called invisible (or IRO).

Progress Guarantees. A TM is *strongly progressive* [17] if *i)* transactions that do not encounter any conflict must be able to commit; and *ii)* at least one transaction among a set of transactions that only conflict on one common object must be able to commit. A weaker form of this progress condition, i.e., *weak progressiveness*, has also been defined in [17], which requires that a transaction can only abort if it experiences a conflict.

We consider two additional liveness properties, namely *obstruction-freedom* and *wait-freedom*. A TM is *obstruction-free* [15] if for every history $\mathcal{H}$ executed by the TM, a transaction $T_i \in \mathcal{H}$ is forcefully aborted only if T_i encounters *step contention*. We have *step contention* for a transaction T_i if a process different from the one running T_i executes a step after the first operation of T_i and before its completion (whether commit or abort). As for *wait-freedom* we adopt the definition adapted for TM that was introduced by Attiya et al. [4]: a TM is *wait-free* [19] if any transaction executed by a non-faulty process eventually commits in a finite number of steps despite the behavior of concurrent transactions[2]. We consider processes to be non-parasitic, i.e., they eventually request the commit of every transaction that they start unless they crash or the transaction is aborted by the TM [9]. Hereafter, we refer to a read-only transaction that guarantees wait-freedom as WFRO; also, if such a read-only transaction also provides invisible reads, then we name it WFIRO (i.e., the union of WFRO and IRO).

Correctness guarantees. Consistent View proscribes the anomalies *G1a*, *G1b*, *G1c*, and *G-single* as defined in [1]. In particular, proscribing *G1a* means that values created by transactions that abort cannot be observed. Proscribing *G1b* does not allow the observation of intermediate non-committed values. *G1c* is not allowed when there is no oriented cycle of all dependence edges in the $DSG(\mathcal{H}^c)$ graph built on the history $\mathcal{H}^c$, where $\mathcal{H}^c$ is derived from $\mathcal{H}$ by removing aborted and executing transactions. Consistent

[2]We adopt the definition provided in [4] because we want to relate the results presented in this paper with the ones presented in [4]. For a formal definition of the strongest progress condition specifically defined for (S)TM, i.e., *local progress*, the reader can refer to the work in [9].

View prevents the G-single anomaly, hence it avoids that $DSG(\mathcal{H})$ contains an oriented cycle with exactly one anti-dependence edge.

Extended Update Serializability (EUS) [27] is stronger than Consistent View, and it can be seen as the union of Consistent View and Serializability of committed write transactions. EUS proscribes the anomalies *G1a*, *G1b*, and *G1c*, as well as the anomaly *Extended G-update*, such that the $DSG(\mathcal{H}^{upc}_{T_k})$ graph built on the committed write transactions in $\mathcal{H}$ plus a generic transaction T_k in $\mathcal{H}$ contains an oriented cycle with one or more anti-dependence edges.

The graph considered in the Extended G-update anomaly only includes committed write transactions and at most one additional transaction T_k belonging to one among the following categories: aborted, executing or read-only transactions. EUS admits non-serializable histories, as illustrated in history $\mathcal{H}_{NO-RTO}$ of Figure 1, in which two read-only/executing/aborted transactions (e.g., T_4 and T_1 in $\mathcal{H}_{NO-RTO}$) are allowed to observe in different orders the commits of non-conflicting write transactions (e.g., T_2 and T_3 in $\mathcal{H}_{NO-RTO}$).

Real-Time Order (RTO) is a partial order defined over a transaction history $\mathcal{H}$, noted $\prec^{RTO}_{\mathcal{H}}$, which reflects the happened-before relations among transactions in a history. A transaction T_q is ordered before T_k in RTO, $T_q \prec^{RTO}_{\mathcal{H}} T_k$, if the commit operation c_q of T_q precedes the begin operation b_k of T_k in $\mathcal{H}$. We introduce a weaker variant of RTO, which we call *Witnessable Real-Time Order* (WRTO), which tracks happened-before relations exclusively between directly conflicting transactions and transactions executed by the same process. Formally $T_q \prec^{WRTO}_{\mathcal{H}} T_k$ if $T_q \prec^{RTO}_{\mathcal{H}} T_k$, and T_q and T_k are connected by a direct dependence edge in $DSG(\mathcal{H})$. A history $\mathcal{H}$ preserves RTO (respectively WRTO) if, after having included in DSG($\mathcal{H}$) a direct edge $\forall T_q, T_k$ in $\mathcal{H}$, such that $T_q \prec^{RTO}_{\mathcal{H}} T_k$ (respectively $T_q \prec^{WRTO}_{\mathcal{H}} T_k$), then the resulting graph does not contain cycles involving T_q and T_k.

An example history ensuring WRTO but not RTO is the history $\mathcal{H}_{WRTO}$ shown in Figure 1, where transaction T_4 runs concurrently with two write transactions T_3 and T_2, and T_2 runs sequentially after T_3. Since T_2 and T_3 neither conflict nor are executed by the same process, then $T_3 \prec^{RTO}_{\mathcal{H}} T_2$ holds. RTO is not ensured because T_4 observes the committed versions of T_2 but not those of T_3, and hence DSG($\mathcal{H}_{WRTO}$) plus the RTO edge from T_3 to T_2 contains a cycle that includes T_3 and T_2. On the contrary, a history that does not ensure WRTO and RTO is the history $\mathcal{H}_{NO-RTO}$ in Figure 1. Transaction T_1 runs sequentially after transaction T_2, and the two transactions conflict, hence $T_2 \prec^{WRTO}_{\mathcal{H}} T_1$ holds. However, T_1 does not observe the version of x committed by T_2, and thus DSG($\mathcal{H}_{NO-RTO}$) plus the WRTO edge from T_2 to T_1 contains a cycle that includes T_2 and T_1.

3. IMPOSSIBILITY RESULTS ON DAP AND RTO

In this section we seek an answer to the following question: *consider a DAP TM that guarantees RTO; can such a TM provide WFRO and IRO?* We do so by proving in Theorem 1 that a DAP TM cannot guarantee both RTO and WFRO if write transactions are obstruction-free. The result assumes only the RTO relation as the correctness guarantee and it is independent of the visibility of read-only transactions. In Theorem 2 we show that the impossibility of combining RTO and WFRO holds if the progress requirement of write transactions is weak progressiveness and read-only transactions are invisible (IRO). The intuition to prove these two results is the following: we show that any DAP TM that guarantees WRTO must accept a history that violates RTO. This history is illustrated in Figure 1 through $\mathcal{H}_{WRTO}$, where the RTO between the two non-conflicting transactions T_2 and T_3 is violated due to the return values of T_4's read operations. To show that $\mathcal{H}_{WRTO}$ is accepted by any DAP TM that guarantees WRTO and WFRO, we prove that such a TM must produce the return values of the read operations in $\mathcal{H}_{WRTO}$.

The proofs of the theorems rely on the following lemmas. In Lemma 1 we prove that in a WDAP TM two concurrent disjoint-access transactions cannot (even non-concurrently) contend on a common base object. It is worth noting that this result is not directly entailed by the definition of WDAP, because WDAP only precludes such transactions to *concurrently* contend on a common base object. The proof of Lemma 1 (which is provided in [26] due to space constraints) is based on the indistinguishability of detecting if the two *concurrent* disjoint-access transactions are *concurrently* contending on a common base object. In addition, this result differs from the result of Lemma 2 in [4], which proves that in a WDAP TM two disjoint-access transactions cannot contend on a common base object if they are *non-concurrent.*

Then Lemma 2 (whose proof is still provided in [26] due to space constraints) uses the result of Lemma 1 to prove that in a WDAP TM two conflicting transactions cannot contend on a common base object before the conflict actually occurs. Finally Lemma 3 (whose proof is still provided in [26]) relies on Lemma 2 to show why the read-only transaction T_4 in $\mathcal{H}_{WRTO}$ must execute as shown in Figure 1 in a WDAP TM that guarantees WRTO and WFRO. An interesting study on the relation between the impossibility results proved in this section and the existing impossibility results in literature is reported in Section 6.

LEMMA 1. *In a WDAP TM two concurrent disjoint-access transactions cannot contend on a common base object.*

As said, Lemma 2 asserts that in a WDAP TM, two transactions that conflict (either directly or transitively) cannot contend on a common base object before the time in which a path connecting the two transactions in the conflict graph is created. The proof is based on the indistinguishability of the following two scenarios: one where a conflict actually occurs; and the other where one of the two operations generating the conflict never occurs.

LEMMA 2. *Let T_i and T_j be two transactions in a history $\mathcal{H}$ generated by a WDAP TM. Assume that there exists only one path connecting T_i and T_j in DSG($\mathcal{H}$), which consists of a direct edge connecting T_i and T_j corresponding to two conflicting operations op_i and op_j, issued respectively by T_i and T_j. The operation op_i generates the event ϕ_i, and op_j generates ϕ_j. Further, assume that T_i executes ϕ_i after the commit of T_j. Then, if T_i and T_j contend on a common base object at time t, the conflict between them must occur at time $t' \leq t$.*

Lemma 3 asserts that a read operation of a wait-free read-only transaction has to always return at least the latest version of an object committed at the time the read operation on that object started. As before, the proof is based on indistinguishability arguments. Its core argument is that, in a WDAP TM a read operation of a read-only transaction T_i, which reads a version preceding the latest committed version x_j, is not able to distinguish whether x_j has been committed before T_i began or not.

LEMMA 3. *Given a WDAP TM that guarantees WRTO and WFRO, for each read-only transaction T_i executed by the TM, a read operation $R_i(x)$ by T_i returns the last version x_j committed on x at the time $R_i(x)$ starts its execution, if x_j has been committed by a transaction T_j that conflicts with T_i only due to the operations $R_i(x)$ and $W_j(x)$.*

We now prove Theorem 1, which states that a DAP TM cannot guarantee both RTO and WFRO if the progress requirement of write transactions is obstruction-freedom.

THEOREM 1. *No WDAP, obstruction-free TM that guarantees WFRO can ensure RTO.*

PROOF. The proof follows by contradiction and we assume that two different transactions are executed by two distinct processes. By contradiction, we assume that there exists a TM providing WDAP, obstruction-free write transactions, WFRO and such that $\forall \mathcal{H}$ accepted by the TM, $\mathcal{H}$ preserves RTO, and hence WRTO. Consider the history $\mathcal{H}_{WRTO}$ as executed in Figure 1. T_3 is a write transaction that runs solo and writes the version y_3 of y and then commits. T_2 begins after T_3, runs solo, writes x_2 of x, and then commits. T_4 is a read-only transaction that reads the initial version of y, i.e., y_0, before T_3 begins, and executes a read operation $R_4(x)$ on x, after T_2's commit. Both T_2 and T_3 cannot be aborted in $\mathcal{H}_{WRTO}$ because the TM is obstruction-free.

Since x_2 is the last version of x committed before the execution of $R_4(x)$, and the only path connecting T_2 and T_4 in DSG($\mathcal{H}_{WRTO}$) is the edge associated with the conflict of $R_4(x)$ and $W_2(x)$, then $R_4(x)$ has to return the version x_2 of T_2 by the result of Lemma 3. That is because the assumed WDAP TM provides WFRO and WRTO, which is implied by RTO (assumed by contradiction). Note that, even assuming the visibility of T_4's reads, T_3 can neither abort due to the detection of the conflict with $R_4(y_0)$, which is now visible, (as T_3 runs solo), nor wait for the completion of T_4 (as T_3 could be indefinitely blocked if the process executing T_4 crashed).

However, history $\mathcal{H}_{WRTO}$ does not preserve RTO because: *i)* $T_3 \prec^{RTO}_{\mathcal{H}_{WRTO}} T_2$; and *ii)* there exists the oriented path $T_2 \xrightarrow{wr} T_4 \overset{rw}{\dashrightarrow} T_3$ from T_2 to T_3 in $DSG(\mathcal{H}_{WRTO})$.

Therefore we have shown that a WDAP, obstruction-free TM, that guarantees WFRO and WRTO necessarily violates RTO (as the TM cannot reject the history $\mathcal{H}_{WRTO}$). But WRTO is strictly weaker than RTO, which means that to guarantee RTO the TM should guarantee WRTO, and thus there cannot exist a WDAP, obstruction-free TM that guarantees WFRO and RTO. □

Next we question the possibility to ensure RTO in a WDAP TM when considering weak progressiveness as the progress guarantee for write transactions. The answer is still negative (as we show in Theorem 2, whose formal proof is still in [26]) if we require WFIRO, which includes invisible read-only transactions. The proof is analogous to the one of Theorem 1, but further takes into account that write transactions cannot detect a conflict with read-only transactions due to the invisibility of the latter. To do so, we rely on the indistinguishability between the execution in Figure 1 and an analogous execution where T_4 does not take any step.

THEOREM 2. *No WDAP, weakly progressive TM that guarantees WFIRO can ensure RTO.*

It is interesting to relate the above results to at least two existing DAP TM algorithms, namely TLC [5] and the SDAP TM proposed in [3]. The latter TM guarantees opacity (and hence RTO) and can be easily shown to ensure WFRO. However, this TM adopts visible read-only transactions (hence not contradicting Theorem 2), because their execution needs to block the commit of concurrent and conflicting write transactions. For this reason, write transactions are not obstruction-free and, hence, the TM in [3] does not contradict Theorem 1. TLC [5] is another SDAP TM implementation that guarantees invisible read-only and strongly progressive transactions. However, TLC does not guarantee WFRO, thus again one of the hypothesis of Theorem 2 is not met.

4. A SDAP TM WITH WITNESSABLE REAL-TIME ORDER

In Section 3 we have shown that RTO cannot be guaranteed by a WDAP TM that provides WFIRO. Here we provide a possibility result by adopting WRTO: it is possible to implement a WFIRO TM that guarantees the strongest variant of DAP, strong progressiveness for write transactions, and a correctness criterion whose semantics is very close to those provided by opacity or virtual world consistency. This consistency criterion, known in the literature as Extended Update Serializability (EUS) [1, 27], guarantees the serializability of the history of committed write transactions — hence ensuring that the state of the TM is updated without anomalies. Further, analogously to opacity, virtual world consistency, and TMS1, EUS provides Consistent View.

The details of such a TM are shown in the technical report [26] and are omitted from this paper for space constraints, although we provide an overview in the next Section 4.1. However intuitively the above properties are achieved as follows. Committed write transactions can be guaranteed to be serializable without sharing any global information but just leveraging meta data associated with transactional objects, by adopting a scheme similar to the DAP version of TL2 [5]. On the other hand, Consistent View and WRTO can be ensured by combining a multi-version scheme that allows a read operation by a transaction T to never incur wait conditions, and to always return the right version v such that v was not committed by a transaction T' that causally follows T, i.e., v is a correct state observable by T. This is achievable without sharing any global information (e.g., a global clock, which would violate DAP) and without applying any modification during the execution of a read operation (invisible read-only transactions) by just exploiting meta data associated with the committed versions, in order to detect the causal dependencies of commit events.

4.1 Algorithm Overview

Data structures. The proposed algorithm relies on vector clocks as identifiers of the snapshots committed and as references to determine which of the available object versions should be returned by read operations.

Each process p_i maintains a scalar, tc, that stores the timestamp associated with the last commit of process p_i; and a vector clock of size N_p, $maxS$, where $maxS[k]$ records the maximum value of process p_k's tc as known by p_i. Intuitively, at each step of the execution of a transaction T processed by p_i, $maxS$ identifies the commit events of the transactions serialized before T. Further, each transaction T maintains a vector clock, $upperS$, which identifies the commit events of the transactions serialized after T.

Commit events. In order to univocally identify the commit events in a totally decentralized way, the versions created upon commit are associated with two identifiers, i.e., cid and S. The former is the identifier of the process having committed those versions, while the latter is the vector clock that identifies the committed snapshot containing the versions created by this commit event. Therefore the cid-th entry of vector S associated with a version ver is the value of tc at the time ver was committed by p_{cid}. Intuitively, the remaining entries $S[j]$, with $j \neq cid$, capture the causal dependencies developed by the transaction that committed ver with the transactions executed by the other processes.

Read logic. The version visibility logic relies on both $upperS$ and $maxS$ to determine whether a commit event should be visible by a transaction T. As already mentioned, the commit events that precede or are equal to $maxS$ correspond to transactions that were already serialized before T, and are hence considered as visible by T; the commit events that do not precede or are equal to $upperS$ correspond to transactions that were already serialized after T, and are hence non-visible by T. Finally, the remaining commit events can be potentially visible by T and are said to be *uncertain*.

As an example, we provide in Figure 2 a graphical representation of the meaning of $maxS$ and $upperS$ for a transaction T at a certain point of its execution by process p_0 in a configuration of three processes p_0, p_1 and p_2. Given the current value of $maxS$, transaction T can determine that the transactions that generated the commit events having $S \in$\{ \{1,0,0\}, \{0,2,0\}, \{0,1,2\} \} are serialized before T. They are therefore in the *past* of T. On the contrary, due to the value of $upperS$, T cannot observe the commit events with $S \in$ \{ \{0,5,3\}, \{0,4,3\} \}, as their vector clocks S are concurrent with T's $upperS$. This is because, as a result of the values observed by T's read operations so far, T has been serialized before the transactions that generated these commit events. These transactions are therefore in T's future.

Upon each read operation on a transactional object, the corresponding set of versions is retrieved and the uncertain ones are analyzed to determine whether the corresponding commit is visible to T, i.e., serialized before T. If an uncertain version ver is not visible, the transaction creating ver is serialized after T, therefore T moves its $upperS$ backwards so as to exclude the vector clock S of ver. Otherwise, that transaction creating ver has to be serialized before T. The latter case will trigger an advancement of $maxS$ only when T completes, in order to include the vector clock S of ver in the visible snapshot of the transactions executing after T on the same process.

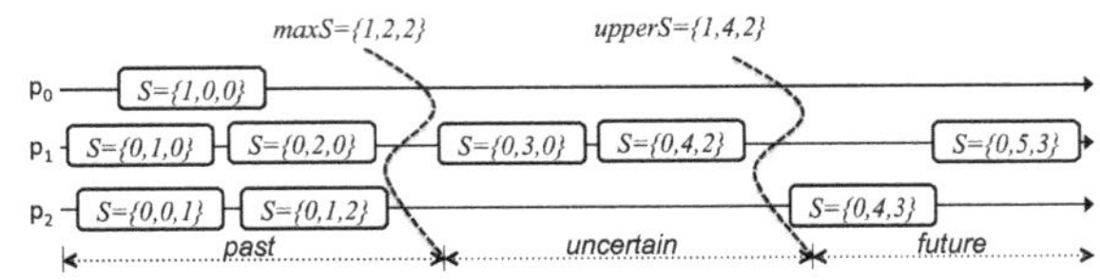

Figure 2: Example of usage of vectors $maxS$ and $upperS$ for a transaction T. A rectangle at process p_i identifies a commit event by process p_i and is tagged with the corresponding vector clock S.

In order to determine the visibility of an uncertain version ver, if any exists, the transaction read-set is re-validated to verify whether it is safe to serialize the transaction that committed ver before the reading transaction. An uncertain version ver of object o is non-visible to transaction T, if T has read a version ver_1 of object o', and: *i)* a version ver_2 of o' exists that is more recent than ver_1; *ii)* the commit of ver causally depends on the commit of ver_2 (the vector clock S of ver is greater than or equal to the vector clock S of ver_2). If the two conditions above are met, and ver had been serialized before T since its beginning, then T should have observed ver_2 (and not ver_1) at the time it issued a read on o'.

Finally, the version returned by a read operation is the most recent of the visible versions.

Commit phase. The algorithm allows a write transaction T to commit only if *i)* it is able to acquire all locks on the objects read and written by T; and *ii)* T's read-set has not been invalidated by a concurrent transaction, i.e., for each version read by T, that version is still the last committed version of the corresponding object. This is sufficient to guarantee the serializability of the history of the write transactions, as required by EUS. Furthermore, the S vector clock associated with a snapshot committed by T is set to be greater than any of the S vector clocks of the objects read and overwritten by T. This allows to track causality dependencies among transactions, which is necessary to guarantee the correct execution of read operations.

5. TIME AND SPACE COMPLEXITY OF DAP TM IMPLEMENTATIONS

Despite the theoretical relevance of the algorithm in Section 4, we note that it comes with a non-negligible overhead: each version of a transactional object has to keep a vector clock as big as the maximum number of concurrent processes N_p; a read operation of a read-only transaction may accomplish $k \cdot N_o$ steps in order to return the correct value, where k is the number of versions of a transactional object, and N_o is the total number of transactional objects. In the following we prove that these costs are necessary even considering only Consistent View and WRTO.

5.1 Time Complexity

In this section we investigate the costs a WDAP TM has to pay if it guarantees WFIRO when the correctness guarantee is Consistent View. Roughly, this means that every read operation does not observe any incorrect state as long as write transactions produce correct states. Note that the latter is needed because Consistent View does not enforce write transactions to always produce correct states (unlike EUS). We also suppose that the TM guarantees WRTO, in order to rule out any trivial implementation of WFIRO, in which the read-only transactions only observe the initial version of the transactional objects.

The intuition behind the result is that such a TM cannot always ensure a constant cost for handling any read operation because a read cannot rely on any shared timestamp to determine the correct state to be observed (as for TL2 [12] or LSA [29]). In fact, if that was the case, then the TM would trivially violate DAP. In particular, what we show is that, the maximum number of steps performed by any read operation of read-only transactions for determining whether a version can be observed without violating Consistent View is $\Omega(N_o)$. Let us introduce the definition of read-only time complexity of a TM.

Definition 1. *The read-only time complexity of a TM is the maximum number of steps performed by any read operation of any read-only transaction executed by the TM.*

Given the previous definition, we show that the read-only time complexity of the above TM is $\Omega(k \cdot N_o)$, where k is the maximum number of versions associated with any transactional object. For convenience in the proof we rely on the function CheckVersion, which determines whether a live read-only transaction that executes a read operation on an object x is allowed to observe the version x_i of x. More formally, given a configuration Ψ_k, a read-only transaction T_{ro} live in Ψ_k, and a version x_i that exists in Ψ_k, CheckVersion(Ψ_k,T_{ro},x_i) returns true if T_{ro} can return x_i by executing a read operation on x without violating Consistent View; it returns false otherwise.

The proof is based on the following scenario: a read-only transaction T_{ro} whose read-set has been invalidated by a write transaction T_i and such that it executes a read operation on an object x after the invalidation. Here, we focus on how to determine the correct version of x to be observed. Clearly, T_{ro} cannot observe the version x_i if x_i has been written by T_i because the resulting DSG would contain the following cycle: $T_{ro} \overset{rw}{\dashrightarrow} T_i \xrightarrow{wr} T_{ro}$. In addition, T_{ro} cannot arbitrarily decide not to observe x_i because it could have been written by a transaction committed before T_{ro}'s begin, hence violating WRTO.

To determine this, the function CheckVersion(Ψ_k,T_{ro},x_i) executed by a WDAP TM has to apply trivial primitives on the base objects associated with the objects that T_{ro} already read (i.e., the validation of T_{ro}'s read-set). Let us assume that at the time T_{ro} executes its read operation on x, it has already executed read operations on all the other objects, then the number of steps performed by CheckVersion(Ψ_k,T_{ro},x_i) is $\Omega(N_o)$. Now, if we suppose that there are k versions associated with any transactional object, the number of steps performed by the T_{ro}'s read operation on x is equal to $\Omega(k \cdot N_o)$, which is also the read-only time complexity of the TM. In the following proof we assume either obstruction-free or weakly progressive write transactions.

Theorem 3. *Given a WDAP multi-version TM that guarantees WFIRO, Consistent View, WRTO, and either obstruction-freedom or weak progressiveness for write transactions, the read-only time complexity of the TM is $\Omega(k \cdot N_o)$, where k is the number of versions a transactional object can have, and N_o is the total number of transactional objects.*

Proof. By hypothesis we consider a WDAP multi-version TM that guarantees WFIRO, Consistent View, WRTO, and either weakly progressive or obstruction-free write transactions. Also, let $E = E_1 \cdot E_2 \cdot E_3 \cdot E_4$ be the following execution of the TM in which only the processes p_1 and p_2 take steps. E_1: transaction T_1, executed by process p_1, writes to all the N_o shared objects some values and then it commits. E_2: transaction T_{ro}, executed by process p_2, performs $\Theta(N_o)$ read operations on $\Theta(N_o)$ different objects from some set Q_{RO}. Due to WRTO, these operations return the last available versions (the ones committed by T_1). E_3: transaction T_i, executed by process p_1, performs $\Theta(N_o)$ write operations on $\Theta(N_o)$ different objects from some set $Q_{WR} = Q_1 \cup \{y\}$, such that $Q_1 \cap Q_{RO} = \emptyset$ and $y \in Q_{RO}$. Then T_i commits. E_4: transaction T_{ro} performs a read operation on object $x \in Q_1$ (thus $x \notin Q_{RO}$) and it returns the version x_j such that $x_j \ll x_i$ and x_i is the version of x committed by T_i. We also assume that the process running in an execution interval (i.e., E_1, E_2, E_3, E_4) runs solo in that interval.

E is an admissible execution for the assumed TM because no transaction in E violates neither the liveness nor the correctness properties guaranteed by the TM. Regarding the former, no read operation of T_{ro} can generate an abort since read-only transactions are wait-free; and both the write transactions T_1 and T_i have to commit in E because of the following. T_1 has to commit in E because it runs solo (as required by obstruction-freedom) and it does not encounter any conflict (as required by weak progressiveness); T_i has to commit under obstruction-freedom because it runs solo, and it has to commit under weak progressiveness (even though it encounters a conflict with T_{ro}) for the following reason: T_i has to commit also in an execution $E' = E_1 \cdot E_3$, where T_{ro} is not processed, and E' and E are indistinguishable to p_1 since T_{ro} is invisible. Regarding the correctness guarantee, the history $E|\mathcal{H}$ does not violate Consistent View since the graph $DSG(E|\mathcal{H})$ does not contain any oriented cycle (including those with exactly one anti-dependence edge) and transactions only observe committed values. The graph is the union of the paths $T_1 \xrightarrow{wr} T_{ro} \overset{rw}{\dashrightarrow} T_i$ and $T_1 \xrightarrow{ww} T_i$.

We define the configuration Ψ_k as the result of the processing of $E_1 \cdot E_2 \cdot E_3$. Now, by contradiction we assume that the number of steps for executing CheckVersion(Ψ_k,T_{ro},x_i) is $\mathcal{O}(N_o)$. Our assumption means that, when T_{ro} executes the read operation on x in E_4, p_2 executes $\mathcal{O}(N_o)$ steps by applying trivial primitives on $\mathcal{O}(N_o)$ base objects, in order to determine that x_i cannot be visible. In fact, if that read operation returned x_i, then Consistent View would be violated. Our assumption also entails that T_i has to apply non-trivial primitives on $\mathcal{O}(N_o)$ base objects among the ones accessed by T_{ro} to guarantee the correct execution of CheckVersion(Ψ_k,T_{ro},x_i) in E. In fact, if that is not the case and T_i's execution applies non-trivial primitives on $N_o - \mathcal{O}(N_o)$ base objects among the ones that are not accessed by T_{ro}, then $E|\mathcal{H}$ can violate Consistent View because CheckVersion(Ψ_k,T_{ro},x_i) can return true by erroneously applying trivial primitives on only $\mathcal{O}(N_o)$ base objects.

We now show that our assumption leads us to a contradiction since either the worst case of $\mathcal{O}(N_o)$ steps is not enough to preserve Consistent View or WDAP is not guaranteed. To do that, let us consider an execution $E'' = E_1 \cdot E_2 \cdot \bar{E}_3 \cdot E_4$, where $\bar{E}_3$ differs from E_3 only because Q_{WR} is equal to $Q_1 \cup \{z\}$ in $\bar{E}_3$, where $z \in Q_{RO}$. First, we have to notice that E'' is admissible for the assumed TM because of the same arguments provided for E. Then, since T_i does not write on y in $\bar{E}_3$, but it writes on z, it has to apply non-trivial primitives on the $\mathcal{O}(N_o)$ base objects which T_{ro} applies trivial primitives on. In fact, if that is not the case and T_i's execution applies non-trivial primitives on $N_o - \mathcal{O}(N_o)$ base objects among the ones that are not accessed by T_{ro}, then $E''|\mathcal{H}$ can violate Consistent View because CHECKVERSION(Ψ_k,T_{ro},x_i) can return true by erroneously applying trivial primitives on only $\mathcal{O}(N_o)$ base objects.

However, if that is the case, we can build $\Theta(N_o)$ executions like E'', i.e., E^*, where z is replaced by an object among the ones in Q_{RO}, and T_i's execution in E^* performs its write operations by applying non-trivial primitives on $\mathcal{O}(N_o)$ base objects among the ones accessed by T_{ro}. Since the executions are $\Theta(N_o)$ and the base objects accessed by T_{ro} are only $\mathcal{O}(N_o)$, there exist at least two executions of them where the transactions T_i in the two executions access at least one common base object among the $\mathcal{O}(N_o)$ previously accessed by T_{ro}. Without loss of generality we assume that those two executions are E and E''.

Therefore T_i in E and T_i in E'' access at least one common base object among the $\mathcal{O}(N_o)$ previously accessed by T_{ro}, and the access to that base object depends on the write operations on y and z respectively, in order to be distinguishable to the process executing T_{ro} from an execution where T_i does not write any object in Q_{RO} (T_i does not invalidate T_{ro}'s read-set). Consequently, such a TM must accept an execution with two concurrent non-conflicting transactions T_i^* and T_i^+, one writing only y and the other writing only z, which both access at least one common base object among the $\mathcal{O}(N_o)$ previously accessed by T_{ro}, thus violating WDAP due to Lemma 1.

Therefore, since the assumption on the cost of $\mathcal{O}(N_o)$ for CHECKVERSION(Ψ_k,T_{ro},x_i) entails a TM that violates either WDAP or Consistent View, then CHECKVERSION(Ψ_k,T_{ro},x_i) must have a cost equal to $\Omega(N_o)$. Thus the maximum number of steps performed by any read operation of read-only transactions for determining whether a version can be observed without violating Consistent View is $\Omega(N_o)$. If we suppose that there are k versions of any transactional object, then the read-only time complexity of the assumed TM is equal to $\Omega(k \cdot N_o)$. ☐

5.2 Space Complexity

We now investigate the space complexity of a SDAP multi-version TM that guarantees WFIRO, namely the necessary meta data associated with each version of a transactional object. We prove a lower bound that holds assuming Consistent View as correctness guarantee, WRTO, and assuming either weak progressiveness or obstruction-freedom for write transactions. Note that in this lower bound we consider SDAP, which matches also the variant of DAP ensured by the algorithm in Section 4, rather than WDAP as before.

As in the proof of the time complexity, we assume that the TM also guarantees WRTO to rule out any trivial implementation of WFIRO, in which the read-only transactions only observe the initial transactional state. In order to derive an implementation-independent proof, we use an innovative technique, which shows an equivalence between the problem of detecting cycles containing exactly one anti-dependence edge using a SDAP TM, and determining causality in a distributed message passing system. The intuition behind the proof is that whenever a read-only transaction executes a read operation, it needs to detect whether that operation creates a cycle with one anti-dependence edge in the conflict graph associated with the current history. Due to the existence of the SDAP requirement, this check has to be performed without indiscriminately accessing all the information associated with the conflict graph, but only extracting this information via the base objects associated with the accessed transactional objects.

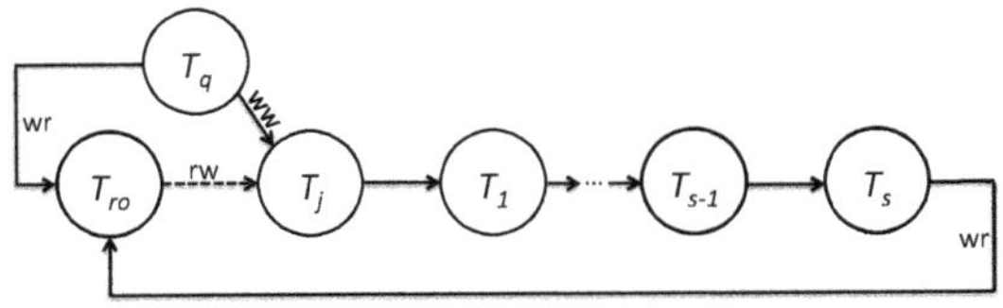

Figure 3: T_{ro} creating a cycle C with exactly one anti-dependence edge in $DSG(\mathcal{H})$.

THEOREM 4. *Given a SDAP TM that guarantees WFIRO, Consistent View, WRTO and either obstruction-freedom or weak progressiveness for the write transactions, then the space complexity for each version of a transactional object is $\Omega(m)$, where $m = min(N_o, N_p)$.*

PROOF. To guarantee Consistent View, the TM has to ensure that every accepted history $\mathcal{H}$ does not contain a cycle C with exactly one anti-dependence edge in the $DSG(\mathcal{H})$. We assume that an initial version of each transactional object d exists in the TM, which we denote with d_0. Now consider the history $\mathcal{H}$ whose $DSG(\mathcal{H})$ is shown in Figure 3, in which the first transaction to execute in absence of concurrency is T_q, which commits the version x_q. As we assume obstruction-freedom or weak progressiveness, the TM cannot refuse T_q's commit.

After T_q's commit a read-only transaction T_{ro} issues a read on object x. As we assume WFRO, the read operation of T_{ro} must eventually return some value, and by WRTO, the value returned has to be x_q. Before T_{ro} takes any other step, transaction T_j starts, writes x_j and d_j^1 (where we assume object $d^1 \neq x$) and commits (we will shortly prove that this commit cannot be rejected by the TM). Following the commit of T_j, the set of write transactions $\mathcal{T}=\{T_1,\ldots,T_i,\ldots,T_{s-1},T_s\}$ is executed sequentially. Each transaction $T_i \in \mathcal{T}$ issues the following operations in $\mathcal{H}$: T_i starts, reads an object d^i, writes a different object d^{i+1}, and requests to commit. We further assume that each transaction T_i runs solo, i.e., T_{i+1} starts only after T_i commits. As we assume that transaction T_1 and the transactions in $\mathcal{T}$ run solo, they must commit if we assume obstruction-freedom. On the other hand, if we assume weak progressiveness, T_j may abort due to the presence of an anti-dependency on T_{ro}. However, since we assume invisible read-only transactions, T_j cannot detect the occurrence of this conflict and, also in this case, it cannot abort.

Now, let us assume that T_{ro} issues a read operation on object d^{s+1}. At this point, as T_s committed version d_s^{s+1}, T_{ro} needs to decide whether to observe this version or not. Note that, since T_{ro} has already developed an anti-dependence towards T_j, if T_{ro} observed d_s^{s+1}, Consistent View would be violated, as a cycle with exactly one anti-dependence would be created. Also, since we assume that the TM ensures WRTO, it cannot deterministically return the initial version d_0^{s+1}. In fact, using such a deterministic policy, it is straightforward to show that a read-only transaction T' may trivially miss the version committed by a write transaction that commits before T''s begin. Also, in the assumed history, T_{ro} cannot be aware of having developed an anti-dependence towards T_j, as we assume IRO. Hence, by no means, T_{ro} could have transmitted any information to T_j on the execution of its read on x_q. Further, no other transaction could have notified T_{ro} of the existence of such anti-dependence.

Note that if T_{ro} ignored the possibility of having developed new anti-dependences when determining the visibility of d_s^{s+1}, it could miss the existence of the cycle C, and violate Consistent View. It follows that T_{ro} has to first validate its current read-set, which comprises only x_q. This allows T_{ro} to detect the anti-dependence with T_j, and poses T_{ro} with the problem to determine whether there exists an oriented path from T_j to T_s (in which case d_s^{s+1} should not be observed). Note that since we assume a SDAP TM, T_{ro} needs to detect the existence of a path of direct dependencies from T_j to T_s, without however being able to apply trivial operations to any of the base objects that the transactions $T_1,\ldots,T_{s-1}$ accessed (as T_{ro} accesses a disjoint data set with respect to these transactions).

We now assume a total number of transactional objects greater than the maximum number of concurrent processes (i.e., $N_o \geq N_p$). In a SDAP TM, the only way for transactions to transmit information concerning the conflicts that they develop is via the base objects associated with the transactional objects that they access. The transmission of this information can be emulated considering a distributed message passing system (DS) comprising the same number of processes considered in the TM, namely N_p. Consider, in particular, the following simulation: for each direct read-dependence edge $T_i \xrightarrow{wr} T_{i+1} \in$DSG($\mathcal{H}$) developed by a pair of write/read operations on version d_i^{i+1} of transactional object d^{i+1}, we can associate the events of send, respectively receive, of a message $m_{i,i+1}$ in DS from p_i, respectively to p_{i+1}. Since the communication of any type of information on the ordering of events in a SDAP TM can only take place via base objects, this can be simulated in the DS by assuming that $m_{i,i+1}$ can only be tagged with the information that T_i had stored in the base object associated with version d_i^{i+1}, at the time in which T_i created it. Analogously for the direct anti-dependence edge $T_{ro} \overset{rw}{\dashrightarrow} T_j \in$DSG($\mathcal{H}$) developed by the operations $R(x_q)$ and $W(x_j)$, we can associate the events of send, respectively receive, of a message $m_{j,ro}$ in DS from p_j, respectively to p_{ro}. What triggers the sending of this message in this history is the fact that T_{ro} has to access the base object of x_j (and of all existing versions of x) in order to validate its read-set.

With this simulation we transformed the problem of determining if there exists a path from T_j to T_s in DSG($\mathcal{H}$) based on the information available to T_{ro}, to the problem of having the process p_{ro} (that executes transaction T_{ro}) in DS to determine if the two messages $m_{j,ro}$ and $m_{s,ro}$ are causally ordered [23], namely $m_{j,ro} \prec_{DS} m_{s,ro}$. Thanks to the result in [24], in a distributed system of N_p processes such as DS, given two events e and e', $e \prec_{DS} e'$ iff $\mathcal{V}(e) < \mathcal{V}(e')$, where $\mathcal{V}(e)$ (respectively $\mathcal{V}(e')$) is the vector clock of size N_p associated to e (respectively e'). Hence the base objects need to have a space capacity equal [10] to $\Omega(N_p)$.

We now go over the case where the total number of transactional objects is lesser than the maximum number of concurrent processes (i.e., $N_o < N_p$). In this case, each version encodes the most recent state of the TM at the time the version is created. By doing so, a transaction has all the sufficient information to decide whether a version can be read or not. Note that, storing the most recent state of the whole TM in each version is also (trivially) necessary in this case because keeping the entire state but one transactional object could let the TM miss a dependency on that object, thus generating a violation of Consistent View. For instance, a TM that follows this intuition has been provided by Ardekani et al. in [2].

We showed that a lower bound on the space complexity of each version of a SDAP TM that guarantees Consistent View, WFIRO, WRTO and obstruction-freedom (or weak progressiveness), is $\Omega(m)$, where $m = min(N_o, N_p)$. □

6. RELATED RESULTS

Theorem 1 has relations with a lower bound [4] defined on the number of non-trivial primitives applied by read-only transactions in a Strict Serializable and DAP TM (where DAP here is the one defined in [22]) that ensures minimal progressiveness for write transactions. This lower bound defines a necessary condition for the visibility of the read-only transactions to ensure WFRO and Strict Serializability, that is not sufficient in the case of obstruction-free write transactions because it is superseded by Theorem 1 in that case (since Strict Serializability demands RTO [25, 16]).

On the other hand, that necessary condition is also a sufficient condition in case write transactions are weakly progressive. As an evidence of that, Attiya and Hillel proposed such a TM in [3], which is even able to guarantee opacity.

If we suppose a parasitic-free TM, the impossibility presented by Perelman et al. [28] uses the same assumptions of Theorem 2, and proves that such a TM cannot guarantee Strict Serializability. In fact, it is easy to prove that, in a parasitic-free TM, MV-permissiveness may imply wait-free and invisible read-only transactions, and weakly progressive write transactions. However, the result is weaker than the one of Theorem 2, since Strict Serializability demands RTO.

The impossibility result by Guerraoui and Kapalka [15] rules out the possibility to combine a SDAP TM and obstruction-free transactions if the target correctness guarantee is Serializability. The authors prove the result by only considering write transactions, and therefore we can consider their impossibility still valid if the target correctness guarantee is EUS. Later this same impossibility result [15] has been superseded by the results of the PCL theorem [8], which relaxes the correctness guarantee assumed in [15]. Our algorithm overcomes those two results by assuming a different progress guarantee for write transactions.

Our lower bound on the time complexity is related to the lower bound presented in [16] where the authors prove that the maximum number of steps performed by any operation of any transaction executed by a progressive (which is stronger than weakly progressive) single-version TM is $\Omega(N_o)$ if the TM guarantees opacity.

7. CONCLUSIONS

In this paper we enriched the literature on impossibility, possibility, and lower bound results of DAP TM. We presented two impossibility results ruling DAP TM that guarantees real-time order relations and a set of desirable progress properties. Furthermore, we provided a possibility result: an algorithm that circumvents the existing DAP limitations by providing a strong correctness property (i.e., EUS), a variant of the real-time order we introduced in this paper (i.e., *Witnessable Real-Time Order*), and the same set of progress properties as before. We also provided two lower bounds on the space and time complexity of such a DAP TM, which highlight that efficient DAP TM implementations should necessarily sacrifice either invisible reads or wait-freedom for read-only transactions because lowering the correctness level is not enough.

8. ACKNOWLEDGMENTS

The authors thank Rachid Guerraoui and Srivatsan Ravi for the useful feedbacks. Peluso, Palmieri and Ravindran are supported in part by US Air Force Office of Scientific Research under grants FA9550-14-1-0143 and FA9550-14-1-0187, and US National Science Foundation under grant CNS-1217385. Romano is supported in part by FCT projects UID/CEC/50021/2013 and EXPL/EEI-ESS/0361/2013.

9. REFERENCES

[1] A. Adya. *Weak Consistency: A Generalized Theory and Optimistic Implementations for Distributed Transactions*. PhD thesis, 1999.

[2] M. S. Ardekani, P. Sutra, and M. Shapiro. Non-monotonic snapshot isolation: Scalable and strong consistency for geo-replicated transactional systems. In *SRDS*, pages 163–172, 2013.

[3] H. Attiya and E. Hillel. A single-version STM that is multi-versioned permissive. *Theory Comput. Syst.*, 51(4):425–446, 2012.

[4] H. Attiya, E. Hillel, and A. Milani. Inherent limitations on disjoint-access parallel implementations of transactional memory. *Theory Comput. Syst.*, 49(4):698–719, 2011.

[5] H. Avni and N. Shavit. Maintaining Consistent Transactional States Without a Global Clock. In *SIROCCO*, pages 131–140, 2008.

[6] H. Berenson, P. Bernstein, J. Gray, J. Melton, E. O'Neil, and P. O'Neil. A Critique of ANSI SQL Isolation Levels. In *SIGMOD*, pages 1–10, 1995.

[7] P. A. Bernstein, V. Hadzilacos, and N. Goodman. *Concurrency Control and Recovery in Database Systems*. Addison-Wesley, 1987.

[8] V. Bushkov, D. Dziuma, P. Fatourou, and R. Guerraoui. The PCL Theorem. Transactions cannot be Parallel, Consistent and Live. In *SPAA*, pages 178–187, 2014.

[9] V. Bushkov, R. Guerraoui, and M. Kapalka. On the liveness of transactional memory. In *PODC*, pages 9–18, 2012.

[10] B. Charron-Bost. Concerning the size of logical clocks in distributed systems. *Inf. Process. Lett.*, 39(1):11–16, 1991.

[11] T. David, R. Guerraoui, and V. Trigonakis. Everything you always wanted to know about synchronization but were afraid to ask. In *SOSP*, pages 33–48, 2013.

[12] D. Dice, O. Shalev, and N. Shavit. Transactional Locking II. In *DISC*, pages 194–208, 2006.

[13] S. Doherty, L. Groves, V. Luchangco, and M. Moir. Towards formally specifying and verifying transactional memory. *Formal Asp. Comput.*, 25(5):769–799, 2013.

[14] F. Ellen, P. Fatourou, E. Kosmas, A. Milani, and C. Travers. Universal constructions that ensure disjoint-access parallelism and wait-freedom. In *PODC*, pages 115–124, 2012.

[15] R. Guerraoui and M. Kapalka. On Obstruction-free Transactions. In *SPAA*, pages 304–313, 2008.

[16] R. Guerraoui and M. Kapalka. On the correctness of transactional memory. In *PPoPP*, pages 175–184, 2008.

[17] R. Guerraoui and M. Kapalka. The Semantics of Progress in Lock-based Transactional Memory. In *POPL*, 2009.

[18] R. Guerraoui and P. Romano. *Transactional Memory. Foundations, Algorithms, Tools, and Applications*. Springer, 2015.

[19] M. Herlihy. Wait-free synchronization. *ACM TOPLAS*, 13(1), 1991.

[20] M. Herlihy, V. Luchangco, and M. Moir. Obstruction-Free Synchronization: Double-Ended Queues As an Example. In *ICDCS*, pages 522–529, 2003.

[21] D. Imbs and M. Raynal. Virtual World Consistency: A Condition for STM Systems (with a Versatile Protocol with Invisible Read Operations). *Theoretical Computer Science*, 444:113–127, July 2012.

[22] A. Israeli and L. Rappoport. Disjoint-access-parallel Implementations of Strong Shared Memory Primitives. In *PODC*, pages 151–160, 1994.

[23] L. Lamport. Time, clocks, and the ordering of events in a distributed system. *Communications of the ACM*, 21(7):558–565, 1978.

[24] F. Mattern. Virtual time and global states of distributed systems. In *Parallel and Distributed Algorithms*, pages 215–226, 1989.

[25] C. H. Papadimitriou. The Serializability of Concurrent Database Updates. *Journal of the ACM*, 26(4):631–653, Oct. 1979.

[26] S. Peluso, R. Palmieri, P. Romano, B. Ravindran, and F. Quaglia. Disjoint-Access Parallelism: Impossibility, Possibility, and Cost of Transactional Memory Implementations. Technical report, Virginia Tech, 2015.

[27] S. Peluso, P. Ruivo, P. Romano, F. Quaglia, and L. Rodrigues. When Scalability Meets Consistency: Genuine Multiversion Update-Serializable Partial Data Replication. In *ICDCS*, pages 455–465, 2012.

[28] D. Perelman, R. Fan, and I. Keidar. On maintaining multiple versions in STM. In *PODC*, pages 16–25, 2010.

[29] T. Riegel, P. Felber, and C. Fetzer. A Lazy Snapshot Algorithm with Eager Validation. In *DISC*, pages 284–298, 2006.

[30] N. Shavit and D. Touitou. Software transactional memory. In *PODC*, pages 204–213, 1995.

Safety-Liveness Exclusion in Distributed Computing

Victor Bushkov
EPFL, IC, LPD
victor.bushkov@epfl.ch

Rachid Guerraoui
EPFL, IC, LPD
rachid.guerraoui@epfl.ch

ABSTRACT

The history of distributed computing is full of trade-offs between safety and liveness. For instance, one of the most celebrated results in the field, namely the impossibility of consensus in an asynchronous system basically says that we cannot devise an algorithm that deterministically ensures consensus agreement and validity (i.e., safety) on the one hand, and consensus wait-freedom (i.e., liveness) on the other hand.

The motivation of this work is to study the extent to which safety and liveness properties inherently exclude each other. More specifically, we ask, given any safety property S, whether we can determine the strongest (resp. weakest) liveness property that can (resp. cannot) be achieved with S. We show that, maybe surprisingly, the answers to these safety-liveness exclusion questions are in general negative. This has several ramifications in various distributed computing contexts. In the context of consensus for example, this means that it is impossible to determine the strongest (resp. the weakest) liveness property that can (resp. cannot) be ensured with linearizability.

However, we present a way to circumvent these impossibilities and answer positively the safety-liveness question by considering a restricted form of liveness. We consider a definition that gathers generalized forms of obstruction-freedom and lock-freedom while enabling to determine the strongest (resp. weakest) liveness property that can (resp. cannot) be implemented in the context of consensus and transactional memory.

Categories and Subject Descriptors

D.1.3 [**Programming Techniques**]: Concurrent Programming

General Terms

Theory

Keywords

Concurrency, Safety, Liveness, Impossibility Results, Consensus, Transactional Memory

Permission to make digital or hard copies of all or part of this work for personal or classroom use is granted without fee provided that copies are not made or distributed for profit or commercial advantage and that copies bear this notice and the full citation on the first page. Copyrights for components of this work owned by others than ACM must be honored. Abstracting with credit is permitted. To copy otherwise, or republish, to post on servers or to redistribute to lists, requires prior specific permission and/or a fee. Request permissions from permissions@acm.org.
PODC'15, July 21–23, 2015, Donostia-San Sebastián, Spain.
Copyright is held by the owner/author(s). Publication rights licensed to ACM.
ACM 978-1-4503-3617-8 /15/07 ...$15.00.
DOI: http://dx.doi.org/10.1145/2767386.2767401.

1. INTRODUCTION

The correctness of a distributed algorithm is expressed through *safety* and *liveness* properties [30, 1, 33, 29]. These properties can be defined as sets of histories (traces). More specifically, a safety property is defined as a prefix-closed and limit-closed set of well-formed histories [29]. Whereas, a liveness property is defined as a set of histories that permits any finite well-formed history, i.e., for every finite history there exists a continuation of that history in the liveness property [29].

Because a liveness property basically states that certain 'good' events should eventually happen while a safety property states that certain 'bad' events should never happen, it occurs sometimes that a safety property makes it impossible to guarantee a liveness property, i.e., when the 'bad' and the 'good' coincide. For example, it is impossible to implement a consensus shared object using only asynchronous read/write shared memory while ensuring both wait-freedom, a liveness property, and agreement and validity, a safety property [9, 28]. The history of distributed computing is full of such trade-offs [8, 19, 37, 22, 14, 15, 7, 13, 5].

We ask the questions of *safety-liveness exclusions*: namely if we can determine, given any safety property S, the strongest (resp. weakest) liveness property that can (resp. cannot) be achieved with S. In the context of consensus for instance, this would mean determining the strongest liveness property that can be ensured while still ensuring consensus safety. Given that consensus is at the heart of state machine replication [26, 32, 12, 27], addressing such questions could enable us to determine the maximum availability (liveness) to be expected if the consistency (safety) of a shared distributed service needs to be preserved. More specifically, given $\mathbb{S}$ and $\mathbb{L}$ the sets of safety and liveness properties respectively, we seek to determine if there is a mapping $f_w : \mathbb{S} \rightarrow \mathbb{L}$ (resp. $f_s : \mathbb{S} \rightarrow \mathbb{L}$) that maps every safety property $S \in \mathbb{S}$ onto the weakest (resp. strongest) liveness property $L \in \mathbb{L}$ that cannot (resp. can) be achieved with S.

When the strongest possible liveness property in a given context is known to be implementable with a given safety property, the answer to the above question is trivial. In many cases, however, the question is more challenging. We show in this paper that, maybe surprisingly, in the general case, it is impossible to determine the strongest (resp. weakest) liveness property that can (resp. cannot) be achieved with a given (non-trivial) safety property. In other words, the safety-liveness exclusion mappings do not exist.

We proceed as follows. We consider a general asynchronous shared-memory distributed system, in which any number of processes can fail by crashing, and we say that a liveness property *excludes* a safety property of a shared object if *every* implementation of that object which ensures the safety property, violates the liveness property. We then show that there is no strongest liveness property that does not exclude a given safety property in a non-trivial case, and give a necessary and sufficient condition when there is a weakest liveness property that excludes a given safety property.

- If L_{max} is the strongest possible liveness property among all liveness properties (L_{max} is a liveness property that requires progress for *all* non-crashed processes), then the first result states the following. If there exists a strongest liveness property that does not exclude a given safety property, then such property must be L_{max}.

- The fact that a liveness property L excludes a safety property S means that there is an adversary w.r.t. L, i.e., an entity that plays against an implementation ensuring S and that decides on the schedule and inputs of processes to win the game by having the implementation violate L. Our second necessary and sufficient condition states that there is a weakest liveness property that excludes safety property S iff for all adversaries w.r.t. L_{max}, the intersection of their behavior is also a behavior of an adversary w.r.t. L_{max}.

For all common safety properties studied in the literature and all common liveness properties, it is possible to find two adversaries the intersection of which behavior is not a behavior of an adversary, e.g. by considering two adversaries that make processes invoke operations with different arguments or different process identifiers, which results in two disjoint behaviors. Thus, for all common safety properties which are impossible to implement together with a corresponding strongest liveness property L_{max}, we have two impossibility results. They basically state that there are no safety-liveness exclusion mappings.

A corollary of our impossibilities is, for instance, that there is no strongest liveness property that can be implemented (resp. no weakest liveness property which is impossible to implement) together with consensus safety, i.e., agreement and validity. Also, we can now answer questions such as the one raised in [5], about the existence of a weakest transactional memory (TM) liveness property which is impossible to implement together with opacity [16] and the existence of a strongest TM liveness property implementable with opacity[1]. We show that there are no such liveness properties. In fact, our impossibilities can be applied to many other contexts, such as k-set agreement [3] or high-level object implementations from registers [19] to show that there is no strongest implementable liveness property (resp. no weakest non-implementable liveness property).

One way to circumvent our impossibilities is to restrict the definitions of liveness and safety, i.e., basically to consider subsets $\mathscr{S} \subseteq \mathbb{S}$ and $\mathscr{L} \subseteq \mathbb{L}$, so that it is possible to find mappings $f_w : \mathbb{S} \rightarrow \mathscr{L}$ and $f_s : \mathbb{S} \rightarrow \mathscr{L}$. We explore a restricted definition of liveness that covers properties of *non-blocking* systems and includes properties that require either *minimal* or *maximal* progress and which are either *dependent* or *independent* of a scheduler.[2] Our restricted definition combines the notions of *k-obstruction-freedom* [35] and *l-lock-freedom*. While k-obstruction-freedom is a dependent maximal progress guarantee that requires progress of every process in a group of less than k processes which execute alone, l-lock freedom is an independent minimal progress guarantee that requires progress of at least l correct processes. We define a liveness property as a union of l-lock-freedom and k-obstruction-freedom, where $l \leq k$, and call such a property *(l,k)-freedom*. Being general enough, (l,k)-freedom covers liveness properties of shared objects considered most commonly used in literature and allows us to positively answer the safety-liveness exclusion question for many common safety properties. For example, considering consensus in a read-write shared memory system of n processes, the strongest implementable liveness property is $(1,1)$-freedom and the weakest non-implementable is $(1,2)$-freedom; while for TM implementations the strongest implementable liveness property is $(1,n)$-freedom and the weakest non-implementable is $(2,2)$-freedom. Finally, we show that (l,k)-freedom has its own limitations by giving an example of a TM safety property for which we cannot find a weakest liveness that excludes the safety property.

The rest of the paper is organized as follows. Section 2 recalls basic definitions of a shared memory system. Section 3 defines safety and liveness properties. Section 4 poses the safety-liveness exclusion problem. There we give our impossibility results for the general case. Section 5 describes one way to circumvent the impossibility results. Section 6 concludes the paper by discussing alternative ways.

2. SYSTEM MODEL

We consider a general shared memory system of n asynchronous *processes* which might stop by crashing. The processes interact with each other only by performing *atomic* primitives on base objects. *Base objects* are shared objects, like read/write registers, test-and-set, compare-and-swap and etc., which are usually provided by the hardware and which are used to implement higher level shared objects. We assume that each process is *sequential* in the sense that after invoking a primitive, the process cannot invoke another primitive until it receives a corresponding response.

A shared object is defined by its type. A shared *object type* Tp is a tuple (St, Inv, Res, Seq), where St is the set of all possible states of the object, Inv is the set of all possible *invocations* on the object, Res is the set of all possible *responses* from the object, and $Seq \subseteq Inv \times St \times St \times Res$ is the *sequential specification* of the object. An *implementation* I of a shared object of type Tp is a set of algorithms $\{I_1, \ldots, I_n\}$ on base objects such that each algorithm I_i corresponds to a process p_i. When process p_i invokes inv_i on I, where inv is some invocation from Inv, it executes algorithm I_i with inv_i as an input of the algorithm. When executing algorithm I_i process p_i performs *steps* which could be an invocation, a response, or an atomic operation on base objects and local computations. The order in which processes take steps is determined by an external entity called a *scheduler* over which processes have no control. The system is *asynchronous* in the sense that a scheduler may delay any process for an arbitrary long period of time and there is no way for one process to determine if some other process is crashed or delayed.

We use the I/O automata model of asynchronous shared memory systems [29] in which invocations and responses are input and output actions of an automaton. The complete model is given in the full version of the paper [4], here we give basic definitions of the model. Implementation $I = \{I_1, \ldots, I_n\}$ is modeled by a com-

[1]It was shown in [5] that in the case of TM shared objects [18, 21, 34], it is impossible to ensure both opacity and local progress, the strongest liveness property. However, the question whether there exists a weakest TM liveness property that excludes opacity or a strongest TM liveness property that does not exclude opacity remained open.

[2]A *non-blocking* system is a one in which no process p can prevent other processes from making progress once p crashes, i.e. stops participating in a computation. A *maximal* [23] progress guarantee requires progress for all processes while a *minimal* [23] progress guarantee requires progress for some processes. A *dependent* [23] progress guarantee depends on the scheduling of processes while an *independent* [23] progress guarantee has the same requirement irrespectively of how processes are scheduled.

position $A_I = A_{I_1} \times \ldots \times A_{I_n} \times A_B$ of I/O automata, where each I/O automaton A_{I_i} corresponds to algorithm I_i and A_B corresponds to all base objects used in I. A sequence of actions and states of an I/O automaton, ending with a state in the case when the sequence is finite, is called an *execution*. A sequence of input $in(A_I)$ and output actions $out(A_I)$ of an I/O automaton A_I is called a *history* (or a trace) of A_I. A history h of an I/O automata A_{I_i} is *well-formed* if h is a sequence of alternating inputs and outputs starting with an input. A history h of an I/O automaton A_I is *well-formed* if for every A_{I_i} history $h|p_i$ is well-formed, where $h|p_i$ is the longest subsequence of h consisting only of actions of A_{I_i}. Herein, we consider only well-formed histories. An action a is *enabled* at a state s of A_I if there exists a transition (s, a, s') to some state s' of A_I. An I/O automaton A_I is *input-enabled* if for every history h of A_I, every process p_i, and every input action inv_i of A_{I_i} the following holds: if $h|p_i$ ends with an output action, then $h \cdot inv_i$ is a history of A_{I_i}. Since I has no control over invocations, A_I should be input-enabled.

To model process crashes, we augment the model with a special input action $crash_i$ [29] and a special state $s_{crashed,i}$ of A_{I_i} corresponding to each process p_i. At state $s_{crashed,i}$, no action of A_{I_i} is enabled, and from every state $s \neq s_{crashed,i}$ of A_{I_i}, there is a transition $(s, crash_i, s_{crashed,i})$. When an I/O automaton A_{I_i} executes action $crash_i$, it means that process p_i *crashes* and stops executing any steps. Process p_i *crashes in history* h, if h has a $crash_i$ action. Otherwise, process p_i is said to be *correct* in history h. For every object type $Tp = (St, Inv, Res, Seq)$ we denote by $ext_i(Tp)$ the set $(\{inv_i | inv \in Inv\} \cup \{crash_i\} \cup \{res_i | res \in Res\})$ and by $ext(Tp)$ the set $\bigcup_{1 \leq i \leq n} ext_i(Tp)$.

3. CORRECTNESS PROPERTIES

3.1 Safety

A safety property states that some 'bad' events will never happen. For example, *linearizability* [24], *serializability* [31], and *opacity* [16], safety properties of shared memory systems, require that processes never receive responses which result in an inconsistent view of a shared memory system. A safety property is defined as a prefix-closed and limit-closed set of histories [1, 29].

DEFINITION 3.1. *A* safety *property S of a shared object of type $Tp = (St, Inv, Res, Seq)$ is a non-empty set of histories consisting of actions from $ext(Tp)$ such that (1) if $h \in S$, then every prefix of h is in S, and (2) if $h_1, h_2, \ldots$ is an infinite sequence of finite histories in S such that h_j is a prefix of h_{j+1}, for every j, then the unique infinite history which is the limit of $h_1, h_2, \ldots$ is also in S. Implementation I of Tp* ensures *safety property S if every finite history of A_I is in S.*

We assume that each safety property does not contain histories which cannot be implemented, i.e. we assume safety properties S such that for any history $h \in S$, there exists an implementation I such that h is a history of A_I and I ensures S. We also make an additional assumption that a safety property should allow at least one response for any invocation that executes sequentially from an initial state. Specifically, we require that for each $inv \in Inv$ and each process p_i there exists $res \in Res$ such that $inv_i \cdot res_i \in S$.

3.2 Liveness

A liveness property states that some 'good' events will eventually happen. For example, wait-freedom [19, 23] states that every operation by a correct process should eventually return a response. Starvation-freedom [2, 23] states that every correct process that tries to acquire a lock should eventually succeed. Local progress [5] states that every correct process should eventually commit its transactions.

A liveness property is a property which permits every finite history [30, 1, 29]. For I/O systems, a liveness property states that an input is eventually returned a corresponding output [33]. In particular, for shared memory systems, a liveness property states that some process is eventually returned a desirable response, i.e. *makes progress* [23, 25, 35]. For each shared object type, there is a property that requires progress for all correct processes, the strongest liveness requirement that can be expected. For example, for shared registers, the strongest liveness requirement is wait-freedom. Starvation-freedom is the strongest liveness requirement for lock-based implementations. For TM objects, the strongest liveness requirement is local progress. Hence, for every shared object type we assume a property L_{max} which states the strongest liveness requirement. Formally, with each shared object type $Tp = (St, Inv, Res, Seq)$ we associate some set L_{max} of histories consisting of actions from $ext(Tp)$ such that every finite history h consisting of actions from $ext(Tp)$ is a prefix of some history in L_{max}, i.e. there exists a history h' such that $h \cdot h' \in L_{max}$. Like fairness properties are defined in [38], we define each liveness property as a weakening of L_{max}:

DEFINITION 3.2. *A set L of histories consisting of actions from $ext(Tp)$ is a* liveness *property of a shared object of type Tp if $L_{max} \subseteq L$.*

Let I be an implementation of an object of type Tp. Intuitively, implementation I ensures liveness property L if every fair history of A_I is in L. The restriction to fair histories is necessary because a liveness property cannot require progress from processes which do not get fair turns from a scheduler to perform steps [11]. An execution e of I/O automaton A_I is *fair* if any of the following holds: (I) if e is finite, then no action, other than *crash* actions, is enabled in the final state of e, or (II) if e is infinite, then for every process p_i execution e has either infinitely many actions of A_{I_i} or infinitely many occurrences of states at which no action, other than $crash_i$, of A_{I_i} is enabled. A history h of A_I is *fair* if there exists a fair execution e of A_I such that h is the longest subsequence of e consisting only of input and output actions. Denote by $fair(A_I)$ the set of all fair histories of A_I. Implementation I *ensures* liveness property L if $fair(A_I) \subseteq L$.

The stronger/weaker relation on properties is defined in the standard way [38]. Property L_1 is *weaker* than property L_2 (L_2 is *stronger* than L_1) if every implementation that ensures L_2 also ensures L_1. It easy to see that L_1 is weaker than L_2 iff $L_2 \subseteq L_1$.

4. SAFETY-LIVENESS EXCLUSION

A liveness property states that some good events should eventually happen, while a safety property states that some bad events should never happen. Safety and liveness properties exclude each other when the bad events of the safety property coincide with the good events of the liveness property. In the case of shared memory systems, this translates into the impossibility of implementing a shared object that ensures both properties. Let S and L be respectively a safety and a liveness properties of a shared object of type Tp.

DEFINITION 4.1. *Liveness property L* excludes *safety property S if there is no implementation I of an object of type Tp such that I ensures both S and L.*

For example, if Tp is the consensus object type and the set of all possible implementations of Tp is restricted to implementations that use only read-write registers as base objects, then the impossibility result in [9, 6, 28] states that wait-freedom excludes agreement and validity. Another example is the exclusion of local progress and opacity for transactional memory object type [5]. Below we address the following questions: when is it possible to determine a weakest (resp. a strongest) liveness property which excludes (resp. does not exclude) a given safety property? Basically we ask the following question: if $\mathbb{S}$ and $\mathbb{L}$ are the sets of all safety and liveness properties under given general definitions, what is the largest subset $\mathscr{S} \subseteq \mathbb{S}$ for which there exists a map $f_w : \mathscr{S} \to \mathbb{L}$ (resp. $f_s : \mathscr{S} \to \mathbb{L}$) that maps every safety property $S \in \mathscr{S}$ onto the weakest (resp. strongest) liveness property $L \in \mathbb{L}$ that excludes (resp. does not exclude) S.

4.1 Weakest non-implementable liveness

DEFINITION 4.2. *A liveness property L is the* weakest *liveness property to exclude a safety property S if (1) L excludes S and (2) for any liveness property L', if L' excludes S then L' is stronger than L.*

In order to reason about the existence of a weakest liveness property that excludes S, we define a subset of S which we call an adversary set. Informally, an adversary set w.r.t. L and S is a set of histories such that for every implementation I ensureing S there exists a history of I which is in the adversary set and not in L. The existence of an adversary set w.r.t. L and S implies that there is an adversary, which decides on a sequence of steps produced by a scheduler and on invocations sent to implementation I, such that for any implementation the adversary makes I produce an execution that violates L.

DEFINITION 4.3. *An* adversary set *w.r.t. L and S is a non-empty set of histories F such that: (1) $F \subseteq S$, (2) $F \subseteq \overline{L}$, where $\overline{L}$ is the complement of L taken over all well-formed histories, and (3) for every implementation I ensureing S there is a history $h \in fair(A_I)$ such that $h \in F$.*

It is easy to see that L excludes S iff there is an adversary set w.r.t. L and S. The following theorem gives a characterization of safety properties for which it is possible to find a weakest liveness property that excludes them.

THEOREM 4.4. *Let $F(L_{max})$ be the set of all adversary sets w.r.t. L_{max} and S, and let $G_{max} = \bigcap_{F \in F(L_{max})} F$. There exists a weakest liveness property that excludes S iff $G_{max} \in F(L_{max})$.*

PROOF. *Necessary condition*: Let L_w be the weakest liveness property that excludes S. Since L_w excludes S, there exists an adversary set F_{L_w} w.r.t. L_w and S.

We first prove that $L_w = \overline{F_{L_w}}$. Assume that $L_w \neq \overline{F_{L_w}}$. By the definition of F_{L_w}, $F_{L_w} \subseteq \overline{L_w}$, and therefore $L_w \subseteq \overline{F_{L_w}}$. Because $L_w \neq \overline{F_{L_w}}$ and $L_w \subseteq \overline{F_{L_w}}$, there is a history h such that $h \in \overline{F_{L_w}}$ and $h \notin L_w$. Because $h \in \overline{F_{L_w}}$ and $L_w \subseteq \overline{F_{L_w}}$, then $L_w \cup \{h\} \subseteq \overline{F_{L_w}}$, and consequently $F_{L_w} \subseteq \overline{L_w \cup \{h\}}$. Consider liveness property $L_w \cup \{h\}$, F_{L_w} is an adversary set w.r.t. $L_w \cup \{h\}$ and S, because $F_{L_w} \subseteq \overline{L_w \cup \{h\}}$. Therefore, $L_w \cup \{h\}$ excludes S and, by the definition of L_w, $L_w \cup \{h\}$ is stronger than L_w, i.e. $L_w \cup \{h\} \subseteq L_w$. This contradicts the fact that $h \notin L_w$.

Next, we prove that for every $F \in F(L_{max})$, $F_{L_w} \subseteq F$. Assume that there is $F \in F(L_{max})$ such that $F_{L_w} \nsubseteq F$. Consider set $\overline{F}$, $\overline{F}$ is a liveness property because $F \subseteq \overline{L_{max}}$ (by the definition of F), and therefore $L_{max} \subseteq \overline{F}$. Since $F \subseteq \overline{\overline{F}}$, then F is an adversary set w.r.t. $\overline{F}$ and S, i.e., $\overline{F}$ excludes S. Since $\overline{F}$ excludes S, $\overline{F}$ is stronger than L_w, i.e. $\overline{F} \subseteq L_w$. Since $F_{L_w} \nsubseteq F$ and $L_w = \overline{F_{L_w}}$, then there exists a history h' such that $h' \notin L_w$ and $h' \in \overline{F}$. This contradicts the fact that $\overline{F} \subseteq L_w$.

Since $F_{L_w} \subseteq F$ for every $F \in F(L_{max})$, then $F_{L_w} \subseteq G_{max}$. By the definition of F_{L_w}, for every implementation I there is $h'' \in fair(A_I)$ such that $h'' \in F_{L_w} \subseteq G_{max}$. Thus, G_{max} is an adversary set w.r.t. L_{max} and S.

Sufficient condition: Because $G_{max} \subseteq \overline{L_{max}}$ (by the definition of an adversary set G_{max}), then $L_{max} \subseteq \overline{G_{max}}$, i.e. $\overline{G_{max}}$ is a liveness property. Since $G_{max} \subseteq \overline{\overline{G_{max}}}$ and $G_{max} \in F(L_{max})$, then G_{max} is an adversary set w.r.t. $\overline{G_{max}}$ and S. Hence, $\overline{G_{max}}$ excludes S.

Consider some liveness property L which excludes S. There is an adversary set F_L w.r.t. L and S. Since $L_{max} \subseteq L$ and $F_L \subseteq \overline{L}$, then $F_L \subseteq \overline{L_{max}}$. Therefore, F_L is an adversary set w.r.t. L_{max} and S. Since G_{max} is the intersection of all adversary sets w.r.t. L_{max} and S, G_{max} is a subset of every adversary set w.r.t. L_{max} and S. From $G_{max} \subseteq F_L \subseteq \overline{L}$ it follows that $L \subseteq \overline{G_{max}}$. Thus, we showed that every liveness property that excludes S is stronger than $\overline{G_{max}}$. By definition, $\overline{G_{max}}$ is the weakest liveness property that excludes S. □

For every object type Tp and most symmetric safety properties S of Tp, i.e. safety properties the requirements of which are the same for all processes irrespectively of process identifiers, it is possible to find two adversary sets F_1 and F_2 w.r.t. L_{max} and S such that $F_1 \cap F_2 = \emptyset$, and consequently $G_{max} \notin F(L_{max})$. Therefore, Theorem 4.4 means that for most safety properties there is no weakest liveness property that excludes the given safety property. We have the following two corollaries:

Corollary: consensus implementations from registers. A consensus shared object is used by processes to agree on some value from a set of proposed values. Each process proposes its own value v by invoking operation $propose(v)$ on a consensus object and receives as a response some value v' (decides value v'). Formally, *agreement and validity*, a safety property of consensus objects, states that all processes decide the same value and the decided value is the value proposed by one of the processes. *Wait-freedom* [19], a liveness property of consensus objects, states that every correct process eventually decides. Consider implementations of consensus that use only read/write registers as base objects. In that case, it is shown in [6] that if two processes propose different values, then there is an execution in which both of them take infinite number of steps without ever deciding a value. Hence, there exists an adversary set $F_1 = \{propose_1(v) \cdot propose_2(v')\}$ w.r.t. wait-freedom and agreement and validity. The proof of the impossibility result does not depend on whether process p_1 invokes the $propose_1(v)$ operation first or not, consequently, $F_2 = \{propose_2(v') \cdot propose_1(v)\}$ is also an adversary set. Since $F_1 \cap F_2 = \emptyset$, it follows that $G_{max} = \emptyset$.

COROLLARY 4.5. *There is no weakest liveness property of consensus objects which excludes agreement and validity when these objects are implemented only from read/write registers.*

Corollary: transactional memory. Transactional memory (TM) allows to enclose sequential code within atomic transactions which are executed concurrently. Transactional code contains accesses to transactional variables which can be read or written, these variables can be accessed only within transactions. Each transaction is executed only by one process. Processes in a TM implementation can invoke the following transactional operations: *start* which requests to start a new transaction and returns either *ok* or an abort event A, $x.write(v)$ which writes value v to transactional variable x within a transaction and returns either *ok* or an abort event A; $x.read$ which reads a value from transactional variable x within a transaction and returns either a value v or an abort event A; $tryC$ which requests to commit a transaction and returns a commit event C or an abort event A. The sequential specification *Seq* of a TM object is such that if a transaction commits, then all the changes made to transactional variables within the transaction are made visible to other processes, and if a transaction aborts, then all the changes are discarded.

Opacity [16], a safety property of TM implementations, states that every transaction, even aborted, observes a consistent state of the system. Specifically, history h ensures opacity if for every finite prefix h' of h there exists a sequential history s such that s is equivalent to some completion $comp(h')$ of h', s preserves the real time order of $comp(h')$, and s respects the sequential specification *Seq*. A *completion* $comp(h)$ of history h is any history derived from h by appending $tryC \cdot A$ for every transaction which does not invoke a commit request in h and by appending either an abort event A or a commit event C for every transaction which invokes a commit request but does not receive a corresponding response in h. Two histories h_1 and h_2 are *equivalent* if for every process p_i, $h_1|p_i = h_2|p_i$. History h_1 *preserves the real time order* of history h_2 if for any two transaction T_1 and T_2 in h_2 if T_1 receives an abort or a commit event, i.e. completes, before T_2 invokes *start* in h_2, then T_1 completes before T_2 starts in h_1. In TM implementations requiring that each operation returns a response is not enough because such requirement can be trivially ensured simply by aborting every transaction. To make progress transactions should be able to eventually commit. Therefore, the set of 'good' events is restricted to commit events. *Local progress* [5], the strongest liveness property of TM implementations, requires that every correct process is eventually given a chance to invoke a commit request $tryC()$ and eventually one of the commit requests $tryC()$ is returned a commit response C. In other words local progress requires that for every correct process eventually there is a transaction which is not aborted. It was shown in [5] that it is impossible to implement a TM object which ensures both opacity and local progress. Consider the adversary set defined by the following strategy [5]:

1. **Step 1.** Process p_1 invokes $start_1$ and waits until it receives as a response ok_1 or A_1. If the response is A_1 the adversary repeats Step 1. Otherwise, process p_1 invokes $x.read_1()$ and waits until it receives as a response v'_1 or A_1. If the response is A_1 the adversary repeats Step 1. Otherwise, the adversary goes to Step 2.

2. **Step 2.** Process p_2 invokes $start_2$ and waits until it receives as a response ok_2 or A_2. If the response is A_2 the adversary repeats Step 2. Otherwise, process p_2 invokes $x.read_2()$ and waits until it receives as a response v''_2 or A_2. If the response is A_2, the adversary repeats Step 2. Otherwise p_2 invokes $x.write_2(v'+1)$, and waits until it receives as a response ok_2 or A_2. If the response is A_2, then the adversary repeats Step 2. Otherwise, p_2 invokes $tryC_2()$ operation and waits until it receives a response C_2 or A_2. If the response is A_2, the adversary repeats Step 2. Otherwise the strategy goes to Step 3.

3. **Step 3.** Process p_1 invokes $x.write_1(v''+1)$ and waits until it receives as a response ok_1 or A_1. If the response is A_1, then the adversary goes to Step 1. Otherwise p_1 invokes $tryC_1()$ operation and waits until it receives a response C_1 or A_1. If the response is A_1, the adversary goes to Step 1. Otherwise the adversary stops.

Let F_1 be the set of all histories produced by the adversary set described by the above strategy, i.e. the set of histories that result from applying the strategy to every possible TM object implementation that ensures opacity. In [5] it is shown that every history which ensures opacity and which is produced by the above strategy violates local progress. Therefore, F_1 is an adversary set w.r.t. local progress and opacity. Let us exchange processes in the above strategy so that process p_1 plays the role of p_2 and vice versa and let F_2 be the set of all possible histories produced by the resulting adversary. Set F_2 is an adversary set w.r.t. local progress and opacity since the impossibility result does not depend on process identifiers. Since local progress is the strongest liveness property of TM objects, then $F_1, F_2 \in F(L_{max})$. However $F_1 \cap F_2 = \emptyset$, because every history from F_1 begins with $start_1$ invocation and every history from F_2 begins with $start_2$. Since $F_1 \cap F_2 = \emptyset$, it follows that $G_{max} = \emptyset$.

COROLLARY 4.6. *There is no weakest liveness property of TM objects which excludes opacity.*

4.2 Strongest implementable liveness

DEFINITION 4.7. *Liveness property L is the* strongest *liveness property that does not exclude a given safety property S if (1) L does not exclude S, and (2) for any liveness property L' if L' does not exclude S then L' is weaker than L.*

Before proving the theorem which states that L_{max} is the only possible strongest liveness property that does not exclude S in case when such a property exists, we prove the following lemma first.

LEMMA 4.8. *The strongest liveness property that an implementation I ensures is $L_{max} \cup fair(A_I)$.*

PROOF. By contradiction, assume that there is a liveness property L such that I ensures L and $L_{max} \cup fair(A_I)$ is not stronger than L, i.e., $L_{max} \cup fair(A_I) \not\subseteq L$. Because L is a liveness property, $L_{max} \subseteq L$. And because I ensures L, then $fair(A_I) \subseteq L$. From $L_{max} \subseteq L$ and $fair(A_I) \subseteq L$ it follows that $L_{max} \cup fair(A_I) \subseteq L$. This contradicts the fact that $L_{max} \cup fair(A_I) \not\subseteq L$.

□

THEOREM 4.9. *If there is a strongest liveness property that does not exclude S, then it should be L_{max}.*

PROOF. Let L_s be the strongest liveness property that does not exclude S. By definition, there is an implementation I_s which ensures both L_s and S. By Lemma 4.8, $L_s = L_{max} \cup fair(A_{I_s})$.

Assume that $L_s \neq L_{max}$, i.e. $fair(A_{I_s}) \setminus L_{max} \neq \emptyset$. We first prove that every history in $fair(A_{I_s}) \setminus L_{max}$ does not include responses. Assume, by contradiction, that there is history $h \in fair(A_{I_s}) \setminus L_{max}$ which includes a response. Let res_k be the first response in h, i.e. $h = h' \cdot res_k \cdot h''$ and h' does not include any responses. Consider a trivial implementation I_t which does not return responses for any invocation. Let A_{I_t} be an I/O automaton that models I_t. Notice that since the implementation is trivial it does not require any base objects. Because I_t does not return responses, then every history of A_{I_t} consists only of invocations and probably some *crash* events, and therefore, history h is not a history of $fair(A_{I_t})$. By Lemma 4.8, implementation I_t ensures liveness property $L_t = L_{max} \cup fair(A_{I_t})$, note that L_t is not weaker than L_s since $h \notin fair(A_{I_t})$ and $h \in fair(A_{I_s}) \setminus L_{max}$. Let h_t be some history of A_{I_t}. Because h_t consists only of invocations and probably some *crash* events, which are input actions of A_{I_s}, and A_{I_s} is input-enabled, h_t is also a history of A_{I_s}. Because I_s ensures S, $h_t \in S$. Thus, every history of A_{I_t} is in S and therefore I_t ensures S. Hence, L_t does not exclude S. This contradicts the facts that L_s is the strongest liveness property that does not exclude S and L_t is not weaker than L_s.

Next we prove that for any history $h \in fair(A_{I_s}) \setminus L_{max}$, for any process p_l, and for any response res_l, $h \cdot res_l \notin S$ holds. Assume, by contradiction, that there is a history $h \in fair(A_{I_s}) \setminus L_{max}$, a process p_l, a response res_l such that $h \cdot res_l \in S$. Let inv_l be the invocation in h corresponding to response res_l, i.e. $h \cdot res_l | p_l = inv_l \cdot res_l$. Consider history $inv_l \cdot res_l \in S$. Let I be an implementation such that I ensures S and $inv_l \cdot res_l$ is a history of A_I.

Consider a trivial implementation I_b such that: (1) when algorithm I_l^b, corresponding to p_l, receives invocation inv_l the first time it returns res_l, and for the second instance of inv_l it stops without returning any response, (2) when I_l^b receives an invocation other than inv_l it stops without returning any response, and (3) every algorithm I_j^b, where $j \neq l$, once it receives any invocation, it stops without returning any response. Formally, implementation I_b can be described by an I/O automaton $A_{I_b} = A_{I_1^b} \times \ldots \times A_{I_n^b}$ (because I does not use any base objects A_B is omitted from the composition) such that:

- for every $1 \leq i \leq n$, $in(A_{I_i^b}) = \{inv_i | inv \in Inv\} \cup \{crash_i\}$ and $out(A_{I_i^b}) = \{res_i | res \in Res\}$;
- when $A_{I_l^b}$ executes inv_l from an initial state, $A_{I_l^b}$ changes its state to a state s^l at which only $crash_l$ and output action res_l are enabled. Let s^l_{en} be a state of $A_{I_l^b}$ such that there is a transition (s^l, res_l, s^l_{en}) in $A_{I_l^b}$; note that from state s^l_{en} every invocation is enabled. For every invocation $inv' \in Inv$, when $A_{I_l^b}$ executes inv'_l from s^l_{en}, $A_{I_l^b}$ changes its state to a state s^l_1 at which only $crash_l$ action is enabled;
- for every invocation $inv'' \in Inv$, such that $inv'' \neq inv$, when $A_{I_l^b}$ executes inv''_l from an initial state $A_{I_l^b}$ changes its state to a state s^l_2 at which only $crash_l$ action is enabled;
- for every $j \neq l$ and for every invocation $inv' \in Inv$, when $A_{I_j^b}$ executes inv'_j from an initial state, $A_{I_j^b}$ changes its state to a state s^j_1 at which only $crash_j$ action is enabled.

Let h' be any history of A_{I_b} such that h' contains a response. Because I_b returns a response only for the first instance of inv_l, it follows that the response in h' is res_l and $h'|p_l = inv_l \cdot res_l$. Because $inv_l \cdot res_l$ is a history of A_I and A_I is input-enabled, then every history h' such that h' contains a single response and $h'|p_l = inv_l \cdot res_l$ is also a history of A_I. Because I ensures S, it follows that every such history h' is in S. Let h'' be any history of A_{I_b} such that h' contains a response. Because A_I is input-enabled, h'' is also a history of A_I and, consequently, $h'' \in S$. Hence, every history of A_{I_b} is in S and, consequently, I_b ensures S. Because (1) $h|p_l = inv_l$, and (2) state s^l of I/O automaton $A_{I_l^b}$ is reachable by executing inv_l from an initial state, and (3) at s^l output action res_l is enabled then every execution of A_{I_b}, to which history h corresponds, is not fair, and consequently $h \notin fair(A_{I_b})$.

By Lemma 4.8, implementation I_b ensures liveness property $L_b = L_{max} \cup fair(A_{I_b})$. Hence, L_b does not exclude S. Because $h \in L_s$ and $h \notin L_b$, liveness property L_b is not weaker than liveness property L_s. This contradicts the facts that L_s is the strongest liveness property that does not exclude S and L_b does not exclude S.

We proved that for every history $h \in fair(A_{I_s}) \setminus L_{max}$ the following holds: (1) h does not contain any responses and (2) there is no process p_i and response res such that $h \cdot res_i \in S$.

Let h be any history in $fair(A_{I_s}) \setminus L_{max}$ and let inv_i be some invocation in h by a process p_i which does not crash in h. Let res_i be a response such that $inv_i \cdot res_i \in S$ and let I' be an implementation which ensures S and which has $inv_i \cdot res_i$ as its history. Because $A_{I'}$, an I/O automata model of I', is input-enabled, it follows that every history h' such that h' includes a single response and $h'|p_i = inv_i \cdot res_i$ is a history of $A_{I'}$. Because I' ensures S, it follows that every such history $h' \in S$. This contradicts the fact that $h \cdot res_i \notin S$. □

Corollary: consensus objects. Consider those implementations of consensus that use only read/write registers as base objects. Since L_{max}, which is wait-freedom, is impossible [6] to ensure together with agreement and validity using only registers, then we have the following corollary:

COROLLARY 4.10. *There is no strongest liveness property of consensus objects which does not exclude agreement and validity when these objects are implemented only from read/write registers.*

Corollary: transactional memory. Because L_{max}, which is local progress, is impossible [5] to ensure together with opacity, then we have the following corollary:

COROLLARY 4.11. *There is no strongest liveness property of TM objects which does not exclude opacity.*

5. CIRCUMVENTING THE IMPOSSIBILITIES

In this section we show that if we restrict the space of liveness properties, then it is possible to determine weakest (strongest) liveness property that excludes (does not exclude) a safety property in certain cases.

5.1 (l,k)-Freedom

Instead of giving a general set-theoretic definition of liveness, we give a definition based on the notion of progress [23]. Accordingly, liveness properties can be classified into properties which require either *maximal* or *minimal* progress and which are either *dependent* or *independent* of a scheduler. *Maximal* progress properties require progress for *every* correct process, while minimal progress properties require progress for *some* correct processes. *Wait-freedom*, which requires progress for every correct process, and *obstruction-freedom*, which requires progress only for processes that eventually run without step contention, are examples of maximal progress properties. *Lock-freedom*, which requires progress for at least one correct process, is an example of a minimal progress property. Wait-freedom and lock-freedom are examples of independent progress properties, while obstruction-freedom is an example of dependent progress property. We give a definition of liveness that encompasses both maximal and minimal progress and dependent and independent guarantees.

Intuitively, we say that a process makes progress in an execution if it eventually receives 'good' responses in that execution for its invocations. However, for different object types, the notion of a 'good' response might be different. For example, for objects like consensus or registers, any response is a 'good' response; but for TM objects 'good' responses are those which do not abort transactions. Therefore, we assume that for each object type $Tp = (St, Inv, Res, Seq)$ there is a fixed subset of responses $G_{Tp} \subseteq Res$ which are necessary to make progress. We say that a correct process p_i *makes progress* in a fair execution e if e contains infinitely many responses from $\{res_i | res \in G_{Tp}\}$.

Between the independent progress guarantee of wait-freedom and the dependent progress guarantee of obstruction-freedom lie intermediate maximal progress guarantees that can be satisfied only when up to k processes are scheduled to take steps. Such progress guarantees are grouped into k-obstruction-freedom properties. *k-Obstruction-freedom* [35] states that if at any point in an execution there are at most k processes taking steps, then all these processes should make progress. Likewise, between the maximal progress guarantee of wait-freedom and the minimal progress guarantee of lock-freedom lie intermediate independent progress guarantees that require progress for at least l processes. We introduce the notion of l-lock-freedom to group such guarantees. *l-Lock-freedom* states that at least l processes should make progress if there are at least l correct processes in an execution or all processes should make progress if there are less than l correct processes in an execution.

l-Lock-freedom and k-obstruction-freedom are different kinds of progress requirements. We combine these two kinds of requirements into a more general one. Specifically, we define *(l,k)-freedom*, where $l \leq k$.

DEFINITION 5.1. *A fair execution e ensures (l,k)-freedom if the following holds. If at most k processes take infinitely many steps in e, then*

- *if at least l processes are correct in e, then at least l processes make progress in e,*
- *if less than l processes are correct in e, then all correct processes make progress in e.*

Observe that if a process is correct in e (i.e. it does not crash) it does not necessary mean that it takes infinitely many steps in e, e.g. a correct process might be prevented from taking steps by the implementation which does not enable steps after certain state. Notice that if LF_l is the set of all executions that ensure l-lock-freedom and OF_k is the set of all executions that ensure k-obstruction-freedom, then $LF_l \cup OF_k$ is the set of all executions that ensure (l,k)-freedom. An implementation I is (l,k)-free if every fair execution of I ensures (l,k)-freedom.

Liveness properties defined as (l,k)-freedom are not totally ordered. For example, consider $(1,3)$-freedom and $(2,2)$-freedom properties. An execution in which only two processes take steps and only one of those two processes makes progress ensures $(1,3)$-freedom but does not ensure $(2,2)$-freedom. An execution in which only three processes take steps and none of those three processes makes progress ensures $(2,2)$-freedom but does not ensure $(1,3)$-freedom. Therefore, $(1,3)$-freedom and $(2,2)$-freedom are incomparable to each other. However, despite the fact that (l,k)-freedom properties are not totally ordered, it is possible to find weakest non-implementable and strongest implementable (l,k)-freedom properties in most cases.

5.2 Consensus and TM examples

Consider implementations of consensus that use only read/write registers as base objects. The impossibility of consensus from registers [6] says that if two processes invoke two *propose*(v) operations with different arguments, then there is an adversary set that produces a fair execution in which none of the two processes ever decides a value. Consequently, $(1,2)$-freedom excludes agreement and validity in the case of implementations from registers. Because $(1,1)$-freedom, which is obstruction-freedom, is the only consensus liveness property which is weaker than $(1,2)$-freedom and which is possible [20, 17] to implement using registers, we have the following theorem.

THEOREM 5.2. *For implementations of consensus from read/write registers $(1,1)$-freedom is the strongest (l,k)-freedom property that does not exclude agreement and validity and $(1,2)$-freedom is the weakest (l,k)-freedom property that excludes agreement and validity.*

As another example, consider TM shared objects. In [5] it is shown that any non-blocking liveness property which is *biprogressing* is impossible to implement in the TM context with safety properties like *strict serializability* [31] or *opacity* [16] in a system of two processes. A *biprogressing* liveness property is a property which requires progress for at least two correct processes. In the case of (l,k)-freedom properties, the weakest biprogressing property is $(2,2)$-freedom. Since in the TM context it is possible [10] to implement $(1,n)$-freedom, which is the strongest property that requires progress for at most one process, together with opacity, we have the following theorem.

THEOREM 5.3. *For TM implementations $(1,n)$-freedom is the strongest (l,k)-freedom property that does not exclude opacity and $(2,2)$-freedom is the weakest (l,k)-freedom property that excludes opacity.*

It is worth noting that in case of (l,k)-freedom liveness properties, the strongest implementable TM liveness property, $(1,n)$-freedom, is not weaker than the weakest non-implementable TM liveness property, $(2,2)$-freedom. In fact, these two properties are incomparable.

5.3 Limitations of (l,k)-freedom: a counterexample

Even though (l,k)-freedom allows to circumvent the safety-liveness exclusion impossibility for consensus and TM from Section 4, there are still some safety properties for which it is not the case. For instance, consider the following safety property S of TM. A TM history h ensures S if the following hold:

1. h ensures opacity, and
2. for any three (or more) concurrent transactions $T_1, T_2, T_3, \ldots$ in h, executed by different processes $p_1, p_2, p_3, \ldots$, respectively, if (1) there exists a number t s.t. for each process $p_i \in \{p_1, p_2, p_3, \ldots\}$, T_i is the t-th transactions in $h|p_i$ and (2) each T_i invokes *tryC*$()_i$ *after* at least other two transactions from $\{T_1, T_2, T_3, \ldots\}$ receive a response for a *start*$()_j$ operation in h, where $j \neq i$, then $T_1, T_2, T_3, \ldots$ should be aborted in h.

In other words, safety property S requires opacity plus an additional requirement that if three or more transactions have the same timestamp t and invoke a commit request *tryC*$()$ after any two of them receive a response for starting a transaction request *start*$()$, then such transactions should be aborted. In [5] it is shown that $(2,2)$-freedom is impossible to implement together with opacity. Because S includes the requirement of opacity, then in the TM context $(2,2)$-freedom excludes S. In order to show that $(1,3)$-freedom excludes S, consider the following adversary:

1. **Step 1.** Processes p_1, p_2, p_3 concurrently invoke *start*$()$ request to start a transaction and each waits for a response which should be either *ok* or A. Once each of the three processes receives a response, the adversary goes to Step 2.
2. **Step 2.** Processes which did not receive an abort event A at Step 1, concurrently invoke *tryC*$()$ request to commit their transaction and each waits for a response which should be either C or A. If each process receives an abort event A, the adversary goes to Step 1. Otherwise the adversary stops.

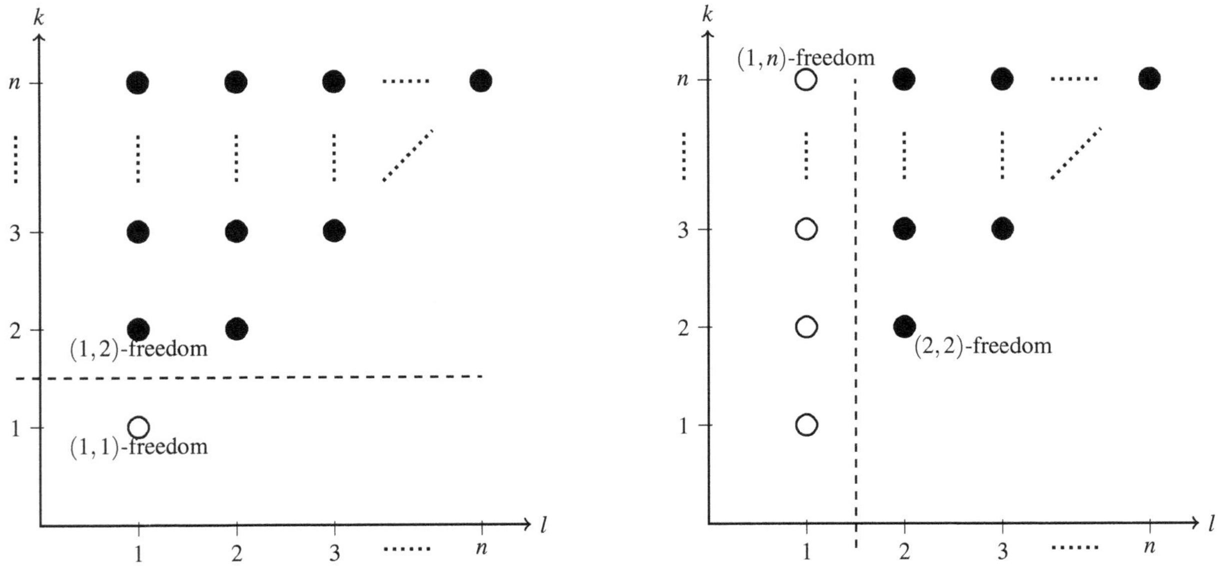

(a) S is agreement and validity of consensus.

(b) S is opacity of TM.

Figure 1: (l,k)-Freedom properties can be represented as points on a two-dimensional plane. The more a point located to the right and the higher it is, the stronger the corresponding (l,k)-freedom property is. White points indicate (l,k)-freedom properties that do not exclude a given safety property S, and black ones exclude S.

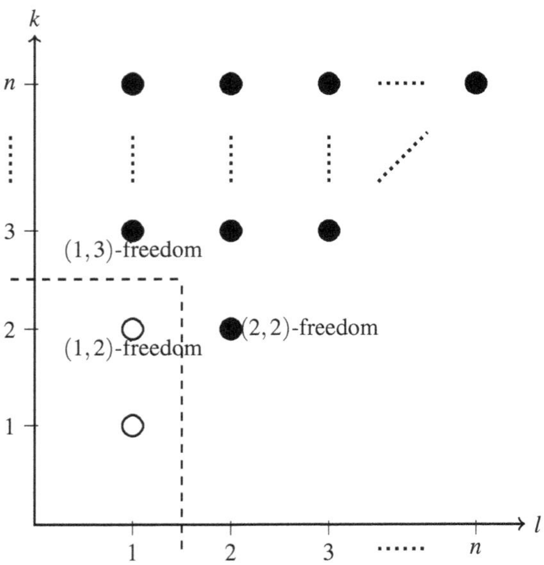

Figure 2: The case when $S = S_e$.

Assume that the adversary terminates, i.e. there exists a history h such that some process commits in h. Without loss of generality assume this process to be p_1. Let the committing transaction T_1 be a t-th transaction of p_1. According to the adversary, the three processes invoke new transactions concurrently to each other, and consequently the committing transaction is concurrent to the other two t-th transactions of p_2 and p_3. According to the adversary, T_1 invokes *tryC*() only after p_2 and p_3 receive responses for *start*() at Step 1 (which eventually happens because of $(1,3)$-freedom). Thus the conditions of the second requirement of property S are satisfied, and consequently, transactions T_1, T_2, T_3 should be aborted - a contradiction. Since the adversary never terminates, none of the three correct processes receives a commit response. Therefore every history produced by the adversary violates $(1,3)$-freedom.

In order to show that there is no weakest (l,k)-freedom property non-implementable with S we show that $(1,2)$-freedom, which is weaker than both $(1,3)$-freedom and $(2,2)$-freedom, is implementable with S. Below we give a simple TM implementation the purpose of which is to show that $(1,2)$-freedom does not exclude S.

The main idea of the implementation is the following. The implementation uses a single shared compare-and-swap object which holds a version number and a value of each transactional variable. Additionally, it uses a shared snapshot object of n registers, where n is the total number of processes. When a process p_i starts a new transaction, it increments its local timestamp, writes the new timestamp to the i-th register, and copies the content of the compare-and-swap object to its local memory. The process performs transactional reads and writes using only the local memory. When the process invokes a commit request it first takes the snapshot of the registers and checks if at least two other processes have a greater timestamp. If so, the transaction is aborted. Otherwise, the process tries to update the compare-and-swap object with a new version number and new values from its local memory. The version numbers are used to ensure opacity, while the timestamps are used to ensure the second requirement of S.

The algorithm uses a shared compare-and-swap object C initialized to $(1,(0,\dots,0))$, array of shared registers R[1, ..., n] (initially $(0,\dots,0)$) which supports an atomic *scan* operation. Also each process has local variables *timestamp*, *count* (both are initially 0), and *version* (initially $\perp$). Below we show that the algorithm ensures the second requirement of S and $(1,2)$-freedom, the proof of opacity is given in the full version of the paper [4].

LEMMA 5.4. *Algorithm $I_{(1,2)}$ implements a TM that ensures S and $(1,2)$-freedom.*

operation $start()_i$
$timestamp \leftarrow timestamp + 1$
$R[i] \leftarrow timestamp$
$(version, oldval) \leftarrow C.read$
$values \leftarrow oldval$
return ok_i

operation $x_m.read()_i$
return $values[m]_i$

operation $x_m.write(v)_i$
$values[m] \leftarrow v$
return ok_i

operation $tryC()_i$
$snapshot \leftarrow R.scan()$
for $j \leftarrow 1$ **to** n **do**
if $snapshot[j] \geq timestamp$ **then** $count \leftarrow count + 1$
if $count \geq 3$ **then**
$count \leftarrow 0$
return A_i
$count \leftarrow 0$
if $C.C\&S((version, oldval), (version + 1, values))$ **then**
$version \leftarrow \bot$
return C_i
else
$version \leftarrow \bot$
return A_i

Algorithm 1: Algorithm $I_{(1,2)}$ implementing a TM that ensures S and $(1,2)$-freedom.

PROOF. *The second requirement of S.* Observe that each time a process starts a new transaction it increments its timestamp by 1 and announces the new timestamp to other processes by updating the corresponding register $R[i]$. Let h be any history of $I_{(1,2)}$ and let $T_1, T_2, T_3, \ldots$ be any three (or more) concurrent transactions in h, executed by different processes $p_1, p_2, p_3, \ldots$, respectively, s.t. there exists number t s.t. for each $p_i \in \{p_1, p_2, p_3, \ldots\}$, T_i is the t-th transactions in $h|p_i$ and each T_i invokes $tryC_i$ *after* some other two transactions are returned a response for a $start()_j$, where $j \neq i$ and $j \in \{1,2,3,\ldots\}$.

Because each $T_1, T_2, T_3, \ldots$ is the t-th transaction of a corresponding process, when $T_1, T_2, T_3, \ldots$ execute $start()$, the timestamps of each process becomes t and is written to the corresponding register. Since each T_1, T_2, T_3 invokes $tryC()$ after some other two processes get responses for $start()$, each transaction observes the new timestamps of the other two transactions. Therefore, *count* becomes at least 3 during the execution of $tryC()$ of each of the transaction. And consequently, each of the transaction aborts in h.

$(1,2)$-*Freedom.* Consider a fair execution e of $I_{(1,2)}$ and its corresponding history h such that only two processes take infinitely many steps (and therefore only two processes are correct). Consider any live, i.e. transaction which is not aborted or committed, transaction T_k executed by a correct process in history h. A transaction T_k can be aborted by $I_{(1,2)}$ only if T_k either encounters that some other transaction has a higher timestamp tm or T_k reads some version w and then fails to commit version $w+1$. Since eventually there are only two processes that take steps, eventually transactions can be aborted only when T_k reads some version w and then fails to commit version $w+1$; this can happen only if some other transaction by the second correct process commits version $w+1$. Since a transaction that commits any version cannot be aborted, there are infinitely many transactions in h that are not aborted, and so history h, and thus also TM implementation $I_{(1,2)}$, ensures $(1,2)$-freedom. □

6. CONCLUDING REMARKS

Our impossibility results mean that if we consider too general definitions of liveness, then it is impossible to answer questions about strongest (weakest) implementable (non-implementable) liveness property. To circumvent these impossibility results it is necessary to consider more restricted definitions of liveness. We have considered one such restriction in the previous section. Here we discuss alternative ones.

For example, we may consider the notion of S-freedom [36], which states that for every set of correct processes P, where S is a set containing some natural numbers and $|P| \in S$, every process in P should make progress as long as it does not encounter step contention with processes outside P. A characterization of liveness properties of consensus objects is given in [36] which partitions liveness properties into implementable (using registers only) and non-implementable properties; S-freedom is then shown to be implementable iff $|S| = 1$. However, even such restricted definition of liveness does not allow to determine a strongest (or a weakest) implementable (or non-implementable) liveness property with a safety property like consensus agreement and validity. Because none of the S-freedom properties with $|S| = 1$ is comparable to each other, there is no strongest S-freedom consensus liveness property implementable using only registers.

One way to circumvent the issue is to consider a restricted definition of liveness which totally orders all liveness properties. For example, the notion of (n,x)-liveness [25] states that x processes should be wait-free and $n-x$ processes should be obstruction-free. It is shown [25] that if $x \geq 1$, then it is impossible to implement a consensus object from registers. Since the set of all (n,x)-liveness properties is totally ordered, then the strongest (and the only) implementable liveness property is $(n,0)$-liveness, and the weakest non-implementable liveness property is $(n,1)$-liveness. Liveness properties can also be defined based on the notion of k-obstruction-freedom [35] which states that if processes from a set P, where $|P| \leq k$, do not encounter step contention with processes outside of P, then every process from P should make progress. According to this definition, the strongest implementable liveness property of a consensus object is 1-obstruction-freedom and the weakest non-implementable is 2-obstruction-freedom. However, the definitions of liveness in [25, 35] do not include some common liveness properties, e.g. lock-freedom that requires progress for at least one process. There is a compromise between how general a definition of liveness should be and the possibility of totally ordering the defined liveness properties.

7. ACKNOWLEDGEMENTS

We wish to thank the anonymous reviewers for their helpful comments. This work has been supported by the European Commission under the 7th Framework Program through the TransForm (FP7-MC-ITN-238639) project and by the European Research Council under the Adversary-Oriented Computing project (ERC-2013-AdG-339539-AOC).

References

[1] B. Alpern and F. B. Schneider. Defining liveness. *Information Processing Letters*, 21(4), 1985.

[2] H. Attiya and J. Welch. *Distributed Computing: Fundamentals, Simulations and Advanced Topics*. John Wiley & Sons, 2004.

[3] E. Borowsky and E. Gafni. Generalized flp impossibility result for t-resilient asynchronous computations. In *ACM STOC*, 1993.

[4] V. Bushkov and R. Guerraoui. Safety-liveness exclusion in distributed computing. Technical Report 207929, EPFL, 2015.

[5] V. Bushkov, R. Guerraoui, and M. Kapałka. On the liveness of transactional memory. In *ACM PODC*, 2012.

[6] B. Chor, A. Israeli, and M. Li. On processor coordination using asynchronous hardware. In *ACM PODC*, 1987.

[7] F. Ellen, P. Fatourou, E. Kosmas, A. Milani, and C. Travers. Universal constructions that ensure disjoint-access parallelism and wait-freedom. In *ACM PODC*, 2012.

[8] F. Fich and E. Ruppert. Hundreds of impossibility results for distributed computing. *Distrib. Comput.*, 16(2-3), 2003.

[9] M. J. Fischer, N. A. Lynch, and M. S. Paterson. Impossibility of distributed consensus with one faulty process. *J. ACM*, 32(2), 1985.

[10] K. Fraser. Practical lock freedom. In *PhD thesis, Cambridge University Computer Laboratory*, 2003.

[11] P. Ganty, R. Majumdar, and A. Rybalchenko. Verifying liveness for asynchronous programs. In *ACM POPL*, 2009.

[12] S. Gilbert and N. Lynch. Brewer's conjecture and the feasibility of consistent, available, partition-tolerant web services. *SIGACT News*, 33(2), 2002.

[13] S. Gilbert and N. A. Lynch. Perspectives on the cap theorem. *Computer*, 45(2), 2012.

[14] D. S. Greenberg, G. Taubenfeld, and D.-W. Wang. Choice coordination with multiple alternatives (preliminary version). In *WDAG*, 1992.

[15] R. Guerraoui and M. Kapalka. On obstruction-free transactions. In *ACM SPAA*, 2008.

[16] R. Guerraoui and M. Kapalka. On the correctness of transactional memory. In *ACM PPoPP*, 2008.

[17] R. Guerraoui and E. Ruppert. Anonymous and fault-tolerant shared-memory computing. *Distributed Computing*, 20(3):165–177, 2007.

[18] T. Harris, J. R. Larus, and R. Rajwar. *Transactional Memory, 2nd edition*. Morgan and Claypool, 2010.

[19] M. Herlihy. Wait-free synchronization. *ACM Trans. Program. Lang. Syst.*, 13(1), 1991.

[20] M. Herlihy, V. Luchangco, and M. Moir. Obstruction-free synchronization: Double-ended queues as an example. In *IEEE ICDCS*, 2003.

[21] M. Herlihy, V. Luchangco, M. Moir, and W. N. Scherer, III. Software transactional memory for dynamic-sized data structures. In *ACM PODC*, 2003.

[22] M. Herlihy and N. Shavit. The topological structure of asynchronous computability. *J. ACM*, 46(6), 1999.

[23] M. Herlihy and N. Shavit. On the nature of progress. In *OPODIS*, 2011.

[24] M. P. Herlihy and J. M. Wing. Linearizability: a correctness condition for concurrent objects. *ACM Trans. Program. Lang. Syst.*, 12(3), 1990.

[25] D. Imbs, M. Raynal, and G. Taubenfeld. On asymmetric progress conditions. In *ACM PODC*, 2010.

[26] L. Lamport. Using time instead of timeout for fault-tolerant distributed systems. *ACM Trans. Program. Lang. Syst.*, 6(2), 1984.

[27] B. W. Lampson. How to build a highly available system using consensus. In *WDAG*, 1996.

[28] M. C. Loui and H. H. Abu-Amara. *Memory requirements for agreement among unreliable asynchronous processes*, volume 4. JAI press, 1987.

[29] N. A. Lynch. *Distributed Algorithms*. Morgan Kaufmann Publishers Inc., 1996.

[30] S. Owicki and L. Lamport. Proving liveness properties of concurrent programs. *ACM Trans. Program. Lang. Syst.*, 4(3), 1982.

[31] C. H. Papadimitriou. The serializability of concurrent database updates. *J. ACM*, 26(4), 1979.

[32] F. B. Schneider. Implementing fault-tolerant services using the state machine approach: a tutorial. *ACM Comput. Surv.*, 22(4), 1990.

[33] R. Segala, R. Gawlick, J. Søgaard-Andersen, and N. Lynch. Liveness in timed and untimed systems. *Inf. Comput.*, 141(2), 1998.

[34] N. Shavit and D. Touitou. Software transactional memory. In *ACM PODC*, 1995.

[35] G. Taubenfeld. On the computational power of shared objects. In *OPODIS*, 2009.

[36] G. Taubenfeld. The computational structure of progress conditions. In *DISC*, 2010.

[37] G. Taubenfeld and S. Moran. Possibility and impossibility results in a shared memory environment. *Acta Inf*, 33, 1996.

[38] H. Völzer and D. Varacca. Defining fairness in reactive and concurrent systems. *J. ACM*, 59(3), 2012.

Brief Announcement: Eventually Consistent Linearizability*

Maciej Kokociński Tadeusz Kobus Paweł T. Wojciechowski
Institute of Computing Science
Poznan University of Technology
{Maciej.Kokocinski, Tadeusz.Kobus, Pawel.T.Wojciechowski}@cs.put.edu.pl

ABSTRACT

Eventually consistent linearizability (ec-linearizability) is a new correctness condition for eventually consistent distributed systems (modeled as shared objects). Unlike the existing definitions of eventual consistency, ec-linearizability is suitable for describing the behaviour of some popular eventually consistent systems, such as Cassandra. It is because ec-linearizability allows for certain types of phenomena, such as lost updates. Similarly to linearizability, ec-linearizability is a safety property and is both local and nonblocking. Thus, ec-linearizability is a property that is both easy to use and reason about.

Categories and Subject Descriptors

D.1.3 [**Programming Techniques**]: Concurrent Programming; D.2.4 [**Software Engineering**]: Software/Program Verification

Keywords

Eventual consistency; correctness condition; linearizability

1. INTRODUCTION

Modern distributed applications often trade strong consistency for higher performance and increased availability. Development of such applications is difficult (and thus costly), because the programmer has to account for various artifacts caused by reading stale (inconsistent) data. Usually it is assumed that inconsistencies can occur only temporarily and over time servers running the distributed application converge to a consistent state. Hence, such an approach is often described as eventually consistent.

Surprisingly, relatively little attention has been devoted to formally describing the way in which such systems function and the guarantees they offer (for a broader discussion see Section 2). Some authors provide only a very vague specification of the system's behaviour [1] [14]. The more formal ones lack the description of the system properties from the client's point of view ([13] [5] [3] among others), or assume stronger guarantees than some popular eventually consistent systems, such as Cassandra ([4], [12]). Alternatively, some definitions assume that the system becomes strongly consistent at some point in the future [11] [7]. It means that systems that satisfy these properties are as difficult to implement, as if they were strongly consistent.

In this paper, we propose *eventually consistent linearizability (ec-linearizability)*, a new correctness condition for distributed systems (modeled as shared objects). Ec-linearizability relaxes linearizability [8] by allowing for a certain amount of inconsistency between operation executions on the same object. However, ec-linearizability retains the two fundamental properties of linearizability: locality and nonblocking. The former requires that the system is ec-linearizable if and only if every object is ec-linearizable. The latter states that every ec-linearizable history of some ec-linearizable object has an extension that is also ec-linearizable. Ec-linearizability is non-empty as well as prefix- and limit-closed. Therefore, it is a safety property [9].

Ec-linearizability is defined using a more basic property, called Δ*-ec-linearizability*. Roughly speaking, Δ corresponds to the level of inconsistency that each operation can encounter. For $\Delta = 0$, Δ-ec-linearizability reduces to linearizability.

2. RELATED WORK

Below we give a succinct survey on the literature relevant to our work. There is no single definition of *eventual consistency* that the community agrees upon. Informal definitions state that in a system that is eventually consistent, updates to the system's state are not necessarily immediately visible to subsequent read operations. On the other hand, if no new update operations are issued, eventually all read operations will return a value produced by the most recent update operation [1] [14] [2].

This formulation of eventual consistency is to some extent reflected by *eventual linearizability*, first defined in [11] and later refined in [7]. Eventual linearizability models intermittent inconsistencies (as in self-stabilizing systems) that may occur in a system only up to a certain point in time (measured in terms of elapsed time or the number of events from the beginning of computation). As noted by the authors, providing eventual linearizability is as difficult as providing linearizability itself, because, from some moment on, all pro-

*The project was funded from National Science Centre funds granted by decision No. DEC-2012/07/B/ST6/01230.

Permission to make digital or hard copies of part or all of this work for personal or classroom use is granted without fee provided that copies are not made or distributed for profit or commercial advantage, and that copies bear this notice and the full citation on the first page. Copyrights for third-party components of this work must be honored. For all other uses, contact the owner/author(s). Copyright is held by the author/owner(s).
PODC'15, July 21–23, 2015, Donostia-San Sebastián, Spain.
ACM 978-1-4503-3617-8 /15/07.
http://dx.doi.org/10.1145/2767386.2767448.

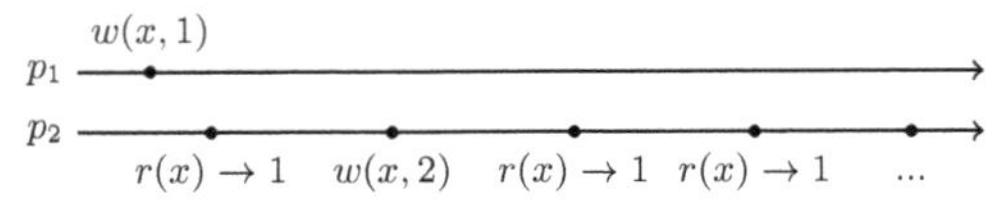

Figure 1: An example execution history in Cassandra with a lost update (p_1's clock drifts into future).

cesses have to work in a fully coordinated fashion (no further inconsistencies are allowed).

Contrary to eventual linearizability, ec-linearizability does not require the system to exhibit strong consistency at any point during the (possibly infinite) execution. Instead, ec-linearizability makes some weak assumptions on the history of operations already submitted to the system. In this sense, ec-linearizability is similar to approaches described below.

In some definitions, such as those in [13] [5] [3] [10] [4], processes in a system are guaranteed to eventually agree on some common prefix of (updating) operations. It means that the system *converges* over time to a consistent state. In some cases, as in [13], [3] or [4], all operations executed by any process have to be eventually visible to all operations that arrive after some point in the future. However, such a requirement can be deemed too strong. In fact, Cassandra, a popular eventually consistent replicated data storage system, allows some updates to be lost (and thus not visible) under certain circumstances (see Figure 1). Moreover, ensuring such a guarantee is not possible for some operations. For example, consider two concurrent *pop* operations executed on a stack. The stack has an invariant: no element can be returned when the stack is empty. If the stack has only one element and partition occurs, both *pop* operations will return the same last element. During convergence, the invariant will be broken, leading to a corrupt -1 sized stack. Inevitably, the next *push* operation performed on it will be lost (the pushed value will never be visible to any other operation). In principle, eventual-visibility of every operation is easy to ensure with updating operations that do not return a value or operations that commute [4] [12].

Ec-linearizability maintains a common prefix of operations but allows some operations to be omitted from it (and thus, it allows to model lost updates). Additionally, ec-linearizability is a correctness condition that, similarly to linearizability [8], concentrates on the interaction between the clients (processes) and the system, and intends to be as general as possible. In this way, it significantly differs from definitions in [13] [5] [3] [10], which put an emphasis on the properties of the systems' internal state, not on the correctness from the clients' point of view.

3. THE DEFINITION

We reuse the notation and basic definitions (such as completion of a history, legal history, etc.) from [6], but we only consider deterministic and finitely nondeterministic shared objects. Otherwise, neither linearizability, nor ec-linearizability, is a safety property.

For any complete sequential history S, S' is a *complete prefix* (or a *complete subsequence*) of S, if S' is a prefix (or a subsequence) of S, such that it contains an invocation event of some operation op_k, if and only if it contains the response event of op_k. We use S^k to denote a prefix consisting of the first k operation executions in S, and $S^{k,k+l}$ to denote a contiguous subsequence consisting of l consecutive operation executions in S starting from the k-th one. Let $fluctus(S)$ be a function that returns the set of all possible complete subsequences of any permutation of operation executions in S, e.g., $fluctus(\langle op_1, op_2\rangle) = \{\langle\rangle, \langle op_1\rangle, \langle op_2\rangle, \langle op_1, op_2\rangle, \langle op_2, op_1\rangle\}$, where $op_k = \langle inv[op_k], resp[op_k]\rangle$. Additionally, by $S_1 \cdot S_2$ we denote the concatenation of S_1 and S_2.

We are now ready to present our correctness condition. We define ec-linearizability using Δ-ec-linearizability. This way we ensure that the size of the inconsistency window, denoted Δ, is unknown but finite.

Definition 1. A history H is Δ-*ec-linearizable* for some natural number Δ, if:

1. there exists a sequential history $S = \langle op_1, op_2, ...\rangle$ equivalent to some completion of H, such that $\rightarrow_H \subseteq \rightarrow_S$, and

2. there exists L, a legal complete subsequence of S, such that for every operation execution op_k in S, there exists a legal history $V = P \cdot F \cdot \langle op_k\rangle$, such that:
   - P is a complete prefix of L and P is a subsequence of $S^{k-1-\Delta}$ (or P is empty, if $\Delta \geq k-1$),
   - $F \in fluctus(S^{k-\Delta,k})$,
   - if $k > \Delta$, then there exists an operation op_l in F, such that op_l is in L, or op_k is in L.

Definition 2. A history is *ec-linearizable* if it is Δ-ec-linearizable for some Δ.

Δ-ec-linearizability defines a *view* V for every operation in a given history. The view V represents the subjective perspective (from the operation's point of view) on the operations processed by the system. More precisely, V is composed of two parts: the common prefix P and the *fluctus* part F. P is a prefix of the sequence L, which consists of operations that are agreed upon. Since L is shared between the views of operations (each operation observes a prefix of L), the amount of inconsistencies each operation observes is limited. The inconsistencies observed by the operations are modeled by the fluctus part F. It may consist of up to Δ operation executions that directly precede the considered operation in S. These operations may appear in F in any order (not consistent with the order they appear in S).

Note that our definition assumes that some operations may never be included in L. This way, we model the possibility that some conflicting operations are rolled-back or overwritten. More precisely, an operation may never appear in L even though it completed correctly and returned results to the issuing process. It can, however, appear in fluctus parts of views of the next Δ operations processed by the system. This trait reflects the *update semantics* of eventually consistent systems that ec-linearizability models. In such systems, when there are two operations performed on independent sites, they are executed locally, and their updates are propagated asynchronously. Whenever any process receives updates to the same object coming from two different sites, it may try to merge them or, if the updates do not commute (conflict), it may discard (or overwrite) one of them (the winning update is chosen deterministically).

Δ-ec-linearizability ensures progress by requiring that at least one operation from the fluctus part or the operation itself is in L. Without this requirement, satisfying Δ-ec-linearizability would be trivial: an implementation that never

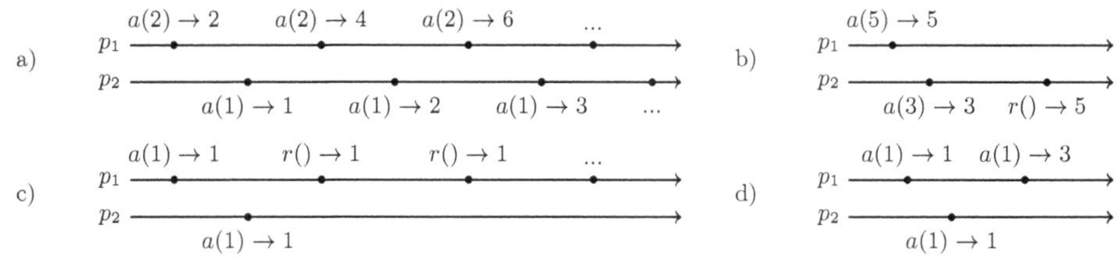

history	ecl	wc	tl	el	bec
a	0	1	0	0	0
b	1	0	0	0	0
c	1	1	0	0	0
d	0	1	1	1	1

Figure 2: Incomparability of properties.

conducts any communication between processes would suffice. It is therefore imperative that L increases over time. Moreover, it is guaranteed that for every operation in L, only a finite number of operations can be excluded from L. In particular, given $\Delta+1$ conflicting operations, at least one of them has to be recognized by all processes.

It is easy to show that ec-linearizability ensures eventual consistency in its most basic formulation: "if writes stop, then, processes will—at some point in time and forever afterwards—all agree on the same value for each object in the system."[2] Consider a history H. Let op_k be the last update operation in H included in L. If H is infinite, then there exists a finite Δ, such that the view of every operation in H, invoked Δ events after the response of op_k, contains op_k as the last update operation.

4. RESULTS

In this section, we present a few results regarding ec-linearizability. We begin with some easy observations. Firstly, a history that is Δ-ec-linearizable is also Δ'-ec-linearizable for some $\Delta' > \Delta$. Larger Δ means that we require even weaker consistency for the history. Secondly, Δ-ec-linearizability reduces to linearizability for $\Delta = 0$. In this case, the size of inconsistency window is zero, and the progress condition enforces every operation to be included in L. Additionally, as in case of linearizablilty, ec-linearizability requires that S respects the real-time order of H.

Now we compare ec-linearizability (ecl) with weak-consistency (wc), t-linearizablity for some t (tl), eventual linearizability (el) [7] and basic eventual consistency (bec) [4]. We show that ec-linearizability is incomparable with the rest of the properties by producing a few simple histories, which are shown in Figure 2. In each history two processes p_1 and p_2 execute operations on the same shared object that holds a single integer register and exports two operations: $a(u) \to v$ which adds u to the register and returns its current value, and $r() \to v$ which returns the current value of the register.

The infinite history a is trivially weakly consistent, because each process observes only all its previous operations. This history is not ec-linearizable, because processes never agree on a common prefix of operations (Δ has to be finite). On the other hand, in history b the opposite is true. From p_2's point of view, operation $a(5) \to 5$ overrides operation $a(3) \to 3$. It is an example of a lost update history acceptable by ec-linearizability, but not a weakly consistent one (p_2 does not recognize its own update operation).

History c also contains a lost update. It is not t-linearizable for any t, because p_1 never recognizes p_2's operation. For the same reason history c is neither eventually linearizable, nor (basically) eventually consistent. History d is not ec-linearizable, because there is no legal view of operation $a(1) \to 3$. However, it is t-linearizable for $t = 2$. It is also eventually linearizable and (basically) eventually consistent.

It is possible to show that ec-linearizability is both prefix- and limit-closed. It is also non-empty, therefore it is a safety property (unlike eventual linearizability) [9]. Two fundamental properties of linearizability are *locality* and *nonblocking* [8]. Both are preserved by ec-linearizability, what makes it an easy to reason about correctness condition.

5. REFERENCES

[1] P. Bailis and A. Ghodsi. Eventual consistency today: Limitations, extensions, and beyond. *Queue*, 11(3), Mar. 2013.

[2] P. Bailis, A. Ghodsi, J. M. Hellerstein, and I. Stoica. Bolt-on causal consistency. In *Proc. of SIGMOD '13*, June 2013.

[3] A. Bouajjani, C. Enea, and J. Hamza. Verifying eventual consistency of optimistic replication systems. In *Proc. of POPL '14*, Jan. 2014.

[4] S. Burckhardt, A. Gotsman, and H. Yang. Understanding eventual consistency. Technical Report MSR-TR-2013-39, March 2013.

[5] A. Fekete, D. Gupta, V. Luchangco, N. Lynch, and A. Shvartsman. Eventually-serializable data services. In *Proc. of PODC '96*, May 1996.

[6] R. Guerraoui and E. Ruppert. Linearizability is not always a safety property. In *Proc. of NETYS '14*. May 2014.

[7] R. Guerraoui and E. Ruppert. A paradox of eventual linearizability in shared memory. In *Proc. of PODC '14*, July 2014.

[8] M. P. Herlihy and J. M. Wing. Linearizability: A correctness condition for concurrent objects. *ACM TOPLAS*, 12(3), 1990.

[9] N. A. Lynch. *Distributed Algorithms*. Morgan Kaufmann Publishers Inc., 1996.

[10] Y. Saito and M. Shapiro. Optimistic replication. *ACM Comput. Surv.*, 37(1), Mar. 2005.

[11] M. Serafini, D. Dobre, M. Majuntke, P. Bokor, and N. Suri. Eventually linearizable shared objects. In *Proc. of PODC '10*, July 2010.

[12] M. Shapiro, N. Preguiça, C. Baquero, and M. Zawirski. Conflict-free replicated data types. In *Proc. of SSS '11*, May 2011.

[13] D. Terry, M. Theimer, K. Petersen, A. Demers, M. Spreitzer, and C. Hauser. Managing update conflicts in Bayou, a weakly connected replicated storage system. In *Proc. of SOSP '95*, Dec. 1995.

[14] W. Vogels. Eventually consistent. *Commun. ACM*, 52(1), Jan. 2009.

Help!

[Extended Abstract]

Keren Censor-Hillel
Department of Computer Science, Technion
ckeren@cs.technion.ac.il

Erez Petrank
Department of Computer Science, Technion
erez@cs.technion.ac.il

Shahar Timnat
Department of Computer Science, Technion
stimnat@cs.technion.ac.il

ABSTRACT

A fundamental challenge in designing concurrent data structures is obtaining efficient wait-free implementations, in which each operation completes regardless of the behavior of other operations in the system. The most common paradigm for guaranteeing wait-freedom is to employ a helping mechanism, in which, intuitively, fast processes help slow processes complete their operations. Curiously, despite its abundant use, to date, helping has not been formally defined nor was its necessity rigorously studied.

In this paper we initiate a rigorous study of the interaction between wait-freedom and helping. We start with presenting a formal definition of help, capturing the intuition of one thread helping another to make progress. Next, we present families of object types for which help is necessary in order to obtain wait-freedom. In other words, we prove that for some types there are no linearizable wait-free help-free implementations. In contrast, we show that other, simple types, can be implemented in a linearizable wait-free manner without employing help. Finally, we provide a universal strong primitive for implementing wait-free data structures without using help. Specifically, given a wait-free help-free fetch&cons object, one can implement any type in a wait-free help-free manner.

Categories and Subject Descriptors

D.1.3 [**Programming Techniques**]: Concurrent Programming

Keywords

Parallel Algorithms; Concurrent Data Structures; Progress Guarantees; Wait-Freedom; Help

1. INTRODUCTION

The era of multi-core architectures has been having a huge impact on software development: exploiting parallelism has become the main challenge of today's programming. With multiple processors communicating by accessing shared memory, the behavior of concurrent algorithms is measured by both *safety/correctness* and *progress* conditions.

Permission to make digital or hard copies of all or part of this work for personal or classroom use is granted without fee provided that copies are not made or distributed for profit or commercial advantage and that copies bear this notice and the full citation on the first page. Copyrights for components of this work owned by others than ACM must be honored. Abstracting with credit is permitted. To copy otherwise, or republish, to post on servers or to redistribute to lists, requires prior specific permission and/or a fee. Request permissions from permissions@acm.org.
PODC'15, July 21–23, 2015, Donostia-San Sebastián, Spain.
Copyright © 2015 ACM 978-1-4503-3617-8 /15/07 ...$15.00.
DOI: http://dx.doi.org/10.1145/2767386.2767415.

Most of the code written today is lock-based, but this is shifting towards codes without locks [14]. The holy grail of designing concurrent data structures is in obtaining efficient *wait-free* implementations, with research dating back to some of the most important studies in distributed computing [21, 10, 17]. Wait-freedom refers to implementations in which each operation terminates in a finite, preferably small, number of steps and, in particular, without dependence on the behavior of other processes in the system.

While the goal is fundamental [14, 4], wait-free implementations are often more complicated than non wait-free designs such as *lock-free* implementations, which only require that some operation makes progress but not necessarily all. In practice, sometimes all processes complete their operations in a timely manner despite following a code that only guarantees lock-freedom. A line of work orthogonal to the one in this paper attempts to explain this behavior by the fact that the worst-case adversarial schedules are of low probability in practice. Such studies describe benevolent adversaries under which it is sufficient to design lock-free algorithms [9, 15, 2].

Nevertheless, wait-freedom captures progress against the worst possible behavior, and as such is vital for real-time systems. Previous work identifies relations of other properties of implementations to the possibility of being wait-free. For example, no universal construction can be wait-free and satisfy disjoint-access parallelism [6].

One common approach used in order to guarantee wait-freedom is to employ some *helping* mechanism [23, 17, 12, 13, 14, 19, 8, 20, 25, 26]. Loosely speaking, in helping mechanisms, apart from completing their own operation, processes perform some additional work whose goal is to facilitate the work of others. Curiously, despite being a crucial ingredient, whether explicitly or implicitly, in many implementations of concurrent data structures, the notion of helping has been lacking thorough study as a concept.

Intrigued by the tools needed in order to achieve wait-freedom, we offer in this work a rigorous study of the interaction between the helping paradigm and wait-freedom. In particular, we are interested in the following question: Does wait-freedom require help? To this end, we start by proposing a formal definition of help. The proposed definition is based on linearization order of histories of an implementation rather than on a semantic description. We give evidence that the proposed definition matches the intuitive notion. We then present and analyze properties of types for which any wait-free implementation necessitates help. Such types includes popular data structures such as the stack and the queue. In contrast, we show that other types can be implemented in a wait-free help-free manner. A natural example is an implementation of a set (with the INSERT, DELETE, and CONTAINS operations) with a bounded range of possible values.

1.1 Our Contributions

Our first contribution is definitial: we propose a formal definition of the existing intuitive concept of helping in Definition 3.3. Roughly speaking, a process p helps an operation of another process q if a step of p determines that q's operation is linearized before some other operation.

We note that there is some ambiguity in the literature regarding the concept of help; it is used informally to describe two different things. One usage of help is in the common case where processes of lock-free algorithms coordinate access to a shared location. Here, one process p_1 completes the (already ongoing) operation of another process p_2 in order to enable access to shared data and to allow p_1 to complete its operation. Barnes [5] uses this practice as a general technique to achieve lock-freedom. This is also the case for the queue of [22], where processes sometimes need to fix the tail pointer to point to the last node (and not the one before last) before they can execute their own operation. Loosely speaking, the purpose of the above practice is not "altruistic". A process fixes the tail pointer because otherwise it would not be able to execute its own operation.

This is very different from the usage of help in, e.g., UPDATE operations in [1], which perform embedded scans for the sole "altruistic" purpose of enabling concurrent SCAN operations. It also differs from reading a designated announcements array, whose sole purpose is to allow processes to ask other processes for help, such as in [17]. In [17], a process could have easily completed its operation without helping any other operation (by proposing to the consensus object used in this build a value that consists only the process's own value, without values of other processes viewed in the announcements array). Our definition of help deliberately excludes the former concept (where a process simply enables data access for its own operation), and captures only the latter "altruistic" form of help.

Having a formal notion of helping, we turn to study the interaction between wait-freedom and help. We look into characterizing properties of types that require help in any wait-free implementation. We define and analyze two general types of objects. The first type, which we call *Exact Order Types*, consists of types in which the order of operations affects the result of future operations. That is, for some operations sequences, every change in the order of operations influences the final state of the object. Natural examples of exact order types are FIFO queues and LIFO stacks.

Exact order types bear some similarity to previously defined objects, such as *perturbable objects* [18] and *class G objects* [7], since all definitions deal with an operation that needs to return different results in several different executions. However, these definitions are not equivalent. For example, queues are exact order types, but are not perturbable objects, while a max-register is perturbable but not exact order. We mention perturbable objects in Section 8.

The second type, which we call *Global View Types*, consists of types which support an operation that obtains the entire state of the object. Examples of global view types are snapshot objects, increment objects, and fetch&add. For instance, in an increment object that supports the operations GET and INCREMENT, the result of a GET depends on the exact number of preceding INCREMENTS. However, unlike the queue and stack, the result of an operation is not necessarily influenced by the internal order of previous operations. Notice that global view types are not equivalent to *readable objects* as defined by Ruppert [24], since for some global view types any applicable operation must change the state of the object. For example, a fetch&increment object is a global view type, but is not a readable object.

We prove that every wait-free implementation of any exact order type and any global view type requires help. Furthermore, when the CAS primitive is not available, we show that a max register [3] requires help even in order to provide lock-freedom.

Theorems 4.18, 5.1 (rephrased).
A linearizable implementation of a wait-free exact order type or a wait-free global view type using READ, WRITE, and CAS, or a lock-free max register using READ and WRITE, cannot be help-free.

We prove the above by constructing infinite executions in which some operation never completes unless helping occurs. This is done by carefully combining the definition of help with the attributes of the type.

We then show positive results, i.e., that some types can be implemented in a wait-free help-free manner. This is trivial for a *vacuous* type whose only operation is a NO-OP, but when CASes are available this also holds for a max register and for a *set* type, which supports the operations INSERT, DELETE and CONTAINS[1].

The proof that these types have wait-free help-free implementations can be generalized to additional types, provided they have an implementation in which every operation is linearized in a specific step of the same operation. Intuitively, these are implementations in which the result of an operation "does not depend too strongly" on past operations.

Naturally, the characterization of types which require help depends on the primitives being used, and while our results are generally stated for READ, WRITE, and CAS, we discuss additional primitives as well. In particular, we show that exact order types cannot be both help-free and wait-free even if the FETCH&ADD primitive is available, but the same statement is not true for global view types. Finally, we show that a fetch&cons primitive is universal for wait-free help-free objects. This means that given a wait-free help-free fetch&cons object, one can implement any type in a wait-free help-free manner.

Due to lack of space, some parts are omitted and can be found in the full paper. This includes some of the detailed proofs, and the discussion about max registers where only READ and WRITE primitives are allowed.

1.2 Additional Related Work

Helping mechanisms come in different forms. Some wait-free implementations use a designated `announcement` array, with a slot for each process. Each process uses its slot to describe the operation it is currently seeking to execute, and other processes read this announcement and help complete the operation. This is perhaps the most widely used helping mechanism, appearing in specific designs, as well as in universal constructions [17], and in general techniques, such as for converting any lock-free data structure to a wait-free data structure [26].

But other forms of help exist. Consider, for example, the form of help that is used for the double-collect snapshot algorithm of [1]. In this wait-free snapshot object, each UPDATE operation starts by performing an embedded SCAN and adding it to the updated location. A SCAN operation op_1 that checks the object twice and sees no change can safely return this view. If a change has been observed, then the UPDATE operation op_2 that caused it also writes the view of its embedded SCAN, allowing op_1 to adopt this view and return it, despite the object being, perhaps constantly, changed. Thus, intuitively, the UPDATES help the SCANS.

[1]A degenerated set, in which the INSERT and DELETE operations do not return a boolean value indicating whether they succeeded can also be implemented without CASes.

2. MODEL AND DEFINITIONS

We consider a standard shared memory setting with a fixed set of processes P. In each computation step, a process executes a single atomic primitive on a shared memory register, possibly preceded with some local computation. The set of atomic primitives contains READ, WRITE primitives, and usually also CAS. Where specifically mentioned, it is extended with the FETCH&ADD primitive.

A CAS primitive is defined by a triplet, consisting of a target register, an expected-value, and a new-value. When a CAS step is executed, the value stored in the target register is compared to the expected-value. If they are equal, the value in the target register is replaced with the new-value, and the Boolean value true is returned. In such a case we say that the CAS is *successful*. Otherwise, the shared memory remains unchanged, and false is returned. We stress that a CAS is executed atomically.

A FETCH&ADD primitive is defined by a target register and an integer value. An execution of the FETCH&ADD primitive atomically returns the value previously stored in the target register and replaces it with the sum of the previous value and the FETCH&ADD's integer value.

A *type* (e.g., a FIFO queue) is defined by a state machine, and is accessed via *operations*. An operation receives zero or more input parameters, and returns one result, which may be null. The state machine of a type is a function that maps a state and an operation (including input parameters) to a new state and a result of the operation.

An *object*, is an implementation of a type using atomic primitives. An implementation specifies the primitives and local computation to be executed for each operation. The local computation can influence the next chosen primitive step. When the last primitive step of an operation is finished, the operation's result is computed locally and the operation is completed.

In the current work, we consider only executions of objects. Thus, a *program* of a process consists of operations on an object that the process should execute. The program may include local computations, and results of previous operations may affect the chosen future operations and their input parameters. A program can be finite (consisting of a finite number of operations) or infinite. This may also depend on the results of operations.

A *history* is a log of an execution (or a part of an execution) of a program. It consists of a finite or infinite sequence of computation steps. Each computation step is coupled with the specific operation that is being executed by the process that executed the step. The first step of an operation is also coupled with the input parameters of the operation, and the last step of an operation is also associated with the operation's result. A single computation step is also considered a history (of length one).

A *schedule* is a finite or infinite sequence of process ids. Given a schedule, an object, and a program for each process in P, a unique matching history corresponds. For a given history, a unique schedule corresponds. Given two histories, h_1, h_2, we denote by $h_1 \circ h_2$ the history derived from the concatenation of history h_2 after h_1. Given a program $prog$ for each process in P, and a history h, for each $p \in P$ we denote by $h \circ p$ the history derived from scheduling process p to take another single step following its program immediately after h.

The *set of histories created by an object O* is the set that consists of every history h created by an execution of any fixed set of processes P and any corresponding programs on object O, in any schedule S.

A history defines a partial order on the operations it includes. An operation op_1 is before an operation op_2 (denoted: $op_1 \prec op_2$) if op_1 is completed before op_2 begins. A sequential history is a history in which this order is a total order. A linearization [16] L of a history h is a sequence of operations (including their input parameters and results) such that 1) L includes all the operations that are completed in h, and may include operations that are started but are not completed in h, 2) the operations in L have the same input parameters as the operations in h, and also the same output results for operations that are completed in h, 3) for every two operations op_1 and op_2, if $op_1 \prec op_2$ in h, and op_2 is included in L, then $op_1 \prec op_2$ in L, and 4) L is consistent with the type definition of the object creating history h. An object O is a linearizable implementation of type T if each history in the set of histories created by O has a linearization.

Lock-freedom and wait-freedom are forms of progress guarantees. In the context of our work, they apply to objects (which are, as mentioned above, specific implementations of types). An object O is lock-free if there is no history h in the set of histories created by O such that 1) h is infinite and 2) only a finite number of operations is completed in h. That is, an object is lock-free if at least one of the executing processes must make progress and complete its operation in a finite number of steps. Wait-freedom is a strictly stronger progress guarantee. An object O is wait-free if there is no history h in the set of histories created by O such that 1) h includes an infinite number of steps by some process p and 2) the same process p completes only a finite number of operations in h. That is, O is wait-free if every process that is scheduled to run infinite computation steps must eventually complete its operation, regardless of the scheduling.

3. WHAT IS HELP?

The main contribution of this work is in establishing that many types cannot be implemented in a linearizable wait-free manner without employing a helping mechanism. To establish such a conclusion, it is necessary to accurately define help. In this section we discuss help intuitively, define it formally, and consider examples showing that the formal definition expresses the intuitive concept of help. Additionally, we will establish two general facts about help-free wait-free implementations.

3.1 Intuitive Discussion

Many wait-free algorithms employ an array with a designated entry for each process. A process announces in this array what operation it wishes to execute, and other processes that see this announcement might help and execute this operation for it. Such mechanisms are used in most wait-free universal constructions, dating back to [17] and many other constructions since. These mechanisms are probably the most explicit way to offer help, but not the only one possible. Considering help in a more general form, we find it helpful[2] to think of the following scenario.

Consider a system of three processes, p_1, p_2, p_3, and an object that implements a FIFO queue. The program of p_1 is ENQUEUE(1), the program of p_2 is ENQUEUE(2), and the program of p_3 is DEQUEUE(). First consider a schedule in which p_3 starts running solo until completing its operation. The result of the dequeue, regardless of the implementation of the FIFO queue, is null. If before scheduling p_3, we schedule p_1 and let it complete its operation, and only then let p_3 run and complete its own operation, p_3 will return 1. If we schedule p_1 to start executing its operation, and stop it at some point (possibly before its completion) and then run p_3 solo until completing its operation, it may return either null or 1. Hence, if we consider the execution of p_1 running solo, there is (at least) one computation step S in it, such that if we stop p_1 immediately

[2]Pun intended.

before S and run p_3 solo, then p_3 returns null, and if we stop p_1 immediately after S and run p_3 solo, p_3 returns 1.

Similarly, if we consider the execution of p_2 running solo, there is (at least) one computation step that "flips" the value returned by p_3 when running solo from null to 2. We now consider a schedule that interleaves p_1 and p_2 until one of them completes. In any such execution, there is (at least) one computation step that "flips" the result of p_3 from null to either 1 or 2. If a step taken by p_2 "flips" the result of p_3 and causes it to return 1 (which is the value enqueued by p_1) we say that p_2 helped p_1. Similarly, if a step taken by p_1 "flips" the result of p_3 and causes it to return 2, then p_1 helped p_2.

This is the intuition behind the help notion that is defined below. Some known lock-free queue algorithms do not employ help, such as the lock-free queue of Michael and Scott [22]. However, we prove in Section 4 that any *wait-free* queue algorithm must employ help.

3.2 Help Definition

We say that an operation *op* belongs to history h if h contains at least one computation step of *op*. Note that *op* is a specific instance of an operation on an object, which has exactly one invocation, and one result. We say that the *owner* of *op* is the process that executes *op*.

DEFINITION 3.1. (Linearization Function.) *We say that f is a linearization function over a set of histories H, if for every $h \in H$, $f(h)$ is a linearization of h.*

DEFINITION 3.2. (Decided Operations Order.) *For a history h in a set of histories H, a linearization function f over H, and two operations op_1 and op_2, we say that op_1 is* decided before *op_2 in h with respect to f and the set of histories H, if there exists no $s \in H$ such that h is a prefix of s and $op_2 \prec op_1$ in $f(s)$.*

DEFINITION 3.3. (Help-Free Implementation.) *A set of histories H is without help, or help-free, if there exists a linearization function f over H such that for every $h \in H$, every two operations op_1, op_2, and a single computation step γ such that $h \circ \gamma \in H$ it holds that if op_1 is decided before op_2 in $h \circ \gamma$ and op_1 is not decided before op_2 in h, then computation step γ is a step in the execution of op_1 by the owner of op_1*[3].

An object is a help-free implementation, if the set of histories created by it is help-free.

To better understand this definition, consider an execution of an object. When considering two concurrent operations, the linearization of these operations dictates which operation comes first. The definition considers the specific step, γ, in which it is decided which operation comes first. In a help-free implementation, γ is always taken by the process whose operation is decided to be the one that comes first.

Consider the wait-free universal construction of Herlihy [17]. One of the phases in this construction is a wait-free reduction from a *fetch-and-cons* list to consensus. A fetch-and-cons (or a fetch-and-cons list) is a type that supports a single operation, *fetch-and-cons*, which receives a single input parameter, and outputs an ordered list of the parameters of all the previous invocations of *fetch-and-cons*. That is, conceptually, the state of a fetch-and-cons type is a list. A *fetch-and-cons* operation returns the current list, and adds (hereafter, cons) its input operation to the head of the list.

[3]For readers familiar with the concept of strong linearization [11], we note that a set of histories can be strongly linearizable yet not help-free, and can also be help-free yet not strongly linearizable.

The reduction from fetch-and-cons to consensus is as follows. A special announce array, with a slot for each process, is used to store the input parameter of each ongoing *fetch-and-cons* operation. Thus, when a process desires to execute a *fetch-and-cons* operation, it first writes its input value to its slot in the announce array.

Next, the process reads the entire announce array. Using this information, it calculates a *goal* that consists of all the operations recently announced in the array. The process will attempt to cons *all* of these operations into the fetch-and-cons list. It reads the current state of the fetch-and-cons list, and appends this list to the end of its own goal (removing duplications.) Afterwards, the process starts executing (at most) n instances of consensus (n is the number of processes). In each instance of consensus, a process proposes its own process id.

The goal of the process that wins the consensus represents the updated state of the fetch-and-cons list. Thus, if the process wins a consensus instance, it returns immediately (as its own operation has definitely been applied). If it loses a consensus, it updates its goal again to be its original goal (minus duplications that already appear it the updated state) followed by the new list, which is the goal of the last winner. After participating in n instances of consensus, the process can safely return, since at least one of the winners in these instances already sees the process's operation in the announces array, and includes it in its goal.

This is a classic example of help. Wait-freedom is obtained due to the fact that the effect of process p winning an instance is adding to the list all the items it saw in the announce array, not merely its own item. To see that this algorithm is not help-free according to Definition 3.3 consider a system of three processes. Each process first announces its wanted item in the ANNOUNCE array, and then reads all of the array. Assume p_1's place in the array is before p_2's, but that p_2 writes to the announce array first. p_3 then reads the announce array and sees p_2's item. Then p_1 writes to the announce array, and afterwards continue to read the entire array.

At this point p_2 is stalled, while p_1 and p_3 start competing in consensus. If the winner is p_1, then p_1's item is added to the list before p_2's item (since p_1's place in the list is before p_2's). If the winner is p_3, then the item of p_2 is added to the list, but the item of p_1 not as yet. Thus, a step of p_3 can decide that the item of p_2 is before that of p_1, and thus the fetch-and-cons operation of p_2 comes before that of p_1. This contradicts help-freedom.

A system of two processes.

In general, help is not required in a system with only two processes. The universal construction of [17] is help-free in such a system, and can be used to implement any type in a help-free wait-free manner. Accordingly, we concentrate on proving that help is required for systems with at least three processes.

3.3 General Observations

In this subsection we point out two facts regarding the decided operations order (Definition 3.2) that are useful to prove that some types cannot be both wait-free and help-free. The first fact is true for non help-free implementations as well, as it is derived directly from the linearizability criteria. It states that for completed operations, the decided order must comply with the partial order a history defines, and for future operations, the decided order cannot contradict partial orders that may apply later on.

OBSERVATION 3.4. *In any history h:*
(1) Once an operation is completed it must be decided before all operations that have not yet started.
(2) While an operation has not yet started it cannot be decided before any operation of a different process.

(3) In particular, the order between two operations of two different processes cannot be decided as long as none of these operations have started.

The second fact is an application of the first observation for help-free implementations.

CLAIM 3.5. *In a help-free implementation in a system that includes at least three processes, for a given history h and a linearizarion function f, if an operation op_1 of a process p_1 is decided before an operation op_2 of a process p_2, then op_1 must be decided before any future (not yet started) operation of any process.*

PROOF. Immediately following h, allow p_2 to run solo long enough to complete the execution of op_2. By Observation 3.4, op_2 must now be decided before any future operation. Thus, by transitivity, op_1 must be decided before any future operation as well. In a help-free implementation, op_1 cannot be decided before a different operation as a result of a step of p_2. Thus, op_1 must be decided before future operations already at h. □

4. EXACT ORDER TYPES

In this section we prove that some types cannot be implemented in a linearizable, wait-free, and help-free manner. Simply put: for some types, wait-freedom requires help. We first prove this result for systems that support only READ, WRITE, and CAS primitives. In the full paper we also extend the proof to hold for systems that support the FETCH&ADD primitive as well. This section focuses on exact order types. Roughly speaking, these are types in which switching the order between two operations changes the results of future operations. An intuitive example for such a type is the FIFO queue. The exact location in which an item is enqueued is important, and will change the results of future dequeues operations.

In what follows we formally define exact order types. This definition uses the concept of a sequence of operations. If S is a sequence of operations, we denote by $S(n)$ the first n operations in S, and by S_n the n-th operation in S. We denote by $(S + op?)$ a sequence that contains S and possibly also the operation op. That is, $(S + op?)$ is in fact a set of sequences that contains S, and also sequences that are similar to S, except that a single operation op is inserted in somewhere between (or before or after) the operations of S.

DEFINITION 4.1. (Exact Order Types.) *An exact order type t is a type for which there exists an operation op, an infinite sequence of operations W, and a (finite or an infinite) sequence of operations R, such that for every integer $n \geq 0$ there exists an integer $m \geq 1$, such that for at least one operation in $R(m)$, the result it returns in any execution in $W(n+1) \circ (R(m) + op?)$ differs from the result it returns in any execution in $W(n) \circ op \circ (R(m) + W_{n+1}?)$.*

Examples of such types are a queue, a stack, and the fetch-and-cons used in [17]. To gain some intuition about the definition, consider the queue. Let op be an ENQUEUE(1) operation, W be an infinite sequence of ENQUEUE(2) operations, and R be an infinite sequence of DEQUEUE operations. The queue is an exact order type, because the $(n+1)$-st dequeue returns a different result in any execution that starts with $n+1$ ENQUEUE(2) operations compared to any execution that starts with n ENQUEUE(2) operations and then an ENQUEUE(1).

More formally, let n be an integer, and set m to be $n+1$. Executions in $W(n+1) \circ (R(m) + op?)$ start with $n+1$ ENQUEUE(2) operations, followed by $n+1$ DEQUEUE operations. (There is possibly an ENQUEUE(1) somewhere between the dequeues, but not before any of the ENQUEUE(2).) Executions in $W(n) \circ op \circ (R(m) + W_{n+1}?)$ start with n ENQUEUE(2) operations, then an ENQUEUE(1) operation, and then $n+1$ DEQUEUE operations. (Again, there is possibly an ENQUEUE(2) somewhere between the dequeues.) From the specification of the FIFO queue, the last DEQUEUE must return a different result in the first case (in which it must return 2) than in the second case (in which it must return 1).

We now turn to prove that any exact order type cannot be both help-free and wait-free. Let Q be a linearizable, help-free implementation of an exact order type. The reader may find it helpful to consider a FIFO queue as a concrete example throughout the proof. We will prove that Q is not wait-free. For convenience, we assume Q is lock-free, as otherwise, it is not wait-free and we are done. Let op_1, W, and R be the operation and sequences of operations, respectively, guaranteed in the definition of exact order types. Consider a system of three processes, p_1, p_2, and p_3. The program of process p_1 is the operation op_1. The program of process p_2 is the infinite sequence W. The program of process p_3 is the (finite or infinite) sequence R. The operation of p_1 is op_1, an operation of p_2 is denoted op_2, and the first operation of p_3 is denoted op_3.

We start by proving two claims that are true for any execution of Q in which p_1, p_2, and p_3 follow their respective programs. These claims are the only ones that directly involve the definition of exact order types. The rest of the proof considers a specific execution, and builds on these two claims.

CLAIM 4.2. *Let h be a history such that the first n operations are already decided to be the first n operations of p_2 (which are $W(n)$), and p_3 has not yet taken any step. (Denote the $(n+1)$-st operation of p_2 by op_2.)*
(1.) If in h op_1 is decided before op_3, then the order between op_1 and op_2 is already decided.
(2.) Similarly, if in h op_2 is decided before op_3, then the order between op_1 and op_2 is already decided.

PROOF. For convenience, we prove (1). The proof of (2) is symmetrical. Assume that in h op_1 is decided before op_3, and let m be the integer corresponding to n by the definition of exact order types. Immediately after h, let p_3 run in a solo execution until it completes exactly m operations. Denote the history after this solo execution of p_3 by h', and consider the linearization of h'.

The first n operations in the linearization must be $W(n)$. The linearization must also include exactly m operations of p_3 (which are $R(m)$), and somewhere before them, it must also include op_1. The linearization may or may not include op_2. There are two cases. If the $(n+1)$-st operation in the linearization is op_1, then the linearization is in $W(n) \circ op_1 \circ (R(m) + W_{n+1}?)$, while if the $n+1$-st operation in the linearization is op_2, then the linearization must be exactly $W(n+1) \circ op_1 \circ R(m)$ which is in $W(n+1) \circ (R(m) + op_1?)$. We claim that whichever is the case, the order between op_1 and op_2 is already decided in h'.

To see this, consider any continuation $h' \circ x$ of h'. Consider the linearization of $h' \circ x$. This linearization must also start with $W(n)$, must also include $R(m)$, and somewhere before $R(m)$ it must include op_1. It may or may not include op_2 somewhere before R_m. All the rest of the operations in $h' \circ x$ must be linearized after R_m, because they where not yet started when R_m was completed. Thus, the linearization of $h' \circ x$ must begin with a prefix that belongs to either $W(n) \circ op_1 \circ (R(m) + W_{n+1}?)$ or $W(n+1) \circ (R(m) + op_1?)$. Mark this prefix as Prefix(Lin($h' \circ x$)).

So far we have obtained that for every x such that $h' \circ x$ is a continuation of h', Prefix(Lin($h' \circ x$)) belongs to either $W(n) \circ op_1 \circ (R(m) + W_{n+1}?)$ or $W(n+1) \circ (R(m) + op_1?)$. The next step is to show that for every x, Prefix(Lin($h' \circ x$)) belongs to the same one of these sets. To do this, we consider the results of $R(m)$ in h'.

In h', the operations $R(m)$ are already completed, and their results are set. By definition of exact order types, these results cannot be consistent with both $W(n) \circ op_1 \circ (R(m) + W_{n+1}?)$ and $W(n+1) \circ (R(m) + op_1?)$. Thus, if the linearization of h' is in $W(n) \circ op_1 \circ (R(m) + W_{n+1}?)$, then the results of $R(m)$ mean that for every x, Prefix(Lin($h' \circ x$)) cannot be in $W(n+1) \circ (R(m) + op_1?)$, and thus must belong to $W(n) \circ op_1 \circ (R(m) + W_{n+1}?)$. Similarly, if the linearization of h' is in $W(n+1) \circ (R(m) + op_1?)$, then for every x, Prefix(Lin($h' \circ x$)) must be in $W(n+1) \circ (R(m) + op_1?)$ as well.

Since the order between op_1 and op_2 is the same for each continuation of h', it follows by definition that the order between op_1 and op_2 is already decided in h'. Since Q is a help-free implementation, then the order between op_1 and op_2 cannot be decided during the solo execution of p_3 which is the delta between h and h'. Thus, the order between op_1 and op_2 is already decided in h. □

CLAIM 4.3. *Let h, h', and h'' be three histories, such that in all of them the first n operations are already decided to be the first n operations of p_2 (which are $W(n)$), and p_3 has not yet taken any step. (Denote the $(n+1)$-st operation of p_2 by op_2.) Furthermore, in h the order between op_1 and op_2 is not yet decided, in h' op_1 is decided before op_2, and in h'' op_2 is decided before op_1.*
(1.) h' and h'' are distinguishable by p_3.
(2.) h and h' are distinguishable by at least one of p_2 and p_3.
(3.) h and h'' are distinguishable by at least one of p_1 and p_3.

REMARK 4.4. *(3.) is not needed in the proof, but is stated for completeness.*

PROOF. Let m be the integer corresponding to n by the definition of exact order types. We start by proving (1). Since in h' op_1 is decided before op_2, then in h' op_1 must also be decided before op_3 by Claim 3.5. Assume that immediately after h' p_3 is run in a solo execution until it completes exactly m operations. The linearization of this execution must start with $W(n)$, followed by op_1. This linearization must also include the first m operations of p_3 (which are $R(m)$, and it may or may not include op_2. Thus, the linearization must be in $W(n) \circ op_1 \circ (R(m) + W_{n+1}?)$.

Now assume that immediately after h'' p_3 is run in a solo execution until it completes exactly m operations. This time, the linearization must be in $W(n+1) \circ (R(m) + op_1?)$. By the definition of exact order types, there is at least one operation in $R(m)$, that is, at least one operation of p_3, which returns a different result in these two executions. Thus, h' and h'' are *distinguishable* by process p_3.

We turn to prove (2). Assume that immediately after h' p_2 is run until it completes op_2, and then p_3 is run in a solo execution until it completes exactly m operations. The linearization of this execution must be exactly $W(n) \circ op_1 \circ W_{n+1} \circ R(m)$ which is in $W(n) \circ op_1 \circ (R(m) + W_{n+1}?)$.

Now assume that immediately after h p_2 is run until it completes op_2 and then p_3 is run in a solo execution until it completes exactly m operations. At the point in time exactly after op_2 is completed, and exactly before p_3 starts executing op_3, op_2 is decided before op_3 (Observation 3.4). Thus, by Claim 4.2, the order between op_1 and op_2 is already decided. Since the order is not decided in h, the implementation is wait-free, and p_1 has not taken another step since h, it follows that op_2 must be decided before op_1.

In other words, in the execution in which after h p_2 completes op_2 and then p_3 completes exactly m operations, op_2, which is W_{n+1}, is decided before both op_3 and op_1. Thus, the linearization of this execution must be in $W(n+1) \circ (R(m) + op_1?)$.

```
 1: h = ε;
 2: op1 = the single operation of p1;
 3: while (true)                                              ▷ main loop
 4:    op2 = the first uncompleted operation of p2;
 5:    while (true)                                           ▷ inner loop
 6:       if op1 is not decided before op2 in h ∘ p1
 7:          h = h ∘ p1;
 8:          continue;                                        ▷ goto line 5
 9:       if op2 is not decided before op1 in h ∘ p2
10:          h = h ∘ p2;
11:          continue;                                        ▷ goto line 5
12:       break;                                              ▷ goto line 13
13:    h = h ∘ p2;            ▷ this step will be proved to be a CAS
14:    h = h ∘ p1;     ▷ this step will be proved to be a failed CAS
15:    while (op2 is not completed in h)                      ▷ complete op2
16:       h = h ∘ p2;
```

Figure 1: The algorithm for constructing the history in the proof of Theorem 4.18.

By the definition of exact order types, there is at least one operation in $R(m)$, that is, at least one operation of p_3, which returns a different result in these two executions. Thus, h and h' are *distinguishable* by at least one of the processes p_2 and p_3. The proof of (3) is similar. □

In the rest of the proof of the main theorem we build an infinite history h, such that the processes p_1, p_2, and p_3 follow their respective programs, and p_1 executes infinitely many (failed) CAS steps, yet never completes its operation, contradicting wait-freedom. The algorithm for constructing this history is depicted in Figure 1. In lines 5–12, p_1 and p_2 are scheduled to run their programs as long as it is not yet decided which of their operations comes first. Afterwards, the execution of Q is in a critical point. If p_1 were to take a step, then op_1 will be decided before op_2, and if p_2 were to take a step, then op_2 will be decided before op_1. We prove using indistinguishability arguments, that the next step by both p_1 and p_2 is a CAS (and that both steps access the same target register). Next (line 13), p_2 executes its CAS, and then (line 14) p_1 attempts a CAS as well, which is going to fail. Afterwards, p_2 is scheduled to complete its operation, and then the above is repeated with p_2's next operation.

It is shown that in iteration $n+1$ of the algorithm for constructing h, the n first operations are already decided to be the first n operations of p_2 (that is, $W(n)$), and iteration $n+1$ is a "competition" between op_1 and W_{n+1}. Exact order types are used to show that the two possible results of this competition must be distinguishable from one another.

We prove a series of claims on the execution of history h, which is a history of object Q. Most claims refer to the state of the execution of Q in specific points in the execution, described by a corresponding line in the algorithm given in Figure 1. These claims are proved by induction, where the induction variable is the iteration number of the main loop (lines 3–16). The induction hypothesis is that claims (4.5–4.16) are correct. Claim 4.5 is the only one to use the induction hypothesis directly. The other claims follow from Claim 4.5.

CLAIM 4.5. *Immediately after line 4, it holds that 1) the order between op_1 and op_2 is not yet decided, and 2) all the operations of p_2 prior to op_2 are decided before op_1.*

PROOF. For the first iteration of the main loop, this is trivial because h is empty (Observation 3.4). For iteration $i \geq 2$, it follows from the induction hypothesis, Observation 4.13, and Claim 4.16. □

OBSERVATION 4.6. *The order between op_1 and op_2 cannot be decided during the inner loop (lines 5–12).*

This follows from the fact that Q is help-free, and from inspecting the conditions in lines 6 and 9.

OBSERVATION 4.7. *Process p_3 never takes a step in h.*

CLAIM 4.8. *The order between op_1 and op_2 must be decided before any one of op_1 and op_2 is completed.*

PROOF. If op_1 is completed, then op_1 must be decided before all future operations of p_3 (Observation 3.4). All the operations of p_2 prior to op_2 are already decided before op_1 (Claim 4.5), and by Observation 4.7, p_3 hasn't taken any steps. Thus, by Claim 4.2, the order between op_1 and op_2 is already decided.

Similarly, if op_2 is completed, then op_2 must be decided before all future operations of p_3 (Observation 3.4). Again, all the operations of p_2 prior to op_2 are already decided before op_1 (Claim 4.5), and by Observation 4.7, p_3 hasn't taken any steps. Thus, by Claim 4.2, the order between op_1 and op_2 is already decided. □

CLAIM 4.9. *The execution of the inner loop (lines 5–12) is finite.*

PROOF. By combining Observation 4.6 and Claim 4.8, no operation in Q is completed in h during the execution of the inner loop. Since Q is lock-free, and each loop iteration adds a single step to h, this cannot last infinitely. □

OBSERVATION 4.10. *Immediately before line 13 op_1 is decided before op_2 in $h \circ p_1$, op_2 is decided before op_1 in $h \circ p_2$, and, hence, the order of op_1 and op_2 is not decided in h.*

From observing the code, the inner loop exits and line 13 is reached only if the next step of either p_1 or p_2 will decide the order. Since the queue algorithm is help-free, in $h \circ p_1$, op_1 is decided before op_2, and in $h \circ p_2$, op_2 is decided before op_1.

CLAIM 4.11. *Immediately before line 13 the following holds.*
(1.) The next primitive step in the programs of both p_1 and p_2 is to the same memory location.
(2.) The next primitive step in the programs of both p_1 and p_2 is a CAS.
(3.) The expected-value of both the CAS *operations of p_1 and p_2 is the value that appears in the designated address.*
(4.) The new-value of both the CAS *operations is different than the expected-value.*

PROOF. By Observation 4.10, in $h \circ p_1$, op_1 is decided before op_2. It follows that op_1 is decided before op_2 in $h \circ p_1 \circ p_2$ as well. Similarly, op_2 is decided before op_1 in $h \circ p_2 \circ p_1$. By Claim 4.3 (1), it follows that $h \circ p_1 \circ p_2$ must be *distinguishable* from $h \circ p_2 \circ p_1$ by process p_3. It immediately follows that the next primitive step of both p_1 and p_2 is to the same memory location. Furthermore, the next step of both p_1 and p_2 cannot be a READ primitive. Also, it cannot be a CAS that does not change the shared memory, i.e., a CAS in which the expected-value is different than the value in the target address, or a CAS in which the expected-value and new-value are the same.

Thus, the next step by both p_1 and p_2 is either a WRITE primitive or a CAS which satisfies conditions (3) and (4) of the claim. It remains to show the next step is not a WRITE. Assume by way of contradiction the next step by p_1 is a WRITE. Then, $h \circ p_1$ is indistinguishable from $h \circ p_2 \circ p_1$ to all process excluding p_2, again contradicting Claim 4.3 (1). A similar argument also shows that the next step of p_2 cannot be a WRITE. □

Claim 4.11 immediately implies:

COROLLARY 4.12. *The primitive step p_2 takes in line 13 is a successful* CAS*, and the primitive step p_1 takes in line 14 is a failed* CAS.

OBSERVATION 4.13. *Immediately after line 13, op_2 is decided before op_1.*

This follows immediately from Observation 4.10, and from line 13 of the algorithm for constructing h. Next, for convenience, we denote the first operation of p_3 as op_3.

CLAIM 4.14. *Immediately before line 13, the order between op_1 and op_3 is not yet decided.*

PROOF. Process p_3 has not yet taken any steps (Observation 4.7), and thus its operation cannot be decided before op_1 (Observation 3.4). Assume by way of contradiction that op_1 is decided before op_3. All the operations of p_2 prior to op_2 are already decided before op_1 (Claim 4.5) and thus by Claim 4.2, the order between op_1 and op_2 is already decided. But the order between op_1 and op_2 is not yet decided before line 13 (Claim 4.5 and Observation 4.6), yielding contradiction. □

CLAIM 4.15. *Immediately after completing line 16, the order between op_1 and op_3 is not yet decided.*

PROOF. By Claim 4.14, the order between op_1 and op_3 is not yet decided before line 13. Steps by p_2 cannot decide the order between op_1 and op_3 in a help-free algorithm, and thus the only step which could potentially decide the order until after line 16 is the step p_1 takes in line 14. Assume by way of contradiction this step decides the order between op_1 and op_3.

If this step decides the order between op_1 and op_3 then after this step op_1 must be decided before op_3. By Corollary 4.12, this step is a failed CAS. Thus, the state immediately before this step and the state immediately after this step are indistinguishable to all processes other than p_1. This contradicts Claim 4.3 (2). □

CLAIM 4.16. *Immediately after line 16, the order between op_1 and the operation of p_2 following op_2 is not yet decided.*

PROOF. The operation of p_2 following op_2 has not yet begun, and thus it cannot be decided before op_1 (Observation 3.4). Assume by contradiction that op_1 is decided before the next operation of p_2. Thus, by Claim 3.5, op_1 must be decided before all future operations of p_3, including op_3. But by Claim 4.15, op_1 is not yet decided before op_3, yielding a contradiction. □

COROLLARY 4.17. *Q is not wait-free.*

PROOF. By Claim 4.9, each execution of the inner loop is finite. Thus, there are infinitely many executions of the main loop. In each such execution, p_1 takes at least a single step in line 14. Thus p_1 takes infinitely many steps. Yet, by combining Claims 4.5, and 4.8, op_1 is not completed in any iteration of the main loop, which implies it is never completed. Thus, Q is not wait-free. □

Since the assumptions on Q were that it is linearizable, help-free, and lock-free, we can rephrase Corollary 4.17 as follows.

THEOREM 4.18. *A wait-free linearizable implementation of an exact order type cannot be help-free.*

It is interesting to note that in history h built in this proof, process p_3 never takes a step. Nevertheless, its existence is necessary for the proof. History h demonstrates that in a lock-free help-free linearizable implementation of an exact order type, a process may fail a CAS infinitely many times, while competing processes complete infinitely many operations. This is indeed a possible scenario in the lock-free help-free linearizable queue of Michael and Scott [22], where a process may never successfully ENQUEUE due to infinitely many other ENQUEUE operations.

5. GLOBAL VIEW TYPES

In this section we investigate a different set of types, that can also not be obtained in a wait-free manner without using help. These are types that support an operation that returns some kind of a global view. We start by addressing a specific example: a single-scanner snapshot. We later identify accurately what other types belong to this group. The technique of the proof used here is similar to that of Section 4, but the details are different and more complicated.

The single scanner snapshot type supports two operations: UPDATE and SCAN. Each process is associated with a single register entry, which is initially set to $\perp$. An UPDATE operation modifies the value of the register associated with the updater, and a SCAN operation returns an atomic view (snapshot) of all the registers. This variant is referred to as a single-writer snapshot, unlike a mulit-writer snapshot object that allows any process to write to any of the shared registers. In a single scanner snapshot, only a single SCAN operation is allowed at any given moment[4].

Let S be a linearizable, help-free implementation of a single scanner snapshot. We prove that S is not wait-free. For convenience, we assume S is lock-free, as otherwise, it is not wait-free and we are done. Consider a system of three processes, p_1, p_2, and p_3. The program of p_1 is a single UPDATE(0) operation, the program of p_2 is an infinite sequence alternating between UPDATE(0) and UPDATE(1) operations, and the program of process p_3 is an infinite sequence of SCAN operations.

Again, we build an infinite history h, such that processes p_1, p_2, and p_3 follow their respective programs. This time, we show that in h either p_1 executes infinitely many (failed) CAS steps, yet never completes its operation (as before), or alternatively, that starting at some point, neither p_1 nor p_2 complete any more operations, but at least one of them executes infinitely many steps.

The algorithm for constructing this history is depicted in Figure 2. In every iteration, the operations of p_1, p_2, p_3 are denoted op_1, op_2, op_3 respectively. In lines 6–11, processes p_1 and p_2 are scheduled to run their programs as long as neither op_1 nor op_2 is decided before op_3. After the loop is ended, if p_1 takes another step op_1 will be decided before op_3, and if p_2 takes another step then op_2 will be decided before op_3.

Then, in lines 12–13, p_3 is run as much as possible without changing the property achieved at the end of the previous loop. That is, when the loop of lines 12–13 is stopped, it is still true that 1) if p_1 takes another step then op_1 will be decided before op_3, and 2) if p_2 takes another step then op_2 will be decided before op_3. However, if p_3 will take another step, then at least one of (1) and (2) will no longer hold.

Now, the execution is divided into two cases. The first possibility is that if p_3 takes another step, both (1) and (2) will cease to hold simultaneously. In this case, similarly to the proof of Theorem 4.18, we show that both the CAS operations of p_1 and p_2 are to the same address, we allow p_2 to successfully executes its CAS, and let p_1 attempt its CAS and fail. Afterwards both op_2 and op_3

1: $h = \epsilon$;
2: while (true) ▷ main loop
3: op_1 = the first uncompleted operation of p_1;
4: op_2 = the first uncompleted operation of p_2;
5: op_3 = the first uncompleted operation of p_3; ▷ a scan
6: while (true) ▷ first inner loop
7: if op_1 is not decided before op_3 in $h \circ p_1$
8: $h = h \circ p_1$; continue; ▷ goto line 6
9: if op_2 is not decided before op_3 in $h \circ p_2$
10: $h = h \circ p_2$; continue; ▷ goto line 6
11: break; ▷ goto line 12
12: while (op_1 is decided before op_3 in $h \circ p_3 \circ p_1$ and op_2 is decided before op_3 in $h \circ p_3 \circ p_2$) ▷ second inner loop
13: $h = h \circ p_3$
14: if (op_1 is not decided before op_3 in $h \circ p_3 \circ p_1$ and op_2 is not decided before op_3 in $h \circ p_3 \circ p_2$)
15: $h = h \circ p_2$; ▷ this step will be proved to be a CAS
16: $h = h \circ p_1$; ▷ this step will be proved to be a failed CAS
17: while (op_2 is not completed in h) ▷ complete op_2
18: $h = h \circ p_2$;
19: else
20: Let $k \in \{1, 2\}$ satisfy op_k is not decided before op_3 in $h \circ p_3 \circ p_k$
21: Let $j \in \{1, 2\}$ satisfy op_j is decided before op_3 in $h \circ p_3 \circ p_j$
22: $h = h \circ p_3$;
23: $h = h \circ p_k$;
24: while (op_3 is not completed in h) ▷ complete op_3
25: $h = h \circ p_3$;

Figure 2: The algorithm for constructing the history in the proof of Theorem 5.1.

are completed, and we repeat the process with the next operations of p_2 and p_3.

The other possibility is that the next step of p_3 only causes one of the conditions (1) and (2) to cease to hold. Then, we allow p_3 to take the next step, and afterwards schedule the process (either p_1 or p_2) that can take a step without causing its operation to be decided before op_3. We prove this step is not a "real" progress, and cannot be the last step in the operation. Afterwards we allow op_3 to be completed, and repeat the process with the next operation of p_3.

The proof is available in the full paper. The full paper also formally defines a family of types, global view types, for which the proof applies. Natural examples of global view types are all variants of the snapshot, an increment object, and the fetch-and-cons.

THEOREM 5.1. *A global view type has no linearizable, wait-free, help-free implementation.*

6. TYPES THAT DO NOT REQUIRE HELP

In this section, we establish that some types can be implemented in a wait-free manner without using help. Loosely speaking, if the type operations dependency is weak enough then no help is required. As a trivial example, consider the *vacuous type*. A vacuous object supports only one operation, NO-OP, which receives no input parameters and returns no output parameters (void). Thus, the result of a NO-OP does not depend on the execution of any previous operations. Consequently, there is no operations dependency at all in the vacuous type. It can trivially be implemented by simply returning void without executing any computation steps, and without employing help.

6.1 A Help-Free Wait-Free Set

As a more interesting example, consider the *set* type of a finite domain. The set type supports three operations, INSERT, DELETE,

[4] Formally, the type is a snapshot, and a single-scanner implementation is a constrained implementation of it, in the sense that its correctness is only guaranteed as long as no two SCAN operations are executed concurrently.

```
bool insert(int key) {
    bool result = CAS(A[key],0,1);          ▷ linearization point
    return result; }
bool delete (int key) {
    bool result = CAS(A[key],1,0);          ▷ linearization point
    return result; }
bool contains (int key) {
    bool result = (A[key] == 1);            ▷ linearization point
    return result; }
```

Figure 3: A help-free wait-free set implementation

and CONTAINS. Each of the operations receives a single input parameter which is a key in the set domain, and returns a boolean value. An INSERT operation adds the given key to the set and returns true if the key is not already in the set, otherwise it does nothing and returns false. A DELETE operation removes a key from the set and returns true if the key is present in the set, otherwise it does nothing and returns false. A CONTAINS operation returns true if and only if the input key exists in the set.

Consider the following wait-free help-free set implementation given in Figure 3. The implementation uses an array with a bit for every key in the set domain. Initially, all bits are set to zero, and the set is empty. To insert a key, a process performs a CAS operation that changes the bit from zero to one. If the CAS succeeds, the process returns true. If the CAS fails, that means that the key is already in the set, and the process returns false. Deletion is executed symmetrically by CASing from one to zero, and contains reads the appropriate bit and returns true if and only if it is set to one.

In this set algorithm, it is easy to specify the linearization point of each operation. In fact, every operation consists of only a single computation step, which is the linearization point of that operation. For any type, an obstruction-free implementation in which the linearization point of every operation can be specified as a step in the execution of *the same* operation is help-free.

The function f that proves such an implementation is help-free is derived naturally from the linearization points. For each given history, the operations are ordered according to the order of the execution of their linearization points. Consider a type T, an obstruction-free implementation of it O, and the corresponding set of histories H. Assume the code of O specifies the linearization point of each operation at the execution of a specific computation step of the same operation. Let f be the linearization function derived from this specification.

CLAIM 6.1. *For every $h \in H$, every two operations op_1, op_2, and a single computation step γ such that $h \circ \gamma \in H$, it holds that if op_1 is decided before op_2 in $h \circ \gamma$ and op_1 is not decided before op_2 in h, then γ is the linearization point of op_1.*

As a direct result, γ is executed by the owner of op_1, and thus O is help-free.

PROOF. First, we observe that op_1 is not yet linearized in h. If it were, then the order between op_1 and op_2 would have already been decided: were op_2 linearized before op_1 then op_2 would have been decided before op_1, and were op_1 linearized before op_2 or op_1 is linearized and op_2 not, then op_1 would have been decided before op_2. Thus, op_1 cannot be linearized in h.

Second, we observe that op_1 is linearized in $h \circ \gamma$. Were it not, then a solo execution of the owner of op_2 until the linearization of op_2 would have linearized op_2 before op_1, contradicting the assumption that op_1 is decided before op_2 in $h \circ \gamma$. □

```
void WriteMax(int key) {
    while(true) {
        int local = value;          ▷ linearization point if value ≥ key
        if (local ≥ key)
            return;
        if (CAS(value, local, key));        ▷ l.p. if the CAS succeeds
            return;
} }
int ReadMax() {
    int result = value;                     ▷ linearization point
    return result;
}
```

Figure 4: A help-free wait-free max register implementation

6.2 A Help-Free Wait-Free Max Register

In the full paper we prove that a lock-free max register cannot be help-free if only READS and WRITES are available. In this subsection we show that a help-free wait-free max register is possible when using the CAS primitive. The implementation uses a shared integer, denoted `value`, initialized to zero. This integer holds the current max value. The implementation is given in Figure 4.

A WRITEMAX operation first reads the shared integer `value`. If it is greater than or equal to the input key, then the operation simply returns. Otherwise it tries by a CAS to replace the old (smaller) value with the operation's input key. If the CAS succeeds, the operation returns. Otherwise the operation starts again from the beginning. This implementation is wait-free because each time the CAS fails, the shared `value` grows by at least one. Thus, a WRITEMAX(x) operation is guaranteed to return after a maximum of x iterations. A READMAX operation simply reads the `value` and returns it.

Help-Freedom is proved similarly to the wait-free help-free set, using Claim 6.1. In the given max register implementation, the linearization point of every operation can be specified as a step in the execution of *the same* operation, and thus it is help-free. The linearization point of a WRITEMAX operation is always its last computation step. This is either reading the `value` variable (if the read value is greater than the key), or the CAS (if the CAS succeeds). The linearization point of a READMAX is reading the `value`.

7. A UNIVERSALITY OF FETCH-AND-CONS

A fetch-and-cons object allows a process to atomically add an item to the beginning of a list and return the items following it. We show that given a help-free wait-free fetch-and-cons primitive, one can implement any type in a linearizable wait-free help-free manner. Not surprisingly for a universal object, both Theorems 4.18 and 5.1 hold for fetch-and-cons and show it cannot be implemented in a help-free wait-free manner.

To show that fetch-and-cons is indeed universal, we use a known wait-free reduction from any sequential object to fetch-and-cons, described in detail in [17]. We claim that the reduction is help-free. In essence, each process executes every operation in two parts. First, the process calls fetch-and-cons to add the description of the operation (such as ENQUEUE(2)) to the head of the list, and gets all the operations that preceded it. This fetch-and-cons is the linearization point of the operation.

Second, the process computes the results of its operation by examining all the operations from the beginning of the execution, and thus determining the "state" prior to its own operation and the appropriate result. Note that since every operation is linearized in its own fetch-and-cons step, this reduction is help-free by Claim 6.1.

8. DISCUSSION

This paper studies the fundamental notion of help for wait-free concurrent algorithms. It formalizes the notion, and presents conditions under which concurrent data structures must use help to obtain wait-freedom.

We view our contribution as a lower-bound type of result, which sheds light on a key element that implementations of certain object types must contain. As such, we hope it will have a significant impact on both research and design of concurrent data structures. First, we believe it can lead to modularity in designs of implementations that are shown to require a helping mechanism in order to be wait-free, by allowing to pinpoint the place where help occurs.

Second, we ask whether our definition of help can be improved in any sense, and expect this to be an important line of further research. We think that our proposed definition is a good one, but there exist other possible definitions as well. An open question is how various formalizations of this notion relate to each other. Another important open problem is to find a definition for the other notion of help, as we distinguish in the introduction. Such a definition should capture the mechanisms that allow a process to set the ground for its own operation by possibly assisting another operation, for the sole purpose of completing its own operation. In this paper we do not refer to the latter as help, as captured by our definition.

An additional open problem is the further characterizations of families of data structures that require help to obtain wait-freedom. For example, we conjecture that *perturbable objects* [18] cannot have wait-free help-free implementations when using only READ and WRITE primitives, but the proof would need to substantially extend our arguments for the max register type.

Acknowledgements.

The authors thank Nir Shavit for intriguing discussions, and the anonymous referees of a previous version of the paper for helpful comments. The first author is supported in part by ISF Grant 1696/14. The second and third authors are supported in part by ISF Grant 274/14.

9. REFERENCES

[1] Y. Afek, H. Attiya, D. Dolev, E. Gafni, M. Merritt, and N. Shavit. Atomic snapshots of shared memory. *J. ACM*, 40(4):873–890, Sept. 1993.

[2] D. Alistarh, K. Censor-Hillel, and N. Shavit. Are lock-free concurrent algorithms practically wait-free? In *Symposium on Theory of Computing, (STOC)*, pages 714–723, 2014.

[3] J. Aspnes, H. Attiya, and K. Censor-Hillel. Polylogarithmic concurrent data structures from monotone circuits. *J. ACM*, 59(1):2:1–2:24, Mar. 2012.

[4] H. Attiya and J. Welch. *Distributed Computing: Fundamentals, Simulations and Advanced Topics (2nd edition)*. John Wiley Interscience, March 2004.

[5] G. Barnes. A method for implementing lock-free shared-data structures. In *SPAA*, pages 261–270, 1993.

[6] F. Ellen, P. Fatourou, E. Kosmas, A. Milani, and C. Travers. Universal constructions that ensure disjoint-access parallelism and wait-freedom. In *Proceedings of the 31st ACM Symposium on Principles of Distributed Computing (PODC)*, pages 115–124, 2012.

[7] F. Ellen, D. Hendler, and N. Shavit. On the inherent sequentiality of concurrent objects. *SIAM J. Comput.*, 41(3):519–536, 2012.

[8] P. Fatourou and N. D. Kallimanis. A highly-efficient wait-free universal construction. In *SPAA*, pages 325–334, 2011.

[9] F. E. Fich, V. Luchangco, M. Moir, and N. Shavit. Obstruction-free algorithms can be practically wait-free. In *19th International Symposium on Distributed Computing (DISC)*, pages 78–92, 2005.

[10] M. J. Fischer, N. A. Lynch, and M. S. Paterson. Impossibility of distributed consensus with one faulty process. *J. ACM*, 32(2):374–382, Apr. 1985.

[11] W. M. Golab, L. Higham, and P. Woelfel. Linearizable implementations do not suffice for randomized distributed computation. In *Proceedings of the 43rd ACM Symposium on Theory of Computing, STOC 2011, San Jose, CA, USA, 6-8 June 2011*, pages 373–382, 2011.

[12] M. Herlihy. A methodology for implementing highly concurrent data structures. In *Proceedings of the Second ACM SIGPLAN Symposium on Principles & Practice of Parallel Programming (PPOPP)*, pages 197–206, 1990.

[13] M. Herlihy. Wait-free synchronization. *ACM Trans. Program. Lang. Syst.*, 13(1):124–149, Jan. 1991.

[14] M. Herlihy and N. Shavit. *The Art of Multiprocessor Programming*. Morgan Kaufmann, 2008.

[15] M. Herlihy and N. Shavit. On the nature of progress. In *Proceedings of the 15th International Conference on Principles of Distributed Systems (OPODIS)*, pages 313–328, 2011.

[16] M. Herlihy and J. M. Wing. Linearizability: A correctness condition for concurrent objects. *ACM Trans. Program. Lang. Syst.*, 12(3):463–492, 1990.

[17] M. P. Herlihy. Impossibility and universality results for wait-free synchronization. In *Proceedings of the Seventh Annual ACM Symposium on Principles of Distributed Computing (PODC)*, pages 276–290, 1988.

[18] P. Jayanti, K. Tan, and S. Toueg. Time and space lower bounds for nonblocking implementations. *SIAM J. Comput.*, 30(2):438–456, 2000.

[19] A. Kogan and E. Petrank. Wait-free queues with multiple enqueuers and dequeuers. In *PPOPP*, pages 223–234, 2011.

[20] A. Kogan and E. Petrank. A methodology for creating fast wait-free data structures. In *PPOPP*, pages 141–150, 2012.

[21] L. Lamport. A new solution of dijkstra's concurrent programming problem. *Commun. ACM*, 17(8):453–455, Aug. 1974.

[22] M. M. Michael and M. L. Scott. Simple, fast, and practical non-blocking and blocking concurrent queue algorithms. In *Proceedings of the Fifteenth Annual ACM Symposium on Principles of Distributed Computing, Philadelphia, Pennsylvania, USA, May 23-26, 1996*, pages 267–275, 1996.

[23] S. A. Plotkin. Sticky bits and universality of consensus. In *Proceedings of the Eighth Annual ACM Symposium on Principles of Distributed Computing (PODC)*, pages 159–175, 1989.

[24] E. Ruppert. Determining consensus numbers. *SIAM J. Comput.*, 30(4):1156–1168, 2000.

[25] S. Timnat, A. Braginsky, A. Kogan, and E. Petrank. Wait-free linked-lists. In *OPODIS*, 2012.

[26] S. Timnat and E. Petrank. A practical wait-free simulation for lock-free data structures. In *ACM SIGPLAN Symposium on Principles and Practice of Parallel Programming (PPOPP)*, pages 357–368, 2014.

Lock-Free Algorithms under Stochastic Schedulers

Dan Alistarh
Microsoft Research
Cambridge
dan.alistarh@microsoft.com

Thomas Sauerwald
Computer Laboratory
University of Cambridge
tms41@cam.ac.uk

Milan Vojnović
Microsoft Research
Cambridge
milanv@microsoft.com

ABSTRACT

In this work, we consider the following random process, motivated by the analysis of lock-free concurrent algorithms under high memory contention. In each round, a new scheduling step is allocated to one of n threads, according to a distribution $\mathbf{p} = (p_1, p_2, \ldots, p_n)$, where thread i is scheduled with probability p_i. When some thread first reaches a set threshold of executed steps, it registers a *win*, completing its current operation, and resets its step count to 1. At the same time, threads whose step count was close to the threshold also get reset because of the win, but to 0 steps, being penalized for *almost* winning. We are interested in two questions: how often does *some* thread complete an operation (*system latency*), and how often does a *specific* thread complete an operation (*individual latency*)?

We provide asymptotically tight bounds for the system and individual latency of this general concurrency pattern, for arbitrary scheduling distributions $\mathbf{p}$. Surprisingly, a simple characterization exists: in expectation, the system will complete a new operation every $\Theta(1/\|\mathbf{p}\|_2)$ steps, while thread i will complete a new operation every $\Theta(\|\mathbf{p}\|_2/p_i^2)$ steps. The proof is interesting in its own right, as it requires a careful analysis of how the higher norms of the vector $\mathbf{p}$ influence the thread step counts and latencies in this random process. Our result offers a simple connection between the scheduling distribution and the average performance of concurrent algorithms, which has several applications.

Categories and Subject Descriptors

E.1 [**Data Structures**]: Distributed Data Structures; F.2.2 [**Analysis of Algorithms and Problem Complexity**]: Nonnumerical Algorithms and Problems

General Terms

Theory

Permission to make digital or hard copies of all or part of this work for personal or classroom use is granted without fee provided that copies are not made or distributed for profit or commercial advantage and that copies bear this notice and the full citation on the first page. Copyrights for components of this work owned by others than ACM must be honored. Abstracting with credit is permitted. To copy otherwise, or republish, to post on servers or to redistribute to lists, requires prior specific permission and/or a fee. Request permissions from permissions@acm.org.
PODC'15, July 21–23, 2015, Donostia-San Sebastián, Spain.
Copyright © 2015 ACM 978-1-4503-3617-8 /15/07 ...$15.00.
DOI: http://dx.doi.org/10.1145/2767386.2767430 .

Keywords

Shared memory; lock-free algorithms; scheduling

1. INTRODUCTION

One of the main computing trends of the last decade has been increased pressure on concurrent algorithms and data structures to *scale* under concurrency. *Lock-free (non-blocking)* data structures [15] represent a promising solution to this problem, thanks to their good performance and relatively simple structure. Unlike lock-based approaches, these data structures follow the principle that some operation should always complete every finite number of steps; the blocking of a single execution thread should never prevent the whole system from progressing. Efficient lock-free implementations are now known for many classic data structures, such as counters, stacks, queues, lists, or trees [10,15, 16,18,22,24].

Recently, there has been increased interest in the analytical properties of lock-free data structures [1,9,16]. Herlihy and Shavit [16] suggested that, on realistic schedules, lock-free algorithms ensure that *each* operation completes in a finite number of its own steps, i.e., that lock-free algorithms are in fact *wait-free* [13]. Alistarh, Censor-Hillel, and Shavit [1] extended this idea and gave a simple stochastic condition on schedules under which any lock-free algorithm becomes wait-free with probability 1: roughly, it is enough for the schedule to have some non-zero probability of picking each thread i in each step. They also gave evidence that such schedules are common in *high memory contention scenarios*, and characterized the performance of a general family of lock-free algorithms, called *Single-CAS Universal (SCU)*,[1] under an idealized *uniform stochastic scheduler*, which picks the next processor to schedule in each step with uniform probability.

More precisely, any algorithm in *SCU* follows a classic *scan-and-validate* pattern: a *scan* region designed to assess the state of the concurrent data structure and to locally compute an updated state, ending with a *validate* step consisting of a read-modify-write operation which atomically checks that the state of the data structure is still consistent with the scan, and, if so, commits the updated state. Crucially, this last validation step may fail if the data structure state changes between the scan and the validation step,

[1]The SCU algorithmic pattern is *lock-free universal* [1,13] in the sense that it can be used to provide a lock-free concurrent implementation for every object that can be specified sequentially.

meaning that some other operation succeeded in the meantime. If validation fails, the current operation restarts. This pattern is common in lock-free algorithms, e.g., [18,24], and in databases with optimistic concurrency control [21].

The Stochastic Game. The analysis of algorithms in *SCU* under stochastic schedulers reduces to the following process [1]: we are given constant operation length $k \geq 2$, n bins (each associated with a thread), and probability distribution $\mathbf{p} = (p_1, p_2, \dots, p_n)$. In each step, we allocate one new ball (scheduler step) into one of the bins, according to the distribution $\mathbf{p}$, where bin i gets the ball with probability p_i. Bins continue to acquire balls, until one of them first reaches a threshold of $k+1$ balls. At this time, the corresponding bin registers a *win* (its thread completes its operation), and gets reset to containing a single ball. Moreover, bins which contain k balls at this time get *reset* to having 0 balls, being penalized for *almost* winning. All other bins maintain their ball count. The rationale for this modeling choice is as follows. A newly completed operation changes the shared state; therefore, any thread that was *about to win*, i.e., within a step of performing its validation will have to first *fail* its validation, after which it must restart its current operation.

Given this process, we are interested in two questions: how often does *some bin* register a win (*system latency*), and how often does *a specific bin i* register a win (*individual latency*)?

The Question. Reference [1] gave bounds for these parameters under a *uniform scheduler distribution* $\mathbf{p} = (1/n, \dots, 1/n)$. However, their technique hinges on the symmetry of the distribution, and does not apply to non-uniform scheduling, leaving open the question of performance under non-uniform contention.

Bounding latencies for general $\mathbf{p}$ is important for several reasons. First, modern processors exhibit consistently non-uniform scheduling, due to non-uniform memory access times. (See references [8, 17] for examples.) Second, key questions remain unsolved: what is the relative *performance advantage* of a thread that gets scheduled with higher probability? What is the *worst-case* scheduling distribution for lock-free algorithms? What is the *optimal* system latency achievable, while guaranteeing some minimal progress guarantees for individual threads?

Contribution. In this paper, we give asymptotically tight bounds on the performance of lock-free algorithms following the universal lock-free *SCU* pattern, in the common case where operations have constant length, with respect to any *arbitrary* sequence of scheduling distributions $\mathbf{p}(n)$, where n is the number of processors.[2]

THEOREM 1. *Given an arbitrary scheduling distribution $\mathbf{p} = (p_1, p_2, \dots, p_n)$, and constant operation length k, algorithms in* SCU *have system latency $\Theta(1/\|\mathbf{p}\|_2)$. Each process i has individual latency $\Theta(\|\mathbf{p}\|_2/p_i^2)$.*

Given the relatively complex structure of the algorithms, we find it surprising that such a simple characterization exists for general $\mathbf{p}$, and that this characterization does not depend on any higher norm of $\mathbf{p}$. By contrast, we also show that simple modifications of the pattern, where all bins get reset to one ball upon reset, induce system latency system latency $\Theta(1/\|\mathbf{p}\|_k)$ and individual latency $\Theta(p_i^k/\mathbf{p}\|_k)$. (These modifications correspond to obstruction-free algorithms [4, 14].)

Analysis Overview. The technical argument behind these bounds is quite non-trivial. We express the balls-into-bins game corresponding to an algorithm as a Markov chain, where each state is a possible configuration of occupancies of the bins, and each transition corresponds to a new ball being placed. An interesting feature of this chain is that a win by bin i also affects the state of bins containing k balls before i's win, which induces non-trivial correlations between occupancies of the bins. It would be enough to characterize the stationary distribution of this chain: the rate at which bin i wins is the stationary probability of bin i transitioning from k balls to 1 ball, while the win rate of the system is the sum of individual rates. These win rates are the reciprocals of individual and system latencies, respectively.

Computing the stationary distribution of such a process for general $\mathbf{p}$, n, and k is infeasible, so we adopt a more elaborate strategy. We begin by bounding the system latency. Our main gadget for this part of the argument is to analyze a simplified chain, where all bin loads are considered modulo k. This choice is somewhat unintuitive, since this simplification obscures exactly the probability that a bin has k balls, which directly determines the bin winning rates. However, the stationary distribution of this simpler chain is easier to compute, and we show that it implies a clean $\sqrt{k}/\|\mathbf{p}\|_2$ lower bound on the expected system latency.

The system latency upper bound is more involved. We split the execution into phases, where a phase is the interval between two wins. (The expected length of this interval is the system latency.) We consider the state of the chain at a *random* time t, and wish to bound the *residual* (remaining) phase length from such a time. We partition bins according to the number of balls they contain at t, where a bin is at level $1 \leq \ell \leq k+1$ if it still needs ℓ balls to reach $k+1$ and win the phase. Ideally, we would like to argue that there are many bins at low levels, and that these bins will dominate the phase competition, winning within a small number of steps.

However, since the distribution $\mathbf{p}$ may be unbalanced, the probability weight contained by each level ℓ at time t might not be well-concentrated. We overcome this technical obstacle by a careful argument which merges the Hoeffding bounds for each level ℓ, showing that the expected residual phase length has to be $O(1/\|\mathbf{p}\|_2)$, irrespective of the structure of $\mathbf{p}$. We prove high probability bounds similarly.

We then focus on bounding individual latencies, and in particular on upper and lower bounds on the probability w_i that a specific bin (thread) i wins a *random* phase. While the $\Omega(p_i^2/\|\mathbf{p}\|_2^2)$ lower bound on w_i is relatively simple, following by the previous analysis, the upper bound on w_i is non-standard.

To obtain the bound, we characterize the occupancies of *all* bins at the beginning of a random phase, to ensure that bin i gets enough competition. These occupancies are complex, and not well-concentrated, as we do not restrict $\mathbf{p}$ and k. We circumvent this problem by first considering the occupancy distribution at a random time step. Then we build a connection between the probability that the bin occupancies are unbalanced at *a random time* and the probability that the bin occupancies are unbalanced at *the beginning of*

[2]We express complexity in terms of the number of threads n, as is standard; throughout, we write $\mathbf{p}$ instead of $\mathbf{p}(n)$ for brevity.

a random phase. The proof of this relation employs an interesting adversarial counting argument. We roughly show that bin i gets a lot of competition on average, which implies a matching upper bound of $O(p_i^2/\|\mathbf{p}\|_2^2)$ on i's winning probability, implying individual latency bounds.

Applications. Our result relates the scheduling distribution $\mathbf{p}$ with the average performance of a lock-free algorithm in *SCU*, and provides simple answers to the questions on the relative latency advantage of processors (*ratio of scheduling probabilities squared*), and the worst-case scheduling distribution (*uniform*).

It has two additional practical applications: given the simple relation between $\mathbf{p}$ and the performance metrics, determining the scheduling probabilities which minimize system latency, i.e., the optimal backoff scheme, under a set of individual latency constraints, becomes a well-defined optimization problem.

Second, a useful by-product of our technical framework is that we can understand the average-case behavior of various other concurrency patterns under arbitrary scheduling distributions. A particularly interesting pattern is when, on a win by thread i, *all* threads get reset to 1, irrespective of their current step count, which corresponds to the general family of *obstruction-free* concurrent algorithms, e.g. [4, 14], and to database transactions with optimistic concurrency control, e.g., [21, Chapter 7]. Our framework shows that the system latency of such algorithms is $\Theta(1/\|\mathbf{p}\|_k)$. This implies a separation in terms of average complexity between this algorithmic class and lock-free algorithms, for virtually any scheduling distribution $\mathbf{p}$.

2. RELATED WORK

Aspnes [3] was the first to consider distributed algorithms under randomized schedulers, solving consensus efficiently under a scheduler model different from the one we consider. Alistarh, Censor-Hillel, and Shavit [1] introduced the *stochastic* scheduler model, and isolated the *SCU* algorithmic pattern.

Their work implies bounds on the system and individual latencies for *SCU* given $\mathbf{p} = (1/n, 1/n, \ldots, 1/n)$. Specifically, they showed that system latency is $O(\sqrt{n})$ steps, while individual latency is $O(n\sqrt{n})$ steps. In brief, their analysis works by expressing the algorithm as a Markov chain, and noticing that, since both the operation code and the scheduling distribution are *symmetric*, the general Markov chain can be collapsed onto a simpler chain, called the *global* chain. This mapping is a proper *lifting* [7, 12] of the general chain, and characterizing the stationary distribution of the global chain is enough to bound the latency of the algorithm. One main technical step is bounding the stationary probabilities of the global chain; this works by carefully characterizing the chain for $k = 2$, and then generalizing to general constants k by symmetry.

We analyze algorithms in *SCU* under *arbitrary distributions* $\mathbf{p}$, which requires us to take a different approach. We cannot employ Markov chain lifting, since states that are symmetric in terms of bin occupancies may now have completely different probabilities in the stationary distribution of the chain. Similarly, we can no longer reduce the system latency analysis to the case $k = 2$, since the generalization to arbitrary k relies on symmetry of the distribution. Finally, in the symmetric case, system latency immediately determines the individual latencies, as two bins have exactly the same probability of winning an arbitrary phase. This is clearly no longer the case for non-uniform $\mathbf{p}$, and, in fact, determining the individual winning probabilities given the system latency is one of the main technical components of our argument. For uniform $\mathbf{p}$, we obtain the same asymptotic bounds as [1], although their lifting argument yields tighter constants.

Balls-into-bins processes [5] are popular abstractions for resource allocation problems, where balls (tasks, requests) are randomly allocated to bins (resources, processors). Such processes are relatively well understood in the uniform setting [5, 19], but recently there has been a growing interest in non-uniform settings, where either balls have different weights [23] or bins have correlated probabilities to be picked [11].

3. PRELIMINARIES

3.1 Modeling

The Shared Memory Model. In this model, n processes (threads) communicate through registers, on which they perform read, write, or compare-and-swap(CAS) atomic operations. A CAS operation takes three arguments (R, *expectedVal*, *newVal*), where R is the register on which it is applied, *expectedVal* is the expected value of the register, and *newVal* is the new value to be written. The operation compares *expVal* with the current value v of R, and atomically updates R to *newVal* if the expected value matches the current value, i.e. $expVal = v$. In this case, we say that the CAS *succeeds*. Otherwise, the value of R is not updated, and the CAS *fails*.

Each algorithm implements a shared object, which is an abstraction providing a set of methods, each given by its sequential specification. The algorithm is composed of shared-memory steps and local computation. The order in which these steps are performed is controlled by a *scheduler*.

Stochastic Schedulers. In general, a scheduler for n processes can be defined by a triple (Π_t, A_t, θ). For each time step $t \geq 1$, Π_t is a probability distribution for scheduling the n processes at time t, and A_t is the subset of *possibly active* processes at time step t. At time step $t \geq 1$, the distribution Π_t gives, for every $i \in \{1, \ldots, n\}$ a probability p_i^t, with which process i is scheduled. The distribution Π_t may depend on arbitrary outside factors, such as the current state of the algorithm being scheduled. For every $t \geq 1$, the parameters ensure the following: *(i)* $\sum_{i=1}^n p_i^t = 1$; *(ii)* For every process $i \in A_t$, $p_i^t \geq \theta$; *(iii)* For every process $i \notin A_t$, $p_i^t = 0$; *(iv)* $A_{t+1} \subseteq A_t$. A scheduler (Π_t, A_t, θ) is *stochastic* if $\theta > 0$. We consider a static *non-uniform* scheduler, which picks the next process to schedule using a fixed distribution $\mathbf{p} = (p_1, p_2, \ldots, p_n)$ at every time t.

Executions and Schedules. An execution is a sequence of operations performed by the processes. Since process steps are atomic, we can assume discrete time, where at every time unit a single process is scheduled. In a time unit, a process performs any number of local computations or coin flips, after which it issues a *step*, which consists of a single shared memory operation. Whenever a process is scheduled to take a new step by the scheduler, it performs its local computation and then executes its next step, as dictated by the algorithm. Thus, the *schedule* is a possibly infinite sequence of process identifiers. If process i is in position t in the sequence, then it is active at time t.

```
1 Shared: registers R1, R2, ..., Rk
2    procedure operation()
3    while true do
4       v1 ← R1.read(); v2 ← R2.read(); ...;
        vk−1 ← Rk−1.read()
5       vk ← Rk.read() /* Scan region */
6       v' ← new proposed state based on
        v1, v2, ..., vk
7       flag ← CAS(Rk, vk, v')  /* Validation
        step */
8       if flag = true then
9          output success
```

Algorithm 1: The structure of the lock-free algorithms in *SCU*.

Progress Guarantees. An implementation is *lock-free (non-blocking)* if, for each time t in the execution, there exists a finite bound T_t such that *some* operation returns within the next T_t steps. An implementation is *wait-free* if, for every operation, there exists a finite bound T on the number of steps that the operation can take before returning.

3.2 Algorithmic Pattern and Complexity Measures

We now describe the *Single-CAS Universal* algorithmic pattern which is the focus of our analysis. This pattern can be used to provide a lock-free concurrent implementation of any sequential object, via a straightforward extension of Herlihy's universal construction [13]. This pattern is also the basis for several efficient implementations of shared objects, such as counters, lists, stacks, queues, or skip-lists, e.g. [10, 15, 24].

An operation using the *SCU* pattern consists of a *scan-and-validate* loop consisting of k steps reading shared registers $R_1, R_2, \ldots, R_k$, ending with a *validation* step which performs a *compare-and-swap* operation on the last read location R_k. (Please see Algorithm 1.) If this compare-and-swap operation succeeds, then the operation returns successfully. Otherwise, if the operation fails, and the process re-issues the operation.

Complexity Metrics. We address the following question: what is the performance of an arbitrary algorithm A in *SCU*, under an arbitrary non-uniform stochastic scheduler given by the distribution $\mathbf{p} = (p_1, p_2, \ldots, p_n)$?

We consider two natural performance measures. The first is *system latency*, i.e., the expected number of time steps between two completed operations by the system. The second is *individual latency*, i.e., the expected number of time steps between two committed operations by a *specific* process i. Individual latency is the correspondent of the *step complexity* metric, which measures the number of individual steps taken by an operation in order to complete.

3.3 Markov Chain Formulation and Preliminary Results

In the following, we fix an algorithm A in *SCU*, whose structure is fixed, and follows the pattern in Algorithm 1. We assume that each process executes an infinite number of operations, and that each process executes its next operation as soon as it completes the current one.

Modeling the Algorithm. First, notice that we can reduce A to the following balls-into-bins game. Consider a system of n bins, representing the processes, each starting with one ball. This state corresponds to the process being about to read the value of R_1. In each scheduling round, the scheduler allocates a new ball (i.e., a step) into one of the n bins: bin i gets the ball with probability p_i. Bins continue to receive balls until reaching k balls, which corresponds to being about to perform the CAS operation in line 7 in Algorithm 1.

Following the algorithm, whenever the scheduler places a ball into a bin that already contains k balls, a new operation gets completed and we therefore record a *win* by the system and by the corresponding process. Crucially, on a win by process i, the bin corresponding to the process is reset to having one ball, whereas all the other bins which had exactly k balls before i's win will be reset to 0 balls.

Markov Chain Formulation. It is easy to see that the system can be modeled as a discrete-time Markov chain. At the arrival of the t-th ball, a bin $I(t)$ is selected at random by drawing a sample from the distribution $\mathbf{p} = (p_1, p_2, \ldots, p_n)$. The state of the system is defined by the bin occupancies $X(t) = (X_1(t), X_2(t), \ldots, X_n(t))$ before the arrival of the t-th ball. If the selected bin has less than k balls, i.e., $X_{I(t)}(t) \in \{0, \ldots, k-1\}$, then we simply increment $X_{I(t)}$ by 1 and continue. Otherwise, if $X_{I(t)}(t) = k$, we reset $I(t)$ to one ball, i.e., $X_{I(t)}(t+1) = 1$. Further, we reset all other bins $j \neq I(t)$ with $X_j(t) = k$ so that $X_j(t+1) = 0$.[3] The process of bin occupancies $\{X(t)\}_{t\geq 0}$ is a discrete-time Markov chain with the finite state space $\{0, 1, \ldots, k\}^n$.

Stationary Distribution and Ergodicity. Under the assumption $p_i > 0$ for each bin i, the transition matrix of the Markov chain $\{X(t)\}_{t\geq 0}$ is irreducible, and thus, has a unique stationary distribution π (see, e.g., [6]).

The chain $\{X(t)\}_{t\geq 0}$ is not aperiodic. To resolve this issue, we simply consider a perturbed version that is parameterized with $\delta \in (0, 1)$ such that at each time step a new ball arrives with probability $1 - \delta$ and is assigned to one of the bins according to the given distribution $\mathbf{p}$, and otherwise no ball arrives in the given time step and the occupancies of the bins remain unchanged. Such a perturbation results in a "lazy" Markov chain $\{X^{\delta}(t)\}_{t\geq 0}$ that has the same stationary distribution, but unlike the original chain, it is aperiodic, and hence, ergodic. The increase of the system and individual expected latencies is only for a factor $1/(1-\delta)$, which can be made arbitrarily close to 1 by taking δ small enough. In what follows, we will tacitly assume that the given vector $\mathbf{p}$ is already chosen so that the chain $\{X(t)\}_{t\geq 0}$ is ergodic, i.e., irreducible and aperiodic.

Win Points, Phases, and Latencies. For the Markov chain $\{X(t)\}_{t\geq 0}$, we say that a time-step t is a *win point* if at time-step t bin i is selected such that $X_i(t-1) = k$. The win points are technically reset points of the *point process* $T_0 \leq 0 < T_1 < T_2 < \ldots$ where T_r is the time-step of the r-th win point.

A *phase* corresponds to the interval of time-steps starting at a win point and ending in the time-step just before the next win point. The phases are enumerated such that the 0-th phase corresponds to the interval of time-steps $[T_0, T_1)$, first phase corresponds to the interval of time-steps $[T_1, T_2)$ and so on. The length of the r-th phase is denoted by S_r. Since we are interested in the long-run average performance,

[3]The winning bin is reset to one ball since its next step is the first step in the next operation, whereas all other bins with $X_j(t) = k$ get reset to 0 since they must fail their validation (CAS operation) before being able to restart their operation.

we shall consider expected values with respect to the stationary distribution of the bin occupancies. We refer to a *random time* t to be an arbitrary time t under the assumption that the initial bin occupancies at time 0 are according to the stationary distribution. Under this assumption, the distribution of the bin occupancies at any given time $t \geq 0$ is the stationary distribution.

We shall also consider the state of the bin occupancies embedded at the win points. We refer to a *random phase* r to be an arbitrary phase r under assumption that the initial bin occupancies at time 0 are according to the stationary distribution of the bin occupancies at a win point. We are interested in characterizing system latency τ, defined as the expected number of time-steps between two consecutive win points, i.e., $\tau = \mathbf{E}[S_r]$. By the Palm inversion formula (see Lemma 1), the rate of win points λ satisfies $\lambda = 1/\tau$. The individual latency τ_i for bin i is the expected number of time steps between two consecutive win points in which bin i wins. Again, by the Palm inversion formula, the rate of wins of bin i, λ_i, satisfies $\lambda_i = 1/\tau_i$. The rates of system win points and individual win points satisfy $\lambda = \sum_{i=1}^{n} \lambda_i$. The winning probability of bin i in a random phase r is denoted with w_i. By the Palm inversion formula, $\lambda_i = \lambda w_i$, for every bin i. The rate of win points for a bin i satisfies $\lambda_i = p_i \cdot \mathbf{Pr}[X_i(t) = k]$, where t is a random time step.

Helper Results. We now state a couple of results which are used throughout the analysis. Their proofs are deferred to the full version of the paper [2].

The first is the Palm inversion formula. This is a well-known relation in the context of renewal and regenerative processes, which relates expectations of a stochastic process with respect to the stationary distribution of the state at an arbitrary time and the stationary distribution of the state at a special point in time. Please see e.g. [6] for further background and for a proof.

LEMMA 1 (PALM INVERSION FORMULA). *Let $X(t)$ be a regenerative process (e.g. see [6]) on the state space E with regeneration points $\cdots < T_{-1} < T_0 = 0 < T_1 < \cdots$ and the let $S_r = T_{r+1} - T_r$ for $r \in \mathbf{Z}$. Suppose that $f : E \to \mathbf{R}$ is such that*

$$\mathbf{E}\left[\sum_{t=0}^{S_0-1} |f(X(t))|\right] < \infty.$$

Suppose π is the stationary distribution of the process $X(t)$. Then, we have

$$\sum_{\mathbf{x}\in E} f(\mathbf{x})\pi(\mathbf{x}) = \frac{\mathbf{E}\left[\sum_{t=0}^{S_0-1} f(X(t))\right]}{\mathbf{E}[S_0]}.$$

If the distribution of S_0 is proper and non-lattice, then for any initial state $\mathbf{x} \in E$,

$$\lim_{t\to\infty} \mathbf{E}[f(X(t)) \mid X(0) = \mathbf{x}] = \sum_{\mathbf{x}\in E} f(\mathbf{x})\pi(\mathbf{x}).$$

The second auxiliary result characterizes the stationary distribution of a simplified stochastic process.

LEMMA 2. *Let $Y(t) = (X_1(t) \bmod k,\ X_2(t) \bmod k,\ \ldots,\ X_n(t) \bmod k)$. Then, $Y(t)$ is an ergodic, discrete-time Markov chain on the state space $\{0, 1, \ldots, k-1\}^n$ with uniform stationary distribution π, i.e.*

$$\lim_{t\to\infty} \mathbf{Pr}[Y(t) = \mathbf{x} \mid Y(0) = \mathbf{y}] = \pi(\mathbf{x}) = 1/k^n,$$
$$\text{for any } \mathbf{x}, \mathbf{y} \in \{0, 1, \ldots, k-1\}^n.$$

The second result characterizes the system latency and probability of winning a random phase for a simpler process, where all bins get reset to 1 on a win. Due to space limitations, the analysis of this process is given in the full version of this paper [2]. This result may be of independent interest, as it is related to non-uniform birthday processes, e.g. [20].

THEOREM 2. *The length S_r of a random phase r and the probabilities w_i that bin i wins an arbitrary phase, in the process where all bins reset to one ball on a win, satisfy: $\mathbf{E}[S_r] \in \left[\frac{(k!/2)^{1/k}}{2\|\mathbf{p}\|_k}, \frac{8ek^k}{\|\mathbf{p}\|_k}\right]$ and $w_i = \Theta\left(\frac{p_i^k}{\|\mathbf{p}\|_k^k}\right)$.*

4. ANALYSIS OF SYSTEM LATENCY

Proof Strategy. We are interested in upper and lower bounds on system latency τ, assuming that the operation length k is a constant. Determining these quantities from the stationary distribution of the Markov chain described in the previous section would be sufficient. Unfortunately, we will not be able to determine such bounds directly, as the occupancies of individual bins are highly correlated. Instead, we take a more roundabout approach: we first consider the stationary distribution of the simplified random process described in Lemma 2, in which bin occupancies are taken modulo k. Analyzing such a process may appear useless at first, as it obscures the probability that a bin contains k balls, which is essential for determining λ. However, we show that a characterization of this simplified process is a clean $\sqrt{k}/\|\mathbf{p}\|_2$ lower bound on system latency τ for the complete stochastic process.

THEOREM 3. *The expected system latency satisfies*

$$\tau \geq \sqrt{k}/\|\mathbf{p}\|_2.$$

PROOF. Fix an arbitrary bin i. By the definition of the Markov chain $\{X(t)\}_{t\geq 0}$, we have that the probability that a bin i contains 0 balls at time $t+1$ is

$$\mathbf{Pr}[X_i(t+1) = 0] = (1-p_i)\mathbf{Pr}[X_i(t) = 0] + \sum_{j\neq i} p_j \mathbf{Pr}[X_j(t) = k, X_i(t) = k],$$

since the bin's state either did not change, or some other bin $j \neq i$ won in the previous step, while i also contained k balls.

Hence, for the expected values with respect to the stationary distribution we have

$$p_i \mathbf{Pr}[X_i(t) = 0] = \sum_{j\neq i} p_j \mathbf{Pr}[X_j(t) = k, X_i(t) = k].$$

By Lemma 2, $\mathbf{Pr}[X_i(t) = 0] + \mathbf{Pr}[X_i(t) = k] = 1/k$. Therefore, we can rewrite the previous relation as

$$\sum_{j=1}^{n} p_j \mathbf{Pr}[X_i(t) = k, X_j(t) = k] = \frac{1}{k} p_i.$$

Using this identity, we obtain

$$\frac{1}{k}\sum_{i=1}^{n} p_i^2 = \sum_{i=1}^{n} p_i \sum_{j=1}^{n} p_j \mathbf{Pr}[X_i(t) = k, X_j(t) = k]$$
$$= \mathbf{E}\left[\left(\sum_{i=1}^{n} p_i \mathbf{1}_{X_i(t)=k}\right)^2\right]$$
$$\geq \left(\sum_{i=1}^{n} p_i \mathbf{Pr}[X_i(t) = k]\right)^2 = \left(\sum_{i=1}^{n} \lambda_i\right)^2 = \lambda^2,$$

where the last inequality is by Jensen's inequality and we use the fact that for every bin i, $\lambda_i = p_i \mathbf{Pr}[X_i(t) = k]$. We have thus showed that $\lambda \leq \sqrt{\sum_{i=1}^{n} p_i^2}/\sqrt{k} = \|\mathbf{p}\|_2/\sqrt{k}$. The proof is completed by recalling that $\tau = 1/\lambda$. □

The proof of the upper bound is more complex, and works as follows. We pick a random time t, and bound the *residual phase length* $S(t)$, i.e., the remaining number of steps until an operation completes. The second step is to bound the length of a phase depending on this quantity; in fact bounding the residual phase length gives a *stronger* measure of performance.

To bound the residual phase length, our starting tool is Lemma 2, which provides a handle on the occupancy distribution modulo k at time t. However, the main difficulty with bounding $S(t)$ is that the occupancy distribution at time t may be quite irregular depending on the "shape" of the vector $\mathbf{p}$. We will take into account these possibilities, merging the Hoeffding bounds at each occupancy level to show that the residual phase length is always $O(1/\|\mathbf{p}\|_2)$.

LEMMA 3. *For a random time t, the residual phase length $S(t)$ satisfies $\mathbf{E}[S(t)] = O(1/\|\mathbf{p}\|_2)$. Moreover, for constant $C > 0$, $\mathbf{Pr}[S(t) \leq C \cdot (\log n)^{1+\frac{\log k}{2}}/\|\mathbf{p}\|_2] \geq 1 - 1/n$.*

PROOF. We partition the bins into *levels* $1, 2, \ldots, k+1$, where a bin is at level ℓ at time t if it needs to acquire ℓ balls in order to win, i.e., it contains $k+1-\ell$ balls at t. Since we are interested in upper bounding the phase length, we can assume that there are no bins at level 1 at time t, as those could only shorten the phase.

For each bin i and level $2 \leq \ell \leq k+1$, we define the indicator random variable $Z_{\ell,i}(t)$ to equal p_i^ℓ if bin i is at level ℓ at time t, and 0, otherwise. Further, define $Z_\ell(t) = \sum_{i=1}^{n} Z_{\ell,i}(t)$. By Lemma 2, we know that $\mathbf{E}[Z_\ell(t)] = \frac{1}{k}\|\mathbf{p}\|_\ell^\ell$ and that $Z_{\ell,1}(t), Z_{\ell,2}(t), \ldots, Z_{\ell,n}(t)$ are independent events for every $2 \leq \ell \leq k+1$. Hence, for fixed ℓ, we apply Hoeffding's inequality to variables $(Z_{\ell,i}(t))_i$ to obtain the following bound

$$\mathbf{Pr}\left[Z_\ell(t) \leq \|\mathbf{p}\|_\ell^\ell/(2k)\right] \leq \exp\left(-\frac{1}{2k^2}\frac{(\sum_{i=1}^{n} p_i^\ell)^2}{\sum_{i=1}^{n} p_i^{2\ell}}\right) =$$
$$\exp\left(-\frac{1}{2k^2}\frac{\|\mathbf{p}\|_\ell^{2\ell}}{\|\mathbf{p}\|_{2\ell}^{2\ell}}\right). \quad (1)$$

Recall that the phase ends as soon as, for some level ℓ, a bin that is at level ℓ at time t acquires ℓ balls. By Theorem 2, we have that, conditional on the values of $(Z_{\ell,i}(t))_{\ell,i}$ the expected residual phase length is

$$\mathbf{E}[S(t) \mid (Z_{\ell,i}(t))_{\ell,i}] = O\Big(\min_{2\leq\ell\leq k+1} \frac{1}{Z_\ell(t)^{1/\ell}}\Big). \quad (2)$$

We now focus on bounding the left-hand side quantity in terms of $1/\|\mathbf{p}\|_2$.

For $2 \leq \ell \leq k$, let $\mathcal{E}_\ell$ be the event that $Z_\ell(t) \leq \|\mathbf{p}\|_\ell^\ell/(2k)$. Let j be the index of the first event $\mathcal{E}_\ell$ that holds when we consider the events $\mathcal{E}_2, \mathcal{E}_3, \ldots, \mathcal{E}_k$ in increasing order of parameter ℓ if any exists, and let j be equal to $k+1$, otherwise. In other words, the norm bounds for all levels $< j$ have failed, and the bound holds at j. Combining the resulting bound on the norm with Equation (2), it follows that $\mathbf{E}[S(t) \mid \overline{\mathcal{E}_2} \wedge \overline{\mathcal{E}_3} \wedge \ldots \wedge \overline{\mathcal{E}_{j-1}} \wedge \mathcal{E}_j] = O(1/\|\mathbf{p}\|_j)$.

Applying the law of total expectation, it follows that there exists a constant $C > 0$ such that

$$\mathbf{E}[S(t)] \leq C\Big(\frac{1}{\|\mathbf{p}\|_2} + \sum_{\ell=2}^{k} \mathbf{Pr}\left[\overline{\mathcal{E}_2} \wedge \overline{\mathcal{E}_3} \wedge \ldots \wedge \overline{\mathcal{E}_\ell}\right] \frac{1}{\|\mathbf{p}\|_{\ell+1}}\Big). \quad (3)$$

Bounding the probability term for fixed ℓ and applying the bound (1) we obtain

$$\mathbf{Pr}\left[\overline{\mathcal{E}_2} \wedge \overline{\mathcal{E}_3} \wedge \ldots \wedge \overline{\mathcal{E}_\ell}\right] \leq \min_{j=2}^{\ell}\Big\{\mathbf{Pr}[\overline{\mathcal{E}_j}]\Big\}$$
$$\leq \Big(\prod_{j=2}^{\ell} \mathbf{Pr}[\overline{\mathcal{E}_j}]\Big)^{1/(\ell-1)} \leq \prod_{j=2}^{\ell} \exp\left(-\frac{1}{2k^2(\ell-1)}\frac{\|\mathbf{p}\|_j^{2j}}{\|\mathbf{p}\|_{2j}^{2j}}\right).$$

Bounding the last term using the fact that $\exp(-x) \leq 1/x$ for $x > 0$, and $\|\mathbf{p}\|_j/\|\mathbf{p}\|_{j+1} \geq 1$, we have

$$\prod_{j=2}^{\ell} \exp\Big(-\frac{1}{2k^2(\ell-1)}\frac{\|\mathbf{p}\|_j^{2j}}{\|\mathbf{p}\|_{2j}^{2j}}\Big) \leq \prod_{j=2}^{\ell} 2(\ell-1)k^2\frac{\|\mathbf{p}\|_{j+1}}{\|\mathbf{p}\|_j}$$
$$\leq (2(\ell-1)k^2)^{\ell-1}\frac{\|\mathbf{p}\|_{\ell+1}}{\|\mathbf{p}\|_2}.$$

Combining with Equation (3), it follows that there exists a constant $C' > 0$ such that

$$\mathbf{E}[S(t)] \leq C'\Big(\frac{1}{\|\mathbf{p}\|_2} + \sum_{\ell=2}^{k}\frac{\|\mathbf{p}\|_{\ell+1}}{\|\mathbf{p}\|_2}\cdot\frac{1}{\|\mathbf{p}\|_{\ell+1}}\Big)$$
$$\leq C' \cdot \frac{k}{\|\mathbf{p}\|_2} = O\Big(\frac{1}{\|\mathbf{p}\|_2}\Big).$$

The proof of the high probability bound is similar, and can be found in the full version of the paper [2]. □

Final Step. To obtain the upper bounds on the phase length, we relate the residual phase length $S(t)$ at a random time t to the expected phase length S_r of a random phase r.

LEMMA 4. *Let S_r be the length of a random phase r, and let $S(t)$ be the residual length of the phase at a random time t. Then the following relations hold: $\mathbf{E}[S_r] \leq 2\,\mathbf{E}[S(t)]$ and $\mathbf{Pr}[S_r > 2\theta] \leq 2\,\mathbf{Pr}[S(t) > \theta]$, for $\theta \geq 0$.*

PROOF. The first claim is showed as follows. By the Palm inversion formula, we have

$$\mathbf{E}[S(t)] = \frac{\mathbf{E}[\sum_{s=0}^{S_r-1}(S_r - s)]}{\mathbf{E}[S_r]} = \frac{\mathbf{E}[S_r(S_r+1)]}{2\,\mathbf{E}[S_r]}$$
$$\geq \frac{\mathbf{E}[S_r^2]}{2\,\mathbf{E}[S_r]} \geq \frac{1}{2}\mathbf{E}[S_r]$$

where the last inequality is by Jensen's inequality.

The second claim is showed as follows. Again, by the Palm inversion formula we have

$$\begin{aligned}\mathbf{Pr}[S(t)>\theta] &= \frac{\mathbf{E}[\sum_{s=0}^{S_r-1}\mathbf{1}_{S_r-s>\theta}]}{\mathbf{E}[S_r]} = \\ \frac{\mathbf{E}[\max\{S_r-\theta,0\}]}{\mathbf{E}[S_r]} &\geq \frac{\mathbf{E}[\max\{S_r-\theta,0\}\mathbf{1}_{S_r>2\theta}]}{\mathbf{E}[S_r]} = \\ \frac{\mathbf{E}[S_r\mathbf{1}_{S_r>2\theta}]}{2\,\mathbf{E}[S_r]} &\geq \frac{\mathbf{E}[S_r]\,\mathbf{E}[\mathbf{1}_{S_r>2\theta}]}{2\,\mathbf{E}[S_r]} = \frac{1}{2}\mathbf{Pr}[S_r>2\theta]\end{aligned}$$

where the last inequality follows by Harris' inequality, as S_r is a real-valued random variable and

$$\mathbf{E}[S_r\mathbf{1}_{S_r>2\theta}] = \mathbf{E}[f(S_r)g(S_r)]$$

for two non-decreasing functions f and g defined by $f(x)=x$ and $g(x)=\mathbf{1}_{x>2\theta}$ for $x\in\mathbf{R}$. □

The proof of the phase upper bound therefore follows by combining Lemma 3 and Lemma 4.

THEOREM 4. *The expected system latency satisfies* $\tau = O(1/\|\mathbf{p}\|_2)$.

5. ANALYSIS OF INDIVIDUAL LATENCIES

5.1 Upper Bound for Winning Probabilities

We prove the following bound on the probability that bin i wins a phase, which will imply an individual latency bound of $\Omega(\|\mathbf{p}\|_2/p_i^2)$ for bin i.

THEOREM 5. *For every bin* i, *the winning probability satisfies* $w_i = O(p_i^2/\|\mathbf{p}\|_2^2)$.

Proof Outline. The proof of this result is quite involved, so we first provide an outline for the case $k=2$. Fix an arbitrary bin i. Let W_r be the event that in a random phase r bin i wins, so $w_i = \mathbf{Pr}[W_r]$. A time step t is defined to be bad if $\sum_{i=1}^n p_i^2\mathbf{1}_{Y_i(t)=1}\leq\|\mathbf{p}\|_2^2/16$. Similarly, a phase r is defined to be bad if its first time step is bad. Intuitively, if a phase is not bad, then there is "enough competition" which limits the winning probability of i. Let B_r denote the event that phase r is bad. By a simple conditioning, we have $\mathbf{Pr}[W_r]=\mathbf{Pr}[\overline{B}_r]\cdot\mathbf{Pr}[W_r\mid\overline{B}_r]+\mathbf{Pr}[B_r]\cdot\mathbf{Pr}[W_r\mid B_r]$. We shall establish the following three claims:

$$\mathbf{Pr}[B_r]\leq\exp\left(-C\frac{\|\mathbf{p}\|_2^2}{\|\mathbf{p}\|_3^2}\right),\ \text{for a constant } C>0, \tag{4}$$

$$\mathbf{Pr}[W_r\mid\overline{B}_r]=O\left(\frac{p_i^2}{\|\mathbf{p}\|_2^2}\right)\ \text{and}$$
$$\mathbf{Pr}[W_r\mid B_r]=O\left(\frac{p_i^2}{\|\mathbf{p}\|_3^2}\right). \tag{5}$$

The asserted upper bound follows then by combining these bounds and the fact that $\exp(-x)\leq 1/x$ for $x>0$,

$$\mathbf{Pr}[W_r]\leq\exp\left(-C\frac{\|\mathbf{p}\|_2^2}{\|\mathbf{p}\|_3^2}\right)\cdot\frac{p_i^2}{\|\mathbf{p}\|_3^2}+\frac{p_i^2}{\|\mathbf{p}\|_2^2}=O\left(\frac{p_i^2}{\|\mathbf{p}\|_2^2}\right).$$

The inequality in (4) is obtained by showing first that the probability that a random time t is bad is at most $\exp(-C'\|\mathbf{p}\|_2/\|\mathbf{p}\|_3)$ for a constant $C'>0$, and then showing that the probability that a random phase r is bad is upper bounded by a similar bound. The first upper bound in (5) is obtained by conservatively assuming that at the beginning of phase r, bin i has one ball and exploiting that the probability mass on the bins having one ball is large enough, and then applying Theorem 2. The second upper bound in (5) is obtained by assuming that bin i has one ball and all other bins have zero balls, and again applying Theorem 2.

For $k\geq 3$, we need a more careful analysis, as the (conditional) winning probabilities could lie between any of the values $p_i^2/\|\mathbf{p}\|_j^2$ for $2\leq j\leq k+1$. Corresponding to these values, we define different gradients of "badness", and derive bounds as in (4) and (5) for each gradient separately. Then all these bounds are charged against each other and the proof is completed in a similar way as in Lemma 3. We give the full proof of Theorem 5 in the full version of our paper [2], and focus here on establishing the key step, Eq. (4), and its version for $k\geq 3$.

Probability of a Bad Phase. Our goal is to show that the probability that a random phase is bad is small. In order to capture the general case $k\geq 3$, we first have to formalize the notion of ℓ-badness of a time step and introduce some further pieces of notation. Similar to the proof of Lemma 3, we partition bins into levels $1,2,\ldots,k+1$, where bins at level ℓ need to acquire ℓ balls in order to win. For each bin i and level $2\leq\ell\leq k+1$, we define the indicator random variable $Z_{\ell,i}(t)$ to equal p_i^ℓ if bin i is at level ℓ at time t, and 0, otherwise. Further, define $Z_\ell(t)=\sum_{i=1}^n Z_{\ell,i}(t)$.

DEFINITION 1. *For every level* $2\leq\ell\leq k$, *a time step* t *is (i)* ℓ-bad *if* $Z_\ell(t)<\|\mathbf{p}\|_\ell^\ell/(8k)$, *(ii)* ℓ-good *if* $Z_\ell(t)\geq\|\mathbf{p}\|_\ell^\ell/(8k)$, *(iii)* ℓ-perfect *if all time steps in* $[t,t+1/(32k\|\mathbf{p}\|_2)]$ *are* ℓ-*good.*

As before, a phase is ℓ-bad, ℓ-good or ℓ-perfect if the first time step of that phase is ℓ-bad, ℓ-good or ℓ-perfect. The idea behind the definition of ℓ-perfect is that it enforces a particular structure on the time steps; every block of ℓ-perfect time steps is followed up with exactly $1/(32k\|\mathbf{p}\|_2)$ rounds which are ℓ-good (but not ℓ-perfect), after which there is at least one ℓ-bad round. The next lemma is the key ingredient of the proof.

LEMMA 5 (KEY LEMMA). *For every* $2\leq\ell\leq k$, *a random phase is* ℓ-*bad w. p.* $\leq\exp(-\Omega((\frac{\|\mathbf{p}\|_\ell}{\|\mathbf{p}\|_{\ell+1}})^4))$.

PROOF. Let $B^\ell(T)$ be the number of ℓ-bad phases and let $N(T)$ be the number of phases in the time interval $[0,T)$. By the ergodicity of the Markov chain of bin occupancies and Theorem 4,

$$\mathbf{Pr}[\text{phase } r \text{ is } \ell\text{-bad}] = \lim_{T\to\infty} B^\ell(T)/N(T)$$
$$\text{and}\quad \lim_{T\to\infty} N(T)/T=\Omega(\|\mathbf{p}\|_2),$$

where the limits hold with probability 1.

Let $L^\ell(T)$ be the number of non-perfect times steps in the time interval $[0,T)$. From Lemma 7 below it follows that $\lim_{T\to\infty}B^\ell(T)/L^\ell(T)=O(\|\mathbf{p}\|_2)$ with probability 1. Combining these relations with the relation below which comes from Lemma 6 completes the proof:

$$\lim_{T\to\infty}\frac{L^\ell(T)}{T}\leq\exp\Big(-\Omega\big((\frac{\|\mathbf{p}\|_\ell}{\|\mathbf{p}\|_{\ell+1}})^4\big)\Big)\quad\text{w.p. 1}$$

□

LEMMA 6. *For every level $2 \le \ell \le k$, a random time t is ℓ-perfect w. p. at least $1 - \exp\Big(-\Omega\big((\frac{\|\mathbf{p}\|_\ell}{\|\mathbf{p}\|_{\ell+1}})^4\big)\Big)$.*

The proof of Lemma 6 follows by first exploiting that for a random time t, the occupancy distribution modulo k is uniform, which allows us to apply Hoeffding's bound to lower bound $Z_\ell(t)$. Then we lower bound the set of bins at level ℓ at time step t which do not receive any ball until time $t+1/(32k\|\mathbf{p}\|_2)$. Combining these two parts yields the statement of the lemma, whose complete proof is deferred to the full version of this paper [2].

LEMMA 7. *For every level $2 \le \ell \le k$ and random time t,*

$$\mathbf{Pr}[\text{ time step } t \text{ is beginning of a } \ell\text{-bad phase }] \le O(\|\mathbf{p}\|_2) \cdot \mathbf{Pr}[\text{ time step } t \text{ is not } \ell\text{-perfect }].$$

The proof of this lemma relies on a careful comparison between the point process associated to ℓ-bad phases, and the point process associated to ℓ-(non-)perfect time steps. Intuitively, we will show that, on average, every bad phase can be charged $\Omega(1/\|\mathbf{p}\|_2)$ non-perfect time steps, which then implies Lemma 7.

Proof of Lemma 7. We will relate ℓ-non-perfect time steps and ℓ-bad phases (since $2 \le \ell \le k-1$ is fixed throughout this part, we will often simply say non-perfect and bad). To this end we will consider a specific process which in parallel counts the number of bad phases and lower bounds the number of non-perfect time steps. This process will use a (non-complete) partitioning of phases into set of phases, called epochs.

DEFINITION 2. *An epoch is defined to be an interval of consecutive phases that starts at the beginning of a bad phase and ends at the end of the first occurance of a phase that contains at least one perfect time step.*

Starting from a fixed perfect time step (w.l.o.g. time 0), we can enumerate all epochs by $E_1, E_2, \ldots$. The j-th phase of the e-th epoch is denoted by $E_{e,j}$, whose length is $|E_{e,j}|$. Finally, $|E_e| \ge 1$ denotes the size of epoch e, i.e., the number of phases it contains. An illustration of these definitions can be found in Figure 1.

Counting the Ratio Phase-by-Phase. Figure 1 suggests a link between the phase lengths and the number of non-perfect time steps. In particular, every phase of an epoch except for the last one contains only non-perfect time steps. To elaborate on this link, we next describe a process which follows the partitioning into epochs to update two counters. First, a counter B adds up all phases which are part of the e-th epoch. Simultaneously, a second counter L adds up all phase lengths $|E_{e,j}|$ except the last one as well as the $1/(32k\|\mathbf{p}\|_2)$ good but non-perfect time steps that prelude any new epoch. The precise description can be found in Process 2.

The next lemma shows that the counters B and L are indeed related to the number of bad phases and the number of non-perfect rounds. It basically follows from the definition of an epoch.

LEMMA 8. *Consider Process 2 running until the f-th epoch is completed, and let $B = B(f)$ and $L = L(f)$ be the values of the counters B and L at this time. Then the following two statements hold. First, $B(f)$ counts exactly the total number of bad phases that occur until the last time step of the*

$e = 0,\ j = 0$ `/* counters for epoch and phase */`
$L = 0,\ B = 0$ `/* counters for non-perfect rounds and bad phases */`
while true **do**
  Jump to the next bad phase, $e = e + 1,\ j = 0$
  repeat
    $j = j + 1$
    Allocate balls until phase j of epoch i ends
    if $j = 1$ **then** $L = L + 1/(32k\|\mathbf{p}\|_2)$, $B = B + 1$
    if $j \ge 2$ **then** $L = L + |E_{e,j-1}|$, $B = B + 1$
  until *phase j contained a perfect time step*

Process 2: The original counting process and its phase-based updates.

f-th epoch. Second, the expression $L(f) = \sum_{e=1}^{f}\big(\frac{1}{32k\|\mathbf{p}\|_2} + \sum_{j=1}^{|E_e|-1} |E_{e,j}|\big)$ lower bounds the number of non-perfect time steps which belong to a phase of the first f epochs.

Counting the Ratio Epoch-by-Epoch. The problem with analyzing Process 2 is that we do not have a good control on its actual length in terms of phases or time steps. We could think of it as facing an online adversary who is allowed to see the evolution of all phase lengths and then able to end the epoch after an arbitrary phase. However, we know that every phase will take $\Omega(1/\|\mathbf{p}\|_2)$ with constant prob. > 0, regardless of the occupancy distribution at the beginning of that phase. This motivates the definition of a modified process, where the epoch length is the maximum number x so that more than half of its phase lengths are less than some threshold $1/(16k\|\mathbf{p}\|_2)$. If $x > 0$, then we conservatively assume that the epoch runs for x phases all of which have length 0. If $x = 0$, then we assume that the epoch consists of one phase of length $1/(128k\|\mathbf{p}\|_2)$.

For the modified process we generate for the e-th epoch with phase j a separate infinite sequence of bin samples denoted by $M_{e,j} \in \{1, \ldots, n\}^{\mathbb{N}}$. Here, $M_{e,j}(t)$ is the bin where the t-th ball of phase j in epoch E_e is placed, where for any bin i, $\mathbf{Pr}[M_{e,j}(t) = i] = p_i$. Further, for every pair e, j, we use an indicator variable $Z_{e,j}$ which is one iff the bin samples $M_{e,j}$ ensure that no bin gets two balls within $1/(16k\|\mathbf{p}\|_2)$ time steps.

$e = 0,\ \widetilde{L} = 0,\ \widetilde{B} = 0$ `/* counters for epoch, non-perfect rounds and bad phases */`
$M_{e,j} \in \{1, \ldots, n\}^{\mathbb{N}}$ `/* random sequence for bin samples in phase` j `of the` e`-th epoch */`
while true **do**
  $e = e + 1$
  $\widetilde{S}_e = \max\{x \ge 1 : \sum_{j=1}^{x} Z_{e,j} < x/2\}$
    `/* defined by` $M_{e,j}$ `for` $j = 1, 2, \ldots$ `*/`
  if $\widetilde{S}_e = 0$ **then** $\widetilde{L} = \widetilde{L} + 1/(128k\|\mathbf{p}\|_2)$, $\widetilde{B} = \widetilde{B} + 1$
  if $\widetilde{S}_e \ne 0$ **then** $\widetilde{L} = \widetilde{L} + 0,\ \widetilde{B} = \widetilde{B} + \widetilde{S}_e$

Process 3: The modified process and its epoch-based updates.

We proceed to establish a coupling which implies that L/B majorises $\widetilde{L}/\widetilde{B}$. A random variable X is stochastically

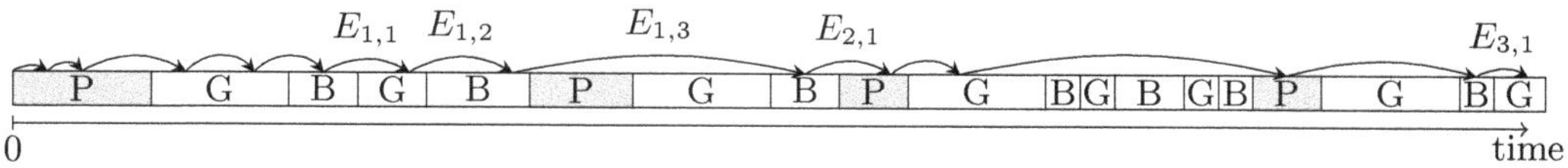

Figure 1: Illustration of phases viewed as a point process in time, which can be of three different types: P (perfect), G (good but not perfect) and B (bad). Arrows with a label $E_{e,j}$ form phase j in epoch e. Phases without a label do not belong to any epoch.

smaller (is majorized by) Y, in symbols $X \preceq Y$, if $\mathbf{Pr}[X \geq \theta] \leq \mathbf{Pr}[Y \geq \theta]$ for every θ.

LEMMA 9. *Consider the original process and modified process both running until epoch f is completed, and let $B(f)$, $L(f)$, $\widetilde{B}(f)$, $\widetilde{L}(f)$ be the value of the four counters at this time. Then $L(f)/B(f) \succeq \widetilde{L}(f)/\widetilde{B}(f)$.*

The proof of this lemma is based on a coupling where the original process uses the same bin samples $M_{e,j}$ as the modified process. Finally, we study the distribution of the counters $\widetilde{B}$ and $\widetilde{L}$.

LEMMA 10. *For the modified process (Process 3), the following statements holds.*

- *For any $\theta \geq 1$ and epoch e, $\mathbf{Pr}[\widetilde{S}_e \geq \theta] \leq (1/4)2^{-\theta}$, thus, in particular, $\mathbf{Pr}[\widetilde{S}_e < \infty] = 1$.*
- *Let $\widetilde{B} = \widetilde{B}(f)$ and $\widetilde{L} = \widetilde{L}(f)$ be the values of the counters $\widetilde{B}$ and $\widetilde{L}$ until epoch f is completed. Then, $\widetilde{L}(f) \succeq \mathsf{Bin}(f, 1/2)/(128k\|\mathbf{p}\|_2)$, and $\widetilde{B}(f) \preceq \mathsf{Geo}(1/2) \cdot f$.*

PROOF COMPLETING THE PROOF OF LEMMA 7. First, we consider $\widetilde{L}(f)/\widetilde{B}(f)$ for a large value of epoch f. By Lemma 10, $\mathbf{E}[\widetilde{L}(f)] \geq (f/2)/(128k\|\mathbf{p}\|_2)$ and $\mathbf{E}[\widetilde{B}(f)] \leq 2f$. Hence by ergodicity, the following limits hold w.p. 1:

$$\lim_{f\to\infty} \widetilde{L}(f) \geq f \cdot \frac{1}{192k\|\mathbf{p}\|_2} \text{ and } \lim_{f\to\infty} \widetilde{B}(f) \leq 3f,$$

$$\text{implying } \lim_{f\to\infty} \frac{L(f)}{B(f)} \geq \lim_{f\to\infty} \frac{\widetilde{L}(f)}{\widetilde{B}(f)} \geq \frac{1}{576k\|\mathbf{p}\|_2},$$

where the first inequality follows from Lemma 9. By Lemma 8, we know that $L(f)$ is a lower bound on the number of non-perfect time steps until the end of epoch f, and $B(f)$ counts the number of bad phases until the end of epoch f. Hence considering the beginning steps of bad phases as a separate process, we have

$$\mathbf{Pr}[\text{ time step } t \text{ is beginning of a bad phase }] \leq$$
$$576k \cdot \|\mathbf{p}\|_2 \cdot \mathbf{Pr}[\text{ time step } t \text{ is not perfect }].$$

□

Lower Bound on Winning Probabilities. Finally, we prove a lower bound on the winning probability exploiting the fact that at a random time t, any bin i has $k-2$ balls with probability $1/k$.

THEOREM 6. *For any bin i, the winning probability satisfies $w_i = \Omega(p_i^2/\|\mathbf{p}\|_2^2)$.*

Due to space limitations, we only present an outline of the proof. We know that for a random time t the probability that bin i has $k-2$ balls is exactly $1/k$. We show that this condition continues to hold from time t until the end of the current phase with a constant probability. This will follow by considering the additional events that (i) bin i does not receive a ball in the time interval $[t, t+s]$ where $s = \Theta(1/\|\mathbf{p}\|_2)$ and (ii) the event that the next phase starts in that interval. By reasoning about the point process, we can deduce that for a constant fraction of phases, bin i has $k-2$ balls, and the claim then follows by Theorem 2 which shows that bin i has a probability of $\Omega(p_i^2/\|\mathbf{p}\|_2^2)$ for winning such a phase.

6. APPLICATIONS AND FUTURE DIRECTIONS

Our characterization has two non-trivial applications. The first is given by the following practical question: given a set of lower bound constraints on the performance of individual threads (individual latency upper bounds), what is the scheduling distribution which minimizes *system* latency? Modifying the scheduling distribution is commonly done through back-offs. By Theorem 1, this now corresponds to the simple optimization problem of maximizing the 2-norm of the scheduling probabilities $\mathbf{p}$, subject to a set of lower bounds on the scheduling probabilities.

The second application comes by noticing that the simple process where all bins are reset to 1 on a win models *obstruction-free* concurrent algorithms, which guarantee progress only in the absence of contention, and may abort operations otherwise. Theorem 2 implies that the system latency of an obstruction-free algorithm is $\Theta(1/\|\mathbf{p}\|_k)$, where k is the operation length. This provides a complexity separation between obstruction-free and lock-free algorithms, under stochastic schedulers, for most values of the scheduling distribution $\mathbf{p}$.

Summing up, we have given general framework for competitive non-uniform balls-into-bins processes. While we focused on a particular application, lock-free algorithms, we believe that our techniques can be used to model a broader class of algorithms and processes related to scheduling contended applications. Hence, a natural but challenging question would be to find a general characterization, which parameterizes the winning probabilities and phase lengths in terms of the reset policies. Further, it would be interesting if a similar model applies to *transactions* (either in hardware or in software), and if similar performance bounds can be derived.

7. REFERENCES

[1] Dan Alistarh, Keren Censor-Hillel, and Nir Shavit. Are lock-free concurrent algorithms practically wait-free? In *Proceedings of the 46th ACM Symposium on Theory of Computing*, STOC'14, pages 714–723, 2014. Full version containing measurements available at: http://arxiv.org/abs/1311.3200.

[2] Dan Alistarh, Thomas Sauerwald, and Milan Vojnovic. Lock-free algorithms under stochastic schedulers. Technical Report MSR-TR-2015-41, May 2015.

[3] James Aspnes. Fast deterministic consensus in a noisy environment. *J. Algorithms*, 45(1):16–39, 2002.

[4] Hagit Attiya, Rachid Guerraoui, Danny Hendler, and Petr Kuznetsov. The complexity of obstruction-free implementations. *J. ACM*, 56(4):24:1–24:33, July 2009.

[5] Yossi Azar, Andrei Z. Broder, Anna R. Karlin, and Eli Upfal. Balanced allocations. *SIAM J. Comput.*, 29(1):180–200, 1999.

[6] Pierre Bremaud. *Markov Chains: Gibbs Fields, Monte Carlo Simulation, and Queues (Text in Applied Mathematics)*. Springer, 2nd edition, 2001.

[7] Fang Chen, László Lovász, and Igor Pak. Lifting markov chains to speed up mixing. In *Proceedings of the 31st Annual ACM Symposium on Theory of Computing*, STOC'99, pages 275–281.

[8] Dave Dice, Virendra J. Marathe, and Nir Shavit. Brief announcement: Persistent unfairness arising from cache residency imbalance. In *Proceedings of the 26th ACM Symposium on Parallelism in Algorithms and Architectures*, SPAA'14, pages 82–83, 2014.

[9] Faith Ellen, Panagiota Fatourou, Joanna Helga, and Eric Ruppert. The amortized complexity of non-blocking binary search trees. In *Proceedings of the 2014 ACM Symposium on Principles of Distributed Computing*, PODC '14, pages 332–340, New York, NY, USA, 2014. ACM.

[10] Keir Fraser and Timothy L. Harris. Concurrent programming without locks. *ACM Trans. Comput. Syst.*, 25(2), 2007.

[11] Brighten Godfrey. Balls and bins with structure: balanced allocations on hypergraphs. In *Proceedings of the 19th ACM-SIAM Symposium on Discrete Algorithms*, SODA'08, pages 511–517, 2008.

[12] Thomas P. Hayes and Alistair Sinclair. Liftings of tree-structured markov chains. In *Proceedings of the 13th International Conference on Approximation, and 14th International Conference on Randomization, and Combinatorial Optimization: Algorithms and Techniques*, APPROX/RANDOM'10, pages 602–616, 2010.

[13] Maurice Herlihy. Wait-free synchronization. *ACM Transactions on Programming Languages and Systems*, 13(1):123–149, January 1991.

[14] Maurice Herlihy, Victor Luchangco, and Mark Moir. Obstruction-free synchronization: Double-ended queues as an example. In *Proceedings of the 23rd International Conference on Distributed Computing Systems*, ICDCS'03, pages 522–529, 2003.

[15] Maurice Herlihy and Nir Shavit. *The art of multiprocessor programming*. Morgan Kaufmann, 2008.

[16] Maurice Herlihy and Nir Shavit. On the nature of progress. In *Proceedings of the 15th International Conference on Principles of Distributed Systems*, OPODIS'11, pages 313–328, 2011.

[17] Christoph Lameter. Numa (non-uniform memory access): An overview. *Queue*, 11(7):40:40–40:51, July 2013.

[18] Maged M. Michael and Michael L. Scott. Simple, fast, and practical non-blocking and blocking concurrent queue algorithms. In *Proceedings of the 15th ACM Symposium on Principles of Distributed Computing*, PODC'96, pages 267–275, 1996.

[19] Michael Mitzenmacher and Eli Upfal. *Probability and Computing: Randomized Algorithms and Probabilistic Analysis*. Cambridge University Press, New York, NY, USA, 2005.

[20] Thomas S. Nunnikhoven. A birthday problem solution for nonuniform birth frequencies. *The American Statistician*, 46(4):270–274, 1992.

[21] Raghu Ramakrishnan and Johannes Gehrke. *Database Management Systems*. McGraw-Hill, Inc., New York, NY, USA, 3rd edition, 2003.

[22] Michael L. Scott. *Shared-Memory Synchronization*. Synthesis Lectures on Computer Architecture. Morgan & Claypool Publishers, 2013.

[23] Kunal Talwar and Udi Wieder. Balanced allocations: the weighted case. In *Proceedings of the 39th ACM Symposium on Theory of Computing*, STOC'07, pages 256–265, 2007.

[24] R. K. Treiber. Systems programming: Coping with parallelism. Technical Report RJ 5118, IBM Almaden Research Center, 1986.

Reclaiming Memory for Lock-Free Data Structures: There has to be a Better Way

Trevor Brown
Department of Computer Science
University of Toronto
tabrown@cs.toronto.edu

ABSTRACT

Memory reclamation for sequential or lock-based data structures is typically easy. However, memory reclamation for lock-free data structures is a significant challenge. Automatic techniques such as garbage collection are inefficient or use locks, and non-automatic techniques either have high overhead, or do not work for many reasonably simple data structures. For example, subtle problems can arise when hazard pointers, one of the most common non-automatic techniques, are applied to many natural lock-free data structures. Epoch based reclamation (EBR), which is by far the most efficient non-automatic technique, allows the number of unreclaimed objects to grow without bound, because one slow or crashed process can prevent all other processes from reclaiming memory.

We develop a more efficient, distributed variant of EBR that solves this problem. It is based on signaling, which is provided by many operating systems, such as Linux and UNIX. Our new scheme takes O(1) amortized steps per high-level operation on the lock-free data structure and O(1) steps in the worst case each time an object is removed from the data structure. At any point, $O(mn^2)$ objects are waiting to be freed, where n is the number of processes and m is a small constant for most data structures. Experiments show that our scheme has very low overhead: on average 10%, and at worst 28%, for a balanced binary search tree over many thread counts, operation mixes and contention levels. Our scheme also outperforms a highly efficient implementation of hazard pointers by an average of 75%.

Typically, memory reclamation code is tightly woven into lock-free data structure code. To improve modularity and facilitate the comparison of different memory reclamation schemes, we also introduce a highly flexible abstraction. It allows a programmer to easily interchange schemes for reclamation, object pooling, allocation and deallocation with virtually no overhead, by changing a single line of code.

Categories and Subject Descriptors

D.1.3 [**Programming Techniques**]: Concurrent Programming—*Parallel programming*; D.4.2 [**Operating Systems**]: Storage Management—*Allocation/deallocation strategies*

Permission to make digital or hard copies of all or part of this work for personal or classroom use is granted without fee provided that copies are not made or distributed for profit or commercial advantage and that copies bear this notice and the full citation on the first page. Copyrights for components of this work owned by others than ACM must be honored. Abstracting with credit is permitted. To copy otherwise, or republish, to post on servers or to redistribute to lists, requires prior specific permission and/or a fee. Request permissions from permissions@acm.org.
PODC'15, July 21–23, 2015, Donostia-San Sebastián, Spain.
Copyright © 2015 ACM 978-1-4503-3617-8 /15/07 ...$15.00.
DOI: http://dx.doi.org/10.1145/2767386.2767436.

General Terms

Algorithms, Performance, Reliability

Keywords

Memory reclamation; lock-free; non-blocking; epoch-based reclamation; hazard pointers; signals; fault-tolerance

1. INTRODUCTION

In concurrent data structures that use locks, it is typically straightforward to free memory to the operating system after a node is removed from the data structure. For example, consider a singly-linked list implementation of the set abstract data type using hand-over-hand locking. Hand-over-hand locking allows a process to lock a node (other than the head node) only if it holds a lock on the node's predecessor. To traverse from a locked node u to its successor v, the process first locks v, then it unlocks u. To delete a node u, a process first locks the head node, then performs hand-over-hand locking until it reaches u's predecessor and locks it. The process then locks u (to ensure no other process holds a lock on u), removes it from the list, frees it to the operating system, and finally unlocks u's predecessor. It is easy to argue that no other process has a pointer to u when u is freed.

In contrast, memory reclamation is one of the most challenging aspects of lock-free data structure design. Lock-free algorithms (also called non-blocking algorithms) guarantee that as long as some process continues to take steps, eventually some process will complete an operation. The main difficulty in performing memory reclamation for a lock-free data structure is that a process can be sleeping while holding a pointer to an object that is about to be freed. Thus, carelessly freeing an object can cause a sleeping process to access freed memory when it wakes up, crashing the program or producing subtle errors. Since nodes are not locked, processes must coordinate to let each other know which nodes are safe to reclaim, and which might still be accessed. (This is also a problem for data structures with lock-based updates and lock-free queries. The solutions presented hererin apply equally well to lock-based data structures with lock-free queries.)

Techniques for determining which nodes are safe to reclaim can be divided into *automatic techniques*, which do not require a programmer to specify when an object has been removed from the data structure, and *non-automatic techniques*, which do. It is conceptually useful to divide the work of reclaiming an object into two parts: determining when an object is removed from the data structure, and determining when this object can be freed to the operating system. The former is the responsibility of either an *automatic* memory reclamation scheme, or a lock-free data structure. The latter is always the responsibility of the memory reclamation scheme. Automatic techniques offer a significantly simpler programming environment, but can be inefficient. Non-automatic techniques are particularly useful when developing data structures for software libraries, since optimization can pay large dividends when code is reused. Additionally, non-automatic techniques can be used to build data structures that serve as building blocks to construct new automated techniques.

Garbage collectors comprise the largest class of automated techniques. The literature on garbage collection is vast, and lies outside the scope of this paper. Garbage collection schemes are surveyed in [16, 22]. Reference counting is another technique that can be automated. Limited forms of reference counting are also used to construct non-automatic techniques.

Non-automatic techniques can broadly be grouped into four categories: *object pools*, *hazard pointers*, *epoch based reclamation* and *transactional memory assisted reclamation*. As will be discussed in Section 3, these techniques either do not work for, or are inefficient for, many natural lock-free data structures.

In epoch based reclamation (EBR), the execution is divided into epochs. Each object removed from the data structure in epoch e is placed into a shared *limbo bag* for epoch e. Limbo bags are maintained for the last three epochs. Each time a process starts an operation, it reads and announces the current epoch, and checks the announcements of other processes. If all processes have announced the current epoch, then a new epoch begins, and the contents of the oldest limbo bag can be reclaimed. If a process sleeps or crashes during an operation, then no memory can be reclaimed, so EBR is not fault tolerant.

We begin by developing a more efficient, distributed variant of EBR, called DEBRA. DEBRA replaces the shared limbo bags of EBR with per-process bags, and amortizes the checking of processes' announced epochs by reading only one announcement at the start of each operation. Each limbo bag is implemented as a singly-linked list of *blocks*, which each contain 256 pointers to objects. Whenever a process announces a new epoch, it appends its oldest limbo bag to a local object pool in constant time. Whenever local pools grow too large or small, entire blocks are moved to or from a shared object pool. Operating on blocks instead of individual objects significantly reduces overhead. DEBRA performs O(1) steps at the beginning and end of each operation supported by the lock-free data structure and O(1) steps each time an object is removed from the data structure.

Our main contribution is DEBRA+, the first fault tolerant epoch based reclamation scheme. The primary challenge was to find a way to allow a process to advance the current epoch without waiting for another process, which may have crashed. In order to advance the epoch, we must ensure that such a process will not access any retired object if it takes another step. The technique we introduce for adding fault tolerance to DEBRA uses signals, an interprocess communication mechanism supported by many operating systems (e.g., Linux and UNIX). With DEBRA+, the number of objects waiting to be freed is $O(mn^2)$, where n is the number of processes and m is the largest number of objects removed from the data structure by one operation.

A major problem arises when auditioning non-automatic techniques to see which performs best for a given lock-free data structure. The set of operations exposed to the programmer by non-automatic techniques varies widely. This is undesirable for several reasons. First, from a theoretical standpoint, there is no reason that a data structure should have to be aware of how its objects are allocated and reclaimed. Second, it is difficult to interchange memory reclamation schemes to determine which performs best in a given situation. Presently, doing this entails writing many different versions of the data structure, each version tailored to a specific memory reclamation scheme. Third, as new advancements in memory reclamation appear, existing data structures have to be reimplemented (and their correctness painstakingly re-examined) before they can reap the benefits. Updating lock-free data structures in this way is non-trivial. Fourth, moving code to a machine with a different memory consistency model can require changes to the memory reclamation scheme, which currently requires changing the code for the lock-free data structure as well. Fifth, if several instances of a data structure are used for very different purposes (e.g., many small trees with strict memory footprint requirements and one large tree with no such requirement), then it may be appropriate to use different memory reclamation schemes for the different instances. Currently, this requires writing and maintaining code for different versions of the data structure.

These issues were all considered in the context of sequential data structures when the C++ standard template libraries were implemented. Their solution was to introduce an *Allocator* abstraction, which allows a data structure to perform *allocate* and *deallocate* operations. With this abstraction, the memory allocation scheme for a data structure can easily be changed without modifying or compiling (or even having access to) the data structure code. Unfortunately, the Allocator abstraction cannot be applied directly to lock- free programming, since its operations do not align well with the operations of lock-free memory reclamation schemes. (For example, it requires the data structure to know when an object can be freed.) The main challenge in developing an appropriate generalization of the Allocator abstraction is to find the right set of operations to expose to the data structure implementation, so that the result is simultaneously highly efficient, versatile and easy to program. In Section 6, we present the first generalization of the Allocator abstraction for lock-free programming.

Experiments on C++ implementations of DEBRA and DEBRA+ show that overhead is very low. Compared with performing no reclamation at all, DEBRA is on average 4% slower, and at worst 21% slower, over a wide variety of thread counts and workloads. In some experiments, DEBRA actually *improves* performance by as much as 20%. Although it seems impossible to achieve better performance when computation is spent reclaiming objects, DEBRA reduces the memory footprint of the data structure, which improves memory locality and cache performance. Adding fault tolerance to DEBRA adds 2.5% overhead, on average.

2. MODEL

We consider an asynchronous shared memory system with n processes. Each process has local memory that is not accessible by any other process, and there is a shared memory accessible by all processes. Memory is divided into primitive objects, which have atomic operations that are provided directly by the hardware. Examples include read/write registers, compare-and-swap (CAS) objects, and double-wide compare-and-swap (DWCAS) objects. A *record* is a collection of primitive objects, which we refer to as *fields*. A data structure consists of a fixed set of *entry points*, which are pointers to records, and the records that are reachable by following one or more pointers from an entry point. A record is *retired from a data structure* when it changes from being in the data structure to not being in the data structure. A record is *inserted into a data structure* when it changes from being not in the data structure to being in the data structure. The system is equipped with a *memory allocator*. Initially, no record is accessible to any process. *Allocating* a record makes it accessible and provides the process that requested it with a pointer to the record. A record can also be *freed*, which makes it inaccessible. Accessing a freed record results in the failure of the entire system.

3. RELATED WORK

There are many existing techniques for reclaiming memory in lock-free data structures. However, all of these techniques have some disadvantages.

Object Pools (OP). A particularly simple way to prevent processes from accessing a freed record is to never free any record, but allow processes to reuse retired records. Whenever a record is retired, it is returned to a pool of records (of the same type), from which it can be retrieved by any process that wants to allocate a record. Implementations of shared object pools are described in [14, 24]. If a shared pool is highly contended, then per-process pools can be added, so each process synchronizes on the shared pool only when one of its local pools is either empty or larger than some threshold.

Reference Counting (RC). RC augments each record o with a counter that records the number of pointers that processes, entry points and records have to r. An record can safely be freed once its reference count becomes zero. Reference counts are updated every time a pointer to a record is created or destroyed. Naturally, a process must first read a pointer to reach a record before it can increment the record's reference counter. This window between when a record is reached and when its reference counter is updated reveals the main challenge in designing a RC scheme: the reference count of a freed record must not be accessed. However, the reference count of a retired record can be accessed.

Detlefs et al. [6] introduced lock-free reference counting (LFRC), which is applicable to arbitrary lock-free data structures. LFRC uses the double compare-and-swap (DCAS) synchronization primitive, which atomically modifies two arbitrary words in memory, to change the reference count of a record only if a certain pointer still points to it. DCAS is not natively available in modern hardware, but it can be implemented from CAS. Herlihy et al. [15] subsequently improved LFRC to single-word lock-free reference counting (SLFRC), which uses single-word CAS instead of DCAS. To prevent the reference count of a freed record from being accessed, the implementation of SLFRC uses a variant of Hazard Pointers (described below) to prevent records from being freed until any pending accesses have finished. Lee [17] developed a distributed reference counting scheme from fetch-and-increment and swap. Each node contains several limited reference counts, and the true reference count for a node is distributed between itself and its parent. The scheme was developed for in-trees (wherein each node has a pointer only to its parent), but it may be generalizable.

RC requires extra memory for *each record* and it cannot reclaim records whose pointers form a cycle (since their reference counts will never drop to zero). Manually breaking cycles to allow reclamation requires knowledge of a data structure and adds more overhead. RC has high overhead, since following a pointer involves (at least) two costly atomic synchronization primitives; experiments confirm that RC is less efficient than other techniques [13].

Hazard Pointers (HPs). Michael introduced HPs [20], and provided a wait-free implementation from atomic read/write registers. (Herlihy et al. [15] independently developed another version of HPs, providing a lock-free implementation from CAS, and a wait-free implementation from double-wide CAS.) HPs track which records might be accessed by each process. Before a process can access a field of a record r, or use a pointer to r as the expected value for a CAS, it must first acquire a hazard pointer to r. To correctly use HPs, one must satisfy the following constraint. Suppose a record r is retired at time t_r and later accessed by a process p at time t_a. If r remains retired between t_r and t_a, then one of p's HPs must continuously point to r from before t_r until after t_a. It is easy to verify that, after a record r is retired and is not pointed to by any HP, no process can obtain a HP to r until it is next inserted into the data structure. Therefore, a process can safely free a retired record after scanning all HPs and seeing that none point to r.

To acquire a HP to r, a process first announces the HP by writing a pointer to r in a shared *announce* array with one part for each process. This announces to all processes that r might be accessed and cannot safely be freed. Then, the process verifies that r is in the data structure. If the record is not in the data structure, then the process can behave as if its operation had failed due to contention (typically by aborting and restarting its operation), without threatening the progress guarantees of the data structure. For many data structures, a process cannot easily determine whether a record is in the data structure, and they are modified in an ad-hoc way to allow operations to restart whenever they cannot tell. This requires reproving the data structures' progress guarantees.

Many lock-free algorithms require only a small constant number k of HPs per process, since a HP can be released once a process will no longer access the record to which it points during an operation. Scanning the HPs of all processes takes $\Theta(nk)$ steps, so doing this each time a record is retired would be costly. However, with a small modification, the expected amortized cost to retire an object is $O(1)$. Each process maintains a local collection of retired records. When a collection contains $nk + \Omega(nk)$ objects, the process creates a hash table T containing every HP, and, for each object o in its collection, checks whether o is in T. If not, o is freed. Since there are at most nk records in T, $\Omega(nk)$ records can be freed. Thus, the number of records waiting to be freed is $O(kn^2)$.

Problems with Hazard Pointers and marking. Many lock-free data structures use *marking* to prevent processes from erroneously performing modifications to records just before, or after, they are removed from the data structure. Specifically, before a record is removed from the data structure, all of its pointers are marked, and a process is allowed to change a pointer only if it is not marked. A subtle, but significant problem arises when one considers the interaction between HPs and marking in lock-free data structures that can contain a marked node that points to another marked node (e.g., [4, 5, 7, 10, 21, 23]). Specifically, it occurs when a process reads a marked pointer to a record and attempts to acquire a HP to it.

For example, consider a lock-free singly-linked list that marks a node's next pointer before removing it from the list. (It is easy to see that two consecutive nodes u and u' can be marked if one process marks u, in preparation to delete it, and another process simultaneously marks u'.) Suppose that, while searching this list, a process p has acquired a HP to node u and needs to obtain a HP to the next node, u'. To acquire the HP to u', p reads and announces the pointer to u', and must then verify that u' is in the list. If the pointer to u' is unmarked, then u is in the list, and, consequently, so is u'. If this pointer is marked and u' is not in the list, then p can behave as if its operation had failed, without threatening the progress guarantees of the list. However, behaving as if its operation had failed when this pointer is marked and u' is in the list might invalidate the progress guarantees of the list. If one does not want to reprove the data structure's progress guarantees, then p must find some way to determine whether u' is actually in the list.

By definition, u' is in the list if and only if it is reachable from an entry point or an unmarked node. One option is for p to traverse the list backwards from u until it reaches an unmarked node, and then search for u' from there. However, unless p has already acquired HPs to every node it will return to, it can encounter the same problem while moving backwards in the list. Furthermore, even after p reaches an unmarked node, it can encounter the same problem while searching for u' from that node. Each time p reads and announces a marked pointer, and recursively starts a search, its set of announcements grows. Consequently, the number of HPs p must hold at once (and, hence, the number of retired nodes that cannot be freed) can be arbitrarily large. This problem also occurs if p searches for u' from the beginning of the list, instead of traversing backwards. Additionally, for some data structures, the amortized cost of operations depends on the number of marked nodes they traverse. Searching from an entry point can provably increase the amortized cost of operations [9].

More about Hazard Pointers. Aghazadeh et al. [1] recently introduced an improved version of HPs with a worst case constant time procedure for scanning HPs each time a record is retired. Their algorithm maintains two queues of length nk for each process. These queues are used to incrementally scan HPs as records are retired. The algorithm adds a limited type of reference count to each record that tracks the number of incoming references from one of the queues. Note that $\Theta(\log nk)$ bits are reserved in each record for the reference count.

A technique called *Beware & Cleanup* (B&C) was introduced by Gidenstam et al. [12] to allow processes to acquire hazard pointers to retired records. A limited form of RC is added to HPs to ensure that a retired record is freed only when no other record points to it. The reference count of a record counts incoming pointers from other records, but does not count incoming pointers from processes' local memories. Before reclaiming a retired record, a process must check that its reference count is zero, and that no HP points to it. Consequently, after announcing a HP to a record r, it suffices to check that another record points to r. It follows that operations do not have to restart when they reach a retired record. The goal of the work was to optimize the performance of algorithms with searches that frequently encounter retired records and, consequently, have to restart. They do not identify the problem with HPs described above, but their technique solves it. However, B&C's algorithm for retiring records is very complicated, and the technique has higher overhead than either RC or HPs.

Hardware transactional memory (HTM). Dragojević et al. [8] explored simple schemes for memory reclamation using HTM. Alistarh et al. [2] introduced an elegant algorithm called StackTrack (ST). The key idea is to execute each operation of the lock-free data structure in a transaction, and use the implementation of HTM to automatically monitor all pointers stored in the private memory of processes without having to explicitly announce pointers before they are accessed. The HTM system will abort any transaction that accesses a record which is freed during the transaction. To decrease the probability of aborting transactions, each operation is split into many small transactions. This takes advantage of the fact that lock-free algorithms do not depend on transactions for correctness. Splitting operations into small transactions introduces overhead, and also causes some problems whose solutions introduce further overhead. For example, at the end of each transaction, any pointers that will be used by the next transaction are announced, so that they are not freed before the next transaction begins. Any time a process wants to free a record r, it must first verify that r is not announced.

Since currently available implementations of HTM do not offer progress guarantees, a *fallback path* that does not use HTM must be provided to make the algorithm lock-free. ST falls back to HPs. The paper does not give an upper bound on the number of retired records that are not freed. Although no such constraint is stated in the paper, ST cannot be applied to any data structure with an operation that atomically removes two or more records from the data structure [18]. Currently, ST requires a programmer to insert code before and after each operation, and after every few lines of lock-free data structure code (although, it should be possible to write a compiler to automate much of this).

Epochs. A process is in a *quiescent state* whenever it does not have a pointer to any record in the data structure. A grace period is any time interval during which every process has a point when it is in a quiescent state. Quiescent state-based reclamation (QSBR) [19] uses the fact that a record retired by a process can safely be freed after any subsequent grace period. Applying QSBR to a data structure requires manually identifying quiescent states, which may be impractical for some data structures. Additionally, QSBR is not fault-tolerant, because a stalled process can indefinitely prevent reclamation of any memory.

Fraser [11] described epoch based reclamation (EBR), which is similar to QSBR, but assumes that a process is in a quiescent state between its successive data structure operations. More specifically, EBR can be applied only if processes cannot save pointers read during an operation and access them during a later operation. EBR uses a single global counter, which records the current *epoch*, and an announce array. Each data structure operation first reads and announces the current epoch ε, and then checks whether all processes have announced the current epoch. If so, it increments the current epoch using CAS. The key observation is that the period of time starting from when the epoch was changed from $\varepsilon - 2$ to $\varepsilon - 1$ until it was changed from $\varepsilon - 1$ to ε is a grace period (since each process announced a new value, and, hence, started a new operation). So, any records retired in epoch $\varepsilon - 2$ can safely be freed in epoch ε. Whenever a record is retired in epoch ε, it is appended to a *limbo bag* for that epoch. It is sufficient to maintain three limbo bags (for epochs ε, $\varepsilon - 1$ and $\varepsilon - 2$, respectively). Whenever the epoch changes, every record in the oldest limbo bag is freed, and that limbo bag becomes the limbo bag for the current epoch.

Since EBR introduces overhead per *operation*, it is significantly more efficient than HPs, which requires costly synchronization for each pointer read. However, synchronizing on shared limbo bags makes it significantly less efficient than DEBRA. The penalty for writing to memory on a per operation basis, rather than a per pointer basis, is that processes have little information about which records might be accessed by a process that is suspected to have crashed. Consequently, EBR is not fault tolerant; no memory can be reclaimed after a process crash, and a slow process can prevent an unbounded number of retired records from being freed.

Drop the Anchor (DTA). Braginsky, Kogan and Petrank [3] introduced DTA, a specialized technique for singly-linked lists, which explores a middle ground between HPs and EBR. Instead of acquiring a HP each time a pointer to a node is read, a HP is acquired only once for every c pointers read. If another process q suspects that p has crashed, then q will *cut p out of the list* by replacing all nodes that p might access with new copies, and marking the old nodes so that p can tell what has happened if it eventually wakes up. This allows memory reclamation to continue, even if processes crash.

DTA has been shown to be efficient [2, 3]. However, it is not clear how it could be extended to work for other data structures. Additionally, DTA needs to be integrated with the mechanism for synchronizing updates to the linked list, because processes are cut out of the list concurrently with updates.

4. DEBRA: DISTRIBUTED EPOCH BASED RECLAMATION

Our new memory reclamation scheme, DEBRA, provides four operations: *leaveQstate*(), *enterQstate*(), *retire*(r) and *isQuiescent*(), where r is a record. Each of these operations runs in worst-case constant time. Let T be a lock-free data structure. To use DEBRA,

T simply invokes *leaveQstate* at the beginning of each operation, *enterQstate* at the end of each operation, and *retire*(r) each time a record r is retired (i.e., removed from T). Like EBR, DEBRA assumes that a process does not hold a pointer to any record between successive operations on T. Another constraint is that *retire*(r) can be invoked only once each time r is retired. Each process alternates invocations of *leaveQstate* and *enterQstate*, beginning with an invocation of *leaveQstate*. Each process is said to be quiescent initially and after invoking *enterQstate*, and is said to be non-quiescent after invoking *leaveQstate*. An invocation of *isQuiescent* by a process returns true if it is quiescent, and false otherwise.

In DEBRA, each process p has three limbo bags, denoted bag_0, bag_1 and bag_2, which contain records that it removed from the data structure. At any point, one of these bags is designated as p's limbo bag for the current epoch, and is pointed to by a local variable *currentBag*. Whenever p removes a record from the data structure, it simply adds it to *currentBag*. Each process has a *quiescent bit*, which indicates whether the process is currently quiescent. The only thing p does when it enters a quiescent state is set its quiescent bit. Whenever p *leaves* a quiescent state, it reads the current epoch e and announces it in $announce_p$. If this changes the value of $announce_p$, then the contents of the oldest limbo bag can be reused or freed. In this case, p changes *currentBag* to point to the oldest limbo bag, and then moves the contents of *currentBag* to an object pool. (Alternatively, the records in *currentBag* could be freed.) Next, p attempts to determine whether the epoch can be advanced, which is the case if each process is either quiescent or has announced e. Process p incrementally scans the announcements and quiescent bits of all processes, amortizing the cost over n *leaveQstate* operations. A local variable *checked* keeps track of the number of processes that p has verified are quiescent or have announced e since p last announced a new epoch. Once *checked* is n, p performs a CAS to increment the current epoch.

DEBRA reclaims a record only when no process has a pointer to it: Suppose p places a record r in limbo bag b at time t_1, and moves r from b to the pool at time t_2. Assume, to obtain a contradiction, that a process q has a pointer to r at time t_2. At time t_1, b is p's current limbo bag, and just before time t_2, b is changed from being p's oldest limbo bag to being p's current limbo bag, again. Thus, *currentBag* must be changed at least three times between t_1 and t_2. Since p changes *currentBag* only in an invocation of *leaveQstate* that changes $announce_p$, p must perform at least three such invocations between t_1 and t_2. The current epoch must change between any pair of invocations of *leaveQstate* that change $announce_p$, so the current epoch must change at least twice between t_1 and t_2. By definition, at some time between two changes of the current epoch, say from e to e' and from e' to e'', q must either be quiescent or have announced e'. Process q cannot announce e' prior to the current epoch changing to e', thus, it must announce e' between these two epoch changes. Since q can only announce an epoch when it is in a quiescent state, q must be quiescent at some point between t_1 and t_2. This means q must obtain its pointer to r by following pointers from an entry point after it was quiescent, which is after t_1. However, r is removed from the data structure before t_1, and, hence, it is no longer reachable by following pointers from an entry point, which is a contradiction.

The object pool shared by all processes is implemented as a collection of n *pool bags*, one per process, and one shared bag. Whenever a process moves a record to the pool, it places the record in its pool bag. If its pool bag is too large, it moves some records to the shared bag. Whenever a process wants to allocate a record, it first attempts to remove one from its pool bag. If its pool bag is empty, it attempts to take some records from the shared bag. If the process fails to take any record from the shared bag, then it will allocate a new record.

For efficiency, each pool bag and limbo bag is implemented as a *blockbag*, which is a singly-linked list of *blocks*. Each block contains a *next* pointer and up to B records. (In our experiments, $B = 256$.) The head block in a blockbag always contains fewer than B records, and every subsequent block contains B records. With this invariant, it is straightforward to design constant time operations to add and remove records in a blockbag, and to move all full blocks from one blockbag to another. This allows a process to move all full blocks of records in its oldest limbo bag to the pool highly efficiently after announcing a new epoch. However, if the process only moves *full* blocks to the pool, then this limbo bag may be left with some records in its head block. These records *could* be moved to the pool immediately, but it is more efficient to leave them in the bag, and simply move them to the pool later, once the block that contains them is full. One consequence of not moving these records to the pool is that each limbo bag can contain at most $B-1$ records that were retired two or more epochs ago. This does not affect correctness. The shared bag is implemented as a lock-free singly-linked list of blocks with operations to add and remove a full block. Moving entire blocks to and from the shared bag reduces the frequency with which processes must synchronize on the shared bag.

Operating on blocks instead of individual records significantly reduces overhead. However, it also requires a process to allocate and deallocate blocks. To reduce the number of blocks that are allocated and deallocated during an execution, each process has a bounded *block pool* that is used by all of its blockbags. Instead of deallocating a block, a process returns the block to its block bool. If the block pool is already full, then the block is freed. Experiments show that allowing each process to keep up to 16 blocks in its block pool reduces the number of blocks allocated by more than 99.9%. No blocks are allocated for the shared bag, since blocks are simply moved between pool bags and the shared bag.

Two additional optimization are made. First, the least significant bit of $announce_p$ is used as p's quiescent bit. This allows both values to be read and written atomically, which reduces the number of reads and writes to shared memory. Second, a process increments the current epoch only after invoking *leaveQstate* at least MIN_CALLS times, where MIN_CALLS is a constant (100 in our experiments). This is especially helpful when the number of processes is small. For example, in a single process system, without this optimization, the process will advance the epoch and try to move records to the pool at the beginning of every single operation, introducing unnecessary overhead.

5. ADDING FAULT TOLERANCE

The primary disadvantage of DEBRA is that a crashed or slow process can stay in a non-quiescent state for an arbitrarily long time. This prevents any other processes from freeing memory. Although we did not observe this pathological behaviour in our experiments, many applications require a bound on the number of records waiting to be freed.

Lock-free data structures are ideal for building fault tolerant systems, because they are designed to be provably fault tolerant. If a process crashes while it is in the middle of any lock-free operation, and it leaves the data structure in an inconsistent state, other processes can always repair that state. The onus is on a process that wants to access part of a data structure to restore that part of the data structure to a consistent state before using it. Consequently, a lock-free data structure always provides procedures to repair and access parts of the data structure that are damaged (by a process

```
1  process local variables:
2     descriptor *desc;
3  void signalHandler(args):
4    if (isQuiescent()) then
5      enterQstate();
6      siglongjmp(...);            // jump to recovery code
7  int doOperationXYZ(args):
8    ...                           // quiescent preamble
9    while (!done)
10     if (sigsetjmp(...))         // begin recovery code
11       if (isRProtected(desc)) done = help(desc);
12       RUnprotectAll();
13     else                        // end recovery code
14       leaveQstate();            // begin body
15       do search phase
16       initialize *desc
17       RProtect each record will be accessed, or used
             as the old value of a CAS, by help(desc)
18       RProtect(desc);
19       done = help(desc);
20       enterQstate();            // end body
21       RUnprotectAll();
22   ...                           // quiescent postamble
23   perform retire() calls
```

Figure 1: Applying DEBRA+ to a typical lock-free operation. Lines 14 and 20 are necessary for both DEBRA and DEBRA+. Gray lines are necessary for fault tolerance (DEBRA+).

crash) or undergoing changes. (Furthermore, these procedures are necessarily designed so that processes can crash while executing them, and other processes can still repair the data structure and continue to make progress.) We use these procedures to design a mechanism that allows a process to *neutralize* another process that is preventing it from advancing the epoch.

A novel aspect of DEBRA+ is our use of two features offered by Unix, Linux and other POSIX-compliant operating systems. The first is *signaling*, an inter-process communication mechanism. Signals can be sent to a process by the operating system, and by other processes. When a process receives a signal, the code it was executing is interrupted, and the process begins executing a *signal handler*, instead. When the process returns from the signal handler, it resumes executing from where it was interrupted. A process can specify what action it will take when it receives a particular signal by registering a function as its signal handler.

The second feature is *non-local goto*, which allows a process to begin executing from a different instruction, *outside* of the current function, by using two procedures: *sigsetjmp* and *siglongjmp*. A process first invokes *sigsetjmp*, which saves its local state and returns false. Later, the process can invoke *siglongjmp*, which restores the state saved by *sigsetjmp* immediately prior to its return, but causes it to return true instead of false. The standard way to use these primitives is with the idiom: "if (sigsetjmp(...)) alternate(); else usual();". A process that executes this code will save its state and execute usual(). Then, if the process later invokes *siglongjmp*, it will restore the state saved by *sigsetjmp* and immediately begin executing alternate().

At the beginning of each operation by a process q, q invokes *sigsetjmp*, following the idiom described above, and then proceeds with its operation. Another process p can interrupt q by sending a signal to q. We design q's signal handler so that, if q was interrupted while it was in a quiescent state, then q will simply return from the signal handler and resume its regular execution from wherever it was interrupted. However, if q was interrupted in a non-quiescent state, then it is neutralized: it will enter a quiescent state and perform a *siglongjmp*. Then, q will execute special *recovery code*, which allows it to clean up any mess it left because it was neutralized. Since q's signal handler performs *siglongjmp* only if q was interrupted in a non-quiescent state, q will not perform *siglongjmp* while it is executing recovery code. Hence, if q receives a signal while it is executing recovery code, it will simply return from the signal handler and resume executing wherever it left off.

Our technique requires the operating system to guarantee that, after a process p sends q a signal, the next time process q takes a step, it will execute its signal handler. (This requirement can be weakened with small modifications to DEBRA+, which are discussed in the full version of this paper.) With this guarantee, after p has sent a signal to q, it knows that q will not access any retired record until q has executed its recovery code and subsequently executed *leaveQstate*. Thus, as soon as p has sent q a signal, p can immediately proceed as if q is quiescent.

Recovery code must be tailored to the data structure, but it is straightforward for lock-free operations of the following form. Each operation is divided into three parts: a quiescent bookkeeping *preamble*, a non-quiescent *body*, and a quiescent bookkeeping *postamble*. Processes can be neutralized while executing in the body, but cannot be neutralized while executing in the preamble or postamble (because a process will not call *siglongjmp* while it is quiescent). Consequently, processes should not do anything in the body that will corrupt the data structure if they are neutralized part way through. Allocation, deallocation, manipulation of process-local data structures that persist between operations, and other non-reentrant actions should occur only in the preamble and postamble. Figure 1 shows how to apply DEBRA+ to such an operation. The remainder of this section explains the steps shown there.

The body proceeds by first reading some records, then initializing and announcing a special record (allocated in the preamble) called a *descriptor*, which describes how to perform the operation. It then executes a *help* procedure, which uses the information in the descriptor to perform the operation. We assume that the descriptor includes all pointers that the *help* procedure will follow (or use as the expected value of a CAS). The *help* procedure can also be used by other processes to help the operation complete. In a system where processes may crash, a process whose progress is blocked by another operation cannot simply wait for the operation to complete, so helping is necessary. The *help* procedure for any lock-free algorithm is always reentrant and idempotent, because, at any time, one process can pause, and another process can begin helping. Likewise, *enterQstate* must be both reentrant and idempotent.

We now describe recovery for an operation O performed by a process p. Suppose p receives a signal, enters a quiescent state, and then performs *siglongjmp* to begin executing its recovery code. Although there are many places where p might have been executing when it was neutralized, it is fairly simply to determine what action it should take next. The main challenge is determining whether another process already performed O on p's behalf. To do this, p checks whether it announced a descriptor for O before it was neutralized. If it did, then some other process might have seen this descriptor and started helping O. So, p invokes *help* (which is safe even if another process already helped O, since *help* is idempotent). Otherwise, p can simply restart the body of O.

DEBRA allows a non-quiescent process executing an operation to safely access any record that it reached by following pointers from an entry point during the operation. However, DEBRA does *not* allow quiescent processes to safely access any records. Once a process p has been sent a signal, other processes treat p as if were quiescent. Furthermore, p enters a quiescent state before executing recovery code, and it remains in a quiescent state throughout the recovery code. Consequently, after p starts executing its signal handler, it cannot safely access any records it has pointers to, since they might already have been freed. However, the help procedure in the recovery code must access the descriptor record, and possibly some of the records to which it points. We use HPs in a very limited way to prevent these records from being freed by other processes before p has finished either its operation or its recovery code. This lets p safely run its recovery code in a quiescent state, so that other processes can continue to advance the current epoch and reclaim memory.

We now describe how HPs are used. Before p invokes *help* for a descriptor d, it must acquire HPs by invoking *RProtect* for each record that $help(d)$ will access, and finally invoking $RProtect(d)$. At the end of each operation (just after performing *enterQstate*), and at the end of its recovery code, p invokes *RUnprotectAll* to release all of its HPs. Before p can move a record r to the pool, it must first verify that no HP points to it by invoking $isRProtected(r)$, which returns true if some HP points to r, and false otherwise. When executing recovery code, p first invokes *isRProtected* to determine whether the last descriptor it announced is protected. If so, then each r in S is also protected, and p is ready to safely execute $help(d)$. Otherwise, p has not yet invoked $help(d)$, so no other process is aware of p's operation, and p can simply terminate its recovery code and restart its operation. Note that, since *RProtect* is performed while a process is non-quiescent, p might be neutralized while executing it. Hence, it must be reentrant and idempotent.

Using our new *neutralizing* mechanism, we can bound the number of records waiting to be freed. Each time a process p performing *leaveQstate* encounters a process q that is not quiescent and has not announced epoch e, p checks whether the size of its own current limbo bag exceeds some constant c. If so, p neutralizes q. After p's current limbo bag contains at least c elements, and p performs n more data structure operations, it will have performed *leaveQstate* n times, and each non-quiescent process will either have announced the current epoch or been neutralized by p. Consequently, p will advance the current epoch, and, the next time it performs *leaveQstate*, it will announce the new epoch and reclaim records. It follows that p's current limbo bag can contain at most $c+O(nm)$ elements, where m is the largest number of records that can be removed from the data structure by a high-level operation. Therefore, the total number of records waiting to be freed is $O(n(nm+c))$.

In DEBRA, all full blocks in a limbo bag are moved to the pool in constant time. In DEBRA+, records can be moved to the pool only if no HP points to them, so this is no longer possible. One way to move records from a limbo bag b to the pool is to iterate over each record r in b, and check if a HP points to r. To make this more efficient, we move records from b to the pool only when b contains $nk+\Omega(nk)+B$ records, where k is the number of HPs needed per process, and B is the maximum number of records in a block. Before we begin iterating over records in b, we create a hash table containing every HP. Then, we can check whether a HP points to r in O(1) expected time. We can further optimize by rearranging records in b so that we can still move full blocks to the pool, instead of individual records. To do this, we iterate over the records in b, and move all records that are pointed to by HPs to the beginning of the blockbag. All full blocks that do not contain a record pointed to by a HP are then moved to the pool (in constant time). Since there are at most nk HPs, and we scan only when b contains at least $nk+B+\Omega(nk)$ records, we will be able to move at least $max\{B,\Omega(nk)\}$ records to the pool. Thus, the expected amortized cost to move a record to the pool (or free it) is O(1).

One problem with DEBRA+ is that it seems difficult to apply to lock-based data structures, because it is dangerous to interrupt a process and force it to restart while it holds a lock. Of course, there is little reason to use DEBRA+ for a lock-based data structure, since locks can cause deadlock if processes crash. For lock-based data structures, DEBRA can be used, instead.

6. A LOCK-FREE MEMORY MANAGEMENT ABSTRACTION

There are many compelling reasons to separate memory allocation and reclamation from data structure code. Although the steps that a programmer must take to apply a non-automatic technique to a data structure vary widely, it is possible to find a small, natural set of operations that allows a programmer to write data structure code once, and easily plug in many popular memory reclamation schemes. In this section, we describe a record management abstraction, called a Record Manager, that is easy to use, and provides sufficient flexibility to support (all three versions of) HPs, DTA, EBR, DEBRA and DEBRA+. (ST is not supported because it currently requires a programmer to insert transactions throughout the code, and annotate the beginning and end of each stack frame.)

A Record Manager has three components: an Allocator, a Reclaimer and a Pool. The Allocator determines how records will be allocated (e.g., by individual calls to *malloc* or by handing out records from a large range of memory) and freed. The Reclaimer is given records after they are removed from the data structure, and determines when they can be safely handed off to the Pool. The Pool determines when records are handed to the Allocator to be freed, and whether a process actually uses the Allocator to allocate a new record.

We implement data structures, Allocators, Reclaimers and Pools in a modular way, so that they can be combined without recompiling them. This clean separation into interchangeable components allows, e.g., the same Pool implementation to be used with both a HP Reclaimer and a DEBRA Reclaimer. Modularity is typically achieved with inheritance, but inheritance introduces significant runtime overhead. For example, when the precompiled data structure invokes *retire*, it does not know which of the precompiled versions of *retire* it should use, so it must perform work at runtime to choose the correct implementation. In C++, this can be done more efficiently with *template parameters*, which allow a compiler to reach into compiled code and replace placeholder calls with calls to the correct implementations. Unlike inheritance, templates introduce no overhead, since the correct implementation is compiled into the code. Furthermore, if the correct implementation is a small function, the compiler can simply insert its code directly into the calling function (eliminating the function call altogether).

A programmer interacts with the Record Manager, which exposes the operations of the Pool and Reclaimer. A Pool provides *allocate* and *deallocate* operations. A Reclaimer provides operations for the basic events that memory reclamation schemes are interested in: starting and finishing data structure operations (*leaveQstate* and *enterQstate*), reaching a new pointer and disposing of it (*protect* and *unprotect*), and retiring a record (*retire*). It also provides operations to check whether a process is quiescent (*isQuiescent*) and whether a pointer can be followed safely (*isProtected*). Finally, it provides operations for making information available to recovery code (*RProtect*, *RUnprotectAll*, *isRProtected*).

Most of these are described in Section 4 and Section 5. We describe the rest here. *protect*, which must be invoked on a record r before accessing any field of r, returns true if the process successfully protects r (and, hence, is permitted to access its fields), and returns false otherwise. Once a process has successfully protected r, it remains protected until the process invokes $unprotect(r)$ or becomes quiescent. $isProtected(r)$ returns true if r is currently protected by the process.

Reclaimers for DEBRA and DEBRA+ are effectively described in Section 4 and Section 5. For these techniques, *unprotect* does nothing, and *protect* and *isProtected* simply return true. (Consequently, these calls are optimized out of the code by the compiler.) For HPs, *leaveQstate*, *RProtect* and *RUnprotectAll* all do nothing, and *isQuiescent* and *isRProtected* simply return false. *unprotect*(r) releases a HP to r, and *enterQstate* clears all announced HPs. *protect* announces a HP to a record and executes a function, which determines whether that record is in the data structure. *retire*(r) places r in a bag, and, if the bag contains sufficiently many records, it constructs a hash table T containing all HPs, and moves all records not in T to the Pool (as described in Section 3).

A predicate called *supportsCrashRecovery* is added to Reclaimers to allow a programmer to add crash recovery to a data structure without imposing overhead for Reclaimers that do not support crash recovery. For example, a programmer can check whether *supportsCrashRecovery* is true before invoking *RProtect*. The code statement "if (*supportsCrashRecovery*)" statically evaluates to "if (true)" or "if (false)" at compile time, once the Reclaimer template has been filled in. Consequently, these if-statements are completely eliminated by the compiler. In our experiments, this predicate is used to invoke *sigsetjmp* only for DEBRA+ (eliminating overhead for the other techniques).

7. EXPERIMENTS

We did experiments to compare the performance of various Reclaimers: DEBRA, DEBRA+, HP, ST and no reclamation (None). We used the Record Manager abstraction to perform allocation and reclamation for a lock-free balanced binary search tree [4]. This BST can contain marked nodes that point to other marked nodes, so ST cannot be used, and we must confront the problems described in Section 3 to apply HP. Properly dealing with HP's problems would be highly complex and inefficient, so we simply restart any operation that encounters a marked node. Consequently, applying HP causes the BST to lose its lock-free progress guarantee. To determine whether this significantly affects the performance of HP, we added the same restarting behaviour to DEBRA, and observed that its impact on performance was small.

Code for ST was graciously provided by its authors. They used a lock-based skip list to compare None, HP and ST. We modified their code to use a Record Manager for allocating and pooling nodes, and used it to compare None, DEBRA, HP and ST. The actual reclamation code for HP and ST is due to the authors of ST. Since the skip list uses locks, it cannot use DEBRA+.

We ran our experiments on an Intel i7 4770 machine with 4 cores, 8 hardware threads and 16GB of memory, running Ubuntu 14.04. (There is currently no system with more than 4 cores that provides HTM and, hence, supports ST.) All code was compiled with GCC 4.9.1-3 and the highest optimization level (-O3). Google's high performance Thread Caching malloc (tcmalloc-2.4) was used.

Our first experiment compared the overhead of performing reclamation for the various Reclaimers. In this experiment, each Reclaimer performed all the work necessary to reclaim nodes, but nodes were not actually reclaimed (and, hence, were not reused). The Record Manager used a *Bump Allocator*: each process requests a large region of memory from the operating system at the beginning of an execution, and then divides that region into nodes, which it allocates in sequence. Since nodes were not actually reclaimed, we eliminated the Pool component of the Record Manager. In this experiment, a data structure suffers the overhead of reclamation, but does *not* enjoy its benefits (namely, a smaller memory footprint and fewer cache misses).

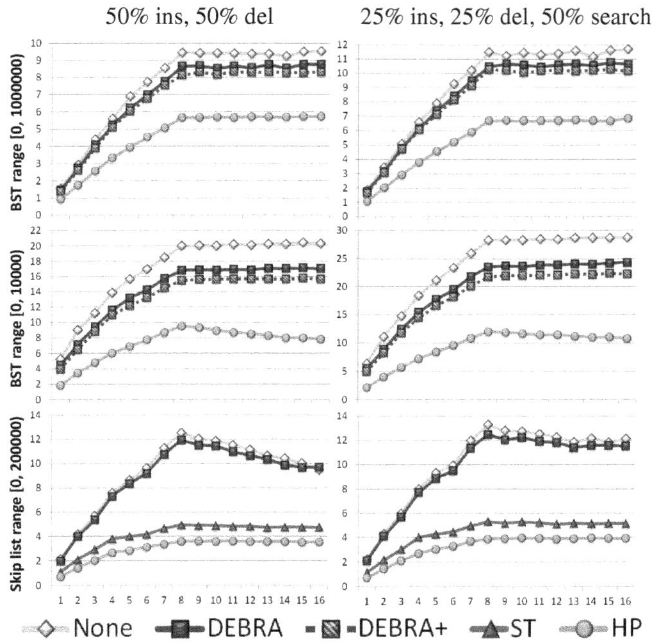

Figure 2: Results for Experiment 1 (Overhead of reclamation). The x-axis shows the number of processes. The y-axis shows throughput, in millions of operations per second.

For the balanced BST, we ran eight *trials* for each combination of Reclaimers in {None, DEBRA, DEBRA+, HP}, thread counts (in {1, 2, ..., 16}), operation mixes in {25i-25d, 50i-50d} (where xi-yd means x% insertions, y% deletions and $(100 - x - y)$% searches) and key ranges in {[0, 10000), [0, 1000000)}. For the skip list, the thread counts and operation mixes were the same, but ST was used instead of DEBRA+, and there was only one key range, [0, 200000). In each trial, the data structure was first prefilled to half of the key range, then the appropriate number of threads performed random operations (according to the operation mix) on uniformly random keys from the key range for two seconds. The average of each set of eight trials became a data point in a graph. (Unfortunately, the system quickly runs out of memory when nodes are not reclaimed, so it is not possible to run all trials for longer than two seconds. However, we ran long trials for many cases to verify that the results do not change.)

The results in Figure 2 show that DEBRA and DEBRA+ have extremely low overhead. In the BST, DEBRA has between 5% and 22% overhead (averaging 12%), and DEBRA+ has between 7% and 28% overhead (averaging 17%). Compared to HP, on average, DEBRA performs 94% more operations and DEBRA+ performs 83% more. This is largely because DEBRA and DEBRA+ synchronize once *per operation*, whereas HP synchronizes each time a process reaches a new node. In the skip list, DEBRA has up to 6% overhead (averaging 4%), outperforms HP by an average of 200%, and also outperforms ST by between 93% and 168% (averaging 133%). ST has significant overhead. For instance, on average, it starts almost four transactions per operation (each of which announces one or more pointers), and runtime checks are frequently performed to determine if a new transaction should be started.

In our second experiment, nodes were actually reclaimed. The Reclaimers were each paired with the same Pool as DEBRA. The only exception was None, which does not use a Pool. (Thus, None is the same as in the first experiment.)

The results appear in Figure 3. In the BST, DEBRA is only 8% slower than None on average, and, for some data points, DEBRA actually improves performance by up to 12%. This is possible be-

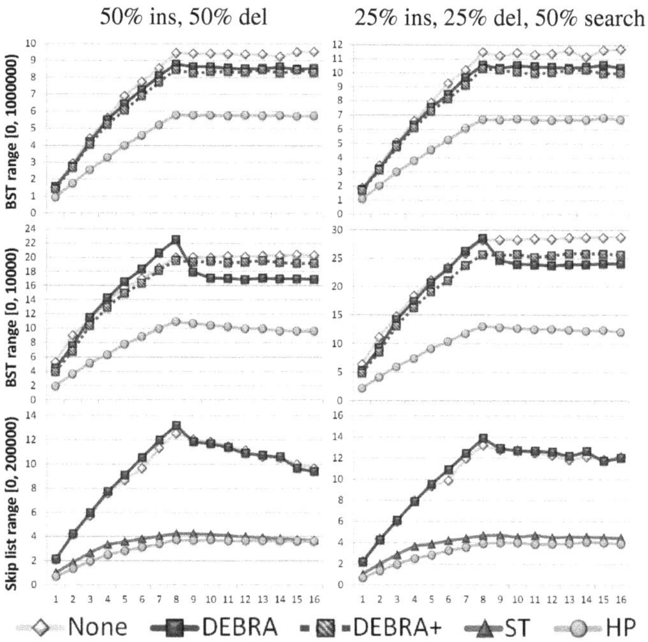

Figure 3: Experiment 2 (Using a Bump Allocator and a Pool).

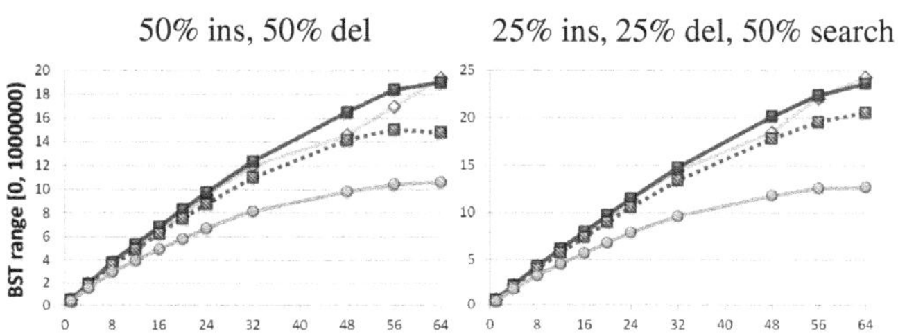

Figure 4: Extra results for Experiment 2 on Oracle T4-1.

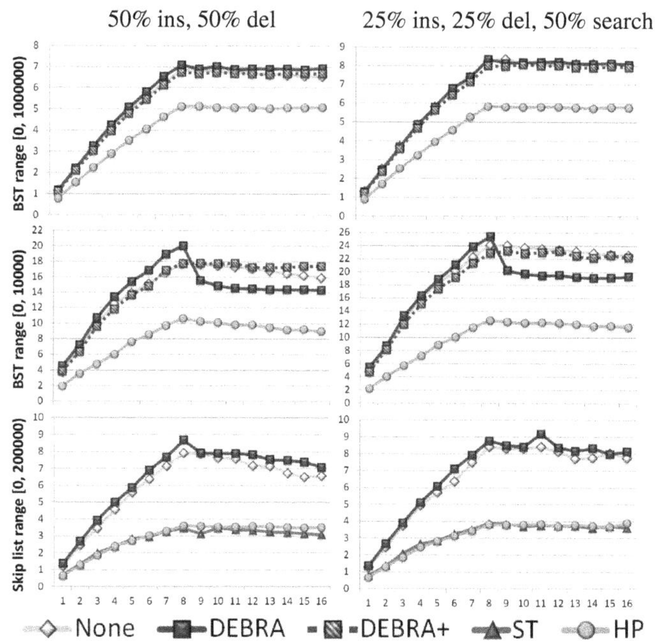

Figure 5: Experiment 3: (Using malloc and a Pool).

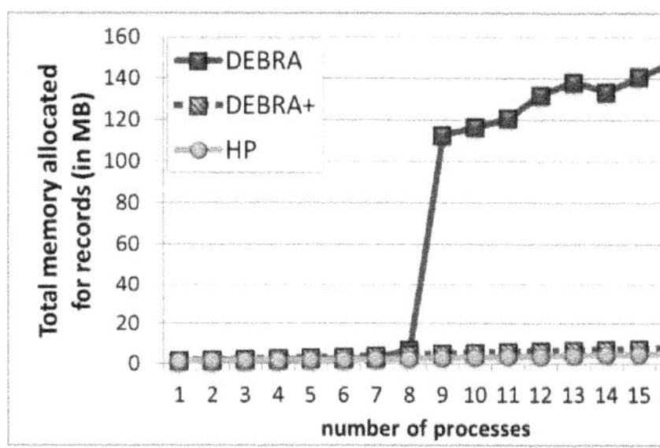

Figure 6: Memory allocated for records in Experiment 2 in the BST with keyrange 10,000 and workload 50i-50d.

cause DEBRA reduces the memory footprint of the data structure, which allows a larger fraction of the allocated nodes to fit in cache and, hence, reduces the number of cache misses. DEBRA+ is between 2% and 25% slower than None, averaging 10%. Compared to HP, DEBRA is between 48% and 145% faster, averaging 80%, and DEBRA+ is between 43% and 123% faster, averaging 76%. In the skip list, DEBRA performs *as well as None*. DEBRA also *outperforms* ST by between 108% and 211%, averaging 160%.

To measure the benefit of neutralizing slow processes, we tracked the total amount of memory allocated for records in each trial. Since we used bump allocation, this simply required determining how far each bump allocator's pointer had moved during the execution. Thus, we were able to compute the total amount of memory allocated *after* each trial had finished (without having any impact on the trial while it was executing). Figure 6 shows the total amount of memory allocated for records in the second experiment in the BST with key range 10,000 and workload 50i-50d. (The other cases were similar.) DEBRA, DEBRA+ and HP all perform similarly up to eight processes. However, for more than eight processes, some processes are always context switched out, and they often prevent DEBRA from advancing the epoch in a timely manner. DEBRA+ fixes this issue. With 16 processes, DEBRA+ neutralizes processes an average of 935 times per trial, reducing memory usage by an average of 94% over DEBRA.

We also ran the second experiment on a NUMA Oracle T4-1 system with 8 cores and 64 hardware contexts. Figure 4 shows a subset of the results (which is limited due to lack of space).

Our third experiment is like the second, except we used a different Allocator, which does not preallocate memory. The Allocator's *allocate* operation simply invokes *malloc* to request memory from the operation system (and its *deallocate* operation invokes *free*).

The results (in Figure 5) are similar to the results for the second experiment. However, the absolute throughput is significantly smaller than in the previous experiments, because of the overhead of invoking *malloc*. Although HP and ST are negatively affected, proportionally, they slow down less than None, DEBRA and DEBRA+. This illustrates an important experimental principle: *uniformly adding overhead to an experiment disproportionately impacts low-overhead algorithms, and obscures their advantage.*

8. CONCLUSION

In this work, we presented a distributed variant of EBR, called DEBRA. Compared to EBR, DEBRA significantly reduces synchronization overhead and offers high performance even with many more processes than physical cores. Our experiments show that, compared with performing no reclamation at all, DEBRA is 4% slower on average, 21% slower at worst, and up to 20% *faster* in some cases. Moreover, DEBRA outperforms StackTrack by an average of 138%. DEBRA is easy to use, and only adds O(1) steps per data structure operation and O(1) steps per retired record.

We also presented DEBRA+, the first epoch based reclamation scheme that allows processes to continue reclaiming memory after a process has crashed. In an n process system, the number of objects waiting to be freed is $O(mn^2)$, where m is the largest number of objects retired by one data structure operation. The cost to reuse or free a record is O(1) expected amortized time. In our experiments, DEBRA+ reduced memory consumption over DEBRA by 94%. Compared with performing no reclamation, DEBRA+ is only 10% slower on average. DEBRA+ also outperforms a highly efficient implementation of hazard pointers by an average of 70%.

We introduced the *Record Manager*, the first generalization of the C++ *Allocator* abstraction that is suitable for lock-free programming. A Record Manager separates memory reclamation code from lock-free data structure code, which allows a dynamic data structure to be implemented without knowing how its records will be allocated, reclaimed and freed. This abstraction adds virtually no overhead. It is highly flexible, allowing a programmer to interchange techniques for reclamation, object pooling, allocation and deallocation by changing one line of code.

Besides DEBRA and DEBRA+, the neutralizing technique introduced in this work is of independent interest. It would be useful to find different ways to neutralize processes, so, for example, the neutralizing technique could be used with different operating systems. There may also be opportunities to apply neutralizing in other contexts, such as garbage collection. Finally, it would also be interesting to understand whether these ideas can be extended to lock-based algorithms (even for a restricted class, such as reentrant and idempotent algorithms).

Acknowledgments

I would like to acknowledge my supervisor Faith Ellen for her insightful suggestions. I also extend my thanks to Ryan Johnson, whose advice and detailed knowledge of operating system mechanisms was invaluable to me. I thank Dave Dice for kindly running my experiments on the Oracle machine. Lastly, I thank the authors of StackTrack for sharing their code, and the anonymous reviewers for their helpful comments. This research was supported by the National Science and Engineering Research Council of Canada.

9. REFERENCES

[1] Z. Aghazadeh, W. Golab, and P. Woelfel. Making objects writable. In *Proceedings of the 2014 ACM symposium on Principles of distr. comp.*, pages 385–395. ACM, 2014.

[2] D. Alistarh, P. Eugster, M. Herlihy, A. Matveev, and N. Shavit. Stacktrack: An automated transactional approach to concurrent memory reclamation. In *Proceedings of the 9th European Conference on Comp. Sys.*, page 25. ACM, 2014.

[3] A. Braginsky, A. Kogan, and E. Petrank. Drop the anchor: lightweight memory management for non-blocking data structures. In *Proceedings of the 25th ACM symposium on Parallelism in alg. and arch.*, pages 33–42. ACM, 2013.

[4] T. Brown, F. Ellen, and E. Ruppert. A general technique for non-blocking trees. In *Proceedings of the 19th ACM SIGPLAN symposium on Principles and practice of parallel programming*, pages 329–342. ACM, 2014.

[5] T. Brown and J. Helga. Non-blocking k-ary search trees. In *Principles of Distr. Sys.*, pages 207–221. Springer, 2011.

[6] D. L. Detlefs, P. A. Martin, M. Moir, and G. L. Steele Jr. Lock-free reference counting. *Distributed Computing*, 15(4):255–271, 2002.

[7] D. Drachsler, M. Vechev, and E. Yahav. Practical concurrent binary search trees via logical ordering. In *Proceedings of the 19th annual ACM symposium on Principles and practice of parallel programming*, pages 343–356. ACM, 2014.

[8] A. Dragojević, M. Herlihy, Y. Lev, and M. Moir. On the power of hardware transactional memory to simplify memory management. In *Proceedings of the 30th annual ACM SIGACT-SIGOPS symposium on Principles of distributed computing*, pages 99–108. ACM, 2011.

[9] F. Ellen, P. Fatourou, J. Helga, and E. Ruppert. The amortized complexity of non-blocking binary search trees. In *Proc. of ACM Symp. on Princ. of Distr. Comp.*, PODC '14, pages 332–340, New York, NY, USA, 2014. ACM.

[10] F. Ellen, P. Fatourou, E. Ruppert, and F. van Breugel. Non-blocking binary search trees. In *Proceedings of the 29th ACM SIGACT-SIGOPS symposium on Principles of distributed computing*, pages 131–140. ACM, 2010.

[11] K. Fraser. *Practical lock-freedom*. PhD thesis, University of Cambridge, 2004.

[12] A. Gidenstam, M. Papatriantafilou, H. Sundell, and P. Tsigas. Efficient and reliable lock-free memory reclamation based on reference counting. *Parallel and Distributed Systems, IEEE Transactions on*, 20(8):1173–1187, 2009.

[13] T. E. Hart, P. E. McKenney, A. D. Brown, and J. Walpole. Performance of memory reclamation for lockless synchronization. *Journal of Parallel and Distributed Computing*, 67(12):1270–1285, 2007.

[14] M. Herlihy. A methodology for implementing highly concurrent data objects. *ACM Trans. Program. Lang. Syst.*, 15(5):745–770, Nov. 1993.

[15] M. Herlihy, V. Luchangco, P. Martin, and M. Moir. Nonblocking memory management support for dynamic-sized data structures. *ACM Transactions on Computer Systems (TOCS)*, 23(2):146–196, 2005.

[16] R. Jones and R. Lins. Garbage collection: Algorithms for automatic dynamic memory management. *John Wiliey & Sons Ltd., England*, 1996.

[17] H. Lee. Fast local-spin abortable mutual exclusion with bounded space. In *Principles of Distributed Systems*, pages 364–379. Springer, 2010.

[18] A. Matveev. Private communication.

[19] P. E. McKenney and J. D. Slingwine. Read-copy update: Using execution history to solve concurrency problems. In *Parallel and Distr. Comp. and Sys.*, pages 509–518, 1998.

[20] M. Michael. Hazard pointers: Safe memory reclamation for lock-free objects. *Parallel and Distributed Systems, IEEE Transactions on*, 15(6):491–504, 2004.

[21] A. Natarajan and N. Mittal. Fast concurrent lock-free binary search trees. In *Proceedings of the 19th annual ACM symposium on Principles and practice of parallel programming*, pages 317–328. ACM, 2014.

[22] M. Schoeberl and W. Puffitsch. Nonblocking real-time garbage collection. *ACM Transactions on Embedded Computing Systems (TECS)*, 10(1):6, 2010.

[23] N. Shafiei. Non-blocking patricia tries with replace operations. In *Distributed Comp. Sys. (ICDCS), 2013 IEEE 33rd Int. Conf. on*, pages 216–225. IEEE, 2013.

[24] R. K. Treiber. *Systems programming: Coping with parallelism*. International Business Machines Incorporated, Thomas J. Watson Research Center, 1986.

On the Space Complexity of Set Agreement*

Carole Delporte-Gallet
LIAFA, Université Paris-Diderot

Hugues Fauconnier
LIAFA, Université Paris-Diderot

Petr Kuznetsov
Télécom ParisTech

Eric Ruppert
York University

ABSTRACT

The k-set agreement problem is a generalization of the classical consensus problem in which processes are permitted to output up to k different input values. In a system of n processes, an m-obstruction-free solution to the problem requires termination only in executions where the number of processes taking steps is eventually bounded by m. This family of progress conditions generalizes wait-freedom ($m = n$) and obstruction-freedom ($m = 1$). In this paper, we prove upper and lower bounds on the number of registers required to solve m-obstruction-free k-set agreement, considering both one-shot and repeated formulations. In particular, we show that repeated k-set agreement can be solved using $n + 2m - k$ registers and establish a nearly matching lower bound of $n + m - k$.

Categories and Subject Descriptors

F.2.2 [**Analysis of Algorithms and Problem Complexity**]: Nonnumerical Algorithms; D.4.1 [**Operating Systems**]: Process Management—*concurrency, multiprocessing/multiprogramming, synchronization*

Keywords

space complexity; k-set agreement; m-obstruction-freedom

1. INTRODUCTION

Algorithms that allow processes to reach agreement are one of the central concerns of the theory of distributed computing, since some kind of agreement underlies many tasks that require processes to coordinate with one another. In the classical consensus problem, each process begins with an input value, and all processes must agree to output one of those input values. Chaudhuri [3] introduced the k-set agreement problem, which generalizes the consensus problem by allowing processes to output up to k different input values in any execution. Consensus is the special case where $k = 1$. Set agreement is trivial for n processes if $k \geq n$: each process can simply output its own input value.

We consider the k-set agreement problem for $k < n$ in an asynchronous system equipped with shared read/write registers. To satisfy *wait-free* termination, non-faulty processes must terminate even if an arbitrary number of processes fail. The impossibility of solving wait-free k-set agreement using registers was a landmark result proved by three groups of researchers [2, 11, 12]. However, Herlihy, Luchangco and Moir [10] observed that k-set agreement *is* solvable (even for $k = 1$) under a weaker termination property, known as *obstruction-freedom* or *solo-termination*, which requires that a process must eventually terminate if it takes enough steps without interruption from other processes. Obstruction-freedom was introduced as a way of separating concerns: obstruction-free algorithms maintain safety properties in all possible executions, but make progress only when one process can run for long enough without encountering contention. Various scheduling mechanisms designed to reduce contention (such as backing off) can then be used to satisfy this condition.

Taubenfeld [13] introduced the m-obstruction-freedom progress property, which requires that, in any execution where at most m processes take infinitely many steps, each process that continues to take steps will eventually terminate successfully. Wait-freedom and obstruction-freedom are special cases, with the extreme values $m = n$ and $m = 1$, respectively. Like ordinary obstruction-freedom, m-obstruction-free algorithms guarantee safety in all runs. However, m-obstruction-freedom provides a stronger progress property: larger values of m require less rigid constraints on the scheduler in order to ensure progress. Since k-set agreement has no wait-free solution among $k + 1$ processes, it follows that there is no m-obstruction free solution when $m > k$. The converse follows from the work of Yang, Neiger and Gafni [15]: m-obstruction-free k-set agreement *can* be solved if $m \leq k$. In this paper, we study how the number of registers required to solve m-obstruction-free k-set agreement among n processes depends on the parameters m, k and n.

Previously, the only non-trivial space lower bound was for the very special case where $m = k = 1$. In this case, Fich,

*The first two authors were supported by the Agence Nationale de la Recherche, project DISPLEXITY, the third author was supported by the Agence Nationale de la Recherche, under grant agreement ANR-14-CE35-0010-01, project DISCMAT, and the fourth author by the Fondation Sciences Mathématiques de Paris and the Natural Sciences and Engineering Research Council of Canada.

Permission to make digital or hard copies of all or part of this work for personal or classroom use is granted without fee provided that copies are not made or distributed for profit or commercial advantage and that copies bear this notice and the full citation on the first page. Copyrights for components of this work owned by others than ACM must be honored. Abstracting with credit is permitted. To copy otherwise, or republish, to post on servers or to redistribute to lists, requires prior specific permission and/or a fee. Request permissions from permissions@acm.org.
PODC'15, July 21–23, 2015, Donostia-San Sebastián, Spain.
Copyright © 2015 ACM 978-1-4503-3617-8/15/07 ...$15.00.
DOI: http://dx.doi.org/10.1145/2767386.2767406.

	Repeated		One-shot	
Non-Anonymous	**lower**: $n+m-k$	(Section 3)	lower: 2	[4]
	upper: $\min(n+2m-k, n)$	(Section 4)	upper: $\min(n+2m-k, n)$	(Section 4)
Anonymous	lower: $n+m-k$	(Section 3)	**lower**: $\sqrt{m(\frac{n}{k}-2)}$ for $D = \mathbb{N}$	(Section 5)
	upper: $(m+1)(n-k)+m^2+1$	(Section 6)	upper: $(m+1)(n-k)+m^2$	(Section 6)

Figure 1: Lower and upper bounds on the number of registers to solve m-obstruction-free k-set agreement among n processes, where $1 \leq m \leq k < n$ and input values are from domain D (with $|D| > k$). Our main results appear in boldface; the others are corollaries.

Herlihy and Shavit [7] showed $\Omega(\sqrt{n})$ registers are needed. The best upper bound for this case is the trivial one of n registers, which comes from the fact that n (large) single-writer registers can implement any number of multi-writer registers [14]. Closing the gap between the linear upper bound and the $\Omega(\sqrt{n})$ lower bound is a major open problem. Unfortunately, there has been no progress on this gap in the past two decades.

We first prove nearly tight linear upper and lower bounds on the number of registers required for *repeated* set agreement. In many applications, such as Herlihy's universal construction [9], there is a sequence of (independent) agreement tasks that must be solved, rather than just one. We define the repeated k-set agreement problem to model this situation. Processes access an infinite sequence of instances k-set agreement in order. For all executions and for all i, processes accessing the ith instance of k-set agreement may output at most k of the values that are used as inputs to that instance.

We prove that any m-obstruction-free solution to repeated k-set agreement among n processes requires at least $n+m-k$ registers. We also give a novel algorithm for this task using $\min(n+2m-k, n)$ registers. Previously, the only known set agreement algorithm that uses fewer than n registers was a 1-obstruction-free k-set agreement algorithm that uses $2n-2k$ registers [4]. Our algorithm generalizes that algorithm (to handle any value of m) and improves the number of registers used in the case where $m = 1$ from $2(n-k)$ to $n-k+2$. For the case where $m = k = 1$, our results establish that obstruction-free repeated consensus requires exactly n registers. Thus, the gap between the $\Omega(\sqrt{n})$ lower bound and the $O(n)$ upper bound is closed when we consider the *repeated* version of the problem.

For the one-shot version of k-set agreement, we focus on the restricted case of anonymous systems, where processes do not have unique identifiers and are all programmed identically. We prove that any anonymous algorithm must use more than $\sqrt{m(\frac{n}{k}-2)}$ registers. The $\Omega(\sqrt{n})$ lower bound of Fich, Herlihy and Shavit [7] (for the anonymous case) is a special case of our result with $m = k = 1$, but the new result gives additional insight into the problem by showing a dependence on m and k. Moreover, the technique used in our proof is somewhat different, since it requires building an execution involving many different input values where each process is prevented from learning about any input value different from its own. We also prove that it is possible to solve the problem anonymously. Our algorithm for the repeated version of the problem uses $(m+1)(n-k)+m^2+1$ registers. (The usual construction using n single-writer registers is not applicable, since it presupposes unique identifiers.)

Figure 1 summarizes our results. Our four main results are in boldface; the others are corollaries.

2. PRELIMINARIES

We consider the standard asynchronous shared-memory model, in which $n > 1$ processes $p_1, \ldots, p_n$ communicate by applying read and write operations to shared *registers*. The registers are *multi-writer* and *multi-reader*, i.e., there are no restrictions on which processes may access which registers.

Each process has a local state that consists of the values stored in its local variables and a programme counter. A computation of the system proceeds in *steps* performed by the processes. Each step is one of the following: (1) an invocation of an operation, (2) a read or write operation on a shared register, (3) local computation that results in a change of a process's state, or (4) a response of an operation. Writes update the state of a shared register. All steps may update the local state of the process that performs it. A *configuration* specifies the state of each register and the local state of each process at one moment. In an *initial configuration*, all registers have the initial values specified by the algorithm and all processes are in their initial states.

A process is *active* if an operation has been invoked on the process but the operation has not yet produced a matching response; otherwise the process is called *idle*. We assume that an operation can only be invoked on an idle process and only active processes take steps. We focus on deterministic algorithms. Thus, given the current local state of an active process, the algorithm for this process stipulates the unique next *step* the process can perform. An *execution fragment* of an algorithm is a (possibly infinite) sequence of steps starting from some configuration that "respects" the algorithm for each process. An *execution* is an execution fragment that starts from the initial configuration. An operation is completed if its invocation is followed by a matching response. In an infinite execution, a process is *correct* if it takes an infinite number of steps or is idle from some point on.

Our algorithms make use of multi-writer *snapshot objects* [1], which can be implemented from registers. A snapshot object stores a vector of r values and provide two atomic operations: *update*(i, v) ($i \in \{1, \ldots, r\}$), which writes value v to component i, and *scan*(), which returns the vector of the most recently written values to components $1, \ldots, r$.

2.1 Set agreement

We begin with a formal definition of the *repeated k-set agreement* problem. Processes may perform PROPOSE(v) operations, where v is drawn from an input domain D. Each PROPOSE operation outputs a response from D when it terminates. For an execution α, let $In_i(\alpha)$ be the set of values that are used as the argument to some process's ith invocation of PROPOSE and let $Out_i(\alpha)$ be the set of values that are the response of some process's ith PROPOSE operation. Then, in every execution α of an algorithm that solves repeated k-set agreement the following properties must hold.

- *Validity*: $\forall i,\ Out_i(\alpha) \subseteq In_i(\alpha)$.
- *k-Agreement*: $\forall i,\ |Out_i(\alpha)| \leq k$.

An m-obstruction-free algorithm must additionally satisfy the following termination condition.

- *m-Obstruction-Freedom*: in every execution in which at most m processes take infinitely many steps, every correct process completes each of its operations.

The special case when $k = 1$ is called *consensus*. In the *(one-shot) k-set agreement problem*, every process invokes PROPOSE at most once.

It is known that wait-free $(k+1)$-process k-set agreement cannot be solved using registers [2, 11, 12]. This implies the following lemma, which we shall use to prove our space lower bounds.

LEMMA 1. *Let A be any algorithm that solves m-obstruction-free k-set agreement using registers. For any set V of m input values and any set Q of m processes, there is an execution of A in which only processes in Q take steps and all values in V are output.*

PROOF. Suppose the opposite for some sets V and Q and consider all executions of A in which only processes in Q with inputs in V take steps. By the assumption, at most $m-1$ distinct values are decided in each of these executions, which implies a wait-free m-process $(m-1)$-set agreement algorithm, violating [2, 11, 12]. □

Lemma 1 implies that no algorithm can solve m-obstruction-free k-set agreement using registers if $k < m$. In the rest of the paper, we derive lower and upper bounds on the space complexity of m-obstruction-free k-set agreement for n processes, where $m \leq k < n$. (If $k \geq n$, the problem is trivial and no registers are required: each process can simply output its own input value.)

3. LOWER BOUND FOR REPEATED SET AGREEMENT

In this section, we prove that solving m-obstruction-free repeated k-set agreement among n processes requires at least $n+m-k$ registers. Since the proof is technical, we first provide a brief overview. For simplicity, assume for now that $k+1$ is a multiple of m. We assume that there is an algorithm that uses fewer than $n+m-k$ registers, and construct an execution in which processes return $k+1$ different values in some instance of set agreement, contradicting the k-agreement property. The proof first constructs $c = \frac{k+1}{m}$ disjoint sets $Q_1, Q_2, \ldots, Q_c$ of m processes each, and an execution α that passes through a sequence of configurations $D_1, D_2, \ldots, D_c$ with the following property. For $1 \leq i < c$, *every possible* execution fragment by the processes in Q_i starting from D_i writes only to registers that are overwritten immediately after D_i in α. Moreover, processes in Q_i take no more steps after D_i in α. We can then splice into α any execution fragment by processes in Q_i at D_i, knowing that the rest of α will not be affected, since all evidence of the inserted steps will be overwritten. For each group Q_i, the fragment we splice into α accesses a "fresh" instance of set agreement that was never accessed during α. (In each fragment that is spliced in, only the m processes in Q_i take steps, so all PROPOSE operations terminate and the processes will eventually reach and complete the fresh instance of set agreement.) We ensure that these groups of m processes output disjoint sets of m different values each for this one instance of set agreement, for a total of $c \cdot m = k+1$ different outputs, a contradiction.

THEOREM 2. *Any algorithm for m-obstruction-free repeated k-set agreement among n processes requires at least $n+m-k$ registers.*

PROOF. To derive a contradiction, assume there exists an algorithm for m-obstruction-free repeated k-set agreement using $r = n+m-k-1$ registers. Let $c = \lceil \frac{k+1}{m} \rceil$. Since $k \geq m$, we have $c \geq 2$. We define a *block write* to a set A of registers by a set P of processes to be an execution fragment in which each process of P takes a single step, such that the set of registers written during the fragment is A.

We first construct an execution

$$C_0 \overset{\alpha_1}{\rightsquigarrow} D_1 \overset{\beta_1}{\rightsquigarrow} C_1 \overset{\alpha_2}{\rightsquigarrow} D_2 \overset{\beta_2}{\rightsquigarrow} C_2 \overset{\alpha_3}{\rightsquigarrow} \cdots \overset{\beta_{c-1}}{\rightsquigarrow} C_{c-1} \qquad (1)$$

and sets $A_1, \ldots, A_{c-1}$ of registers such that C_0 is the initial configuration and for all j,

1. α_j is an execution fragment containing only steps by two disjoint sets P_j and Q_j of processes that goes from configuration C_{j-1} to configuration D_j,
2. β_j is a block write to A_j by P_j that goes from configuration D_j to configuration C_j,
3. $|Q_1| = k+1-(c-1)m$,
4. if $j > 1$, $|Q_j| = m$,
5. $|P_j| = |A_j|$,
6. $Q_j \cap Q_{j'} = \emptyset$ for $j' \neq j$,
7. $Q_j \cap P_{j'} = \emptyset$ for $j' > j$, and
8. there is no execution fragment starting from D_j in which only processes in Q_j take steps and some process writes outside A_j.

BASE CASE ($j = 0$): Let C_0 be the initial configuration.

INDUCTIVE STEP: Let $1 \leq j \leq c-1$. Assume we have constructed the execution from C_0 to C_{j-1} satisfying all the properties. The algorithm in Figure 2 constructs the execution fragment α_j and the sets P_j, Q_j and A_j. Then, let β_j be the execution fragment starting from D_j where each process in P_j takes a single step and let C_j be the resulting configuration.

1 let α_j be the empty execution fragment
2 $D_j \leftarrow C_{j-1}$
3 $P_j \leftarrow \emptyset$
4 $A_j \leftarrow \emptyset$
5 if $j > 1$ then $size \leftarrow m$ else $size \leftarrow k + 1 - (c-1)m$
6 let Q_j be a set of $size$ processes disjoint from $Q_1 \cup Q_2 \cup \cdots \cup Q_{j-1}$
7 loop until no execution fragment starting from D_j by Q_j writes outside A_j
8   let δ be an execution fragment starting from D_j by Q_j until some process $q \in Q_j$ is poised for the first time to write to a register that is not in A_j and let R be that register
9     $\alpha_j \leftarrow \alpha_j \cdot \delta$
10   let D_j be the configuration reached from C_{j-1} by performing α_j
11   let q' be some process outside $Q_1 \cup Q_2 \cup \cdots \cup Q_j \cup P_j$
12     $A_j \leftarrow A_j \cup \{R\}$
13     $P_j \leftarrow P_j \cup \{q\}$
14     $Q_j \leftarrow (Q_j - \{q\}) \cup \{q'\}$
15 end loop
16 output $\alpha_j, D_j, P_j, Q_j, A_j$

Figure 2: Algorithm used in the proof of Theorem 2 to construct α_j, D_j, P_j, Q_j and A_j.

Observe that the construction algorithm terminates: each loop iteration adds a new register to A_j, so it terminates after at most r iterations. We next check that the required processes on line 6 and 11 exist. When $j = 1$, we have $size = k+1-(c-1)m = k+1-\lceil\frac{k+1}{m}\rceil \cdot m + m \leq m < n$, so one can choose the required processes on line 6. For $j > 1$, one can choose the process on line 6 because

$$\begin{aligned} |Q_1 \cup \cdots \cup Q_{j-1}| &= k+1-(c-1)m+(j-2)m \\ &\quad \text{(by induction hypothesis 3, 4 and 6)} \\ &\leq k+1-(c-1)m+(c-3)m \\ &\quad \text{(since } j \leq c-1) \\ &= k+1-2m \leq n-2m \\ &\quad \text{(since } k < n). \end{aligned}$$

Similarly, one can choose the required process q' at line 11 because

$$\begin{aligned} &|Q_1 \cup \cdots \cup Q_j \cup P_j| \\ \leq\ & k+1-2m+|Q_j|+|P_j| \\ & \text{(since } |Q_1 \cup \cdots \cup Q_{j-1}| \leq k+1-2m) \\ \leq\ & k+1-m+r-1 \\ & \text{(since } |Q_j| = m \text{ and } |P_j| = |A_j| \leq r-1) \\ =\ & n-1 \\ & \text{(since } r = n+m-k-1). \end{aligned}$$

We verify the construction satisfies all of the properties. Line 10 of the algorithm updates D_j each time α_j is updated, to ensure property 1. Property 2 is true by definition of β_j and C_j. Q_j is initialized to a set whose size satisfies property 3 or 4 on line 6 and the size of this set is preserved whenever Q_j is altered on line 14. P_j and A_j are initialized to be empty, and both are updated by adding one element to each on line 12 and 13, so they remain the same size after every iteration of the loop. (Note that P_j and Q_j are disjoint at the beginning of each iteration of the loop, so line 13 does add a new process to P_j.) Every process placed in Q_j at line 6 or 14 was chosen to be outside $Q_1 \cup \ldots \cup Q_{j-1}$, guaranteeing property 6. Similarly, processes added to P_j are always outside $Q_1 \cup \ldots \cup Q_{j-1}$, and whenever a process is added to P_j, it is removed from Q_j, so property 7 is satisfied. Finally, property 8 is guaranteed by the exit condition of the loop. This completes the inductive construction.

Now, let s be the maximum number of invocations of PROPOSE by any process in the execution that takes the system to configuration C_{c-1}. Let Q_c be a set of m processes disjoint from $Q_1 \cup \cdots \cup Q_{c-1}$. (These m processes exist since $|Q_1 \cup \cdots \cup Q_{c-1}| = k+1-m \leq n-m$.) Let $D_c = C_{c-1}$.

For each $j \in \{1, \ldots, c\}$, we now construct an execution fragment γ_j by the processes in Q_j starting from D_j. Since $|Q_j| \leq m$, each PROPOSE in γ_j must terminate. First, the processes in Q_j run one by one until each completes its first s invocations of PROPOSE. Then, the processes of Q_j run their $(s+1)$th invocation of PROPOSE, each using its own id as its input value so that they decide $|Q_j|$ different output values. By Lemma 1, such an execution fragment exists. Note that for $j < c$, γ_j cannot write outside of A_j, by property 8. So, all traces of γ_j's activity are obliterated by the block write β_j. Thus, we can insert $\gamma_1, \ldots, \gamma_c$ into execution (1) at $D_1, \ldots, D_c$, respectively, and the resulting execution is still legal. In the resulting execution, the number of distinct outputs for the $(s+1)$th instance of set agreement is $\sum_{j=1}^{c} |Q_j| = k+1$, violating k-agreement. This completes the proof. □

4. ALGORITHM FOR REPEATED SET AGREEMENT

4.1 One-shot k-set agreement

We first give an algorithm that uses a snapshot object of $r = n + 2m - k$ components to solve (one-shot) m-obstruction-free k-set agreement, and then describe how to extend it to solve repeated set agreement. The one-shot algorithm is shown in Figure 3. Roughly speaking, the first $k - m$ processes to decide can output arbitrary values, but we ensure that the last $\ell = n - k + m$ processes all agree on at most m different values (for a total of at most k different values).

Each process stores its preferred value in its local variable *pref*. Initially, it prefers its own input value. Each process executes a loop in which it stores its *pref* and identifier into

```
1   Shared variable:
2       A: snapshot object with r = n + 2m − k components, each initially ⊥
3   PROPOSE(v)
4       pref ← v
5       i ← 0
6       loop
7           update ith component of A with (pref, id)
8           s ← scan of A
9           if |{s[j] : 0 ≤ j < r}| ≤ m and ∀j, s[j] ≠ ⊥ then
10              let j1 ← min{j1 : ∃j2 > j1 such that s[j1] = s[j2]}, output value in s[j1] and halt
11          if ∀j ≠ i, s[j] ∉ {⊥, (pref, id)} and ∃j1 ≠ j2 such that s[j1] = s[j2] then
12              j1 ← min{j1 : ∃j2 > j1 such that s[j1] = s[j2]}
13              pref ← value in s[j1]
14          else i ← (i + 1) mod r
15      end loop
16  end PROPOSE
```

Figure 3: Algorithm for m-obstruction-free k-set agreement. Code for a process with identifier id.

a component of the snapshot object, takes a scan of the snapshot object and updates its *pref* variable based on the scan. The location i that the process updates advances in each iteration of the loop, as long as the process's *pref* value remains the same. When the process updates its *pref*, it does not advance to the next location: instead it updates the same location during the next iteration of the loop.

The process repeats this loop until a scan returns a vector containing at most m different value-id pairs, at which point it returns one of those values. In each iteration, a process updates its *pref* value when it does not see any copies of its current value-id pair anywhere in the vector returned by the scan, except for the component it just updated, *and* it does see two copies of some other pair. In this case, it adopts the value of the pair that appears twice as its *pref*.

The algorithm in Figure 3 is an improvement on the algorithm of [4], which was designed for the special case where $m = 1$ and uses $2(n-k)$ registers, compared to the $n-k+2$ registers used by ours.

We now prove that the algorithm in Figure 3 indeed solves m-obstruction-free k-set agreement. It is easy to see that **validity** holds: the only values that can appear in the snapshot object or in a process's local *pref* variable are input values. Thus, only input values can be produced as outputs.

Before proving k-agreement and termination, we first establish the following invariant.

LEMMA 3. *For each process identifier id, all the pairs in A with identifier id have the same value.*

PROOF. To derive a contradiction, assume there is an execution that reaches a configuration C in which $A[i_1] = (v_1, id)$ and $A[i_2] = (v_2, id)$ where $v_1 \neq v_2$. Let p_{id} be the process with identifier id. Let u_1 and u_2 be the last steps before C in which p_{id} updates $A[i_1]$ and $A[i_2]$, respectively. Without loss of generality, assume u_1 is before u_2. Then, between u_1 and u_2, p_{id} changes its *pref* variable at line 13. Consider the first time after u_1 that p_{id} performs such a change, and let i^* and s^* be the values of p_{id}'s local variables i and s at that time. Since s^* was obtained from a scan between u_1 and C and $A[i_1] = (v_1, id)$ throughout that interval, $s^*[i_1]$ is (v_1, id). Thus, $i^* = i_1$; otherwise the test on line 11 would not be satisfied, and p_{id} would not change *pref* at line 13. Therefore, in the next iteration of the loop, p_{id} will update location $A[i_1]$. This update is after u_1 and no later than u_2 (and hence before C), which contradicts the definition of u_1 as the last update performed by p_{id} on $A[i_1]$ before C. □

To prove **k-agreement**, let $\ell = n - k + m$. If at most $n - \ell$ processes decide, then k-agreement is trivial since $n - \ell = k - m < k$. So, consider an execution in which more than $n - \ell$ processes decide. Order the processes that decide according to the times when each performs its last scan, and let q_0 be the $(n-\ell+1)$th process in this ordering. Let X be the set of at most m different pairs that appear in the vector that q_0's final scan returns. Let V be the set of values that appear in pairs of X. Then, $|V| \leq |X| \leq m$. We prove that q_0 and all processes that come later in the ordering output values in V. Thus, the total number of values output is at most $(n - \ell) + |V| \leq n - (n - k + m) + m = k$.

LEMMA 4. *In any configuration after q_0 performs its final scan, only pairs with values in V can appear in two or more locations of A.*

PROOF. Let C_0 be the configuration just after q_0's final scan. We shall show by induction that in each configuration reachable from C_0, only pairs with values in V can appear in two or more locations of A. For the base case, consider the configuration C_0. By the definition of V, A contains only pairs with values in V, so the claim holds.

For the induction step, suppose the claim holds in all configurations from C_0 to some configuration C_1 reachable from C_0. Let st be a step that takes the system from C_1 to another configuration C_2. We show that the claim holds in configuration C_2. We need only consider the case where st is an update by some process p_{id}. Let (v, id) be the pair that st stores in a component of A.

CASE 1: st is the first update by p_{id} after C_0. If $v \in V$, then st cannot cause a violation of the claim. If $v \notin V$, then A contains exactly one copy of (v, id) in configuration C_2, since $(v, id) \notin X$, so again st preserves the claim.

CASE 2: st is not the first update by p_{id} after C_0. Let s_{id} be the vector obtained by p_{id}'s last scan before st. We show that $v \in V$, and hence st preserves the claim, by considering two subcases.

CASE 2A: s_{id} satisfies the condition on line 11. Then, p_{id} updates its *pref* variable at line 13, so the value v is the value of a pair that appears twice in s_{id}. By the induction hypothesis, $v \in V$.

CASE 2B: s_{id} does not satisfy the condition on line 11. We first argue that at least one pair appears twice in s_{id}. Recall that there are at most $\ell - 1$ undecided processes in C_0. Since A contains at most m distinct pairs ($|X| \leq m$) in C_0 and at most $\ell - 1$ processes update A after C_0, Lemma 3 implies that, when the scan s_{id} is performed, A contains at most $m + \ell - 1 = n + 2m - k - 1$ distinct pairs. Since there are $r = n + 2m - k$ locations in A, at least one pair appears twice in s_{id}.

Since q_0 has previously output a value, s_{id} contains no $\perp$ elements. Thus, the reason that s_{id} does not satisfy the condition on line 11 must be that for some j different from p_{id}'s position i, $s_{id}[j] = (pref, id)$. Just before taking the scan s_{id}, p_{id} stores (v, id) in location i. This update occurs after C_0, since *st* is not the first update by p_{id} after C_0. In the configuration after this update of location i, both $s_{id}[j]$ and $s_{id}[i]$ contain (v, id). So, by the induction hypothesis, $v \in V$. □

Lemma 4 implies that all processes after the $(n - \ell)$th in the ordering can only decide one of the (at most) m values in V and, thus, k-**agreement** is ensured.

To prove m-**obstruction-freedom**, consider an execution where the set P of processes that take infinitely many steps has size at most m. To derive a contradiction, assume some process in P never decides. In each loop iteration, a process either keeps its preferred value and increments i (its location to update) modulo r or sets its preferred value without modifying i. We partition P into two subsets: the set NS of "non-stabilizing" processes that modify i infinitely often and the set S of "stabilizing" processes that eventually get stuck updating the same location i forever.

LEMMA 5. *There is at least one process in NS.*

PROOF. To derive a contradiction, assume the claim is false (i.e., $P = S$). Let μ be a time after which only processes in P take steps and no process changes its local variable i. Then there is a set M of at most m locations whose contents are updated after μ. Let NM be the set of at least $n + m - k \geq 2$ locations that are not updated after μ. Let μ' be any time when each process in P has performed at least one update after μ. Thus, at μ', every location in M contains a pair stored by a process in P.

Let p be a process in P that performs a scan that returns a vector s_p after μ'. By the hypothesis, p changes its preferred value in every iteration after μ', so s_p satisfies the condition on line 11. Process p then changes *pref* to a value v in a pair (v, k) that appears twice in s_p. Since each component in M is updated by different processes, no two can contain the same pair after μ'. We consider two cases.

CASE 1: in s_p, (v, k) appears in one component of M and one of NM. As (v, k) is read from a component in M after μ', $p_k \in P$. Consider the time (after μ) at which p_k stores (v, k) in a component in M. Since no register in NM ever changes its value after μ, in p_k's subsequent scan, (v, k) is in some register of NM and p_k will not change its preferred value, contradicting the fact that $P = S$.

CASE 2: in s_p, (v, k) appears in two components of NM. By the definitions of NM and μ', (v, k) is found twice in NM at all times after μ. As p changes its preferred value after its next update, it must have found another pair that appears twice and was not in A previously. Then this new pair cannot be in two locations in NM. The pair cannot be in two locations in M either because all the locations of M are updated by different processes. Thus, this new pair is in one location of M and one location of NM. But, as we have seen in Case 1, this leads to a contradiction. □

Thus, some process updates each component of A infinitely often, yielding the following corollary.

COROLLARY 6. *There is a time after which A contains only pairs stored by processes in P.*

By Corollary 6, there is a time ν after which (1) A contains only pairs stored by processes in P. By Lemma 3, (2) all pairs in A with the same id have the same value. By the assumption, (3) $|P| \leq m$. (1), (2) and (3) imply that after ν, each time a process $p \in P$ performs a scan it finds at most m different pairs in the snapshot and decides. This contradiction establishes the m-obstruction-freedom property.

THEOREM 7. *For $1 \leq m \leq k < n$, there is an m-obstruction-free algorithm that solves k-set agreement among n processes using* $\min(n + 2m - k, n)$ *registers.*

PROOF. We established above that the algorithm in Figure 3 solves the problem using a snapshot object of $n+2m-k$ components. If $n + 2m - k \leq n$, the snapshot object can be implemented from $n + 2m - k$ registers [6]. Otherwise, the snapshot can be implemented from n single-writer registers [1, 14]. □

4.2 Repeated k-set agreement

The one-shot k-set agreement algorithm can be transformed into an algorithm for repeated set agreement with the same space complexity to prove the following theorem.

THEOREM 8. *For $1 \leq m \leq k < n$, there is an m-obstruction-free algorithm that solve repeated k-set agreement among n processes using* $\min(n + 2m - k, n)$ *registers.*

Since the algorithm for repeated set agreement is quite similar to the one-shot algorithm, we describe it briefly here. A detailed proof the algorithm's correctness can be found in the companion technical report [5].

The pseudocode for our m-obstruction-free repeated k-set agreement algorithm is given in Figure 4. It essentially follows the pseudocode of the one-shot algorithm (Figure 3), with additional "shortcuts" which a process may use to adopt a value output previously by another process that has already reached a higher instance of repeated set agreement. Also, a value stored by a process in a lower instance is treated as $\perp$. Thus, a process decides in instance t only if all tuples found in A are stored by processes in instance t and there are at most m distinct tuples, or if another process has reached an instance higher than t.

Each process p maintains a local variable *history* that stores a sequence of output values that have been produced in the all instances of repeated k-set agreement p has completed so far. In the current instance t, p essentially follows the one-shot algorithm (Figure 3), except that it appends the current instance number t and *history* to each value it stores in the shared memory. Thus, each element of the vector returned by a scan of A contains either $\perp$ or a tuple of

```
Shared variable:
    A: snapshot object with r = n + 2m − k components, each initially ⊥
Persistent local variables:
    i ← 0
    t ← 0
    history ← empty sequence
Propose(v)
    t ← t + 1
    if |history| ≥ t then
        output the t-th value in history and halt
    pref ← v
    loop
        update ith component of A with (pref, id, t, history)
        s ← scan of A
        if ∃j such that s[j] = (w, id′, t′, his) with t′ > t then
            history ← his
            output the t-th value in his and halt
        if |{s[j] : 0 ≤ j < r}| ≤ m and ∀j, s[j] is neither ⊥ nor of the form (w, q, t′, his) with t′ < t then
            let j1 ← min{j1 : ∃j2 > j1 such that s[j1] = s[j2]}
            let w be the value in s[j1]
            history ← history · w
            output w and halt
        if ∀j ≠ i, s[j] ∉ {⊥, (pref, id, t, history)} and ∃j1 ≠ j2 such that s[j1] and s[j2] contain
                identical t-tuples then
            j1 ← min{j1 : ∃j2 > j1 such that s[j1] and s[j2] contain identical t-tuples}
            pref ← value in s[j1]
        else i ← (i + 1) mod r
    end loop
end Propose
```

Figure 4: Algorithm for m-obstruction-free repeated k-set agreement.

the form (id, v, t', his). If $t' > t$, then p_{id} has already completed instance t and his contains the corresponding output value. If this is the case, p adopts all the values output by p_{id} for instances from t to $t'-1$. If $t' < t$, indicating that p_{id} has not yet reached instance t, then the position of A is treated as if it were $\perp$ in the one-shot algorithm.

To prove k-**agreement**, we focus on processes that produce their output for instance t without adopting a value from the history that another process stored in A. We call these *t-deciding processes.* Since each other processes that completes its tth Propose adopts one of the value of a t-deciding process, it suffices to prove that t-deciding processes output at most k different values. As in the proof for the one-shot case, we show that the last $\ell = n-k+m$ t-deciding processes output at most m values. There is one complication in the argument: after the $(n-\ell+1)$th t-deciding process performs its last scan during instance t, processes may store a t'-tuple with $t' < t$. We show that each process can do this only in a single location, which ensures the agreement property for instance t is not disrupted.

To show m-**obstruction-freedom**, consider an execution where the set P of processes that take infinitely many steps has size at most m. To derive a contradiction, assume some process in P does not complete a Propose. Let t be the smallest number for which some process does not complete its tth Propose and let P' be the set of processes that do not complete their tth Propose. Since the processes in P' never witness the presence of a process in a higher instance of set-agreement, the argument for the one-shot case can be applied to this set P' to obtain the desired contradiction.

5. LOWER BOUND FOR ANONYMOUS ONE-SHOT AGREEMENT

We now turn to anonymous algorithms, where processes are not equipped with identifiers and are programmed identically. We also assume that the domain of possible input values is $\mathbb{N}$. In this section, we show that any n-process anonymous algorithm for m-obstruction-free (one-shot) k-set agreement requires $\Omega(\sqrt{\frac{nm}{k}})$ registers. Note that this bound on space complexity reflects all three parameters: increasing n or m makes the problem harder and increasing k makes the problem easier. It also generalizes the anonymous result of Fich, Herlihy and Shavit [7] (which is the special case when $m = k = 1$) by showing the dependence on two additional parameters m and k. The assumption of anonymity allows us to add *clones* to an execution. A clone of a process p is another process p' that has the same input as p. Whenever p takes a step, p' takes an identical step immediately afterwards.

Let A be an anonymous algorithm that solves m-obstruction-free k-set agreement among n processes using finitely many registers. For each set V of m distinct input values, fix an execution $\alpha(V)$ such that at most m processes take steps during α and output all values in V. (Such an execution exists, by Lemma 1.) Let $\mathbf{R}(V)$ be the sequence of distinct registers written during $\alpha(V)$ in the order they are first written in $\alpha(V)$. For any sequence $\mathbf{R}$ of distinct registers, define $\mathfrak{V}(\mathbf{R}) = \{V \subset \mathbb{N} : |V| = m \text{ and } \mathbf{R} \text{ is a prefix of } \mathbf{R}(V)\}$.

LEMMA 9. *Let $r > 0$ and suppose $n \geq \lceil \frac{k+1}{m} \rceil (m + \frac{r^2-r}{2})$. Then, for $i = 0, \ldots, r+1$, there is a sequence $\mathbf{R}_i$ of length i such that $\mathfrak{V}(\mathbf{R}_i)$ is an infinite set.*

PROOF. We prove the claim by induction on i.

Base case ($i = 0$): $\mathbf{R}_0$ is the empty sequence and $\mathfrak{V}(\mathbf{R}_0) = \{V \subset \mathbb{N} : |V| = m\}$ is infinite.

Induction step: Let $i \in \{1, 2, \ldots, r+1\}$. Assume there is a sequence $\mathbf{R}_{i-1} = \langle R_1, R_2, \ldots, R_{i-1}\rangle$ such that $\mathfrak{V}(\mathbf{R}_{i-1})$ is infinite.

The induction step is technical, so we begin with an informal overview. Let $c = \lceil \frac{k+1}{m} \rceil$. We first show that there cannot be c disjoint sets $V_1, \ldots, V_c$ in $\mathfrak{V}(\mathbf{R}_{i-1})$ such that each $\alpha(V_\ell)$ writes only to registers in $\mathbf{R}_{i-1}$; otherwise, we could glue together the $\alpha(V_\ell)$'s so that each $\alpha(V_\ell)$ is invisible to all the others, and the number of output values in this glued-together execution would be $|V_1 \cup V_2 \cup \cdots \cup V_c| = mc > k$. Then, the rest of the argument is easy: infinitely many sets in $\mathfrak{V}(\mathbf{R}_{i-1})$ must have register sequences of length at least i. Since there are only finitely many registers, infinitely many of those sets have the same register R in position i of their sequence. These form the infinite set $\mathfrak{V}(\mathbf{R}_i)$, where $\mathbf{R}_i = \mathbf{R}_{i-1} \cdot R$.

Now, we give the detailed argument. To derive a contradiction, assume that (*) there exist c disjoint sets $V_1, \ldots, V_c$ in $\mathfrak{V}(\mathbf{R}_{i-1})$ such that for all ℓ, $\alpha(V_\ell)$ writes only to registers in $\mathbf{R}_{i-1}$. Let $P_1, \ldots, P_c$ be c disjoint sets of m processes each. The following claim describes how we can glue together the $\alpha(V_\ell)$'s. If β is an execution and P is a set of processes, $\beta|P$ denotes the subsequence of β consisting of steps taken by processes in P.

CLAIM: For $j = 0, 1, \ldots, i-1$, there exists an execution β_j with the following properties.

1. Exactly $\frac{cj(j-1)}{2}$ processes outside of $P_1 \cup \ldots \cup P_c$ take steps during β_j.
2. For $\ell = 1, \ldots, c$, there is a write by some process in P_ℓ to each of $R_1, R_2, \ldots, R_j$ during β_j.
3. No process writes to any register outside of $\{R_1, R_2, \ldots, R_j\}$ during β_j.
4. For $\ell = 1, \ldots, c$, $\beta_j|P_\ell$ is the prefix of $\alpha(V_\ell)$ up to but not including the first write to R_{j+1} (or the entire execution $\alpha(V_\ell)$ if $j = i-1$).

We prove the claim by inductively constructing the executions β_j.

BASE CASE ($j = 0$): We build β_0 by concatenating the maximal prefixes of $\alpha(V_1), \alpha(V_2), \ldots, \alpha(V_c)$ that do not contain any writes, performed by process sets $P_1, \ldots, P_c$, respectively. No processes outside $P_1 \cup \cdots \cup P_c$ take steps in β_0. Property 2 is vacuously satisfied. Properties 3 and 4 follow immediately from the definition of β_0.

INDUCTIVE STEP: Let $j \in \{1, \ldots, i-1\}$. Assume that there is a β_{j-1} satisfying the four properties. We describe how to construct β_j.

For each ℓ, we insert $j-1$ clones of processes in P_ℓ, and we pause one clone just before the last write by a process in P_ℓ to each of $R_1, \ldots, R_{j-1}$. Such a write exists, by property 2 of the induction hypothesis. Moreover, there are enough processes to create these clones, since the number of processes that take steps in β_{j-1} plus the $c(j-1)$ additional clones needed to construct β_j total at most $mc + \frac{c(j-1)(j-2)}{2} + c(j-1) = mc + \frac{cj(j-1)}{2} \leq mc + \frac{c(i-1)(i-2)}{2} \leq mc + \frac{cr(r-1)}{2} = \lceil \frac{k+1}{m} \rceil (m + \frac{r^2-r}{2})$ and by the hypothesis of the lemma, there are this many processes in the system.

Let β'_{j-1} be the execution that results from adding all of the clones to β_{j-1}. We add some more steps to the end of β'_{j-1} as follows. For each $\ell = 1, \ldots, c$, we add a block write by the clones of processes in P_ℓ followed by steps of processes in P_ℓ continuing the steps of $\alpha(V_\ell)$ until some process is poised to write to R_{j+1} for the first time (or until the end of $\alpha(V_\ell)$ if $j = i-1$). (This is legal, because the block write ensures that all registers have the same state as they would have after $\beta_{j-1}|P_\ell$, which is a prefix of $\alpha(V_\ell)$, by induction hypothesis 4.) Thus, we ensure that β_j satisfies property 4.

By property 4 of the inductive hypothesis, the first newly added step by a process in P_ℓ writes to R_j. Combined with induction hypothesis 2, this proves property 2. For $j < i-1$, property 3 holds because we stop the processes in P_ℓ just before they write to any register outside of $\{R_1, \ldots, R_j\}$. For $j = i-1$, property 3 follows from our assumption (*) that $\alpha(V_\ell)$ writes only to registers in $\mathbf{R}_{i-1}$.

The processes outside $P_1 \cup \cdots \cup P_c$ that take steps in β_j are the $\frac{c(j-1)(j-2)}{2}$ processes that take steps in β_{j-1} plus the $c(j-1)$ clones that we added when constructing β'_{j-1}. So the total number of such processes is $\frac{cj(j-1)}{2}$, satisfying property 1. This completes the proof of the claim.

In β_{i-1} processes in P_ℓ output all m values in V_ℓ (for all ℓ). Since $V_1, \ldots, V_c$ are disjoint sets, there are at least $cm = \lceil \frac{k+1}{m} \rceil \cdot m \geq k+1$ different output values in β_{i-1}. This contradicts the k-agreement property. Thus, assumption (*) is false, so there are fewer than c disjoint sets in $\mathfrak{V}(\mathbf{R}_{i-1})$ such that $\alpha(V_\ell)$ writes only to registers in $\mathbf{R}_{i-1}$. Thus, there are infinitely many sets V in $\mathfrak{V}(\mathbf{R}_{i-1})$ such that $\alpha(V)$ writes outside of $\mathbf{R}_{i-1}$. Since there are only finitely many registers, there must be infinitely many of these sets V such that the first register outside of $\mathbf{R}_{i-1}$ written during $\alpha(V)$ is the same for all V. Call that register R. Let $\mathbf{R}_i$ be obtained by concatenating R to the end of $\mathbf{R}_{i-1}$. Then, there are infinitely many sets V such that $\mathbf{R}_i$ is a prefix of $\mathbf{R}(V)$. This completes the proof. □

THEOREM 10. *Any anonymous algorithm that solves m-obstruction-free k-set agreement among n processes using registers must use more than $\sqrt{m(\frac{n}{k} - 2)}$ registers.*

PROOF. Assume an algorithm solves the problem using r registers where $r \leq \sqrt{m(\frac{n}{k} - 2)}$. Then,

$$\begin{aligned} r &\leq \sqrt{m\left(\frac{n}{k} - 2\right)} \\ &\leq \sqrt{m\left(\frac{2n}{k+m} - 2\right)} \\ &\quad \left(\text{since } m \leq k \Rightarrow \frac{2n}{k+m} \geq \frac{n}{k}\right) \\ &= \sqrt{\frac{2m(n-k-m)}{k+m}} \end{aligned}$$

```
Shared variables:
      A: snapshot object with r = (m+1)(n−k) + m² components, each initially ⊥
      H: register, initially the empty sequence
Persistent local variables:
      i ← 0
      t ← 0
      history ← empty sequence
PROPOSE(v)
      write history into H
      t ← t + 1
      if |history| ≥ t then
            output the tth value in history and halt
      run the following two threads in parallel until one of them produces an output
      thread 1:
            pref ← v
            ℓ ← n + m − k
            loop
                  update ith component of A with value (pref, t, history)
                  s ← scan of A
                  if ∃j such that s[j] = (w, t', his) with t' > t then
                        history ← his
                        output the t-th value in his and halt
                  if |{s[j] : 0 ≤ j < r}| ≤ m and every entry of s is a t-tuple then
                        let w be the most common frequent value in s
                        history ← history · w
                        output w and halt
                  if |{j : s[j] = (pref, t, ∗)}| < ℓ and ∃new such that |{j : s[j] = (new, t, ∗)}| ≥ ℓ then
                        pref ← new
                  i ← (i + 1) mod r
            end loop
      thread 2:
            loop
                  if |H| ≥ t then
                        let w be the tth element of H
                        history ← history · w
                        output w and halt
            end loop
end PROPOSE
```

Figure 5: Anonymous algorithm for m-obstruction-free repeated k-set agreement.

$$\begin{aligned} \Rightarrow \quad r^2 - r &\le \frac{2m(n-k-m)}{k+m} \\ \Rightarrow \quad \frac{k+m}{m} \cdot \frac{r^2-r}{2} &\le n-k-m \\ \Rightarrow \quad n &\ge \frac{k+m}{m}\left(m + \frac{r^2-r}{2}\right) \\ &\ge \left\lceil \frac{k+1}{m} \right\rceil \left(m + \frac{r^2-r}{2}\right). \end{aligned}$$

So, by Lemma 9 there exists a sequence of $r+1$ registers used in some executions of A, which is impossible since there are only r registers. □

6. ANONYMOUS ALGORITHM FOR REPEATED SET AGREEMENT

THEOREM 11. *There is an algorithm that solves m-obstruction-free repeated k-set agreement among n processes (for $m \le k$) using $(m+1)(n-k)+m^2+1$ registers.*

The algorithm is shown in Figure 5. Its proof of correctness appears in [5]. The algorithm employs the same basic strategy as the one in Section 4. It uses a snapshot object A with $r = (m+1)(n-k)+m^2$ components, which can be built anonymously and non-blocking using r registers [8]. Again, the idea is to allow the first $\ell = n+m-k$ processes to choose arbitrary outputs and then ensure that the last $n-\ell = k-m$ processes output at most m different values, for a total of at most k different values.

For one-shot k-set agreement, processes alternate between storing their preferred value in a component of the snapshot object A and performing a scan of A. The conditions for outputting a value and adopting a new preference differ from the algorithm in Section 4 to compensate for the lack of identifiers. Whenever a process observes m or fewer different values in a scan, it can output the one that occurs most frequently. Otherwise, if a process sees fewer than ℓ copies of its own preference and at least ℓ copies of another value, it adopts this other value as its preference.

The adaptation of this algorithm to repeated consensus is similar to the technique used for the non-anonymous case. There is one additional complication: there is no known space-efficient wait-free anonymous snapshot implementation from registers, so we use a non-blocking implementation. Therefore, some processes may *starve* while accessing the snapshot object, under the condition that at least one process manages to complete infinitely many instances of k-set agreement.

To ensure that starving processes also complete their PROPOSE operations we use one additional register H where "fast" processes write their outputs. Every process periodically checks H in a parallel thread (lines 32-32) and if it finds out that $|H| \geq t$, where t is the instance of agreement the process is working on, it outputs the t-th value found in H. As in the non-anonymous case, the sequence of values that have been output in the instances of repeated k-set agreement the process has completed so far is stored in a local variable *history*. To ensure that *history* is updated exactly once per instance of k-set agreement, we require that the threads of a process are scheduled so that the pairs of lines 21–22, 25–26, and 35–36 are executed without interruption from the process's other thread.

7. CONCLUDING REMARKS

A small gap remains between the upper and lower bounds for non-anonymous repeated set agreement. The one-shot algorithm of [4] uses fewer registers than ours for one special case: when $m = 1$ and $k = n - 1$, it uses two registers compared to our three. This suggests the upper bound could perhaps be improved to $n + m - k$. The gaps are larger for the other scenarios shown in Figure 1. It would be interesting to see if there is an anonymous algorithm that uses linear space, rather than quadratic space. Another natural continuation of this work would be to extend the one-shot anonymous lower bound to the non-anonymous setting. However, closing the gap for the one-shot setting eludes us still.

Acknowledgements.

We thank the anonymous referees for their helpful comments.

8. REFERENCES

[1] Yehuda Afek, Hagit Attiya, Danny Dolev, Eli Gafni, Michael Merritt, and Nir Shavit. Atomic snapshots of shared memory. *Journal of the ACM*, 40(4):873–890, September 1993.

[2] Elizabeth Borowsky and Eli Gafni. Generalized FLP impossibility result for t-resilient asynchronous computations. In *Proc. 25th ACM Symposium on Theory of Computing*, pages 91–100, 1993.

[3] Soma Chaudhuri. More choices allow more faults: Set consensus problems in totally asynchronous systems. *Information and Computation*, 105(1):132–158, July 1993.

[4] Carole Delporte-Gallet, Hugues Fauconnier, Eli Gafni, and Sergio Rajsbaum. Black art: Obstruction-free k-set agreement with $|MWMR\ registers| < |proccesses|$. In *Proc. 1st International Conference on Networked Systems*, volume 7853 of *LNCS*, pages 28–41, 2013.

[5] Carole Delporte-Gallet, Hugues Fauconnier, Petr Kuznetsov, and Eric Ruppert. On the space complexity of set agreement. *CoRR*, abs/1505.02690, 2015.

[6] Faith Ellen, Panagiota Fatourou, and Eric Ruppert. Time lower bounds for implementations of multi-writer snapshots. *Journal of the ACM*, 54(6), December 2007.

[7] Faith Ellen Fich, Maurice Herlihy, and Nir Shavit. On the space complexity of randomized synchronization. *Journal of the ACM*, 45(5):843–862, September 1998.

[8] Rachid Guerraoui and Eric Ruppert. Anonymous and fault-tolerant shared-memory computing. *Distributed Computing*, 20(3):165–177, October 2007.

[9] Maurice Herlihy. Wait-free synchronization. *ACM Transactions on Programming Languages and Systems*, 13(1):124–149, January 1991.

[10] Maurice Herlihy, Victor Luchangco, and Mark Moir. Obstruction-free synchronization: Double-ended queues as an example. In *Proc. 23rd International Conference on Distributed Computing Systems*, pages 522–529, 2003.

[11] Maurice Herlihy and Nir Shavit. The topological structure of asynchronous computability. *Journal of the ACM*, 46(6):858–923, November 1999.

[12] Michael Saks and Fotios Zaharoglou. Wait-free k-set agreement is impossible: The topology of public knowledge. *SIAM Journal on Computing*, 29(5):1449–1483, 2000.

[13] Gadi Taubenfeld. Contention-sensitive data structures and algorithms. In *Proc. 23rd International Symposium on Distributed Computing*, volume 5805 of *LNCS*, pages 157–171, 2009.

[14] Paul M. B. Vitányi and Baruch Awerbuch. Atomic shared register access by asynchronous hardware. In *Proc. 27th Symposium on Foundations of Computer Science*, pages 233–243, 1986.

[15] Jiong Yang, Gil Neiger, and Eli Gafni. Structured derivations of consensus algorithms for failure detectors. In *Proc. 17th ACM Symposium on Principles of Distributed Computing*, pages 297–306, 1998.

How Fair is Your Protocol? A Utility-based Approach to Protocol Optimality

Juan Garay
Yahoo Labs
garay@yahoo-inc.com

Jonathan Katz
University of Maryland
jkatz@cs.umd.edu

Björn Tackmann*
UC San Diego
btackmann@eng.ucsd.edu

Vassilis Zikas†
ETH Zurich
vzikas@inf.ethz.ch

ABSTRACT

Security of distributed cryptographic protocols usually requires *privacy* (inputs of the honest parties remain hidden), *correctness* (the adversary cannot improperly affect the outcome), and *fairness* (if the adversary learns the output, all honest parties do also). Cleve's seminal result (STOC '86) implies that satisfying these properties simultaneously is impossible in the presence of dishonest majorities, and led to several proposals for relaxed notions of fairness. While these works also suggest completeness results (i.e., the ability to design protocols which achieve their fairness notion), their assessment is typically of an all-or-nothing nature.

In this work we put forth a new approach for defining relaxed fairness guarantees that allows for a quantitative comparison between protocols with regard to the level of fairness they achieve. The basic idea is to use an appropriate utility function to express the preferences of an adversary who wants to violate fairness. We also show optimal protocols with respect to our notion, in both the two-party and multiparty settings.

Categories and Subject Descriptors

C.2.0 [**Computer-Communication Networks**]: General—*Security and Protection*

General Terms

Security, Theory

1. INTRODUCTION

Two parties p_1 and p_2 wishing to sign a contract are considering the following two protocols, Π_1 and Π_2 (communication is done over secure channels):

- In Π_1, p_1 and p_2 locally digitally sign the contract, compute commitments c_0 and c_1 on the signed versions, and exchange these commitments. Subsequently, p_1 opens its commitment to p_2, and then p_2 opens his commitment to p_1. If during any of the above steps p_i, $i \in \{1, 2\}$, observes that p_{3-i} sends him an inconsistent message, then he aborts.
- Π_2 starts off similarly to Π_1, except that to determine who opens his commitment first, the parties execute a coin tossing protocol [4]: p_1 and p_2 locally commit to random bits b_1 and b_2, exchange the commitments, and then in a single round they open them. For each p_i, if the opening of b_{3-i} is valid then p_i computes $b = b_1 \oplus b_2$; otherwise p_i aborts. The parties then use b to determine which party opens the committed signed contract first.

Which protocol should the parties use? Intuitively, and assuming a party is honest, the answer should be clear: Π_2, since the cheating capabilities of a corrupt party are reduced in comparison to Π_1. Indeed, the probability of a corrupted p_i forcing an unfair abort (i.e., receiving the contract signed by p_{3-i} while preventing p_{3-i} from also receiving it) in protocol Π_2 is roughly half of the probability in protocol Π_1. In other words, one would simply say that protocol Π_2 is "twice as fair as" protocol Π_1.

Yet, most existing cryptographic security definitions, including those specifically intended to model relaxed notions of fairness in an effort to circumvent Cleve's impossibility result [10], would simply say that both protocols are unfair and make no further statement about their relative fairness. For example, both protocols would be considered unfair with respect to *resource fairness* [16], which formalizes the intuition of the *gradual release* paradigm [4, 2, 11, 5, 23] in a simulation-based framework. Indeed, a resource-fair protocol should ensure that, upon abort, the amount of computation that the honest party needs for producing the output is comparable to the adversary's for the same task; this is clearly not the case for either of the protocols, as with probability at least one-half the adversary might learn the output (i.e., receive the signed contract) when it is infeasible for the other party to compute it. The same holds for "rational" definitions of fairness [1, 20], which require the protocol to be an equilibrium strategy with respect to a preference/utility function for rational agents. We stress that some of these definitional frameworks show that one *can* construct pro-

*Research partly done at ETH Zurich.

†Research partly done at University of Maryland and UCLA.

Permission to make digital or hard copies of all or part of this work for personal or classroom use is granted without fee provided that copies are not made or distributed for profit or commercial advantage and that copies bear this notice and the full citation on the first page. Copyrights for components of this work owned by others than ACM must be honored. Abstracting with credit is permitted. To copy otherwise, or republish, to post on servers or to redistribute to lists, requires prior specific permission and/or a fee. Request permissions from permissions@acm.org.
PODC'15, July 21–23, 2015, Donostia-San Sebastián, Spain.
Copyright is held by the owner/author(s). Publication rights licensed to ACM.
ACM 978-1-4503-3617-8 /15/07 ...$15.00.
http://dx.doi.org/10.1145/2767386.2767431.

tocols that are fair with respect to the given framework; nevertheless, none of them provide a way to quantify the "amount" of fairness achieved by an arbitrary cryptographic protocol.

Motivated by the above observation, in this paper we put forth quantitative definitions of fairness for two-party and multi-party protocols. Our notions are based on the idea that we can use an appropriate utility function to express the preferences of an adversary who wants to break fairness. Our definitions allow for comparing protocols with respect to how fair they are, placing them in a partial order according to a relative-fairness relation. We then investigate the question of finding maximal elements in this partial order (which we refer to as *optimally fair* protocols) for the case of two-party and multi-party secure function evaluation (SFE). Importantly, our quantitative fairness and optimality approach is fully composable (cf. [8]) with respect to standard secure protocols, in the sense that we can replace a "hybrid" in a fair/optimal protocol with a protocol which securely implements it without affecting its fairness/optimality.

Our approach builds on machinery developed in the recently proposed *Rational Protocol Design* (RPD) framework, by Garay *et al.* [14]. In more detail, [14] describes how to design protocols which keep the utility of an attacker aiming at provoking certain security breaches as low as possible. At a high level, we use RPD as follows: first, we specify the class of utility functions that naturally capture an adversary attacking a protocol's fairness, and then we interpret the actual utility that the best attacker (i.e., the one maximizing its respective utility) obtains against a given protocol as a measure of the protocol's fairness. The more a protocol limits its best attacker with respect to our fairness-specific utility function, the fairer the protocol is. Going back to the Π_1 vs. Π_2 example at the beginning of the section, we can now readily use this utility function to formally express that protocol Π_2 is fairer than protocol Π_1, because Π_1 allows the adversary to *always* obtain maximum utility, whereas Π_2 reduces this utility by a factor of $1/2$.

Related work. There is a considerable amount of work on fairness, and on defining relaxed notions of fairness. After Cleve's impossibility result [10], perhaps the most notable line of work is on "gradual release" of information [4, 2, 11, 5, 23, 16]. More recently, Gordon and Katz [18] proposed the notion of *1/p-security*. Roughly, their definition guarantees that fairness holds except with probability $1/p$, for some specified polynomial p. One could adopt the parameter p as a measure of a protocol's fairness, although Gordon and Katz show some fundamental limits regarding what functions can be securely computed with regard to their definition. In our work we design protocols for evaluating *arbitrary* functions. At a definitional level, we observe that our definition always (except with negligible probability) guarantees privacy and correctness, which is not the case for $1/p$-security; see Section 5. Interestingly, we also show that for an appropriate choice of the utility function, our utility-based fairness notion implies $1/p$-security for some p.

A different line of work tries to capture relaxed notions of fairness by assuming that protocol participants are rational agents with a fairness-related utility function [1, 20]. This approach is incomparable to ours, or to any other existing notion of fairness in the non-rational setting where the honest parties are *not* rational and follow the protocol as specified. In particular, the optimal protocols suggested here (and in other fairness notions in the non-rational setting) do not imply an equilibrium in the sense of [1, 20].[1] We stress also that the definitions from [1, 20] do not imply a comparative notion of fairness, as a protocol either induces an equilibrium or it does not.

Organization of the paper. The remainder of the paper is organized as follows. In Section 2 we describe notation and the very basics of the RPD framework [14] that are needed for understanding and evaluating our results. In Section 3 we define the utility function of attackers who aim to violate fairness, which enables the relative assessment of protocols as well as the notions of "optimal" fairness which we use in this work. In Section 4 we present optimally fair protocols for two-party and multi-party ($n > 2$ parties) secure function evaluation (SFE) (Sections 4.1 and 4.2, resp.) Our protocols are not only optimally fair but also optimal with respect to the number of *reconstruction rounds*—a measure formalized here which has been implicit in the fairness literature. Furthermore, for the case of multi-party SFE, we also provide an alternative (incomparable) notion of optimality that relates to how costly corruptions might be for the adversary.[2] Finally, in Section 5 we compare our utility-based fairness notion to $1/p$-security (aka "partial fairness") as developed by Gordon and Katz [18]. Detailed constructions, proofs, and other complementary material appear in the full version of this work [15].

2. PRELIMINARIES

We first establish some notational conventions. For an integer $n \in \mathbb{N}$, the set of positive numbers smaller or equal to n is $[n] := \{1, \ldots, n\}$. In the context of two-party protocols, we will always refer to the parties as p_1 and p_2, and for $i \in \{1, 2\}$ the symbol $\neg i$ refers to the value $3-i$ (so $p_{\neg i} \neq p_i$). Most statements in this paper are actually asymptotic with respect to an (often implicit) security parameter $k \in \mathbb{N}$. Hence, $f \leq g$ means that $\exists k_0\ \forall k \geq k_0 : f(k) \leq g(k)$, and a function $\mu : \mathbb{N} \to \mathbb{R}$ is *negligible* if for all polynomials p, $\mu \leq 1/p$, and *noticeable* if there exists a polynomial p with $\mu \geq 1/p$. We further introduce the symbols $f \overset{\text{negl}}{\approx} g :\Leftrightarrow \exists$ negligible $\mu : |f - g| \leq \mu$, and $f \overset{\text{negl}}{\geq} g :\Leftrightarrow \exists$ negligible $\mu : f \geq g - \mu$, with $\overset{\text{negl}}{\leq}$ defined analogously.

For the model of protocol composition, we follow Canetti's adaptive simulation-based model for multi-party computation [6]. The protocol execution is formalized by collections of interactive Turing machines (ITMs); the set of all *efficient* ITMs is denoted by ITM. We generally denote our protocols by Π and our (ideal) functionalities (which are also referred to as the trusted party [6]) by $\mathcal{F}$ both with descriptive super- or subscripts, the adversary by $\mathcal{A}$, the simulator by $\mathcal{S}$, and the environment by $\mathcal{Z}$. The random variable ensemble $\{\text{EXEC}_{\Pi,\mathcal{A},\mathcal{Z}}(k,z)\}_{k\in\mathbb{N},z\in\{0,1\}^*}$, which is more compactly often written as $\text{EXEC}_{\Pi,\mathcal{A},\mathcal{Z}}$, describes the contents of $\mathcal{Z}$'s output tape after an execution with Π, $\mathcal{F}$, and $\mathcal{A}$, on auxiliary input $z \in \{0,1\}^*$.

[1] We note in passing that our protocols do, in fact, imply an equilibrium, but in the attack "meta-game" defined in [14]. Interested readers are referred to [14] for more details.

[2] Secure multi-party computation with costly corruptions was first studied in [13].

Rational Protocol Design. Our results utilize the *Rational Protocol Design* (RPD) framework [14]. Here we review the basic elements that are needed to motivate and express our definitions and results; we refer to the framework paper [14] for further details. In RPD, security is defined via a two-party sequential zero-sum game with perfect information, called the *attack game*, between a protocol *designer* D and an *attacker* A. The designer D plays first by specifying a protocol Π for the (honest) participants to run; subsequently, the attacker A, who is informed about D's move (i.e., learns the protocol) plays by specifying a polynomial-time attack strategy $\mathcal{A}$ by which it may corrupt parties and try to subvert the execution of the protocol (uncorrupted parties follow Π as prescribed). Note that it suffices to define the utility $u_{\mathtt{A}}$ of the adversary as the game is zero-sum. (The utility $u_{\mathtt{D}}$ of the designer is then $-u_{\mathtt{A}}$.)

The utility definition relies on the simulation paradigm[3] in which a real-world execution of protocol Π in the presence of attack strategy (or adversary) $\mathcal{A}$ is compared to an ideal-world execution involving an ideal-world attack strategy (that is, a simulator $\mathcal{S}$) interacting with a functionality $\mathcal{F}$ which models the task at hand. Roughly speaking, the requirement is that the two worlds be indistinguishable to any environment $\mathcal{Z}$ which provides the inputs and obtains the outputs of all parties, and interacts arbitrarily with the adversary $\mathcal{A}$.

For defining the utilities in RPD, however, the real world is compared to an ideal world in which $\mathcal{S}$ gets to interact with a *relaxed* version of the functionality which, in addition to implementing the task as $\mathcal{F}$ would, also allows the simulator to perform the attacks we are interested in capturing. For example, an attack to the protocol's correctness is modeled by the functionality allowing the simulator to modify the outputs (even of honest parties). Given such a functionality, the utility of any given adversary is defined as the expected utility of the best simulator for this adversary, where the simulator's utility is defined based on which weaknesses of the ideal functionality the simulator is forced to exploit.

3. UTILITY-BASED FAIRNESS AND PROTOCOL OPTIMALITY

In this section, we make use of the RPD framework to introduce a natural fairness relation (partial order) to the space of efficient protocols. Specifically, we consider an instantiation of RPD with an attacker who obtains utility for violating fairness. The RPD machinery can be applied to most simulation-based security frameworks; however, for the sake of clarity we restrict ourselves to the technically simpler framework of Canetti [6] (allowing sequential and modular composition), which considers synchronous protocols with guaranteed termination. Our definitions can be extended to Universally Composable (UC) security [7] using the approach of Katz *et al.* [21] to model terminating synchronous computation in UC.

Now to our approach. We follow the three-step process described in [14] for specifying an adversary's utility, instantiating this process with parameters that capture a fairness-targeted attacker:

[3]In RPD the statements are formalized in Canetti's Universal Composition (UC) framework [7]; however, one could in principle use any other simulation-based model such as Canetti's MPC framework [6].

Step 1: Relaxing the ideal experiment to allow attacks on fairness. First, we relax the ideal world to allow the simulator to perform fairness-related attacks. In particular, we consider the experiment corresponding to standard ideal SFE with abort experiment [6, 17] with the difference that the simulator only receives the outputs of corrupted parties *if he asks for them* (we denote the corresponding trusted-party/functionality as $\mathcal{F}^{\perp}_{\text{SFE}}$). In a nutshell, $\mathcal{F}^{\perp}_{\text{SFE}}$ is similar to standard SFE but allows the simulator to ask for corrupted parties' outputs, and, subsequently, to send $\mathcal{F}^{\perp}_{\text{SFE}}$ a special (`abort`)-message even after having received these outputs (but before some honest parties receive the output). Upon receiving such an abort message, the functionality sets the output of every (honest) party to $\perp$. We refer to the above ideal world as the $\mathcal{F}^{\perp}_{\text{SFE}}$*-ideal world.* We point out that the functionality $\mathcal{F}^{\perp}_{\text{SFE}}$ is as usually parametrized by the actual function f to be evaluated; when we want to make this function f explicit we will write $\mathcal{F}^{f,\perp}_{\text{SFE}}$.

Step 2: Events and payoffs. Next, we specify a set of events in the experiment corresponding to the ideal evaluation of $\mathcal{F}^{\perp}_{\text{SFE}}$ which capture whether or not a fairness breach occurs, and assign to each such event a "payoff" value capturing the severity of provoking the event. The relevant questions to ask with respect to fairness are:

1. Does the adversary learn "noticeable" information about the output of the corrupted parties?
2. Do honest parties learn their output?

The events used to describe fairness correspond to the four possible combinations of answers to the above questions. In particular, we define the events indexed by a string $ij \in \{0,1\}^2$, where i (resp., j) equals 1 if the answer to the first (resp., second) question is yes and 0 otherwise. The events are then as follows:

E_{00}: The simulator does not ask functionality $\mathcal{F}^{\perp}_{\text{SFE}}$ for any of the corrupted parties' outputs and instructs it to abort before all honest parties receive their output. (Thus, neither the simulator nor the honest parties will receive their outputs.)

E_{01}: The simulator does not ask $\mathcal{F}^{\perp}_{\text{SFE}}$ for any of the corrupted parties' outputs and does not abort. (When the protocol terminates, then only the honest parties will receive the output. This event also accounts for cases where the adversary does not corrupt *any* party.)

E_{10}: The simulator asks $\mathcal{F}^{\perp}_{\text{SFE}}$ for some corrupted party's output and instructs it to abort before any honest party receives the output.

E_{11}: The simulator asks $\mathcal{F}^{\perp}_{\text{SFE}}$ for some corrupted party's output and does not abort. (When the protocol terminates, both the honest parties and the simulator will receive their outputs. This event also accounts for cases where the adversary corrupts *all* parties.)

We remark that our definition does not give any advantage to an adversary corrupting all parties. This is consistent with the intuitive notion of fairness, as when there is no honest party, the adversary has nobody to gain an unfair advantage over.

To each of the events E_{ij} we associate a real-valued *payoff* γ_{ij} which captures the adversary's utility when provoking this event. Thus, the adversary's payoff is specified by vector $\vec{\gamma} = (\gamma_{00}, \gamma_{01}, \gamma_{10}, \gamma_{11})$, corresponding to events $\vec{E} = (E_{00}, E_{01}, E_{10}, E_{11})$.

Finally, we define the expected payoff of a given simulator $\mathcal{S}$ (for an environment $\mathcal{Z}$) to be[4]:

$$U_I^{\mathcal{F}_{\text{SFE}}^{\perp}, \vec{\gamma}}(\mathcal{S}, \mathcal{Z}) \quad := \quad \sum_{i,j \in \{0,1\}} \gamma_{ij} \Pr[E_{ij}]. \tag{1}$$

Step 3: Defining the attacker's utility. Given the expected payoff $U_I^{\mathcal{F}_{\text{SFE}}^{\perp}, \vec{\gamma}}(\mathcal{S}, \mathcal{Z})$, the utility $u_{\mathtt{A}}(\Pi, \mathcal{A})$ for a pair $(\Pi, \mathcal{A})$ is defined following the methodology in [14] as the expected payoff of the *best* simulator[5] that simulates $\mathcal{A}$ in the $\mathcal{F}_{\text{SFE}}^{\perp}$-ideal world in presence of the least favorable environment, i.e., the one that is *most* favorable to the attacker. To make the payoff vector $\vec{\gamma}$ explicit, we sometimes denote the above utility as $\hat{U}^{\Pi, \mathcal{F}_{\text{SFE}}^{\perp}, \vec{\gamma}}(\mathcal{A})$ and refer to it as the *payoff of strategy* $\mathcal{A}$ (for attacking Π).

More formally, for a protocol Π, denote by $\mathtt{SIM}_{\mathcal{A}}$ the class of simulators for $\mathcal{A}$, i.e, $\mathtt{SIM}_{\mathcal{A}} = \{\mathcal{S} \in \mathtt{ITM} \mid \forall \mathcal{Z} : \text{EXEC}_{\Pi, \mathcal{A}, \mathcal{Z}} \approx \text{EXEC}_{\mathcal{F}_{\text{SFE}}^{\perp}, \mathcal{S}, \mathcal{Z}}\}$. The payoff of strategy $\mathcal{A}$ (for attacking Π) is then defined as:

$$u_{\mathtt{A}}(\Pi, \mathcal{A}) := \hat{U}^{\Pi, \mathcal{F}_{\text{SFE}}^{\perp}, \vec{\gamma}}(\mathcal{A}) := \sup_{\mathcal{Z} \in \mathtt{ITM}} \inf_{\mathcal{S} \in \mathtt{SIM}_{\mathcal{A}}} \{U_I^{\mathcal{F}_{\text{SFE}}^{\perp}, \vec{\gamma}}(\mathcal{S}, \mathcal{Z})\}. \tag{2}$$

To complete our formalization, we now describe a natural relation among the values in $\vec{\gamma}$ which is both intuitive and consistent with existing approaches to fairness, and which we will assume to hold for the remainder of the paper. Specifically, we will consider attackers whose least preferred event is that the honest parties receive their output while the attacker does not, i.e., we assume that $\gamma_{01} = \min_{\gamma \in \vec{\gamma}}\{\gamma\}$. Furthermore, we will assume that the attacker's favorite choice is that he receives the output and the honest parties do not, i.e., $\gamma_{10} = \max_{ij \in \{0,1\}^2}\{\gamma_{ij}\}$. Lastly, we point out that for an arbitrary payoff vector $\vec{\gamma}$, one can assume without loss of generality that any one of its values equals zero, and, therefore, we can set $\gamma_{01} = 0$. This can be seen immediately by setting $\gamma'_{ij} = \gamma_{ij} - \gamma_{01}$. We denote the set of all payoff vectors adhering to the above restrictions by $\Gamma_{\text{fair}} \subseteq \mathbb{R}^4$. Summarizing, our fairness-specific payoff ("preference") vector $\vec{\gamma}$ satisfies

$$0 = \gamma_{01} \leq \min\{\gamma_{00}, \gamma_{11}\} \quad \text{and} \quad \max\{\gamma_{00}, \gamma_{11}\} < \gamma_{10}.$$

Optimally fair protocols. We are now ready to define our partial order relation for protocols with respect to fairness. Informally, a protocol Π will be *at least as fair* as another protocol Π' if the utility of the best adversary $\mathcal{A}$ attacking Π (i.e, the adversary which maximizes $u_{\mathtt{A}}(\Pi, \mathcal{A})$) is no larger than the utility of the best adversary attacking Π' (except for some negligible quantity). Our notion of fairness is with respect to the above natural class Γ_{fair}; for conciseness, we will abbreviate and say that a protocol is "$\vec{\gamma}$-fair," for $\vec{\gamma} \in \Gamma_{\text{fair}}$. Formally:

Definition 1. *Let Π and Π' be protocols, and $\vec{\gamma} \in \Gamma_{fair}$ be a preference vector. We say that Π is* at least as fair as Π' *with respect to $\vec{\gamma}$ (i.e., it is at least as $\vec{\gamma}$-fair), denoted $\Pi \overset{\vec{\gamma}}{\succeq} \Pi'$, if*

$$\sup_{\mathcal{A} \in \mathtt{ITM}} u_{\mathtt{A}}(\Pi, \mathcal{A}) \quad \overset{\text{negl}}{\leq} \quad \sup_{\mathcal{A} \in \mathtt{ITM}} u_{\mathtt{A}}(\Pi', \mathcal{A}). \tag{3}$$

We will refer to a protocol which is a maximal element according to the above fairness relation as an *optimally fair* protocol.

Definition 2. *Let $\vec{\gamma} \in \Gamma_{fair}$. A protocol Π is* optimally $\vec{\gamma}$-fair *if it is at least as $\vec{\gamma}$-fair as any other protocol Π'.*

Definition 2 presents our most basic notion of utility-based fairness. With foresight, one issue that arises with this definition in the multi-party setting is that it is not sensitive to the number of corrupted parties, so when an adversary is able to corrupt parties for free, he is better off corrupting all $n-1$ parties. In Section 4.2 we also present an alternative notion of fairness suitable for situations where the number of corrupted parties does matter, as, for example, when corrupting parties carries some cost (cf. [13]).

4. UTILITY-BASED FAIR SFE

In this section we investigate the question of finding optimally $\vec{\gamma}$-fair protocols for secure two-party and multi-party function evaluation, for any $\vec{\gamma} \in \Gamma_{\text{fair}}$. (Recall that Γ_{fair} is a class of natural preference vectors for fairness—cf. Section 3.) In addition, for the case of multi-party protocols, we also suggest an alternative, incomparable notion of fairness that is sensitive to the number of corrupted parties and is therefore relevant when this number is an issue. As we describe our protocols in the model of [6], the protocols are synchronous and parties communicate with each other via bilateral secure channels. We point out that the protocols described here are secure against adaptive adversaries [9].

4.1 The Two-Party Setting

In this section we present an optimally $\vec{\gamma}$-fair protocol, $\Pi_{2\text{SFE}}^{\text{Opt}}$, for computing any given function. Its optimality is established by proving a general upper bound on the utility $u_{\mathtt{A}}(\Pi, \mathcal{A})$ of an adversary $\mathcal{A}$ attacking it, and then presenting a specific function f and an adversary who attacks the protocol $\Pi_{2\text{SFE}}^{\text{Opt}}$ for computing f that obtains a utility which matches the above upper bound.

4.1.1 The Protocol (Upper Bound)

Our protocol makes use of a well-known cryptographic primitive called *authenticated secret sharing.* An authenticated additive (two-out-of-two) secret sharing scheme is an additive sharing scheme augmented with a message authentication code (MAC) to ensure verifiability. (See the Appendix for a concrete instantiation.) Protocol $\Pi_{2\text{SFE}}^{\text{Opt}}$ works in two phases as follows; f denotes the function to be computed:

1. In the first phase, $\Pi_{2\text{SFE}}^{\text{Opt}}$ invokes an adaptively secure unfair SFE protocol (e.g., the protocol in [17]—call it Π_{GMW})[6] to compute the following function f': f' takes as input the inputs of the parties to f, and outputs an authenticated sharing of the output of f along with an

[4]Refer to [14, Section 2] for the rationale behind this formulation.

[5]The best simulator is taken to be the one that minimizes his payoff [14].

[6]Note that assuming ideally secure channels, the protocol Π_{GMW} is adaptively secure [9].

index $i \in_R \{1,2\}$ chosen uniformly at random. In case the protocol aborts, the honest party takes a default value as the input of the corrupted party and locally computes the function f.

2. In the second phase, if Π_{GMW} did not abort, the protocol continues in two more rounds. In the first round, the output (sharing) is reconstructed towards p_i, and in the second round it is reconstructed towards $p_{\neg i}$. In case $p_{\neg i}$ does not send a valid share to p_i in the first round, p_i again takes a default value as the input of the (corrupted) party $p_{\neg i}$ and computes the function f locally (the second round is then omitted).

As we show in the following theorem, the adversary's payoff in the above protocol is upper-bounded by $\frac{\gamma_{10}+\gamma_{11}}{2}$. The intuition behind the proof is as follows: If the adversary corrupts the party that first receives the output, then he can provoke his most preferred event E_{10} by aborting before sending his last message. However, because this party is chosen at random, this happens only with probability 1/2; with the remaining 1/2 probability the honest party receives the output first, in which case the best choice for the adversary is to allow the protocol to terminate and provoke the event E_{11}.

Without loss of generality, we assume that the function f has a single global output; indeed, a protocol that can compute any such function f can be easily extended to compute functions with multiple, potentially private outputs by using standard techniques, e.g., see [22].

THEOREM 3. *Let $\vec{\gamma} \in \Gamma_{fair}$ and $\mathcal{A}$ be an adversary. Then* $u_A(\Pi^{Opt}_{2SFE}, \mathcal{A}) \overset{\text{negl}}{\leq} \frac{\gamma_{10}+\gamma_{11}}{2}$.

PROOF (SKETCH). We prove the statement for $\Pi^{\text{Opt}}_{\text{2SFE}}$ in the $\mathcal{F}^{f',\perp}_{\text{SFE}}$-hybrid model. The theorem then follows by applying the RPD composition theorem [14, Theorem 5], which extends to the case where the framework is instantiated with the model of Canetti [6].

First we remark that if the adversary corrupts both parties or no party, then the theorem follows directly from the definition of the payoff and the properties of Γ_{fair}, as in these cases the payoff the adversary obtains equals γ_{11} or γ_{01}, respectively. Assume for the remainder of the proof that the adversary corrupts p_1 (the case where the adversary corrupts p_2 is dealt with symmetrically). To complete the proof it suffices to provide a simulator $\mathcal{S}_{\mathcal{A}}$ for any adversary $\mathcal{A}$, such that $\mathcal{S}_{\mathcal{A}}$ has expected payoff at most $\frac{\gamma_{10}+\gamma_{11}}{2}$. Such a (black-box straight-line) simulator $\mathcal{S}_{\mathcal{A}}$ for an adversary $\mathcal{A}$ works as follows.

To emulate the output of $\mathcal{F}^{f',\perp}_{\text{SFE}}$, $\mathcal{S}_{\mathcal{A}}$ does the following (recall that the output consists of a share for p_1 and a uniformly chosen index $i \in \{1,2\}$): $\mathcal{S}_{\mathcal{A}}$ randomly picks an index $\hat{i} \in_R \{1,2\}$ along with the element $\hat{s}_1, \hat{k}_1$ and a random MAC-tag $\hat{t}_2$; $\mathcal{S}_{\mathcal{A}}$ hands to the adversary the (simulated) share $(\hat{s}_1, \hat{t}_2)$, the key $\hat{k}_1$, and the index $\hat{i}$. Subsequently, $\mathcal{S}_{\mathcal{A}}$ simulates the opening stage of $\Pi^{\text{Opt}}_{\text{2SFE}}$:

- If $\hat{i} = 1$, then $\mathcal{S}_{\mathcal{A}}$ sends $\hat{x}_1$ (which it obtained because of the $\mathcal{F}^{f',\perp}_{\text{SFE}}$-hybrid model) to $\mathcal{F}^{f,\perp}_{\text{SFE}}$ and asks for the output[7]; let y denote this output. $\mathcal{S}_{\mathcal{A}}$ computes a share for p_2 which, together with the simulated share of p_1, results in a valid sharing of y, as follows: set $t'_1 := \mathsf{tag}(y, \hat{k}_1)$ and $t'_2 := \mathsf{tag}(y, \hat{k}_2)$ for a uniformly chosen k_2. Set $\hat{s}_2 := (y, t'_1, t'_2) - s_1$ and $\hat{t}_1 := \mathsf{tag}(\hat{s}_2, \hat{k}_1)$. Send $(\hat{s}_2, \hat{t}_1)$ to p_1 for reconstructing the sharing of y. In the next round, receive from $\mathcal{A}$ p_1's share; if $\mathcal{S}_{\mathcal{A}}$ receives a share other than $(\hat{s}_1, \hat{t}_2)$, then it sends `abort` to $\mathcal{F}^{f,\perp}_{\text{SFE}}$, before the honest party is allowed to receive its output.
- If $\hat{i} = 0$ then $\mathcal{S}_{\mathcal{A}}$ receives from $\mathcal{A}$ p_1's share. If $\mathcal{S}_{\mathcal{A}}$ receives a share other than $(\hat{s}_1, \hat{t}_2)$, then it sends a default value to $\mathcal{F}^{f,\perp}_{\text{SFE}}$ (as p_1's input). Otherwise, it asks $\mathcal{F}^{f,\perp}_{\text{SFE}}$ for p_1's output y, and computes a share for p_2 which, together with the simulated share of p_1, results in a valid sharing of y (as above). $\mathcal{S}_{\mathcal{A}}$ sends this share to $\mathcal{A}$.

It is straightforward to verify that $\mathcal{S}_{\mathcal{A}}$ is a good simulator for $\mathcal{A}$, as the simulated keys and shares are distributed identically to the actual sharing in the protocol execution.

We now argue that for any adversary $\mathcal{A}$ corrupting p_1, the payoff of $\mathcal{S}_{\mathcal{A}}$ is (at most) $\frac{\gamma_{10}+\gamma_{11}}{2} + \mu$ for some negligible function μ. If $\mathcal{A}$ makes the evaluation of the function f' in the first phase to abort, the simulator sends $\mathcal{F}^{f,\perp}_{\text{SFE}}$ a default input and delivers to the honest party, which provokes the event E_{01}; hence the payoff of this adversary will be $\gamma_{01} < \frac{\gamma_{10}+\gamma_{11}}{2}$. Otherwise, i.e., if $\mathcal{A}$ allows the parties to receive their f'-outputs/shares in the first phase, then we consider the following two cases: (1) if $\hat{i} = 1$ (i.e., the corrupted party gets the value first), then $\mathcal{A}$ can always provoke his most preferred event by receiving the output in the first round of the opening stage and then aborting, which will make $\mathcal{S}_{\mathcal{A}}$ provoke the event E_{10}. (2) if $\hat{i} = 2$ the adversary's choices are to provoke the events E_{01} or E_{11}, out of which his more preferred one is E_{11}. Because $\hat{i}$ is uniformly chosen, each of the cases (1) and (2) occurs with probability 1/2; hence, the payoff of the adversary is $\frac{\gamma_{10}+\gamma_{11}}{2} + \mu$ (where the negligible quantity μ comes from the fact that there might be a negligible error in the simulation of $\mathcal{S}_{\mathcal{A}}$). Therefore, in any case the utility of the attacker choosing adversary $\mathcal{A}$ is $u_A(\Pi^{\text{Opt}}_{\text{2SFE}}, \mathcal{A}) \overset{\text{negl}}{\leq} \frac{\gamma_{10}+\gamma_{11}}{2}$ which concludes the proof. □

4.1.2 Optimality of the Protocol (Lower Bound)

Next, we show that the above bound is tight for protocols that evaluate *arbitrary* functions. We remark that, for specific classes of functions—such as those with polynomial-size range or domain—one is able to obtain fairer protocols. For example, it is easy to verify that for functions which admit $1/p$-secure solutions [18] for an arbitrary polynomial p, we can reduce the upper bound in Theorem 3 to $\frac{\gamma_{10}+\gamma_{11}}{p}$. (Refer to Section 5 for a detailed comparison of our notion to $1/p$-security). Thus, an interesting future direction is to find optimally fair solutions for computing primitives such as random selection [19] and set intersection [12] which could then be used in higher-level constructions.

The general result shows that there are functions for which $\frac{\gamma_{10}+\gamma_{11}}{2}$ is also a lower bound on the adversary's utility for *any* protocol, independently of the number of rounds. Here we prove this for the particular "swap" function $f_{\mathsf{swp}}(x_1, x_2) = (x_2, x_1)$; the result carries over to a large class of functions (essentially those where $1/p$-security is proved impossible in [18]).

At a high level, the proof goes as follows: First, we observe that in any protocol execution there must be one round

[7]Recall that we assume wlog that f has one global output.

(for each of the parties p_i) in which p_i "learns the output of the evaluation." An adversary corrupting one of the parties at random has probability 1/2 of corrupting the party that receives the output first; in that case the adversary learns the output and can abort the computation, forcing the other party to not receive it, which results in a payoff γ_{10}. With the remaining 1/2 probability, the adversary does not corrupt the correct party. In this case, finishing the protocol and obtaining payoff γ_{11} is the best strategy.[8]

We first show an intermediate result, where we consider two specific adversarial strategies $\mathcal{A}_1$ and $\mathcal{A}_2$, which are valid against any protocol. In strategy $\mathcal{A}_1$, the adversary (statically) corrupts p_1, and proceeds as follows: In each round ℓ, receive all the messages from p_2. Check whether p_1 holds his actual output ($\mathcal{A}_1$ generates a copy of p_1, simulates to this copy that p_2 aborted the protocol, obtains the output of p_1 and checks whether the output of p_1 is the default output—this strategy works since the functionality is secure with abort); if so, record the output and abort the execution before sending p_1's ℓ-round message(s).[9] Otherwise, let p_1 correctly execute its instructions for round ℓ. The strategy $\mathcal{A}_2$ is defined analogously with roles for p_1 and p_2 exchanged.

LEMMA 4. *Let f_{swp} be the swap function, $\mathcal{A}_1$ and $\mathcal{A}_2$ be the strategies defined above, and $\vec{\gamma} \in \Gamma_{fair}$. Every protocol Π which securely realizes functionality $\mathcal{F}_{\text{SFE}}^{f_{\mathsf{swp}},\perp}$ satisfies:*

$$u_{\mathsf{A}}(\Pi, \mathcal{A}_1) + u_{\mathsf{A}}(\Pi, \mathcal{A}_2) \overset{\text{negl}}{\geq} \gamma_{10} + \gamma_{11}.$$

PROOF (SKETCH). For $i \in \{1,2\}$ we consider the environment $\mathcal{Z}_i$ that is executed together with $\mathcal{A}_i$ corrupting p_i. The environment $\mathcal{Z}_i$ will choose a fixed value $x_{\neg i}$, which it provides as an input to $p_{\neg i}$.

For compactness, we introduce the following two events in the protocol execution: We denote by L the event that the adversary aborts in a round where the honest party holds the actual output (in other words the honest party's output is "locked"), and by $\bar{L}$ the event that the adversary aborts at a round where the honest party does not hold the actual output (i.e., if the corrupt party aborts, the honest party outputs some value other than $f(x_1, x_2)$). Observe that, in cases corresponding to the real-world event $\bar{L}$, with overwhelming probability the simulator needs to send to the functionality the "`abort`" messages, provoking γ_{10}; indeed, because Π is secure with abort, in that case $p_{\neg i}$ needs to output $\perp$ with overwhelming probability (otherwise, there is a noticeable probability that he will output a wrong value, which contradicts security with abort of Π). On the other hand, in cases corresponding to L, the simulator must (with overwhelming probability) allow $p_{\neg i}$ to obtain the output from $\mathcal{F}_{\text{SFE}}^{f,\perp}$, provoking the event γ_{11}. Hence, except with negligible error, the adversary obtains γ_{11} and γ_{10} for provoking the events L and $\bar{L}$, respectively. Therefore, the payoff of these adversaries is (at least) $\gamma_{11}\Pr[L] + \gamma_{10}\Pr[\bar{L}] - \mu''$, where μ'' is a negligible function (corresponding to the difference in the payoff that is created due to the simulation error of the optimal simulator).

To complete the proof, we compute the probability of each of the events L and $\bar{L}$ for $\mathcal{A}_1$ and $\mathcal{A}_2$. One important observation for both strategies $\mathcal{A}_1$ and $\mathcal{A}_2$, the adversary instructs the corrupted party to behave honestly until the round when it holds the actual output, hence all messages in the protocol execution have exactly the same distribution as in an honest execution until that round. For each party p_i, the protocol implicitly defines the rounds in which the output of honest, hence also of honestly behaving, parties are "locked." In such an execution, let R_i denote the first round where p_i holds the actual output. There are two cases: (i) $R_1 = R_2$ and (ii) $R_1 \neq R_2$. In case (i), both $\mathcal{A}_1$ and $\mathcal{A}_2$ provoke the event $\bar{L}$. In case (ii), if $R_1 < R_2$, then $\mathcal{A}_1$ always provokes the event $\bar{L}$, while for $\mathcal{A}_2$, with some probability (denoted as $q_{\bar{L}}$), the honest party does not hold the actual output when the $\mathcal{A}_2$ aborts, and with probability $1 - q_{\bar{L}}$ it does.[10] (Of course, the analogous arguments with switched roles hold for $R_1 > R_2$.

For the particular adversaries $\mathcal{A}_1$ and $\mathcal{A}_2$, the considered values R_1 and R_2 are indeed relevant, since the adversaries both use the honest protocol machine as a "black box" until it starts holding the output. The probability of $\bar{L}$ for $\mathcal{A}_1$ is $\Pr[R_1 = R_2] + \Pr[R_1 < R_2] \cdot (1 - q_L)$, and the overall probability of L is $\Pr[R_1 < R_2] \cdot q_L + \Pr[R_1 < R_2]$, the probabilities for $\mathcal{A}_2$ are analogous. Hence, we obtain

$$\begin{aligned}
&u_{\mathsf{A}}(\Pi, \mathcal{A}_1) + u_{\mathsf{A}}(\Pi, \mathcal{A}_2) \\
&\geq \gamma_{11}\Pr{}^{\mathcal{A}_1}[L] + \gamma_{10}\Pr{}^{\mathcal{A}_1}[\bar{L}] + \gamma_{11}\Pr{}^{\mathcal{A}_2}[L] + \gamma_{10}\Pr{}^{\mathcal{A}_2}[\bar{L}] \\
&\geq \gamma_{10} \cdot (2 \cdot \Pr[R_1 = R_2] + (1 + q_{\bar{L}}) \cdot \Pr[R_1 \neq R_2]) \\
&\quad + \gamma_{11} \cdot (1 - q_{\bar{L}}) \cdot \Pr[R_1 \neq R_2] \\
&\geq \gamma_{10} \cdot (\Pr[R_1 = R_2] + \Pr[R_1 < R_2] + \Pr[R_1 > R_2]) \\
&\quad + \gamma_{11} \cdot (\Pr[R_1 = R_2] + \Pr[R_1 < R_2] + \Pr[R_1 > R_2]) \\
&\geq \gamma_{10} + \gamma_{11} - \mu,
\end{aligned}$$

which was exactly the statement we wanted to prove. □

Lemma 4 provides a bound involving two adversaries. (It can be viewed as a statement that "one of $\mathcal{A}_1$ and $\mathcal{A}_2$ must be good"). However, we can use it to prove our lower bound on the payoff by considering the single adversarial strategy, call it $\mathcal{A}_{\text{gen}}$, that is the "mix" of the two strategies $\mathcal{A}_1$ and $\mathcal{A}_2$ described above: The adversary corrupts one party chosen at random, checks (in each round) whether the protocol would compute the correct output on abort, and stops the execution as soon as it obtains the output. In the sequel, for a given function f we say that a protocol securely realizes the functionality $\mathcal{F}_{\text{SFE}}^{f,\perp}$ if it securely evaluates f in the $\mathcal{F}_{\text{SFE}}^{f,\perp}$-ideal world.

THEOREM 5. *Let $\vec{\gamma} \in \Gamma_{fair}$, f_{swp} be the swap function. There exists an adversary $\mathcal{A}$ such that for every protocol Π which securely realizes functionality $\mathcal{F}_{\text{SFE}}^{f_{\mathsf{swp}},\perp}$, it holds that* $u_{\mathsf{A}}(\Pi, \mathcal{A}) \overset{\text{negl}}{\geq} \frac{\gamma_{10}+\gamma_{11}}{2}$.

PROOF. Let $\mathcal{A}$ be the adversary $\mathcal{A}_{\text{gen}}$ described above. As adversary $\mathcal{A}_{\text{gen}}$ chooses one of the strategies $\mathcal{A}_1$ or $\mathcal{A}_2$ uniformly at random, it obtains the average of the utilities of $\mathcal{A}_1$ and $\mathcal{A}_2$. Indeed, using Lemma 4, we obtain

$$u_{\mathsf{A}}(\Pi, \mathcal{A}_{\text{gen}}) = \frac{1}{2} \cdot u_{\mathsf{A}}(\Pi, \mathcal{A}_2) + \frac{1}{2} \cdot u_{\mathsf{A}}(\Pi, \mathcal{A}_2) \overset{\text{negl}}{\geq} \frac{1}{2} \cdot (\gamma_{10} + \gamma_{11} - \mu),$$

which completes the proof. □

[8]The adversary could also obtain γ_{01} by aborting, but will not play this strategy as, by assumption, $\gamma_{01} \leq \min\{\gamma_{00}, \gamma_{11}\}$.

[9]This attack is possible because the adversary is rushing.

[10]The reason is that we don't exclude protocols in which the output of a party which has been "locked" in some round gets "unlocked" in a future round.

The above theorem establishes that $\Pi^{\text{Opt}}_{\text{2SFE}}$ is optimally γ-fair. We also remark that the protocol is optimal with respect to the number of reconstruction rounds. See Appendix 4.1.3 for details.

4.1.3 Round Complexity of the Reconstruction Phase

Most, if not all, protocols in the literature designed to achieve a (relaxed) notion of fairness have a similar structure: They first invoke a general (unfair) SFE protocol for computing a sharing of the output, and then proceed to a reconstruction phase where they attempt to obtain the output by reconstructing this sharing. Since the first (unfair SFE) phase is common in all those protocols, the number of rounds of the reconstruction phase is a reasonable complexity measure for such protocols.

As we show below, protocol $\Pi^{\text{Opt}}_{\text{2SFE}}$ is not only optimally $\vec{\gamma}$-fair but is also optimal with respect to the number of reconstruction rounds, i.e., the number of rounds it invokes after the sharing of the output has been generated. To demonstrate this we first provide a formal definition of reconstruction rounds. Note that also the notion of reconstruction rounds is implicit in many works in the fairness literature, to our knowledge, a formal definition such as the one described here has not been provided elsewhere.

Intuitively, a protocol has ℓ reconstruction rounds if up to ℓ rounds before the end, the adversary has not gained any advantage in learning the output, but the next round is the one where the reconstruction starts. Formally,

DEFINITION 6. *Let Π be an SFE protocol for evaluating the (multi-party) function $f : (\{0,1\}^*)^n \to (\{0,1\}^*)^n$ which terminates in m rounds. We say that Π has ℓ* reconstruction-rounds *if it implements the (fair) functionality $\mathcal{F}^f_{\text{SFE}}$ in the presence of any adversary who aborts in any of the rounds $1, \ldots, m-\ell$, but does not implement it if the adversary aborts in round $m-\ell+1$.*

LEMMA 7. *Π^{Opt}_{2SFE} has two reconstruction rounds.*

PROOF (SKETCH). The security of the protocol used in phase 1 of $\Pi^{\text{Opt}}_{\text{2SFE}}$ and the privacy of the secret sharing, ensures that the view of the adversary during this phase (including his output) can be perfectly simulated without ever involving the functionality. Thus if the adversary corrupting, say, p_1 (the case of a corrupted p_2 is symmetric) aborts during this phase, then p_2 can simply locally evaluate the function on his input and a default input by the adversary. To simulate this, the simulator will simply hand the default input to the fair functionality. However, as implied by the lower bound in Theorem 5, this is not the case if the adversary aborts in the first round of phase 2. □

LEMMA 8. *Assuming $\vec{\gamma} \in \Gamma_{fair}$, there exists no optimally $\vec{\gamma}$-fair protocol for computing the swap function f_{swp} (see Lemma 4) with a single reconstruction round.*

PROOF (SKETCH). Assume towards contradiction that a protocol Π with a single reconstruction round exists. Clearly, before the last round the output should not be "locked" for neither of the parties. Indeed, if this is the case the adversary corrupting this party can, as in the proof of Lemma 4, force an unfair abort which cannot be simulated in the $\mathcal{F}^{f_{\mathsf{swp}}}_{\text{SFE}}$-ideal model. Now, in the (single) reconstruction round, a rushing adversary receives the message from the honest party but does not send anything, which can only be simulated by making the honest party abort. This adversary obtains maximum payoff, γ_{10} (except with negligible probability). Thus Π is less $\vec{\gamma}$-fair than $\Pi^{\text{Opt}}_{\text{2SFE}}$ and hence is not optimally $\vec{\gamma}$-fair. □

4.2 The Multi-Party Setting

Throughout this section, we make the simplifying assumption that the attacker prefers learning the output over not learning it, i.e., $\gamma_{00} \leq \gamma_{11}$. Although this assumption is natural and standard in the rational fairness literature, it is *not* without loss of generality. It is, however, useful in proving multi-party fairness statements, as it allows us to compute the utility of the attacker for a protocol which is fully secure for $\mathcal{F}_{\text{SFE}}$, including fairness. Indeed, while such a protocol might still allow the attacker to abort and hence obtain utility γ_{00}, in this case the optimal utility is γ_{11} as the event E_{11} is the "best" event which $\mathcal{A}$ can provoke. Combined with the inequalities from Section 3, the entries in vector $\vec{\gamma}$ satisfy $0 = \gamma_{01} \leq \gamma_{00} \leq \gamma_{11} < \gamma_{10}$. We denote by $\Gamma^+_{\text{fair}} \subseteq \Gamma_{\text{fair}}$ the class of payoff vectors with the above restriction.

The intuition behind protocol $\Pi^{\text{Opt}}_{\text{2SFE}}$ can be extended to also work in the multi-party ($n > 2$) setting. The idea for the corresponding multi-party protocol $\Pi^{\text{Opt}}_{\text{nSFE}}$, which is described below in more detail, is as follows: In a first phase, $\Pi^{\text{Opt}}_{\text{nSFE}}$ computes the private output function $f'(x_1, \ldots, x_n) = (y_1, \ldots, y_n)$, where for some random $i^* \in [n]$, y_{i^*} equals the output of the function f we wish to compute, whereas for all $i \in [n] \setminus \{i^*\}$, $y_i = \bot$; in addition to y_i, every party p_i receives an authentication tag on y_i.[11] If this phase aborts then the protocol also aborts. In phase 2, all parties announce their output y_i (by broadcasting them). If a validly authenticated message $y \neq \bot$ is broadcast, then the parties adopt it; otherwise, they abort.

Functionality $\langle \mathcal{F}^{f,\bot}_{\text{PRIV-SFE}} \rangle$

1. Compute the function f on the given inputs and store the (public) output in variable y.
2. Chose $(\mathsf{sk}, \mathsf{vk}) \xleftarrow{\$} \mathtt{Gen}(1^k)$ and compute a signature $\sigma = \mathtt{Sign}(y, \mathsf{sk})$.
3. Choose a uniformly random $i^* \in [n]$ and set $y_{i^*} = (y, \sigma)$ and for each $i \in [n] \setminus \{i^*\}$, set y_i to a default value (e.g., $y_j = \bot$).
4. Each $p_j \in \mathcal{P}$ receives as (private) output the value (y_j, vk).

Protocol $\Pi^{\text{Opt},f}_{\text{nSFE}}$

1. The parties use protocol Π_{GMW} [17] to evaluate the functionality $\mathcal{F}^{f,\bot}_{\text{PRIV-SFE}}$. If Π_{GMW} aborts then $\Pi^{\text{Opt},f}_{\text{nSFE}}$ also aborts' otherwise every party p_i denotes its output by (y_j, vk).
2. Every party broadcasts y_j. If no party broadcast a pair $y_j = (y, \sigma)$ where σ is a valid signature on y for the key vk then every party aborts. Otherwise, every party output y.

As proven in the full version of this work [15], the utility that any adversary $\mathcal{A}$ accrues against $\Pi^{\text{Opt}}_{\text{nSFE}}$ is

$$u_{\mathsf{A}}(\Pi^{\text{Opt}}_{\text{nSFE}}, \mathcal{A}) \overset{\text{negl}}{\leq} \frac{(n-1)\gamma_{10} + \gamma_{11}}{n},$$

which is in fact optimal (also proven there).

[11] In fact, we do not need to authenticate the default value.

Utility-balanced fairness. A closer look at the above results shows that an adversary who is able to corrupt parties for free is always better off corrupting $n-1$ parties. While this is natural in the case of two parties, in the multi-party case one might be interested in more "fine-grain" optimality notions, which are sensitive to the number of corrupted parties. One such natural notion, which we now present, requires that the allocation of utility to adversaries corrupting different numbers of parties be tight, in the sense that the utility of a best t-*adversary*—i.e., any adversary that optimally attacks the protocol while corrupting up to t parties—cannot be decreased unless the utility of a best t'-adversary increases, for $t' \neq t$.[12] This leads to the notion of *utility-balanced* fairness.

Definition 9. *Let* $\vec{\gamma} \in \Gamma^{+}_{fair}$. *A multi-party protocol* Π *is* utility-balanced $\vec{\gamma}$-fair (w.r.t. corruptions) *if for any protocol* Π', *for every* $(\mathcal{A}_1, \ldots, \mathcal{A}_{n-1})$ *and* $(\mathcal{A}'_1, \ldots, \mathcal{A}'_{n-1})$ *the following holds:*

$$\sum_{t=1}^{n-1} u_{\mathtt{A}}(\Pi, \mathcal{A}_t) \overset{\text{negl}}{\leq} \sum_{t=1}^{n-1} u_{\mathtt{A}}(\Pi', \mathcal{A}'_t),$$

where for $t = 1, \ldots, n-1$, $\mathcal{A}_t$ *and* $\mathcal{A}'_t$ *are* t*-adversaries attacking protocols* Π *and* Π', *respectively.*[13]

In the full version, we show that protocol $\Pi^{\text{Opt}}_{\text{nSFE}}$ is in fact utility-balanced $\vec{\gamma}$-fair. To this end, we first prove that the sum of the expected utilities of the different t-adversaries is

$$\sum_{t=1}^{n-1} u_{\mathtt{A}}(\Pi^{\text{Opt}}_{\text{nSFE}}, \mathcal{A}_t) \overset{\text{negl}}{\leq} \frac{(n-1)}{2}(\gamma_{10} + \gamma_{11}), \quad (4)$$

which we then show to be tight for certain functions. In fact, our upper bound provides a good criterion for checking whether or not a protocol is utility-based $\vec{\gamma}$-fair: if for a protocol there are t-adversaries, $1 \leq t \leq n-1$, such that the sum of their utilities non-negligibly exceeds this bound, then the protocol is not utility-balanced $\vec{\gamma}$-fair. We observe that protocols that are fair according to the traditional fairness notion [17] are not necessarily utility-balanced $\vec{\gamma}$-fair—the reason is that they "give up" completely for $n/2$ parties if n is even. Furthermore, although the protocol $\Pi^{\text{Opt}}_{\text{nSFE}}$ presented above satisfies both utility-based notions (optimal and utility-balanced), these two notions are in fact incomparable; separating examples are given in the full version.

Utility-balanced fairness as optimal fairness with corruption costs. As discussed above, the notion of utility-balanced fairness connects the ability (or willingness) of the adversary to corrupt parties with the utility he obtains. Thus, a natural interpretation of utility-balanced $\vec{\gamma}$-fairness is as a desirable optimality notion when some information about the cost of corrupting parties is known; for example, it is known that certain sets of parties might be easier to corrupt than others. We now show that if we associate a cost to party corruption (as a negative utility for the adversary) then there is a natural connection between utility-balanced $\vec{\gamma}$-fairness and optimal $\vec{\gamma}$-fairness. We first slightly modify the definition of an attacker's utility to account for corruption cost, along the lines of [14].

Specifically, in addition to the events E_{ij} specified in Section 3, we also define, for each subset $\mathcal{I} \subseteq [n]$ of parties, the event $E_{\mathcal{I}}$ that occurs when the adversary corrupts *exactly* the parties in $\mathcal{I}$. The cost of corrupting each such set $\mathcal{I}$ is specified via a function $\mathcal{C} : 2^{\mathcal{P}} \rightarrow \mathbb{R}$, where for any $\mathcal{I} \subseteq \mathcal{P}$, $\mathcal{C}(\mathcal{I})$ describes the cost associated with corrupting the players in $\mathcal{I}$. We generally let the corruption costs $\mathcal{C}(\mathcal{I})$ be non-negative. Thus, the adversary's payoff is specified by the events $\vec{E}^{\mathcal{C}} = (E_{00}, E_{01}, E_{10}, E_{11}, \{E_{\mathcal{I}}\}_{\mathcal{I} \subseteq \mathcal{P}})$ and by the corresponding payoffs $\vec{\gamma}^{\mathcal{C}} = (\gamma_{00}, \gamma_{01}, \gamma_{10}, \gamma_{11}, \{-\mathcal{C}(\mathcal{I})\}_{\mathcal{I} \subseteq \mathcal{P}})$. The expected payoff of a given simulator $\mathcal{S}$ (for an environment $\mathcal{Z}$) is redefined as:

$$U_I^{\mathcal{F}^{\perp}_{\text{SFE}}, \vec{\gamma}^{\mathcal{C}}}(\mathcal{S}, \mathcal{Z}) := \sum_{i,j \in \{0,1\}} \gamma_{ij} \Pr[E_{ij}] - \sum_{\mathcal{I} \subseteq \mathcal{P}} \mathcal{C}(\mathcal{I}) \Pr[E_{\mathcal{I}}]. \quad (5)$$

We write $\vec{\gamma}^{\mathcal{C}} \in \Gamma^{+\mathcal{C}}_{\text{fair}}$ to denote the fact that for the sub-vector $\vec{\gamma} = (\gamma_{00}, \gamma_{01}, \gamma_{10}, \gamma_{11})$ of $\vec{\gamma}^{\mathcal{C}}$, $\vec{\gamma} \in \Gamma^{+}_{\text{fair}}$. Given that the adversary incurs a cost for corrupting parties, we can show that protocols are *ideally* $\vec{\gamma}^{\mathcal{C}}$*-fair* which, roughly speaking, means that the protocol restricts its adversary as much as a completely fair protocol—according to the standard notion of fairness—would. We show that utility-balanced fairness implies an optimality (with respect to the cost function) on ideal $\vec{\gamma}^{\mathcal{C}}$-fairness. (See Definition 19 in [15].) For cost functions that only depend on the number of parties (i.e., $\mathcal{C}(\mathcal{I}) = c(|\mathcal{I}|)$ for $c : [n] \rightarrow \mathbb{R}$), we show the following theorem in the full version.

Theorem 10. *Let* $\vec{\gamma} = (\gamma_{00}, \gamma_{01}, \gamma_{10}, \gamma_{11}) \in \Gamma^{+}_{fair}$. *For a protocol* Π *that is utility-balanced* $\vec{\gamma}$*-fair, the following two statements hold:*

1. Π *is ideally* $\vec{\gamma}^{\mathcal{C}}$*-fair with respect to cost vector* $\vec{\gamma}^{\mathcal{C}} = (\gamma_{00}, \gamma_{01}, \gamma_{10}, \gamma_{11}, \{-\mathcal{C}(\mathcal{I})\}_{\mathcal{I} \subseteq \mathcal{P}}) \in \Gamma^{+\mathcal{C}}_{fair}$ *for the function* $\mathcal{C}(\mathcal{I}) = c(|\mathcal{I}|) = u_{\mathtt{A}}(\Pi, \mathcal{A}_{|\mathcal{I}|})$, *where* $\mathcal{A}_{|\mathcal{I}|}$ *is the best adversary strategy corrupting up to* $|\mathcal{I}|$ *parties.*

2. *The cost function* $\mathcal{C}$ *above is optimal in the sense that there is no protocol which is ideally* $\vec{\gamma}^{\mathcal{C}'}$*-fair with a cost function* $\mathcal{C}'$ *that is strictly dominated by* $\mathcal{C}$ *(see full version for formal definition).*

5. UTILITY-BASED VS. PARTIAL FAIRNESS

A notion that is closely related to our fairness notion is the concept of $1/p$-security—also called *partial fairness*—introduced by Gordon and Katz [18]. Roughly speaking, the notion allows a "distinguishing gap" of at most $1/p$ (for a polynomial p) between the real-world protocol execution and the ideal-world evaluation of the function. Furthermore, all statements discussed informally in this section are proven in the full version of this work.

At a high level, $1/p$-security appears to correspond to bounding the adversary's utility to $\frac{p-1}{p} \cdot \gamma_{11} + \frac{1}{p} \cdot \gamma_{10}$, since the protocol leads to a "fair" outcome with probability $1 - 1/p$ and to an "unfair" outcome with probability $1/p$. This is a better bound than proven in Theorem 3 for our "optimal" protocol—which appears to be a contradiction to our

[12] One can define an even more fine-grain notion of utility balancing, which explicitly puts a bound on the utility of the best t-adversary $\mathcal{A}_t$ *for every* t (instead of bounding the sum). See next subsection and the full version.

[13] Note that we exclude from the sum the utilities of adversaries that do not corrupt any party ($t = 0$) or corrupt every party ($t = n$), since by definition for every protocol these utilities are γ_{01} and γ_{11}, respectively.

optimality result. The protocols of Gordon and Katz [18], however, only apply to functions for which the size of either one party's input domain or one party's output range is bounded by a polynomial. Our protocols do not share this restriction, and the impossibility result in Lemma 5 is shown using a function which has exponential input domains and output ranges.

A weakness of $1/p$-security. In general, $1/p$-security allows privacy (and not only fairness) to be violated with probability $1/p$. Noticing this, Gordon and Katz [18] already suggested that one might additionally require that a $1/p$-protocol be *private*. We point out, however, that even protocols that are both $1/p$-secure and private may have subtle problems. Intuitively, the issue is that privacy and correctness are considered separately, rather than jointly as in standard simulation-based security definitions. For example, consider the following protocol $\tilde{\Pi}$ for computing the logical "and" of two parties' inputs x_1 and x_2:

- The first message is a 0-bit sent from p_2 to p_1.
- If p_2 sent a 1-bit instead of a 0-bit, then p_1 tosses a biased coin C with $\Pr[C = 1] = \frac{1}{4}$, and sends its input x_1 to p_2 if $C = 1$ (or otherwise an empty message).
- Then, p_1 and p_2 engage in any $\frac{1}{4}$-secure protocol to compute $x_1 \wedge x_2$.

In the full version of this work, we show that this protocol is private; this is because p_2 can learn x_1 even in the ideal world (by sending a 1 to the ideal functionality). We also show that the protocol is 1/2-secure. Yet it allows p_2 to learn x_1 and simultaneously force p_1 to output 0.

Analysis of the Gordon-Katz protocols using our approach. Gordon and Katz [18] propose two protocols: one for functions that have (at least) one domain of polynomial size, and one for functions in which (at least) one range is polynomial size. The underlying idea of the protocols is to reconstruct the output in multiple rounds and to provide the actual output starting at a round chosen at random. In all previous rounds, a random output is given. We stress that the protocols are proven secure only with respect to static corruptions; all the statements we make in this section are in this setting.

The protocols described by Gordon and Katz do not realize functionality $\mathcal{F}_{\text{SFE}}^{f,\perp}$, as the correctness of the honest party's output is not guaranteed. In fact, it is inherent to their protocols that if the adversary aborts early, then the honest party may output a random output instead of the correct one. Hence, to formalize the guarantees achieved by those protocols, we weaken our definition by modifying the functionality $\mathcal{F}_{\text{SFE}}^{f,\perp}$ to allow for a correctness error; specifically, the weakened functionality allows the adversary to replace the honest party's output by a randomly chosen output. The original protocol for functions with one polynomial domain (see [18, Section 3.2]) achieves this functionality and bounds the adversary's payoff. The statements about the protocol for functions with polynomial size range transfer analogously.

Comparing $1/p$-security with our notion. Our definition as described in the previous paragraph is *strictly stronger* than $1/p$-security, even if the latter notion is strengthened by additionally requiring privacy as suggested in [18]. Indeed, for the payoff vector $\vec{\gamma} = (0, 0, 1, 0)$ a security statement in our model implies $1/p$-security, and protocol $\tilde{\Pi}$ described above shows that our notion is strictly stronger.

6. ACKNOWLEDGMENTS

Jonathan Katz was supported by NSF grants #0830464, #1111599, and #1223623. Björn Tackmann was supported by the Swiss National Science Foundation (SNF) via the Fellowship no. P2EZP2-155566 and the NSF grant CNS-1228890. Vassilis Zikas was supported by the Swiss National Science Foundation (SNF) via the Ambizione grant PZ00P-2142549.

7. REFERENCES

[1] Gilad Asharov, Ran Canetti, and Carmit Hazay. Towards a game theoretic view of secure computation. In Kenneth G. Paterson, editor, *EUROCRYPT 2011*, volume 6632 of *LNCS*, pages 426–445, Heidelberg, 2011. Springer.

[2] Donald Beaver and Shafi Goldwasser. Multiparty computation with faulty majority. In *Proceedings of the 30th Symposium on Foundations of Computer Science*, pages 468–473. IEEE, 1989.

[3] Amos Beimel, Yehuda Lindell, Eran Omri, and Ilan Orlov. $1/p$-secure multiparty computation without honest majority and the best of both worlds. In Phillip Rogaway, editor, *CRYPTO 2011*, volume 6841 of *LNCS*, pages 277–296, Heidelberg, 2011. Springer.

[4] Manuel Blum. How to exchange (secret) keys. *ACM Transactions on Computer Science*, 1:175–193, 1984.

[5] Dan Boneh and Moni Naor. Timed commitments. In Mihir Bellare, editor, *CRYPTO 2000*, volume 1880 of *LNCS*, pages 236–254, Heidelberg, 2000. Springer.

[6] Ran Canetti. Security and composition of multiparty cryptographic protocols. *Journal of Cryptology*, 13:143–202, April 2000.

[7] Ran Canetti. Universally composable security: A new paradigm for cryptographic protocols. In *Proceedings of the 42nd IEEE Symposium on Foundations of Computer Science*, pages 136–145. IEEE, 2001.

[8] Ran Canetti. Universally composable security: A new paradigm for cryptographic protocols. Cryptology ePrint Archive, Report 2000/067, December 2005. A preliminary version of this work appeared in [7].

[9] Ran Canetti, Uri Feige, Oded Goldreich, and Moni Naor. Adaptively secure multi-party computation. In *Twenty-Eighth Annual ACM Symposium on Theory of Computing*, pages 639–648. ACM, ACM Press, 1995.

[10] Richard E. Cleve. Limits on the security of coin flips when half the processors are faulty. In *Proceedings of the 18th Annual ACM Symposium on Theory of Computing*, pages 364–369, Berkeley, 1986. ACM.

[11] Ivan Damgård. Practical and provably secure release of a secret and exchange of signatures. *Journal of Cryptology*, 8(4):201–222, 1995.

[12] Michael J. Freedman, Kobbi Nissim, and Benny Pinkas. Efficient private matching and set intersection. In Christian Cachin and Jan Camenisch, editors, *Advances in Cryptology - EUROCRYPT 2004, International Conference on the Theory and Applications of Cryptographic Techniques, Interlaken, Switzerland, May 2-6, 2004, Proceedings*, volume 3027 of *Lecture Notes in Computer Science*, pages 1–19. Springer, 2004.

[13] Juan A. Garay, David S. Johnson, Aggelos Kiayias, and Moti Yung. Resource-based corruptions and the combinatorics of hidden diversity. In Robert D. Kleinberg, editor, *Innovations in Theoretical Computer Science, ITCS '13, Berkeley, CA, USA*, pages 415–428. ACM, 2013.

[14] Juan A. Garay, Jonathan Katz, Ueli Maurer, Björn Tackmann, and Vassilis Zikas. Rational protocol design: Cryptography against incentive-driven adversaries. In *54th*

Annual Symposium on Foundations of Computer Science. IEEE, 2013.

[15] Juan A. Garay, Jonathan Katz, Björn Tackmann, and Vassilis Zikas. How fair is your protocol? Cryptology ePrint Archive, Report 2015/187, March 2015.

[16] Juan A. Garay, Philip MacKenzie, Manoj Prabhakaran, and Ke Yang. Resource fairness and composability of cryptographic protocols. In Shai Halevi and Tal Rabin, editors, *TCC 2006*, volume 3876 of *LNCS*, pages 404–428. Springer, 2006.

[17] Oded Goldreich, Silvio Micali, and Avi Wigderson. How to play any mental game—A completeness theorem for protocols with honest majority. In *Proceedings of the 19th Annual ACM Symposium on Theory of Computing*, pages 218–229. ACM, 1987.

[18] Dov Gordon and Jonathan Katz. Partial fairness in secure two-party computation. In Henry Gilbert, editor, *EUROCRYPT 2010*, volume 6110 of *LNCS*, pages 157–176. Springer, 2010.

[19] Ronen Gradwohl, Salil Vadhan, and David Zuckerman. Random selection with an adversarial majority. In *Proceedings of the 26th Annual International Conference on Advances in Cryptology*, CRYPTO'06, pages 409–426, Berlin, Heidelberg, 2006. Springer-Verlag.

[20] Adam Groce and Jonathan Katz. Fair computation with rational players. In David Pointcheval and Thomas Johansson, editors, *EUROCRYPT 2012*, volume 7237 of *LNCS*, pages 81–98. Springer, 2012.

[21] Jonathan Katz, Ueli Maurer, Björn Tackmann, and Vassilis Zikas. Universally composable synchronous computation. In Amit Sahai, editor, *TCC 2013*, volume 7785 of *LNCS*, pages 477–498, Heidelberg, 2013. Springer.

[22] Yehuda Lindell and Benny Pinkas. A proof of security of Yao's protocol for two-party computation. *Journal of Cryptology*, 22(2):161–188, April 2009.

[23] Benny Pinkas. Fair secure two-party computation. In Eli Biham, editor, *EUROCRYPT 2003*, volume 2656 of *LNCS*, pages 87–105, Heidelberg, 2003. Springer.

APPENDIX

This section contains material deferred from Section 4.1.

An authenticated secret sharing scheme. The sharing of a secret s (field element) is a pair (s_1, s_2) of random field elements (in some larger field) with the property that $s_1 + s_2 = (s, \mathsf{tag}(s, k_1), \mathsf{tag}(s, k_2))$, where k_1 and k_2 are MAC keys associated with the parties p_1 and p_2, respectively, and $\mathsf{tag}(x, k)$ denotes a MAC tag for the value x computed with key k. We refer to the values s_1 and s_2 as the *summands*. Each $p_i \in \{p_1, p_2\}$ holds his *share* $(s_i, \mathsf{tag}(s_i, k_{\neg i}))$ along with the MAC key k_i which is used for the generation of the MAC tags he is supposed to verify. We denote by $\langle s \rangle$ a sharing of s and by $\langle s \rangle_i$ party p_i's share. The above sharing can be reconstructed towards any of the parties p_i as follows: $p_{\neg i}$ sends his share $\langle s \rangle_{\neg i} = (s_{\neg i}, t_{\neg i})$ to p_i who, using k_i, verifies that $t_{\neg i}$ is a valid MAC for $s_{\neg i}$. Subsequently, p_i reconstructs the authenticated secret s by computing $s_1 + s_2 := (s, t'_1, t'_2)$ and verifying, using key k_i, that t'_i is a valid MAC for s. If any of the MAC verifications fails then p_i aborts and outputs $\bot$.

Adaptively Secure Computation with Partial Erasures

[Extended Abstract] *

Carmit Hazay†
Bar-Ilan University
carmit.hazay@biu.ac.il

Yehuda lindell‡
Bar-Ilan University
yehuda.lindell@biu.ac.il

Arpita Patra§
Indian Institute of Science
arpita@csa.iisc.ernet.in

ABSTRACT

Adaptive security is a strong corruption model that captures "hacking" attacks where an external attacker breaks into parties' machines in the midst of a protocol execution. There are two types of adaptively-secure protocols: *adaptive with erasures* and *adaptive without erasures*. Achieving adaptivity without erasures is preferable, since secure erasures are not always trivial. However, it seems far harder. We introduce a new model of adaptive security called *adaptive security with partial erasures* that allows erasures, but only assumes them in a minimal sense. Specifically, if all parties are corrupted then security holds as long as *any single party* successfully erases. In addition, security holds if any proper subset of the parties is corrupted without erasures. We initiate a *theoretical study* of this new notion and demonstrate that secure computation in this setting is as efficient as static secure computation. In addition, we study the relations between semi-adaptive security [GWZ09], adaptive security with partial erasures, and adaptive security without any erasures. We prove that the existence of semi-adaptive OT implies secure computation in all these settings.

Categories and Subject Descriptors

F.m [**Theory of Computation**]: Miscellaneous

Keywords

Secure Computation, Adaptive Security, Erasure, Non-committing Encryption, Oblivious Transfer

†Work partially supported by a grant from the Israel Ministry of Science and Technology (grant No. 3-10883).

‡Work supported by the Israel Science Foundation (grant No. 189/11).

§Work partially supported by INSPIRE Faculty Fellowhsip (DST/INSPIRE/04/2014/015727) from Department of Science & Technology, India.

*A full version of this paper is available at `https://eprint.iacr.org/2015/450.pdf`.

Permission to make digital or hard copies of all or part of this work for personal or classroom use is granted without fee provided that copies are not made or distributed for profit or commercial advantage and that copies bear this notice and the full citation on the first page. Copyrights for components of this work owned by others than ACM must be honored. Abstracting with credit is permitted. To copy otherwise, or republish, to post on servers or to redistribute to lists, requires prior specific permission and/or a fee. Request permissions from Permissions@acm.org.

PODC'15, July 21–23, 2015, Donostia-San Sebastián, Spain.

Copyright © 2015 ACM 978-1-4503-3617-8 /15/07 ...$15.00.

DOI: http://dx.doi.org/10.1145/2767386.2767400.

1. INTRODUCTION

1.1 Background

Secure multi-party computation (MPC). In the setting of MPC, a set of parties with private inputs wish to jointly compute some function of their inputs while preserving certain security properties. Two of these properties are *privacy*, meaning that the output is learned but nothing else, and *correctness*, meaning that no corrupted party or parties can cause the output to deviate from the specified function. Security is formally defined by saying that no adversary attacking a real protocol can do more harm than an adversary in an ideal world where an incorruptible trusted third party computes the function for the parties and provides them their output. The adversary may be *semi-honest* (meaning that it follows the protocol specification but tries to learn more than allowed) or *malicious* (meaning that it can run any arbitrary polynomial-time attack strategy). Despite the stringent security requirements on such protocols, it is known that *any* multi-party function can be securely computed in the presence of semi-honest and malicious adversaries [Yao82, GMW87].

Adaptive security. The initial model considered for secure computation was one of a *static adversary* where the adversary controls a subset of the parties (who are called *corrupted*) before the protocol begins, and this subset cannot change. A stronger corruption model that allows the adversary to choose which parties to corrupt throughout the protocol execution, and as a function of its view; such an adversary is called *adaptive*. Adaptive corruptions model "hacking" attacks where an external attacker breaks into parties' machines in the midst of a protocol execution. In the case where protocols run over a long period of time (e.g., consider a "secure database search protocol" where a party can ask queries over time without revealing the query to the database), such attacks are very realistic. We remark that there are two types of adaptively-secure protocols: *adaptive with erasures*, where the honest parties may erase intermediate data as part of the protocol specification, and *adaptive without erasures* where no such erasures are assumed. It is clear that achieving adaptivity without erasures is preferable, since secure erasures are not always trivial (e.g., parts of memory can find their way to the swap file of a machine; if memory is not zeroed then "erased data" can remain in memory for a long time until garbage collection takes place). However, achieving adaptive security without erasures seems far harder than with erasures. First, protocols that achieve adaptivity without erasures are more complex and the computational hardness assumptions needed seem stronger; see [CLOS02, KO04, CDD+04, IPS08]. In contrast, protocols that assume erasures are simpler and require seemingly weaker assumptions [BH92, Lin09, IPS09]. Furthermore, achieving efficiency seems also to be much harder. In particular, constant-round two-party computation that is adaptively secure with erasures is known [Lin09], but no analogous result is known for the case of no erasures. In addition, highly efficient protocols exist with erasures [BDOZ11, DPSZ12, NNOB12], but not without.[1] We conclude that there is a high price of working with a model where no erasures are assumed. However, assuming that all parties successfully erase all data, as specified by the protocol, is also not desirable. This dilemma is the starting point of our work.

1.2 Our Results

1.2.1 Adaptive Security with Partial Erasures

In light of the above dilemma, we introduce a new model of adaptive security that allows erasures, but only assumes them in a minimal sense. Specifically, all parties may be given instructions to erase data (as in the model with erasures). However, security holds as long as *any single party* successfully erases. We stress that the identity of the party that successfully erases is not known, and this means that security is maintained as long as one of the parties' erase mechanism works, and even if all other parties' do not. We also remark that if any proper subset of the parties is corrupted (and so at least one of the parties remains uncorrupted), then all of the corruptions may be without erasures. We formalize this by having two corruption commands that can be issued in the real world: "corrupt-with-erase" (where the party is corrupted and has erased all data as specified by the protocol) and "corrupt-without-erase" (where the party is corrupted and erases nothing). Then, the requirement is that any adversary that corrupts *all* the parties must issue at least one "corrupt-with-erase" command. This elegantly captures the intuitive notion discussed above; no other changes to the standard definition of adaptive security are needed.

We initiate a *theoretical study* of this new notion of adaptivity, with the following results. On the one hand, the cryptographic hardness assumptions needed to achieve this notion of adaptivity *in general* are the same as needed for achieving full adaptivity without erasures. Thus, our goal of reducing the hardness assumptions is not achieved, at least for the general case. On the other hand, we do show that secure channels that are adaptively secure with partial erasures (via non-committing encryption) can be achieved with assumptions that are seemingly weaker than those used in all previous constructions. In addition, we show that adaptivity with partial erasures can yield more efficient and much simpler protocols. We demonstrate this for non-committing encryption, oblivious transfer and secure two-party computation protocol.

Modular composition. One important goal with respect to notions of security is that of composition. Specifically, it is highly desirable that protocols can be composed together in different ways in order to modularly construct more complex protocols. Our new model enables such composition, as long as the number of parties is preserved. Specifically, it is possible to combine a number of two-party (resp., m-party) protocols in order to obtain a more complex two-party (resp., m-party) protocol (this follows from [Can00] who shows that protocols that are adaptively secure with and without erasures compose sequentially). However, it is *not* possible to combine two-party protocols in order to obtain an m-party protocol with $m > 2$. This is because in the setting with m parties, security is guaranteed as long as one party successfully erases, even if the rest do not. Now, if each pair runs two-party protocols between them, then in many pairs neither party may successfully erase. Thus, if the two-party protocols are only secure as long as one party erases, then they may not maintain security. This is certainly a drawback of our model. However, we believe that the advantages (regarding assumptions and efficiency) outweigh this disadvantage. In particular, this is not of concern in the two-party setting (which is in many real-world cases the most interesting). Also, multiparty protocols can be designed from scratch for the desired number of parties in order to bypass this issue.

[1]Observe that the protocols of [BDOZ11, DPSZ12, NNOB12] all have a preprocessing phase followed by an online phase. The online phase is adaptively secure if all of the secrets used to generate the results of the preprocessing phase are erased. Since the preprocessing phase is independent of the inputs, it is also adaptively secure if corruptions take place during this phase.

1.2.2 Relations Amongst Different Security Notions

Recently, [GWZ09] introduced the notion of *two-party semi-adaptive security* in which one of the parties is statically corrupted (i.e., corrupt from the onset) and the other can be adaptively corrupted. This is a strictly weaker notion than adaptive security with partial erasures since the statically-corrupted party can always be viewed as the party that was corrupted "with erasures" (since at the onset there is nothing to erase). Thus, any protocol that is adaptively secure with partial erasures is semi-adaptively secure. We study the relation between semi-adaptive security, adaptive security with partial erasures, and adaptive security without any erasures.

We prove that any semi-adaptive oblivious transfer (OT) can be transformed into an adaptively secure OT with partial erasures by sending the messages of the semi-adaptive OT protocol using a non-committing encryption scheme (NCE) that is adaptively secure with partial erasures. (A similar transform was used by [GWZ09] who showed that adaptively secure OT without erasures can be achieved by sending the messages of a semi-adaptive OT protocol with an NCE scheme that is adaptively secure without any erasures.) In addition, we show that NCE that is adaptively secure without any erasures (and thus with partial erasures as well) can be constructed from any semi-adaptive OT. We therefore have the following theorem:

THEOREM 1.1. *The following statements are equivalent:*

1. *There exists an OT protocol that is semi-adaptively secure;*
2. *There exists an OT protocol that is adaptively secure with partial erasures;*
3. *There exists an OT protocol that is adaptively secure without any erasures.*

The above holds for semi-honest and malicious adversaries.

This shows that our weaker notion of adaptive security (and the even weaker notion of semi-adaptivity) does not allow the construction of secure protocols that rely on weaker cryptographic hardness assumptions. This deepens our understanding of adaptive security. An important corollary of this result implies that MPC with adaptive security is reduced to semi-adaptive OT. This follows by combining our result with the [GWZ09] transformation specified above, and the fact that the [GMW87] protocol is adaptively secure when instantiated with adaptively secure OT. Namely:

COROLLARY 1.2. (Informal.) *Assume the existence of semi-adaptive OT. Then, there exists a multi-party protocol with semi-honest and adaptive security.*

We summarize this discussion in Figure 1.

Our next result studies NCE. Informally, NCE implements secure channels in the presence of adaptive adversaries. NCE is achieved by having an additional property where "dummy" ciphertexts can be generated and later decrypted into any plaintext. This is a strong security requirement and as such NCE schemes are

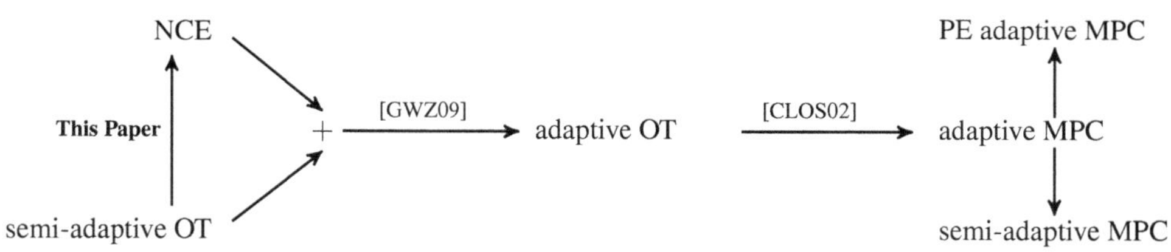

Figure 1: Notation $a \to b$ implies that b exists relying on the assumption that a exists. Notation $+$ implies that both primitives are needed to build the third primitive. In addition, PE denotes partial erasures.

relatively complicated, inefficient, and rely on seemingly stronger cryptographic hardness assumptions. We show that NCE in the partial erasures model can be achieved with a seemingly weaker assumption of public-key encryption with ciphertext samplability (NCE without any erasures is known to be achieved with ciphertext and public-key samplability; here we remove the latter assumption, and rely on the same assumption required for an NCE where *at most one party* is adaptively corrupted [DN00]). Specifically, we show the following in semi-honest and malicious settings:

THEOREM 1.3. (Informal.) *Assume the existence of public-key encryption with oblivious and invertible sampling of ciphertexts. Then, there exists an NCE that is secure with partial erasures.*

1.2.3 Efficient Constructions with Partial Erasures

We also study the efficiency of basic primitives with partial erasures and design strictly better constructions than in the adaptive setting, where the first two results hold in the *malicious* setting.

Non-committing encryption. We first construct NCE with partial erasures that is far more efficient than standard NCE without erasures. In particular, known constructions induce overhead of $\mathcal{O}(1)$ public-key operations for every transmitted bit [CFGN96, DN00, CDSMW09], while our protocol implies a constant number of such operations per polynomial-length message.

THEOREM 1.4. (Informal.) *Under the standard assumptions for achieving adaptive security, there exists an NCE with partial erasures security, where the sender and receiver compute $\mathcal{O}(1)$ public-key operations to transmit a message of length n.*

Our construction is a slightly modified version of the NCE construction that appears in [HP14].

Oblivious transfer. OT is one of the most fundamental and important primitives used for secure computation. Prior work on adaptively secure OT includes [Bea97, CLOS02, Lin09, GWZ09]. The most efficient protocol achieving adaptively-secure OT without any erasures is due to [GWZ09], who transform a semi-adaptive OT to an adaptive OT without any erasures using NCE, as described above. Their construction transfers ℓ-bit strings using $\mathcal{O}(\ell)$ public-key operations and is built on an extension of the OT of [PVW08] that requires only a constant number of public-key operations, but is only statically secure. We construct OT that is adaptively secure with partial erasures, and requires only a *a constant number* of public-key operations to transfer a string, like the protocol of [PVW08]. We achieve this by constructing a semi-adaptive OT with a constant number of public-key operations, and then apply the constant-overhead NCE with partial erasures mentioned above. This transformation was already mentioned above and yields adaptively secure OT with partial erasures.

THEOREM 1.5. (Informal.) *Under the standard assumptions for achieving adaptive security, there exists an adaptively secure OT protocol with partial erasures, where the sender and receiver compute $\mathcal{O}(1)$ public-key operations in order to obliviously transfer a message of length n.*

Secure two-party computation. We show that the [GMW87] protocol is adaptively secure with partial erasures in the semi-honest setting when using OT with partial erasures. This implies that when plugging in our OT from above, the overall time complexity of [GMW87] is $O(|C|)$ public-key operations. This overhead matches its overhead in the static setting but with stronger security.

2. PRELIMINARIES

We denote the security parameter by n. A function $\mu(\cdot)$ is *negligible* if for every polynomial $p(\cdot)$ there exists a value N such that for all $n > N$ it holds that $\mu(n) < \frac{1}{p(n)}$. We write PPT for (non-uniform) probabilistic polynomial-time and PKE for public-key encryption scheme. $a \leftarrow A$ to denote the uniform random sampling of a from a set A.

Simulatable PKE. Informally, a simulatable PKE is an IND-CPA PKE that consists of four additional algorithms specified as follows. An oblivious public-key generator (also denoted by oblivious sampler) $\widetilde{\mathsf{Gen}}$ and a corresponding key faking algorithm (also denoted by invertible sampler) $\widetilde{\mathsf{Gen}}^{-1}$, an oblivious ciphertext generator $\widetilde{\mathsf{Enc}}$ and a corresponding ciphertext faking algorithm $\widetilde{\mathsf{Enc}}^{-1}$. Intuitively, the key faking algorithm is used to explain a legitimately generated public-key as an obliviously generated public-key. Similarly, the ciphertext faking algorithm is used to explain a legitimately generated ciphertext as an obliviously generated ciphertext. The formal definition is omitted.

3. SECURITY DEFINITIONS

In this section we introduce a new model of adaptive security that allows erasures, but only assumes them in a minimal sense. Specifically, all parties may be given instructions to erase data (as in the model with erasures). However, security holds as long as *any single party* successfully erases. We stress that the identity of the party that successfully erases is not known, and this means that security is maintained as long as one of the partys erase mechanism works, and even if all other parties' do not. We also remark that if any proper subset of the parties is corrupted (and so at least one of the parties remains uncorrupted), then all of the corruptions may be without erasures. In this section, we also recall the existing notion of semi-adaptive [GWZ09] and adaptive security. We introduce our definitions in the universal composability framework in the two-party setting [Can01], which we briefly recall below.

3.1 The Universal Composability Framework

The universal composability (UC) [Can01] framework was proposed by Canetti for defining security and composition of protocols. In this framework, one first defines an "ideal functionality" of a protocol and then proves that a particular implementation of this protocol operating in a given computational environment securely realizes the ideal functionality. The basic entities involved are two parties P_0 and P_1, a PPT adversary $\textsc{Adv}$ and a PPT environment $\textsc{Env}$. The real execution of a protocol Π, run by the parties in the presence of $\textsc{Adv}$ and $\textsc{Env}$, with input z, is modeled by a sequence of activations of the entities. The environment $\textsc{Env}$ is activated first, generating the inputs to the other parties. Then the protocol proceeds by having $\textsc{Adv}$ exchange messages with the parties and $\textsc{Env}$. Finally, the environment outputs one bit, which is the output of the protocol. The security of the protocols is defined by comparing the real execution of the protocol to an ideal process in which an additional entity, the ideal functionality $\mathcal{F}$ is introduced. $\mathcal{F}$ is an incorruptible trusted party that is programmed to produce the desired functionality of the given task. The parties are replaced by dummy parties who do not communicate with each other; whenever a dummy party is activated, it forwards its input to $\mathcal{F}$. Let $\textsc{Sim}$ denote the PPT adversary in this idealized execution. As in the real-life execution, the output of the protocol execution is the one bit output of $\textsc{Env}$. Now a protocol Π securely realizes an ideal functionality $\mathcal{F}$ if for any real-life adversary $\textsc{Adv}$ there exists an ideal execution adversary $\textsc{Sim}$ such that no $\textsc{Env}$, on any input, can tell with non-negligible probability whether it is interacting with adversary $\textsc{Adv}$ and parties running protocol Π in the real execution or with $\textsc{Sim}$ and the ideal functionality $\mathcal{F}$ in the ideal execution. More precisely, a protocol Π securely realizes $\mathcal{F}$ if the two binary distribution ensembles, $\{\mathbf{REAL}_{\Pi,\textsc{Adv},\textsc{Env}}(n, x_0, x_1, z)\}_{x_0,x_1,z\in\{0,1\}^*,n\in\mathbb{N}}$ and $\{\mathbf{IDEAL}_{\mathcal{F},\textsc{Sim},\textsc{Env}}(n, x_0, x_1, z)\}_{x_0,x_1,z\in\{0,1\}^*,n\in\mathbb{N}}$ are computationally indistinguishable. The first ensemble describes $\textsc{Env}$'s output after interacting with $\textsc{Adv}$ and the parties P_0, P_1 running protocol Π with inputs x_0, x_1 respectively. The second ensemble describes $\textsc{Env}$'s output after interacting with adversary $\textsc{Sim}$, ideal functionality $\mathcal{F}$ and dummy parties P_0, P_1 interacting with $\mathcal{F}$ with inputs x_0, x_1 respectively. Namely,

$$\{\mathbf{IDEAL}_{\mathcal{F},\textsc{Sim},\textsc{Env}}(n, x_0, x_1, z)\}_{x_0,x_1,z\in\{0,1\}^*,n\in\mathbb{N}} \approx_c \{\mathbf{REAL}_{\Pi,\textsc{Adv},\textsc{Env}}(n, x_0, x_1, z,)\}_{x_0,x_1,z\in\{0,1\}^*,n\in\mathbb{N}}.$$

The $\mathcal{F}$-hybrid model. In order to construct some of our protocols, we will use secure two-party protocols as subprotocols. The standard way of doing this is to work in a "*hybrid model*" where both the parties interact with each other (as in the real model) in the outer protocol and use ideal functionality calls (as in the ideal model) for the subprotocols. Specifically, when constructing a protocol Π that uses a subprotocol for securely computing some functionality $\mathcal{F}$, the parties run Π and use "ideal calls" to $\mathcal{F}$ (instead of running the subprotocols implementing $\mathcal{F}$). The execution of Π that invokes $\mathcal{F}$ every time it requires to execute the subprotocol implementing $\mathcal{F}$ is called the *$\mathcal{F}$-hybrid execution of* Π and is denoted as $\Pi^{\mathcal{F}}$. The hybrid ensemble $\mathbf{HYBRID}_{\Pi^{\mathcal{F}},\textsc{Adv},\textsc{Env}}(n, x_0, x_1, z)$ describes $\textsc{Env}$'s output after interacting with $\textsc{Adv}$ and the parties P_0, P_1 running protocol $\Pi^{\mathcal{F}}$ with inputs x_0, x_1 respectively. By UC definition, the hybrid ensemble should be indistinguishable from the real ensemble with respect to protocol Π where the calls to $\mathcal{F}$ are instantiated with a realization of $\mathcal{F}$.

3.2 Defining Security

We begin with the formal definition of semi-adaptive security as stated in [GWZ09]. Loosely speaking, a protocol is semi-adaptively secure if it is secure with respect to *second-corruption adaptive adversarial strategy* as defined below.

DEFINITION 3.1. *An adversarial strategy is second-corruption adaptive if either at least one of the parties is corrupted prior to the protocol execution or no party is ever corrupted. In the former case, the other party can be adaptively corrupted at any point during or after protocol execution. I.e, the first corruption (if at all it occurs) must be static and the second corruption can be adaptive.*

Intuitively, a semi-adaptive simulator should be able to equivocate the internal state of the party that is adaptively corrupted. There are two subtleties regarding the construction of such a simulator. First, since most functionalities require a trusted setup in order to be realized in UC settings, it must be ensured that this setup is generated independently of the identity of the corrupted party (which is not the case for all statically secure protocols). [GWZ09] denote this property by *setup-adaptive simulation*. Formally stated,

DEFINITION 3.2. *A simulator* $\textsc{Sim} = (\textsc{Sim}_s, \textsc{Sim}_p)$ *is setup-adaptive if it first runs* $\textsc{Sim}_s$ *to simulate all the trusted setup and then runs* $\textsc{Sim}_p$ *(which is given any output generated by* $\textsc{Sim}_s$*) to simulate the protocol execution. While* $\textsc{Sim}_s$ *does not get to see which party is corrupted,* $\textsc{Sim}_p$ *gets to see it.*

Another subtlety that is formalized by *input-preserving* simulation is defined below.

DEFINITION 3.3. *An adversary is protocol-honest if it corrupts one of the parties P prior to protocol execution and then follows the honest protocol specification using some input x on behalf of the corrupted party. A simulator* $\textsc{Sim}$ *is input-preserving if during the simulation of a protocol-honest adversary that corrupts party P and runs the honest protocol with input x,* $\textsc{Sim}$ *submits the same input x to the ideal functionality $\mathcal{F}_f$ on behalf of P.*

We are now ready to define semi-adaptive security.

DEFINITION 3.4. *A protocol Π semi-adaptively realizes functionality $\mathcal{F}$ if for every* PPT *semi-honest (malicious) adversary* $\textsc{Adv}$*, and for every* PPT *environment* $\textsc{Env}$ *that follow a second-corruption adaptive adversarial strategy, there exists a non-uniform setup-adaptive and input-preserving* PPT *ideal adversary* $\textsc{Sim}$ *such that for $|x_0| = |x_1|$:*

$$\{\mathbf{IDEAL}_{\mathcal{F},\textsc{Sim},\textsc{Env}}(n, x_0, x_1, z)\}_{x_0,x_1,z\in\{0,1\}^*,n\in\mathbb{N}} \approx_c \{\mathbf{REAL}_{\Pi,\textsc{Adv},\textsc{Env}}(n, x_0, x_1, z)\}_{x_0,x_1,z\in\{0,1\}^*,n\in\mathbb{N}}.$$

Next, we recall adaptive security. A protocol is adaptively secure if it is secure with respect to an adversary who non-restrictively corrupts any party any time during or after the protocol execution.

DEFINITION 3.5. *A protocol Π adaptively realizes the functionality $\mathcal{F}$ if for every* PPT *semi-honest (malicious) adversary* $\textsc{Adv}$ *that can corrupt the parties adaptively during or after the protocol execution, and for every* PPT *environment* $\textsc{Env}$*, there exists a* PPT *ideal adversary* $\textsc{Sim}$ *such that for $|x_0| = |x_1|$:*

$$\{\mathbf{IDEAL}_{\mathcal{F},\textsc{Sim},\textsc{Env}}(n, x_0, x_1, z)\}_{x_0,x_1,z\in\{0,1\}^*,n\in\mathbb{N}} \approx_c \{\mathbf{REAL}_{\Pi,\textsc{Adv},\textsc{Env}}(n, x_0, x_1, z)\}_{x_0,x_1,z\in\{0,1\}^*,n\in\mathbb{N}}.$$

We refer to adaptive security as *fully-adaptive* security in order to distinguish this notion from semi-adaptive security, or as *adaptive security without erasures* whenever we wish to distinguish this notion from adaptive security with partial erasures.

Finally, we describe the new notion of security introduced in this work, *adaptive security with partial erasures*, starting with the definition of adaptive with partial erasures adversarial strategy.

DEFINITION 3.6. *An adaptive with partial erasures adversarial strategy implies that an adversary adaptively corrupts a party* *by either issuing a "corrupt-with-erase" or a "corrupt-without-erase" command. If it corrupts P_i issuing a "corrupt-with-erase" command in ith step of the protocol, then upon corruption it does not see the random inputs of P_i used up and until $(i-1)$th step of the protocol. On the other hand, if it corrupts P_i issuing a "corrupt-without-erase" command, then it sees the entire memory of P_i that includes the random inputs used in the protocol execution. If the adversary corrupts both the parties, then it must issue at least one "corrupt-with-erase" command.*

DEFINITION 3.7. *A protocol Π adaptively realizes the functionality $\mathcal{F}$ with partial erasures if for every* PPT *semi-honest (malicious) adversary* ADV *that follows the adaptive with partial erasures adversarial strategy, and for every* PPT *environment* ENV, *there exists a* PPT *ideal adversary* SIM *such that for $|x_0| = |x_1|$:*

$$\{\mathbf{IDEAL}_{\mathcal{F}_f,\mathrm{SIM},\mathrm{ENV}}(n, x_0, x_1, z)\}_{x_0,x_1,z\in\{0,1\}^*,n\in\mathbb{N}}$$
$$\approx_c \{\mathbf{REAL}_{\Pi,\mathrm{ADV},\mathrm{ENV}}(n, x_0, x_1, z)\}_{x_0,x_1,z\in\{0,1\}^*,n\in\mathbb{N}}.$$

3.3 Concrete Functionalities

Secure communication (SC). We define the functionality $\mathcal{F}_{\mathrm{SC}}$ for securely communicating a message m from SEN to REC, following the notations from [GWZ09]. To handle the appropriate leakage to the adversary in the ideal setting, the functionality is parameterized using a non-information oracle $\mathcal{O}$ which gets the values of the exchanged messages m and outputs some side information to the adversary. The security of this functionality depends on the security properties required for the oracle and thus can capture several notions such as NCE and ℓ-equivocal NCE. Specifically, for NCE the oracle only leaks the length of the message, whereas for ℓ-equivocal NCE with equivocality parameter ℓ the oracle leaks an ℓ-length vector such that the ith element in the vector depends on m, for some $i \in \{1, \ldots, \ell\}$. In Figure 2 we define the message communication functionality with respect to oracle $\mathcal{O}$. Next, we define the oracles for the cases of NCE and ℓ-equivocal NCE, starting with the former.

Functionality $\mathcal{F}_{\mathrm{SC}}^{\mathcal{O}}$

Functionality $\mathcal{F}_{\mathrm{SC}}^{\mathcal{O}}$ communicates with sender SEN and receiver REC, and adversary SIM. The functionality starts with a channel-setup phase after which the two parties can send arbitrary many messages from one to another. The functionality is parameterized by a non-information oracle $\mathcal{O}$.

1. **Channel Setup.** Upon receiving input (ChSetup, sid, SEN) from SEN, initialize the machine $\mathcal{O}$ and record the tuple (sid, $\mathcal{O}$). Pass the message (ChSetup, SEN) to REC. In addition pass this message to $\mathcal{O}$ and forward its output to SIM.
2. **Message Transfer.** Upon receiving an input (send, sid, SEN, m) from party SEN, find a tuple (sid, $\mathcal{O}$), and, if none exits, ignore the message. Otherwise, send the message (send, sid, SEN, m) to REC. In addition invoke $\mathcal{O}$ with (send, sid, SEN, m) and forward its output to SIM.
3. **Corruption.** Upon receiving message (corrupt, sid, P) from SIM where $P \in \{\text{SEN}, \text{REC}\}$, send (corrupt, sid, P) to $\mathcal{O}$ and forward its output to the adversary. After the first corruption, stop the execution of $\mathcal{O}$ and give SIM complete control over the functionality to let it learn all inputs and specify any outputs.

Figure 2: The message communication functionality.

DEFINITION 3.8. *$\mathcal{O}$, on input* (send, sid, SEN, m), *produces the output* (send, sid, SEN, $|m|$), *and on any inputs corresponding to the* ChSetup, Corrupt *commands produces no output. We call the functionality $\mathcal{F}_{\mathrm{SC}}^{\mathcal{O}}$ or just $\mathcal{F}_{\mathrm{SC}}$ for brevity, an NCE functionality. A real world protocol which realizes $\mathcal{F}_{\mathrm{SC}}$ is called an NCE scheme.*

In order to define $\mathcal{O}$ for ℓ-equivocal NCE, we present the following definition first.

DEFINITION 3.9. *An oracle $\mathcal{I}$ is called message-ignoring oracle if, on any input* (send, sid, SEN, m), *it ignores the message value m and processes only the input* (send, sid, SEN, $|m|$). *An oracle $\mathcal{M}$ is called message-processing oracle if it has no such restrictions. We call a pair of oracles $(\mathcal{M}, \mathcal{I})$ well-matched if no* PPT *distinguisher $\mathcal{D}$ (with oracle access to either $\mathcal{M}$ or $\mathcal{I}$) can distinguish the message-processing oracle $\mathcal{M}$ from the message-ignoring oracle $\mathcal{I}$.*

DEFINITION 3.10. *Let $(\mathcal{M}, \mathcal{I})$ be a well-matched pair which consists of a message-processing and a message-ignoring oracle respectively. Then we define $\mathcal{O}$ for ℓ-equivocal NCE as $\mathcal{O}^\ell$ with the following structure. Note that $\mathcal{O}^\ell$ is a (stateful) oracle.*

- *Upon initialization, $\mathcal{O}^\ell$ chooses a uniformly random index $i \leftarrow \{1, \ldots, \ell\}$. In addition it initializes a tuple of ℓ independent oracles: $(\mathcal{O}_1, \ldots, \mathcal{O}_\ell)$, where $\mathcal{O}_i = \mathcal{M}$ and for $j \neq i$, the oracles $\mathcal{O}_j$ are independent copies of $\mathcal{I}$.*
- *Whenever $\mathcal{O}^\ell$ receives inputs of the form* (ChSetup, sid, SEN) *or* (send, sid, SEN, m), *it passes the input to each $\mathcal{O}_i$ receiving an output y_i. It then outputs the vector $(y_1, \ldots, y_\ell)$.*
- *Upon receiving an input* (corrupt, sid, P), *the oracle reveals the internal state of the message-processing oracle $\mathcal{O}_i$ only.*

For any such oracle $\mathcal{O}^\ell$, we call $\mathcal{F}_{\mathrm{SC}}^{\mathcal{O}^\ell}$ an ℓ-equivocal NCE functionality. For brevity, we will also use the notation $\mathcal{F}_{\mathrm{SC}}^{\ell}$ to denote $\mathcal{F}_{\mathrm{SC}}^{\mathcal{O}^\ell}$. Lastly, a real world protocol which realizes $\mathcal{F}_{\mathrm{SC}}^{\ell}$ is called an ℓ-equivocal NCE scheme.

As before, no information about message m is revealed during the 'message transfer' stage. However, the internal state of the message-processing oracle $\mathcal{O}_i$, which is revealed upon corruption, might be "committing". Nevertheless, a simulator can simulate the communication between two honest parties over a secure channel, as modeled by $\mathcal{F}_{\mathrm{SC}}^{\ell}$, in a way that allows it to explain later this communication as any one of ℓ possibilities.

On semi-honest and malicious realizations of $\mathcal{F}_{\mathrm{SC}}$. Notably, a semi-honest secure realization of $\mathcal{F}_{\mathrm{SC}}$ (or $\mathcal{F}_{\mathrm{SC}}^{\ell}$) implies malicious security. This is because when the sender is statically corrupted (or before the message has been transferred), the simulator can extract the message by playing the role of the honest receiver (which does not introduce any input to the protocol), and then forward to $\mathcal{F}_{\mathrm{SC}}$ whatever the emulated receiver outputs. On the other hand, in case the receiver is statically corrupted the simulator obtains m from $\mathcal{F}_{\mathrm{SC}}$ and perfectly emulates the communication with the corrupted receiver. Moreover, adaptive corruptions that occur after the message has been transferred are easily simulated as in the semi-honest case. Consequently, we only realize $\mathcal{F}_{\mathrm{SC}}$ in the presence of semi-honest adversaries, regardless of the corruption strategy.

Oblivious transfer (OT). The 1-out-of-2 OT functionality is defined in Figure 3. In a bit OT $x_0, x_1 \in \{0,1\}$, whereas in a string OT $x_0, x_1 \in \{0,1\}^n$.

Secure computation. In Figure 4, we define $\mathcal{F}$ that computes a general function with two inputs and two outputs $f : \{0,1\}^* \times$

Functionality $\mathcal{F}_{\mathrm{OT}}$

Functionality $\mathcal{F}_{\mathrm{OT}}$ communicates with with sender SEN and receiver REC, and adversary SIM.

1. Upon receiving input $(\mathsf{sender}, sid, x_0, x_1)$ from SEN where $x_0, x_1 \in \{0,1\}^n$, record (sid, x_0, x_1).
2. Upon receiving $(\mathsf{receiver}, sid, \sigma)$ from REC, where a tuple (sid, x_0, x_1) is recorded and $\sigma \in \{0,1\}$, send (sid, x_σ) to REC and sid to SIM. Otherwise, abort.

Figure 3: The oblivious transfer functionality.

$\{0,1\}^* \to \{0,1\}^* \times \{0,1\}^*$, where $f = (f_0, f_1)$ maps pairs of inputs (x_0, x_1) to pairs of outputs $\big(f_0(x_0,x_1), f_1(x_0,x_1)\big)$.

Functionality $\mathcal{F}_f$

$\mathcal{F}_f$ communicates with two parties P_0 and P_1, and adversary SIM.

1. Upon receiving input $(\mathsf{Input}_0, sid, x_0)$ from P_0, record the value (P_0, x_0) and send the message (Input_0, sid) to SIM. Ignore future $(\mathsf{Input}_0, ...)$ inputs. Similarly, upon receiving input $(\mathsf{Input}_1, sid, x_1)$ from P_1, record the value (P_1, x_1) and send the message (Input_1, sid) to SIM. Ignore future $(\mathsf{Input}_1, ...)$ inputs.
2. Upon receiving (Output_0, sid) from SIM, if either (P_0, x_0) and (P_1, x_1) are not recorded, ignore the message. Else if (y_0, y_1) is not recorded, then compute $(y_0, y_1) \leftarrow f(x_0, x_1)$ and record (y_0, y_1); send $(\mathsf{Output}_0, sid, y_0)$ to P_0. Ignore future $(\mathsf{Output}_0, ...)$ inputs from SIM. Similarly, upon receipt of (Output_1, sid) from SIM, send $(\mathsf{Output}_1, sid, y_1)$ to P_1. Ignore future $(\mathsf{Output}_1, ...)$ inputs from SIM.

Figure 4: The two-party computation functionality for function $f : \{0,1\}^* \times \{0,1\}^* \to \{0,1\}^* \times \{0,1\}^*$.

Setup generation. As noted in the literature, most functionalities cannot be realized in the UC framework without a trusted setup. One common form of setup is the common reference string (CRS) which is modeled by a functionality $\mathcal{F}^{\mathcal{D}}_{\mathrm{CRS}}$, defined in Figure 5.

Functionality $\mathcal{F}^{\mathcal{D}}_{\mathrm{CRS}}$

$\mathcal{F}^{\mathcal{D}}_{\mathrm{CRS}}$ is parameterized by a PPT sampling algorithm $\mathcal{D}$.

On input CRS, sid from P, if there is no value crs recorded then choose $crs \leftarrow \mathcal{D}()$ and record it. Send $(\mathrm{CRS}, sid, crs, P)$ to SIM and P.

Figure 5: The common reference string ideal functionality.

4. RELATIONS AMONGST THE DIFFERENT SECURITY NOTIONS

In this section, we study the relations between semi-adaptive security, adaptive security with partial erasures and adaptive security. Our first transformation shows that semi-adaptive OT implies NCE (Section 4.1). This further implies that the security of adaptively secure NCE without any erasures can be reduced to the security of semi-adaptive OT. Combining this result with the [GWZ09] compiler that transforms semi-adaptive OT to fully-adaptive OT using NCE, and the fact that the [GMW87] is adaptively secure when instantiated with (fully) adaptively secure OT, the following important theorem is concluded:

THEOREM 4.1. *Assume the existence of semi-adaptive semi-honest OT. Then, there exists a multi-party protocol that adaptively (respectively, with partial erasures or semi-adaptively) realizes any well-formed multi-party efficient functionality f in the presence of semi-honest adversaries.*

We refer to [CLOS02] regarding the formal definition of well-formed functionalities. In the second part of this section we demonstrate the feasibility of adaptively secure NCE with partial erasures under *strictly weaker* hardness assumptions than simulatable PKE (Section 4.2), where all known NCE constructions are based on (a variant) of this assumption. Finally, we prove that any semi-adaptive protocol can be transformed into an adaptively secure protocol with partial erasures by encrypting the messages of the semi-adaptive protocol using adaptively secure NCE with partial erasures. This result is given in Section 4.3.

4.1 NCE from Semi-Adaptive OT

Security in the semi-adaptive setting requires that one of the parties is statically corrupted, which implies a weaker notion of security than adaptive. In the following, we show that NCE, that is adaptively secure *without any erasures* (and thus secure with partial erasures as well), can be constructed from any semi-adaptive OT. Namely, recalling the OT functionality from Figure 3, we exploit the fact that a semi-adaptive OT implies a simulator that either equivocates the receiver's input bit σ (in case the sender is statically corrupted) or $x_{1-\sigma}$ (in case the receiver is statically corrupted), but never both. Our protocol is described in the $\mathcal{F}_{\mathrm{OT}}$-hybrid setting.

PROTOCOL 1 (NCE FROM SEMI-ADAPTIVE OT).

- **Inputs:** *Sender* SEN *is given input message* $m \in \{0,1\}$.
- **The Protocol:**
  1. **Executing semi-adaptive OT on random inputs.** *The parties invoke $\mathcal{F}_{\mathrm{OT}}$ on random inputs, where* SEN *plays the receiver on a random bit σ and* REC *plays the sender on random bits r_0, r_1. Let r denote the output of* SEN.
  2. **Message from the sender.** SEN *sends c to* REC *where $c = \sigma \oplus m$ if $r = \sigma$. Otherwise, $c \leftarrow_R \{0,1\}$.*
  3. **Output.** *Upon receiving c,* REC *recovers the message by computing $m = c \oplus r_0$.*

THEOREM 4.2. *Assume that $\mathcal{F}_{\mathrm{OT}}$ is implemented in the presence of semi-adaptive semi-honest adversaries. Then, Protocol 1 adaptively realizes $\mathcal{F}_{\mathrm{SC}}$ in the presence of semi-honest adversaries, where correctness holds with probability* $5/8$.

We note that by repeating Protocol 1 sufficiently many times, one obtains a protocol Π_{NCE} where the probability of correctness is arbitrarily close to 1. The above theorem implies a simpler NCE protocol assuming the Quadratic Residuosity (QR) assumption (based on the semi-adaptive OT of [GWZ09] that is proven under the QR assumption). We further demonstrate the first realization under the DCR hardness assumption. The proof is given in the full version.

4.2 NCE with Partial Erasures under Weaker Assumptions

In this section we construct an NCE scheme with partial erasures security based on PKE with oblivious ciphertexts generation. This is in contrast to fully adaptive NCE constructions that require simulatable PKE, which implies the oblivious generation of *both* public-keys and ciphertexts. Our construction follows the NCE approach of [DN00] with the difference that instead of locally generating the public-keys, they are now being generated via a two-party protocol π_{KeySetup} that realizes functionality,

$$\mathcal{F}_{\text{KeySetup}} : (\alpha, \beta) \mapsto ((\text{PK}_0^1, \text{PK}_1^1, \text{PK}_0^2, \text{PK}_1^2, \text{SK}_\alpha^1), (\text{PK}_0^1, \text{PK}_1^1, \text{PK}_0^2, \text{PK}_1^2, \text{SK}_\beta^2))$$

Namely, the parties first agree on two public messages $m_0, m_1 \in \mathcal{M}$ and invoke π_{KeySetup}. Next, REC picks a random bit δ and encrypts m_δ under PK_δ^1, and obliviously samples the $(1-\delta)$th ciphertext. Similarly, SEN picks a random bit γ and encrypts m_γ under PK_γ^2, and obliviously samples the $(1-\gamma)$th ciphertext. The parties exchange ciphertexts and decrypt them using the secret keys that they possess. Note that if $\mathcal{M}$ is super polynomial then it is unlikely that an obliviously sampled ciphertext is decrypted into $m_{1-\delta}$, and thus SEN can correctly conclude whether $\alpha = \delta$ with very high probability. Similarly, REC correctly concludes whether $\beta = \gamma$. If both equalities hold SEN sends its message blinded with $\alpha \oplus \gamma$. Otherwise, the parties make another attempt, running the protocol again. This implies that an expected number of four attempts yields a successful attempt since the two pairs of bits equal with probability $1/4$. We observe that a single attempt of our protocol is composed of two attempts of the [DN00] protocol, where the local key generation is replaced by a two-party protocol. Specifically, combining two such attempts enables to equivocate either (α, δ) or (β, γ), which implies message equivocation.

Note that it is sufficient to realize $\mathcal{F}_{\text{KeySetup}}$ using a *statically* secure protocol that can be implemented under the same assumption of PKE with oblivious ciphertexts generation. This is because any PKE with this property implies oblivious transfer [EGL85] which, in turn, implies general secure computation in the presence of semi-honest adversaries [Yao82]. We stress that the parties cannot simply choose the public and secret keys by themselves since that would require the additional assumption of oblivious public-key generation, that we wish to avoid here. Formally, denoting by $\Pi = (\mathsf{Gen}, \mathsf{Enc}, \mathsf{Dec}, \widetilde{\mathsf{Enc}}, \widetilde{\mathsf{Enc}}^{-1})$ a PKE with oblivious ciphertexts generation, we implement functionality $\mathcal{F}_{\text{SC}}$ as follows.

PROTOCOL 2 (NCE WITH PARTIAL ERASURES).

- **Inputs:** *Sender* SEN *is given input message* $m \in \{0, 1\}$.
- **The Protocol:**

1. **Agreeing on messages** m_0 **and** m_1**.** *The parties publicly agree on messages* m_0 *and* m_1.
2. **Invoking** π_{KeySetup}**.** SEN *and* REC *pick random bits* α *and* β, *respectively, and invoke* π_{KeySetup} *on these bits. Denote by* $(\text{PK}_0^1, \text{PK}_1^1, \text{PK}_0^2, \text{PK}_1^2, \text{SK}_\alpha^1)$ *the output of* SEN *and by* $(\text{PK}_0^1, \text{PK}_1^1, \text{PK}_0^2, \text{PK}_1^2, \text{SK}_\beta^2)$ *the output of* REC.
3. **Exchanging ciphertexts.** *Next,* SEN *picks a uniform bit* γ *and sends* c_0^2, c_1^2 *where* $c_\gamma^2 \leftarrow \mathsf{Enc}_{\text{PK}_\gamma^2}(m_\gamma; r_\gamma^2)$ *and* $c_{1-\gamma}^2 \leftarrow \widetilde{\mathsf{Enc}}_{\text{PK}_{1-\gamma}^2}(r_{1-\gamma}^2)$. *Moreover,* REC *picks a random bit* δ *and sends* c_0^1, c_1^1 *where* $c_\delta^1 \leftarrow \mathsf{Enc}_{\text{PK}_\delta^1}(m_\delta; r_\delta^1)$ *and* $c_{1-\delta}^1 \leftarrow \widetilde{\mathsf{Enc}}_{\text{PK}_{1-\delta}^1}(r_{1-\delta}^1)$.
4. **Checking for equality of bits.** *Upon receiving* (c_0^1, c_1^1), SEN *checks whether* $m_\alpha = \mathsf{Dec}_{\text{SK}_\alpha^1}(c_\alpha^1)$ *and sends* $s_0 = 1$ *if equality holds, and* $s_0 = 0$ *otherwise. Similarly, upon receiving* (c_0^2, c_1^2), REC *checks whether* $m_\beta = \mathsf{Dec}_{\text{SK}_\beta^2}(c_\beta^2)$ *and sends* $s_1 = 1$ *if equality holds, and* $s_1 = 0$ *otherwise.*
   If one of the parties sent the bit 0 *the parties return to Step 2.*
5. **Message from SEN.** *Otherwise,* SEN *computes* $z = m \oplus \alpha \oplus \gamma$ *and sends* z.
6. **Output.** REC *computes* $m = z \oplus \delta \oplus \beta$ *and outputs* m.

THEOREM 4.3. *Assume* $\Pi = (\mathsf{Gen}, \mathsf{Enc}, \mathsf{Dec}, \widetilde{\mathsf{Enc}}, \widetilde{\mathsf{Enc}}^{-1})$ *is IND-CPA secure PKE with oblivious ciphertexts generation and let* π_{KeySetup} *be a protocol that statically realizes* $\mathcal{F}_{\text{KeySetup}}$ *in the presence of semi-honest adversaries. Then, Protocol 2 adaptively realizes* $\mathcal{F}_{\text{SC}}$ *with partial erasures in the presence of semi-honest adversaries.*

The security proof relies on the ability of a party to erase its randomness within π_{KeySetup}. Specifically, if a party is corrupted before the execution of π_{KeySetup} is completed then the simulator completes the execution as in the real setting. Otherwise, the input/output within π_{KeySetup} of the corrupted party that uses erasures can be equivocated. Combining these observations with oblivious ciphertexts generation enables the simulator to equivocate the common bit that masks the message. Furthermore, unsuccessful attempts (Steps 2-4) are perfectly simulated. The proof is given in the full version.

4.3 From Semi-Adaptive to Adaptive Security with Partial Erasures

We show how to transform any semi-adaptive protocol into an adaptively secure protocol with partial erasures. This transformation essentially encrypts all the messages of the semi-adaptive protocol using NCE with partial erasures (similarly to the [GWZ09] transformation from semi-adaptive to fully adaptive that uses fully adaptive NCE; see Theorem 2.10). Recall first that semi-adaptive security assumes that the first corruption occurs statically. Therefore, the corruption case that is not addressed here is when the first party is adaptively corrupted. Security against this corruption case is obtained (with or without erasures) by relying on the security of the NCE with partial erasures. Namely, upon adaptively corrupting the first party, the simulator explains the communication between the parties as if that party was statically corrupted. The complete proof of the following theorem is given in the full version.

THEOREM 4.4. *Let* Π *semi-adaptively realizes the functionality* $\mathcal{F}$. *Then protocol* Π', *in which the parties send the messages of* Π *using NCE with partial erasures adaptively realizes* $\mathcal{F}$ *with partial erasures.*

5. EFFICIENT SECURE COMPUTATION WITH PARTIAL ERASURES

In this section we study the efficiency of secure two-party computation with partial erasures. Towards defining a generic protocol we study the efficiency of NCE and OT primitives with partial erasures security, and demonstrate that they can be designed with constant overhead. Concretely, we first build NCE with partial erasures for exponentially large plaintext spaces using only *a constant number* of public-key encryption (PKE) operations (Section 5.1). Note that this is significantly better than the overhead of fully adaptive NCE constructions that require $O(1)$ PKE operations per bit. In Section 5.2 we demonstrate the feasibility of string OT, again with constant overhead, which is significantly better than prior work in the fully adaptive setting. These two results are demonstrated in the malicious setting. We conclude this section with the feasibility of generic secure two-party computation with partial erasures and semi-honest security. Our results imply that the [GMW87] protocol achieves $O(|C|)$ time complexity when the OT functionality is implemented with our protocol from this section, such that C is the boolean circuit that computes the specified functionality. This result is demonstrated in Section 5.3.

5.1 String NCE with Partial Erasures

In this section we prove that a slightly modified version of the NCE construction from [HP14] is NCE with partial erasures, which only requires a constant number of PKE operations per polynomial-length message. This construction is built on two IND-CPA secure primitives with an additional equivocation property. (1) NCE for the receiver (NCER) that implies that one can *efficiently* generate a secret key that decrypts a simulated ciphertext into any plaintext. (2) NCE for the sender (NCES) that implies that one can *efficiently* generate randomness for proving that a ciphertext, encrypted under a fake key, encrypts an arbitrary plaintext.

The idea of this protocol is to have the receiver create two public/secret key pairs where the first pair is for NCES and the second pair is for NCER. The receiver sends the public-keys and the sender encrypts two shares of its message m, each share with a different key. Upon receiving the ciphertexts the receiver recovers the message by decrypting the ciphertexts. We stress that this idea only works if the simulator knows the identity of the corrupted party prior to the protocol execution, since the simulator must decide in advance whether the keys or the ciphertexts should be explained as valid upon corruption (as we cannot have both generated in a fake mode). Nevertheless, in the one-sided setting we cannot tell which party will be adaptively corrupted prior to the execution. We thus resolve this issue using ℓ-equivocal NCE in order to commit to *the choice* of having fake/valid keys and ciphertexts (so the simulator can postpone its decision regarding having either fake keys or ciphertexts to the point where corruption occurs). The fact that this choice induces a binary equivocation space enables to design a protocol with a constant overhead.

The proof from [HP14] is shown in the one-sided setting where either the sender or the receiver are corrupted, but *not both*. In case both parties are corrupted it seems infeasible to prove security since the parties are required to use fake keys/ciphertexts for equivocation, but at the same time explain the keys and ciphertexts as valid. It turns out that the assumption where one of the parties erases its randomness plays a key role in resolving this technicality. That is, if the randomness used for creating the fake key/ciphertext is erased, then it is computationally hard to distinguish a fake key/ciphertext from a valid one. We are now ready to introduce the protocol in the $\mathcal{F}^{\ell}_{\rm SC}$-hybrid model (for $\ell = 2$). Formally, let $\Pi_{\rm NCES} = (\mathsf{Gen}, \mathsf{Gen}^*, \mathsf{Enc}, \mathsf{Dec}, \mathsf{Equivocate})$ denote NCES and $\Pi_{\rm NCER} = (\mathsf{Gen}, \mathsf{Enc}, \mathsf{Enc}^*, \mathsf{Dec}, \mathsf{Equivocate})$ denote NCER for a plaintext space $\{0,1\}^n$.

PROTOCOL 3 (NCE FOR EXPONENTIAL MESSAGE SPACES).

- **Inputs:** *Sender* SEN *is given input message* $m \in \{0,1\}^n$. *Both parties are given security parameter* 1^n.
- **The Protocol:**
  1. **Message from REC.** REC *invokes* $\mathsf{Gen}(1^n)$ *of* $\Pi_{\rm NCES}$ *and* $\Pi_{\rm NCER}$ *and obtains two public/secret key pairs* $(\mathrm{PK}_S, \mathrm{SK}_S)$ *and* $(\mathrm{PK}_R, \mathrm{SK}_R)$*, respectively.* REC *then sends* $(\mathsf{ChSetup}, sid, \mathrm{REC})$ *and* $(\mathsf{send}, sid, \mathrm{REC}, \mathrm{PK}_S)$ *to* $\mathcal{F}^{\ell}_{\rm SC}$*, and the message* PK_R *to* SEN.
  2. **Sending first share.** *Upon receiving* $(\mathsf{send}, sid, \mathrm{REC}, \mathrm{PK}_S)$ *from* $\mathcal{F}^{\ell}_{\rm SC}$ *and* PK_R *from* REC, SEN *picks* m_S *randomly and encrypts it using* PK_S*, creating ciphertext* c_S. SEN *forwards* $(\mathsf{ChSetup}, sid', \mathrm{SEN})$, $(\mathsf{send}, sid', \mathrm{SEN}, c_S)$ *to* $\mathcal{F}^{\ell}_{\rm SC}$.
  3. **Receiving first share.** *Upon receiving* $(\mathsf{send}, sid', \mathrm{SEN}, c_S)$ *from* $\mathcal{F}^{\ell}_{\rm SC}$, REC *decrypts* c_S *and records* m_S.
  4. **Sending second share.** SEN *fixes* m_R *such that* $m = m_S \oplus m_R$ *and encrypts it using* PK_R*, creating ciphertext* c_R. SEN *sends* $(\mathsf{ChSetup}, sid'', \mathrm{SEN})$, $(\mathsf{send}, sid'', \mathrm{SEN}, c_S)$ *to* $\mathcal{F}^{\ell}_{\rm SC}$.
  5. **Receiving the second share and output computation.** *Upon receiving* $(\mathsf{send}, sid'', \mathrm{SEN}, c_S)$ *from* $\mathcal{F}^{\ell}_{\rm SC}$, REC *decrypts* c_S *and records* m_S. *It then outputs* $m = m_S \oplus m_R$.

Note that the plaintext space of our NCE is equivalent to the plaintext spaces of the NCES/NCER. Thus, our protocol transmits n-bits messages using a *constant number of PKE operations*, as opposed to fully adaptive NCE that require $O(n)$ such operations. The following theorem is proved in the full version.

THEOREM 5.1. *Assume the existence of NCER and NCES and ℓ-equivocal NCE. Then Protocol 3 adaptively realizes $\mathcal{F}_{\rm SC}$ with partial erasures in the $\mathcal{F}^{\ell}_{\rm SC}$-hybrid model (for $\ell = 2$) in the presence of semi-honest adversaries.*

5.2 String OT with Partial Erasures

In this section we prove the feasibility of string OT with partial erasures using only a constant number of public-key operations. We recall first that OT with partial erasures can be obtained by encrypting the communication of a semi-adaptive OT using NCE with partial erasures. Therefore, in order to construct a string OT with partial erasures we need to design semi-adaptive *string* OT and *string* NCE with partial erasures, both with a constant overhead. The later is already demonstrated in Section 5.1. We thus focus below on designing semi-adaptive *string* OT with constant overhead. Combining the two results we obtain the following theorem.

THEOREM 5.2. *There exists a protocol that realizes $\mathcal{F}_{\rm OT}$ with partial erasures in the presence of malicious adversaries that requires $\mathcal{O}(1)$ PKE operations to transmit a message of length n.*

We recall that [GWZ09] presented a generic construction for semi-adaptive OT based on a coin tossing protocol and an enhanced dual-mode PKE for a *binary plaintext space*, where the dual-mode plaintext space size determines the size of the sender's message space in the OT. [GWZ09] left the feasibility of string semi-adaptive OT with constant overhead open. In what follows, we resolve this question. We first present a slightly different security definition for enhanced dual-mode PKE. Next, we build a semi-adaptive OT from our modified enhanced dual-mode PKE (which is similar to the construction of [GWZ09]). In the full version of the paper, we further instantiate our modified enhanced dual-mode PKE with a special type of NCES that requires an extra property. Finally, we build such an NCES based on a construction taken from [HP14] under the hardness of the DCR assumption. Combined together, these results imply semi-adaptive string OT using a constant number of PKE operations for exponential size message domains.

5.2.1 A New Enhanced Dual-Mode PKE

Loosely speaking, a dual-mode PKE is a PKE that is initialized with system parameters that can be defined in two modes. For each mode it is possible to generate public and secret keys that are associated with a branch $\sigma \in \{0,1\}$. Similarly, the encryption algorithm generates ciphertexts with respect to a branch $\beta \in \{0,1\}$. Moreover, if the key branch matches the ciphertext branch (that is, $\sigma = \beta$), then the ciphertext can be correctly decrypted. The security of dual-mode PKE relies on the indistinguishability of the two system parameters modes, which are denoted by *messy* and *decryption*. In messy mode the system parameters are generated together with a messy trapdoor, which imply that any public-key (even malformed keys) can be associated with any branch. Moreover, when the key branch does not match the ciphertext branch then the ciphertext becomes statistically independent of the plaintext. On the other hand, in decryption mode the system parameters allow to generate two secret keys that correctly decrypt the two ciphertexts.

In order to construct a semi-adaptive OT based in the [PVW08] OT, [GWZ09] extended the dual-mode notion and define an *enhanced* dual-mode primitive that captures a number of additional requirements. Specifically, it should be possible to equivocate either the receiver's input or the sender's input (depends on which party is statically corrupted). To achieve that, [GWZ09] split the system parameters into two parts; system and temporal. The system part is the same in both modes and is generated prior to the protocol execution. The temporal part defines the mode and is generated during the protocol execution using a coin tossing protocol. The idea is to fix the mode during the simulation depending on which party is statically corrupted.

In this work, we propose a slightly modified definition of enhanced dual-mode encryption, which is different due to the following reasons. First, we consider a primitive where the system parameters (CRS) are identical in both modes, implying that the temporal part is empty. Moreover, the mode is not determined by the temporal part of the CRS, but by the subkey that is used to encrypt $x_{1-\sigma}$. Namely, a public-key consists of two subkeys where the left subkey is used to compute a left ciphertext and the right subkey is used for the right ciphertext, such that each subkey is generated by a different algorithm. This separation is similar to the partition of the system parameters in [GWZ09] into two parts. In addition, the trapdoor that is associated with the CRS is only useful to distinguish the left and right public-keys in the messy mode. The decryption mode has no trapdoor. Finally, in contrast to the [GWZ09] definition, we do not define a fake ciphertext generation algorithm. The formal definition is given below.

DEFINITION 5.3. Enhanced dual-mode PKE *for plaintext space* $\{0,1\}^n$ *consists of a tuple of probabilistic algorithms* ($\mathsf{dSetupGen}$, $\mathsf{dKeyGen}$, dEnc, dDec, $\mathsf{dFindBranch}$, $\mathsf{dEquivocate}$) *specified as follows:*

- $\mathsf{dSetupGen}$, *given a security parameter* n, *output* $(\mathbb{G}, \mathrm{CRS}, \tau)$, *where* CRS *is a common reference string,* τ *is the corresponding trapdoor information and* $\mathbb{G}$ *is a group description.*
- $\mathsf{dKeyGen}$, *consists of the following sub-algorithms such that the former is mode-independent and the latter takes the mode as an input:*
  - $\mathsf{dKeyGenMI}$*: Given* CRS *and a key type* $\alpha \in \{0,1\}$, *output* $(\mathrm{PK}_\alpha, \mathrm{SK}_\alpha)$.
  - $\mathsf{dKeyGenMD}$*: Given* CRS, α *and* $\mu = \mathrm{dec}$, *output* $(\mathrm{PK}_{1-\alpha}, \mathrm{SK}_{1-\alpha})$. *Otherwise, given* CRS, α *and* $\mu = \mathrm{mes}$, *output* $\mathrm{PK}_{1-\alpha}$.

Output $\mathrm{PK} = (\mathrm{PK}_0, \mathrm{PK}_1)$ *and* $\mathrm{SK} = \mathrm{SK}_\alpha$. *In a decryption mode,* SK_0 *and* SK_1 *decrypt left and right ciphertexts, respectively.*
- dEnc, *given* $\mathrm{CRS}, \mathrm{PK} = (\mathrm{PK}_0, \mathrm{PK}_1)$, *an encryption type* $\beta \in \{0,1\}$ *and a plaintext* m, *output* (c, t), *where* c *is the encryption of* m *under key* PK_β *and* t *is the random coins used for encryption.*
- dDec, *given* $\mathrm{CRS}, \mathrm{PK}, \mathrm{SK}$ *and a ciphertext* c, *output* m.
- $\mathsf{dFindBranch}$, *given* $\mathrm{CRS}, \tau, \mathrm{PK}$, *output the key type* ρ *of* PK.
- $\mathsf{dEquivocate}$, *given* $\mathrm{CRS}, \tau, \mathrm{PK}, \alpha, c, m', t', m$ *for a public-key* $\mathrm{PK} = (\mathrm{PK}_0, \mathrm{PK}_1)$ *of type* α *in a messy mode, ciphertext and randomness* c, t' *such that* $(c, t') \leftarrow \mathsf{dEnc}(\mathrm{CRS}, \mathrm{PK}, 1-\alpha, m')$ *and a plaintext* m, *output random coins* t *such that the first output of* $\mathsf{dEnc}(\mathrm{CRS}, \mathrm{PK}, 1-\alpha, m; t)$ *is* c.

DEFINITION 5.4. *A dual-mode PKE* $\Pi_{\mathrm{DUAL}} =$ ($\mathsf{dSetupGen}$, $\mathsf{dKeyGen}$, dEnc, dDec, $\mathsf{dFindBranch}$, $\mathsf{dEquivocate}$) *is* secure *if it satisfies the following:*

Completeness. *For every* $\mu \in \{\mathrm{mes}, \mathrm{dec}\}$, $(\mathbb{G}, \mathrm{CRS}, \tau) \leftarrow \mathsf{dSetupGen}(1^n)$, $m \in \{0,1\}^n$, $\alpha \in \{0,1\}$ *and* $(\mathrm{PK}, \mathrm{SK}) \leftarrow \mathsf{dKeyGen}(\mathrm{CRS}, \mu, \alpha)$, *the decryption on a branch* α *is correct except with negligible probability. Namely, for* $(c, t) \leftarrow \mathsf{dEnc}(\mathrm{CRS}, \mathrm{PK}, \alpha, m)$, $m = \mathsf{dDec}(\mathrm{CRS}, \mathrm{PK}, \mathrm{SK}, c)$.

Enhanced mode indistinguishability. *The subkeys generated by* $\mathsf{dKeyGenMD}$ *in a messy mode and in a decryption modes are computationally indistinguishable for* $\alpha \in \{0,1\}$. *Furthermore, they are computationally indistinguishable from a random element in* $\mathbb{G}$.

Messy branch identification and ciphertext equivocation. *For every* $(\mathbb{G}, \mathrm{CRS}, \tau) \leftarrow \mathsf{dSetupGen}(1^n)$ *and every* $(\mathrm{PK}, \mathrm{SK}) \leftarrow \mathsf{dKeyGen}(\mathrm{CRS}, \mathrm{mes}, \cdot)$, $\mathsf{dFindBranch}(\mathrm{CRS}, \tau, \mathrm{PK})$ *outputs a branch* ρ *such that for every* $m \in \{0,1\}^n$, $\mathsf{dEnc}(\mathrm{CRS}, \mathrm{PK}, 1-\rho, \cdot)$ *is simulatable. Namely,*

$$\{c, t\}_{(c,t) \leftarrow \mathsf{dEnc}(\mathrm{CRS},\mathrm{PK},1-\rho,m)} \approx_s$$
$$\{c, t\}_{(c,t') \leftarrow \mathsf{dEnc}(\mathrm{CRS},\mathrm{PK},1-\rho,m'), t \leftarrow \mathsf{dEquivocate}(\mathrm{CRS},\tau,\mathrm{PK},\rho,c,m',t',m)}$$

Decryption mode key indistinguishability. *For every* $(\mathbb{G}, \mathrm{CRS}, \tau) \leftarrow \mathsf{dSetupGen}(1^n)$, *a left subkey is statistically indistinguishable from a right subkey in a decryption mode.*

5.2.2 *Semi-Adaptive String OT*

Given an enhanced dual-mode scheme $\Pi_{\mathrm{DUAL}} =$ ($\mathsf{dSetupGen}$, $\mathsf{dKeyGen}$, dEnc, dDec, $\mathsf{dFindBranch}$, $\mathsf{dEquivocate}$) as above for a plaintext space $\{0,1\}^n$, we construct a semi-adaptive OT following a similar approach to the semi-adaptive protocol of [GWZ09]. Namely, the receiver runs $\mathsf{dKeyGenMI}$ locally with σ and CRS, and obtains $(\mathrm{PK}_\sigma, \mathrm{SK}_\sigma)$. The parties then run a coin-tossing protocol in order to mutually generate the output of $\mathsf{dKeyGenMD}$, denoted by $\mathrm{PK}_{1-\sigma}$ (in some unknown mode), where only the receiver learns the outcome. REC then sets $\mathrm{PK} = (\mathrm{PK}_0, \mathrm{PK}_1)$ and $\mathrm{SK} = \mathrm{SK}_\sigma$. The coin tossing protocol ensures that the receiver does not learn both secret keys. In order to prevent a corrupted receiver from cheating, we require that it proves that either PK_0 or PK_1 was generated via the coin-tossing protocol. In the full version we explain about the special property we need from the ZK proof used by the receiver (denoted by witness equivocal ZK). Informally, in this type of proofs for compound statements, the simulator knows both witnesses but not which witness will be used. This notion allows to build weaker, yet meaningful ZK proofs that are secure in the presence of adaptive prover corruption. Formally,

PROTOCOL 4 (OT FOR EXPONENTIAL MESSAGE SPACES).

- **CRS:** *A group description* $\mathbb{G}$ *and* CRS *output by* $\mathsf{dSetupGen}(1^n)$.
- **Inputs:** *Sender* SEN *is given input messages* x_0, x_1 *and Receiver* REC *is given a bit* σ.
- **The Protocol:**
  1. REC *runs* $\mathsf{dKeyGenMI}$ *locally and obtains* $(\mathrm{PK}_\sigma, \mathrm{SK}_\sigma)$. *The parties also run a coin tossing protocol in order to mutually generate* $\mathrm{PK}_{1-\sigma}$. *Specifically,* REC *selects a random element* r *from* $\mathbb{G}$ *and sends* SEN *a commitment to* r.
  2. SEN *selects a random element* s *from* $\mathbb{G}$ *and sends* s *to* REC.
  3. REC *sets* $\mathrm{PK}_{1-\sigma} = r \cdot s$, $\mathrm{PK} = (\mathrm{PK}_0, \mathrm{PK}_1)$ *and* $\mathrm{SK} = \mathrm{SK}_\sigma$ *and sends* PK *to* SEN. REC *proves in ZK that either* PK_0/s *or* PK_1/s *was committed by* REC.
  4. *If* SEN *verifies the proof correctly, it computes* $(c_i, t_i) \leftarrow \mathsf{dEnc}(\mathrm{CRS}, \mathrm{PK}, i, x_i)$ *for all* $i \in \{0,1\}$, *and sends* (c_0, c_1) *to* REC.
  5. REC *decrypts* c_σ *using* $\mathsf{dDec}_{\mathrm{SK}}$ *and outputs the result.*

THEOREM 5.5. *Assume the existence of adaptively secure UC commitment schemes, witness equivocal zero-knowledge and the existence of enhanced dual-mode PKE* Π_{DUAL}. *Then, Protocol 4 realizes* $\mathcal{F}_{\mathrm{OT}}$ *with malicious semi-adaptive security in the* $\mathcal{F}_{\mathrm{CRS}}^{\mathcal{D}}$*-hybrid model, where the parties compute* $\mathcal{O}(1)$ *public-key operations to transmit a message of length* n.

We note that adaptive UC commitment schemes [DN02] are sufficient for implementing a coin-tossing protocol in the UC setting (and can be realized under the DCR hardness assumption that is used for our concrete instantiation). Intuitively, the security of Protocol 4 when the sender is statically corrupted follows by ensuring that the simulator knows both secret keys in a decryption mode, implying that it can equivocate σ and decrypt the $(1-\sigma)$th ciphertext. Also, when the receiver is statically corrupted, the simulator enforces a messy mode and thus is able to equivocate $x_{1-\sigma}$. The complete proof is given in the full version.

5.3 General 2PC with Partial Erasures

In this section we show a general result, demonstrating that efficient secure two-party computation (2PC) in the presence of semi-honest adversaries can be achieved using our oblivious transfer protocol from Section 5.2. Concretely, the efficiency of this protocol is as in the static setting and implies $O(|C|)$ time complexity, for C the boolean circuit that computes the specified functionality. That is, we consider the [GMW87] protocol and plug-in our efficient OT protocol with partial erasures. Relying on the UC composition theorem from [Can01] we conclude that the combined protocol is adaptively secure with partial erasures. We note that the theorem from [Can01] is stated in the adaptive setting and holds even in the presence of erasures, assuming that the same party in all sub-protocols is always corrupted with erasures. Next, denote the [GMW87] protocol when combined with the oblivious transfer protocol from Section 5.2 by $\Pi^{\rm OT}$. We claim that $\Pi^{\rm OT}$ adaptively realizes any efficient two-party well-formed functionality f in the presence of semi-honest adversaries. More formally,

THEOREM 5.6. *Let f be a well-formed two-party functionality. Then, Protocol $\Pi^{\rm OT}$ adaptively realizes f with partial erasures in the presence of semi-honest adversaries.*

6. CONCLUSIONS

We introduce the notion of adaptive security with partial erasures and show that it has the potential to yield simpler and more efficient protocols. We believe that it is a natural security guarantee that provides a good tradeoff between paying the price of achieving adaptive security without any erasures and trusting that all honest parties erase securely. Our work leaves a number of interesting questions open. Most notably, the question whether there exists a constant round generic two-party protocol with partial erasures.

7. REFERENCES

[BDOZ11] Rikke Bendlin, Ivan Damgård, Claudio Orlandi, and Sarah Zakarias. Semi-homomorphic encryption and multiparty computation. In *EUROCRYPT*, pages 169–188, 2011.

[Bea97] Donald Beaver. Plug and play encryption. In *CRYPTO*, pages 75–89, 1997.

[BH92] Donald Beaver and Stuart Haber. Cryptographic protocols provably secure against dynamic adversaries. In *EUROCRYPT*, pages 307–323, 1992.

[Can00] Ran Canetti. Security and composition of multiparty cryptographic protocols. *J. Cryptology*, 13(1):143–202, 2000.

[Can01] Ran Canetti. Universally composable security: A new paradigm for cryptographic protocols. In *FOCS*, pages 136–145, 2001.

[CDD+04] Ran Canetti, Ivan Damgård, Stefan Dziembowski, Yuval Ishai, and Tal Malkin. Adaptive versus non-adaptive security of multi-party protocols. *J. Cryptology*, 17(3):153–207, 2004.

[CDSMW09] Seung Geol Choi, Dana Dachman-Soled, Tal Malkin, and Hoeteck Wee. Improved non-committing encryption with applications to adaptively secure protocols. In *ASIACRYPT*, pages 287–302, 2009.

[CFGN96] Ran Canetti, Uriel Feige, Oded Goldreich, and Moni Naor. Adaptively secure multi-party computation. In *STOC*, pages 639–648, 1996.

[CLOS02] Ran Canetti, Yehuda Lindell, Rafail Ostrovsky, and Amit Sahai. Universally composable two-party and multi-party secure computation. In *STOC*, 2002.

[DN00] Ivan Damgård and Jesper Buus Nielsen. Improved non-committing encryption schemes based on a general complexity assumption. In *CRYPTO*, pages 432–450, 2000.

[DN02] Ivan Damgård and Jesper Buus Nielsen. Perfect hiding and perfect binding universally composable commitment schemes with constant expansion factor. In *CRYPTO*, pages 581–596, 2002.

[DPSZ12] Ivan Damgård, Valerio Pastro, Nigel P. Smart, and Sarah Zakarias. Multiparty computation from somewhat homomorphic encryption. In *CRYPTO*, pages 643–662, 2012.

[EGL85] S. Even, O. Goldreich, and A. Lempel. A randomized protocol for signing contracts. *Commun. ACM*, 28(6):637–647, 1985.

[GMW87] Oded Goldreich, Silvio Micali, and Avi Wigderson. How to play any mental game or a completeness theorem for protocols with honest majority. In *STOC*, pages 218–229, 1987.

[GWZ09] Juan A. Garay, Daniel Wichs, and Hong-Sheng Zhou. Somewhat non-committing encryption and efficient adaptively secure oblivious transfer. In *CRYPTO*, pages 505–523, 2009.

[HP14] Carmit Hazay and Arpita Patra. One-sided adaptively secure two-party computation. In *TCC*, pages 368–393, 2014.

[IPS08] Yuval Ishai, Manoj Prabhakaran, and Amit Sahai. Founding cryptography on oblivious transfer - efficiently. In *CRYPTO*, pages 572–591, 2008.

[IPS09] Yuval Ishai, Manoj Prabhakaran, and Amit Sahai. Secure arithmetic computation with no honest majority. In *TCC*, pages 294–314, 2009.

[KO04] Jonathan Katz and Rafail Ostrovsky. Round-optimal secure two-party computation. In *CRYPTO*, pages 335–354, 2004.

[Lin09] Yehuda Lindell. Adaptively secure two-party computation with erasures. In *CT-RSA*, pages 117–132, 2009.

[NNOB12] Jesper Buus Nielsen, Peter Sebastian Nordholt, Claudio Orlandi, and Sai Sheshank Burra. A new approach to practical active-secure two-party computation. In *CRYPTO*, pages 681–700, 2012.

[PVW08] Chris Peikert, Vinod Vaikuntanathan, and Brent Waters. A framework for efficient and composable oblivious transfer. In *CRYPTO*, pages 554–571, 2008.

[Yao82] Andrew Chi-Chih Yao. Protocols for secure computations (extended abstract). In *FOCS*, pages 160–164, 1982.

Improved Analysis of Deterministic Load-Balancing Schemes

Petra Berenbrink
Simon Fraser University
Burnaby, Canada
petra@sfu.ca

Ralf Klasing
CNRS – LaBRI – Université de Bordeaux
Bordeaux, France
ralf.klasing@labri.fr

Adrian Kosowski
Inria – LIAFA – Université Paris Diderot
Paris, France
adrian.kosowski@inria.fr

Frederik Mallmann-Trenn
Simon Fraser University
Burnaby, Canada
École Normale Supérieure
Paris, France
fmallman@sfu.ca

Przemysław Uznański
Helsinki Institute for Information Technology HIIT – Aalto University
Helsinki, Finland
przemyslaw.uznanski@aalto.fi

ABSTRACT

We consider the problem of deterministic load balancing of tokens in the discrete model. A set of n processors is connected into a d-regular undirected network. In every time step, each processor exchanges some of its tokens with each of its neighbors in the network. The goal is to minimize the discrepancy between the number of tokens on the most-loaded and the least-loaded processor as quickly as possible.

Rabani *et al.* (1998) present a general technique for the analysis of a wide class of discrete load balancing algorithms. Their approach is to characterize the deviation between the actual loads of a discrete balancing algorithm with the distribution generated by a related Markov chain. The Markov chain can also be regarded as the underlying model of a continuous diffusion algorithm. Rabani *et al.* showed that after time $T = \mathcal{O}(\log(Kn)/\mu)$, any algorithm of their class achieves a discrepancy of $\mathcal{O}(d \log n/\mu)$, where μ is the spectral gap of the transition matrix of the graph, and K is the initial load discrepancy in the system.

In this work we identify some natural additional conditions on deterministic balancing algorithms, resulting in a class of algorithms reaching a smaller discrepancy. This class contains well-known algorithms, *e.g.*, the ROTOR-ROUTER. Specifically, we introduce the notion of *cumulatively fair* load-balancing algorithms where in any interval of consecutive time steps, the total number of tokens sent out over an edge by a node is the same (up to constants) for all adjacent edges. We prove that algorithms which are cumulatively fair and where every node retains a sufficient part of its load in each step, achieve a discrepancy of $\mathcal{O}(\min\{d\sqrt{\log n/\mu}, d\sqrt{n}\})$ in time $\mathcal{O}(T)$. We also show that in general neither of these assumptions may be omitted without increasing discrepancy. We then show by a combinatorial potential reduction argument that any cumulatively fair scheme satisfying some additional assumptions achieves a discrepancy of $\mathcal{O}(d)$ almost as quickly as the continuous diffusion process. This positive result applies to some of the simplest and most natural discrete load balancing schemes.

Permission to make digital or hard copies of all or part of this work for personal or classroom use is granted without fee provided that copies are not made or distributed for profit or commercial advantage and that copies bear this notice and the full citation on the first page. Copyrights for components of this work owned by others than ACM must be honored. Abstracting with credit is permitted. To copy otherwise, or republish, to post on servers or to redistribute to lists, requires prior specific permission and/or a fee. Request permissions from permissions@acm.org.
PODC'15, July 21–23, 2015, Donostia-San Sebastián, Spain.
Copyright © 2015 ACM 978-1-4503-3617-8 /15/07 ...$15.00.
DOI: http://dx.doi.org/10.1145/2767386.2767413.

Categories and Subject Descriptors

F.2 [**Analysis of Algorithms and Problem Complexity**]: General; C.2.4 [**Computer Systems Organization**]: Computer-Communication Networks—*distributed systems*

General Terms

Theory, Algorithms

Keywords

Deterministic Load-Balancing, Mixing time, Rotor-Router

1. INTRODUCTION

In this paper, we analyze *diffusion-based load balancing algorithms*. We assume that the processors are connected by an arbitrary d-regular graph G. At the beginning, every node has a certain number of tokens, representing its initial load. In general, diffusion-based load balancing algorithms operate in parallel, in synchronous steps. In each step, every node balances its load with *all* of its neighbors. The goal is to distribute the tokens in the network graph as evenly as possible. More precisely, we aim at minimizing the *discrepancy* (also known as *smoothness*), which is defined as the difference between the maximum load and the minimum load, taken over all nodes of the network.

One distinguishes between *continuous* load balancing models, in which load can be split arbitrarily, and the much more realistic *discrete* model, in which load is modeled by tokens which cannot be split. In the former case, the standard continuous diffusion algorithm works as follows. Every node u having load $x(u)$ considers all of its neighbors at the same time, and sends $x(u)/(d+1)$ load to each of its d neighbors, keeping $x(u)/(d+1)$ load for itself. This process may also be implemented more efficiently: for each neighbor v of u, node u sends exactly $\max\{0, (x(u) - x(v))/(d+1)\}$ load to v. It is well-known (*cf. e.g.* [19]) that the load in the continuous model will eventually be perfectly balanced. In the discrete case with indivisible tokens, exact simulation of the continuous process is not possible. A node u may instead try to round the amount of load sent to its neighbor up or down to an integer. Discrete balancing approaches are, in general, much harder to analyze than continuous algorithms.

In [17], Rabani *et al.* suggest a framework to analyze a wide class of discrete neighborhood load balancing algorithms in regular graphs (it can be adapted to non-regular graphs). The scheme compares the discrete balancing algorithm with its continuous version, and the difference is used to bound the so-called error that occurs due to the rounding. Their results hold for *round-fair* algorithms where any node u having load $x_t(u)$ at time t sends either $\lfloor x_t(u)/(d+1) \rfloor$ or $\lceil x_t(u)/(d+1) \rceil$ tokens over its edges. They show that the discrepancy is bounded by $\mathcal{O}(d \log n/\mu)$ after $T = \mathcal{O}(\log(Kn)/\mu)$ steps, where μ is the eigenvalue gap of the transition matrix of the underlying Markov chain and K is the initial load discrepancy. The scheme applies to any discrete load balancing scheme which, at every time step, rounds the load which would be exchanged in the continuous diffusion process by a given pair of nodes to one of the nearest integers, either up or down.

The time T in the above bound is also the time in which a continuous algorithm balances the system load (more or less) completely. T is closely related to the *mixing time* of a random walk on G, which is the time it takes for a random walk to be on every node with almost the same probability. Within the class of schemes considered in [17], the bound of $\mathcal{O}(d \log n/\mu)$ on discrepancy cannot be improved for many important graph classes, such as constant-degree expanders. Since the work [17], many different refinements and variants of this approach have been proposed [4, 9, 10, 18], as well as extensions to other models, including systems with non-uniform tokens [4] and non-uniform machines [2].

1.1 Our Contribution

The main goal of this paper is to continue the work of [17] by analyzing properties/classes of deterministic algorithms that balance better in the diffusive model than the class defined in [17]. We suggest and analyze two general classes of balancing algorithms (called cumulatively fair balancers and good balancers) that include many well-known diffusion algorithms and we bound the discrepancy they achieve after $\mathcal{O}(T)$ time steps. Within the framework of schemes which are deterministic and pose no major implementation challenges (i.e., do not generate negative load and do not rely on additional communication), we obtain a number of significant improvements with respect to the state-of-the-art, cf. Table 1.

For our algorithms we assume that every node of the graph has in addition to its d original edges $d^\circ \geq d$ many self-loops. We define $d^+ = d^\circ + d$ as the degree of the graph including the self-loops.

Cumulatively δ-fair balancers.

We call an algorithm cumulatively δ-fair if *(i)* for every interval of consecutive time steps, the total number of tokens an algorithm sends over the original edges (non-self-loops) differs by at most a small constant δ and *(ii)* for every time step every edge (original edges and self-loops) of a node receives at least $\lfloor x/d^+ \rfloor$ many tokens, where x is the current load of the node. Cumulatively δ-fair balancers are a subclass of the algorithms studied in [17], which satisfied weaker fairness conditions. We show (Theorem 2.3) that algorithms satisfying these conditions with $d^\circ \geq d$ achieve a discrepancy of $\mathcal{O}(d \cdot \min\{\sqrt{\log n/\mu}, \sqrt{n}\})$ in $\mathcal{O}(T)$ time steps. The restrictions result in deterministic balancing schemes with an improved discrepancy after $\mathcal{O}(T)$ time steps. For example, for expanders, the achieved discrepancy after time $\mathcal{O}(T)$ is $\mathcal{O}(\sqrt{\log n})$, as opposed to $\Theta(\log n)$.

Additionally to the upper bound, we show that the discrepancy can be of order $\Omega(d \cdot \text{diam})$ (diam is the diameter of the graph) if we drop the condition of cumulative fairness (Theorem 4.1) or remove self-loops completely (Theorem 4.3). In more detail, Theorem 4.1 shows that there are round-fair balancers that satisfy the constraints of [17] and that have $\Omega(d \cdot \text{diam})$ discrepancy nonetheless. Such discrepancy is worse than the one we obtain for cumulatively fair balancers (Theorem 2.3) for many graph classes. In Theorem 4.3 we show for a specific cumulatively 1-fair balancer not using any self-loops (ROTOR-ROUTER), that it cannot achieve discrepancy better than $\Omega(n)$ on a cycle with n nodes.

The class of cumulatively fair balancers contains many well-known deterministic algorithms. In particular, many of these algorithms are *stateless*, meaning the load any node sends over edges in any step depends solely on the load of the node at this time step. An example for a stateless cumulatively fair balancer is SEND ($\lfloor x/d^+ \rfloor$), where a node with load x sends $\lfloor x/d^+ \rfloor$ many tokens to every original edge (non-self-loop). The remaining $x - \lfloor x/d^+ \rfloor$ tokens are distributed over self-loops such that every self-loop receives at least $\lfloor x/d^+ \rfloor$ many tokens. Similarly, the algorithm SEND ($\lceil x/d^+ \rceil$) is cumulatively fair. Here $\lceil x/d^+ \rceil$ rounds x/d^+ to the next integer and a node with load x sends $\lceil x/d^+ \rceil$ tokens over every original edge. Another well-known algorithm in this class is the so-called ROTOR-ROUTER model (also referred to in the literature as the Propp model, [3, 6, 11]) which uses a simple round-robin approach to distribute the tokens to the d^+ neighbors, i.e., over all its edges.

Good s-balancers.

The class of good s-balancers can be regarded as a restriction of cumulatively 1-fair balancers. A cumulatively 1-fair balancer is a good s-balancer if it *(i)* is round-fair (every edge receives $\lfloor x/d^+ \rfloor$ or $\lceil x/d^+ \rceil$ many tokens, where x is the current load of a node) *(ii)* sends over at least s self-loops $\lceil x/d^+ \rceil$ many tokens in every round. We show that algorithms of this class achieve a $\mathcal{O}(d)$-discrepancy within $\mathcal{O}(T + d \log^2 n/\mu)$ time steps. Moreover, if $s = \Omega(d)$, then the same discrepancy of $\mathcal{O}(d)$ is reached within $\mathcal{O}(T + \log^2 n/\mu)$ time steps. The class of good s-balancers contains many well-known algorithms. For example, the algorithm SEND ($\lceil x/d^+ \rceil$) is a good s-balancer for $d^+ > 2d$. If $d^+ \geq 3d$, then it achieves a $\mathcal{O}(d)$ discrepancy in $\mathcal{O}(T + \log^2 n/\mu)$ time. Additionally, the class contains some variants of the rotor-router approach, *e.g.*, one variant which we denote by ROTOR-ROUTER*. This algorithm maintains $d-1$ self-loops, together with one special self-loop, which always receives $\lceil x_t(u)/(2d) \rceil$ tokens. The remaining tokens are distributed fairly using a rotor-router on the original edges and the $d-1$ self-loops.

Algorithm	Discrepancy after time $\mathcal{O}(T)$	Time to reach $O(d)$ discrepancy	Ref.	D	SL	NL	NC
Discrete diffusion with arbitrary rounding on edges	$\mathcal{O}\left(\frac{d \log n}{\mu}\right)$	✗ (in general)	[17]	(✓)	(✓)	(✓)	(✓)
Randomized distribution of extra tokens by vertices	$\mathcal{O}\left(\min\left\{d^2, d + \sqrt{\frac{d \log d}{\mu}}\right\} \sqrt{\log n}\right)$	✗	[5, 18]	✗	✓	✓	✓
Randomized rounding to nearest integers on edges	$\mathcal{O}\left(\sqrt{d \log n}\right)$	✗	[18]	✗	✓	✗	✓
Computation based on continuous diffusion	$\Theta(d)$	$\mathcal{O}(T)$	[4]	✓	✗	✗	✗
Cumulatively fair balancers	$\mathcal{O}\left(d \min\left\{\sqrt{\frac{\log n}{\mu}}, \sqrt{n}\right\}\right)$	✗ (in general)	Thm 2.3	(✓)	(✓)	(✓)	(✓)
• ROTOR-ROUTER	"	✗	Thm 2.3	✓	✗	✓	✓
• SEND ($\lfloor x/d^+ \rfloor$)	"	open	Thm 2.3	✓	✓	✓	✓
• **Good s-balancers**	"	$\mathcal{O}\left(T + \frac{d \log^2 n}{\mu}\right)$	Thm 3.3	(✓)	(✓)	(✓)	(✓)
• ROTOR-ROUTER*	"	"	Thm 3.3	✓	✗	✓	✓
• SEND ($[x/d^+]$), for any $d^+ > 2d$	"	"	Thm 3.3	✓	✓	✓	✓
• SEND ($[x/d^+]$), for any $d^+ \geq 3d$	"	$\mathcal{O}\left(T + \frac{\log^2 n}{\mu}\right)$	Thm 3.3	✓	✓	✓	✓

Legend: D — Deterministic process; SL — Stateless process; NL — Cannot produce negative loads;
NC — No additional communication required; (✓) denotes properties achieved for some implementations;
$[\cdot]$ denotes rounding to the nearest integer.

Table 1: A comparison of the discrepancy of load-balancing algorithms in the diffusive model for d-regular graphs. In all result statements, if not specified otherwise, we assume that the graph is augmented with at least d self-loops per node ($d^+ \geq 2d$).

The only other result in the literature known to the authors which achieves a discrepancy of $\mathcal{O}(d)$ in $\mathcal{O}(T)$ steps in the *diffusive model* is the one of [4] (see [18] for $\mathcal{O}(d)$ discrepancy in the dimension exchange model where nodes balance with only one neighbor per round). Their algorithms use discrete tokens to simulate and mimic continuous flow.

Technical contributions.
Our techniques for the analysis of cumulatively fair balancers rely on a comparison between our discrete process and the continuous process. The latter can also be regarded as a Markovian process (random walk) which is governed by the transition matrix of the graph. We calculate the total deviation (of any cumulatively fair balancer) to the continuous process as done in [17]. However, instead of doing it step-by-step as in [17], the comparison is done over long time intervals. This was done in, *e.g.*, [13, 22], in the context of the graph exploration problem. Our analysis of this class connects this deviation to the value $\mathcal{O}(\log n/\mu)$, which is a natural upper bound on the mixing time. For the analysis of good s-balancers we combine the algebraic techniques used for the analysis of cumulatively fair balancers with a potential function approach. Whereas all cumulatively 1-fair balancers admit a natural potential function, which is (weakly) monotonous throughout the balancing process, for the narrower class of good s-balancers we can define time phases so that in each time phase, the process exhibits a strict potential drop in each phase of balancing, up to a balancing discrepancy of $\mathcal{O}(d)$. Even though we limit ourselves to regular graphs in this paper, our results can be extended to non-regular graphs.

1.2 Related Work

Herein we only consider related results for load balancing in the discrete diffusive and balancing circuit models, and some results for the rotor-router model which are relevant to our work.

Diffusive load balancing.
Discrete load balancing has been studied in numerous works since [17]. The authors of [9] propose a deterministic load balancing process in which the continuous load transferred along each edge is rounded up or down deterministically, such that the sum of the rounding errors on each edge up to an arbitrary step t is bounded by a constant. This property is called the *bounded-error property.* Then they show that after T steps any process with bounded-error property achieves a discrepancy of $\mathcal{O}(\log^{3/2} n)$ for hypercubes and $\mathcal{O}(1)$ for constant-degree tori. There are no similar results for other graph classes. Note that the algorithm of [9] has the problem that the original demand of a node might exceed its available load, leading to so-called *negative load.*

In [3], the authors consider ROTOR-ROUTER-type walks as a model for load balancing. It is assumed that half of the edges of every node are self-loops. The authors present an algorithm which falls in the class of *bounded-error diffusion processes* introduced in [9]. This results in discrepancy bounds of $\mathcal{O}(\log^{3/2} n)$ and $\mathcal{O}(1)$ for hypercube and r-dimensional torus with $r = \mathcal{O}(1)$. In [2], the authors consider the diffusion algorithms that always round down for heterogeneous networks. They also show that a better load balance can be obtained when the algorithm is allowed to run longer than T steps.

In [4], the authors propose an algorithm that achieves discrepancy of $2d$ after T steps for any graph. For every edge e and step t, their algorithm calculates the number of tokens that should be sent over e in t such that the total number of tokens forwarded over e (over the first t steps) stays as close as possible to the amount of load that is sent by the continuous algorithm over e during the first t steps. However, their algorithm can result in negative load when the initial load of any node is not sufficiently large and it has to calculate the number of tokens that the continuous algorithm sends over all edges. Note that the algorithm presented in this paper has to simulate the continuous algorithm in order to calculate the load that it has to transfer over any edge, whereas our algorithms are much easier and they do not need any additional information, not even the load of their neighbors.

There are several publications that suggest randomized rounding schemes [1,3–5,9,18] to convert the continuous load that is transferred over an edge into discrete load. The algorithm of [5] calculates the number of *additional* tokens (the difference between the continuous flow forwarded over edges and the number of tokens forwarded by the discrete algorithm after rounding *down*). All additional tokens are sent to randomly chosen neighbors. Their discrepancy bounds after T steps are $\mathcal{O}(d \log\log n/\mu)$ and $\mathcal{O}(d\sqrt{\log n}+\sqrt{d \log n \log d/\mu})$ for d-regular graphs, $\mathcal{O}(d \log\log n)$ for expanders, $\mathcal{O}(\log n)$ for hypercubes, and $\mathcal{O}(\sqrt{\log n})$ for tori. The authors of [18] present two randomized algorithms for the diffusive model. They achieve after $\mathcal{O}(T)$ time a discrepancy of $\mathcal{O}(d^2\sqrt{\log n})$ by first sending $\lfloor x(u)/(d+1)\rfloor$ tokens to every neighbor and itself, and afterwards by distributing the remaining tokens randomly. Additionally, they provide an algorithm which achieves after $\mathcal{O}(T)$ time a discrepancy of $\mathcal{O}(\sqrt{d \log n})$ by rounding the flow sent over edges randomly to the nearest integers which might cause negative loads. For a comparison with our results see Table 1.

Dimension exchange model.

In the Dimension Exchange model, the nodes are only allowed to balance with one neighbor at a time. Whereas for all diffusion algorithms considered so far the discrepancy in the diffusion model is at least d, dimension exchange algorithms are able to balance the load up to an additive constant. In [10] the authors consider a discrete dimension exchange algorithm for the matching model. Every node i that is connected to a matching edge calculates the load difference over that edge. If that value is positive, the algorithm rounds it up or down, each with probability one half. This result is improved in [18], where the authors show that a constant final discrepancy can be achieved within $\mathcal{O}(T)$ steps for regular graphs in the random matching model, and constant-degree regular graphs in the periodic matching (balancing circuit) model.

Rotor-router walks.

Originally introduced in [16], the *rotor-router walk* model was employed by Jim Propp for derandomizing the random walk, thereby frequently appearing under the alternative names of *Propp machines* and *deterministic random walks* [6,8,11,12]. In the rotor-router model, the nodes send their tokens out in a round-robin fashion. It is assumed that the edges of the nodes are cyclically ordered, and that every node is equipped with a rotor which points to one of its edges. Every node first sends one token over the edge pointed to by the rotor. The rotor is moved to the next edge which will be used by the next token, and so on, until all tokens of the node have been sent out over one of the edges. It has been shown that the rotor walks capture the average behaviour of random walks in a variety of respects such as hitting probabilities and hitting times. The rotor-router model can be used for load balancing, and directly fits into the framework we consider in this paper. The authors of [20] obtain rough bounds on the discrepancy, independently of [17]. In [3], the authors study a lazy version of the rotor-router process (half of the edges are self-loops) for load balancing. They prove that the rotor walk falls in the class of *bounded-error diffusion processes* introduced in [9]. Using this fact they obtain discrepancy bounds of $\mathcal{O}(\log^{3/2} n)$ and $\mathcal{O}(1)$ for the hypercube and r-dimensional torus with $r = \mathcal{O}(1)$, respectively, which improve the best existing bounds of $\mathcal{O}(\log^2 n)$ and $\mathcal{O}(n^{1/r})$ in this graph class.

1.3 Model and Notation

In this section we define our general model, which applies to both classes of studied algorithms.

The input of the load-balancing process is a symmetric and directed regular graph $G = (V, E)$ with n nodes. Every node has out-degree and in-degree d. We have $m \in \mathbf{N}$ indivisible tokens (workload) which are arbitrarily distributed over the nodes of the network. For simplicity of notation only, we assume that initially G does not contain multiple edges. In general, the nodes of the graph may be treated as anonymous, and no node identifiers will be required. The time is divided into synchronized steps. Let $\mathbf{x}_t = (x_t(1), \dots, x_t(n))$ be the *load vector* at the beginning of step t, where $x_t(u)$ corresponds to the load of node u at the beginning of step t. In particular, $\mathbf{x}_1$ denotes the initial load distribution and $\bar{\mathbf{x}}$ is the real-valued vector resulting when every node has achieved average load, $\bar{\mathbf{x}}(u) = \frac{1}{n}\sum_{u\in V} x_1(u) \equiv \bar{x}$, for all $u \in V$. Note that the total load summed over all nodes does not change over time. The *discrepancy* is defined as the load difference between the node with the *highest load* and the node with the *lowest load.* We will denote by K the maximal initial discrepancy in $\mathbf{x}_1$, *i.e.*, $K = \max_{u\in V} x_1(u) - \min_{u\in V} x_1(u)$. The *balancedness* of an algorithm is defined as the gap between the node with the highest load and the *average load.*

In order to introduce self-loops, we transform G into the graph $G^+ = (V, E \cup E^\circ)$ by adding d° self-loops to every node. For a fixed $u \in V$, let $E_u^\circ = \{e_1(u,u), \dots, e_{d^\circ}(u,u)\}$ denote the set of self-loops of u and let E_u denote the original edges of u in G. We assume $d^\circ = \mathcal{O}(d)$. We can now define $E_u^+ = E_u^\circ \cup E_u$ and $E^\circ = \bigcup_{u\in V} E_u^\circ$. In the following, we call G the *original graph* and G^+ the *balancing graph.* The edges E° are called self-loop edges of G^+ and E_u are the original edges. We remark again that the balancing graph is introduced for purposes of analysis, only, and is completely transparent from the perspective of algorithm design. We also define $d^+ = d + d^\circ$ as the degree of any node in G^+. $N(u)$ is the set of direct neighbors of u in G^+, *i.e.*, it contains all neighbors of u in G including u itself (because of the self-loops).

For a fixed edge $e = (u, v) \in E^+$ let $f_t(e)$ be the number of tokens which u sends to v in step t. In particular, let $f_t(u, u) = \sum_{e\in E_u^\circ} f_t(e)$. Let $F_t(e)$ denote the cumulative load sent from u to v in steps $1, \dots, t$, i.e, $F_t(e) = \sum_{\tau\leq t} f_\tau(e)$. For a fixed node $u \in V$, we define $f_t^{out}(u) = \sum_{v\in N(u)} f_t(u, v)$ to be the number of tokens (or flow) leaving u in step t. The incoming flow is then defined as $f_t^{in}(u) = \sum_{\{v:u\in N(v)\}} f_t(v, u)$. We define the cumulative incoming and original flows $F_t^{out}(u)$ and $F_t^{in}(u)$ accordingly, and $\mathbf{F}_t^{out}$ and $\mathbf{F}_t^{in}$ are defined as the vectors of the (cumulative) original and incoming flow. We will say that edge $e = (u, v)$ received x tokens when node u sends x tokens to v.

2. RESULTS FOR CUMULATIVELY FAIR BALANCERS

In this section we present a general class of algorithms, called *cumulative fair* algorithms, and analyze their discrepancy after $T = \mathcal{O}((\log K + \log n)/\mu)$ many time steps. Note that T is the balancing time of the continuous diffusion algorithm if the initial discrepancy is K, and d is the number of original edges (non-self-loops) of each node.

We call an algorithm *cumulatively fair* if the flow that is sent out over every edge of u (including the self-loops) up to step t can differ by at most δ.

DEFINITION 2.1. *Let δ be a constant. An algorithm is called* cumulatively δ-fair *if for all $t \in \mathbf{N}$, $u \in V$*

- *every edge $e \in E_u^+$ receives at least $\lfloor x_t(u)/d^+ \rfloor$ many tokens.*
- *all original edges $e_1, e_2 \in E_u$ satisfy $|F_t(e_1) - F_t(e_2)| \leq \delta$.*

Note that *round-fair* algorithms (defined in [17]) are not necessarily cumulatively δ-fair for any fixed δ.

OBSERVATION 2.2. *The algorithms* SEND $(\lfloor x/d^+ \rfloor)$ *and* SEND $(\lceil x/d^+ \rceil)$ *are 0-cumulatively fair. Furthermore,* ROTOR-ROUTER *is cumulatively 1-fair.*

For cumulatively fair balancers we show the following bound.

THEOREM 2.3. *Let G be any d-regular input graph and let d^+ is the degree of the balancing graph G^+ (including the self-loops). Let δ be a constant. Assume A is a cumulatively δ-fair balancer. Then, after $\mathcal{O}(\log(Kn)/\mu)$ time steps, A achieves a discrepancy of*

(i) $\mathcal{O}\left((\delta+1) \cdot d \cdot \sqrt{\log n/\mu}\right)$ *for* $d^+ \geq 2d$.

(ii) $\mathcal{O}((\delta+1) \cdot d \cdot \sqrt{n})$ *for* $d^+ \geq 2d$.

(iii) $\mathcal{O}((\delta+1) \cdot d \cdot \log n/\mu)$ *for arbitrary* $d^+ \geq d+1$.

For constant δ and at least d self-loops, the results of Claim (i) of the above theorem show a better discrepancy after T steps compared to the result of [17]. Claim (ii) provides an improvement for graphs with a bad expansion (small eigenvalue gap), such as cycles.

The rest of this section is devoted to the proof of Theorem 2.3. The core idea of the proof is to regard the balancing process over several steps and to observe that the cumulative load of the nodes is closely related to a random walk of all tokens. The difference to the random walk can be bounded by a small corrective vector depending on δ. We start by providing some additional definitions.

In the analysis, we change the way the tokens are kept at a node: In addition to sending tokens over self-loop edges we allow a node to retain a remainder (of tokens) of size $r < d^+$ at every node. The reason for this is that the proof requires the cumulative fairness on all edges and not just on original edges. One can show (Proposition A.1) that every cumulatively fair balancer can be transformed (by shifting tokens from self-loops to the remainder) into an algorithm guaranteeing cumulative fairness on all edges and that this transformed algorithm sends exactly the same load over original edges in every round.

Let the remainder $r_t(u)$ of node u in step t be the number of tokens of u that will not participate in the load distribution over its original edges and self-loops. Then, $\mathbf{r}_t = (r_t(1), \ldots, r_t(n))$ denotes the *remainder vector* at step t, where $r_t(i)$ is the number of tokens kept by the i'th node of G in step t. We will denote by r the upper bound on the maximum remainder of an algorithm, satisfying $|r_t(u)| \leq r \leq d^+$ for every time step t and every $u \in V$. For the ease of notation, we assume that $r < d^+$. Note that for all $u \in V$ and all steps t

$$x_1(u) + F_{t-1}^{in}(u) = r_t(u) + F_t^{out}(u). \tag{1}$$

Moreover,

$$x_t(u) = f_t^{out}(u) + r_t(u). \tag{2}$$

Let $\mathbf{P}$ denote the transition matrix of a random walk of G^+. Let $\mathbf{P}(u,v)$ denote the one-step probability for the walk to go from u to v. Then $\mathbf{P}(u,v) = 1/d^+$ if $(u,v) \in E$, $\mathbf{P}(u,v) = d^\circ/d^+$ if $u = v$, and $\mathbf{P}(u,v) = 0$ otherwise.

Let μ be the eigenvalue gap of $\mathbf{P}$, i.e., $\mu = 1 - \lambda_2$, where λ_2 is the second largest eigenvalue. We define $\mathbf{P}^t$ to be the t-steps transition matrix, *i.e.*, $\mathbf{P}^t = \mathbf{P} \cdot \mathbf{P}^{t-1}$. We define the *steady-state* distribution as $\mathbf{P}^\infty = \lim_{t\to\infty} \mathbf{P}^t$. Note that $\forall u, v \in V$, $\mathbf{P}^\infty(u,v) = d^+/(2|E^+|) = 1/n$. Observe that $P^\infty \cdot \mathbf{x}_1 = (\bar{x}, \bar{x}, \ldots, \bar{x})$. We can express $\mathbf{P}^t$ as $\mathbf{P}^t = \mathbf{P}^\infty + \mathbf{\Lambda}_t$, where $\mathbf{\Lambda}_t$ is the error-term calculating the difference between $\mathbf{P}^t$ and the steady-state distribution. Let $p \geq 1$. The p-norm of a vector $\mathbf{r}$ is defined as $\|\mathbf{r}\|_p = \left(\sum_{i=1}^n |r_i|^p\right)^{\frac{1}{p}}$. In particular, $\|\mathbf{r}\|_\infty$ is defined to be $\max\{|r_1|, \ldots, |r_n|\}$.

We are ready to prove the main theorem of this section. The core idea of the proof is to calculate the total deviation between any cumulatively fair balancer and a continuous process, similar to [17]. However, instead of comparing the two processes step-by-step as in [17], the comparison is done over long time intervals similar to [13]. This deviation is then connected to the value $\mathcal{O}(\log n/\mu)$.

PROOF PROOF OF THEOREM 2.3. Fix a node $u \in V$. Note that by the definition of cumulatively δ-fairness and Proposition A.1 we have for all $(u,v) \in E_u^+$ that

$$\left|F_t(u,v) - F_t^{out}(u)/d^+\right| \leq \delta. \tag{3}$$

We will define a corrective vector which at time t measures the difference between the load the nodes sent over original edges at time t and the load the nodes should have sent over these edges in order to ensure that every original edge received the exact same (continuous) load until time t. Formally, we define the n-dimensional corrective vector $\boldsymbol{\delta}_{t,u}$ with $\delta_{t,u}(v) = F_t(v,u) - F_t^{out}(v)/d^+$ for $v \neq u$ and $\delta_{t,u}(u) = F_t(u,u) - d^\circ/d^+ \cdot F_t^{out}(u)$. The entries of the corrective vector satisfy $|\delta_{t,u}(v)| \leq \delta$ for $v \in N(u) \setminus \{u\}$, $|\delta_{t,u}(u)| \leq d^\circ\delta$, and $\delta_{t,u}(v) = 0$ for $v \notin N(u)$. Consequently, $\|\boldsymbol{\delta}_{t,u}\|_1 \leq \delta d^+$. Then we derive from (3) the following bound on the incoming cumulative load of node u

$$\begin{aligned} F_t^{in}(u) &\underset{def.}{=} \sum_{v \in N(u)} F_t(v,u) = \sum_{v \in N(u)\setminus\{u\}} F_t(v,u) + F_t(u,u) \\ &\underset{(3)}{=} \sum_{v \in N(u)\setminus\{u\}} \left(\frac{1}{d^+} F_t^{out}(v) + \delta_{t,u}(v)\right) \qquad (4) \\ &\quad + \frac{d^\circ}{d^+} F_t^{out}(u) + \delta_{t,u}(u) \\ &= \sum_{v \in N(u)\setminus\{u\}} \frac{1}{d^+} F_t^{out}(v) + \frac{d^\circ}{d^+} F_t^{out}(u) + \|\boldsymbol{\delta}_{t,u}\|_1 . \end{aligned}$$

(5)

Rewriting (1) by introducing (5) we get:

$$F_t^{out}(u) = \sum_{v \in N(u)\setminus\{u\}} \frac{1}{d^+} F_{t-1}^{out}(v) + \frac{d^\circ}{d^+} F_{t-1}^{out}(u) + \underbrace{\|\boldsymbol{\delta}_{t,u}\|_1 - r_t(u)}_{\varepsilon_t(u)} + x_1(u). \quad (6)$$

We have $\|\varepsilon_t(u)\|_\infty \leq \delta d^+ + r$. Rewriting (6) in vector form, we obtain

$$\mathbf{F}_t^{out} = \mathbf{x}_1 + \mathbf{P} \cdot \mathbf{F}_{t-1}^{out} + \boldsymbol{\varepsilon}_t = \sum_{0 \leq \tau < t} \mathbf{P}^\tau \mathbf{x}_1 + \sum_{1 \leq \tau \leq t} \mathbf{P}^{t-\tau} \cdot \boldsymbol{\varepsilon}_\tau.$$

For any $\widehat{T} > 0$, the number of tokens leaving node u in the interval $[t+1; t+\widehat{T}]$ is $\mathbf{F}_{t+\widehat{T}}^{out}(u) - \mathbf{F}_t^{out}(u)$. Hence,

$$\mathbf{F}_{t+\widehat{T}}^{out} - \mathbf{F}_t^{out} = \sum_{t \leq \tau < t+\widehat{T}} \mathbf{P}^\tau \mathbf{x}_1 + \sum_{1 \leq \tau \leq t} (\mathbf{P}^{t+\widehat{T}-\tau} - \mathbf{P}^{t-\tau}) \cdot \boldsymbol{\varepsilon}_\tau + \sum_{t < \tau \leq t+\widehat{T}} \mathbf{P}^{t+\widehat{T}-\tau} \cdot \boldsymbol{\varepsilon}_\tau.$$

We set $t^* = t - 4t_\mu$, where $t_\mu = 7\log n/\mu$, and substitute $\mathbf{P}^\tau = \mathbf{P}^\infty + \boldsymbol{\Lambda}_\tau$. We derive

$$\begin{aligned}\mathbf{F}_{t+\widehat{T}}^{out} - \mathbf{F}_t^{out} &= \sum_{t \leq \tau < t+\widehat{T}} \mathbf{P}^\tau \mathbf{x}_1 + \sum_{1 \leq \tau \leq t^*} (\mathbf{P}^{t+\widehat{T}-\tau} - \mathbf{P}^{t-\tau})\boldsymbol{\varepsilon}_\tau \\ &\quad + \sum_{t^* < \tau \leq t} (\mathbf{P}^{t+\widehat{T}-\tau} - \mathbf{P}^{t-\tau})\boldsymbol{\varepsilon}_\tau + \sum_{t < \tau \leq t+\widehat{T}} \mathbf{P}^{t+\widehat{T}-\tau}\boldsymbol{\varepsilon}_\tau \\ &= \widehat{T}\mathbf{P}^\infty \mathbf{x}_1 + \sum_{t \leq \tau < t+\widehat{T}} \boldsymbol{\Lambda}_\tau \mathbf{x}_1 + \sum_{1 \leq \tau \leq t^*} (\boldsymbol{\Lambda}_{t+\widehat{T}-\tau} - \boldsymbol{\Lambda}_{t-\tau})\boldsymbol{\varepsilon}_\tau \\ &\quad + \sum_{t^* < \tau \leq t} (\mathbf{P}^{t+\widehat{T}-\tau} - \mathbf{P}^{t-\tau}) \cdot \boldsymbol{\varepsilon}_\tau + \sum_{t < \tau \leq t+\widehat{T}} \mathbf{P}^{t+\widehat{T}-\tau} \cdot \boldsymbol{\varepsilon}_\tau. \quad (7)\end{aligned}$$

In the following we use $\bar{\mathbf{x}} = \mathbf{P}^\infty \mathbf{x}_1$.

$$\begin{aligned}&\left\| \sum_{t < \tau \leq t+\widehat{T}} \mathbf{x}_\tau - \widehat{T} \cdot \bar{\mathbf{x}} \right\|_\infty = \\ &\underset{(2)}{=} \left\| \left(\mathbf{F}_{t+\widehat{T}}^{out} - \mathbf{F}_t^{out} + \sum_{t < \tau \leq t+\widehat{T}} \mathbf{r}_\tau \right) - \widehat{T}\mathbf{P}^\infty \mathbf{x}_1 \right\|_\infty \\ &\underset{(7)}{\leq} \sum_{t \leq \tau < t+\widehat{T}} \|\boldsymbol{\Lambda}_\tau \mathbf{x}_1\|_\infty + \sum_{1 \leq \tau \leq t^*} \left(\left\|\boldsymbol{\Lambda}_{t+\widehat{T}-\tau}\boldsymbol{\varepsilon}_\tau\right\|_\infty + \|\boldsymbol{\Lambda}_{t-\tau}\boldsymbol{\varepsilon}_\tau\|_\infty \right) \\ &\quad + \sum_{t^* < \tau \leq t} \left\| (\mathbf{P}^{t+\widehat{T}-\tau} - \mathbf{P}^{t-\tau})\boldsymbol{\varepsilon}_\tau \right\|_\infty \\ &\quad + \sum_{t < \tau \leq t+\widehat{T}} \left\| \mathbf{P}^{t+\widehat{T}-\tau}\boldsymbol{\varepsilon}_\tau \right\|_\infty + \sum_{t < \tau \leq t+\widehat{T}} \|\mathbf{r}_\tau\|_\infty.\end{aligned}$$

By well-known properties of mixing in graphs (cf. the full version of this paper [21]) it follows for $t \geq 28 \cdot \log(nK)/\mu$ that $\forall_{\tau \geq t} \|\boldsymbol{\Lambda}_\tau \mathbf{x}_1\|_\infty \leq 2^{-4}$, and moreover $\sum_{\tau \geq 4 \cdot t_\mu} \|\boldsymbol{\Lambda}_\tau \boldsymbol{\varepsilon}_\tau\|_\infty \leq n^{-4} \cdot \max_{\tau \geq 4 \cdot t_\mu}\{\|\boldsymbol{\varepsilon}_\tau\|_\infty\}$. This results in

$$\begin{aligned}&\left\| \sum_{t < \tau \leq t+\widehat{T}} \mathbf{x}_\tau - \widehat{T} \cdot \bar{\mathbf{x}} \right\|_\infty \leq \\ &\leq \widehat{T} \cdot 2^{-4} + 2 \cdot n^{-4} \max_{1 \leq \tau \leq t^*} \|\boldsymbol{\varepsilon}_\tau\|_\infty \\ &\quad + \sum_{t^* < \tau \leq t} \left\| (\mathbf{P}^{t+\widehat{T}-\tau} - \mathbf{P}^{t-\tau})\boldsymbol{\varepsilon}_\tau \right\|_\infty + \widehat{T}(\delta d^+ + r) + \widehat{T}r \\ &\leq \frac{\widehat{T}}{4} + (\delta d^+ + r) \\ &\quad + \sum_{t^* < \tau \leq t} \left\| (\mathbf{P}^{t+\widehat{T}-\tau} - \mathbf{P}^{t-\tau})\boldsymbol{\varepsilon}_\tau \right\|_\infty + \widehat{T}(\delta d^+ + 2r).\end{aligned}$$

Dividing the last equation by $\widehat{T}$ yields

$$\begin{aligned}&\left\| \frac{\sum_{t < \tau \leq t+\widehat{T}} \mathbf{x}_\tau}{\widehat{T}} - \bar{\mathbf{x}} \right\|_\infty \leq \frac{1}{4} + (\delta d^+ + 2r) \\ &+ \frac{(\delta d^+ + r) + \sum_{t^* < \tau \leq t} \left\| (\mathbf{P}^{t+\widehat{T}-\tau} - \mathbf{P}^{t-\tau})\boldsymbol{\varepsilon}_\tau \right\|_\infty}{\widehat{T}}. \quad (8)\end{aligned}$$

In this way, in (8) we have derived a bound on the difference between the average load of a node during an interval of length $\widehat{T}$ and the average load $\bar{x}$.

In the remainder we bound (8) for $\widehat{T} = 1$, which describes the load difference to the average. Fix an arbitrary $t \geq 28\log(nK)/\mu$. We define $P_t(u, w)$ to be the probability that a random walk following matrix $\mathbf{P}$, initially located at $u \in V$, is located at w after t time steps. Let w be the i'th node of V, then we define $\mathbf{w}$ to be the vector, such that $\mathbf{w}[i] = 1$ and $\forall_{j \neq i} \mathbf{w}[j] = 0$. Let $a = t - \tau$. Then, we have:

$$\begin{aligned}&\left\| (\mathbf{P}^{t+1-\tau} - \mathbf{P}^{t-\tau})\boldsymbol{\varepsilon}_\tau \right\|_\infty = \left\| (\mathbf{P}^{a+1} - \mathbf{P}^a)\boldsymbol{\varepsilon}_{t-a} \right\|_\infty \\ &= \max_{w \in V} \left| \mathbf{w}^\top \left(\mathbf{P}^{a+1} - \mathbf{P}^a\right) \boldsymbol{\varepsilon}_{t-a} \right| \\ &= \max_{w \in V} \left| \mathbf{w}^\top \left(\mathbf{P}^{a+1} - \mathbf{P}^a\right) \left(\sum_{v \in V} \boldsymbol{\varepsilon}_{t-a}(v)\mathbf{v} \right) \right| \\ &\leq \|\boldsymbol{\varepsilon}_{t-a}\|_\infty \cdot \max_{w \in V} \sum_{v \in V} \left| \mathbf{w}^\top (\mathbf{P}^{a+1} - \mathbf{P}^a)\mathbf{v} \right| \\ &\leq (\delta d^+ + r) \cdot \max_{w \in V} \sum_{v \in V} |P_{a+1}(v, w) - P_a(v, w)| \quad (9)\end{aligned}$$

Since the graph is regular, we have $P_t(v, w) = P_t(w, v)$.[1] From here on, we split the analysis of the claims of the Theorem, proving each of them seperately by combining and bounding equations (8) and (9) in different ways.

(i) $\mathcal{O}\left((\delta+1)d\sqrt{\frac{\log n}{\mu}}\right)$**-discrepancy for** $d^+ \geq 2d$ **:** For regular graphs having $P(u, u) \geq 1/2$ for all $u \in V$, we have by [14] (for $a > 0$)

$$\forall_{w \in V} \sum_{v \in V} |P_{a+1}(w, v) - P_a(w, v)| < \frac{24}{\sqrt{a}}.$$

(For case of $a = 0$, we have $\forall_{w \in V} \sum_{v \in V} |P_1(w, v) - P_0(w, v)| \leq 2$.)

[1]For general graphs, one can use $P_t(v, w) = (d^+(w)/d^+(v))P_t(w, v)$

We obtain by applying $\sum_{a=1}^{t-t^*} 1/\sqrt{a} \leq 2\sqrt{t-t^*}$

$$\sum_{0\leq a<t-t^*} \left\|(\mathbf{P}^{a+1}-\mathbf{P}^{a})\varepsilon_{t-a}\right\|_\infty <$$

$$< (\delta d^+ + r)\left(2+48\sqrt{\underbrace{t-t^*}_{4t_\mu}}\right) \leq 98(\delta d^+ + r)\sqrt{t_\mu}.$$

Introducing this into (8) and setting $\widehat{T}=1$ yields

$$\begin{aligned}\|\mathbf{x}_{t+1}-\bar{x}\|_\infty &= \mathcal{O}\left((\delta d^+ + r)\sqrt{t_\mu}\right)\\ &= \mathcal{O}\left(((\delta+1)d)\sqrt{\frac{\log n}{\mu}}\right)\end{aligned}$$

where we take into account that $t_\mu = 7\log n/\mu$, and that $r \leq d^+$. (Observe that whenever a cumulatively fair balancer has a $\delta = 0$ the bound on the remainder r has to be of order $\Omega(d)$.)

(ii) **$\mathcal{O}((\delta+1)d\sqrt{n})$-discrepancy for $d^+ \geq 2d$:** Let D_{a+1} be the diagonal matrix of $(P_{a+1}-P_a)$ and let X be the corresponding base change matrix.

$$\begin{aligned}\max_{w\in V}\sum_{v\in V}|P_{a+1}(w,v)-P_a(w,v)| &=\\ &= \max_{w\in V}\sum_{v\in V}|\mathbf{v}(P_{a+1}-P_a)\mathbf{w}|\\ &= \max_{w\in V}\|(P_{a+1}-P_a)\mathbf{w}\|_1\\ &\leq \max_{\|\mathbf{w}\|_2=1}\|(P_{a+1}-P_a)\mathbf{w}\|_1\\ &= \max_{\|\mathbf{w}\|_2=1}\left\|X^\top D_{a+1}X\mathbf{w}\right\|_1\\ &\leq \sqrt{n}\left\|X^\top D_{a+1}X\right\|_2\\ &= \sqrt{n}\|D_{a+1}X\|_2. \end{aligned} \quad (10)$$

We have

$$D_{a+1} = \begin{pmatrix} \lambda_1^{a+1}-\lambda_1^a & 0 & \dots & 0\\ 0 & \lambda_2^{a+1}-\lambda_2^a & \dots & 0\\ \vdots & \vdots & \ddots & \vdots\\ 0 & 0 & \dots & \lambda_n^{a+1}-\lambda_n^a\end{pmatrix}.$$

where $\lambda_1,\dots,\lambda_n$ are the eigenvalues of P. We note that $\lambda_1 = 1$ and $\lambda_2,\dots,\lambda_n \in [0,1]$ since $d^\circ \geq d$. Hence by plugging (10) into (9) we derive

$$\begin{aligned}&\sum_{0\leq a<t-t^*}\left\|(\mathbf{P}^{t+\widehat{T}-\tau}-\mathbf{P}^{t-\tau})\varepsilon_\tau\right\|_\infty \leq\\ &\leq (\delta+1)d^+\cdot\sum_{a<t-t^*}\max_{w\in V}\sum_{v\in V}|P_{a+1}(w,v)-P_a(w,v)|\\ &\leq (\delta+1)d^+\cdot\sum_{a<t-t^*}\sqrt{n}\|D_{a+1}X\|_2\\ &\leq (\delta+1)d^+\cdot\sqrt{n}\sum_{a=0}^{t-t^*}|\lambda_2^{a+1}-\lambda_2^a|\\ &= (\delta+1)d^+\cdot\sqrt{n}\cdot(\lambda_2^0-\lambda_2^{t-t^*})\\ &\leq (\delta+1)d^+\cdot\sqrt{n}\end{aligned}$$

Introducing this into (8) and setting $\widehat{T}=1$ yields:

$$\|\mathbf{x}_{t+1}-\bar{x}\|_\infty \leq (\delta+1)d^+\cdot\sqrt{n},$$

which completes the proof.

(iii) **$\mathcal{O}\left((\delta+1)\frac{d\log n}{\mu}\right)$-discrepancy for $d^+ \geq d+1$:** We bound the term $\sum_{t^*<\tau\leq t}\left\|(\mathbf{P}^{t+\widehat{T}-\tau}-\mathbf{P}^{t-\tau})\varepsilon_\tau\right\|_\infty$ of (8):

$$\begin{aligned}&\sum_{t^*<\tau\leq t}\left\|(\mathbf{P}^{t+\widehat{T}-\tau}-\mathbf{P}^{t-\tau})\varepsilon_\tau\right\|_\infty \leq\\ &\leq \sum_{t^*<\tau\leq t}\left(\left\|(\mathbf{P}^{t+\widehat{T}-\tau}\varepsilon_\tau\right\|_\infty + \left\|\mathbf{P}^{t-\tau}\varepsilon_\tau\right\|_\infty\right)\\ &\leq 2\sum_{t^*<\tau\leq t}\|\varepsilon_\tau\|_\infty\\ &\leq 2(\delta d^+ + r)(t-t^*) = 8t_\mu(\delta d^+ + r).\end{aligned}$$

Putting this into (8) and dividing by $\widehat{T}$ gives:

$$\begin{aligned}&\left\|\frac{\sum_{t<\tau\leq t+\widehat{T}}\mathbf{x}_\tau}{\widehat{T}}-\bar{x}\right\|_\infty \leq\\ &\leq \left(\delta d^+ + 2r + \frac{1}{4}\right) + \frac{(8t_\mu+1)(\delta d^+ + r)}{\widehat{T}}. \end{aligned}\quad (11)$$

The claim follows from (11) by setting $\widehat{T}=1$.

We remark that in the above case analysis, we mostly bounded expressions of the form:

$$\sum_{a=0}^{+\infty}\max_{w\in V}\sum_{v\in V}|P_{a+1}(v,w)-P_a(v,w)|.$$

It is not clear if the obtained analysis is asymptotically tight. For example, the question whether it may be possible to replace "$\sqrt{n}$" in claim (ii) by a term which is polylogarithmic in n is an interesting open question in the theory of random walks on graphs (cf. [15] for some recent related results in the area). □

3. RESULTS FOR GOOD s-BALANCERS

In this section, we consider a subclass of cumulatively 1-fair balancers that achieve a better discrepancy compared to the cumulatively fair balancers if the runtime is slightly larger than T. Algorithms of this class are, by definition, a subclass of cumulatively 1-fair balancers. Hence, Theorem 2.3 also applies to Good s-Balancing Algorithms. A cumulatively 1-fair balancer is also a good s-balancer if the algorithm is *(i)* round-fair and *(ii)* self-preferring, *i.e.*, if it favors self-loop edges over original edges. As we will see in Theorem 3.3, the "more self-preferring" an algorithm is, the faster it balances.

DEFINITION 3.1. *Assume δ is an arbitrary constant and $1 \leq s \leq d^\circ$. An algorithm is called a* good s-balancer *if if for $t \in \mathbf{N}$ and $u \in V$ all edges of u (including self-loops) receive $\lfloor x_t(u)/d^+\rfloor$ many tokens in step t. The remaining $e(u) = x_t(u) - d^+\cdot\lfloor x_t(u)/d^+\rfloor$ have to be distributed over the edges such that*

1. *the algorithm is cumulatively 1-fair*

2. *at least* $\min\{s, e(u)\}$ *self-loops receive* $\lceil x_t(u)/d^+ \rceil$ *many tokens. (s-self-preferring)*
3. *every edge* $e \in E_u^+$ *receives at most* $\lceil x_t(u)/d^+ \rceil$ *many tokens.*

Note that, by definition, every good s-balancer is round-fair, meaning that every edge receives either $\lfloor x_t(u)/d^+ \rfloor$ or $\lceil x_t(u)/d^+ \rceil$ many tokens in every round.

OBSERVATION 3.2. *The algorithm* SEND $([^x/_{d^+}])$ *is a good* $(d^+ - 2d)$*-balancer for* $d^+ > 2d$. *Furthermore,* ROTOR-ROUTER* *is a good* 1*-balancer.*

The following theorem shows that good s-balancers achieve a smaller discrepancy of $O(d)$ if they are allowed to run longer than T steps.

THEOREM 3.3. *Let G be any d-regular input graph and let d^+ is the degree of the balancing graph G^+. Let δ be an arbitrary constant and let $1 \le s \le (d^+ - d)$. Assume A is a good s-balancer. Then A achieves a discrepancy of $((2\delta + 1)d^+ + 4d^\circ)$ after time $\mathcal{O}\left(\log K + ds^{-1} \cdot \log^2 n/\mu\right)$.*

We note that large values of s ($s = \Omega(d)$) increase the speed of the balancing process. In Theorem 4.2 (Section 4) we provide a lower bound of $\Omega(d)$ on the discrepancy of any stateless algorithms, the bound is independent of the balancing time. Since the class of good s-balancers contains many stateless algorithms, this also means that the bound on the discrepancy in Theorem 3.3 cannot be improved without further restrictions on the class.

The remainder of this section is devoted to a proof of Theorem 3.3. We first define the following two families of potential functions, parameterized by c:

$$\phi_t(c) = \sum_{v \in V} \max\{x_t(v) - cd^+, 0\} \text{ and}$$

$$\phi'_t(c) = \sum_{v \in V} \max\{cd^+ + s - x_t(v), 0\}.$$

To show the theorem we use Equation 8 of the proof of Theorem 2.3, to derive Lemma 3.4. The lemma shows that, for every node u, there exists a time step t_u in which the load of the node has a certain distance to $\bar{x}$. We will then show that the time step t_u results in a potential drop of $\phi_t(c)$ for u if the load of u was larger than cd^+.

The following lemma gives a bound on the required length of the time interval so that there is a step t_u where u has a load which is sufficiently close to $\bar{x}$. The required time is expressed as a fraction of $\log n/\mu$. The lemma shows a tradeoff (parameter λ) between the required time and the load difference of u to $\bar{x}$. The proof can be found in the full version of the paper.

LEMMA 3.4. *Consider any cumulatively δ-fair balancer with remainder bounded by r, and an initialization of the load balancing process with average load $\bar{x}$ and initial discrepancy K. Let $\lambda \ge 0$, and let $t \ge 16 \cdot \log(nK)/\mu$, and let $\widehat{T} = O\left(d \log n/(\mu \cdot (\lambda + 1))\right)$. Then we have:*
For all $u \in V$ there exists a time step $t' \in [t+1; t+\widehat{T}]$ such that $x_{t'}(u) \le \bar{x} + \delta d^+ + 2r + 1/2 + \lambda$.

The next lemma bounds the one-step potential drop of $\phi_t(c)$ occurring on every node which has a load of more than cd^+ at time $t-1$ and has a smaller load of at most $cd^+ + s$ at time t. The proof can be found in the full version.

LEMMA 3.5 (MONOTONICITY OF POTENTIAL). *Let A be a good s-balancer. The potential $\phi_t(c)$ is non-increasing in time and it satisfies: $\phi_t(c) \le \phi_{t-1}(c) - \sum_{u \in V} \Delta_t(c, u)$, where: $\Delta_t(c, u) = \min\{x_{t-1}(u), cd^+ + s\} - \max\{x_t(u), cd^+\}$ if $x_{t-1}(u) > x_t(u)$ and $x_{t-1}(u) > cd^+$ and $\Delta_t(c, u) = 0$ otherwise.*

The following observation extends Lemma 3.5 to intervals $[t, t']$. It estimates the potential drop of $\phi_t(c)$ for nodes which have a load $\ge cd^+$ at time t and a load $\le cd^+$ during one time step of the interval. The observation follows directly from Lemma 3.5; we omit its proof.

OBSERVATION 3.6. *Let A be a good s-balancer and let $t \le t'$ be two fixed time steps. Denote by U the subset of nodes such that for all $u \in U$ $x_t(u) \ge cd^+ + 1$ and there exists a moment of time $t_u \in [t, t']$ such that $x_{t_u}(u) \le cd^+$. Then $\phi_{t'}(c) \le \phi_t(c) - \sum_{u \in U} \max\{s, x_t(u) - cd^+\}$.*

The potential defined in Lemma 3.5 bounds the number of tokens above certain thresholds. Now we use $\phi'_t(c)$ to show symmetric results measuring the number of 'gaps' below certain thresholds. The proof of Lemma 3.7 is very similar to that of Lemma 3.5, and we provide it for completeness in the full version of this paper.

LEMMA 3.7. *Let A be a good s-balancer. The potential $\phi'_t(c)$ is non-increasing in time and it satisfies: $\phi'_t(c) \le \phi'_{t-1}(c) - \sum_{u \in V} \Delta'_t(c, u)$, where:*
$\Delta'_t(c, u) = \min\{x_t(u), cd^+ + s\} - \max\{x_{t-1}(u), cd^+\}$ if $x_{t-1}(u) < x_t(u)$ and $x_{t-1}(u) < cd^+ + s$ and $\Delta'_t(c, u) = 0$ otherwise.

Before proving the lemma, we remark that the potential admits a drop at node u at time t (*i.e.*, $\Delta'_t(c, u) \ge 1$) for every node u such that $x_{t-1}(u) \le cd^+$ and $x_t(u) \ge cd^+ + 1$, for any algorithm which is at least 1-self-preferring. Again, the following observation follows directly from Lemma 3.7; we omit its proof.

OBSERVATION 3.8. *Let A be a good s-balancer and let $t \le t'$ be two fixed time steps. Denote by U the subset of nodes such that for all $u \in U$ $x_t(u) < cd^+ + s$ and there exists a moment of time $t_u \in [t, t']$ such that $x_{t_u}(u) \ge cd^+ + s$. Then $\phi'_{t'}(c) \le \phi_t(c) - \sum_{u \in U} \max\{s, cd^+ + s - x_t(u)\}$.*

The main idea of the rest of the proof is the following. We will consider the potential functions $\phi_t(c)$ for decreasing values of c and analyze the time T_c it takes to decrease the potentials $\phi_t(c)$. The time bound of Theorem 3.3 is then the sum of the times T_c for suitably chosen values of c. A symmetrical argument can be used to bound $\phi'_t(c)$. Details of the arguments of the proof are provided in the full version.

4. LOWER BOUNDS

We start by showing that the cumulative fairness bounds we introduce cannot be completely discarded when improving upon the discrepancy gaps from [17]. Note that a round-fair balancer is not necessarily cumulatively δ-fair for any constant δ. In the following we show that there are round-fair balancers which have a discrepancy of at least $\Omega(\text{diam}(G) \cdot d)$. The proofs of this section are deferred to the full version.

THEOREM 4.1. *Let G be a d-regular graph. There exists an initial distribution of tokens and a round-fair balancer A, such that A cannot achieve a discrepancy better than $(c \cdot \mathrm{diam}(G) \cdot d)$, for some positive constant $c > 0$.*

The following bound shows that the stateless algorithms we design are asymptotically the best possible in terms of eventual discrepancy. Namely, any stateless algorithm is not able to achieve a discrepancy better than cd, for some constant c. This also means that the bound on the discrepancy, presented in Theorem 3.3, cannot be improved in general for the class of good s-balancers.

THEOREM 4.2. *Let A be an arbitrary deterministic and stateless algorithm. For every even n, there exists a d-regular graph and an initial load distribution such that A cannot achieve discrepancy better than cd, for some positive constant $c > 0$.*

Our final lower bounds concern variants of the ROTOR-ROUTER. The next theorem shows that for a graph without self-loops (*i.e.*, $G = G^+$) the best possible discrepancy of the ROTOR-ROUTER is at least $c \cdot d \cdot \varphi'(G)$, where $\varphi'(G)$ is the odd girth of graph G, *i.e.*, the length of the shortest odd length cycle over all nodes of G. This gives for an odd-length cycle of n nodes a discrepancy of at least $c \cdot n$ for some constant c.

THEOREM 4.3. *Let G be any d-regular and non-bipartite graph, and let $d^+ = d$. Then, there exists an initial load distribution and direction of the rotors such that* ROTOR-ROUTER *cannot achieve discrepancy better than $(c \cdot d\varphi(G))$, for some positive constant $c > 0$, where $(2\varphi(G) + 1)$ is the odd girth of G.*

5. CONCLUSION

We introduced two classes of deterministic load-balancing algorithms: Cumulative δ-fair balancers and good s-balancer. The lower bounds show discrepancies of $\Omega(d \cdot \mathrm{diam})$ for algorithms which are not cumulatively δ-fair or which do not have any self-loops. However, there are two main questions which we leave unanswered: 1) How many self-loops are necessary to obtain our bounds? 2) Are the restrictions imposed by good s-balancers necessary to obtain our bounds?

6. ACKNOWLEDGMENTS

This research was partially supported by the project ANR DISPLEXITY and by the "Investments for the future" Programme IdEx Bordeaux CPU (ANR-10-IDEX-03-02). Part of this work was done while PU was affiliated with Aix-Marseille Université.

7. REFERENCES

[1] C. Adolphs and P. Berenbrink. *Distributed self-prefering load balancing with weights and speeds.* In *PODC*, pages 135–144, 2012.

[2] C. Adolphs and P. Berenbrink. *Improved bounds on diffusion load balancing.* In *IPDPS*, 2012.

[3] H. Akbari and P. Berenbrink. *Parallel rotor walks on finite graphs and applications in discrete load balancing.* In *SPAA*, pages 186–195, 2013.

[4] H. Akbari, P. Berenbrink, and T. Sauerwald. *A simple approach for adapting continuous load balancing processes to discrete settings.* In *PODC*, pages 271–280, 2012.

[5] P. Berenbrink, C. Cooper, T. Friedetzky, T. Friedrich, and T. Sauerwald. *Randomized diffusion for indivisible loads.* In *SODA*, pages 429–439, 2011.

[6] J. Cooper, B. Doerr, T. Friedrich, and J. Spencer. Deterministic random walks on regular trees. *Random Struct. Algorithms*, 37(3):353–366, 2010.

[7] J. Cooper and J. Spencer. Simulating a random walk with constant error. *Combinatorics, Probability and Computing*, 15:815–822, 2006.

[8] B. Doerr and T. Friedrich. Deterministic random walks on the two-dimensional grid. *Combinatorics, Probability and Computing*, 18(1-2):123–144, 2009.

[9] T. Friedrich, M. Gairing, and T. Sauerwald. *Quasirandom load balancing.* In *SODA*, pages 1620–1629, 2010.

[10] T. Friedrich and T. Sauerwald. *Near-perfect load balancing by randomized rounding.* In *STOC*, pages 121–130, 2009.

[11] T. Friedrich and T. Sauerwald. The cover time of deterministic random walks. In *COCOON*, pages 130–139, 2010.

[12] S. Kijima, K. Koga, and K. Makino. *Deterministic random walks on finite graphs.* In *ANALCO*, pages 16–25, 2012.

[13] A. Kosowski and D. Pająk. *Does Adding More Agents Make a Difference? A Case Study of Cover Time for the Rotor-Router.* In *ICALP*, pages 544–555, 2014.

[14] D. Levin, Y. Peres, and E. Wilmer. *Markov chains and mixing times.* American Mathematical Society, 2006.

[15] J. Norris, Y. Peres, A. Zhai. *Surprise probabilities in Markov chains.* In *SODA*, pages 1759–1773, 2015.

[16] V. Priezzhev, D. Dhar, A. Dhar, and S. Krishnamurthy. *Eulerian walkers as a model of self-organized criticality. Phys. Rev. Lett.*, 77:5079–5082, 1996.

[17] Y. Rabani, A. Sinclair, and R. Wanka. *Local divergence of Markov chains and the analysis of iterative load-balancing schemes.* In *FOCS*, pages 694–703, 1998.

[18] T. Sauerwald and H. Sun. *Tight bounds for randomized load balancing on arbitrary network topologies.* In *FOCS*, pages 341–350, 2012. A revised and extended version is available online at: http://arxiv.org/abs/1201.2715.

[19] R. Subramanian and I. Scherson. *An analysis of diffusive load-balancing.* In *SPAA*, pages 220–225, 1994.

[20] T. Shiraga, Y. Yamauchi, S. Kijimam, and M. Yamashita. *Deterministic Random Walks for Rapidly Mixing Chains.* `arXiv:1311.3749`, 2013.

[21] P. Berenbrink, R. Klasing, A. Kosowski, F. Mallmann-Trenn, and P. Uznański. *Improved Analysis of Deterministic Load-Balancing Schemes.* `arXiv:1404.4344`, 2014.

[22] V. Yanovski, I. Wagner, and A. Bruckstein. *A Distributed Ant Algorithm for Efficiently Patrolling a Network Algorithmica*, 37(3):165-186, 2003.

APPENDIX

A. AUXILIARY PROPOSITION

The following proposition shows that the change in the model (the way the tokens are retained) in the preliminaries of Section 2 in comparison to the original model described in Section 1.3 does change the load sent over any original edge in the graph. In particular, every cumulatively fair balancer can be transformed (by shifting tokens from self-loops to the remainder) into an algorithm guaranteeing cumulative fairness on all edges and that this transformed algorithm sends exactly the same load over original edges in every round.

PROPOSITION A.1. *For any cumulatively δ-fair load-balancing algorithm A, there exists an Algorithm A' with remainder $r \leq d^+$ such that for any t and for all $(u, v) \in E_u^+$*

1. $\left|F_t(u,v) - \frac{F_t^{out}(u)}{d^+}\right| \leq \delta.$
2. *the load sent over (u, v) is the same in A and A'.*

PROOF. The reformulation of algorithm A as algorithm A' proceeds as follows. For all edges $e \in E(G)$ (*i.e.*, except for self-loops), in every step A' places the same amount of load on e as A. However, in A' load may be retained on nodes in a different way, being placed in the remainder $r_t(u)$ rather than on self-loops at node $u \in V$. To prove, that it is always possible, we proceed by induction.

Specifically, at a fixed moment of time t, let $f_t(e)$ be the amount of load put on an edge e by algorithm A, and $f_t'(e)$ be the amount of load put on an edge by A', and let $F_t(e)$ and $F_t'(e)$ be the respective cumulative loads for algorithms A and A'. Algorithm A' processes all edges (including self-loops) sequentially and verifies if sending this amount of load along e would satisfy the cumulative fairness condition up to time t with respect to all edges originating from u already processed.

Let e_1 be the edge or self-loop that violates the cumulative load property for A', that is there exists an incident edge or self-loop e_2 such that $|(F_{t-1}'(e_1) + f_t(e_1)) - (F_{t-1}'(e_2) + f_t(e_2))| > \delta$. Since $|f_t(e_1) - f_t(e_2)| \leq 1$, and $|F_{t-1}'(e_1) - F_{t-1}'(e_2)| \leq \delta$ (from inductive assumption), we get that

$$(F_{t-1}'(e_1) + f_t(e_1)) - (F_{t-1}'(e_2) + f_t(e_2)) \in \{\delta + 1, -\delta - 1\} \tag{12}$$

(without loss of generality we can assume that this value is $\delta + 1$). Moreover, we can show that for every e_2' such that the pair e_1, e_2' violates cumulative fairness, the value (12) is $\delta + 1$ (otherwise $F_{t-1}'(e_1) - F_{t-1}'(e_2) = \delta$ and $F_{t-1}'(e_1) - F_{t-1}'(e_2') = -\delta$ imply $F_{t-1}'(e_2') - F_{t-1}'(e_2) = 2\delta$ which contradicts the inductive assumption). We can also observe that e_1 is a loop (attached to vertex u), since non-loop edges satisfy cumulatively fairness for A. Thus it is enough to set $f_t'(e_1) = f_t(e_1) - 1$ and increase $r_t(u)$ by one (in the mirror scenario with a value of $-\delta - 1$ in (12) we would set $f_t'(e_1) = f_t(e_1) + 1$ and decrease $r_t(u)$ by one). It is easy to observe that this makes e_1 satisfy δ-fairness with every other edge incident to u. After processing all edges and self-loops and edges in this way and since every edge receives $\lfloor x_t(u)/d^+ \rfloor$ tokens, we eventually obtain that cumulative fairness is preserved, and moreover $|r_t'(u)| \leq d^+$. □

Brief Announcement: Robust and Private Distributed Shared Atomic Memory in Message Passing Networks

Shlomi Dolev*
Department of Computer Science
Ben-Gurion University of the Negev
84105 Beer-Sheva, Israel
dolev@cs.bgu.ac.il

Thomas Petig
Department of Computer Science and Engineering
Chalmers University of Technology
41296 Gothenburg, Sweden
petig@chalmers.se

Elad M. Schiller
Department of Computer Science and Engineering
Chalmers University of Technology
41296 Gothenburg, Sweden
elad@chalmers.se

ABSTRACT

We study the problem of privately emulating shared memory in message passing networks. The system includes N servers, and at most e semi-Byzantine servers that can deviate from the algorithm by sending corrupted data. Moreover, at most f servers can fail and stop.

The focus is on coded atomic storage (CAS) algorithms. We present a variant that ensures no information leakage by letting the servers store their data as secret shares. Our enhancement to CAS uses $\lceil (N + k + 2e)/2 \rceil$-size quorums and Reed-Solomon codes. This enhancement preserves the algorithm ability to function in asynchronous system settings.

To the best of our knowledge, we are the first to address the privacy issue when emulating shared memory in message-passing systems.

Categories and Subject Descriptors

D.4.2 [**Operating Systems**]: Storage Management—*Distributed memories*; C.4 [**Performance Of Systems**]: Fault tolerance; C.2.4 [**Computer-Communication Networks**]: Distributed Systems—*Distributed applications*

Keywords

shared memory emulation; message passing; network coding; secret sharing; privacy; semi-Byzantine; MRMW; fault tolerance

*Supported by the Rita Altura Trust Chair in Computer Sciences, Israel Science Foundation (grant 428/11), the Israeli Internet Association, and the Israeli Ministry of Science and Technology, Infrastructure Research in the Field of Advanced Computing and Cyber Security.

Permission to make digital or hard copies of part or all of this work for personal or classroom use is granted without fee provided that copies are not made or distributed for profit or commercial advantage, and that copies bear this notice and the full citation on the first page. Copyrights for third-party components of this work must be honored. For all other uses, contact the owner/author(s). Copyright is held by the author/owner(s).

PODC'15, July 21–23, 2015, Donostia-San Sebastián, Spain.
ACM 978-1-4503-3617-8 /15/07.
http://dx.doi.org/10.1145/2767386.2767450.

1. INTRODUCTION

Security and privacy are often imperative for distributed systems. This motivates us to study the problem of emulating shared memory in message passing networks that include N servers, at most f crash-stop failures and e semi-Byzantine servers that can deviate from the algorithm by sending corrupted data. We look at coded atomic storage algorithms that ensure no information leakage by letting the servers store their data as secret shares. We consider an enhancement of the coded atomic storage (CAS) algorithm by Cadambe et al. [3] in which we use $\lceil (N+k+2e)/2 \rceil$-size quorums and (N, k)-Reed-Solomon codes, where k represents the message length.

The first algorithm for emulating a single-writer multi-reader shared memory by Attiya et al. [1], as well as the multi-writer multi-reader version by Fan and Lynch [4], handle link and node failures. Cadambe et al. [3] present the coded atomic storage (CAS) algorithm and improve communication and storage costs by using quorums and (N, k)-maximum distance separable (MDS) codes [7]. The CAS algorithm enables the reader to restore the data under the presence of $\frac{N-k}{2}$ stop-failed servers. We address privacy by storing on each node merely parts of the data, as in Shamir's secret sharing scheme [8], which we can implement using Reed-Solomon codes [5] and a matching error correction algorithm (Berlekamp-Welch [9]). This variation of the CAS algorithm also provides resilience against other errors, for example, data corruption of a bounded number of secret shares. We show how to combine shared-memory emulation with robustness and privacy.

Background

The (N, k)-*threshold scheme* for integers k and N, such that $0 < k \leq N$, is defined by Shamir [8] and splits a secret s into N secret shares $\{s_i\}_{i \in \{1,\ldots,N\}}$. This scheme requires that there exists a mapping from any $S \subseteq \{s_i\}_{i \in \{1,\ldots,N\}}$ with $|S| \geq k$ to the secret s, but it is impossible to determine s from a set of less than k secret shares. Let K be a finite field such that it size $|K|$ is prime. The (N, k)-Reed-Solomon code, $\Phi : \mathcal{S} \to \mathcal{W}$, transforms the input data, i.e., one element of a k dimensional vector space, $\mathcal{S}$, over K, into N dimensional vector space, $\mathcal{W}$, over the same field, K. k and N are as above. We call N the block length and k the message length. The Berlekamp-Welch algorithm, Φ^{-1}, can correct (N, k)-Reed-Solomon codes within $\mathcal{O}(N^3)$

Algorithm 1: The robust and private coded atomic storage algorithm, code for p_i.

Writer: `// Writes secret` s.
Query for the highest finalized tag from a quorum, select the message $((z,k), w, \text{'fin'})$ such that z is max.;
pre-write: Send $((z+1,i), \Phi_{p_j}(s), \text{'pre'})$ to all $p_j \in \mathcal{P}$ and wait until quorum acknowledges;
finalize: Send $((z+1,i), \perp, \text{'fin'})$ to all $p_j \in \mathcal{P}$ and wait until quorum acknowledges;

Reader: `// Returns secret` s, `or` $\perp$ `in case of failure.`
Query for the highest finalized tag from a quorum, select the tag $((z,j), w_{p_j}, \text{'fin'})$ such that z is maximal;
Finalize: Send $(t, \perp, \text{'fin'})$ to all $s \in \mathcal{P}$ and let Q be the response of a quorum ;
if $|\{(t, w, \textit{'fin'}) \in Q : w \neq \perp\}| \geq k + 2e$ **then**
  return $\Phi^{-1}(\{(t, w, s) \in Q : w \neq \perp\})$;
else return $\perp$;

Server: Storage variable: $S \subset \mathcal{T} \times (\mathcal{W} \cup \{\perp\}) \times \{\text{'pre'}, \text{'fin'}\}$;
upon (receive query) **do**
  Reply with highest finalized tag;
upon (receive pre-write $(t, w, \text{'pre'})$) **do**
  if $\nexists(t, \bullet) \in S$ **then** $S \leftarrow S \cup (t, w, \text{'pre'})$;
  Reply with acknowledgement;
upon (receive finalize $(t, \perp, \text{'fin'})$ from writer) **do**
  if $\exists(t, w, \textit{'pre'}) \in S$ **then**
    $S \leftarrow (S \setminus \{(t, w, \text{'pre'})\}) \cup (t, w, \text{'fin'})$;
  else Add $(t, \perp, \text{'fin'})$ to S;
  Reply with acknowledgement;
upon (finalize $(t, \perp, \text{'fin'})$ from reader) **do**
  if $\exists(t, w, \bullet) \in S : w \neq \perp$ **then**
    $S \leftarrow (S \setminus \{(t, w, \bullet)\}) \cup \{(t, w, \text{'fin'})\}$;
    reply $(t, w, \text{'fin'})$;
  else
    $S \leftarrow S \cup \{(t, \perp, \text{'fin'})\}$;
    reply $(t, \perp, \text{'fin'})$;

time in the presence of e errors and f erasures, as long as $2e + f < N - k + 1$ [9]. Note that (N,k)-Reed-Solomon codes are a (N,k)-threshold scheme [5]. For this the input vector $(\sigma_1, \ldots, \sigma_k) \in \mathcal{S}$ consists of the secret σ_1 and randomly chosen values $\sigma_2, \ldots, \sigma_k$ from a uniform distribution over $\mathcal{S}$. We use Φ to map $(\sigma_1, \ldots, \sigma_k)$ to the secret shares $(w_1, \ldots, w_N) \in \mathcal{W}$.

Our contribution

We show how to emulate atomic shared memory in the presence of semi-Byzantine servers. This approach ensures privacy. Namely, no group of up to $k-1$ servers is able to reconstruct the stored data, i.e., the secret. Furthermore, a reader can reconstruct the correct secret even if up to e servers deliver corrupted secret shares. We do that using Reed-Solomon codes [6] and the Berlekamp-Welch error correction algorithm [9]. This works because Cadambe et al. [3] use the class of maximum-distance separable codes for their CAS algorithm, which includes the Reed-Solomon codes.

2. SYSTEM SETTINGS

We consider message passing networks in which nodes exchange messages via communication links. Messages are of the form $(t, w, d) \in \mathcal{T} \times \mathcal{W} \cup \{\perp\} \times \mathcal{D}$, where $\mathcal{T}$ is the set of tag tuples (z, i) that contain an integer z and a node identifier i. With $\mathcal{W}$ we denote, as mentioned, the set of secret shares, where $\perp$ is the invalid share and $\mathcal{D} := \{\text{'pre'}, \text{'fin'}\}$ is the label set. We distinguish among three node types: *server*, *reader* and *writer*. Each writer and each reader is reliably connected to all servers, and with bounded communication delays. Let $\mathcal{P}$ be the *server* set, where $N := |\mathcal{P}|$.

Our settings are motivated by (reliable) servers that stores large secret shares on (unreliable) mass storage systems. We allow at most e semi-Byzantine servers and at most f failures, such as communication delay violation. We assume that semi-Byzantine servers can send corrupted secret shares to readers, but not corrupted tags or labels, i.e., when a semi-Byzantine server replies with a tuple (t, w, d), only w might be corrupted. Writers split secrets using the (N,k)-Reed-Solomon code and submit the resulting secret shares to the servers. Servers store their secret shares and deliver them to the readers upon request. The proposed solution withstands a fault model that includes both server stop-failure and server semi-Byzantine behavior.

We say that a secret sharing protocol is *t-private* when a set of at most t servers cannot compute the secret, as in [2]. Note that a 0-private protocol preserves no privacy. When the presence of at most t semi-Byzantine servers and at most s stop-failed servers does not influence the correctness of secret restored by a reader, we say that the protocol is *(s,t)-robust*, similar to *t-resilience* in [2].

Quorums of $(k + 2e)$-overlap

We define a *quorum* as a server subset $Q \subseteq \mathcal{P}$ with at least $\lceil \frac{N+k+2e}{2} \rceil$ elements, and we write $\mathcal{Q}$ as the all quorum set.

Lemma 1 shows that any two different quorums share at least $k+2e$ servers, rather than just k of them as in Cadambe et al. [3]. These quorums guarantees that once a writer finishes its write operation, any reader can retrieve at least $k+2e$ secret shares and reconstruct the secret.

LEMMA 1. (Variation of [3], Lemma 5.1) *Suppose that* $1 \le k \le N-2f-2e$. ***(1)*** *If* $Q_1, Q_2 \in \mathcal{Q}$, *then* $|Q_1 \cap Q_2| \ge k+2e$. ***(2)*** *The existence of such a* k *implies the existence of* $Q \in \mathcal{Q}$ *such that* Q *has no crashed servers.*

Proof. **(1)** Let $Q_1, Q_2 \in \mathcal{Q}$, then $|Q_1 \cap Q_2| = |Q_1| + |Q_2| - |Q_1 \cup Q_2| \ge 2\lceil \frac{N+k+2e}{2} \rceil - N \ge k+2e$. **(2)** Since there are at most f crashed servers, we can show that without such f servers, there are still enough alive servers for a quorum. It follows that $N-f \ge N - \lfloor \frac{N-k-2e}{2} \rfloor = \lceil \frac{N+k+2e}{2} \rceil$. □

By Lemma 1, the atomicity and liveness analysis in [3, Theorem 5.2 to Lemma 5.9] also holds when the CAS algorithm that uses $(k+2e)$-overlap quorums.

3. THE ALGORITHM

In order to tolerate at most e (secret share corruptions made by) semi-Byzantine servers, we propose Algorithm 1 as a variation of Cadambe et al. [3] CAS algorithm that uses $(k+2e)$-overlap quorums and (N, k)-Reed-Solomon codes [6], which is an (N, k)-MDS [7] code that Cadambe et al. [3] uses. By the atomicity and liveness analysis for the case of $(k+2e)$-overlap quorums (the remark after Lemma 1), the reader retrieves $k+2e$ unique secret shares that include at most e manipulated shares.

COROLLARY 1. *For* $1 \le k \le N-2f-2e$, *Algorithm 1 emulates a shared atomic read/write memory.*

Robustness

Robustness is added by the ability of the Berlekamp-Welch algorithm to correct error in the Reed-Solomon codes. Note that semi-Byzantine servers only introduce corrupted secret shares. Lemma 2 shows the robustness of Algorithm 1 against up to e semi-Byzantine servers and up to f stop-failed servers.

LEMMA 2. *For* $k \in \{1\ldots, N-2f-2e\}$, *Algorithm 1* (f, e)*-robust.*

Proof. If a writer issues a query, pre-write and finalize operations it does not read back the secret from the server. Thus, writers are immune to semi-Byzantine servers. Servers do not exchange secrets with other servers and thus are not directly affected by semi-Byzantine servers. A reader collects secret shares from qourum of servers, but never writes them to servers, since a query and a finalize only contains a $\perp$ in place of a secret share. By Lemma 1 and Corollary 1 follows that a reader p_i receives at least $k+2e$ secret shares from the finalize operation. From these $k+2e$ secret shares at most e are corrupted and, thus, p_i computes the correct secret by applying Berlekamp-Welch. □

Privacy

Our approach ensures privacy of the secret among servers. In Lemma 3 we see that a group of less than k servers are not able to reconstruct the secret by combining the secret shares they have stored locally.

LEMMA 3. *For* $1 \le k \le N-2f-2e$, *Algorithm 1 is* $(k-1)$*-private.*

Proof. Reed-Solomon codes implement the Shamir secret sharing [5] and, thus, $k-1$ servers cannot compute the secret using their $k-1$ local secret shares. □

Note that in the case $k=1$, even if privacy is not protected, it is still possible to correct corrupted memory copies. This holds because the reader reads $1+2e$ secret shares and, thus, the additional $2e$ secret shares contain redundant information for the Berlekamp-Welch error correction.

4. CONCLUSIONS

Interestingly, fundamental building blocks for distributed systems can provide privacy and robustness. We show how to implement a robust and private coded atomic storage protocol, which is resilient to semi-Byzantine servers using shared memory emulation in message passing networks. In addition, our algorithm tolerates server crashes, and at the same time, it ensures the privacy of the stored data. We believe that our approach and techniques are useful for providing robustness and privacy for many more building blocks for distributed systems.

References

[1] H. Attiya, A. Bar-Noy, and D. Dolev. Sharing memory robustly in message-passing systems. *Journal of the ACM (JACM)*, 42(1):124–142, 1995.

[2] M. Ben-Or, S. Goldwasser, and A. Wigderson. Completeness theorems for non-cryptographic fault-tolerant distributed computation (extended abstract). In J. Simon, editor, *Proceedings of the 20th Annual ACM Symposium on Theory of Computing, May 2-4, 1988, Chicago, Illinois, USA*, pages 1–10. ACM, 1988.

[3] V. R. Cadambe, N. A. Lynch, M. Médard, and P. M. Musial. A coded shared atomic memory algorithm for message passing architectures. In *2014 IEEE 13th International Symposium on Network Computing and Applications, NCA 2014, Cambridge, MA, USA, 21-23 August, 2014*, pages 253–260. IEEE Computer Society, 2014.

[4] R. Fan and N. A. Lynch. Efficient replication of large data objects. In F. E. Fich, editor, *Distributed Computing, 17th International Conference, DISC 2003, Sorrento, Italy, October 1-3, 2003, Proceedings*, volume 2848 of *Lecture Notes in Computer Science*, pages 75–91. Springer, 2003.

[5] R. J. McEliece and D. V. Sarwate. On sharing secrets and reed-solomon codes. *Commun. ACM*, 24(9):583–584, Sept. 1981.

[6] I. S. Reed and G. Solomon. Polynomial codes over certain finite fields. *Journal of the Society for Industrial & Applied Mathematics*, 8(2):300–304, 1960.

[7] R. M. Roth. *Introduction to coding theory*. Cambridge University Press, 2006.

[8] A. Shamir. How to share a secret. *Commun. ACM*, 22(11):612–613, 1979.

[9] L. Welch and E. Berlekamp. Error correction for algebraic block codes, Dec. 30 1986. US Patent 4,633,470.

Randomized Proof-Labeling Schemes*

Mor Baruch
School of Electrical Engineering
Tel Aviv University
Tel Aviv, Israel
mor@eng.tau.ac.il

Pierre Fraigniaud[†]
Dept. of Computer Science
CNRS and Univ. Paris Diderot
France
Pierre.Fraigniaud@liafa.univ-paris-diderot.fr

Boaz Patt-Shamir[‡]
School of Electrical Engineering
Tel Aviv University
Tel Aviv, Israel
boaz@tau.ac.il

ABSTRACT

Proof-labeling schemes, introduced by Korman, Kutten and Peleg [PODC 2005], are a mechanism to certify that a network configuration satisfies a given boolean predicate. Such mechanisms find applications in many contexts, e.g., the design of fault-tolerant distributed algorithms. In a proof-labeling scheme, predicate verification consists of neighbors exchanging labels, whose contents depends on the predicate. In this paper, we introduce the notion of *randomized* proof-labeling schemes where messages are randomized and correctness is probabilistic. We show that randomization reduces label size exponentially while guaranteeing probability of correctness arbitrarily close to one. In addition, we present a novel label-size lower bound technique that applies to both deterministic and randomized proof-labeling schemes. Using this technique, we establish several tight bounds on the verification complexity of MST, acyclicity, connectivity, and longest cycle size.

Categories and Subject Descriptors

F.2.2 [**Analysis of Algorithms and Problem Complexity**]: Nonnumerical Algorithms and Problems; G.2.2 [**Discrete Mathematics**]: Graph Theory; B.8.1 [**Performance and Reliability**]: Reliability, Testing, and Fault-Tolerance

General Terms

Algorithms, Reliability, Theory

Keywords

Distributed verification, communication complexity.

*Research supported in part by the Ministry of Science Technology and Space, Israel, French-Israeli project MAIMONIDE 31768XL, and by the French-Israeli Laboratory FILOFOCS.

[†]Additional support from the ANR project DISPLEXITY, and from the INRIA project GANG.

[‡]Supported in part by the Israel Science Foundation (grant No. 1444/14).

Permission to make digital or hard copies of all or part of this work for personal or classroom use is granted without fee provided that copies are not made or distributed for profit or commercial advantage and that copies bear this notice and the full citation on the first page. Copyrights for components of this work owned by others than ACM must be honored. Abstracting with credit is permitted. To copy otherwise, or republish, to post on servers or to redistribute to lists, requires prior specific permission and/or a fee. Request permissions from Permissions@acm.org.
PODC'15, July 21–23, 2015, Donostia-San Sebastián, Spain
© 2015 ACM. ISBN 978-1-4503-3617-8 /15/07 $15.00
DOI:http://dx.doi.org/10.1145/2767386.2767421.

1. INTRODUCTION

Context and Objective.

Deciding the validity of a predicate over a distributed system (e.g., whether the nodes are properly colored, or whether the nodes have reached consensus), in a decentralized fashion, has received much attention over the years due to its applications to various domains, including checking the results obtained from the execution of a distributed program [7, 15, 30], establishing lower bounds on the time required for distributed approximation [10], estimating the complexity of logics required for distributed run-time verification [16], and general distributed complexity theory [14]. In the context of local computing in networks, a distributed decision is typically performed by letting each node inspect its state and the state of its neighbors, and return either TRUE or FALSE depending on whether this local configuration is consistent with a legal (global) state of the network. The decision is correct if all nodes return TRUE on legal states, and if at least one node returns FALSE on every illegal state. (A node returning FALSE could, e.g., launch a recovery procedure). For instance, deciding the correctness of the predicate asserting that the nodes are properly colored is straightforward: every node collects the colors of its neighbors, and returns TRUE if and only if none of these colors is the same as its own color.

Not all distributed network predicates can be decided locally directly. Consider, for example, deciding whether a set of edges constitute a spanning tree: locally, nodes cannot even distinguish between a path and a cycle [14]. To overcome this difficulty, system state is sometimes augmented with some additional information that allows nodes to decide locally the correctness of a global predicate. This is typically the case when checking the correctness of the output of a distributed program: in addition to its required output, each node can compute a local *label* used to verify the correctness of the global output. For instance, in an algorithm computing a spanning tree (i.e., the output at each node v is the identity of its parent in the tree), it is sufficient that every node additionally computes the identity of the root $r(v)$ and the distance from v to $r(v)$ in the tree [7, 22].

The notion of distributed verification as outlined above is formalized by the concept of *proof-labeling scheme*, introduced in [30]. A proof-labeling scheme for a predicate $\mathcal{P}$ consists of a *prover* and a *verifier*. The prover is an oracle which, for every legal state of the network, assigns a *label* $\ell(v)$ to every node v. The verifier is a distributed algorithm whose input, at each node v, consists of the local state of v, its label $\ell(v)$, and the label $\ell(w)$ of each of its neighbors w. The output of the verifier, at each node, is a a boolean value. The proof-labeling scheme is called *correct for predicate* $\mathcal{P}$ if the following two conditions hold: (1) For every legal state, the prover assigns labels to the nodes such that the verifier returns TRUE at every node; (2) For every illegal state, and for every label assignment to the nodes, the verifier returns FALSE in at least one node.

The complexity measure used in evaluating the quality of a proof-labeling scheme is the *label size*. This measure captures the ongoing communication complexity of the scheme: In order to verify that the predicate holds, it is assumed that periodically, nodes transmit their labels to their neighbors, and each node runs the local verification procedure on the complete neighborhood's label set. Some predicates can be verified using labels whose sizes are of the same order of magnitude as the size of a node ID, like, e.g., $O(\log n)$-bit labels for spanning tree in n-node networks. However, some predicates require labels whose sizes are significantly larger than the size of an ID, like, e.g., $\Omega(\log^2 n)$ bits for minimum-weight spanning tree (MST) [28], and even $\Omega(n^2)$ bits for Symmetry (i.e., the existence of a non-trivial automorphism) [20]. Such a high overhead may be considered prohibitively expensive.

The main objective of the paper is to study the effect of randomization on the communication complexity of verification. For this purpose, we present and investigate *randomized* proof-labeling schemes. The idea is as follows. Every node v has a label $\ell(v)$. Using $\ell(v)$ and some coin tosses, node v computes a randomized certificate for each of its neighbors and sends it over. Given the certificates received from all neighbors, and its local label $\ell(v)$, node v executes a local deterministic verification procedure that returns TRUE or FALSE such that the following holds, for some arbitrarily small constant $\epsilon \in (0, \frac{1}{2})$ fixed a priori: (1) For every legal state, the prover assigns labels to the nodes such that the probability that the verifier returns TRUE at all nodes is at least $1 - \epsilon$, and (2) For every illegal state, and for every label assignment to the nodes, the probability that the verifier returns FALSE in at least one node is at least $1 - \epsilon$. We also consider the stronger 1-sided error scenario, in which the scheme is not allowed to err on legal instances, that is, in one-sided error schemes (2) remains the same, but we replace (1) with the requirement that for every legal state, the prover assigns labels to the nodes such that the verifier returns TRUE at all nodes with probability 1. We note that schemes with one-sided error may be preferable to those with two-sided errors if false alarms (i.e., a detection of error in a perfectly legal state) have very high cost. (All schemes we present in this paper have one-sided error.)

Intuitively, in the framework of checking the validity of outputs produced by an algorithm that is not completely trustworthy, or whose outputs may be corrupted somehow, a randomized proof-labeling scheme can be used to make sure that if the output is incorrect, then collectively, the nodes will be able to detect it. For that purpose, in addition to the output required by some problem specification (e.g., select an edge subset which forms an MST), the algorithms must also produce a label at each node, from which certificates are generated randomly. After exchanging the certificates between all pairs of neighbors, the randomized proof-labeling scheme is guaranteed (probabilistically) to return TRUE everywhere if and only if the outputs are correct w.r.t. the predicate describing the problem specification. This guarantee holds even in the face of adversarial labels in the following sense: if the outputs are incorrect, then there is no label assignment that guarantees (probabilistically) that the certificates will be accepted everywhere, while if the outputs are correct, and the labels are according to the specification, then with good probability, all local verification procedures will accept. If some node v returns FALSE (which occurs with small—0 in the one-sided case—probability on a legal instance, but with high probability on an illegal instance), then v may launch a recovery procedure or restart the algorithm.

Let us make a few remarks before summarizing our main results. First, observe that a randomized proof-labeling scheme does not exchange the labels between the nodes, but only the randomized certificates. It is thus expected that the communication complexity of randomized proof-labeling schemes be significantly reduced compared to the communication complexity of deterministic ones. Second, the exact value of the probability parameter ϵ is typically not very important. In particular, the correctness of all the schemes in this paper is oblivious to ϵ, in the sense that ϵ can be chosen as close to 0 as desired by straightforward adjustments of our schemes. In term of complexity, when ϵ is constant, the dependence on ϵ is confined to constant factors hidden by our asymptotic notation. Therefore, for the sake of concreteness, we present our schemes with success guarantee at least $\frac{2}{3}$ (i.e., for $\epsilon = \frac{1}{3}$).

Our Contributions.

In this paper we introduce and formalize the concept of *randomized* proof-labeling as outlined above. For this model we give the following universal result. Consider an n-node system, where each node has a k-bit state (a node state includes its identity, input, output and maybe more). We show that every predicate over such system has 1-sided error randomized proof-labeling scheme with certificates of $O(\log n + \log k)$ bits. Hence, assuming that states of nodes require $\text{poly}(n)$ bits to describe, our scheme insures that by exchanging only $O(\log n)$ bits, every (sequentially decidable) property can be probabilistically verified with success probability at least $\frac{2}{3}$. (In contrast, there are natural properties that require the exchange of $\omega(\log n)$ bits to be verified deterministically). Our universal logarithmic bound is tight, as we show by exhibiting a property for which any randomized proof-labeling scheme requires certificates of $\Omega(\log n + \log k)$ bits to verify. Our next generic constructions provides, by using randomization, an exponential improvement over deterministic schemes. More precisely, we prove that for any property that can be verified by a deterministic proof-labeling scheme using κ-bit messages, there is a randomized proof-labeling scheme using only $O(\log \kappa)$-bit messages. A nice corollary of this result is that there exists a randomized proof-labeling scheme for MST using $O(\log \log n)$-bit certificates.

In addition, we provide a general lower bound technique for the certificate size of a proof-labeling scheme. This technique is based on the novel notion called *graph crosses*. It applies to both deterministic and probabilistic schemes, generalizing known lower bounds for specific proof-labeling schemes. The probabilistic version applies to any 1-sided error randomized proof-labeling scheme. It also applies to 2-sided error schemes, under some additional constraints regarding the way the certificates are randomly generated by the nodes. Under these assumptions, the upper bound $O(\log \log n)$ bits on the certificate size for MST is tight.

Finally, we consider a few natural problems and properties and provide randomized proof-labeling schemes for them, with optimal or close-to-optimal certificate sizes. In particular, we show that the randomized verification complexity of acyclicity (and hence also a lower bound for MST), as well as the verification complexity of biconnectivity, is $\Theta(\log \log n)$. We also consider the randomized verification complexity of two versions of the longest cycle problem. For the question of deciding whether there is a cycle of length at least c, we give an upper bound of $O(\log \log n)$ and a lower bound of $\Omega(\log \log c)$. For the complementary question ("yes" if all cycles are smaller than c), we show that $\Omega(\log \frac{n}{c})$ and of $\Omega(\log \log \frac{n}{c})$ bits are required for certificates in deterministic and randomized proof-labeling schemes, respectively.

Related Work.

Labeling schemes were studied extensively in the past, in two directions: *informative labeling schemes*, and *proof-labeling schemes*.

In the framework of informative labeling schemes, one is given a function f on pairs (or sets) of nodes, and $(\mathcal{M}, \mathcal{D})$ is an f-labeling scheme for a graph family $\mathcal{F}$ if $\mathcal{M}$, the *marker*, is an algorithm that, given a graph $G = (V, E)$ in $\mathcal{F}$, assigns a label $\ell(v)$ to every $v \in V$, and $\mathcal{D}$, the *decoder*, is an algorithm that satisfies $\mathcal{D}(\ell(u), \ell(v)) = f(u, v)$ for every pair of nodes in G. The main performance criterion is the size of the labels, which should be as small as possible. Since the seminal work of Kannan, Naor, and Rudich [23] on adjacency-labeling, there have been quite a lot of investigations, for a large set of functions f, including the following: adjacency [4, 23], distance [2, 9, 18, 17, 19, 24, 26, 34, 36], connectivity and flow [25, 27], nearest common ancestor [3, 35], etc. In particular, the notion of universal f-matrices for several functions f was introduced in [31], and used to construct upper and lower bounds on the sizes of the corresponding f-labeling schemes. Most investigations related to the design of compact routing tables can also be placed in the framework of informative labeling. This includes, e.g., the papers [11, 12, 37] on routing in trees.

Proof-labeling schemes are not dealing with computing a function, but with verifying a proof that the given instance satisfies some given boolean predicate. This proof is distributed among the nodes under the form of labels assigned to the node by a *prover* which assigns a label to every node. The *verifier* is a distributed algorithm in charge of verifying the distributed proof. As for informative labeling scheme, the main performance criterion is the size of the labels. This concept was introduced by Korman, Kutten, and Peleg in [30]. Among the results that were presented in this paper, it is worth mentioning the $\Theta(\log n)$ bit bound on the verification complexity of acyclicity and the upper bound $O(\log^2 n + \log n \log W)$ bits for MST, where W is the maximal possible weight of an edge. This bound was improved to $O(\log n \log W)$ bits in [28], where a matching lower bound of $\Omega(\log n \log W)$ bits is established for $W > \log n$. It is worth noticing that proof-labeling schemes are closely related to self stabilizing algorithms, that is, algorithms which have to periodically verify the correctness of the system state. See, e.g., [1] where the notion of local detection was introduced and used for designing a self stabilizing protocol constructing a spanning tree, and [29] for another example of using distributed local verification of proofs for the design of self stabilizing algorithms. The reader interested in the tight connections between proof-labeling schemes and self-stabilization is referred to the recent paper [8]. Proof-labeling schemes, where nodes may communicate at distance greater than 1, i.e., may take their individual decision based on the labels of the nodes in their vicinity at distance $t > 1$, was recently studied in [20]. Finally, distributed decision and verification processes in which the global interpretation of the collection of individual outputs is not restricted to be the logical conjunction of these outputs has been studied in [5, 6].

To our knowledge, there are very few papers dealing with randomization in the framework of informative labeling schemes, or proof-labeling schemes. Randomized informative schemes for trees, including randomized schemes for adjacency and ancestry, were presented in [13]. The crucial difference between our work and this latter work is the following. In our approach, a label is stored at every node, based on which each node produces a random certificate, and we are interested in minimizing the size of the certificates. Instead, the approach in [13] is more restrictive, as each node label is randomly computed and stored at each node, and the measure is the size of these labels. More recently, [14] provided a framework that could be used for setting up a complexity theory for local distributed computing. This framework includes several complexity classes, including NLD (for non-deterministic local decision) and BPNLD (for bounded probability NLD). The former is a generalization of proof-labeling schemes (with slight differences, including the fact that certificates should be independent of the IDs), and the latter is a randomized version of the former. Nevertheless, in both cases, the emphasis was put on the existence of a proof, and not on its size. In fact, it is proved that all (decidable) languages are in BPNLD, but the proof of this result involves labels as large as poly(n) bits. In contrast, the randomized proof-labeling schemes described in this paper involve labels of poly-logarithmic size.

The conceptual difference between our approach and the approach of [13, 14] is significant. In [13, 14], the prover is randomized, while the verifier is deterministic, and the measure is *space complexity* (the size of the labels). Instead, in this paper, the randomization part is also delegated to the verifier, and the measure is *communication complexity* (the size of the exchanged certificates).

2. MODEL AND DEFINITIONS

2.1 Computational Framework

A network is modeled as a connected graph $G = (V, E)$, without self-loops or multiple edges. Recall that two graphs $G_1 = (V_1, E_1)$ and $G_2 = (V_2, E_2)$ are *isomorphic* if there exists a bijection $\sigma : V_1 \to V_2$ such that: $\{u, v\} \in E_1 \iff \{\sigma(u), \sigma(v)\} \in E_2$. We assume that the edges incident to a node v are numbered in sequence $1, \dots, \deg(v)$, where $\deg(v)$ is the *degree* of v. The number of e at v is the *port number* of e at v. An edge may have different port numbers on its two endpoints.

In a *configuration* G_s, we are given a graph $G = (V, E)$, a *state* space S, and a state assignment function $s : V \to S$. The state of a node v, denoted $s(v)$, includes all local input to v. In particular, the state may include the node identity $\mathrm{Id}(v)$ (if the network is not anonymous) and weights of its incident edges (for edge-weighted networks). The state of v may also include other data like, e.g., the result of an algorithm.

Mechanisms such as proof-labeling schemes involve simple distributed algorithms, acting in one synchronous communication round and computation, in which every node sends a value to each of its neighbors, and, upon reception of the values from all its neighbors, every node computes an output. In the context of proof-labeling schemes, this output is either TRUE or FALSE.

Unless specified otherwise, we always assume non-anonymous networks, i.e., every node v is provided with an identity $\mathrm{Id}(v)$, that is part of the state of v. All identities in the same network are pairwise distinct. Nevertheless, the definition of proof-labeling schemes does not need the presence of identities.

2.2 Deterministic and Randomized Proof-Labeling Schemes

We first recall the definition of deterministic proof-labeling schemes (abbreviated PLS henceforth), as introduced in [30]. Given a family $\mathcal{F}$ of configurations, and a boolean predicate $\mathcal{P}$ over $\mathcal{F}$, a PLS for $(\mathcal{F}, \mathcal{P})$ is a mechanism for deciding $\mathcal{P}(G_s)$ for every $G_s \in \mathcal{F}$. A PLS consists of two components: a *prover* **p**, and a *verifier* **v**. The prover is an oracle which, given any configuration $G_s \in \mathcal{F}$, assigns a bit string $\ell(v)$ to every node v, called the *label* of v. The verifier is a decentralized algorithm running concurrently at every node. At each node v, it takes as input the state $s(v)$ of v, its label $\ell(v)$ and the labels of all its neighbors, i.e., the ordered set $\{\ell(w_i) \mid i = 1, \dots, \deg(v)\}$ where w_i is the neighbor reachable from v through the edge with port number i. The verifier **v** at each node outputs a boolean. If the outputs are TRUE at all nodes, **v** is said to *accept* the configuration, and otherwise (i.e., **v** outputs FALSE in at least one node) **v** is said to *reject* the configuration. For correctness, a proof-labeling scheme $(\mathbf{p}, \mathbf{v})$ for $(\mathcal{F}, \mathcal{P})$ must satisfy the following requirements, for every $G_s \in \mathcal{F}$:

- If $\mathcal{P}(G_s) = \text{TRUE}$ then, using the labels assigned by $\mathbf{p}$, the verifier $\mathbf{v}$ accepts G_s.
- If $\mathcal{P}(G_s) = \text{FALSE}$ then, for every label assignment, the verifier $\mathbf{v}$ rejects G_s.

The *verification complexity* of a deterministic proof-labeling scheme $(\mathbf{p}, \mathbf{v})$, denoted by κ, is the maximal length of the labels assigned by the prover $\mathbf{p}$ on a legal configuration $G_s \in \mathcal{F}$ (i.e., a configuration satisfying $\mathcal{P}$).

In this paper we extend the above definition to *randomized proof labeling schemes* (RPLS). The idea is to allow randomization in the verification part of the scheme. Specifically, an RPLS is defined as follows. The goal and the prover in an RPLS remain exactly as defined for PLS. However, in an RPLS the verifier $\mathbf{v}$ has access to a source of independent random bits at each node. At node v, using the label $\ell(v)$ and the private random bits available at v, the verifier produces a random bit string, called *certificate*, for each of its neighbors. The random certificate of v for w_i, the neighbor reachable through port i, is denoted by $c_i(v)$. In an RPLS, *only the certificates are communicated for verification.* More precisely, the input of the verifier at node v consists of its state $s(v)$, its label $\ell(v)$, and all the certificates received from its neighbors, i.e., the collection $\{c_{p_i}(w_i),\ i = 1, \ldots, \deg(v)\}$ where w_i is the neighbor reachable from v through the edge e_i with port number i at v, and p_i is the port number of e_i at w_i. A randomized scheme $(\mathbf{p}, \mathbf{v})$ for $(\mathcal{F}, \mathcal{P})$ must satisfy the following requirements, for every $G_s \in \mathcal{F}$:

- If $\mathcal{P}(G_s) = \text{TRUE}$ then, using the labels assigned by $\mathbf{p}$, $\Pr[\mathbf{v} \text{ accepts } G_s] \geq p_{\text{accept}}$.
- If $\mathcal{P}(G_s) = \text{FALSE}$ then, for every label assignment, $\Pr[\mathbf{v} \text{ rejects } G_s] \geq p_{\text{reject}}$.

Following the sequential complexity classes RP and BPP (see, e.g., [33]), we define two flavors of RPLSs: in *one-sided error* RPLS, we have $p_{\text{accept}} = 1$ and $p_{\text{reject}} = \frac{1}{2}$; and in *two-sided error* RPLS, we have $p_{\text{accept}} = p_{\text{reject}} = \frac{2}{3}$.[1] Unless explicitly stated otherwise, in this paper we refer by RPLS to two-sided RPLS.

Clearly, RPLSs give weaker guarantees than deterministic PLSs. The main reason to prefer an RPLS over a PLS is the possible saving in verification complexity, defined next.

DEFINITION 2.1. *The* verification complexity *of a randomized proof-labeling scheme $(\mathbf{p}, \mathbf{v})$, denoted by κ, is the maximal length of the (random) certificates generated by the (randomized) verifier $\mathbf{v}$ based on the labels assigned to the nodes by the prover $\mathbf{p}$ on a legal configuration $G_s \in \mathcal{F}$ (i.e., a configuration satisfying $\mathcal{P}$).*

3. UNIVERSAL SCHEMES

In this section we show that in RPLS, one can save exponentially in the verification complexity w.r.t. PLS. Using this result, we derive a universal RPLS and prove that there is no better one. We start with a reduction from RPLS to PLS.

THEOREM 3.1. *Let $\mathcal{F}$ be a family of configurations, and let $\mathcal{P}$ be a boolean predicate over $\mathcal{F}$. If there is a PLS for $(\mathcal{F}, \mathcal{P})$ with verification complexity κ, then there is a one-sided RPLS for $(\mathcal{F}, \mathcal{P})$ with verification complexity $O(\log \kappa)$.*

The proof of this theorem uses a result about (2-party) communication complexity. In a 2-party communication complexity problem there are two players, Alice and Bob. Alice receives as input a λ-bit string x and Bob receives another λ-bit string y. The goal is for Alice and Bob to compute a certain function $f(x, y)$ by exchanging the smallest possible number of bits. For any two λ-bit strings x and y, let $\text{EQ}(x, y)$ denote the equality predicate. The following fact is well known (see [32]).

LEMMA 3.2. *The randomized communication complexity of deciding EQ over λ-bit strings is $\Theta(\log \lambda)$.*

This lemma implies the following upper bound.

LEMMA 3.3 (BASED ON [32]). *There exists a 2-party randomized protocol π for EQ over λ-bit strings, in which one side sends $O(\log \lambda)$ bits, and the other side then decides the outcome, such that for any input strings a, b we have that $\Pr[\pi(a, b) = \text{TRUE} \mid a = b] = 1$ and $\Pr[\pi(a, b) = \text{FALSE} \mid a \neq b] > 2/3$.*

Proof of Theorem 3.1: Let $(\mathbf{p}, \mathbf{v})$ be a proof-labeling scheme for $(\mathcal{F}, \mathcal{P})$ with verification complexity κ. We construct a randomized proof-labeling scheme $(\mathbf{p}', \mathbf{v}')$ for $(\mathcal{F}, \mathcal{P})$ as follows. Let $G_s \in \mathcal{F}$ be a configuration satisfying predicate $\mathcal{P}$. For every node v, the prover $\mathbf{p}'$ sets the label of v as the vector of labels

$$\ell'(v) = \big(\ell(v), \ell(w_1), \ldots, \ell(w_d)\big)$$

where $w_1, \ldots, w_d$ are the $d = \deg(v)$ neighbors of v in G ordered by port number, and $\ell(\cdot)$ is the label assignment for G_s as provided by $\mathbf{p}$. Next, let π be the protocol for EQ from Lemma 3.3. Recall that in π, there is a *sender* and a *decider*. The certificate sent by node v to each of its neighbors under $(\mathbf{p}', \mathbf{v}')$ is defined to be exactly the message sent by the "sender" under π on input $\ell(v)$. The decision of the local verifier $\mathbf{v}'$ is as follows. If the format of the local label is not as expected, the local verifier outputs FALSE immediately. Otherwise, given the received certificates, the local verifier runs the "decider" part of π for each neighbor. If any of these instances of π returns FALSE, then the local verifier returns FALSE. Otherwise, the complete label $\ell'(v)$ (which is a vector) is fed into the local deterministic verifier $\mathbf{v}$ (assumed to be given), and the output of $\mathbf{v}'$ will be in this case the output of $\mathbf{v}(\ell'(v))$. This concludes the construction of $(\mathbf{p}', \mathbf{v}')$.

The logarithmic verification complexity of $(\mathbf{p}', \mathbf{v}')$ follows directly from the construction and from Lemma 3.3. We now show correctness of the scheme. Suppose first that G_s satisfies the predicate. Then, with the labels assigned by $\mathbf{p}'$, we have that, for every node v, $\ell'(v) = \big(\ell(v), \ell(w_1), \ldots, \ell(w_d)\big)$, with the labels $\ell(\cdot)$ assigned by $\mathbf{p}$. Therefore, by Lemma 3.3 and by construction, π returns TRUE with probability 1 in all d instances run by v. It follows that $\mathbf{v}'$ applies $\mathbf{v}$ at node v on $\ell'(v)$, for which $\mathbf{v}$ returns TRUE at v. Hence, $\mathbf{v}'$ returns TRUE at v as well.

Suppose now that G_s does not satisfy the predicate. If any node v has a label that does not comply with the expected format, the verifier $\mathbf{v}'$ returns FALSE at v and we are done. So assume that every node v has a label of the form $\big(\ell_0^v, \ell_1^v, \ldots, \ell_d^v\big)$ where $d = \deg(v)$. We first note that if the labels are *consistent* in the sense that, for every node v and its ith neighbor w, $\ell_i^v = \ell_0^w$, then $\mathbf{v}'$ returns the value returned by $\mathbf{v}$, which must be FALSE at some node by correctness of $\mathbf{v}$. If the labels are not consistent in the above sense, then there is at least one pair of adjacent nodes $\{v, w\}$ such that w is the ith neighbor of v, and $\ell_i^v \neq \ell_0^w$. In this case, by Lemma 3.3, the local verifier at v outputs FALSE with probability at least $2/3$, as required. ∎

Next, we note the existence of a universal PLS construction, where the label of every node is a representation of the graph configuration, summarized in the following lemma.

[1] The choice of $1/2$ and $2/3$ is somewhat arbitrary. The idea is that we can boost the probability of correctness to $1 - \delta$ by repeating the verification procedure $O(\log(1/\delta))$ times independently and outputting the majority of outcomes.

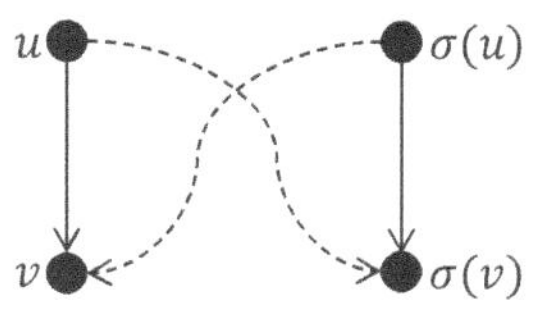

Figure 1: *Crossing two edges under an isomorphism σ. Solid edges are the edges of G, and dashed edged are the edges of $\sigma_{\bowtie}(G)$.*

LEMMA 3.4 ([20, 30]). *Let $\mathcal{F}$ be a family of configurations with states in S, and let $\mathcal{P}$ be a boolean predicate over $\mathcal{F}$. Assume that every state in S can be represented using $k = k(n)$ bits in n-node networks. There exists a PLS for $(\mathcal{F}, \mathcal{P})$ with verification complexity $O(nk + \min\{n^2, m \log n\})$, where m is the number of edges in the network.*

Combining Theorem 3.1 and Lemma 3.4 we obtain the following universal result for RPLSs.

COROLLARY 3.5. *Let $\mathcal{F}$ be a family of configurations with states in S, and let $\mathcal{P}$ be a boolean predicate over $\mathcal{F}$. Assume that every state in S can be represented using $k = k(n)$ bits in n-node networks. There exists a randomized proof-labeling scheme for $(\mathcal{F}, \mathcal{P})$ with verification complexity $O(\log n + \log k)$.*

The upper bound in Corollary 3.5 is tight, as stated below.

THEOREM 3.6. *For any function $k(n)$, there exist a family $\mathcal{F}$ of configurations with states on $k = k(n)$ bits in n-node graphs, and a predicate $\mathcal{P}$ over $\mathcal{F}$ such that any randomized proof-labeling scheme for $(\mathcal{F}, \mathcal{P})$ has verification complexity $\Omega(\log n + \log k)$.*

The proof, which is omitted from this extended abstract, is by reduction from 2-party EQ. The idea is that for any function $k(n)$, we can show a family $\mathcal{F}$ of configurations with states on $k = k(n)$ bits in n-node graphs, and a predicate $\mathcal{P}$ over $\mathcal{F}$ such that the following holds. Any randomized proof-labeling scheme for $(\mathcal{F}, \mathcal{P})$, with verification complexity κ, can be used to construct a 2-party communication protocol for EQ of n-bit strings and of k-bit strings, with error probability of at most $1/3$, using κ bits of communication. Then, from Lemma 3.2, we get the desired lower bound.

4. GENERIC LOWER BOUNDS

In this section we formalize a general tool that can be used to prove lower bounds for both deterministic and randomized proof-labeling schemes. The general idea was used many times in the past, most relevantly in [30].

4.1 A General Tool: Edge Crossing

We start with a technical definition, and then define our main concept.

DEFINITION 4.1. *Let $G = (V, E)$ be a graph and let $H_1 = (V_1, E_1)$ and $H_2 = (V_2, E_2)$ be two subgraphs of G. H_1 and H_2 are* independent *if and only if $V_1 \cap V_2 = \emptyset$ and $E \cap (V_1 \times V_2) = \emptyset$.*

The following definition is illustrated in Figure 1.

DEFINITION 4.2 (CROSSING). *Let $G = (V, E)$ be a graph, and let $H_1 = (V_1, E_1)$ and $H_2 = (V_2, E_2)$ be two independent isomorphic subgraphs of G with isomorphism $\sigma : V_1 \to V_2$. The* crossing *of G induced by σ, denoted by $\sigma_{\bowtie}(G)$, is the graph obtained from G by replacing every pair of edges $\{u, v\} \in E_1$ and $\{\sigma(u), \sigma(v)\} \in E_2$, by the pair $\{u, \sigma(v)\}$ and $\{\sigma(u), v\}$.*

Crossing can be very useful in proving lower bounds on the verification complexity of both deterministic and randomized proof labeling schemes. We start by showing the simpler case of deterministic PLSs.

PROPOSITION 4.3. *Let $(\mathbf{p}, \mathbf{v})$ be a deterministic PLS for $(\mathcal{F}, \mathcal{P})$ with verification complexity κ. Suppose that there is a configuration $G_s \in \mathcal{F}$ where G contains r pairwise independent isomorphic subgraphs $H_1, \dots, H_r$ with s edges each, and let $\sigma_i : H_1 \to H_i$ be a port-preserving isomorphism for $i \in \{1, \dots, r\}$. If $\kappa < \frac{\log r}{2s}$, then there are $1 \leq i < j \leq r$ such that G_s is accepted by $(\mathbf{p}, \mathbf{v})$ if and only if $(\sigma_j \circ \sigma_i^{-1})_{\bowtie}(G)_s$ is accepted by $(\mathbf{p}, \mathbf{v})$.*

Proof: Let G_s be a configuration as described in the statement. Assume that $\kappa < \frac{\log r}{2s}$, and consider a collection $\{\sigma_i : V(H_1) \to V(H_i), i = 1, \dots, r\}$ of r port-preserving isomorphisms. Order the nodes of H_1 arbitrarily. This order induces an order on the nodes of H_i thanks to σ_i. For every i, consider the bit-string L_i constructed by concatenating the labels given by $\mathbf{p}$ to the nodes of H_i, in the order induced by σ_i. We have $|L_i| < \log r$ for every i because $|V(H_i)| \leq 2s$, and thus there are less than r possible distinct L_i's in total. Therefore, by the pigeonhole principle, there are $i \neq j$ such that $L_i = L_j$. Define $\sigma = \sigma_j \circ \sigma_i^{-1}$, and consider the output of the verifier $\mathbf{v}$ in G_s and in $\sigma_{\bowtie}(G)_s$.

Suppose G_s is accepted by $(\mathbf{p}, \mathbf{v})$, i.e., with the labels provided by $\mathbf{p}$, the verifier $\mathbf{v}$ outputs TRUE at all nodes of G. Therefore, all nodes outside H_i and H_j also output TRUE in $\sigma_{\bowtie}(G)_s$. Now, let v be a node in H_i. Each neighbor w of v from H_i is replaced in $\sigma_{\bowtie}(G)_s$ by the node $\sigma(w)$ from H_j. Since w and $\sigma(w)$ have the same label, the verifier acts the same at v in both G_s and $\sigma_{\bowtie}(G)_s$. Therefore $\mathbf{v}$ outputs TRUE at every node of H_i in $\sigma_{\bowtie}(G)_s$. For the same reason, the verifier acts the same at every node v of H_j, in both G_s and $\sigma_{\bowtie}(G)_s$. Therefore, the verifier also outputs TRUE at all nodes in $\sigma_{\bowtie}(G)_s$, which implies that $\sigma_{\bowtie}(G)_s$ is accepted by $(\mathbf{p}, \mathbf{v})$.

Similarly, if G_s is rejected by $(\mathbf{p}, \mathbf{v})$ then, for any label-assignment to the nodes, the verifier $\mathbf{v}$ outputs FALSE in at least one node v of G. If this node v is not in H_i or H_j, then $\mathbf{v}$ also outputs FALSE at v in $\sigma_{\bowtie}(G)_s$. If this node v belongs to one of the two subgraph H_i or H_j, then, since the verifier acts the same at v in both G_s and $\sigma_{\bowtie}(G)_s$, $\mathbf{v}$ also outputs FALSE at this node in $\sigma_{\bowtie}(G)_s$, which implies that $\sigma_{\bowtie}(G)_s$ is rejected by $(\mathbf{p}, \mathbf{v})$. The proposition follows. ∎

Proposition 4.3 has the following useful consequence.

THEOREM 4.4. *Let $\mathcal{F}$ be a family of configurations, and let $\mathcal{P}$ be a boolean predicate over $\mathcal{F}$. Suppose that there is a configuration $G_s \in \mathcal{F}$ satisfying that (1) G contains as subgraphs r pairwise independent isomorphic copies $H_1, \dots, H_r$ with s edges each, and (2) there exist r port-preserving isomorphisms $\sigma_i : V(H_1) \to V(H_i)$ such that for every $i \neq j$, the isomorphism $\sigma^{ij} = \sigma_j \circ \sigma_i^{-1}$ satisfies $\mathcal{P}(G_s) \neq \mathcal{P}({\sigma^{ij}}_{\bowtie}(G)_s)$. Then the verification complexity of any proof-labeling scheme for $(\mathcal{F}, \mathcal{P})$ is $\Omega(\frac{\log r}{s})$.*

Remark: Note that Theorem 4.4 cannot yield lower bounds greater than $\Omega(\log n)$, because $r = O(n)$.

4.2 Generic Lower Bounds for Randomized Proof-Labeling Schemes

We now proceed with a generalization of Theorem 4.4 to randomized proof-labeling schemes. First we define *edge-independent* RPLSs.

DEFINITION 4.5. *An RPLS* $(\mathbf{p},\mathbf{v})$ *is called* edge-independent *if the verifier* $\mathbf{v}$ *uses independent random bits for each certificate* $c_i(v)$, *for all edges* e_i *incident to* v, $i = 1,\ldots,\deg(v)$.

We can prove the following result for edge-independent two-sided error RPLSs.

PROPOSITION 4.6. *Let* $(\mathbf{p},\mathbf{v})$ *be an edge-independent RPLS for* $(\mathcal{F},\mathcal{P})$ *with verification complexity* κ. *Assume that there is a configuration* $G_s \in \mathcal{F}$ *with* $\mathcal{P}(G_s) =$ TRUE *such that* G *contains* r *pairwise independent isomorphic subgraphs* $H_1,\ldots,H_r$ *with* s *edges each, and let* $\sigma_i : H_1 \to H_i$ *be a port-preserving isomorphism for each* $i \in \{1,\ldots,r\}$. *If* $\kappa < (\frac{1}{2s} - o(1)) \log\log r$, *then there are* $1 \le i < j \le r$ *such that* G_s *is accepted by* $(\mathbf{p},\mathbf{v})$ *if and only if* $(\sigma_j \circ \sigma_i^{-1})_{\bowtie}(G)_s$ *is accepted by* $(\mathbf{p},\mathbf{v})$.

Proof: We start the proof by a collection of technical preliminary results. Given a real number x and $0 < \epsilon \le 1$, we denote by $\lfloor x \rfloor_\epsilon$ the value of x rounded down to the closest integer multiple of ϵ, i.e., $\lfloor x \rfloor_\epsilon \stackrel{\text{def}}{=} \lfloor \frac{x}{\epsilon} \rfloor \epsilon$. Given a real function $f : X \to \mathbb{R}$ over a set X, and $\epsilon > 0$, we define the *ϵ-rounded* $f_\epsilon : X \to \mathbb{R}$ of f by $f_\epsilon(x) \stackrel{\text{def}}{=} \lfloor f(x) \rfloor_\epsilon$ for every $x \in X$.

We shall consider ϵ-rounded probability distributions. Note that an ϵ-rounded probability distribution is not necessarily a probability distribution, because it may not sum up to 1. However, it has the following probabilistic interpretation. Let X be a set, and let $\Pr$ and $\Pr'$ be two probability distributions over X. Then

$$\Pr_\epsilon = \Pr'_\epsilon \;\Rightarrow\; \forall Y \subseteq X, \left|\Pr[Y] - \Pr'[Y]\right| \le \epsilon |X|\,. \quad (1)$$

Indeed, if $\Pr_\epsilon[x] = \Pr'_\epsilon[x]$ for every $x \in X$, then we have that $\left|\Pr[x] - \Pr'[x]\right| < \epsilon$ for every x. Using the triangle inequality we thus get $\left|\Pr[Y] - \Pr'[Y]\right| \le \sum_{x \in Y} \left|\Pr[x] - \Pr'[x]\right| < \epsilon|Y| \le \epsilon|X|$.

The advantage of ϵ-rounded distributions is that there are not too many. Indeed, let X be a finite set, and let $\mathcal{D}$ be the set of all probability distributions over X. The number of distinct ϵ-rounded distributions over X is at most $2^{|X|}\epsilon^{-|X|}$, that is,

$$|\{\Pr_\epsilon \mid \Pr \in \mathcal{D}\}| \le (2/\epsilon)^{|X|}. \quad (2)$$

This is because the set of ϵ-rounded distributions is a subset of the functions from X to $\{\epsilon i, i = 0, 1\ldots, \lfloor 1/\epsilon \rfloor\}$, which implies that their number is at most $(1 + \frac{1}{\epsilon})^{|X|} \le 2^{|X|}\epsilon^{-|X|}$.

We now have all the ingredients we need to prove the proposition. Let G_s be a configuration and $\{\sigma_i\}_{i=1}^r$ be the isomorphisms as described in the proposition. Note that for any $i \ne j$, if G_s is labeled by $\mathbf{p}$ and the crossing with $\sigma = \sigma_j \circ \sigma_i^{-1}$ satisfies

$$\left|\Pr[\mathbf{v} \text{ accepts } G_s] - \Pr[\mathbf{v} \text{ accepts } \sigma_{\bowtie}(G)_s]\right| < \frac{1}{3}, \quad (3)$$

then G_s is accepted by $(\mathbf{p},\mathbf{v})$ if and only if $\sigma_{\bowtie}(G)_s$ is accepted by $(\mathbf{p},\mathbf{v})$. We prove that if $\kappa < (\frac{1}{2s} - o(1)) \log\log r$, then there exist $i \ne j$ that satisfy Eq. (3). We use a counting argument. Order the edges of H_1 arbitrarily, and obtain, using σ_i, an ordering for each H_i. Assume w.l.o.g. that all certificates are exactly κ bits long. Then, using the order we defined, there is a 1-1 correspondence between each $2\kappa s$ bit string and each particular choice of certificates communicated in any H_i. Let $\mathcal{D}$ denote the set of distributions over $2\kappa s$-long bit strings, and define

$$\epsilon = 1/(12s \cdot 2^{2s\kappa})\,.$$

Consider the set of distributions in $\mathcal{D}$, ϵ-rounded. Since there are at most $2^{2s\kappa}$ bit strings of length $2\kappa s$, from Eq. (2) we conclude that there are no more than $(2/\epsilon)^{(2^{2s\kappa})}$ such ϵ-rounded distributions. Let us now make the following technical observation. Let $\alpha \ge 1$, $\beta \ge 1$ and $\gamma \ge 2$ be such that $\log(\beta + \log\alpha) = o(\log\log\gamma)$. Then

$$\beta < (1 - o(1)) \log\log\gamma \;\Rightarrow\; \gamma > (\alpha 2^\beta)^{(2^\beta)}.$$

This follows from the fact that

$$\beta < \log\log\gamma - \log(\beta + \log\alpha) \iff 2^\beta(\beta + \log\alpha) < \log\gamma \iff (\alpha 2^\beta)^{(2^\beta)} < \gamma.$$

By setting $\alpha = 24s$ and $\beta = 2s\kappa$ we obtain that the number of ϵ-rounded distributions satisfies

$$(2/\epsilon)^{(2^{2s\kappa})} = \left(24s \cdot 2^{2s\kappa}\right)^{(2^{2s\kappa})} < r.$$

Therefore, by the pigeonhole principle, it must be the case that among $H_1,\ldots,H_r$ there are H_i and H_j, where $i \ne j$, with identical ϵ-rounded distributions over the certificates.

Now, let $\sigma = \sigma_j \circ \sigma_i^{-1}$. For any $u \in H_i$, we say that u and $\sigma(u) \in H_j$ are *siblings*. Consider running $\mathbf{v}$ on G_s and on $\sigma_{\bowtie}(G)_s$, where, in both cases, we assume that the correct labels are given to the nodes by prover $\mathbf{p}$ applied to G_s. This means that in both G_s and $\sigma_{\bowtie}(G)_s$, the distributions of certificates sent by sibling nodes are the same. However, the distributions of certificates *received* by sibling nodes may have changed (albeit only slightly, as we show next), due to crossing H_i with H_j.

To analyze $\mathbf{v}$ on G_s and $\sigma_{\bowtie}(G)_s$, we change the certificates sent in G_s to those sent in $\sigma_{\bowtie}(G)_s$ inductively, and show that each such modification results only in a small change in the probability of acceptance. We view $G = (V,E)$ as a symmetric directed graph, i.e., each edge $e = \{u,v\} \in E$ is viewed as two symmetric arcs (u,v) and (v,u). Let us order these arcs in G arbitrarily, and let $\mathcal{C}$ denote the set of certificate vectors $\vec{c}$ for which the verifier $\mathbf{v}$ accepts G_s, with coordinates ordered according to the fixed order of the arcs. Consider a node v in H_i, and one of its incoming arcs (u,v) in H_i. Let u' and v' in H_j be the respective siblings of u and v. Assume, w.l.o.g., that $(u,v) = e_1$. Let $\vec{c} \in \mathcal{C}$. The certificate sent to v by u along e_1 is therefore c_1. Let $\vec{c}_{-1}$ be the vector $\vec{c}$ with the first coordinate c_1 omitted, i.e., $\vec{c}_{-1}$ is one dimension less than $\vec{c}$. Denote by A the event where V sends $\vec{c}_{-1}$ on $E \setminus \{e_1\}$. Using the above notations, we have:

$$\begin{aligned}
&\Pr[\mathbf{v} \text{ accepts } G_s] \\
&\quad= \sum_{\vec{c} \in \mathcal{C}} \Pr[\text{nodes in } V \text{ send } \vec{c} \text{ on } E] && (4)\\
&\quad= \sum_{\vec{c} \in \mathcal{C}} \Big(\Pr[u \text{ sends } c_1 \text{ on } e_1] \cdot \Pr[A]\Big) && (5)\\
&\quad> \sum_{\vec{c} \in \mathcal{C}} \Big(\big(\Pr[u' \text{ sends } c_1 \text{ on } (u',v')] - \epsilon\big) \cdot \Pr[A]\Big) && (6)
\end{aligned}$$

Eq. (4) is by definitions. Eq. (5) follows from the independence of c_1 from $\vec{c}_{-1}$ by our assumption of edge independence of $\mathbf{v}$. Eq. (6) follows from Eq. (1) since u and u' have the same ϵ-rounded distribution over their certificates. Let G'_s be the virtual labeled configuration consisting of G_s labeled by $\mathbf{p}$ but where the certificate distribution sent by u along e_1 is changed to the distribution of certificates sent by u' along (u',v') in G_s. We get that

$$\begin{aligned}
\Pr[\mathbf{v} \text{ accepts } G_s] &> \Pr[\mathbf{v} \text{ accepts } G'_s] - \epsilon \sum_{\vec{c} \in \mathcal{C}} \Pr[A] && (7)\\
&\ge \Pr[\mathbf{v} \text{ accepts } G'_s] - \epsilon\, 2^\kappa && (8)
\end{aligned}$$

Eq. (7) is by definition of G'_s, and Eq. (8) follows from the observation that the second sum in Eq. (7) is at most 2^κ since the number of distinct c_1 values is at most 2^κ, and, for any fixed certificate value γ,

$$\sum_{\vec{c}\in\mathcal{C},c_1=\gamma} \Pr[V \text{ sends } \vec{c}_{-1} \text{ on } E\setminus\{e_1\}] \le 1.$$

We repeat the same process for the certificate sent along another arc (a,b) of H_i, resulting in a virtual configuration G''_s in which we replace the distribution of the certificates sent by a to b by the distribution of the certificates sent by a' to b', where a' and b' are the respective siblings of a and b in H_j. Again, we get

$$\Pr[\mathbf{v} \text{ accepts } G'_s] > \Pr[\mathbf{v} \text{ accepts } G''_s] - \epsilon 2^\kappa.$$

By repeating the process $4s$ times, once for every arc in H_i and in H_j, we eventually get

$$\Pr[\mathbf{v} \text{ accepts } G_s] > \Pr[\mathbf{v} \text{ accepts } \sigma_{\bowtie}(G)_s] - 4\epsilon s 2^\kappa.$$

Moreover, by switching the roles of G_s and $\sigma_{\bowtie}(G)_s$ in the analysis, we also get that,

$$\Pr[\mathbf{v} \text{ accepts } \sigma_{\bowtie}(G)_s] > \Pr[\mathbf{v} \text{ accepts } G_s] - 4\epsilon s 2^\kappa.$$

I.e., $\Pr[\mathbf{v}$ accepts $\sigma_{\bowtie}(G)_s]$ and $\Pr[\mathbf{v}$ accepts $G_s]$ differ by less than $\pm 4\epsilon s 2^\kappa$. By the choice of ϵ, we conclude that

$$\Big|\Pr[\mathbf{v} \text{ accepts } G_s] - \Pr[\mathbf{v} \text{ accepts } \sigma_{\bowtie}(G)_s]\Big| < \frac{1}{3},$$

which completes the proof. ∎

The following corollary of Proposition 4.6 is the way we use to bound the verification complexity of two-sided error, edge independent RPLSs.

THEOREM 4.7. *Let $\mathcal{F}$ be a family of configurations, and let $\mathcal{P}$ be a boolean predicate over $\mathcal{F}$. If there is a configuration $G_s \in \mathcal{F}$ satisfying that (1) G contains r pairwise independent isomorphic subgraphs $H_1,\ldots,H_r$ with s edges each, and (2) there exist r port-preserving isomorphisms $\sigma_i : V(H_1) \to V(H_i)$ such that $\mathcal{P}(G_s) \ne \mathcal{P}(\sigma_{\bowtie}(G)_s)$ for every isomorphism $\sigma = \sigma_j \circ \sigma_i^{-1}$ between H_i and H_j, for $1 \le i \ne j \le r$, then the verification complexity of any edge-independent RPLS for $(\mathcal{F},\mathcal{P})$ is $\Omega(\frac{\log\log r}{s})$.*

Again, we note that since $r = O(n)$, Theorem 4.7 cannot be used to prove lower bounds greater than $\Omega(\log\log n)$.

Lower bounds for one-sided RPLSs.

We can replace the assumption of edge-independent RPLS in Theorem 4.7 by the requirement that the RPLS is *one sided* and obtain essentially the same lower bound. Recall that in one-sided RPLS we insist that if $\mathcal{P}(G_s) =$ TRUE, then the verifier $\mathbf{v}$ must accept *always*, i.e., with probability 1. For this case we have the following proposition, whose proof is much simpler.

PROPOSITION 4.8. *Let $(\mathbf{p},\mathbf{v})$ be a one-sided RPLS for $(\mathcal{F},\mathcal{P})$ with verification complexity κ. Assume that there is a configuration $G_s \in \mathcal{F}$ with $\mathcal{P}(G_s) =$ TRUE such that G contains r pairwise independent isomorphic subgraphs $H_1,\ldots,H_r$ with s edges each, and let $\sigma_i : H_1 \to H_i$ be a port-preserving isomorphism for each $1 \le i \le r$. If for any isomorphism $\sigma^{ij} = \sigma_j \circ \sigma_i^{-1}$ we have that $\mathcal{P}(\sigma_{\bowtie}(G)_s) =$ FALSE, then $\kappa \ge \frac{1}{2s}\log\log r$.*

Proof: Fix G_s as in the statement, and let $(\mathbf{p},\mathbf{v})$ be a one-sided RPLS for $(\mathcal{F},\mathcal{P})$. Assume w.l.o.g. that all certificates under $(\mathbf{p},\mathbf{v})$ have length exactly κ. For each edge $e=\{u,v\}$, let $x(u,v)$ denote the support of the certificates sent over e by u, i.e., all bit strings of length κ with positive probability to be sent from u to v under G_s and $(\mathbf{p},\mathbf{v})$. Since there are κ bits in each certificate, the number of distinct certificates is at most 2^κ, and hence the number of distinct supports is $2^{(2^\kappa)}$. Ordering the nodes of H_1 somehow and using the order induced by the port-preserving isomorphisms, we can represent each specific setting of the $2s$ certificates sent over the edges of H_i as a $2s\kappa$-long bit string. Now, if $\kappa < \frac{1}{2s}\log\log r$, then $2^{(2^{2s\kappa})} < r$, and hence, by the pigeonhole principle, there are $1 \le i < j \le r$ such that the supports of all the $2s$ respective (directed) edges in H_i and H_j are identical. Define $\sigma = \sigma_j \circ \sigma_i^{-1}$, and let $u' = \sigma(u)$ for some node u in H_i. Let v be a neighbor of u in H_i and let $v' = \sigma(v)$.

Fix an arbitrary global certificate $\underline{c}$ assignment (assigning a certificate to each direction of each edge of G) that can be generated in G_s by $(\mathbf{p},\mathbf{v})$ with positive probability. Note that since $\mathcal{P}(G_s) =$ TRUE and the RPLS is one sided, and since the probability of generating $\underline{c}$ is strictly positive, it must be the case that under $\underline{c}$, the verifier accepts at all nodes (deterministically). Now, let c_1 denote the coordinate of (u,v) in $\underline{c}$, i.e., the certificate sent by u to v in $\underline{c}$. Similarly let c_2 denote the certificate sent by u' to v' in $\underline{c}$. Let $\underline{c}'$ denote the global certificate obtained from $\underline{c}$ by switching c_1 and c_2, i.e., under $\underline{c}'$, u sends c_1 to v' and u' sends c_2 to v' (cf. Figure 1).

We claim that the verifier $\mathbf{v}$ accepts at all nodes under $\underline{c}'$. To see that, note that since $\mathcal{P}(G_s) =$ TRUE, it must be the case (by the independence of certificates received at a node, given the labels) that *any* certificate in $x(u',v')$ sent to v' results in the verifier $\mathbf{v}$ at v' outputting TRUE: otherwise, there will be a non-zero probability that $\mathbf{v}$ rejects at v', resulting in rejecting a "yes" instance. Therefore, the fact that $x(u,v) = x(u',v')$ (by our choice) necessarily implies that if v' receives $c_1 \in x(u,v) = x(u',v')$, the verifier $\mathbf{v}$ at v' outputs TRUE. Similarly for v accepting c_2.

Continuing inductively in this fashion we switch the certificates edge by edge, and arrive at the conclusion that the verifier $\mathbf{v}$ accepts $\sigma_{\bowtie}(G)_s$. Moreover, since we can apply the switching procedure described above to *any* legal certificate assignment $\underline{c}$ for G_s, we have that if $\kappa < \frac{1}{2s}\log\log r$, then $\sigma_{\bowtie}(G)_s$ is accepted by the RPLS with probability 1, contradicting our assumption that $\mathcal{P}(\sigma_{\bowtie}(G)_s) =$ FALSE and the requirement that a one-sided RPLS rejects a "no" instance with probability at least $\frac{1}{2}$. ∎

We note that all the upper bounds we derive in Section 5 are both edge-independent and one-sided.

5. VERIFICATION COMPLEXITY OF SOME SPECIFIC PREDICATES

We now bound, from above and from below, the deterministic and randomized verification complexity of a few specific problems using the tools developed in Sections 3 and 4. We study three important problems of independent interest. Each of these problems has received attention in the framework of (deterministic) proof-labeling schemes, as well as in other frameworks like distributed algorithm design, property testing, etc. We note that all RPLSs constructed in this section are edge-independent and one-sided, and that all lower bounds here are for RPLSs which are either edge independent or one-sided.

In the following, let $\mathcal{F}_{con}$ be the family of all connected graphs, and let $G_e\{x,y\}$ denote the graph over the set of nodes $\{x,y\}$ and an edge connecting x and y.

5.1 Minimum-Weight Spanning Tree (MST)

Recall that a Minimum-weight Spanning Tree (MST) of a weighted n-node graph G is a spanning tree of G whose sum of all its edge-weights is minimum among all spanning trees of G. In this setting, we assume that every node is aware of the weights of its incident edges (i.e., these weights, indexed by port numbers, are part of its state).

THEOREM 5.1. *The randomized verification complexity of* $(\mathcal{F}_{con}, MST)$ *is* $\Theta(\log\log n)$.

Proof: The upper bound follows from combining Theorem 3.1 with the proof-labeling scheme for MST in [30], whose verification complexity is $O(\log^2 n)$ (assuming polynomial edge weights). For the lower bound, we will show that any randomized proof-labeling scheme for the much simpler predicate of *acyclicity* has verification complexities as stated. Let $\mathcal{F}$ be the family of graphs that consist of lines and cycles, i.e., if $G \in \mathcal{F}$ then G is a line or G is a cycle, where all edges have weight 1. Let $P = (u_1, u_2, \ldots, u_n)$ be the n-node path, with port numbers consistently ordered. We define $H_1, \ldots, H_r$, for $r = \lfloor \frac{n}{3} \rfloor - 1$, as follows. Let $H_1 = G_e\{u_1, u_2\}$. For $i = 2, \ldots, \lfloor \frac{n}{3} \rfloor - 1$, let $H_i = G_e\{u_{3i}, u_{3i+1}\}$, and $\sigma_i : V(H_1) \to V(H_i)$ satisfying $\sigma_i(u_1) = u_{3i}$ and $\sigma_i(u_2) = u_{3i+1}$. For any $1 \le i < j \le \lfloor \frac{n}{3} \rfloor - 1$, let $\sigma^{ij} = \sigma_j \circ \sigma_i^{-1}$. We get that $\sigma^{ij}{}_{\bowtie}(P)$ consists of removing edges $\{u_{3i}, u_{3i+1}\}$ and $\{u_{3j}, u_{3j+1}\}$ from P, and replacing them by $\{u_{3i}, u_{3j+1}\}$ and $\{u_{3j}, u_{3i+1}\}$, creating the cycle $C = (u_{3i+1}, u_{3i+2}, \ldots, u_{3j-1}, u_{3j})$. Note that $\sigma^{ij}{}_{\bowtie}(P) \notin \mathcal{F}$, but C is a connected component of $\sigma^{ij}{}_{\bowtie}(P)$ and $C \in \mathcal{F}$. Moreover, C is a cycle, i.e., not satisfying the predicate. Therefore, by Theorem 4.7, the verification complexity of $(\mathcal{F}, acyclicity)$ is $\Omega(\log\log n)$. Hence, since $\mathcal{F} \subset \mathcal{F}_{con}$, the verification complexity of $(\mathcal{F}_{con}, \text{MST})$ is $\Omega(\log\log n)$. ∎

5.2 Vertex Bi-Connectivity

A connected graph G is called vertex-biconnected if the result of removing any node from G is a connected graph.

In [30], the authors proved a $\Theta(\log n)$ bound on the deterministic verification complexity of the s-t connectivity problem. In this problem, given a connected graph $G = (V, E)$ and two specified nodes $s, t \in V$, the goal is for all nodes to agree on a natural number k, where k is the vertex connectivity between s and t in G. Note that this is not a decision problem as it was presented. Slightly modified, where k is a parameter of the problem, we obtain the problem s-t k-connectivity, where the goal is to decide whether the vertex connectivity between s and t is exactly k, and the $\Theta(\log n)$ bound still holds. This problem is closely related to vertex-biconnectivity, with the main differences that in the latter we consider the connectivity between *all* pairs of nodes and we only check whether it is at least 2. Let v2con denote the predicate of vertex-biconnectivity. We have the following result.

THEOREM 5.2. *The deterministic verification complexity of* $(\mathcal{F}_{con}, v2con)$ *is* $\Theta(\log n)$*, and its randomized verification complexity is* $\Theta(\log\log n)$.

Proof: The upper bounds follow from the observation that we can encode all relevant information used in the biconnectivity algorithm of Tarjan [21] using $O(\log n)$ bits. For the lower bounds, let G be a graph that consists of an n-node cycle, with port numbers consistently ordered, and additional edges from one node to all other nodes. (See Figure 2a for illustration). That is,
$G = (\{v_0, \ldots, v_{n-1}\}, E_c \cup E_0)$ where

$$E_c = \{\{v_i, v_{(i+1) \bmod n}\} \mid i = 0, \ldots, n-1\} \text{ and}$$
$$E_0 = \{\{v_0, v_j\} \mid j = 2, \ldots, n-2\}.$$

We have v2con$(G) = $ TRUE. Now, let $H_1 = G_e\{v_1, v_2\}$. For $i = 2, \ldots, \lfloor \frac{n}{3} \rfloor - 1$, let $H_i = G_e\{v_{3i}, v_{3i+1}\}$, and $\sigma_i : V(H_1) \to V(H_i)$ satisfying $\sigma_i(v_1) = v_{3i}$ and $\sigma_i(v_2) = v_{3i+1}$. For any $1 \le i < j \le \lfloor \frac{n}{3} \rfloor - 1$, let $\sigma^{ij} = \sigma_j \circ \sigma_i^{-1}$. We get that $\sigma^{ij}{}_{\bowtie}(G)$ consists of two disjoint cycles with some edges in E_0 between them, and v_0 is an articulation point. Therefore, v2con$(\sigma^{ij}{}_{\bowtie}(G)) = $ FALSE. Hence, the conditions of Theorems 4.4 and 4.7 are satisfied, and the lower bounds follow. ∎

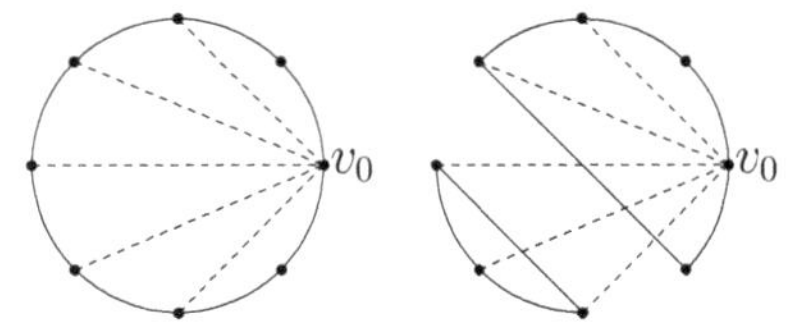

Figure 2: *(a): The graph G in the proof of Theorem 5.2, and restricted to nodes $\{v_0, \ldots, v_{c-1}\}$ in the proof of Theorem 5.4. Dashed edges are E_0. (b): The graph $\sigma^{ij}{}_{\bowtie}(G)$.*

Another result in [30] regarding connectivity is an upper bound of $O(k \log n)$ on the deterministic verification complexity of the k-flow problem. In this problem, the goal is to decide whether the value of the maximum flow between s and t is exactly k. Using Theorem 3.1 on that result, we get an upper bound of $O(\log k + \log\log n)$ on the randomized verification complexity of the k-flow problem.

5.3 Longest Cycle Size

For any positive integer c, we define the predicate "cycle-at-most-c" over graphs, which is true for G if and only if all simples cycle in G contain at most c nodes. We also define the predicate "cycle-at-least-c" over graphs, which is true for G if and only if there is a simple cycle in G with at least c nodes. Note that due to the asymmetry between acceptance and rejection in verification schemes, these are different questions despite their complementary nature. Similarly, note that for $c = n$, cycle-at-least-c is NP-complete and cycle-at-most-c is coNP-complete. We have the following upper bounds for cycle-at-least-c.

THEOREM 5.3. *The deterministic verification complexity of* $(\mathcal{F}_{con}$, *cycle-at-least-c*$)$ *is* $O(\log n)$*, and its randomized verification complexity is* $O(\log\log n)$.

The upper bounds follow by marking the cycle nodes using $O(\log n)$ bits (details omitted). The following theorem states lower bounds for cycle-at-least-c.

THEOREM 5.4. *The deterministic verification complexity of* $(\mathcal{F}_{con}$, *cycle-at-least-c*$)$ *is* $\Omega(\log c)$*, and its randomized verification complexity is* $\Omega(\log\log c)$.

Proof: Let G be a graph that consists of a c-node cycle, with port numbers consistently ordered, and additional edges from one to all other nodes of the graph (see Figure 2). Formally,

$$G = (\{v_0, \ldots, v_{n-1}\}, E_c \cup E_0)\text{ , where}$$
$$E_c = \{\{v_i, v_{(i+1) \bmod c}\} \mid i = 0, \ldots, c-1\}\text{ , and}$$
$$E_0 = \{\{v_0, v_j\} \mid j = 2, \ldots, n-1\, ,\, j \ne c-1\}\,.$$

Clearly, cycle-at-least-$c(G) = $ TRUE. Let $H_1 = G_e\{v_0, v_1\}$. For $i = 2, \ldots, \lfloor \frac{c}{3} \rfloor - 1$, let $H_i = G_e\{v_{3i}, v_{3i+1}\}$, and $\sigma_i : V(H_1) \to V(H_i)$ satisfying $\sigma_i(v_0) = v_{3i}$ and $\sigma_i(v_1) = v_{3i+1}$. For any $1 \le i < j \le \lfloor \frac{c}{3} \rfloor - 1$, let $\sigma^{ij} = \sigma_j \circ \sigma_i^{-1}$. We get that

$\sigma^{ij}{}_{\bowtie}(G)$ consists of two disjoint cycles of size strictly less than $c-1$ each, with some edges in E_0 between them. The size of every simple cycle in $\sigma^{ij}{}_{\bowtie}(G)$ is strictly less than c, and therefore, cycle-at-least-$c(\sigma^{ij}{}_{\bowtie}(G))$ = FALSE. Hence, the conditions of Theorems 4.4 and 4.7 are satisfied, and the lower bounds follow. ∎

The lower bound in Theorem 5.4 shows the hardness of distinguishing between graphs which contain a cycle of length c and ones which contain only cycles of length up to $c-1$. We now present an alternative technique, which shows that this lower bound holds also in the case where the question is to distinguish between graphs with a cycle of size n and graphs where all cycles are strictly smaller than c. Formally, let $\mathcal{F} = \mathcal{F}_1 \cup \mathcal{F}_2$, where $\mathcal{F}_1$ is the family of all connected graphs over $n \geq c$ nodes that contains an n-node cycle, and $\mathcal{F}_2$ is the family of all connected graphs over $n \geq c$ nodes where all cycles have size at most $c-1$.

THEOREM 5.5. *The deterministic verification complexity of* $(\mathcal{F}$, *cycle-at-least-c*$)$ *is* $\Omega(\log c)$.

Proof: Let G be as described in the lower bound part of the proof of Theorem 5.2 (see Figure 2a), where $n \geq c$. This graph satisfies $G \in \mathcal{F}$ and cycle-at-least-$c(G)$ = TRUE. Let $(\mathbf{p}, \mathbf{v})$ be a proof-labeling scheme for cycle-at-least-c over $\mathcal{F}$. Assume, for the purpose of contradiction, that the verification complexity of that scheme is less than $\frac{1}{2}\log(\lfloor\frac{c-1}{3}\rfloor)$. Let $\{H_1, \ldots, H_r\}$, for $r = \lfloor\frac{c-1}{3}\rfloor$, be a set of pairwise independent subgraphs, each consists of exactly one cycle edge and its two endpoints. This set exists since $n \geq c-1$. For each edge, there are less than $\log(\lfloor\frac{c-1}{3}\rfloor)$ bits in the sequence of both labels of the extremities of the edge. Hence, there are less than $\lfloor\frac{c-1}{3}\rfloor$ possible sequences. Therefore, by the pigeonhole principle, there are two independent cycle edges, say e_1 and e_2, that have exactly the same labels. Recall that the port numbers of the cycle edges are consistently ordered. Hence, for the corresponding isomorphism, $\sigma_{\bowtie}(G)$ consists of two disjoint cycles of size strictly less than n each, with only edges in E_0 between them. Note that possibly $\sigma_{\bowtie}(G) \notin \mathcal{F}$. We apply this crossing inductively as long as there is a cycle of size at least $c-1$. This process terminates when we eventually get at a graph G' which consists of a set $\mathcal{C}$ of disjoint cycles, all of size less than $c-1$, with only edges in E_0 connecting them (see Figure 2b). Note that at most two E_0 edges can participate in any simple cycle in G'. Since there are no other connections between the cycles in $\mathcal{C}$, both edges in E_0 have to be connected to the same cycle in $\mathcal{C}$. Therefore, a simple cycle of maximum length in G' is a simple cycle of maximum length in $\mathcal{C}$, with two edges from E_0 instead of just one, and its size is strictly less than c. Hence, $G' \in \mathcal{F}$ and cycle-at-least-$c(G')$ = FALSE. On the other hand, the verifier accepts G', a contradiction. This concludes the proof of the theorem. ∎

Finally, consider now the problem of deciding the predicate cycle-at-most-c. We note that it is co-NP hard, because for $c = n-1$, cycle-at-most-c is the complement of Hamiltonian Cycle. Observe that a proof-labeling scheme for $(\mathcal{F}_{con}$, cycle-at-most-$c)$, with polynomial verification complexity and polynomial computation at each node can be translated into a sequential verifiable proof of polynomial size, and hence the existence of such a PLS would imply that NP = co-NP. Therefore, we do not expect to find an efficient PLS (let alone RPLS) for this problem. The universal scheme, in which the computation complexity at each node is unbounded, is the best scheme we know for this problem from the viewpoint of verification complexity. A lower bound on the verification complexity is presented in the following theorem.

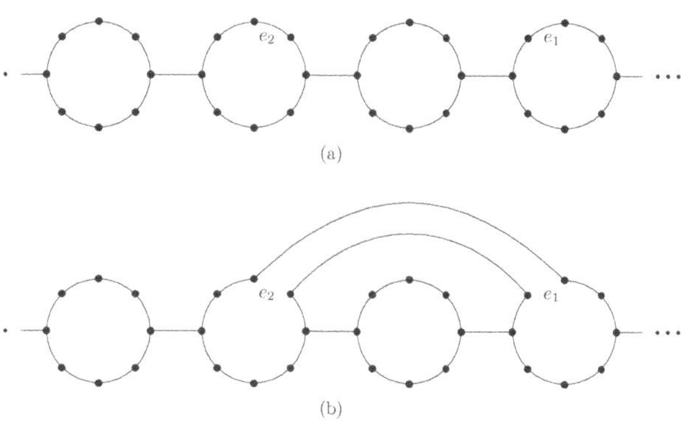

Figure 3: *(a) the graph* G *in the proof of Theorem 5.6 for* $c = 8$. *(b)* $\sigma_{\bowtie}(G)$.

THEOREM 5.6. *The deterministic verification complexity of* $(\mathcal{F}_{con}$, *cycle-at-most-c*$)$ *is* $\Omega(\log\frac{n}{c})$, *and its randomized verification complexity is* $\Omega(\log\log\frac{n}{c})$.

Proof: Let G be a chain of $\lceil\frac{n}{c}\rceil$ disjoint cycles of c nodes each (except one of at most c nodes), where every two neighboring cycles are connected by an edge (see Figure 3a). It obviously holds that cycle-at-most-$c(G)$ = TRUE. Let $\{H_1, \ldots, H_r\}$, for $r = \lceil\frac{n}{c}\rceil$, be a set of pairwise independent subgraphs, each consists of an edge from different cycle and its two endpoints. This set exists since there are $\lceil\frac{n}{c}\rceil$ cycles. For every two independent edges from different cycles, say $e_1 = \{u, v\}$ from cycle i and $e_2 = \{u', v'\}$ from cycle j, where $i \neq j$, we have that cycle-at-most-$c(\sigma_{\bowtie}(G))$ = FALSE for any isomorphism σ (see Figure 3). Therefore, the conditions of Theorems 4.4 and 4.7 are satisfied, and the lower bounds follow. ∎

6. CONCLUSION

In this paper we introduced the concept of randomized proof-labeling schemes (RPLS) and derived a few fundamental results and a few concrete results. The main message of the paper is that randomizing proof-labeling schemes reduces communication complexity exponentially. We also formalized the crossing technique which allows one to obtain lower bounds on the communication complexity of proof labeling schemes, both deterministic and randomized. Many interesting questions remain open. We list a few below.

- What is the relation between one-sided and two-sided RPLSs?
- Can the crossing technique (Theorem 4.7) be extended to show lower bounds on the verification complexity of two-sided RPLSs which are not edge independent? Can it be extended to the case where nodes have access to shared randomness?
- What are the relations between RPLS and the different complexity classes in [14], including LD, BPLD, NLD, and BPNLD?
- Can the complexity of the prover $\mathbf{p}$ be also accounted for in proof-labeling scheme? In particular, what is the effect of randomization on the prover complexity?

7. REFERENCES

[1] Y. Afek, S. Kutten, and M. Yung. The local detection paradigm and its application to self-stabilization. *Theor. Comput. Sci.*, 186(1-2):199–229, 1997.

[2] S. Alstrup, P. Bille, and T. Rauhe. Labeling schemes for small distances in trees. In *14th ACM-SIAM Symposium on Discrete Algorithms (SODA)*, pages 689–698, 2003.

[3] S. Alstrup, C. Gavoille, H. Kaplan, and T. Rauhe. Nearest common ancestors: a survey and a new distributed algorithm. In *14th ACM Symp. on Parallelism in Algorithms and Architectures (SPAA)*, pages 258–264, 2002.

[4] S. Alstrup and T. Rauhe. Small induced-universal graphs and compact implicit graph representations. In *43rd Symposium on Foundations of Computer Science (FOCS)*, pages 53–62, 2002.

[5] H. Arfaoui, P. Fraigniaud, D. Ilcinkas, and F. Mathieu. Distributedly testing cycle-freeness. In *40th Int. Workshop on Graph-Theoretic Concepts in Computer Science (WG)*, LNCS, pages 15–28. Springer, 2014.

[6] H. Arfaoui, P. Fraigniaud, and A. Pelc. Local decision and verification with bounded-size outputs. In *15th Symp. on Stabilization, Safety, and Security of Distributed Systems (SSS)*, LNCS, pages 133–147. Springer, 2013.

[7] B. Awerbuch, B. Patt-Shamir, and G. Varghese. Self-stabilization by local checking and correction. In *32nd Symposium on Foundations of Computer Science (FOCS)*, pages 268–277. IEEE, 1991.

[8] L. Blin, P. Fraigniaud, and B. Patt-Shamir. On proof-labeling schemes versus silent self-stabilizing algorithms. In *16th Int. Symp. on Stabilization, Safety, and Security of Distributed Systems (SSS)*, LNCS, pages 18–32. Springer, 2014.

[9] E. Cohen, E. Halperin, H. Kaplan, and U. Zwick. Reachability and distance queries via 2-hop labels. In *13th ACM-SIAM Symposium on Discrete Algorithms (SODA)*, pages 937–946, 2002.

[10] A. Das Sarma, S. Holzer, L. Kor, A. Korman, D. Nanongkai, G. Pandurangan, D. Peleg, and R. Wattenhofer. Distributed verification and hardness of distributed approximation. *SIAM J. Comput.*, 41(5):1235–1265, 2012.

[11] P. Fraigniaud and C. Gavoille. Routing in trees. In *28th International Colloquium on Automata, Languages and Programming (ICALP)*, LNCS, pages 757–772. Springer, 2001.

[12] P. Fraigniaud and C. Gavoille. A space lower bound for routing in trees. In *19th Symp. on Theoretical Aspects of Computer Science (STACS)*, LNCS, pages 65–75. Springer, 2002.

[13] P. Fraigniaud and A. Korman. On randomized representations of graphs using short labels. In *21st ACM Symp. on Parallelism in Algorithms and Architectures (SPAA)*, pages 131–137, 2009.

[14] P. Fraigniaud, A. Korman, and D. Peleg. Towards a complexity theory for local distributed computing. *J. ACM*, 60(5):35, 2013.

[15] P. Fraigniaud, S. Rajsbaum, and C. Travers. Locality and checkability in wait-free computing. *Distributed Computing*, 26(4):223–242, 2013.

[16] P. Fraigniaud, S. Rajsbaum, and C. Travers. On the number of opinions needed for fault-tolerant run-time monitoring in distributed systems. In *5th International Conference on Runtime Verification (RV)*, LNCS, pages 92–107. Springer, 2014.

[17] C. Gavoille, M. Katz, N. A. Katz, C. Paul, and D. Peleg. Approximate distance labeling schemes. In *9th European Symposium on Algorithms (ESA)*, pages 476–487, 2001.

[18] C. Gavoille and C. Paul. Split decomposition and distance labelling: An optimal scheme for distance hereditary graphs. *Electronic Notes in Discrete Mathematics*, 10:117–120, 2001.

[19] C. Gavoille, D. Peleg, S. Perennes, and R. Raz. Distance labeling in graphs. In *12th ACM Symposium on Discrete Algorithms (SODA)*, pages 210–219, 2001.

[20] M. Göös and J. Suomela. Locally checkable proofs. In *30th ACM Symp. on Principles of Distributed Computing (PODC)*, pages 159–168, 2011.

[21] J. E. Hopcroft and R. E. Tarjan. Efficient algorithms for graph manipulation. *Commun. ACM*, 16(6):372–378, 1973.

[22] G. Itkis and L. A. Levin. Fast and lean self-stabilizing asynchronous protocols. In *35th Annual Symposium on Foundations of Computer Science (FOCS)*, pages 226–239. IEEE, 1994.

[23] S. Kannan, M. Naor, and S. Rudich. Implicit representation of graphs. *SIAM J. Discrete Math.*, 5(4):596–603, 1992.

[24] H. Kaplan and T. Milo. Short and simple labels for small distances and other functions. In *7th Int. Workshop on Algorithms and Data Structures (WADS)*, pages 246–257, 2001.

[25] M. Katz, N. A. Katz, A. Korman, and D. Peleg. Labeling schemes for flow and connectivity. In *13th ACM-SIAM Symposium on Discrete Algorithms (SODA)*, pages 927–936, 2002.

[26] M. Katz, N. A. Katz, and D. Peleg. Distance labeling schemes for well-separated graph classes. *Discrete Applied Mathematics*, 145(3):384–402, 2005.

[27] A. Korman. Labeling schemes for vertex connectivity. *ACM Transactions on Algorithms*, 6(2), 2010.

[28] A. Korman and S. Kutten. Distributed verification of minimum spanning trees. *Distributed Computing*, 20:253–266, 2007.

[29] A. Korman, S. Kutten, and T. Masuzawa. Fast and compact self stabilizing verification, computation, and fault detection of an MST. In *30th Annual ACM Symposium on Principles of Distributed Computing (PODC)*, pages 311–320, 2011.

[30] A. Korman, S. Kutten, and D. Peleg. Proof labeling schemes. *Distributed Computing*, 22(4):215–233, 2010.

[31] A. Korman, D. Peleg, and Y. Rodeh. Constructing labeling schemes through universal matrices. *Algorithmica*, 57(4):641–652, 2010.

[32] E. Kushilevitz and N. Nisan. *Communication complexity*. Cambridge University Press, 1997.

[33] C. H. Papadimitriou. *Computational Complexity*. Addison Wesley Longman, 1994.

[34] D. Peleg. Proximity-preserving labeling schemes and their applications. In *25th International Workshop Graph-Theoretic Concepts in Computer Science (WG)*, pages 30–41, 1999.

[35] D. Peleg. Informative labeling schemes for graphs. *Theor. Comput. Sci.*, 340(3):577–593, 2005.

[36] M. Thorup. Compact oracles for reachability and approximate distances in planar digraphs. In *42nd Symp. on Foundations of Computer Science (FOCS)*, pages 242–251, 2001.

[37] M. Thorup and U. Zwick. Compact routing schemes. In *13th ACM Symp. on Parallelism in Algorithms and Architectures (SPAA)*, pages 1–10, 2001.

Distributed Convex Thresholding

Ran Wolff
Yahoo Labs
Haifa, Israel
ranw@yahoo-inc.com

ABSTRACT

Over the last fifteen years, a large group of algorithms emerged which compute various predicates from distributed data with a focus on communication efficiency. These algorithms are often called "communication-efficient", "geometric-monitoring", or "local" algorithms. We jointly call them *distributed convex thresholding* algorithms, for reasons which will be explained in this work. Distributed convex thresholding algorithms have found their applications in domains in which bandwidth is a scarce resource, such as wireless sensor networks and peer-to-peer systems, or in scenarios in which data rapidly streams to the different processors but outcome of the predicate rarely changes. Common to all of these algorithms is the use of a data dependent criteria to determine when further messaging is required.

This work presents two very simple yet exceedingly general theorems from which the correctness of all distributed convex thresholding algorithms can be elicited, and demonstrates that for key examples. Because the theorems are general, they extend the range of predicates which can be computed in a communication efficient manner beyond what is currently known. Unlike the previous correction proofs given to these algorithms, the proofs of the theorems presented here do not depend on the communication infrastructure. So the correctness of any distributed convex thresholding algorithm is immediately extended from broadcast enabled networks or from cycle free networks to general networks. Inspecting existing algorithms in light of the new theorems reveals that they contain redundant requirements, which cause them to send messages when indeed none are needed.

Categories and Subject Descriptors

F.1.2 [**Modes of Computation**]: Parallelism and concurrency

General Terms

Thresholding; Ordering; Convexity

Permission to make digital or hard copies of all or part of this work for personal or classroom use is granted without fee provided that copies are not made or distributed for profit or commercial advantage and that copies bear this notice and the full citation on the first page. Copyrights for components of this work owned by others than the author(s) must be honored. Abstracting with credit is permitted. To copy otherwise, or republish, to post on servers or to redistribute to lists, requires prior specific permission and/or a fee. Request permissions from Permissions@acm.org.
PODC'15, July 21 - 23, 2015, Donostia-San Sebastián, Spain.
Copyright is held by the owner/author(s). Publication rights licensed to ACM.
ACM ACM 978-1-4503-3617-8/15/07 ... $15.00
DOI: http://dx.doi.org/10.1145/2767386.2767387.

Keywords

Local algorithms; Geometric monitoring; Communication efficient algorithms; Wireless sensor networks; Peer-to-peer systems

1. INTRODUCTION

Over the last fifteen years there has been an increasing interest in a group of distributed algorithms which are often called "communication-efficient" [22], "local" [27], or "geometric-monitoring" [24] algorithms. This interest is fueled by three main application areas: Distributed high speed streams, in which a model of the data needs to be monitored without sending messages too frequently; wireless sensor networks, in which every message sent or received shortens the lifetime of the system; and peer-to-peer networks in which the sheer enormity of the system would easily chock the limited bandwidth of every peer unless communication efficiency is maintained. In such scenarios, traditional centralized sum reduction algorithms and decentralized gossip algorithms are often deemed too wasteful.

Overall, several dozens of distributed convex thresholding algorithms were presented and many of them are widely cited. At the center of these algorithm lays a *data dependent* criteria which can be computed by every processor and under which the processor can stop sending updates about its local statistics. Whenever a processor stops, it is guaranteed that it either computes the correct output or there has to be at least one processor which has not stopped updating. The ability to stop sending messages at a data dependent condition is the key property which makes those algorithms so efficient in terms of their message use. When this ability is complemented by a mechanism which assures consensus among processors and a mechanism which assures that messaging leads to convergence, the algorithm guarantees the *eventual accuracy* of the local output of each processor.

The stopping criteria itself is rarely complex. Usually, it involve comparing a local statistics which is known only to the processor, a joint statistics known to some or all the processors, and some target decision range for the statistics. One example [22] calculates a majority by comparing a local "Yes" or "No" vote of a processor (a local statistic) to the vote on a subset of processors whose vote has been shared with all processors (a joint statistics). Each processor abstains from sending its vote if the joint statistics and a weighted average of the local vote and the joint statistics both have more "Yes" votes than "No" votes (a decision range).

Still, the theory behind stopping rules, the proof of their correctness (i.e., that if in the example above all processors stop then the global vote must be "Yes"), and the characterization of their expected performance, can be very complex. Moreover, while some of the algorithms presented are clearly derived from previous ones, an overarching perspective of all of them is still missing. Without such perspective it is hard to explain the relation between algorithms which solve the same problem using different communication infrastructures (e.g. [24] in broadcast enabled networks vs. [27] in cycle-free networks), between algorithms handling different data types (e.g., [29] which thresholds the average in the segment $[0,1]$ vs. [27] which defines a similar thresholding problem in $\mathbb{R}^d$), and between algorithms computing related predicates (such as the absolute majority [29] and the relative majority [20]). Because a joint perspective is missing, it is also hard to understand the scope of problems for which such algorithms are suitable and where those algorithms stand in relation with well known algorithmic families such as gossip-based algorithms. Last, although problem convexity clearly has a major role in all those algorithms, we claim that its full gravity has yet not been appreciated.

This paper defines the family of *distributed convex thresholding* algorithms which includes all of the algorithms mentioned above, and many more. Our main result is a pair of simple theorems which can be used to prove all of those algorithms. Because the theorems are stated in a very general setting, they apply to any vector space with corresponding scalar weights, and are independent of the communication infrastructure (unlike previous work whose correctness relied on cycle freedom or on central coordination.) Furthermore, they allow exploring the limitations of distributed convex thresholding. They explain, for instance, why computing the relative order of averages is problematic when inputs have varying weights. Given this analysis, we are able to work around the problem in at least some cases. Returning to previous work, we find that key algorithms include redundant restrictions or overlook important optimization. That is, they send messages based on the stopping criteria they define where they would avoid messaging if they used our theorems. Looking forward, we believe our results greatly simplify the development of new efficient algorithms for a variety of distributed problems. We exemplify that by presenting an algorithm for a problem which, as best we know, was not yet addressed by a communication efficient algorithm.

The rest of this paper is structured as follows: The next section provides the notations and some basic definitions. Section 3 then proves our main results concerning distributed convex thresholding. It is followed by a reduction from distributed ordering to distributed convex thresholding which is presented in Section 4. We present an example for deriving an algorithm based on distributed convex thresholding in Section 5. Section 6 provides a broad review of related work, focusing on some of their inefficiencies. Some conclusions and research goals are depicted in the last section. To simplify reading, proofs are moved to Appendix A.

2. NOTATIONS

A weighted vector X is a pair of a vector and a weight. For every $X \in \mathbb{W}$ we denote the *vector* by $\overrightarrow{X}$ in the vector field $\overrightarrow{\mathbb{W}}$ and the *weight* $|X|$ in the matching[1] scalar field $|\mathbb{W}|$. The vector field $\overrightarrow{\mathbb{W}}$ is typically $\mathbb{R}^d$ and the scalar field $|\mathbb{W}|$ is often the positive reals, $\mathbb{R}^+$. However, the case where $|\mathbb{W}|$ is the field of positive semi-definite matrices is also important because it lends itself to expressing vector of random variables with inverse covariance weights. The multiplicative inverse of $|X|$ is denoted $|X|^{-1}$ or $\frac{1}{|X|}$ and is defined for all $|X| \neq 0$. We distinguish weighted vector by their capital letter name, X, Y, or Z, or by upper indices X^1, X^2 and X^n. Lower indices are used strictly in case the vectors X_1 and X_2 reside on different processors (p_1 and p_2, respectively), meaning that processor p_i can access X_i but not X_j.

DEFINITION 1. *[Weighted Vector Addition] Let $\mathbb{W}$ be a space of weighted vectors. The addition operator $X \oplus Y$ is defined as the weighted vector with weight $|X \oplus Y| = |X| + |Y|$ and value $\overrightarrow{X \oplus Y} = |X \oplus Y|^{-1}\left(|X| \cdot \overrightarrow{X} + |Y| \cdot \overrightarrow{Y}\right)$.*

If $|\mathbb{W}|$ are the real positive numbers then $X \oplus Y$ is simply the weighted average of $\overrightarrow{X}$ and $\overrightarrow{Y}$. If $|\mathbb{W}|$ are inverse covariance matrices (a.k.a., precision matrix) then $\overrightarrow{X \oplus Y}$ is the maximum likelihood estimation of two noisy measurements $\overrightarrow{X}$ and $\overrightarrow{Y}$ with precision (inverse variance) $|X|$ and $|Y|$, respectively. $|X \oplus Y|$ is then the precision of this estimation. We shorthand $\bigoplus$ for the iteration operator:

$$\bigoplus_{i\in\{1\ldots n\}} X^i = \left(\ldots\left(\left(X^1 \oplus X^2\right) \oplus X^3\right) \oplus \cdots \oplus X^n\right).$$

DEFINITION 2. *[Weight division] Let $|\mathbb{W}|$ a space of scalars and $\alpha \in [0,1]$. For every $|X| \in |\mathbb{W}|$ the weight division operator $\alpha \odot |X|$ is defined by $|\alpha \odot X| + |(1-\alpha) \odot X| = \alpha |X| + (1-\alpha)|X| = |X|$.*

DEFINITION 3. *Let $\preceq$ be an order on the vector field $\overrightarrow{\mathbb{W}}$. A scalar $\omega \in |\mathbb{W}|$ is* positive *if for all $\overrightarrow{X}, \overrightarrow{Y} \in \overrightarrow{\mathbb{W}}$ we have that $\overrightarrow{X} \preceq \overrightarrow{Y} \Leftrightarrow \omega\overrightarrow{X} \preceq \omega\overrightarrow{Y}$.*

The identity element $1 \in |\mathbb{W}|$ does not affect the order of any two vectors and is, by definition, positive. The multiplicative inverse of every positive scalar must also be positive because $\omega\omega^{-1} = 1$. It easily follows that if $|X|$ and $|Y|$ are positive then $\frac{|X|}{|X \oplus Y|}$ and $\frac{|Y|}{|X \oplus Y|}$ are both positive. Additionally positivity in the context of an order on $\overrightarrow{\mathbb{W}}$ induces an order on $|\mathbb{W}|$: For any positive $|X|, |Y| \in |\mathbb{W}|$ we say $|X| < |Y|$ if and only if $|Y| - |X|$ is positive. As their name applies, positive semi-definite matrices such as the covariance are positive.

DEFINITION 4. *[Convexity] Let $\mathbb{W}$ be the space of weighted vectors and let $R \subseteq \overrightarrow{\mathbb{W}}$ then R is convex if and only if for all $X, Y \in \mathbb{W}$ such that $\overrightarrow{X}, \overrightarrow{Y} \in R$ the vector $\overrightarrow{X \oplus Y}$ is in R as well.*

In the following two sections we focus on a single convex region R. However, in many problems the accepted algorithmic approach is to cover $\overrightarrow{\mathbb{W}}$ with convex regions and then have processors consent on one of them.

[1] By matching we mean that the multiplication of each vector by every scalar must be defined.

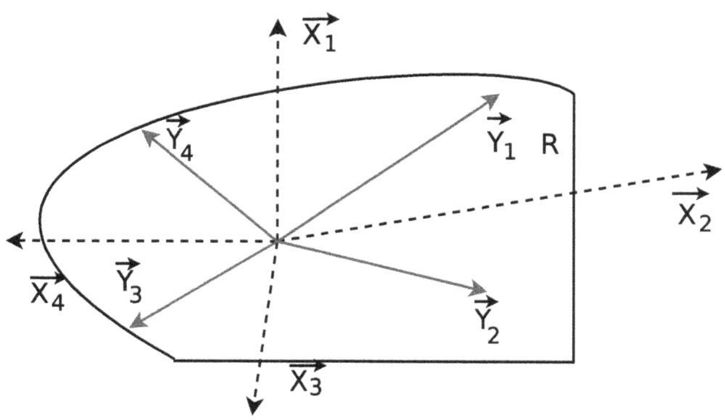

Figure 1: Example for Thm 6

DEFINITION 5. *[Preserving statistics (adapted from [12])] A set of weighted vector, Y^1 through Y^n, are a preserving statistics of another set of weighted vectors, X^1 through X^m, if and only if $\overrightarrow{\bigoplus_{i\in\{1,\ldots,n\}} Y^i} = \overrightarrow{\bigoplus_{j\in\{1,\ldots,m\}} X^j}$. If additionally $\left|\bigoplus_{i\in\{1,\ldots,n\}} Y^i\right| = \left|\bigoplus_{j\in\{1,\ldots,m\}} X^j\right|$ then Y^1 through Y^n are a mass preserving statistics of X^1 through X^m.*

3. DISTRIBUTED CONVEX THRESHOLDING

Based on the definitions in the previous section, we turn to the the first contribution of this paper: Two theorems which can be used to prove the the correctness of the stopping rules used by all convex thresholding algorithms.

THEOREM 6. *[Distributed convex thresholding] Given a set of processors $P = \{p_1, \ldots, p_n\}$ with corresponding inputs X_1 through X_n and a preserving statistics Y_1 through Y_n of those inputs and given any convex region $R \subseteq \vec{\mathbb{W}}$, if for all $p_i \in P$ it holds that $\vec{Y_i} \in R$ then $\overrightarrow{\bigoplus_{p_i\in P} X_i} \in R$ as well.*

PROOF. See Thm. 16 in Appendix A. □

An example for this theorem can be seen in Fig. 1. If for some arbitrary convex R in $\mathbb{R}^2$ we have that a preserving statistics of the inputs are a set of vectors which all reside in R then we are guaranteed that the weighted average of the inputs is in R as well.

As we show in Section 6, the simple proof of Theorem 6 suffices to replace the proofs of a large group of distributed data mining algorithms. To prove the correctness of another set of related algorithms we need to allow non-convex regions R which contain an agreed upon point $\vec{r} \in R$.

DEFINITION 7. *[Bounding sphere (adapted from [24])] Let $\vec{X}$ and $\vec{r}$ be vectors in $\vec{\mathbb{W}}$. The bounding sphere of $\vec{X}$ and $\vec{r}$ is defined by*

$$BSph\left(\vec{X}, \vec{r}\right) = \left\{\vec{Z} \in \vec{\mathbb{W}} : \left\|\vec{Z} - \frac{\vec{X} + \vec{r}}{2}\right\| < \left\|\vec{X} - \frac{\vec{X} + \vec{r}}{2}\right\|\right\}$$

where $\|\cdot\|$ is the L2 norm.

THEOREM 8. *[Geometric thresholding] Given a set of processors $P = \{p_1, \ldots, p_n\}$ with inputs X_1 through X_n with a preserving statistics Y_1 through Y_n, a region $R \subset \vec{\mathbb{W}}$ (convex or non-convex) and a reference vector $\vec{r} \in R$, if for all $p_i \in P$ the bounding sphere $BSph\left(\vec{Y_i}, \vec{r}\right) \subseteq R$ then $\overrightarrow{\bigoplus_{p_i\in P} X_i} \in R$ as well.*

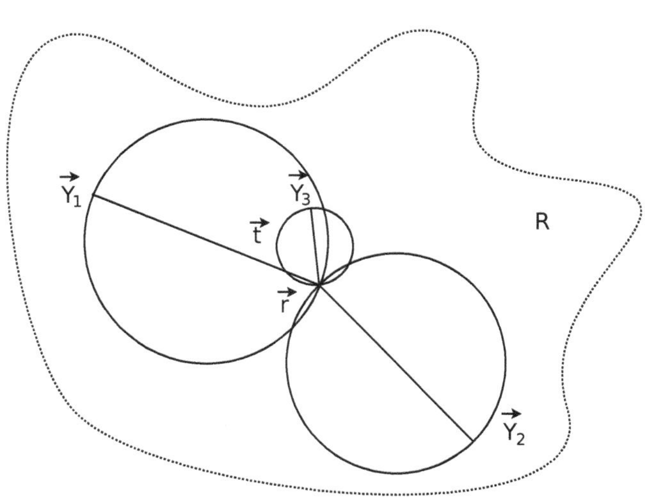

Figure 2: Example for Thm. 8

PROOF. See Thm. 17 in Appendix A. □

An example for the use of Thm 8 can be seen in Fig. 2. Since the three bounding spheres defined by $\vec{Y_1}, \vec{Y_2}, \vec{Y_3}$ and $\vec{r}$ are all subsets of R it is guaranteed that their weighted average $\vec{t}$ is in R.

Notice that Theorem 6 and Theorem 8 do not restrict the choice of a statistics Y_i beyond the necessity of value preservation. There is also no restriction on the mechanism by which it is validated that all $\vec{Y_i}$ are in R (respectively, that $BSph\left(\vec{Y_i}, \vec{r}\right) \subseteq R$, in the case of Theorem 8). In Section 5 below we demonstrate that the properties of mass preservation, consensus, and convergence are quite simple to achieve in both broadcast enabled network and general networks.

4. DISTRIBUTED CONVEX ORDERING

Distributed ordering of averages is closely related to distributed thresholding. For instance, a majority vote, deciding if the average is higher than 50 percent, can be easily reduced to the relative majority, deciding which of two averages is higher. We now show that for some order relations $\preceq$ on $\mathbb{R}^n$ it is possible to reduce distributed ordering of the averages, $\overrightarrow{\bigoplus_{p_i\in P} X_i} \preceq \overrightarrow{\bigoplus_{p_i\in P} Y_i}$, to distributed convex thresholding.

4.1 Order which is preserved under $\oplus$

The key property of an order which reduction to distributed convex thresholding is whether it is preserved under the $\oplus$ operator, in at least some of the cases.

DEFINITION 9. *Given two regions $R, Q \subseteq \mathbb{W}$ the order $\preceq$ is preserved under $\oplus$ on R, Q if for all $X^1, X^2 \in R$ and $Y^1, Y^2 \in Q$ such that $\vec{X_1} \preceq \vec{Y_1}$ and $\vec{X_2} \preceq \vec{Y_2}$ we have that $\overrightarrow{X_1 \oplus X_2} \preceq \overrightarrow{Y_1 \oplus Y_2}$ as well.*

For such orders, if a preserving statistics of the inputs can be limited to within R and Q then Theorem 6 can be applied to solve the ordering problem using the following corollary.

COROLLARY 10. *Let $\preceq$ be an order relation on $\vec{\mathbb{W}}$ and let $R, Q \subseteq \mathbb{W}$ be two regions such that $\preceq$ is preserved under $\oplus$ on R, Q. Given a set of processors $P = \{p_1, \ldots, p_n\}$ such that each p_i has a pair of inputs X_i^1 and X_i^2 and a pair of preserving statistics Y_i^1 and Y_i^2, respectively. If for all p_i we have that $\vec{Y_i^1} \preceq \vec{Y_i^2}$ then $\overrightarrow{\bigoplus_{p_i\in P} X_i^1} \preceq \overrightarrow{\bigoplus_{p_i\in P} X_i^2}$.*

PROOF. See Cor. 18 in Appendix A. □

Cor. 10 has a great simplifying power: If for a given order $\preceq$ we can show that it is preserved under $\oplus$ when the preserving statistics lay in two specific regions R and Q then the problem is instantly reducible to distributed convex thresholding on $RQ_{\preceq}$.

4.2 Order by an inner-product

Previous work on distributed decision tree induction and clustering have often used the fact that important metrics by which candidates are ordered in these domains (e.g., the information gain) grow monotonously in a specific direction in at least sections of $\mathbb{R}^d$. We now focus on such metrics to derive some general results on order preservation under $\oplus$. For a given pair $\overrightarrow{r}, \overrightarrow{s} \in \mathbb{R}^d$ we consider the order $\preceq_{\overrightarrow{r},\overrightarrow{s}}$ which orders any two weighted vectors $X, Y \in \mathbb{W}$ according to the inner products of their vector part with $\overrightarrow{r}$ and with $\overrightarrow{s}$:

$$X \preceq_{\overrightarrow{r},\overrightarrow{s}} Y \Leftrightarrow \left\langle \overrightarrow{X}, \overrightarrow{r} \right\rangle \leq \left\langle \overrightarrow{Y}, \overrightarrow{s} \right\rangle.$$

THEOREM 11. *Let* $RQ = \left\{(X, Y) \in \mathbb{W}^2 : 0 < |X| = \alpha |Y|\right\}$ *then the order* $\preceq_{\overrightarrow{r},\overrightarrow{s}}$ *is preserved under* $\oplus$ *on* RQ.

PROOF. See The. 19 in Appendix A. □

The result in Theorem 11 already extend beyond previous art by allowing the compared variables to have different weights (so long as their proportion is a constant). However, often the problem at hand does not permit a fixed proportion. On the other hand, it is simple to show examples in which $X^1 \preceq_{\overrightarrow{r},\overrightarrow{s}} Y^1$ and $X^2 \preceq_{\overrightarrow{r},\overrightarrow{s}} Y^2$ and yet $X^1 \oplus X^2 \npreceq_{\overrightarrow{r},\overrightarrow{s}} Y^1 \oplus Y^2$. Consider positive real weights and $\overrightarrow{r} = \overrightarrow{s}$ and imagine choosing $X^1 \preceq_{\overrightarrow{r},\overrightarrow{r}} Y^1 \preceq_{\overrightarrow{r},\overrightarrow{r}} X^2 \preceq_{\overrightarrow{r},\overrightarrow{r}} Y^2$ such that their weights are $0 < \left|X^1\right| \ll \left|X^2\right|$ and $0 < \left|Y^2\right| \ll \left|Y^1\right|$. It is easy to see that in this case $\left\langle \overrightarrow{X^1 \oplus X^2}, \overrightarrow{r} \right\rangle \rightarrow \left\langle \overrightarrow{X^2}, \overrightarrow{r} \right\rangle$ and $\left\langle \overrightarrow{Y^1 \oplus Y^2}, \overrightarrow{r} \right\rangle \rightarrow \left\langle \overrightarrow{Y^1}, \overrightarrow{r} \right\rangle$. Hence, for the right weights we have that $Y^1 \oplus Y^2 \preceq_{\overrightarrow{r},\overrightarrow{r}} X^1 \oplus X^2$.

The solution we propose for the problem of ordering weighted vectors of arbitrary weights is to define a stricter order which takes into account both their weights and their vector parts. We show that this stricter order is preserved under $\oplus$ and that when weighted vectors are ordered by the strict order, their vector parts are respectively ordered by the original order.

DEFINITION 12. *[Strict ordering] Given a space of weighted vectors* $\mathbb{W}$ *with positive weights* $|\mathbb{W}|$ *and given an order* $\preceq_{\overrightarrow{r},\overrightarrow{s}}$ *on* $\overrightarrow{\mathbb{W}}$ *which induces the order* $\leq$ *on* $|\mathbb{W}|$, *the strict order* $\underline{\preceq}_{\overrightarrow{r},\overrightarrow{s}}$ *on* $\mathbb{W}$ *is*

$$X \underline{\preceq}_{\overrightarrow{r},\overrightarrow{s}} Y \Leftrightarrow |Y| \leq |X| \wedge |X| \overrightarrow{X} \preceq_{\overrightarrow{r},\overrightarrow{s}} |Y| \overrightarrow{Y}.$$

THEOREM 13. *The strict order* $\underline{\preceq}_{\overrightarrow{r},\overrightarrow{s}}$ *is preserved under* $\oplus$ *for any* $\overrightarrow{r}, \overrightarrow{s} \in \mathbb{R}^d$ *and* $X, Y \in \mathbb{W}$.

PROOF. See The. 20 in Appendix A. □

THEOREM 14. *Given an order* $\preceq_{\overrightarrow{r},\overrightarrow{s}}$ *on* $\overrightarrow{\mathbb{W}}$ *and* $X, Y \in \mathbb{W}$ *such that according to the strict order* $X \underline{\preceq}_{\overrightarrow{r},\overrightarrow{s}} Y$ *it follows* $\overrightarrow{X} \preceq_{\overrightarrow{r},\overrightarrow{s}} \overrightarrow{Y}$ *as well.*

PROOF. See The. 21 in Appendix A. □

5. CLOSEST SENSOR ALGORITHM

As an example for the use of our results we present algorithms for a problem from the wireless sensor network domain. Consider a field of randomly located sensors, each of whom can reliably communicate with nearby sensors using short range radio. Assume there are one or more targets in the sensor field, and that the sensors can each measure range and angle to every target (e.g., using acoustic sensors), as well as separate the target (e.g., according to pitch). The goal of the sensors is to identify which of them is the nearest to each target. That nearest sensor can then escalate its measurements (e.g., by increasing its sample rate or by photographing the target and relaying the photograph to a control center).

Sensor readings are necessarily noisy. We assume the measured range is $\hat{r} \sim N\left(r, \sigma_r^2\right)$, where r is the true value and σ_r a known constant, and the measured angle is, likewise, $\hat{\theta} \sim N\left(\theta, \sigma_\theta^2\right)$. As a local pre-processing stage, each sensor translates its reading to Cartesian coordinates based on its location $s_i = \begin{bmatrix} x_i \\ y_i \end{bmatrix}$ on a joint Cartesian coordinate system. This means the noisy polar measurement of the jth signal source is translated to X^j with $\overrightarrow{X_i^j} = \begin{bmatrix} x_i^j + \hat{r}^j \cos \hat{\theta}^j \\ y_i^j + \hat{r}^j \sin \hat{\theta}^j \end{bmatrix}$ and $\left|X_i^j\right| = \left(\begin{bmatrix} \cos \hat{\theta}^j & -\sin \hat{\theta}^j \\ \sin \hat{\theta}^j & \cos \hat{\theta}^j \end{bmatrix} \begin{bmatrix} \sigma_r^2 & 0 \\ 0 & \sigma_\theta^2 \end{bmatrix} \begin{bmatrix} \cos \hat{\theta}^j & -\sin \hat{\theta}^j \\ \sin \hat{\theta}^j & \cos \hat{\theta}^j \end{bmatrix}^{-1}\right)^{-1}$.

It is natural to describe algorithms intended for wireless sensor networks in terms of event handling. The algorithm described in Alg. 1 handles three different events: A new measurement event which is triggered by the sensor mechanism and which provides p_i with a new measurement $\begin{bmatrix} \hat{r}^j \\ \hat{\theta}^j \end{bmatrix}$ for the jth signal source, a clock event in which it evaluates its current status, computes the current estimated solution, and decides whether any messages need to be sent, and an incoming message event in which it handles the messages send by its neighbors.

We assume every processor is aware of the set of neighbors with whom it can communicate symmetrically and reliably, N_i. We also assume the processor is given the measurement errors of its range and angle sensors (which can vary individually, although we ignore this aspect). Last, we assume every processor p_i is given both its location $\overrightarrow{s_i} \in \mathbb{R}^2$ and the pre-computed partitioning $R_V = \{R_1, \ldots, R_n\}$ of $\mathbb{R}^2$ according to closeness to the different processors (i.e., the processors' Voronoi diagram).

Each processor p_i will maintain a weighted vector Y_i^j which will preserve the statistics for the measurements of the jth signal source and another vector Z_i^j which will preserve the last value of Y_i^j which it sent to its neighbors. Additionally, for every $p_\ell \in N_i$ the processor p_i maintains the last value T_ℓ^j which p_ℓ reported for the jth signal source.

When a new measurement $\begin{bmatrix} \hat{r}^j \\ \hat{\theta}^j \end{bmatrix}$ arrives, p_i compute the weighted vector X_i^j which corresponds to that measurement in Cartesian space. Then, it sets Y_i^j to $Y_i^j \oplus X_i^j$. Likewise, when a message arrives from some $p_\ell \in N_i$ which contains an update U_ℓ^j to the Y_i^j statistics p_i sets Y_i^j to $Y_i^j \oplus U_\ell^j$. In this case, p_i also logs U_ℓ^j in T_ℓ^j for future use.

Periodically, p_i is triggered to compute the nearest sensor to every signal source. When it does, it computes the R_k^j which contains every $\overrightarrow{Y_i^j}$ and states p_k is the nearest to the jth signal source. Then,

Algorithm 1 Closest sensor

Constants for sensor p_i:
– Its location $\overrightarrow{s_i}$ and a pre-computed Voronoi diagram $R_V = \{R_1, \ldots, R_n\}$ based on all sensor locations
– The set N_i of sensors in range
– The measurement error of the range sensor σ_r and of the angle σ_θ sensor
Local status at p_i:
– The current statistics Y_i^j and the last sent vector $\overrightarrow{Z_i^j}$ for every signal source j
– Last received statistics T_k^j for every signal source j and every sensor $p_k \in N_i$ in range
Algorithm:
On new measurement $\begin{bmatrix} \hat{r^j} \\ \hat{\theta^j} \end{bmatrix}$ ***of source*** j***:***
– Compute X_i^j and update $Y_i^j \leftarrow Y_i^j \oplus X_i^j$
On incoming update message from sensor $p_\ell \in N_i$:
– For every U_ℓ^j pertaining to source j in the message
– – Set $Y_i^j \leftarrow Y_i^j \oplus U_\ell^j$
– – Set $T_\ell^j \leftarrow U_\ell^j$
Periodically:
– Compute R_k^j for every source j
– Output that sensor p_k is closest to the signal source j
– For every signal source j and neighbor $p_\ell \in N_i$
– – If $\overrightarrow{Z_i^j}, \overrightarrow{T_\ell^j} \in R_k^j$ then no update is needed
– – Otherwise
– – – Add $\frac{1}{2|N_i|} \odot Y_i^j$ to the update message
– – – Set $Y_i^j \leftarrow \frac{1}{2} \odot Y_i^j$
– – – Set $Z_i^j \leftarrow Y_i^j$
– If the update message is not empty
– – Broadcast the update message to N_i

p_i validates all processors compute the same R_k^j and for the jth signal source by checking that both $\overrightarrow{Z_i^j}$ and each $\overrightarrow{T_\ell^j}$ are in the R_k^j. If for all signal sources and all neighbors p_ℓ this stopping condition holds then p_i does not update in this period. Otherwise, for every signal source j requiring an update, p_i sets Y_i^j to half its weight. Then, p_j builds a message which contains the update $\frac{1}{2|N_i|} \odot Y_i^j$ for each such signal. That message is broadcasted to the neighbors in N_i.

5.1 Eventual correctness

First, we notice that Y_1^j through Y_n^j are a mass preserving statistics of all of the measurements of the jth signal source: They are initialized with a zero weight. Whenever a new measurement is taken, it is included into the Y_i^j of exactly one processor, and updates subtract half the weight of one Y_i^j in p_i only to add $|N_i|$ copies of $\frac{1}{2|N_i|} \odot Y_i^j$ to its neighbors. Additionally, we notice that updates are a repeated averaging process. Therefore, known results [6, 14, 9] guarantee that if updates persist indefinitely then every $\overrightarrow{Y_i^j}$ will converge to the best estimator of the location of the jth signal source based on all of the measurements taken by all of the sensors. Thus, we only need to prove that the condition in which all processors stop updating assures correctness of their local outputs.

THEOREM 15. *If for every p_i and each $p_\ell \in N_i$ and for every signal source j $\overrightarrow{Y_i^j}, \overrightarrow{Z_i^j}, \overrightarrow{T_\ell^j} \in R_k^j$ then $\overrightarrow{\bigoplus_{p_i \in P} X_i^j} \in R_k^j$.*

PROOF. For every p_i, $\overrightarrow{Y_i^j}, \overrightarrow{Z_i^j} \in R_k^j$ as computed by p_i, and $\overrightarrow{T_i^j}, \overrightarrow{Y_\ell^j} \in R_k^j$ as computed by p_ℓ we have that on termination, $\overrightarrow{Z_i^j} = \overrightarrow{T_i^j}$. Thus, assuming the network is connected, all processors must compute the same R_k^j to terminate. Since each R_k^j is, by definition, convex it follows from Thm. 6 that $\overrightarrow{\bigoplus_{p_i \in P} Y_i^j} \in R_k^j$. last, we already saw that Y_i^j for $i = 1, \ldots, n$ is a mass preserving statistics of all of the measurements X_i^j for $i = 1, \ldots, n$. Therefore, $\overrightarrow{\bigoplus_{p_i \in P} X_i^j} \in R_k^j$. □

6. RELATED WORK

The origins of the class of distributed algorithms we refer to as distributed convex thresholding algorithms can be traced back to two papers: The first [22] describes a communication efficient algorithm for broadcast-based cluster systems and the second [29] a fully decentralized algorithm for tree-based peer-to-peer networks. Both algorithms compute a majority vote, arguably the most fundamental predicate there is. They then reduce a high level data mining concept – association rules – to a large set of asynchronous majority votes. Two tracks of research followed from those two papers which are best discriminated by the underlying communication infrastructure.

6.1 Broadcast based algorithms

In broadcast based systems, coordination among processors allows establishing a joint reference statics which can be used by all processors. Distributed convex thresholding algorithms such as [22, 23] which are intended for broadcast enabled networks and whose objective is to compute the majority use broadcast messages to establish an estimation of the global frequency of yes votes. Processors are divided to two sets: those which contributed their inputs by sending a broadcast, C, and those which have yet not, $P \setminus C$. Each processor in the latter set needs to decide if the support he has for the majority vote, s_i yes votes out of c_i total votes, should be shared. It does so by computing the average of the the votes which have been shared, $\frac{\sum_{p_j \in C} s_j}{\sum_{p_j \in C} c_j}$, and the potential average if all of the processors which have not shared their votes have the same vote as it does, $\frac{|P \setminus C| s_i + \sum_{p_j \in C} s_j}{|P \setminus C| c_i + \sum_{p_j \in C} c_j}$. If both are greater than half then p_i assume the majority is of yes votes and in both are less than half it assumes the majority is of no votes. If the averages do not agree, then p_i shares his vote.

To see this is a special case of distributed convex thresholding designate that the input of p_i is X_i with $|X_i| = c_i$ and $\overrightarrow{X_i} = \frac{s_i}{c_i}$. The criteria for not sending messages becomes that $\overrightarrow{\bigoplus_{p_j \in C} X_j}$ and $\overrightarrow{(|P \setminus C| \odot X_i) \oplus \left(\bigoplus_{p_j \in C} X_j\right)}$ are both in $\left[0, \frac{1}{2}\right]$ or both in $\left(\frac{1}{2}, 1\right]$. Define $\overrightarrow{r} = \overrightarrow{\bigoplus_{p_j \in C} X_j}$ and Y_i with $\overrightarrow{Y_i} = \overrightarrow{(|P \setminus C| \odot X_i) \oplus \left(\bigoplus_{p_j \in C} X_j\right)}$ and with $|Y_i| = |X_i| + \frac{\left|\bigoplus_{p_j \in C} X_j\right|}{|P \setminus C|}$ for $p_i \in P \setminus C$ and with $\overrightarrow{Y_i} = \overrightarrow{\bigoplus_{p_j \in C} X_j}$ and $|Y_i| = 0$ for $p_i \in C$. Notice that $\bigoplus_{p_i \in P} Y_i = \bigoplus_{p_i \in P \setminus C} Y_i = \bigoplus_{p_i \in P} X_i$ and hence Y_i is a mass preserving statistic. Further notice that the requirement that for each processor $\overrightarrow{Y_i}$ and $\overrightarrow{r}$ be in the same region, is a special case of Thm. 8.

The one dimensional framework of a majority vote was generalized to $\mathbb{R}^d$ in [24] and denoted *geometrical monitoring*. Geometric monitoring became a very influential concept which was followed by dozens of applications of which [10, 5, 15, 1, 7, 25, 17, 11, 16, 19] is a mere sample. The basic theorem of geometric monitoring, often denoted *the bounding lemma* compares a reference point p, known to all processors, and a locally known drift vector d_i known to just p_i. It states that the convex-hull of the vectors $p, p+d_1, \ldots p+d_n$ is a subset of the union of the bounding spheres defined by p and the various $p + d_i$. If the bounding sphere of p_i extends beyond the decision area then p_i sends its drift data d_i to the coordinator which then initiates a balancing process to compute a new p.

Obviously, Thm. 8 is a generalization of the bounding lemma, which connect it to previous work in [22]. However, this generalization carries two benefits: Firstly, it uncovers that, unlike [22], work on geometric monitoring does not take into account the accumulation of weight at the coordinator, but rather just its vector value. This could lead to great inefficiencies: Consider the three processors depicted in Fig. 3 and assume each already communicated one data point which the coordinator, $\overrightarrow{d_1^1}$, $\overrightarrow{d_2^1}$, and $\overrightarrow{d_3^1}$, respectively, such that the current location of $\overrightarrow{p}$ is $\overrightarrow{p} = \frac{\overrightarrow{d_1^1}+\overrightarrow{d_2^1}+\overrightarrow{d_3^1}}{3}$. Now, each processor experienced drift $\overrightarrow{d_1^2}$, $\overrightarrow{d_2^2}$, and $\overrightarrow{d_3^2}$. According to the accepted in geometric monitoring, they each will be in violation if $BSph\left(\overrightarrow{p}, \overrightarrow{d_i^2}\right)$ extends outside R. This would lead to another round which would end with $\overrightarrow{p} = \frac{\overrightarrow{d_1^1}+\overrightarrow{d_2^1}+\overrightarrow{d_3^1}+\overrightarrow{d_1^2}+\overrightarrow{d_2^2}+\overrightarrow{d_3^2}}{6}$.

What Thm. 8 suggests, which concurs with [22], is that $\overrightarrow{p}$ can be a zero weight reference point, and that each processor can set its local statistics to the $\oplus$ of its input and a unit weight, $\overrightarrow{p}$ valued, weighted vector. This way, the average of $\overrightarrow{p}$ and the statistics at the processors remains the same. Often, this average statistics would not extend outside R and no messaging would be needed.

Taking this idea further, the second contribution of Thm. 8 is that if $\overrightarrow{p}$ is merely a zero weight reference point then there is no need for central coordination. When a violation occurs processors can just as well balance their statistics asynchronously with their neighbors, as they do in the k-means algorithm in [27]. Combining these two ideas we get a recipe for turning each algorithm which has been suggested for the coordinated framework of geometric monitoring into one which works just as well in a decentralized peer-to-peer framework.

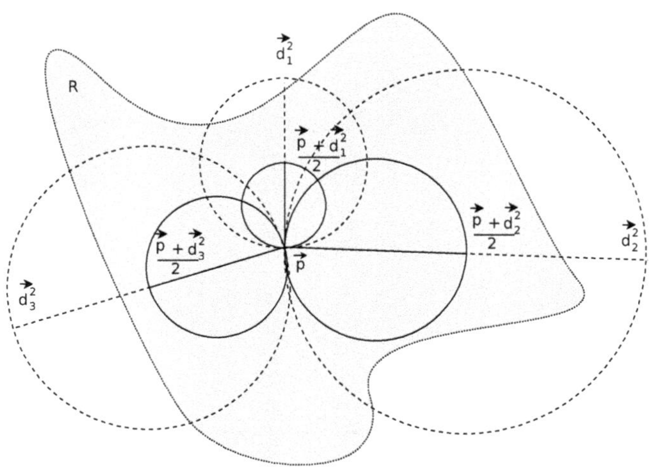

Figure 3: Sharing weight from the coordinator to the processors reduces the volumes of the bounding spheres.

6.2 Fully decentralized algorithms

Parallel to the development of coordinator based algorithms, there has been similar progress in fully decentralized ones. Similarly, majority voting was generalized to thresholding in $\mathbb{R}^d$ [27] and was shown to benefit for a variety of data mining related problems [27, 2, 8, 28]. Initially, progress has been limited to systems in which the communication network is a tree. Deriving that tree in a decentralized manner was part of the algorithm (e.g., in [3]) or it was left to an auxiliary algorithm. A key example, [27] denotes the average of the data collected at p_i by $\overrightarrow{\mathcal{K}_i}$ and the agreement of p_i and its tree-neighbor p_j by $\overrightarrow{\mathcal{A}_{i,j}}$ and then denotes the weighted difference of $\overrightarrow{\mathcal{K}_i}$ and $\overrightarrow{\mathcal{A}_{i,j}}$ the withheld knowledge $\overrightarrow{\mathcal{W}_{i,j}}$. It then proves that if for all p_i and their neighbors p_j $\overrightarrow{\mathcal{K}_i}$, $\overrightarrow{\mathcal{A}_{i,j}}$, and $\overrightarrow{\mathcal{W}_{i,j}}$ resides in the same convex region R then the global average is in R as well.

To show this result a special case of Thm. 6, select an arbitrary p_i and connect it to a virtual root p_{root}. Now, let $\overrightarrow{\mathcal{W}_{j,\uparrow}}$ denote the withheld knowledge of p_j with respect to the neighbor which connects it to the root. At p_i, $\overrightarrow{\mathcal{W}_{i,\uparrow}}$ is $\overrightarrow{\mathcal{K}_i}$ by definition, because no message was sent from p_i to p_{root}. It is easy to see that the different $\overrightarrow{\mathcal{W}_{i,\uparrow}}$ are a mass preserving statistics of the inputs X_i because each portion of every input is counted at only one $\overrightarrow{\mathcal{W}_{i,\uparrow}}$.

Recently, the limitation of tree networks has been lifted with the description of L2 thresholding in general undirected graphs [26]. The basis idea behind that work is to keep track, at both p_i and its neighbor p_j, of the statistics that is sent from one to the other $X_{i,j}$ and compute at p_i a statistics S_i such that $S_i \oplus \bigoplus_{p_j \in N_i} X_{i,j} = X_i \oplus \bigoplus_{p_j \in N_i} X_{j,i}$ [2]. To see that this is a special case of Thm. 6 we note that S_1 through S_n is mass preserving statistics of X_1 through X_n. Which can be proved by iterating for all $p_i \in P$ on

[2]The original notation is $S_i = X_i \oplus \bigoplus_{p_j \in N_i} X_{j,i} \ominus X_{i,j}$. But we find the definition of $\ominus$ superfluous.

both sides of the equation.

$$S_i \oplus \bigoplus_{p_j \in N_i} X_{i,j} = X_i \oplus \bigoplus_{p_j \in N_i} X_{j,i}$$

$$\bigoplus_{p_i \in P} \left(S_i \oplus \bigoplus_{p_j \in N_i} X_{i,j} \right) = \bigoplus_{p_i \in P} \left(X_i \oplus \bigoplus_{p_j \in N_i} X_{j,i} \right)$$

$$\left(\bigoplus_{p_i \in P} S_i \right) \oplus \left(\bigoplus_{p_i \in P} \bigoplus_{p_j \in N_i} X_{i,j} \right) =$$

$$\left(\bigoplus_{p_i \in P} X_i \right) \oplus \left(\bigoplus_{p_i \in P} \bigoplus_{p_j \in N_i} X_{j,i} \right)$$

Since eventually $X_{i,j} = X_{j,i}$ it follows that

$$\bigoplus_{p_i \in P} S_i = \bigoplus_{p_i \in P} X_i$$

We notice, however, that [26] requires that both $\overrightarrow{A_{i,j}}$ and the weighted difference $\overrightarrow{S_i \ominus A_{i,j}}$ are in the same R with $\overrightarrow{S_i}$. In truth, less demanding requirements (e.g., that $\overrightarrow{A_{i,j}}$ is in the same R as $\overrightarrow{S_i}$) would work just as well. The excess requirement sometimes trigger messages where none are needed.

6.3 Distributed ordering

Related to distributed thresholding, the problem of distributed ordering was also addressed by convex thresholding algorithms. Firstly, through a reduction to majority voting was suggested [18] in which the difference in frequency is computed for every pair of inputs $\overrightarrow{Y_i^{j,k}} = \overrightarrow{X_i^j} - \overrightarrow{X_i^k}$. The differences are thresholded with respect to the regions $[-1, 0]$ and $(0, 1]$ to conclude which has the greater average, $\overrightarrow{X_i^j}$ or $\overrightarrow{X_i^k}$. Then, the order is determined from the full matrix of differences. An algorithm with greater efficiency was then presented in [20]. Related to [20], an algorithm was described in [4] which computes the most outlaid sample. Due to the specific characteristic of the problem that algorithm was suitable to general networks, although it utilized communication inefficient flooding. Overall, progress on ordering problems has been limited to orders which can be reduced to an inner product and in which all inputs have the same weights. This paper explains why these restrictions emerge from convexity and presents a way in which they can sometimes be avoided.

7. CONCLUSIONS AND FURTHER RESEARCH

This paper presents a unified theoretical basis for a large group of algorithms which were shown to have multiple applications in distributed data mining and in distributed system monitoring. This new theory places all those algorithms within a single family, that of distributed convex thresholding algorithms. It allows simple proofs of correctness which consist of the identification of a preserving statistics and of a mechanism for convergence to the mean. Most importantly, the new theorems open the door for the integration of results from the very broad field of distributed algorithms, specifically including algorithm for speeding convergence to the mean. As a side benefit, the general applicability of the new result allow broadening the scope of distributed convex thresholding algorithms to new and interesting data types such as probability vectors and covariance matrices.

The concept of consensus appears many times in this work. However, the most important aspect of consensus, which was not covered by this or any previous work, is consensus among independent agents rather than the cooperative ones. We intend to look into distributed convex thresholding where rather than reducing messaging the objective of each agents is to contribute as little weight as possible.

In terms of applications, we leave out due to page limitation a demonstration of applying this new framework to one of the most important algorithms in wireless sensor networks – the distributed Kalman filter [21, 13]. Indeed, the algorithm described in Section 5 goes a long way towards that goal. But we feel a followup work is needed to show how performance of current distributed Kalman filtering algorithms can be improved by distributed convex thresholding.

8. REFERENCES

[1] B. Babcock and C. Olston. Distributed top-k monitoring. In *Proceedings of the 2003 ACM SIGMOD International Conference on Management of Data*, SIGMOD '03, pages 28–39, San Diego, California, 2003.

[2] K. Bhaduri, R. Wolff, C. Giannella, and H. Kargupta. Distributed Decision-Tree Induction in Peer-to-Peer Systems. *Stat. Anal. Data Min.*, 1(2):85–103, June 2008.

[3] Y. Birk, L. Liss, A. Schuster, and R. Wolff. A Local Algorithm for Ad Hoc Majority Voting via Charge Fusion. In *Proceedings of DISC*, Amsterdam , October 2004.

[4] J. W. Branch, C. Giannella, B. Szymanski, and R. W. andWolff2009 Hillol Kargupta. In-Network Outlier Detection in Wireless Sensor Networks. *Knowledge and Information Systems*, 34(1):23–54, 2013.

[5] S. Burdakis and A. Deligiannakis. Detecting outliers in sensor networks using the geometric approach. In *Data Engineering (ICDE), 2012 IEEE 28th International Conference on*, pages 1108–1119, April 2012.

[6] S. Chatterjee and E. Seneta. Towards consensus: Some convergence theorems on repeated averaging. *Journal of Applied Probability*, pages 89–97, 1977.

[7] G. Cormode, S. Muthukrishnan, and K. Yi. Algorithms for distributed functional monitoring. In *Proceedings of the Nineteenth Annual ACM-SIAM Symposium on Discrete Algorithms*, SODA '08, pages 1076–1085, Philadelphia, PA, USA, 2008.

[8] S. Datta, K. Bhaduri, C. Giannella, R. Wolff, and H. Kargupta. Distributed Data Mining in Peer-to-Peer Networks. *IEEE Internet Computing*, 10(4):18–26, July 2006.

[9] I. Eyal, I. Keidar, and R. Rom. LiMoSense - Live Monitoring in Dynamic Sensor Networks. In *Proceedings of ALGOSENSOR*, 2011.

[10] M. Garofalakis, D. Keren, and V. Samoladas. Sketch-based geometric monitoring of distributed stream queries. *Proc. VLDB Endow.*, 6(10):937–948, Aug. 2013.

[11] N. Giatrakos, A. Deligiannakis, M. Garofalakis, I. Sharfman, and A. Schuster. Prediction-based geometric monitoring over distributed data streams. In *Proceedings of the 2012 ACM SIGMOD International Conference on Management of Data*, SIGMOD '12, pages 265–276, Scottsdale, Arizona, USA, 2012.

[12] M. Jelasity, A. Montresor, and O. Babaoglu. Gossip-Based Aggregation in Large Dynamic Networks. *ACM Transactions on Computer Systems*, 23(3):219–252, August 2005.

[13] S. Kar and J. M. F. Moura. Gossip and Distributed Kalman Filtering: Weak Consensus under Weak Detectability. *IEEE Transactions on Signal Processing*, 59(4):1766 – 1784, 2011.

[14] D. Kempe, A. Dobra, and J. Gehrke. Gossip-Based Computation of Aggregate Information. In *Proceedings of Foundations of Computer Science (FOCS)*, pages 482–491, 2003.

[15] D. Keren, G. Sagy, A. Abboud, D. Ben-David, A. Schuster, I. Sharfman, and A. Deligiannakis. Geometric monitoring of heterogeneous streams. *IEEE Transactions on Knowledge and Data Engineering – preprint*, 2014.

[16] D. Keren, G. Sagy, A. Abboud, D. Ben-David, A. Schuster, I. Sharfman, and A. Deligiannakis. Geometric monitoring of heterogeneous streams. *Knowledge and Data Engineering, IEEE Transactions on*, 26(8):1890–1903, Aug 2014.

[17] J. Kogan. Feature selection over distributed data streams through convex optimization. In *Proceedings of the 2012 SIAM International Conference on Data Mining*, pages 475–484.

[18] D. Krivitski, A. Schuster, and R. Wolff. A Local Facility Location Algorithm for Sensor Networks. In *Proceedings of DCOSS'05*, pages 368–375, Marina del Rey, California, June 2005.

[19] A. Lazerson, I. Sharfman, D. Keren, A. Schuster, M. Garofalakis, and V. Samoladas. Monitoring distributed streams using convex decompositions. *Proceedings of the VLDB Endowment*, 8(5), 2015.

[20] P. Luo, H. Xiong, K. , Lü, and Z. Shi. Distributed Classification in Peer-to-Peer Networks. In *Proceedings of ACM SIGKDD*, pages 968–976, 2007.

[21] R. Olfati-Saber. Distributed Kalman Filter with Embedded Consensus Filters. In *Proceedings of CDC-ECC*, pages 8179 – 8184, 2005.

[22] A. Schuster and R. Wolff. Communication-Efficient Distributed Mining of Association Rules. In *Proceedings of ACM-SIGMOD'01*, pages 473–484, Santa Barbara, California, May 2001.

[23] A. Schuster, R. Wolff, and D. Trock. A High-Performance Distributed Algorithm for Mining Association Rules. In *Proceedings of ICDM*, pages 291–298, Melbourne, Florida, November 2003.

[24] I. Sharfman, A. Schuster, and D. Keren. A geometric approach to monitoring threshold functions over distributed data streams. *ACM Transactions on Database Systems (TODS)*, 32(4):23, 2007.

[25] I. Sharfman, A. Schuster, and D. Keren. Shape sensitive geometric monitoring. In *Proceedings of the Twenty-seventh ACM SIGMOD-SIGACT-SIGART Symposium on Principles of Database Systems*, PODS '08, pages 301–310, Vancouver, Canada, 2008.

[26] R. Wolff. Local thresholding in general network graphs. *IEEE Transactions on Knowledge and Data Engineering*, 26:916 – 928, 2014.

[27] R. Wolff, K. Bhaduri, and H. Kargupta. Local L2 Thresholding Based Data Mining in Peer-to-Peer Systems. In *Proceedings of SDM*, pages 430–441, 2006.

[28] R. Wolff, K. Bhaduri, and H. Kargupta. A generic local algorithm for mining data streams in large distributed systems. 21(4):465–478, April 2009.

[29] R. Wolff and A. Schuster. Mining Association Rules in Peer-to-Peer Systems. In *Proceedings of ICDM*, pages 363–370, Melbourne, Florida, November 2003.

APPENDIX

A. PROOFS

THEOREM 16. *[Distributed convex thresholding] Given a set of processors $P = \{p_1, \ldots, p_n\}$ with corresponding inputs X_1 through X_n and a preserving statistics Y_1 through Y_n of those inputs and given any convex region $R \subseteq \overrightarrow{\mathbb{W}}$, if for all p_i it holds that $\overrightarrow{Y_i} \in R$ then $\overrightarrow{\bigoplus_{p_i \in P} X_i} \in R$ as well.*

PROOF. Since all $\overrightarrow{Y_i} \in R$ convexity dictates $\overrightarrow{\bigoplus_{p_i \in P} Y_i} \in R$ and since Y_1 through Y_n is a preserving statistics of X_1 through X_n $\overrightarrow{\bigoplus_{p_i \in P} Y_i} = \overrightarrow{\bigoplus_{p_i \in P} X_i}$. It follows that $\overrightarrow{\bigoplus_{p_i \in P} X_i} \in R$ as well. □

THEOREM 17. *[Geometric thresholding] Given a set of processors $P = \{p_1, \ldots, p_n\}$ with inputs X_1 through X_n with a preserving statistics Y_1 through Y_n, a region $R \subset \overrightarrow{\mathbb{W}}$ (convex or non-convex) and a reference vector $\overrightarrow{r} \in R$, if for all $p_i \in P$ the bounding sphere $BSph\left(\overrightarrow{Y_i}, \overrightarrow{r}\right) \subseteq R$ then $\overrightarrow{\bigoplus_{p_i \in P} X_i} \in R$ as well.*

PROOF. We first show that the convex hull of $\overrightarrow{Y_1}$ through $\overrightarrow{Y_n}$ and of $\overrightarrow{r}$ is a subset of the union of the bounding spheres $BSph\left(\overrightarrow{Y_1}, \overrightarrow{r}\right)$ through $BSph\left(\overrightarrow{Y_n}, \overrightarrow{r}\right)$.

A simple geometric proof suffices for $n = 2$ (see Figure 4): Firstly, the three vectors $\overrightarrow{Y_1}$, $\overrightarrow{Y_2}$ and $\overrightarrow{r}$ define a plane, which is bound to contain $\overrightarrow{Y_1 \oplus Y_2}$. It suffices, therefore, to prove the theorem in $\mathbb{R}^2$, regardless of the original dimension d. Since in $\mathbb{R}^2$ $\left(\overrightarrow{Y_1}, \overrightarrow{r}\right)$ and $\left(\overrightarrow{Y_2}, \overrightarrow{r}\right)$ are diameters of $BSph\left(\overrightarrow{Y_1}, \overrightarrow{r}\right)$ and $BSph\left(\overrightarrow{Y_2}, \overrightarrow{r}\right)$, respectively, Thale's theorem states both $\Delta\overrightarrow{Y_1}, \overrightarrow{r}, \overrightarrow{s}$ and $\Delta\overrightarrow{Y_2}, \overrightarrow{r}, \overrightarrow{s}$ are right triangles. It follows that the line $\left(\overrightarrow{Y_1}, \overrightarrow{Y_2}\right)$ passes through $\overrightarrow{s}$. Therefore, the triangle $\Delta\overrightarrow{Y_1}, \overrightarrow{r}, \overrightarrow{Y_2}$, which is the convex hull of $\overrightarrow{Y_1}$, $\overrightarrow{Y_2}$, and $\overrightarrow{r}$, is contained in the unification of $BSph\left(\overrightarrow{Y_1}, \overrightarrow{r}\right)$ and $BSph\left(\overrightarrow{Y_2}, \overrightarrow{r}\right)$.

Adding a third vector, Y_3, we notice that each of the facets $\Delta\overrightarrow{Y_1}, \overrightarrow{r}, \overrightarrow{Y_2}$, $\Delta\overrightarrow{Y_1}, \overrightarrow{r}, \overrightarrow{Y_3}$, $\Delta\overrightarrow{Y_2}, \overrightarrow{r}, \overrightarrow{Y_3}$, of the resulting pyramid is contained in a pair of bounding spheres. Picking any point $\overrightarrow{t}$ in the pyramid, we notice that it can be described as the weighted average of $\overrightarrow{r}$, $\overrightarrow{Y_2}$, $\overrightarrow{s_1}$ and $\overrightarrow{s_3}$, which are all points on $BSph\left(\overrightarrow{Y_2}, \overrightarrow{r}\right)$. Therefore, it resides in that bounding box. Adding further vectors $\overrightarrow{Y_4}$, $\overrightarrow{Y_5}$, etc. will add more facets to the convex hull and hence additional $\overrightarrow{s_i}$ points on the bounding spheres, without changing the fact that any point in the convex hull resides inside at least one of the bounding spheres.

Last, $\overrightarrow{\bigoplus_{p_i \in P} Y_i}$ must reside in the convex hull of the $\overrightarrow{Y_i}$, and hence in the convex hull of the $\overrightarrow{Y_i}$ and of $\overrightarrow{r}$. Because each bounding sphere is a subset of R and because the $\overrightarrow{Y_i}$ are a preserving statistics of the $\overrightarrow{X_i}$ this means $\overrightarrow{\bigoplus_{p_i \in P} X_i} \in R$ as well. □

COROLLARY 18. *Let $\preceq$ be an order relation on $\overrightarrow{\mathbb{W}}$ and let $R, Q \subseteq \mathbb{W}$ be two regions such that $\preceq$ is preserved under $\oplus$ on*

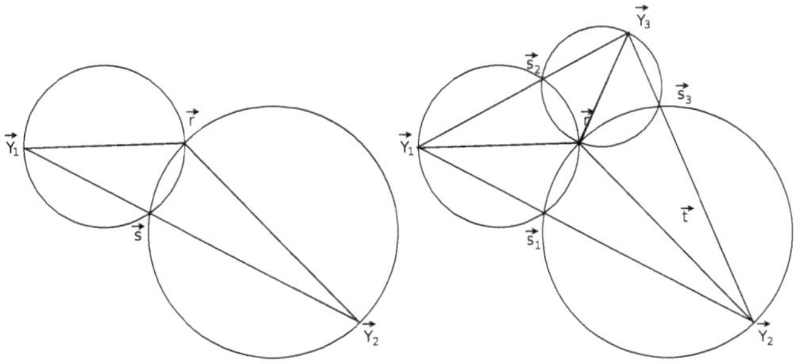

(a) Two vectors (b) Three vectors

Figure 4: Proof of Theorem 17

R, Q. Given a set of processors $P = \{p_1, \ldots, p_n\}$ such that each p_i has a pair of inputs X_i^1 and X_i^2 and a pair of preserving statistics Y_i^1 and Y_i^2, respectively, if for all p_i we have that $\overrightarrow{Y_i^1} \preceq \overrightarrow{Y_i^2}$ then $\overrightarrow{\bigoplus_{p_i \in P} X_i^1} \preceq \overrightarrow{\bigoplus_{p_i \in P} X_i^2}$.

PROOF. Define the region $RQ_{\preceq} \subseteq \mathbb{W}^2$ by $(Z,T) \in RQ_{\preceq} \Leftrightarrow \overrightarrow{Z} \preceq \overrightarrow{T}$. Because $\preceq$ is preserved under $\oplus$ we have that for each $(Z^1, T^1), (Z^2, T^2) \in RQ_{\preceq}$ the vector $(Z^1 \oplus Z^2, T^1 \oplus T^2)$ is in $RQ_{\preceq}$ as well. Hence, $RQ_{\preceq}$ is convex. Since it is given that for all $p_i \in P$ we have that $(Y_i^1, Y_i^2) \in RQ_{\preceq}$, it follows from Theorem 6 that $\left(\bigoplus_{p_i \in P} Y_i^1, \bigoplus_{p_i \in P} Y_i^2\right) = \left(\bigoplus_{p_i \in P} X_i^1, \bigoplus_{p_i \in P} X_i^2\right) \in RQ_{\preceq}$ as well. Hence, $\overrightarrow{\bigoplus_{p_i \in P} X_i^1} \preceq \overrightarrow{\bigoplus_{p_i \in P} X_i^2}$. $\square$

THEOREM 19. *Let $RQ = \{(X,Y) \in \mathbb{W}^2 : 0 < |X| = \alpha |Y|\}$ then the order $\preceq_{\vec{r},\vec{s}}$ is preserved under $\oplus$ on RQ.*

PROOF. We need to show that for every $(X^1, Y^1), (X^2, Y^2) \in RQ$ it holds that $(X^1 \oplus X^2, Y^1 \oplus Y^2) \in RQ$ and that if $X^1 \preceq_{\vec{r},\vec{s}} Y^1$ and $X^2 \preceq_{\vec{r},\vec{s}} Y^2$ then $X^1 \oplus X^2 \preceq_{\vec{r},\vec{s}} Y^1 \oplus Y^2$ as well. The former follows from

$$|X_1 \oplus X_2| = |X_1| + |X_2| = \alpha |Y_1| + \alpha |Y_2| = \alpha |Y_1 \oplus Y_2|.$$

For the latter, we rewrite the requirement in terms of the inner product: From $\left\langle \overrightarrow{X^1}, \vec{r} \right\rangle \leq \left\langle \overrightarrow{Y^1}, \vec{s} \right\rangle$ and $\left\langle \overrightarrow{X^2}, \vec{r} \right\rangle \leq \left\langle \overrightarrow{Y^2}, \vec{s} \right\rangle$ we need to derive that

$$\left\langle \overrightarrow{X^1 \oplus X^2}, \vec{r} \right\rangle \leq \left\langle \overrightarrow{Y^1 \oplus Y^2}, \vec{s} \right\rangle.$$

Since the inner product is linear in the first component we have that

$$\left\langle \overrightarrow{X^1 \oplus X^2}, \vec{r} \right\rangle = \left\langle \frac{|X^1|}{|X^1 \oplus X^2|} \overrightarrow{X^1} + \frac{|X^2|}{|X^1 \oplus X^2|} \overrightarrow{X^2}, \vec{r} \right\rangle$$

$$= \left\langle \frac{|X^1|}{|X^1 \oplus X^2|} \overrightarrow{X^1}, \vec{r} \right\rangle + \left\langle \frac{|X^2|}{|X^1 \oplus X^2|} \overrightarrow{X^2}, \vec{r} \right\rangle$$

and that

$$\left\langle \overrightarrow{Y^1 \oplus Y^2}, \vec{s} \right\rangle = \left\langle \frac{|Y^1|}{|Y^1 \oplus Y^2|} \overrightarrow{Y^1}, \vec{s} \right\rangle + \left\langle \frac{|Y^2|}{|Y^1 \oplus Y^2|} \overrightarrow{Y^2}, \vec{s} \right\rangle.$$

Noting $0 < |X^1| = \alpha |Y^1|$, etc., we have that $0 < \frac{|X^1|}{|X^1 \oplus X^2|} = \frac{|Y^1|}{|Y^1 \oplus Y^2|}$. By definition of positive weights, $\left\langle \overrightarrow{X^1}, \vec{r} \right\rangle \leq \left\langle \overrightarrow{Y^1}, \vec{s} \right\rangle$ if and only if

$$\left\langle \frac{|X^1|}{|X^1 \oplus X^2|} \overrightarrow{X^1}, \vec{r} \right\rangle \leq \left\langle \frac{|X^1|}{|X^1 \oplus X^2|} \overrightarrow{Y^1}, \vec{s} \right\rangle$$
$$= \left\langle \frac{|Y^1|}{|Y^1 \oplus Y^2|} \overrightarrow{Y^1}, \vec{s} \right\rangle.$$

Replacing x^1 for $\left\langle \frac{|X^1|}{|X^1 \oplus X^2|} \overrightarrow{X^1}, \vec{r} \right\rangle$, x^2 for $\left\langle \frac{|X^2|}{|X^1 \oplus X^2|} \overrightarrow{X^2}, \vec{r} \right\rangle$, y^1 for $\left\langle \frac{|X^1|}{|X^1 \oplus X^2|} \overrightarrow{Y^1}, \vec{s} \right\rangle$ and y^2 for $\left\langle \frac{|X^2|}{|X^1 \oplus X^2|} \overrightarrow{Y^2}, \vec{s} \right\rangle$ we can finally write the requirement as proving that if $x^1 \leq y^1$ and $x^2 \leq y^2$ then $x^1 + x^2 \leq y^1 + y^2$, which is trivial since they are all real numbers. $\square$

THEOREM 20. *The strict order $\preceq_{\vec{r},\vec{s}}$ is preserved under $\oplus$ for any $\vec{r}, \vec{s} \in \mathbb{R}^d$ and $X, Y \in \mathbb{W}$.*

PROOF. Consider X^1, X^2, Y^1, Y^2 such that $X^1 \preceq_{\vec{r},\vec{s}} Y^1$ and $X^2 \preceq_{\vec{r},\vec{s}} Y^2$. By definition of the order $\preceq_{\vec{r},\vec{s}}$,

$$|Y^1 \oplus Y^2| = |Y^1| + |Y^2| \leq |X^1| + |X^2| < |X^1 \oplus X^2|.$$

Define $Z^1, Z^2, T^1, T^2 \in \mathbb{W}$ with $|Z^1| = |Z^2| = |T^1| = |T^2| = 1$ and with $\overrightarrow{Z^1} = |X^1| \overrightarrow{X^1}$, $\overrightarrow{Z^2} = |X^2| \overrightarrow{X^2}$, $\overrightarrow{T^1} = |Y^1| \overrightarrow{Y^1}$ and $\overrightarrow{T^2} = |Y^2| \overrightarrow{Y^2}$. By definition of $\preceq_{\vec{r},\vec{s}}$, $\overrightarrow{Z^1} \preceq_{\vec{r},\vec{s}} \overrightarrow{T^1}$ and $\overrightarrow{Z^2} \preceq_{\vec{r},\vec{s}} \overrightarrow{T^2}$ and since $|Z^1| = |Z^2| = |T^1| = |T^2|$ if follows from Theorem 11 that $\overrightarrow{Z^1 \oplus Z^2} \preceq_{\vec{r},\vec{s}} \overrightarrow{T^1 \oplus T^2}$. I.e., $\frac{|X^1|\overrightarrow{X^1} + |X^2|\overrightarrow{X^2}}{2} \preceq_{\vec{r},\vec{s}} \frac{|Y^1|\overrightarrow{Y^1} + |Y^2|\overrightarrow{Y^2}}{2}$. Since $|Y^1 \oplus Y^2|$ is positive we can write

$$\frac{|X^1|\overrightarrow{X^1} + |X^2|\overrightarrow{X^2}}{|Y^1 \oplus Y^2|} = \frac{|X^1 \oplus X^2|}{|Y^1 \oplus Y^2|} \frac{|X^1|\overrightarrow{X^1} + |X^2|\overrightarrow{X^2}}{|X^1 \oplus X^2|}$$
$$\preceq_{\vec{r},\vec{s}} \frac{|Y^1|\overrightarrow{Y^1} + |Y^2|\overrightarrow{Y^2}}{|Y^1 \oplus Y^2|}.$$

Since $|Y^1 \oplus Y^2| \leq |X^1 \oplus X^2|$ we know $1 \leq \frac{|X^1 \oplus X^2|}{|Y^1 \oplus Y^2|}$. It follows that $\frac{|X^1|\overrightarrow{X^1} + |X^2|\overrightarrow{X^2}}{|X^1 \oplus X^2|} \preceq_{\vec{r},\vec{s}} \frac{|Y^1|\overrightarrow{Y^1} + |Y^2|\overrightarrow{Y^2}}{|Y^1 \oplus Y^2|}$ which is equivalent to $\overrightarrow{X^1 \oplus X^2} \preceq_{\vec{r},\vec{s}} \overrightarrow{Y^1 \oplus Y^2}$. Hence, $X^1 \oplus X^2 \preceq_{\vec{r},\vec{s}} Y^1 \oplus Y^2$. $\square$

THEOREM 21. *Given an order $\preceq_{\vec{r},\vec{s}}$ on $\overrightarrow{\mathbb{W}}$ and $X, Y \in \mathbb{W}$ such that according to the strict order $X \preceq_{\vec{r},\vec{s}} Y$ it follows $\overrightarrow{X} \preceq_{\vec{r},\vec{s}} \overrightarrow{Y}$ as well.*

PROOF.

$$X \preceq_{\vec{r},\vec{s}} Y \Leftrightarrow |Y| \leq |X| \wedge \left\langle |X| \overrightarrow{X}, \vec{r} \right\rangle \leq \left\langle |Y| \overrightarrow{Y}, \vec{s} \right\rangle$$

and therefore $\left\langle \overrightarrow{X}, \vec{r} \right\rangle \leq \left\langle \frac{|X|}{|Y|} \overrightarrow{X}, \vec{r} \right\rangle \leq \left\langle \overrightarrow{Y}, \vec{s} \right\rangle$. $\square$

Brief Announcement: Average Complexity for the LOCAL Model

Laurent Feuilloley*
École Normale Supérieure de Cachan, France
laurent.feuilloley@ens-cachan.fr

ABSTRACT

A standard model in network synchronised distributed computing is the LOCAL model [5]. In this model, the processors work in rounds and, in the classic setting, they know the number of vertices of the network, n. Using n, they can compute the number of rounds after which they must all stop and output. It has been shown recently that for many problems, one can basically remove the assumption about the knowledge of n, without increasing the asymptotic running time [2][4]. In this case, it is assumed that different vertices can choose their final output at different rounds, but continue to transmit messages. In both models, the measure of the running time is the number of rounds before the last node outputs. In this brief announcement, the vertices do not have the knowledge of n, and we consider an alternative measure: the average, over the nodes, of the number of rounds before they output. We prove that the complexity of a problem can be exponentially smaller with the new measure, but that Linial's lower bound for colouring [3] still holds.

1. INTRODUCTION

In the LOCAL model [5], the processors are located at the nodes of the network, have distinct identifiers, and work in rounds. At each round, each processor sends messages to its direct neighbours, receives messages from them, and computes its new state. In some variants of this model, e.g., when n is not known [2, 4], every node can choose its output at an arbitrary round, yet it must continue to transmit the messages it receives. The classic measure of the running time is the number of rounds before all the nodes have output. We consider an alternative measure which is the average, over the nodes, of the running time before they output.

An equivalent way to describe the LOCAL model is to consider that every node gathers all the information in a ball around itself and output a function of this ball. For example a node can increment the radius of the ball it sees, until it has enough information to output. This second vision of the LOCAL model is more convenient for this paper. Therefore, in the following, we mostly consider radiuses, and not rounds. When the algorithm, the graph, and the identifiers are set, the "radius of the node v" refers to the radius at which the algorithm chooses to output, and we denote it by $r(v)$. From this point of view, the classic measure of the running time is the maximum of the radiuses of these balls, and the alternative measure is the average of these radiuses. More precisely for a given size n, the running time is usually:

$$\max_{G:|G|=n} \left(\max_{v \in G} r(v) \right),$$

and, in this paper, we consider:

$$\max_{G:|G|=n} \left(\sum_{v \in G} r(v)/n \right).$$

In this brief announcement, the computation is always deterministic, and the average is always over the nodes. In particular, remark that we consider the worst case for the distribution of the identifiers.

On one hand, we show that there is a natural problem for which there exists an algorithm with average running time exponentially smaller than the worst case complexity. In this problem, called *largest ID*, every vertex of a cycle must decide if it has the largest ID or not, which is a classic way to elect a leader. On the other hand, we show that Linial's lower bound on colouring [3] holds for the average node measure, i.e. the vertices need an average radius of $\Omega(\log^* n)$ to compute a valid 3-colouring. Note that this lower bound matches the upper bound as it is possible to 3-colour the n-node ring in $O(\log^* n)$ rounds even without the knowledge of n [2][4].

The goal of this work is to continue the study of locality by proposing a new measure of the running time. This measure is suited to algorithms in which some vertices may stop very early. An example of application is in the context of dynamic networks. The average time to update the labels of the graph after a change at a random node, can be estimated using the average measure. Also in the context of parallel computations that simulate distributed computations, we can take advantage of the fact that a job is finished earlier to process an other job, and then the average running time is the relevant measure.

**Part of this work was done while the author was visiting LIAFA at university Paris Diderot, with additional support from ANR project DISPLEXITY.*

Permission to make digital or hard copies of part or all of this work for personal or classroom use is granted without fee provided that copies are not made or distributed for profit or commercial advantage and that copies bear this notice and the full citation on the first page. Copyrights for third-party components of this work must be honored. For all other uses, contact the Owner/Author. Copyright is held by the owner/author(s).
PODC'15, July 21–23, 2015, Donostia-San Sebastián, Spain.
Copyright © 2015 ACM 978-1-4503-3617-8 /15/07 ...$15.00.
DOI:http://dx.doi.org/10.1145/2767386.2767446 .

2. ALGORITHM FOR THE LARGEST ID IN A CYCLE

In this section, we show that the *largest ID* problem on a cycle has a linear worst case complexity, and that there exists an algorithm with logarithmic average radius. In this problem, each vertex must output *Yes* if it has the largest identifier in the graph, and *No* otherwise. The worst case complexity of the problem is linear because, for any algorithm, the vertex with the maximum ID needs to see all the cycle. The following straightforward algorithm gives a linear upper bound: each node increases its radius until it discovers an ID that is larger than its own ID, or until it has seen all the cycle. We show that the average running time of this algorithm is logarithmic in n.

The vertex with the maximum identifier needs $n/2$ rounds to discover that it has the largest ID. We can consider that the other vertices are in a path, and that reaching an endpoint is sufficient to stop and output *No*. The radius needed by these other vertices is the minimum distance to a vertex with larger ID or an endpoint. Note that the vertex with largest ID of the segment must reach an endpoint. We can then subdivide the vertices of the segment into three parts: the one with the largest ID, the ones in the segment on the left, and the ones on the right. Let $a(p)$ be the maximum (over the permutations of the identifiers) sum of radiuses in a segment with p vertices. Then the following recurrence relation follows from the decomposition into three pieces, and from the symmetry:

$$a(p) = \max_{1 \leq k \leq \lceil p/2 \rceil} \{k + a(k-1) + a(p-k)\}.$$

This sequence $a(n)$, with initial values $a(0) = 0$, and $a(1) = 1$, is known to be in $\theta(n \ln(n))$ (see for example the sequence A000788 of the OEIS [6]). Thereafter, the average radius is logarithmic in n, which is exponentially smaller than the worst case complexity.

3. LOWER BOUND FOR COLOURING

The classic algorithm for distributed 3-colouring a ring is the Cole-Vishkin algorithm [1], that uses $O(\log^* n)$ rounds for every vertex. This is basically optimal for the classic measure, as Linial proved that this task requires $\Omega(\log^* n)$ rounds[3]. One could try to improve the average complexity, using less rounds for some vertices. In this section, we show that this is useless: Linial's lower bound also holds for this new measure.

THEOREM 1. *The average complexity of 3-colouring a ring with n nodes is $\Omega(\log^* n)$.*

We say that an algorithm A for 3-colouring is minimal, if there is no other algorithm A' that behaves strictly better. More precisely, A is minimal if there does not exist A' that uses at most the same radius as A for every neighbourhood, and a strictly smaller radius for at least one neighbourhood. Without loss of generality we prove the theorem only for minimal algorithms. We first prove two lemmas about the regularity of the distribution of the radiuses. For technical reasons, we begin with 4-colouring and then come back to 3-colouring.

LEMMA 2. *In a graph G with identifiers, given two arbitrary vertices x and y, separated by k vertices, if an algorithm A is minimal for 4-colouring, then the radiuses of the vertices between x and y are at most $\max\{r(x), r(y)\} + k$.*

PROOF. For the sake of contradiction, suppose that there exists G, x, y, k and A as in the lemma, and some vertices between x and y with radiuses strictly larger than the threshold, $\max\{r(x), r(y)\} + k$. Let N be the slice of identifiers that contains x, y, the vertices between them, and the views of x and y. We show how to transform A into a strictly smaller algorithm A', by decreasing the radiuses of some vertices in the neighbourhood N. For every vertex v, if when running A, v discovers that it is not in the neighborhood N between x and y, or if it stops before reaching the threshold, then it does the same with A'. Otherwise, v knows that it is in this particular neighbourhood, stops at radius $\max\{r(x), r(y)\} + k$, and outputs obeying two simple rules that depend only on the two direct neighbours. Assume without loss of generality that $ID(x) > ID(y)$, and let d, be the distance between v and x. First, if a neighbour has stopped strictly before the threshold, choose a different colour. Second, if a neighbour has not stopped before the threshold, then if d is even, v outputs a colour in $\{1, 2\}$, else v outputs a colour in $\{3, 4\}$. One can check that this new algorithm A' produces a valid 4-colouring for every graph and identifiers. Moreover for every neighbourhood the radius given by A' is at most the one given by A, and, for at least one neighbourhood, strictly smaller. This contradicts the fact that A is minimal. □

We use lemma 2 to prove the following more practical result.

LEMMA 3. *If a vertex v uses radius r, in a minimal algorithm A for 3-colouring, then the average of the radiuses of the vertices at distance at most $r/2$ from v, is $\Omega(r)$.*

PROOF. First note that it is sufficient to prove the result for 4-colouring, as it implies the result for 3-colouring. Let d in $\{1, 2, ..., \lfloor r/2 \rfloor\}$, and let u_d and w_d be the two vertices at distance d from v on the cycle. Lemma 2 implies

$$r \leq \max\{r(u_d), r(w_d)\} + 2d - 1,$$

then

$$r - 2d + 1 \leq r(u_d) + r(w_d).$$

Then by summing over d:

$$\sum_{d=1}^{\lfloor r/2 \rfloor} (r - 2d + 1) \leq \sum_{d=1}^{\lfloor r/2 \rfloor} r(u_d) + r(w_d).$$

If we add r on both side of the equation, the right-hand term is the sum of the radiuses of the vertices at distance at most $r/2$ from v, and the left-hand term is quadratic in r. The lemma follows. □

The end of the proof of theorem 1 uses the following corollary of Linial's lower bound as a black box. For every algorithm that 3-colours a cycle of length larger than $n/2$, there exists a permutation of the node identifiers such that at least one vertex needs a radius of $\frac{1}{2}.\log^*(n/2)$. Given a minimal algorithm A, we show that we can build a permutation π of the identifiers that leads to an average running time in $\Omega(\log^* n)$.

First, consider an n-cycle and a permutation of the identifiers, such that one vertex has radius at least $\frac{1}{2}.\log^*(n/2)$. We take the slice of identifiers that are in the ball of radius $\frac{1}{2}.\log^*(n/2)$ around this vertex, and put it at the beginning of π. Then, consider the rest of the identifiers, and repeat the operation: remove from the original set of identifier a $\frac{1}{2}.\log^*(n/2)$-ball around a vertex with large radius, and concatenate it to π. We do it until there are less than $n/2$ vertices remaining in the original set. Finally, we put the rest of the identifiers at the end of π in an arbitrary order.

The vertex at the centre of each slice has exactly the same $\frac{1}{2}\log^*(n/2)$-neighbourhood as when it was removed from the original set of identifiers, hence its radius in π, with the same algorithm A, is at least $\frac{1}{2}\log^*(n/2)$. Thanks to lemma 3, the average radius in each slice is $\Omega(\log^*(n/2))$, that is $\Omega(\log^*(n))$. Then the average radius in π is $\Omega(\log^*(n))$. This concludes the proof of the theorem.

4. CONCLUSION AND FURTHER WORK

This paper presents a new measure of the locality. It is close to the classic measure for some problems, and very different for others. It would be interesting to characterise the problems of the first and second types. Also, we only consider the cycle topology, and results for more general graphs are missing. Last, as the average we consider is over the nodes, but it would also be interesting to begin to study the expectancy of the running time on graphs where the permutation of the identifiers is taken uniformly at random, for both the classic and the new measure.

Acknowledgements

I would like to thank Pierre Fraigniaud, Juho Hirvonen, Tuomo Lempiäinen and Jukka Suomela for helpful discussions.

5. REFERENCES

[1] Richard Cole, and Uzi Vishkin. Deterministic Coin Tossing with Applications to Optimal Parallel List Ranking. *Information and Control*, 70(1):32–53,1986.

[2] Amos Korman, Jean-Sébastien Sereni, and Laurent Viennot. Toward more localized local algorithms: removing assumptions concerning global knowledge. *Distributed Computing*, 26(5-6):289–308, 2013.

[3] Nathan Linial. Locality in distributed graph algorithms. *SIAM J. Comput.*, 21(1):193–201, 1992.

[4] Topi Musto. Knowledge of degree bounds in local algorithms. Master's thesis, University of Helsinki, 2011.

[5] David Peleg. Distributed Computing: A Locality-Sensitive Approach. SIAM, Philadelphia, PA, 2000.

[6] N. J. A. Sloane. The On-Line Encyclopedia of Integer Sequences. A000788.

Brief Announcement: Investigating the Cost of Anonymity on Dynamic Networks

Giuseppe Antonio Di Luna Roberto Baldoni
Dipartimento di Ingegneria Informatica, Automatica e Gestionale Antonio Ruberti
Università degli Studi di Roma La Sapienza, Via Ariosto 25, Rome, Italy
{diluna,baldoni}@dis.uniroma1.it

ABSTRACT

In this paper we study the problem of counting processes in a synchronous dynamic network where a distinguished leader is available and other nodes share the same identifier. The network topology may change at each synchronous round and each node communicates with its neighbors by broadcasting messages. In such networks it is well known that counting requires $\Omega(D)$ rounds where D is the network diameter. We identify a non-trivial subset of dynamic networks where counting requires $\Omega(\log |V|)$ rounds even when the dynamic diameter, D, is constant with respect to the network size and the bandwidth is unlimited.

1. INTRODUCTION

Computing over a dynamic distributed system has become mainstream in the recent years, this has been due to advent of peer-to-peer systems and the capillary distribution of mobile devices. In this paper we consider a dynamic system where processes do not leave the computation while there is an adversary that continuously changes the communication graph connecting such processes. We assume a strong adversary that is able to access nodes' local variables in order to deploy at each computational round the worst possible network topology to contrast the convergence of the counting algorithm. The adversary is only constrained to maintain at each round a connected topology, i.e. 1-interval connectivity [1]. In this setting, it has been shown in [5] that counting cannot be solved without a leader and, recently, counting algorithms have been provided that minimize the nodes' knowledge about the moves of the adversary (e.g., [4]).

We show that counting on graphs where $D > 3$ requires at least $\Omega(\log |V|)$ rounds. We prove this bound on a family of dynamic graphs, namely $\mathcal{G}(\mathrm{PD})_2$ graphs, in which each node has a persistent distance from the leader across rounds and such distance is at most 2. From this bound is immediate to see that on dynamic graphs with constant dynamic diameter D the cost of counting is $D+\Omega(\log |V|)$ rounds, showing that any algorithm has to pay at least a factor of $\Omega(\log |V|)$ to overcome nodes' anonymity. Due to lack of space proofs are omitted, the interested reader can refer to [3].

Related Work: The problem of counting in an anonymous network with worst-case adversary and broadcast communication has been investigated in [5] where authors conjectured impossibility of counting despite the presence of a leader node. [2] considers directed static network with IDs with bandwidth limited to $\Omega(\log |V|)$-bits, it shows that the time needed to solve counting is function of the network size even when $D = 2$, specifically $\Omega(\frac{|V|}{\log |V|})$ rounds. When considering unlimited bandwidth in either static networks with IDs, dynamic network with IDs or anonymous static networks, there are algorithms showing that the cost of counting is at most of the same order of information dissemination which is $\Omega(D)$ [1, 5]. The lower bound presented in this paper shows that in a non-trivial set of anonymous dynamic (1-interval connected) networks, even when D is constant with respect to V, there is at least a gap of $\Omega(\log |V|)$ rounds between counting and information dissemination, identifying thus a cost of handling anonymity in such networks.

2. SYSTEM MODEL

We consider a synchronous system composed by a finite static set of processes $V : \{v_0, \ldots, v_n\}$ (also called *nodes*). Nodes in $V \setminus \{v_l\}$ are *anonymous*, i.e., they initially have no identifiers and execute a deterministic *round-based* computation. Node v_l is a special leader node that has a different unique state. Processes communicate through a communication network which is *dynamic*. We assume at each round r the network is stable and represented by a graph $G_r = (V, E(r))$ where $E(r) \subseteq V \times V$ is the set of bidirectional links at round r connecting processes in V. A *dynamic graph* $G = \{G_0, G_1, \ldots, G_r, \ldots\}$ is an infinite sequence of graphs one at each round r of the computation. We denote as $d_r(v_0, v_1)$ the distance between v_0, v_1 on graph G_r. Every round is divided in a *send phase* where processes send the messages for the current round and a *receive phase* where nodes process received messages for preparing messages to be sent in the next round. Each Process communicates with its neighbors through an *anonymous broadcast* primitive: a message m sent by node v_i in the send phase of round r will be delivered to all its neighbors during the receive phase of r. The message m initially sent by node v at round r is disseminated though G at round r' if all nodes in the networks received a copy of m by round r'. The dynamic diameter of the network, D, is the maximum numbers of rounds needed to disseminate a message in G.

Permission to make digital or hard copies of part or all of this work for personal or classroom use is granted without fee provided that copies are not made or distributed for profit or commercial advantage, and that copies bear this notice and the full citation on the first page. Copyrights for third-party components of this work must be honored. For all other uses, contact the owner/author(s). Copyright is held by the author/owner(s).
PODC'15, July 21–23, 2015, Donostia-San Sebastián, Spain.
ACM 978-1-4503-3617-8 /15/07.
http://dx.doi.org/10.1145/2767386.2767442.

DEFINITION 1. *Given a dynamic network G with $|V|$ processes, a distributed algorithm $\mathcal{A}$ solves the counting on G if it exists a round r at which the leader outputs $|V|$ and terminates.*

In the rest of the paper we consider a specific set of dynamic graphs, namely $\mathcal{G}(\text{PD})_2$, a each node of a graph belonging to $\mathcal{G}(\text{PD})_2$ has distance either 2 or 1 from the leader and such distance does not change across rounds (an example of a graph belonging to $\mathcal{G}(\text{PD})_2$ is shown of the right part of Figure 1). Formally:

DEFINITION 2. *A graph G belongs to $\mathcal{G}(PD)_2$, iff $\forall v \in V \setminus \{v_l\}$, $\exists d \in [1,2]$ such that $\forall r :: d_r(v, v_l) = d$.*

3. LOWER BOUND FOR $\mathcal{G}$(PD)$_2$

The bound is computed by introducing a *Dynamic Bipartite Labeled k-Multigraphs* ($\mathcal{M}(\text{DBL}_k)$), by showing that counting on $\mathcal{G}(\text{PD})_2$ requires at least the same number of rounds as counting over $\mathcal{M}(\text{DBL}_k)$ and by finally showing a lower bound for counting over $\mathcal{M}(\text{DBL}_k)$.

3.1 Counting in $\mathcal{M}$(DBL$_k$)

Let consider a dynamic connected multigraph M defined as follows $M = \cup_{r=0}^{\infty}\{(\{v_l\} \cup W, E(r), f_r, l_r)\}$ where $E(r)$ is a set of edges at round r, W a set of nodes, $f_r : E(r) \rightarrow \{v_l\} \times W$ a function that maps each edge to the endpoints nodes and $l_r : E(r) \rightarrow \{1, 2, \ldots, k\}$ a function labeling edges. M belongs to $\mathcal{M}(\text{DBL}_k)$ if for each round r the number of edges connecting a node $v \in W$ to v_l is less than $k+1$. We have that two edges connected to the same non leader node have different labels, more formally defined $E^v(r) = f_r^{-1}(v_l, v)$ we have that $l_r(e') \neq l_r(e'')$, $\forall e', e'' \in E^v(r)$. We additionally denote as M_r the instance of M at round r. When a node belonging to M receives a broadcast message m from edge e, m brings to the node the label of the edge $l(e)$.

LEMMA 1. *Let us consider a dynamic connected multigraph M in $\mathcal{M}(DBL_k)$. If any counting algorithm takes more than T rounds to complete on M, then there exists a graph G in $\mathcal{G}(PD)_2$ such that any counting algorithm requires more than T rounds to complete on G.*

As a consequence of the lemma, it follows that a lower bound for counting on $\mathcal{M}(\text{DBL}_k)$ holds also for graphs in $\mathcal{G}(\text{PD})_2$. Let us now introduce the following notions on $M \in \mathcal{M}(\text{DBL}_k)$:

DEFINITION 3. *Given a node $v \in W$ at round r we define the set of edge labels $L(v,r) : \{l_1, \ldots, l_j\}$ with $l_i \in L(v,r)$ iff $\exists e \in E(r)$ and $l_r(e) = l_i$ and $f_r(e) = (v, v_l)$.*

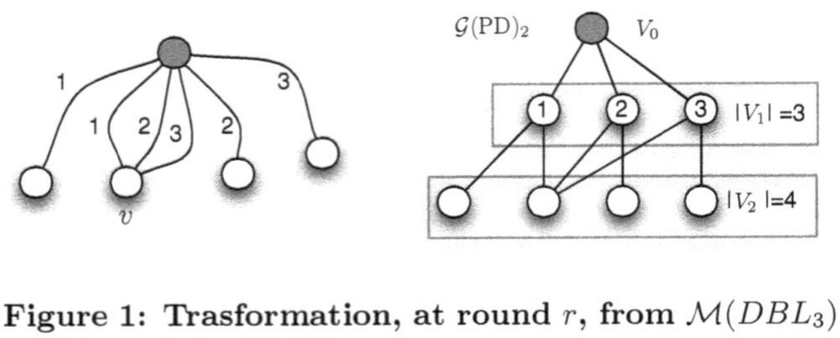

Figure 1: Trasformation, at round r, from $\mathcal{M}(DBL_3)$ multigraph to $\mathcal{G}(\text{PD})_2$.

As an example in Figure 1, the edge label set of node v at round r is $\{1, 2, 3\}$.

DEFINITION 4. *Given a node $v \in W$ at round r, we define the state $S(v,r)$ as an ordered list $S(v,r) : [(\bot), L(v,0), \ldots, L(v, r-1)]$ where $(\bot)$ is the first state of any non-leader node*[1].

Given a list $A : [L_0, \ldots, L_{r-1}]$ we have that $|A|$ denotes the number of nodes with the same state $S(v,r) = A$ at round r. Considering Figure 1, we have $S(v, r+1) = [\bot, \ldots, \{1,2,3\}]$ and $|S(v, r+1)| = 1$ since v is the only node connected to v_l by $\{1,2,3\}$ at round r.

DEFINITION 5. *Given the leader v_l at round r we define the leader state $S(v_l, r)$ as $[C(v_l, 0), \ldots, C(v_l, r-1)]$ where $C(v_l, i)$ with $i < r$ is a multiset of elements. Element $(j, S(v,i)) \in C(v_l, i)$ iff it exists a node v with state $S(v,i)$ connected to v_l by an edge with label j.*

As for states of local nodes, $|(j, S(v,r))|$ denotes the number of nodes with state equal to $S(v,r)$ connected to v_l by an edge with label j at round r.

3.2 Lower Bound for $\mathcal{M}$(DBL$_k$)

The proof is based on linear algebra concepts. We introduce some notation on vectors and matrices used in this section.

Linear algebra notation: Given a vector $\mathbf{a} \in \mathbb{Z}^n$, we denote as $(\mathbf{a})_j$ the j-th component of $\mathbf{a}$ (with $1 \leq j \leq n$) and as $\sum \mathbf{a}$ the sum of all components of $\mathbf{a}$. Additionally, $\sum^+ \mathbf{a}$ (resp. $\sum^- \mathbf{a}$) denotes the sum of only the positive (resp. negative) components. Given two vectors $\mathbf{a}, \mathbf{b}$ we have $\begin{bmatrix}\mathbf{a} & \mathbf{b}\end{bmatrix}^\intercal$ is the vector obtained by appending vector $\mathbf{b}$ after vector $\mathbf{a}$. Given a matrix $\mathbf{M} \in \mathbb{N}^{n,m}$ we denote as $(\mathbf{M})_j$ its j-th row (with $1 \leq j \leq n$) and as $ker(\mathbf{M})$ the set of vectors $\mathbf{a} \in \mathbb{Z}^m$ such that $\mathbf{Ma} = \mathbf{0}$. We also consider the set of vectors $B = \{\mathbf{a}^1, \ldots, \mathbf{a}^\ell\}$ that form a basis for $ker(\mathbf{M})$, i.e., $ker(\mathbf{M}) = SPAN(B)$. Finally we denote as $\mathbf{a}_r$ the instance of vector $\mathbf{a}$ at round r.

We prove the bound for the family $\mathcal{M}(\text{DBL}_k)$ by first proving the lower bound for $\mathcal{M}(\text{DBL}_2)$. Considering the latter proof, we first introduce a system of equations that characterizes the states of the nodes of the multigraph at round zero. The lower bound for $\mathcal{M}(\text{DBL}_2)$ is then proved by studying the evolution of this system of equations through the rounds.

Consider $M \in \mathcal{M}(\mathbf{DBL}_2)$ and $r = 0$: At the end of round 0 the leader has state $S(v_l, 0) : [\{(1, [\bot]), (2, [\bot])\}]$, this leader state can be generated by many different configurations of nodes and edges in M. Such configurations are determined by the number of non leader processes with states $[\{1\}], [\{2\}], [\{1,2\}]$ and they are solutions of the following system of equations at round 0:

$$\begin{cases} |(1, [\bot])| = |[\{1\}]| + |[\{1,2\}]| \\ |(2, [\bot])| = |[\{2\}]| + |[\{1,2\}]| \end{cases}_{r=0} \qquad (1)$$

with the additional constraint that any variable in the solution cannot assume a negative value. When the leader updates its state, in successive rounds, we have a new system of equations. The system of equations 1 can be written in a matrix form as follows: $\mathbf{m}_0 = \mathbf{M}_0 \mathbf{s}_0$. Where $\mathbf{M}_0 : \begin{bmatrix} 1 & 0 & 1 \\ 0 & 1 & 1 \end{bmatrix}$

[1]For simplicity whenever not necessary we omit the presence of $(\bot)$ as first element of $S(v,r)$.

represents the matrix of coefficients of the system at round 0, $\mathbf{m}_0$ is the column vector of constant terms (each component of $\mathbf{m}_r$ represents the multiplicity of a certain element in the state of the leader at round r) and $\mathbf{s}_0$ is a solution vector. Let us remark that $\mathbf{M}_r$ depends of the round only while $\mathbf{m}_r$ depends of the leader state at round r.

The matrix $\mathbf{M}_0$ is characterized by $ker(\mathbf{M}_0) = SPAN(\{\mathbf{k}_0 : [1 \;\; 1 \;\; -1]^\intercal\})$. Solutions of the matrix equation for round 0 are related by the following linear combination $\mathbf{k}_0$: $\mathbf{s}'_0 = \mathbf{s}_0 + t\mathbf{k}_0$ with $t \in \mathbb{N}$ and such that each component of $\mathbf{s}'_0$ is non negative. From the point of view of the leader each solution represents a distinct graph belonging to $\mathcal{M}(\mathrm{DBL}_2)$ with a different number of processes: $\sum \mathbf{s}'_0 - \sum \mathbf{s}_0 = t \sum \mathbf{k}_0 = t$.

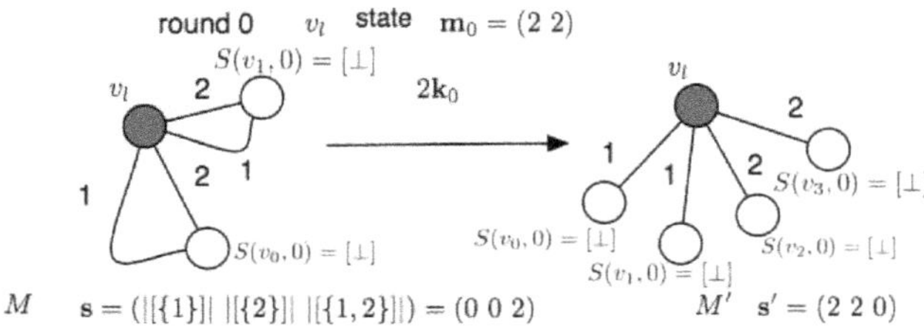

Figure 2: Two dynamic multigraphs $M, M' \in \mathcal{M}(\mathbf{DBL}_2)$ of different size that are indistinguishable at round $r = 0$, the relationship among M, M' is given by the kernel vector $\mathbf{k}_0$

Considering the example of Figure 2, the system of equations at round 0 for the multigraph M is the following

$$\begin{cases} 2 = |[\{1\}]| + |[\{1,2\}]| \\ 2 = |[\{2\}]| + |[\{1,2\}]| \end{cases}_{r=0} \quad (2)$$

where $\mathbf{m}_0 : [2 \;\; 2]^\intercal$. For such system of equations a solution is $\mathbf{s}_0 : [0 \;\; 0 \;\; 2]^\intercal$, then using the kernel transformation another solution is $\mathbf{s}'_0 = \mathbf{s}_0 + 2\mathbf{k}_0 : [2 \;\; 2 \;\; 0]^\intercal$, these two solutions correspond to two $M, M' \in \mathcal{M}(\mathrm{DBL}_2)$ of different size that generate the same state $S(v_l, 0)$. Each solution vector $\mathbf{s}_r$ corresponds to a run of the dynamic multigraph M until round r. The idea that we will use to show the lower bound is to characterize how the kernel space of $\mathbf{M}_r$ evolves and under which conditions we have an unique solution, that corresponds to an unique size $|W|$.

General structure of $\mathbf{M}_r$: At round r we have $\mathbf{m}_r = \mathbf{M}_r\mathbf{s}_r$. The number of columns of $\mathbf{M}_r$ is equal to the number of all possible states of non-leader nodes, at round $r+1$, which is $column(r) = 3^{r+1}$. Each row of $\mathbf{M}_r$ corresponds to a possible connection $(j, S(v, r'))$ of v_l at some round $0 \le r' \le r$. Thus the number of rows at round r is two times the number of existent states in $[0, r]$: $row(r) = 2\sum_{k=0}^{r} 3^k$. The leader connection $(j, [x_0, \ldots, x_{r'-1}])$ with $j \in \{1, 2\}$ introduces at round r' an equation in the system, and thus a row in $\mathbf{M}_{r'}$, that is $|(j, [x_0, \ldots, x_{r'-1}])|$ $= |[x_0, \ldots, x_{r'-1}, \{j\}]| + |[x_0, \ldots, x_{r'-1}, \{1,2\}]$. This equation at round r becomes:

$$|(j, [x_0, \ldots, x_{r'}])| = \sum_{\forall s \in (\{1\}|\{2\}|\{1,2\})^{r-r'}} |[x_0, \ldots, x_{r'-1}, \{j\}, s]| + \sum_{\forall s \in (\{1\}|\{2\}|\{1,2\})^{r-r'}} [x_0, \ldots, x_{r'-1}, \{1,2\}, s]| \quad (3)$$

where $(\{1\}|\{2\}|\{1,2\})^{r-r'}$ is the set of all possible lists with elements in $\{\{1\}, \{2\}, \{1,2\}\}$ and size $r - r'$. In the following lemmas we specifically characterize the structure of the kernel space of $\mathbf{M}_r$.

LEMMA 2. *Let us consider the matrix $\mathbf{M}_r$ of the family $\mathcal{M}(DBL_2)$ at round r. The dimension of the kernel space of $\mathbf{M}_r$ is one (i.e., $ker(\mathbf{M}_r) = SPAN(\{\mathbf{k}_r\})$).*

LEMMA 3. *Let us consider the matrix $\mathbf{M}_r$ of the family $\mathcal{M}(DBL_2)$ at round r. We have $\mathbf{k}_r = [\mathbf{k}_{r-1} \;\; \mathbf{k}_{r-1} \;\; -\mathbf{k}_{r-1}]^\intercal$ with $\mathbf{k}_{-1} = 1$.*

LEMMA 4. *Let consider the matrix $\mathbf{M}_r$ of the family $\mathcal{M}(DBL_2)$ at round r.*

We have: $\begin{cases} min(\sum^+ \mathbf{k}_r, \sum^- \mathbf{k}_r) = \sum^- \mathbf{k}_r = \frac{1}{2}(3^r + 1) - 1 \\ \sum \mathbf{k}_r = 1 \end{cases}$

Intuitively if we have a system with n nodes and $n \ge \sum^- \mathbf{k}_r$ then there exist at least two possible distinct solution $\mathbf{s}_r$ and $\mathbf{s}'_r = \mathbf{s}_r + \mathbf{k}_r$ that gives the same $\mathbf{m}_r = \mathbf{M}_r\mathbf{s}_r$ and with $\sum \mathbf{s}_r \ne \sum \mathbf{s}'_r$ therefore counting is impossible.

LEMMA 5. *Let us consider $M, M' \in \mathcal{M}(DBL_2)$ such that their sizes are: $|W| = n$ and $|W'| = n + 1$. Does not exist an algorithm $\mathcal{A}_l$ that at round $r \le \lfloor log_3(2|n| + 1) \rfloor$ is able to distinguish if it is running on multigraph M or M'.*

Considering that $\mathcal{M}(\mathrm{DBL}_2) \subseteq \mathcal{M}(\mathrm{DBL}_k)$, we can state the following theorem whose proof is straightforward.

THEOREM 1. *Any algorithm $\mathcal{A}$ cannot solve the counting on an instance $M \in \mathcal{M}(DBL_k)$ at round $r < \lfloor log_3(2|W| + 1) \rfloor - 1$.*

From Theorem 1 and Lemma 1 we have

THEOREM 2. *Given an instance $G \in \mathcal{G}(PD)_2$ any counting algorithm $\mathcal{A}$ on G requires $\Omega(log|V|)$ rounds.*

Acknowledgements: The work has been partially supported by the Italian PRIN Project TENACE "Protecting National Critical Infrastructures from Cyber Threats".

4. REFERENCES

[1] F. Kuhn, N. Lynch, and R. Oshman. Distributed computation in dynamic networks. In *STOC '10*, pages 513–522. ACM, 2010.

[2] F. Kuhn and R. Oshman. The complexity of data aggregation in directed networks. In *DISC' 11*, pages 416–431, 2011.

[3] G. D. Luna and R. Baldoni. Investigating the cost of anonymity on dynamic networks. `http://arxiv.org/abs/1505.03509`.

[4] G. D. Luna, R. Baldoni, S. Bonomi, and I. Chatzigiannakis. Counting in anonymous dynamic networks under worst case adversary. In *ICDCS '14*, pages 338–347. IEEE, 2014.

[5] O. Michail, I. Chatzigiannakis, and P. Spirakis. Brief announcement: Naming and counting in anonymous unknown dynamic networks. In *DISC '12*, pages 437–438. Springer, 2012.

Online Resource Leasing*

Christine Markarian & Friedhelm Meyer auf der Heide
Heinz Nixdorf Institute & Computer Science Department
University of Paderborn
Fürstenallee 11, 33102 Paderborn, Germany
{christine.markarian,fmadh}@uni-paderborn.de

ABSTRACT

Many markets have seen a shift from the idea of *buying* and moved to *leasing* instead. Arguably, the latter has been the major catalyst for their success. Ten years ago, research realized this shift and initiated the study of 'online leasing problems' by introducing leasing to online optimization problems. Resources required to provide a service in an 'online leasing problem' are no more *bought* but *leased* for different durations. In this paper, we provide an overview of results that contribute to the understanding of 'online resource leasing problems'.

1. INTRODUCTION

Decisions regarding which resources to acquire in order to provide services comprise the core of many optimization problems. Examples of such resources include servers in a network, machines in the Cloud, and warehouses in a company. Classical problems which fall into this category of problems are Facility Location, Steiner Tree, and Set Cover. Such problems have been widely studied in both offline and online settings. Traditionally, these decisions are considered to be final: we *buy* the resources. Once a resource is bought, it can be used any time in the future without inducing further costs that can be influenced by time or number of uses. In pursuit of better economies of scale, a number of models were introduced. In the Buy-at-Bulk model [3], number of uses matter, such that cost varies with the capacity a resource provides (the larger the capacity the cheaper per unit). Another well studied model is the Rent-or-Buy model [4], where apart from buying resources for various capacities, a resource can be bought and used forever at a larger cost. None of these models, however, consider the effect of time on the cost. In fact, deploying a server for a long period, for example, incurs maintenance and update costs which must be taken care of. Moreover, consider the Cloud Computing market, which among many others have shifted from *buying* to *leasing*. The latter has seen a huge jump in the past years and arguably, the major catalyst for its success is the flexibility it has been offering to its users. Cloud users are now able to access resources in the Cloud for reasonable prices whenever they need without the urge to make huge investments like before. In the light of realizing this shift and influence of time on the cost of resources, Meyerson introduced the *leasing* model [1]. In this model, resources are leased for different periods of time and expire afterwards, such that the cost paid for a resource depends on the duration of its lease. Naturally, a longer duration induces a more expensive but cheaper-per-unit-time leasing cost. He illustrated leasing with the Parking Permit Problem. Here, each day, we either use the car if it is rainy or walk if it is sunny. If we take the car, we must have a valid parking permit, and there are K different types of parking permits (leases), each with its own duration (e.g., one day, one week, one month) and cost. The goal is to buy a set of parking permits in order to cover all rainy days and minimize the total cost of purchases without using weather forecasts. This simple problem has inspired a significant literature about optimization problems that were previously studied in an online setting and are now defined with a leasing aspect as well. The rest of this paper gives an overview of this literature.

*This work was partially supported by the German Research Foundation (DFG) within the Collaborative Research Center 'On-The-Fly Computing' (SFB 901) and the International Graduate School 'Dynamic Intelligent Systems'.

Permission to make digital or hard copies of part or all of this work for personal or classroom use is granted without fee provided that copies are not made or distributed for profit or commercial advantage and that copies bear this notice and the full citation on the first page. Copyrights for third-party components of this work must be honored. For all other uses, contact the Owner/Author.
Copyright is held by the owner/author(s).
PODC '15, July 21-23, 2015, Donostia-San SebastiÃạn, Spain.
ACM 978-1-4503-3617-8/15/07.
http://dx.doi.org/10.1145/2767386.2767454

2. STATE OF THE ART: FROM 'BUYING' TO 'LEASING'

Ever since the leasing model was introduced, many online optimization problems were extended, by including a leasing aspect. In this section, we summarize the most prominent of these results. The standard measure of *competitiveness* is used to give the quality of online algorithms.

From 'Online Facility Location' to 'Facility Leasing'. One of the most well-known online problems appearing as a sub-problem in many applications is Online Facility Location. Here, a set of m facilities (each with a setup cost) is given. A set of n clients arrive (each with a connection cost for each facility) and must be connected to some facility. An online algorithm must connect arriving clients by opening facilities, while minimizing the total setup and connection costs. Meyerson [7] presented a randomized $O(\log n)$-competitive algorithm for Online Facility Location which was improved to a deterministic $O(\log n/ \log \log n)$-competitive algorithm by Fotakis [6] (who also showed that this bound is optimal). Motivated to keep up with current markets and inspired by Meyerson's Parking Permit Problem, Anthony et al. [8] extended Online Facility Location to Facility Leasing. Here, unlike Online Facility Location in which facilities can be used forever once they are opened, we must pick one of K different lease types when opening a facility. An online algorithm must connect arriving clients by leasing facilities, while minimizing the total leasing and connection costs. Facility Leasing is in fact a generalization of Online Facility Location if we allow only one type of lease having an infinite period of time ($K = 1$). Anthony and Gupta [8] showed an interesting relationship between infrastructure leasing problems and stochastic optimization that led to an $O(K)$-approximation for Facility Leasing in the offline setting. Nagarajan and Williamson [9] later improved the $O(K)$-approximation to a 3-approximation and gave an $O(K \log n)$-competitive algorithm for metric Facility Leasing in the online setting. In [10], we improved the results by Nagarajan and Williamson [9] by removing the dependency on n (and thereby on time) from the competitive factor. We gave an $O(l_{max} \log(l_{max}))$-competitive algorithm where l_{max} is the maximum lease length.

From 'Online Set Cover' to 'Set Cover Leasing'. OnlineSetCover is a special case of non-metric Online Facility Location. Here, elements from a set U ($|U| = n$) arrive over time and must be covered by sets from a family F ($|F| = m$) of subsets of U (each with a cost). Alon et al. [2] gave an $O(\log m \log n)$-competitive and an $O(\log n \log d)$-competitive deterministic algorithm for weighted and unweighted Online Set Cover, respectively (where d is the maximum number of sets an element belogs to). They also showed that their bounds are nearly tight due to a lower bound $O(\log m \log n / (\log \log m + \log \log n))$ which they give for a wide range of relations among m and n. In [12], we gave the first online algorithm for the leasing variant of Online Set Cover: Set Cover Leasing. Set Cover Leasing was introduced along with Facility Leasing by Anthony and Gupta [8], who gave an optimal $O(\log n)$-approximation offline algorithm for Set Cover Leasing. Unlike Online Set Cover in which sets are paid for once and can be used forever, each set in Set Cover Leasing can be leased for K different periods of time with different costs. An online algorithm is asked to minimize the total leasing costs of sets, such that elements arriving at any time t are covered by sets which contain them and are leased during time t.

Online leasing with deadlines. The leasing model by Meyerson [1] makes the assumption that demands need to be served as soon as they arrive. In many real-world applications, however, this need not be true. Consider Cloud users, for example, who are flexible regarding when to use the resources (e.g., any day within two weeks will do). Such users will be happy to wait and be offered better resource prices for a later day. To capture such scenarios, we introduced, in a recent work [11], a new model for online leasing problems such that demands can be postponed up to some fixed period of time resulting in a deadline for each demand. Each demand i can be served anytime between its arrival a_i and its deadline $a_i + d_i$ by a leased resource. The objective is to meet all deadlines while minimizing the total leasing costs. This model is a natural generalization of Meyerson's Parking Permit Problem in which $d_i = 0$ for all i. We proposed an online algorithm that is $\Theta\left(K + \frac{d_{max}}{l_{min}}\right)$-competitive where d_{max} and l_{min} denote the largest d_i and the shortest available lease length, respectively. We also extended the SetCoverLeasing problem by deadlines and gave an $\mathcal{O}\left(\log(m \cdot (K + \frac{d_{max}}{l_{min}})) \log l_{max}\right)$-competitive online algorithm which also implies an improvement for Set Cover Leasing [12] by removing time dependency from the competitive factor.

3. REFERENCES

[1] A. Meyerson *The parking permit problem. In Proceedings of the 46th Annual IEEE Symposium on Foundations of Computer Science (FOCS)*, pp. 274 - 284, 2005.

[2] N. Alon, B. Awerbuch, Y. Azar, N. Buchbinder, and J. Naor *The online set cover problem. In Proceedings of the 35th Annual ACM Symposium on the Theory of Computation (STOC)*, pp. 100 - 105, 2003.

[3] M. Andrews and L. Zhang *Wavelength assignment in optical networks with fixed fiber capacity. In Proceedings of the 31st International Colloquium (ICALP)*, pp. 134 - 145, 2004.

[4] A. Gupta, A. Kumar, M. P'al, and Roughgarden *Approximation via cost sharing: Simpler and better approximation algorithms for network design. Journal of the ACM (JACM)* 54 (3), No. 11, 2007.

[5] D. Fotakis *A primal-dual algorithm for online non-uniform facility location. Journal of Discrete Algorithms*, 5 (1), pp. 141 - 148, 2007.

[6] D. Fotakis *On the competitive ratio for online facility location. Algorithmica*, 50 (1), pp. 1 - 57, 2008.

[7] A. Meyerson *Online facility location. In Proceedings of the 42nd Annual IEEE Symposium on Foundations of Computer Science (FOCS)*, pp. 426 - 431, 2001.

[8] B. M. Anthony and A. Gupta *Infrastructure leasing problems. In Proceedings of the 12th International Conference on Integer Programming and Combinatorial Optimization (IPCO)*, pp. 424 - 438, 2007.

[9] C. Nagarajan and D. Williamson *Offline and online facility leasing. In Proceedings of the 13th International Conference on Integer Programming and Combinatorial Optimization (IPCO), 5035*, pp. 303 - 315, 2008.

[10] P. Kling, F. Meyer auf der Heide, and P. Pietrzyk *An Algorithm for online facility leasing. In Proceedings of the 19th International Colloquium on Structural Information and Communication Complexity (SIROCCO)*, pp. 61 - 72, 2012.

[11] S. Li, A. Mäcker, C. Markarian, F. Meyer auf der Heide, and Sören Riechers *Towards flexible demands in pnline leasing problems. In 21st International Computing and Combinatorics Conference (COCOON)*, to appear, 2015.

[12] S. Abshoff, C. Markarian, and F. Meyer auf der Heide *Randomized Online algorithms for set cover leasing problems. In Proceedings of the 8th Annual International Conference on Combinatorial Optimization and Applications (COCOA)*, pp 25 - 34, 2014.

Deterministic $(\Delta + 1)$-Coloring in Sublinear (in Δ) Time in Static, Dynamic and Faulty Networks

Leonid Barenboim*
Open University of Israel
Department of Mathematics and Computer Science
leonidb@openu.ac.il

ABSTRACT

In the distributed message passing model a communication network is represented by an n-vertex graph $G = (V, E)$ of maximum degree Δ. Computation proceeds in discrete synchronous rounds consisting of sending and receiving messages and performing local computations. The running time of an algorithm is the number of rounds it requires. In the *static setting* the network remains unchanged throughout the entire execution. In the *dynamic setting* the topology of the network changes, and a new solution has to be computed after each change. In the *faulty setting* the network is static, but some vertices or edges may lose the computed solution as a result of faults. The goal of an algorithm in this setting is fixing the solution.

The problems of $(\Delta + 1)$-vertex-coloring and $(2\Delta - 1)$-edge-coloring are among the most important and intensively studied problems in distributed computing. Despite a very intensive research in the last 30 years, no deterministic algorithms for these problems with sublinear (in Δ) time have been known so far. Moreover, for more restricted scenarios and some related problems there are lower bounds of $\Omega(\Delta)$ [13, 14, 20, 27]. The question of the possibility to devise algorithms that overcome this challenging barrier is one of the most fundamental questions in distributed symmetry breaking [4, 6, 13, 14, 19, 24]. In this paper we settle this question for $(\Delta+1)$-vertex-coloring and $(2\Delta-1)$-edge-coloring by devising deterministic algorithms that require $O(\Delta^{3/4} \log \Delta + \log^* n)$ time in the static, dynamic and faulty settings. (The term $\log^* n$ is unavoidable in view of the lower bound of Linial [21].) Moreover, for $(1 + o(1))\Delta$-vertex-coloring and $(2 + o(1))\Delta$-edge-coloring we devise algorithms with $\tilde{O}(\sqrt{\Delta} + \log^* n)$ deterministic time. This is roughly a quadratic improvement comparing to the state-of-the-art that requires $O(\Delta + \log^* n)$ time [4, 19, 24]. Our results are actually more general than that since they apply also to a variant of the list-coloring problem that generalizes ordinary coloring.

Our results are obtained using a novel technique for coloring partially-colored graphs (also known as *fixing*). We partition the uncolored parts into a small number of subgraphs with certain helpful properties. Then we color these subgraphs gradually using a technique that employs *constructions of polynomials* in a novel way. Our construction is inspired by the algorithm of Linial [21] for ordinary $O(\Delta^2)$-coloring. However, it is a more sophisticated construction that differs from [21] in several important respects. These new insights in using systems of polynomials allow us to significantly speed up the $O(\Delta)$-coloring algorithms. Moreover, they allow us to devise algorithms with the same running time also in the more complicated settings of dynamic and faulty networks.

*Part of this work has been performed while the author was a postdoctoral fellow at a joint program of the Simons Institute for the Theory of Computing at UC Berkeley and I-Core at Weizmann Institute.

Permission to make digital or hard copies of all or part of this work for personal or classroom use is granted without fee provided that copies are not made or distributed for profit or commercial advantage and that copies bear this notice and the full citation on the first page. Copyrights for components of this work owned by others than ACM must be honored. Abstracting with credit is permitted. To copy otherwise, or republish, to post on servers or to redistribute to lists, requires prior specific permission and/or a fee. Request permissions from permissions@acm.org.

PODC'15, July 21–23, 2015, Donostia-San Sebastián, Spain.

Copyright © 2015 ACM 978-1-4503-3617-8 /15/07 ...$15.00.

DOI: http://dx.doi.org/10.1145/2767386.2767410 .

Categories and Subject Descriptors

G.2.2 [**Graph Theory**]: Network Problems

General Terms

Algorithms

Keywords

Distributed Algorithms; Coloring; Partitions; Polynomials

1. INTRODUCTION

1.1 The Settings

In the distributed message passing model a communication network is represented by an n-vertex graph $G = (V, E)$. The vertices of G host processors, and communication is performed over the edges. Each vertex has a unique identity number (ID) consisting of $O(\log n)$ bits. Computation starts simultaneously and proceeds in discrete synchronous rounds. In each round vertices send messages, receive messages and perform local computations. The number of rounds required for all vertices to arrive at a solution is the *running time* of the algorithm.

In *static graphs* the input graph never change. However, in order to deal with dynamic networks, such as mobile networks or networks with unreliable links we need a more appropriate model. To this end we consider also the *dynamic graphs* model. In this model the input graph changes gradually. Specifically, in each step a subset of vertices $W \subseteq V$ is removed from the graph, and a new set of vertices U is added. (The number of vertices in the network is upper-bounded by n.) In addition, the vertices of U become connected in a certain way in $U \cup V \setminus W$. Consequently, the set of edges changes as well. Hence a new graph $G' = (V', E')$ is produced. The goal of a dynamic distributed algorithm is to compute a solution for G' given a solution for G. The running time of a dynamic distributed algorithm is the worst-case number of rounds required for finding such a solution. (Once the graph G' is provided as an input to the algorithm, no additional changes are made until the algorithm completes its task.) This model is a natural extension of the sequential dynamic model and has been widely used. See, e.g., [9] and the references therein.

In *faulty graphs* the input graph is static, but a subset $U \subseteq V$ (respectively, $E' \subseteq E$) may lose the computed solution as a result of faults. The goal of a distributed algorithm for a faulty network is to compute a new solution for U (resp., E'), such that it is consistent with the solution of $V \setminus U$ (resp., $E \setminus E'$). The worst case number of rounds required for such a solution (given that no new faults occur during the execution of the algorithm) is the running time. Systems with faulty memory have been intensively studied in various settings. See, e.g., the survey of [12].

1.2 Our Results and Comparison with Related Work

Static Networks: Vertex coloring and edge coloring are among the most fundamental problems in the area of distributed algorithms. These problems are very well motivated by real-life tasks such as scheduling, resource allocation, channel assignment, work-load balancing, medium access control, etc. Moreover, these problems are of great importance from the theoretical point of view. They have been very intensively studied since the eighties, but the gaps between the best currently-known upper and lower bounds are enormous. This is especially true in the study of *deterministic algorithms.* In terms of the maximum degree Δ of the graph, the best known algorithms for $(\Delta + 1)$-vertex-coloring and $(2\Delta - 1)$-edge-coloring have running time $O(\Delta + \log^* n)$ [24, 4, 19]. In the general cases there are no known lower bounds in terms of Δ. The best currently-known deterministic upper bound in terms of n is $2^{O(\sqrt{\log n})}$ [25]. The best currently-known lower bound is $\Omega(\log^* n)$ [21]. The algorithm of [25], however, requires collecting a network topology of radius $2^{O(\sqrt{\log n})}$ in the worst case. In some networks this may require learning the entire input graph. In other words, messages of size $O(n^2)$ may be required. Remarkably, prior to our current work no deterministic algorithms that have both sublinear running time and sublinear message size have been known.

Despite the absence of strong lower bounds in the general case, there were several intriguing developments in the study of *local iterative coloring algorithms.* In these algorithms the only operation that is allowed in each round for each vertex is studying the colors of the neighbors and computing a new color based on these colors and the previous color. In STOC'93 [27] Szegedy and Vishwanathan presented a heuristic argument showing that such algorithms require $\Theta(\Delta \log \Delta)$ rounds. In PODC'06 [20] Kuhn and Wattenhofer devised an explicit local iterative coloring algorithm with time $O(\Delta \log \Delta + \log^* n)$, and proved a lower bound of $\Omega(\Delta / \log^2 \Delta + \log^* n)$ for this type of algorithms.

The $O(\Delta \log \Delta)$ barrier of Szegedy and Vishwanathan was broken by Barenboim and Elkin in STOC'09 [4], and independently by Kuhn in SPAA'09 [19]. (See also [7].) Specifically, a deterministic $(\Delta + 1)$-vertex-coloring algorithm with time $O(\Delta + \log^* n)$ was devised. (This algorithm is not locally iterative.) However, breaking the *linear in* Δ barrier remained a challenging goal up until now. The challenge is related to the fact that for certain types of algorithms and certain more restricted scenarios lower bounds of $\Omega(\Delta)$ are known. Besides the aforementioned results of Szegedy and Vishwanathan and Kuhn and Wattenhofer, there are also lower bounds for closely related problems of maximal matching and fractional matching. (Note that in a proper edge coloring each color class is a matching.) Maximal matching requires $\Omega(\Delta)$ rounds in the more restricted setting in which there are no distinct IDs, but instead edges are properly $O(\Delta)$-colored [14]. Fractional matching requires $\Omega(\Delta)$ rounds in the strongest $\mathcal{LOCAL}$ setting (stronger than the one employed in our current paper) using general algorithms.

The $\Omega(\Delta)$ lower bound of [14] for $O(\Delta)$-edge-colored graphs with no IDs implies that the simple well-known greedy $O(\Delta)$-time algorithm that iterates over all colors is optimal in that setting. A similar greedy algorithm is known for transforming $O(\Delta)$-edge-coloring into $(2\Delta - 1)$-edge coloring and $O(\Delta)$-vertex coloring into $(\Delta + 1)$-coloring in $O(\Delta)$ time. However, for the coloring problems it is unknown whether this is optimal or not. Moreover, for the general case in which vertices have distinct IDs with no initial colors the question of whether linear in Δ time is optimal remained wide open. In the current paper we break the linear in Δ barrier, and thus address this question. Specifically, we devise $(\Delta + 1)$-vertex-coloring and $(2\Delta - 1)$-edge-coloring deterministic algorithms that require $O(\Delta^{3/4} \log \Delta + \log^* n)$-time. This improves upon the state-of-the-art of [4, 19] for vertex coloring, and the long-standing result of Panconesi and Rizzi [24] for edge coloring. By slightly increasing the number of colors we obtain $(1 + o(1))\Delta$-vertex-coloring and $(2 + o(1))\Delta$-edge-coloring in $\tilde{O}(\sqrt{\Delta} + \log^* n)$ time. Our vertex-coloring algorithms send messages of size $O(\log n)$. Thus we obtain the first deterministic $(\Delta + 1)$-coloring algorithm that has both *sublinear running time* and *sublinear message complexity.* Our edge-coloring algorithms may have to send messages of greater size by a multiplicative factor of $O(\Delta)$.

Our results illustrate a separation between the deterministic edge coloring and maximal matching problems. While maximal matching in anonymous $O(\Delta)$-edge-colored graphs requires $\Omega(\Delta)$ time [14], a $(2\Delta - 1)$-edge-coloring can be computed in $o(\Delta)$ time. (Our algorithms are applicable not only to graphs with distinct IDs, but also to (anonymous) properly-colored graphs. If the graph is initially $O(D)$-colored, then the factor of $\log^* n$ in our algorithms is replaced by $O(\log^* D)$.) Using the reduction of Luby [22] the lower bound of [14] can be applied to the maximal independent set problem in anonymous $O(\Delta)$-vertex-colored graphs. Hence, there is a similar separation between the deterministic maximal independent set problem and the deterministic $(\Delta + 1)$-vertex coloring problem. Up until now such separations were only known for randomized algorithms. Specifically, Elkin et al. [10] showed a separation between randomized edge coloring and maximal matching in a more general setting of graphs with unique IDs.

Our results are actually more general than that. They also apply to partially colored graphs. In other words, some vertices or edges are already colored, and all vertices have distinct IDs. In this case our algorithms compute a proper coloring of the uncolored parts that is consistent with the coloring of the colored ones. To the best of our knowledge, prior to our work this could be done only by coloring the uncolored parts using the linear-time algorithm and a fresh palette (e.g., $\{\Delta + 2, \Delta + 3, ..., 2\Delta + 2\}$), and reducing the number of colors in linear time via the aforementioned greedy algorithm. (Note that a proper partial $(\Delta+1)$-vertex-coloring can be always extended to a proper $(\Delta + 1)$-vertex-coloring of the entire graph. Similarly, a proper partial $(2\Delta - 1)$-edge coloring can be always extended to a proper $(2\Delta - 1)$-edge-coloring of the entire graph.) In the current work we introduce a new technique that allows one to achieve this in sublinear time.

Our results also give rise to an algorithm for the *list-coloring problem*. This problem generalizes standard colorings. In list-coloring each vertex (respectively, edge) is provided with a list of at least $\Delta + 1$ colors, and the goal of each vertex (resp., edge) is to select a color from its own list, such that the entire vertex coloring (resp., edge coloring) is proper. If all vertex-lists have at least $(\Delta + 1)$ colors (resp., all edge-lists have at least $(2\Delta - 1)$ colors), then this is always possible. We employ our techniques for coloring partially colored graphs in order to devise list-coloring algorithms. Specifically, suppose that each vertex (resp., edge) is provided with a list of at least $\Delta + 1$ colors (resp., $2\Delta - 1$ colors) taken from a range of size $d \geq \Delta + 1$. Then our algorithm computes a proper vertex- (resp., edge-) list-coloring within $O(d^{3/4} \log d + \log^* n)$ deterministic time. Whenever $d = O(\Delta)$ the running time becomes $O(\Delta^{3/4} \log \Delta + \log^* n)$. Prior to our work the best result for deterministic list-coloring was [7] in conjunction with the standard reduction from list coloring to $(\Delta + 1)$-coloring. It required $O(\Delta + \log^* n)$ time.

We remark that our algorithms for static networks assume that all vertices know Δ and n, similarly to most previously-known results. However, this assumption can be dropped using the technique of Korman et al. [17]. The latter technique allows one to transform a quite wide family of algorithms that require the knowledge of n and Δ into algorithms that do not require this knowledge, while the running time is affected only by constant factors. Our algorithms have the properties of being "locally checkable" and "gluable" required by [17], and thus the technique of [17] is applicable to them.

Dynamic and Faulty Networks: We use our algorithms for coloring partially colored graphs in order to devise dynamic algorithms for $(\Delta + 1)$-vertex-coloring and $(2\Delta - 1)$-edge-coloring. Since the dynamic setting incur changes in the topology that result in partially colored graphs, our algorithms for the static setting turn out to be very useful for the dynamic setting as well. Specifically, our dynamic vertex- and edge-coloring algorithms have deterministic update time $O(\Delta^{3/4} \log \Delta + \log^* n)$. Moreover, our static algorithms are very useful in the scenario when vertices lose colors due to faults. Again, this results in partially colored networks that can be fixed using our new techniques, also within deterministic time $O(\Delta^{3/4} \log \Delta + \log^* n)$. Prior to our work the best results of deterministic dynamic algorithms and algorithms for faulty networks had running time $O(\Delta + \log^* n)$. These algorithms consist of defining new parts that have to be colored or recolored, coloring them using a fresh palette of size $O(\Delta)$ using the algorithm of [7], and reducing the number of colors via the standard color reduction.

1.3 Our Techniques

In this section we describe our techniques and high-level ideas. For simplicity we focus here only on the static setting. The main idea in our algorithms is a quick coloring of partially-colored graphs. Specifically, the uncolored parts are colored in such a way that is consistent with the colored ones. This approach in which a full solution is obtained given a partial one is also known as *fixing*. (See, e.g., [16] where it is applied to other problems and scenarios. The ideas of [16], however, are very different from the ones presented in our paper.) The high-level idea of our approach is as follows. We partition the (uncolored parts of the) input graph G into subgraphs $G_1, G_2, ..., G_p$ where $p = o(\Delta)$. The subgraphs have some helpful properties that allow us to handle them extremely quickly. (We elaborate on these properties shortly.) Specifically, after a short preprocessing phase that requires $O(\log^* n)$ time and is performed on all subgraphs in parallel, each subgraph is handled just within a single round! Consequently, within $p = o(\Delta)$ rounds we are done. We start by computing a proper coloring of G_1. Then we compute a proper coloring of G_2 that is consistent with that of G_1. Next, we compute a coloring of G_3 that is consistent with the colorings of G_1 and G_2, etc. In each iteration the new coloring is consistent with the previously computed ones. Finally, after p iterations we obtain a proper coloring of the entire graph G.

In order to compute a coloring of each subgraph within a single round we employ the helpful properties of our partition. It is related to two previously known partitions:
(1) a partition into p subgraphs, each with *maximum degree* $O((\Delta/p)^2)$ [4, 19], and
(2) a partition into p subgraphs, each with *arboricity*[1] $O(a/p)$ [5]. (a is the arboricity of the input graph.)
Each of these two previously-known partitions has a major disadvantage, if used in our current scheme. Therefore, we employ a new partition instead. Our new partition consists of p subgraphs with *arboricity* $O(\Delta/p)$. Thus the product of parameters is linear in the maximum degree, but not necessarily linear in the arboricity. Still, this is sufficiently good for our goals. Moreover, this new partition can be computed in $o(\Delta) + O(\log^* n)$ time.

We select the parameter p in such a way that the arboricity of the subgraphs in our partitions is at most $\sqrt{\Delta}$ and

[1] The arboricity $a = a(G)$ is the minimum number of forests into which the edge set can be partitioned. Note that given two subgraphs $G' = (V, E')$ and $G'' = (V, E'')$, the arboricity of $\tilde{G} = (V, E' \cup E'')$ is at most $a(G') + a(G'')$.

the number of subgrpahs is $o(\Delta)$. Thus, in our partitions it always holds that $p > \sqrt{\Delta}$ and $p = o(\Delta)$. Moreover, each vertex in each subgraph knows who its parents are. The number of parents is $O(\Delta/p)$, since there is at most one parent per forest. In the preprocessing stage each subgraph is colored with $O((\Delta/p)^2) = O(\Delta)$ colors using the algorithm Arb-Linial [3] within $O(\log^* n)$ time. (The time is $O(\log^* n)$ rather than $O(\log n)$ since the latter bound is required only if vertices do not know who their parents are. Otherwise, algorithm Arb-Linial is a simple extension of Linial algorithm [21], where the only difference is that vertices consider their parents instead of all their neighbors. See [3].) Consequently, each subgraph is colored properly, but there may be monochromatic edges that cross between subgraphs. This is corrected gradually by iterating over $G_1, G_2, ..., G_p$. In iteration i, $1 \leq i \leq p$, we recolor G_i in such a way that the coloring in the subgraph induced by vertices of $G_1, G_2, ..., G_i$ is proper. To this end we employ *constructions of polynomials*. Constructions of polynomials were employed by Linial [21] (using a construction of Erdős, Frankel and Füredi [11]), and by Barenboim and Elkin [3] that adapted the algorithm of Linial to graphs of bounded arboricity (cf. Algorithm Arb-Linial in [3]). In the current work, however, our construction is more sophisticated, and differs from that of [21, 11, 3] in two important respects. Specifically, while the constructions of [21, 11, 3] assign each old color a *single distinct polynomial* in an *arbitrary fashion*, our technique assigns each old color *numerous distinct polynomials* that are *carefully selected*. This allows us to minimize the number of conflicts with colors in $G_1, G_2, ..., G_{i-1}$. Consequently, among the large number of polynomials assigned to a vertex we can find one with sufficiently few conflicts. Then it is used to find a color that is not taken by any neighbor in $G_1, G_2, ..., G_{i-1}$ and does not cause conflicts with neighbors in G_i.

1.4 Related Work on Randomized Algorithms

In the eighties several randomized $O(\log n)$-time algorithms were devised for a variety of problems. In particular, Luby [22] and Alon, Babai and Itai [1] devised an $O(\log n)$-time algorithm that computes a maximal independent set, with high probability. A few years later Luby [23] extended this result also to the $(\Delta + 1)$-vertex-coloring problem. Israeli and Itai devised an $O(\log n)$-time algorithms that computes a maximal matching, with high probability. These algorithms are the best currently-known ones for general graphs. However, for very wide families of graphs significant progress has been made recently. Specifically, Kothapalli et al. [18] devised an $O(\Delta)$-vertex-coloring algorithm that requires $O(\log \Delta + \sqrt{\log n})$ time, with high probability. This result was significantly improved by Barenboim, Elkin, Pettie and Schneider [8] who devised a $(\Delta + 1)$-vertex-coloring algorithm that requires $O(\log \Delta + 2^{\sqrt{\log \log n}})$ time, with high probability. This algorithm, however, employs messages of polylogarithmic size.

Since running times of our algorithms are affected by the number of vertices n only in the unavoidable $\log^* n$ term, in graphs with reasonably small maximum degree Δ our algorithms outperform not only all previously-known deterministic algorithms, but also the randomized ones.

2. PRELIMINARIES

For a positive integer k, we denote $[k] = \{0, 1, ..., k-1\}$. A *proper k-coloring* φ of a graph $G = (V, E)$ is a function $\varphi : V \rightarrow [k]$, such that for each $(u, v) \in E$ it holds that $\varphi(u) \neq \varphi(v)$. The set of vertices of a graph G is denoted $V(G)$. The set of edges is denoted $E(G)$. For a subset $U \subseteq V$, $G(U)$ denotes the subgraph induced by U. For a subset $E' \subseteq E$, $G(E')$ denotes the subgraph induced by E'. For a vertex v in a graph $G = (V, E)$, the set of *neighbors* of v is denoted $\Gamma(v)$. An *oriented forest* is an acyclic subgraph with orientation on the edges with out-degree at most 1. Each edge in an oriented forest is directed towards the parent. A *k-forest-decomposition* is a partition of the edge set E of a graph G into at most k sets, such that each set is an oriented forest. Hence, the out-degree of each vertex in this case is at most k. For a vertex $v \in V$, the endpoints of outgoing edges of v are its *parents* in the k forests. This set of parents is denoted by $\Pi(v)$.

3. COLORING IN STATIC GRAPHS

3.1 High-Level Description

In this section we describe the high-level approach of our algorithm (called Procedure Color). Specifically, we employ two helper procedures that are defined and analyzed in the sequel. One of the procedures (Procedure Partition; see Section 3.3) accepts as input[1] a graph $G = (V, E)$, and computes a vertex-disjoint partition into subgraphs $G_1, G_2, ..., G_p$, such that each subgraph has arboricity $O(\Delta/p)$, for an integer p, $1 \leq p \leq \Delta$. Moreover, the subgraphs are provided with an orientation towards parents, and therefore, each vertex knows who its $O(\Delta/p)$ parents are. The other procedure (Procedure Recolor; see Section 3.2) accepts as input a graph G in which some G_i, $i \in \{1, 2, ..., p\}$, is properly colored (by the preprocessing phase), and recolors G_i in such a way that colors of vertices in G_i do not conflict with final colors of their neighbors in G. More precisely, Procedure Recolor accepts a coloring φ of G, a list of forbidden colors $L(v)$ for each $v \in V$ (representing the final colors already taken by neighbors of v in G), and computes a new proper coloring ψ of G_i, such that $\psi(v) \notin L(v)$ for all $v \in V$. Each time Procedure Recolor is executed (except for the first time) a subset of neighbors of each vertex has been already colored by ψ. These subsets determine the sets $L(v)$. In order to represent G_i the procedure accepts a subset of parents $\bar{\Gamma}(v) \subseteq \Gamma(v)$ that belong to G_i. It also accepts a list $B(v)$ of colors φ of these parents. Finally, it accepts upper bounds ℓ and β on the sizes of $L(v)$ and $\bar{\Gamma}(v)$, respectively. To summarize, the arguments of Procedure Recolor (invoked on each vertex $v \in V(G_i)$ in parallel) are: φ,v,$L(v)$,$\bar{\Gamma}(v)$,$B(v)$,ℓ, β. (By passing a vertex v as an argument to a procedure we mean that the identity number of v is passed to the procedure.)

Our main algorithm (Procedure Color) is presented below. It accepts a graph G and two positive integer parameters $p < q$ as input, and proceeds as follows. First, it computes a partition of the graph G into subgraphs

[1]The procedures in this paper accept input in a distributed manner. In particular, accepting a graph as input means that the input of each vertex is the vertex identity and the identities of its neighbors.

$G_1, G_2, ..., G_p$ with arboricity $a = O(\Delta/p)$ each. (Some variants of our algorithm will produce subgraphs with slightly larger arboricity. We explain this in the sequel.) To this end, our algorithm employs Procedure Partition that accepts the parameters p, q. The parameter q affects the running time and the quality of the result. (We elaborate on this later.) Next, in parallel, we compute colorings φ of the subgraphs $G_1, G_2, ..., G_p$ using $O(a^2)$ colors per subgraph, by the algorithm Arb-Linial [3]. (In this preprocessing stage the vertices haven't been assigned a color ψ yet.) Then our algorithm performs p phases. In phase $i = 1, 2, ..., p$, for each vertex $v \in V(G_i)$, we compute the set $L(v)$ of colors of neighbors of v in G that already have a color ψ, the set $\bar{\Gamma}(v)$ of *parents* of v in G_i, and the set $B(v)$ of colors of vertices in $\bar{\Gamma}(v)$ (colored by φ). Then we set $\ell = \Delta$ and $\beta = a$. Note that indeed $L(v)$ has at most Δ elements, and the number of parents of v in G_i is at most a, i.e., $|\bar{\Gamma}(v)| \leq a$. These parameters are used in the invocation of Procedure Recolor in phase i. Once the last phase p terminates we obtain a coloring ψ for the entire graph G. This completes the description of the algorithm. Next, we we describe and analyze our helper procedures in Sections 3.2 - 3.3. Then we analyze the entire algorithm (Procedure Color) and prove its correctness in Section 3.4.

Algorithm 1 Color(G, v, p, q)

A procedure to be executed by each vertex $v \in V$

```
⟨G_1, G_2, ..., G_p, a⟩ := Partition(G,p, q)
for i = 1, 2, ..., p in parallel do
    φ_i := Arb-Linial(G_i)    /* φ_i employs c · a^2 colors,
        for a universal constant c > 0 */
    if v ∈ V(G_i) then
        φ(v) := φ_i(v)
    end if
end for
ψ(v) := ⊥
for i = 1, 2, ..., p do
    /* The p iterations are performed one after another,
       each iteration in a separate round */
    if v ∈ V(G_i) then
        L(v) := {ψ(u) | u ∈ Γ(v) ∧ ψ(u) ≠ ⊥}
        Γ̄(v) := {u | u ∈ V(G_i) ∧ u ∈ Π(v)}
        B(v) := {φ(u) | u ∈ Γ̄(v)
        ψ(v) : = Recolor(v, φ, L(v), Γ̄(v), B(v), ℓ :=
            Δ, β := a)
    end if
end for
return ψ(v)
```

3.2 Procedure Recolor

In this section we devise a procedure that computes a proper coloring taking into account lists of forbidden colors. The procedure employs an initial proper coloring φ that does not take into account these lists, and computes a new coloring ψ that does so. The input of the procedure consists of a graph $G = (V, E)$. In addition, for each vertex $v \in V$ the input consists of a color $\varphi(v)$, a list of forbidden colors $L(v)$, and a list of neighbors $\bar{\Gamma}(v) \subseteq \Gamma(v)$, such that $\varphi(u) \neq \varphi(v)$ for each $u \in \bar{\Gamma}(v)$. Denote $B(v) = \{\varphi(u) \mid u \in \bar{\Gamma}(v)\}$. The maximum size of a set $L(v)$ is bounded by an integer parameter ℓ, and the maximum size of $\bar{\Gamma}(v)$ (and hence, also of $B(v)$) is bounded by an integer parameter β. The elements in $L(v)$ belong to $[\ell + (2\beta+1) \cdot \mu]$, where $\mu = O(\sqrt{\ell} + \beta)$ (defined precisely in the next paragraph), and the elements in $B(v)$ belong to $[c \cdot \beta^2]$, for a universal constant $c > 4$. For each $v \in V$, it holds that $\varphi(v) \in [c \cdot \beta^2]$ and $\varphi(v) \notin B(v)$. (But it may hold that $\varphi(v) \in L(v)$.) The procedure computes a new coloring ψ, such that for each $v \in V$ it holds that $\psi(v) \in [\ell + (2\beta+1) \cdot \mu]$, $\psi(v) \neq \psi(u)$ for each $u \in \bar{\Gamma}(v)$, and $\psi(v) \notin L(v)$.

The computation requires just a single round and proceeds as follows. Each vertex $v \in V$ constructs a set of μ polynomials $p_{0_v}(x), p_{1_v}(x), ..., p_{\mu-1_v}(x)$, where μ is a prime such that $\lceil\sqrt{\ell}\rceil + \lceil\sqrt{c}\rceil \cdot \beta \leq \mu \leq 2 \cdot (\lceil\sqrt{\ell}\rceil + \lceil\sqrt{c}\rceil \cdot \beta)$. (Such a prime exists by the Bertrand-Chebyshev postulate.) These polynomials are defined over the field $\mathbb{Z}_\mu$ of integers modulo μ. The polynomial $p_{i_v}(x)$, $i = 0, 1, ...\mu - 1$, is of the form $i + a \cdot x + b \cdot x^2$, where a and b are deduced from $\varphi(v)$ as follows.

$$a = \left\lfloor \varphi(v) / \left\lceil \sqrt{c \cdot \beta^2} \right\rceil \right\rfloor \quad ; \quad b = \varphi(v) \bmod \left\lceil \sqrt{c \cdot \beta^2} \right\rceil.$$

The pair $\langle a, b \rangle$ can be seen as a representation of $\varphi(v)$. Note that if for a pair of vertices $u, v \in V$ it holds that $\varphi(u) \neq \varphi(v)$, then either $\left\lfloor \varphi(u) / \left\lceil \sqrt{c \cdot \beta^2} \right\rceil \right\rfloor \neq \left\lfloor \varphi(v) / \left\lceil \sqrt{c \cdot \beta^2} \right\rceil \right\rfloor$ or $\left(\varphi(u) \bmod \left\lceil \sqrt{c \cdot \beta^2} \right\rceil\right) \neq \left(\varphi(v) \bmod \left\lceil \sqrt{c \cdot \beta^2} \right\rceil\right)$. Therefore, for each $u, v \in V$, such that $\varphi(u) \neq \varphi(v)$, the set of polynomials constructed by u and the set of polynomials constructed by v are disjoint.

We say that a polynomial p has a *conflict* with a color $\gamma \in [\mu^2]$, if the representation $\langle x, y \rangle = \langle \lfloor \gamma/\mu \rfloor, \gamma \bmod \mu \rangle$ of γ by two elements $x, y \in \mathbb{Z}\mu$ satisfies $y = p(x)$. We aim at finding a polynomial for each $v \in V$ with minimum number of conflicts with $L(v)$. (Later it will be used to find a color that conflicts neither with $L(v)$ nor with colors found by neighbors of v in $\bar{\Gamma}(v)$ using their polynomials.) To this end, each $v \in V$ finds an index $i \in [\mu]$, such that the polynomial $p_{i_v}(x)$ of v satisfies the following: the set $L_i(v) = L(v) \cap \{p_{i_v}(k) + k \cdot \mu \mid k = 0, 1, ..., \mu - 1\}$ has the minimum size among the sets $L_0(v), L_1(v), ..., L_{\mu-1}(v)$. Here $p_{i_v}(k)$ is computed over $\mathbb{Z}_\mu$, and thus, $0 \leq p_{i_v}(k) \leq \mu - 1$. But the rest of the expression is computed over the integers, and thus, $0 \leq p_{i_v}(k) + k \cdot \mu \leq \mu^2 - 1$. The expression can be seen as an ordered pair $\langle k, p_{i_v}(k) \rangle$. By Pigeonhole principle, the size of $L_i(v)$ is at most ℓ/μ. (Note that $L_i(v) \cap L_j(v) = \emptyset$ for any pair of integers $i \neq j, 0 \leq i, j \leq \mu - 1$. This is because $p_{i_v}(k) \neq p_{j_v}(k)$ for $k = 0, 1, ..., \mu - 1$, and $p_{i_v}(k) + k \cdot \mu \neq p_{j_v}(k') + k' \cdot \mu$ for $k' \neq k$.)

Since $\mu - \ell/\mu \geq \mu - \sqrt{\ell} \geq \sqrt{\ell} + \sqrt{c} \cdot \beta - \sqrt{\ell} > 2\beta$, the set $\hat{L}_i(v) = \{p_{i_v}(k) + k \cdot \mu \mid k = 0, 1, ..., \mu - 1\} \setminus L(v)$ contains more than 2β elements. For each $u \in \bar{\Gamma}(v)$, an index j that satisfies the aforementioned condition is found (i.e., the polynomial p_{j_u} of u satisfies that $L_j(u)$ has minimum size among $L_0(u), L_1(u), ..., L_{\mu-1}(u)$). The polynomials $p_{i_v}(x)$ of v and $p_{j_u}(x)$ of u intersect in at most 2 points, since they are of degree 2. Since $|\bar{\Gamma}(v)| \leq \beta$ and $\hat{L}_i(v) > 2\beta$, there exists $k \in \{0, 1, ., ., \mu - 1\}$, such that $p_{i_v}(k) + k \cdot \mu \in \hat{L}_i(v)$ and $p_{i_v}(k) \neq p_{j_u}(k)$ for all $u \in \bar{\Gamma}(v)$. The color $\psi(v)$ is set as $p_{i_v}(k) + k \cdot \mu$ for the smallest k as above. Note that for each $u \in \bar{\Gamma}(v)$ it holds that $\psi(v) \neq \psi(u)$. Indeed, for any integer $k' \in \{0, 1, ...\mu - 1\}$ it holds that $p_{i_v}(k) + k \cdot \mu \neq p_{j_u}(k') + k' \cdot \mu$. Note that the inequality holds in particular for $k' = k$. Moreover, since k is selected as the smallest appropriate integer, it holds that $k \leq |L_i(v)| + 2|\bar{\Gamma}(v)| \leq \ell/\mu + 2\beta$. This completes the description of Procedure Recolor. See pseudocode below. Next, we prove the correctness of Procedure Recolor.

Algorithm 2 Procedure Recolor(φ,v,$L(v)$,$\bar{\Gamma}(v)$,$B(v)$,ℓ, β)

A procedure to be executed by each vertex $v \in V$

1: $a := \left\lfloor \varphi(v) / \left\lceil \sqrt{c \cdot \beta^2} \right\rceil \right\rfloor$
2: $b := \varphi(v) \bmod \left\lceil \sqrt{c \cdot \beta^2} \right\rceil$
3: μ := a prime such that $\left\lceil \sqrt{\ell} \right\rceil + \lceil \sqrt{c} \rceil \cdot \beta \leq \mu \leq 2 \cdot (\left\lceil \sqrt{\ell} \right\rceil + \lceil \sqrt{c} \rceil \cdot \beta)$
4: **for** $i := 0, 1, ..., \mu - 1$ **do**
5:     **define** $p_{i_v}(x) = i + a \cdot x + b \cdot x^2$
6: **end for**
7: **find** $i \in \{0, 1, ..., \mu - 1\}$ **such that** $L_i(v) = L(v) \cap \{p_{i_v}(k) + k \cdot \mu \mid k = 0, 1, ..., \mu - 1\}$ has minimum size among $L_0(v), L_1(v), ..., L_{\mu-1}(v)$.
8: **send** $p_{i_v}(x)$ to all neighbors in $\Gamma(v)$
9: **receive** $p_{j_u}(x)$ from all neighbors $u \in \Gamma(v)$
10: **find** smallest $k \in \{0, 1, ..., \mu - 1\}$ **such that** $p_{i_v}(k) + k \cdot \mu \notin L(v)$ and $p_{i_v}(k) \neq p_{j_u}(k)$ for all $u \in \bar{\Gamma}(v)$
11: $\psi(v) := p_{i_v}(k) + k \cdot \mu$

Lemma 3.1. *Procedure Recolor computes a coloring ψ, such that for any $v \in V$ and $u \in \bar{\Gamma}(v)$, it holds that $\psi(v) \neq \psi(u)$. The coloring ψ employs $\ell + (2\beta + 1) \cdot \mu = \ell + O(\sqrt{\ell} \cdot \beta + \beta^2)$ colors.*

PROOF. Let $u \in \bar{\Gamma}(v)$ be a neighbor of v. By the discussion preceding the pseudococde of Procedure Recolor, the search in line 10 of the procedure succeeds. Hence, it finds an integer $k \in \{0, 1, ..., \mu - 1\}$ such that $p_{i_v}(k) \neq p_{j_u}(k)$. Thus, $p_{i_v}(k) + k \cdot \mu \neq p_{j_u}(k') + k' \cdot \mu$ for all $k' \in \{0, 1, ..., \mu - 1\}$, i.e., for all possible choices of k' by u. (This is because either $k = k'$, and then $p_{i_v}(k) + k \cdot \mu \neq p_{j_u}(k) + k \cdot \mu$, or $k \neq k'$, and then $|k \cdot \mu - k' \cdot \mu| \geq \mu$ while $|p_{i_v}(k) - p_{j_u}(k')| \leq \mu - 1$.) Therefore, $\psi(v) = p_{i_v}(k) + k \cdot \mu \neq p_{j_u}(k') + k' \cdot \mu = \psi(u)$.

Next, we analyze the number of colors of ψ. Since $p_{i_v}(k) + k \cdot \mu \neq p_{j_v}(k') + k' \cdot \mu$ for $i \neq j$ and any $k, k' \in \{0, 1, ..., \mu - 1\}$, it holds that $L_i(v) \cap L_j(v) = \emptyset$. Hence by the Pigeonhole principle the set $L_i(v)$ with minimum size is of cardinality at most ℓ/μ. Therefore, there are at least $2\beta + 1$ elements $k' \in \{0, 1, ..., \lfloor \ell/\mu \rfloor + 2\beta\}$ such that $p_{i_v}(k') + k' \cdot \mu \notin L_i(v)$. Among those $2\beta + 1$ elements at most 2β are such that $p_{i_v}(k') = p_{j_u}(k')$, for some $u \in \bar{\Gamma}(v)$. Thus, there exists $k \in \{0, 1, ..., \lfloor \ell/\mu \rfloor + 2\beta\}$, such that $p_{i_v}(k) + k \cdot \mu \notin L(v)$ and $p_{i_v}(k) \neq p_{j_u}(k)$ for all $u \in \bar{\Gamma}(v)$. Therefore, $\psi(v) = p_{i_v}(k) + k \cdot \mu \leq (\mu - 1) + (2\beta + \ell/\mu) \cdot \mu < \ell + (2\beta + 1) \cdot \mu$. □

Lemma 3.2. *For each $v \in V$ it holds that $\psi(v) \notin L(v)$.*

PROOF. The proof is immediate by the success of the search in line 10. (See the paragraph preceding the pseudocode of Procedure Recolor.) □

Lemma 3.3. *Procedure Recolor requires a single communication round.*

PROOF. The communication steps of the procedure are in lines 8-9 only, which require just one round. □

3.3 Procedure Partition

In this section we devise a procedure that accepts as input a graph G and positive integer parameter $p < q$, and computes a vertex-disjoint partition $G_1, G_2, ..., G_p$, such that each subgraph in the partition has arboricity $O(\Delta/p)$. We employ an auxiliary procedure devised in [5], called Procedure Simple-Arbdefective. It accepts as input a graph G with an acyclic orientation of the edges, and an integer parameter $k > 0$. Suppose that the longest consistently oriented path in G has length λ, and the maximum out-degree is d. Then Procedure Simple-Arbdefective computes a partition of G into k subgraphs, each with arboricity $\lfloor d/k \rfloor$. The running time of Procedure Simple-Arbdefective is $O(\lambda)$. (We note that we use here an even simpler version of Procedure Simple-Arbdefective. Specifically, the original procedure is applicable even when not all edges are oriented. In the current paper we invoke it only on graphs and subgraphs in which all edges are oriented.)

Procedure Simple-Arbdefective is employed in our Procedure Partition as follows. Procedure Partition starts by coloring the input graph $G = (V, E)$ properly with $O(\Delta^2)$ colors using Linial's algorithm [21]. Denote by τ_0 the resulting coloring. We orient the edges of G towards endpoints of greater color. Note that the resulting orientation is acyclic, it has out-degree at most Δ, and its length is $O(\Delta^2)$. Then, for a parameter $q > p$, the procedures groups the $O(\Delta^2)$ colors of the coloring into $t = O(\Delta^2/q)$ disjoint color classes, each with at least q colors and at most $2q$ colors. (Specifically, the first $t - 1$ color classes consist of q colors each, and the last color class has between q and $2q$ colors.) Let $G_1, G_2, ..., G_t$, be the subgraphs induced by vertices of the t color classes. (For $i = 1, 2, ..., t$, the subgraph G_i is induced by vertices of the color class i.) The orientation restricted to each subgraph has length at most $2q$. We invoke Procedure Simple-Arbdefective in parallel on the subgraphs $G_1, G_2, ..., G_t$ with the input parameter $k = p$. As a result we obtain a vertex labeling using p labels in each subgraph. The union of all labels of vertices results in a $(p \cdot t)$-labeling of $G = (V, E)$. It holds that each vertex $v \in V$ has at most $\lfloor \Delta/p \rfloor$ outgoing-edge neighbors in G with the same label as that of v.

Removing the edges with endpoints of the same label results in a subgraph G' of G that is colored using $t \cdot p < t \cdot q$ colors. (The labeling is a proper coloring now since all remaining edges are bi-chromatic.) In other words, we have reduced the number of colors by a factor of at least q/p at the price of removing some edges. Denote this coloring by τ_1. Repeating this for $r = O(\log_{q/p} \Delta)$ iteration results in a coloring τ_r that employs p colors. (Note that orientations of removed edges will not change once they have been removed, but may change as long as the edges are present.) Once we arrive at a p-coloring, the number of colors cannot be improved further using this technique, and we stop. The coloring τ_r is a proper coloring of some subgraph of G, but not necessarily a proper coloring of G itself. Nevertheless, we next prove that each subgraph of G induced by vertices of the same color of τ_r has arboricity $O((\Delta/p) \cdot \log_{q/p} \Delta)$. Moreover, the orientation of the edges of this subgraph has out-degree $O((\Delta/p) \cdot \log_{q/p} \Delta)$, and it is oriented towards the parents. This completes the description of Procedure Partition. Its pseudocode and analysis are provided below.

Algorithm 3 Procedure Partition(G,p,q)

1: $\tau_0 := (c \cdot \Delta^2)$-coloring of G using the algorithm of Linial [21]
2: $s = c \cdot \Delta^2$ /* an upper bound on the number of colors used */
3: $i = 0$ /* i is the index of τ_i */
4: $E' = E$ /* E' is the set of edges that have not been removed yet */
5: **while** $s > p$ **do**
6: $t := \lfloor s/q \rfloor$
7: group the vertices of G into t disjoint subsets $V_1, V_2, ..., V_t$, where $V_j = \{v \mid (j-1) \cdot q \leq \tau_i(v) < j \cdot q\}$ for $j = 1, 2, ..., t-1$, and $V_t = \{v \mid (t-1) \cdot q \leq \tau_i(v)\}$.
8: **for** $j := 1, 2, ..., t$ **in parallel do**
9: $G_j := (V_j,\ E_j := \{(v,u) \mid v,u \in V_j \wedge (v,u) \in E' \wedge \tau_i(v) \neq \tau_i(u)\})$
10: orient E_j towards endpoints of greater τ_i-color
11: $\tau_{i+1} :=$ Simple-Arbdefective(G_j,$k := p$) /* G_j is labeled using the labels $0, 1, ..., p-1$ */
12: **for each** $v \in V_j$ **in parallel do** $\tau_{i+1}(v) := \tau_{i+1}(v) + p \cdot (j-1)$ **end for**
13: **end for**
14: $s := t \cdot p$
15: $i := i + 1$
16: remove from E' all monochromatic edges with respect to τ_i, in parallel
17: **end while**
18: $\alpha := \lfloor i \cdot \Delta/p \rfloor$
19: **for** $j := 1, 2, ..., p$ **in parallel do**
20: $V'_j := \{v \mid \tau_i(v) = j\}$
21: **end for**
22: **return** $\langle G(V'_1), G(V'_2), ..., G(V'_p), \alpha \rangle$
23: /* The structure is returned in a distributed manner, i.e., each vertex knows the index j of the set $G(V'_j)$ it belongs to, and the value α. */

Lemma 3.4. *For $i = 0, 1, 2, ..., r$ let τ_i denote the coloring produced by Procedure Partition (invoked with integer parameters $p > 0$ and $q > p$) after i iterations of the procedure (lines 5 - 17). Then the number of colors of τ_i is at most $\max\{(p/q)^i \cdot c \cdot \Delta^2), p\}$, for a universal constant $c > 0$, and vertices of each color of τ_i induce subgraphs of arboricity at most $(i \cdot \Delta/p)$ each. (Moreover, vertices know who their parents are.)*

The correctness of Lemma 3.4 follows by induction on i using the fact that the subset of removed edges in each iteration forms a subgraph of arboricity at most Δ/p, and vertices know who their parents are (since the orientation of removed edges is towards the parents). Therefore, the union of these i removed edge-subsets induces a subgraph of arboricity at most $(i \cdot \Delta/p)$. Next, we analyze the running time of the procedure.

Lemma 3.5. *Procedure Partition (invoked with parameters $p > 0$ and $q > p$) arrives to a p-coloring of the input graph G within $r = O(\log_{q/p} \Delta)$ iteration. (This coloring is not necessarily proper, but has the properties of Lemma 3.4.) The overall running time of Procedure Partition is $O(q \cdot \log_{q/p} \Delta + \log^* n)$.*

PROOF. Set $r = \left\lceil \log_{q/p}(c \cdot \Delta^2) \right\rceil$. It holds that $(p/q)^r \cdot c \cdot \Delta^2 \leq 1$, and thus $\max\{(p/q)^r \cdot c \cdot \Delta^2), p\} = p$. Therefore, at most r iterations are required to arrive to a p coloring. In each iteration an orientation of length at most $2q$ is computed, and employed to produce a new coloring. The running time is proportional to the length of the orientation. Therefore, each iteration requires $O(q)$ rounds. Since the initial $O(\Delta^2)$-coloring requires $O(\log^* n)$ time, the overall running time is $O(q \log_{q/p} \Delta + \log^* n)$. □

3.4 Analysis

In this section we analyze Procedure Color (Algorithm 1) and prove its correctness. We start by showing that the procedure computes a proper coloring of G, and analyzing the number of colors it employs.

Lemma 3.6. *Suppose that Procedure Color is invoked on an input graph G and the parameters p, q, $1 \leq p < q \leq \Delta$. Then the procedure computes a proper coloring ψ of G that employs at most*
$\Delta + O(\sqrt{\Delta} \cdot \log_{q/p} \Delta \cdot \Delta/p + (\log_{q/p} \Delta \cdot \Delta/p)^2)$ colors.

PROOF. We start by proving that the coloring is proper. Line 1 of Procedure Color computes a partition of G into vertex-disjoint subgraphs $G_1, G_2, ..., G_p$, each with arboricity $a \leq r \cdot \Delta/p = O(\log_{q/p} \Delta \cdot \Delta/p)$. (See Lemma 3.4.) Lines 2 - 6 of Procedure Color compute proper colorings $\varphi_1, \varphi_2, ..., \varphi_p$ of $G_1, G_2, ..., G_p$, respectively, using $O(a^2) = O((\log_{q/p} \Delta \cdot \Delta/p)^2)$ colors per subgraph.

Next, we prove by induction on i that the loop in lines 9 - 17 of Procedure Color computes a proper coloring of the graph induced by $V(G_1) \cup V(G_2) \cup ... \cup V(G_i)$.
Base (i = 0): Before the loop starts the assertion holds trivially.
Step: Suppose that the assertion holds for $i-1$. We prove it for i. By the induction hypothesis, in the beginning of the ith iteration the graph induced by $V(G_1) \cup V(G_2) \cup ... \cup V(G_{i-1})$ is properly colored. Note that in this stage vertices that do not belong to this graph haven't been assigned a color ψ yet. In line 12 a list of forbidden colors $L(v)$ is computed. For each $v \in V(G_i)$ this is a list of colors of all neighbors of v that have already obtained a color ψ. In other words, this is the list of colors of neighbors of v in the subgraph induced by $V(G_1) \cup V(G_2) \cup ... \cup V(G_{i-1})$. By Lemma 3.2, line 15 computes a color $\psi(v)$ for v that is distinct from all colors in $L(v)$. Moreover, for each neighbor u of v in $G(V_i)$, either u is the parent of v, or v is the parent of u (in the orientation produced by Procedure Partition), i.e., $u \in \bar{\Gamma}(v)$ or $v \in \bar{\Gamma}(u)$. In either case it holds that $\psi(u) \neq \psi(v)$, by Lemma 3.1. Consequently, for $v \in V_i$, it holds that $\psi(v)$ is distinct from $\psi(u)$ for any $u \in V_1 \cup V_2, \cup ... \cup V_i$. Since vertices of $V_1 \cup V_2 \cup ... \cup V_{i-1}$ have retained their colors, the coloring ψ in $V_1 \cup V_2 \cup ... \cup V_i$ is proper. This completes the inductive proof.

Next, we analyze the number of colors used by ψ. By Lemma 3.1, procedure Recolor computes a coloring with $\ell + O(\beta \cdot \mu) = \ell + O(\sqrt{\ell} \cdot \beta + \beta^2)$ colors. Since $\ell = \Delta$ and $\beta = \alpha = O(\log_{q/p} \Delta \cdot \Delta/p)$, the number of colors is $\Delta + O(\sqrt{\Delta} \cdot \log_{q/p} \Delta \cdot \Delta/p + (\log_{q/p} \Delta \cdot \Delta/p)^2)$. Since all invocations of Procedure Recolor employ the same palette of colors, this is also the final number of colors used by ψ once Procedure Color terminates. □

Lemma 3.7. *Procedure Color requires $O(q \cdot \log_{q/p} \Delta + \log^* n)$ rounds.*

PROOF. Line 1 of Procedure Color (i.e., the execution of Procedure Partition) requires $O(q \cdot \log_{q/p} \Delta + \log^* n)$ rounds. (See Lemma 3.5.) The parallel executions of Procedure Arb-Linial [3] in lines 2 -7 of Procedure Color require $O(\log^* n)$ time. Each iteration of lines 9 -17 requires a constant number of rounds. (Learning the neighborhoods in lines 12 - 14 requires one round, and invoking Procedure Recolor in line 15 requires one round.) Since there are p iterations, the overall running time of Procedure Color is $O(q \cdot \log_{q/p} \Delta + \log^* n + p) = O(q \cdot \log_{q/p} \Delta + \log^* n)$. □

Set $p = \lfloor \Delta^{3/4} \rfloor$ and $q = 2p$ in Lemmas 3.6 - 3.7. By using a standard reduction that reduces one color per round, we obtain the following result.

Theorem 3.8. *A proper $(\Delta+1)$-coloring of an input graph G can be computed in $O(\Delta^{3/4} \log \Delta + \log^* n)$ deterministic time.*

Another useful result is obtained when setting $p = \lfloor \sqrt{\Delta} \log^2 \Delta \rfloor$ and $q = 2p$ in Lemmas 3.6 - 3.7. This, however, results in slightly more than $(\Delta + 1)$ colors.

Corollary 3.9. *A proper $(1+o(1))\Delta$-coloring (specifically, a $(\Delta + O(\Delta/\log \Delta))$-coloring) of an input graph G can be computed in $O(\sqrt{\Delta} \log^3 \Delta + \log^* n)$ deterministic time.*

It is well known that an $f(\Delta)$-vertex-coloring algorithm gives rise to an $f(2\Delta - 2)$-edge-coloring algorithms, for any function $f()$. (This is done using line graphs. See, e.g., [6].) Thus, we obtain the following theorem.

Theorem 3.10. *(1) A proper $(2\Delta - 1)$-edge-coloring of an input graph G can be computed in $O(\Delta^{3/4} \log \Delta + \log^* n)$ deterministic time. (2) A proper $(2 + o(1))\Delta$-edge-coloring of an input graph G can be computed in $O(\sqrt{\Delta} \log^3 \Delta + \log^* n)$ deterministic time.*

3.5 Coloring Partially-Colored Graphs and List Coloring

In this section we present a generalization of $(\Delta + 1)$-vertex-coloring. Specifically, consider the following problem. We are given an input graph $G = (V, E)$ and a coloring φ_0 of a subset $U \subseteq V$. Our goal is to complete the coloring, i.e., color the set $V \setminus U$ such that the entire graph G is properly colored. Obviously, this is a generalization of the standard vertex coloring problem, in which $U = \emptyset$.

In order to solve this more general problem we make a modification in Procedure Color (Algorithm 1), and then invoke it on the induced subgraph $G' = G(V \setminus U)$, but with the parameter Δ of the original graph G. The modification is performed in line 8 of Procedure Color. Instead of always setting $\psi(v) := \perp$, we do it only if $v \in V \setminus U$. Otherwise, we set $\psi(v) := \varphi_0(v)$. This completes the description of the modification. The modified procedure will be henceforth referred to as *Procedure Mod-Color.* Obviously, the running time of the modified procedure is at most the running time of Procedure Color. We next prove that it indeed produces a proper coloring of G', and moreover, for any $u, v \in V$ it holds that $\psi(u) \neq \psi(v)$.

Theorem 3.11. *Suppose that we are given a graph $G = (V, E)$ with maximum degree $\Delta = \Delta(G)$, and a subset $U \subseteq V$ that is already properly $(\Delta+1)$-vertex-colored. Then Procedure Mod-Color invoked on G' (but with the parameter Δ set as $\Delta(G)$, rather than $\Delta(G')$) results in a proper coloring of the entire graph G.*

PROOF. The proof is by induction on the number of iterations, similarly to the proof of Lemma 3.6. Specifically, we would like to show that after i iterations of lines 9 - 17 (where $0 \leq i \leq p$) the set $U \cup V(G'_1) \cup V(G'_2) \cup ... \cup V(G'_i)$ is properly colored. The main difference is in the base case. While in the proof of Lemma 3.6 the base case is an empty coloring, here we have the coloring φ_0 of U. But this is a proper coloring of U, so we are done.
For the inductive step, observe that the set $L(v)$ never contains more that $\Delta = \Delta(G)$ forbidden colors. Hence, invoking Procedure Recolor on $V(G'_i)$ results in a proper coloring in $V(G'_i)$ that has no conflicts with vertices that have already obtained a color ψ in previous iterations. (This follows directly from the correctness of Procedure Recolor.) Thus, $U \cup V(G'_1) \cup V(G'_2) \cup ... \cup V(G'_i)$ is properly colored after i iterations. □

Note that the bounds on the number of colors of Procedure Color hold also for Procedure Mod-Color (when invoked on the same graph G and the same parameters p, q), since these bounds depend only on the parameters Δ, p and q. Hence, we obtain the following result.

Theorem 3.12. *Suppose that we are given an input graph $G = (V, E)$ in which a subset $U \subseteq V$ of vertices is already colored. Then Procedure Mod-Color produces a proper coloring of $V \setminus U$ that is consistent with U, i.e., a proper coloring of the entire graph G. The bounds on the number of colors and running time of Procedure Mod-Color are the same as those of Procedure Color given in Lemmas 3.6-3.7.*

Next we use Procedure Mod-Color in order to devise an algorithm for *List Coloring.* Specifically, we consider the following variant of the problem. Suppose that we are given a graph G and an integer $d = O(\Delta)$. Moreover, each vertex $v \in V$ holds a list $R(v)$ of at least $(\Delta + 1)$ *permitted colors* taken from the range $[d]$. Our goal is to compute a proper coloring ψ of G where each color $\psi(v)$ belongs to the list of colors $R(v)$ of v. To solve this problem we perform a reduction from the List Coloring problem to the problem of coloring partially colored graphs. Specifically, we construct a graph $\hat{G}$ from G by adding new vertices as follows. For each vertex $v \in V$ we construct the set of forbidden colors $L(v) = [d] \setminus R(v)$. Then, for each color $c \in L(v)$, we add a new vertex v_c and a new edge (v, v_c). Then, for each such vertex v_c, we color v_c by c. Consequently, each vertex $v \in V$ has an additional set of neighbors colored by all the forbidden colors. The set of free colors that can still be used by v is exactly the set of colors in $R(v)$. Note that $\Delta(\hat{G}) < d$. (We will prove this shortly.) We invoke procedure Mod-Color on $\hat{G}$, where each vertex v simulates the vertices v_c locally. Finally, reduce the number of colors to d by the standard reduction, a color per round. Next, we show that this results in a proper list-coloring of G.

Lemma 3.13. *The reduction from list coloring to coloring partially colored graphs produces a proper list coloring.*

PROOF. First, we prove that the maximum degree of $\hat{G}$ is indeed at most $d-1$. Since each list $R(v)$ of a vertex $v \in V$ contains at least $(\Delta+1)$ colors, the size of $L(v)$ is at most $d-\Delta-1$. Since each vertex $v \in V$ has at most Δ neighbors in G, the degree of v in $\hat{G}$ is at most $d-1$. Hence $\Delta(\hat{G}) < d$.

Now, consider an invocation of Procedure Mod-Color on the Graph $\hat{G}$ followed by the standard reduction that produces a d-coloring. Let $\psi(v)$ be the resulting color of a vertex $v \in V(G)$. By the correctness of procedure Mod-Color, $\psi(v)$ is distinct from the colors of all neighbors $v_c \in V(\hat{G}) \setminus V(G)$ of v and all neighbors $u \in V(G)$ of v. Moreover, the colors of the vertices in $V(\hat{G}) \setminus V(G)$ remain unchanged throughout the entire execution. Therefore, $\psi(v) \notin L(v)$. On the other hand, $\psi(v) \in [d]$, and thus $\psi(v) \in [d] \setminus L(V) = R(v)$. □

We summarize this section with the following theorem obtained from Theorem 3.12 and Lemma 3.13.

Theorem 3.14. *Suppose that we are given a graph $G = (V, E)$ and a list of colors for each $v \in V$, and each list consists of at least $(\Delta+1)$-colors taken from the range $[d]$, for some integer $d \geq \Delta+1$. Then a list coloring of G can be computed within $O(d^{3/4} \log d + \log^* n)$ time. If $d = O(\Delta)$ then the running time is $O(\Delta^{3/4} \log \Delta + \log^* n)$.*

4. DYNAMIC AND FAULTY GRAPHS

In this section we employ the techniques introduced in Section 3 in order to devise algorithms for *dynamic and faulty networks*. We say that a graph $G = (V, E)$ encounters a *fault* if a subset of vertices $U \subseteq V$ lose their colors (i.e., become uncolored). This situation can be repaired directly by invoking Procedure Mod-Color. (See Theorem 3.12.) A more delicate situation occurs with *dynamic graphs*, i.e., when the graph topology changes. Specifically, suppose that we are given a graph $G = (V, E)$ that is properly colored. The graph may be required to change in one of the following ways. Each such change is called *an update*.
(1) A subset of vertices W of V (and the edges adjacent on these vertices) are removed.
(2) A new set of vertices W' is added. The vertices in W' are allowed to connect to vertices in $V \cup W'$ in any way.
(3) A subset of edges of E is removed.
(4) A new set of edges between vertices of V is added.
For simplicity we assume that all vertices know an upper bound on the maximum number of vertices that are present after the change. However, note that the number of colors is not affected by the number of vertices, and the running time is only affected by an additive factor of $\log^* n$. Hence, even if the upper bound is exponential in the actual size, this will only affect the running time by a single additional round. Next, we describe how to handle each case in order to obtain a proper coloring after an update.

Case (1) - A subset of vertices W of V is removed: If a subset of vertices is removed, the new graph G' remains properly colored. However, the number of colors may be too large, if the update has significantly reduced the maximum degree. To solve this, each vertex $v \in V \setminus W$ can calculate the maximum degree $d(v, k)$ in its k-hop neighborhood in the new graph $G' = G(V \setminus W)$, where k is in the order of the running time of (the other steps) of the algorithm. If the color of v is outside of the required range defined by $d(v, k)$, then this color is discarded. Note that this way we may discard some appropriate colors, since $d(v, k)$ may be smaller than the maximum degree of G'. However, any inappropriate (i.e., too large) color will be discarded, since $d(v, k)$ is not larger than the maximum degree. Thus, we are left with a subset of vertices that are appropriately colored and vertices that still have to be colored. This is done using Procedure Mod-Color. (See Theorem 3.12).

To have an accurate number of colors we employ the technique of [17]. Specifically, we start with an estimate $\delta = O(1)$ of the maximum degree. (This initial estimate may be much smaller than the actual degree). We invoke Procedure Mod-Color with this estimate. Consequently, if the estimate is too low, some vertices may fail to execute the procedure. But the set of failed vertices is a subset of the yet uncolored vertices, since colored vertices retain their colors. Then we double δ and perform another invocation of Procedure Mod-Color. This process is repeated as long as there are uncolored vertices. Once δ becomes larger than Δ we can be confident that all vertices have succeeded (by the correctness of Procedure Mod-Color), and the process terminates. The running time is affected only by a constant factor. (The additive $\log \Delta \log^* n$ term can be saved by invoking the algorithm of Linial that requires $O(\log^* n)$ time in parallel for all estimations of the degree, i.e., for $\delta = 1, 2, 4, 8, 16, ..., n$. See [3] for more details.)

Case (2) - A new set of vertices W' is added: Let $G' = (V', E')$ be the graph after an update. It consists of a subset of colored vertices V and a subset of uncolored vertices W'. Hence we invoke Procedure Mod-Color with the parameters $V' = V \cup W'$ and $U = V$ (see Theorem 3.12) that produces a proper coloring of the entire graph G'. Moreover, the colors of vertices of the original graph G are retained. If the update has increased the maximum degree we will need to apply the technique of [17] as in case (1). However, note that in the current case the maximum degree may only grow, and therefore all colors of V are appropriate, and we do not discard any of them.

Case (3) - A subset of edges of E is removed: This case is very similar to case (1). The only problem occurs if the maximum degree is reduced, and some colors become too large. This is solved as in case (1).

Case (4) - A new set of edges between vertices of V is added: This case consists of adding new edges between colored vertices. This may cause conflicts. To solve this, for each monochromatic edge (u, v) we discard the color of the endpoint with a greater ID. (Note that this may cause some edges to lose both colors.) Then we are left with a subset of uncolored vertices. To correct this we proceed as in step (1). This completes the description of the cases.

In some occasions vertices may know the maximum degree after each update. For example, this is the case if we start with an initial graph G_0 that changes in such a way that preserves the maximum degree of G_0. In other words, the series of graphs $G_0, G_1, G_2, ...$ that is produced satisfy $\Delta(G_0) = \Delta(G_1) = \Delta(G_2) = ... = \Delta$. In this way the technique of [17] is not required, and we can come up with exactly $(\Delta+1)$-colors after each update.

We summarize this discussion with the next theorem.

Theorem 4.1. *(1) Suppose that a $(\Delta+1)$-vertex-colored graph G encounters a fault in which a subset of vertices lose their colors. Then the coloring can be corrected by assigning colors to uncolored vertices. This results in a proper $(\Delta+1)$-coloring in $O(\Delta^{3/4}\log\Delta+\log^* n)$ time or a proper $(1+o(1))\Delta$-coloring in $O(\sqrt{\Delta}\log^3\Delta+\log^* n)$ time.*
(2) Suppose that a $(\Delta+1)$-vertex colored graph changes dynamically. Then an $O(\Delta)$-coloring can be computed within $O(\sqrt{\Delta}\log^3\Delta+\log^* n)$ update-time. If the vertices know the maximum degree after each change, then a $(\Delta+1)$-coloring can be computed in $O(\Delta^{3/4}\log\Delta+\log^* n)$ time.

We remark that the results of this section are applicable also to edge coloring, since edge coloring is vertex coloring of the line graph, and line graphs can be simulated locally.

Acknowledgments
The author is grateful to the anonymous reviewers for very helpful comments.

5. REFERENCES

[1] N. Alon, L. Babai, and A. Itai. A fast and simple randomized parallel algorithm for the maximal independent set problem. *Journal of Algorithms*, 7(4):567–583, 1986.
[2] B. Awerbuch, A. V. Goldberg, M. Luby, and S. Plotkin. Network decomposition and locality in distributed computation. In *Proc. of the 30th Annual Symposium on Foundations of Computer Science*, pages 364–369, 1989.
[3] L. Barenboim, and M. Elkin. Sublogarithmic distributed MIS algorithm for sparse graphs using Nash-Williams decomposition. In *Proc. of the 27th ACM Symp. on Principles of Distributed Computing*, pages 25–34, 2008.
[4] L. Barenboim, and M. Elkin. Distributed $(\Delta+1)$-coloring in linear (in Δ) time. In *Proc. 41th ACM Symp. on Theory of Computing*, pp. 111-120, 2009.
[5] L. Barenboim, and M. Elkin. Deterministic distributed vertex coloring in polylogarithmic time. In *Proc. 29th ACM Symp. on Principles of Distributed Computing*, pages 410-419, 2010.
[6] L. Barenboim, and M. Elkin. Distributed deterministic edge coloring using bounded neighborhood independence. In *Proc. of the 30th ACM Symp. on Principles of Distributed Computing*, pages 129 - 138, 2011.
[7] L. Barenboim, M. Elkin, and F. Kuhn. Distributed (Delta+1)-Coloring in Linear (in Delta) Time. *SIAM Journal on Computing*, 43(1): 72-95, 2014.
[8] L. Barenboim, M. Elkin, S. Pettie, and J. Schneider. The locality of distributed symmetry breaking. In *Proc. of the 53rd Annual Symposium on Foundations of Computer Science*, pages 321-330, 2012.
[9] M. Elkin. A near-optimal distributed fully dynamic algorithm for maintaining sparse spanners. In *Proc. of the 26th ACM Symp. on Principles of Distributed Computing*, page 185-194, 2007.
[10] M. Elkin, S. Pettie, and H. Su. $(2\Delta-1)$-Edge-Coloring is Much Easier than Maximal Matching in the Distributed Setting. In *Proc. of the 26th ACM-SIAM Symp. on Discrete Algorithms*, pages 355-370, 2015.
[11] P. Erdős, P. Frankl, and Z. Füredi. Families of finite sets in which no set is covered by the union of r others. *Israel J. of Mathematics*, 51:79–89, 1985.
[12] I. Finocchi, F. Grandoni, G. Italiano. Designing Reliable Algorithms in Unreliable Memories. In *Proc. of the 13th European Symposium on Algorithms*, pages 1-8, 2005.
[13] M. Göös, J. Hirvonen, and J. Suomela. Linear-in-delta lower bounds in the LOCAL model. In *proc. of the 33th ACM Symp. on Principles of Distributed Computing*, pages 86-95, 2014.
[14] J. Hirvonen, and J. Suomela. Distributed maximal matching: greedy is optimal. In *Proc. of the 31th ACM Symp on Principles of Distributed Computing*, pages 165-174, 2012.
[15] A. Israeli, and A. Itai. A fast and simple randomized parallel algorithm for maximal matching. *Information Processing Letters*, 22(2):77-80, 1986.
[16] M. König, and R. Wattenhofer. On local fixing. In *Proc. of the 17th International Conf. on Principles of Distributed Systems*, pages 191 - 205, 2013.
[17] A. Korman, J. Sereni, and L. Viennot. Toward more localized local algorithms: removing assumptions concerning global knowledge. In *Proc. of the 30th ACM Symp. on Principles of Distributed Computing*, pages 49-58, 2011.
[18] K. Kothapalli, C. Scheideler, M. Onus, and C. Schindelhauer. Distributed coloring in $O(\sqrt{\log n})$ bit rounds. In *Proc. of the 20th International Parallel and Distributed Processing Symposium*, 2006.
[19] F. Kuhn. Weak graph colorings: distributed algorithms and applications. In *Proc. of the 21st ACM Symposium on Parallel Algorithms and Architectures*, pages 138–144, 2009.
[20] F. Kuhn, and R. Wattenhofer. On the complexity of distributed graph coloring. In *Proc. 25th ACM Symp. Principles of Distributed Computing*, pp. 7–15, 2006.
[21] N. Linial. Distributive graph algorithms: Global solutions from local data In *Proc. 28th Symp. on Foundation of Computer Science*, pp. 331–335, 1987.
[22] M. Luby. A simple parallel algorithm for the maximal independent set problem. *SIAM Journal on Computing*, 15:1036-1053, 1986.
[23] M. Luby. Removing randomness in parallel computation without a processor penalty. In *Proc. of the 29th Annual Symposium on Foundations of Computer Science*, pages 162-173, 1988.
[24] A. Panconesi, and R. Rizzi. Some simple distributed algorithms for sparse networks. *Distributed Computing*, 14(2):97–100, 2001.
[25] A. Panconesi, and A. Srinivasan. On the complexity of distributed network decomposition. *Journal of Algorithms*, 20(2):581-592, 1995.
[26] D. Peleg. *Distributed Computing: A Locality-Sensitive Approach.* SIAM, 2000.
[27] M. Szegedy, and S. Vishwanathan. Locality based graph coloring. In *Proc. 25th ACM Symposium on Theory of Computing*, pages 201-207, 1993.

On Information Complexity in the Broadcast Model

Mark Braverman*
Department of Computer Science
Princeton University
mbraverm@cs.princeton.edu

Rotem Oshman†
Department of Computer Science
Tel Aviv University
roshman@tau.ac.il

ABSTRACT

Information complexity is the extension of classical information theory to the *interactive* setting, where instead of one-way transmission we are interested in back-and-forth communication. This approach has been very influential in communication complexity, where it enables us to prove powerful lower bounds by quantifying the amount of information the participants in the computation must reveal about their inputs. In this paper we study information complexity in the classical broadcast model: k parties with private inputs wish to compute some function of their inputs, and they communicate by sending messages (one at a time) over a broadcast channel. We measure how much information the players reveal about their inputs to an external observer. This is called *external information cost*.

Using this approach, we prove a tight lower bound of $\Omega(n \log k + k)$ on the communication complexity of *set disjointness*, a fundamental problem in communication complexity. We also give a deterministic matching upper bound.

Next we study *compression*, a central question in information complexity: given a protocol with low information cost (but possibly high communication), can we *compress* the protocol so that its communication cost matches its information cost? In the two-player setting, it is known that every protocol can be compressed to roughly its external information cost. We show that for the multi-party case this is no longer true: there is a gap of at least $\Omega(k/\log k)$ between external information and communication. However, if we wish to compress *many* independent instances of the same protocol, then it is possible to do so with an amortized per-copy cost that approaches the information cost as the number of copies goes to infinity.

*Research supported in part by an NSF CAREER award (CCF-1149888), a Turing Centenary Fellowship, a Packard Fellowship in Science and Engineering, and the Simons Collaboration on Algorithms and Geometry.

†Research supported in part by the I-CORE Program of the Planning and Budgeting Committee and the Israel Science Foundation, Grant No. 4/11.

Permission to make digital or hard copies of all or part of this work for personal or classroom use is granted without fee provided that copies are not made or distributed for profit or commercial advantage and that copies bear this notice and the full citation on the first page. Copyrights for components of this work owned by others than ACM must be honored. Abstracting with credit is permitted. To copy otherwise, or republish, to post on servers or to redistribute to lists, requires prior specific permission and/or a fee. Request permissions from permissions@acm.org.
PODC'15, July 21–23, 2015, Donostia-San Sebastián, Spain.
Copyright is held by the owner/author(s). Publication rights licensed to ACM.
ACM 978-1-4503-3617-8 /15/07 ...$15.00.
DOI: http://dx.doi.org/10.1145/2767386.2767425.

1. INTRODUCTION

Classical information theory studies the cost of transmitting information from a sender to a receiver, over a channel which may be subject to various types of noise. The traditional focus is on *amortized cost in the limit*: the sender has many messages $\boldsymbol{X}_1, \ldots, \boldsymbol{X}_n$ drawn independently from the same distribution, and we are interested in the amortized number of bits it must communicate per message (that is, the total communication required to send all n messages, divided by n), in the limit as n grows to infinity. This question was addressed by Shannon in his seminal work [27], where he showed that in the noiseless case the amortized per-copy cost is exactly $H(\boldsymbol{X})$, the entropy of the distribution from which the messages are drawn. Later, Huffman showed [20] that a *single* copy of $\boldsymbol{X}$ can be sent in $H(\boldsymbol{X}) + 1$ bits, so for (noiseless) one-way transmission, the single-shot cost and the cost-in-the-limit are essentially the same.

The emerging field of *information complexity* seeks to extend the ideas of classical information theory to an interactive setting, where the parties involved in the computation communicate back-and-forth in order to achieve some shared goal. The basic two-party setup has two players, Alice and Bob, who receive private inputs $\boldsymbol{X}, \boldsymbol{Y}$ respectively, and wish to compute some function $f(\boldsymbol{X}, \boldsymbol{Y})$ (or more generally, perform some task that depends on the inputs). We are interested in characterizing the amount of information the players must reveal about their inputs in order to compute f; this is called the *information cost* of f. In this paper we work with *external information cost* [7], which measures the amount of information revealed to an external observer who initially does not know the inputs to the protocol. (See [7] for alternative ways to measure information cost.)

Information cost turns out to be a natural lower bound on *communication cost*, the number of bits that the players need to send to compute f, so a lower bound on information cost translates immediately to a lower bound on communication. In addition, information cost has some nice properties, such as additivity, that can make it easier to work with than communication. Consequently, information lower bounds have been very useful in proving communication lower bounds (e.g., [2, 17, 5, 29]).

One can also ask whether, as is true for one-way transmission, any protocol can be *compressed* to its information cost. This question has not been fully resolved yet, but the answer will have deep implications in theoretical computer science [7, 3, 15]. Both single-shot compression [3] and amortized cost in the limit [7] are of great interest, and they appear to have very different costs [15]. In the two-party setting it is known that any protocol can be compressed almost all the way down to its external information cost, with a logarithmic dependence on the communication complexity of the original, uncompressed protocol [3].

The broadcast model. In this paper we study the classical broadcast model of communication (also called the *shared blackboard model* in communication complexity literature [22]). We have k players, each with a private input $X_i \in \{0,1\}^n$, and the players wish to compute a joint function $f(X_1, \ldots, X_k)$ of their inputs. The players communicate by "writing messages on a blackboard" that all players can read for free (i.e., they communicate by broadcasting messages to each other). We allow the players to use randomization when deciding what to write on the board. This model is widely studied in theoretical computer science, in areas ranging from streaming [1, 2, 17] to cryptography [16] and mechanism design [13]. Beyond being a fundamental model of communication complexity, the broadcast model can also be viewed as an abstract model of single-hop wireless networks, which abstracts away the details of contention management.

We study two fundamental questions in the broadcast model: the communication complexity of set disjointness, and the question of whether interactive protocols can be compressed.

Set disjointness in the broadcast model. Set disjointness is one of the most fundamental problems in communication complexity; it has been studied in the classical two-player model [21, 25], in the number-on-forehead model (e.g., [28]), and in many other settings (see [11] for a survey); it has applications in various areas ranging from streaming [1] to data structures [23], distributed computing [26], circuit lower bounds [10] and many other examples. In multi-party (number-in-hand) set disjointness, each of the k players receives a subset $X_i \subseteq [n]$, and the players need to determine whether $\bigcap_{i=1}^{n} X_i = \emptyset$; formally, we shall denote

$$\textsc{Disj}_{n,k}(X_1, \ldots, X_k) = \neg \bigvee_{j=1}^{n} \bigwedge_{i=1}^{k} X_i^j,$$

where X_i^j is coordinate j of player i's input. Set disjointness reduces to many natural problems, so a lower bound on its communication complexity implies lower bounds on many other problems as well.

It is known that for two players, set disjointness requires $\Omega(n)$ bits of communication [21, 25], and a trivial reduction shows that $\Omega(n)$ is also a lower bound for k players. It is not difficult to see that $\Omega(k)$ is also a lower bound, as intuitively, each player must speak at least once to solve the problem. As for upper bounds, there is a simple protocol with communication complexity $O(n \log n + k)$: the players go in order, with each player i writing on the board the coordinates j where $X_i^j = 0$, unless they already appear on the board. A player that has no new zero coordinates to contribute writes a single bit to indicate this. After all players have taken their turn, if there is some coordinate that does not appear on the board, then this coordinate is in the intersection; otherwise the intersection is empty.

A-priori, it is not obvious whether the "right answer" is $\Theta(n+k)$, $\Theta(n \log n + k)$, or somewhere in between. After all, in some cases where one might naively expect a logarithmic factor to arise, it does not: a famous example is the randomized protocol of Håstad and Wigderson [19], which solves two-player set disjointness under the promise that $|X| = |Y| = s$ in $O(s)$ bits, instead of the naive $O(s \log n)$. (In fact, two players can even *compute the exact intersection* of their sets X, Y using $O(s)$ bits when $|X| = |Y| = s$ [6, 8].)

In this paper we show that the randomized communication complexity of set disjointness with k players is actually $\Theta(n \log k + k)$. Intuitively, the factor $\log k$ arises because the protocol must "find", for each $j \in [n]$, some player i with $X_i^j = 0$, before it can declare that $\bigcap_{i=1}^{k} X_i = 0$. The index of such a player is "worth" $\log k$ bits of information, as this is how many bits we require to encode it. We are able to formalize this intuition using notions from information theory and prove a lower bound of $\Omega(n \log k + k)$ on the information cost of set disjointness

To our knowledge, ours is the first communication lower bound on a decision problem in the broadcast model that grows with the number of players. This serves as evidence that while reductions from two-party communication complexity are incredibly useful [12, 24], additional benefit can be derived from directly considering multi-party models. Although an additional factor of $\log k$ in the lower bound may not seem large, communication complexity lower bounds are often applied in distributed computing to prove lower bounds on the number of rounds required to solve some task, and in that context one divides by the number of bits that can be sent per round, which can end up being linear in the number of participants (see, e.g., [14]). So for instance, when $k = \Theta(n)$, the difference between a lower bound of $\Omega(n \log k)$ and a lower bound of $\Omega(n)$ on the total communication complexity can end up being the difference between a logarithmic round lower bound and a constant (i.e., trivial) bound.

We remark that a *promise* version of set disjointness has received significant attention in the broadcast model ([2, 17] and others), due to its connections to streaming lower bounds [1]. Set disjointness and other problems have also recently been investigated in a *point-to-point* model of multi-party communication ([5, 29] and others). And finally, in [24], a technique called *symmetrization* is introduced to obtain multi-party lower bounds on several pointwise-Boolean functions, such as pointwise-OR, where the output is a vector Y such that $Y_i = \bigvee_j X_i^j$ for each $i \in [n]$. Although symmetrization can prove a lower bound of $\Omega(n \log k)$ on pointwise-OR, this technique seems too weak to prove a lower bound of $\Omega(n \log k)$ on set disjointness.

Compressing multi-party broadcast protocols. For two players, it is known that any interactive protocol can be compressed to roughly its external information cost [3], which is the amount of information revealed to an external observer about the players' inputs. We observe that for multiple parties this no longer holds: for the function $\bigwedge_{i=1}^{k} X_i$, the information cost under any distribution is bounded by $O(\log k)$, but we show that there is a distribution under which the communication cost is $\Omega(k)$. This shows that there is a gap of at least $\Omega(k/\log k)$ between external information and communication in the k-player broadcast model. However, while a *single* instance cannot be compressed, we do show that for many instances we can achieve compression: the *amortized* cost per-copy as the number of copies tends to infinity is bounded by the external information cost, generalizing the result of [7] for two players. We note that while [7] deals with *internal information*, which measures what the players learn about each others' inputs, here are we concerned with *external information*, which measures what an external observer learns. External information is generally an easier quantity to work with, and consequently we are able to simplify the protocol from [7].

Organization. The remainder of the paper is organized as follows. Before diving into the technical details, we give an informal overview of the set disjointness lower bound in Section 2. In Section 3 we review some basic notions from communication complexity and information theory, and in Section 4 we prove the two lower bounds on set disjointness, of $\Omega(n \log k)$ and $\Omega(k)$ respectively. A matching deterministic upper bound, with communication complexity $O(n \log k + k)$, is presented in Section 5. In Section 6 we discuss the issue of compression, prove that there is a gap of $\Omega(k/\log k)$ between information and communication, and show that computation involving many independent instances of the same problem can be compressed such that in the limit as the number of instances goes to infinity, the per-instance cost tends to the information cost of the problem.

2. HIGH-LEVEL OVERVIEW OF THE SET DISJOINTNESS LOWER BOUND

Our lower bound follows the information-theoretic approach [9, 2]: in order to prove a lower bound on the communication complexity of set disjointness, we will show that any protocol that solves it with small (constant) error must reveal a lot of information about the players' inputs, in the information-theoretic sense: the entropy of the inputs (i.e., our uncertainty about them) is significantly reduced once the transcript of the protocol is observed. Each bit the protocol communicates can reveal at most one bit of information about the inputs, so we immediately obtain a lower bound on communication as well.

The precise notion of information cost we use in this paper was introduced in [2], and is called *conditional information cost.* We will work with a distribution $(\boldsymbol{X}, \boldsymbol{D}) \sim \mu$ on two variables: the input the players, $\boldsymbol{X} = \boldsymbol{X}_1, \ldots, \boldsymbol{X}_k$, and an auxiliary variable $\boldsymbol{D}$. The essential property of the distribution is that conditioned on $\boldsymbol{D}$, the inputs $\boldsymbol{X}_1, \ldots, \boldsymbol{X}_k$ are independent, and this will be crucial to our proof. Conditional information cost measures the information an external observer learns about the inputs, conditioned on $\boldsymbol{D}$.

One of the advantages of the information-based approach is that it allows us to decompose the problem into many small problems, prove that each small problem is "a little bit hard", and obtain a lower bound for the overall problem that is equal to the sum of the bounds on the smaller problems. This is called *direct sum* [2]. In our case, as in [2], since $\text{DISJ}_{n,k} = \neg \bigvee_{j=1}^{n} \bigwedge_{i=1}^{k} X_i^j$, we will break the problem up into n instances of one-bit AND. We prove a lower bound of $\Omega(\log k)$ on AND, and obtain a lower bound of $\Omega(n \log k)$ for disjointness.

In order to show that any protocol computing AND must reveal $\Omega(\log k)$ bits of information about the input, we argue that whenever the output of the protocol is 0, the protocol's transcript must "point" to some player i whose input is zero. The notion of "pointing to a player" is formalized using the *posterior probability* that $X_i = 0$ after the transcript is observed. Under our input distribution, the prior probability that $X_i = 0$ is only $O(1/k)$, but we will show that for "most" transcripts, there is a player i with a *constant* posterior probability of $X_i = 0$ given the transcript. Intuitively, since a-priori we had $X_i = 0$ with probability only $O(1/k)$, we are "very surprised" to learn that $X_i = 0$ with constant probability, and this "surprise" is worth $\Omega(\log k)$ bits of information. Viewed another way: a-priori, since each player receives 0 with probability roughly $1/k$, we expect a small (constant) number of players to receive 0, but we have no idea who they are. Once the transcript is revealed, we can "point" to a player that probably received 0, so our uncertainty about the input is greatly reduced. Since the identify of the player requires $\Omega(\log k)$ bits to write down, this is the amount of information we have learned about the input.

We proceed to review the definitions and notions required to make this outline formal.

3. PRELIMINARIES

Notation. We use bold-face letters to denote random variables. For variables $\boldsymbol{A}_1, \ldots, \boldsymbol{A}_\ell$ with joint distribution μ, we let $\mu(\boldsymbol{A}_i)$ denote the marginal distribution of $\boldsymbol{A}_i$, and $\mu(\boldsymbol{A}_i | \boldsymbol{A}_j = a_j)$ denote the distribution of $\boldsymbol{A}_i$ conditioned on $\boldsymbol{A}_j = a_j$ (and similarly for more variables). For a string S, we let $|S|$ denote the length of S.

The broadcast model. In the *broadcast model*, also called the *shared blackboard model* [22], we have k players. Each player i receives a private input X_i, and the players wish to compute a joint function $f(X_1, \ldots, X_n)$ of their inputs. Communication is via a shared blackboard (or broadcast channel) that all players can read for free. At each point in the protocol, the current contents of the blackboard determine whose turn it is to speak next, and that player generates a message using its input, private and public randomness, and the contents of the blackboard, and writes it on the board. Then the next player speaks, and so on, until eventually the protocol halts and the players output some values (for which they are not charged).

Communication complexity. For a protocol Π, we define the *communication complexity of* Π, denoted $\text{CC}(\Pi)$, as the worst-case number of bits that are written on the board in any execution of Π. The *communication complexity of a problem f with error ϵ*, denoted $\text{CC}_\epsilon(f)$, is the minimum communication complexity of any protocol Π that solves f on any input with error probability at most ϵ over the protocol's randomness.

In Section 6 we shall also study *distributional* (or *average-case*) communication complexity. Given an input distribution μ, we define the *distributional complexity of f with error ϵ*, denoted $\text{D}_\epsilon^\mu(f)$, to be the minimum communication complexity of a protocol that solves f with error probability at most ϵ when inputs are drawn from μ (i.e., the probability is over both the input and the protocol's randomness).

Information theory. We require the following notions from classical information theory.

The *entropy* of a random variable measures how much uncertainty we have about it, and corresponds to the number of bits required to encode the variable (in a lossless encoding).

Definition 1. The *entropy* of a random variable $\boldsymbol{X} \sim \mu$ with support $\mathcal{X}$ is given by

$$H(\boldsymbol{X}) = \sum_{x \in \mathcal{X}} \Pr_{\mu}[\boldsymbol{X} = x] \log \frac{1}{\Pr_\mu[\boldsymbol{X} = x]}.$$

We also define *conditional entropy*, which measure the average uncertainty that remains about a random variable $\boldsymbol{X}$, after we observe the value of another random variable $\boldsymbol{Y}$.

Definition 2. For two random variables $\boldsymbol{X}, \boldsymbol{Y}$ with joint distribution μ, the *conditional entropy of $\boldsymbol{X}$ given $\boldsymbol{Y}$* is

$$H(\boldsymbol{X} \mid \boldsymbol{Y}) = \mathop{\mathbb{E}}_{\boldsymbol{y} \sim \mu(\boldsymbol{Y})} H(\boldsymbol{X} \mid \boldsymbol{Y} = \boldsymbol{y}),$$

where $H(\boldsymbol{X} \mid \boldsymbol{Y} = a)$ denotes the entropy of $\boldsymbol{X}$ with respect to the distribution $\mu(\boldsymbol{X} \mid \boldsymbol{Y} = a)$.

To quantify the amount of information we have learned about a random variable $\boldsymbol{X}$ from observing another variable $\boldsymbol{Y}$, we use *mutual information*, which measures the "loss of uncertainty" about $\boldsymbol{X}$ when given $\boldsymbol{Y}$ (or, symmetrically, $\boldsymbol{Y}$ when given $\boldsymbol{X}$):

Definition 3. The *mutual information* between two random variables $\boldsymbol{X}, \boldsymbol{Y}$ is given by

$$\text{I}(\boldsymbol{X}; \boldsymbol{Y}) = H(\boldsymbol{X}) - H(\boldsymbol{X} \mid \boldsymbol{Y}) = H(\boldsymbol{Y}) - H(\boldsymbol{Y} \mid \boldsymbol{X}).$$

The *conditional mutual information between $\boldsymbol{X}$ and $\boldsymbol{Y}$ given $\boldsymbol{Z}$* is

$$\begin{aligned} \mathrm{I}(\boldsymbol{X};\boldsymbol{Y}\mid\boldsymbol{Z}) &= H(\boldsymbol{X}\mid\boldsymbol{Z}) - H(\boldsymbol{X}\mid\boldsymbol{Y},\boldsymbol{Z}) \\ &= H(\boldsymbol{Y},\boldsymbol{Z}) - H(\boldsymbol{Y}\mid\boldsymbol{X},\boldsymbol{Z}). \end{aligned}$$

For clarity, the distribution on the variables may sometimes be included as a subscript ("$\mathrm{I}_\mu(\boldsymbol{X};\boldsymbol{Y})$"), but we generally omit it when clear from the context.

Intuitively, the mutual information between two variables $\boldsymbol{A},\boldsymbol{B}$ should also correspond to how much the distribution of $\boldsymbol{A}$ is distorted from its prior distribution when the value of $\boldsymbol{B}$ is revealed. This relationship is captured using *Kullback-Leibler divergence* (also known as *relative entropy*) to measure the distance (or difference) between two distributions.

Definition 4. Given two distributions μ_1,μ_2 with support $\mathcal{X}$, the *KL divergence* of μ_1 from μ_2 is

$$\mathsf{D}\left(\frac{\mu_1}{\mu_2}\right) = \sum_{x\in\mathcal{X}} \mu_1(x)\log\frac{\mu_1(x)}{\mu_2(x)}.$$

KL divergence is not a metric: it is non-negative and it equals zero only when $\mu_1 = \mu_2$, but it is not symmetric. It is helpful to think of μ_1 as the "true" or posterior distribution, and of μ_2 as our prior belief.

Mutual information and KL divergence are related as follows:

$$\begin{aligned} \mathrm{I}(\boldsymbol{X};\boldsymbol{Y}) &= \mathop{\mathbb{E}}_{y\sim\mu(\boldsymbol{Y})} \mathsf{D}\left(\frac{\mu(\boldsymbol{X}\mid\boldsymbol{Y}=y)}{\mu(\boldsymbol{X})}\right) \\ &= \mathop{\mathbb{E}}_{x\sim\mu(\boldsymbol{X})} \mathsf{D}\left(\frac{\mu(\boldsymbol{Y}\mid\boldsymbol{X}=x)}{\mu(\boldsymbol{Y})}\right), \end{aligned} \tag{1}$$

and similarly for conditional mutual information. In words: the information $\boldsymbol{Y}$ conveys about $\boldsymbol{X}$ is the expected divergence between the posterior distribution of $\boldsymbol{X}$ when the value of $\boldsymbol{Y}$ is revealed, and the prior distribution of $\boldsymbol{X}$ when $\boldsymbol{Y}$ is not known (or vice-versa).

External information cost. Given a protocol Π, we use $\boldsymbol{\Pi}$ to denote the random variable representing the transcript of Π. (The randomness arises both from the input distribution and the protocol's own private and public randomness.) *External information cost* is defined, by extension of the two-party case [9, 2], as follows:

Definition 5. Given a protocol Π and distribution μ, we define the *external information cost of Π under μ* by

$$\mathop{\mathrm{IC}}_\mu(\Pi) := \mathrm{I}(\boldsymbol{\Pi};\boldsymbol{X}),$$

where $\boldsymbol{X}\sim\mu$ is the joint input to the protocol.

For a problem f, distribution μ and error parameter $\epsilon\in(0,1)$, the *external information cost of f under μ with error ϵ* is defined to be

$$\mathop{\mathrm{IC}}_\mu(f,\epsilon) := \inf_\Pi \mathop{\mathrm{IC}}_\mu(\Pi),$$

where the infimum is taken over all protocols that solve f with worst-case error probability at most ϵ (for any input, over the protocol's randomness).

Observe that $\mathrm{IC}_\mu(\Pi) := \mathrm{I}(\boldsymbol{\Pi};\boldsymbol{X}) \le H(\boldsymbol{\Pi}) \le |\boldsymbol{\Pi}|$, so any lower bound on the information cost immediately translates to a communication lower bound.

For our lower bound we use the notion of *conditional information cost*, introduced in [2]. It generalizes the usual information cost by introducing conditioning on an auxiliary variable.

Definition 6. Let Π be a randomized protocol, and let μ be a distribution on $\mathcal{X}\times\mathcal{D}$ for some $\mathcal{X},\mathcal{D}$. The *conditional information cost* of Π with respect to μ is given by

$$\mathop{\mathrm{CIC}}_\mu(\Pi) = \mathop{\mathrm{I}}_{(\boldsymbol{X},\boldsymbol{D})\sim\mu}(\boldsymbol{\Pi};\boldsymbol{X}\mid\boldsymbol{D}).$$

For a problem f and an error parameter $\epsilon\in(0,1)$, we define

$$\mathop{\mathrm{CIC}}_\mu(f,\epsilon) = \inf_\Pi \mathop{\mathrm{CIC}}_\mu(\Pi),$$

where the infimum is taken over all protocols that solve P with worst-case error ϵ on any input.

As with external information, conditional information is a lower bound on communication complexity.

Now we are ready to prove our main lower bound.

4. SET DISJOINTNESS LOWER BOUND

Following the approach of [2], in order to prove a lower bound of $\Omega(n\log k)$ on the communication complexity of $\textsc{Disj}_{n,k}$, we decompose the disjointness problem into n copies of k-player $\textsc{And}_k$ on a single bit, and argue that the cost adds up linearly.

LEMMA 1 ([2]). *Let μ be a distribution on $\{0,1\}^k\times\mathcal{D}$, such that*

(1) For any (X,D) in the support of μ, $\bigwedge_{i=1}^k X_i = 0$,[1] and

(2) For any $d\in\mathcal{D}$, when we draw $(\boldsymbol{X},\boldsymbol{D})\sim\mu$ conditioned on $\boldsymbol{D}=d$, the variables $\boldsymbol{X}_1,\ldots,\boldsymbol{X}_k$ are independent.

Then $\mathrm{CIC}_{\mu^n}(\textsc{Disj}_{n,k},\epsilon) \ge n\cdot\mathrm{CIC}_\mu(\textsc{And}_k,\epsilon)$.

Therefore, to obtain a lower bound of $\Omega(n\log k)$ on $\textsc{Disj}_{n,k}$, it is sufficient to prove a lower bound of $\Omega(\log k)$ on $\textsc{And}_k$, and this is is what we shall do next. We will separately show that $\Omega(k)$ is also a lower bound on the communication complexity of $\textsc{And}_k$, but this is an easy argument that does not require information theory.

4.1 Lower Bound for Single-Bit AND

For this lower bound we must exhibit a "hard distribution" μ on inputs $\{0,1\}^k$, which satisfies the conditions of Lemma 1, and on which $\textsc{And}_k$ has information cost $\Omega(\log k)$. Our considerations in choosing the distribution μ are as follows:

- To satisfy condition (1) of Lemma 1, the distribution must always assign zero to at least one player. We ensure this by choosing one uniformly random player $\boldsymbol{Z}\in[k]$ and assigning it zero. We will satisfy condition (2) by designing our distribution such that conditioned on the value of $\boldsymbol{Z}$, the players' inputs will be independent. Our analysis will be conditioned on $\boldsymbol{Z}$ (that is, $\boldsymbol{Z}$ will serve as our "auxiliary variable" previously denoted by $\boldsymbol{D}$).
- For the remaining players, intuitively we wish to have as few zeroes as possible, to make it hard for the protocol to find a player that received zero. One might even be tempted to assign one to all players other than $\boldsymbol{Z}$, but since $\mathrm{CIC}(\Pi) = \mathrm{I}(\boldsymbol{\Pi};\boldsymbol{X}\mid\boldsymbol{Z}) \le H(\boldsymbol{X}|\boldsymbol{Z})$, we cannot do this—we must ensure that the input has residual entropy at least $\Omega(\log k)$ even conditioned on $\boldsymbol{Z}$. (If all players other than $\boldsymbol{Z}$ receive 1, the residual entropy would be 0.)

[1]This requirement may seem odd: if we fix the output of $\textsc{And}_k$ to zero, how can the distribution be hard for the protocol? The answer is that the protocol must be correct w.h.p. on *any* input, even inputs that are not in the support. The distribution is used only to analyze the *information cost* of the protocol, not its correctness.

- Ideally, then, one would choose a single player other than $\boldsymbol{Z}$, assign it zero, and assign everyone else one. But this would not be a product distribution, even conditioned on $\boldsymbol{Z}$.

- We can come close to the ideal above by assigning each player other than $\boldsymbol{Z}$ a zero with probability $1/k$, independent of the other players.

Formally, the distribution μ is defined as follows: first we select a uniformly random player $\boldsymbol{Z} \in [k]$; we set $\boldsymbol{X_Z} = 0$. For each $i \neq \boldsymbol{Z}$ we have $\Pr[\boldsymbol{X}_i = 0 \mid \boldsymbol{Z}] = 1/k$ independent of all the other inputs.

Under the distribution μ described above, it is somewhat likely (constant probability) that besides the special player $\boldsymbol{Z}$, exactly one other player receives zero. In our analysis we condition on this event, which makes the distribution symmetric: a uniformly random pair of players receive zero, and the others receive one. Notice that conditioned on exactly two players receiving zero and on $\boldsymbol{Z}$, the identity of the other player that received zero is uniform in $[k] \setminus \{\boldsymbol{Z}\}$, so it is worth roughly $\log k$ bits of information. Our proof argues that the protocol must *find* some player that received zero, and since, due to the symmetry, it cannot tell which is the special player $\boldsymbol{Z}$, it finds the *other* player that got zero with probability $1/2$. This will show that the conditional information cost of the protocol is $\Omega(\log k)$.

Posterior probabilities. What does it mean for the protocol to "find a player that received zero"? We formalize this in terms of the *posterior probability distribution* of the input $\boldsymbol{X}$ given the transcript and $\boldsymbol{Z}$. "Finding a zero" will mean that for some $i \in [k]$, the posterior probability of $\boldsymbol{X}_i = 0$ given the transcript is *constant* (whereas the prior was only $O(1/k)$).

Recall that the conditional information cost can be re-phrased in terms of the KL-divergence between the posterior and prior of $\boldsymbol{X}$:

$$\mathrm{I}(\boldsymbol{\Pi}; \boldsymbol{X} \mid \boldsymbol{Z}) = \mathop{\mathbb{E}}_{\boldsymbol{\ell}, \boldsymbol{z}} \mathsf{D}\left(\frac{\mu(\boldsymbol{X} \mid \boldsymbol{\Pi} = \boldsymbol{\ell}, \boldsymbol{Z} = \boldsymbol{z})}{\mu(\boldsymbol{X} \mid \boldsymbol{Z} = \boldsymbol{z})} \right).$$

It is more convenient to work with the distributions of the individual inputs $\boldsymbol{X}_i$ rather than the distribution of the entire input $\boldsymbol{X}$. And this will be sufficient to prove the lower bound:

LEMMA 2.

$$\mathrm{I}(\boldsymbol{\Pi}; \boldsymbol{X} \mid \boldsymbol{Z}) \geq \sum_{i=1}^{k} \mathop{\mathbb{E}}_{\boldsymbol{\ell}, \boldsymbol{z}} \mathsf{D}\left(\frac{\mu(\boldsymbol{X}_i \mid \boldsymbol{\Pi} = \boldsymbol{\ell}, \boldsymbol{Z} = \boldsymbol{z})}{\mu(\boldsymbol{X}_i \mid \boldsymbol{Z} = \boldsymbol{z})} \right).$$

In other words, it is enough to show that for "many" transcripts ℓ there is *some* player i whose posterior distribution given $\boldsymbol{\Pi} = \ell$ is very different from his prior distribution (all conditioned on $\boldsymbol{Z}$). In general, when $i = \boldsymbol{Z}$, the divergence is zero: we know in advance that $\boldsymbol{X}_i = 0$, so the posterior and the prior are the same. So in fact we are interested in bounding

$$\mathrm{I}(\boldsymbol{\Pi}; \boldsymbol{X} | \boldsymbol{Z}) \geq \frac{1}{k} \sum_{i=1}^{k} \sum_{z \neq i} \mathop{\mathbb{E}}_{\boldsymbol{\ell} \sim \pi | \boldsymbol{Z} = z} \mathsf{D}\left(\frac{\mu(\boldsymbol{X}_i \mid \boldsymbol{\Pi} = \boldsymbol{\ell}, \boldsymbol{Z} = z)}{\mu(\boldsymbol{X}_i \mid \boldsymbol{Z} = z)} \right). \tag{2}$$

As we said, we will show that for many transcript ℓ, some player has "shown his hand" and revealed that its input was probably 0: for some $i \neq z$, the posterior probability of $\boldsymbol{X}_i = 0$ given $\boldsymbol{\Pi} = \ell, \boldsymbol{Z} = z$ is constant. Since the prior is only $O(1/k)$, this gives us a divergence of $\Omega(\log k)$: specifically, if the posterior probability of 0 is p, then

$$\mathsf{D}\left(\frac{\mu(\boldsymbol{X}_i \mid \boldsymbol{\Pi} = \ell, \boldsymbol{Z} = z)}{\mu(\boldsymbol{X}_i \mid \boldsymbol{Z} = z)} \right) \tag{3}$$

$$= \sum_{b=0,1} \Bigg(\Pr[\boldsymbol{X}_i = b \mid \boldsymbol{\Pi} = \ell, \boldsymbol{Z} = z] \cdot \cdot \log \frac{\Pr[\boldsymbol{X}_i = b \mid \boldsymbol{\Pi} = \ell, \boldsymbol{Z} = z]}{\Pr[\boldsymbol{X}_i = b \mid \boldsymbol{Z} = z]} \Bigg)$$

$$= p \log \frac{p}{\frac{1}{k}} + (1-p) \log \frac{1-p}{1-\frac{1}{k}} \geq p \log k - H(p)$$

$$\geq p \log(k) - 1. \tag{4}$$

(As usual, we assume the convention that $0 \log 0 = 0$.) Plugging (4) into (2), with constant p, yields the lower bound. But first we must show that indeed many transcripts "point" to a player that received zero.

Finding zeroes. In order to analyze the posterior probabilities, we examine the structure of the protocol. As usual for this kind of proof, we use the fact that for any transcript, the probability of getting this transcript can be broken up into the product of functions that each depend only on the input to a single player:

LEMMA 3 ([2]). *For any transcript ℓ, there exist functions $\{q_{i,b}^{\ell}\}_{i \in [k], b \in \{0,1\}}$ s.t. $\Pr[\boldsymbol{\Pi}(X) = \ell] = \prod_{i=1}^{k} q_{i,X_i}^{\ell}$.*

This is proven by an easy induction on rounds: at each point in the protocol, some player i is next to speak. If the transcript so far is ℓ, the probability of getting a particular extension ℓm depends only on player i's random choices and its input X_i. Therefore we set $q_{i,X_i}^{\ell m} = q_{i,X_i}^{\ell} \cdot \Pr[\text{player } i \text{ sends } m \text{ on inputs } X_i \text{ after seeing } \ell]$, and for each $j \neq i$ we set $q_{j,X_j}^{\ell m} = q_{j,X_j}^{\ell}$.

The probability that a particular transcript ℓ is generated when $\boldsymbol{X}_i = b$ is proportional to $q_{i,b}^{\ell}$. Therefore, the posterior probability that $\boldsymbol{X}_i = 0$ given transcript ℓ is related to the ratio between $q_{i,0}^{\ell}$ and $q_{i,1}^{\ell}$: intuitively, the larger $q_{i,0}^{\ell}$ is with respect to $q_{i,1}^{\ell}$, the more we are inclined to believe that $\boldsymbol{X}_i = 0$ if we observe transcript ℓ. Indeed, using Bayes' rule we can show:

LEMMA 4. *Suppose that $q_{i,1} \neq 0$, and let $\alpha_i^{\ell} := q_{i,0}^{\ell}/q_{i,1}^{\ell}$. For any transcript ℓ we have*

$$\Pr[\boldsymbol{X}_i = 0 \mid \boldsymbol{\Pi} = \ell, \boldsymbol{Z} \neq i] = \frac{q_{i,0}^{\ell}}{q_{i,0}^{\ell} + (k-1) q_{i,1}}$$

$$= \frac{\alpha_i^{\ell}}{\alpha_i^{\ell} + k - 1} \geq \frac{\alpha_i^{\ell}}{\alpha_i^{\ell} + k}. \tag{5}$$

When $q_{i,1} = 0$, the posterior is of course 1.

Notice that when $\alpha_i^{\ell} = \Omega(k)$ this posterior probability becomes constant. The factor of $\Omega(k)$ is needed to overcome the prior probability that $\boldsymbol{X}_i = 0$, which is only $1/k$.

"Good transcripts". Our task now is to show that for "many" transcripts ℓ we indeed have $\alpha_i^{\ell} = \Omega(k)$ for some $i \in [k]$. Not all transcripts satisfy this property: for example, the protocol can decide with probability ϵ to throw its hands up and do nothing. However, we will show that transcripts that do not point to a player that received zero contribute to the error of the protocol, and therefore the total probability of getting such a transcript cannot be large.

We focus our attention on inputs that have exactly two zeroes, and our "good transcripts" will also be chosen with respect to their behavior on these inputs. Let $\mathcal{X}_c$ denote the set of inputs with c zeroes for $c \in [k]$. Note that the correct answer for AND_k is 1 on inputs in $\mathcal{X}_0$ (there is only one such input, 1^k) and 0 on inputs in $\mathcal{X}_c$ for $c \geq 1$.

Let π_2 be the distribution of transcripts conditioned on the input being in $\mathcal{X}_2$:

$$\pi_2(\ell) = \sum_{X \in \mathcal{X}_2} \left[\mu(X|_{\mathcal{X}_2}) \prod_{i=1}^{k} q^{\ell}_{i,X_i} \right].$$

Let L be the set of transcripts satisfying the following constraints: for each $\ell \in L$, the output of the protocol is 0, and also

$$\pi_2(\ell) \geq C \cdot \prod_{i=1}^{k} q^{\ell}_{i,1},$$

where C is some large constant whose value will be chosen later. In other words, L is the set of transcripts with output 0 which "strongly prefer" inputs with two zeroes over 1^k. (In particular, these transcripts do not contribute much to the error of the protocol.)

To show that L has large mass under π_2, let us partition the complement of L into two sets B_0, B_1 based on the output value on each transcript. Neither set can be large:

- The transcripts in B_1 cannot have large mass under π_2 because they yield the wrong output (1) on all inputs in $\mathcal{X}_2$:

$$\begin{aligned}
\pi_2(B_1) &= \sum_{\ell \in B_1} \sum_{X \in \mathcal{X}_2} \mu(X|_{\mathcal{X}_2}) \Pr[\mathbf{\Pi} = \ell \mid \mathbf{X} = X] \\
&= \frac{1}{\mu(\mathcal{X}_2)} \sum_{X \in \mathcal{X}_2} \mu(X) \sum_{\ell \in B_1} \Pr[\mathbf{\Pi} = \ell \mid \mathbf{X} = X] \\
&\leq \frac{1}{\mu(\mathcal{X}_2)} \sum_{X \in \mathcal{X}_{\geq 1}} \mu(X) \sum_{\ell \in B_1} \Pr[\mathbf{\Pi} = \ell \mid \mathbf{X} = X] \\
&\leq \frac{1}{\mu(\mathcal{X}_2)} \Pr_{\mu}[\Pi \text{ outputs } 1] \leq \frac{\delta}{\mu(\mathcal{X}_2)}.
\end{aligned}$$

- B_0 contains transcripts on which the output is 0, but

$$\pi_2(\ell) < C \cdot \prod_{i=1}^{k} q^{\ell}_{i,1}.$$

These transcripts contribute to the error of the protocol on 1^k at least in proportion to their mass under π_2, and therefore they also cannot have large mass:

$$\begin{aligned}
\Pr\left[\mathbf{\Pi}(1^k) \text{ outputs } 0\right] &\geq \sum_{\ell \in B_0} \Pr\left[\mathbf{\Pi}(1^k) = \ell\right] \\
&= \sum_{\ell \in B_0} \prod_{i=1}^{k} q^{\ell}_{i,1} \\
&> \sum_{\ell \in B_0} \pi_2(\ell)/C = \pi_2(B_0)/C,
\end{aligned}$$

and therefore $\pi_2(B_0) < C \cdot \delta$.

Together we have that assuming $C \cdot \delta < 1/200$ and $\delta/\mu(\mathcal{X}_2) < 1/200$ (both constant requirements), $\pi_2(B_0 \cup B_1) < 1/100$. Note that we can choose C arbitrarily large, and compensate by assuming a smaller error probability δ.

For any transcript $\ell \in L$, we have

$$\pi_2(\ell) = \sum_{X \in \mathcal{X}_2} \mu(X|_{\mathcal{X}_2}) \prod_{i=1}^{k} q^{\ell}_{i,X_i} \geq C \prod_{i=1}^{k} q^{\ell}_{i,1}.$$

Given membership in $\mathcal{X}_2$, all two-zero inputs are equally likely, so $\mu(X|_{\mathcal{X}_2}) = \frac{1}{\binom{k}{2}}$ for any $X \in \mathcal{X}_2$. Note that for each $X \in \mathcal{X}_2$ we can write $\prod_{i=1}^{k} q^{\ell}_{i,X_i} = q^{\ell}_{j_1,0} q^{\ell}_{j_2,0} \cdot \prod_{i \neq j_1,j_2} q^{\ell}_{i,1}$, where $j_1 \neq j_2$ are the two indices where X has zero. Dividing both sides by $\prod_{i=1}^{k} q^{\ell}_{i,1}$ (and renaming the indices for convenience), we obtain

$$\frac{1}{\binom{k}{2}} \sum_{i<j} \alpha^{\ell}_i \alpha^{\ell}_j \geq C.$$

Because $\sum_{i<j} a_i a_i \leq (\sum_i a_i)^2$ for any sequence $a_1, \ldots, a_N$, we get that

$$\sum_i \alpha^{\ell}_i \geq \sqrt{\frac{k(k-1)}{2} \cdot C} \geq \sqrt{\frac{k^2}{4} \cdot C} = \frac{\sqrt{C}}{2} k. \tag{6}$$

That is, the *sum* of the coefficients is linear for each $\ell \in L$. However, we need to show that for many transcripts the *maximum* coefficient is linear, and this does not necessarily hold for all of L; for example, it could be that for half the values of i we have $\alpha^{\ell}_i = \Omega(1)$, instead of having one value of i for which $\alpha^{\ell}_i = \Omega(k)$. To eliminate such transcripts, we further restrict our attention to transcripts that are somewhat likely to appear when there are exactly two zeroes in the input, not more. For such transcripts, there are only two players that can be "pointed to", so only two coefficients can be large.

Formally, we focus our attention on the subset $L' \subseteq L$ of transcripts ℓ satisfying

$$\Pr[\mathbf{\Pi} = \ell \mid \mathbf{X} \in \mathcal{X}_2] \geq \frac{1}{2} \Pr[\mathbf{\Pi} = \ell \mid \mathbf{X} \in \mathcal{X}_3],$$

that is, transcripts that "like" inputs with two zeroes not much less than inputs with three zeroes. We have $\pi_2(L') \geq \pi_2(L) - 1/2$, because

$$\begin{aligned}
\pi_2(L \setminus L') &= \sum_{\ell \in L \setminus L'} \Pr[\mathbf{\Pi} = \ell \mid \mathbf{X} \in \mathcal{X}_2] \\
&\leq \frac{1}{2} \sum_{\ell \in L \setminus L'} \Pr[\mathbf{\Pi} = \ell \mid \mathbf{X} \in \mathcal{X}_3] \leq \frac{1}{2}.
\end{aligned}$$

Now fix $\ell \in L'$, and let us show that for some $i \in [k]$, the posterior probability of $X_i = 0$ given ℓ is $\Omega(k)$ times the posterior probability of 1. If there is some i for which $q^{\ell}_{i,1} = 0$, then we are done, so assume that this is not the case. Because $\ell \in L'$,

$$\sum_{X \in \mathcal{X}_2} \mu(X|_{\mathcal{X}_2}) \prod_{i=1}^{k} q^{\ell}_{i,X_i} \geq \frac{1}{2} \sum_{X \in \mathcal{X}_3} \mu(X|_{\mathcal{X}_3}) \prod_{i=1}^{k} q^{\ell}_{i,X_i},$$

that is,

$$\frac{1}{\binom{k}{2}} \sum_{i<j} \alpha^{\ell}_i \alpha^{\ell}_j \geq \frac{1}{2\binom{k}{3}} \sum_{i<j<m} \alpha^{\ell}_i \alpha^{\ell}_j \alpha^{\ell}_m. \tag{7}$$

Now assume for the sake of contradiction that for a constant C' whose value will be fixed later, we have $\alpha^{\ell}_i < C'k$ for each $i \in [k]$. Then

$$\begin{aligned}
6 \sum_{i<j<m} \alpha^{\ell}_i \alpha^{\ell}_j \alpha^{\ell}_m &= \left(\sum_i \alpha^{\ell}_i \right)^3 - 3 \sum_{i \neq j} \left(\alpha^{\ell}_i \right)^2 \alpha^{\ell}_j - \sum_i \alpha^3_i \\
&> \left(\sum_i \alpha^{\ell}_i \right)^3 - 3C'k \sum_{i \neq j} \alpha^{\ell}_i \alpha^{\ell}_j - (C')^2 k^2 \sum_i \alpha_i \\
&\geq \left(\sum_i \alpha^{\ell}_i \right)^3 - 3C'k \left(\sum_i \alpha^{\ell}_i \right)^2 - (C')^2 k^2 \sum_i \alpha_i.
\end{aligned}$$

From (6) we know that $k \leq 2\sum_i \alpha_i^\ell/(\sqrt{C})$, so

$$6\sum_{i<j<m} \alpha_i^\ell \alpha_j^\ell \alpha_m^\ell \geq \left(\sum_i \alpha_i^\ell\right)^3 - 6\frac{C'}{\sqrt{C}}\left(\sum_i \alpha_i^\ell\right)^3 - 4\frac{(C')^2}{C}\left(\sum_i \alpha_i\right)^3.$$

If we choose, e.g., $C' < \sqrt{C}/100$, we get that

$$6\sum_{i<j<m} \alpha_i^\ell \alpha_j^\ell \alpha_m^\ell \geq \frac{1}{2}\left(\sum_i \alpha_i^\ell\right)^3 \overset{(6)}{\geq} \frac{1}{4}\sqrt{C}k\left(\sum_i \alpha_i^\ell\right)^2,$$

and therefore

$$\frac{1}{2\binom{k}{3}}\sum_{i<j<m} \alpha_i^\ell \alpha_j^\ell \alpha_m^\ell \geq \frac{\sqrt{C}}{16k^2}\left(\sum_i \alpha_i^\ell\right)^2.$$

This gives us a lower bound on the right-hand side in (7). The left-hand side is bounded from above by

$$\frac{1}{\binom{k}{2}}\sum_{i<j} \alpha_i^\ell \alpha_j^\ell \leq \frac{4}{k^2}\left(\sum_i \alpha_i^\ell\right)^2.$$

If we choose C sufficiently large we obtain a contradiction to (7). Note that the value of C' is constrained only by the value of C, so by increasing C (which requires only assuming a smaller error probability δ for the protocol) we can obtain an arbitrarily large lower bound $\max_i \alpha_i^\ell \geq C'k$.

All together, we have now shown the following:

LEMMA 5. *Fix a constant probability $p \in (0,1)$, and let $c > 0$ be a constant such that $c/(c+1) \geq p$. Then there exist constants $\delta, p \in (0,1)$ such that for any k, any protocol that solves* AND_k *with error at most δ has a set L of transcripts such that $\pi_2(L) \geq p$, and for each $\ell \in L$ there is a player $i = i(\ell)$ with $\alpha_i^\ell \geq ck$.*

Notice that by (5), for the player $i(\ell)$ from the lemma we have $\Pr\left[\boldsymbol{X}_{i(\ell)} = 0 \mid \boldsymbol{\Pi} = \ell, \boldsymbol{Z} \neq i\right] \geq \alpha_{i(\ell)}^\ell/(\alpha_{i(\ell)}^\ell + k) \geq (ck)/(ck + k) \geq p$, i.e., the posterior is constant. From (4), assuming $k \geq 2^{2/p}$, for any $z \neq i(\ell)$,

$$\mathsf{D}\left(\frac{\mu(\boldsymbol{X}_{i(\ell)} \mid \boldsymbol{\Pi} = \ell, \boldsymbol{Z} = z)}{\mu(\boldsymbol{X}_{i(\ell)} \mid \boldsymbol{Z} = z)}\right) \geq p\log k - 1 \geq (p/2)\log k, \tag{8}$$

so we are "very surprised" by the posterior distribution of $\boldsymbol{X}_{i(\ell)}$ given $\boldsymbol{\Pi}$. Now recall that this is lower bound on the divergence is what we needed to show: by Lemma 2, together with some technical details that are omitted here, we obtain $\mathrm{I}_\mu(\boldsymbol{\Pi}; \boldsymbol{X} \mid \boldsymbol{Z}) \geq \Omega(\log k)$, completing the proof.

THEOREM 1. *For the distribution μ we described and a sufficiently small δ,* $\text{CIC}_\mu(\text{AND}_k, \delta) \geq \Omega(\log k)$.

COROLLARY 1. *By Lemma 1 we have* $\text{CIC}_{\mu^n}(\text{DISJ}_{n,k}, \delta) \geq \Omega(n\log k)$, *and hence* $\text{CC}_\delta(\text{DISJ}_{n,k}) \geq \Omega(n\log k)$.

We now show that computing AND_k requires $\Omega(k)$ bits of communication, which also implies a lower bound of $\Omega(k)$ on $\text{DISJ}_{n,k}$. This is an easy argument which does not require information complexity.

LEMMA 6. *For any constant error parameter $\epsilon \in (0, 1/3)$ we have* $\text{CC}_\epsilon(\text{AND}_k) = \Omega(k)$.

PROOF. By the easy direction of Yao's minimax principle [30], it is sufficient to show that for some input distribution μ we have $\mathrm{D}_\epsilon^\mu(\text{AND}_k) = \Omega(k)$, that is, any deterministic protocol that errs with probability at most ϵ on inputs drawn from μ uses $\Omega(k)$ bits of communication.

Fix $\epsilon' > \epsilon$ such that $\epsilon/(1-\epsilon') < 1/2$. Consider the following input distribution μ: with probability $\epsilon' > \epsilon$, all players receive 1, and with probability $1-\epsilon'$, one random player receives 0 and the other players receive 1.

Fix a deterministic protocol Π for AND_k. Let $p_1, \ldots, p_\ell$ be the order in which players speak when the input is 1^k, and assume for the sake of contradiction that $\ell < (1 - \epsilon/(1-\epsilon')) \cdot k$.

If $\Pi(1^k) = 0$, then Π's error under μ is $\epsilon' > \epsilon$, so we can assume that $\Pi(1^k) = 1$. Let $\mathcal{E}$ be the event that the input is not 1^k, but all of the players $p_1, \ldots, p_\ell$ receive 1. We have $\Pr_\mu[\mathcal{E}] = (1-\epsilon') \cdot (1 - \ell/k) > \epsilon$. But when $\mathcal{E}$ occurs, the transcript of Π is identical to its transcript on 1^k, as Π is deterministic and all players that speak when the input is 1^k still receive 1 (in particular, the order of players that speak also remains the same under $\mathcal{E}$). Therefore with probability $> \epsilon$ the protocol outputs the wrong answer. □

5. MATCHING UPPER BOUND FOR SET DISJOINTNESS

We now describe a deterministic protocol for $\text{DISJ}_{n,k}$ with communication complexity $O(n\log k + k)$, which, in light of the lower bounds above, is optimal even for randomized algorithms. The protocol improves upon the naive version described in the introduction: the players attempt to convince themselves that $\bigcap_{i=1}^k X_i = \emptyset$ by writing on the board the indices of coordinates $i \in [n]$ where their input is zero; these coordinates cannot be in the intersection. To reduce the amount of communication, players never write on the board a coordinate that already appears on the board, and we also "pack together" coordinates: instead of writing them one-by-one, which requires $\Theta(\log n)$ bits per coordinate, we write batches of many coordinates simultaneously, encoding them as a set. This reduces the amortized cost per coordinate to $\Theta(\log k)$.

The protocol runs in *cycles*, where in each cycle some prefix of the players $1, \ldots, k$ each speak exactly once, in order, and the remaining players do not speak. Let Z_i be the set of coordinates that do not appear on the board at the beginning of cycle i, and let $z_i := |Z_i|$. Notice that if the input sets are indeed disjoint, then by the pigeonhole principle, at least one player has at least z_i/k zero coordinates that do not appear on the board ("new zeroes").

Suppose that at the beginning of cycle i we still have $z_i \geq k^2$. When it is the turn of player j to speak, if player j has at least z_i/k new zeroes, then it chooses z_i/k of them and writes them on the board, encoded as a subset of Z_i. The number of possible subsets is $\binom{z_i}{z_i/k} \leq ((z_i e)/(z_i/k))^{z_i/k} = (ek)^{z_i/k}$, so encoding one subset requires $(z_i/k)\log(ek)$ bits (i.e., the amortized cost per coordinate written is $\log(ek)$). If player j does not have z_i/k new zeroes to contribute, it writes a single bit on the board indicating this ("pass"), and we move on to the next player.

When at the beginning of some cycle i we have $z_i < k^2$, each player simply writes all its new zeroes on the board in the naive encoding (as elements of Z_i). This requires $O(\log k)$ bits per coordinate.

The protocol ends when one of the following occurs: if at any point all coordinates appear on the board, then the players halt and output "disjoint". Otherwise, if a complete cycle goes by in which all players pass, then the players halt and output "non-disjoint". Also, if we reach a cycle i with $z_i < k^2$, and at the end of the cycle not all coordinates appear on the board, then the players output "non-disjoint".

THEOREM 2. *The protocol describes above solves* $\text{DISJ}_{n,k}$ *in* $O(n \log k + k)$ *bits of communication.*

6. ON INTERACTIVE COMPRESSION FOR THE BROADCAST MODEL

The issue of *compression* is at the heart of information theory: can we condense messages (or, in the interactive case, protocols) to their information content? For the case of one-way transmission we know that the answer is yes, both for the amortized per-message cost in the limit as the number of messages (called the *block size*) goes to infinity [27] and also for just a single message [20].

In the interactive setting, it is known that a single instance of any protocol can be compressed to nearly its external information cost [3], while for amortized compression with an infinite block size (i.e., as the number of copies goes to infinity) we can achieve even better compression, to a measure called the *internal* information cost [7].[2] Let us discuss each of these goals in the k-party broadcast model.

Single-shot compression. In [3] it is shown that a two-party protocol Π with communication complexity C and external information cost I can be simulated (compressed) by a protocol with communication $O(I \cdot \log C)$. (External information for two players is given by Definition 6 for $k = 2$.) However, we observe that we cannot achieve such compression for the general multiparty case in the blackboard model: we already noted that the function AND_k requires $\Omega(k)$ bits of communication under some distribution. We now observe that $\text{IC}_\mu(\text{AND}_k) \le O(\log k)$ for any distribution μ: we can solve AND_k by a protocol Π, where the players go in order and write their input on the board, until we find a player whose input was 0 (in which case we halt), or have seen that all players had 1. The entropy of the transcript of Π is $O(\log k)$, because we can encode it by writing the index of the first player that wrote 0, or $\perp$ if there is no such player. Therefore $\text{IC}_\mu(\text{AND}_k) \le \text{I}(\mathbf{\Pi}; \boldsymbol{X}) \le H(\mathbf{\Pi}) \le O(\log k)$.

This demonstrates that the AND_k function *cannot be compressed* to its external information cost: there is a gap of $\Omega(k/\log(k))$ between its communication and information complexity. It is not clear whether or not this gap is the largest possible, but it seems reasonable that any function can be compressed to no more than k times its external information cost, with a possible polylogarithmic dependence on the communication complexity (as in [3]).

Amortized compression. Let $T(f^n, \epsilon)$ be the task of computing f on n independent inputs with marginal error ϵ on each instance. It is not difficult to extend the compression protocol from [7] (which is designed for a different notion of information cost, *internal* information [4]) to the external information of protocols in the k-party broadcast model, obtaining the following result:

[2]*Compressing a protocol* Π *to some cost* T means constructing another protocol Θ, whose communication complexity is T, such that given inputs $\boldsymbol{X}, \boldsymbol{Y}$, the players can use Θ to sample from a distribution close to the distribution of Π's transcript $\mathbf{\Pi}(\boldsymbol{X}, \boldsymbol{Y})$. The players are not charged for writing out the transcript of Π that they sampled, only for the communication they exchange in order to agree on the sample. This is generalized to multiple players in the natural way.

THEOREM 3. *For any function* f*, error parameter* $\epsilon \in (0,1)$ *and distribution* μ*,*

$$\lim_{n \to \infty} \frac{\text{D}_{\mu^n}(T(f^n, \epsilon))}{n} \le \text{IC}_\mu(f, \epsilon).$$

(For two players, external information is bounded from below by internal information, the notion used in [7], so our result does not improve on theirs for the two-party case. However, the notion used in [7] does not extend to the multiparty broadcast model for $k > 2$.)

We give a high-level overview of the compression scheme. This is a simplified version of the protocol from [7]. A similar but somewhat less explicit construction is given in [18].

Fix a protocol Π, and assume for simplicity that it has a fixed number of rounds and the players speak in an order that is fixed in advance (our result does not require these assumptions). Let $\boldsymbol{M}_1, \ldots, \boldsymbol{M}_r$ be random messages representing the messages of the protocol, where each message $\boldsymbol{M}_j$ is sent by player i_j. The randomness is over both the input distribution and the private and public randomness of the protocol.

Using the chain rule for mutual information, the information cost of Π can be seen to accumulate over rounds as follows:

$$\text{IC}(\Pi) = \text{I}(\mathbf{\Pi}; \boldsymbol{X}) = \sum_{j=1}^{r} \text{I}(\boldsymbol{M}_j; \boldsymbol{X} \mid \boldsymbol{M}_{<j}),$$

in other words, the information we learn from observing $\mathbf{\Pi}$ is the information we learn from the first message, plus the information we learn from the second message given what we already learned from the first, and so on. Moreover, since message $\boldsymbol{M}_j$ is sent by player i_j and depends only on i_j's input and the transcript so far, $\boldsymbol{M}_j$ conveys no information about the other players' inputs given $\boldsymbol{M}_{<j}$, so in fact

$$\begin{aligned} \text{IC}(\Pi) &= \sum_{j=1}^{r} \text{I}(\boldsymbol{M}_j; \boldsymbol{X}_{i_j} \mid \boldsymbol{M}_{<j}) \\ &\stackrel{(1)}{=} \sum_{j=1}^{r} \mathop{\mathbb{E}}_{\boldsymbol{m}_{<j}, \boldsymbol{x}_{i_j}} \text{D}\left(\frac{\mu(\boldsymbol{M}_j \mid \boldsymbol{X}_{i_j} = \boldsymbol{x}_{i_j}, \boldsymbol{M}_{<j} = \boldsymbol{m}_{<j})}{\mu(\boldsymbol{M}_j \mid \boldsymbol{M}_{<j} = \boldsymbol{m}_{<j})} \right). \end{aligned}$$

We can interpret this as follows: in each round j, player i_j generates message $\boldsymbol{M}_j$ from a distribution η that depends on the transcript so far, $\boldsymbol{M}_{<j}$, and on its input $\boldsymbol{X}_{i_j}$. An external observer who has seen $\boldsymbol{M}_{<j}$ but does not know $\boldsymbol{X}$ can try to predict the next message $\boldsymbol{M}_j$; let ν be the distribution representing the external observer's prediction.[3] The information revealed about $\boldsymbol{X}_{i_j}$ in round j corresponds to the observer's ability to predict $\boldsymbol{M}_j$: the closer ν is to η, the less "surprised" the observer is when it sees $\boldsymbol{M}_j$, and the less information it learns. Therefore, in protocols that do not reveal a lot of information, the observer knows a prior distribution ν that is already fairly close to the true distribution η of the next message, and we can use this fact to *compress* the next message. Note that all players are able to compute the prior ν of the external observer (it depends only on $\boldsymbol{M}_{i_j}$). However, only player i_j knows the true distribution η.

Before proceeding it will be useful to review an elementary form of *rejection sampling*. Suppose we have a distribution η over some domain U, and we wish to sample from η, but we are only able to sample uniform random variables. One way to sample from η is to generate an infinite sequence of two-dimensional points $(\boldsymbol{x}_1, \boldsymbol{p}_1), (\boldsymbol{x}_2, \boldsymbol{p}_2), \ldots$ uniformly distributed in $U \times [0,1]$, select

[3]Formally, to sample from ν, one samples $\boldsymbol{X}_{i_j}$ from its distribution given $\boldsymbol{M}_{<j}$ and then computes $\boldsymbol{M}_j$.

the first point i that falls under the curve of η — that is, satisfies $\eta(\boldsymbol{x}_i) > \boldsymbol{p}_i$ — and output $\boldsymbol{x}_i$. It is not difficult to see that this generates the correct distribution η, since given $\boldsymbol{x}_i = x$, the probability that point i falls under the curve of η is exactly $\eta(x)$. Moreover, the probability for any given point to fall under the curve is $1/|U|$, so the expected number of points we need before finding a good point is U.

In the compressed protocol we simulate round j as follows. We let U be the set of possible next messages (the domain of $\boldsymbol{M}_j$), and we publicly sample points $(\boldsymbol{x}_1, \boldsymbol{p}_1), (\boldsymbol{x}_2, \boldsymbol{p}_2), \ldots$ uniformly distributed in $U \times [0,1]$ using public randomness. Player i_j, who knows the true distribution η of the next message, selects the first point that falls under the curve of η. The other players do not know η, but they do know some prior ν, which is also known to player i_j. If ν is close to η, then the other players already have some idea of which points player i_j might have selected. Instead of writing the message on the board as it would in the original protocol, player i_j writes some information on the board to help the other players learn exactly which point it selected, using its knowledge of both η and ν. The closer ν is to the true distribution η, the less player i_j will need to write on the board.

Let $a_\ell = (x_\ell, p_\ell)$ be the point selected by player i_j. First, player i_j writes on the board the value $\lceil i/|U| \rceil$. This requires a small number of bits, because $\boldsymbol{i}$ is a binomial random variable with expectation $|U|$. Let P be the set of points with indices i' such that $\lceil i'/|U| \rceil = \lceil i/|U| \rceil$; all players restrict their attention to points in the set P, whose size is $|U|$.

Next player i_j writes the log-ratio $s = \lceil \log(\eta(x_\ell)/\nu(x_\ell)) \rceil$.[4] This requires roughly $\log\log(\eta(x_\ell)/\nu(x_\ell))$ bits, using a variable-length encoding. All other players now scale up their prior ν by 2^s, and eliminate all points that do not fall under the scaled curve $2^s \cdot \nu$ from consideration, since we know that $p_\ell < \eta(x_\ell) \le 2^s \cdot \nu(x_\ell)$. Let $P' \subseteq P$ be the remaining set (see Figure 1).

This is not sufficient to narrow the candidate pool down to a single point; indeed, the expected number of points in P' is 2^s, because there are $|U|$ points in P and each one falls under the curve $2^s \cdot \nu$ with probability $2^s/|U|$. However, player i_j knows the set P', and it now simply writes the index of the point it selected inside the set P' (that is, if $P' = \{a_{t_1}, \ldots, a_{t_m}\}$ then player i_j writes the index c such that $t_c = \ell$). Since we expect that $|P'| \approx 2^s$, this requires roughly s bits. Now all players know which point was selected by player i_j, and we can continue on to the next round.

More formally, the sampling procedure can be summarized as follows:

LEMMA 7. *Suppose that all players are given a distribution η over some universe $\mathcal{U}$, and in addition, player i is given a distribution ν over $\mathcal{U}$. Fix $\epsilon \in (0,1)$. Then there is a protocol Θ, at the end of which player i outputs an element $\boldsymbol{X} \sim \eta$, and the other players all output the same element $\boldsymbol{Y}$, with the property that for each $x \in \mathcal{U}$, $\Pr[\boldsymbol{X} = \boldsymbol{Y} \mid \boldsymbol{X} = x] \ge 1 - \epsilon$. The expected communication of Θ is $\mathsf{D}(\nu \parallel \eta) + O(\log \mathsf{D}(\nu \parallel \eta) + \log(1/\epsilon))$.*

As mentioned above, this result is proven slightly differently in [18].

Using this lemma repeatedly, we can sample an entire transcript of Π using communication $\mathrm{IC}(\Pi) + O(\log \mathrm{IC}(\Pi)) + O(r \cdot \log(1/\epsilon))$, where r is the number of rounds in Π. (The cost is obtained by summing over the costs of the individual rounds as bounded in Lemma 7, using the log-sum inequality to move the sum inside the log in the second term.)

Now suppose we are given n independent inputs drawn from μ, and we solve $T(f^n, \delta)$ by running n independent instances of Π

[4]It may happen that $\nu(x_\ell) < \eta(x_\ell)$ and the logarithm is negative, but this will not be a problem.

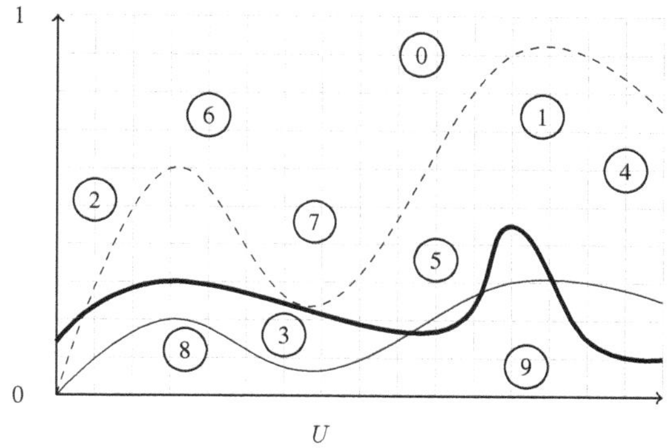

Figure 1: Illustration for the sampling procedure. The thick curve is the true distribution η, the thin curve is the prior ν, and the dashed curve is the scaled prior $2^s \cdot \nu$. In this example, player i_j will select point 3 to output, and the candidates that will be considered by the other players are $P' = \{1, 3, 4, 5, 8, 9\}$. Player i_j will send '2' to indicate that the second point in P', point 3, should be selected.

in parallel: first we execute the first round of Π on each of the instances, then the next round, and so on. The resulting protocol has the same number of rounds r that Π has, and since the copies are independent, its information cost is $n \cdot \mathrm{IC}(\Pi)$. (It is crucial that when we execute Π in parallel on the different instances so that the number of rounds does not increase.) We can compress the n-fold protocol using the scheme outlined above, reducing its communication complexity to

$$C := n \cdot \mathrm{IC}(\Pi) + r \cdot O(\log(n \cdot \mathrm{IC}(\Pi)) + \log(1/\epsilon)),$$

and $C/n \to \mathrm{IC}(\Pi)$ as n tends to infinity, as desired. (This informal presentation glosses over many details, including how to handle the additional error incurred during compression. They will appear in the full version of the paper.)

It is not clear whether the compression result of Theorem 3 is tight in general, but it is tight for product distributions.

THEOREM 4. *For any function f, error parameter $\epsilon \in (0,1)$ and product distribution μ,*

$$\lim_{n \to \infty} \frac{\mathrm{D}_{\mu^n}(T(f^n, \epsilon))}{n} = \mathrm{IC}_\mu(f, \epsilon).$$

PROOF SKETCH. Since $\mathrm{D}_\eta(g, \epsilon) \ge \mathrm{IC}_\eta(g, \epsilon)$ for any task g and distribution η, to prove the theorem it suffices to show that $\mathrm{IC}_{\mu^n}(T(f^n, \epsilon)) \ge n \cdot \mathrm{IC}_\mu(T(f^n, \epsilon))$ when μ is a product distribution. (The other direction is given by Theorem 3.) This is very similar to the direct sum result from [2], given in Lemma 1: indeed, it is even simpler to show than the statement in Lemma 1, because here we compare the information cost of actually solving n independent copies to the cost of solving one copy, whereas in Lemma 1 we compared the cost of computing the *disjunction* on n copies to the cost of solving a single copy. To show that $\mathrm{IC}_{\mu^n}(T(f^n, \epsilon)) \ge n \cdot \mathrm{IC}_\mu(T(f^n, \epsilon))$ for a product distribution μ we can apply the same proof used to show Lemma 1 in [2], using an "empty variable" as our auxiliary variable $\boldsymbol{D}$. $\square$

Characterizing the exact cost of one-shot compression and of compression with infinite block length in the broadcast model remain open questions.

7. REFERENCES

[1] Noga Alon, Yossi Matias, and Mario Szegedy. The space complexity of approximating the frequency moments. *Journal of Computer and System Sciences*, 58(1):137 – 147, 1999.

[2] Ziv Bar-Yossef, T. S. Jayram, Ravi Kumar, and D. Sivakumar. An information statistics approach to data stream and communication complexity. *J. Comput. Syst. Sci.*, 68(4):702–732, 2004.

[3] Boaz Barak, Mark Braverman, Xi Chen, and Anup Rao. How to compress interactive communication. *SIAM J. Comput.*, 42(3):1327–1363, 2013.

[4] Mark Braverman. Interactive information complexity. In *Proceedings of the 44th Symposium on Theory of Computing Conference, STOC 2012, New York, NY, USA, May 19 - 22, 2012*, pages 505–524, 2012.

[5] Mark Braverman, Faith Ellen, Rotem Oshman, Toniann Pitassi, and Vinod Vaikuntanathan. A tight bound for set disjointness in the message-passing model. In *54th Annual IEEE Symposium on Foundations of Computer Science, FOCS 2013, 26-29 October, 2013, Berkeley, CA, USA*, pages 668–677, 2013.

[6] Mark Braverman, Ankit Garg, Denis Pankratov, and Omri Weinstein. From information to exact communication. In *Proceedings of the forty-fifth annual ACM symposium on Theory of computing*, pages 151–160. ACM, 2013.

[7] Mark Braverman and Anup Rao. Information equals amortized communication. In *Proceedings of the 2011 IEEE 52nd Annual Symposium on Foundations of Computer Science*, FOCS '11, pages 748–757, 2011.

[8] Joshua Brody, Amit Chakrabarti, Ranganath Kondapally, David P. Woodruff, and Grigory Yaroslavtsev. Beyond set disjointness: The communication complexity of finding the intersection. In *Proceedings of the 2014 ACM Symposium on Principles of Distributed Computing*, PODC '14, pages 106–113, 2014.

[9] Amit Chakrabarti, Yaoyun Shi, Anthony Wirth, and Andrew Chi-Chih Yao. Informational complexity and the direct sum problem for simultaneous message complexity. In *42nd Annual Symposium on Foundations of Computer Science, FOCS 2001*, pages 270–278, 2001.

[10] Ashok K. Chandra, Merrick L. Furst, and Richard J. Lipton. Multi-party protocols. In *Proceedings of the Fifteenth Annual ACM Symposium on Theory of Computing*, STOC '83, pages 94–99, 1983.

[11] Arkadev Chattopadhyay and Toniann Pitassi. The story of set disjointness. *SIGACT News*, 41(3):59–85, 2010.

[12] Atish Das Sarma, Stephan Holzer, Liah Kor, Amos Korman, Danupon Nanongkai, Gopal Pandurangan, David Peleg, and Roger Wattenhofer. Distributed verification and hardness of distributed approximation. In *Proceedings of the Forty-third Annual ACM Symposium on Theory of Computing*, pages 363–372, 2011.

[13] Shahar Dobzinski, Noam Nisan, and Sigal Oren. Economic efficiency requires interaction. In *Proceedings of the 46th Annual ACM Symposium on Theory of Computing*, STOC '14, pages 233–242, 2014.

[14] Andrew Drucker, Fabian Kuhn, and Rotem Oshman. On the power of the congested clique model. In *ACM Symposium on Principles of Distributed Computing, PODC '14, Paris, France, July 15-18, 2014*, pages 367–376, 2014.

[15] Anat Ganor, Gillat Kol, and Ran Raz. Exponential separation of information and communication. In *55th IEEE Annual Symposium on Foundations of Computer Science, FOCS 2014, Philadelphia, PA, USA, October 18-21, 2014*, pages 176–185, 2014.

[16] Oded Goldreich and A Warning. Secure multi-party computation. unpublished manuscript, 1998.

[17] André Gronemeier. Asymptotically optimal lower bounds on the NIH-multi-party information complexity of the AND-function and disjointness. In *Proc. 26th Symp. on Theor. Aspects of Comp. Sc. (STACS)*, pages 505–516, 2009.

[18] Prahladh Harsha, Rahul Jain, David McAllester, and Jaikumar Radhakrishnan. The communication complexity of correlation. In *Computational Complexity, 2007. CCC'07. Twenty-Second Annual IEEE Conference on*, pages 10–23. IEEE, 2007.

[19] Johan Håstad and Avi Wigderson. The randomized communication complexity of set disjointness. *Theory of Computing*, 3(11):211–219, 2007.

[20] D.A. Huffman. A method for the construction of minimum-redundancy codes. *Proceedings of the IRE*, 40(9):1098–1101, 1952.

[21] Bala Kalyanasundaram and Georg Schnitger. The probabilistic communication complexity of set intersection. *SIAM J. Discrete Math.*, 5(4):545–557, 1992.

[22] Eyal Kushilevitz and Noam Nisan. *Communication complexity*. Cambridge University Press, 1997.

[23] Mihai Patrascu. Unifying the landscape of cell-probe lower bounds. *SIAM J. Comput.*, 40(3):827–847, 2011.

[24] Jeff M. Phillips, Elad Verbin, and Qin Zhang. Lower bounds for number-in-hand multiparty communication complexity, made easy. SODA '12, pages 486–501, 2012.

[25] A. A. Razborov. On the distributional complexity of disjointness. *Theor. Comput. Sci.*, 106:385–390, 1992.

[26] Atish Das Sarma, Stephan Holzer, Liah Kor, Amos Korman, Danupon Nanongkai, Gopal Pandurangan, David Peleg, and Roger Wattenhofer. Distributed verification and hardness of distributed approximation. *SIAM J. Comput.*, 41(5):1235–1265, 2012.

[27] C. E. Shannon. A mathematical theory of communication. *Bell System Technical Journal*, 27(3):379–423, 1948.

[28] Alexander A. Sherstov. Communication lower bounds using directional derivatives. In *Proc. 45th Symp. on Theory of Comp. (STOC)*, pages 921–930, 2013.

[29] David P. Woodruff and Qin Zhang. An optimal lower bound for distinct elements in the message passing model. In *Proceedings of the Twenty-Fifth Annual ACM-SIAM Symposium on Discrete Algorithms, SODA 2014, Portland, Oregon, USA, January 5-7, 2014*, pages 718–733, 2014.

[30] Andrew Chi-Chin Yao. Probabilistic computations: Toward a unified measure of complexity. SFCS '77, pages 222–227, 1977.

How to Elect a Leader Faster than a Tournament

Dan Alistarh
Microsoft Research
dan.alistarh@microsoft.com

Rati Gelashvili
MIT
gelash@mit.edu

Adrian Vladu
MIT
avladu@mit.edu

ABSTRACT

The problem of electing a leader from among n contenders is one of the fundamental questions in distributed computing. In its simplest formulation, the task is as follows: given n processors, all participants must eventually return a *win* or *lose* indication, such that a single contender may *win*. Despite a considerable amount of work on leader election, the following question is still open: can we elect a leader in an asynchronous fault-prone system faster than just running a $\Theta(\log n)$-time tournament, against a strong adaptive adversary?

In this paper, we answer this question in the affirmative, improving on a decades-old upper bound. We introduce two new algorithmic ideas to reduce the time complexity of electing a leader to $O(\log^* n)$, using $O(n^2)$ point-to-point messages. A non-trivial application of our algorithm is a new upper bound for the *tight renaming* problem, assigning n items to the n participants in expected $O(\log^2 n)$ time and $O(n^2)$ messages. We complement our results with lower bound of $\Omega(n^2)$ messages for solving these two problems, closing the question of their message complexity.

Categories and Subject Descriptors

F.2.2 [**Analysis of Algorithms and Problem Complexity**]: Nonnumerical Algorithms and Problems

General Terms

Theory, Algorithms

Keywords

Leader election; randomized algorithms; message-passing; asynchronous; message complexity; lower bound.

1. INTRODUCTION

The problem of picking a leader from among a set of n contenders in a fault-prone system is among the most well-studied questions in distributed computing. In its simplest form, *leader election (test-and-set)* [1] is stated as follows. Given n participating processors, each of the contenders must eventually return either a *win* or *lose* indication, with the property that a single participant may *win*. Leader election is one of a set of canonical problems, or *tasks*, whose solvability and complexity are the focus of distributed computing theory, along with *consensus (agreement)* [24, 26], *mutual exclusion* [15], *renaming* [10], or *task allocation (do-all)* [23]. These problems are usually considered in *asynchronous* models, such as message-passing or shared-memory [25].

We focus on leader election in the *asynchronous message-passing* model, in which each of n processors is connected to every other processor via a point-to-point channel. Communication is asynchronous, i.e., messages can be arbitrarily delayed. Moreover, local computation of processors is also performed in asynchronous steps. The scheduling of computation steps and message deliveries in the system is controlled by a *strong (adaptive) adversary*, which can examine local state, including random coin flips, and crash $t < n/2$ of the participants at any point during the computation. The natural complexity metrics are *message complexity*, i.e., total number of messages sent by the protocol, and *time complexity*, i.e. the number of times a processor relies on the adversary to schedule a computation step or to deliver messages.

Many fundamental results in distributed computing are related to the complexity of canonical tasks in asynchronous models. For example, Fisher, Lynch, and Patterson [16] showed that it is impossible to solve consensus deterministically in an asynchronous system if one of the n participants may fail by crashing. This deterministic impossibility extends to leader election [21]. Since the publication of the FLP result, a tremendous amount of research effort has been invested into overcoming this impossibility for canonical tasks. Seminal work by Ben-Or [13] showed that relaxing the problem specification to allow probabilistic termination can circumvent FLP, and obtain efficient distributed algorithms.

Consequently, the past three decades have seen a continuous quest to improve the randomized upper and lower bounds for canonical tasks, and in fact tight (or almost tight) complexity bounds are now known, against a strong adversary, for consensus [11, 5], mutual exclusion [19, 20, 18], renaming [4], and task allocation [14, 7].

For leader election against a strong adversary, the situation is different. The fastest known solution is more than

Permission to make digital or hard copies of all or part of this work for personal or classroom use is granted without fee provided that copies are not made or distributed for profit or commercial advantage and that copies bear this notice and the full citation on the first page. Copyrights for components of this work owned by others than ACM must be honored. Abstracting with credit is permitted. To copy otherwise, or republish, to post on servers or to redistribute to lists, requires prior specific permission and/or a fee. Request permissions from Permissions@acm.org.
PODC'15, July 21–23, 2015, Donostia-San Sebastián, Spain.
ACM 978-1-4503-3617-8 /15/07 ...$15.00
DOI: http://dx.doi.org/10.1145/2767386.2767420.

two decades old [1], and is a *tournament tree*: build a binary tree with n leaves, and pair up the participants, which start at the leaves, into two-processor "matches," whose winner is decided by two-processor randomized consensus; winners of such matches continue to compete, while losers drop out, until a single winner prevails. Time complexity is logarithmic, as the winner has to communicate at each tree level. No time lower bounds are known. Despite significant recent interest and progress on this problem in weaker adversarial models [6, 3, 17], the question of whether a tournament is optimal when electing a leader against a strong adversary is surprisingly still open.

Contribution: In this paper, we show that it is possible to break the logarithmic barrier in the classic asynchronous message-passing model, against an adaptive adversary. We present a new randomized algorithm which elects a leader in expected $O(\log^* n)$ time, sending $O(n^2)$ messages.

The algorithm is based on two new ideas, which we briefly describe below. The general structure is rather simple: computation occurs in *phases*, where each phase is designed to drop as many participants as possible, while ensuring that at least one processor survives.

Consider a simple implementation: each processor flips a biased coin at the beginning of the phase, to decide whether to give up (value 0) or continue (value 1), and communicates its choice to others. If at least one processor out of the n_r participants in phase r flips 1, all processors which flipped 0 can safely drop from contention. We could aim for $o(\log n)$ iterations by setting the probabilities to obtain less than a constant fraction of survivors in each phase. Unfortunately, a strong adversary easily breaks such a strategy: since it can see the flips, it can schedule all the processors that flipped 0 to complete the phase *before* any processor that flipped 1, forcing *everyone* to continue.

Techniques: Our first algorithmic idea is a way to *hide* the processor coin flips during the phase, handicapping the adaptive adversary. In each phase, each processor first takes a "poison pill" (moves to *commit* state), and broadcasts this to all other processors. The processor then flips a biased local coin to decide whether to drop out of contention (*low* priority) or to take an "antidote" (*high* priority), broadcasts its new state, and checks the states of other processors. Crucially, if it has flipped low priority, and sees *any other processor* either in *commit* state or in *high priority* state, the processor returns *lose*. Otherwise, it survives to the next phase.

The above mechanics guarantee at least one survivor (in the unlikely event where all processors flip *low* priority, they all survive), but can lead to few survivors in each phase. The insight is that, to ensure many survivors, the adversary must examine the processors' coin flips. But to do so, the adversary must first allow it to take the poison pill (state *commit*). Crucially, any low-priority processor observing this *commit* state automatically drops out. We prove that, because of this catch-22, the adversarial scheduler can do no more than to let processors execute each phase sequentially, one-by-one, hoping that the first processor flipping high priority, which eliminates all later low-priority participants, comes as late as possible in the sequence.

Now we can bias the flips such that a group of at most $O(\sqrt{n_r})$ processors survive because they flipped high priority, and $O(\sqrt{n_r})$ processors survive because they did not observe any high priority. This choice of bias seems hard to improve, as it yields the perfect balance between the sizes of the two groups of survivors.

Our second algorithmic idea breaks this roadblock. Consider two extreme scenarios for a phase: first when all participants communicate with each other, leading to similar views and second, when processors see fragmented views, observing just a subset of other processors. In the first case, each processor can safely set a low probability of surviving. This does not work in the second case since processor views have a lot of variance. We exploit this variance to break symmetry. Our technical argument combines these two strategies such that we obtain at most $O(\log^2 n_r)$ expected survivors in a phase, under *any* scheduling.

The final algorithm has additional useful properties. It is *adaptive*, meaning that, if $k \leq n$ processors participate, its complexity becomes $O(\log^* k)$. Moreover, since most participants drop in the first round of broadcast, the message complexity is $O(kn)$, which we shall prove is asymptotically optimal.

Renaming: Based on these properties we design a message-optimal algorithm for *strong renaming*, which assigns distinct items (or names) labeled from 1 to n to the n processors, using expected $O(n^2)$ messages and $O(\log^2 n)$ time. We employ a simple strategy: each processor repeatedly picks a random name that it sees as available, announces it, and competes for it via an instance of leader election. If the processor wins, it returns the name; otherwise, it tries again. The algorithm can be seen as a balls-into-bins game, in which n balls are the processors and bins are the names. We need to characterize two parameters: the maximum number of trials by a single processor, and the maximum contention on a single bin, as they are linked with message and time complexity. The critical difficulty is that, since rounds are not synchronised, the bin occupancy views perceived by the processors are effectively under adversarial control and out-of-date or incoherent views can lead to wasted trials and increased contention on the bins.

Our task is to prove that, in fact, this balls-into-bins process is robust to the correlations and skews in the trial probability distributions caused by asynchrony. Our approach is to carefully bound the evolution of processors' views and their trial distributions as more and more trials are performed. Roughly, for $j \geq 1$, we split the execution into time intervals, where at most $n/2^{j-1}$ names are available at the beginning of the interval j, and focus on bounding the number of wasted trials in each interval. The main technical difficulty that we overcome is that the views corresponding to these trials could be highly correlated, as the adversary may delay messages to increase the probability of a collision.

Lower bound: We match the message complexity of our algorithms with an $\Omega(n^2)$ lower bound on the expected message complexity of any leader election or renaming algorithm. The intuition behind the bound is that no processor should be able to decide without receiving a message, as the others might have already elected a winner; since the adversary can fail up to $n/2$ processors, it should be able to force each processor to either send or receive $n/2$ messages. However, this intuition is not entirely correct, as groups of processors could employ complex gossip-like message distribution strategies to guarantee that at least *some* processors receive *some* messages while keeping the total message count

$o(n^2)$. We thwart such strategies with a non-trivial indistinguishability argument, showing that in fact there must exist a group of $\Theta(n)$ processors, each of which either sends or receives a total of $\Theta(n)$ messages. A similar argument yields the $\Omega(n^2)$ lower bound for renaming, and in fact for any object with strongly non-commutative operations [12].

Related Work: We focus on previous work on the complexity of randomized leader election[1] and renaming, most of which considered the asynchronous shared-memory. However, one option is to emulate efficient shared-memory solutions via simulations between shared-memory and message-passing [9]. This preserves time complexity, but communication may be increased by at most a linear factor.

We classify previous solutions according to their adversarial model. Against a strong adversary, the fastest known leader election algorithm is the tournament tree of Afek et al. [1], whose contention-adaptive variant was given in [6]. For n participants, these algorithms require $\Theta(\log n)$ time, and $\Theta(n^2 \log n)$ messages using a careful simulation. *PoisonPill* is contention-adaptive, improves time complexity (more than) exponentially, and gives tight message complexity bounds.

For renaming, fastest known shared-memory algorithm [4] can be simulated with $O(\log n)$ time, and $\Theta(n^2 \log n)$ messages. (The latter bounds are obtained by simulating an AKS sorting network [2]; constructible solutions pay an extra logarithmic factor in both measures.) Our balls-into-bins approach is simpler and message-optimal, at the cost of an extra logarithmic factor in the time complexity. Reference [6] uses a simpler balls-into-bins approach for renaming, where each processor tries all the names, in random order, until acquiring some one. Despite the similarity, this algorithm has expected time complexity $\Omega(n)$, as a late processor may try out a linear number of spots before succeeding.

References [3, 17] considered the complexity of leader election against a weak (oblivious) adversary, which fixes the schedule in advance. The structure of splitting the computation into sifting rounds, eliminating more than a constant factor of the participants per round, was introduced in [3], where the authors give an algorithm with $O(\log \log n)$ time complexity. Giakkoupis and Woelfel [17] improved this to $O(\log^* k)$, where k is the number of participants. These algorithms yield the same bounds in asynchronous message-passing, but their complexity bounds only hold against a *weak* adversary, which fixes the schedule in advance.

The *consensus* problem can be stated as leader election if we ask processors to return the *identifier* of the winner, as opposed to a win/lose indication. As such, consensus solves leader election, but not vice-versa [21]. In fact, randomized consensus has $\Omega(n)$ time complexity [11]. Recent work [5] considered the message complexity of randomized consensus in the same model, achieving $O(n^2 \log^2 n)$ message complexity, and $O(n \log^3 n)$ time complexity, using completely different techniques.

2. DEFINITIONS AND NOTATION

System Model: We consider classic asynchronous message-passing model [9]. Here, n processors communicate with each other by sending *messages* through *channels*. There is one channel from each processor to every other processor; the channel from i to j is independent from the channel from j to i. Messages can be arbitrarily delayed by a channel, but do not get corrupted.

Computations are modeled as sequences of steps of the processors, which can be either *delivery steps*, representing the delivery of a new message, or *computation steps*. At each computation step, the processor receives all messages delivered to it since the last computation step, and, unless it is *faulty*, it can perform local computation and send new messages. A processor is *non-faulty*, if it is allowed to perform local computations and send messages infinitely often and if all messages it sends are eventually delivered. Notice that messages are also delivered to *faulty* processors, although their outgoing messages may be dropped.

We consider algorithms that tolerate up to $t \leq \lceil n/2 \rceil - 1$ processor failures. That is, when more than half of the processors are non-faulty, they all return an answer from the protocol with probability one. A standard assumption in this setting is that all non-faulty processors always take part in the computation by replying to the messages, irrespective of whether they participate in a certain algorithm or even after they return a value—otherwise, the $t \leq \lceil n/2 \rceil - 1$ condition may be violated.

The Communicate Primitive: Our algorithms use a procedure called communicate, defined in [9] as a building block for asynchronous communication. The call communicate(m) sends the message m to all n processors and waits for at least $\lfloor n/2 \rfloor + 1$ acknowledgments before proceeding with the protocol. The communicate procedure can be viewed as a best-effort broadcast mechanism; its key property is that any two communicate calls intersect in at least one recipient. In the following, a processor i will communicate messages of the form (*propagate*,v_i) or (*collect*,v). For the first message type, each recipient j updates its view of the variable v and acknowledges by sending back an ACK message. In the second case, the acknowledgement is a pair (ACK,v_j) containing j's view of the variable for the receiving process. In both cases, processor i waits for $> n/2$ ACK replies before proceeding with its protocol. In the case of *collect*, the communicate call returns an array of at least $\lfloor n/2 \rfloor + 1$ views that were received.

Adversary: We consider strong adversarial setting where the scheduling of processor steps, message deliveries and processor failures are controlled by an adaptive adversary. At any point, the adversary can examine the system state, including the outcomes of random coin flips, and adjusts the scheduling accordingly.

Complexity Measures: We consider two worst-case complexity measures against the adaptive adversary. *Message complexity* is the maximum expected number of messages sent by all processors during an execution. When defining *time complexity*, we need to take into account the fact that, in asynchronous message-passing, the adversary schedules both message delivery and local computation.

Definition (Time Complexity). *Assume that the adversary fixes two arbitrarily large numbers t_1 and t_2 before an execution, and these numbers are unknown to the algorithm. Then, during the execution, the adversary delivers every message of a non-faulty processor within time t_1 and sched-*

[1]Some older references, e.g. [1], employ the name *test-and-set* exclusively for this task, and use leader election for the consensus (agreement) problem, while more recent ones [17] equate test-and-set and leader election.

ules a subsequent step of any non-faulty processor in time at most t_2.[2] *An algorithm has time complexity* $O(T)$ *if the maximum expected time before all non-faulty processors return that the adversary can achieve is* $O(T(t_1 + t_2))$.[3]

For instance, in our algorithms, all messages are triggered by the communicate primitive. A processor depends on the adversary to schedule a step in order to compute and call communicate, and then depends on the adversary to deliver these messages and acknowledgments. In the above definition, if all processors call communicate at most T times, then all non-faulty processors return in time at most $2T(t_1+t_2) = O(T(t_1+t_2))$: each communicated message reaches destination in time t_1, gets processed within time t_2, at which point the acknowledgment is sent back and delivered after t_1 time. So, after $2t_1 + t_2$ time responses from more than half processors are received, and in at most t_2 time the next step of the processor is scheduled when it again computes and communicates. This implies the following.

Claim 2.1. *For any algorithm, if the maximum expected number of* communicate *calls by any processor that the adversary can achieve is* $O(T)$, *then time complexity is also* $O(T)$.

Problem Statements: In *leader election (test-and-set)*, each processor may return either *WIN* or *LOSE*. Every (correct) processor should return (*termination*), and only one processor may return *WIN* (*unique winner*). No processor may lose before the eventual winner starts its execution. The goal is to ensure that operations are *linearizable*, i.e., can be ordered such that (1) the first operation is *WIN* and every other return value is *LOSE*, and (2) the order of non-overlapping operations is respected. *Strong (tight) renaming* requires every (correct) processor to eventually return a *unique* name between 1 and n.

3. LEADER ELECTION ALGORITHM

Our leader election algorithm guarantees that if k processors participate, the maximum expected number of communicate calls by any processor that the *strong adaptive* adversary can achieve is $O(\log^* k)$, and the maximum expected total number of messages is $O(nk)$. We start by illustrating the main algorithmic idea.

3.1 The PoisonPill Technique

Consider the protocol specified in Figure 1 from the point of view of a participating processor. The procedure receives the id of the processor as an input, and returns a *SURVIVE*/*DIE* indication. All n processors react to received messages by replying with acknowledgments according to the communicate procedure. In the following, we call a *quorum* any set of more than $n/2$ processors.

[2]Note that the adversary can set t_1 or t_2 arbitrarily large, unknown to the algorithm, so the guarantees from the algorithm's perspective are still only that messages are *eventually* delivered and steps are *eventually* scheduled.

[3]Applied to asynchronous shared-memory, this yields an alternative definition of *step (time) complexity*, taking t_2 as an upper bound on the time for a thread to take a shared-memory step (and ignoring t_1). Counting all the delivery and non-trivial computation *steps* in message-passing gives an alternative definition of message complexity, corresponding to shared-memory *work complexity*.

Each processor stores the current status of other processors in a *Status* array, which we also call its *view*. During the round, the processor will ask all other processors for their *Status* array. The contents are merged into the *Views* matrix, where *Views*[i][j] is processor j's status, as seen by processor i.

```
   Input: Unique identifier i of the participating processor
   Output: SURVIVE or DIE
   Local variables:
      Status[n] = {⊥};
      Views[n][n];
      int coin;
1  procedure PoisonPill⟨i⟩
2     Status[i] ← Commit
                                          /* commit to coin flip */
3     communicate(propagate, Status[i])
                                          /* propagate status */
4     coin ← random(1 with probability 1/√n, 0 otherwise)
                                          /* flip coin */
5     if coin = 0 then Status[i] ← Low-Pri
6     else Status[i] ← High-Pri
7     communicate(propagate, Status[i])
                                          /* propagate updated status */
8     Views ← communicate(collect, Status)
                                          /* collect status from > n/2 */
9     if Status[i] = Low-Pri then
10        if ∃proc. j : (∃k : Views[k][j] ∈ {Commit, High-Pri}
          and ∀k′ : Views[k′][j] ≠ Low-Pri) then
11           return DIE
             /* i has low priority, sees processor j
                with either high priority or
                committed and not low priority, and
                dies */
12    return SURVIVE
```

Figure 1: PoisonPill **Technique**

Each participating processor first announces that it is about to flip a random coin by moving to state *Commit* (lines 2-3), then obtains either low or high priority based on the outcome of a biased coin flip. (As the name suggests, a high priority processor will survive the round, whereas a low priority may drop from contention in the round.) The processor then propagates its priority information to a quorum via the communicate procedure (line 7). More precisely, the processor i sends messages to all other processors, asking them to update their *Status*[i] entries to the new value, and awaits acknowledgments from a quorum.

Next, processor i collects the status of other processors from a quorum using the communicate(*collect*, *Status*) call on line 8, which requests views of the *Status* array from each processor j. Note that the resulting *Views* matrix will contain replies (rows) from at least $n/2$ processors.

The crux of the round procedure is the *DIE* condition on line 11. A processor i returns *DIE* at this line if *both* of the following occur: (1) the processor i has low priority, *and* (2) it observes another processor j that does not have low priority in any of the views, but j has either high priority or is committed to flipping a coin (state *Commit*) in some view. Otherwise, processor i survives. The first key observation is that

Claim 3.1. *If all processors participating in* PoisonPill *return, at least one processor survives.*

Proof. Assume the contrary. Since processors with high priority always survive, all participating processors must have a low priority. All participants propagate their low priority information to a quorum by calling the communicate procedure on line 7. Let i be the last processor that completes this communicate call. At this point, the status information of all participants is already propagated to a quorum. More precisely, for every participating processor j, more than half of the processors have a view $Status[j] = Low\text{-}Pri$.

Therefore, when processor i proceeds to line 8 and collects the *Status* arrays from more than half of the processors, then, since any two quorums intersect, for every participating processor j, there will be a view of some processor k' showing j's low priority. All non-participating processors will have priority $\bot$ in all views. But given the structure of the protocol, processor i will *not* return on line 11 and will survive. This contradiction completes the proof. □

On the other hand, we can bound the expected number of processors that survive:

Claim 3.2. *The expected number of processors that return SURVIVE is* $O(\sqrt{n})$.

Proof. Consider the random coin flips on line 4 and let us highlight the first time when some processor i flips value 1. We will argue that no other processor j that subsequently (or simultaneously) flips value 0 can survive. Consider such a state. When processor j flips 0, processor i has already propagated its *Commit* status to a quorum of processors. Furthermore, processor i has a high priority, thus no processor can ever view it as having a low priority. Hence, when processor j collects views from a quorum, because every two quorums have an intersection, some processor k will definitely report the status of processor i as *Commit* or *High-Pri* and no processor will report *Low-Pri*. Thus, processor j will have to return *DIE* on line 11.

The above argument implies that processors survive either if they flip 1 and get a high priority, or if they flip 0 strictly before any other processor flips 1. Each of the at most n processors independently flips a biased coin on line 4 and hence, the number of processors that flip 1 is at most the number of 1's in n Bernoulli trials with success probability $1/\sqrt{n}$, in expectation $\sqrt{n}$. Processors that flip 0 at the same time as the first 1 do not survive, and it also takes $\sqrt{n}$ trials in expectation before the first 1 is flipped, giving an upper bound $\sqrt{n}$ on the maximum expected number of processors that can flip 0 and survive. □

It is possible to apply this technique recursively with some extra care and construct an algorithm with an expected $O(\log\log n)$ time complexity. But we do not want to stop here.

3.2 Heterogeneous PoisonPill

Building a more efficient algorithm based on the PoisonPill technique requires reducing the number of survivors beyond $\Omega(\sqrt{n})$ without violating the invariant that not all participants may die. We control the coin flip bias, but setting the probability of flipping 1 to $1/\sqrt{n}$ is provably optimal. Let the adversary schedule processors to execute PoisonPill sequentially. With a larger probability of flipping 1, more than $\sqrt{n}$ processors are expected to get a high priority and survive. With a smaller probability, at least the first $\sqrt{n}$ processors are expected to all have low priority and survive. There are always $\Omega(\sqrt{n})$ survivors.

To overcome the above lower bound, after committing, we make each processor record the list ℓ of all processors including itself, that have a non-$\bot$ status in some view collected from the quorum. Then we use the size of list ℓ of a processor to determine its probability bias. Each processor also augments priority with its ℓ and propagates that as a status. This way, every time a high or low priority of a processor p is observed, ℓ of processor p is also known. Finally, the survival criterion is modified: each processor first computes set L as the union of all processors whose non-$\bot$ statuses it ever observed itself, and of the ℓ lists it has observed in priority informations in these statuses. If there is a processor in L for which no reported view has low priority, the current processor drops.

The algorithm is described in Figure 2. The particular choice of coin flip bias is influenced by factors that should become clear from the analysis. Despite modifications, the

```
   Input: Unique identifier i of the participating processor
   Output: SURVIVE or DIE
   Local variables:
       Status[n] = {⊥};
       Views[n][n];
       int coin;
1  procedure HeterogeneousPoisonPill⟨i⟩
2      Status[i] ← {.stat = Commit, .list = {}}
                                        /* commit to coin flip */
3      communicate(propagate, Status[i])
                                         /* propagate status */
4      Views ← communicate(collect, Status)
                                      /* collect status from > n/2 */
5      ℓ ← {j | ∃k : Views[k][j] ≠ ⊥}
                                       /* record participants */
6      if |ℓ| = 1 then prob ← 1                      /* set bias */
7      else prob ← log|ℓ| / |ℓ|                        /* set bias */
8      coin ← random(1 with probability prob, 0 otherwise)
                                                  /* flip coin */
9      if coin = 0 then Status[i] ← {.stat = Low-Pri, .list = ℓ}
                                  /* record priority and list */
10     else Status[i] ← {.stat = High-Pri, .list = ℓ}
                                  /* record priority and list */
11     communicate(propagate, Status[i])
                               /* propagate priority and list */
12     Views ← communicate(collect, Status)
                                      /* collect status from > n/2 */
13     if Status[i].stat = Low-Pri then
14         L ← ∪_{k,j: Views[k][j]≠⊥} Views[k][j].list
                                     /* union all observed lists */
15         L ← L ∪ {j | ∃k : Views[k][j] ≠ ⊥}
                                   /* record new participants */
16         if ∃proc. j ∈ L : ∀k : Views[k][j].stat ≠ Low-Pri
           then
17             return DIE
           /* i has low priority, learns about
              processor j participating whose low
              priority is not reported, and dies
              */
18     return SURVIVE
```

Figure 2: Heterogeneous PoisonPill

same argument as in Claim 3.1 still guarantees at least one survivor. Let us now prove that the views of the processors have the following interesting *closure property*, which will be critical to bounding the number of survivors with low priority.

Claim 3.3. *Consider any set S of processors that each flip 0 and survive. Let U be the union of all L lists of processors in S. Then, for $p \in U$ and every processor q in the ℓ list of p, q is also in U.*

Proof. In order for processors in S to survive, they should have observed a low priority for each of the processors in their L lists. Thus, every processor $p \in U$ must flip 0, as otherwise it would not have a low priority. However, the low priority of p observed by a survivor was augmented by the ℓ list of p. According to the algorithm, the survivor includes in its own L all processors q from this ℓ list of p, implying $q \in U$. □

Next, let us prove a few other useful claims:

Claim 3.4. *If processor q completed executing line 3 no later than processor p completed executing line 3, then q will be included in the ℓ list of p.*

Proof. When p collects statuses on line 4 from a quorum, q is already done propagating its *Commit* on line 3. As every two quorum has an intersection, p will observe a non-$\perp$ status of q on line 5. □

Claim 3.5. *The probability of at least z processors flipping 0 and surviving is $O(1/z)$.*

Proof. Let S be the set of the z processors that flip 0 and survive and let us define U as in Claim 3.3. For any processor $p \in U$ and any processor q that completes executing line 3 no later than p, by Claim 3.4 processor q has to be contained in the ℓ list of p, which by the closure property (Claim 3.3) implies $q \in U$. Thus, if we consider the ordering of processors according to the time they complete executing line 3, all processors not in U must be ordered strictly after all processors in U.

Therefore, during the execution, first $|U|$ processors that complete line 3 must all flip 0. The adversary may influence the composition of U, but by the closure property, each ℓ list of processors in U contains only processors in U, meaning $|\ell| \leq |U|$. So the probability for each processor to flip 0 is at most $(1 - \frac{\log |U|}{|U|})$ and for all processors in U to flip 0's is at most $(1 - \frac{\log |U|}{|U|})^{|U|} = O(1/|U|)$. This is $O(1/z)$ since all z survivors from S are included in their own lists and hence also in U. □

We have never relied on knowing n. If $k \leq n$ processors participate in the heterogeneous PoisonPill, we get

Lemma 3.6. *The maximum expected number of processors that flip 0 and survive is $O(\log k) + O(1)$.*

Lemma 3.7. *The maximum expected number of processors that flip 1 is $O(\log^2 k) + O(1)$.*

Proof. Consider the ordering of processors according to the time they complete executing line 3, breaking ties arbitrarily. Due to Claim 3.4, the processor that is ordered first always has $|l| \geq 1$, the second processor always computes $|l| \geq 2$, and so on. The probability of flipping 1 decreases as $|l|$ increases, and the best expectation achievable by adversary is $1 + \sum_{l=2}^{k} \frac{\log l}{l} = O(\log^2 k) + O(1)$ as desired. □

3.3 Final construction

The idea of implementing leader election is to have rounds of heterogeneous PoisonPill, where all processors participate in the first round and only the survivors of round r participate in round $r+1$. Each processor p, before participating in round r_p, first propagates r_p as its current round number to a quorum, then collects information about the rounds of other processors from a quorum. Let R be the maximum round number of a processor in all views that p collected. To determine the winner, we use the idea from [27]: if $R > r_p$, then p loses and if $R < r_p - 1$ then p wins. We also use a standard doorway mechanism [1] to ensure linearizability. The pseudocode of the final construction is given in the full version of this paper [8], along with the complete proof of the following statement:

Theorem 3.8. *Our leader election algorithm is linearizable. If there are at most $\lceil n/2 \rceil - 1$ processor faults, all non-faulty processors terminate with probability 1. For k participants, it has time complexity $O(\log^* k)$ and message complexity $O(kn)$.*

The performance guarantees follow from Lemma 3.6 and from Lemma 3.7 with some careful analysis. In particular, later rounds in which maximum expected number of participants is constant require special treatment.

4. THE RENAMING ALGORITHM

```
Input: Unique identifier i from a large namespace
Output: int name ∈ [n]
Local variables:
    bool Contended[n] = {false};
    bool Views[n][n];
    int coin, spot, outcome;
procedure getName⟨i⟩
    while true do
        Views ← communicate(collect, Contended)
        /* collect contention information */
        for j ← 1 to n do
            if ∃k : Views[k][j] = true then
                Contended[j] ← true
                /* mark names that became contended
                   */
        communicate(propagate, {Contended[j] |
        Contended[j] = true})            /* propagate */
        spot ← random(j | Contended[j] = false)
                /* pick random uncontended name */
        Contended[spot] ← true
        outcome ← LeaderElect_spot(i)
                        /* contend for a new name */
        communicate(propagate, Contended[spot])
                        /* propagate contention */
        if outcome = WIN then
            return spot /* win iff you are leader */
```

Figure 3: Pseudocode of the renaming algorithm for n processors.

The algorithm is described in Figure 3. There is a separate leader election protocol for each name; which a processor must win in order to claim the name. Each processor repeatedly chooses a new name and contends for it by participating in the corresponding leader election, until it eventually wins. Processors keep track of contended names and use this information to choose the next name to compete for: in particular, the next name is selected uniformly at random from the uncontended names.

We now give a detailed overview of the proof. The full proof is given in the technical report version of our paper [8]. First, we show that the algorithm is correct.

Lemma 4.1. *No two processors return the same name from the* getName *call and if there are at most* $\lceil n/2 \rceil - 1$ *processor faults, all non-faulty processors terminate with probability 1.*

Let us now introduce some notation. For an arbitrary execution, and for every name u, consider the first time when more than half of processors have $Contended[u] = \mathsf{true}$ in their view (or time ∞, if this never happens). Let $\prec$ denote the name ordering based on these times, and let $\{u_i\}$ be the sequence of names sorted according to increasing $\prec$. Among the names with time ∞, sort later the ones that are never contended by the processors. Resolve all the remaining ties according to the order of the names. This ordering has the following useful temporal property.

Lemma 4.2. *In any execution, if a processor views* $Contended[i] = \mathsf{true}$ *in some while loop iteration, and in some subsequent iteration on line 8 the same processor views* $Contended[j] = \mathsf{false}$, $i \prec j$ *has to hold.*

Let X_i be a random variable, denoting the number of processors that ever contend in a leader election for the name u_i. The following holds.

Lemma 4.3. *The message complexity of our renaming algorithm is* $O(n \cdot \mathbb{E}[\sum_{i=1}^{n} X_i])$.

We partition names $\{u_i\}$ into $\log n$ *groups*, where the first group G_1 contains the first $n/2$ names, second group G_2 contains the next $n/4$ names, etc. We use notation $G_{j' \geq j}$, $G_{j'' > j}$ and $G_{j''' < j}$ to denote the union of all groups $G_{j'}$ where $j' \geq j$, all groups $G_{j''}$ where $j'' > j$, and all groups $G_{j'''}$ where $j''' < j$, respectively. We can now split any execution into at most $\log n$ phases. The first phase starts when the execution starts and ends as soon as for each $u_i \in G_1$ more than half of the processors view $Contended[u_i] = \mathsf{true}$ (the way $\{u\}$ is sorted, this is the same as when the contention information about $u_{n/2}$ is propagated to a quorum). At this time, the second phase starts and ends when for each $u_i \in G_2$ more than half of the processors view $Contended[u_i] = \mathsf{true}$. When the second phase ends, the third phase starts, and so on.

Consider any loop iteration of some processor p in some execution. We say that an iteration *starts* at a time instant when p executes line 2 and reaches line 3. Let V_p be p's view of the *Contended* array right before picking a spot on line 8 in the given iteration. We say that an iteration is *clean*(j), if the iteration starts during phase j and no name from later groups $G_{j''>j}$ is contended in V_p. We say that an iteration is *dirty*(j), if the iteration starts during phase j and some name from a later group $G_{j''>j}$ is contended in V_p.

Observe that any iteration that starts in phase j can be uniquely classified as *clean*(j) or *dirty*(j) and in these iterations, processors view all names $u_i \in G_{j'''<j}$ from previous groups as contended.

Lemma 4.4. *In any execution, at most* $\frac{n}{2^{j-1}}$ *processors ever contend for names from groups* $G_{j' \geq j}$.

Lemma 4.5. *For any fixed* j, *the total number of clean*(j) *iterations is larger than or equal to* $\alpha n + \frac{n}{2^{j-1}}$ *with probability at most* $e^{-\frac{\alpha n}{16}}$ *for all* $\alpha \geq \frac{1}{2^{j-5}}$.

Proof. Fix some j. Consider a time t when the first *dirty*(j) iteration is completed. At time t, there exists an i such that $u_i \in G_{j''>j}$ and a quorum of processors view $Contended[i] = \mathsf{true}$, so all iterations that start later will set $Contended[i] \leftarrow \mathsf{true}$ on line 6. Therefore, any iteration that starts after t must observe $Contended[i] = \mathsf{true}$ on line 8 and by definition cannot be *clean*(j). By Lemma 4.4, at most $\frac{n}{2^{j-1}}$ processors can have active *clean*(j) iterations at time t. The total number of *clean*(j) iterations is thus upper bounded by $\frac{n}{2^{j-1}}$ plus the number of *clean*(j) iterations completed before time t, which we denote as *safe* iterations.[4] Safe iterations all finish before any iteration where a processor contends for a name in $G_{j''>j}$ is completed. By Lemma 4.4, at most $\frac{n}{2^j}$ different processors can ever contend for names in $G_{j''>j}$, therefore, αn safe iterations can occur only if in at most $\frac{n}{2^j}$ of them processors choose to contend in $G_{j''>j}$. Otherwise, some processor would have to complete an iteration where it contended for a name in $G_{j''>j}$.

In every *clean*(j) iteration, on line 8, any processor p contends for a name in $G_{j' \geq j}$ uniformly at random among non-contended spots in its view V_p. With probability at least $\frac{1}{2}$, p contends for a name from $G_{j''>j}$, because by definition of *clean*(j), all spots in $G_{j''>j}$ are non-contended in V_p.

Let us describe the process by considering a random variable $Z \sim \mathrm{B}(\alpha n, \frac{1}{2})$ for $\alpha \geq \frac{1}{2^{j-5}}$, where each success event corresponds to an iteration contending in $G_{j''>j}$. By the end, the probability of αn iterations with at most $\frac{n}{2^j}$ processors contending in $G_{j''>j}$ is:

$$\Pr\left[Z \leq \frac{n}{2^j}\right] = \Pr\left[Z \leq \frac{\alpha n}{2}\left(1 - \frac{2^{j-1}\alpha - 1}{2^{j-1}\alpha}\right)\right]$$
$$\leq \exp\left(-\frac{\alpha n (2^{j-1}\alpha - 1)^2}{2(2^{j-1}\alpha)^2}\right) \leq e^{-\frac{\alpha n}{8}}$$

So far, we have assumed that the set of names belonging to the later groups $G_{j''>j}$ was fixed, but the the adversary controls the execution. Luckily, what happened before phase j (i.e. the actual names that were acquired from $G_{j'''<j}$) is irrelevant, because all the names from the earlier phases are viewed as contended by all iterations that start in phases $j' \geq j$. Unfortunately, however, the adversary also influences what names belong to group j and to groups $G_{j''>j}$. There are $\binom{2^{1-j}n}{2^{-j}n}$ different possible choices for names in G_j, and by a union bound, the probability that αn iterations can occur even for one of them is at most:

$$e^{-\frac{\alpha n}{8}} \cdot \binom{2^{1-j}n}{2^{-j}n} \leq e^{-\frac{\alpha n}{8}} \cdot (2e)^{2^{-j}n} \leq e^{-n(2^{-3}\alpha - 2^{1-j})}$$
$$\leq e^{-\frac{\alpha n}{16}}, \text{ proving the claim.}$$

□

Plugging $\alpha = \beta - \frac{1}{2^{j-1}} \geq \frac{1}{2^{j-5}}$ in the above lemma, we obtain that the total number of *clean*(j) iterations is larger than or equal to βn with probability at most $e^{-\frac{\beta n}{32}}$ for all $\beta \geq \frac{1}{2^{j-6}}$. Let $X_i(clean)$ be the number of processors that ever contend for $u_i \in G_j$ in some *clean*(j) iteration and define $X_i(dirty)$ analogously: as the number of processors that ever contend for $u_i \in G_j$ in some *dirty*(j) iteration. Relying on the above bound on the number of *clean*(j) iterations, we get the following result:

[4] If no *dirty*(j) iteration ever completes, then we call all *clean*(j) iterations safe.

Lemma 4.6. $\mathbb{E}[\sum_{i=1}^{n} X_i(clean)] = O(n)$.

Each iteration where a processor contends for a name $u_i \in G_j$ is by definition either as $clean(j)$, $dirty(j)$ or starts in a phase $j''' < j$. Let us call these $cross(j)$ and denote by $X_i(cross)$ the number of such iterations. We show that in any execution, for each j, any processor participates in at most one $dirty(j)$ and at most one $cross(j)$ iteration. This allows us to prove with some work the following lemma:

Lemma 4.7. $\mathbb{E}[\sum_{i=1}^{n} X_i(dirty)] = O(n)$ *and* $\mathbb{E}[\sum_{i=1}^{n} X_i(cross)] = O(n)$.

The message complexity upper bound then follows by piecing together the previous claims.

Theorem 4.8. *The expected message complexity of our renaming algorithm is* $O(n^2)$.

Proof. We know $X_i = X_i(clean) + X_i(dirty) + X_i(cross)$ and by Lemma 4.6, Lemma 4.7 we get $\mathbb{E}[\sum_i X_i] = O(n)$. Combining with Lemma 4.3 gives the desired result. □

The time complexity upper bound exploits a trade-off between the probability that a processor collides in an iteration (and must continue) and the ratio of available slots which must be assigned during that iteration.

Theorem 4.9. *The time complexity of the the renaming algorithm is* $O(\log^2 n)$.

Proof Sketch. We fix an arbitrary processor p, and upper bound the number of loop iterations it performs during the execution. Let M_i be the set of free slots that p sees when performing its random choice in the ith iteration of the loop, and let $m_i = |M_i|$.

Assuming that p does not complete in iteration i, let $Y_i \subseteq M_i$ be the set of *new* slots that p finds out have become contended at the beginning of iteration $i+1$, and let $y_i = |Y_i|$. We define an iteration as *low-information* if $y_i/m_i < 1/\log m_i$. Intuitively, in a high-information iteration, the processor collides, but at least reduces its random range for choices by a significant factor.

We then focus on a low-information iteration i. We model the interaction between the processor and the adversary as follows: p first makes a random choice among m_i slots. The adversary can then schedule $m_i - 1$ other processors to make choices in M_i. Importantly, we note that the adversary can schedule some processors several times; however, for each such re-scheduling, it must announce the previously chosen slot. A balls-into-bins argument yields that the adversary can obtain at most m_i extra choices for the iteration to stay *low-information*, with probability at least $1 - 1/m_i$.

Recall that the goal of the adversary is to cause a collision with p's random choice r. We reduce this to a balls-into-bins game in which the adversary throws at most $2m_i - 1$ initial balls into a set of $m_i(1 - 1/\log m_i)$ bins, with the goal of hitting a specific bin, corresponding to p's random choice. However, the probability that an arbitrary bin gets hit in this game is at most a constant.

By the above, processor p terminates in each low-information iteration with constant probability. Putting it all together, we obtain that, for $c \geq 4$ constant, after $c \log^2 n$ iterations, any processor p will terminate with probability $1 - 1/n^{c-1}$, either because m_i reaches 1, or because one of its probes was successful in an low-information phase, which occurs with high probability. □

5. COMMUNICATION LOWER BOUND

In this section, we prove that our algorithms are message-optimal by showing a lower bound of expected $\Omega(n^2)$ messages on any algorithm implementing leader election or renaming in an asynchronous message-passing system where $t < n/2$ processors may fail by crashing. In fact, we prove such a lower bound for any object which exports *strongly non-commutative* methods [12].

Definition 5.1. *Given an object O, a method M of this object is* strongly non-commutative *if there exists some state S of O for which an instance m_1 of M executed sequentially by processor p changes the result of an instance m_2 of M executed by processor $q \neq p$, and vice-versa, i.e. m_2 changes the result of m_1 from state S.*

We now give a message complexity lower bound for objects with non-commutative operations.

Theorem 5.2. *Any implementation of an object O with a strongly non-commutative operation M by $k \leq n$ processors guaranteeing termination with at least constant probability $\alpha > 0$ in an asynchronous message-passing system where $t < n/2$ processors may fail by crashing must have worst-case expected message complexity $\Omega(\alpha k n)$.*

Proof. Let A be an algorithm implementing a shared object O with a strongly non-commutative method M, in asynchronous message-passing with $t < n/2$, guaranteeing termination with probability α. We define an adversarial strategy for which we will argue that all the resulting terminating executions (regardless of their probability) must cause $\Omega(kn)$ messages to be sent. This clearly implies our claim. The strategy proceeds as follows.

Assume that each processor is executing an instance of M. The adversary picks a subset S of $k/4$ participants, and places them in a "bubble:" for each such processor q, the adversary suspends all its incoming and outgoing messages in a buffer, until there are at least $n/4$ such messages in the buffer. At this point, the processor is freed from the bubble, and is allowed to take steps synchronously, together with other processors. Processors outside S execute in lock-step, and their messages outside the bubble are delivered in a timely fashion.

Note that this strategy induces a family of executions $\mathcal{E}$, each of which is defined by the set of coin flips made by the processors. We can assume that there exists a time τ after which in all executions in $\mathcal{E}$ with non-zero probability no processors send any more messages. Otherwise, the adversary can always wait for another message that must be sent, then for the next message, and so on, until $\Omega(kn)$ messages.

Let us prove that in each execution $E \in \mathcal{E}$ every processor in the bubble must eventually leave the bubble before returning, which implies $\Omega(kn)$ messages in executions in which all processors return. Towards this goal, we first show that a processor cannot return while still in the bubble. Then we prove that all processors in the bubble are forced to either return while still in the bubble (which cannot happen) or leave the bubble, completing the proof.

For the first part, assume for the sake of contradiction that there exists an execution $E \in \mathcal{E}$ and a processor $p \in S$ that decides in E while still being in the bubble. Practically, this implies that p has returned from its method invocation without receiving any messages, and without any of its messages being received. To obtain a contradiction, we build two alternate executions E' and E'', both of which are indistinguishable to p, but in which p must return different outputs.

In execution E', we run all processors outside the bubble until one of them returns–this must eventually occur with constant probability, since this execution is indistinguishable to these processors from an execution in which all (at most $k/4 < n/2$) processors in the bubble are initially crashed. We suspend messages sent to the processors inside the bubble. We then run processor p, which flips the same coins as in E (the execution exists as this happens with probability > 0), observes the same emptiness and therefore eventually returns with constant probability, without having received any messages. We deliver p's messages and suspended messages as soon as p decides.

In execution E'', we first run p in isolation, suspending its messages. With probability > 0, p flips the same coins as in E, and must eventually decide with constant probability without having received any messages. We then run all processors outside the bubble in lock-step. One of these processors must eventually return with constant probability, since to these processors, the execution is indistinguishable from an execution in which p (and other processors in the bubble) has crashed initially. We deliver p's messages after this decision. Since both E' and E'' are indistinguishable to p, it has to return the same value in both executions with constant probability. However, this cannot be the case because instances of method M are strongly non-commutative, the two returning instances are not concurrent, and occur in opposite orders in the two executions. This correctness requirement is enforced *deterministically*. Therefore, p must return distinct values in executions E' and E'', which is a contradiction. Hence, p cannot return in E.

To complete the argument, we prove that p has to eventually return or leave the bubble, with probability $\geq \alpha$. We cannot directly require this of the execution prefix E since not all messages by correct processors have been delivered in this prefix. For this, we consider time τ, at which we crash all recipients of messages by p, and all processors that sent messages to p in E. By the definition of the bubble, the number of crashes we need to expend is $< n/4$. Therefore, by definition of τ, there exists a valid execution, in which no more messages will be sent and p must eventually decide with probability $\geq \alpha$. From p's prospective, the current execution in the bubble can be this execution, and if the adversary keeps p in the bubble for long enough, it has to decide with probability $\geq \alpha$. However, from the previous argument, we know that p cannot decide while in the bubble, therefore p has to eventually leave the bubble in order to be able to decide and return.

This shows that a specific processor p must eventually leave the bubble. The final difficulty is in showing that we can apply the same argument to *all* processors in the bubble at the same time without exceeding the failure budget. Notice however that we could apply the following strategy: for each processor q in the bubble, we could fail all senders and recipients of q ($< n/4$), and also all other processors in the bubble ($< n/4$) at time τ. This can be applied without exceeding the failure budget. Since any processor q could be the sole survivor from the bubble to which we have applied the buffering strategy, and since q does not see a difference from an execution in which it has to return, analogously to the previous case, we obtain that each q in the bubble has to eventually leave the bubble with probability $\geq \alpha$.

Therefore, we obtain that at least $\alpha kn/16$ messages have to be exchanged during the execution, which implies the claim. □

It is easy to check that the *elect* procedure of a leader election algorithm and the *rename* procedure of a strong renaming algorithm are both non-commutative. (In the case of renaming, consider $n+1$ distinct processors executing the rename procedure. By the pigeonhole principle, there exists some non-zero probability that two processors choose the same name in solo executions. Therefore, these two operations do not commute, and therefore the *rename* procedure is strongly non-commutative.) We therefore obtain the following corollary.

Corollary 5.3. *Any implementation of leader election or renaming by $k \leq n$ processors which ensures termination with probability at least $\alpha > 0$ in an asynchronous message-passing system where $t < n/2$ processors may fail by crashing must have worst-case expected message complexity $\Omega(\alpha kn)$.*

6. DISCUSSION AND FUTURE WORK

We have given the first sub-logarithmic leader election algorithm against a strong adversary, and asymptotically tight bounds for the message complexity of renaming and leader election. Our results also limit the power of topological lower bound techniques, e.g. [22], when applied to randomized leader election, since these techniques allow processors to communicate using unit-cost broadcasts or snapshots. Our algorithm shows that no bound stronger than $\Omega(\log^* n)$ time is possible using such techniques, unless the cost of information dissemination is explicitly taken into account.

Determining the tight time complexity bounds for leader election remains an intriguing open question. Another interesting research direction would be to apply the tools we developed to obtain time- and message-efficient implementations of other fundamental distributed tasks, such as task allocation or mutual exclusion, and to explore solutions optimizing bit complexity.

7. ACKNOWLEDGMENTS

Support is gratefully acknowledged from the National Science Foundation under grants CCF-1217921, CCF-1301926, and IIS-1447786, the Department of Energy under grant ER26116/DE-SC0008923, and the Oracle and Intel corporations.

The authors would like to thank Prof. Nir Shavit for advice and encouragement during this work, and the anonymous reviewers for their very useful suggestions.

8. REFERENCES

[1] Y. Afek, E. Gafni, J. Tromp, and P. M. B. Vitányi. Wait-free test-and-set (extended abstract). In *Proceedings of the 6th International Workshop on Distributed Algorithms*, WDAG '92, pages 85–94, London, UK, UK, 1992. Springer-Verlag.

[2] M. Ajtai, J. Komlós, and E. Szemerédi. An $O(n \log n)$ sorting network. In *Proceedings of the Fifteenth Annual ACM Symposium on Theory of Computing*, STOC '83, pages 1–9, New York, NY, USA, 1983. ACM.

[3] D. Alistarh and J. Aspnes. Sub-logarithmic test-and-set against a weak adversary. In *Distributed Computing: 25th International Symposium, DISC 2011*, volume 6950 of *Lecture Notes in Computer Science*, pages 97–109. Springer-Verlag, Sept. 2011.

[4] D. Alistarh, J. Aspnes, K. Censor-Hillel, S. Gilbert, and R. Guerraoui. Tight bounds for asynchronous renaming. Accepted to JACM, Sept. 2013.

[5] D. Alistarh, J. Aspnes, V. King, and J. Saia. Communication-efficient randomized consensus. In *Distributed Computing*, pages 61–75. Springer, 2014.

[6] D. Alistarh, H. Attiya, S. Gilbert, A. Giurgiu, and R. Guerraoui. Fast Randomized Test-and-Set and Renaming. In *Proceedings of DISC 2010*, Lecture Notes in Computer Science. Springer-Verlag New York, Ms Ingrid Cunningham, 175 Fifth Ave, New York, Ny 10010 Usa, 2010.

[7] D. Alistarh, M. A. Bender, S. Gilbert, and R. Guerraoui. How to allocate tasks asynchronously. In *53rd Annual IEEE Symposium on Foundations of Computer Science, FOCS 2012, New Brunswick, NJ, USA, October 20-23, 2012*, pages 331–340, 2012.

[8] D. Alistarh, R. Gelashvili, and A. Vladu. How to elect a leader faster than a tournament. Technical report, http://arxiv.org/abs/1411.1001.

[9] H. Attiya, A. Bar-Noy, and D. Dolev. Sharing memory robustly in message-passing systems. *Journal of the ACM (JACM)*, 42(1):124–142, 1995.

[10] H. Attiya, A. Bar-Noy, D. Dolev, D. Peleg, and R. Reischuk. Renaming in an asynchronous environment. *J. ACM*, 37(3):524–548, July 1990.

[11] H. Attiya and K. Censor. Tight bounds for asynchronous randomized consensus. *J. ACM*, 55(5):20:1–20:26, Nov. 2008.

[12] H. Attiya, R. Guerraoui, D. Hendler, P. Kuznetsov, M. M. Michael, and M. Vechev. Laws of order: expensive synchronization in concurrent algorithms cannot be eliminated. In *ACM SIGPLAN Notices*, volume 46, pages 487–498. ACM, 2011.

[13] M. Ben-Or. Another advantage of free choice (extended abstract): Completely asynchronous agreement protocols. In *Proceedings of the Second Annual ACM Symposium on Principles of Distributed Computing*, PODC '83, pages 27–30, New York, NY, USA, 1983. ACM.

[14] J. F. Buss, P. C. Kanellakis, P. L. Ragde, and A. A. Shvartsman. Parallel algorithms with processor failures and delays. *J. Algorithms*, 20:45–86, January 1996.

[15] E. W. Dijkstra. Solution of a problem in concurrent programming control. *Commun. ACM*, 8(9):569–, Sept. 1965.

[16] M. J. Fischer, N. A. Lynch, and M. S. Paterson. Impossibility of distributed consensus with one faulty process. *J. ACM*, 32(2):374–382, Apr. 1985.

[17] G. Giakkoupis and P. Woelfel. On the time and space complexity of randomized test-and-set. In *Proceedings of the 2012 ACM Symposium on Principles of Distributed Computing*, PODC '12, pages 19–28, New York, NY, USA, 2012. ACM.

[18] G. Giakkoupis and P. Woelfel. A tight rmr lower bound for randomized mutual exclusion. In *Proceedings of the Forty-fourth Annual ACM Symposium on Theory of Computing*, STOC '12, pages 983–1002, New York, NY, USA, 2012. ACM.

[19] D. Hendler and P. Woelfel. Randomized mutual exclusion in o(log n / log log n) rmrs. In *Proceedings of the 28th ACM Symposium on Principles of Distributed Computing*, PODC '09, pages 26–35, New York, NY, USA, 2009. ACM.

[20] D. Hendler and P. Woelfel. Adaptive randomized mutual exclusion in sub-logarithmic expected time. In *Proceedings of the 29th ACM SIGACT-SIGOPS Symposium on Principles of Distributed Computing*, PODC '10, pages 141–150, New York, NY, USA, 2010. ACM.

[21] M. Herlihy. Wait-free synchronization. *ACM Trans. Program. Lang. Syst.*, 13(1):124–149, Jan. 1991.

[22] M. Herlihy and N. Shavit. The topological structure of asynchronous computability. *Journal of The ACM*, 46:858–923, 1999.

[23] P. C. Kanellakis and A. A. Shvartsman. Efficient parallel algorithms can be made robust. *Distrib. Comput.*, 5(4):201–217, Apr. 1992.

[24] L. Lamport, R. Shostak, and M. Pease. The byzantine generals problem. *ACM Trans. Program. Lang. Syst.*, 4(3):382–401, July 1982.

[25] N. Lynch. *Distributed Algorithms*. Morgan Kaufmann, 1997.

[26] M. Pease, R. Shostak, and L. Lamport. Reaching agreement in the presence of faults. *J. ACM*, 27(2):228–234, Apr. 1980.

[27] M. Saks, N. Shavit, and H. Woll. Optimal time randomized consensus – making resilient algorithms fast in practice. In *Proceedings of the second annual ACM-SIAM symposium on Discrete algorithms*, pages 351–362. Society for Industrial and Applied Mathematics, 1991.

The Weakest Failure Detector for Eventual Consistency

Swan Dubois
Sorbonne Universités, UPMC
Univ Paris 06, CNRS, INRIA,
LIP6 UMR 7606

Rachid Guerraoui
EPFL

Petr Kuznetsov*
Télécom ParisTech

Franck Petit
Sorbonne Universités, UPMC
Univ Paris 06, CNRS, INRIA,
LIP6 UMR 7606

Pierre Sens
Sorbonne Universités, UPMC
Univ Paris 06, CNRS, INRIA,
LIP6 UMR 7606

ABSTRACT

In its classical form, a *consistent* replicated service requires all replicas to witness the same evolution of the service state. Assuming a message-passing environment with a majority of correct processes, the necessary and sufficient information about failures for implementing a general state machine replication scheme ensuring consistency is captured by the Ω failure detector.

This paper shows that in such a message-passing environment, Ω is also the weakest failure detector to implement an *eventually consistent* replicated service, where replicas are expected to agree on the evolution of the service state only after some (*a priori* unknown) time.

In fact, we show that Ω is the weakest to implement eventual consistency in *any* message-passing environment, *i.e.*, under any assumption on when and where failures might occur. Ensuring (strong) consistency in any environment requires, in addition to Ω, the quorum failure detector Σ. Our paper thus captures, for the first time, an exact computational difference between building a replicated state machine that ensures consistency and one that only ensures eventual consistency.

Categories and Subject Descriptors

C.2.4 [**Computer-Communication Networks**]: Distributed Systems; F.1.1 [**Computation by Abstract Devices**]: Models of Computation—*relations between models*

Keywords

eventual consistency, failure detectors

1. INTRODUCTION

State machine replication [21, 26] is the most studied technique to build a highly-available and consistent distributed service. Roughly speaking, the idea consists in replicating the service, modeled as a state machine, over several processes and ensuring that all replicas behave like one correct and available state machine, despite concurrent invocations of operations and failures of replicas. This is typically captured using the abstraction of a *total order broadcast* [3], where messages represent invocations of the service operations from clients to replicas (server processes). Assuming that the state machine is deterministic, delivering the invocations in the same total order ensures indeed that the replicas behave like a single state machine. Total order broadcast is, in turn, typically implemented by having the processes agree on which batch of messages to execute next, using the *consensus* abstraction [22, 3]. (The two abstractions, consensus and total order broadcast, were shown to be equivalent [3].)

Replicas behaving like a single one is a property generally called *consistency*. The sole purpose of the abstractions underlying the state machine replication scheme, namely consensus and total order broadcast, is precisely to ensure this consistency, while providing at the same time *availability*, namely that the replicated service does not stop responding. The inherent costs of these abstractions are sometimes considered too high, both in terms of the necessary computability assumptions about the underlying system [12, 2, 1], and the number of communication steps needed to deliver an invocation [22, 23].

An appealing approach to circumvent these costs is to trade consistency with what is sometimes called *eventual consistency* [25, 29]: namely to give up the requirement that the replicas *always* look the same, and replace it with the requirement that they only look the same *eventually*, *i.e.*, after a finite but not *a priori* bounded period of time. Basically, *eventual consistency* says that the replicas can diverge for some period, as long as this period is finite.

Many systems claim to implement general state machines that ensure eventual consistency in message-passing systems, *e.g.*, [20, 7]. But, to our knowledge, there has been no theoretical study of the exact assumptions on the information about failures underlying those implementations. This paper is the first to do so: using the formalism of failure detectors [3, 2], it addresses the question of the minimal information about failures needed to implement an eventually consistent replicated state machine.

It has been shown in [2] that, in a message-passing environment with a majority of correct processes, the weakest failure detector to implement consensus (and, thus, total order broadcast [5]) is the *eventual leader* failure detector, denoted Ω. In short, Ω outputs, at every process, a *leader*

*The research leading to these results has received funding from the Agence Nationale de la Recherche, under grant agreement N ANR-14-CE35-0010-01, project DISCMAT.

Permission to make digital or hard copies of all or part of this work for personal or classroom use is granted without fee provided that copies are not made or distributed for profit or commercial advantage and that copies bear this notice and the full citation on the first page. Copyrights for components of this work owned by others than ACM must be honored. Abstracting with credit is permitted. To copy otherwise, or republish, to post on servers or to redistribute to lists, requires prior specific permission and/or a fee. Request permissions from permissions@acm.org.
PODC'15, July 21–23, 2015, Donostia-San Sebastián, Spain.
Copyright © 2015 ACM 978-1-4503-3617-8 /15/07 ...$15.00.
DOI: http://dx.doi.org/10.1145/2767386.2767404.

process so that, eventually, the same correct process is considered leader by all. Ω can thus be viewed as the weakest failure detector to implement a generic replicated state machine ensuring consistency and availability in an environment with a majority of correct processes.

We show in this paper that, maybe surprisingly, the weakest failure detector to implement an *eventually consistent* replicated service in this environment (in fact, in *any* environment) is still Ω. We prove our result via an interesting generalization of the celebrated "CHT proof" by Chandra, Hadzilacos and Toueg [2]. In the CHT proof, every process periodically extracts the identifier of a process that is expected to be correct (the *leader*) from the *valencies* of an ever-growing collection of locally simulated runs. We carefully adjust the notion of valency to apply this approach to the weaker abstraction of *eventual consensus*, which we show to be necessary and sufficient to implement eventual consistency.

Our result becomes less surprising if we realize that a correct majority prevents the system from being *partitioned*, and we know that both consistency and availability cannot be achieved while tolerating partitions [1, 14, 8]. Therefore, in a system with a correct majority of processes, there is no gain in weakening consistency: (strong) consistency requires the same information about failures as eventual one. In an arbitrary environment, however, *i.e.*, under any assumptions on when and where failures may occur, the weakest failure detector for consistency is known to be $\Omega + \Sigma$, where Σ [8] returns a set of processes (called a *quorum*) so that every two such quorums intersect at any time and there is a time after which all returned quorums contain only correct processes. We show in this paper that ensuring eventual consistency does not require Σ: only Ω is needed, even if we do not assume a majority of correct processes. Therefore, Σ represents the exact difference between consistency and eventual consistency. Our result thus theoretically backs up partition-tolerance [1, 14] as one of the main motivations behind the very notion of eventual consistency.

We establish our results through the following steps:

- We give precise definitions of the notions of *eventual consensus* and *eventual total order broadcast*. We show that the two abstractions are equivalent. These underlie the intuitive notion of eventual consistency implemented in many replicated services [7, 6, 4].
- We show how to extend the celebrated CHT proof [2], initially establishing that Ω is necessary for solving consensus, to the context of eventual consensus. Through this extension, we indirectly highlight a hidden power of the technique proposed in [2] that somehow provides more than was used in the original CHT proof.
- We present an algorithm that uses Ω to implement, in any message-passing environment, an eventually consistent replicated service. The algorithm features three interesting properties: (1) An invocation can be performed after the optimal number of two communication steps, even if a majority of processes is not correct and even during periods when processes disagree on the leader, i.e., partition periods; [1] (2) If Ω outputs the same leader at all processes from the very beginning, then the algorithm implements total order broadcast and hence ensures consistency; (3) *Causal* ordering is ensured even during periods where Ω outputs different leaders at different processes.

[1]Note that three communication steps are, in the worst case, necessary when strong consistency is required [23].

The rest of the paper is organized as follows. We present our system model and basic definitions in Section 2. In Section 3, we introduce abstractions for implementing eventual consistency: namely, eventual consensus and eventual total order broadcast, and we prove them to be equivalent. We show in Section 4 that the weakest failure detector for eventual consensus in any message-passing environment is Ω. We present in Section 5 our algorithm that implements eventual total order broadcast using Ω in any environment. Section 6 discusses related work, and Section 7 concludes the paper.

2. PRELIMINARIES

We adopt the classical model of distributed systems provided with the failure detector abstraction proposed in [3, 2]. In particular we employ the simplified version of the model proposed in [15, 18].

We consider a message-passing system with a set of processes $\Pi = \{p_1, p_2, \ldots, p_n\}$ ($n \geq 2$). Processes execute steps of computation asynchronously, *i.e.*, there is no bound on the delay between steps. However, we assume a discrete global clock to which the processes do not have access. The range of this clock's ticks is $\mathbb{N}$. Each pair of processes are connected by a reliable link.

Processes may fail by *crashing*. A *failure pattern* is a function $F : \mathbb{N} \rightarrow 2^{\Pi}$, where $F(t)$ is the set of processes that have crashed by time t. We assume that processes never recover from crashes, *i. e.*, $F(t) \subseteq F(t+1)$. Let $faulty(F) = \bigcup_{t \in \mathbb{N}} F(t)$ be the set of *faulty* processes in a failure pattern F; and $correct(F) = \Pi - faulty(F)$ be the set of *correct* processes in F. An *environment*, denoted $\mathcal{E}$, is a set of failure patterns.

A *failure detector history* H *with range* $\mathcal{R}$ is a function $H : \Pi \times \mathbb{N} \rightarrow \mathcal{R}$, where $H(p,t)$ is interpreted as the value output by the failure detector module of process p at time t. A *failure detector* $\mathcal{D}$ *with range* $\mathcal{R}$ is a function that maps every failure pattern F to a nonempty set of failure detector histories. $\mathcal{D}(F)$ denotes the set of all possible failure detector histories that may be output by $\mathcal{D}$ in a failure pattern F.

For example, at each process, the *leader failure detector* Ω outputs the id of a process; furthermore, if a correct process exists, then there is a time after which Ω outputs the id of the same correct process at every correct process. Another example is the *quorum failure detector* Σ, which outputs a set of processes at each process. Any two sets output at any times and by any processes intersect, and eventually every set output at any correct process consists of only correct processes.

An *algorithm* $\mathcal{A}$ is modeled as a collection of n deterministic automata, where $\mathcal{A}(p)$ specifies the behavior of process p. Computation proceeds in *steps* of these automata. In each step, identified as a tuple $(p, m, d, \mathcal{A})$, a process p atomically (1) receives a single message m (that can be the empty message λ) or accepts an *input* (from the external world), (2) queries its local failure detector module and receives a value d, (3) changes its state according to $\mathcal{A}(p)$, and (4) sends a message specified by $\mathcal{A}(p)$ for the new state to every process or produces an *output* (to the external world). Note that the use of λ ensures that a step of a process is always enabled, even if no message is sent to it.

A *configuration* of an algorithm $\mathcal{A}$ specifies the local state of each process and the set of messages in transit. In the *initial* configuration of $\mathcal{A}$, no message is in transit and each process p is in the initial state of the automaton $\mathcal{A}(p)$. A *schedule* S of $\mathcal{A}$ is a finite or infinite sequence of steps of $\mathcal{A}$ that respects $\mathcal{A}(p)$ for each p.

Following [18], we model inputs and outputs of processes using *input histories* H_I and *output histories* H_O that specify the inputs each process receives from its application and the outputs each process returns to the application over time. A *run of algorithm* $\mathcal{A}$ *using failure detector* $\mathcal{D}$ *in environment* $\mathcal{E}$ is a tuple $R = (F, H, H_I, H_O, S, T)$, where F is a failure pattern in $\mathcal{E}$, H is a failure detector history in $\mathcal{D}(F)$, H_I and H_O are input and output histories of $\mathcal{A}$, S is a schedule of $\mathcal{A}$, and T is a list of increasing times in $\mathbb{N}$, where $T[i]$ is the time when step $S[i]$ is taken. $H \in \mathcal{D}(F)$, the failure detector values received by steps in S are consistent with H, and H_I and H_O are consistent with S. An infinite run of $\mathcal{A}$ is *admissible* if (1) every correct process takes an infinite number of steps in S; and (2) each message sent to a correct process is eventually received.

We then define a distributed-computing *problem*, such as consensus or total order broadcast, as a set of tuples (H_I, H_O) where H_I is an input history and H_O is an output history. An algorithm $\mathcal{A}$ using a failure detector $\mathcal{D}$ solves a problem P in an environment $\mathcal{E}$ if in every admissible run of $\mathcal{A}$ in $\mathcal{E}$, the input and output histories are in P. Typically, inputs and outputs represent invocations and responses of *operations* exported by the implemented abstraction. If there is an algorithm that solves P using $\mathcal{D}$, we sometimes, with a slight language abuse, say that $\mathcal{D}$ *implements* P.

Consider two problems P and P'. A *transformation from* P *to* P' *in an environment* $\mathcal{E}$ [17] is a map $T_{P \to P'}$ that, given any algorithm $\mathcal{A}_P$ solving P in $\mathcal{E}$, yields an algorithm $\mathcal{A}_{P'}$ solving P' in $\mathcal{E}$. The transformation is *asynchronous* in the sense that $\mathcal{A}_P$ is used as a "black box" where $\mathcal{A}_{P'}$ is obtained by feeding inputs to $\mathcal{A}_P$ and using the returned outputs to solve P'. Hence, if P is solvable in $\mathcal{E}$ using a failure detector $\mathcal{D}$, the existence of a transformation $T_{P \to P'}$ in $\mathcal{E}$ establishes that P' is also solvable in $\mathcal{E}$ using $\mathcal{D}$. If, additionally, there exists a transformation from P' to P in $\mathcal{E}$, we say that P and P' are *equivalent in* $\mathcal{E}$.

Failure detectors can be partially ordered based on their "power": failure detector $\mathcal{D}$ is *weaker than* failure detector $\mathcal{D}'$ in $\mathcal{E}$ if there is an algorithm that *emulates* the output of $\mathcal{D}$ using $\mathcal{D}'$ in $\mathcal{E}$ [2, 18]. If $\mathcal{D}$ is weaker than $\mathcal{D}'$, any problem that can be solved with $\mathcal{D}$ can also be solved with $\mathcal{D}'$. For a problem P, $\mathcal{D}^*$ is the *weakest* failure detector to solve P in $\mathcal{E}$ if (a) there is an algorithm that uses $\mathcal{D}^*$ to solve P in $\mathcal{E}$, and (b) $\mathcal{D}^*$ is weaker than any failure detector $\mathcal{D}$ that can be used to solve P in $\mathcal{E}$.

3. ABSTRACTIONS FOR EVENTUAL CONSISTENCY

We define two basic abstractions that capture the notion of eventual consistency: eventual total order broadcast and eventual consensus. We show that the two abstractions are equivalent: each of them can be used to implement the other.

Eventual Total Order Broadcast (ETOB).

The *total order broadcast* (TOB) abstraction [17] exports one operation *broadcastTOB(m)* and maintains, at every process p_i, an output variable d_i. Let $d_i(t)$ denote the value of d_i at time t. Intuitively, $d_i(t)$ is the sequence of messages p_i *delivered* by time t. We write $m \in d_i(t)$ if m appears in $d_i(t)$.

A process p_i *broadcasts a message* m *at time* t by a call to *broadcastTOB(m)*. We say that a process p_i *stably delivers a message* m *at time* t if p_i appends m to $d_i(t)$ and m is never removed from d_i after that, *i.e.*, $m \notin d_i(t-1)$ and $\forall t' \geq t$: $m \in d_i(t')$. Note that if a message is delivered but not *stably* delivered by p_i at time t, it appears in $d_i(t)$ but not in $d_i(t')$ for some $t' > t$.

Assuming that broadcast messages are distinct, the TOB abstraction satisfies:

TOB-Validity If a correct process p_i broadcasts a message m at time t, then p_i eventually stably delivers m, i.e., $\forall t'' \geq t' : m \in d_i(t'')$ for some $t' > t$.

TOB-No-creation If $m \in d_i(t)$, then m was broadcast by some process p_j at some time $t' < t$.

TOB-No-duplication No message appears more than once in $d_i(t)$.

TOB-Agreement If a message m is stably delivered by some correct process p_i at time t, then m is eventually stably delivered by every correct process p_j.

TOB-Stability For any correct process p_i, $d_i(t_1)$ is a prefix of $d_i(t_2)$ for all $t_1, t_2 \in \mathbb{N}$, $t_1 \leq t_2$.

TOB-Total-order Let p_i and p_j be any two correct processes such that two messages m_1 and m_2 appear in $d_i(t)$ and $d_j(t)$ at time t. If m_1 appears before m_2 in $d_i(t)$, then m_1 appears before m_2 in $d_j(t)$.

We then introduce the *eventual total order broadcast* (ETOB) abstraction, which maintains the same inputs and outputs as TOB (messages are broadcast by a call to *broadcastETOB(m)*) and satisfies, in every admissible run, the TOB-Validity, TOB-No-creation, TOB-No-duplication, and TOB-Agreement properties, plus the following relaxed properties for some $\tau \in \mathbb{N}$:

ETOB-Stability For any correct process p_i, $d_i(t_1)$ is a prefix of $d_i(t_2)$ for all $t_1, t_2 \in \mathbb{N}$, $\tau \leq t_1 \leq t_2$.

ETOB-Total-order Let p_i and p_j be correct processes such that messages m_1 and m_2 appear in $d_i(t)$ and $d_j(t)$ for some $t \geq \tau$. If m_1 appears before m_2 in $d_i(t)$, then m_1 appears before m_2 in $d_j(t)$.

As we show in this paper, satisfying the following optional (but useful) property in ETOB does not require more information about failures.

TOB-Causal-Order Let p_i be a correct process such that two messages m_1 and m_2 appear in $d_i(t)$ at time $t \in \mathbb{N}$. If m_2 depends causally of m_1, then m_1 appears before m_2 in $d_i(t)$.

Here we say that a message m_2 *causally depends* on a message m_1 in a run R, and write $m_1 \to_R m_2$, if one of the following conditions holds in R: (1) a process p_i sends m_1 and then sends m_2, (2) a process p_i receives m_1 and then sends m_2, or (3) there exists m_3 such that $m_1 \to_R m_3$ and $m_3 \to_R m_2$.

Eventual Consensus (EC).

The *consensus* abstraction (C) [12] exports, to every process p_i, a single operation *proposeC* that takes a binary argument and returns a binary response (we also say *decides*) so that the following properties are satisfied:

C-Termination Every correct process eventually returns a response to *proposeC*.

C-Integrity Every process returns a response at most once.

C-Agreement No two processes return different values.

C-Validity Every value returned was previously proposed.

The *eventual consensus* (EC) abstraction exports, to every process p_i, operations $proposeEC_1$, $proposeEC_2$, ... that take binary arguments and return binary responses. Assuming that, for all $j \in \mathbb{N}$, every process invokes $proposeEC_j$ as soon as it returns a response to $proposeEC_{j-1}$, the abstraction guarantees that, in every admissible run, there exists $k \in \mathbb{N}$, such that the following properties are satisfied:

EC-Termination Every correct process eventually returns a response to $proposeEC_j$ for all $j \in \mathbb{N}$.

EC-Integrity No process responds twice to $proposeEC_j$ for all $j \in \mathbb{N}$.

EC-Validity Every value returned to $proposeEC_j$ was previously proposed to $proposeEC_j$ for all $j \in \mathbb{N}$.

EC-Agreement No two processes return different values to $proposeEC_j$ for all $j \geq k$.

It is straightforward to transform the binary version of EC into a multivalued one with unbounded set of inputs [24]. In the following, by referring to EC we mean a multivalued version of it.

Equivalence between EC *and* ETOB.

It is well known that, in their classical forms, the consensus and the total order broadcast abstractions are equivalent [3]. In this section, we show that a similar result holds for our eventual versions of these abstractions.

The intuition behind the transformation from EC to ETOB is the following. Each time a process p_i wants to ETOB-broadcast a message m, p sends m to each process. Periodically, every process p_i proposes its current sequence of messages received so far to EC. This sequence is built by concatenating the last output of EC(stored in a local variable d_i) to the batch of all messages received by the process and not yet present in d_i. The output of EC is stored in d_i, i.e., at any time, each process delivers the last sequence of messages returned by EC.

The correctness of this transformation follows from the fact that ECeventually returns consistent responses to the processes. Thus, eventually, all processes agree on the same linearly growing sequence of stably delivered messages. Furthermore, every message broadcast by a correct process eventually appears either in the delivered message sequence or in the batches of not yet delivered messages at all correct processes. Thus, by EC-Validity of EC, every message ETOB-broadcast by a correct process is eventually stored in d_i of every correct process p_i forever. By construction, no message appears in d_i twice or if it was not previously ETOB-broadcast. Therefore, the transformation satisfies the properties of ETOB.

The transformation from ETOB to EC is as follows. At each invocation of the EC primitive, the process broadcasts a message using the ETOB abstraction. This message contains the proposed value and the index of the consensus instance. As soon as a message corresponding to a given eventual consensus instance is delivered by process p_i (appears in d_i), p_i returns the value contained in the message.

Since the ETOB abstraction guarantees that every process eventually stably delivers the same sequence of messages, there exists a consensus instance after which the responses of the transformation to all alive processes are identical. Moreover, by ETOB-Validity, every message ETOB-broadcast by a correct process p_i is eventually stably delivered. Thus, every correct process eventually returns from any EC-instance it invokes. Thus, the transformation satisfies the EC specification.

THEOREM 1. *In any environment $\mathcal{E}$,* EC *and* ETOB *are equivalent.*

From EC *to* ETOB. To prove this result, it is sufficient to provide a protocol that implements ETOB in an environment $\mathcal{E}$ knowing that there exists a protocol that implements EC in this environment. This transformation protocol $\mathcal{T}_{EC \rightarrow ETOB}$ is stated in Algorithm 1. Now, we are going to prove that $\mathcal{T}_{EC \rightarrow ETOB}$ implements ETOB. Assume that there exists a message m broadcast by a correct process p_i at time t. As p_i is correct, every correct process receives the message $push(m)$ in a finite time. Then, m appears in the set $toDeliver$ of all correct processes in a finite time. Hence, by the termination property of EC and the construction of the function $NewBatch$, there exists ℓ such that m is included in any sequence submitted to $proposeEC_\ell$. By the EC-Validity and the EC-Termination properties, we deduce that p_i stably delivers m in a finite time, that proves that $\mathcal{T}_{EC \rightarrow ETOB}$ satisfies the TOB-Validity property. If a process p_i delivers a message m at time t, then m appears in the sequence responded by its last invocation of $proposeEC_\ell$. By construction and by the EC-Validity property, this sequence contains only messages that appear in the set $toDeliver$ of a process p_j at the time p_j invokes $proposeEC_\ell$. But this set is incrementally built at the reception of messages $push$ that contains only messages broadcast by a process. This implies that $\mathcal{T}_{EC \rightarrow ETOB}$ satisfies the TOB-No-creation. As the sequence outputted at any time by any process is the response to its last invocation of $proposeEC$ and that the sequence submitted to any invocation of this primitive contains no duplicated message (by definition of the function $NewBatch$), we can deduce from the EC-Validity property that $\mathcal{T}_{EC \rightarrow ETOB}$ satisfies the TOB-No-duplication. Assume that a correct process p_i stably delivers a message m, i.e., there exists a time after which m always appears in d_i. By the algorithm, m always appears in the response of $proposeEC$ to p_i after this time. As EC-Agreement property is eventually satisfied, we can deduce that m always appears in the response of $proposeEC$ for any correct process after some time. Thus, any correct process stably delivers m, and $\mathcal{T}_{EC \rightarrow ETOB}$ satisfies the TOB-Agreement. Let τ be the time after which the EC primitive satisfies EC-Agreement and EC-Validity. Let p_i be a correct process and $\tau \leq t_1 \leq t_2$. Let ℓ_1 (respectively ℓ_2) be the integer such that $d_i(t_1)$ (respectively $d_i(t_2)$) is the response of $proposeEC_{\ell_1}$ (respectively $proposeEC_{\ell_2}$). By construction of the protocol and the EC-Agreement and EC-Validity properties, we know that, after time τ, the response of $proposeEC_\ell$ to correct processes is a prefix of the response of $proposeEC_{\ell+1}$. As we have $\ell_1 \leq \ell_2$, we can deduce that $\mathcal{T}_{EC \rightarrow ETOB}$ satisfies the ETOB-Stability property. Let p_i and p_j be two correct processes such that two messages m_1 and m_2 appear in $d_i(t)$ and $d_j(t)$ at time $t \geq \tau$. Let ℓ be the smallest integer such that m_1 and m_2 appear in the response of $proposeEC_\ell$. By the EC-Agreement property, we know that the response of $proposeEC_\ell$ is identical for all correct processes. Then , by the ETOB-Stability property proved above, that implies that, if m_1 appears before m_2 in $d_i(t)$, then m_1 appears before m_2 in $d_j(t)$. In other words, $\mathcal{T}_{EC \rightarrow ETOB}$ satisfies the ETOB-Total-order property. In conclusion, $\mathcal{T}_{EC \rightarrow ETOB}$ satisfies the ETOB specification in an environment $\mathcal{E}$ provided that there exists a protocol that implements EC in this environment.

Algorithm 1 $\mathcal{T}_{\mathsf{EC}\rightarrow\mathsf{ETOB}}$: transformation from EC to ETOB for process p_i

PROOF. **Output variable:**
d_i: sequence of messages of M (initially empty) outputted at any time by p_i

Internal variables:
$toDeliver_i$: set of messages of M (initially empty) containing all messages received by p_i
$count_i$: integer (initially 0) that stores the number of the last instance of consensus invoked by p_i

Messages:
$push(m)$ with m a message of M

Functions:
$Send(message)$ sends $message$ to all processes (including p_i)
$NewBatch(d_i, toDeliver_i)$ returns a sequence containing all messages from the set $toDeliver_i \setminus \{m | m \in d_i\}$

On reception of $broadcastETOB(m)$ **from the application**
$Send(push(m))$

On reception of $push(m)$ **from** p_j
$toDeliver_i := toDeliver_i \cup \{m\}$

On reception of d **as response of** $proposeEC_\ell$
$d_i := d$
$count_i := count_i + 1$
$proposeEC_{count_i}(d_i.NewBatch(d_i, toDeliver_i))$

On local timeout
If $count_i = 0$ then
$count_i := 1$
$proposeEC_1(NewBatch(d_i, toDeliver_i))$

From ETOB *to* EC.

To prove this result, it is sufficient to provide a protocol that implements EC in an environment $\mathcal{E}$ given a protocol that implements ETOB in this environment. This transformation protocol $\mathcal{T}_{\mathsf{ETOB}\rightarrow\mathsf{EC}}$ is stated in Algorithm 2. Now, we are going to prove that $\mathcal{T}_{\mathsf{ETOB}\rightarrow\mathsf{EC}}$ implements EC.

Let p_i be a correct process that invokes $proposeEC_\ell(v)$ with $\ell \in \mathbb{N}$. Then, by fairness and the TOB-Validity property, the construction of the protocol implies that the ETOB primitive delivers the message (ℓ, v) to p_i in a finite time. By the use of the local timeout, we know that p_i returns from $proposeEC_\ell(v)$ in a finite time, that proves that $\mathcal{T}_{\mathsf{ETOB}\rightarrow\mathsf{EC}}$ satisfies the EC-Termination property.

The update of the variable $count_i$ to ℓ for any process p_i that invokes $proposeEC_\ell$ and the assumptions on operations $proposeEC$ ensure us that p_i executes at most once the function $DecideEC(\ell, received_i[\Omega_i, \ell])$. Hence, $\mathcal{T}_{\mathsf{ETOB}\rightarrow\mathsf{EC}}$ satisfies the EC-Integrity property.

Let τ be the time after which the ETOB-Stability and the ETOB-Total-order properties are satisfied. Let k be the smallest integer such that any process that invokes $proposeEC_k$ in run r invokes it after τ.

If we assume that there exist two correct processes p_i and p_j that return different values to $proposeEC_\ell$ with $\ell \geq k$, we obtain a contradiction with the ETOB-Stability, ETOB-Total-order, or TOB-Agreement property. Indeed, if p_i returns a value after time τ, that implies that this value appears in d_i and then, by the TOB-Agreement property, this value eventually appears in d_j. If p_j returns a different value from p_i, that implies that this value is the first occurrence of a message associated to $proposeEC_\ell$ in d_j at the time of the return of $proposeEC_\ell$. After that, d_j cannot satisfy simultaneously the ETOB-Stability and the ETOB-Total-order properties. This contradiction shows that $\mathcal{T}_{\mathsf{ETOB}\rightarrow\mathsf{EC}}$ satisfies the EC-Agreement property.

If we assume that there exists a process p_i that returns to $proposeEC_\ell$ with $\ell \in \mathbb{N}$ a value that was not proposed to $proposeEC_\ell$, we obtain a contradiction with the TOB-No-creation property. Indeed, the return of p_i from $proposeEC_\ell$ is chosen in d_i that contains the output of the ETOB primitive and processes broadcast only proposed values. This contradiction shows that $\mathcal{T}_{\mathsf{ETOB}\rightarrow\mathsf{EC}}$ satisfies the EC-Validity property.

In conclusion, $\mathcal{T}_{\mathsf{ETOB}\rightarrow\mathsf{EC}}$ satisfies the EC specification in an environment $\mathcal{E}$ provided that there exists a protocol that implements ETOB in this environment. □

Algorithm 2 $\mathcal{T}_{\mathsf{ETOB}\rightarrow\mathsf{EC}}$: transformation from ETOB to EC for process p_i

Internal variables:
$count_i$: integer (initially 0) that stores the number of the last instances of consensus invoked by p_i
d_i: sequence of messages (initially empty) outputted to p_i by the ETOB primitive

Functions:
$First(\ell)$: returns the value v such that (ℓ, v) is the first message of the form $(\ell, *)$ in d_i if such messages exist, $\perp$ otherwise
$DecideEC(\ell, v)$: returns the value v as response to $proposeEC_\ell$

On invocation of $proposeEC_\ell(v)$
$count_i := \ell$
$broadcastETOB((\ell, v))$

On local time out
If $First(count_i) \neq \perp$ then
$DecideEC(count_i, First(count_i))$

4. THE WEAKEST FAILURE DETECTOR FOR EC

In this section, we show that Ω is necessary and sufficient for implementing the eventual consensus abstraction EC:

THEOREM 2. *In any environment $\mathcal{E}$, Ω is the weakest failure detector for* EC.

Ω is necessary for EC.

Let $\mathcal{E}$ be any environment. We show below that Ω is weaker than any failure detector $\mathcal{D}$ that can be used to solve EC in $\mathcal{E}$. Recall that implementing Ω means outputting, at every process, the identifier of a *leader* process so that eventually, the same correct leader is output permanently at all correct processes.

First, we briefly recall the arguments use by Chandra et al. [2] in the original CHT proof deriving Ω from any algorithm solving consensus (to get a more detailed survey of the proof please rever to [13, Chapter 3]). The basic observation there is that a run of any algorithm using a failure detector induces a *directed acyclic graph* (DAG). The DAG contains a sample of failure detector values output by $\mathcal{D}$ in the current run and captures causal relations between them. Each process p_i maintains a local copy of the DAG, denoted by G_i: p_i periodically queries its failure detector module, updates G_i by connecting every vertex of the DAG with the vertex containing the returned failure-detector value with an edge, and broadcasts the DAG. An edge from vertex $[p_i, d, m]$ to vertex $[p_j, d', m']$ is thus interpreted as "p_i queried $\mathcal{D}$ for the mth time and obtained value d and after that p_j queried $\mathcal{D}$ for the m'th time and obtained value d'". Whenever p_i receives a DAG G_j calculated earlier by p_j, p_i merges G_i with G_j. As a result, DAGs maintained by the correct processes converge to the same infinite DAG G. The DAG G_i is then used by p_i to simulate a number of runs of the given consensus algorithm $\mathcal{A}$ for all possible inputs to the processes. All these runs are organized in the form of a *simulation tree* Υ_i. The simulation trees Υ_i maintained by the correct processes converge to the same infinite simulation tree Υ.

The outputs produced in the simulated runs of Υ_i are then used by p_i to compute the current estimate of Ω. Every vertex σ of Υ_i is assigned a valency tag based on the decisions taken in all its *extensions* (descendants of σ in Υ_i): σ is assigned a tag $v \in \{0,1\}$ if σ has an extension in which some process decides v. A vertex is bivalent if it is assigned both 0 and 1. It is then shown in [2] that by locating the same bivalent vertex in the limit tree Υ, the correct process can eventually extract the identifier of the same correct process. (More details can be found in [2, 13].)

We show that this method, originally designed for consensus, can be extended to eventual consensus (i.e., to the weaker EC abstraction). The extension is not trivial and requires carefully adjusting the notion of valency of a vertex in the simulation tree.

LEMMA 3. *In every environment $\mathcal{E}$, if a failure detector $\mathcal{D}$ implements* EC *in $\mathcal{E}$, then Ω is weaker than $\mathcal{D}$ in $\mathcal{E}$.*

PROOF. Let $\mathcal{A}$ be any algorithm that implements EC using a failure detector $\mathcal{D}$ in an environment $\mathcal{E}$. As in [2], every process p_i maintains a failure detector sample stored in DAG G_i and periodically uses G_i to simulate a set of runs of $\mathcal{A}$ for all possible sequence of inputs of EC. The simulated runs are organized by p_i in an ever-growing *simulation tree* Υ_i. A vertex of Υ_i is the schedule of a finite run of $\mathcal{A}$ "triggered" by a path in G_i in which every process starts with invoking $proposeEC_1(v)$, for some $v \in \{0,1\}$, takes steps using the failure detector values stipulated by the path in G_i and, once $proposeEC_\ell(v)$ is complete, eventually invokes $proposeEC_{\ell+1}(v')$, for some $v' \in \{0,1\}$. (For the record, we equip each vertex of Υ_i with the path in G_i used to produce it.) A vertex is connected by an edge to each one-step extension of it. [2]

Note that in every admissible infinite simulated run, EC-Termination, EC-Integrity and EC-Validity are satisfied and that there is $k > 0$ such that for all $\ell \geq k$, the invocations and responses of $proposeEC_\ell$ satisfy the EC-Agreement.

Since processes periodically broadcast their DAGs, the simulation tree Υ_i constructed locally by a correct process p_i *converges* to an infinite simulation tree Υ, in the sense that every finite subtree of Υ is eventually part of Υ_i. The infinite simulation tree Υ, starting from the initial configuration of $\mathcal{A}$ and, in the limit, contains all possible schedules that can triggered by the paths DAGs G_i.

Consider a vertex σ in Υ identifying a unique finite schedule of a run of $\mathcal{A}$ using $\mathcal{D}$ in the current failure pattern F. For $k > 0$, we say that σ is *k-enabled* if $k = 1$ or σ contains a response from $proposeEC_{k-1}$ at some process. Now

[2]In [2], the simulated schedules form a *simulation forest*, where a distinct simulation tree corresponds to each initial configuration encoding consensus inputs. Here we follow [18]: there is a single initial configuration and inputs are encoded in the form of input histories. As a result, we get a single simulation tree where branches depend on the parameters of $proposeEC_\ell$ calls.

Algorithm 3 Locating a bivalent vertex in Υ.

```
k := 1
σ := root of ϒ
while true do
    if σ is k-bivalent then break
    σ1 := a descendant of σ in which
          EC-Agreement does not hold for proposeEC_k
    σ2 := a descendant of σ1 in which every correct process
          completes proposeEC_k and receives
          all messages sent to it in σ
    choose k' > k and σ3, a descendant of σ2, such that
          k'-tag of σ3 contains {0, 1}
    k := k'
    σ := σ3
```

we associate each vertex σ in Υ with a set of *valency tags* associated with each "consensus instance" k, called the *k-tag* of σ, as follows:

- If σ is k-enabled and has a descendant (in Υ) in which $proposeEC_k$ returns $x \in \{0,1\}$, then x is added to the k-tag of σ.
- If σ is k-enabled and has a descendant in which two different values are returned by $proposeEC_k$, then $\perp$ is added to the k-tag of σ.

If σ is not k-enabled, then its k-tag is empty. If the k-tag of σ is $\{x\}$, $x \in \{0,1\}$, we say that σ is *(k,x)-valent* (*k-univalent*). If the k-tag is $\{0,1\}$, then we say that σ is *k-bivalent*. If the k-tag of σ contains $\perp$, we say that σ is *k-invalid*

Since $\mathcal{A}$ ensures EC-Termination in all admissible runs extending σ, each k-enabled vertex σ, the k-tag of σ is non-empty. Moreover, EC-Termination and EC-Validity imply that a vertex in which no process has invoked $proposeEC_k$ yet has a descendant in which $proposeEC_k$ returns 0 and a descendant in which $proposeEC_k$ returns 1. Indeed, a run in which only v, $v \in \{0,1\}$ is proposed in instance k and every correct process takes enough steps must contain v as an output. Thus:

(*) For each vertex σ, there exists $k \in \mathbb{N}$ and σ', a descendant of σ, such that k-tag of σ' contains $\{0,1\}$.

If the "limit tree" Υ contains a k-bivalent vertex, we can apply the arguments of [2] to extract Ω. Now we show that such a vertex exists in Υ. Then we can simply let every process locate the "first" such vertex in its local tree Υ_i. To establish an order on the vertices, we can associate each vertex σ of Υ with the value m such that vertex $[p_i, d, m]$ of G is used to simulate the last step of σ (recall that we equip each vertex of Υ with the corresponding path). Then we order vertices of Υ in the order consistent with the growth of m. Since every vertex in G has only finitely many incoming edges, the sets of vertices having the same value of m are finite. Thus, we can break the ties in the m-based order using any deterministic procedure on these finite sets.

Eventually, by choosing the first k-bivalent vertex in their local trees Υ_i, the correct processes will eventually stabilize on the same k-bivalent vertex $\tilde{\sigma}$ in the limit tree Υ and apply the CHT extraction procedure to derive the same correct process based on k-tags assigned to $\tilde{\sigma}$'s descendants.

It remains to show that Υ indeed contains a k-bivalent vertex for some k. Consider the procedure described in Algorithm 3 that intends to locate such a vertex, starting with the root of the tree.

For the currently considered k-enabled vertex σ that is *not* k-bivalent (if it is k-bivalent, we are done), we use (*) to locate σ_3, a descendant of σ, such that (1) in σ_3, two processes return different values in $proposeEC_k$ in σ_3, (2) in σ_3, every correct process has completed $proposeEC_k$ and has received every message sent to it in σ, and (3) the k'-tag of σ_3 contains $\{0, 1\}$.

Thus, the procedure in Algorithm 3 either terminates by locating a k-bivalent tag and then we are done, or it never terminates. Suppose, by contradiction, that the procedure never terminates. Hence, we have an infinite admissible run of $\mathcal{A}$ in which no agreement is provided in infinitely many instances of consensus. Indeed, in the constructed path along the tree, every correct process appears infinitely many times and receives every message sent to it. This admissible run violated the EC-Agreement property of EC—a contradiction.

Thus, the correct processes will eventually locate the same k-bivalent vertex and then, as in [2], stabilize extracting the same correct process identifier to emulate Ω. □

Ω is sufficient for EC.

Chandra and Toueg proved that Ω is sufficient to implement the classical version of the consensus abstraction in an environment where a majority of processes are correct [3]. In this section, we extend this result to the eventual consensus abstraction for any environment.

The proposed implementation of EC is very simple. Each process has access to an Ω failure detector module. Upon each invocation of the EC primitive, a process broadcasts the proposed value (and the associated consensus index). Every process stores every received value. Each process p_i periodically checks whether it has received a value for the current consensus instance from the process that it currently believes to be the leader. If so, p_i returns this value. The correctness of this EC implementation relies on the fact that, eventually, all correct processes trust the same leader (by the definition of Ω) and then decide (return responses) consistently on the values proposed by this process.

LEMMA 4. *In every environment $\mathcal{E}$,* EC *can be implemented using Ω.*

PROOF. We propose such an implementation in Algorithm 4. Then, we prove that any admissible run r of the algorithm in any environment $\mathcal{E}$ satisfies the EC-Termination, EC-Integrity, EC-Agreement, and EC-Validity properties.

Assume that a correct process never returns from an invocation of *proposeEC* in r. Without loss of generality, denote by ℓ the smallest integer such that a correct process p_i never returns from the invocation of $proposeEC_\ell$. This implies that p_i always evaluates $received_i[\Omega_i, count_i]$ to $\bot$. We know by definition of Ω that, eventually, Ω_i always returns the same correct process p_j. Hence, by construction of ℓ, p_j returns from $proposeEC_0$,..., $proposeEC_{\ell-1}$ and then sends the message $promote(v, \ell)$ to all processes in a finite time. As p_i and p_j are correct, p_i receives this message and updates $received_i[\Omega_i, count_i]$ to v in a finite time. Therefore, the algorithm satisfies the EC-Termination property.

The update of the variable $count_i$ to ℓ for any process p_i that invokes $proposeEC_\ell$ and the assumptions on operations *proposeEC* ensure us that p_i executes at most once the function $DecideEC(\ell, received_i[\Omega_i, \ell])$. Hence, the EC-Integrity property is satisfied.

Let τ_Ω be the time from which the local outputs of Ω are identical and constants for all correct processes in r. Let k be the smallest integer such that any process that invokes $proposeEC_k$ in r invokes it after τ_Ω.

Let ℓ be an integer such that $\ell \geq k$. Assume that p_i and p_j are two processes that respond to $proposeEC_\ell$. Then, they respectively execute the function $DecideEC(\ell, received_i[\Omega_i, \ell])$ and $DecideEC(\ell, received_j[\Omega_j, \ell])$. By construction of k, we can deduce that $\Omega_i = \Omega_j = p_l$. That implies that p_i and p_j both received a message $promote(v, \ell)$ from p_l. As p_l sends such a message at most once, we can deduce that $received_i[p_l, \ell] = received_j[p_l, \ell]$, that proves that ensures the EC-Agreement property.

Let ℓ be an integer such that $\ell \geq k$. Assume that p_i is a process that respond to $proposeEC_\ell$. The value returned by p_i was previously received from Ω_i in a message of type *promote*. By construction of the protocol, Ω_i sends only one message of this type and this latter contains the value proposed to Ω_i, hence, the EC-Validity property is satisfied.

Thus, Algorithm 4 indeed implements EC in any environment using Ω. □

Algorithm 4 EC using Ω: algorithm for process p_i

Local variables:
  $count_i$: integer (initially 0) that stores the number of the last instances of consensus invoked by p_i
  $received_i$: two dimensional tabular that stores a value for each pair of processes/integer (initially $\bot$)
Functions:
  $DecideEC(\ell, v)$ returns the value v as a response to $proposeEC_\ell$
Messages:
  $promote(v, \ell)$ with $v \in \{0, 1\}$ and $\ell \in \mathbb{N}$
On invocation of $proposeEC_\ell(v)$
  $count_i := \ell$
  Send $promote(v, \ell)$ to all
On reception of $promote(v, \ell)$ **from** p_j
  $received_i[j, \ell] := v$
On local time out
  If $received_i[\Omega_i, count_i] \neq \bot$ do
    $DecideEC(count_i, received_i[\Omega_i, count_i])$

5. AN EVENTUAL TOTAL ORDER BROADCAST ALGORITHM

We have shown in the previous section that Ω is the weakest failure detector for the EC abstraction (and, by Theorem 1, the ETOB abstraction) in any environment. In this section, we describe an algorithm that directly implements ETOB using Ω and which we believe is interesting in its own right.

The algorithm has three interesting properties. First, it needs only two communication steps to deliver any message when the leader does not change, whereas algorithms implementing classical TOB need at least three communication steps in this case. Second, the algorithm actually implements total order broadcast if Ω outputs the same leader at all processes from the very beginning. Third, the algorithm additionally ensures the property of TOB-Causal-Order, which does not require more information about faults.

The intuition behind this algorithm is as follows. Every process that intends to ETOB-broadcast a message sends it to all other processes. Each process p_i has access to an Ω failure detector module and maintains a DAG that stores the set of messages delivered so far together with their causal

Algorithm 5 $\mathcal{ETOB}$: protocol for process p_i

Output variable:
  d_i: sequence of messages $m \in M$ (initially empty) output by p_i

Internal variables:
  $promote_i$: sequence of messages $m \in M$ (initially empty) promoted by p_i when $\Omega_i = p_i$
  CG_i: directed graph on messages of M (initially empty) that contains causality dependencies known by p_i

Messages:
  $update(CG_i)$ with CG_i a directed graph on messages of M
  $promote(promote_i)$ with $promote_i$ a sequence of messages $m \in M$

Functions:
  $UpdateCG(m, C(m))$ adds the node m and the set of edges $\{(m', m) | m' \in C(m)\}$ to CG_i
  $UnionCG(CG_j)$ replaces CG_i by the union of CG_i and CG_j
  $UpdatePromote()$ replaces $promote_i$ by one of the sequences of messages s such that $promote_i$ is a prefix of s, s contains once all messages of CG_i, and for every edge (m_1, m_2) of CG_i, m_1 appears before m_2 in s

On $broadcastETOB(m, C(m))$ **from the application**
  $UpdateCG(m, C(m))$
  Send $update(CG_i)$ to all

On reception of $update(CG_j)$ **from** p_j
  $UnionCG(CG_j)$
  $UpdatePromote()$

On reception of $promote(promote_j)$ **from** p_j
  If $\Omega_i = p_j$ then
    $d_i := promote_j$

On local time out
  If $\Omega_i = p_i$ then
    Send $promote(promote_i)$ to all

dependencies. As long as p_i considers itself the leader (its module of Ω outputs p_i), it periodically sends to all processes a sequence of messages computed from its DAG so that the sequence respects the causal order and admits the last delivered sequence as a prefix. A process that receives a sequence of messages delivers it only if it has been sent by the current leader output by Ω. The correctness of this algorithm directly follows from the properties of Ω. Indeed, once all correct processes trust the same leader, this leader promotes its own sequence of messages, which ensures the ETOB specification.

The pseudocode of the algorithm is given in Algorithm 5). Below we present the proof of its correctness, including the proof that the algorithm additionally ensures TOB-Causal-Order.

LEMMA 5. *In every environment $\mathcal{E}$, Algorithm $\mathcal{ETOB}$ implements* ETOB *using Ω.*

PROOF. First, we prove that any run r of $\mathcal{ETOB}$ in any environment $\mathcal{E}$ satisfies the TOB-Validity, TOB-No-creation, TOB-No-duplication, and TOB-Agreement properties.

Assume that a correct process p_i broadcasts a message m at time t for a given $t \in \mathbb{N}$. We know that Ω outputs the same correct process p_j to all correct processes in a finite time. As p_j is correct, it receives the message $update(CG_i)$ from p_i (that contains m) in a finite time. Then, p_j includes m in its causality graph (by a call to $UnionCG$) and in its promotion sequence (by a call to $UpdatePromote$). As p_j never removes a message from its promotion sequence and is outputted by Ω, p_i adopts the promotion sequence of p_j in a finite time and this sequence contains m, that proves that $\mathcal{ETOB}$ satisfies the TOB-Validity property.

Any sequence outputted by any process is built by a call to $UpdatePromote$ by a process p_i. This function ensures that any message appearing in the computed sequence appears in the graph CG_p. This graph is built by successive calls to $UnionCG$ that ensure that the graph contains only messages received in a message of type *update*. The construction of the protocol ensures us that such messages have been broadcast by a process. Then, we can deduce that $\mathcal{ETOB}$ satisfies the TOB-No-creation property.

Any sequence outputted by any process is built by a call to $UpdatePromote$ that ensures that any message appears only once. Then, we can deduce that $\mathcal{ETOB}$ satisfies the TOB-No-duplication property.

Assume that a correct process p_i stably delivers a message m at time t for a given $t \in \mathbb{N}$. We know that Ω outputs the same correct process p_j to all correct processes after some finite time. Since m appears in every $d_i(t')$ such that $t' \geq t$, we derive that m appears infinitely in $promote_j$ from a given point of the run. Hence, the construction of the protocol and the correctness of p_j implies that any correct process eventually stably delivers m, and $\mathcal{ETOB}$ satisfies the TOB-Agreement property.

We now prove that, for any environment $\mathcal{E}$, for any run r of $\mathcal{ETOB}$ in $\mathcal{E}$, there exists a $\tau \in \mathbb{N}$ satisfying ETOB-Stability, ETOB-Total-order, and TOB-Causal-Order properties in r. Hence, let r be a run of $\mathcal{ETOB}$ in an environment $\mathcal{E}$. Let us define:

- τ_Ω the time from which the local outputs of Ω are identical and constant for all correct processes in r;
- Δ_c the longest communication delay between two correct processes in r;
- Δ_t the longest local timeout for correct processes in r;
- $\tau = \tau_\Omega + \Delta_t + \Delta_c$

Let p_i be a correct process and p_j be the correct elected by Ω after τ_Ω. Let t_1 and t_2 be two integers such that $\tau \leq t_1 \leq t_2$. As the output of Ω is stable after τ_Ω and the choice of τ ensures us that p_i receives at least one message of type *promote* from p_j, we can deduce from the construction of the protocol that there exists $t_3 \leq t_1$ and $t_4 \leq t_2$ such that $d_i(t_1) = promote_j(t_3)$ and $d_i(t_2) = promote_j(t_4)$. But the function $UpdatePromote$ used to build $promote_j$ ensures that $promote_j(t_3)$ is a prefix of $promote_j(t_4)$. Then, $\mathcal{ETOB}$ satisfies the ETOB-Stability property after time τ.

Let p_i and p_j be two correct processes such that two messages m_1 and m_2 appear in $d_i(t)$ and $d_j(t)$ at time $t \geq \tau$. Assume that m_1 appears before m_2 in $d_i(t)$. Let p_k be the correct elected by Ω after τ_Ω. As the output of Ω is stable after τ_Ω and the choice of τ ensures us that p_i and p_j receive at least one message of type *promote* from p_j, the construction of the protocol ensures us that we can consider t_1 and t_2 such that $d_i(t) = promote_k(t_1)$ and $d_j(t) = promote_k(t_2)$. The definition of the function $UpdatePromote$ executed by p_k allows us to deduce that either $d_i(t)$ is a prefix of $d_j(t)$ or $d_j(t)$ is a prefix of $d_i(t)$. In both cases, we obtain that m_1 appears before m_2 in $d_j(t)$, that proves that $\mathcal{ETOB}$ satisfies the ETOB-Total-order property after time τ.

Let p_i be a correct process such that two messages m_1 and m_2 appear in $d_i(t)$ at time $t \geq 0$. Assume that $m_1 \in C(m_2)$ when m_2 is broadcast. Let p_j be the process trusted by Ω_i at the time p_i adopts the sequence $d_i(t)$. If m_2 appears in

$d_i(t)$, that implies that the edge (m_1, m_2) appears in CG_j at the time p_j executes $UpdatePromote$ (since p_j previously executed $UnionCG$ that includes at least m and the set of edges $\{(m', m)|m' \in C(m)\}$ in CG_j). The construction of $UpdatePromote$ ensures us that m_1 appears before m_2 in $d_i(t)$, that proves that $\mathcal{ETOB}$ satisfies the TOB-Causal-Order property.

In conclusion, $\mathcal{ETOB}$ is an implementation of ETOB assuming that processes have access to the Ω failure detector in any environment. □

6. RELATED WORK

Modern data service providers such as Amazon's Dynamo [7], Yahoo's PNUTs [6] or Google Bigtable distributed storage [4] are intended to offer highly available services. They consequently replicate those services over several server processes. In order to tolerate process failures as well as partitions, they consider eventual consistency [25, 29, 28].

The term *eventual* consensus was introduced in [19]. It refers to one instance of consensus which stabilizes at the end; not multiple instances as we consider in this paper. In [9], a self-stabilizing form of consensus was proposed: assuming a self-stabilizing implementation of $\diamond S$ (also described in the paper) and executing a sequence of consensus instances, validity and agreement are eventually ensured. Their consensus abstraction is close to ours but the authors focused on the shared-memory model and did not address the question of the weakest failure detector.

In [11], the intuition behind eventual consistency was captured through the concept of eventual serializability. Two kinds of operations were defined: (1) a "stable" operation of which response needs to be totally ordered after all operations preceding it and (2) "weak" operations of which responses might not reflect all their preceding operations. Our ETOB abstraction captures consistency with respect to the "weak" operations. (Our lower bound on the necessity of Ω naturally extends to the stronger definitions.)

Our perspective on eventual consistency is closely related to the notion of *eventual linearizability* discussed recently in [27] and [16]. It is shown in [27] that the weakest failure detector to boost eventually linearizable objects to linearizable ones is $\diamond P$. We are focusing primarily on the weakest failure detector to *implement* eventual consistency, so their result is orthogonal to ours.

In [16], eventual linearizability is compared against linearizability in the context of implementing specific objects in a shared-memory context. It turns out that an eventually linearizable implementation of a *fetch-and-increment* object is as hard to achieve as a linearizable one. Our ETOB construction can be seen as an *eventually linearizable universal construction*: given any sequential object type, ETOB provides an eventually linearizable concurrent implementation of it. Brought to the message-passing environment with a correct majority, our results complement [16]: we show that in this setting, an eventually consistent replicated service (eventually linearizable object with a sequential specification) requires exactly the same information about failures as a consistent (linearizable) one.

7. CONCLUDING REMARKS

This paper defined the abstraction of eventual total order broadcast and proved its equivalence to eventual consensus: two fundamental building blocks to implement a general replicated state machine that ensures eventual consistency. We proved that the weakest failure detector to implement these abstractions is Ω, in any message-passing environment. We could hence determine the gap between building a general replicated state machine that ensures consistency in a message-passing system and one that ensures only eventual consistency. In terms of information about failures, this gap is precisely captured by failure detector Σ [8]. In terms of time complexity, the gap is exactly one message delay: an operation on the strongly consistent replicated must, in the worst case, incur three communication steps [23], while one build using our eventually total order broadcast protocol completes an operation in the optimal number of two communication steps.

Our ETOB abstraction captures a form of eventual consistency implemented in multiple replicated services [7, 6, 4]. In addition to eventual consistency guarantees, such systems sometimes produce indications when a prefix of operations on the replicated service is *committed*, i.e., is not subject to further changes. A prefix of operations can be committed, *e.g.*, in sufficiently long periods of synchrony, when a majority of correct processes elect the same leader and all incoming and outgoing messages of the leader to the correct majority are delivered within some fixed bound. We believe that such indications could easily be implemented, during the stable periods, on top of ETOB. Naturally, our results imply that Ω is necessary for such systems too.

Our EC abstraction assumes eventual agreement, but requires integrity and validity to be always ensured. Other definitions of eventual consensus could be considered. In particular, we have studied an eventual consensus abstraction assuming, instead of eventual agrement, *eventual integrity*, *i.e.*, a bounded number of decisions in a given consensus instance could be revoked a finite number of times. In the companion technical report [10], we define this abstraction of eventual *irrevocable* consensus (EIC) more precisely and show that it is equivalent to our EC abstraction.

8. REFERENCES

[1] E. A. Brewer. Towards robust distributed systems (abstract). In *Proceedings of the Nineteenth Annual ACM Symposium on Principles of Distributed Computing*, PODC '00, pages 7–, 2000.

[2] T. D. Chandra, V. Hadzilacos, and S. Toueg. The weakest failure detector for solving consensus. *J. ACM*, 43(4):685–722, July 1996.

[3] T. D. Chandra and S. Toueg. Unreliable failure detectors for reliable distributed systems. *J. ACM*, 43(2):225–267, Mar. 1996.

[4] F. Chang, J. Dean, S. Ghemawat, W. C. Hsieh, D. A. Wallach, M. Burrows, T. Chandra, A. Fikes, and R. E. Gruber. Bigtable: A distributed storage system for structured data. *ACM Trans. Comput. Syst.*, 26(2):4:1–4:26, June 2008.

[5] B. Charron-Bost and G. Tel. Approximation d'une borne inférieure répartie. Technical Report LIX/RR/94/06, Laboratoire d'Informatique LIX, École Polytechnique, Sept. 1994.

[6] B. F. Cooper, R. Ramakrishnan, U. Srivastava, A. Silberstein, P. Bohannon, H.-A. Jacobsen, N. Puz, D. Weaver, and R. Yerneni. Pnuts: Yahoo!'s hosted data serving platform. *Proc. VLDB Endow.*, 1(2):1277–1288, Aug. 2008.

[7] G. DeCandia, D. Hastorun, M. Jampani, G. Kakulapati, A. Lakshman, A. Pilchin, S. Sivasubramanian, P. Vosshall, and W. Vogels. Dynamo: Amazon's highly available key-value store.

In *Proceedings of Twenty-first ACM SIGOPS Symposium on Operating Systems Principles*, SOSP '07, pages 205–220, New York, NY, USA, 2007. ACM.

[8] C. Delporte-Gallet, H. Fauconnier, and R. Guerraoui. Tight failure detection bounds on atomic object implementations. *J. ACM*, 57(4), 2010.

[9] S. Dolev, R. I. Kat, and E. M. Schiller. When consensus meets self-stabilization. *Journal of Computer and System Sciences*, 76(8):884 – 900, 2010.

[10] S. Dubois, R. Guerraoui, P. Kuznetsov, F. Petit, and P. Sens. The weakest failure detector for eventual consistency. *CoRR*, abs/X.X, 2015.

[11] A. Fekete, D. Gupta, V. Luchangco, N. Lynch, and A. Shvartsman. Eventually-serializable data services. In *Proceedings of the Fifteenth Annual ACM Symposium on Principles of Distributed Computing*, PODC '96, pages 300–309, New York, NY, USA, 1996. ACM.

[12] M. J. Fischer, N. A. Lynch, and M. S. Paterson. Impossibility of distributed consensus with one faulty process. *J. ACM*, 32(2):374–382, Apr. 1985.

[13] F. C. Freiling, R. Guerraoui, and P. Kuznetsov. The failure detector abstraction. *ACM Comput. Surv.*, 43(2):9:1–9:40, Feb. 2011.

[14] S. Gilbert and N. Lynch. Brewer's conjecture and the feasibility of consistent, available, partition-tolerant web services. *SIGACT News*, 33(2):51–59, June 2002.

[15] R. Guerraoui, V. Hadzilacos, P. Kuznetsov, and S. Toueg. The weakest failure detectors to solve quittable consensus and nonblocking atomic commit. *SIAM J. Comput.*, 41(6):1343–1379, 2012.

[16] R. Guerraoui and E. Ruppert. A paradox of eventual linearizability in shared memory. In *Proceedings of the 2014 ACM Symposium on Principles of Distributed Computing*, PODC '14, pages 40–49, 2014.

[17] V. Hadzilacos and S. Toueg. A modular approach to fault-tolerant broadcasts and related problems. Technical Report TR 94-1425, Department of Computer Science, Cornell University, May 1994.

[18] P. Jayanti and S. Toueg. Every problem has a weakest failure detector. In *PODC*, pages 75–84, 2008.

[19] F. Kuhn, Y. Moses, and R. Oshman. Coordinated consensus in dynamic networks. In *Proceedings of the 30th Annual ACM Symposium on Principles of Distributed Computing (PODC)*, pages 1–10. ACM, 2011.

[20] A. Lakshman and P. Malik. Cassandra: A decentralized structured storage system. *SIGOPS Oper. Syst. Rev.*, 44(2):35–40, Apr. 2010.

[21] L. Lamport. Proving the correctness of multiprocessor programs. *Transactions on software engineering*, 3(2):125–143, Mar. 1977.

[22] L. Lamport. The Part-Time parliament. *ACM Transactions on Computer Systems*, 16(2):133–169, May 1998.

[23] L. Lamport. Lower bounds for asynchronous consensus. *Distributed Computing*, 19(2):104–125, 2006.

[24] A. Mostefaoui, M. Raynal, and F. Tronel. From binary consensus to multivalued consensus in asynchronous message-passing systems. *Inf. Process. Lett.*, 73(5-6):207–212, Mar. 2000.

[25] Y. Saito and M. Shapiro. Optimistic replication. *ACM Comput. Surv.*, 37(1):42–81, Mar. 2005.

[26] F. B. Schneider. Implementing fault-tolerant services using the state machine approach: A tutorial. *ACM Computing Surveys*, 22(4):299–319, Dec. 1990.

[27] M. Serafini, D. Dobre, M. Majuntke, P. Bokor, and N. Suri. Eventually linearizable shared objects. In A. W. Richa and R. Guerraoui, editors, *Proceedings of the 29th Annual ACM Symposium on Principles of Distributed Computing*, pages 95–104. ACM, 2010.

[28] A. Singh, P. Fonseca, P. Kuznetsov, R. Rodrigues, and P. Maniatis. Zeno: Eventually consistent byzantine-fault tolerance. In *Proceedings of the 6th USENIX Symposium on Networked Systems Design and Implementation*, NSDI'09, pages 169–184, Berkeley, CA, USA, 2009. USENIX Association.

[29] W. Vogels. Eventually consistent. *Commun. ACM*, 52(1):40–44, Jan. 2009.

Limitations of Highly-Available Eventually-Consistent Data Stores

Hagit Attiya
Computer Science Department
Technion

Faith Ellen
Department of Computer Science
University of Toronto

Adam Morrison
Computer Science Department
Technion

ABSTRACT

Modern *replicated data stores* aim to provide high availability, by immediately responding to client requests, often by implementing objects that expose concurrency. Such objects, for example, multi-valued registers (MVRs), do not have sequential specifications. This paper explores a recent model for replicated data stores that can be used to precisely specify *causal consistency* for such objects, and liveness properties like *eventual consistency*, without revealing details of the underlying implementation. The model is used to prove the following results:

- An eventually consistent data store implementing MVRs cannot satisfy a consistency model strictly stronger than *observable causal consistency* ($\mathcal{OCC}$). $\mathcal{OCC}$ is a model somewhat stronger than causal consistency, which captures executions in which client observations can use causality to infer concurrency of operations. This result holds under certain assumptions about the data store.
- Under the same assumptions, an eventually consistent and causally consistent replicated data store must send messages of unbounded size: If s objects are supported by n replicas, then, for every $k > 1$, there is an execution in which an $\Omega(\min\{n, s\}k)$-bit message is sent.

Categories and Subject Descriptors

C.2.4 [**Computer Systems Organization**]: Distributed Systems

Keywords

Replicated data store; causal consistency; eventual consistency

1. INTRODUCTION

Distributed data storage provides fault-tolerant access to objects by replicating them over a wide-area network. A *replicated data store* needs to balance between *availability* of data (i.e. accesses to data return without delay), and its *consistency*, while tolerating message delays. The *CAP theorem* [8,18] demonstrates the difficulty of achieving this balance, showing that strong *C*onsistency (i.e. *atomicity*) cannot be satisfied together with high *A*vailability and *P*artition tolerance.

One aspect of data consistency is a safety property restricting the possible values observed by clients accessing different replicas. The set of possible executions is called a *consistency model*. For example, *causal consistency* [2] ensures that the causes of an operation are visible at a replica no later than the operation itself. (A precise definition appears in Section 3.) A smaller set of possible executions means that there is less uncertainty about the data. So, one consistency model is *strictly stronger* than another if its executions are a proper subset of the executions of the other.

Some weak consistency models can be trivially satisfied by never updating the data. Therefore, another aspect of data consistency is a liveness property, ensuring that updates are applied at all replicas. The designers of many systems, e.g., Dynamo [13] and Cassandra [1], opt for a very weak liveness property called, somewhat confusingly, *eventual consistency* [5,9,10,29]. Eventual consistency only ensures that each replica eventually observes all updates to the object, a property also referred to as *update propagation* [11].

Several data stores [4,6,16,21,22] satisfy causal consistency, motivated by the assumption that it is the strongest consistency model possible with eventual consistency. Towards resolving this assumption, this paper shows that an eventually consistent data store cannot satisfy a consistency model strictly stronger than *observable causal consistency* ($\mathcal{OCC}$). This is done within a precise model of replicated data stores, exposing assumptions and inherent costs.

A challenge in modeling replicated data stores is that many of them implement objects that cannot be specified sequentially. For example, in a *multi-value register* (MVR) [13], a read returns the set of values written by currently conflicting writes, i.e., writes that are not causally related. Similarly, an *observed-remove set* (ORset) [27] specifies that whenever a `remove` and an `add` of the same element are concurrent, the `add` "wins." By exposing concurrency in the specification, such objects are leaking low-level scheduling details to the client.

Specifying these objects independently of their implementation is particularly challenging in the context of causal consistency, whose definition relies on *visibility* of operations. Visibility of operations, in turn, depends on message sending and delivery, which are governed by the implemen-

Permission to make digital or hard copies of all or part of this work for personal or classroom use is granted without fee provided that copies are not made or distributed for profit or commercial advantage and that copies bear this notice and the full citation on the first page. Copyrights for components of this work owned by others than ACM must be honored. Abstracting with credit is permitted. To copy otherwise, or republish, to post on servers or to redistribute to lists, requires prior specific permission and/or a fee. Request permissions from permissions@acm.org.
PODC'15, July 21–23, 2015, Donostia-San Sebastián, Spain.
Copyright is held by the owner/author(s). Publication rights licensed to ACM.
ACM 978-1-4503-3617-8 /15/07 ...$15.00.
http://dx.doi.org/10.1145/2767386.2767419.

tation. Following [10], we separate the *abstract execution*, as observed by clients of the replicated data store, from the *concrete execution*, which happens "under the hood" of the system.

This paper shows that a consistency model strictly stronger than $\mathcal{OCC}$ cannot be satisfied by an eventually consistent data store implementing MVRs. $\mathcal{OCC}$ captures executions in which client observations can use causality to infer concurrency of operations (see Section 5). This result holds under certain assumptions about the data store: read operations do not modify the state, and messages are generated only following an operation. Without these assumptions, a data store may trivially satisfy a consistency model stronger than $\mathcal{OCC}$ (and causal consistency) by ruling out some causally consistent executions. For example, a data store in which reads may modify replica state can prevent the execution in which replica R writes a value v to an MVR and then another replica R' reads this value, by not exposing v at R' until K additional operations have been applied at R'.

Our result is related to the *CAC theorem* [23,24], showing that natural causal *C*onsistency is the strongest model that can be satisfied together with high *A*vailability and one-way *C*onvergence. (One-way convergence is a stronger liveness property than eventual consistency.) Our proof, and the assumptions it exposes, show that the CAC theorem has an implicit model for the way implementations are structured. Counter-example implementations like the one mentioned above demonstrate that deviating from this structure allows a consistency model stronger than causal consistency to be satisfied. (A detailed comparison appears in Section 5.3.)

We also prove that causally consistent and eventually consistent stores implementing MVRs require messages of unbounded length. Specifically, if s objects are supported by n replicas, then, for every $k > 1$, there is an execution, whose length grows with k, in which an $\Omega(\min\{n, s\} \lg k)$-bit message is sent. This extends a result of Charron-Bost [12], showing that ordering $\Omega(n^2)$ events on n nodes using m-tuples (i.e. vector clocks [17,25]) requires $m \geq n$. In contrast, our result does not assume that messages have a particular format, and we show that, even for a fixed number of replicas and objects, the message length is unbounded.

2. MODEL

We model a highly-available replicated data store as a message-passing system, consisting of *replicas* that handle client operations on the replicated objects, and communicate the changes to each other with messages. We assume replicas *broadcast* their messages to all other replicas; replicas can implement point-to-point communication by ignoring messages for which they are not the intended recipient. Our model is mostly standard, with the following exception: Replicas handle client operations *immediately*, without communicating with other replicas. This models the crucial *high-availability* property of the data store—completion of a client operation must not depend on communication with another replica, so that the data store remains available despite network failures.

Replicas: We model a replica as a state machine $R = (\Sigma, \sigma_0, E, \Delta)$, where Σ is a set of *states*, $\sigma_0 \in \Sigma$ is the *initial state*, E is a set of possible *events*, and $\Delta : \Sigma \times E \to \Sigma$ is a (partial) *transition function*. We say that an event e is enabled in state σ if $\Delta(\sigma, e)$ is defined. A state transition is a local step of a replica, describing how the state of the replica changes in response to an enabled event. Three kinds of events model interactions of the replica with its clients and with other replicas:

- *do(o,op,v)*: a client of the replica invokes operation *op* on replicated object o and immediately receives response v from the replica,
- *send(m)*: the replica broadcasts message m, and
- *receive(m)*: the replica receives message m.

The *action*, act(e), of an event e specifies which kind of event (*do*, *send*, or *receive*) it is. Each *send(m)* and *receive(m)* event e has message attribute msg(e) $= m$. Each *do(o,op,v)* event e has attributes obj(e) $= o$, which is the object the client is operating on, op(e) $=$ *op*, which is the operation of the client, and rval(e) $= v$, which is the response the client receives.

We assume that the content of a message sent by a replica is a deterministic function of its state: if $\Delta(\sigma, \mathit{send}(m_1)) = \sigma_1$ and $\Delta(\sigma, \mathit{send}(m_2)) = \sigma_2$, then $m_1 = m_2$ and hence, $\sigma_1 = \sigma_2$.

Executions: An *execution* is a (possibly infinite) sequence of events occurring at the replicas. It is an interleaving of a sequence of events occurring at each replica. We denote by $R(e)$ the replica at which an event e occurs. A (finite or infinite) sequence of events, $e_1, e_2, \ldots$, occurring at a replica $R = (\Sigma, \sigma_0, \Delta)$ is *well-formed* if there is a sequence of states, $\sigma_1, \sigma_2, \ldots$, such that $\sigma_i = \Delta(\sigma_{i-1}, e_i)$ for all $1 \leq i \leq$ the length of the sequence. If this sequence has length n, then σ_n is the *state of R at the end of the sequence.*

We consider only well-formed executions.

DEFINITION 1. *An execution α is* well-formed *if for every replica $R = (\Sigma, \sigma_0, \Delta)$, (1) the subsequence of events at R, denoted $\alpha|_R$, is well-formed, and (2) for every receive(m) event e at R, a send(m) event at replica $R' \neq R$ precedes e in α. If α is finite then* the state of replica R at the end of α *is the state of R at the end of $\alpha|_R$.*

Well-formed executions only prohibit messages from appearing out of thin air or being received before they are sent. Messages may be dropped, delivered out of order, or delivered multiple times.

Recall the happens-before relation [20]:

DEFINITION 2. *Let α be an execution. Event $e \in \alpha$ happens before event $e' \in \alpha$ (written $e \xrightarrow{hb(\alpha)} e'$, or simply $e \xrightarrow{hb} e'$ if the context is clear) if one of the following conditions holds:*

(1) Thread of execution: $R(e) = R(e')$ *and e precedes e' in α.*

(2) Message delivery: $e = \mathit{send}(m)$ *and* $e' = \mathit{receive}(m)$.

(3) Transitivity: *There is an event $f \in \alpha$, such that $e \xrightarrow{hb} f$ and $f \xrightarrow{hb} e'$.*

PROPOSITION 1. *Let α be an execution, and e an event in α. Then the following sequences of events are well-formed executions:*

1. *β, the subsequence of α consisting of all events e' such that $e \stackrel{hb}{\not\to} e'$.*

2. γ, *the subsequence of* α *consisting of all events* e' *such that* $e' \xrightarrow{hb} e$.

Further, for any replica R, $\beta|_R$ *and* $\gamma|_R$ *are prefixes of* $\alpha|_R$.

Network partitions: *Eventually consistent* data stores require that every operation *eventually* propagates to every other replica. To facilitate eventual consistency, we must require that the network is not partitioned from some point on. We assume that this cannot occur in *infinite* executions. Specifically, we consider only infinite executions in which the network is *sufficiently connected*, as defined below.

We say that a replica *has a message pending in state* σ if some event e with $\text{act}(e) = \textit{send}$ is enabled in σ. We assume that a replica does not have a message pending following a send event. In other words, a send event relays everything the replica has to send. Given an execution α and an event $e \in \alpha$, we say that a replica R *has a message pending in* e if R has a message pending in the state at the end of $\alpha'|_R$, where α' is the prefix of α ending with e.

DEFINITION 3. *The network is* sufficiently connected *in an infinite well-formed execution* α *if the following conditions hold:*

(1) Eventual transmission: *no replica has a message pending in all events of some (infinite) suffix of* α*, and*

(2) Eventual delivery: *if replica* R *sends message* m*, then every replica* $R' \neq R$ *eventually receives* m.

Thus, if a replica wants to send a message, i.e. it has a message pending in some state, then either it eventually broadcasts the message *or* it transitions into a state with no message pending without sending the message. This could happen, for example, if a client invokes an operation which cancels a previous operation that had not yet propagated to other replicas.

3. REASONING ABOUT REPLICATED DATA STORES

This section describes a framework for reasoning about highly-available replicated data stores, following Burckhardt et al. [10].

3.1 Specifying Replicated Objects

Replicated data stores are often used to implement objects which have some underlying notion of concurrency, and so cannot be specified sequentially. They generalize standard sequential specifications [19] as follows. A sequential specification of a deterministic object determines the return value of an operation from the sequence of prior operations applied to the object. However, with a replicated object, operations executing at different replicas might have inconsistent notions of "prior operations", e.g., because updates made on one side of a partition do not propagate to the other side. We therefore specify the return value of an operation based on operations that are *visible* to it: prior operations at the same replica, and remote operations whose effects have propagated to the replica through the network.

Visibility is defined in the context of an *abstract execution*. An abstract execution contains only the *histories* of operations invoked by the clients, i.e., only *do* events:

DEFINITION 4. *An* abstract execution *is a tuple* (H, vis)*, where* H *is a sequence of do events and* $vis \subseteq H \times H$ *is an acyclic* visibility relation *(where* $(e_1, e_2) \in vis$ *is denoted by* $e_1 \xrightarrow{vis} e_2$*) that satisfies (1) if* e_1 *precedes* e_2 *in* H *and* $R(e_1) = R(e_2)$*, then* $e_1 \xrightarrow{vis} e_2$*, (2) if* $e_1 \xrightarrow{vis} e_2$*,* e_2 *precedes* e_3 *in* H*, and* $R(e_2) = R(e_3)$*, then* $e_1 \xrightarrow{vis} e_3$*, and (3) if* $e_1 \xrightarrow{vis} e_2$ *then* e_1 *precedes* e_2 *in* H.

We decouple visibility—when an operation becomes *observable* by the client—from the low-level happens-before relation (Definition 2), defined for receiving and sending messages between replicas, because having happens-before imply observability of an operation would place excessively strict demands on the data store. It would mean that receiving a message sent after an operation *op* makes *op* and *all its transitive dependencies* observable. This disallows, for example, buffering received information and not "exposing" it immediately, an implementation technique used in many causally consistent data stores to avoid sending the dependencies with each message [4,6,16,21,22] and to satisfy consistency conditions [11,15,26].

The reason for including both the visibility relation, *vis*, and a total order of the events, H, is that some specifications need a total order on events to resolve conflicts created by concurrent operations, i.e., those that are not related by visibility.

DEFINITION 5. *Let* $A = (H, vis)$ *be an abstract execution. An abstract execution* $A' = (H', vis')$ *is a* prefix *of* A *if (1)* H' *is a prefix of* H *and (2)* $vis' = vis \cap (H' \times H')$*. A set* $\mathcal{S}$ *of abstract executions is* prefixed-closed *if* $A \in \mathcal{S}$ *implies that* $A' \in S$ *for every prefix* A' *of* A.

An abstract execution $A = (H, vis)$ is *o-only* if $\text{obj}(e) = o$, for all $e \in H$.

DEFINITION 6. *A* replicated object specification *of an object o is a prefix-closed set* $\mathcal{S}(o)$ *of o-only abstract executions.*

The specification, $\mathcal{S}(o)$, of an object o is defined using the notion of an *operation context* [10]. The *operation context* of an operation on an object o consists of the prior operations on o that are visible to the operation:

DEFINITION 7. *Let* $A = (H, vis)$ *be an abstract execution, and* $e \in H$*. The* operation context of e in A *is the abstract execution* $ctxt(A, e) = (H', vis \cap (V_e \times V_e))$*, where* $V_e = \left\{e' \in H \mid e' \xrightarrow{vis} e \wedge obj(e') = obj(e)\right\} \cup \{e\}$*, and* H' *is the subsequence of* H *containing only events in* V_e*. If* $e' \in H$*, we say that* $e' \in ctxt(A, e)$ *iff* $e' \in H'$.

We specify the return value, $rval(e)$, of a *do* event e applying an operation to object o as a function of its operation context, $ctxt(A, e)$:

$$\text{rval}(e) = f_o(ctxt(A, e)).$$

Figure 1 shows examples of such functions, including those of the *multi-value register* (MVR) and the *observed-remove set* (ORset). In an MVR, a read returns the set of values written by currently conflicting writes—i.e. writes that are not causally related. Similarly, an ORset specifies that whenever a `remove` and `add` are concurrent, the `add` "wins"—i.e., `remove` only removes items that it observes.

The specification $\mathcal{S}(o)$ contains abstract executions in which every operation's response is as specified above:

$$f_{\text{r/w reg}}(H', vis', e) = \begin{cases} \texttt{ok} & \text{if op}(e)\text{=write}(v) \\ v, \text{ where the last write event in } H \text{ is write}(v) & \text{if op}(e)\text{=read} \end{cases}$$

(a) Read/write register

$$f_{\text{MVR}}(H', vis', e) = \begin{cases} \texttt{ok} & \text{if op}(e)\text{=write}(v) \\ \{v \mid \exists e_1 \in H \text{ op}(e_1) = \text{write}(v) \wedge \neg\exists e_2 \in H \text{ op}(e_2) = \text{write}(\cdot) \wedge e_1 \xrightarrow{vis} e_2\} & \text{if op}(e)\text{=read} \end{cases}$$

(b) Multi-valued register (MVR)

$$f_{\text{ORset}}(H', vis', e) = \begin{cases} \texttt{ok} & \text{if op}(e)\text{=add}(v) \\ \texttt{ok} & \text{if op}(e)\text{=remove}(v) \\ \{v \mid \exists e_1 \in H \text{ op}(e_1) = \text{add}(v) \wedge \neg\exists e_2 \in H \text{ op}(e_2) = \text{remove}(v) \wedge e_1 \xrightarrow{vis} e_2\} & \text{if op}(e)\text{=read} \end{cases}$$

(c) Observed-remove set (ORset)

Figure 1: Functions specifying replicated objects: $ctxt(A, e) = (H', vis', e)$.

$$\mathcal{S}(o) = \{ A \mid A = (H, vis) \text{ is an } o\text{-only abstract execution, and } \forall e \in H, \text{rval}(e) = f_o(ctxt(A, e)) \}$$

3.2 Consistency Models

Informally, a *safety property* ensures that nothing "bad" happens in an execution, and hence, the same is true for any of its prefixes. We are interested in safety properties of abstract executions, e.g. *correctness*, which says that all objects conform to their specification.

DEFINITION 8. *An abstract execution $A = (H, vis)$ is* correct *if for every object o,*

$$A|_o = (H|_o, vis \cap (H|_o \times H|_o)) \in \mathcal{S}(o),$$

where $H|_o$ is the subsequence of H consisting of events e with obj(e) = o, and $\mathcal{S}(o)$ is the specification of o.

The definition of correctness, like other definitions soon to follow, aims to restrict the responses returned by a data store to high-level object operations, while leaving the low-level details of message transmissions unspecified. We can apply these definitions to a data store execution by considering the abstract execution in which the high-level operations occur in the same order on each replica and return the same responses:

DEFINITION 9. *Execution α* complies with *an abstract execution $A = (H, vis)$ if for every replica R, $H|_R = \alpha|_R^{do}$, where $\alpha|_R^{do}$ denotes the subsequence of do events by replica R.*

DEFINITION 10. *A data store D is* correct *if every execution α of D complies with a correct abstract execution.*

Henceforth, we consider only correct data stores.

We say that abstract executions $A = (H, vis)$ and $A' = (H', vis')$ are *equivalent*, or $A \equiv A'$, if for every replica R, $H|_R = H'|_R$. (Notice that if an execution α complies with A, then any abstract execution A' that α complies with it is equivalent to A.) A *consistency model* is a prefix-closed set of abstract executions that is closed under equivalence. It extends the concept of object specification to handle multiple objects. Analogously, *satisfying a consistency model* extends the concept of correctness for a data store:

DEFINITION 11. *A data store D* satisfies *a consistency model* $\mathcal{C}$ *if every execution α of D complies with some $A \in \mathcal{C}$.*

Causal consistency guarantees that effects are visible only after their causes. In other words, if e_1 is visible to e_2 and e_2 is visible to e_3, then e_1 is visible to e_3:

DEFINITION 12. *A correct abstract execution $A = (H, vis)$ is* causally consistent *if vis is transitive: if $e_1 \xrightarrow{vis} e_2$ and $e_2 \xrightarrow{vis} e_3$, then $e_1 \xrightarrow{vis} e_3$.*

Causal memory [2] can be seen as a special case of this definition, capturing only read/write registers. It has been widely adopted in distributed key/value stores [4, 6, 14, 16, 21, 22, 30], but extending to general, replicated data types seems to require using a framework like the one used here.

3.3 Eventual Consistency

Informally, a *liveness property* promises that something "good" eventually happens in an execution. The distinguishing feature of liveness is that it cannot be violated by any finite execution [3]—it is always possible that the required "good thing" will occur in the future. In our context, a "good thing" is an operation becoming visible.

DEFINITION 13. *An infinite abstract execution $A = (H, vis)$ is* eventually consistent *if for every event $e \in H$, there are only finitely many events $e' \in H$ such that obj(e') = obj(e) and $e \not\xrightarrow{vis} e'$.*

Observe that eventual consistency is a property of abstract executions because *visibility* is defined for abstract executions only. In other words, while our network model guarantees eventual message delivery, the delivery of a message about some operation does not guarantee that the data store will *choose* to make that operation visible. As with consistency models, we bridge the high-level and low-level worlds using compliance:

DEFINITION 14. *A data store D is* eventually consistent *if, for every infinite execution α of D, every abstract execution that α complies with is eventually consistent.*

3.4 Exposing Concurrency in Specifications

Perrin et al. have shown that a replicated object can be implemented so that client operations appear to be totally ordered (by breaking ties between concurrent operations in the same manner in every replica). They thus argue that replicated objects should be specified with sequential specifications [26]. Indeed, with a single object, concurrency can be "hidden," in the sense that the client cannot detect that concurrent operations exist and are being arbitrarily ordered.

Imagine that a data store implementing a single MVR object arbitrarily orders concurrent writes and exposes only one of them to the clients—in effect, implementing a read-/write register instead of an MVR. The clients cannot detect that this is happening, because there is always an MVR abstract execution consistent with their observations.

In contrast, with *multiple* objects, the combination of causal and eventual consistency allows clients to infer concurrency of operations even if the data store tries to "hide" it by ordering them. Figure 2 shows how the causal and eventual consistency requirements enable the client to infer concurrency of operations if multiple objects are supported. In the execution depicted, there are three MVRs shown as differently shaded circles. The data store must return $\bot$ as a response to r_z since $w_z \not\xrightarrow{hb} r_z$ (Proposition 2 in Section 4), and similarly for r_y. Suppose the data store orders w_x^1 before w_x^2, and thus reads from x return w_x^2. The client can still infer w_x^1 and w_x^2 are concurrent, because had w_x^1 been visible at R_2 when w_x^2 was executed, r_y should have returned w_y. (A symmetric argument applies if w_x^2 is ordered before w_x^1.)

Therefore, wince we consider multiple objects and causal consistency, we use replicated object specifications that incorporate concurrency.

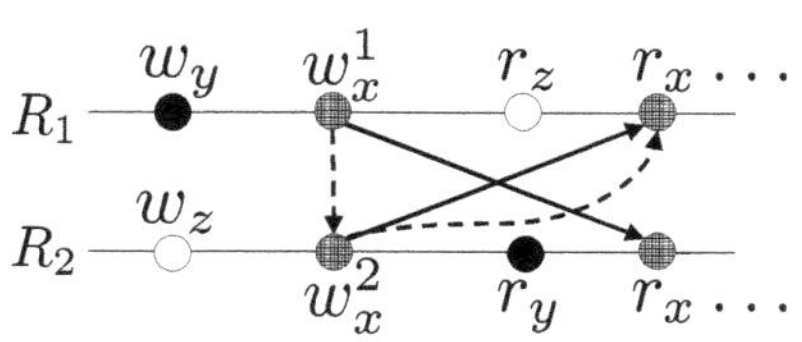

Figure 2: Causal links (dashed arrows) implied by r_x returning only the value of w_x^2 contradict information flow in messages (solid arrows), since they imply that r_y should return w_y's value.

4. WRITE-PROPAGATING DATA STORES

A *write-propagating* data store is an eventually consistent data store whose implementation (i.e., replica state machine) satisfies two properties, *invisible reads* and *op-driven messages*, defined next. Every highly-available replicated data storage system we are aware of [6,10,13,14,16,21,28,30] has these properties, when viewed in our model (i.e., ignoring issues such as timeouts for retransmitting dropped messages).

A data store has *op-driven messages* if it generates messages only as a result of a client operation, and not in response to a received message:

DEFINITION 15. *A data store D has* op-driven messages *if for any replica $R = (\Sigma, \sigma_0, E, \Delta)$, (1) R does not have a message pending in σ_0, and (2) if $\Delta(\sigma_1, receive(m)) = \sigma_2$ and R does not have a message pending in σ_1, then R does not have a message pending in σ_2.*

A data store has *invisible reads* if a client read operation does not change the state of the replica:

DEFINITION 16. *A data store D has* invisible reads *if for any replica $R = (\Sigma, \sigma_0, E, \Delta)$, if $\Delta(\sigma_1, e) = \sigma_2$ and $op(e) = read$, then $\sigma_1 = \sigma_2$.*

In this paper, we concentrate on data stores providing MVRs, as they expose concurrency and are used in real systems [10, 13, 21]. To simplify notation, we begin the names of events invoking write operations with w and begin the names of events invoking read operations with r. We assume that each write event writes a different value, so we do not distinguish between the event $w = do(o, write, v)$ and its value v; e.g., we say that $w \in \text{rval}(r)$, instead of saying that the value written by the event w is in $\text{rval}(r)$.

We proceed to prove several key properties of write-propagating data stores, which serve as building blocks for the proofs of our main results.

A basic property, which holds for *any* data store providing MVRs, is that if read r returns some write w, then w happens before r.

PROPOSITION 2. *Let D be a data store providing MVRs and α be an execution of D. Let $A = (H, vis)$ an abstract execution that α complies with. Let r be a $do(o, read, V)$ event and w be a $do(o, write, v)$ event such that $v \in V$. Then $w \xrightarrow{hb} r$.*

We show (in Corollary 4 below) that write-propagating data stores, i.e. with invisible reads and op-driven messages, satisfy the original definition of eventual consistency [29], i.e., that "if clients stop issuing update requests, then the replicas will eventually reach a consistent state." We first define *quiescent executions*, in which no message is "in flight."

DEFINITION 17. *A finite execution α is* quiescent *if for every replica R, (1) R does not have a message pending after its last event in α, and (2) every message R sends in α is received by every replica $R' \neq R$.*

Now we show that if the execution is quiescent, then all replicas are in a consistent state, in the sense that a client operation receives the same response regardless of the replica that executes it.

LEMMA 3. *Let D be an eventually consistent data store with invisible reads. Let α be a quiescent execution of D. If two reads of the same MVR at different replicas are appended to α, then both reads return the same response.*

Finally, we show that if D has op-driven messages, we can extend a finite execution α of D into a quiescent execution α' by (1) sending any message pending at any replica, and then (2) delivering each message in flight to every replica but its sender. There are no messages pending at the end of α', since D has op-driven messages. Therefore, α' is quiescent. This establishes the following corollary of Lemma 3.

COROLLARY 4. *Let D be an eventually consistent data store with invisible reads and op-driven messages. Let α be a finite execution of D. Then α can be extended to an execution in which, for any object o, a read of o that occurs at the end of the extended execution returns the same response no matter at which replica it is performed.*

In most real data store systems, a replica generates a message following a client write operation to propagate the write to remote replicas. We show that a write-propagating data store *must*, in fact, do this, if the execution appears quiescent from the replica's perspective. To reason about individual messages that a replica receives in a given execution, we use the notation $e \xrightarrow{rcv} e'$ to denote that the first message sent by $R(e)$ after e is received by $R(e')$ before e'.

LEMMA 5. *Let D be an eventually consistent data store with invisible reads and op-driven messages. Let α be an execution of D whose last event is a write w at replica R. Suppose that in α, $e \xrightarrow{hb} w \implies e \xrightarrow{rcv} w$ for any do event e. Then R has a message pending following w.*

5. LIMITS OF SATISFIABLE CONSISTENCY MODELS

We explore the *strength* of consistency models satisfiable by eventually consistent replicated data stores. A consistency model $\mathcal{C}'$ is *stronger* than consistency model $\mathcal{C}$ if $\mathcal{C}' \subset \mathcal{C}$, that is, $\mathcal{C}'$ prohibits some abstract executions that $\mathcal{C}$ admits, but not vice versa. We show that a strengthening of causal consistency, *observable causal consistency* ($\mathcal{OCC}$), is the strongest consistency model satisfiable by a write-propagating data store implementing MVRs. To prove that no consistency model stronger than $\mathcal{C}$ is satisfied by a data store D, it suffices to show that, for every $A \in \mathcal{C}$, at least one execution α of D complies with A. (This is because any execution A' that α complies with is equivalent to A. Since $A \in \mathcal{C}$ and $\mathcal{C}$ is closed under equivalence, $A' \in \mathcal{C}$. Thus, it cannot be that D satisfies a stronger consistency model $\mathcal{C}' \subset \mathcal{C}$.)

5.1 Observable causal consistency

Intuitively, in an MVR abstract execution $A = (H, vis)$, vis specifies some information flow between replicas that dictates which prior writes are visible to each executed read, which dictates the return value of each read given this available information. Indeed, for write-propagating data stores, one can construct an execution in which, for each (non-transitive) vis edge (w, r) between events in distinct replicas, $R(w)$ transmits a message after w and $R(r)$ receives this message before r (Section 5.2). In other words, we can reconstruct the information flow given in any MVR abstract execution.

A data store wishing to avoid generating an execution that complies with $A = (H, vis)$ (e.g, to implement a stronger consistency model that does not include A) must return different responses for some of the reads in this execution. How can this be achieved? One way, for example, is to ignore the received information (for a while). However, a data store with invisible reads cannot do this (Section 5.3).

Another option is to "hide" concurrency. For example, if read r returns $\{w_0, w_1\}$ in A, the execution we construct will have w_0 and w_1 concurrent according to happens-before. The data store could still have r return just w_1, but it must make sure that the response it generates complies with *some* abstract execution. As Figure 3a shows, this means finding an abstract execution in which these writes are *ordered*. Intuitively, the data store is pretending that w_0 is visible to w_1 even though $w_0 \not\xrightarrow{hb} w_1$.

This kind of pretense has casuality implications, as demonstrated in Figure 3b. If $w_0 \xrightarrow{vis} w_1$, then w_1' should be visible to r' because of transitivity. However, r' does not know about w_1'. To remain correct, there has to be a write $\hat{w}$ visible to r' which can be artificially ordered after w_1', just like w_0 and w_1 were ordered.

Observable causal consistency ($\mathcal{OCC}$) contains abstract executions whose induced information flow is such that concurrent writes cannot be "hidden" in this way. $\mathcal{OCC}$ contains causally consistent abstract executions that expose concurrency between operations only when the clients can infer this concurrency from their observations, and so it cannot be hidden. $\mathcal{OCC}$ achieves this by requiring that whenever a read returns $\{w_0, w_1\}$, there must exist writes w_0' and w_1' to different objects, such that w_1' is visible to w_0 but not to w_1 (and w_0' is visible to w_1 but not to w_0), and any write $\hat{w}$ to $obj(w_1')$ that is visible to w_1 cannot be concurrent with w_1', i.e., must be visible to w_1' (again, symmetrically for w_0'). This guarantees that w_1 cannot be ordered after w_0 nor w_0 ordered after w_1, as shown in Figure 3c.

DEFINITION 18. *A causally consistent abstract execution $A = (H, vis)$ is* observably causally consistent *($\mathcal{OCC}$) if for any read r of some MVR o for which $rval(r) \supseteq \{w_0, w_1\}$, there exist w_0' and w_1' such that the following conditions hold:*

1. *w_i' is a write that is visible to w_{1-i} but to a different object than o: $w_i' \xrightarrow{vis} w_{i-1}$ and $obj(w_i') \neq o$,*
2. *w_0' and w_1' are writes to different objects: $obj(w_0') \neq obj(w_1')$,*
3. *w_i' is not visible to w_i: $w_i' \not\xrightarrow{vis} w_i$,*
4. *no write to $obj(w_i')$ occurring concurrently with w_i' is visible to w_i: for any $\hat{w}$, if $obj(\hat{w}) = obj(w_i')$ and $\hat{w} \xrightarrow{vis} w_i$, then $\hat{w} \xrightarrow{vis} w_i'$.*

5.2 Impossibility of Stronger Consistency than $\mathcal{OCC}$

THEOREM 6. *Let D be an eventually consistent data store, providing MVRs, with invisible reads and op-driven messages. Then D does not satisfy a consistency model stronger than observable causal consistency ($\mathcal{OCC}$).*

To prove the theorem it suffices to show that for any abstract execution $A \in \mathcal{OCC}$, there is an execution α of D that complies with A. Thus, let $A = (H, vis) \in \mathcal{OCC}$ be an observably causally consistent execution. (In particular, A is causally consistent.) We will construct an execution α that complies with A. We obtain α by a recursive process, in which we deliver messages generated after events to ensure that $hb(\alpha) \subseteq vis$. The crux of the proof is to show that D cannot add "fake" visibility edges, and, hence, every read returns the same response in α as it does in A.

5.2.1 Revealing Executions

An MVR abstract execution $A = (H, vis)$ is *revealing*, if for every write operation $w \in H$, the operation $R(w)$ performs immediately before w is a read operation r_w of the same object and, for every $e \in H$, $r_w \xrightarrow{vis} e \implies w \xrightarrow{vis} e$ if $e \neq w$, and $e \xrightarrow{vis} w \implies e \xrightarrow{vis} r_w$ if $e \neq r_w$. That is, w and r_w are identical with respect to the visibility relation. Consequently, r_w "reveals" the state of the MVR when the write w is applied. This enables us to reason about the write operations that are visible to w, which is otherwise difficult. (In contrast, writes visible to a read can be inferred from the read's response.) The following lemma, proved in the full version, formalizes this intuition:

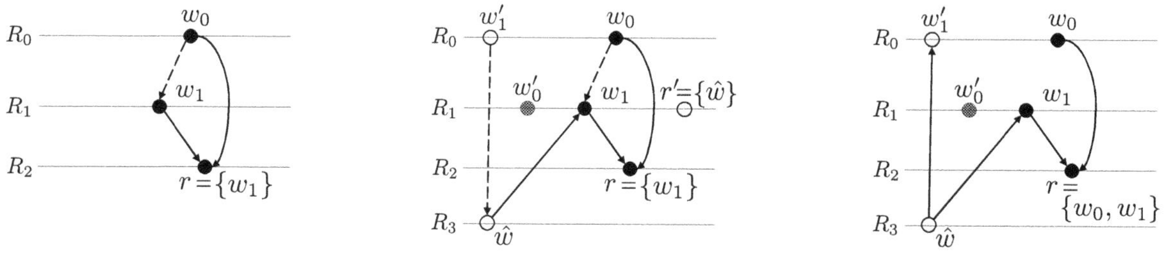

(a) If r returns only w_1, the data store effectively "pretends" that $w_0 \xrightarrow{vis} w_1$.

(b) $w_0 \xrightarrow{vis} w_1$ implies that w_1' should be visible to r'. Here, the data store can pretend that $w_1' \xrightarrow{vis} \hat{w}$ to make the return value of r' valid.

(c) An $\mathcal{OCC}$ execution prevents pretending that $w_1' \xrightarrow{vis} \hat{w}$. In turn, this prevents pretending that $w_0 \xrightarrow{vis} w_1$. Thus r is required to return $\{w_0, w_1\}$.

Figure 3: **Observable causal consistency:** motivation for definition. Circles of the same color correspond to operations on the same MVR object. Solid arrows represent $\xrightarrow{vis}$ edges induced by information flow in messages (i.e., are also $\xrightarrow{hb}$ edges). Dashed arrows represent additional $\xrightarrow{vis}$ edges required to make the execution comply with the MVR specification.

LEMMA 7. *Let $A = (H, vis)$ be a causally consistent revealing MVR abstract execution, $r \in H$ be a read operation in A, and $A' = (H', vis')$, be the operation context of r in A (Definition 7). Let β be an execution of D such that, for all $w \in H'$, $r_w, w \in \beta$. Then for any causally consistent MVR abstract execution $\hat{A} = (\hat{H}, \hat{vis})$ that β complies with, $w' \xrightarrow{vis} w \implies w' \xrightarrow{\hat{vis}} w$ for any $w', w \in H'$.*

Without loss of generality, we assume the $\mathcal{OCC}$ abstract execution A we consider in our proof is revealing. (Due to invisible reads, we can always obtain a revealing abstract execution A' by adding the appropriate r_w operations and vis edges to A, without affecting the response of existing reads in A. Then, for any execution α' of D that complies with A', the execution α obtained by removing the r_w operations from α' is an execution of D that complies with A.)

5.2.2 Recursive Construction of α

We construct the execution α by induction on the length of H. In the base case, $H = \varepsilon$, we take $\alpha = \varepsilon$. For the recursive step, let $H = H'\,e$, and let $R = R(e)$. That is, $op = \text{op}(e)$ is the last high-level operation invoked in α, and it is invoked at replica R on the MVR obj(e). Let $A' = (H', vis')$ be a prefix of A. (By Definition 5, if $e_1 \xrightarrow{vis} e_2$, either $e_1 \xrightarrow{vis'} e_2$ or $e_2 = e$.) Let α' be the execution of D our construction returns for A'. We define α by extending α' in three steps:

(1) Message delivery. Consider the events e' such that $e' \xrightarrow{vis} e$, in the order they occur in H. Let $m_{e'}$ be the first message sent by $R(e')$ after e' in α', if such a message exists. If $m_{e'}$ is not delivered to R in α', we deliver it to R in α by appending a *receive*$(m_{e'})$ event at R.

(2) Invoking op(e). Let $\hat{e}$ be the transition in which op(e) is invoked at R on obj(e). We append $\hat{e}$. (The crux of the proof will be to show that $\hat{e} = e$, i.e., that rval$(\hat{e})$ = rval(e).)

(3) Message sending. If R has a message m pending as a result of $\hat{e}$, we append a *send*(m) event at R.

Before proving that $\hat{e} = e$, we state some properties of α.

PROPOSITION 8. *For any do events $e_0, e_1 \in \alpha$, $e_0 \xrightarrow{hb} e_1 \implies e_0 \xrightarrow{vis} \pi(e_1)$ and, if e_0 and e_1 are at different replicas, then $e_0 \xrightarrow{hb} e_1 \implies e_0 \xrightarrow{rcv} \pi(e_1)$, where $\pi(e_1) = e$ if $e_1 = \hat{e}$, or e_1 otherwise.*

Write operations have an even stronger property: if a write w is visible to some operation e' in A, then $w \xrightarrow{hb} e'$ in α:

PROPOSITION 9. *Let $w, e' \in H$. If $w \xrightarrow{vis} e'$ then $w \xrightarrow{hb} \pi^{-1}(e')$, where $\pi^{-1}(e') = \hat{e}$ if $e' = e$ or e' otherwise.*

5.2.3 α Complies with A

We prove by induction on A that the constructed execution α of D complies with A. The base case, $H = \varepsilon$, is vacuously true. For the inductive step, let $H = H'\,e$, $A' = (H', vis')$ be a prefix of A, and α' the output of our construction on A'. From the induction hypothesis, α' complies with A'. We must therefore prove that $\hat{e}$, the *do* event we invoke at replica R when extending α' to α, returns the same response as the event e in A. If op(e) = write, then rval(e) = ok because the only response the MVR specification allows for a write is `ok`. Thus, because D is correct, it is also the case that rval$(\hat{e})$ = ok. The remaining case, when op(e) = read, follows from the next two lemmas.

LEMMA 10. *$w \in rval(\hat{e}) \implies w \in rval(e)$.*

PROOF. Suppose that $w \in \text{rval}(\hat{e})$ but $w \notin \text{rval}(e)$. Then $w \xrightarrow{hb} \hat{e}$ (Proposition 2) and thus $w \xrightarrow{vis} e$ (Proposition 8). But, as $w \notin \text{rval}(e)$, there exists some $w_1 \in \text{rval}(e)$ such that $w \xrightarrow{vis} w_1 \xrightarrow{vis} e$. Then $w_1 \xrightarrow{hb} \hat{e}$ by Proposition 9.

Let α_0 be the execution obtained by removing from α any event e' such that $e' \not\xrightarrow{hb} \hat{e}$. (By Proposition 1, α_0 is an execution of D.) Let $\alpha_1 = \alpha_0\,\hat{e}$. Then α_1 is an execution of D. R does not have a message pending at the end of α_1 (by construction of α and since D has invisible reads and op-driven messages). If $R' \neq R$ sends a message m in α_1, R receives m in α_1 (by Proposition 8). Let $\beta = \alpha_1\,\alpha_2$ be an execution of D obtained by appending *receive* events to α_1 in some arbitrary order, so that, in β every replica receives every message sent by another replica in α_1. Then β is a quiescent execution, and R receives no messages in α_2, so its state at the of β is the same as its state at the end of α_1.

Now, consider the execution $\beta_\infty = \beta\,\hat{r}_1\,\hat{r}_2\,\ldots$ in which we append to β a sequence of read operations of the MVR obj($\hat{e}$) at R. Then β_∞ is an execution of D and $\hat{r}_i = \hat{e}$ for all $i \geq 1$ (as D has invisible reads). Since D is eventually consistent, β_∞ complies with some causally consistent MVR abstract execution $\hat{A} = (\hat{H}, \hat{vis})$ such that, for some $j \geq 1$, for any *do* event $e' \in \beta$, $e' \xrightarrow{\hat{vis}} \hat{r}_j$.

By Proposition 9, for any $w \in ctxt(A, e)$, $w \xrightarrow{hb} \hat{e}$, and so $r_w \xrightarrow{hb} \hat{e}$ (since $r_w \xrightarrow{hb} w$). Thus, $r_w, w \in \beta$ (and so $r_w, w \in \beta_\infty$). Since $w \xrightarrow{vis} w_1$, Lemma 7 implies that $w \xrightarrow{\hat{vis}} w_1$. Yet $w \in \text{rval}(\hat{r}_j) = \text{rval}(\hat{e})$, although $w \xrightarrow{\hat{vis}} w_1 \xrightarrow{\hat{vis}} r_j$, which contradicts the MVR specification. $\square$

LEMMA 11. $w_0 \in rval(e) \implies w_0 \in rval(\hat{e})$.

PROOF. Suppose that $w_0 \in \text{rval}(e)$ but $w_0 \notin \text{rval}(\hat{e})$. Let $\text{rval}(\hat{e}) = \{w_1, \ldots, w_k\}$. Observe that $w_0, w_1, \ldots, w_k \in ctxt(A, e)$. This follows because (1) for any $w' \in \text{rval}(e)$, $w' \xrightarrow{vis} e$ (MVR specification), (2) $w_0 \in \text{rval}(e)$ by definition, and (3) for $1 \leq i \leq k$, $w_i \in \text{rval}(e)$ by Lemma 10.

Now, for any $1 \leq i \leq k$, $\{w_0, w_i\} \subseteq \text{rval}(e)$, and $A \in \mathcal{OCC}$, so, by Definition 18, there exists a write w_i' by $R(w_0)$ preceding w_0 such that $\text{obj}(w_i') \neq \text{obj}(w_0)$ and $w_i' \not\xrightarrow{vis} w_i$. Notice that $w_i' \in ctxt(A, e)$ since $w_i' \xrightarrow{vis} w_0 \xrightarrow{vis} e$.

Let α_0 be the execution obtained by removing from α any event e' such that $e' \not\xrightarrow{hb} \hat{e}$. (By Proposition 1, α_0 is an execution of D.) Let $\alpha_1 = \alpha_0\,\hat{e}$. Then α_1 is an execution of D. R does not have a message pending at the end of α_1 (by construction of α and since D has invisible reads and op-driven messages). If $R' \neq R$ sends a message m in α_1, R receives m in α_1 (by Proposition 8). Let $\beta = \alpha_1\,\alpha_2$ be an execution of D obtained by appending *receive* events to α_1 in some arbitrary order, so that, in β every replica receives every message sent by another replica in α_1. Then β is a quiescent execution, and R receives no messages in α_2, so its state at the of β is the same as its state at the end of α_1.

Let β' be the execution obtained from β by adding a read r_i' of the MVR $\text{obj}(w_i')$ at $R(w_i)$ immediately after w_i. (Since D has invisible reads, β' is a quiescent execution of D.)

Now, consider the execution $\beta_\infty = \beta'\,\hat{r}_1\,\hat{r}_2\,\ldots$ in which we append to β' a sequence of read operations of the MVR obj($\hat{e}$) at R. Then β_∞ is an execution of D and $\hat{r}_i = \hat{e}$ for all $i \geq 1$ (as D has invisible reads). Since D is eventually consistent, β_∞ complies with some causally consistent MVR abstract execution $\hat{A} = (\hat{H}, \hat{vis})$ such that for some $j \geq 1$, for any *do* event $e' \in \beta'$, $e' \xrightarrow{\hat{vis}} \hat{r}_j$.

Notice that for any $w \in ctxt(A, e)$, $w \xrightarrow{hb} \hat{e}$ (by Proposition 9), and so $r_w \xrightarrow{hb} \hat{e}$ (since $r_w \xrightarrow{hb} w$). Thus, $r_w, w \in ctxt(A, e) \implies r_w, w \in \beta \implies r_w, w \in \beta' \implies r_w, w \in \beta_\infty$. We can thus apply Lemma 7 to β_∞.

Since $R(w_i)$ does not receive any messages between w_i and r_i', $w_i' \xrightarrow{hb(\beta')} r_i' \iff w_i' \xrightarrow{hb(\beta)} w_i \iff w_i' \xrightarrow{hb} w_i$. However, $w_i' \in \text{rval}(r_i')$ implies $w_i' \xrightarrow{hb(\beta')} r_i'$ (by Proposition 2), which implies $w_i' \xrightarrow{hb} w_i$ and, thus, $w_i' \xrightarrow{vis} w_i$ (by Proposition 8), which is impossible since $w_i' \not\xrightarrow{vis} w_i$. Thus $w_i' \notin \text{rval}(r_i')$ for all $1 \leq i \leq k$.

Now, since $w_0 \xrightarrow{\hat{vis}} \hat{r}_j$ yet $w_0 \notin \text{rval}(\hat{r}_j) = \text{rval}(\hat{e})$, it must be that $w_0 \xrightarrow{\hat{vis}} w_i \xrightarrow{\hat{vis}} \hat{r}_j$ for some $1 \leq i \leq k$ (by the MVR specification). However, $w_i' \xrightarrow{\hat{vis}} w_0$ (from $w_i' \xrightarrow{vis} w_0$ and Lemma 7). Since $\hat{A}$ is causally consistent and $w_0 \xrightarrow{\hat{vis}} w_i$, $w_i' \xrightarrow{\hat{vis}} w_i \xrightarrow{\hat{vis}} r_i'$. Yet $w_i' \notin \text{rval}(r_i')$. Hence, there must exist a write $\hat{w}$ such that $w_i' \xrightarrow{\hat{vis}} \hat{w} \xrightarrow{\hat{vis}} r_i'$, for some $\hat{w} \in \text{rval}(r_i')$. Thus, $\hat{w} \xrightarrow{hb(\beta')} r_i'$ (Proposition 2), implying $\hat{w} \xrightarrow{hb(\beta)} r_i'$, which in turn implies $\hat{w} \xrightarrow{hb} w_i$ (as $R(w_i)$ receives no messages between w_i and r_i). Thus, $\hat{w} \xrightarrow{vis} w_i$ (Proposition 9).

Then $\hat{w} \xrightarrow{vis} w_i'$ by the definition of $\mathcal{OCC}$ (Definition 18). Lemma 7 implies that $\hat{w} \xrightarrow{\hat{vis}} w_i'$. But $w_i' \xrightarrow{\hat{vis}} \hat{w}$ (by definition of $\hat{w}$ above), which means that $\hat{vis}$ is cyclic—a contradiction. $\square$

This implies that $\hat{e} = e$, proving Theorem 6.

5.3 Comparison to the CAC Theorem

Mahajan, Alvisi and Dahlin's CAC theorem [23,24] shows that a certain class of data stores cannot implement a consistency model stronger than *natural causal consistency*, in which the causal order (i.e., visibility) does not violate the real-time order of operations. Respecting real-time order is a stronger demand than we make: interpreted in our framework, natural causal consistency requires that an execution complies with an abstract executions in which events occur in exactly the same order, as opposed to our requirement for identical *per-replica* order.

Our result applies to eventually consistent data stores, whereas the CAC theorem applies to *one-way convergent* data stores. These satisfy a stronger liveness property, essentially stating that any pair of replicas can converge to the same state with two steps of one-way communication. This difference is relevant in practice, as some systems weaken their liveness guarantee to satisfy stronger consistency than natural causal consistency—e.g., GSP, which globally orders write operations [9,11].

Both proofs construct an execution meant to comply with a specific abstract execution, by delivering messages according to the visibility relation. Both proofs require invisible reads; ours also requires op-driven messages.

Having invisible reads is inherently required for Theorem 6 and the CAC theorem to hold. Without invisible reads, the data store D can avoid producing certain causally consistent executions and thus satisfy a consistency model which is stronger than causal consistency (and $\mathcal{OCC}$). For example, suppose that D does not "expose" a write by returning it in response to a read until K read operations have been applied locally. This is illustrated in the top figure, where a *vis* edge is shown as a dashed arrow and an *hb* edge that is not a *vis* edge is shown as a solid arrow. Then D still satisfies eventual consistency, but no execution of D complies with the causally consistent abstract execution in which

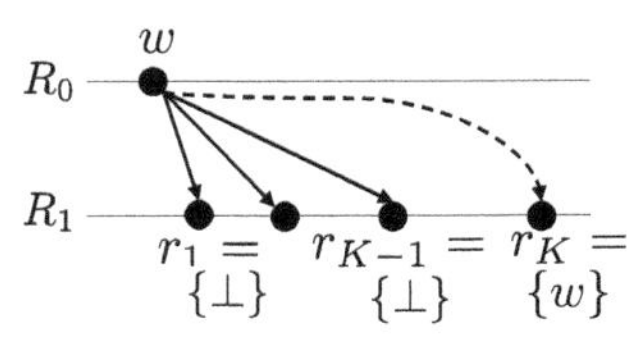

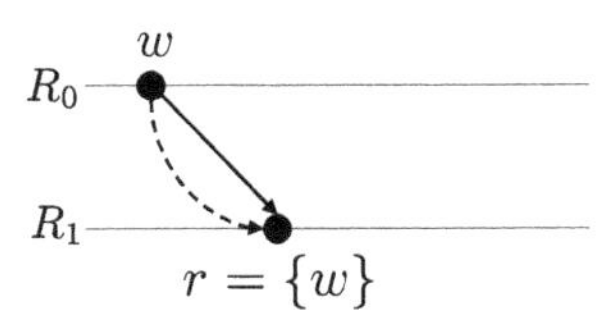

```
for all i ∈ [1,...,n']
  for all j ∈ [1,...,k]
    do_i(x_i, write(⟨j,i⟩), ok)
    send_i(m_j^i)
```

(a) β

```
for all i ∈ [1,...,n']
  for all j ∈ [1,...,g(i)]
    receive_{n-1}(m_j^i)
    do_{n-1}(x_i, read, v) // v = ⟨j,i⟩

do_{n-1}(y, write(1), ok)
send_{n-1}(m_y)
```

(b) γ_g

```
for all p ≠ i, 1 ≤ p ≤ n'
  for all j ∈ [1,...,k]
    receive_n(m_j^p)
receive_n(m_y)
for all j ∈ [1,...,k]
  receive_n(m_{i,j})
  do_n(y, read, v)
  if v = 1
    do_n(x_i, read, ⟨u,i⟩) // u = g(i)
    output g(i) = u
```

(c) d_i

Figure 4: Generating execution $\alpha_g = \beta\gamma_g$, which encodes g, and the transition sequence d_i, which decodes $g(i)$. We subscript an event with the id of its replica, e.g., do_i for a *do* event at R_i.

R_0 writes and R_1 immediately reads the value written (illustrated in the bottom figure). In contrast, we do not have an example of a data store without op-driven messages that satisfies a stronger consistency model than $\mathcal{OCC}$. Whether this assumption can be relaxed is an interesting question.

6. LOWER BOUND ON MESSAGE SIZE

We bound the size of messages used by write-propagating eventually consistent data stores. If s MVRs are supported by n replicas, then, for every $k > 1$, there is an execution in which an $\Omega(\min\{n, s\}k)$-bit message is sent. When $s \geq n$, this matches the complexity of the causal consistency algorithm of [2]. Messages in their algorithm contain vector timestamps [17, 25] of n components, each of which is logarithmic in the number of operations in the respective replica, yielding messages of size $O(nk)$, when there are 2^k operations. This leaves open the question of designing a data store using $O(sk)$-bit messages, when $s \in o(n)$.

THEOREM 12. *Let D be a causally consistent and eventually consistent data store with invisible reads and op-driven messages. Suppose that D provides s MVRs and has n replicas. Then for every $k \geq min\{n-2, s-1\}$ there is an execution α_k in which D sends a message containing $min\{n-2, s-1\} \lg k$ bits.*

PROOF. Let $n' = \min\{n-2, s-1\}$. For every $g : [n'] \mapsto [k]$, we construct an execution α_g that ends with a message m_g being sent. We prove that g can be decoded given m_g, which implies that for some g, m_g contains at least $n' \lg k$ bits. The basic idea is that, in α_g, each replica R_i, $1 \leq i \leq n'$, performs k writes, $w_1^i, \ldots, w_k^i$ to the MVR x_i. R_{n-1} performs a write w_y to the MVR y after observing the $g(i)$-th write of R_i, for every $1 \leq i \leq n'$. The message R_{n-1} subsequently broadcasts is m_g. We can decode g using m_g as follows. To output $g(i)$ for some i, we start with all replicas in their initial state, and execute the writes $w_1^i, \ldots, w_k^i$ for all i. (They are independent of g.) We deliver to R_n all messages but those sent by R_i, followed by m_g. Due to causal consistency, R_n cannot return w_y in response to a read of y, since w_y depends on $w_{g(i)}^i$, and R_n does not "know" this value. But if we now deliver R_i's messages to R_n, reading y after each message is received, the result of the read of y will contain w_y after the $g(i)$-th message has been delivered. Thus, we can find $g(i)$ given only m_g.

Now we describe the construction and decoding procedure more formally.

Construction of α_g: For any g, $\alpha_g = \beta\gamma_g$, where β is independent of g, and γ_g ends with R_{n-1} sending m_g. In β (Figure 4a), the sequence of events for each replica R_i consists of a write operation w_j^i writing $\langle j, i\rangle$ to MVR x_i followed by broadcasting a message m_i^j, for $1 \leq j \leq k$. (Lemma 5 implies each m_i^j exists.) In γ_g (Figure 4b), R_{n-1} receives, for each R_i, the messages $m_1^i, \ldots, m_{g(i)}^i$, while performing a read r_i^j of x_i after receiving each message. In the full version, we prove that $w_j^i \in \text{rval}(r_j^i)$. Finally, by Lemma 5, R_{n-1} writes 1 to register y and broadcasts m_g.

Decoding g from m_g (Figure 4c): Decoding $g(i)$ given m_g is performed by going through a sequence of transitions at R_n that ends with a $do(x_i, \text{read}, \langle g(i), i\rangle)$, which provides $g(i)$. We begin by having R_n receive the messages $m_1^p, \ldots, m_k^p$ for each $p \neq i$. (These messages can be obtained from β, which does not depend on g, so do not need to be provided explicitly.) We then obtain $g(i)$ by delivering m_j^i for j in increasing order, performing a read of y after each message delivery. If R_n reads 1, we read $\langle u, i\rangle$ from x_i and return $g(i) = u$. Let $d_i = e_1, \ldots, e_l$ be this sequence of transitions at R_n. To show that the execution $\alpha' = \beta\gamma_g d_i$ is well-formed, we prove in the full version that $\alpha'|R_n = d_i$. Thus, $g(i)$ can be computed given m_g, which implies g can be computed given m_g, and the theorem follows. □

One can prove Proposition 2, Lemma 3, and Lemma 5 for read/write registers (see Section 4), and these imply analogs of Theorem 12 for a data store providing read/write registers, as well as a combination of MVRs and registers.

7. SUMMARY

We present a framework for specifying highly-available replicated data stores, for objects that can expose concurrency. For write-propagating data stores, representing many real systems, we show that an eventually consistent data store cannot satisfy a consistency model strictly stronger than $\mathcal{OCC}$. An important open question is to implement an eventually consistent $\mathcal{OCC}$ data store, which will show that $\mathcal{OCC}$ is the strongest possible consistency model for eventually consistent data stores. We also prove that the data store must send messages whose size grows with the number of replicas and the number of operations.

In the full version of the paper, we also extend the space lower bounds proved by Burckhardt et al. [10] for replicas implementing certain objects, like MVRs and ORsets. While their results seemingly imply the space optimality of existing implementations of these objects [7,27], they hinge on properties that many networks do not exhibit: *redelivery* and *reordering* of messages. We extend these lower bound proofs so that they do not require message redelivery and reordering. Thus, they hold even for relatively well-behaved networks that only delay or delete messages.

We have focused on MVRs, and left other objects, like read/write (last-writer wins) registers and ORsets, to future work. It would be interesting to determine whether Theorem 12 applies to ORsets, and more importantly, if Theorem 6 holds for other objects besides MVRs.

Acknowledgements: This work is supported by the Israel Science Foundation (grants 1227/10 and 1749/14), by Yad HaNadiv foundation, and by the Natural Science and Engineering Research Council of Canada. Faith Ellen was supported in part at the Technion by a Lady David Fellowship. Adam Morrison was supported in part at the Technion by an Aly Kaufman Fellowship.

8. REFERENCES

[1] *The Apache Cassandra Project.*

[2] M. Ahamad, G. Neiger, J. E. Burns, P. Kohli, and P. W. Hutto. Causal memory: definitions, implementation, and programming. *Dist. Comp.*, 9(1), 1995.

[3] B. Alpern and F. B. Schneider. Defining liveness. *Inf. Process. Lett.*, 21:181–185, October 1985.

[4] P. Bailis, A. Fekete, A. Ghodsi, J. M. Hellerstein, and I. Stoica. The Potential Dangers of Causal Consistency and an Explicit Solution. In *SoCC '12*, pages 22:1–22:7.

[5] P. Bailis and A. Ghodsi. Eventual consistency today: Limitations, extensions, and beyond. *Commun. ACM*, 56(5):55–63, May 2013.

[6] P. Bailis, A. Ghodsi, J. M. Hellerstein, and I. Stoica. Bolt-on Causal Consistency. In *SIGMOD '13*, pages 761–772.

[7] A. Bieniusa, M. Zawirski, N. Preguiça, M. Shapiro, C. Baquero, V. Balegas, and S. Duarte. An Optimized Conflict-free Replicated Set. Technical Report RR-8083, INRIA, Oct. 2012.

[8] E. A. Brewer. Towards robust distributed systems. In *PODC '00*, page 7.

[9] S. Burckhardt. *Principles of Eventual Consistency.* Found. and Trends in Programming Languages, 2014.

[10] S. Burckhardt, A. Gotsman, H. Yang, and M. Zawirski. Replicated data types: Specification, verification, optimality. In *POPL '14*, pages 271–284.

[11] S. Burckhardt, D. Leijen, J. Protzenko, and M. Fähndrich. Global Sequence Protocol: A Robust Abstraction for Replicated Shared State. In *ECOOP '15*.

[12] B. Charron-Bost. Concerning the Size of Logical Clocks in Distributed Systems. *Inf. Process. Lett.*, 39(1):11–16, July 1991.

[13] G. DeCandia, D. Hastorun, M. Jampani, G. Kakulapati, A. Lakshman, A. Pilchin, S. Sivasubramanian, P. Vosshall, and W. Vogels. Dynamo: Amazon's Highly Available Key-value Store. In *SOSP '07*, pages 205–220.

[14] J. Du, S. Elnikety, A. Roy, and W. Zwaenepoel. Orbe: Scalable causal consistency using dependency matrices and physical clocks. In *SOCC '13*, pages 11:1–11:14.

[15] J. Du, C. Iorgulescu, A. Roy, and W. Zwaenepoel. GentleRain: Cheap and Scalable Causal Consistency with Physical Clocks. In *SoCC '14*, pages 4:1–4:13.

[16] J. Du, C. Iorgulescu, A. Roy, and W. Zwaenepoel. Closing The Performance Gap between Causal Consistency and Eventual Consistency. In *Proceedings of the 1st Workshop on Principles and Practice of Eventual Consistency*, 2014.

[17] C. J. Fidge. Partial orders for parallel debugging. *ACM SIGPLAN Notices*, 24(1):183–194, 1989.

[18] S. Gilbert and N. Lynch. Brewer's conjecture and the feasibility of consistent, available, partition-tolerant web services. *SIGACT News*, 33(2):51–59, June 2002.

[19] M. P. Herlihy and J. M. Wing. Linearizability: a correctness condition for concurrent objects. *ACM Trans. Prog. Lang. Syst.*, 12:463–492, July 1990.

[20] L. Lamport. Time, Clocks, and the Ordering of Events in a Distributed System. *Commun. ACM*, 21(7):558–565, July 1978.

[21] W. Lloyd, M. J. Freedman, M. Kaminsky, and D. G. Andersen. Don't Settle for Eventual: Scalable Causal Consistency for Wide-area Storage with COPS. In *SOSP '11*, pages 401–416.

[22] W. Lloyd, M. J. Freedman, M. Kaminsky, and D. G. Andersen. Stronger Semantics for Low-Latency Geo-Replicated Storage. In *NSDI '13*, pages 313–328.

[23] P. Mahajan. *Highly Available Storage with Minimal Trust.* PhD thesis, The University Of Texas at Austin, Austin, TX, USA, May 2012.

[24] P. Mahajan, L. Alvisi, and M. Dahlin. Consistency, Availability, and Convergence. Technical Report TR-11-22, The University of Texas at Austin, 2011.

[25] F. Mattern. Virtual time and global states of distributed systems. In M. Consard and P. Quinton, editors, *Parallel and Distributed Algorithm*, pages 215–226. North-Holland, 1989.

[26] M. Perrin, A. Mostéfaoui, and C. Jard. Brief Announcement: Update Consistency in Partitionable Systems. In *DISC '14*, pages 546–547.

[27] M. Shapiro, N. Preguiça, C. Baquero, and M. Zawirski. A comprehensive study of Convergent and Commutative Replicated Data Types. Technical Report RR-7506, INRIA, Jan. 2011.

[28] M. Shapiro, N. Preguiça, C. Baquero, and M. Zawirski. Conflict-free Replicated Data Types. In *SSS '11*, pages 386–400.

[29] W. Vogels. Eventually consistent. *Commun. ACM*, 52(1):40–44, Jan. 2009.

[30] M. Zawirski, A. Bieniusa, V. Balegas, S. Duarte, C. Baquero, M. Shapiro, and N. Preguiça. SwiftCloud: Fault-Tolerant Geo-Replication Integrated all the Way to the Client Machine. Technical Report RR-8347, INRIA, Aug. 2013.

Computing Weak Consistency in Polynomial Time

[Extended Abstract]

Wojciech Golab[*] [†]
Dept. of Electrical and Computer Engineering
University of Waterloo, Canada
wgolab@uwaterloo.ca

Xiaozhou (Steve) Li[‡]
Google Inc.
Mountain View, CA, USA
xzli@google.com

Alejandro López-Ortiz[†]
School of Computer Science
University of Waterloo, Canada
alopez-o@uwaterloo.ca

Naomi Nishimura[†]
School of Computer Science
University of Waterloo, Canada
nishi@uwaterloo.ca

ABSTRACT

The k-atomicity property can be used to describe the consistency of data operations in large distributed storage systems. The weak consistency guarantees offered by such systems are seen as a necessary compromise in view of Brewer's CAP principle. The k-atomicity property requires that every read operation obtains a value that is at most k updates (writes) old, and becomes a useful way to quantify weak consistency if k is treated as a variable that can be computed from a history of operations. Specifically, the value of k quantifies how far the history deviates from Lamport's atomicity property for read/write registers. We address the problem of computing k indirectly by solving the k-atomicity verification problem (k-AV): given a history of read/write operations and a positive integer k, decide whether the history is k-atomic. Gibbons and Korach showed that in general this problem is NP-complete when $k = 1$, and hence not solvable in polynomial time unless P = NP. In this paper we present two algorithms that solve the k-AV problem for any $k \geq 2$ in special cases. Similarly to known solutions for $k = 1$ and $k = 2$, both algorithms assume that all the values written to a given object are distinct. The first algorithm places an additional restriction on the structure of the input history and solves k-AV in $O(n^2 + n \cdot k \log k)$ time. The second algorithm does not place any additional restrictions on the input but is efficient only when k is small and when concurrency among write operations is limited. Its time complexity is $O(n^2)$ if both k and our particular measure of write concurrency are bounded by constants.

Categories and Subject Descriptors

F.2 [**Theory of Computation**]: Analysis of Algorithms and Problem Complexity; D.2.4 [**Software**]: Software Engineering—*Software/Program Verification*

General Terms

Algorithms, theory, verification

Keywords

Consistency; atomicity; verification; distributed storage

1. INTRODUCTION

Distributed storage and data management systems empower a broad range of data-intensive services today including social networking, web search, e-mail, calendars, and online auctions. In an effort to cope with web-scale workloads in the face of immense competitive pressures, the designs of such services have shifted away from conventional relational databases and towards simpler but more scalable solutions. As a result, many practical systems offer simple key-value operations and BASE (Basically Available, Soft state, Eventual consistency) properties either instead of or side-by-side with conventional transactions and more powerful ACID (Atomicity/Consistency/Isolation/Durability) properties.

Eventually consistent key-value stores are an important breed of distributed storage systems that provide BASE properties [7, 25, 27]. Their distinguishing characteristic is the ability to remain available in the face of network partitions, in which disjoint subsets of hosts become isolated from one another and are unable to communicate. To ensure that storage operations can proceed despite such partitions, specialized replication techniques such as *sloppy quorums* [7, 17, 23] are used. As a side effect, eventually-consistent systems can only provide weak consistency guarantees—a necessary compromise according to Brewer's CAP principle [5], which states that a distributed storage system cannot simultaneously provide strong consistency (C), high availabil-

[*]Author supported in part by the Google Faculty Research Awards Program.
[†]Author supported in part by the Natural Sciences and Engineering Research Council (NSERC) of Canada.
[‡]Part of this research was conducted while this author was at Hewlett-Packard Labs.

Permission to make digital or hard copies of part or all of this work for personal or classroom use is granted without fee provided that copies are not made or distributed for profit or commercial advantage, and that copies bear this notice and the full citation on the first page. Copyrights for third-party components of this work must be honored. For all other uses, contact the owner/author(s). Copyright is held by the author/owner(s).
PODC'15, July 21–23, 2015, Donostia-San Sebastián, Spain.
ACM 978-1-4503-3617-8/15/07.
http://dx.doi.org/10.1145/2767386.2767407.

ity (A), and partition-tolerance (P). This observation has been formalized by Lynch and Gilbert as the impossibility of implementing an atomic read/write register object in an asynchronous message passing system with unreliable communication channels [11]. A read/write register object in this context corresponds to a key-value pair as follows: the key is the object's name and is immutable, whereas the value is the object's state and can be accessed using read and write operations.

As defined by Vogels [27], eventual consistency means that if an object is not updated and no failures occur for a sufficiently long period of time, then eventually all read operations on the object return the last updated value of that object. Although this definition captures nicely the essence of eventual consistency, it also leaves open important questions regarding the behavior of key-value stores in practice: how long is "eventual", and how consistent are reads when objects are updated continuously? In an attempt to answer the latter question, various notions of *data staleness* have been defined and analyzed. In this context, a value written to a key is considered stale once it is overwritten by another value, and so the staleness of a particular read is a measure of the "distance" between two write operations: the write that assigned the value read (called the *dictating write* of the read), and the write that assigned the latest value to the object under consideration.

In this paper, we focus on a formal notion of *version-based staleness*, which is defined by counting write operations. Specifically, we consider the *k-atomicity* property of Aiyer et al. [1], which is a generalization of Lamport's atomicity property for read/write registers [18]. Both properties are defined over an *execution history*, which is a collection of read/write operations tagged with distinct start and finish times. An operation in such a history "happens before" another operation if the former finishes before the latter starts, and a history is called k-atomic if there exists a total order over the operations that extends the "happens before" partial order, and in which every read returns a value written by one of the last k writes preceding the read in the total order.

The k-atomicity verification (k-AV) problem is to decide for a given execution history and integer $k \geq 1$ whether the history is k-atomic. An efficient solution to this problem makes it possible to compute the smallest k for which a given history is k-atomic, which quantifies the maximum degree of staleness observed by clients accessing an eventually consistent storage system. Thus, solving k-AV makes it possible to analyze the actual consistency provided by such systems in arbitrary workloads, including ones where writes occur continuously and concurrently with each other.

Our main contribution in this paper is a pair of algorithms that solve the k-AV problem for arbitrary $k \geq 2$ and address the previously unsolved case $k \geq 3$. Both algorithms assume that all the values written to a given object in a history are distinct, which makes 1-AV solvable in $O(n \log n)$ time for a history of n operations. The first algorithm, called GPO ("greedy plus obligations"), places an additional restriction on the structure of the input history and solves k-AV for arbitrary k in $O(n^2 + n \cdot k \log k)$ time. The second algorithm, called CGS ("configuration graph search"), does not place any additional restrictions on the input but is efficient only when k is small and when concurrency among write operations is restricted. Its time complexity is $O(n^2)$ if both k and our specific measure of write concurrency are bounded by constants. As explained in Section 7, we expect these algorithms to perform efficiently in the vast majority of cases encountered in practice.

2. RELATED WORK

The fundamental problem of defining consistency properties for shared objects was first addressed by Misra [20] and Lamport [18]. Lamport defined a number of key concepts in this area, including the *happens before* and $\longrightarrow$ (i.e., precedes) relations, and the atomicity property for registers [18]. The "happens before" relation is an irreflexive partial order over instantaneous events that captures the following notion of causality: given two events e_1, e_2 in Einstein's four-dimensional space-time, we say that e_1 happens before e_2 if it is possible for a pulse of light emitted at A to arrive at B, and hence for A to physically cause B. Operations on objects are modeled as collections of events, and given two operations op_1, op_2 we say that $op_1 \longrightarrow op_2$ if every event of op_1 happens before every event of op_2. In the presence of a global clock events can be totally ordered according to time, in which case $op_1 \longrightarrow op_2$ means that op_1 finishes before op_2 starts. Lamport's atomic read/write register satisfies the property that any collection of operations applied to the object can be arranged (conceptually) in some total order that extends $\longrightarrow$ and in which every read returns the value assigned by the latest write [18]. Misra's axioms provide an alternative definition of such a register, and explicitly address the case of multiple concurrent writers [20], whereas Lamport's definitions are given for the single-writer case but generalize easily to multiple writers. Herlihy and Wing's *linearizability* property is a generalization of Lamport's atomicity property to arbitrary typed shared objects, and to scenarios that include pending (i.e., incomplete) operations that may appear to take effect before they finish [15]. Herlihy and Wing's *happens before* relation over pairs of operations is a special case of Lamport's $\longrightarrow$ relation when events are totally ordered.

Several relaxed consistency properties have been defined in an attempt to describe the behavior of weakly consistent distributed storage systems. In general these properties capture the staleness of the values returned by read operations, which we can think of more precisely as the "distance" between operations, as explained in Section 1. Two notions of staleness have been defined in literature: *time-based* and *version-based*. A time-based staleness of t time units means that a read returned a value that was considered fresh at most t time units earlier. Torres-Rojas et al. formalize this notion by defining *timed consistency* properties in distributed message passing systems as generalizations of sequential consistency and causal consistency [26]. Similarly, Golab et al. generalize Lamport's atomicity property for read/write registers [18] by defining Δ-atomicity [13] and Γ-atomicity [14]. On the other hand a version-based staleness of k versions means that a read returned the value assigned by one of the last k writes in some total ordering of the write operations. Aiyer et al. formalize this notion as the *k-atomicity* property, which is also inspired by Lamport's atomic register. A collection of read/write operations is k-atomic if the operations can be arranged in some total order that extends $\longrightarrow$ and in which every read returns the value assigned by one of the k latest writes.

Several storage systems and modeling frameworks incorporate relaxed consistency properties. The TACT (Tunable Availability/Consistency Tradeoffs) framework of Yu and Vahdat defines version-based and time-based staleness informally as *order error* and *staleness* [29]. Lee and Welch describe a probabilistic consistency framework in the context of *randomized registers* implemented using probabilistic quorums [19]. Their analysis refers implicitly to version-based staleness by deriving bounds on the probability that a stale replica exists for a data item that has been overwritten a certain number of times. The Probabilistically Bounded Staleness (PBS) framework of Bailis et al. uses similar principles to derive bounds on time-based and version-based staleness [3]. They formalize both notions of staleness in the simplified model where write operations do not overlap in time with other read or write operations. Ardekani and Terry as well as Terry et al. propose storage systems that can be configured using service level agreements (SLAs) to provide bounds on time-based staleness [2, 24]. Our contributions complement this body of work in the following way: our techniques for computing version-based staleness from observed histories could be used to validate frameworks like TACT and PBS, and verify the correctness of storage systems that support staleness-based SLAs, provided that technical differences among various definitions of staleness can be reconciled. This approach stands in contrast to the technique used by Wada et al., and by Bermbach and Tai, which measures the convergence time of the replication protocol of a distributed system rather than capturing the staleness actually observed by clients [4, 28].

Decision problems pertaining to the consistency properties discussed herein were first studied in the context of verifying shared memories. The input to the decision problem is an *execution history*—a sequence of invocation and response events corresponding to operations applied to a collection of shared objects. The events in a history define the invocations and responses of operations on objects. Gibbons and Korach showed that deciding whether such a history is atomic is NP-complete in the general case [10]. However, in the special case when each write operation on a given object assigns a distinct value, polynomial-time decision algorithms for atomicity have been developed. Under this assumption, Misra's axioms can be used to characterize atomicity as the absence of cycles in a *conflict graph* whose vertices represent values and whose edges represent precedence constraints imposed by the ordering of reads and writes in the history [20]. For a history with n operations the time complexity of this algorithm is $O(n^2)$. Gibbons and Korach instead followed the approach of clustering operations according to the value read or written, and characterized atomicity as the absence of conflicts between pairs of such clusters [10]. Their algorithm has time complexity $O(n \log n)$.

The decision problem for the k-atomicity property is called the k-atomicity verification (k-AV) problem. Given a history and an integer $k \geq 1$, the objective is to decide whether the history is k-atomic. The *locality* property of k-atomicity states that the input history is k-atomic if and only if for each object accessed, the subhistory of operations on that specific object is k-atomic [12, 15]. Accordingly, solutions to k-AV assume without loss of generality that all operations are applied to the same object. A solution to k-AV can be used to compute the *k-value* of a history: the smallest k for which the history is k-atomic. The k-value equals 1 if and only if the history is atomic in Lamport's sense [18], and larger k-values indicate deviation from atomicity and hence from linearizability; the higher the k the greater the deviation.

The k-AV problem was first considered by Golab et al. [13]. Like the problem of deciding atomicity, k-AV is NP-complete in the general case, assuming that k is part of the input. Golab et al. present the first polynomial-time solutions to 2-AV under the assumption that each write operation on a given object assigns a distinct value, which is the same assumption that makes 1-AV tractable [12]. One algorithm, called LBT, runs in $O(n^2)$ time for a history with n operations. It leverages ideas inspired by Misra [20], as well as the technique of limited backtracking [8]. The other algorithm, called FZF, runs in $O(n \log n)$ time, and borrows the clustering idea of Gibbons and Korach [10].

The k-AV problem is somewhat similar to the graph bandwidth problem (GBW). Given a graph G and a positive integer k, the GBW problem is to decide whether it is possible to arrange the vertices of G at distinct positions on a line such that any two vertices that are adjacent in G are separated by at most $k-1$ other vertices on the line. GBW is NP-complete when k is part of the input [21], and is solvable in polynomial time when k is fixed [9, 22]. The algorithm of Saxe uses dynamic programming and runs in $O(n^{k+1})$ time where n is the number of vertices [22]. Kleitman and Vohra [16] present a GBW algorithm that runs in $O(n \log n)$ time, but is correct only for interval graphs.

Our graph-theoretic characterization of k-AV presented in Section 2 (see Lemma 2) has a similar flavor to GBW in the sense that it refers to a linear arrangement of vertices that is constrained by edges. The main difference is that we consider constraints with respect to two different but related sets of edges, with one set imposing "hard" constraints similarly to edges in a topological ordering, and the other set imposing "soft" constraints similarly to edges in GBW. Furthermore, our edges are directed and the union of the two edge sets has a structure similar to an interval graph, whereas GBW is defined over arbitrary undirected graphs. As regards time complexity, we are not aware of a polynomial time Turing reduction from GBW to k-AV or vice versa. Such a reduction from k-AV to GBW would imply that k-AV is solvable in polynomial time for fixed k.

3. PRELIMINARIES

Following the model of Herlihy and Wing [15], we define an *execution history* (or *history* for short) as a sequence of *events* where each event is either the invocation or the response of an operation on a read/write register. Each operation in the history has both an invocation and a response event, and all operations are applied to the same object (see discussion of locality in Section 2). Each event is tagged with a unique time, and events appear in the history in increasing order of their times. The exact values of these times are not important, only their relative order, and so we assume without loss of generality that the ith event (counting from $i = 1$) occurs at time i. Each event also records the operation type (i.e., read vs. write), its argument (for writes only) and its return value (for reads only). The *value* of an operation *op* is its argument if *op* is a write, and its response if *op* is a read. Given a read r and a write w we call w a *dictating write* of r if r and w share the same value. In that case we call r a *dictated read* of w. In the remainder of the paper, the number of operations in H and the number of writes in H are denoted by n and n_w, respectively.

Given an operation op, we denote by $s(op)$ and $f(op)$ the start time and finish time of op, respectively. Given a pair of operations op_1, op_2 in a history H we denote Herlihy and Wing's *happens before* relation by $<_H$ (i.e., $op_1 <_H op_2$ if and only if $f(op_1) < s(op_2)$). We say that op_1 and op_2 are *concurrent* if neither $op_1 <_H op_2$ nor $op_2 <_H op_1$. A total order $<_T$ over the operations in a history H *extends* the partial order $<_H$, denoted $<_T \supseteq <_H$, if every pair of operations op_1, op_2 in H satisfies $op_1 <_H op_2 \Rightarrow op_1 <_T op_2$. We call $<_T$ a *k-atomic total order for H* if $<_T \supseteq <_H$ and every read operation returns the value assigned by one of the last k writes that precede it in $<_T$. A history H is k-atomic if and only if there exists a k-atomic total order $<_T$ for H. Mathematically a total order $<_T$ over the values in H is a relation, but for convenience we often treat it as the corresponding sequence of values and refer to it as T.

In the remainder of the paper, we make the following assumption to circumvent the NP-completeness of k-AV:

Assumption 1. *For any history H, every read operation in H has exactly one dictating write.*

Without Assumption 1 the k-AV problem is NP-complete, assuming that k is part of the input, because 1-AV is NP-complete [10]. Assumption 1 can be enforced in practical storage systems by embedding a unique identifier, for example based on the current time and client ID, in each value.

Under Assumption 1 we adopt the following notational convention: for any history H and any value v read or written in H, $w(v)$ denotes the unique dictating write of v in H. Similarly we use $r(v)$ to denote a read of v in H. If more than one read of v exists in H then the particular operation corresponding to $r(v)$ is specified in the context.

We make two additional assumptions to simplify our algorithms and their analysis. First, we assume that a value cannot be read before it is written:

Assumption 2. *For any history H, if r is a read in H and w is its dictating write then $r <_H w$ is false.*

Any history H that violates Assumption 2 automatically fails to satisfy k-atomicity for any $k \geq 1$. Assumption 2 can be tested in $O(n \log n)$ steps by clustering operations by their value, and checking for each value that no read precedes its dictating write.

Second, we assume that a read never finishes before its dictating write:

Assumption 3. *For any history H, if r is a read and w is its dictating write then $f(w) < f(r)$.*

Assumption 3 implies no loss of generality because any history H that satisfies Assumptions 1 and 2 can be transformed efficiently into a history H' that in addition satisfies Assumption 3 in a manner that preserves k-atomicity. This is done using the normalization procedure presented as Algorithm 1. Theorem 1 asserts the correctness of this procedure, and its proof is omitted due to lack of space.

Theorem 1. *If the input history H of the normalization procedure (Algorithm 1) satisfies the pre-conditions (Assumptions 1–2) then the output history H' satisfies the post-conditions (Assumptions 1–3, H is k-atomic if and only if H' is k-atomic).*

```
Input: history H that satisfies Assumptions 1–2.
Output: history H' that satisfies Assumptions 1–3,
        and is k-atomic if and only if H is.
H' := H
for every value v in H do
    r(v) := read of v with earliest finish time in H
    if f(r(v)) < f(w(v)) then
        shift the response event for w(v)'s
        counterpart in H' to the position
        immediately preceding the response event of
        r(v)'s counterpart in H'
    end
end
```

Algorithm 1: Normalization procedure for histories.

In general our algorithms assume that $2 \leq k \leq n$. For $k = 1$ the algorithm of Gibbons and Korach can be used instead [10], and its time complexity is $O(n \log n)$. For $k > n$ one can decide k-atomicity efficiently by verifying that each read has a dictating write and that no read precedes any of its dictating writes. These conditions are implied by Assumptions 1 and 2, and can be verified in $O(n \log n)$ time.

To simplify the presentation and analysis of our k-AV algorithms we first describe two graph-theoretic representations of the input history. These are given in Definition 1, which is inspired by Misra's *before* relation on values [20], and in Definition 2. We use both definitions to characterize k-atomicity in Lemma 2, which we use extensively later in Sections 4 and 5. The proof of Lemma 2 is omitted due to lack of space.

Definition 1. *The* read value graph *for a history H, denoted $G_R(V, E_R)$, is a directed graph where V is the set of values written in H, and E_R contains an edge (v, v') if and only if $v \neq v'$ and there exists a read $r(v')$ in H such that $w(v) <_H r(v')$.*

Definition 2. *The* write graph *for a history H, denoted $G_W(V, E_W)$, is a directed graph where V is the set of values written in H, and E_W contains an edge (v, v') if and only if $w(v) <_H w(v')$.*

Lemma 2. *A history H is k-atomic if and only if its corresponding write graph $G_W(V, E_W)$ has a topological ordering $T = \langle v_1, v_2, \ldots, v_{|V|} \rangle$, such that for any two vertices v_i and v_j in T, if the read value graph $G_R(V, E_R)$ for H contains an edge (v_i, v_j) then $j > i - k$.*

Informally speaking, G_R and G_W both capture constraints on the order in which writes may appear to take effect. Lemma 2 then asserts that H is k-atomic if and only if there is an ordering of the writes that is consistent with G_W and in which the edges of G_R never point "backward" by more than $k - 1$ positions.

Examples of G_R and G_W are presented in Figure 1 with respect to a small input history. Operations in the history are illustrated as intervals of time following the style of diagrams used by Herlihy and Wing [15]. The horizontal dimension represents time and the vertical dimension is used only to separate the intervals visually. The history has two 3-atomic total orders, namely $\langle 5, 2, 1, 3, 4 \rangle$ and $\langle 5, 2, 3, 1, 4 \rangle$, but fails to satisfy 2-atomicity because $w(1)$ and $w(3)$ both separate $w(2)$ from $r(2)$. Consequently, the history is not 1-atomic either.

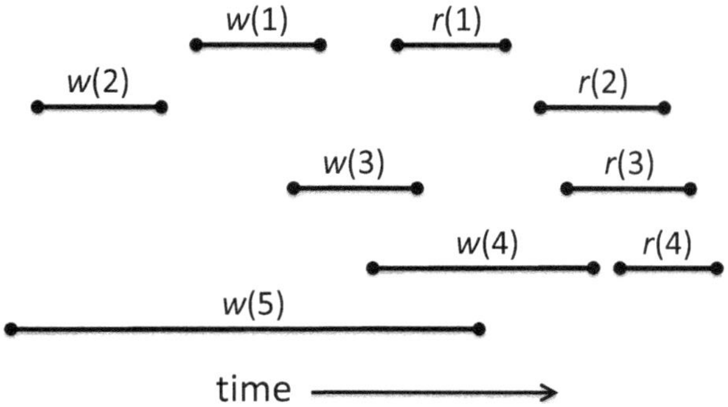

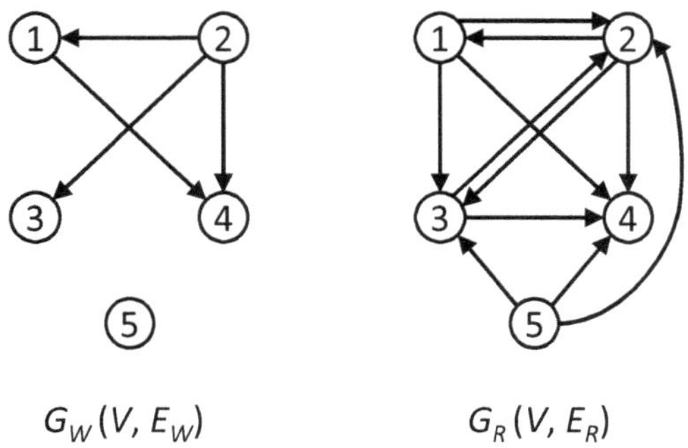

Figure 1: Example execution history (top) and corresponding graph representation (bottom).

4. AN EFFICIENT ALGORITHM FOR A RESTRICTED CLASS OF HISTORIES

In this section, we present an efficient algorithm called GPO ("greedy plus obligations") that solves k-AV for arbitrary k in the special case when the input history satisfies Assumptions 1–3 as well as the following:

ASSUMPTION 4. *For any history H and for any value v written in H, the write $w(v)$ has a dictated read $r(v)$ such that $w(v) <_H r(v)$.*

Using the terminology of Gibbons and Korach, Assumption 4 implies that every zone in the history is a forward zone [10]. Intuitively, this requirement constrains the k-AV problem by ensuring the presence of certain edges in the representation of a history H as a write graph G_W and a read value graph G_R. Specifically, for every pair of values v and v', Assumption 4 ensures that G_R contains the edge (v, v') if $f(w(v)) < f(w(v'))$, or the edge (v', v) if $f(w(v')) < f(w(v))$. In contrast, Assumptions 1–3 alone do not imply that v and v' are ordered by G_W or G_R in the case when $w(v)$ and $w(v')$ are concurrent.

4.1 Algorithm description

The main idea behind GPO is "greedy plus obligations;" hence the name. Like the LBT algorithm for 2-AV [12], GPO constructs a k-atomic total order in reverse. For each value placed in the k-atomic total order the algorithm evaluates any constraints this placement imposes on the choice of subsequent values, and records these constraints using internal data structures.

Given multiple candidates for the next value to be placed, GPO greedily picks the one whose dictating write has the largest finish time. In some cases this choice is narrowed down to a subset of values that must be placed within the next $k-1$ (or fewer) positions in the k-atomic total order due to constraints imposed on them by values that were placed earlier. Once GPO chooses the next value v, it identifies two types of constraints imposed by v: (i) if the write of v happens before the read of some value v' that has not yet been placed then v' must be placed in one of the next $k-1$ positions; and (ii) if the write of such a value v' happens before the write of another value v'' that has not yet been placed then v'' must also be placed in the next $k-1$ positions.

The constraints are tracked using $k-1$ sets of values called *obligation sets*, denoted by $B[1]$ to $B[k-1]$, initially all empty. The purpose of $B[i]$ is to record the values that must be placed in the next i positions of the k-atomic total order, and so naturally GPO must maintain the invariant $B[1] \subseteq B[2] \subseteq \cdots \subseteq B[k-1]$. An obligation set $B[i]$ is called *overfull*, *full*, or *underfull* if $|B[i]| > i$, $|B[i]| = i$, or $|B[i]| < i$, respectively. As GPO decides the next value to be placed it faces three possibilities. If there exists an overfull obligation set then GPO simply outputs NO because it is impossible to place more than i values in the next i positions. If no obligation sets are overfull but at least one of them is full then GPO first identifies the smallest full set, and then among the values in that set it greedily picks the one whose dictating write has the largest finish time. Otherwise all obligation sets are underfull, and GPO greedily chooses a value that has not yet been placed and whose dictating write has the largest finish time.

Having chosen the next value v, GPO updates the obligation sets by removing the value that was just placed, and then copying the remaining values from $B[i+1]$ to $B[i]$. Intuitively, if a value was supposed to be placed in the next $i+1$ positions at the beginning of a given iteration and is not chosen in the same iteration then it must be placed in the next i positions at the beginning of the next iteration. In addition, GPO updates $B[k-1]$ by adding values determined according to the two types of constraints imposed by v, as described earlier. As long as no overfull obligation set is encountered the algorithm continues to choose values and update the obligation sets until it has constructed a k-atomic total order for the input history. At that point GPO returns YES. The full procedure is presented as Algorithm 2.

The intuition underling lines 7 and 9 of GPO, which choose a value v with maximum finish time over any other candidate value v', follows from two observations. First, $w(v)$ happens before a subset of the operations that $w(v')$ happens before, and hence the choice of v as the next value in the reverse k-atomic order is the least constraining with respect to other values that have not yet been chosen. Second, choosing v in an earlier iteration than v' positions v' before v in the k-atomic total order, which tends to be consistent with the direction of edges in G_R because $f(w(v')) < f(w(v))$ implies that G_R contains the edge (v', v) under Assumption 4. Given that this edge exists, choosing v' instead in an earlier iteration than v would open the possibility that v precedes

v' by more than $k-1$ positions in the chosen total order over values, which precludes such an order being k-atomic (see Lemma 2).

4.2 Examples

With respect to the example history presented in Figure 1, GPO works correctly only if we remove $w(5)$, which lacks a dictated read and hence violates Assumption 4. Consider the case $k=3$ with $w(5)$ removed. The algorithm chooses 4 at line 9 in the first iteration, which imposes no additional constraints. It then chooses 3 at line 9 in the second iteration, and adds the values $\{1,2\}$ to $B[2]$. In the third iteration it chooses 1 from $B[2]$ at line 7, and then copies 2 to $B[1]$. In the fourth iteration it chooses 2 from $B[1]$ at line 7. Thus, GPO computes the total order $\langle 2,1,3,4\rangle$ and returns YES. This response is correct because the input history without $w(5)$ is 3-atomic.

Next, consider the case $k=2$ with $w(5)$ removed. As before the algorithm chooses 4 in the first iteration. In the second iteration it chooses 3 at line 9, and adds the values $\{1,2\}$ to $B[1]$, causing a return of NO at line 19 because $|B[1]| = 2 > 1$. This response is correct because the input history is not 2-atomic, even without $w(5)$.

Finally, consider the full history in Figure 1 with $w(5)$ included. The algorithm chooses 4 at line 9 in the first iteration, which imposes no additional constraints. It then chooses 5 at line 9 in the second iteration, and adds the values $\{1,2,3\}$ to $B[2]$, causing a return of NO at line 19 because $|B[2]| = 3 > 2$. This response is incorrect because the input history is 3-atomic. Thus, GPO breaks because the input history fails to satisfy Assumption 4.

4.3 Analysis

References to $G_R(V, E_R)$ and $G_W(V, E_W)$ in our analysis pertain to the read value graph and the write graph for the input history H (Definitions 1 and 2). These structures are needed only for analysis and therefore do not appear in the pseudo-code of Algorithm 2. The symbols T_x, U_x, and $B_x[i]$ denote the values of T, U, and $B[i]$ at the end of iteration x of the outer loop. Detailed proofs of correctness are omitted due to lack of space.

LEMMA 3. *The outer loop of the algorithm provides the following invariant:*

(a) for every value v accessed in H, v is either in T_x or in U_x (but not in both); and

(b) for every i, $1 \le i \le k-1$, if there exists a value $v \in B_x[i]$ and a value $v' \in U_x$ such that $w(v) <_H w(v')$ then $v' \in B_x[i]$.

LEMMA 4. *Suppose that the algorithm outputs YES. Then the sequence of values T obtained when line 22 is reached is a topological ordering of G_W.*

LEMMA 5. *If the algorithm outputs YES then H is k-atomic.*

LEMMA 6. *If H is k-atomic then the algorithm outputs YES.*

PROOF SKETCH. Suppose that H is k-atomic. We show that the algorithm outputs YES by proving the following predicate $P(x)$ for all $x \le n_w$, where n_w denotes the number of writes in H:

```
   Input: history H and integer k, 2 ≤ k ≤ n.
   Output: YES if H is k-atomic, NO otherwise.
   // suffix of k-atomic total order for H
1  T := empty sequence
   // set of values that have not yet been added
      to T
2  U := set of values written in H
3  for i := 1 to k − 1 do  B[i] := ∅
4  while U ≠ ∅ do
      // apply greedy heuristic
5     if ∃ i : |B[i]| = i then
6        ℓ := smallest such i
7        v := value in B[ℓ] such that w(v) has the
         largest finish time
8     else
9        v := value in U such that w(v) has the
         largest finish time
10    end
11    remove v from U and pre-pend it to T
      // update obligation sets
12    W := subset of values v′ ∈ U such that some
      read r(v′) satisfies w(v) <_H r(v′)
13    W′ := subset of values v′ ∈ U such that some
      value v″ ∈ W satisfies w(v″) <_H w(v′)
14    for j := 1 to k − 2 do
15       B[j] := B[j + 1] \ {v}
16    end
17    B[k − 1] := (B[k − 1] ∪ W ∪ W′) \ {v}
18    if ∃ i : |B[i]| > i then
19       return NO
20    end
21 end
22 return YES
```

Algorithm 2: The GPO algorithm.

(a) the algorithm executes line 11 at least x times and computes a sequence $T_x = \langle v_1, v_2, \ldots, v_x\rangle$ that is the suffix of some k-atomic total order for H;

(b) for any i such that $1 \le i \le k-1$ and for any value v, if $v \in B_x[i]$ then v is one of the i immediate predecessors of v_1 in any k-atomic total order for which T_x is a suffix, and hence $|B_x[i]| \le i$; and

(c) for any value v, if G_R contains an edge (a, b) such that a is $i \ge 0$ positions to the right of v_1 in T_x and b is not in T_x, then $b \in B_x[k-1-j]$ for all j such that $0 \le j \le i$.

Part (b) of the predicate $P(x)$ ensures that the algorithm never exits at line 19, and therefore outputs YES at line 22, as wanted. The predicate is proved by induction on x, and the most technically challenging aspect of the induction step is to establish $P(x+1)$-(a). To that end, we show that no matter which value v the algorithm chooses during iteration $x+1$ (at line 7 or 9), there is some k-atomic total order T for H such that T_x is a suffix of T. □

THEOREM 7. *The algorithm outputs YES if and only if H is k-atomic. Furthermore, the algorithm has time complexity $O(n^2 + n \cdot k \log k)$ where n is the number of operations in the input history H.*

PROOF SKETCH. Correctness of the return value follows from Lemmas 5 and 6. Assuming that U and $B[1]$ to $B[k-1]$ are represented using balanced trees, each iteration can be completed in $O(n+k\log k)$ steps: $O(n)$ to remove v from U as well as to compute W and W', and $O(k\log k)$ to update $B[i]$ for all i. We assume that each set $B[i]$ is implemented using a balanced tree, and that Algorithm 2 is optimized to return NO at line 15 or 17 if the size of $B[i]$ exceeds i, in accordance with lines 18–19. This optimization ensures that $B[\ell]$ at line 7 can be scanned in $O(k)$ time, that deletions from $B[i]$ at line 15 or 17 complete in $O(\log k)$ time, and that the set unions at line 17 complete in $O(k\log k)$ time. The total number of iterations is bounded by n and hence the overall time complexity is $O(n^2+n\cdot k\log k)$. □

5. A GENERAL ALGORITHM

In this section we present a k-AV algorithm called CGS ("configuration graph search") that is correct for any history satisfying Assumptions 1–3, and whose worst case time complexity is polynomial only in the special case when both k and our specific measure of write concurrency are bounded by constants.

5.1 Algorithm description

The algorithm uses the graph-theoretic representations of the input history H described in Section 3 as Definitions 1 and 2. Its complexity depends on both the size of these graph structures and on a formal notion of concurrency among write operations captured in Definition 3.

DEFINITION 3. *The* write concurrency *of a history H is the maximum number of writes that any one write overlaps with, including itself.*

The algorithm works by analyzing possible topological orderings of G_W starting with small permutations of values called *configurations*, which are formalized in Definition 4. Intuitively, each configuration is a candidate contiguous subsequence of a k-atomic total order for H, and must therefore satisfy constraints related to edges of G_W and G_R in accordance with Lemma 2. Furthermore, it must be possible to compose smaller configurations to form larger contiguous subsequences of a k-atomic total order for H. These requirements have two implications regarding the size of a configuration S. First, for Lemma 2 the order of the $k-1$ immediate predecessors of at least one value in S (i.e., the last one) must be fixed, and so S must contain at least k values. Second, for composability the set of values outside of S must be partitioned into those that can only precede S in a topological ordering of G_W, and those that can only follow S. As a result, the number of values in S must be greater than or equal to the write concurrency of H, denoted in this section by m. Thus, S must have size at least $\max(m,k)$.

DEFINITION 4. *An* (m,k)-configuration with respect to a read value graph $G_R(V,E_R)$ and write graph $G_W(V,E_W)$ *is any sequence $S=\langle v_1,v_2,\ldots,v_l\rangle$ of $l=\max(m,k)$ values that satisfies the following properties:*

(a) S is a contiguous subsequence of some topological ordering of G_W;

(b) if G_R contains an edge (v,v') such that both v and v' are values in S, say $v=v_i$ and $v'=v_j$, then $j>i-k$; and

(c) if G_R contains an edge (v,v') such that v is the last value in S and v' is not in S, then S contains a value v'' such that G_W contains the edge (v'',v').

The algorithm attempts to find a k-atomic total order for the input history by stringing together (m,k)-configurations. To that end, the algorithm searches for a sufficiently long path in a directed graph of configurations where the edge set represents the *extends* relation formalized in Definition 5.

DEFINITION 5. *For any (m,k)-configurations C and C' with respect to a read value graph $G_R(V,E_R)$ and write graph $G_W(V,E_W)$, we say that C'* extends *C if and only if C' is obtained from C by removing the first value v and appending a value $v'\neq v$ such such that $(v',v)\notin E_W$.*

As we show later on in Lemma 8, a path through the directed graph of configurations induces a non-repeating sequence of values whose order obeys the constraints imposed by the happens before relation $<_H$ for the input history H. As a result, the length of the longest path in this graph can be used to decide k-atomicity. The full procedure is presented as Algorithm 3, where the parameter k is given as input and the write concurrency of the input history, denoted by m, is computed explicitly at line 8.

Input: history H and integer k, $2\leq k\leq n$.
Output: YES if H is k-atomic, NO otherwise.
1 $G_R(V,E_R)$:= read value graph for H
2 $G_W(V,E_W)$:= write graph for H
3 **if** $|V|\leq k$ **then**
4 | **return** YES
5 **else if** $\exists v\in V$ s.t. $|\{v'\in V \mid (v',v)\in E_W \wedge (v,v')\in E_R\}|\geq k$ **then**
6 | **return** NO
7 **else**
8 | m := write concurrency of H
9 | $\mathcal{C}$:= set of (m,k)-configurations with respect to G_R and G_W
10 | $E_C := \{(c,c')\subseteq \mathcal{C}\times\mathcal{C} \mid$ configuration c' extends configuration $c\}$
11 | G_C := configuration graph $(\mathcal{C},E_C)$
12 | **if** G_C is non-empty and contains a path with $|V|-\max(m,k)$ edges **then**
13 | | **return** YES
14 | **else**
15 | | **return** NO
16 | **end**
17 **end**

Algorithm 3: The CGS algorithm.

5.2 Examples

With respect to the example history presented in Figure 1, CGS works correctly for all $k\geq 1$. The write concurrency for this particular input is $m=5$. Recall from Section 3 that the input history is 3-atomic but not 1-atomic or 2-atomic. For $k=1$ the condition at line 5 holds with $v=1$ and $v'=2$, and so the algorithm correctly returns NO at line 6.

For $k=2$ the condition at line 5 is false and so the algorithm proceeds to build the set $\mathcal{C}$ of $(5,2)$-configurations at line 9. According to Definition 4 there are no possible $(5, 2)$-configurations because it is impossible to satisfy clause (b). As a result, the configuration graph G_C computed at line 11 is empty. Thus, the condition at line 12 is false and CGS correctly returns NO at line 15.

For $k = 3$ the condition at line 5 is false and so the algorithm proceeds to build the set $\mathcal{C}$ of $(5, 3)$-configurations at line 9. According to Definition 4 the only possible $(5, 3)$-configurations are $\langle 5, 2, 1, 3, 4\rangle$ and $\langle 5, 2, 3, 1, 4\rangle$, which are the two possible 3-atomic total orders for H. The configuration graph G_C computed at line 11 is therefore non-empty and contains a path with $|V| - \max(m, k) = 5 - 5 = 0$ edges. Thus, the condition at line 12 holds and CGS correctly returns YES at line 13.

Finally, consider the case when $w(5)$ is removed from the input. In that case the write concurrency becomes $m = 3$. For $k = 2$ the condition at line 5 is false and so the algorithm proceeds to build the set $\mathcal{C}$ of $(3, 2)$-configurations at line 9. The possible $(3, 2)$-configurations are: $\langle 2, 1, 4\rangle$, $\langle 2, 3, 4\rangle$, $\langle 1, 3, 4\rangle$, $\langle 1, 4, 3\rangle$, and $\langle 3, 1, 4\rangle$. However, the configuration graph G_C computed at line 11 does not contain any edges, and hence does not contain a path with $|V| - \max(3, 2) = 4 - 3 = 2$ edges. Thus, the condition at line 12 is false and CGS correctly returns NO at line 15. For $k = 3$ the condition at line 5 is again false and the possible $(3, 3)$-configurations include $\langle 2, 1, 3\rangle$, $\langle 1, 3, 4\rangle$, and several others. Since $\langle 1, 3, 4\rangle$ extends $\langle 2, 1, 3\rangle$ it follows that the graph G_C computed at line 11 is non-empty and contains a path with $|V| - \max(3, 3) = 4 - 3 = 1$ edges. Thus, the condition at line 12 holds and CGS correctly returns YES at line 13.

5.3 Analysis

In this section we suppose that Assumptions 1–3 hold and we show that the algorithm returns YES if and only if the input history H is k-atomic. In our analysis any references to the *configuration graph* G_C pertain to the graph structure computed at line 11 of the algorithm. Detailed proofs of correctness are omitted due to lack of space.

DEFINITION 6. *Let $P = \langle C_1, C_2, C_3, \ldots, C_l\rangle$ be a finite path in the configuration graph G_C. The* sequence S of values induced by P *is defined recursively as follows: if $l = 1$ then $S = C_1$, otherwise S is the sequence of values induced by $\langle C_1, C_2, C_3, \ldots, C_{l-1}\rangle$ followed by the last value of C_l.*

LEMMA 8. *For any finite path $P = \langle C_1, C_2, C_3, \ldots, C_l\rangle$ in the configuration graph G_C, the sequence S of values induced by P is a subsequence of some topological ordering of G_W.*

COROLLARY 9. *Suppose that H contains $n_w \geq k$ writes. Then any path P through the configuration graph G_C has length (number of edges) at most $n_w - \max(m, k)$.*

LEMMA 10. *Suppose that H contains $n_w \geq k$ writes. Then H is k-atomic if and only if the configuration graph G_C is non-empty and has a path with exactly $n_w - \max(m, k)$ edges.*

THEOREM 11. *The algorithm returns YES if H is k-atomic, and NO otherwise.*

PROOF SKETCH. If $|V| \leq k$ then any topological ordering of G_W shows that H is k-atomic (Lemma 2) under Assumptions 1–3, and so the algorithm returns YES at line 4. Otherwise if the condition at line 5 holds then H is not k-atomic because in any topological ordering of G_W one of the vertices v' precedes v by more than $k - 1$ positions (Lemma 2), and so the algorithm returns NO at line 6. Finally, if the algorithm reaches line 12 then k-atomicity is decided using Lemma 10 and the algorithm returns the correct response at line 13 or line 15. □

LEMMA 12. *The graph G_C of (m, k)-configurations for a history H with n_w writes has at most $n_w \cdot (2m - 1)^{\max(m,k)-1}$ vertices and at most $n_w \cdot (2m - 1)^{\max(m,k)}$ edges.*

PROOF SKETCH. In each (m, k)-configuration there are at most n_w choices for the first value, and for each value v there are at most $2m - 1$ choices for the successor of v: at most $m - 1$ values whose writes overlap with $w(v)$, and an independent set of at most m out-neighbors of v in G_W. □

THEOREM 13. *The time complexity of the algorithm is $O(n^2 + n \cdot \max(m, k)^2 \cdot (2m - 1)^{\max(m,k)-1})$ where n denotes the number of operations in the input history H, and m is the write concurrency of H.*

PROOF SKETCH. $O(n^2)$ steps are required to construct G_R and G_W, as well as some intermediate structures that speed up the construction of G_C. Computing m at line 8 requires $O(n^2)$ steps. The total number of vertices in G_C is at most $n \cdot (2m - 1)^{\max(m,k)-1}$ by Lemma 12 and each vertex can be identified along with its in-edges in $O(\max(m, k)^2)$ steps given that the condition tested at line 5 of the algorithm is false. □

6. PRACTICAL APPLICABILITY

In this section we investigate the time complexity of algorithm CGS (Section 5) in practice by computing the parameters n (number of operations) and m (write concurrency, see Definition 3) from experimental data. The data set is borrowed from the experimental study of Γ-atomicity [14].

Experimental environment.

The experiments were conducted using ten 64-bit 2.2 GHz dual-core AMD Opteron servers equipped with 7200 RPM SATA disks and Gigabit Ethernet. Five servers were used to execute Cassandra 1.2.4 [17] and another five to run the Yahoo Cloud Serving Benchmark (YCSB) 0.1.4 [6]. The software environment included CentOS 5.5 Linux and OpenJDK 1.7.0_19. Clocks skew across servers was estimated using the `ntpq` command as less than 10ms.

Translation of execution histories into k-AV test cases.

The data set includes five sets of experiments, where each experiment comprises multiple (3-9) runs with different combinations of storage system settings and workload parameters. In each run the benchmark (YCSB) applies operations to the storage system (Cassandra) for 60 seconds, usually at the peak throughput level of approximately 1000 operations/s/server, which yields an execution history containing hundreds of thousands of operations.

Although the history generated by each of the 49 experimental runs could be used directly as an instance of k-AV, each object accessed in the history can be analyzed separately thanks to the locality property of k-atomicity, as explained in Section 2. Therefore, we first project the history obtained from a given run into a set of sub-histories corresponding to distinct objects. Furthermore, each of these sub-histories can often be decomposed into smaller fragments

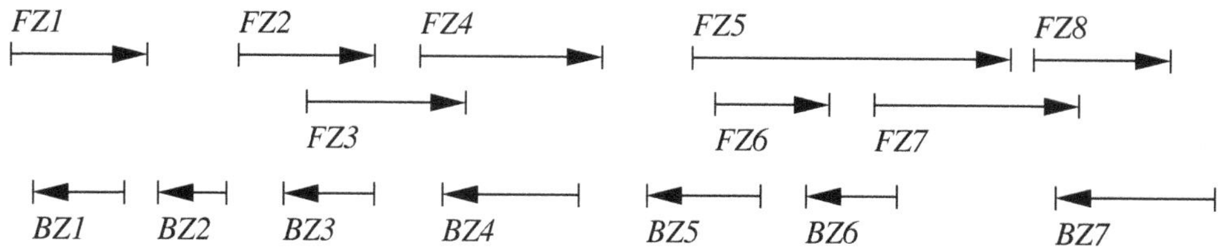

Figure 2: Example of zones in a history, reproduced from [12].

that can be analyzed separately—a technique used by the FZF algorithm for solving 2-AV [12]. The decomposition is based upon Gibbons and Korach's method of clustering operations into *zones*, each of which comprises a write operation and its dictated reads [10]. A zone is represented as the time interval from the minimum finish time of any operation in the zone to the maximum start time of any operation in the zone. A *forward zone* occurs when the minimum finish time is less than the maximum start time, meaning that at least one dictated read starts after some other operation in the zone finishes. A *backward zone* occurs when the minimum finish time is greater than or equal to the maximum start time, meaning that all operations in the zone overlap at a common point in time. For completeness we include in Figure 2 a copy of Figure 3 from [12], which illustrates a possible combination of zones in one history. In this figure *FZx* and *BZx* indicate forward and backward zones, respectively, and time increases from left to right.

The decomposition procedure groups zones into maximal subsets called *chunks* such that (i) two forward zones are in the same chunk if they intersect, and (ii) a backward zone belongs to a chunk if its time interval is contained entirely in the union of the time intervals of the forward zones in that chunk. As an example, in Figure 2 there are three chunks: $\{FZ_1, BZ_1\}$, $\{FZ_2, FZ_3, FZ_4, BZ_3, BZ_4\}$, and $\{FZ_5, FZ_6, FZ_7, FZ_8, BZ_6\}$. The remaining zones BZ_2, BZ_5 and BZ_7 can be ignored in the context of k-AV, intuitively because their operations can be linearized easily in-between chunks. It is straightforward to show that under Assumptions 1–2 an execution history is k-atomic if and only if each chunk of that history is k-atomic.

Experimental results.

We applied the above translation procedure to the 49 execution histories in the data set, which generated more than two million chunks. For each history we computed the total number of chunks, total number of zones, total number of operations, maximum number of operations per chunk, maximum write concurrency, number of chunks with $m \leq 5$, number of chunks that satisfy Assumption 4, and number of chunks where $m > 5$ and Assumption 4 is not satisfied.

The detailed results, which we omit due to lack of space, show that the chunks are quite small, generally comprising fewer than 200 operations and 4-5 operations per zone on average. Thus, the problem instances are fairly small but not small enough to permit solving k-AV by brute force. More than 99.3% of the chunks satisfy Assumption 4 and can therefore be analyzed efficiently using the GPO algorithm from Section 4. More than 99.9% of the chunks have write concurrency $m \leq 5$, and hence they are likely good candidates for the CGS algorithm from Section 5 provided that k is similarly small. The remaining chunks, where $m > 5$ and Assumption 4 does not hold, account for fewer than 0.1% of the test cases. These inputs may be too complex for our CGS algorithm.

7. CONCLUSION AND DISCUSSION

In this paper we have presented two algorithms that solve the k-AV problem for arbitrary $k \geq 2$ in special cases. Our algorithms assume that each read has exactly one dictating write (Assumption 1), which circumvents NP-completeness when $k \leq 2$. The first algorithm (GPO) places an additional restriction on the structure of the execution history but always runs in polynomial time. The second algorithm (CGS) does not place any additional restrictions on the input but its running time is polynomial only if both k and our measure of write concurrency (Definition 3) are bounded by constants. The time complexity of k-AV under Assumption 1, with no additional restrictions, remains unsettled.

Our algorithms enable precise measurement of version-based staleness, which in turn has several applications: (i) analyzing and understanding the behavior of eventually consistent storage systems (e.g., [7, 17, 23]); (ii) validating mathematical models of consistency (e.g., [3]); as well as (iii) verifying that a storage system or consistency tuning framework (e.g., [2, 24, 29]) delivers a promised level of consistency, and quantifying the severity of any consistency violations observed.

Measurement of version-based staleness entails computing the k-value of a history H, denoted k_H, which is the smallest integer $k \geq 1$ for which H is k-atomic. This value can be computed by a brute force method where k-AV is solved for consecutive values of k starting at $k = 1$, or by executing a binary search over $1 \leq k \leq n_w$ where n_w is the number of writes in H. When k_H is sufficiently large compared to m, the brute force approach is optimal for an exponential time algorithm such as CGS because the time complexity is dominated by the cost of solving k-AV for $k = k_H + 1$. Otherwise the computation may benefit from binary search with the overall time complexity bounded by $O(\log n_w)$ times the cost of solving k-AV for $k = n_w$.

Given that our k-AV algorithms do not guarantee polynomial running time without additional restrictions, their practical value depends on how often these restrictions hold in real data sets. To shed light on this point we analyzed the execution histories from [14] to determine representative values of n (number of operations) and m (write concurrency, Definition 3). The results suggest that in practice n is typically small (<1000), and the vast majority (>99%) of k-AV instances satisfy Assumption 4, which makes GPO applicable. In most of the remaining cases m is small (≤ 5) and hence CGS is efficient for small k (e.g., $k \leq m$). A very small fraction of cases (<0.1%) fail to satisfy both Assumption 4 and $m \leq 5$, and may be too complex for CGS.

8. REFERENCES

[1] A. Aiyer, L. Alvisi, and R. A. Bazzi. On the availability of non-strict quorum systems. In *Proc. of the 19th International Symposium on Distributed Computing (DISC)*, pages 48–62, September 2005.

[2] M. S. Ardekani and D. B. Terry. A self-configurable geo-replicated cloud storage system. In *Proc. of the 11th USENIX Symposium on Operating Systems Design and Implementation (OSDI)*, pages 367–381, 2014.

[3] P. Bailis, S. Venkataraman, M. J. Franklin, J. M. Hellerstein, and I. Stoica. Probabilistically bounded staleness for practical partial quorums. *PVLDB*, 5(8):776–787, 2012.

[4] D. Bermbach and S. Tai. Eventual consistency: How soon is eventual? An evaluation of Amazon S3's consistency behavior. In *Proc. of the 6th Workshop on Middleware for Service Oriented Computing (MW4SOC)*, 2011.

[5] E. A. Brewer. Towards robust distributed systems (abstract). In *Proc. of the 19th ACM Symposium on Principles of Distributed Computing (PODC)*, 2000.

[6] B. F. Cooper, A. Silberstein, E. Tam, R. Ramakrishnan, and R. Sears. Benchmarking cloud serving systems with YCSB. In *ACM Symposium on Cloud Computing (SoCC)*, pages 143–154, June 2010.

[7] G. DeCandia, D. Hastorun, M. Jampani, G. Kakulapati, A. Lakshman, A. Pilchin, S. Sivasubramanian, P. Vosshall, and W. Vogels. Dynamo: Amazon's highly available key-value store. In *Proc. of the 21st ACM Symposium on Operating System Principles (SOSP)*, pages 205–220, October 2007.

[8] S. Even, A. Itai, and A. Shamir. On the complexity of timetable and multicommodity flow problems. *SIAM Journal on Computing*, 5(4):691–703, December 1976.

[9] M. R. Garey, R. L. Graham, D. S. Johnson, and D. E. Knuth. Complexity results for bandwidth minimization. *SIAM Journal on Applied Mathematics*, 34(3):477–495, May 1978.

[10] P. Gibbons and E. Korach. Testing shared memories. *SIAM Journal on Computing*, 26:1208–1244, August 1997.

[11] S. Gilbert and N. A. Lynch. Brewer's conjecture and the feasibility of consistent, available, partition-tolerant web services. *SIGACT News*, 33(2):51–59, 2002.

[12] W. Golab, J. Hurwitz, and X. Li. On the k-atomicity-verification problem. In *Proc. of the 33rd International Conference on Distributed Computing Systems (ICDCS)*, 2013.

[13] W. Golab, X. Li, and M. A. Shah. Analyzing consistency properties for fun and profit. In *Proc. of the 30th ACM Symposium on Principles of Distributed Computing (PODC)*, pages 197–206, June 2011.

[14] W. Golab, M. R. Rahman, A. AuYoung, K. Keeton, and I. Gupta. Client-centric benchmarking of eventual consistency for cloud storage systems. In *Proc. of the 34th International Conference on Distributed Computing Systems (ICDCS)*, pages 493–502, 2014.

[15] M. Herlihy and J. M. Wing. Linearizability: A correctness condition for concurrent objects. *ACM Transactions on Programming Languages and Systems*, 12(3):463–492, July 1990.

[16] D. J. Kleitman and R. V. Vohra. Computing the bandwidth of interval graphs. *SIAM Journal on Discrete Mathematics*, 3(3):373–375, August 1990.

[17] A. Lakshman and P. Malik. Cassandra: A decentralized structured storage system. *SIGOPS Oper. Syst. Rev.*, 44(2):35–40, Apr. 2010.

[18] L. Lamport. On interprocess communication, Part I: Basic formalism and Part II: Algorithms. *Distributed Computing*, 1(2):77–101, June 1986.

[19] H. Lee and J. L. Welch. Randomized registers and iterative algorithms. *Distributed Computing*, 17(3):209–221, 2005.

[20] J. Misra. Axioms for memory access in asynchronous hardware systems. *ACM Transactions on Programming Languages and Systems*, 8(1):142–153, January 1986.

[21] C. H. Papadimitriou. The NP-completeness of the bandwidth minimization problem. *Computing*, 16(3):263–270, September 1976.

[22] J. Saxe. Dynamic-programming algorithms for recognizing small-bandwidth graphs in polynomial time. *SIAM Journal on Algebraic and Discrete Methods*, 1(4):363–369, December 1980.

[23] R. Sumbaly, J. Kreps, L. Gao, A. Feinberg, C. Soman, and S. Shah. Serving large-scale batch computed data with project Voldemort. In *Proc. of the 10th USENIX Conference on File and Storage Technologies (FAST)*, 2012.

[24] D. B. Terry, V. Prabhakaran, R. Kotla, M. Balakrishnan, M. K. Aguilera, and H. Abu-Libdeh. Consistency-based service level agreements for cloud storage. In *Proc. of the 24th ACM Symposium on Operating Systems Principles (SOSP)*, pages 309–324, 2013.

[25] D. B. Terry, M. M. Theimer, K. Petersen, A. J. Demers, M. J. Spreitzer, and C. H. Hauser. Managing update conflicts in Bayou, a weakly connected replicated storage system. In *Proc. of the 15th ACM Symposium on Operating Systems Principles (SOSP)*, pages 172–182, 1995.

[26] F. J. Torres-Rojas, M. Ahamad, and M. Raynal. Timed consistency for shared distributed objects. In *Proc. of the 18th ACM Symposium on Principles of Distributed Computing (PODC)*, pages 163–172, 1999.

[27] W. Vogels. Eventually consistent. *Queue*, 6(6):14–19, Oct. 2008.

[28] H. Wada, A. Fekete, L. Zhao, K. Lee, and A. Liu. Data consistency properties and the trade-offs in commercial cloud storages: the consumers' perspective. In *Proc. of the 5th Biennial Conference on Innovative Data Systems Research (CIDR)*, January 2011.

[29] H. Yu and A. Vahdat. Design and evaluation of a conit-based continuous consistency model for replicated services. *ACM Trans. Comput. Syst.*, 20(3):239–282, 2002.

On the Push&Pull Protocol for Rumour Spreading

[Extended Abstract] *

Hüseyin Acan
School of Mathematical Sciences
Monash University
Clayton, Australia
huseyin.acan@monash.edu

Andrea Collevecchio
School of Mathematics
Monash University
Clayton, Australia
and Ca' Foscari University
Venice, Italy
andrea.collevecchio@monash.edu

Abbas Mehrabian
Department of Combinatorics and Optimization
University of Waterloo
Waterloo, Canada
amehrabi@uwaterloo.ca

Nick Wormald
School of Mathematical Sciences
Monash University
Clayton, Australia
nick.wormald@monash.edu

ABSTRACT

The asynchronous push&pull protocol, a randomized distributed algorithm for spreading a rumour in a graph G, is defined as follows. Independent exponential clocks of rate 1 are associated with the vertices of G, one to each vertex. Initially, one vertex of G knows the rumour. Whenever the clock of a vertex x rings, it calls a random neighbour y: if x knows the rumour and y does not, then x tells y the rumour (a push operation), and if x does not know the rumour and y knows it, y tells x the rumour (a pull operation). The average spread time of G is the expected time it takes for all vertices to know the rumour, and the guaranteed spread time of G is the smallest time t such that with probability at least $1 - 1/n$, after time t all vertices know the rumour. The synchronous variant of this protocol, in which each clock rings precisely at times $1, 2, \dots$, has been studied extensively.

We prove the following results for any n-vertex graph: in either version, the average spread time is at most linear even if only the pull operation is used, and the guaranteed spread time is within a logarithmic factor of the average spread time, so it is $O(n \log n)$. In the asynchronous version, both the average and guaranteed spread times are $\Omega(\log n)$. We give examples of graphs illustrating that these bounds are best possible up to constant factors.

We also prove the first theoretical relationships between the guaranteed spread times in the two versions. Firstly, in all graphs the guaranteed spread time in the asynchronous version is within an $O(\log n)$ factor of that in the synchronous version, and this is tight. Next, we find examples of graphs whose asynchronous spread times are logarithmic, but the synchronous versions are polynomially large. Finally, we show for any graph that the ratio of the synchronous spread time to the asynchronous spread time is $O(n^{2/3})$.

Categories and Subject Descriptors

C.2.0 [**Computer-Communication Networks**]: General—*data communications*; F.2.2 [**Analysis of Algorithms and Problem Complexity**]: Nonnumerical Algorithms and Problems—*computations on discrete structures*; G.2.2 [**Discrete Mathematics**]: Graph Theory—*network problems*

General Terms

Algorithms, Performance, Theory

Keywords

randomized rumour spreading; push&pull protocol; asynchronous time model

1. INTRODUCTION

Randomized rumour spreading is an important primitive for information dissemination in networks and has numerous applications in network science, ranging from spreading information in the WWW and Twitter to spreading viruses and diffusion of ideas in human communities. A well studied rumour spreading protocol is the *(synchronous) push&pull protocol*, introduced by Demers et al. [6] and popularized by Karp et al. [20]. Suppose that one node in a network is aware of a piece of information, the 'rumour', and wants to spread it to all nodes quickly. The protocol proceeds in rounds. In each round, every *informed* node contacts a random neighbour and sends the rumour to it ('pushes' the rumour), and every *uninformed* nodes contacts a random neighbour and gets the rumour if the neighbour knows it ('pulls' the rumour).

*A full version of this paper is available at `http://arxiv.org/abs/1411.0948`.

Permission to make digital or hard copies of all or part of this work for personal or classroom use is granted without fee provided that copies are not made or distributed for profit or commercial advantage and that copies bear this notice and the full citation on the first page. Copyrights for components of this work owned by others than ACM must be honored. Abstracting with credit is permitted. To copy otherwise, or republish, to post on servers or to redistribute to lists, requires prior specific permission and/or a fee. Request permissions from permissions@acm.org.
PODC'15, July 21–23, 2015, Donostia-San Sebastián, Spain.
Copyright is held by the owner/author(s). Publication rights licensed to ACM.
ACM 978-1-4503-3617-8 /15/07 ...$15.00.
DOI: http://dx.doi.org/10.1145/2767386.2767416.

A point to point communication network can be modelled as an undirected graph: the nodes represent the processors and the links represent communication channels between them. Studying rumour spreading has several applications to distributed computing in such networks, of which we mention just two. The first is in broadcasting algorithms: a single processor wants to broadcast a piece of information to all other processors in the network (see [17] for a survey). There are at least four advantages to the push&pull protocol: it puts much less load on the edges than naïve flooding, it is simple (each node makes a simple local decision in each round; no knowledge of the global topology is needed; no state is maintained), scalable (the protocol is independent of the size of network: it does not grow more complex as the network grows) and robust (the protocol tolerates random node/link failures without the use of error recovery mechanisms, see [11]). A second application comes from the maintenance of databases replicated at many sites, e.g., yellow pages, name servers, or server directories. There are updates injected at various nodes, and these updates must propagate to all nodes in the network. In each round, a processor communicates with a random neighbour and they share any new information, so that eventually all copies of the database converge to the same contents. See [6] for details. Other than the aforementioned applications, rumour spreading protocols have successfully been applied in various contexts such as resource discovery [16], distributed averaging [5], data aggregation [21], and the spread of computer viruses [3].

In this paper we only consider simple, undirected and connected graphs. Given a graph and a starting vertex, the *spread time* of a certain protocol is the time it takes for the rumour to spread in the whole graph, i.e. the time difference between the moment the protocol is initiated and the moment when everyone learns the rumour. For the synchronous push&pull protocol, it turned out that the spread time is closely related to the *expansion profile* of the graph. Let $\Phi(G)$ and $\alpha(G)$ denote the conductance and the vertex expansion of a graph G, respectively. After a series of results by various scholars, Giakkoupis [14, 15] showed the spread time is $O\left(\min\{\Phi(G)^{-1} \cdot \log n, \alpha(G)^{-1} \cdot \log^2 n\}\right)$. This protocol has recently been used to model news propagation in social networks. Doerr et al. [7] proved an upper bound of $O(\log n)$ for the spread time on Barabási-Albert graphs, and Fountoulakis et al. [13] proved the same upper bound (up to constant factors) for the spread time on Chung-Lu random graphs.

All the above results assumed a synchronized model, i.e. all nodes take action simultaneously at discrete time steps. In many applications and certainly in real-world social networks, this assumption is not very plausible. Boyd et al. [5] proposed an asynchronous time model with a continuous time line. Each node has its own independent clock that rings at the times of a rate 1 Poisson process. (Since the times between rings is an exponential random variable, we shall call this an *exponential clock*.) The protocol now specifies for every node what to do when its own clock rings. The rumour spreading problem in the asynchronous time model has so far received less attention. Rumour spreading protocols in this model turn out to be closely related to Richardson's model for the spread of a disease [10] and to first-passage percolation [18] with edges having i.i.d. exponential weights. The main difference is that in rumour spreading protocols each vertex contacts one neighbour at a time. So, for instance in the 'push only' protocol, the net communication rate outwards from a vertex is fixed, and hence the rate that the vertex passes the rumour to any one given neighbour is inversely proportional to its degree (the push&pull protocol is a bit more complicated). Hence, the degrees of vertices play a crucial role not seen in Richardson's model or first-passage percolation. However, on regular graphs, the asynchronous push&pull protocol, Richardson's model, and first-passage percolation are essentially the same process, assuming appropriate parameters are chosen. In this sense, Fill and Pemantle [12] and Bollobás and Kohayakawa [4] showed that a.a.s. the spread time of the asynchronous push&pull protocol is $\Theta(\log n)$ on the hypercube graph. Janson [19] and Amini et al. [2] showed the same results (up to constant factors) for the complete graph and for random regular graphs, respectively. These bounds match the same order of magnitude as in the synchronized case. Doerr et al. [9] experimentally compared the spread time in the two time models. They state that 'Our experiments show that the asynchronous model is faster on all graph classes [considered here].' However, a general relationship between the spread times of the two variants has not been proved theoretically.

Fountoulakis et al. [13] investigated the asynchronous push&pull protocol on Chung-Lu random graphs with exponent between 2 and 3. For these graphs, they showed that a.a.s. after some constant time, $n - o(n)$ nodes are informed. Doerr et al. [8] showed that for the preferential attachment graph (the non-tree case), a.a.s. all but $o(n)$ vertices receive the rumour in time $O\left(\sqrt{\log n}\right)$, but to inform all vertices a.a.s., $\Theta(\log n)$ time is necessary and sufficient. Panagiotou and Speidel [22] studied this protocol on Erdős-Renyi random graphs and proved that if the average degree is $(1 + \Omega(1)) \log n$, a.a.s. the spread time is $(1 + o(1)) \log n$.

1.1 Our contribution

In this paper we answer a fundamental question about the asynchronous push&pull protocol: what are the minimum and maximum spread times on an n-vertex graph? Our proof techniques yield new results on the well studied synchronous version as well. We also compare the performances of the two protocols on the same graph, and prove the first theoretical relationships between their spread times.

We now formally define the protocols. In this paper G denotes the ground graph which is simple and connected, and n counts its vertices, and is assumed to be sufficiently large.

Definition 1. (Asynchronous push&pull protocol) Suppose that an independent exponential clock of rate 1 is associated with each vertex of G. Suppose that initially, some vertex v of G knows a piece of information, the so-called *rumour*. The rumour spreads in G as follows. Whenever the clock of a vertex x rings, this vertex performs an 'action': it calls a random neighbour y; if x knows the rumour and y does not, then x tells y the rumour (a *push* operation), and if x does not know the rumour and y knows it, y tells x the rumour (a *pull* operation). Note that if both x and y know the rumour or neither of them knows it, then this action is useless. Also, vertices have no memory, hence x may call the same neighbour several consecutive times. The *spread time* of G starting from v, written $\mathrm{ST_a}(G, v)$, is the first time that all vertices of G know the rumour. Note that this is a continuous random variable, with two sources of randomness: the Poisson processes associated with the vertices, and random neighbour-selection of the vertices. The *guaranteed spread time* of G, written $\mathrm{gst}_a(G)$, is the smallest deterministic number t such that for every $v \in V(G)$ we have $\mathbb{P}[\mathrm{ST}_a(G,v) > t] \leq 1/n$. The *worst average spread time* of G, written $\mathrm{wast}_a(G)$, is the smallest deterministic number t such that for every $v \in V(G)$ we have $\mathbb{E}[\mathrm{ST}_a(G,v)] \leq t$.

Definition 2. (Synchronous push&pull protocol) Initially some vertex v of G knows the rumour, which spreads in G in a round-robin manner: in each round $1, 2, \ldots$, all vertices perform actions simultaneously. That is, each vertex x calls a random neighbour y; if x knows the rumour and y does not, then x tells y the rumour (a *push* operation), and if x does not know the rumour and y knows it, y tells x the rumour (a *pull* operation). Note that this is a synchronous protocol, e.g. a vertex that receives a rumour in a certain round cannot send it on in the same round. The *spread time* of G starting from v, $\mathrm{ST}_s(G,v)$, is the first time that all vertices of G know the rumour. Note that this is a discrete random variable, with one source of randomness: the random neighbour-selection of the vertices. The *guaranteed spread time* of G, written $\mathrm{gst}_s(G)$, and the *worst average spread time* of G, written $\mathrm{wast}_s(G)$, are defined in an analogous way to the asynchronous case.

We remark that the notion of 'guaranteed spread time' was first defined by Feige et al. [11] under the name 'almost sure rumor coverage time' for the 'push only' protocol. (In this protocol, which was studied prior to push&pull, the informed nodes push the rumour, but the uninformed ones do nothing. The 'pull only' protocol is defined conversely.)

It turns out that changing the starting vertex affects the spread time by at most a multiplicative factor of 2. Specifically, in [1] we prove that for any two vertices u and v,

$$\mathrm{ST}_s(G,u) \overset{s}{\leq} 2\,\mathrm{ST}_s(G,v) \text{ and } \mathrm{ST}_a(G,u) \overset{s}{\leq} 2\,\mathrm{ST}_a(G,v)\,. \quad (1)$$

(For random variables X and Y, $X \overset{s}{\leq} Y$ means X is *stochastically dominated by* Y, that is, for any t we have $\mathbb{P}[X \geq t] \leq \mathbb{P}[Y \geq t]$.) These imply that $\mathrm{wast}_s(G) \leq 2\mathbb{E}[\mathrm{ST}_s(G,v)]$ and $\mathrm{wast}_a(G) \leq 2\mathbb{E}[\mathrm{ST}_a(G,v)]$ for any vertex v.

Our first main result is the following theorem.

THEOREM 1. *The following hold for any n-vertex graph G.*

$$(1-1/n)\,\mathrm{wast}_a(G) \leq \mathrm{gst}_a(G) \leq e\,\mathrm{wast}_a(G)\log n\,, \quad (2)$$
$$\mathrm{wast}_a(G) = \Omega(\log n) \text{ and } \mathrm{wast}_a(G) = O(n)\,, \quad (3)$$
$$\mathrm{gst}_a(G) = \Omega(\log n) \text{ and } \mathrm{gst}_a(G) = O(n\log n)\,. \quad (4)$$

Moreover, these bounds are asymptotically best possible, up to the constant factors.

Our proof of the right-hand bound in (3) is based on the pull operation only, so this bound applies equally well to the 'pull only' protocol.

The arguments for (2) and the right-hand bounds in (3) and (4) can easily be extended to the synchronous variant, giving the following theorem. The bound (7) below also follows from [11, Theorem 2.1], but here we also show its tightness.

THEOREM 2. *The following hold for any n-vertex graph G.*

$$(1-1/n)\,\mathrm{wast}_s(G) \leq \mathrm{gst}_s(G) \leq e\,\mathrm{wast}_s(G)\log n\,, \quad (5)$$
$$\mathrm{wast}_s(G) = O(n)\,, \quad (6)$$
$$\mathrm{gst}_s(G) = O(n\log n)\,. \quad (7)$$

Moreover, these bounds are asymptotically best possible, up to the constant factors.

Open problem 1. Find the best possible constants factors in Theorems 1 and 2.

We next turn to studying the relationship between the asynchronous and synchronous variants on the same graph.

THEOREM 3. *For any G we have*

$$\mathrm{gst}_a(G) = O\left(\mathrm{gst}_s(G)\log n\right)\,,$$

and this bound is best possible, up to the constant factor.

For all graphs we examined a stronger result holds, which suggests the following conjecture.

Conjecture 1. For any n-vertex graph G we have $\mathrm{gst}_a(G) \leq \mathrm{gst}_s(G) + O(\log n)$.

Our last main result is the following theorem, whose proof is somewhat technical, and uses couplings with the sequential rumour spreading protocol.

THEOREM 4. *For any $\alpha \in [0,1)$ we have*

$$\mathrm{gst}_s(G) \leq n^{1-\alpha} + O(\mathrm{gst}_a(G)n^{(1+\alpha)/2})\,. \quad (8)$$

COROLLARY 1. *We have*

$$\frac{\mathrm{gst}_s(G)}{\mathrm{gst}_a(G)} = \Omega(1/\log n) \text{ and } \frac{\mathrm{gst}_s(G)}{\mathrm{gst}_a(G)} = O(n^{2/3})\,,$$

and the left-hand bound is asymptotically best possible, up to the constant factor. Moreover, there exist infinitely many graphs for which this ratio is $\Omega\left(n^{1/3}(\log n)^{-4/3}\right)$.

Open problem 2. What is the maximum possible value of the ratio $\mathrm{gst}_s(G)/\mathrm{gst}_a(G)$ for an n-vertex graph G?

The parameters $\mathrm{wast}_s(G)$ and $\mathrm{wast}_a(G)$ can be approximated easily using the Monte Carlo method: simulate the protocols several times, measuring the spread time of each simulation, and output the average. Another open problem is to design a *deterministic* approximation algorithm for any one of $\mathrm{wast}_a(G)$, $\mathrm{gst}_a(G)$, $\mathrm{wast}_s(G)$ or $\mathrm{gst}_s(G)$.

For the proofs we use standard graph theoretic arguments and well known properties of the exponential distribution and Poisson processes, in particular the memorylessness, and the fact that the union of two Poisson processes is another Poisson process. For proving Theorem 4 we define a careful coupling between the synchronous and asynchronous protocols.

Previous work on the asynchronous push&pull protocol has focused on special graphs. This paper is the first systematic study of this protocol on all graphs. We believe this protocol is fascinating and is quite different from its synchronous variant, in the sense that different techniques are required for analyzing it, and the spread times of the two versions can be quite different. Our work makes significant progress on better understanding of this protocol, and will hopefully inspire further research on this problem.

In Section 2 we prove some preliminary results and study some examples, which demonstrate tightness of some of the above bounds. Theorems 1 and 2 are proved in Section 3. Theorems 3 and 4 and Corollary 1 are proved in Section 4. All proofs omitted from this extended abstract can be found in the full version [1].

2. PRELIMINARIES AND EXAMPLES

Let $\mathrm{Geo}(p)$ denote a geometric random variable with parameter p; namely for any $k \in \{0,1,\dots\}$, $\mathbb{P}[\mathrm{Geo}(p)=k] = (1-p)^k p$. Let $\mathrm{Exp}(\lambda)$ denote an exponential random variable with parameter λ and mean $1/\lambda$. For random variables X and Y, $X \overset{d}{=} Y$ means X and Y have the same distribution. All logarithms are natural. We say an event happens *asymptotically almost surely (a.a.s.)* if the probability that it happens approaches 1 as n grows. For functions f and g, the notation $f \sim g$ means $f(n)/g(n)$ approaches 1 as n grows.

We start by making a few observations valid for all graphs.

Observation 1. Consider the asynchronous variant. Let uv be an edge. Whenever v's clock rings, it calls u with probability $1/\deg(v)$. Hence, for each vertex v, we can replace v's clock by one exponential clock for each incident edge, these clocks being independent of all other clocks and having rate $1/\deg(v)$.

Observation 2. Whenever a new vertex is informed, by memorylessness of the exponential random variable, we may imagine that all clocks are restarted.

The following definition will be used throughout.

Definition 3. (Communication time) For an edge $e = uv$, the *communication time via edge e*, written $T(e)$, is defined as follows. Suppose τ is the first time that one of u and v learns the rumour, and ρ is the first time after τ that one of u and v calls the other one. Then $T(e) = \rho - \tau$, which is nonnegative. Note that after time ρ, both u and v know the rumour.

Observation 3. Let $uv \in E(G)$. In the synchronous version,

$$T(uv) \overset{d}{=} 1 + \min\{\mathrm{Geo}(1/\deg(u)), \mathrm{Geo}(1/\deg(v))\}\,.$$

Using Observations 1 and 2 we obtain a nicer formula for the asynchronous version.

PROPOSITION 1. *Let $uv \in E(G)$. In the asynchronous version,*

$$T(uv) \overset{d}{=} \mathrm{Exp}(1/\deg(u) + 1/\deg(v))\,. \qquad (9)$$

Moreover, the random variables $\{T_e\}_{e\in E(G)}$ are mutually independent.

We next study some important graphs and bound their spread times, partly for showing tightness of some of the bounds obtained, and partly to serve as an introduction to the behaviour of the protocols.

2.1 The complete graph

For the complete graph, K_n, we have $\mathrm{wast_a}(K_n) = \log n + O(1)$ (see [1]). In fact, Janson [19] showed that a.a.s. we have $\mathrm{ST_a}(K_n, v) \sim \log n$. Moreover, it is implicit in his proof that $\mathrm{gst_a}(K_n) \sim (3/2)\log n$. For the synchronous version, Karp et al. [20] showed that a.a.s. $\mathrm{ST_s}(K_n, v) \sim \log_3 n$. It follows that $\mathrm{wast_s}(K_n) \sim \log_3 n$. It is implicit in their proof that $\mathrm{gst_s}(K_n) = O(\log n)$.

2.2 The star

The star G_n^* with n vertices has $n-1$ leaves and a central vertex that is adjacent to every other vertex. It is clear that $\mathrm{ST_s}(G_n^*, v) = 1$ if v is the central vertex and $\mathrm{ST_s}(G_n^*, v) = 2$ otherwise. So we have $\mathrm{wast_s}(G_n^*) = \mathrm{gst_s}(G_n^*) = 2$. In the asynchronous case, we have that $\mathrm{wast_a}(G_n^*) \sim \log n$ and $\mathrm{gst_a}(G_n^*) \sim 2\log n$ (see [1]). This graph gives that the left-hand bounds in (2), (3), (4), (5) and Corollary 1, and Theorem 3, are tight, up to constant factors.

2.3 The path

For the path graph P_n, we have $\mathrm{wast_a}(P_n) \sim n$, which shows that the right-hand bound in (3) is tight, up to the constant factor. Moreover, $\mathrm{gst_a}(P_n) \sim n$. For the synchronous protocol, we have $\mathrm{wast_s}(P_n) = (4/3)n - 2$, which shows that the right-hand bound in (6) is tight, up to the constant factor. Finally, we have $\mathrm{gst_s}(P_n) \sim (4/3)n$. See [1] for details.

2.4 The double star

Consider the tree DS_n consisting of two adjacent vertices of degree $n/2$ and $n-2$ leaves, see Figure 1(Top). In [1] we show that $\mathrm{gst_a}(DS_n)$ and $\mathrm{gst_s}(DS_n)$ are both $\Theta(n\log n)$, while the average times $\mathrm{wast_a}(DS_n)$ and $\mathrm{wast_s}(DS_n)$ are $\Theta(n)$. This example hence shows tightness of the right-hand bounds in (2), (4), (5) and (7) up to constant factors. The main delay in spreading the rumour in this graph comes from the edge joining the two centres. The idea is that it takes $O(n)$ units of time on average for this edge to pass the rumour, but to be sure that this has happened with probability $1-1/n$, we need to wait $O(n\log n)$ units of time.

2.5 The necklace graph

Let m and $k \ge 2$ be positive integers, and let G be the necklace graph given in Figure 1(Bottom), where there are m diamonds, each consisting of k edge-disjoint paths of length 2 with the same end vertices, which we call *hubs*. The number of vertices is $n = km + m + 1$. Let us analyze the average spread time.

Consider the asynchronous case first. Proposition 1 gives that for each edge e,

$$T(e) \overset{d}{=} \mathrm{Exp}(1/2 + 1/k) \overset{s}{\le} \mathrm{Exp}(1/2)$$

and that the $\{T(e)\}_{e\in E}$ are independent. Between any two consecutive hubs there are k disjoint paths of length 2, so the communication time between them is stochastically dominated by $Z := \min\{Z_1, \dots, Z_k\}$, where the Z_i are independent random variables equal in distribution to the sum of two independent $\mathrm{Exp}(1/2)$ random variables.

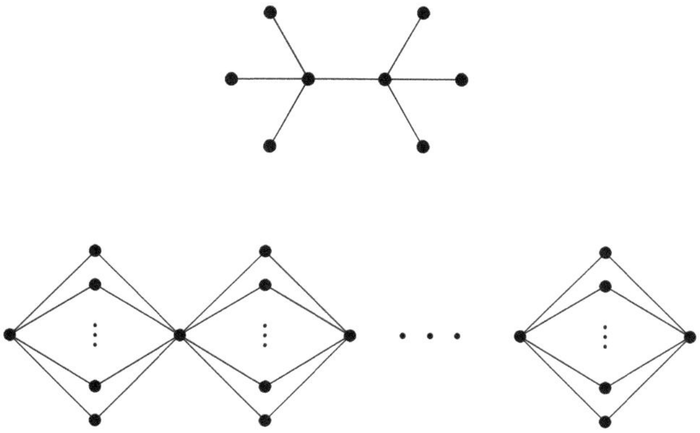

Figure 1: Top: the double star graph DS_8, which has a large guaranteed spread time in both variants. Bottom: a necklace graph, on which the asynchronous push&pull protocol is much quicker than its synchronous variant.

LEMMA 1. *We have* $\mathbb{E}[Z] = O(1/\sqrt{k})$.

PROOF. For any $t \geq 0$ we have

$$\begin{aligned}\mathbb{P}[Z > t] &= \prod_i \mathbb{P}[Z_i > t] = \mathbb{P}[Z_1 > t]^k \\ &\leq \left(1 - \mathbb{P}[\mathrm{Exp}(1/2) \leq t/2]^2\right)^k \\ &= \left(2e^{-t/4} - e^{-t/2}\right)^k .\end{aligned}$$

Thus, using the inequality $2e^{-t/4} - e^{-t/2} \leq e^{-t^2/64}$ valid for $t \in [0, 4]$, we find

$$\begin{aligned}\mathbb{E}[Z] &= \int_0^\infty \mathbb{P}[Z > t]\,\mathrm{d}t \\ &\leq \int_0^4 e^{-kt^2/64}\mathrm{d}t + \int_4^\infty (2e^{-t/4})^k \mathrm{d}t \\ &\leq 8\sqrt{\pi/k} + \frac{2^{k+2}}{ke^k} = O(1/\sqrt{k}) . \quad \square\end{aligned}$$

By Lemma 1, the expected time for all the hubs to learn the rumour is $O(mk^{-1/2})$. Once all the hubs learn the rumour, a degree 2 vertex pulls the rumour in Exp(1) time. The expected value of the maximum of at most km independent Exp(1) variables is $O(\log km)$. So by linearity of expectation, $\mathrm{wast_a}(G) = O(\log n + mk^{-1/2})$.

In the synchronous case, for any G we have $\mathrm{wast_s}(G) \geq \mathrm{diam}(G)$. For this graph, we get $\mathrm{wast_s}(G) \geq 2m$. Choosing $k = \Theta\left((n/\log n)^{2/3}\right)$ and $m = \Theta\left(n^{1/3}(\log n)^{2/3}\right)$ gives

$$\mathrm{wast_a}(G) = O(\log n) \text{ and } \mathrm{wast_s}(G) = \Omega(n^{1/3}(\log n)^{2/3}) .$$

This graph has $\mathrm{wast_s}(G)/\mathrm{wast_a}(G) = \Omega\left((n/\log n)^{1/3}\right)$ and is the example promised by Corollary 1.

3. EXTREMAL SPREAD TIMES

In this section we prove Theorems 1 and 2.

3.1 Proof of (2) and its tightness

For a given $t \geq 0$, consider the protocol which is the same as push&pull except that, if the rumour has not spread to all vertices by time t, then the new process reinitializes. Coupling the new process with push&pull, we obtain for any $k \in \{0, 1, 2, \dots\}$ that

$$\mathbb{P}[\mathrm{ST_a}(G, v) > kt] \leq \mathbb{P}[\mathrm{ST_a}(G, v) > t]^k . \qquad (10)$$

and

$$\mathbb{P}[\mathrm{ST_s}(G, v) > kt] \leq \mathbb{P}[\mathrm{ST_s}(G, v) > t]^k . \qquad (11)$$

Combining (10) with

$$\mathbb{P}[\mathrm{ST_a}(G, v) > e\mathbb{E}[\mathrm{ST_a}(G, v)]] < 1/e,$$

which comes directly from Markov's inequality, we obtain

$$\mathbb{P}[\mathrm{ST_a}(G, v) > e \log n\, \mathbb{E}[\mathrm{ST_a}(G, v)]] < 1/n.$$

Since $\mathbb{E}[\mathrm{ST_a}(G, v)] \leq \mathrm{wast_a}(G)$ for all v, this gives the right-hand inequality in (2) directly from the definition of $\mathrm{gst_a}$. This inequality is tight up to the constant factor, as the double star has $\mathrm{wast_a}(DS_n) = \Theta(n)$ and $\mathrm{gst_a}(DS_n) = \Theta(n \log n)$ (see Section 2.4).

To prove the left-hand inequality, let $\tau = \mathrm{gst_a}(G)$ and let v be a vertex such that $\mathbb{E}[\mathrm{ST_a}(G, v)] = \mathrm{wast_a}(G)$. Then

$$\begin{aligned}\mathrm{wast_a}(G) &= \int_0^\infty \mathbb{P}[\mathrm{ST_a}(G, v) > t]\,dt \\ &= \sum_{i=0}^\infty \int_{i\tau}^{(i+1)\tau} \mathbb{P}[\mathrm{ST_a}(G, v) > t]\,dt \\ &\leq \sum_{i=0}^\infty \frac{\tau}{n^i}\end{aligned}$$

by (10) with $t = \tau$. Hence $\mathrm{wast_a}(G) \leq \tau/(1 - 1/n)$. This inequality is tight up to a constant factor, as the star has $\mathrm{wast_a}(G_n^*) = \Theta(\mathrm{gst_a}(G_n^*)) = \Theta(\log n)$ (see Section 2.2).

3.2 Proof of the right-hand bound in (3) and its tightness

We will actually prove this using pull operations only. Indeed we will show $\mathrm{wast_a^{pull}}(G) \leq 4n$, where the superscript pull means the 'pull only' protocol. Since the path has $\mathrm{wast_a^{pull}}(P_n) \geq \mathrm{wast_a}(P_n) = \Theta(n)$ (see Section 2.3), this bound would be tight up to the constant factor.

The proof is by induction: we prove that when there are precisely m uninformed vertices, just b of which have informed neighbours (we call these b vertices the *boundary vertices*), the expected remaining time for the rumour to reach all vertices is at most $4m - 2b$. The inductive step is proved as follows. Let I denote the set of informed vertices, B the set of boundary vertices, and R the set of the remaining vertices. Let $|B| = b$ and $|B| + |R| = m$. Let $d(v)$ denote the degree of v in G and, for a set S of vertices, let $d_S(v)$ count the number of neighbours of v in S. We consider two cases.

Firstly, suppose that there exists a boundary vertex v with $d_R(v) \geq d_B(v)$ (see Figure 2(Left)). We can for the next step ignore all calls from vertices other than v, so the process is forced to wait until v is informed before any other vertices. This clearly gives an upper bound on the spread time. The expected time taken for v to pull the rumour from vertices in I is

$$\begin{aligned}\frac{d(v)}{d_I(v)} &= \frac{d_I(v) + d_R(v) + d_B(v)}{d_I(v)} \\ &\leq 1 + \frac{2d_R(v)}{d_I(v)} \leq 1 + 2d_R(v) .\end{aligned}$$

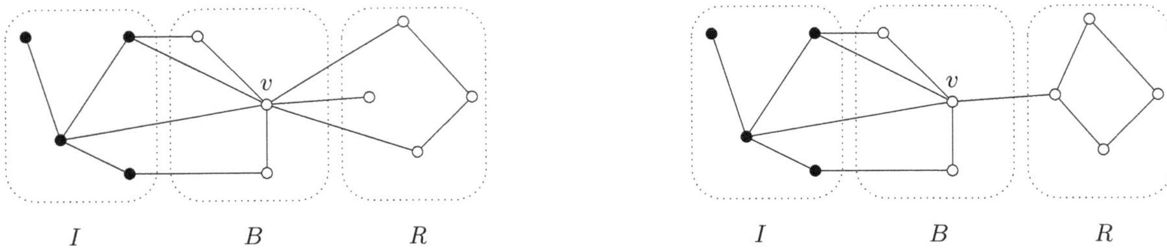

Figure 2: Left: first case in the proof of the right-hand bound in (3): there exists a boundary vertex v with $3 = d_R(v) \geq d_B(v) = 2$. Right: second case in the proof of the right-hand bound in (3): for all boundary vertices v we have $d_R(v) < d_B(v)$ (informed vertices are black, uninformed vertices are white).

Once v is informed, the number of uninformed vertices decreases by 1, and the number of boundary vertices increases by $d_R(v) - 1$. The inductive hypothesis concludes this case since

$$1 + 2d_R(v) + 4(m-1) - 2(b + d_R(v) - 1) < 4m - 2b.$$

Otherwise, if there is no such v (as in Figure 2(Right)), then any boundary vertex v has a 'pulling rate' of

$$\frac{d_I(v)}{d_I(v) + d_R(v) + d_B(v)} \geq \frac{1}{1 + d_R(v) + d_B(v)} \geq \frac{1}{2d_B(v)} \geq \frac{1}{2b}.$$

Since there are b boundary vertices, together they have a pulling rate of at least $1/2$, so the expected time until a boundary vertex is informed is at most 2. Once this happens, m decreases by 1 and b either does not decrease or decreases by 1, and the inductive hypothesis concludes the proof.

3.3 Proof of the left-hand bound in (3) and its tightness

In this section we show for any vertex v_0 of a graph G we have $\mathbb{E}[\mathrm{ST}_a(G, v_0)] = \Omega(\log n)$. This is tight as the star has $\mathrm{wast}_a(G_n^*) = O(\log n)$ (see Section 2.2). We give an argument for an equivalent protocol, defined below.

Definition 4. (Two-clock-per-edge protocol) On each edge place two exponential clocks, one near each end vertex. All clocks are independent. On an edge joining vertices u and v, the clocks both have rate $\deg(u)^{-1} + \deg(v)^{-1}$. Note that this is the rate of calls along that edge, combined, from u and v (see Proposition 1). At any time that the clock near u on an edge uv rings, and v knows the rumour but u does not, the rumour is passed to u.

LEMMA 2. *The two-clock-per-edge protocol is equivalent to the asynchronous push&pull protocol.*

PROOF. Consider an arbitrary moment during the execution of the two-clock-per-edge protocol. Let I denote the set of informed vertices. For any edge uv with $u \in I$ and $v \notin I$, the rate of calls along uv is $\deg(u)^{-1} + \deg(v)^{-1}$. Moreover, the edges act independently. So, the behaviour of the protocol at this moment is exactly the same as that of the asynchronous push&pull protocol. Hence, the two protocols are equivalent. □

In view of Lemma 2, we may work with the two-clock-per-edge protocol instead. Let X_v be the time taken for the first clock located near v to ring. Then X_v is distributed as $\mathrm{Exp}(f(v))$ where $f(v) = 1 + \sum \deg(u)^{-1}$, the sum being over all neighbours u of v. Hence, $\sum f(v) = 2n$.

On the other hand, for a vertex $v \neq v_0$ to learn the rumour, at least one of the clocks located near v must ring. Thus

$$\max\{X_v : v \in V(G)\backslash\{v_0\}\} \overset{s}{\leq} \mathrm{ST}_a(G, v_0).$$

Let $X = \max\{X_v : v \in V(G)\backslash\{v_0\}\}$. Hence to prove $\mathbb{E}[\mathrm{ST}_a(G, v_0)] = \Omega(\log n)$ it suffices to show $\mathbb{E}[X] = \Omega(\log n)$.

Let $\tau = \log(n-1)/3$ and $A = V(G) \setminus \{v_0\}$, Then we have

$$\begin{aligned}
\mathbb{P}[X < \tau] &= \prod_{v \in A}(X_v < \tau) = \prod_{v \in A}(1 - e^{-\tau f(v)}) \\
&\leq \exp\left(-\sum_{v \in A} e^{-\tau f(v)}\right) \\
&\leq \exp\left(-(n-1)e^{-\tau \sum_v f(v)/(n-1)}\right) \\
&\leq \exp\left(-(n-1)e^{-3\tau}\right) = e^{-1}.
\end{aligned}$$

Here the first inequality follows from $1 - x \leq e^{-x}$, the second from the arithmetic-geometric mean inequality, and the last one from $2n = \sum_v f(v) \leq 3(n-1)$ which holds for any $n \geq 3$. Consequently,

$$\mathbb{E}[X] \geq \mathbb{P}[X \geq \tau]\,\tau \geq (1 - e^{-1})\log(n-1)/3 = \Omega(\log n),$$

as required.

3.4 Proof of (4) and its tightness

The bounds in (4) follow immediately from (2) and (3). The left-hand bound is tight as the star has $\mathrm{gst}_a(G_n^*) = \Theta(\log n)$ (see Section 2.2), and the right-hand bound is tight as the double star has $\mathrm{gst}_a(DS_n) = \Theta(n \log n)$ (see Section 2.4).

3.5 Proof of Theorem 2

The proof of (5) and its tightness are exactly the same as that for (2). The proof for (6) is similar to the one for the right-hand bound in (3) given in Section 3.2, and can be found in [1]. This gives $\mathrm{wast}_s(G) = O(n)$, which is tight up to the constant factor, as the path has diameter $n-1$ and hence $\mathrm{wast}_s(P_n) \geq n-1$. Finally, the bound $\mathrm{gst}_s(G) = O(n \log n)$ is a direct consequence of (5) and (6), and it is tight as the double star has guaranteed spread time $\Theta(n \log n)$ (see Section 2.4).

4. COMPARISON OF THE TWO PROTOCOLS

We first prove Corollary 1 assuming Theorems 3 and 4, and in the following subsections we prove these theorems. The left-hand bound in Corollary 1 follows from Theorem 3; it is tight, up to the constant factor, as the star graph has $\mathrm{gst_a}(G_n^*) = \Theta(\log n)$ and $\mathrm{gst_s}(G_n^*) = 2$ (see Section 2.2). The right-hand bound in Corollary 1 follows from Theorem 4 by choosing $\alpha = 1/3$. A graph G was given in Section 2.5 having $\mathrm{wast_s}(G)/\mathrm{wast_a}(G) = \Omega\left((n/\log n)^{1/3}\right)$. Using (2) and (5), we get $\mathrm{gst_s}(G)/\mathrm{gst_a}(G) = \Omega\left(n^{1/3}(\log n)^{-4/3}\right)$ for this G.

4.1 The lower bound

In this section we prove Theorem 3. Let G be an n-vertex graph and let s denote the vertex starting the rumour. We build a coupling between the two versions. Consider a 'collection of calling lists for vertices': for every vertex u, we have an infinite list of vertices, each entry of which is a uniformly random neighbour of u, chosen independently from other entries. The coupling is built by using the same collection of calling lists for the two versions of the push&pull protocol. Note that $\mathrm{ST_s}(G,s)$ is determined by this collection, but to determine $\mathrm{ST_a}(G,s)$ we also need to know the Poisson processes associated with the vertices.

Let B denote the event '$\mathrm{ST_s}(G,s) \le 2\,\mathrm{gst_s}(G)$', which depends on the calling lists only. Inequality (11) gives $\mathbb{P}[B^c] \le 1/n^2$. (Here, B^c denotes the complement of B.) Partition the time interval $[0, 2\,\mathrm{gst_s}(G) \times 4\log n)$ into subintervals $[0, 4\log n)$, $[4\log n, 8\log n)$, etc. Consider a 'decelerated' variant of the asynchronous push&pull protocol in which each vertex makes a call the first time its clock rings in each subinterval (if it does), but ignores later clock rings in that subinterval (if any). The spread time in this protocol is stochastically larger than that in the asynchronous push&pull protocol, so without loss of generality we may and will work with the decelerated variant. Let A denote the event 'during each of these $2\,\mathrm{gst_s}(G)$ subintervals, all clocks ring at least once.' If A happens, then an inductive argument gives that for any $1 \le k \le 2\,\mathrm{gst_s}(G)$, the set of informed vertices in the decelerated variant at time $4k\log n$ contains the set of informed vertices after k rounds of the synchronous version. Hence, if both A and B happen, then we would have

$$\mathrm{ST_a}(G,s) \le (4\log n)\,\mathrm{ST_s}(G,s) \le (8\log n)\,\mathrm{gst_s}(G)\,.$$

Hence to complete the proof, we need only show that $\mathbb{P}[A^c] < 1/n - 1/n^2$.

Let I denote a given subinterval of length $4\log n$. In the asynchronous version, the clock of any given vertex rings with probability at least $1 - n^{-4}$ during I. By the union bound, all clocks ring at least once during I, with probability at least $1-n^{-3}$. The number of subintervals in the definition of A is $2\,\mathrm{gst_s}(G)$, which is $O(n\log n)$ by (7). By the union bound again, $\mathbb{P}[A^c] = O\left(\log n/n^2\right)$, as required.

Theorem 3 is tight, up to the constant factor, as the star has $\mathrm{gst_a}(G_n^*) = \Theta(\log n)$ and $\mathrm{gst_s}(G_n^*) = 2$ (see Section 2.2).

4.2 The upper bound

The proof of Theorem 4 can be found in [1]. Here we sketch the proof. The main ingredients in the proof are a coupling between the two protocols, and sharp concentration bounds. Consider the asynchronous version. List the vertices in the order their clocks ring. The list ends once all the vertices are informed. Now consider the natural coupling between the two protocols, the synchronous actions follow the same ordering as in the list. We partition the list into blocks according to a certain rule in such a way that the blocks have the following property: the synchronous protocol in each round will inform a superset of the set of vertices informed by the asynchronous variant in any single block. For example, if we require that in each block each vertex communicates with the others at most once, then we would have this property. However, in order to get our bound, we need to use a more delicate rule for building the blocks. To conclude, we find an upper bound for the number of blocks, which coincides with the right-hand side of (8).

5. ACKNOWLEDGEMENTS

Andrea Collevecchio was supported by ARC Discovery Project grant DP140100559 and STREP project MATHEMACS. Abbas Mehrabian was supported by the Vanier Canada Graduate Scholarships program; most of this work was done while he was visiting Monash University. Nick Wormald was supported by Australian Laureate Fellowships grant FL120100125.

6. REFERENCES

[1] H. Acan, A. Collevecchio, A. Mehrabian, and N. Wormald. On the push&pull protocol for rumour spreading. *arXiv*, 1411.0948 [cs.DC], 2014.

[2] H. Amini, M. Draief, and M. Lelarge. Flooding in weighted sparse random graphs. *SIAM J. Discrete Math.*, 27(1):1–26, 2013.

[3] N. Berger, C. Borgs, J. Chayes, and A. Saberi. On the spread of viruses on the Internet. In *Proc. 16th Symp. Discrete Algorithms (SODA)*, pages 301–310, 2005.

[4] B. Bollobás and Y. Kohayakawa. On Richardson's model on the hypercube. In *Combinatorics, geometry and probability (Cambridge, 1993)*, pages 129–137. Cambridge Univ. Press, Cambridge, 1997.

[5] S. Boyd, A. Ghosh, B. Prabhakar, and D. Shah. Randomized gossip algorithms. *IEEE Transactions on Information Theory*, 52(6):2508–2530, 2006.

[6] A. Demers, D. Greene, C. Hauser, W. Irish, J. Larson, S. Shenker, H. Sturgis, D. Swinehart, and D. Terry. Epidemic algorithms for replicated database maintenance. In *Proc. 6th Symp. Principles of Distributed Computing (PODC)*, pages 1–12, 1987.

[7] B. Doerr, M. Fouz, and T. Friedrich. Social networks spread rumors in sublogarithmic time. In *Proc. 43th Symp. Theory of Computing (STOC)*, pages 21–30, 2011.

[8] B. Doerr, M. Fouz, and T. Friedrich. Asynchronous rumor spreading in preferential attachment graphs. In *Proc. 13th Scandinavian Workshop Algorithm Theory (SWAT)*, pages 307–315, 2012.

[9] B. Doerr, M. Fouz, and T. Friedrich. Experimental analysis of rumor spreading in social networks. In *Design and analysis of algorithms*, volume 7659 of *Lecture Notes in Comput. Sci.*, pages 159–173. Springer, Heidelberg, 2012.

[10] R. Durrett. Stochastic growth models: recent results and open problems. In *Mathematical approaches to problems in resource management and epidemiology (Ithaca, NY, 1987)*, volume 81 of *Lecture Notes in Biomath.*, pages 308–312. Springer, Berlin, 1989.

[11] U. Feige, D. Peleg, P. Raghavan, and E. Upfal. Randomized broadcast in networks. *Random Struct. Algorithms*, 1(4):447–460, 1990.

[12] J. A. Fill and R. Pemantle. Percolation, first-passage percolation and covering times for Richardson's model on the n-cube. *Ann. Appl. Probab.*, 3(2):593–629, 1993.

[13] N. Fountoulakis, K. Panagiotou, and T. Sauerwald. Ultra-fast rumor spreading in social networks. In *Proc. 23th Symp. Discrete Algorithms (SODA)*, pages 1642–1660, 2012.

[14] G. Giakkoupis. Tight bounds for rumor spreading in graphs of a given conductance. In *28th International Symposium on Theoretical Aspects of Computer Science (STACS 2011)*, volume 9, pages 57–68, 2011.

[15] G. Giakkoupis. Tight bounds for rumor spreading with vertex expansion. In *Proc. 25th Symp. Discrete Algorithms (SODA)*, pages 801–815, 2014.

[16] M. Harchol-Balter, F. T. Leighton, and D. Lewin. Resource discovery in distributed networks. In *Proc. 18th Symp. Principles of Distributed Computing (PODC)*, pages 229–237, 1999.

[17] S. M. Hedetniemi, S. T. Hedetniemi, and A. L. Liestman. A survey of gossiping and broadcasting in communication networks. *Networks*, 18(4):319–349, 1988.

[18] C. D. Howard. Models of first-passage percolation. In *Probability on discrete structures*, volume 110 of *Encyclopaedia Math. Sci.*, pages 125–173. Springer, Berlin, 2004.

[19] S. Janson. One, two and three times $\log n/n$ for paths in a complete graph with random weights. *Combin. Probab. Comput.*, 8(4):347–361, 1999.

[20] R. Karp, C. Schindelhauer, S. Shenker, and B. Vöcking. Randomized Rumor Spreading. In *Proc. 41st Symp. Foundations of Computer Science (FOCS)*, pages 565–574, 2000.

[21] D. Kempe, A. Dobra, and J. Gehrke. Gossip-based computation of aggregate information. In *Proc. 44th Symp. Foundations of Computer Science (FOCS)*, pages 482–491, 2003.

[22] K. Panagiotou and L. Speidel. Asynchronous rumor spreading on random graphs. In L. Cai, S.-W. Cheng, and T.-W. Lam, editors, *Algorithms and Computation*, volume 8283 of *Lecture Notes in Computer Science*, pages 424–434. Springer Berlin Heidelberg, 2013.

Distributed Resource Discovery in Sub-Logarithmic Time

Bernhard Haeupler*
School of Computer Science
Carnegie Mellon University
Pittsburgh, PA 15213, USA
haeupler@cs.cmu.edu

Dahlia Malkhi
VMware Research
Palo Alto, CA 94304, USA
dmalkhi@vmware.com

ABSTRACT

We present a new distributed algorithm for the resource discovery problem introduced by Harchol-Balter, Leighton, and Levin in PODC'99.

The resource discovery problem consists of a synchronous network with n machines in which at any timestep any machine v can PUSH or PULL a message to/from any other machine u whose (IP) address is known to v. Messages can contain addresses which then change the "topology". The goal of a distributed resource discovery problem is to enable all machines to learn the addresses of all other machines as fast as possible while keeping the number of messages sent low.

We present a randomized distributed algorithm that achieves this goal in $O(\log D \log \log n)$ rounds using $O(n)$ messages, where D is the strong diameter of the initial topology. Up to the $\log \log n$ factor, our round complexity is best possible given the trivial $\Omega(\log D)$ lower bound. For many typical networks with $D = o(n)$, our running time is a drastic improvement over prior $O(\log n)$ round algorithms. In particular, for networks with polylogarithmic diameter an $O(\log^2 \log n)$ running time and thus an almost exponential speedup is obtained.

Categories and Subject Descriptors

F.2.2 [**Theory of Computation**]: ANALYSIS OF ALGORITHMS AND PROBLEM COMPLEXITY—*Nonnumerical Algorithms and Problems*; F.1.2 [**Theory of Computation**]: COMPUTATION BY ABSTRACT DEVICES—*Modes of Computation* Parallelism and concurrency

General Terms

Algorithms, Theory, Performance, Reliability

*Research supported in part by NSF award "AF:Small:Distributed Algorithms for Near-Planar Networks".

Permission to make digital or hard copies of all or part of this work for personal or classroom use is granted without fee provided that copies are not made or distributed for profit or commercial advantage and that copies bear this notice and the full citation on the first page. Copyrights for components of this work owned by others than the author(s) must be honored. Abstracting with credit is permitted. To copy otherwise, or republish, to post on servers or to redistribute to lists, requires prior specific permission and/or a fee. Request permissions from permissions@acm.org.
PODC'14, July 21 – 23, 2015, Donostia-San SebastiÃąn, Spain.
Copyright is held by the owner/author(s). Publication rights licensed to ACM.
ACM 978-1-4503-3617-8/15/07 ...$15.00.
http://dx.doi.org/10.1145/2767386.2767435.

Keywords

resource discovery; direct addressing; gossip; information dissemination; rumor spreading

1. INTRODUCTION

We give a new distributed algorithm for the classical *resource discovery* problem introduced in [11] that features drastically improved running time on typical networks while maintaining an optimal message complexity.

Resource discovery is a basic task in distributed networks that is concerned with informing all participants in a network about each other in a fast and communication efficient way. It can be used as a coordination mechanism, e.g., in networks with somewhat frequent joins and leaves, and often forms the first step for implementing further distributed functionalities. As such, it has been intensely studied from both a practical and theoretical perspective.

1.1 Formal Problem Definition

The mathematical definition as a distributed problem goes back to the work of Harchol-Baler et al. [11] and arose in the context of building a large-scale distributed cache for their newly founded company Akamai:

Machines are abstracted as nodes in a directed graph $G = (V, E)$ with n nodes in which a directed edge $(u, v) \in E$ means that machine u knows (the IP address of) v and can thus contact v. We write $\Gamma(u)$ to denote set of nodes that node u can contact. Communication proceeds in synchronous rounds in which each node u can PUSH or PULL a message to/from any nodes in $\Gamma(u)$. Each such operation gets counted as one message. In a message a node can communicate any desired information but typically a node simply sends the set of IDs it knows and possibly some small amount of control information, e.g., $O(\log n)$ bits. Once a node has received a message containing addresses it can contact the respective nodes in subsequent rounds and the network graph G changes accordingly. This network model has also been called the DIRECT ADDRESSING or DA model [8].

The goal of distributed resource discovery algorithms in the DA model is to guarantee that for a given initial network topology all nodes learn about each other as quickly as possible without sending too many messages.

1.2 Prior Work on Resource Discovery

The trivial resource discovery algorithm in the DA model is flooding. Flooding simply has every node forward its knowledge to *all* nodes it knows about. It is easy to see that this flooding algorithm terminates in $\log D + 1$ time where D is the (weak) diameter[1] of the initial network topology and that this running time bound is optimal. On the other hand, the flooding algorithm has a horrible message complexity and sends up to $\Theta(n^2)$ messages in a single round. This is even true for sparse networks as they become dense quickly.

The idea of Harchol-Balter et al. was to leverage randomization in achieving more communication efficient information dissemination. They introduced the NameDropper gossip algorithm in which each node sends the addresses it knows solely to a uniformly random contact. They proved that $O(\log D \log n)$ rounds each using n messages are sufficient for this algorithm to solve the resource discovery problem. Subsequently Law and Siu [18] gave a simple randomized resource discovery algorithm requiring $O(\log n)$ rounds and Kutten, Peleg, and Vishkin [17] building on a connectivity algorithm of Shiloach and Vishkin [20] gave a deterministic algorithm that uses $O(\log n)$ rounds and sends only $O(n \log n)$ messages in total.

1.3 Our Result

While these $O(\log n)$ running times match the trivial $\Omega(\log D)$ lower bound for networks with a linear (or polynomial) diameter, such networks are arguably not the setting of interest. Indeed the networks topologies one would expect to encounter in a resource discovery setting are typically well connected and have a small, e.g., at most (poly-)logarithmic, strong diameter[2]. In those networks, the $\Omega(\log D)$ lower bound merely excludes the existence of sub-log-logarithmic algorithm thus leaving open the question whether such exponentially faster algorithms are achievable. In this work we answer this question in the affirmative by giving an algorithm that matches the $\Omega(\log D)$ lower bound for the strong diameter up to an $O(\log \log n)$ factor:

THEOREM 1. *Suppose a network in the DA model with n nodes and a strong diameter of D. There is a distributed randomized algorithm that, with high probability, completes a resource discovery in any such network in $O(\log D \cdot \log \log n)$ rounds using a total of $\Theta(n)$ messages.*

Remarks:

- Like all previous works we do not attempt to give any formal failure model and prove robustness results for our algorithm with respect to any permanent or temporary failure or interleaved join and leaves. This said, we believe that the randomized GOSSIP nature of our algorithm (similar to [11]) actually makes the algorithm quite robust at least to random failures or leaves (which, e.g., are unlikely to specifically delete cluster-centers). More over the (almost) exponentially faster running time guarantee on typical networks compared to prior approaches drastically reduces the timeframe in which the network needs to be (sufficiently) stable and allows the rebuilding process to be run more frequently.
- Like [18] but in contrast to [11, 17] we give running time guarantees with respect to the strong diameter. We postulate this diameter to be small for instances of interest. We also remark that it is generally impossible to have GOSSIP algorithms that perform well in graphs with low weak-diameter while having nodes send at most c messages per round. In fact such algorithms cannot run in less than $\log_c n = \log n / \log c$ rounds on the star-network in which one center node knows about all other n nodes (but not vice versa) even though this network has a weak diameter of 2. Thus the only way to even achieve sub-logarithmic running time in this network is to have a single node send at least polynomially many messages in one round.

1.4 More Prior Work

In addition to the results of [11, 17, 18] on the resource discovery problem (see Section 1.2) the techniques used in our algorithm are also closely related to [8, 2]. These works show that one can achieve sub-logarithmic running times for the global broadcast problem if one considers a communication model that allows for DIRECT ADDRESSING and also for contacting a random participating node in each round. In particular, Avin and Elsässer[2] gave an algorithm with $O(\sqrt{\log n})$ round complexity while Haeupler and Malkhi [9] showed that even a $\Theta(\log \log n)$ running time is achievable and optimal. These results can be interpreted as running times of resource discovery algorithms on random topologies in which each node has many directed links to independently chosen nodes. Since such topologies have a logarithmic diameter Theorem 1 implies an $O(\log^2 \log n)$ running time for this setting as well. The setting in this paper however is significantly more involved because no randomness or even expansion in the topology is assumed. The one (and only) crucial idea we managed to carry over from [8] is to organize nodes in clusters and try to achieve a doubly exponential growing process by having clusters of size s reach out to $O(s)$ clusters for merging thus leading to s^2 size clusters in one step.

We also remark that there are many parallels between this work and gossip algorithms for the LOCAL model [19], which features a fixed undirected topology. There too the resource discovery or global broadcast problem can be solved via flooding in an optimal time complexity, which is $O(D)$ in the LOCAL model. This however requires up to $\Theta(n^2)$ messages per round. Demers et al. [6] were the first to introduce randomized gossip algorithm to achieve fast and reliable information dissemination. Since then uniform gossip has been shown to work well on complete graphs [12] and random and expanding topologies [4, 7]. Similar to this work more recent non-uniform gossip algorithms [3, 8] even achieve $O(D + \text{poly} \log n)$ running times, which are close to the trivial $\Omega(D)$ lower bound achieved by flooding albeit

[1]The weak diameter of a network is the smallest integer for which every node has a path of length at most D to any other node when directions of edges are ignored.

[2]The strong diameter of a network is the smallest integer for which every node has a directed path of length at most D to any other node.

while using only $O(1)$ communication (instead of $O(n)$) per node.

Beyond these works, owing to the high practical relevance of the topic, many works have studied variants of the resource discovery problem. We mention [15, 1, 16] which consider resource discovery in an asynchronous setting, [10, 13] which considers communication efficient resource discovery gossip with small messages and refer to [14] and the recent PhD thesis of Davtya [5] for a broader overview and further references.

2. RESOURCE DISCOVERY

2.1 Clusters

In this section we introduce clusters, a simple tool used in this paper to achieve efficient exploration. Briefly, a cluster is a set of nodes that have a designated cluster-center known to all nodes in the cluster. All nodes within a cluster can exchange information via the center using only a constant number of rounds and messages per node. This allows a cluster to act in a coordinated manner.

More precisely, a cluster is a set S of nodes, with each node $v \in S$ containing a variable $follow_v = \ell_S$ set to the address of the cluster leader. Initially all nodes form their own cluster and have $follow$ set to their own address. For a node v, we denote its cluster by $C(v)$ (or simply C when clear from context).

Having a central leader which is known to all nodes in a cluster allows a cluster to coordinate using only a constant number of communication rounds. In particular, in one communication round followers may PUSH information to the leader and thus have the leader collect inputs from the entire cluster. In a second round, followers may PULL a response from the leader. Throughout the rest of this paper we implicitly assume that information is exchanged within each cluster before external communication steps as needed. This allows us to treat clusters as indivisible entities which act as a unit and share full information, while omitting the details concerning PUSHing and PULLing messages.

We furthermore use the following notation: For two clusters C_1, C_2, if there is an edge from a node $v \in C_1$ to a node $w \in C_2$ we say that C_2 is a *cneighbor* of C_1. Clusters generally do not know which clusters are cneighbors. For this reason any cluster C maintains a set $A(C)$ in which it keeps track of clusters that it knows to be current cneighbors.

Remark:
A cluster can easily find out, using two cluster internal PUSH/PULL rounds, which nodes $\Gamma(C)$ the nodes in C are connected to. However, it is much harder (or message intensive) to find out what its distinct cneighbors are, i.e., which nodes in $\Gamma(C)$ belong to the same cluster. In particular, as clusters merge these clusterings change and it is generally too message expensive to keep a complete list of cneighbors updated. This is the reason for having $A(C)$. It also means that after every round of cluster merging the list $A(C)$ becomes outdated and is thus set to be the empty set.

2.2 The Resource Discovery Algorithm

We next give a high level description of our algorithm: The algorithm first calls the INITIALIZATION sub-routine which reduces the number of clusters by a polylogarithmic factor, bringing the average cluster size to $s = \log^{O(1)} n$. This is done in $\Theta(\log\log n)$ rounds via a merging process that guarantees singly exponential reduction process in the number of clusters.

The main loop of the algorithm then employs iterations with a doubly exponential growth progress by roughly squaring the average size s of a cluster in each iteration. For this, each iteration begins with using the DISCOVERCNEIGHBORS routine to have clusters explore their neighborhood and discover at least $d \approx s$ cneighbors as potential merging partners.

Clusters that do not have enough cneighbors use INFLATEOUTDEGREE to perform a local flooding procedure until at least d clusters are reached. This requires at most $\log D$ flooding steps and does not lead to a large message overhead because only clusters with less then d cneighbors participate.

The SAMPLEMERGE routine then randomly sub-samples roughly a $1/d \approx 1/s$ fraction of clusters to be the new cluster-centers and assigns each non-selected cluster to a cluster center. With high probablity, the number of clusters is thus reduced roughly by factor s, which leads to a new average cluster size of about $s \cdot d \approx s^2$.

This doubly exponential merging process is performed for $O(\log\log n)$ iterations until the average cluster size reaches at least $\sqrt{n}\log n$. A final INFLATEOUTDEGREE guarantees that every cluster becomes aware of any other cluster. The cluster centers then inform all their nodes about all other nodes, which completes the resource discovery process.

Algorithm 1 Log-logarithmic resource discovery algorithm

INITIALIZATION($\Theta(\log\log n)$)
$\epsilon \leftarrow 1/2$
$s \leftarrow \log^{2/\epsilon} n$
Clusters of size $s' > s$ split into $\lceil s'/s \rceil$ clusters of size between $s/2$ and s

repeat
▷ explore/expand neighbors to discover $s^{1-\epsilon}$ cneighbors
    DISCOVERCNEIGHBORS($s, 2/\epsilon$)
    $d \leftarrow s^{1-\epsilon}$
    INFLATEOUTDEGREE(d)

▷ sample-merge phase to reduce number of clusters by roughly $1/d$
    SAMPLEMERGE(s, d)
    $s \leftarrow \Theta(s \cdot d/\log n)$ ▷ $\Theta(s \cdot d/\log n) = \Omega(s^{2-1.5\epsilon})$
    Clusters of size $s' > s$ split into $\lceil s'/s \rceil$ clusters of size between $s/2$ and s

until $s \geq \sqrt{n}\log n$ ▷ $\Theta(\log\log n)$ repetitions

INFLATEOUTDEGREE($\sqrt{n}$) ▷ all clusters become aware of all clusters
Cluster centers inform all nodes in their cluster about all other nodes

2.3 Analysis

Next we prove our main theorem:

THEOREM 1 (repeated). *Suppose a network in the DA model with n nodes and a strong diameter of D. There is a distributed randomized algorithm that, with high probability, completes a resource discovery in any such network in $O(\log D \cdot \log\log n)$ rounds using a total of $\Theta(n)$ messages.*

The proof relies on the following guarantees about the subroutines referenced in Algorithm 1. We give their statements here and provide their implementations and proofs in subsequent subsections.

LEMMA 2. *Assume that there are at least $\Omega(\log n)$ clusters before a call to* INITIALIZATION. *For every r, with high probability,* INITIALIZATION*(r) reduces the number of clusters by a factor of $c = e^{\Theta(r)}$ using $O(r)$ rounds and $\Theta(n)$ messages in total.*

LEMMA 3. *Assume each cluster is of size at most s and suppose that $s \geq \log^2 n$. With high probability after a call of* DISCOVERCNEIGHBORS*(s,r) each cluster C knows either all or at least $|A(C)| \geq \Theta(s^{1-(2/r)})$ distinct cneighbors. The routine furthermore requires at most $O(r)$ rounds with at most $O(rs^{1-(1/r)})$ messages being sent by each cluster.*

LEMMA 4. *Assume that each cluster has outgoing edges to either to all of its cneighbors or to at least d of them. Assume further that the underlying network has a strong diameter of at most D. Then, at the end of* INFLATEOUTDEGREE*(d) a cluster C is aware of either all clusters or at least d cneighbors, i.e, $|A(C)| \geq d$. Furthermore, only $O(\log D)$ rounds and $O(d \cdot \log D)$ messages per cluster are required.*

LEMMA 5. *Assuming that at the beginning of* SAMPLEMERGE*(d) every cluster C is aware of at least $d \geq \log^2 n$ cneighbors, i.e., $|A(C)| \geq d$, then with high probability* SAMPLEMERGE*(d) reduces the number of clusters by a factor of $\Theta(\log n/d)$. Furthermore, only $O(1)$ rounds and $O(d)$ messages per cluster are required.*

PROOF OF THEOREM 1. We first prove the correctness of Algorithm 1. Initially each node forms its own cluster so there are n clusters. Theorem 2 now guarantees that the initialization step ends with at most $n/\log^{2/\epsilon} n = n/s$ clusters. The splitting of clusters of size larger than s leads to at most n/s further clusters for a total of at most $2n/s$ clusters each of size at most s.

We prove by induction that this guarantee of at most $2n/s$ clusters of size at most s holds whenever the beginning or end of the main loop is reached.

In particular, Theorem 3 guarantees for all $eps > 0$, that during DISCOVERCNEIGHBORS$(s, 2/\epsilon)$ every cluster discovers at least $d = s^{1-\epsilon}$ or all its cneighbors and Theorem 4 guarantees that after INFLATEOUTDEGREE(d) every node has at least d cneighbors in its $A(C)$ set. Theorem 5 shows that SAMPLEMERGE(d) then reduces the number of clusters by a $\Theta(\log n/d)$ factor thus decreasing the number of clusters to at most $\Theta(n/(\frac{s \cdot d}{\log n}))$ or n/s after the parameter s is updated. Splitting clusters larger than s again at most doubles the number of clusters to $2n/s$ and leads to clusters of size at most s as postulated.

Once the main loop terminates this leads to at most $2\sqrt{n}/\log n$ clusters. A final call to INFLATEOUTDEGREE$(\sqrt{n})$, according to Theorem 4, then leads to all clusters being aware of all other clusters which allows the cluster centers to inform all nodes in their cluster about all other nodes. The algorithm thus terminates correctly.

Next we analyze the number rounds and number of messages required for this process. Theorem 2 guarantees that the initialization takes $\Theta(\log\log n)$ rounds and $\Theta(n)$ messages. For the main loop we claim that there are at most $4\log\log n$ iterations of the main loop of Algorithm 1 and that each such iteration uses only $O(\log D)$ rounds and at most $O(n/\log n)$ messages. The number of iterations follows simply from the observation that each iteration increases s to $\Theta(s^{2-\epsilon}/\log n) \geq \Theta(s^{2-\epsilon}/s^{\epsilon/2}) = \Theta(s^{2-1.5\epsilon})$. Even for $\epsilon = 1/2$ having $i = 4\log\log n$ iterations s would increase s from $\log^2 n$ to $(\log^2 n)^{1.25^i} \geq 2^{2^{\log\log n}} = n$ which implies that the loop terminates after less than $4\log\log n$ iterations. Regarding the number of messages and rounds, Theorem 3 states that DISCOVERCNEIGHBORS$(s,2/\epsilon)$ uses at most $O(2/\epsilon s^{1-\epsilon/2})$ messages for each of the $2n/s$ clusters for a total of at most $O(n/s^{\epsilon/2}) = O(n/\log n)$ messages per iteration. It also requires only $O(1)$ rounds. Similarly, SAMPLEMERGE(d) uses a total of $2n/s \cdot ds = O(n/s^{\epsilon}) = O(n/\log^2 n)$ messages and $O(1)$ rounds.
Lastly, INFLATEOUTDEGREE(d) uses

$$2n/s \cdot d \log D = O(n \log n/s^{\epsilon}) = O(n/\log n)$$

messages and $\log D$ rounds. This shows that the main loop requires overall at most $O(\log D \log\log n)$ rounds and $o(N)$ messages.

To complete the analysis, note that the final call of INFLATEOUTDEGREE$(\sqrt{n})$ also requires at most $O(\log D)$ rounds and at most $O(\log D\sqrt{n}) \cdot 2n/(\sqrt{n}\log n) = O(n)$ messages. □

2.4 Initialization

The initialization sub-routine brings down the number of clusters in a network by a polylogartihmic factor by having $O(\log\log n)$ rounds in which a constant fraction of the clusters merges.

In a round, the goal is to break symmetry into joiners and joinees, such that sufficiently many joiners merge with joinees. In a full topology, it would suffice to flip a coin to become joiner/joinee and then select a merging partner at random; this would succeed for a constant fraction of the network. In general topologies this simple rule does not work, because some nodes may be more important than others due to the graph structure. For example, in a star graph, the center determines the success/failure of all merging attempts. To address this, we first use a randomized neighbor-selection step which identifies important nodes. After this step, every node which received more than one neighbor-request chooses to be a joinee and immediately accept any joiner request. There will remain a group of nodes which are neither joinees, nor have their requests accepted already. The nice thing is that each one of these nodes will be matched with at most one incoming neighbor request and one outgoing request. Therefore, within this set, flipping a coin to become joiner/joinee will succeed in merging a constant fraction with high probability.

Algorithm 2 INITIALIZATION(r)

```
1: for r iterations do
2:     every cluster C picks one neighbor v ∈ Γ(C) and sends a merge request C(v)
3:     if cluster received more than one merge request then
4:         retract your own merge request          ▷ choose to become joinee
5:         send all (non-retracted) incoming requests a joinee signal
6:         accept any (non-retracted) incoming requests
7:     end if
8:     with probability 1/2 retract your own merge request
9:     if did not receive a joinee signal then
10:        accept any (non-retracted) incoming request
11:    end if
12:    retract any merge requests that have not been accepted yet
13: end for
```

LEMMA 2. *Assume that there are at least $\Omega(\log n)$ clusters before a call to* INITIALIZATION. *For every r, with high probability,* INITIALIZATION*(r) reduces the number of clusters by a factor of $c = e^{\Theta(r)}$ using $O(r)$ rounds and $\Theta(n)$ messages in total.*

PROOF. Suppose that the number of clusters before any of the r iterations is $N = \Omega(\log n)$. We prove that the iteration reduces the number of clusters by a constant factor with high probability. For this we consider the directed request graph which indicates which cluster requested to be merged with which other cluster. The merge requests guarantee that every node has an out-degree of exactly one. Since there are exactly N requests the number of nodes that retract their request because of multiple received requests is at most $N/2$. We want to show that at least a constant fraction of these requests are accepted. Some are already accepted at Line 5 by the nodes that retracted their requests. If these make up $N/8$ requests the claim is proved. If not then there are at least $N/4$ remaining requests.

Since we resolved requests to nodes with an in-degree larger than one we have the guarantee that these remaining requests decompose into directed cycles and directed paths. In these paths and cycles we break symmetries using randomization. In particular, any remaining edge has a probability of $1/4$ of being accepted because with probability $1/2$ it is not retracted by its requester and with an independent probability of $1/2$ it is accepted by the cluster that received the request. Furthermore, due to the paths structure the $N/4$ remaining requests contain at least $N/8$ requests that are accepted independently. Out of these $N/8$ requests we expect $N/32$ to be accepted and a standard Chernoff bound shows that with high probability at least $\Theta(N)$ will be accepted. This proves that every iteration leads with high probability to at least a constant fraction of the clusters merging. Doing this for r rounds leads to the claimed $e^{\Theta(r)}$ overall reduction in the number of clusters.

To determine the message complexity we note that each cluster sends only $O(1)$ messages per iteration. This leads to at most $O(n)$ messages in the first iteration. Since the number of clusters in subsequent iterations decreases geometrically with a factor of $\delta < 1$ the overall message complexity is also $\sum_{i=0}^{r} \delta^i O(n) = O(n)$. □

2.5 Cneighbor Discovery

The cneighbor-discovery sub-routine probes the nodes neighboring a cluster in order to identify sufficiently many distinct cneighbors. At the beginning of sub-routine, a cluster C has a set $\Gamma(C)$ of neighboring nodes which are split, potentially unevenly, among an unknown set of cneighbors. In a round, the cluster probes roughly s neighbors. It stores all the cneighbors it discovered in $A(C)$ and repeats with remaining neighbors. Intuitively, each such round makes progress in one of two ways. One case is that it discovers a large enough number of 'light' cneighbors, which do not contain a lot of neighbors, and we are done. The other case is that it discovers 'heavy' cneighbors, which contain a total large number of neighboring nodes. In this case, in the next round, C has a significantly reduced set of neighbors to work on.

The algorithm is given as Algorithm 3.

Algorithm 3 DISCOVERCNEIGHBORS(s, r)

```
X ← Γ(C)
A(C) = ∅
for 2r repetitions do
    select a random set R ⊆ X of size min{s^{1−(1/r)}, |X|}
    PULL from each v ∈ R the members of C(v)
    A(C) ← A(C) ∪ (⋃_{v∈R} {C(v)})
    X ← X \ (⋃_{v∈R} C(v))
end for
```

LEMMA 3. *Assume each cluster is of size at most s and suppose that $s \geq \log^2 n$. With high probability after a call of* DISCOVERCNEIGHBORS*(s, r) each cluster C knows either all or at least $|A(C)| \geq \Theta(s^{1-(2/r)})$ distinct cneighbors. The routine furthermore requires at most $O(r)$ rounds with at most $O(rs^{1-(1/r)})$ messages being sent by each cluster.*

PROOF. Define $t = s^{1-(1/r)}$. Consider one cluster C and denote $C_1, \ldots, C_m$ its cneighbors. We define the degree $\Delta_C(C_i)$ of a cneighbor C_i to be the number of edges going from C to distinct nodes in C_i. We classify these cneighbors according to this degree into two groups. The first group contains all "heavy" cneighbors whose degree makes up at least a $c\log(n)/t$ fraction of X for some constant $c > 1$, i.e., $\Delta_C(C_i) \geq c|X|\log(n)/t$, while the second group contains all other "light" cneighbors of C.

If at any iteration the size $|X|$ of the remaining neighborhood becomes smaller than t then all neighbors are contacted completing the claim. The remainder of this proof is concerned with the case that $|X|$ remains large and t neighbors get selected in each iteration.

Since the t neighbors in R are chosen independently at random each heavy cneighbor is PULLED in expectation $c\log n$ times and with high probability at least once. In particular the probability of not being PULLed at all is at most $(1 - \frac{c|X|\log(n)/t}{|X|})^t < e^{-c\log n}$.

Conversely, every light cneighbor is hit with at most an expected $c\log n$ PULLs from C and a standard Chernoff bound shows that with high probability at most $O(\log n)$ PULLs go to any such cneighbor.

We consider two cases. If the sum total of degrees going into light cneighbors is at least a $1/t^{(1/r)}$ fraction then the number of edges selected from this set is in expectation and with high probability $\Omega(t^{(1-(1/r))}) = \Omega(s^{(1-(1/r))(1-(1/r))}) = \Omega(t^{(1-(2/r))})$. The number of distinct light cneighbors hit is therefore at least $\Omega(t^{(1-(2/r))})/O(\log n)$ with high probability finishing the claim.

The other possibility is that the total number of edges going into light cneighbors is less than a $1/t^{(1/r)}$ fraction. Since these are the only edges that make up the total degree $|X|$ the new set X' of the next iteration has size $|X'| \leq |X|/t^{(1/r)}$.

Thus each iteration with high probability either discovers enough distinct cneighbors or reduces the total degree by a $t^{(1/r)}$ factor. Furthermore, if the algorithm does succeed in the first round we know that in this iteration at least one cluster of degree $c|X|\log n/t$ existed. Since the degree can be at most the size of the cluster which is assumed to be at most s we get that either the first iteration succeeds or $|X| \leq st/c\log n \leq s^2$. Therefore, failed iterations which reduce $|X|$ by a factor of $1/t^{(1/r)}$ can happen at most $2r$ times before $|X| \leq t$ and all remaining cneighbors are contacted. □

2.6 Degree Inflation

The sub-routine for degree-inflation works to expand the out-degree of all clusters to a desired threshold d. In a round, every 'lean' node, whose degree has not reached the desired threshold, simply PULLs from all of its neighbors their neighbor-sets. This means that a cluster PULLs information about nodes at twice the distance of the previous round. Therefore, in at most $\log D$ rounds, the entire graph can be PULLed.

Algorithm 4 INFLATEOUTDEGREE(d)

```
for log D iterations do
    if |A(C)| < d then
        pull A(C') from every C' ∈ A(C) into A(C)
    end if
end for
```

LEMMA 4. *Assume that each cluster has outgoing edges to either to all of its cneighbors or to at least d of them. Assume further that the underlying network has a strong diameter of at most D. Then, at the end of* INFLATEOUTDEGREE*(d) a cluster C is aware of either all clusters or at least d cneighbors, i.e, $|A(C)| \geq d$. Furthermore, only $O(\log D)$ rounds and $O(d \cdot \log D)$ messages per cluster are required.*

PROOF. For analysis purposes, we fix a distance function $d()$ reflecting the shortest cluster-to-cluster hop length between clusters at the beginning of the procedure. Clearly, $d(C_1, C_2) \leq D$ for every two clusters C_1, C_2. InflateDegree progresses in iterations. At the start of each iteration, a cluster C is called *lean* if $|A(C)| < d$. Clusters continue iterating the loop only as long as they remain lean.

We prove the lemma by induction on the following invariant: For every lean cluster C entering its k'th loop iteration, $A(C)$ contains all clusters W with $d(C, W) \leq 2^{(k-1)}$. The base of the induction for $k = 1$ holds since if C is initially lean then it has outgoing edges to all of its distance-1 cneighbors. Suppose C is lean at the beginning of iteration $k + 1$. Consider any cluster W with $D(C, W) \leq 2^k$. There exists some cluster W' on the path from C to W, such that $D(C, W') \leq 2^{(k-1)}$ and $D(W', W) \leq 2^{(k-1)}$. Let's examine $A(C)$ and $A(W')$ at the k'th iteration. When the iteration starts, we know that C is lean, and by the induction hypothesis $W' \in A(C)$. We know that C remains lean at the end of the k'th iteration after it pulls $A(W')$ into $A(C)$. Therefore, when the k'th iteration starts, W' too is lean, and by the induction hypothesis, $W \in A(W')$. Therefore, W is pulled into $A(C)$ at the k'th iteration. This completes the induction.

Clearly, within $\log(D)$ iterations, C learns about all existing clusters and we are done. Each cluster furthermore only uses less than d connections per iterations for a total of at most $d \cdot \min\{\log d, \log D\}$ connections per cluster. □

2.7 Sample and Merge

A sample-and-merge sub-routine starts with at most N/s clusters all having d out-cneighbors. Then, a fraction of roughly $1/d$ are sampled to become center-clusters (more precisely, we sample with probability $c\log n/d$, to guarantee that every cluster has a cneighbor which is sampled). Each non-center cluster selects one sampled cluster among its d cneighbors to join. At the end of the sub-routine, the number of clusters is reduced by a factor of roughly $d/(c\log n)$).

Algorithm 5 SAMPLEMERGE(d)

```
with probability c log n/d become a cluster-center
if non-center cluster then
    contact d clusters from A(C) to find a center-cluster
    merge with an arbitrary neighboring center-cluster
end if
```

LEMMA 5. *Assuming that at the beginning of* SAMPLEMERGE*(d) every cluster C is aware of at least $d \geq \log^2 n$ cneighbors, i.e., $|A(C)| \geq d$, then with high probability* SAMPLEMERGE*(d) reduces the number of clusters by a factor of $\Theta(\log n/d)$. Furthermore, only $O(1)$ rounds and $O(d)$ messages per cluster are required.*

PROOF. Let x be the number of clusters before SAMPLEMERGE. After sampling, the expected number of center-clusters is $\mu = x \cdot (c\log n/d)$. Since $x \geq |A(C_1)| = d$ we have $\mu \geq \log n$. Since each cluster makes an independent decision, a standard Chernoff bound shows that with high probability there are exactly $\Theta(\mu)$ center-clusters which form the new clusters after SAMPLEMERGE. A similar argument guarantees that with high probability out of the d neighbors contacted by a non-center cluster at least one center-cluster is found. This guarantees that no non-center clusters survive the SAMPLEMERGE procedure. □

3. CONCLUSION AND OPEN PROBLEMS

The work presented in this paper makes a large improvement in the round complexity of resource discovery on instances of interest while maintaining the overall communication optimal. There are a number of compelling problems left to tackle.

First, while the message complexity of our algorithm is $O(n)$ there are nodes that send more than $O(1)$ messages per round. We believe that it is possible to design a gossip algorithm with the same running time guarantees in which nodes send at most one message per round. This requires a modified INITIALIZATION routine which does not just guarantee that the number of clusters is reduced by a polylogarithmic factor but instead guarantees that *each* cluster is of polylogarithmic size. More importantly the SAMPLEMERGE routine needs to be followed by an intricate re-balancing step which guarantees that each cluster-center is joined by sufficiently many clusters. We defer these details to the journal version.

Second, our work leaves open to further improve the network discovery time of graphs with only a weak diameter bound. Our intuition is that a crucial building block for solving this would be a log-logarithmic local-flooding algorithm. Once achieved, it may be repeated $\log D$ times to fold the entire graph into a clique, in a similar manner to the utilization of local broadcast in the gossip techniques of [3].

4. REFERENCES

[1] I. Abraham and D. Dolev. Asynchronous resource discovery. *Computer Networks*, 50(10):1616–1629, 2006.

[2] C. Avin and R. Elsässer. Faster Rumor Spreading: Breaking the $\log n$ Barrier. In *Proceedings of the International Symposium on Distributed Computing*, DISC '13, pages 209–223, 2013.

[3] K. Censor-Hillel, B. Haeupler, J. Kelner, and P. Maymounkov. Global Computation in a Poorly Connected World: Fast Rumor Spreading with no Dependence on Conductance. In *Proceedings of the ACM Symposium on Theory of Computing*, STOC '12, pages 961–970, 2012.

[4] F. Chierichetti, S. Lattanzi, and A. Panconesi. Almost tight bounds for rumour spreading with conductance. In *Proceedings of the 42nd ACM Symposium on Theory of Computing (STOC)*, pages 399–408, 2010.

[5] S. Davtyan. *Resource Discovery and Cooperation in Decentralized Systems*. PhD thesis, University of Connecticut, 2014.

[6] A. Demers, D. Greene, C. Hauser, W. Irish, J. Larson, S. Shenker, H. Sturgis, D. Swinehart, and D. Terry. Epidemic algorithms for replicated database maintenance. In *Proceedings of the sixth Annual ACM Symposium on Principles of Distributed Computing (PODC)*, pages 1–12, 1987.

[7] G. Giakkoupis. Tight bounds for rumor spreading in graphs of a given conductance. In *28th International Symposium on Theoretical Aspects of Computer Science (STACS)*, pages 57–68, Dagstuhl, Germany, 2011. Schloss Dagstuhl–Leibniz-Zentrum fuer Informatik.

[8] B. Haeupler. Simple, fast and deterministic gossip and rumor spreading. In *Proceedings of the ACM-SIAM Symposium on Discrete Algorithms*, SODA '13, pages 705–716, 2013.

[9] B. Haeupler and D. Malkhi. Optimal gossip with direct addressing. In *Proceedings of the 31st ACM Symposium on Principles of Distributed Computing (PODC)*, pages 176–185, 2014.

[10] B. Haeupler, G. Pandurangan, D. Peleg, R. Rajaraman, and Z. Sun. Discovery through gossip. In *Proceedinbgs of the 24th ACM Symposium on Parallelism in Algorithms and Architectures*, SPAA '12, pages 140–149, New York, NY, USA, 2012. ACM.

[11] M. Harchol-Balter, T. Leighton, and D. Lewin. Resource discovery in distributed networks. In *Proceedings of the ACM Symposium on Principles of Distributed Computing*, PODC'99, pages 229–237, 1999.

[12] R. Karp, C. Schindelhauer, S. Shenker, and B. Vocking. Randomized rumor spreading. In *Proceedings of the 41st Annual Symposium on Foundations of Computer Science (FOCS)*, pages 565–574, Washington, DC, USA, 2000. IEEE Computer Society.

[13] S. Kniesburges, A. Koutsopoulos, and C. Scheideler. A deterministic worst-case message complexity optimal solution for resource discovery. *Theoretical Computer Science*, 2014.

[14] K. M. Konwar, D. Kowalski, and A. A. Shvartsman. Node discovery in networks. *Journal of Parallel and Distributed Computing*, 69(4):337–348, 2009.

[15] S. Kutten and D. Peleg. Asynchronous resource discovery in peer to peer networks. In *Reliable Distributed Systems, 2002. Proceedings. 21st IEEE Symposium on*, pages 224–231. IEEE, 2002.

[16] S. Kutten and D. Peleg. Asynchronous resource discovery in peer-to-peer networks. *Computer Networks*, 51(1):190–206, 2007.

[17] S. Kutten, D. Peleg, and U. Vishkin. Deterministic resource discovery in distributed networks. *Theory of Computing Systems*, 36(5):479–495, 2003.

[18] C. Law and K.-Y. Siu. An $O(\log n)$ randomized resource discovery algorithm. In *Brief Announcements of the 14th International Symposium on Distributed Computing, Technical University of Madrid, Technical Report FIM/110.1/DLSIIS*, pages 5–8. Citeseer, 2000.

[19] D. Peleg. *Distributed computing: a locality-sensitive approach*. Society for Industrial and Applied Mathematics, Philadelphia, PA, USA, 2000.

[20] Y. Shiloach and U. Vishkin. An $O(\log n)$ parallel connectivity algorithm. *Journal of Algorithms*, 3(1):57–67, 1982.

The Cost of Synchronizing Multiple-Access Channels*

Tomasz Jurdzinski
Institute of Computer Science
University of Wrocław, Poland
tju@cs.uni.wroc.pl

Grzegorz Stachowiak
Institute of Computer Science
University of Wrocław, Poland
gst@cs.uni.wroc.pl

ABSTRACT

Multiple access channel is a communication model in which many users, also called stations, could exchange information. Since it offers limited capacity, some information sent through it might be lost due to signal interference (collision). Therefore, successful message delivery to a station requires breaking symmetry on the channel. In this work we consider the channel-synchronization problem on non-synchronized channels: assuming stations with messages wake-up dynamically on the channel, what is the minimum (expected) time needed for all stations to receive at least one message each.

Historically, the first considered "classical" channel assu med that whenever two or more stations transmit simultaneously, the transmitted information is lost, otherwise it is delivered to all stations. In the seminal paper, Kushilevitz and Mansour [19] proved that the first successful transmission on the channel with n contending stations may require, in the worst case, $\Omega(\log n)$ expected communication rounds for any protocol. The result, however, holds under assumption that all contenders start their protocols at the same round. We prove that in more general scenario, in which the stations may have different local clocks and start the protocol at arbitrary times, the lower bound increases quadratically to $\Omega(\log^2 n)$ expected rounds. Both lower bounds are matched by corresponding algorithms developed in previous papers. Therefore, our lower bound proves the polynomial impact of synchronization on the classical multiple-access channels.

Recently, more accurate channels based on Signal to Interference and Noise Ratio (SINR) were proposed and studied. The advantage of the SINR-based channel is that, apart of being closer to realistic physical scenario, some more demanding communication patterns could be scheduled in a single round. We support this intuition by showing that on such channel delivery of a message could be done faster than on the classical channel, mainly, in $O(\log^2 n/\log\log n)$ expected number of rounds, thus separating the classical channel model from the SINR one. (The same time bound also holds with high probability.)

Finally, we prove that for *deterministic* protocols receiving a message on the SINR channel requires time $\Omega(n)$, which surprisingly drops nearly exponentially to $O(\log^2 n)$ if the stations have access to the global clock, which also separates SINR channel from the classic one, due to the lower bound $\Omega(n \log n)$ on the latter. We also match the latter bound by corresponding lower bound. This together with our $O(\log^2 / \log\log n)$ round randomized algorithm, also proves a gap between deterministic and randomized solutions to the synchronization problem.

Categories and Subject Descriptors

C.2.1 [**Computer-Communication Networks**]: Network Architecture and Design; F.2.2 [**Analysis of Algorithms and Problem Complexity**]: Nonnumerical Algorithms and Problems

Keywords

multiple-access channel, SINR channel,
synchronization problem, symmetry-breaking

1. INTRODUCTION

In a multiple access channel, n stations (also called users or nodes) communicate by transmitting and receiving messages to/from other stations. Each station knows the upper bound N on the number of stations in the network n, and N is polynomial in n. Each message contains $O(\log N)$ bits. Communication takes place in synchronous rounds (also called steps), in which each station can transmit and receive a message. If two or more stations transmit at the same round, a collision occurs. There are two popular settings defining the behavior of the channel in case of collision.

Classical (radio) channel: In the classical channel, it is assumed that in such case no message is successfully delivered to any station in case of collision, c.f., the survey by Chlebus [4].

SINR channel: In the recently introduced SINR channel, resolving collision at a round is subject to more complex physical rules. Stations are deployed into a metric space with the distance function dist$(\cdot,\cdot)$, more precisely, in a ball of radius $1-\varepsilon$ for some $\varepsilon \in (0,1)$, c.f., [14]. There are three fixed model parameters: path loss α, threshold $\beta \geq 1$, and ambient noise $\mathcal{N} > 0$. W.l.o.g. we assume that β and $\mathcal{N}$ are equal to 1, otherwise a constant scaling in algorithms and

*This work was supported by the Polish National Science Centre grant DEC-2012/07/B/ST6/01534.

Permission to make digital or hard copies of all or part of this work for personal or classroom use is granted without fee provided that copies are not made or distributed for profit or commercial advantage and that copies bear this notice and the full citation on the first page. Copyrights for components of this work owned by others than ACM must be honored. Abstracting with credit is permitted. To copy otherwise, or republish, to post on servers or to redistribute to lists, requires prior specific permission and/or a fee. Request permissions from permissions@acm.org.
PODC'15, July 21–23, 2015, Donostia-San Sebastián, Spain.
Copyright is held by the owner/author(s). Publication rights licensed to ACM.
ACM 978-1-4503-3617-8 /15/07 ...$15.00.
DOI: http://dx.doi.org/10.1145/2767386.2767439 .

lower bound would result in the same asymptotic results (to allow this, model parameters, or at least their good estimates, should be know to the stations). The $SINR(v, u, \mathcal{T})$ ratio, for given stations u, v and a set of (transmitting) stations $\mathcal{T}$, is defined as follows:

$$SINR(v, u, \mathcal{T}) = \frac{P\text{dist}(v, u)^{-\alpha}}{\mathcal{N} + \sum_{w \in \mathcal{T} \setminus \{v\}} P\text{dist}(w, u)^{-\alpha}} \quad (1)$$

where P, the transmission power, is typically set to 1 in case of SINR channel model. In the *Signal-to-Interference-and-Noise-Ratio (SINR) channel* a station u successfully receives a message from a station v (or equivalently, the message from v is successfully delivered to station u) in a round if $v \in \mathcal{T}$, $u \notin \mathcal{T}$, and

$$SINR(v, u, \mathcal{T}) \geq \beta ,$$

where $\mathcal{T}$ is the set of stations transmitting in that round.

In both channels, we do not assume any carrier-sensing capabilities, i.e., no additional feedback (apart of successfully delivered messages, as defined above for each of the two models) is provided to stations.

Communication problem and complexity. Stations wake up in arbitrary rounds, without access to the global clock (unless stated otherwise, see Section 4.2 for results if the global clock is available). A station can transmit only after awakening or receiving a message (i.e., receiving a message awakes a sleeping station). The goal of the synchronization problem which can be viewed as channel-symmetry-breaking problem* is to make every station receiving a message, in other words, to make all stations awaken, i.e., receiving at least one message. This requires breaking symmetry between competing stations, due to collisions that occur if two or more stations transmit simultaneously. We measure time from the first awakening of a station until every station receives a message. Note that in case of the classical multiple access channel, this problem is equivalent with performing the first successful transmission on the channel. Our main focus is on randomized solutions, except of Section 4 when we obtain results for deterministic algorithms on SINR channel.

We distinguish between *expected* time complexity of a randomized algorithm and complexity which holds *with high probability* (whp). By "with high probability" we mean the probability bigger than $1-n^{-a}$, for some constant $a > 1$ that could be made sufficiently large without changing asymptotic time complexity. Both complexities are determined, for a given n, as the maximum over all instances of size n.

The lack of synchronization of nodes of a network denotes in this paper the fact that nodes do not have access to the global clock and they do not start a protocol execution at the same time. However, as pointed out earlier, communication takes place in synchronous rounds.

1.1 Previous results

Previous work on classical multiple access channel. Early work on the classical channel included developing randomized protocols such as Aloha [1] and (binary) exponential backoff [20]. The study of these and other algorithms has been continued in a number of papers since then — here we mentioned only the most relevant once due to limited space (see also the survey by Chlebus [4] for more thorough description of results). Under assumption that all stations are awaken simultaneously, Bar-Yehuda, Goldreich and Ittai [3] gave the solution in expected $O(\log n)$ number of rounds (in fact, their solution guaranteed constant probability of successful submission in the sequence of $O(\log n)$ rounds, but it can be naturally extended to Las Vegas algorithm by repeating the sequence until the first successful submission). Kushilevitz and Mansour [19] proved the matching lower bound $\Omega(\log n)$, that holds even with constant probability. This bound has been later strengthened by Farach-Colton and Mosteiro [8] in the case of uniform algorithms and by Daum et al. [7] for arbitrary algorithms (see also [21] for further generalizations). The above papers, and many follow-up works, delivered also results for Monte Carlo algorithms.

In general setting without synchronized start-up, Gasieniec, Pelc and Peleg [9] were the first to study this problem. They also picked the name "wake-up" for the problem in general setting. Among others, they proposed randomized Monte Carlo algorithm guarantying the first successful transmission in $O(n \log n)$ rounds with high probability. (Here by "high probability" we understand probability bigger than $1 - n^{-a}$, for some constant $a > 1$ that could be made sufficiently large depending on needs.) In the follow-up paper, Jurdzinski and Stachowiak [15] improved that result to $O(\log^2 n)$ rounds with high probability.

Gasieniec, Pelc and Peleg [9] also studied deterministic solutions, among others, they proved that there exists a deterministic solution guarantying first successful transmission in $O(n \log^2 n)$ rounds for arbitrary wake-up times. Chrobak et al. [5] introduced the notion of synchronizers — deterministic transmission schedules that try to minimize time of the first successful transmission adaptively for unknown number of awakening stations. The recent advances on deterministic algorithms can be found in [17]. It is worth mentioning that for simplified setting in which all stations are awaken at the same time, the problem is already solved by Clementi et al. [6], who proved the lower bound $\Omega(n \log n)$, and Komlos and Greenberg [16] who proved existence of matching algorithm (see also Indyk [12] and Kowalski [18] for constructive approach).

Closing the logarithmic gap between the "static case" in which all stations are awaken at the same time and the general case is a long standing open problem, in both cases of randomized Las Vegas and deterministic algorithms,. In this work we solve the randomized one.

SINR channel. Symmetry-breaking problems have not been studied on the SINR channel so far. Other related problems are usually more expensive in terms of time complexity, for instance, local broadcast [10], in which every node has to inform its neighbors about its rumor, was done in time $O(\Delta\text{polylog}(n))$, where Δ is the local density of a network. Another related problem studied in the SINR model is link scheduling, where *particular* direct connections have to be done (see e.g., [11]); because of specific links to be realized, scheduling often depends on so called "affectance" of the set of links, which might be large with respect to n. In [22], throughput optimization was challenged in the presence of jamming. Our solutions of symmetry-breaking problem on the SINR channel are much faster than the above solutions to related problems, which yields complexity sep-

*In the literature, this problem was also known under different names, such as collision solving, wake-up, selection, as it was considered independently for slightly different channels and settings.

aration between these problems and the one considered in this work

Related work. The problem has much faster solution in the model with collision detection: the matching bounds $\Omega(\log\log n)$ (but only for "fair" protocols) and $O(\log\log n)$ expected time were proved in [23] (analyzed only for "static" case). Recently, Fernandez Anta et al. [2] showed how to reach a relatively large constant throughput (i.e., the rate of successful transmissions) on the channel with collision detection and in the static case without any bounds on contention or even distinct ids. Removing the remaining assumptions (about static case and/or collision detection capability) without harming complexity is a challenging open problem.

1.2 Our contribution

We start with proving a lower bound $\Omega(\log^2 n)$ on expected time of any symmetry-breaking protocol on the classical multiple access channel, c.f., Section 2. Our result works for *any* randomized protocol, understood as a probabilistic distribution over all possible deterministic executions. We do not assume any restrictions such as fairness or independent random choices at different rounds.

Comparing our result with well studied $\Theta(\log n \log(1/\zeta))$ complexity for Monte Carlo (MC) solutions guarantying symmetry breaking with probability at least $1-\zeta$, we observe that the lack of synchronization creates a real challenge for designing Las Vegas (LV) algorithms. Mainly, it is no longer possible to repeat an MC solution until the first success — if it was the case, we could obtain an LV solution working in expected $O(\log n)$ number of rounds, by simply applying the bounds on the process of waiting for the first success. Our lower bound says that such a solution — natural in a "synchronized" world — is not the case in more realistic scenarios with non-synchronized wake-up times.

Next we show in Section 3 that SINR channel is provably faster, in terms of receiving first message, than the classical channel. More precisely, we show an algorithm - first MC with high probability and next LV with the same expected number of rounds $O(\log^2 n/\log\log n)$. The algorithm is oscillating transmission probabilities based on the feedback from the channel: if there was a transmission (received or done by the considered station) then transmission probability drops substantially by factor 2, otherwise it grows mildly by factor $g = (\log n)^{c/\log n}$, where $c > 0$ is a suitable constant. All these modifications are done only within some range of transmission probabilities. The main argument in the analysis is similar to those used before on the classical channel: trying to assure that there will be $\Omega(\log n)$ rounds with a constant sum of transmission probabilities, which translates into high probability of getting a round with a single transmitter. However, knowing from the previous section that this technique is limited by lower bounds on LV, and also on MC algorithms whp, we explore the properties of SINR. Mainly, if the sum of transmission probabilities grow beyond some constant, some small regions of frequent transmitters (i.e., containing nodes with relatively high sum of transmission probabilities) become hearing each other due to the fact that their signal is not affected by other faraway transmissions. In this way not only successful transmissions occur, but also transmission probabilities of many stations will drop by factor 2, and the sum of transmission probabilities of all awakened stations will quickly return to the "safe" range of $[1/2, 2]$, in which a single transmission occurs with a constant probability.

Table 1: Complexity of symmetry breaking in various settings

Random.	Global clock	SINR channel	Classical channel
yes	yes/no	$O(\frac{\log^2 n}{\log\log n})$	$\Theta(\log^2 n)$, [15, 8]
no	yes	$\Theta(\log^2 N)$	$O(n\log N)$, $\Omega(n\log(N/n))$, [6]
no	no	$\Omega(n)$	$O(n\log^2 N)$, [9]

Finally, because the SINR is a relatively new model and not yet explored in depth, we study the impact of randomization and access to global clock on the time of symmetry breaking. In Section 4.1 we show an adaptive scenario that finds channel set-up (i.e., location of stations) enforcing symmetry-breaking time $\Omega(n)$ in the model without global clock. On the other hand, we already know that there is a deterministic solution in the model with global clock that accomplishes even stronger leader election task in $O(\log^2 n)$ rounds, c.f., [14]. In Section 4.2 we match this bound from below, showing a strategy to enforce $O(\log^2 n)$ rounds against any deterministic solution to the symmetry-breaking problem.

Due to limited space, some proofs are omitted, they will be presented in the full version of the paper.

1.3 Technical preliminaries

FACT 1. *The following hold:*

1. $1 - x \le e^{-x}$ *for every* $0 < x < 1$.
2. *If* $x \in [0, 1/2)$, *then* $(1/4)^x < 1 - x$.
3. $f(x) = xe^{-x}$ *is a decreasing function for* $x > 1$.

FACT 2 ([15]). *Assume that* k *awake stations transmit in a round with probabilities* $p_1, \ldots, p_k$ *such that* $p_i \le 1/2$ *for each* $i \in [1, k]$. *Let* $y = \sum_{i=1}^{k} p_i$. *Then, the probability that exactly one station is transmitting is at least* $y\left(\frac{1}{4}\right)^y$.

LEMMA 1. *Let* $Y_1, \ldots, Y_n$ *be 0/1 random variables such that* $P(Y_i = 1) \ge p_i$ *regardless of the values of* $Y_1, \ldots, Y_{i-1}$ *for each* $i \in [n]$. *Then,* $\Pr(\sum_{i=1}^{n} Y_i > a) \ge \Pr(\sum_{i=1}^{n} X_i > a)$ *for each* a, *where* $X_1, \ldots, X_n$ *are* independent *0/1 random variables such that* $P(X_i = 1) = p_i$.

Assumptions and notation. To avoid rounding, we assume that n is a power of 2. The notation $\log x$ denotes the logarithm of x to the base 2, unless the base is stated explicitly.

2. LOWER BOUND FOR RANDOMIZED SYMMETRY BREAKING ON THE CLASSICAL CHANNEL

In this section we prove the lower bound on the expected running time of probabilistic Las Vegas algorithms for synchronization on a classical multiple access channel. The result is proved for the non-synchronized channel (with no global clock), and even if stations know their exact number n and are equipped with different IDs (though first we prove a version without ID's).

This model was considered in the Jurdzinski and Stachowiak paper [15] where an algorithm called *Probability Increase* achieving the running time $O(\log n \log(1/\varepsilon))$ was shown for wakeup with probability at least $1 - \varepsilon$. This algorithm can be modified for $\varepsilon = 1/n^2$ by adding transmissions with probability $1/n$ after (a very unlikely) unsuccessful wakeup. (That is, a node starts transmitting with probability $1/n$ after $t(n) = O(\log^2 n)$ rounds from its spontaneous wake-up, if no there was no wake-up round before. Here, $t(n)$ is time bound in which the original wake-up is finished when it does not succeed.) It is easy to show that such a modified algorithm achieves the expected waking time $O(\log^2 n)$. We will prove a matching lower bound.

THEOREM 1. *The lower bound for the expected time of randomized Las Vegas solutions for the synchronization problem is* $\Omega(\log^2 n)$.

We carry out the proof in scenario without IDs. The more general variant with IDs can be then reduced to the one without IDs.

For the proof we assume that n is big enough to carry out all estimations. For the sake of contradiction, we assume that there exists a synchronization algorithm $\mathcal{A}$, which has expected running time $o(\log^2 n)$. We will prove that this time has to be $\Omega(\log^2 n)$, thus obtaining a contradiction. Unlike in the paper of Farach-Colton and Mosteiro [8], we prove the lower bound not only for uniform algorithms but for *any* randomized algorithms.

2.1 The sketch of the proof

For the algorithm $\mathcal{A}$, let p_i be the probability that the first transmission of a node is in the ith round according to its inner clock. We call p_i the *initial broadcast probability* of a node in round i (note that a round which we denote by i for the purpose of analysis can have different local clock states for different nodes participating in the protocol). Moreover, let $s_i = p_1 + \ldots + p_i$. We also assume that n is large enough to guarantee that the expected time in which $\mathcal{A}$ wakes up all nodes is larger than $\log^2 n$ (recall that our contrary assumption states that the expected time is $o(\log^2 n)$).

Let *probability mass* in a round i be the sum of probabilities of transmission over all nodes which are awake in that round. Using Fact 2, one can quite accurately estimate the probability that exactly one node transmits in the round i as a function of the probability mass of that round. Actually, the optimal probability mass is $\Theta(1)$. However, as $\mathcal{A}$ is not an oblivious algorithm, it is not obvious how to estimate the value of probability mass in various rounds.

Observe also that, if we knew the number of currently awake nodes, the broadcast probabilities could be adjusted to maximize the probability that exactly one node transmits. Thus, the actual difficulty which causes large time of the algorithm follows from uncertainty about the number of currently awake nodes and their broadcast probabilities.

Although $\mathcal{A}$ is adaptive and therefore the probabilities p_i do not characterize its full behavior, we can infer some properties of probabilities p_i from the assumption that $\mathcal{A}$ finishes in $o(\log^2 n)$. By considering a scenario that only one node is waken up spontaneously, we obtain the following result.

PROPOSITION 1. *If the expected wake up time of $\mathcal{A}$ is $o(\log^2 n)$ then $s_t > 1/2$ for $s_t = p_1 + \cdots + p_t$, $t = \log^2 n$ and n large enough.*

Based on the algorithm $\mathcal{A}$, we define the "game" $\mathcal{A}'$, a "simplified version" of the algorithm $\mathcal{A}$ in which each node behaves as in $\mathcal{A}$ up to its first transmission (ignoring received messages) and does not transmit at all after its first transmission†. Because $\mathcal{A}'$ is almost uniform (behavior of each node in each round depends merely on one bit of information), it is easier for analysis. In particular, its behavior is *fully* characterized by the probabilities p_i.

On the other hand, the following relationship between $\mathcal{A}$ and $\mathcal{A}'$ holds.

PROPOSITION 2. *Consider executions of $\mathcal{A}$ and $\mathcal{A}'$ on a fixed pattern of spontaneous wake ups and for fixed values of all random bits. Assume that, in the execution of $\mathcal{A}'$, no node transmits in each round $i < t_0$ and at least two nodes transmit in each round $t_0 \leq i \leq T$ for some $T \in \mathbb{N}$. Then, no wake up message occurs in the corresponding execution of $\mathcal{A}$ in rounds $1, 2, \ldots, T$.*

Another helpful property of $\mathcal{A}'$ is that, if the sum of initial broadcast probabilities of awake stations in a round is large, the probability that the number of transmitters in that round is 0 or 1 is small.

PROPOSITION 3. *There exists a constant c such that if the sum of initial broadcast probabilities S in round i is bigger than $c \log n$, the probability of no or one transmitting node in round i of $\mathcal{A}'$ is smaller than $1/n^2$.*

The above property combined with Proposition 1 leads to the following conclusion.

PROPOSITION 4. *If we wake spontaneously at least $2c\log n$ nodes in each of the rounds: $i-t+1, i-t+2, \ldots, \ldots, i-1, i$, then the probability of no or one transmitting node in round i of $\mathcal{A}'$ is smaller than $1/n^2$.*

Given the above observations, we build wake up patterns which are somehow "difficult" for $\mathcal{A}'$. More precisely, we will analyze behavior of $\mathcal{A}'$ on $\Theta(\log n)$ waking patterns I_k that specify how nodes wake up spontaneously during the algorithm execution. The *pattern* I_k for $k \in [0.2 \log n, 0.9 \log n]$ is defined as follows:

- In each of rounds $1, 2, 3, \ldots, t$ we wake up spontaneously 2^k nodes.
- In each of rounds $t+1, t+2, t+3, \ldots, T = \frac{n}{4c \log n}$, $2c \log n$ nodes are woken spontaneously up, where c is the constant from Proposition 3.

where $t = \log^2 n$. Intuitively, the nodes waken up in rounds $1, \ldots, t$ introduce uncertainty about the actual probability mass while the nodes waken up later guarantee that a successful round is very improbable in rounds $[t, T]$ (see Proposition 4).

Let S_i be the sum of initial broadcast probabilities in round i for the pattern I_k. Note that $S_i = 2^k(p_1 + p_2 + \cdots + p_i) = 2^k s_i$ for each $i \leq t$.

†We call $\mathcal{A}'$ a *game* in order to emphasize that it is not an alternative synchronization algorithm. In particular, in $\mathcal{A}'$, nodes do not finish an "execution" after a round with successful transmission. The game $\mathcal{A}'$ is just a tool for simplifying analysis of $\mathcal{A}$.

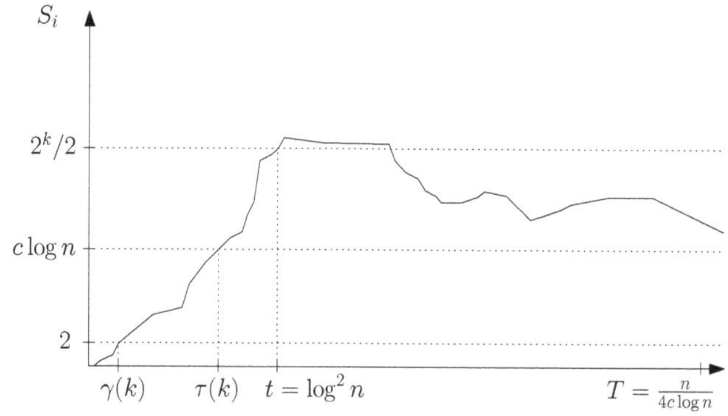

Figure 1: An illustration of changes of the sum S_i of transmission probabilities of spontaneously awaken nodes for the pattern I_k. As the goal is to illustrate introduced notations and the dynamics of change of S_i, we do not care about scaling of values.

The construction of the patterns I_k assures that for each k (and n large enough), there is the round $\gamma(k)$ such that $S_i < 2$ for $i \le \gamma(k)$ and $S_i \ge 2$ for $\gamma(k) < i \le T$. Moreover, there is also the round $\gamma(k) \le \tau(k) \le t$ such that $S_i < c\log n$ for $i \le \tau(k)$ and $S_i \ge c\log n$ for $\tau(k) < i \le T$. The reader can see these observations depicted on Figure 1 as well.

We consider the following events in the game:

- $Z_{\gamma(k)}$: no node transmits in rounds $1, 2, 3, \ldots, \gamma(k)$.
- A_i for $\gamma(k) < i \le T$: the number of transmitting nodes in round i is at least 2.

The following fact is a simple corollary from Proposition 2.

FACT 3. *If X, the conjunction of events*

$$Z_{\gamma(k)}, A_{\gamma(k)+1}, A_{\gamma(k)+2}, \ldots A_T$$

holds in the game $\mathcal{A}'$, then no wake up occurs in the corresponding execution of the algorithm $\mathcal{A}$ in rounds $1, 2, \ldots, T$.

If we assume that the actual probability mass in the round i is close to S_i, $Z_{\gamma(k)}$ is quite probable due to the fact that $S_i < 2$ for each $i \le \gamma(k)$. Simultaneously, there are at least two transmitters in each round $i > \tau(k)$ with high probability (this corresponds to the conjunction of $A_{\tau(k)+2}, \ldots A_T$), by Proposition 4.

Moreover, observe that $S_i = s_i \cdot 2^k$ for $i \le t$, where S_i is the sum of initial broadcast probabilities of awake nodes in round i for the pattern I_k. Recall also that the probability mass maximizing the chance that exactly one node transmits in a round is $\Theta(1)$. Thus, assuming that S_i accurately estimates probability mass in an execution of $\mathcal{A}'$ in rounds up to t, A_i is not satisfied for I_k with non neglibile probability for such rounds i that s_i is smaller than $1/2^k$.

The above intuitions are formalized as follows. First, we show that rounds $i > \tau(k)$ have meaningless impact on the probability of X, i.e., the conjunction of

$$Z_{\gamma(k)}, A_{\gamma(k)+1}, A_{\gamma(k)+2}, \ldots A_T.$$

Then, taking advantage of the fact that $\mathcal{A}$ accomplishes channel synchronization in $o(\log^2 n)$ rounds in expectation, we derive an upper bound on the probability

$$P_k = \text{Prob}\left(Z_{\gamma(k)}, A_{\gamma(k)+1}, A_{\gamma(k)+2}, \ldots A_\tau(k)\right)$$

that holds irrespective of a spontaneous wake-up pattern of the adversary (i.e., irrespective of the actual value of k). Using the fact that unique transmissions in rounds $\tau(k)+1, \ldots, T$ are very improbable, we get $P_k = O(\log^3 n/n)$ using Markov inequality.

On the other hand, for each $k \in [0.2\log n, 0.9\log n]$ we also bound the probability P_k from below. To this aim, we first show that the actual probability mass in each round $i \le \tau(k)$ may be well approximated by the sum of initial broadcast probabilities of spontaneously awaken stations in that round. The lower bound on P_k is expressed in terms of sizes of sets of rounds $l_j = |L_j|$, where

$$L_j = \left\{ i \,|\, 2^{-j} < \sum_{l=1}^{i} p_i = l_j \le 2^{-j+1}, \right\}$$

This lower bound states that

$$P_k > (1/4)^{\Theta(\sum_{j\in[0.1\log n, \log n]} l_j 2^{k-j})}.$$

Given the lower and the upper bounds on probabilities P_k, we derive lower and the upper bounds on the product $\prod_k P_k$ over considered values of k. This way we get the inequality:

$$(1/4)^{0.3\log^2 n} > \prod_{k\in[0.1\log n, \log n]} P_k > (1/4)^{\Theta(\sum_j l_j)}.$$

Thus, $\sum_{j\in[0.1\log n, \log n]} l_j = \Omega(\log^2 n)$. Finally, note that the rounds from the set L_{j+1} are before the rounds from L_j for each j. Therefore, for

$$t' = \sum_{j\in[0.1\log n, \log n]} l_j$$

we have $s_{t'} \le 1/n^{0.1} < 1/2$. So for the pattern in which only one station is woken up spontaneously (see Proposition 1), the expected waking time is $\Omega(\log^2 n)$.

2.2 The scenario with IDs

Finally, we consider the case that nodes have unique IDs from the range $[1, n]$. We show that even with IDs expected waking time time is $\Omega(\log^2 n)$. Contrary, assume that an algorithm $\mathcal{A}$ finishes wake up is expected $f(n) = o(\log^2 n)$ rounds when nodes are equipped with IDs. Now, consider the following algorithm $\mathcal{B}$ for the scenario without IDs and $\sqrt{n}$ nodes. We already proved, that the expected waking time for $\sqrt{n}$ nodes is $\Omega(\log^2 n)$. After waking up, each node repeats the following procedure as long as wake up is not finished: choose randomly ID in the range $[1, n]$; execute the algorithm $\mathcal{A}$ with chosen ID for $2f(n) = o(\log^2 n)$ rounds. Then, the wake up round appears in rounds $[1, 2f(n)]$ with probability $> 1/4$ as the IDs are unique with probability at least $1/2$ and the probability of wake up with unique IDs in $2f(n)$ rounds is at least $1/2$. If unfortunately the IDs of nodes woken up in rounds from the range $[1, n]$ are not unique, all these nodes assign themselves new IDs up to round $4f(n)$. Thus, if there is no wake up round up to $4f(n)$ (which happens with probability $< 3/4$), such a round it appears in the period $[4f(n)+1, 6f(n)]$ with probability $> \frac{3}{4} \cdot \frac{1}{4}$. By continuing this reasoning further, we see that the expected running time of $\mathcal{B}$ is at most

$$f(n) \cdot \sum_i (2+4i)(3/4)^{i-1}(1/4) = o(f(n^2)) = o(\log^2 n).$$

This result contradicts the lower bound $\Omega(\log^2 n)$ for algorithms in the scenario without IDs.

3. RANDOMIZED SYMMETRY-BREAKING ON THE SINR CHANNEL

In this section we provide a symmetry-breaking algorithm on the SINR channel and show that it solves the synchronization problem in $O(\log^2 n/\log\log n)$ rounds with high probability and in expectation. Thus, we obtain a gap in complexity of the problem between the traditional multiple-access channel and its SINR counterpart. As pointed out in Section 1.2, the solution in the SINR channel benefits from the fact that some nodes can receive messages from close neighbors despite the fact that there are many transmitters in a round. Using information inferred from such messages, nodes can adjust their broadcast probabilities appropriately.

3.1 Idea of the algorithm

Let a *successful round* be a round in which exactly one node transmits a message. Unlike in the classic channel, one can imagine that an algorithm for the SINR channel can succeed without a successful round. However, due to scalability of SINR model (see e.g., Section 4.2 where we use the scalability property), a universal algorithm for the SINR channel requires a successful round as well. In order to achieve this goal faster than in the classical multiple access channel, we should make use of the fact that nodes can receive messages even in rounds which are not successful.

For a given round t of an execution of a randomized algorithm, let $P(t)$ denote the sum of transmission probabilities p_v off all awake nodes v. By Fact 2, if $P(t) = \Theta(1)$ then the probability of success is $\Theta(1)$ as well. Therefore, logarithmic number of such rounds is sufficient to get a successful round whp. To achieve this goal, we start from the following algorithm working in $\Theta(\log^2 n)$ rounds also in the classical channel [15]. Each node v assigns $p_v = 1/n^2$ directly after its (spontaneous) wakeup. Then, it transmits with probability p_v in each round and increases p_v twice in each $r = \Theta(\log n)$ rounds until $p_v > 1/4$.

One can observe that, regardless of the wake-up pattern, $P(t') = \Theta(1)$ in some round $t' = O(\log^2 n)$, where 0 is the number of the round in which the first wakeup appears. Moreover, $P(t + r) \leq 2P(t) + 1/n$ since each node v increases p_v only once in each r rounds and $p_v = 1/n^2$ at the beginning. Therefore, each of rounds $t', t'+1, \ldots, t'+r$ are successful with probability $\Theta(1)$ and the algorithm is successful with high probability in $O(\log^2 n)$ rounds. As confirmed by the lower bounds, the complexity of this algorithm is $\Omega(\log^2 n)$ as well.

The above scenario works as well if the rapid increase of p_v by the factor 2 once in each $r = \Theta(\log n)$ rounds is replaced with the gradual increase $p_v \leftarrow p_v \cdot g$ in each round, where $g = g(n)$ is chosen such that $g^r = 2$. For technical reasons, we apply this modification in our algorithm. In order to achieve a better solution for the SINR channel, we also do the following:

(a) the rate g of increase of p_v is chosen larger than that in the algorithm for the classical channel;

(b) a node which is transmitting or receiving a message in a round decreases its probability p_v twice after that round (i.e., $p_v \leftarrow p_v/2$).

Point (a) alone would mean that the number of rounds t such that $P(t) = \Theta(1)$ becomes $o(\log n)$ as the probabilities increase faster. This in turn would mean that we can not rely only on rounds t such that $P(t) = \Theta(1)$ in order to prove success of the algorithm with high probability. The goal of point (b) is to guarantee that, after getting t such that $P(t) = \Theta(1)$, some nodes decrease their probabilities ensuring that the rate of increase g is balanced by these reductions of p_v's.

It turns out that there exist constants x, p depending merely on the SINR parameters such that, if $P(t) > 1$ then the set of nodes S such that each $v \in S$ either transmits in t or receives a message in t satisfies $\sum_{v\in S} p_v \geq x$ with probability at least p.[‡] As a result, the expectation of $P(t+1)$ is at most $gP(t) - px$ provided $P(t) > 1$. Thus, the goal is to choose g small enough to guarantee that the multiplicative increase g is balanced by the subtrahend px in the long run with high probability. On the other hand, we want to choose g large enough to achieve $P(t) = \Theta(1)$ for t as small as possible, even in the case that the adversary wakes up spontaneously only one node.

As we show in the next subsection, the value

$$g = 2^{\Theta\left(\frac{\log\log n}{\log n}\right)},$$

e.g., g such that $g^r = \log n$ for $r = \Theta(\log n)$, gives the algorithm which succeeds in $O(\log^2 / \log\log n)$ with high probability. Interestingly, higher values of g do not guarantee wakeup with high probability (at least using our analysis) while smaller values of g give larger time complexity. Thus, $O(\log^2 n/\log\log n)$ is the optimal time for such approach parameterized by the value of $g = g(n)$.

3.2 The algorithm

We consider the following randomized algorithm SINGLEHOPWAKEUP:

Algorithm 1 SINGLEHOPWAKEUP {p is a local variable for each v}

```
upon wakeup of v set p ← 1/n^2
for each round do
    v transmits with probability p
    if v receives a message then
        p ← p/2
    else
        p ← min{1/2, p · g}
```

Upon a spontaneous wake-up, a node v sets up transmission probability $p = 1/n^2$. In each of T round following its wake-up, the node transmits with probability p, which is updated as follows: if the node transmitted or heard other transmitting node in the current round then $p_v \leftarrow p/2$ at the end of the round, otherwise $p \leftarrow p{\cdot}g$, where $g = (\log n)^{c/\log n}$ for some fixed positive constant c to be specified later in the analysis. However, if the new value of p would be bigger than $1/2$ after a round, we do not update its value.

THEOREM 2. *Algorithm* SINGLEHOPWAKEUP *guarantees that each node receives a message in $O(\log^2 n/\log\log n)$ rounds, with high probability.*

[‡]This is the key property showing difference between radio channel and SINR channel. In radio channel, a node receives a message only when there is exactly one transmitter in the whole network in the given round.

Sketch of the proof

For the purpose of analysis, let fix the wake-up pattern and locations of nodes (defined by the adversary). Let 1 be the first round in the beginning of each some node(s) is awaken spontaneously, and let $T = c_1 \log^2 n / \log \log n$ be the end of the period in which we want to prove a successful reception of a message by each node whp, for some sufficiently large constant c_1 specified later in the analysis. Let $p_v(t)$ be the transmission probability of the node v at round t, and let $P(t) = \sum_v p_v(t)$. For technical reason, if a node v has not been awaken spontaneously by round t then we set $p_v(t) = 0$. We also say that a round t is *successful* if exactly one node transmits at t (and the algorithm succeeds in such a round). A round t is called *optimistic* if either $P(t) \in [1/2, 2]$ or $P(t) \leq 1/2$ and at least one node transmits in t.

LEMMA 2. *If a round t is optimistic then the (conditional) probability that a single node transmits in t is at least $1/16$.*

COROLLARY 1. *If there are at least $c_3 \log n$ optimistic rounds in an execution of the algorithm for some sufficiently large constant $c_3 > 0$ then the algorithm succeeds whp*

In view of the above corollary, it is sufficient to analyze such a scenario in which there are less than $c_3 \log n$ rounds t inside first T rounds such that $P(t) \leq 2$ and at least one node transmits in round t. One can show that there are many "loud" rounds t in such a case, i.e., with $P(t) > 2$. This is due to the fact that the sum of probabilities increases g times in a round without any transmission.

LEMMA 3. *Given any values $c_3, c_5, c > 0$, one can choose c_1 such that at least one of the following statement holds:*

(a) there are at least $c_3 \log n$ optimistic rounds,

(b) there are at least $c_5 \log n$ rounds t such that $P(t) > 2$.

Thanks to the above observations, we can restrict from now on to the case that there are at least $c_5 \log n$ rounds t such that $P(t) > 2$, for any chosen $c_5 > 0$.

LEMMA 4. *For every round t of an execution, if $P(t) > 1$ then $P(t+1) \leq gP(t) - x$ with probability at least $8r$, for some constants $x, r > 0$ which depend merely on the parameters of the SINR model.*

PROOF. More exactly, we find a constant x' such that $P(t+1) \leq g(P(t) - x') - x'/2$ with probability at least r' for some $x', r' \in (0, 1)$, provided $P(t) > 1$. This will give the result of the lemma for $x = x'(g + 1/2)$ and $r = r'/8$. The idea is to show that nodes with transmission probability at least x' decrease their probabilities in round t.

Consider a round t in which $P(t) > 1$ and a constant $x' < 1/2$. Let B be the smallest ball such that the sum of transmission probabilities in B is larger or equal to x' and let ρ be the radius of B. We limit from below the probability that each node in B decreases its transmission probability in round t by the value equal to the probability of the conjunction of three independent events:

- E_1: exactly one node from B transmits in round t; the probability of E_1 is at least $x'(1/4)^{x'}/2 \geq x'/4$ if $x' \leq 1/2$ by Fact 2;
- E_2: no other node in a box B' transmits such that B' is concentric with B and the radius of B' is $a\rho$, for some constant a; the probability of E_2 is bounded from below by a function which is (conversely) exponential wrt a^2 and x', since B' may be covered by $O(a^2)$ boxes of radius ρ and each such box contains nodes with transmission probability at most x'; (thus, the nodes located in $B' \setminus B$ can be split in $O(a^2)$ disjoint sets such that the sum of probabilities in each set is at most x');
- E_3: the interference in B received from nodes located outside of B' is as small as it cannot make a transmission inside B impossible; this could be achieved by the fact that the expected interference from nodes in distance $d \in [i\rho, (i+1)\rho)$ is $O(i \cdot x'/i^{\alpha})$ as one can cover them by $O(i)$ boxes of radius ρ; thus, the expected interference from nodes located outside of B' is $O(\sum_{i=a}^{\infty} 1/i^{\alpha-1})$; as $\lim_{a \to \infty} \sum_{i=a}^{\infty} 1/i^z = 0$, the expected interference can be arbitrarily small for large enough a; then, using Markov inequality, the probability of E_3 is at least some constant.

It is sufficient to choose any r' which is larger than the probability of the conjunction of the events E_1, E_2 and E_3. □

Let us conceptually split each round t into two sub-rounds. In the first sub-round each node that decides to change its transmission probability according to the rule $p \leftarrow p \cdot g$ applies that rule. In the second sub-round, the nodes which transmitted or heard a message in the actual round change their transmission probabilities according to the rule $p \leftarrow p/2$. Note that, by Lemma 4, the second sub-round of each round satisfies $P(t+1) \leq P(t) - x$ with probability at least $8r$.

Let us partition all sub-rounds from the beginning of an execution until time T into three types: a sub-round t is of type A if $P(t) > 1$ and $P(t+1) \leq P(t) - x$, of type B if $P(t) > 1$ and $P(t+1) > P(t) - x$, and of type C if $P(t) \leq 1$. Here the constant x is the one claimed in Lemma 4.

Consider a $\langle 2, 1 \rangle$*-decreasing sequence* of consecutive sub-rounds $[t, t']$ defined as follows: $t' \leq T$, each sub-round in $[t, t']$ is of type A or B and additionally $P(t) > 2$. A *maximal* $\langle 2, 1 \rangle$-decreasing sequence is a $\langle 2, 1 \rangle$-decreasing sequence which cannot be extended. Note that, given a maximal $\langle 2, 1 \rangle$-decreasing sequence with the last sub-round $t' < T$, the following statements hold: $P(t') \in (1, 2]$, $P(t'+1) < 1 < P(t')$ and at least one node transmits in t' (otherwise we would have $P(t'+1) \geq P(t')$ by the rules of updating transmission probabilities). Thus, the round t' is optimistic. Hence, it is sufficient to show that there are at least $c_3 \log n$ disjoint $\langle 2, 1 \rangle$-decreasing sequences. One can observe that maximal $\langle 2, 1 \rangle$-decreasing sequences satisfy the following conditions.

CLAIM 1. *1. A partition of an execution in maximal $\langle 2, 1 \rangle$-decreasing sequences is unique.*
2. Each two maximal $\langle 2, 1 \rangle$-decreasing sequences are disjoint.
3. Each sub-round t such that $P(t) \geq 2$ belongs to some maximal $\langle 2, 1 \rangle$-decreasing sequence.

Let us concatenate all maximal disjoint $\langle 2, 1 \rangle$-decreasing sequence up to time T; this corresponds to removing all rounds of type C and rounds of type A and B that do not belong to any $\langle 2, 1 \rangle$-decreasing sequence. Claim 1.3

and Lemma 3 imply that such a sequence has length at least $c_5 \log n$, provided c_1 is large enough. Consider the first $c_5 \log n$ rounds in the obtained sequence, for sufficiently large constant $c_5 > 0$. We refer to this sequence as σ (note that consecutive rounds in σ do not necessarily correspond to consecutive rounds in the execution).

The sequence σ might be considered as a sequence of letters A and B corresponding to the types of consecutive sub-rounds in σ such that:

- Every sub-round in the odd position is of type B (since, according to the definition, we defer decrease of transmission probabilities to the second sub-round of each round).
- the type of each sub-round in the even position is A with probability at least $8r$ and B with probability at most $1 - 8r$, regardless of types of other sub-rounds.

In the following, we formalize a proof that σ contains $\Omega(\log n)$ maximal $\langle 2, 1\rangle$-decreasing sequences, based on the following intuition. In order to finish a maximal $\langle 2, 1\rangle$-decreasing sequence ending at round $t' < T$, we have to decrease the sum of transmission probabilities of active nodes by factor around 2, since $2P(t'+1) \leq 2 \leq P(t)$ for a maximal $\langle 2, 1\rangle$-decreasing sequence $[t, t']$. As the decrease of the sum of transmission probabilities made in a sub-round of type A is much larger than the increase of this sum made in a sub-round of type B,[§] a maximal $\langle 2, 1\rangle$-decreasing sequence has to contain very large number of sub-rounds B compared to the number of sub-rounds A (see Lemma 6). On the other hand, by the fact that every sub-round in the even position in the sequence is of type A with probability at least $8r$, such dominance of sub-rounds B can happen with small probability (getting smaller on long sequences), and therefore σ contains many maximal $\langle 2, 1\rangle$-decreasing sequences.

First, let us make an observation bounding from below the fraction of sub-rounds A in σ.

LEMMA 5. *For each $\eta > 0$ one can choose sufficiently large constant $c_5 > 0$ such that the probability of the following event is smaller than $1/n^{\eta}$: there are at most $2rc_5 \log n$ sub-rounds of type A among the first $c_5 \log n$ sub-rounds of σ.*

Next, we fix the constant c in $g = (\log n)^{c/\log n}$ in such a way that the increase of the sum of probabilities in $c_5 \log n$ rounds of σ caused by applying the rule $p \leftarrow p \cdot g$ is not too large. Now, assume that the constant c_5 is fixed and chosen such that Lemma 5 holds. Let the constant c be chosen such that

$$g^{c_5 \log n} \leq \frac{1}{4} rxc_5 \log n \tag{2}$$

for $g = g(n) = (\log n)^{c/\log n}$. In this way, even if there are only rounds of type B in σ then the largest probability sum which appears in σ is at most $2g \cdot g^{c_5 \log n} \leq rxc_5 \log n$. On the other hand, if at least $2rc_5 \log n$ rounds of type A appear in σ (which holds whp by Lemma 5), the decrease of probability sum is at least $2rxc_5 \log n$. Note that, thanks to concavity of an exponential function, (2) implies

$$g^b \leq 1 + \frac{1}{4} c_5 rx \log n \cdot \frac{b}{c_5 \log n} = 1 + \frac{1}{4} brx \tag{3}$$

[§]This claim holds provided the sum of transmission probabilities is not too large. We assure that this is true by choosing g sufficiently small.

for each natural $b \leq c_5 \log n$.

Now, in contrast to Lemma 5, we bound the number of sub-rounds of type A from above.

LEMMA 6. *Consider a maximal $\langle 2, 1\rangle$-decreasing sequence of length at most $c_5 \log n$, and let r be as specified in Lemma 4. Then $a \leq br + c'$, where a is the number of rounds of type A, b is the number of rounds of type B in the sequence and c' is a constant dependent on x only.*

Now we conclude the proof of Theorem 2. It follows from Lemma 6 that in every $\langle 2, 1\rangle$-decreasing sequence containing a rounds of type A and b rounds of type B we have $a \leq br + c'$. Assume, that σ corresponds to an execution in which there are at least $c_5 \log n$ rounds t in which $P(t) > 2$. Let a^* be the total number of rounds of type A in σ and let b^* be the total number of rounds of type B in σ. Let i^* be the number of maximal $\langle 2, 1\rangle$-decreasing sequences contained in σ. By applying Lemma 6 to each of these $\langle 2, 1\rangle$-decreasing sequences, we get $a^* \leq b^* r + i^* c'$. Observe also that, straight from the definition, $a^* + b^* = c_5 \log n$. Consequently,

$$a^* \leq b^* r + i^* c' \leq (a^* + b^*) r + i^* c' = rc_5 \log n + i^* c'.$$

On the other hand, by Lemma 5, the inequality

$$a^* < 2rc_5 \log n$$

holds with negligible probability. Thus $i^* < \frac{rc_5 \log n}{c'} = c_3 \log n$ with negligible probability. The only case when we can have less than $c_3 \log n$ optimistic rounds is possible when there are at least $c_5 \log n$ rounds t in which $P(t) > 2$, AND, we have $i^* < c_3 \log n$ in the sequence σ . Since the probability of such an event is negligible, there are at least $c_3 \log n$ optimistic rounds whp. Therefore the algorithm is successful whp. As r and c' are constants which depend merely on the SINR parameters, one can obtain large enough value of i^* by setting c_5 large enough.

3.3 Optimizing expected time

As the lower bound $\Omega(\log^2 n)$ is known for single-hop symmetry-breaking whp in classical channel [8], Theorem 2 exhibits the gap between SINR and classical channel in this case. However, as we have shown in Theorem 1, the lower bound in classical channel extends to the scenario, when complexity is defined as an expected execution time until success for algorithms which finish successfully with probability 1 (i.e., Las Vegas algorithms).

Consider a modified algorithm SINGLEHOPWAKEUP, where each node works as before in its first T rounds after waking up spontaneously and transmits a message with probability $1/n$ in each round afterwards. By choosing the constant c_1 large enough, we can guarantee that modified SINGLEHOPWAKEUP succeeds with probability $1 - 1/n^3$ in first T rounds. Observe that in each but nT remaining rounds, all awake nodes transmit with probability $1/n$. Then, the success probability in each such round t is at least $p_s = \frac{k}{n}(1 - 1/n)^{k-1}$, where $1 \leq k \leq n$ is the number of awake nodes in the round. As $\min_{i \in [1,n]} (\frac{k}{n}(1 - 1/n)^{k-1}) \geq 1/n$, the algorithm succeeds with probability at least $1/n$ in each such round. One can easily check that this gives an algorithm which succeeds with expected time

$$O(T) = O(\log^2 n / \log \log n).$$

Indeed, the algorithm finishes in T rounds with pbb $1 - 1/n^3$. Moreover, for each $t \geq n^c$ and $c > 2$, the probability that the algorithm does not finish in at most t rounds is at most $(1-1/n)^{n^c/2} \leq 1/n^{2c}$ for n large enough.

This gives the following corollary showing a gap in complexity of single-hop symmetry-breaking between classical channel and SINR.

Corollary 2. *Modified* SingleHopWakeUp *is a Las Vegas algorithm which accomplishes synchronization in expected time $O(\log^2 n/\log\log n)$.*

4. LOWER BOUNDS FOR DETERMINISTIC SYNCHRONIZATION ON THE SINR CHANNEL

In this section, we consider deterministic algorithms. We assume that each station has assigned unique ID in the range $[N]$ for $N = n^c$, where $c \geq q$ is a fixed constant.

Assume that A is a symmetry-breaking protocol working in time $f(n)$. Let *oblivious schedule* OS_i for $i \in [N]$ corresponding to A be a 0/1 vector of length $f(n)$ describing behaviour of a station with ID equal i in rounds $t = 1, \ldots, f(n)$ provided i has not received a message from any other station: $OS_i[t] = 1$ iff i transmits in round t according to A.

We say that a station v sends a message *spontaneously* in round t if it has not received a message up to t and it sends a message in t (according to its oblivious schedule).

For the model without global clock, we count rounds starting from the round in which the first station is waken up spontaneously.

4.1 The model without global clock

Theorem 3. *Each deterministic symmetry-breaking protocol in the model without global clock works in time $\Omega(n)$ even in networks with polynomial granularity.*

Sketch of the proof Contrary, assume that a symmetry-breaking protocol A works in time $o(n)$. We consider networks where all stations are located at points

$$(id, 0), (id, \delta d), (id, 2\delta d)$$

for $i = 1, 2, \ldots, n/3$, where $d = 1/n$ and δ is a small constant. We say that positions $(id, 0), (id, \delta d), (id, 2\delta d)$ form *slot i*. The constant δ is chosen such that if all three stations from slot i transmit a message simultaneously and no station from slots $i' > i$ transmits a message at the same time, then no station from slots $i+1, \ldots, n/3$ receives a message[¶].

Then, we assign IDs for consecutive slots and wake-up patterns such that:

- no station transmits a message until round t for some $t \geq 0$;
- all stations from the slot i transmit a message in round $t+i$ for $i = 1, \ldots, cn$;

[¶]If the background noise $\mathcal{N}$ is greater than 0 or $\beta > 1$, then it is sufficient that a slot contains two positions in order to guarantee the property that no stations to the right of slot i can hear a message from the slot i if all its elements transmit simultaneously. The only reason for which slots have three (not two) elements here is to assure that the proof works for $\mathcal{N} = 0$ and $\beta = 1$ as well.

Figure 2: A network family for a lower bound in the model without global clock.

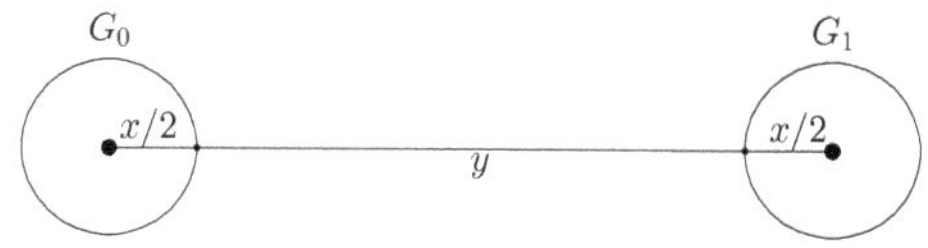

Figure 3: A union of networks in the recursive construction from the proof of Theorem 4.

- no station from the slot i transmits a message before round $t+i$ for $i = 1, \ldots, cn$.

where $0 < c < 1$ is a constant. If the above properties are ensured the stations from slot cn cannot hear a message until the round $t + cn$. Now, if we change the wake-up pattern such that they are not awake spontaneously, the protocol requires $t + cn$ which contradicts the contrary assumption. Below, we describe details of the above scenario.

4.2 The model with global clock

Theorem 4. *Each deterministic symmetry-breaking protocol in the model with global clock works in time $\Omega((\log n) \cdot (\log N))$.*

Sketch of the proof We prove the theorem by contradiction. A network giving contradiction with the contrary assumption is build recursively (see Figure 3). For consecutive $i = 1, 2, \ldots, \log n$, we build network families F_i, where the elements of F_i have size 2^i and require $\Omega(i \log N)$ rounds for symmetry-breaking. In fact, we assure even more: in each network G from F_i, there is no round t in the period $[\frac{1}{2} i \log N]$ such that exactly one station from F_i transmits a message in t.Simultaneously, we assure that the size of F_i is sufficiently large. Given F_i, we obtain elements of F_{i+1} by carefully joining pairs of elements of F_i. If F_i is sufficiently large, it contains many pairs G_0, G_1 of networks such that in each round in $[1 + \frac{1}{2} i \log N, \frac{1}{2}(i+1) \log N]$ either no station from both networks transmit or at least one station from each of them transmits. If we choose G_0, G_1 enclosed in very small disks and locate them far away, we can guarantee that G_i is not aware of G_{1-i} until a round in which exactly one element of G_{1-i} transmits and no-one from G_i transmits. (In order to ensure this property, we have also to assure that G_i cannot generate interference which changes perception of messages transmitted inside G_{1-i}.) Thus, we guarantee that the elements of F_{i+1} do not have a round until $\frac{1}{2}(i+1) \log N$ in which exactly one station transmits. If one puts a station v far away from an element of F_{i+1} and does not wake-up v spontaneously, then v is not waken up until round $\frac{1}{2}(i+1) \log N$. Let us make it clear here that "far away" in this context still denotes a distance within a circle of diameter 1. Therefore, we require that the distances in networks of F_1 are at least exponentially small in order to guarantee that after $\log n$ steps of joining smaller networks into larger ones, the obtained network is still contained in a disk of diameter 1.

As the leader election protocol from [13] can be applied as the symmetry-breaking protocol working in time $O((\log n) \cdot (\log N))$, $\Theta((\log n) \cdot (\log N))$ is the actual complexity of the problem.

5. CONCLUSIONS AND OPEN PROBLEMS

We show that there exists a gap of magnitude (at least) $\log\log n$ between complexity of synchronization in classic (radio) MAC channel and its SINR counterpart. This separation result is strengthened by the fact that $\Omega(\log^2 n)$ lower bound for the radio channel holds when the complexity bound has to hold whp as well as when an expected time is considered. Moreover, we show an exponential gap between local and global clocks for deterministic synchronization on the SINR channel.

Among various open problems which remain unsolved, we point out to the fact that no superlogarithmic lower bound on (randomized) synchronization of SINR channel without global clock is known.

Acknowledgments We would like to thank Darek Kowalski for many stimulating discussions on the topic and problems considered in this paper.

6. REFERENCES

[1] N. M. Abramson. Development of the alohanet. *IEEE Transactions on Information Theory*, 31(2):119–123, 1985.

[2] A. F. Anta, M. A. Mosteiro, and J. R. Muñoz. Unbounded contention resolution in multiple-access channels. *Algorithmica*, 67(3):295–314, 2013.

[3] R. Bar-Yehuda, O. Goldreich, and A. Itai. On the time-complexity of broadcast in multi-hop radio networks: An exponential gap between determinism and randomization. *J. Comput. Syst. Sci.*, 45(1):104–126, 1992.

[4] B. Chlebus. Randomized communication in radio networks. In J. R. P.M. Pardalos, S. Rajasekaran and J. Rolim, editors, *Handbook on Randomized Computing*. Kluwer Academic Publishers, 2001.

[5] M. Chrobak, L. Gasieniec, and D. R. Kowalski. The wake-up problem in multihop radio networks. *SIAM J. Comput.*, 36(5):1453–1471, 2007.

[6] A. E. F. Clementi, A. Monti, and R. Silvestri. Distributed broadcast in radio networks of unknown topology. *Theor. Comput. Sci.*, 302(1-3):337–364, 2003.

[7] S. Daum, F. Kuhn, and C. C. Newport. Efficient symmetry breaking in multi-channel radio networks. In M. K. Aguilera, editor, *Distributed Computing - 26th International Symposium, DISC 2012, 2012. Proceedings*, volume 7611 of *Lecture Notes in Computer Science*, pages 238–252. Springer, 2012.

[8] M. Farach-Colton and M. A. Mosteiro. Initializing sensor networks of non-uniform density in the weak sensor model. *Algorithmica*, 2014.

[9] L. Gasieniec, A. Pelc, and D. Peleg. The wakeup problem in synchronous broadcast systems. *SIAM J. Discrete Math.*, 14(2):207–222, 2001.

[10] O. Goussevskaia, T. Moscibroda, and R. Wattenhofer. Local broadcasting in the physical interference model. In M. Segal and A. Kesselman, editors, *DIALM-POMC*, pages 35–44. ACM, 2008.

[11] M. M. Halldórsson and P. Mitra. Nearly optimal bounds for distributed wireless scheduling in the SINR model. In L. Aceto, M. Henzinger, and J. Sgall, editors, *Automata, Languages and Programming - 38th International Colloquium, ICALP 2011, Proceedings, Part II*, volume 6756 of *Lecture Notes in Computer Science*, pages 625–636. Springer, 2011.

[12] P. Indyk. Explicit constructions of selectors and related combinatorial structures, with applications. In D. Eppstein, editor, *Proceedings of the Thirteenth Annual ACM-SIAM Symposium on Discrete Algorithms*, pages 697–704. ACM/SIAM, 2002.

[13] T. Jurdzinski, D. R. Kowalski, and G. Stachowiak. Distributed deterministic broadcasting in uniform-power ad hoc wireless networks. In *Fundamentals of Computation Theory - 19th International Symposium, FCT 2013*, pages 195–209, 2013.

[14] T. Jurdzinski, D. R. Kowalski, and G. Stachowiak. Distributed deterministic broadcasting in wireless networks of weak devices. In F. V. Fomin, R. Freivalds, M. Z. Kwiatkowska, and D. Peleg, editors, *Automata, Languages, and Programming - 40th International Colloquium, ICALP 2013, Proceedings, Part II*, volume 7966 of *Lecture Notes in Computer Science*, pages 632–644. Springer, 2013.

[15] T. Jurdzinski and G. Stachowiak. Probabilistic algorithms for the wake-up problem in single-hop radio networks. *Theory Comput. Syst.*, 38(3):347–367, 2005.

[16] J. Komlós and A. G. Greenberg. An asymptotically fast nonadaptive algorithm for conflict resolution in multiple-access channels. *IEEE Transactions on Information Theory*, 31(2):302–306, 1985.

[17] D. Kowalski. Coordination problems in ad hoc radio networks. In J. D. R. Sotiris Nikoletseas, editor, *Springer Book on Theoretical Aspects of Distributed Computing in Sensor Networks*. Springer, 2010.

[18] D. R. Kowalski. On selection problem in radio networks. In M. K. Aguilera and J. Aspnes, editors, *PODC*, pages 158–166. ACM, 2005.

[19] E. Kushilevitz and Y. Mansour. An omega(d log (n/d)) lower bound for broadcast in radio networks. *SIAM J. Comput.*, 27(3):702–712, 1998.

[20] R. Metcalfe and D. Boggs. Ethernet: Distributed packet switching for local computer networks. *Commun. ACM*, 19(7):395–404, 1976.

[21] C. C. Newport. Radio network lower bounds made easy. In F. Kuhn, editor, *Distributed Computing - 28th International Symposium, DISC 2014, Austin, TX, USA, October 12-15, 2014. Proceedings*, volume 8784 of *Lecture Notes in Computer Science*, pages 258–272. Springer, 2014.

[22] A. Ogierman, A. W. Richa, C. Scheideler, S. Schmid, and J. Zhang. Competitive MAC under adversarial SINR. In *2014 IEEE Conference on Computer Communications, INFOCOM 2014, Toronto, Canada, April 27 - May 2, 2014*, pages 2751–2759. IEEE, 2014.

[23] D. E. Willard. Log-logarithmic selection resolution protocols in a multiple access channel. *SIAM J. Comput.*, 15(2):468–477, 1986.

Leveraging Multiple Channels in Ad Hoc Networks*

Magnús M. Halldórsson
ICE-TCS
School of Computer Science
Reykjavik University
Iceland
mmh@ru.is

Yuexuan Wang
College of Comp. Sci. & Tech.
Zhejiang University, Hangzhou
&
The University of Hong Kong
amywang@hku.hk

Dongxiao Yu
Department of Computer Science
The University of Hong Kong
Hong Kong, P.R. China
dxyu@cs.hku.hk

ABSTRACT

We explore the utility of multiple channels of communication in wireless networks under the SINR model of interference. The central question is whether multiple channels can result in linear speedup, up to some fundamental limit. We answer this question affirmatively for the data aggregation problem, perhaps the most fundamental problem in sensor networks. To achieve this, we form a hierarchical structure of independent interest, and illustrate its versatility by obtaining a new algorithm with linear speedup for the node coloring problem.

Categories and Subject Descriptors

C.2.1 [**Computer-Communication Networks**]: Network Architecture and Design; F.2.2 [**Analysis of Algorithms and Problem Complexity**]: Nonnumerical Algorithms and Problems

General Terms

Algorithms, Design, Theory

Keywords

Ad Hoc wireless networks; Multiple channels; SINR; Data aggregation; Distributed algorithms

1. INTRODUCTION

Diversity in wireless networks – the availability of multiple opportunities for communication – is well known to decrease interference, increase reliability, and improve performance. The question is: how much does it help and what are the limits to such improvements. In particular, we seek an answer to the following fundamental question in the context of the SINR model:

Can we attain linear speedup in distributed wireless algorithms as the number of channels increase up to a fundamental limit?

Thus, we are interested in the fundamental limits of the benefits of diversity. In the best case, the multiple-channel complexity matches the single-channel complexity, scaled with the number of channels, with an unavoidable *additive* polylogarithmic term.

We focus our attention on data dissemination problems, in particular *data aggregation*, sometimes referred to as the "killer-app" for sensor networks: compute a compressible function (e.g., average) of values stored at the nodes.

Multiple channels can be available to nodes due to available frequencies, or modulation schemes. They can also be simulated by time-division multiplexing (TDMA), by assigning time slots to the different channels. The converse does not hold, however, as multiple channels are a strictly more constrained form of communication. Namely, whereas nodes can listen (and even choose to send) in all slots of a TDMA schedule, they can only listen on one of the multiple channels. Thus, multiple channels can be viewed as a form of *parallelism* in wireless communication, and our inquiry involves the parallelizability of the fundamental wireless tasks.

Multiple channels have been found to yield linear speedups in graph-based models, such as for broadcast [8], minimum dominating sets [6] and maximal independent sets [4]. Essentially the only work on multiple channels in the SINR model, however, is [38], that attains a sub-linear speedup for local information exchange, and holds only for a restricted number of channels when each message can carry multiple packets. Thus, little has been known about the limits for leveraging multiple channels in the SINR context.

Model. For a network model, we assume synchronized operation, where nodes have no power control, no collision detection, but have a carrier sense mechanism as in standard signal strength measurements. The SINR model of interference is assumed, but the parameters (α, β, N) are allowed to vary within fixed ranges. We assume for simplicity of exposition that nodes are located in the plane, but the results extend to fading metrics. We also assume for simplicity simultaneous wake-up, although the results can be adapted to other situations. Nodes have no knowledge of the location of other nodes or their distribution, but have a polynomial bound on the number of nodes and are given approximate values of SINR parameters.

*Partially supported by Iceland Research Foundation grants 120032011 and 152679-051, National Natural Science Foundation of China Grant 61073174, 61373027 and HKU Small Project.

Permission to make digital or hard copies of all or part of this work for personal or classroom use is granted without fee provided that copies are not made or distributed for profit or commercial advantage and that copies bear this notice and the full citation on the first page. Copyrights for components of this work owned by others than ACM must be honored. Abstracting with credit is permitted. To copy otherwise, or republish, to post on servers or to redistribute to lists, requires prior specific permission and/or a fee. Request permissions from permissions@acm.org.
PODC'15, July 21–23, 2015, Donostia-San Sebastián, Spain.
Copyright © 2015 ACM 978-1-4503-3617-8 /15/07 ...$15.00.
DOI: http://dx.doi.org/10.1145/2767386.2767437.

Our Results

Let D be the diameter of the reachability graph, Δ be its maximum degree, $\mathcal{F}$ be the number of channels, and n the number of nodes (see Sec. 2 for definitions). We say that an event happens with high probability (with respect to n), if it happens with probability $1 - 1/n^c$ for some constant $c > 0$.

We give a randomized algorithm that achieves data aggregation in $O(D + \Delta/\mathcal{F} + \log n \log\log n)$ time with high probability. Since Δ is a lower bound for aggregation in single-channel networks, even ones with few hops, we achieve linear speedup up to the additive $\log n \log\log n$ term. This is essentially best possible for a setting where high probability guarantees are required.

Our data aggregation algorithm is based on a data aggregation structure that can be constructed in $O(\log^2 n)$ time. If a $\log^{O(1)} n$-approximation of Δ is known, the time for constructing the aggregation structure is $O(\Delta/\mathcal{F} + \log n \cdot \log\log n)$. Hence, in this case, the total time for accomplishing data aggregation (taking into account the time for structure construction) is $O(D + \frac{\Delta}{\mathcal{F}} + \log n \log\log n)$ with high probability.

The aggregation structure is of independent interest, as it can be used to solve other core problems. To illustrate its applicability, we give an algorithm for the node coloring problem that runs in $O(\frac{\Delta}{\mathcal{F}} + \log n \log\log n)$ time with high probability.

Lower Bounds

We indicate here briefly why our bounds are probably the best possible. Any global task involving communication requires at least D steps, which yields a lower bound on every instance. Similarly, $\lceil \log n \rceil$ is a lower bound for data aggregation, since at most half the items can be coalesced in a single round. Also, logarithmic number of steps are necessary for any form of high probability bounds of randomized algorithms. Thus, independent of the parallelization in the form of multiple channels, $\Omega(D + \log n)$ steps are needed.

In a single channel, the term Δ is necessary for any communication task that involves all nodes when using uniform power. In particular, consider the "exponential chain", where point i is located at position 2^i on the real line, $i = 1, 2, \ldots, n$. Then, when using uniform power, at most one successful transmission can occur in a time slot (assuming $\beta \geq 2^{1/\alpha}$) [25]. In particular, aggregation and coloring require Δ steps in single-channel networks, and clearly $\mathcal{F}$ channels can reduce the time requirement at most to $\Delta/\mathcal{F}$. While no proof is known, it is unlikely that power control reduces this bound in the distributed SINR setting; known distributed algorithms all feature time complexity of either the distance diversity (which can be as large as n) [11, 2, 27] or terms corresponding to Δ [21, 10, 12, 34].

Related Work

Data Aggregation. In single-channel networks, there have been a long line of research on data aggregation under different settings in the protocol model [15, 24, 30, 31, 33, 32] and the SINR model [1, 9, 13, 23, 22, 14, 11, 2]. Regarding the distributed solutions under the SINR model, a distributed aggregation algorithm with uniform power assignment is proposed in [23], which achieves a latency upper bound of $O(D+\Delta)$. Assuming a model where every node in the network knows its position, the network diameter and the number of neighbors, Li et al. [22] presented a distributed algorithm with a latency bound of O(K), where K is the logarithm of the ratio between the length of the longest link and that of the shortest link. And this result needs that nodes can adjust the transmission power arbitrarily. In [14], Hobbs et al. gave a deterministic algorithm which can accomplish data aggregation in $O(D + \Delta \log n)$ rounds. An entirely different approach is to use (significant) precomputation to build a fast aggregation structure. In particular, aggregation can be achieved in optimal $O(D + \log n)$ time [11, 2], but this uses $O(K \log^2 n)$ time for precomputation and also relies heavily on arbitrary power control.

In multi-channel networks, the multiple-message broadcast algorithm given in [4] can be adapted to solve the data aggregation problem in $O(D + \Delta + \frac{\log^2 n}{\mathcal{F}} + \log n \log\log n)$ rounds with high probability. But this result is presented in the graph-based interference model and restricts the number of channels to $\log n$. An algorithm for the related broadcast problem was given in [8] for a similar setting but also allowing disruptions on channels. The work closest to ours is a recent treatment of the local information exchange problem in multi-channel SINR networks [38], where Yu et al. gave a distributed algorithm attaining a sub-linear speedup. In the algorithm, the number of channels that can be used effectively is limited to $O(\sqrt{\Delta/\log n})$, resulting in an $\Omega(\log n \cdot \sqrt{\Delta \log n})$ lower bound on the performance of the algorithm.

Coloring. The distributed node coloring problem has been extensively studied since the 1980s, as a classical symmetry breaking paradigm [3]. Most work has been in message passing models that ignore interference and collisions. Assuming a graph based model that defines only direct interference from neighbors, Moscibroda and Wattenhofer [26] gave an $O(\Delta \log n)$ time randomized algorithm using $O(\Delta)$ colors for bounded-independence graphs, This was lated improved to a $\Delta+1$-coloring in $O(\Delta + \log\Delta \log n)$ time [29]. Derbel and Talbi [7] showed that the algorithm of [26] can also work in the SINR model with the same time and color bounds. Yu et al. [37] gave a randomized algorithm with running time $O(\Delta \log n + \log^2 n)$ that achieves a $\Delta + 1$-coloring in the SINR model. All of the above results are for wireless networks with a single channel, and it appears no work has previously addressed the coloring problem in multiple channel networks, let alone in the SINR model.

Backbone Network Construction. Another line of related work is finding dominating sets and/or a broadcast/aggregation network in a multi-hop scenario. The work we directly use is that of [28] with an algorithm that finds a dominating set in the SINR model in $O(\log n)$ time. An algorithm was given in [26] that finds a maximal independent set running in $O(\log^2 n)$ time in the quasi unit disk model; it was converted to the SINR model in [37]. These works do not attempt to construct a network among dominators. Broadcast or aggregation networks among dominators are formed in some works such as [2, 11, 18, 19, 16, 35, 36]. These works either need a large ϵ (at least 2/3) to work [35, 36], use precise location information [18, 19, 16], or arbitrary power adjustment [2, 11]. All these works are only for single-channel networks.

2. MODEL AND PROBLEM FORMULATIONS

The network consists of n nodes (denoted as V) that are

arbitrarily placed on a a plane. Each node is identified by a unique ID. We focus on the setting of a *uniform* power assignment, where all nodes use the same transmission power P. For two nodes u and v, denote by $d(u, v)$ the distance between u and v.

Multiple Communication Channels and Synchronization. Nodes communicate through a shared medium which is divided into $\mathcal{F}$ channels. Time is divided into synchronized rounds, and each may contain a constant number of synchronized slots. All nodes start the algorithm at the same time. In each slot of every round, each node can select one of the $\mathcal{F}$ channels and choose either to transmit or to listen on the selected channel. A node that operates on a channel in a given slot learns nothing about events on other channels.

Interference and SINR model. Simultaneous transmissions on the same channel interfere with each other. The SINR model captures the interference. In particular, a message sent by node u to node v can be correctly received at v iff (i) u and v operate on the same channel and v is not transmitting, and (ii) the following defined SINR ratio $SINR(u, v)$ is above a hardware defined threshold $\beta \geq 1$.

$$SINR(u, v) = \frac{P/d(u, v)^{\alpha}}{N + \sum_{w \in S \setminus \{u,v\}} \frac{P}{d(w,v)^{\alpha}}} \geq \beta, \qquad (1)$$

where $\alpha > 2$ is the path-loss exponent; N is the ambient noise, and S is the set of nodes transmitting simultaneously as u.

In the absence of other simultaneous transmissions on the same channel, the *transmission range* R_T of a node u is the maximum distance at which a node v can receive a clear transmission from u. The SINR condition (1) tells us that $R_T = (\frac{P}{\beta \cdot N})^{1/\alpha}$.

We assume that nodes can measure the SINR (in case of a successful reception), or total received power (in other cases). This power reception feature is comparable to the RSSI function of real wireless motes. Nodes can use this feature to infer (approximate) distances from the sender of a received message. In our algorithm, indeed, it is enough to only measure whether or not the SINR or the total received power crosses a threshold.

It is always of theoretical interest to determine the tradeoffs between different model assumptions, and to identify the least set of primitives that suffice for efficient execution. We posit, however, that the default model for wireless algorithms in physical models should feature carrier sense ability. Given that such a feature is so standard in even the cheapest hardware and so easily implementable, it would be counterproductive to forbid it. Note that we only require receiver-side sensing, but assume no transmitter-side detection ability.

Communication Graph and Notations. Denote by $R_c = (1 - c)R_T$, where $0 < c < 1$ is a constant. The *communication graph* $G(V, E)$ of a given network consists of all network nodes and edges (v, u) such that $d(v, u) \leq R_{\epsilon}$, where $0 < \epsilon < 1$ is a fixed model parameter. Since nodes of distance very close to R_T can only communicate in the absence of other activity in the network arbitrarily far away, the standard assumption is to assume that it suffices to communicate using a slightly smaller range, R_{ϵ} [2, 5, 17].

We use standard graph terminology: $N(u)$ is the set of neighbors of node u; $d_u = |N(u)|$ is the degree of u; and Δ is the maximum degree of a node. The *diameter* D of a graph G is the maximum, over all pairs of nodes u, v, of the shortest number of hops connecting u with v.

A node u is an *r-neighbor* of node v if $d(u, v) \leq r$. An *r-dominating set* is a subset of nodes (*dominators*) such that each node in G is within a distance r from a dominator (possibly itself). An r-ball is a disk in the plane of radius r. The *density* of an r-dominating set is the maximum number of dominators in an r-ball (over all balls in the plane). A set S is called an *r-independent set* if for any two nodes $u, v \in S$, $d(u, v) > r$. An r-independent set M is called an *r-maximal independent set* if for each node w, either $w \in S$ or there is a node $u \in S$ such that $d(w, u) \leq r$.

Denote by E_v^r the disk with radius r centered at node v, and overload the notation to refer also to the set of nodes in the disk.

Knowledge of Nodes. Nodes know a polynomial approximation to n (i.e., the value of $\log n$, up to constant factors), without which there is an $\Omega(n/\log n)$-lower bound [20]. For simplicity of description, we also use n to denote the estimate. We assume that nodes do not know the precise value of the SINR parameters α, β and N but instead know only upper and lower bounds for the parameters (i.e., α_{min} and α_{max}, β_{min} and β_{max}, N_{min} and N_{max}); for simplicity, we perform calculations assuming that exact values of these parameters are known. To deal with uncertainty regarding those parameters, it is sufficient to choose their maximal/minimal values depending on the fact whether upper or lower estimates are provided. Nodes do not have any other information, such as the network topology, their neighbors or their location coordinates.

Data Aggregation. Initially, each node has a data value. The *data aggregation* problem is to compute an aggregate function (e.g., maximum or average) on the input data from all nodes in the network, and inform all nodes of this value as quickly as possible.

Node Coloring. The *node coloring* problem is to compute a proper vertex coloring of the communication graph G, with the objective of minimizing the number of colors used (and the time spent).

3. TECHNICAL OVERVIEW

Our approach is to build a multi-purpose dissemination structure that we then apply to our problems. The structure has two main parts: the global and the local aspects. These are tied together through the set of *dominators*, which play the role of local leaders and collaborate to carry out the global task.

After finding a low-density set of dominators, the other nodes are partitioned into clusters, each headed by a dominator. These clusters are then colored to disperse the clusters of same color, effectively eliminating interference from other clusters. The clusters are arranged into a communication tree to carry out the global task. These constructions are by now all fairly well known, so we build on previous work, in particular using the $O(\log n)$ round clustering process from [28].

Our main contributions are in the treatment of the intra-cluster aspects. We first estimate the size of each cluster, in order to adjust the contention. We divide the cluster nodes randomly into channels, and run leader election processes to elect a *reporter* in each channel in $O(\log n)$ rounds. We then form a binary tree of $O(\log \mathcal{F})$ levels on the reporters, that can be used to aggregate the data to the dominator. The total time needed for reporter election and reporter tree construction is $O(\log^2 n)$, and the aggregation cost in the clusters is $O(\Delta/\mathcal{F}+\log n \log\log n)$. If a $\log^{O(1)} n$-approximation of Δ is known, the reporter election and the reporter tree construction can be done in $O(\Delta/\mathcal{F} + \log n \log\log n)$ time as well.

4. MAXIMAL INDEPENDENT SET ALGORITHM

We next present a maximal independent set algorithm, which will be invoked frequently in the subsequent structure construction. The algorithm can compute an MIS with respect to a specific distance r in $O(\log n)$ rounds.

In particular, there are two phases in the algorithm: in the first phase, a dominating set of constant density is computed; and in the second phase, an MIS will be elected on the dominating set.

The dominating set of constant density can be computed in $O(\log n)$ rounds using the algorithm given by Scheideler et al. [28]. Now assume that we have a dominating set of density μ. Dominators will execute the algorithm in the second phase to compute a maximal independent set. Here we assume that the transmission range of nodes is $(1+\sigma)r$ for some $\sigma > 0$, i.e., the transmission power of nodes is $P = N\beta((1+\sigma)r)^{\alpha}$.

We say that a message from node u is *clearly received* at node v if: a) $d(u,v) \le r$, and b) the interference sensed by v is at most $T_s = \min\{\frac{1}{2^{\alpha}} \cdot ((1+\sigma)^{\alpha} - 1)N, (\frac{1+\sigma}{4})^{\alpha} \cdot N\beta\}$. Clear reception guarantees that no other node in E_v^{4r} had simultaneously transmitted.

The second phase consists of $\gamma_1 \log n$ rounds for a sufficiently large constant γ_1. In each round, there are three slots:

- **Slot 1.** Each node transmits with probability λ/μ, where λ is a small enough constant.
- **Slot 2.** If a node u listened in the first slot and had a clear reception, u transmits with probability λ/μ.
- **Slot 3.** If a node u transmitted in the first slot and received a message in the second slot, u decides to join the MIS and transmits. Otherwise, u listens. If u listened and received a message from a node v within distance r, u stops executing the algorithm.

Analysis. Since it has been shown that a dominating set of constant density can be computed in $O(\log n)$ rounds in [28], we here only need to analyze the algorithm execution of the second phase. In the subsequent analysis, it is assumed that there has been a constant density dominating set being computed.

Using the standard technique of bounding interference within concentric circles (refer to [2, 17, 36]), we obtain the following result.

LEMMA 1. *During the second phase of the algorithm execution, if a node u transmits in the first slot of a round, every node within distance r will get a clear reception from u with constant probability.*

LEMMA 2. *During the second phase of the algorithm execution, if a node u joins the MIS in a round, it will successfully transmit a message to nodes within distance r in the third slot of the round.*

PROOF. Assume that u joins the MIS in a round t. This means that in the first slot, there is a node w within distance r from u clearly receiving a message from u. We claim that each node in E_u^r also receives the transmission of u in the first slot.

Let S be the set of transmitters in round t. For any node $v \in S$, v is not in E_w^{4r}, since if $v \in E_w^{4r}$, w will sense a busy channel by the transmission power and the setting of T_s. For any node $v' \in E_u^r$, the interference at v' caused by v is $I_{vv'} \le \frac{P}{(d_{wv}-2r)^{\alpha}} \le \frac{P}{(d_{wv}/2)^{\alpha}} \le 2^{\alpha} I_{vw}$. Then the interference at v' caused by all nodes in S is $I_S(v') = \sum_{v\in S} I_{vv'} \le \sum_{v \in S} 2^{\alpha} I_{vw} \le ((1+\sigma)^{\alpha} - 1)N$. Hence, u's message can be clearly received by v'.

Finally, note that only nodes that transmitted in the first slot may transmit in the third slot. Hence, u can send a message to all other nodes in E_u^r. ☐

LEMMA 3. *The algorithm can correctly compute a maximal independent set in $O(\log n)$ rounds with high probability.*

PROOF. We first claim that after executing the second phase of the algorithm, with high probability, each node will either join the MIS or receive a message from an MIS node within distance r. For a node w, in the first slot of a round, the probability that w transmits and all other nodes in E_w^r get a clear reception from w is $\lambda/\mu \cdot c'$ for some constant c' by Lemma 1. If w makes a node in E_w^r get a clear reception from w, it can receive a message in the second slot of the round with probability at least $\lambda/\mu \cdot c'$. Hence, with constant probability, w joins the MIS in a round. Then after $\gamma_1 \log n$ rounds for a sufficiently large constant γ_1, if w does not receive a message from a node within distance r that is in the MIS, it will join the MIS with high probability.

We next show that the nodes joining the MIS form an independent set. For a pair of r-neighbors u, v, assume that u, v are both in the MIS. Let t_u and t_v denote the rounds in which u and v join the MIS respectively. Without loss of generality, assume that $t_u \le t_v$. If $t_u < t_v$, by Lemma 2, u will send a message to v in the third slot of t_u and v will not join the MIS. Hence, $t_u = t_v$. By the algorithm, u joins the MIS only if it receives a message from w in the second slot of t_u. This means that w gets a clear reception from u in the first slot of t_u. By the setting of T_s, this occurs only if v does not transmit in the first slot of t_u, which means that v cannot join the MIS in t_u. This contradiction shows that the nodes joining the MIS constitute an independent set.

Note that the above analysis is based on the dominating set of constant density being correctly computed. As shown in [28], such a dominating set can be computed in $O(\log n)$ rounds. Putting everything together, the Lemma follows. ☐

5. AGGREGATION STRUCTURE CONSTRUCTION

As discussed in Section 3, the structure construction consists of two procedures: Clustering and Reporter Tree Construction. In particular, with the proposed algorithm, we have the following result, which can be obtained by Lemma 6, Lemma 7 and Lemma 9 given later.

THEOREM 4. *A hierarchical aggregation structure can be constructed in $O(\log^2 n)$ rounds with high probability. If a polynomial bound on Δ is given, then $O(\Delta/\mathcal{F}+\log n \log\log n)$ rounds suffice.*

5.1 Communication Backbone

To reduce computation and communication, we use an overlay in the form of a connected dominating set. The dominators function as local leaders, managing the local computation, and participate in disseminating the information globally. The dominators are also colored to ensure good spatial separation between clusters of same color, which in turn allows the local computation to ignore interference from other clusters.

We use a frequently-used argument that shows that well separated communication can proceed independently. The proof of this lemma uses the standard technique of bounding interference within concentric circles (refer to [2, 17, 36]).

LEMMA 5. *Let S_F be the set of nodes selecting to operate on a channel F in a given round. Let r_1, r_2 be distance parameters with $r_2 \leq \left(\frac{\alpha-2}{48\beta(\alpha-1)}\right)^{\frac{1}{\alpha}} \cdot r_1$ and $r_2 \leq R_T/2$. Suppose the set Q_F of nodes transmitting on F satisfies $d(u,v) \geq r_1$, for any pair of nodes $u, v \in Q_F$. Then, each transmission of a node $w \in Q_F$ is properly received by every node in $S_F \cap E_w^{r_2}$.*

Computing a Dominating Set

We first form a *clustering*, which is a function assigning each node a dominator within a specified distance r.

Let $t = \left(\frac{\alpha-2}{48\beta(\alpha-1)}\right)^{1/\alpha}$ and $r_c = \min\{\frac{t}{2t+2} \cdot R_{\epsilon/2}, \frac{\epsilon R_T}{4}\}$. Recall that $R_{\epsilon/2} = (1-\frac{\epsilon}{2})R_T$. We adapt the algorithm of Scheideler et al. [28] to compute an r_c-dominating set of constant density. In the algorithm [28], a node becomes a dominatee once it receives a message from a dominator; we simply additionally require that the node receive a message from a dominator within distance r_c. Using the same argument as in [28], we have the following result.

LEMMA 6. *There is a distributed algorithm running in time $O(\log n)$ that produces, with high probability, an r_c-dominating set of constant density μ, along with the corresponding clustering function.*

Cluster Coloring and a TDMA Scheme of Clusters

To produce a spatial separation of clusters, we find a coloring of the dominators such that any two dominators within distance $R_{\epsilon/2}$ are assigned different colors. The coloring can be done using the algorithm given as follows.

The algorithm is divided into ϕ phases, where ϕ is a sufficiently large constant. Then in each phase i, dominators that are still uncolored execute the MIS algorithm given in Section 4 to compute a $R_{\epsilon/2}$-maximal independent set. Nodes in the elected MIS select i as the color.

By Lemma 3 and the fact that the dominating set is of constant density, it is easy to show the following result.

LEMMA 7. *The algorithm produces, with high probability, a proper coloring for dominators with respect to distance $R_{\epsilon/2}$, i.e., such that any pair of dominators within distance $R_{\epsilon/2}$ are assigned with different colors, in $O(\log n)$ rounds. The number of colors used is a (sufficiently large) constant ϕ.*

The coloring on clusters (dominators) naturally implies the following TDMA scheme of ϕ rounds: nodes whose cluster color is i transmit in the i-th round, for $i = 1, 2, \ldots, \phi$.

Lemma 5 and the setting of r_c imply the following result.

LEMMA 8. *If at most one node transmits in each cluster, and only in clusters of a particular color, then the transmissions are received by all nodes within the same cluster.*

Thus, when using the TDMA scheme, communication within clusters can proceed deterministically without concern for outside interference (as long as only one node transmits in a cluster). We will from here on assume that when needed such a property holds, with the understanding that it incurs an overhead of a constant factor ϕ. For simplicity, in the subsequent sections, we implicitly assume that the clusters of the same color execute the algorithm together in the rounds assigned by the TDMA scheme and we only consider the algorithm execution of the clusters with a particular color, which ensures that clusters can execute the algorithm essentially independently. This assumption only incurs an overhead of a constant factor ϕ on the running times, and hence will not affect the asymptotic running times.

5.2 Reporter Tree Construction in Clusters

For a cluster C_v, let $f_v = \min\{\lfloor |C_v|/c_1 \log n \rfloor, \mathcal{F}\}$, where c_1 is a sufficiently large constant for easing the analysis. Nodes in the cluster C_v will use the first f_v channels for data aggregation. The setting of f_v ensures that there are nodes operating on each of these channels when nodes select channel randomly. Hence, there will be f_v reporters elected which will listen on these f_v channels for collecting the data sent by dominatees. The following lemma follows from Lemmas 12, 13, and 14 given later.

LEMMA 9. *In each cluster C_v, with high probability, f_v reporters are elected and a binary tree of $O(\log \mathcal{F})$ layers is constructed on the reporters in $O(\log^2 n)$ rounds. If a $\log^{O(1)} n$-approximation of Δ is given, then $O(\Delta/\mathcal{F} + \log n \cdot \log\log n)$ rounds suffice.*

The number of reporters in each cluster is determined by the size of the cluster. Before electing the reporters and constructing the binary tree, we first need to compute the number of dominatees in each cluster and make this knowledge known to all dominatees.

Cluster Size Computation

Consider the following defined **Cluster-Size-Computation (CSC)** problem: We are given a set of nodes operating, that is partitioned into well-separated clusters. Given is a parameter $\hat{\Delta}$, with the promise that all clusters are of size at most $\hat{\Delta}$. The problem is to compute the estimate of the cluster size and making each node be aware of the (approximate) size of its cluster. In the most general case, $\hat{\Delta}$ can be set as n.

We first present the Cluster-Size-Computation (CSC) algorithm that deal with any given $\hat{\Delta}$.

CSC Algorithm. The algorithm uses only the first channel, i.e., all nodes operate on a single channel. The stage is divided into $\log \hat{\Delta}$ phases, each of which contains $\gamma \log n + 1$ rounds with a sufficiently large constant γ: the first $\gamma \log n$ rounds are for the feedback of the dominatees; and the last round is for the transmissions of the dominators.

In each of the first $\gamma \log n$ rounds of each phase j, each dominatee u transmits with a specified probability p_u. The probability p_u is initially set as $\lambda/\hat{\Delta}$, where λ is a sufficiently small constant for the convenience of the analysis, and after each phase that u receives no message from its dominator, p_u is doubled. During the first $\gamma \log n$ rounds, dominators just listen. If a dominator received at least $\omega \log n$ messages from nodes in its cluster, where $\omega \geq 24$ is a constant, it settles on the estimate $\lceil \hat{\Delta} \cdot 2^{-j+1} \rceil$ for the number of nodes in its cluster. In the last round, each dominator that has obtained an estimate transmits, in order to disseminate the estimate to all dominatees in its cluster. Dominators and dominatees that have obtained estimates will stop executing the algorithm. □

With the CSC Algorithm, we have the following result.

LEMMA 10. *With a known upper bound $\hat{\Delta}$ on the maximum cluster size, there is a constant approximation algorithm that approximates the size of each cluster in $O(\log \hat{\Delta} \cdot \log n)$ steps, with high probability. Using the naive bound of $\hat{\Delta} \leq n$, the running time is $O(\log^2 n)$ steps, with high probability.*

For the case that $\hat{\Delta} \leq \mathcal{F} \log^c n$ for some constant $c \geq 1$, the Cluster-Size-Computation problem can be solved more efficiently. The basic process is as follows: First, dominatees in each cluster first select the channels uniformly at random; Then, on each channel, a leader is elected and nodes execute the CSC algorithm such that the leader can get a constant approximation of the number of dominatees selecting the channel; Finally, the dominator will get a constant approximation of the cluster size by aggregating the estimates from the leaders on each channel and send the estimate to its dominatees on the first channel.

LEMMA 11. *Given knowledge of $\hat{\Delta}$ satisfying $\hat{\Delta} \leq \mathcal{F} \log^c n$ for some constant $c \geq 1$, we can get a constant approximation of the size of each cluster in $O(\log n \cdot \log \log n)$ steps, with high probability.*

We can combine the two cluster size estimation procedures if $\hat{\Delta}$ is a $\log^{\hat{c}} n$-approximation of Δ for some constant $\hat{c} \geq 0$: When $\hat{\Delta}/\mathcal{F} \leq \log^{\hat{c}+2} n$, Lemma 11 gives a bound of $O(\log n \cdot \log \log n)$ rounds, while otherwise the bound of Lemma 10 is $O(\log^2 n) = O(\Delta/\mathcal{F})$ rounds. Hence, based on Lemma 10 and Lemma 11, we have the following result.

LEMMA 12. *There is a constant-approximation algorithm for **Cluster-Size-Computation** that runs in $O(\log^2 n)$ steps, with high probability. If we are given a $\log^{O(1)} n$-approximation of Δ, then there is a constant-approximation algorithm that runs in $O(\Delta/\mathcal{F} + \log n \cdot \log \log n)$ steps, with high probability.*

For simplify, we shall simply use $|C_v|$ to denote the size estimate derived for cluster C_v. Since it is a constant approximation, it will not affect the asymptotic running times.

Reporter Election

In this stage, reporters are elected in each cluster simultaneously. For a cluster C_v, the number of channels used in this stage is $f_v = \min\{\lfloor |C_v|/c_1 \log n \rfloor, \mathcal{F}\}$, with exactly one reporter elected on each channel.

The reporter election stage contains $\gamma \log n$ rounds. The dominatees in C_v operate on the first f_v channels. At the beginning, each dominatee in C_v selects one of the f_v channels uniformly at random. The nodes selecting a channel then execute the MIS algorithm given in Section 4 to elect one of them as reporter by filtering out the messages from senders in other clusters.

LEMMA 13. *In each cluster C_v, with high probability, exactly one reporter is elected on each of the f_v channels in $O(\log n)$ rounds.*

PROOF. For each channel F of the first f_v ones, let C_v^F be the set of dominatees in C_v selecting a channel F. Based on Lemma 3, we only need to show that for each channel F, $|C_v^F| \geq 1$ holds with high probability.

Because nodes select the channels uniformly at random, the number of dominatees in C_v selecting F is $|C_u|/f_v$ in expectation. Because $|C_v| \geq c_1 f_v \log n$, there are at least $c_1 \log n$ nodes selecting F in expectation. Using Chernoff bound and by the union bound on the error probability, if c_1 is large enough, there are nodes electing every channel of the f_v ones with high probability. □

We shall refer to dominatees that are not reporters as *followers*. Thus, C_v is partitioned into one dominator, f_v reporters, and $|C_v| - f_v - 1$ followers. In subsequence, we use $X_v = \{u_1, \ldots, u_{f_v}\}$ and Y_v to denote the sets of reporters and followers in C_v, respectively.

Aggregation Tree on Reporters

Consider a cluster C_v. Let $u_0 = v$ refer to the dominator. We define a complete binary tree rooted at the dominator, with the nodes ordered in level-order, like a binary heap. Thus, $u_{\lfloor k/2 \rfloor}$ is the parent of u_k in the tree, for $k = 1, \ldots, f_v$.

Once the reporters are elected, the aggregation tree is then ready to use.

LEMMA 14. *A complete binary tree of $\lfloor \log(f_v + 1) \rfloor$ levels is constructed on the reporters for each cluster C_v.*

6. DATA AGGREGATION

The data aggregation algorithm consists of two procedures: Intra-cluster aggregation and inter-cluster aggregation. In the former procedure, the data of followers is first collected through the reporters to the dominators, and then the data is disseminated by the dominators in the latter procedure. These two procedures are executed in parallel. Specifically, in each round, there are five slots that are for these two procedures: the first four slots are for the execution of the intra-cluster aggregation and the last slot is for the inter-cluster aggregation.

6.1 Intra-cluster Aggregation

The intra-cluster aggregation contains two processes: collect the data from followers to the reporters and aggregate the data using the reporter tree to the dominator. These two processes are executed in different slots of each round: the first process is executed in the first two slots, while the execution of the second process uses the other two slots.

Aggregation from Followers to Reporters. The algorithm execution of this process is divided into phases synchronously among clusters. Each phase contains $\gamma \log n + 1$ rounds.

For a cluster C_v, the first f_v channels are used for transmissions. In each phase, the operations of nodes are as follows:

(i) For each follower $u \in Y_v$, in each of the first $\gamma \log n$ rounds, it selects a channel from the first f_v ones uniformly at random, and on the selected channel, it transmits with a specified probability p_u in the first slot and listens in the second slot. In a round, if u receives an acknowledgement message from a reporter, it stops executing the process.

In the last round, u listens on the first channel. After each phase, if u receives a controlling message from its dominator in the last round, it keeps p_u unchanged, and doubles p_u otherwise. Initially, p_u is set as $p_u = \lambda f_v / |C_v|$.

(ii) For a reporter $w \in X_v$, it operates on the channel where it is elected. In each of the first $\gamma \log n$ rounds, w listens in the first slot. If it receives a message from a follower u in its cluster, it transmits an acknowledgement message to u in the second slot. In the last round, w does nothing.

(iii) For the dominator v, in the first $\gamma \log n$ rounds, it listens on the first channel; in the last round, if v receives at least $\omega \log n$ messages from followers during the first $\gamma \log n$ rounds, where ω is an appropriate constant, it transmits on the first channel a controlling message to adjust the transmission probabilities of followers. To ease the analysis, we set ω to be a sufficiently large constant while maintaining $16\gamma\lambda > \omega$ here.

Aggregation on Reporter Tree. The algorithm execution of this process is divided into phases synchronously among clusters. Each phase contains $\lfloor \log(\mathcal{F}+1) \rfloor - 1$ rounds.

For a cluster C_v, in a phase, the first f_v channels are used for transmissions. As before, use $X_v = \{u_1, \dots, u_{f_v}\}$ to denote the set of reporters and T_v to denote the reporter tree. We enumerate the levels of T_v from bottom, i.e., with the leaves at level 1.

In the s-th round of a phase, nodes at level s and $s+1$ of T_v execute the algorithm, such that the data is aggregated from level s to level $s+1$. Other nodes keep silent. In particular, for each node u at level $s+1$, it listens on the channel where it is elected. For each reporter u_k at level s, it operates on the same channel as its parent, i.e., the channel $\lfloor k/2 \rfloor$. If k is odd, it transmits its data to its parent in the third slot of round s; otherwise, it transmits in the fourth slot of round s.

6.2 Inter-cluster Aggregation

In this procedure, we use the algorithm given in [2] (refer to Section 5.2 in [2]) to deal with the data dissemination on a backbone network. The basic idea of the algorithm is as follows: on a constant-density network, flooding (using constant probability transmissions) produces a constant-degree aggregation/broadcast tree, with which data can be aggregated and then broadcast to all nodes in $O(D+\log n)$ rounds with high probability.

6.3 Analysis

We will show the following result, that follows from Lemmas 24, 25 and 27 given later.

THEOREM 15. *Data aggregation can be accomplished in* $O(D + \frac{\Delta}{\mathcal{F}} + \log n \log\log n)$ *rounds, with high probability.*

6.3.1 Aggregation from Followers to Reporters

We first present a property on the total transmission probability of nodes in C_v. Denote by $P_c(v) = \sum_{u \in Y_v} p_u$ the total transmission probability of followers in C_v in a round. We prove later (in Lemma 23) that the following property holds.

PROPERTY 16. ***[Bounded Contention]*** *For each cluster* C_v, *during the algorithm execution,* $P_c(v) \leq \lambda f_v$.

Based on Property 16, using an interference bounding technique similar to that used for proving Lemma 5, we can get the following Lemma 17. The difference here is that we need to consider the channel selections of nodes and nodes transmit with probabilities. In particular, in different clusters, the number of channels used may be different in a round. We say a follower *succeeds* (to transmit) if its message is properly received by a reporter on a channel.

LEMMA 17. *If a follower w transmits in a given round, it succeeds with constant probability.*

The TDMA scheme ensures that after a follower succeeds, it can receive the ack message in the subsequent slot.

LEMMA 18. *A follower u that succeeds to transmit its data to a reporter w in the first slot of a round, will receive an ack message from the reporter in the subsequent slot of the round.*

A phase is called an *increasing* one if the transmission probability of the reporters in C_v is doubled after the phase, i.e., the dominator v receives less than $\omega \log n$ messages, otherwise an *unchanging* one. In a phase j, let N_j denote the number of transmissions by the followers in C_v during phase j. A transmission by a follower $u \in Y_v$ is said to be *successful* if u succeeds to transmit the data to a reporter.

LEMMA 19. *For a cluster C_v and a phase j, if $N_j \leq \omega f_v \log n/4$, then with probability $1 - n^{-3}$, phase j is an increasing phase.*

PROOF. For a transmission s by a follower during phase j, let Z_s be the random variable with value 1 if s occurs on the first channel and 0 otherwise. Denote by $Z = \sum_s Z_s$ the number of transmissions occurring on the first channel. Because the followers select the operating channel uniformly at random from f_v ones, $Pr[Z_s = 1] = 1/f_v$. Hence, $E[Z] \leq \omega \log n/4$. Then if ω is large enough, v receives at most $\frac{\omega}{2} \log n$ messages with probability $1 - n^{-3}$ by Chernoff bound, which completes the proof. □

LEMMA 20. *For a cluster C_v and a phase j, if phase j is an unchanging phase, with probability $1 - O(n^{-3})$, there are $\Omega(f_v \log n)$ successful transmissions.*

PROOF. By Lemma 19, during phase j, there are at least $\omega f_v \log n/4$ transmissions. Then by Lemma 17, in expectation, the number of successful transmissions is at least $\omega f_v \log n/4 \cdot c'$ for some constant c'. If ω is large enough, using Chernoff bound, we get that the number of successful transmissions is $\Omega(f_v \log n)$ with probability $1 - O(n^{-3})$. □

A follower $u \in Y_v$ in cluster C_v is called *active* if v still does not receive the ack message from a reporter. We divide the process of the data aggregation from followers to reporters of C_v into two stages. The first stage consists of those phases where the number of active followers is greater than $4 f_v \log n$, and the second consists of the remaining phases. Since $|C_v| \geq c_1 f_v \log n$, where c_1 is sufficiently large, this is well defined.

LEMMA 21. *Let C_v be a cluster. In the first $O(n)$ phases of the first stage for the cluster, with probability $1 - O(n^{-2})$, $P_c(v) \geq \frac{\omega}{16\gamma} \cdot f_v$.*

PROOF. We prove the Lemma by contradiction. Assume that in a phase j of the first stage, there is a round t such that $P_c(v) < \frac{\omega}{16\gamma} \cdot f_v$. By the setting of the initial transmission probability and the values of ω and γ ($\frac{\omega}{16\gamma} < \lambda$), j is not the first phase. Note that at most $\gamma f_v \log n$ nodes may become inactive in phase $j-1$ and j respectively. And all followers of C_v have the same transmission probability, since by Lemma 8, the controlling messages transmitted by the dominator v can be received by all followers in C_v. Then during phase $j-1$, we get that $P_c(v) \leq \frac{\omega}{16\gamma} \cdot f_v \cdot \frac{4}{3} \cdot \frac{4}{3} = \frac{\omega}{9\gamma}$. Hence, during phase $j-1$, in expectation, there are totally $\frac{\omega f_v \log n}{9}$ transmissions by the followers. Using Chernoff bound, there are less than $\frac{\omega f_v \log n}{4}$ transmissions during phase $j-1$ with probability $1-n^{-3}$ if ω is sufficiently large. By Lemma 19, phase $j-1$ is an increasing phase. Hence, during phase j, $P_c(v) \geq \frac{\omega}{16\gamma} \cdot f_v \cdot 2 \cdot \frac{3}{4} > \frac{\omega}{16\gamma} \cdot f_v$. The Lemma now follows by an application of the union bound. □

LEMMA 22. *After the algorithm has been run for $O(\frac{|C_v|}{f_v \log n})$ phases, with probability $1-n^{-2}$, there are at most $5f_v \log n$ followers that are yet to succeed (and receive an ack).*

PROOF. We claim that in a phase j of the first stage, if $P_c(v) \geq \frac{\omega}{16\gamma} \cdot f_v$, there are $\Omega(f_v \log n)$ successful transmissions with probability $1-n^{-3}$. By Lemma 17, in phase j, there are $\frac{\omega}{16} \cdot f_v \log n \cdot c'$ successful transmissions by the followers in expectation for some constant c'. We then can use Chernoff bound to get that there are $\Omega(f_v \log n)$ successful transmissions with probability $1-n^{-3}$ if ω is large enough.

With the above argument and by Lemma 21 and Lemma 18, after at most $O(\frac{|C_v|}{f_v \log n})$ phases, with probability $1-n^{-2}$, the number of followers that still do not succeed in transmitting to the reporters (and receive ack) is reduced to less than $5f_v \log n$. This completes the proof. □

The above analysis is based on Property 16, whose correctness is given as follows.

LEMMA 23. *Property 16 holds with probability $1-n^{-1}$.*

PROOF. We prove the Lemma by contradiction. Assume that cluster C_v is the first one violating Property 16, and the violating phase is j. By the initial setting of the transmission probability of the followers, $j > 1$. And because after each phase, the transmission probability of followers is at most doubled, in phase $j-1$, $P_c(v) \in (\lambda f_v/2, \lambda f_v]$. And we know that cluster C_v is the first violating one. So for each other cluster C_y, we have $P_c(y) \leq \lambda f_y$ in phase $j-1$, where f_y is the number of channels used by C_y in phase $j-1$.

The expected number of transmissions by followers in C_v during phase $j-1$ is at least $\lambda f_v/2 \cdot \gamma \log n$. Based on above argument, it can be seen that we can still use Lemma 17 in phase $j-1$, i.e., each transmission is successful with some constant probability c'. Hence, in expectation, there are $\lambda/2 \cdot \gamma \log n \cdot c'$ successful transmissions on the first channel. If γ is large enough, the dominator receives at least $\omega \log n$ transmissions with probability $1-n^{-2}$. In this case, v can send a controlling message to all the followers by Lemma 8. By the algorithm, all followers in C_v will not change the transmission probability after phase $j-1$. As a result, the λf_v bound will not be broken in phase j. This contradicts with our assumption. So C_v cannot be the first violating cluster with probability $1-n^{-2}$. The Lemma is then proved by the union bound. □

LEMMA 24. *For each cluster C_v, the data of all followers can be aggregated to the reporters in $O(\frac{\Delta}{\mathcal{F}} + \log n \log\log n)$ rounds with probability $1-O(n^{-1})$.*

PROOF. Consider a cluster C_v. By Lemma 22, the time needed to reduce the number of active followers to at most $5f_v \log n$ is $O(\frac{|C_v|}{f_v \log n}) \cdot \gamma \log n = O(\frac{|C_v|}{f_v})$ with probability $1-n^{-2}$. We consider next the time needed to further reduce the number of active followers to 0. Denote by j the last phase in which the number of active followers is at least $5f_v \log n$. Then in phase $j+1$, there are at most $6f_v \log n$ active followers. We consider next the algorithm execution from phase $j+1$ till all followers become inactive.

In each unchanging phase, by Lemma 20 and Lemma 18, at least $\Omega(f_v \log n)$ followers succeed to send the data to the reporters and receive the ack messages. Hence, there are at most $O(\frac{6f_v \log n}{f_v \log n}) \in O(1)$ unchanging phases since phase $j+1$. Furthermore, clearly, phase j is in the first stage. Hence, by Lemma 21, at the beginning of phase $j+1$, the transmission probability of every active follower is $\Omega(1/\log n)$. Then after $O(1)+O(\log\log n)$ phases, there are enough increasing phases such that the transmission probability of active followers is increased to a constant λ'. Then in the subsequent phase, in each round, by Lemma 17, each active follower can succeed to transmit with probability $\lambda' \cdot c'$ for some constant c'. Hence, if γ is large enough, the error probability that a follower u cannot succeed is reduced to n^{-3}.

From above, we have shown that for a cluster C_v, with probability $1-O(n^{-2})$, all followers will succeed to transmit their data to the reporters in $O(\frac{|C_v|}{f_v}) + O(\log n \log\log n) \in O(\frac{\Delta}{\mathcal{F}} + \log n \log\log n)$ rounds by the value of f_v. This is true for every cluster with probability $1-O(n^{-1})$. Note that the above argument is based on Property 16 whose correctness is proved in Lemma 23. Putting everything together, the Lemma follows. □

6.3.2 Aggregation on Reporter Trees

LEMMA 25. *In each cluster C_v, the data aggregation from the reporters to the dominator can be accomplished in $O(\log \mathcal{F})$ rounds.*

PROOF. The construction of the aggregation tree ensures that when a reporter transmits, it is the only one from the same cluster in the same channel. Thus, by Lemma 8, each transmission is successful. The number of rounds equals the height of the tree, or $\lfloor \log(\mathcal{F}+1) \rfloor$. □

6.3.3 Inter-cluster Aggregation

Theorem 3 in [2] can be rephrased as:

LEMMA 26. *There is a distributed algorithm that runs in $O(D+\log n)$ rounds that forms an aggregation network and accomplishes the data aggregation on any given dominating set of constant density with high probability.*

The above Lemma 26 implies the following result.

LEMMA 27. *The global data aggregation task will be completed within $O(D+\log n)$ rounds with high probability after all clusters have completed their intra-cluster aggregations.*

7. COLORING

As shown in Section 6, using the aggregation structure, the data of dominatees can be efficiently aggregated to the dominator. With this property, the aggregation structure can be used to solve fundamental problems other than data aggregation. We take the coloring problem here as an example.

Algorithm. In the constructed aggregation structure, the dominators are colored with cluster colors in $\{1, \ldots, \phi\}$ for some constant ϕ such that dominators within distance $R_{\epsilon/2}$ receive different cluster colors. We then assign each dominator of cluster color i the sequence of colors $k\phi + i : k = 0, 1, 2, \ldots$ to assign to its cluster nodes.

For each cluster C_v, the algorithm consists of four procedures:

1. The followers execute the data aggregation algorithm given in Section 6.1 to send their IDs to the reporters, by which each reporter will acquire the knowledge of the followers following it (i.e., the follower which transmits the ID to it). After this procedure, an aggregation tree on all nodes in C_v is constructed based on the reporter tree by adding links that connect each reporter and the followers following it.

2. Each reporter sends the number of nodes in its subtree (including the reporters and the followers) to its parent via the reporter tree.

3. The color range (the range of k, which determines the set of available colors) of each reporter and its followers is then disseminated to each reporter via the reporter tree. In particular, on the reporter tree, each node u (recall that the root is the dominator) determines the color ranges of its two children based on the color range assigned to u and the number of nodes in the subtree of its children. The distribution of the color range uses an inverse process to the aggregation on the reporter tree given in Section 6.1.

4. For a reporter u, let B_u denote the set of colors assigned to it (which can be derived using the color range assigned to u). Each reporter u then assigns a different color in B_u to each of its followers and sends the color assignment to its followers one by one on the channel where it is elected.

Because the first procedure uses a randomized algorithm, and the other three procedures are done by letting nodes execute the deterministic TDMA scheme given in Section 5.1. To avoid the interference between the executions of different procedures among clusters, we make these procedures be executed in different slots of every round. Specifically, in each round, there are four slots for the execution of each of the four procedures.

As shown in the proof of Lemma 24, the first procedure takes $O(\frac{|C_v|}{f_v} + \log n \log\log n)$ rounds with high probability; the second procedure takes $O(\log \mathcal{F})$ rounds by Lemma 25; the third procedure can be shown to take $O(\log \mathcal{F})$ rounds as well using a similar argument as that for proving Lemma 25; the fourth procedure takes $O(\frac{|C_v|}{f_v} + \log n \log\log n)$ rounds by noting that each reporter can have at most $O(\frac{|C_v|}{f_v} + \log n \log\log n)$ followers and in each round, a reporter can send a message to its followers by Lemma 8, due to the fact that the reporters transmit on different channels. Because nodes have a constant approximation of $|C_v|$, and knowledge of n (a polynomial estimate) and the number of channels $\mathcal{F}$, they can each determine the completion time of each procedure.

Analysis.

LEMMA 28. *For each cluster C_v, after $O(\frac{\Delta}{\mathcal{F}} + \log n \log\log n)$ rounds, each node in C_v will get a different color with high probability. And the total number of colors used is $O(\Delta)$.*

PROOF. The time bound can be obtained by the execution time of each procedure. We next show that each node in C_v gets a different color and the total number of colors used is $O(\Delta)$.

By Lemma 24, each follower can send its ID to a reporter with high probability. We claim that each follower transmits its ID to only one reporter. This follows from Lemma 18. By this Lemma, once a follower transmits a message to a reporter, it will receive an ack message in the same round. Hence, the sets of followers of reporters are disjoint. With this claim, we can see that the aggregation tree on all nodes in C_v is correctly constructed in the first procedure, i.e., every node is in the tree and has exactly one parent. Then in the second procedure, each reporter will get the exact number of nodes in its subtree by Lemma 25. Based on this knowledge and because the aggregation tree is correctly constructed, after the third procedure, reporters will get disjoint color ranges and the number of colors used is $|C_v| \in O(\Delta)$. Hence, after the fourth procedure, each node will get a different color. □

THEOREM 29. *A proper coloring with $O(\Delta)$ colors can be computed in $O(\frac{\Delta}{\mathcal{F}} + \log n \log\log n)$ rounds with high probability.*

PROOF. The total time used for the coloring is given in Lemma 28. By the algorithm, it is easy to see that the total number of colors used is $\phi \cdot O(\Delta) \in O(\Delta)$.

We next show the correctness of the coloring algorithm. For any two neighboring nodes u, v that are in different clusters, their dominators have distance at most $\epsilon R_T/4 + R_\epsilon + \epsilon R_T/4 = R_{\epsilon/2}$. By the algorithm, the color sets given to the clusters in which u, v stays are disjoint. Hence, u, v will not get the same color. For any pair of neighboring nodes in the same cluster, they will also be assigned different colors by Lemma 28. □

8. REFERENCES

[1] M. K. An, N. X. Lam, D. T. Huynh, and T. N. Nguyen. Minimum latency data aggregation in the physical interference model. *Computer Communications*, 35(18):2175–2186, 2012.

[2] M. H. Bodlaender, M. M. Halldórsson, and P. Mitra. Connectivity and Aggregation in Multihop Wireless Networks. In *PODC*, pages 355–364. ACM, 2013.

[3] R. Cole and U. Vishkin. Deterministic Coin Tossing with Applications to Optimal Parallel List Ranking. *Inf. Control*, 70(1):32–53, July 1986.

[4] S. Daum, M. Ghaffari, S. Gilbert, F. Kuhn, and C. Newport. Maximal independent sets in multichannel radio networks. In *PODC*, pages 335–344, 2013.

[5] S. Daum, S. Gilbert, F. Kuhn, and C. Newport. Broadcast in the Ad Hoc SINR Model. In *DISC*, pages 358–372, 2013.

[6] S. Daum, F. Kuhn, and C. Newport. Efficient symmetry breaking in multi-channel radio networks. In *DISC*, pages 238–252, 2012.

[7] B. Derbel and E. Talbi. Distributed Node Coloring in the SINR Model. In *ICDCS*, pages 708–717, 2010.

[8] S. Dolev, S. Gilbert, M. Khabbazian, and C. Newport. Leveraging channel diversity to gain efficiency and robustness for wireless broadcast. In *DISC*, pages 252–267, 2011.

[9] H. Du, Z. Zhang, W. Wu, L. Wu, and K. Xing. Constant-approximation for optimal data aggregation with physical interference. *Journal of Global Optimization*, 56(4):1653–1666, 2013.

[10] M. M. Halldórsson and P. Mitra. Nearly Optimal Bounds for Distributed Wireless Scheduling in the SINR Model. In *ICALP*, pages 625–636, 2011.

[11] M. M. Halldórsson and P. Mitra. Distributed Connectivity of Wireless Networks. In *PODC*, 2012.

[12] M. M. Halldórsson and P. Mitra. Towards tight bounds for local broadcasting. In *FOMC*, 2012.

[13] M. M. Halldórsson and P. Mitra. Wireless connectivity and capacity. In *SODA*, pages 516–526. SIAM, 2012.

[14] N. Hobbs, Y. Wang, Q.-S. Hua, D. Yu, and F. Lau. Deterministic distributed data aggregation under the SINR model. In *TAMC'12*, pages 385–399, 2012.

[15] S. Huang, P.-J. Wan, C. Vu, Y. Li, and F. Yao. Nearly constant approximation for data aggregation scheduling in wireless sensor networks. In *INFOCOM'07*, pages 366–372, 2007.

[16] T. Jurdzinski, D. Kowalski, M. Rozanski, and G. Stachowiak. Distributed randomized broadcasting in wireless networks under the SINR model. In *DISC*, pages 373–387. 2013.

[17] T. Jurdzinski, D. Kowalski, M. Rozanski, and G. Stachowiak. On the impact of geometry on ad hoc communication in wireless networks. In *PODC '14*, 2014.

[18] T. Jurdzinski and D. R. Kowalski. Distributed backbone structure for algorithms in the SINR model of wireless networks. In *DISC*, pages 106–120, 2012.

[19] T. Jurdzinski, D. R. Kowalski, and G. Stachowiak. Distributed Deterministic Broadcasting in Uniform-power Ad Hoc Wireless Networks. In *FCT'13*, pages 195–209, 2013.

[20] T. Jurdzinski and G. Stachowiak. Probabilistic Algorithms for the Wakeup Problem in Single-Hop Radio Networks. In *ISAAC*, pages 535–549, 2002.

[21] T. Kesselheim and B. Vöcking. Distributed contention resolution in wireless networks. In *DISC*, pages 163–178, 2010.

[22] H. Li, Q.-S. Hua, C. Wu, and F. Lau. Minimum-latency Aggregation Scheduling in Wireless Sensor Networks Under Physical Interference Model. In *MSWiM '10*, pages 360–367, 2010.

[23] X.-Y. Li, X. Xu, S. Wang, S. Tang, G. Dai, J. Zhao, and Y. Qi. Efficient data aggregation in multi-hop wireless sensor networks under physical interference model. In *MASS '09*, pages 353–362, 2009.

[24] Y. Li, L. Guo, and S. Prasad. An energy-efficient distributed algorithm for minimum-latency aggregation scheduling in wireless sensor networks. In *ICDCS'10*, pages 827–836, 2010.

[25] T. Moscibroda and R. Wattenhofer. The complexity of connectivity in wireless networks. In *INFOCOM*, pages 1–13, April 2006.

[26] T. Moscibroda and R. Wattenhofer. Coloring unstructured radio networks. *Distributed Computing*, 21(4):271–284, 2008.

[27] G. Pei and A. K. S. Vullikanti. Distributed approximation algorithms for maximum link scheduling and local broadcasting in the physical interference model. In *INFOCOM*, 2013.

[28] C. Scheideler, A. Richa, and P. Santi. An $O(\log N)$ Dominating Set Protocol for Wireless Ad-hoc Networks Under the Physical Interference Model. In *MobiHoc '08*, pages 91–100, 2008.

[29] J. Schneider and R. Wattenhofer. Coloring Unstructured Wireless Multi-hop Networks. In *PODC*, pages 210–219, 2009.

[30] P.-J. Wan, S. C.-H. Huang, L. Wang, Z. Wan, and X. Jia. Minimum-latency aggregation scheduling in multihop wireless networks. In *MobiHoc '09*, pages 185–194, 2009.

[31] X. Xu, M. Li, X. Mao, S. Tang, and S. Wang. A delay-efficient algorithm for data aggregation in multihop wireless sensor networks. *Parallel and Distributed Systems, IEEE Transactions on*, 22(1):163–175, Jan 2011.

[32] B. Yu and J. Li. Minimum-time aggregation scheduling in multi-sink sensor networks. In *SECON'11*, pages 422–430, 2011.

[33] B. Yu, J. Li, and Y. Li. Distributed data aggregation scheduling in wireless sensor networks. In *INFOCOM'09*, pages 2159–2167, 2009.

[34] D. Yu, Q.-S. Hua, Y. Wang, and F. Lau. An $O(\log n)$ Distributed Approximation Algorithm for Local Broadcasting in Unstructured Wireless Networks. In *DCOSS '12*, pages 132–139, 2012.

[35] D. Yu, Q.-S. Hua, Y. Wang, H. Tan, and F. Lau. Distributed multiple-message broadcast in wireless ad-hoc networks under the SINR model. In *SIROCCO'12*, pages 111–122, 2012.

[36] D. Yu, Q.-S. Hua, Y. Wang, J. Yu, and F. Lau. Efficient distributed multiple-message broadcasting in unstructured wireless networks. In *INFOCOM'13*, pages 2427–2435, 2013.

[37] D. Yu, Y. Wang, Q.-S. Hua, and F. Lau. Distributed $(\Delta+1)$-coloring in the physical model. In *ALGOSENSORS'11*, pages 145–160, 2011.

[38] D. Yu, Y. Wang, Y. Yan, J. Yu, and F. Lau. Speedup of information exchange using multiple channels in wireless ad hoc networks. In *INFOCOM'15*, 2015.

Towards Optimal Synchronous Counting

Christoph Lenzen
clenzen@mpi-inf.mpg.de
Max Planck Institute for Informatics

Joel Rybicki
joel.rybicki@aalto.fi
Max Planck Institute for Informatics
Helsinki Institute for Information Technology HIIT, Dept. of Computer Science, Aalto University

Jukka Suomela
jukka.suomela@aalto.fi
Helsinki Institute for Information Technology HIIT, Dept. of Computer Science, Aalto University

ABSTRACT

Consider a complete communication network of n nodes, in which the nodes receive a common clock pulse. We study the synchronous c-counting problem: given any starting state and up to f faulty nodes with arbitrary behaviour, the task is to eventually have all correct nodes count modulo c in agreement. Thus, we are considering algorithms that are self-stabilising despite Byzantine failures. In this work, we give new algorithms for the synchronous counting problem that (1) are deterministic, (2) have linear stabilisation time in f, (3) use a small number of states, and (4) achieve almost-optimal resilience. Prior algorithms either resort to randomisation, use a large number of states, or have poor resilience. In particular, we achieve an *exponential* improvement in the state complexity of deterministic algorithms, while still achieving linear stabilisation time and almost-linear resilience.

Categories and Subject Descriptors

C.2.4 [**Computer-Communication Networks**]: Distributed Systems; F.2.2 [**Analysis of Algorithms and Problem Complexity**]: Nonnumerical Algorithms and Problems

Keywords

synchronous counting; self-stabilisation; Byzantine fault-tolerance

1. INTRODUCTION

In this work, we design space-efficient, self-stabilising, Byzantine fault-tolerant algorithms for the *synchronous counting problem*. We are given a complete communication network on n nodes, with arbitrary initial states. There are up to f faulty nodes. The task is to synchronise the nodes so that all non-faulty nodes will count rounds modulo c in agreement. For example, here is a possible execution for $n = 4$ nodes, $f = 1$ faulty node, and counting modulo $c = 3$; the execution stabilises after $t = 5$ rounds:

	Stabilisation					Counting						
Node 1:	2	2	0	2	0	0	1	2	0	1	2	...
Node 2:	0	2	0	1	0	0	1	2	0	1	2	...
Node 3:	*faulty node, arbitrary behaviour*											...
Node 4:	0	0	2	0	2	0	1	2	0	1	2	...

Synchronous counting is a coordination primitive that can be used e.g. in large integrated circuits to synchronise subsystems so that we can easily implement *mutual exclusion* and *time division multiple access* in a fault-tolerant way. Note that in this context it is natural to assume that a synchronous clock signal is available, but the clocking system usually will not provide explicit round numbers. Solving synchronous counting thus enables us to construct highly dependable round numbers for subcircuits.

Counting modulo $c = 2$ is closely related to *binary consensus*: given a synchronous counting algorithm one can design a binary consensus algorithm and vice versa [3, 4, 5]—in particular, many lower bounds on binary consensus apply here as well [6, 9, 10]. However, the existing implementations of counting from consensus incur a factor-f overhead in space and message size, rendering them very costly even in small systems.

1.1 Prior Work

It is fairly easy to design space-efficient *randomised* algorithms for synchronous counting [3, 7, 8]: as a simple example, the nodes can just pick random states until a clear majority of them has the same state, after which they start to follow the majority. However, this approach yields algorithms with exponential stabilisation time. Given a shared coin, it is possible to obtain fast randomised algorithms by defaulting to the value of the shared coin whenever no clear majority is observed [1]; unfortunately, existing shared coins are highly inefficient in terms of space and communication.

In comparison, it is even more challenging to come up with space-efficient *deterministic* algorithms for synchronous counting [3, 4, 5], and it remains open to what extent randomisation helps in designing space-efficient algorithms that stabilise quickly. Fast-stabilising deterministic algorithms build on a connection to Byzantine consensus, but require a large number of states per node [3, 4].

For small values of the parameters (e.g., $n = 4$ and $f = 1$) the synchronous counting problem is amenable to *algorithm*

Permission to make digital or hard copies of all or part of this work for personal or classroom use is granted without fee provided that copies are not made or distributed for profit or commercial advantage and that copies bear this notice and the full citation on the first page. Copyrights for components of this work owned by others than ACM must be honored. Abstracting with credit is permitted. To copy otherwise, or republish, to post on servers or to redistribute to lists, requires prior specific permission and/or a fee. Request permissions from permissions@acm.org.
PODC'15, July 21–23, 2015, Donostia-San Sebastián, Spain.
Copyright is held by the owner/author(s). Publication rights licensed to ACM.
ACM 978-1-4503-3617-8 /15/07 ...$15.00.
DOI: http://dx.doi.org/10.1145/2767386.2767423.

resilience	stabilisation time	state bits	deterministic	references
$f < n/3$ (*)	$O(1)$	$n^{O(1)}$ (*)	no	[1]
$f < n/3$	$O(f)$	$O(f \log f)$	yes	[4]
$f < n/3$	$2^{2(n-f)}$	2	no	[7, 8]
$f < n/3$	$\min\{2^{2f+2}+1, 2^{O(f^2/n)}\}$	1	no	[3]
$f = 1$, $n \geq 4$	7	2	yes	[3]
$f = 1$, $n \geq 6$	6	1	yes	[3]
$f = 1$, $n \geq 6$	3	2	yes	[3]
$f = n^{1-o(1)}$	$O(f)$	$O(\log^2 f)$	yes	**this work**

Table 1: Summary of synchronous 2-counting algorithms. "(*)" indicates that details vary, but all known shared coins with large resilience require large states and messages. For randomised algorithms, we list the expected stabilisation time. In [3], further trade-offs between n, the stabilisation time, and the number of state bits are given (for $f = 1$).

synthesis: it is possible to use computers to automatically design both space-efficient and time-efficient deterministic algorithms for synchronous counting. For example, there is a computer-designed algorithm that solves the case of $n \geq 4$ and $f = 1$ with only 3 states per node, and another algorithm that solves the case of $n \geq 6$ and $f = 1$ with only 2 states per node; both of these are optimal [3, 5]. Unfortunately, this approach does not scale, as the space of possible algorithms for given parameters n and f grows rapidly with n.

In summary, currently no algorithms for synchronous counting are known that simultaneously scale well in terms of resilience f, stabilisation time t, and the state that needs to be preserved between rounds. Here, it is worth noting that existing deterministic solutions with small state in essence run $\Omega(f)$ concurrent instances of consensus, which implies that the respective overhead extends to message size and the amount of local computations as well.

1.2 Contributions

Our main contribution is a recursive construction that shows how to "amplify" the resilience of a synchronous counting algorithm. Given a synchronous counter for some values of n and f, we will show how to design synchronous counters for larger values of n and f, with a very small increase in time and state complexity. This has two direct applications:

1. From a practical perspective, we can apply existing computer-designed algorithms (e.g. $n = 4$ and $f = 1$) as a building block in order to design efficient deterministic algorithms for a moderate number of nodes (e.g., $n = 36$ and $f = 7$).
2. From a theoretical perspective, we can now design deterministic algorithms for synchronous counting for any n and for $f = n^{1-o(1)}$ faulty nodes, with a stabilisation time of $O(f)$, and with only $O(\log^2 f / \log\log f)$ bits of state per node.

The state complexity is an *exponential* improvement over prior work, and the stabilisation time is asymptotically optimal for deterministic algorithms [9]. A summary of the related work and our contributions is given in Table 1.

In our deterministic algorithms, each node only needs to store a few number of bits between consecutive rounds, and thus, a node can afford to broadcast its entire state to all other nodes in each round. However, the small number of state bits bears the promise that the communication load can be reduced further. To substantiate the conjecture that finding algorithms with small state complexity may lead to highly communication-efficient solutions, we proceed to consider a slightly stronger synchronous *pulling model*. In this model, a node may send a request to another node and receive a response in a single round, based on the state of the responding node at the beginning of the round. The cost for the exchange is then attributed to the pulling node; in a circuit, this translates to each node being assigned an energy budget that it uses to "pay" for the communication it triggers. In this model, it is straightforward to combine our recursive construction with random sampling to obtain the following results:

1. We can achieve the properties of the deterministic algorithm with each node pulling $\operatorname{polylog} n$ messages in each round. The price is that the resulting algorithm retains a probability of $n^{-\operatorname{polylog} n}$ to fail in each round even after stabilisation.
2. If the failing nodes are chosen independently of the algorithm, we can fix the random choices. This results in a pseudo-random algorithm which stabilises with a probability of $1 - n^{-\operatorname{polylog} n}$ and in this case keeps counting correctly.

1.3 Structure

This paper is organised as follows. In Section 2 we formally define the model of computing and the synchronous counting problem. Section 3 gives the main technical result—a construction for creating a synchronous counting algorithm of larger resilience from several copies of an algorithm with smaller resilience. Section 4 uses this construction to derive deterministic synchronous counting algorithms with linear stabilisation time and polylogarithmic state complexity. Finally, in Section 5, we discuss the pulling model and how randomised sampling can be used to reduce the total number of communicated bits.

2. PRELIMINARIES

We consider a fully-connected distributed message-passing system consisting of n processors, also called nodes, with unique identifiers from the set $[n] = \{0, 1, \ldots, n-1\}$. The computation proceeds in synchronous communication rounds, where in each round each processor: (1) *broadcasts* its local state to all processors, (2) *receives* a vector of messages (that is, states) from all other processors, and (3) *updates* its local state according to the received messages. The initial state of every node is arbitrary. Moreover, up to f nodes may be *Byzantine*, i.e., exhibit arbitrary behaviour, including to send *different* messages to every node. Thus, different nodes may receive different vectors depending on what the Byzantine nodes do.

2.1 Algorithms and Executions

A deterministic algorithm in this model is a tuple $\mathbf{A} = (X, g, h)$, where X is the set of all possible states for a node, $g\colon [n] \times X^n \to X$ is the state transition function, and $h\colon [n] \times X \to [c]$ maps the internal state of a node to an output value. That is, when node $i \in [n]$ receives a vector $\mathbf{x} \in X^n$ of messages, it will update its internal state to $g(i, \mathbf{x}) = s$ and output $h(i, s) \in [c]$. The *state complexity* $S(\mathbf{A})$ of an algorithm $\mathbf{A}$ is the total number of bits required to store the state of a node between consecutive rounds. That is, $S(\mathbf{A}) = \lceil \log |X| \rceil$.

For any given set $\mathcal{F} \subseteq [n]$ of faulty nodes, we define a projection $\pi_{\mathcal{F}}$ as follows: for any received message vector $\mathbf{x} \in X^n$, let $\pi_{\mathcal{F}}(\mathbf{x})$ be a vector $\mathbf{e}$ such that $e_i = *$ if $i \in \mathcal{F}$ and $e_i = x_i$ otherwise. We call $\pi_{\mathcal{F}}(X^n) = \{\pi_{\mathcal{F}}(\mathbf{x}) : \mathbf{x} \in X^n\}$ the set of *configurations*. That is, a configuration consists only of the state of all non-faulty nodes.

We say that a configuration $\mathbf{d}$ is *reachable* from configuration $\mathbf{e}$ if for every non-faulty node $i \notin \mathcal{F}$ there exists some $\mathbf{x} \in X^n$ satisfying $\pi_{\mathcal{F}}(\mathbf{x}) = \mathbf{d}$ and $g(i, \mathbf{x}) = d_i$. This means that when the system is in configuration $\mathbf{e}$, the Byzantine nodes can send node i such messages that i chooses to switch to state d_i. Given the set of faulty nodes, an *execution* of an algorithm $\mathbf{A}$ is an infinite sequence of configurations $\xi = \langle \mathbf{e}_0, \mathbf{e}_1, \mathbf{e}_2, \dots \rangle$ such that $\mathbf{e}_{t+1}$ is reachable from $\mathbf{e}_t$.

2.2 Synchronous Counters

We say that an execution ξ of algorithm $\mathbf{A} = (X, g, h)$ *stabilises* in time t if there is some $r_0 \geq 0$ so that for every non-faulty node $i \in [n]$ the output satisfies

$$h(i, x_{t+r,i}) = r - r_0 \bmod c \text{ for all } r \geq 0.$$

That is, within t steps all non-faulty nodes agree on a common output and start incrementing their counters modulo c each round. Moreover, we say that $\mathbf{A}$ is a *synchronous c-counter* with *resilience* f if there exists a t such that for every $\mathcal{F} \subseteq [n]$, $|\mathcal{F}| \leq f$, all executions of $\mathbf{A}$ stabilise in t rounds. We say that the *stabilisation time* $T(\mathbf{A})$ of algorithm $\mathbf{A}$ is the minimal such t. In what follows, we use $\mathcal{A}(n, f, c)$ to denote the family of synchronous c-counters of resilience f that run on n nodes.

3. BOOSTING RESILIENCE

In this section, we show that given a family of synchronous c-counters for a small number of nodes n and resilience f, we can construct a new family of C-counters of a larger resilience without increasing the number of nodes in the network or the stabilisation time by too much. More precisely, we prove the following main result.

THEOREM 1. *Given $n, f \in \mathbb{N}$, pick $N, F, C \in \mathbb{N}$, where*

- *the number of nodes is $N = kn$ for some number of blocks $3 \leq k \in \mathbb{N}$,*
- *the resilience is $F < (f + 1)m$, where $m = \lceil k/2 \rceil$, and*
- *the counter size is $C > 1$.*

Choose any $c \in \mathbb{N}$ that is a multiple of $3(F + 2)(2m)^k$. Then for any $\mathbf{A} \in \mathcal{A}(n, f, c)$ there exists a $\mathbf{B} \in \mathcal{A}(N, F, C)$ with

$$T(\mathbf{B}) \leq T(\mathbf{A}) + 3(F + 2)(2m)^k,$$
$$S(\mathbf{B}) = S(\mathbf{A}) + \lceil \log(C + 1) \rceil + 1.$$

3.1 High-level Idea of the Construction

Given a suitable counter $\mathbf{A} \in \mathcal{A}(n, f, c)$, we construct a larger network with $N = kn$ nodes and divide the nodes in k blocks of n nodes. Each block runs a copy of $\mathbf{A}$ that is used to (1) determine a "leader block" and (2) output a consistent round counter *within* a block.

Due to the bound on F, only a minority of the blocks (fewer than m) contains more than f faulty nodes. Thus, the counters of a majority of the blocks stabilise within $T(\mathbf{A})$ rounds. By dividing the counters within each block, we let them "point" to one of m possible leader blocks for a fairly large number of consecutive rounds. Block i switches through leaders by a factor of $2m$ faster than block $i+1$. This ensures that, eventually, all stabilised counters point to the same leading block for $3(F + 2)$ rounds.

Using a majority vote on the pointers to leader blocks, we can make sure that all correct nodes—also those in blocks with more than f faulty nodes—will recognise the same block as the leader for sufficiently long. In fact, eventually this will happen for each of the m blocks that may become leaders, one of which must have fewer than f faulty nodes. In particular, its counter will be stabilised and can be "read" by all other nodes based on taking the majority value within that block. Hence, we can guarantee that at some point all nodes agree on a common counter value for at least $3(F + 2)$ rounds. This value is used to control an execution of the well-known *phase king protocol* [2], which solves consensus in $\Theta(F)$ rounds in systems of $N > 3F$ nodes. As the constraint $F < (f + 1)m$ also ensures that $F < N/3$, we can use the phase king protocol to let all nodes agree on the current value of the C-counter that is to be computed. It is straightforward to guarantee that, once this agreement is achieved, it will not be lost again and the counter is incremented by one modulo C in each round.

3.2 Setup

Our goal is to construct a synchronous C-counter that runs in a network of $N = kn$ nodes and tolerates $F < (f + 1)m$ faults. We divide the nodes into k blocks, each of size n. We identify each node $v \in [kn]$ with a tuple $(i, j) \in [k] \times [n]$. Thus, node $v = (i, j)$ is the jth node of block i. Blocks that contain more than f faulty nodes are said to be *faulty*. Otherwise, a block is *non-faulty*.

We will have each block i run a synchronous counter $\mathbf{A}_i$ constructed as follows. Define $\tau = 3(F+2)$ and $c_i = \tau(2m)^{i+1}$ for $i \in [k]$. Let $\mathbf{A} = (X, g, h) \in \mathcal{A}(n, f, c)$ be the given synchronous c-counter, where $c = \alpha\tau(2m)^k$ for some integer α. Now for any $i \in [k]$, we obtain a synchronous c_i-counter $\mathbf{A}_i = (X, g, h_i)$ by defining the output function as $h_i(x) = h(x) \bmod c_i$. That is, $\mathbf{A}_i$ outputs the output of $\mathbf{A}$ modulo c_i. It follows that $T(\mathbf{A}_i) = T(\mathbf{A})$ and $S(\mathbf{A}_i) = S(\mathbf{A})$. Thus, if block i is non-faulty, then $\mathbf{A}_i$ will stabilise in $T(\mathbf{A})$ rounds.

We interpret the value of the counter of (non-faulty, stabilised) block i as a tuple $(r, y) \in [\tau] \times [(2m)^{i+1}]$, where r is incremented by one modulo τ each round, and y is incremented by one whenever r "overflows" to 0. We refer to the counter value that node (i, j) currently has according to $\mathbf{A}_i$

as $(r[i,j], y[i,j])$. Note that this value can be directly inferred from its state, so by broadcasting its state (i,j) implicitly announces its current counter value to all other nodes. We stress that there is no guarantee whatsoever on how these variables behave in faulty blocks, even for non-faulty nodes in faulty blocks—the only guarantee is that non-faulty nodes in non-faulty blocks will count correctly after round $T(\mathbf{A})$.

We define the short-hand

$$b[i,j] = \left\lfloor \frac{y[i,j]}{(2m)^i} \right\rfloor \bmod m.$$

The value $b[i,j]$ indicates the block that the nodes in block i currently consider to be the "leader block" by interpreting the counter given by $\mathbf{A}_i$ appropriately.

Let $b_q[i,j]$ and $r_q[i,j]$ denote the values of $b[i,j]$ and $r[i,j]$ in round q. We will now show that after stabilisation, a non-faulty block i will within c_i rounds point to every block $\beta \in [m]$ for at least τ consecutive rounds. For notational convenience, we let $c_{-1} = \tau$.

LEMMA 1. *Let $i \in [k]$ be a non-faulty block and $t \geq T(\mathbf{A})$. For any $\beta \in [m]$, there exists some $t \leq w \leq t + c_i - c_{i-1}$ such that if (i,j) is non-faulty, then $b_q[i,j] = \beta$ for $w \leq q < w + c_{i-1}$.*

PROOF. By round t, the counter $\mathbf{A}_i$ has stabilised and all non-faulty nodes (i,j) agree. First observe that since $\mathbf{A}_i$ is a c_i-counter, $b[i,j]$ cycles through the set $[m]$ twice in c_i rounds. Moreover, once $b[i,j]$ changes its value, it will keep the new value for $c_{i-1} = \tau(2m)^i$ consecutive rounds.

More formally, let (i,j) be a non-faulty node and $u \geq t$ be the minimal u such that $r_u[i,j] = 0$ and $y_u[i,j] \in \{0, c_i/(2\tau)\}$. In particular, at round u we have $b_u[i,j] = 0$. Moreover, $u \leq t + c_i/2$. Since $b[i,j]$ retains the same value for c_{i-1} consecutive rounds, we get that at round $w = u + (\beta - 1)c_{i-1}$ the value $b[i,j]$ changes to β. Now we have that $b_{w'}[i,j] = \beta$ for $w \leq w' < w + c_{i-1}$. A simple check confirms that $w + c_{i-1} \leq t + c_i$. □

Using this lemma, we can show that after stabilisation, all non-faulty nodes in non-faulty blocks will within c_k rounds point to each $\beta \in [m]$ simultaneously for at least τ rounds.

LEMMA 2. *Let $t \geq T(\mathbf{A})$ and $\beta \in [m]$. There exists some $t \leq u \leq t + c_k - \tau$ such that if (i,j) is a non-faulty node in a non-faulty block, then $b_q[i,j] = \beta$ for $u \leq q < u + \tau$.*

PROOF. We prove the statement for the special case that all blocks are non-faulty. As there is no interaction between the algorithm $\mathbf{A}_i$ of different blocks, the lemma then follows by simply excluding all nodes in faulty blocks. We prove the following claim using induction; see Figure 1 for illustration.

Claim: For any round $t \geq T(\mathbf{A})$, block $\beta \in [m]$ and $h \in [k]$, there exists a round $t \leq u(h) \leq t + c_h - \tau$ such that for all non-faulty nodes (i,j) where $i \leq h$ we have $b_q[i,j] = \beta$ for $u(h) \leq q < u(h) + \tau$.

In particular, the lemma follows from the case $h = k$ of the above claim. For the base case of the induction, observe that case $h = 0$ follows from Lemma 1 as $c_{-1} = \tau$. For the inductive step, suppose the claim holds for some $h \in [k-1]$ and consider the non-faulty block $h+1$. By Lemma 1 there exists $t \leq w \leq t + c_{h+1} - c_h$ such that $b_q[h+1,j] = \beta$ for all $w \leq q < w + c_h$ where $(h+1,j)$ is a non-faulty node. Applying the induction hypothesis to w we get $u(h)$. Setting $u(h+1) = u(h)$ yields that $u(h+1) \leq w + c_h - \tau \leq t + c_{h+1} - \tau$. This proves the claim and the lemma follows. □

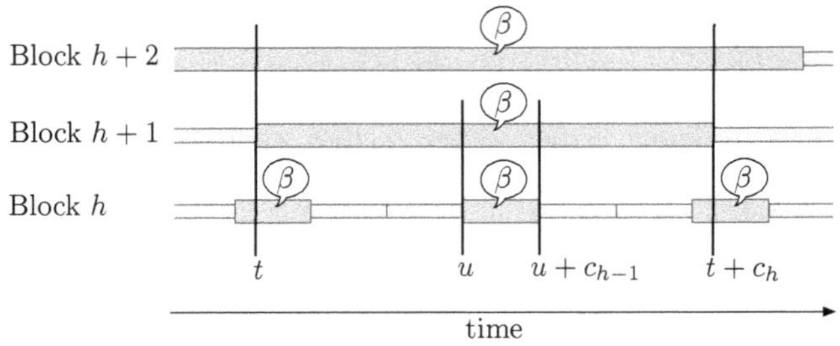

Figure 1: Counters in non-faulty blocks will eventually coincide. The picture illustrates the output of $b[\cdot]$ for three blocks $i \in \{h, h+1, h+2\}$ running $\tau(2m)^{i+1}$-counters with base $2m = 6$. For every $\beta \in [m]$, we can find an interval (highlighted segments) where all non-faulty blocks point to the same value β for sufficiently long, even though the counters may cycle at different time points.

3.3 Voting Blocks

Next, we define the voting scheme for all the blocks. Define the majority operation for every message vector $\mathbf{x} \in X^{kn}$ as follows:

$$\text{majority}\,\mathbf{x} = \begin{cases} a & \text{if } a \text{ appears in } \mathbf{x} \text{ more than } kn/2 \text{ times,} \\ * & \text{otherwise,} \end{cases}$$

where the symbol $*$ indicates that the function may evaluate to an arbitrary value, including different values at different non-faulty nodes. We use the following short-hands as local variables:

$$b^i = \text{majority}\{b[i,j] \mid j \in [n]\},$$
$$B = \text{majority}\{b^i \mid i \in [k]\},$$
$$R = \text{majority}\{r[B,j] \mid j \in [n]\}.$$

Note that these functions can be locally computed from the received state vectors by checking for a majority and defaulting to, e.g., 0, when no such majority is found: by definition, the majority function may return an arbitrary value if $kn/2$ or fewer correct nodes "vote" for the same value; as non-faulty nodes broadcast the same state to all nodes, there can only be one such majority value.

In words, b^i denotes the block which the nodes in block i support as a leader; different correct nodes may "observe" different values of b^i only if i is a faulty block or $\mathbf{A}_i$ has not yet stabilised. As $F < (f+1)m = (f+1)\lceil k/2 \rceil$, majority of the blocks are non-faulty. Hence, if all non-faulty blocks support the same leader block $\beta \in [m]$, then B evaluates to β at all correct nodes. By Lemma 2, this is bound to happen eventually. Finally, R denotes the round counter of block B, which is "read" correctly by all non-faulty nodes if B is non-faulty.

Analogously to before, let $i' \in [k]$ and denote by $B_q[i,j]$ and $R_q[i,j]$, respectively, the values to which the above functions evaluate in round q at node (i,j). Then we can conclude from Lemma 2 that eventually all non-faulty nodes agree on R for τ rounds.

LEMMA 3. *There is a round $t \leq T(\mathbf{A}) + c_k - \tau$ such that:*

(a) $R_q[i,j] = R_q[i',j']$ for any $t \leq q < t + \tau$ and non-faulty nodes (i,j) and (i',j').

(b) $R_{q+1}[i,j] = R_q[i,j] + 1 \bmod \tau$ *for any* $t \le q < t+\tau-1$ *and non-faulty node* (i,j).

PROOF. As $F < (f+1)m$, there is a non-faulty block $\beta \in [m]$. By applying Lemma 2 to round $T(\mathbf{A})$, there is a round $t \le T(\mathbf{A}) + c_k - \tau$ such that $b_q[i,j] = \beta$ for each $t \le q < t+\tau$ and non-faulty node (i,j) in a non-faulty block i. Therefore, $b_q^i = \beta$ for all non-faulty blocks i. As $F < (f+1)m$, the number of faulty blocks is at most $m-1 = \lceil k/2 \rceil - 1 < k/2$, and thus, the majority vote yields $B = \beta$.

Since $T(\mathbf{A}) \le t \le q < t+\tau$, we have that block β has stabilised by round t and therefore, $r_q[\beta,j] = r_q[\beta,j']$ for all non-faulty nodes (β,j), (β,j') in the non-faulty block β. Moreover, as block β is non-faulty, it contains at most f faulty nodes. In particular, it must be that $f < n/3 < n/2$ as otherwise counting cannot be solved and $\mathbf{A} \in \mathcal{A}(n,f,c)$. Hence, a majority vote yields $R = r_q[\beta,j]$, where (β,j) is any non-faulty node in block β proving claim (a).

To show (b), observe that since block β is non-faulty and has stabilised by round t we have that $R_q[i,j] = r_q[\beta,j']$. Moreover, non-faulty nodes in block β increment $r[\beta,j]$ by one modulo τ in the considered interval. □

3.4 Executing the Phase King

We have now built a voting scheme that allows the nodes to eventually agree on common counter for τ rounds. Roughly speaking, what remains is to use this common counter to control a non-self-stabilising F-resilient C-counting algorithm.

We require that this algorithm guarantees two properties. First, all non-faulty nodes reach agreement and start counting correctly within τ rounds provided that the underlying round counter is consistent. Second, if all non-faulty nodes agree on the output, then the agreement persists *regardless* of the round counter's value. It turns out that a straightforward adaptation of the classic phase king protocol [2] does the job.

From now on, we refer to nodes by their indices $v \in [N]$. The phase king protocol (like any consensus protocol) requires that $F < N/3$. It is easy to verify that this follows from the preconditions of Theorem 1.

Denote by $a[v] \in [C] \cup \{\infty\}$ the output register of the algorithm, where ∞ is used as a "reset state". There is also an auxiliary register $d[v] \in \{0,1\}$. Define the following short-hand for the increment operation modulo C:

$$\text{increment } a[v] = \begin{cases} a[v] \leftarrow a[v] + 1 \bmod C & \text{if } a[v] \neq \infty, \\ \text{no action} & \text{if } a[v] = \infty. \end{cases}$$

For $\ell \in [F+2]$, we define the instruction sets listed in Table 2. First, we show that if these instructions are executed in the right order by all non-faulty nodes for a non-faulty leader $\ell \in [F+2]$, then agreement on a counter value is established.

LEMMA 4. *Suppose that for some non-faulty node* $\ell \in [F+2]$ *and a round* q, *all non-faulty nodes execute instruction sets* $I_{3\ell}$, $I_{3\ell+1}$, *and* $I_{3\ell+2}$ *in rounds* $q-2$, $q-1$, *and* q, *respectively. Then* $a_{q+1}[v] = a_{q+1}[u] \neq \infty$ *for any two non-faulty nodes* $u, v \in [N]$. *Moreover,* $d_{q+1}[v] = 1$ *at each non-faulty node.*

PROOF. This is essentially the correctness proof for the phase king algorithm. Without loss of generality, we can assume that the number of faulty nodes is exactly F. By assumption, we have $F < N/3$ and hence $2(N-2F) > N-F$. It follows that it is not possible that two non-faulty nodes $v, u \in [N]$ satisfy both $a_{q-1}[v], a_{q-1}[u] \in [C]$ and $a_{q-1}[v] \neq a_{q-1}[u]$: this would imply that there are at least $N-2F$ non-faulty nodes w that had $a_{q-2}[w] + 1 \bmod C = a_{q-1}[v]$ and the same number of non-faulty nodes w' with $a_{q-2}[w'] + 1 \bmod C = a_{q-1}[u]$; however, there are only $N - F < 2(N-2F)$ non-faulty nodes. Therefore, there is some $x \in [C]$ so that $a_{q-1}[v] \in \{x, \infty\}$ for all non-faulty nodes v. Checking $I_{3\ell+2}$ and exploiting that $2(N-F) > N-F$ once more, we see that this also implies $a_q[v] \in \{x+1 \bmod C, \infty\}$ for any non-faulty node v.

We need to consider two cases. In the first case, all non-faulty nodes execute the first instruction of $I_{3\ell+2}$ in round q. Then $a_{q+1}[v] = \min\{C, a_q[\ell]\} + 1 \bmod C$ for any non-faulty node v. In the second case, there is some node v not executing the first instruction of $I_{3\ell+2}$. Hence, $d_q[v] = 1$, implying that v computed $z_{a_{q-1}[v]} \ge N-F$ in round $q-1$. Consequently, at least $N-2F > F$ non-faulty nodes u satisfy $a_{q-1}[u] = a_{q-1}[v]$. We infer that $a_q[v] = x'$ for all non-faulty nodes v: the third instruction of $I_{3\ell+1}$ must evaluate to $x' \in [C]$ at all non-faulty nodes. Clearly, this implies that $a_{q+1}[v] = a_{q+1}[u] \neq \infty$ for non-faulty nodes v, u, regardless of whether they execute the first instruction of $I_{3\ell+2}$ or not. Trivially, $d_{q+1}[v] = 1$ at each non-faulty node v due to the second instruction of $I_{3\ell+2}$. □

Next, we argue that once agreement is established, it persists—it does not matter any more which instruction sets are executed.

LEMMA 5. *Assume that* $a_q[v] = x \in [C]$ *and* $d_q[v] = 1$ *for all non-faulty nodes* v *in some round* q. *Then* $a_{q+1}[v] = x + 1 \bmod c$ *and* $d_{q+1}[v] = 1$ *for all non-faulty nodes* v.

PROOF. Each node will observe at least $N-F$ nodes with counter value x, and hence at most F nodes with some value $y \neq x$. For non-faulty node v, consider all possible instruction sets it may execute.

First, consider the case where instruction set $I_{3\ell}$ is executed. In this case, v increments x, resulting in $a_{q+1}[v] = x + 1 \bmod C$ and $d_{q+1}[v] = 1$. Second, executing $I_{3\ell+1}$, node v evaluates $z_x \ge N-F$ and $z_y \le F$ for all $y \neq x$. Hence it sets $d_{q+1}[v] = 1$ and $a_{q+1}[v] = x + 1 \bmod C$. Finally, when executing $I_{3\ell+2}$, node v skips the first instruction and sets $d_{q+1}[v] = 1$ and $a_{q+1}[v] = x + 1 \bmod C$. □

3.5 Proof of Theorem 1

We can now prove the main result. As shown in Lemma 3 we have constructed a τ-counter that will remain consistent at least τ rounds. This is a sufficiently long time for the nodes to execute the phase king protocol in synchrony. This protocol will stabilise the C-counter for the network of N nodes. More precisely, each node (i,j) runs the following algorithm:

1. Update the state of algorithm $\mathbf{A}_i$.
2. Compute the counter value R.
3. Update state according to instruction set I_R of the phase king protocol.

By Lemma 3, there is a round $t \le T(\mathbf{A}) + c_k - \tau$ so that the variables $R_q[i,j]$ meet the requirements of τ-counting for rounds $t \le q < t+\tau$. For each round q, all non-faulty nodes execute the same set of instructions. In particular, as $\tau = 3(F+2)$, no matter from which value the τ-counting starts, for at least $F+1$ values $\ell \in [F+2]$ the instruction sets $I_{3\ell}$,

Set	Instructions
$I_{3\ell}$:	1. If fewer than $N-F$ nodes sent $a[v]$, set $a[v] \leftarrow \infty$. 2. increment $a[v]$.
$I_{3\ell+1}$:	1. Let $z_j = \|\{u \in [N] : a[u] = j\}\|$ be the number of j values received. 2. If $z_{a[v]} \geq N-F$, set $d[v] \leftarrow 1$. Otherwise, set $d[v] \leftarrow 0$. 3. Set $a[v] \leftarrow \min\{j : z_j > F\}$. 4. increment $a[v]$.
$I_{3\ell+2}$:	1. If $a[v] = \infty$ or $d[v] = 0$, then set $a[v] \leftarrow \min\{C, a[\ell]\}$. 2. Set $d[v] \leftarrow 1$ and increment $a[v]$.

Table 2: Phase king instruction sets for node $v \in [N]$.

$I_{3\ell+1}$, and $I_{3\ell+2}$, in this order, will be jointly executed by all non-faulty nodes at some point during rounds $t, \ldots, t+\tau-1$.

As there are only F faulty nodes, there are at least two non-faulty nodes $\ell \in [F+2]$. Thus, the prerequisites of Lemma 4 are satisfied in some round $q \leq t+\tau \leq T(\mathbf{A}) + c_k$. By an inductive application of Lemma 5, we conclude that the variables $a_q[v]$ are valid outputs for C-counting, and therefore, we have indeed constructed an algorithm $\mathbf{B} \in \mathcal{A}(N, F, C)$.

The bound on q yields that $T(\mathbf{B}) \leq T(\mathbf{A}) + c_k = T(\mathbf{A}) + 3(F+2)(2m)^k$. Concerning the state complexity, observe that each non-faulty node (i, j) needs the to store the state for executing (1) the algorithm $\mathbf{A}_i$, which needs $S(\mathbf{A}_i) = S(\mathbf{A})$ bits of state, and (2) the phase king protocol, which needs $\lceil \log(C+1) \rceil$ bits to store $a_q[v] \in [C] \cup \{\infty\}$ and one additional bit to store $d_q[v]$. □

4. THE RECURSIVE CONSTRUCTION

In this section, we show how to use Theorem 1 recursively to construct synchronous c-counters with a near-optimal resilience, linear stabilisation time, and a small number of states (see Figure 2 for an illustration). First, we show how to satisfy the preconditions of Theorem 1 in order to start the recursion. Then we demonstrate the principle by choosing a fixed value of k throughout the construction; this achieves a resilience of $\Omega(n^{1-\varepsilon})$ for any constant $\varepsilon > 0$. However, as the number of nodes in the initial applications of Theorem 1 is small, better results are possible by starting out with large values of k and decreasing them later. This yields an algorithm with a resilience of $n^{1-o(1)}$ and $O(f)$ stabilisation time using $O(\log^2 f / \log\log f + \log c)$ state bits.

4.1 The Base Case

To apply Theorem 1, we need counters of resilience $f > 0$. For example, one can use the space-efficient 1-resilient counters from [3] as base of the construction. Alternatively, we can use as a starting point trivial counters for $n = 1$ and $f = 0$. Then we can apply the same construction as in Theorem 1 with the parameters $n = 1$, $f = 0$, $k = N$, and $F < N/3$. The same proof goes through in this case and yields the following corollary. Note that here the resilience is optimal but the algorithm is inefficient with respect to stabilisation time and state complexity.

Corollary 1. *For any $c > 1$, there exists a synchronous c-counter with optimal resilience $f < n/3$ that stabilises in $f^{O(f)}$ rounds and uses $O(f \log f + \log c)$ bits of state.*

Proof. For any $f > 0$, we can construct a f-resilient counter for $3f+1$ nodes. We use the trivial 0-resilient counter for one node as the base case for Theorem 1 and set $k = 3f+1$, that is, each block consists of a single node. Theorem 1 yields an f-resilient algorithm that stabilises in $(3f+2)(2m)^k = f^{O(f)}$ rounds, where the $O(f)$ term is $(3+o(1))f$. □

4.2 Using a Fixed Number of Blocks

For the sake of simplicity, we will first discuss the recursive construction for a fixed value of k here. Improved resilience can be achieved by varying k depending on the level of recursion which we show afterwards.

Theorem 2. *Let $1 > \varepsilon > 0$ and $2 \leq c \in \mathbb{N}$. There exists a synchronous c-counting algorithm with a resilience of $f = \Omega(n^{1-\varepsilon})$ that stabilises in $O(2^{2^{1/\varepsilon}} f)$ rounds and uses $O(2^{1/\varepsilon} \log f + \log^2 f + \log c)$ bits of state per node.*

Proof. Fix $0 < \varepsilon < 1$ and let $k = 2h \geq 4$ be minimal such that $\varepsilon \geq 1/\log h$. Assume $f = 2^j$ for some $j \geq h$ and let $L = \log f / \log h$; w.l.o.g., assume that $L \in \mathbb{N}$. We will analyse how many nodes are required to get to a resilience of $\Omega(n^{1-\varepsilon})$ by applying Theorem 1 for $L \leq \varepsilon \log f$ iterations.

For all $i \geq 0$, let $f_i = h^i$ and $n_i = 4k^i$. At iteration $i+1$ we use Theorem 1 to construct algorithms in $\mathcal{A}(n_{i+1}, f_{i+1}, c)$ (for any c) using n_i and f_i as the input parameters. Since $f_{i+1} = f_i h < (f_i + 1)\lceil k/2 \rceil$ and $n_{i+1} = k n_i$, the conditions of Theorem 1 are satisfied. To start the recursion, we will use an algorithm with parameters $f_0 = 1$ and $n_0 = 4$. By Corollary 1, such an algorithm with a stabilisation time of $T_0 = O(1)$ and a state complexity of $S_0 = O(\log c)$ exists.

Every iteration increases the resilience by a factor of at least $h = k/2$. After L iterations, we tolerate at least $f = f_L = h^L$ failures using $n = n_L = 4k^L$ nodes. This gives

$$\frac{n}{f} = 4\left(\frac{k}{k/2}\right)^L = 4 \cdot 2^L \leq 8 f^{\varepsilon} < 8 n^{\varepsilon}.$$

and it follows that the resilience is $\Omega(n^{1-\varepsilon})$.

It remains to analyse the stabilisation time and state complexity of the resulting algorithm; both follow from Theorem 1. The stabilisation time of layer $i+1$ is

$$T_{i+1} \leq T_i + 3(f_{i+1} + 2)h^k,$$

where $h = \lceil k/2 \rceil$. From the definition of f_i, we get the bound $\sum_{i=0}^{L} f_i = O(f_L) = O(f)$. Hence, overall stabilisation takes

$$T = T_L \leq O\left(h^k \sum_{i=0}^{L} f_i\right) = O(h^k f)$$

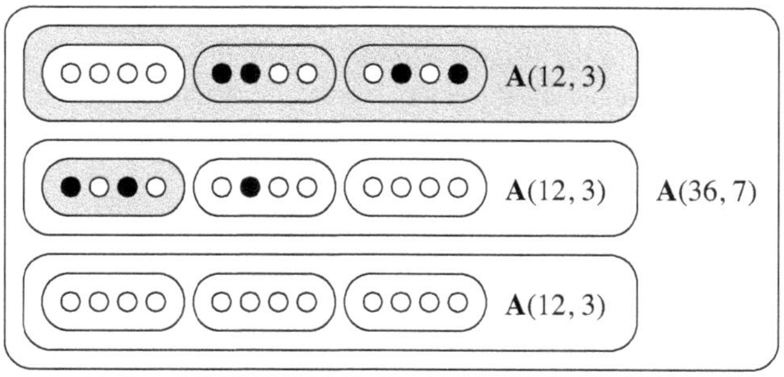

Figure 2: Recursive application of our construction using $k = 3$ blocks. The small circles represent the nodes. Each group of four nodes runs a 1-resilient counter A(4, 1). On top of this, each larger group of 12 nodes runs a 3-resilient counter A(12, 3). At the top-most layer, the nodes run a 7-resilient counter A(36, 7). Faulty nodes are black and faulty blocks are gray.

rounds. From Theorem 1, we get that the state complexity of layer $i+1$ is at most

$$S_i + \lceil \log(3(f_{i+2}+2)h^k+1)\rceil + 1 = S_i + O(k \log h + \log f).$$

As $L \le \varepsilon \log f$, the total number of bits is then bounded by

$$\sum_{i=0}^{L} S_i + O(\log c) = O(\varepsilon k \log h \log f + \log^2 f + \log c).$$

Recall that $h = k/2$ is minimal such that $\varepsilon \ge 1/\log h$. Thus $k = O(2^{1/\varepsilon})$ and $\log h = O(1/\varepsilon)$, yielding the claimed bounds on time and state complexity. □

Choosing a constant ε, we arrive at the following corollary.

COROLLARY 2. *For any constant $1 > \varepsilon > 0$ and any $2 \le c \in \mathbb{N}$, there exists a synchronous c-counter with resilience $f = \Omega(n^{1-\varepsilon})$ that stabilises in $O(f)$ rounds and uses $O(\log^2 n + \log c)$ bits of state.*

4.3 Varying the Number of Blocks

Obviously, the factor $2^{2^{1/\varepsilon}}$ makes the previous construction impractical unless $1/\varepsilon$ is small. However, it turns out that we can still achieve good resilience without a doubly-exponential blow-up in the stabilisation time by carefully varying the number of blocks at each level.

THEOREM 3. *For any $c > 1$, there exist synchronous c-counters with a resilience of $f = n^{1-o(1)}$ that stabilises in $O(f)$ rounds and uses $O(\log^2 f/\log\log f + \log c)$ state bits per node.*

Proving this theorem boils down to choosing k in each iteration as large as possible without violating the bound on the stabilisation time. We again rely on Theorem 1, but instead of using a fixed number of blocks at each iteration, we divide the construction into P *phases*. During each phase, we use a different number of blocks and iterations of Theorem 1. The goal is to have the running time of the last phase dominate the running time of earlier phases.

PROOF. We set each phase $1 \le p \le P$ to use $k_p = 4 \cdot 2^{P-p} > 3$ blocks per layer and then iterate Theorem 1 exactly $R_p = 2k_p$ times. During phase p, we use iteration $1 \le i+1 \le R_p$ to get an algorithm from Theorem 1 that tolerates

$$f_{i+1,p} = \frac{f_{i,p}k_p}{2} < (f_{i,p}+1)\left\lceil \frac{k_p}{2} \right\rceil$$

failures, where $f_{0,p} = f_{R_{p-1},p-1}$ and $f_{R_0,0} = f_{0,0} = 1$. Thus, for any p and i, the values k_p and $f_{i,p}$ satisfy the conditions of Theorem 1. Again, to start the recursion we may use any algorithm tolerating a single fault among 4 nodes giving $f_{0,0} = 1$.

Now, every phase p increases the resilience by a factor of

$$d_p = \left(\frac{f_{i+1,p}}{f_{i,p}}\right)^{R_p} = \left(\frac{k_p}{2}\right)^{R_p}.$$

As there are in total P phases, this means that the total resilience and number of nodes n are given by

$$f = f_P = \prod_{p=1}^{P} d_p = \prod_{p=1}^{P} \left(\frac{k_p}{2}\right)^{R_p} \quad \text{and } n = n_P = 4\prod_{p=1}^{P} k_p^{R_p}.$$

In order to get resilience of $f \ge n^{1-\varepsilon}$, where $\varepsilon = o(1)$, we want to ensure that

$$\frac{n}{f} = 4\prod_{p=1}^{P} 2^{R_p} = 4\prod_{j=0}^{P-1} 2^{2\cdot 2^j} = 2^{2(2^P-1)} \le f^{\varepsilon},$$

which is equivalent to

$$2(2^P-1) = 4\cdot 2^{P-1} - 2 = k_1 - 2 \le \varepsilon \log f.$$

Hence, it is feasible to choose $\varepsilon = k_1/\log f$. Observe that $\sum_{p=1}^{P} k_p = 4(2^P-1) < 2k_1$. It follows that

$$\log f = \log \prod_{p=1}^{P} (k_p/2)^{R_p} = 2\sum_{p=1}^{P} k_p \log(k_p/2) = \Theta(k_1 \log k_1),$$

implying that $k_1 = \Theta(\log f/\log\log f)$. We conclude that $\varepsilon = \Theta(1/\log\log f)$. Note that it is always possible to increase n by letting additional nodes simply adopt the majority counter value among those that execute the "actual" algorithm. Hence, for any sufficiently large n, we can construct an algorithm with resilience $f \ge n^{1-\varepsilon} = n^{1-o(1)}$. □

Let us now analyse the stabilisation time and state complexity of the construction.

LEMMA 6. *The algorithm stabilises in $O(f)$ rounds.*

PROOF. To analyse the stabilisation time, we first bound the stabilisation time of each phase p separately. By Theorem 1, iteration $i+1$ of phase p has stabilisation time

$$T_{i+1,p} = T_{i,p} + O\left(f_{i+1,p}\cdot k_p^{k_p}\right).$$

Analogously to the proof of Theorem 2, we again get a geometric series and the total stabilisation time of phase p is bounded by

$$\sum_{i=1}^{R_p} T_{i+1,p} = O(T_{R_p,p}) = O\left(f_p \cdot k_p^{k_p}\right).$$

Therefore, the total stabilisation time is

$$T = \sum_{p=1}^{P} T_p = O\left(\sum_{p=1}^{P} f_p \cdot k_p^{k_p}\right).$$

For $1 \leq p \leq P-4$, using the shorthand $\lambda = k_{p+1}$, we get

$$\frac{f_{p+1}}{f_p} \cdot \frac{\lambda^\lambda}{k_p^{k_p}} = d_{p+1}\frac{\lambda^\lambda}{(2\lambda)^{2\lambda}} = \frac{\lambda^{2\lambda}}{2^{2\lambda}} \cdot \frac{\lambda^\lambda}{(2\lambda)^{2\lambda}} = \left(\frac{\lambda}{16}\right)^\lambda \geq 2.$$

Thus, we get a geometric series $\sum_{p=1}^{P-3} T_p \leq 2T_{P-2} = O(f)$, and since also $T_{P-2} + T_{P-1} + T_P = O(f)$, the stabilisation time of all phases is bounded by $O(f)$. □

LEMMA 7. *Every node uses at most $O(\log^2 f/\log\log f + \log c)$ bits to encode its state.*

PROOF. By Theorem 1, the number of state bits increases each iteration by $\Theta(\log C_i)$, where C_i is the counter size needed for iteration i. During phase p, the counter size is $O(f \cdot k_p^{k_p})$ in each iteration. There are $R_p = 2k_p$ iterations phase p, and thus the number of bits we need is bounded by

$$S_p = O(k_p(\log f + k_p \log k_p)) = O\big(k_p \log f + k_p^2 \log k_p\big).$$

From earlier computations, we know that $\sum_{i=1}^{P} k_p = O(k_1)$ and $k_1 = O(\varepsilon \log f)$. Thus, we use

$$\begin{aligned} S = \sum_{p=1}^{P} S_p &= O\left(\sum_{p=1}^{P} (k_p \log f + k_p^2 \log k_p)\right) \\ &= O(\varepsilon \log^2 f + \varepsilon^2 \log^2 f (\log \varepsilon + \log\log f)) \\ &= O\left(\frac{\log^2 f}{\log\log f}\right) \end{aligned}$$

bits in total, as $\varepsilon = \Theta(1/\log\log f)$. Storing the output of the resulting c-counter introduces additional $O(\log c)$ bits. □

5. SAVING ON COMMUNICATION USING RANDOMISATION

So far we have considered the model where each node broadcasts its entire state every round. In the case of the algorithm given in Theorem 3, every node will send $S = O(\log^2 f/\log\log f + \log c)$ bits in each round. As there are $\Theta(n^2)$ communication links, the total number of communicated bits in each round is $\Theta(n^2 S)$. In this section, we consider a randomised variant of the algorithm that achieves better message and bit complexities in a slightly different communication model.

5.1 The Pulling Model

Throughout this section we consider the following model, where in every synchronous round: (1) each processor contacts a subset of other nodes by *pulling* their state, (2) each contacted node *responds* by sending their state to the pulling nodes, and (3) all processors update their local state according to the received messages. As before, faulty nodes may respond with arbitrary states that can be different for different pulling nodes. We define the (per-node) message and bit complexities of the algorithm as the maximum number of messages and bits, respectively, pulled by a non-faulty node in any round.

The motivation for this model is that it permits to attribute the energy cost for a message to the pulling node. In a circuit, this means that the pulling node provides the energy for the signal transitions of the communication link: logically, the link is part of the pulling node's circuitry, whereas the "sender" merely spends the energy for writing its state into the register from which all its outgoing links read.

Our goal will be to keep the number of pulls by non-faulty nodes small at all times. This way a small energy budget per round per node suffices in correct operation. By limiting the energy supply of each node, we can also effectively limit the energy consumption of the Byzantine nodes.

5.2 The High-Level Idea

To keep the number of pulls, and thus number of messages sent, small, we modify the construction of Theorem 1 to use random sampling where useful. Essentially, the idea is to show that *with high probability* a small set of sampled messages accurately represents the current state of the system and the randomised algorithm will behave as the deterministic one. There are two steps where the nodes rely on information broadcast by all the nodes: the majority voting scheme over the blocks and our variant of the phase king algorithm. Both can be shown to work with high probability by using concentration bound arguments.

More specifically, for any constant $\kappa \geq 1$ we can bound the probability of failure by $\eta^{-\kappa}$ by sampling $M = \Theta(\log \eta)$ messages; here η denotes the total number of nodes in the system. The idea is to use a union bound over all levels of recursion, nodes, and considered rounds, to show that the sampling succeeds with high probability in all cases. For the randomised variant of Theorem 1, we will require the following additional constraint: when constructing a counter on $N = kn$ nodes, the total number of failures is bounded by $F < \frac{N}{3+\gamma}$, where $\gamma > 0$ is some constant. Since the resilience of the recursive construction is suboptimal anyway, this constraint is always going to be satisfied. This allows us to construct *probabilistic synchronous c-counters* in the sense that the counter stabilises in time T if for all rounds $t \geq T$ all non-faulty nodes count correctly with probability $1 - \eta^{-\kappa}$.

5.3 Sampling Communication Channels

There are two steps in the construction of Theorem 1 where we rely on deterministic broadcasting: the majority sampling for electing a leader block and the execution of the phase king protocol. We start with the latter.

Randomised Phase King. Instead of checking whether at least $N - F$ of all messages have the same value, we check whether at least a fraction of $2/3$ of the sampled messages have the same value. Similarly, when checking for at least $F+1$ values, we check whether a fraction $1/3$ of the sampled messages have this value.

LEMMA 8. *Let $x \in [C] \cup \{\infty\}$ and suppose a node samples M values from the other nodes. Then there exists $M_0(\eta, \kappa, \gamma) = \Theta(\log \eta)$ so that $M \geq M_0$ implies the following with high probability.*

(a) If all non-faulty nodes agree on value x, then x is seen at least $2/3 \cdot M$ times.
(b) If the majority of non-faulty nodes have value x, then more than $1/3 \cdot M$ sampled values will be x.
(c) If at least $2/3 \cdot M$ sampled values have value x, then x is a majority value.

PROOF. Define $\delta = 1 - \frac{2}{3} \cdot \frac{3+\gamma}{2+\gamma}$ and let the random variable X denote the number of x values sampled from *non-faulty* nodes.

(a) If all non-faulty nodes agree on value x, then

$$\mathbf{E}[X] = \left(1 - \frac{F}{N}\right) M > \frac{2+\gamma}{3+\gamma} M.$$

As δ satisfies $(1-\delta)\,\mathbf{E}[X] > 2/3 \cdot M$, Chernoff's bound yields

$$\Pr\left[X < \frac{2}{3}M\right] \leq \Pr[X < (1-\delta)\,\mathbf{E}[X]] \leq \exp\left(-\frac{\delta^2}{2}\,\mathbf{E}[X]\right) \leq \exp\left(-\delta^2 \frac{2+\gamma}{2(3+\gamma)} M_0\right).$$

For sufficiently large $M_0(N,\kappa,\gamma) = \Theta(\log N)$ this probability is bounded by $N^{-\kappa}$.

(b) If a majority of non-faulty nodes have value x, then $\mathbf{E}[X] \geq \frac{1}{2} \cdot \frac{2+\gamma}{3+\gamma} M$. As above, by picking the right constants and using concentration bounds, we get that

$$\Pr\left[X \leq \frac{1}{3}M\right] \leq \Pr[X < (1-\delta)\,\mathbf{E}[X]] \leq \exp\left(-\frac{\delta^2}{2}\,\mathbf{E}[X]\right) \leq \exp\left(-\delta^2 \frac{2+\gamma}{4(3+\gamma)} M_0\right) \leq N^{-\kappa}.$$

(c) Suppose the majority of non-faulty nodes have values different from x. Defining $\bar{X}$ as the random variable counting the number of samples with values different from x and arguing as for (b), we see that

$$\Pr\left[X \geq \frac{2}{3}M\right] = \Pr\left[\bar{X} < \frac{1}{3}M\right] \leq N^{-\kappa},$$

where again we assume that $M_0(N,\kappa,\gamma) = \Theta(\log N)$ is sufficiently large. Thus, $X \geq 2/3 \cdot M$ implies with high probability that the majority of non-faulty nodes have value x. □

As a corollary, we get that when using the sampling scheme, the execution of the phase king essentially behaves as in the deterministic broadcast case.

Corollary 3. *When executing the randomised variant of the phase king protocol from Section 3 for $\eta^{O(1)}$ rounds, the statements of Lemma 4 and Lemma 5 hold with high probability.*

Proof. The algorithm uses two thresholds, $N-F$ and $F+1$. As discussed, these are replaced by $2/3 \cdot M$ and $1/3 \cdot M$ when taking M samples. Using the statements of Lemma 8, we can argue analogously to the proofs of Lemma 4 and Lemma 5; we apply the union bound over all rounds and samples taken by non-faulty nodes ($N-F < \eta$ per round), i.e., over $\eta^{O(1)}$ events. □

Randomised majority voting. It remains to handle the case of majority voting in the construction of Theorem 1. Consider some level of the recursive construction, in which we want to construct a counter of $N = kn$ nodes out of k n-node counters. If $N \ll \log\eta/\log\log\eta$, we can perform the step in the recursive construction using the deterministic algorithm, that is, pulling from all kn nodes. Otherwise, similar to the above sampling scheme for randomised phase king, each node will from each block uniformly sample $M \geq M_0(\eta,\kappa,\gamma) = \Theta(\log\eta)$ states. Again by applying concentration bounds, we can show that with high probability, the non-faulty nodes sample a majority of non-faulty nodes from non-faulty blocks. Thus, we can get a probabilistic version of Lemma 3.

Analogously to Section 3, we define the following local variables at node (i,j) in round q:

$$\begin{aligned} b_q^{i'}[i,j] &= \text{majority}\{b_q[i',j'] : (i',j') \text{ sampled by } (i,j) \text{ in round } q\}, \\ B_q[i,j] &= \text{majority}\{b_q^{i'}[i,j] \mid i' \in [k]\}, \\ R_q[i,j] &= \text{majority}\{r[B_q[i,j],j'] : (i',j') \text{ sampled by } (i,j) \text{ in round } q\}. \end{aligned}$$

Here we sample with repetition and the above sets are multisets; this means all samples from a block are independent and we can readily apply Chernoff's bound.

Lemma 9. *Suppose $x \in [k]$ is a non-faulty block, $M_0 = \Theta(\log\eta)$ is sufficiently large, and all non-faulty blocks count correctly in round q. If for all non-faulty blocks i and non-faulty nodes (i,j) it holds that $b_q[i,j] = x$, then with high probability*

1. *$b_q^{i'}[i,j] = x$ for all non-faulty blocks i',*
2. *$B_q[i,j] = x$, and*
3. *$R_q[i,j] = r_q[x,j']$ for an arbitrary non-faulty node (B,j') in block x.*

Proof. Consider a non-faulty block (recall that a block is non-faulty if it has at most f faulty nodes). Let X denote the number of states of non-faulty nodes sampled from this block by (i,j) in round q. As $f < n/3$, we have that $\mathbf{E}[X] \geq M(n-f)/n > 2/3 \cdot M$. Applying Chernoff's bound for $\delta = 1/4$ and choosing sufficiently large $M_0(\eta,\kappa) = \Theta(\log\eta)$, we obtain that

$$\Pr[X \leq M/2] \leq \Pr[X \leq (1-\delta)\,\mathbf{E}[X]] \leq \exp\left(-\frac{\delta^2}{2}\,\mathbf{E}[X]\right) \leq \eta^{-\kappa}.$$

Applying the union bound to all nodes and all blocks, it follows that, with high probability, non-faulty nodes always sample a majority of non-faulty nodes from non-faulty blocks. The first statement follows, immediately yielding the second as a majority of the blocks is non-faulty. The third statement now holds because we assume that non-faulty blocks count correctly and x is non-faulty. □

5.4 Randomised Resilience Boosting

Define $\mathcal{P}(n,f,c,\eta,\kappa)$ as the family of probabilistic synchronous c-counters on n nodes with resilience f, where probabilistic means that an algorithm $\mathbf{P} \in \mathcal{P}(n,f,c,\eta,\kappa)$ of stabilisation time $T(\mathbf{P})$ merely guarantees that it counts correctly with probability $1-\eta^{-\kappa}$ in rounds $t \geq T(\mathbf{P})$. Thus with high probability, eventually all non-faulty nodes agree on a common counter for sufficiently many rounds. Together with Corollary 3, we get a randomised variant of Theorem 1.

Theorem 4. *Given $n,f,\eta \in \mathbb{N}$, pick $N,F,C \in \mathbb{N}$ and $\kappa > 0$, where*

- *the number of nodes $N = kn \leq \eta$ for some number of blocks $3 \leq k \in \mathbb{N}$,*
- *the resilience $F < (f+1)m$, where $m = \lceil k/2 \rceil$,*
- *$C > 1$ is the new counter size, and*
- *κ is a constant.*

Choose any $c \in \mathbb{N}$ that is an integer multiple of $3(F+2)(2m)^k$. Then for any $\mathbf{A} \in \mathcal{A}(n,f,c)$, there exists $\mathbf{P} \in \mathcal{P}(N,F,C,\eta,\kappa)$ with the following properties.

1. *$T(\mathbf{P}) = T(\mathbf{A}) + 3(F+2)(2m)^k$, and*
2. *$S(\mathbf{P}) = S(\mathbf{A}) + \lceil \log(C+1) \rceil + 1$.*
3. *Each node pulls $O(k \log \eta)$ messages in each round.*

We can choose to replace $\mathbf{A} \in \mathcal{A}(n, f, c)$ by $\mathbf{Q} \in \mathcal{P}(n, f, c, \eta, \kappa)$ when applying this theorem, arguing that with high probability it *behaves* like a corresponding algorithm $\mathbf{A} \in \mathcal{A}(n, f, c)$ for polynomially many rounds. Applying the recursive construction from Section 4 and the union bound, this yields Corollary 4. By always choosing $k = O(\log \eta)$, each node pulls $O(\log^2 \eta)$ messages from other nodes for each layer.

COROLLARY 4. *For any $c > 1$, there exist probabilistic synchronous c-counters with a resilience of $f = n^{1-o(1)}$ that stabilise in $O(f)$ rounds, use $O(\log^2 f / \log \log f + \log c)$ state bits per node, and in which the number of messages pulled by a non-faulty node is $O(\log \eta (\log f / \log \log f)^2)$ per round.*

We note that it is also possible to boost the probability of success, and thus the period of stability, by simply increasing the sample size. For instance, sampling polylog η messages yields an error probability of $\eta^{-\operatorname{polylog} \eta}$ in each round, whereas in the extreme case, by "sampling" all nodes the algorithm reduces to the deterministic case.

5.5 Oblivious Adversary

Finally, we remark that under an *oblivious adversary*, that is, an adversary that picks the set of faulty nodes independently of the randomness used by the non-faulty nodes, we get *pseudo-random* synchronous counters satisfying the following: (1) the execution stabilises with high probability and (2) if the execution stabilises, then all non-faulty nodes will deterministically count correctly. Put otherwise, we can fix the random bits used by the nodes to sample the communication links *once*, and with high probability we sample sufficiently many communication links to non-faulty nodes for the algorithm to (deterministically) stabilise. This gives us the following result.

COROLLARY 5. *For any $c > 1$, there exist pseudo-random synchronous c-counters with a resilience of $f = n^{1-o(1)}$ against an oblivious fault pattern that stabilise in $O(f)$ rounds with high probability, use $O(\log^2 f / \log \log f + \log c)$ state bits per node, and in which the number of messages pulled by a non-faulty node is $O(\log \eta (\log f / \log \log f)^2)$ per round.*

6. CONCLUSIONS

In this work, we showed that there exist (1) *deterministic* algorithms for synchronous counting that have (2) linear stabilisation time, (3) need to store a very small number of state bits between consecutive rounds while still achieving (4) almost-optimal resilience—something no prior algorithms have been able to do. In addition, we discussed how to reduce the total number of communicated bits in the network, while still achieving (2)–(4) by considering probabilistic and pseudo-random synchronous counters.

We conclude by highlighting a few open problems:

1. Are there randomised or deterministic algorithms with optimal resilience of $f < n/3$ that use polylog f state bits and stabilise in $O(f)$ rounds (with small constant factors)?
2. Are there deterministic algorithms that use substantially fewer than $\log^2 f$ state bits?
3. Are there communication-efficient and space-efficient algorithms with high resilience that stabilise quickly in the usual synchronous model?

Acknowledgements

We thank Tuomo Lempiäinen and the anonymous reviewers for helpful comments.

7. REFERENCES

[1] Michael Ben-Or, Danny Dolev, and Ezra N. Hoch. Fast self-stabilizing Byzantine tolerant digital clock synchronization. In *Proc. 27th Annual ACM Symposium on Principles of Distributed Computing (PODC 2008)*, pages 385–394. ACM Press, 2008. doi:10.1145/1400751.1400802.

[2] Piotr Berman, Juan A. Garay, and Kenneth J. Perry. Towards optimal distributed consensus. In *Proc. 30th Annual Symposium on Foundations of Computer Science (FOCS 1989)*, pages 410–415. IEEE, 1989. doi:10.1109/SFCS.1989.63511.

[3] Danny Dolev, Keijo Heljanko, Matti Järvisalo, Janne H. Korhonen, Christoph Lenzen, Joel Rybicki, Jukka Suomela, and Siert Wieringa. Synchronous counting and computational algorithm design, 2015. arXiv:1304.5719v2.

[4] Danny Dolev and Ezra N. Hoch. On self-stabilizing synchronous actions despite Byzantine attacks. In *Proc. 21st International Symposium on Distributed Computing (DISC 2007)*, volume 4731 of *Lecture Notes in Computer Science*, pages 193–207. Springer, 2007. doi:10.1007/978-3-540-75142-7_17.

[5] Danny Dolev, Janne H. Korhonen, Christoph Lenzen, Joel Rybicki, and Jukka Suomela. Synchronous counting and computational algorithm design. In *Proc. 15th International Symposium on Stabilization, Safety, and Security of Distributed Systems (SSS 2013)*, volume 8255 of *Lecture Notes in Computer Science*, pages 237–250. Springer, 2013. doi:10.1007/978-3-319-03089-0_17. arXiv:1304.5719v1.

[6] Danny Dolev and Rüdiger Reischuk. Bounds on information exchange for Byzantine agreement. *Journal of the ACM*, 32(1):191–204, 1985. doi:10.1145/2455.214112.

[7] Shlomi Dolev. *Self-Stabilization*. The MIT Press, Cambridge, MA, 2000.

[8] Shlomi Dolev and Jennifer L. Welch. Self-stabilizing clock synchronization in the presence of Byzantine faults. *Journal of the ACM*, 51(5):780–799, 2004. doi:10.1145/1017460.1017463.

[9] Michael J. Fischer and Nancy A. Lynch. A lower bound for the time to assure interactive consistency. *Information Processing Letters*, 14(4):183–186, 1982. doi:10.1016/0020-0190(82)90033-3.

[10] Marshall C. Pease, Robert E. Shostak, and Leslie Lamport. Reaching agreement in the presence of faults. *Journal of the ACM*, 27(2):228–234, 1980. doi:10.1145/322186.322188.

Fault-Tolerant Consensus in Directed Graphs *

Lewis Tseng
Department of Computer Science
Coordinated Science Laboratory
University of Illinois at Urbana-Champaign
ltseng3@illinois.edu

Nitin H. Vaidya
Department of Electrical and Computer Engineering
Coordinated Science Laboratory
University of Illinois at Urbana-Champaign
nhv@illinois.edu

ABSTRACT

Consider a point-to-point network in which nodes are connected by *directed* links. This paper proves *tight* necessary and sufficient conditions on the underlying communication graphs for solving the following fault-tolerant consensus problems:

- Exact crash-tolerant consensus in *synchronous* systems,
- Approximate crash-tolerant consensus in *asynchronous* systems, and
- Exact Byzantine consensus in *synchronous* systems.

The problem of asynchronous Byzantine consensus in directed graphs remains open.

Prior work has developed analogous necessary and sufficient conditions for *undirected* graphs [11, 3, 9]. However, the conditions for undirected graphs are not adequate to completely characterize these consensus problems in *directed* graphs. Moreover, the algorithms for *directed* graphs presented in this paper are substantially different from those previously developed for *undirected* graphs. Other prior work on directed graphs has explored somewhat different problems than those solved in this paper.

Categories and Subject Descriptors

C.2.4 [**Distributed Systems**]: [Distributed applications]

General Terms

Algorithm, Theory

*This research is supported in part by National Science Foundation awards 1329681, National Science Foundation awards 1421918 and Army Research Office grant W-911-NF-0710287. Any opinions, findings, and conclusions or recommendations expressed here are those of the authors and do not necessarily reflect the views of the funding agencies or the U.S. government.

Permission to make digital or hard copies of all or part of this work for personal or classroom use is granted without fee provided that copies are not made or distributed for profit or commercial advantage and that copies bear this notice and the full citation on the first page. Copyrights for components of this work owned by others than the author(s) must be honored. Abstracting with credit is permitted. To copy otherwise, or republish, to post on servers or to redistribute to lists, requires prior specific permission and/or a fee. Request permissions from Permissions@acm.org.
PODC'15, July 21–23, 2015, Donostia-San Sebastián, Spain.
Copyright is held by the owner/author(s). Publication rights licensed to ACM.
ACM 978-1-4503-3617-8 /15/07 ...$15.00.
DOI: http://dx.doi.org/10.1145/2767386.2767399.

Keywords

Consensus; directed networks; crash and Byzantine faults; asynchronous and synchronous systems

1. INTRODUCTION

Since Lamport, Shostak, and Pease posed the Byzantine *fault-tolerance* problem [19], it has received significant attention over the past three decades [3, 17]. The fault-tolerant consensus problem has been studied extensively in complete networks (e.g., [19, 10, 1]) and in undirected networks (e.g., [11, 9]). This paper addresses the fault-tolerant consensus problem in *incomplete directed* networks, i.e., not every pair of nodes is connected by a communication channel, and the communication channels are not necessarily bi-directional. Our work is motivated by the presence of directed links in wireless networks. However, we believe that the results here are of independent interest as well. There is also work studying directed graphs for similar problems (e.g., [8, 7, 18]), but the formulation is different from our work as elaborated later in Section 2.

The fault-tolerant consensus problem [3, 17] considers n nodes, of which at most f nodes may be faulty. In our work, we address crash faults and Byzantine faults both. Each node is given an *input*, and after a finite amount of time, each fault-free node should produce an *output*, which satisfies appropriate *validity* and *agreement* conditions. We limit our consideration to *scalar* input and output. For synchronous systems, we consider *exact* consensus, where the *agreement* condition requires the fault-free nodes to agree on exactly the *same* output. Since exact consensus is impossible in asynchronous systems [12], we consider *approximate* consensus, where the *agreement* condition requires the fault-free nodes to produce outputs within a certain constant ϵ ($\epsilon > 0$) of each other.

The goal of this paper is to characterize the necessary and sufficient conditions on the underlying communication graph for solving exact and approximate consensus, respectively, in synchronous and asynchronous systems in the presence of *crash* and *Byzantine* faults. Our problem formulation allows nodes to have complete knowledge of the communication graph. Table 1 identifies the results presented in this paper. Where prior work has already obtained the necessary and sufficient conditions, those conditions are also enumerated. Recall that n is the number of nodes in the system. The table on the left is for consensus with up to f crash faults, whereas the table on the right is for consensus with up to f Byzantine faults. The term *connectivity* is used here to

Table 1: Summary of Tight Conditions

Crash-Tolerant Consensus		
	Synchronous	Asynchronous
Undirected graph	$f+1$- connectivity, $n > f$ (follows from well-known results [17, 3])	$f+1$- connectivity, $n > 2f$ (follows from well-known results [17, 3])
Directed graph	*This work*	*This work*

Byzantine Consensus		
	Synchronous	Asynchronous
Undirected graph	$2f+1$- connectivity, $n > 3f$ [11, 9]	$2f+1$- connectivity, $n > 3f$ (follows from [1, 11])
Directed graph	*This work*	Open problem

mean *node connectivity.* We will often use the terms *graph* and *network* interchangeably.

The problem of asynchronous Byzantine consensus in directed graphs remains open. To prove that the necessary conditions presented in the paper are also sufficient, we have developed algorithms that achieve consensus in graphs satisfying those conditions. It turns out that the algorithms required for *directed* graphs are substantially different from those previously developed for *undirected* graphs [11, 3, 9].

As noted above, our problem formulation allows nodes to have complete knowledge of the network topology. It is also possible to achieve consensus when nodes are *constrained* to only have knowledge of the *local* network topology, particularly their immediate neighbors – such algorithms are beyond the scope of this paper. We note, however, that the algorithms using only the *local* neighborhood information require richer communication graphs. Such algorithms have been a topic of prior work [8, 5, 13, 15], including our own work [23, 24, 20].

2. RELATED WORK

Lamport, Shostak, and Pease first addressed the Byzantine fault-tolerance problem in [19]. Subsequent work [11, 9] characterized the necessary and sufficient conditions under which Byzantine consensus is solvable in *undirected* graphs. However, these conditions are not adequate to fully characterize the *directed* graphs in which Byzantine or crash-tolerant consensus is feasible. For synchronous systems, [8] solves *approximate* crash-tolerant consensus in (dynamic) directed networks using local averaging algorithms – on the other hand, we solve *exact* crash-tolerant consensus in directed networks, which requires a different type of algorithm. In the asynchronous setting, [8] addresses approximate consensus with crash faults in *complete* graphs (which are necessarily undirected) – on the other hand, we solve the problem in *incomplete directed* graphs. We also address Byzantine consensus in synchronous systems.

Previous work also studies graph properties for other similar problems. Bansal et al. [4] identified tight conditions for achieving Byzantine consensus in *undirected* graphs using *authentication.* Bansal et al. discovered that all-pair reliable communication is not necessary to achieve consensus when using authentication. Our work differs from Bansal et al. in that our results apply in the absence of authentication or any other security primitives; also our results apply to *directed* graphs. We show that even in the absence of authentication, all-pair reliable communication is not necessary for Byzantine consensus. Alchieri et al. [2] explored the problem of achieving exact consensus in *unknown* networks with Byzantine nodes, but the underlying communication graph is assumed to be *fully-connected.* In our work, the network is assumed to be known to all nodes, and we consider incomplete directed graphs.

Many researchers in the decentralized control area, including Bertsekas and Tsitsiklis [5] and Jadbabaei, Lin and Morse [13], have explored approximate consensus in the absence of faults, using only near-neighbor communication in systems wherein the communication graph may be partially connected and time-varying. Our work considers the case when nodes may suffer crash or Byzantine failures.

Our prior work [23, 24] has considered a restricted class of iterative algorithms for achieving *approximate* Byzantine consensus in directed graphs, where fault-free nodes must agree on values that are approximately equal to each other using iterative algorithms with limited memory (the state carried by the nodes across iterations must be in the convex hull of inputs of the fault-free nodes, which precludes mechanisms such as multi-hop forwarding of messages). The conditions developed in such prior work are *not* necessary when no such restrictions are imposed. Independently, LeBlanc et al. [15, 16], and Zhang and Sundaram [25, 26] have developed results for iterative algorithms for approximate consensus under a *weaker* fault model, where a faulty node must send *identical* messages to all the neighbors.

Recently, researchers have explored consensus problem in directed dynamic networks [6, 7]. The typical fault model in dynamic networks is named *message adversary,* which controls the communication pattern, i.e., the adversary has the power to specify the sets of communication graphs. Biely et al. studied the exact consensus problem [6] and k-set consensus problem [7] (i.e., at most k different outputs at fault-free nodes) in dynamic networks under *message adversary,* and the system is assumed to be synchronous [7]. All the nodes are assumed to be fault-free in [6, 7].

3. MAIN RESULTS

Before presenting our results, we introduce the system model and some terminology to facilitate the discussion.

System Model.

We consider a point-to-point network in which nodes are connected by *directed* links. The communication network is *static,* and it is represented by a simple directed graph $G(\mathcal{V}, \mathcal{E})$, where $\mathcal{V}$ is the set of n nodes, and $\mathcal{E}$ is the set of directed edges between the nodes in $\mathcal{V}$. The communication links are reliable. We assume that $n \geq 2$, since the consensus problem for $n = 1$ is trivial. Node i can transmit messages to another node j if directed edge (i, j) is in $\mathcal{E}$. Each node can send messages to itself as well; however, for convenience, we exclude self-loops from set $\mathcal{E}$. We will often use the terms *edge* and *link* interchangeably.

In the system, up to f nodes may become faulty. A node that suffers crash failure simply stops taking steps. On the other hand, a Byzantine faulty node may misbehave arbitrarily. Possible misbehavior includes sending incorrect and mismatching (or inconsistent) messages to different neighbors. The Byzantine nodes may potentially collaborate with each other. Moreover, the Byzantine nodes are assumed to have a complete knowledge of the execution of the algorithm, including the states of all the nodes, contents of messages the other nodes send to each other, the algorithm specification, and the network topology.

Terminology.

Upper case letters are used to name sets. Lower case italic letters are used to name nodes. All paths used in our discussion are directed paths. Node j is said to be an incoming neighbor of node i if $(j, i) \in \mathcal{E}$. Let N_i^- be the set of incoming neighbors of node i, i.e., $N_i^- = \{j \mid (j, i) \in \mathcal{E}\}$. Define N_i^+ as the set of outgoing neighbors of node i, i.e., $N_i^+ = \{j \mid (i, j) \in \mathcal{E}\}$. For set $B \subseteq \mathcal{V}$, node i is said to be an incoming neighbor of set B if $i \notin B$, and there exists $j \in B$ such that $(i, j) \in \mathcal{E}$. Given subsets of nodes A and B, set B is said to have k incoming neighbors in set A if A contains k distinct incoming neighbors of B.

DEFINITION 1. *Given disjoint non-empty subsets of nodes A and B, $A \stackrel{x}{\Rightarrow} B$ if B has at least x distinct incoming neighbors in A. When it is not true that $A \stackrel{x}{\Rightarrow} B$, we will denote that fact by $A \stackrel{x}{\not\Rightarrow} B$.*

Consider the network in Figure 1, which contains two cliques K_1 and K_2, each consisting of 7 nodes. Within each clique, each node has a directed link to the other 6 nodes in that clique – these links within each clique are not shown in the figure. There are 8 directed links with one endpoint in clique K_1 and the other endpoint in clique K_2. In the network, K_2 has 4 incoming neighbors in K_1, namely u_1, u_2, u_3 and u_4. Thus, $K_1 \stackrel{4}{\Rightarrow} K_2$. Similarly, $K_2 \stackrel{4}{\Rightarrow} K_1$.

Main Results.

The main contribution of this work is to identify necessary and sufficient conditions on the underlying communication graphs $G(\mathcal{V}, \mathcal{E})$ for achieving *consensus* in directed networks. We summarize the main results in three theorems below. Each theorem below requires the graph to satisfy a certain condition: we name the conditions in Theorems 1, 2 and 3 as **CCS** (abbreviating Crash-Consensus-Synchronous), **CCA** (Crash-Consensus-Asynchronous) and **BCS** (Byzantine-Consensus-Synchronous), respectively. Characterization of the necessary and sufficient condition for approximate Byzantine consensus in asynchronous systems remains open.

The precise *validity* conditions that need to be satisfied for different versions of the consensus problem are specified at the start of Sections 4, 5 and 6, respectively. In brief, for Theorem 1, the output at the nodes must equal the input of one of the nodes. For Theorem 2, the output must be in the range of the inputs of all the nodes. For Theorem 3, the validity condition depends on whether the inputs are binary or not: for binary inputs, the output must be the input of a fault-free node, whereas for multi-valued inputs, the output must equal the input of fault-free nodes when they all have the same input. These conditions are standard in the related literature [17, 3, 14].

THEOREM 1. *Exact crash-tolerant consensus in a synchronous system is feasible iff for any partition F, L, C, R of $\mathcal{V}$, where L and R are both non-empty, and $|F| \leq f$, either $L \cup C \stackrel{1}{\Rightarrow} R$ or $R \cup C \stackrel{1}{\Rightarrow} L$.* (Condition CCS)

THEOREM 2. *Approximate crash-tolerant consensus in an asynchronous system is feasible iff for any partition L, C, R of $\mathcal{V}$, where L and R are both non-empty, either $L \cup C \stackrel{f+1}{\Rightarrow} R$ or $R \cup C \stackrel{f+1}{\Rightarrow} L$.* (Condition CCA)

THEOREM 3. *Exact Byzantine consensus in a synchronous system is feasible iff for any partition F, L, C, R of $\mathcal{V}$, where L and R are both non-empty, and $|F| \leq f$, either $L \cup C \stackrel{f+1}{\Rightarrow} R$ or $R \cup C \stackrel{f+1}{\Rightarrow} L$.* (Condition BCS)

The network shown in Figure 1 satisfies Condition BCS for $f = 2$, whereas the network in Figure 2 satisfies Condition CCS for $f = 1$.

Intuitively, for consensus to be achieved, there must be a way for information to "flow between" different subsets of fault-free nodes (subsets L and R in the theorems above), despite the presence of faulty nodes. The different conditions above capture this intuition. Observe that, in each case, for different values of x, we obtain the requirement of the form "either $L \cup C \stackrel{x}{\Rightarrow} R$ or $R \cup C \stackrel{x}{\Rightarrow} L$". Intuitively, information must "flow" either from $L \cup C$ to R, or from $R \cup C$ to L, but it is not necessary that the information flows in both directions – this "asymmetry" in the necessary and sufficient condition is a consequence of the directed nature of the communication network. Note that in Condition CCA (in Theorem 2), the partition does not need set F, unlike Conditions CCS and BCS for the synchronous case.

4. EXACT CRASH-TOLERANT SYNCHRONOUS CONSENSUS

An exact crash-tolerant consensus algorithm must satisfy the following three properties: (i) *Agreement*: the output (i.e., decision) at all the fault-free nodes is identical. (ii) *Validity*: the output of each fault-free node equals the input of one of the nodes. (iii) *Termination*: every fault-free node decides on an output in finite amount of time.

Theorem 1 in Section 3 presents the necessary and sufficient condition (named Condition CCS) for solving the above problem in directed graphs.

4.1 Necessity of Condition CCS

LEMMA 1. *Condition CCS is necessary for exact crash-tolerant consensus in a synchronous system.*

PROOF. The proof is by contradiction. Suppose that there exists a consensus algorithm for graph $G(\mathcal{V}, \mathcal{E})$, but $G(\mathcal{V}, \mathcal{E})$ does not satisfy the condition in the lemma. Thus, there exists a node partition F, L, C, R of $\mathcal{V}$ such that (i) $|F| \leq f$, (ii) L and R are both non-empty, and (iii) $L \cup C \stackrel{1}{\not\Rightarrow} R$ and $R \cup C \stackrel{1}{\not\Rightarrow} L$. The last two assumptions imply that nodes in $L \cup C$ have no links to nodes in R, and nodes in $R \cup C$ have no links to nodes in L.

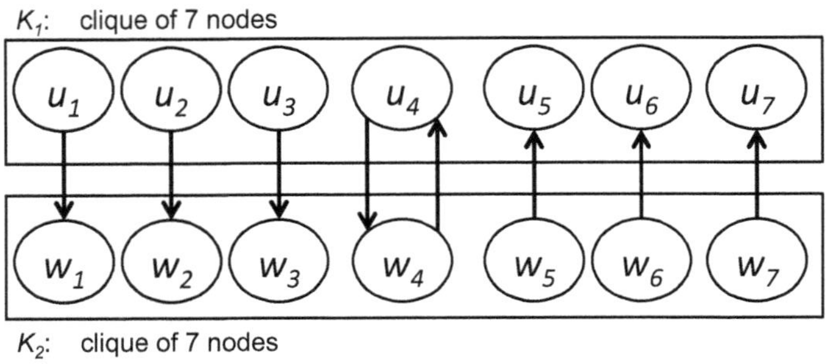

Figure 1: Edges within cliques K_1 and K_2 are not shown.

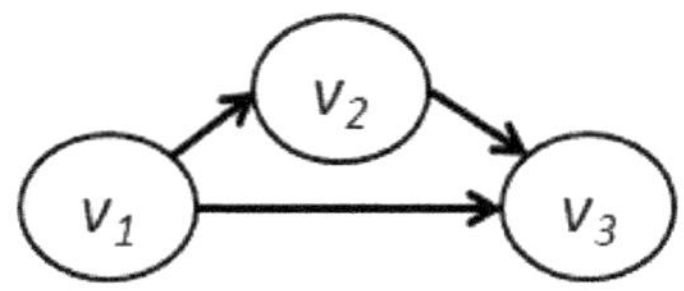

Figure 2: Another example.

Now, consider an execution of the consensus algorithm where F is the set of faulty nodes which crash before the start of the algorithm. All the other nodes are fault-free. This is possible, since by assumption, $|F| \leq f$. Also, suppose that all the nodes in L have input 0, and all the nodes in R have input 1. Nodes in C may have input either 0 or 1.

Consider any node $x \in L$. Since nodes in F fail before taking any steps in the algorithm, and as noted above, there are no links from $C \cup R$ to any node in L, the only input value learned by x throughout the execution of the algorithm is 0. Then to satisfy the validity property, 0 must be the output of node x. Similarly, any node y in R can only learn input values 1 throughout the execution of the algorithm, and thus, 1 must be the output of node y. Since L and R are non-empty and consist of fault-free nodes, the above observations imply that the agreement property is violated. This is a contradiction. □

4.2 Sufficiency of Condition CCS

We prove the sufficiency of Condition CCS constructively by presenting an algorithm, called MVC, and proving its correctness. Algorithm MVC can achieve consensus with multi-valued inputs. MVC uses binary consensus algorithm Min-Max presented below as a component. Algorithm Min-Max can achieve consensus with *binary* inputs (0 or 1). The proposed algorithms prove sufficiency of Condition CCS, but they are not necessarily the most efficient. Development of optimal algorithms needs further research.

4.2.1 Binary Consensus Algorithm Min-Max

Note that Algorithm *Min-Max* has input parameter x_i. To achieve binary consensus, each node i performs Algorithm *Min-Max* passing its binary input value as parameter x_i to Algorithm *Min-Max*. Algorithm Min-Max uses *Compute* as a sub-routine. *Compute* has two parameters: t, which is a binary value, and *Function*, which may be specified as *Min* and *Max*. In the last step of each round in *Compute* at node i, the *Function* is applied to set S_i. $Min(S_i)$ returns minimum of the values in set S_i, and $Max(S_i)$ returns the maximum of the values in set S_i.

Algorithm Min-Max(x_i) for node $i \in \mathcal{V}$

Initialization: $v_i[0]$:= parameter x_i passed to Min-Max

- For phase number $p := 1$ to $2f + 2$:

  If $p \bmod 2 = 0$, then **(Min Phase)**

  $v_i[p]$:= Compute ($v_i[p-1]$, *Min*)

  Else, **(Max Phase)**

  $v_i[p]$:= Compute ($v_i[p-1]$, *Max*)

- Return $v_i[2f + 2]$

Compute(t, *Function*) for node $i \in \mathcal{V}$

- $\tau_i := t$
- Perform $n-1$ rounds, each round consisting of the four steps below:

  Send τ_i to all the nodes in $N_i^+ \cup \{i\}$

  Receive values from $N_i^- \cup \{i\}$

  Denote the set of values received

  in the previous step as S_i

  $\tau_i := Function(S_i)$

- Return τ_i

Note that Algorithm Min-Max may execute for less number of rounds by exploiting the knowledge of topology. For simplicity, we require Algorithm Min-Max to execute for $n - 1$ rounds. In [22], we show that under certain assumptions, usage of both Min and Max functions is necessary.

Correctness of Algorithm Min-Max with Binary Inputs.

We first prove a useful lemma, and introduce the notion of *source* of the graph.

LEMMA 2. *Suppose that graph $G(\mathcal{V}, \mathcal{E})$ satisfies Condition CCS. For any $F \subseteq \mathcal{V}$, such that $|F| \leq f$, let G_F denote the subgraph of G induced by the nodes in $\mathcal{V} - F$. There exists at least one node in G_F that has directed paths in G_F to all nodes in $\mathcal{V} - F$. Such a node is said to be a <u>source</u> for G_F.*

PROOF. The proof of the lemma is by contradiction. Suppose that Graph $G(\mathcal{V}, \mathcal{E})$ satisfies Condition CCS, and for some $F \subseteq \mathcal{V}$, $|F| \leq f$, there exists a pair of nodes $i, j \notin F$ such that there is no node s that has directed paths to both i and j in subgraph G_F induced by nodes in $\mathcal{V} - F$. For the subgraph G_F and a node x in $\mathcal{V} - F$, define S_x as the set of all nodes that have directed paths in G_F to node x. Note that S_x contains x as well, because x trivially has a path to itself.

By assumption, S_i and S_j are disjoint. Moreover, there must be no path from any node in S_i to any node in S_j in G_F, and vice versa, since otherwise, there would exist some node that can reach both nodes i and j, which contradicts our assumption above. Now, define L, C, R as follows: (i) $L := S_i$, (ii) $R := S_j$, and (iii) $C := \mathcal{V} - F - L - R$. We make the following observations:

- *F and C may be empty, but L and R are non-empty*: This is true because $i \in S_i = L$ and $j \in S_j = R$.
- *Nodes in C (if non-empty) have no link to nodes in $L \cup R$*: If some node $c \in C$ has a link to some node $x \in L = S_i$, then c will be able to reach node i on a directed path via node x (since $x \in S_i$ has a path to i, by definition of set S_i). This would then imply that c must be in S_i, however, that contradicts the definition of C as $\mathcal{V} - F - L - R$. By a similar argument, nodes in C cannot have links to nodes in R.
- *There is no link from any node in L to nodes in R, and vice versa*: Recall that $L = S_i$ and $R = S_j$. If some node $x \in L$ has a link to a node $y \in R$, then x will have a directed path to node j via node y. However, this contradicts our assumption above that no node has directed paths to both i and j.

These observations together imply that $L \cup C \overset{1}{\not\Rightarrow} R$ and $C \cup R \overset{1}{\not\Rightarrow} L$. That is, $G(\mathcal{V}, \mathcal{E})$ does not satisfy Condition CCS. This is a contradiction. Thus, Lemma 2 is proved. □

The lemma defines the notion of a *source* node. Essentially, the lemma shows the existence of a directed rooted spanning tree in the induced graph G_F, which has the source node as the root. Presence of such "source" nodes (or root) is crucial in achieving consensus. Similar observations were first made in the context of fault-free consensus [5, 13], and also in the context of other versions of fault-tolerant consensus problems [8, 24, 23, 6] (although the exact manner in which the source node is identified differs for the different problems). The key distinguishing feature of the results presented in this paper is in the algorithms developed to solve the consensus problems. For instance, the structure of the above Min-Max algorithm – making alternating use of Min and Max function – has not been applied for consensus previously, to the best of our knowledge.

LEMMA 3. *Algorithm Min-Max satisfies termination, agreement and validity properties.*

PROOF. The proof of correctness assumes that graph $G(\mathcal{V}, \mathcal{E})$ satisfies Condition CCS. Since Algorithm Min-Max executes a fixed number of phases, its termination occurs in finite time. Validity is satisfied trivially as well. Now we prove that the algorithm satisfies the agreement property when the inputs are binary (0 or 1). We start by observing that $Compute(t, Min)$ never returns a value larger than parameter t passed to *Compute*, and $Compute(t, Max)$ never returns a value smaller than parameter t passed to *Compute*.

Fix an execution of the algorithm. Since there are $2f + 2$ phases. There must exist a pair of consecutive phases p^*, p^*+1 such that *no node crashes* in phases p^* and p^*+1. Without loss of generality, let p^* be the Min Phase (i.e., $p^* \bmod 2 = 0$) and $p^* + 1$ be the Max Phase.

Denote by F the set of nodes that crash before starting phase p^*. Lemma 2 shows the existence of a source node that has directed paths in G_F to all nodes in $\mathcal{V} - F$ (G_F is defined in the Lemma). In general, there may be multiple such source nodes in G_F. Consider the two cases below. In each case, we show that agreement is achieved.

- *Case I: There exists a source s in G_F for which* $v_s[p^* - 1] = 0$: Thus, during the Min Phase p^*, node s will call *Compute(0,Min)*. Then during the first round of *Compute* in phase p^*, those nodes in $\mathcal{V} - F$ with incoming links from node s will update their τ variable (within *Compute*) to be 0. Recall that we are presently assuming binary inputs. Since the source node has directed paths (of length at most $n - 1$) to all the nodes in G_F, it follows by induction that each node i in $\mathcal{V} - F$ will update its state τ_i to be 0 by the end of the $n - 1$ rounds performed within *Compute*. Thus, when *Compute* returns, $v_i[p^*]$ at each $i \in \mathcal{V} - F$ will be set to 0. It should be easy to see that the remaining phases will not change the value of v_i at the fault-free nodes, ensuring agreement when the algorithm terminates.
- *Case II: For each source s in G_F, $v_s[p^* - 1] = 1$*: In this case, we argue that, for each source s, $v_s[p^*] = 1$. Suppose, by way of contradiction, that each source s of G_F has $v_s[p^* - 1] = 1$, but there exists a source node s' for which $v_{s'}[p^*] = 0$. For this to happen, node s' must receive 0 on a path from some other *non-source* node z during phase p^*. This implies that $v_z[p^* - 1] = 0$; additionally, the fact that there exists a path in G_F from z to the source node s' implies that z is also a source in G_F. This contradicts the assumption that all source nodes in G_F have state equal to 1 at the start of phase p^*.

  This shows that, for each source node s, we have $v_s[p^*] = 1$. Now consider Max Phase $p^* + 1$. Recall that no node crashes in Phases p^* and $p^* + 1$. Thus, by an argument analogous to that used for Min Phase p^* in Case I above, it follows that, for all $i \in \mathcal{V} - F$, $v_i[p^* + 1] = 1$, achieving agreement. Any additional phases beyond phase $p^* + 1$ will not result in violation of the agreement, similar to Case I.

□

4.2.2 Multi-Valued Consensus

Algorithm Min-Max is proven correct for binary inputs. We will prove that the Algorithm MVC presented below performs exact consensus with inputs being some integer in the range $[0, K]$, where $K \geq 1$. Algorithm MVC uses Algorithm *Min-Max* as well as *Compute* defined above.

Algorithm MVC for node i

Initialization: $w_i[0] :=$ input of node i

Repeat for $l := 0$ to K

1. $w_i[l + 1] := Compute(w_i[l], Max)$
2. if $w_i[l] = l$, then $y_i[l] := 0$; otherwise, $y_i[l] := 1$
3. if Min-Max($y_i[l]$) returns 0, then
   terminate with output l

Step 3 of the algorithm performs Algorithm Min-Max, with node i passing $y_i[l]$ as the parameter to Min-Max. The "if" statement in step 3 checks the value returned by Algorithm Min-Max, and terminates the algorithm if the returned value is 0. Recall that the system is synchronous. Thus, all fault-free nodes perform *Min-Max* in step 3 in iteration l of the algorithm synchronously. Similarly, all fault-free nodes perform *Compute* (in step 1) in iteration l of the algorithm synchronously.

Correctness of Algorithm MVC.

The proof assumes that graph $G(\mathcal{V}, \mathcal{E})$ satisfies Condition CCS. Observe that Algorithm MVC specifies up to $K+1$ iterations, each iteration consisting of 3 steps enumerated in the algorithm. However, the algorithm may potentially terminate before completing all $K+1$ iterations (due to the check in step 3).

Since Min-Max is a binary consensus algorithm, each node that completes execution of Algorithm Min-Max in iteration l of MVC (i.e., without crashing before this instance of Min-Max) will obtain the same return value from Min-Max in iteration l. This ensures that all fault-free nodes terminate after completing an identical number of iterations. Now we present a lemma that is useful to prove correctness of Algorithm MVC.

LEMMA 4. *If a node i initiates iteration l of Algorithm MVC ($0 \le l \le K$), then (i) $w_i[l] \ge l$, and (ii) $w_i[l]$ equals the input of some node in the system.*

PROOF. The proof is by induction. Consider $l = 0$. $w_i[0]$ is initialized to be the input of node i. All inputs are in the range $[0, K]$, which implies that $w_i[0] \ge 0$. Thus, both parts of the statement of the lemma are true for $l = 0$.

Now assume that the statement of the lemma is true for some l, where $0 \le l < K$. Thus, for each node i that initiates iteration l, $w_i[l] \ge l$ and $w_i[l]$ is the input of some node in the system. Now, if Algorithm MVC terminates without performing iteration $l+1$, the proof of the lemma is complete. Therefore, let us now consider the case that Algorithm MVC is not terminated after completing l iterations. This implies that Min-Max($y_i[l]$) returns 1 in Step 3 of iteration l. Since Algorithm Min-Max is a binary consensus algorithm, the validity condition and the fact that it returns 1 implies that there exists some node j with $y_j[l] = 1$ such that (i) j did not crash before starting the execution of Min-Max($y_j[l]$) in step 3 of iteration l at node j, and (ii) node i has a path from node j consisting only of nodes that have *not* crashed before initiating step 3 of iteration l. Due to the rules for setting the value of $y_j[l]$ in step 2, and the fact that $y_j[l] = 1$, we can infer that that $w_j[l] > l$.

Finally, all nodes that are fault-free at least until initiating step 3 in iteration l must also be fault-free until they finish performing step 1 in iteration l. This implies that when *Compute* is performed in step 1 of iteration l, there exists a path from node j to node i. Existence of this path then ensures that, at node i, *Compute* returns a value $\ge w_j[l] > l$. Thus, $w_i[l+1] > l$. That is, $w_i[l+1] \ge l+1$.

Secondly, *Compute* at node i in iteration l will only return a value that is passed as the first parameter to *Compute* by at least one of the nodes initiating the execution of *Compute* in iteration l. Thus, $w_i[l+1]$ must equal $w_j[l]$ for some node j – by induction basis, $w_j[l]$ must be the input of some node in the syatem, and therefore, $w_i[l+1]$ also equals the input of that node. This concludes the proof. □

LEMMA 5. *Algorithm MVC satisfies termination, agreement and validity properties.*

PROOF. Termination in finite time occurs because Algorithm *Min-Max* and *Compute* return in finite time, and Algorithm MVC performs a finite number of iterations. As discussed earlier, all fault-free nodes terminate after completing an *identical* number of iterations. There are two cases to consider depending on the number of iterations completed before the algorithm is terminated.

Case 1: Algorithm MVC terminates only after completing the last iteration with $l = K$. Due to Lemma 4, for each node j that initiates iteration with $l = K$, we have $w_j[K] \ge K$. However, since all inputs are in the range $[0, K]$, and due to the use of *Compute* to update w_j, we have that $w_j[K] \le K$ as well. This means that $w_j[K] = K$. But by Lemma 4, $w_j[K]$ is also the input of some node in the system; it then follows that some node in the system had value K as the input.

Since $w_j[K] = K$, in iteration $l = K$, $y_j[K] = 0$ for each node j that completes step 2, and thus Min-Max can only return 0 in step 3, resulting in the output value of K at all fault-free nodes. Thus agreement is achieved. As argued above, K is the input of some node, the validity property is also satisfied.

Case 2: Algorithm MVC terminates after completing iteration $l < K$. This implies that all nodes that are fault-free until the end of iteration l must have necessarily obtained the return value of 0 from Min-Max in iteration l, and therefore, they will all terminate with output value l. Thus agreement is achieved. The fact that the return value from Min-Max is 0 implies that at least one node, say node j, must have initiated Min-Max in iteration l with $y_j[l] = 0$, implying (due to step 2) that $w_j[l] = l$. By Lemma 4, $w_j[l] = l$ must be the input of some node. Since l is also the output of the algorithm in this case, validity condition is also satisfied. □

5. APPROXIMATE CRASH-TOLERANT ASYNCHRONOUS CONSENSUS

Approximate crash-tolerant consensus must satisfy the following three properties, where $\epsilon > 0$: (i) *ϵ-agreement*: the difference between outputs at any two fault-free nodes is $< \epsilon$. (ii) *Validity*: the output at any fault-free node is within the range of the inputs at all the nodes. (iii) *Termination:* every fault-free node decides on an output in finite amount of time. For simplicity, we assume that the input at each node is some *real number* in the range $[0, K]$. Note that if $K < \epsilon$, then the problem is trivial, so K is assumed to be $\ge \epsilon$.

Theorem 2 in Section 3 presents the necessary and sufficient condition (named Condition CCA) for solving the above problem in directed graphs.

5.1 Necessity of Condition CCA

LEMMA 6. *Condition CCA is necessary for approximate crash-tolerant consensus in an asynchronous system.*

PROOF. The proof is by contradiction. Suppose that there exists a correct approximate consensus algorithm in $G(\mathcal{V}, \mathcal{E})$, but $G(\mathcal{V}, \mathcal{E})$ does not satisfy the condition in the lemma. That is, there exists a node partition L, C, R such that L and R are non-empty, and $L \cup C \overset{f+1}{\not\Rightarrow} R$ and $C \cup R \overset{f+1}{\not\Rightarrow} L$.

Let $O(L)$ denote the set of nodes in $C \cup R$ that have outgoing links to nodes in L, i.e., $O(L) = \{i \mid i \in C \cup R,\ N_i^+ \cap L \neq \emptyset\}$. Similarly, define $O(R) = \{j \mid j \in L \cup C,\ \ N_j^+ \cap R \neq \emptyset\}$. Since $L \cup C \overset{f+1}{\not\Rightarrow} R$ and $C \cup R \overset{f+1}{\not\Rightarrow} L$, we have $|O(L)| \leq f$ and $|O(R)| \leq f$.

Consider the scenario where (i) each node in L has input 0; (ii) each node in R has input ϵ; (iii) nodes in C (if non-empty) have arbitrary inputs in $[0, \epsilon]$; (iv) no node crashes; and (v) the message delay for communications channels from $O(L)$ to L and from $O(R)$ to R is arbitrarily large compared to all the other channels. Recall that such a scenario is possible, since we have assumed that the input range is $[0, K]$, where $K \geq \epsilon$. Consider nodes in L.

Since messages from the set $O(L)$ take arbitrarily long to arrive at the nodes in L, and $|O(L)| \leq f$, from the perspective of the nodes in L, the nodes in $O(L)$ appear to have crashed. Thus, nodes in L must decide on their output without waiting to hear from the nodes in $O(L)$. Consequently, to satisfy the validity property, the output at each node in L has to be 0, since 0 is the input of all the nodes in L. Similarly, nodes in R must decide their output without hearing from the nodes in $O(R)$; they must choose output as ϵ, because the input at all the nodes in R is ϵ. Thus, the ϵ-agreement property is violated, since the difference between outputs at fault-free nodes is not $< \epsilon$. This is a contradiction. □

5.2 Sufficiency of Condition CCA

We prove the sufficiency of Condition CCA constructively by presenting an algorithm, called Algorithm WA (Wait-and-Average), and proving its correctness. The algorithm, presented below, assumes that each node has the knowledge of the network topology, and the algorithm proceeds in *asynchronous* phases. In each phase, nodes flood messages containing the current value of their state variable v, their identifier, and a phase index. Each node i waits until it has received an "adequate" set of values from other nodes, where "adequate" is made precise by Condition WAIT defined below. Then, node i updates its state variable v to be the *average* of set of values received in the current phase, and then proceeds to the next phase. When node i has finished p_{end} phases, it produces an output that equals the current value of state variable v; p_{end} is an integer $> \log_{n/(n-1)} \frac{K}{\epsilon}$.

In Algorithm WA, observe that $heard_i[p]$ is the set of nodes from which node i has received values during phase p. As seen in the algorithm pseudo-code, node i performs the averaging operation to update its state variable v_i when Condition WAIT below holds for the first time. Algorithm WA is an extension of an approximate consensus algorithm for complete graphs [10]. The key contribution of our work is to identify *Condition WAIT*.

Condition WAIT: For $F_i \subseteq \mathcal{V}$, where $|F_i| \leq f$, denote by $reach_i(F_i)$ the set of nodes that have paths to node i in the subgraph induced by the nodes in $\mathcal{V} - F_i$ (i.e., the paths do not contain nodes in F_i). Condition *WAIT* is satisfied at node i if *there exists* a set $F_i \subseteq \mathcal{V}$, where $|F_i| \leq f$, such that $reach_i(F_i) \subseteq heard_i[p]$. ($reach_i(F_i)$ may be different in each phase, since it depends on the message delays. For simplicity, we ignore the phase index p in the notation.)

Algorithm WA for node $i \in \mathcal{V}$

---

p_{end} is an integer $> \log_{n/(n-1)} \frac{K}{\epsilon}$.

- $v_i[0]$:= input at node i
- For Phase $p := 1$ to p_{end}:
  - On entering phase p:
    $R_i[p] := \{v_i[p-1]\}$
    $heard_i[p] := \{i\}$
    Send message $(v_i[p-1], i, p)$ to
    all the outgoing neighbors
  - When message (h, j, p) is received for the *first time*:
    $R_i[p] := R_i[p] \cup \{h\}$ // $R_i[p]$ is a multiset
    $heard_i[p] := heard_i[p] \cup \{j\}$
    Send message (h, j, p) to
    all the outgoing neighbors
  - When Condition *WAIT* holds for the first time in phase p:
    $v_i[p] := \frac{\sum_{v \in R_i[p]} v}{|R_i[p]|}$
    If $p < p_{end}$, begin the next phase
    Else, output v_i

Note that $R_i[p]$ is a multiset, and thus may contain multiple instances of the same value.

Correctness of Algorithm WA.

We first prove a useful lemma. Let $heard_i^*[p]$ denote the set $heard_i[p]$ when Condition WAIT holds for the first time at node i in phase p. The correctness of Algorithm WA relies on the following lemma, which assumes that graph $G(\mathcal{V}, \mathcal{E})$ satisfies condition CCA. In a given execution, define $F[p]$ as the nodes that have *not* computed value $v[p]$ in phase p, i.e., nodes in $F[p]$ have crashed before computing $v[p]$.

LEMMA 7. *For phase $p \geq 1$, consider two nodes $i, j \in \mathcal{V} - F[p]$. Then, $heard_i^*[p] \cap heard_j^*[p] \neq \emptyset$.*

PROOF. By construction, there exist two sets F_i and F_j such that Condition WAIT holds for sets $heard_i^*[p]$ and F_i at node i, and for sets $heard_j^*[p]$ and F_j at node j. In other words, (i) $F_i \subseteq \mathcal{V}$ and $|F_i| \leq f$, (ii) $F_j \subseteq \mathcal{V}$ and $|F_j| \leq f$, (iii) $reach_i(F_i) \subseteq heard_i^*[p]$, and (iv) $reach_j(F_j) \subseteq heard_j^*[p]$. If $reach_i(F_i) \cap reach_j(F_j) \neq \emptyset$, then the proof is complete, since $reach_i(F_i) \subseteq heard_i^*[p]$ and $reach_j(F_j) \subseteq heard_j^*[p]$. Thus, $heard_i^*[p] \cap heard_j^*[p] \neq \emptyset$.

Now, consider the case when $reach_i(F_i) \cap reach_j(F_j) = \emptyset$. We will derive a contradiction in this case. Recall that $reach_i(F_i)$ is defined as the set of nodes that have paths to node i in the subgraph induced by the nodes in $\mathcal{V} - F_i$. This implies that in graph G, the incoming neighbors of set $reach_i(F_i)$ are contained in set F_i. Similarly, in graph G, the incoming neighbors of set $reach_j(F_j)$ are contained in set F_j.

In graph G, we will find subsets of nodes L, C, R that violate Condition CCA. Let $L = reach_i(F_i)$, $R = reach_j(F_j)$ and $C = \mathcal{V} - L - R$. Observe that since $reach_i(F_i) \cap reach_j(F_j) = \emptyset$, L, C, R form a partition of $\mathcal{V}$. Moreover, $i \in reach_i(F_i)$ and $j \in reach_j(F_j)$; hence, $L = reach_i(F_i)$

and $R = reach_j(F_j)$ are both non-empty. Let $N(L)$ be the set of incoming neighbors of set L. By definition, $N(L)$ is contained in $R \cup C$. Since $L = reach_i(F_i)$, the only nodes that may be in $N(L)$ are also in F_i as argued above, i.e., $N(L) \subseteq F_i$. By assumption, $|F_i| \leq f$. Therefore, $|N(L)| \leq f$, which implies that $R \cup C \overset{f+1}{\not\Rightarrow} L$. Similarly, we can argue that $L \cup C \overset{f+1}{\not\Rightarrow} R$. These two conditions together show that G violates Condition CCA, a contradiction. Thus, $reach_i(F_i) \cap reach_j(F_j) \neq \emptyset$, which implies that $heard_i^*[p] \cap heard_j^*[p] \neq \emptyset$. This completes the proof. □

LEMMA 8. *Algorithm MVC satisfies termination, ϵ-agreement and validity properties.*

PROOF. Validity is trivially true. Denote by F the set of faulty nodes in an execution. Then, observe that Condition WAIT eventually holds at each fault-free node i in each phase $p \leq p_{end}$, because by choosing $F_i = F$, $reach_i(F) \subseteq heard_i[p]$ eventually. This together with the fact that p_{end} is bounded imply termination. Now, we prove that Algorithm WA achieves ϵ-agreement. The methodology in this proof is borrowed from other related work (e.g., [10, 3, 17, 5]).

Recall that $F[p]$ is defined as the nodes that have *not* computed value $v[p]$ in phase p, i.e., nodes in $F[p]$ have crashed before computing $v[p]$. Thus, $\mathcal{V} - F[p]$ is the set of nodes that complete the computation of $v[p]$. In the discussion below, let us denote by $\|x\|$ the absolute value of a real number x. For $p \geq 1$, define

$$M[p] = \max_{i \in \mathcal{V}-F[p]} v_i[p] \quad \text{and} \quad m[p] = \min_{i \in \mathcal{V}-F[p]} v_i[p] \quad (1)$$

With a slight abuse of terminology, let $M[0]$ and $m[0]$ denote the upper bound and the lower bound on the inputs, respectively. Define $\psi[p]$ as the maximum difference between states at nodes in $\mathcal{V} - F[p]$ in the end of phase p. Thus,

$$\psi[p] = \max_{i,j \in \mathcal{V}-F[p]} \|v_i[p] - v_j[p]\| = M[p] - m[p] \quad (2)$$

By definition of $m[p-1]$ and $M[p-1]$, for each node $k \in \mathcal{V} - F[p-1]$, we have

$$m[p-1] \leq v_k[p-1] \leq M[p-1] \quad (3)$$

$$m[p-1] \leq v_k[p-1] \leq M[p-1] \quad (4)$$

Now consider nodes $i, j \in \mathcal{V} - F[p]$. The multiset $R_i[p]$ at node i changes when node i receives new messages. Let $R_i^*[p]$ denote the multiset $R_i[p]$ used by node i to compute $v_i[p]$. Similarly, let $R_j^*[p]$ denote the multiset $R_j[p]$ used by node j to compute $v_j[p]$.

Let $r_i = |R_i^*[p]|$, the size of the multiset $R_i^*[p]$. Similarly, let $r_j = |R_i^*[p]|$. For brevity, the notation r_i and r_j does not include the phase index $[p]$.

By Lemma 7, there exists a common value in $R_i^*[p]$ and $R_j^*[p]$. Denote by c the common value. Note that by construction c is a state of some node in $\mathcal{V} - F[p-1]$. Thus, $m[p-1] \leq c \leq M[p-1]$. Define

$$\gamma = \frac{1}{n}.$$

By Algorithm WA, we have

$$\begin{aligned}
v_i[p] &= \sum_{k \in R_i^*[p]} \frac{1}{r_i} v_k[p-1] \\
&\leq \frac{c}{r_i} + (1 - \frac{1}{r_i})M[p-1] \quad \text{due to (1)} \\
&\leq \gamma c + (\frac{1}{r_i} - \gamma)c + (1 - \frac{1}{r_i})M[p-1] \\
&\leq \gamma c + (1-\gamma)M[p-1] \qquad (5)
\end{aligned}$$

The last inequality is because $\gamma \leq \frac{1}{r_i}$ and $c \leq M[p-1]$.

$$\begin{aligned}
v_j[p] &= \sum_{k \in R_j^*[p]} \frac{1}{r_j} v_k[p-1] \\
&\geq \frac{c}{r_j} + (1 - \frac{1}{r_j})m[p-1] \quad \text{due to (1)} \\
&\geq \gamma c + (\frac{1}{r_j} - \gamma)c + (1 - \frac{1}{r_j})m[p-1] \\
&\geq \gamma c + (1-\gamma)m[p-1] \qquad (6)
\end{aligned}$$

The last inequality is because $\gamma \leq \frac{1}{r_j}$ and $c \geq m[p-1]$. Now, subtracting (6) from (5), we get

$$v_i[p] - v_j[p] \leq (1-\gamma)(M[p-1] - m[p-1]) \quad (7)$$

By swapping the role of i and j above, we can show that

$$v_j[p] - v_i[p] \leq (1-\gamma)(M[p-1] - m[p-1]) \quad (8)$$

(7) and (8) together imply that

$$\begin{aligned}
\|v_i[p] - v_j[p]\| &\leq (1-\gamma)(M[p-1] - m[p-1]) \\
&\leq (1-\gamma)\psi[p-1] \qquad \text{due to (2)}
\end{aligned}$$

Note that the first inequality is because $M[p-1] \geq m[p-1]$. The above inequality holds for each pair of nodes i, j that have computed $v[p]$ in phase p, so we have

$$\max_{i,j \in \mathcal{V}-F[p]} \|v_i[p] - v_j[p]\| \leq (1-\gamma)\psi[p-1]$$

This together with (2) implies that

$$M[p] - m[p] \leq (1-\gamma)(M[p-1] - m[p-1]) \quad (9)$$

By repeated application of (9), we get

$$M[p] - m[p] \leq (1-\gamma)^p (M[0] - m[0]) \quad (10)$$

Therefore, for a given $\epsilon > 0$, if

$$p > \log_{1/(1-\gamma)} \frac{M[0] - m[0]}{\epsilon}, \quad (11)$$

then

$$M[p] - m[p] < \epsilon \quad (12)$$

Recall that we have assumed that the input range is $[0, K]$, where $K \geq \epsilon$. Thus, $M[0] \leq K$ and $m[0] \geq 0$. Also, $\gamma = \frac{1}{n}$ by definition. Then, if we choose

$$p_{end} > \log_{n/(n-1)} \frac{K}{\epsilon},$$

then Algorithm WA satisfies ϵ-agreement property due to (11) and (12). □

6. EXACT BYZANTINE CONSENSUS IN SYNCHRONOUS SYSTEMS

An exact Byzantine consensus algorithm with *binary* inputs must satisfy the following properties: (i) *Agreement*: the output (i.e., decision) at all the fault-free nodes is identical. (ii) *Validity*: the output of every fault-free node equals the input of a fault-free node. (iii) *Termination:* every fault-free node decides on an output in finite amount of time. For multi-valued Byzantine consensus, we consider the weak version of validity [14]: If all fault-free nodes have the same input, then the output of every fault-free node equals its input. Theorem 3 in Section 3 presents the necessary and sufficient condition (named Condition BCS) for solving the above problem in directed graphs.

Due to lack of space, the proofs and the algorithms are presented in [21]. We show [21] that BCS is necessary using the state-machine approach [11, 9]. To prove sufficiency, we first develop an algorithm to achieve Byzantine consensus with *binary* inputs, and then use it to achieve multi-valued Byzantine consensus. We now introduce the notion of *reduced graph* and then present an observation that is useful to construct a Byzantine consensus algorithm in directed graphs that satisfy Condition BCS.

DEFINITION 2. **(Reduced Graph)** *For a given graph $G(\mathcal{V},\mathcal{E})$, and sets $F\subset\mathcal{V}$, $F_1\subset\mathcal{V}-F$, such that $|F|\le f$ and $|F_1|\le f$, reduced graph $G_{F,F_1}(\mathcal{V}_{F,F_1},\mathcal{E}_{F,F_1})$ is defined as follows: (i) $\mathcal{V}_{F,F_1}=\mathcal{V}-F$, and (ii) $\mathcal{E}_{F,F_1}$ is obtained by removing from $\mathcal{E}$ all the links incident on the nodes in F, and all the outgoing links from nodes in F_1. That is, $\mathcal{E}_{F,F_1}=\mathcal{E}-\{(i,j)\mid i\in F \text{ or } j\in F\}-\{(i,j)\mid i\in F_1\}$.*

Observation: Suppose $G(\mathcal{V},\mathcal{E})$ satisfies Condition BCS. Then, for any $F\subset\mathcal{V}$ and $F_1\subset\mathcal{V}-F$, where $|F|\le f$ and $|F_1|\le f$, there exists a set of at least $f+1$ nodes $S\subseteq\mathcal{V}-F$ such that (i) nodes in S are strongly connected in reduced graph G_{F,F_1}, and (ii) for each $j\in\mathcal{V}-F-S$, there exist at least $f+1$ pairwise node-disjoint paths from S to j in G that do not contain any nodes in F.

The proposed algorithm for binary consensus maintains a state variable at each node, with the invariant that this state variables at each fault-free node aways has a "valid" value, where a value is "valid" if it is an input at some fault-free node. Intuitively, the above $f+1$ disjoint paths from the nodes in S to nodes in $\mathcal{V}-F-S$ provide adequate redundancy to allow propagation of values from the nodes in S to the nodes in $\mathcal{V}-F-S$, with the guarantee that any potential message tampering by faulty nodes would not cause the recipients to accept an "invalid" value. In the fortuitous event that the nodes in F are faulty and the nodes in S (which are fault-free) have the same valid state variable, this value is then propagated to all the fault-free nodes, achieving consensus. The algorithm ensures that this fortuitous event occurs at least once during the execution. The rest of the details are presented in [21] for lack of space.

7. DISCUSSION

As noted in Section 3, Condition CCS, CCA, and BCS capture how information can "flow between" different subsets of fault-free nodes despite the presence of faulty nodes under different synchrony assumptions. This section compares the three conditions and the condition for undirected graphs identified in [9, 11].

Comparison of Condition CCS, CCA, and BCS.

LEMMA 9. *Conditions CCS, CCA and BCS are progressively stronger. In particular, (i) Condition BCS implies Condition CCA, but not vice-versa, and (ii) Condition CCA implies Condition CCS, but not vice-versa.*

PROOF.

- Proof of claim (i):

  It should be easy to see that Condition CCA can be viewed as a special case of Condition BCS, if we force set F in Condition BCS to be an empty set. Therefore, Condition BCS implies Condition CCA.

  A clique consisting of $2f+1$ nodes satisfies Condition CCA but not Condition BCS; thus, (not surprisingly) Condition CCA does not imply BCS.

- Proof of claim (ii):

  We will prove that CCA implies CCS by contradiction. Suppose that graph G does not satisfy Condition CCS, i.e., there exists a node partition F,L,C,R of $\mathcal{V}$ such that $L\cup C\overset{1}{\not\Rightarrow}R$ and $R\cup C\overset{1}{\not\Rightarrow}L$. Then, define $C'=C\cup F$. Due to the fact that $|F|\le f$, $L\cup C'\overset{f+1}{\not\Rightarrow}R$ and $R\cup C'\overset{f+1}{\not\Rightarrow}L$, violating Condition CCA. This proves that CCA implies CCS.

  Consider the example network in Figure 2 in Section 3. This network tolerates 1 crash fault in synchronous systems, since it satisfies Condition CCS; however, it does not satisfy Condition CCA when $L=\{v_1\}, C=\emptyset$ and $R=\{v_2,v_3\}$. Thus, CCS does not imply CCA.

□

Comparison of Conditions in Undirected and Directed Graphs.

Previously necessary conditions for undirected graphs [11, 9, 3, 17] all imply that each pair of fault-free nodes can communicate *reliably* despite the presence of f faulty nodes. In particular, this is true due to $f+1$ connectivity in case of crash faults, and $2f+1$ connectivity for Byzantine faults. Specifically, $2f+1$-connectivity implies the presence of $2f+1$ node-disjoint paths between nodes that are not neighbors, allowing each pair of nodes to communicate reliably despite f Byzantine faulty nodes. In contrast, in *directed graphs,* to be able to achieve consensus, it is *not necessary* for **all** node pairs to be able to communicate with each other reliably (even in just one direction). This is a manifestation of the "asymmetry" noted in our discussion above. For instance, the network in Figure 2 can tolerate 1 crash fault in a synchronous setting; however, v_3 does not have paths to the other nodes. Now, consider a network that consists of 6 nodes, 4 of which (say, w_1,w_2,w_3,w_4) form a clique, and also have directed links to nodes w_5 and w_6. Node w_5 has no path to w_6 and vice versa. Yet, Byzantine consensus can be achieved easily by first reaching consensus within the 4-node clique, and then propagating the consensus value (for the 4-node consensus) to nodes w_5 and w_6. Nodes w_5 and w_6 can choose majority of the values received from the nodes in the 4-node clique as its own output. It should be easy to see that this algorithm works correctly for inputs in $\{0,1\}$ as required in the Byzantine consensus formulation considered in this work. However, nodes w_5 and w_6 cannot communicate reliably with each other (in either direction).

There exist graphs that satisfy Condition BCS wherein reliable communication may not be feasible in either direction across a given cut. In particular, consider the network in Figure 1 in Section 3 again. Observe that there are only 4 directed links from K_1 to K_2, and 4 directed links from K_2 to K_1. Thus, reliable communication is *not guaranteed* across the cut (K_1, K_2) in either direction when $f = 2$ (Byzantine faults). Yet, Byzantine consensus is achievable in synchronous systems since this graph satisfies Condition BCS for $f = 2$. We prove this claim in [21].

8. SUMMARY

Necessary and sufficient conditions for solving the following problems in *directed* graphs are presented: (i) exact crash-tolerant consensus in *synchronous* systems, (ii) approximate crash-tolerant consensus in *asynchronous* systems, and (iii) exact Byzantine consensus in *synchronous* systems. Development of efficient algorithms for solving these problems is a topic for future work. Also, tight condition for approximate Byzantine asynchronous consensus in directed graphs remains unknown.

9. REFERENCES

[1] I. Abraham, Y. Amit, and D. Dolev. Optimal resilience asynchronous approximate agreement. In *OPODIS*, pages 229–239, 2004.

[2] E. Alchieri, A. Bessani, J. Silva Fraga, and F. Greve. Byzantine consensus with unknown participants. In T. Baker, A. Bui, and S. Tixeuil, editors, *Principles of Distributed Systems*, volume 5401 of *Lecture Notes in Computer Science*, pages 22–40. Springer Berlin Heidelberg, 2008.

[3] H. Attiya and J. Welch. *Distributed Computing: Fundamentals, Simulations, and Advanced Topics.* Wiley Series on Parallel and Distributed Computing, 2004.

[4] P. Bansal, P. Gopal, A. Gupta, K. Srinathan, and P. K. Vasishta. Byzantine agreement using partial authentication. In *Proceedings of the 25th international conference on Distributed computing*, DISC'11, pages 389–403, Berlin, Heidelberg, 2011. Springer-Verlag.

[5] D. P. Bertsekas and J. N. Tsitsiklis. *Parallel and Distributed Computation: Numerical Methods.* Optimization and Neural Computation Series. Athena Scientific, 1997.

[6] M. Biely, P. Robinson, and U. Schmid. Agreement in directed dynamic networks. In *Structural Information and Communication Complexity*, volume 7355 of *Lecture Notes in Computer Science*, pages 73–84. Springer Berlin Heidelberg, 2012.

[7] M. Biely, P. Robinson, U. Schmid, M. Schwarz, and K. Winkler. Gracefully degrading consensus and k-set agreement in directed dynamic networks. *CoRR*, abs/1408.0620, 2014.

[8] B. Charron-Bost, M. Függer, and T. Nowak. Approximate consensus in highly dynamic networks. *CoRR*, abs/1408.0620, 2014.

[9] D. Dolev. The Byzantine generals strike again. *Journal of Algorithms*, 3(1):14–30, March 1982.

[10] D. Dolev, N. A. Lynch, S. S. Pinter, E. W. Stark, and W. E. Weihl. Reaching approximate agreement in the presence of faults. *J. ACM*, 33:499–516, May 1986.

[11] M. J. Fischer, N. A. Lynch, and M. Merritt. Easy impossibility proofs for distributed consensus problems. In *Proceedings of the fourth annual ACM symposium on Principles of distributed computing*, PODC '85, pages 59–70, NY, USA, 1985. ACM.

[12] M. J. Fischer, N. A. Lynch, and M. S. Paterson. Impossibility of distributed consensus with one faulty process. *J. ACM*, 32:374–382, April 1985.

[13] A. Jadbabaie, J. Lin, and A. Morse. Coordination of groups of mobile autonomous agents using nearest neighbor rules. *Automatic Control, IEEE Transactions on*, 48(6):988–1001, June 2003.

[14] L. Lamport. The weak Byzantine generals problem. *J. ACM*, 30(3):668–676, July 1983.

[15] H. LeBlanc, H. Zhang, X. Koutsoukos, and S. Sundaram. Resilient asymptotic consensus in robust networks. *IEEE Journal on Selected Areas in Communications: Special Issue on In-Network Computation*, 31:766–781, April 2013.

[16] H. LeBlanc, H. Zhang, S. Sundaram, and X. Koutsoukos. Consensus of multi-agent networks in the presence of adversaries using only local information. *HiCoNs*, 2012.

[17] N. A. Lynch. *Distributed Algorithms.* Morgan Kaufmann, 1996.

[18] A. Maurer, S. Tixeuil, and X. Défago. Reliable communication in a dynamic network in the presence of Byzantine faults. *CoRR*, abs/1402.0121, 2014.

[19] M. Pease, R. Shostak, and L. Lamport. Reaching agreement in the presence of faults. *J. ACM*, 27(2):228–234, Apr. 1980.

[20] L. Su and N. Vaidya. Reaching approximate Byzantine consensus with multi-hop communication. *CoRR*, abs/1411.5282, 2014.

[21] L. Tseng and N. H. Vaidya. Exact Byzantine consensus in directed graphs. *CoRR*, abs/1208.5075, 2012.

[22] L. Tseng and N. H. Vaidya. Crash-Tolerant Consensus in Directed Graphs. *CoRR*, abs/1412.8532, 2014.

[23] L. Tseng and N. H. Vaidya. Iterative approximate Byzantine consensus under a generalized fault model. In *International Conference on Distributed Computing and Networking (ICDCN)*, January 2013.

[24] N. H. Vaidya, L. Tseng, and G. Liang. Iterative approximate Byzantine consensus in arbitrary directed graphs. In *Proceedings of the thirty-first annual ACM symposium on Principles of distributed computing*, PODC '12. ACM, 2012.

[25] H. Zhang and S. Sundaram. Robustness of complex networks with implications for consensus and contagion. In *Proceedings of CDC 2012, the 51st IEEE Conference on Decision and Control*, 2012.

[26] H. Zhang and S. Sundaram. Robustness of distributed algorithms to locally bounded adversaries. In *Proceedings of ACC 2012, the 31st American Control Conference*, 2012.

Minimal Synchrony for Byzantine Consensus

Zohir Bouzid
IRISA
Université de Rennes
zohir.bouzid@gmail.com

Achour Mostéfaoui
LINA, Université de Nantes
44322 Nantes, France
Mostefaoui@univ-nantes.fr

Michel Raynal
Institut Universitaire de France
& IRISA, Université de Rennes
raynal@irisa.fr

ABSTRACT

Solving the consensus problem requires in one way or another that the underlying system satisfies some synchrony assumption. Considering an asynchronous message-passing system of n processes where (a) up to $t < n/3$ may commit Byzantine failures, and (b) each pair of processes is connected by two uni-directional channels (with possibly different timing properties), this paper investigates the synchrony assumption required to solve consensus, and presents a signature-free consensus algorithm whose synchrony requirement is the existence of a process that is an *eventual* $\langle t+1\rangle$*bisource*. Such a process p is a correct process that eventually has (a) timely input channels from t correct processes and (b) timely output channels to t correct processes (these input and output channels can connect p to different subsets of processes). As this synchrony condition was shown to be necessary and sufficient in the stronger asynchronous system model (a) enriched with message authentication, and (b) where the channels are bidirectional and have the same timing properties in both directions, it follows that it is also necessary and sufficient in the weaker system model considered in the paper. In addition to the fact that it closes a long-lasting problem related to Byzantine agreement, a noteworthy feature of the proposed algorithm lies in its design simplicity, which is a first-class property.

Categories and Subject Descriptors

C.2.4 [**Computer-Communication Network**]: Distributed Systems *-distributed applications, network operating systems*; D.4.5 [**Operating Systems**] Reliability *-fault-tolerance*; F.1.1 [**Computation by Abstract Devices**]: Models of Computation *-Computability theory*

General Terms: Algorithms, Reliability, Theory

Keywords:
Adopt-commit, Asynchronous message-passing, Byzantine process, Consensus, Distributed algorithm, Eventual timely channel, Feasibility condition, Lower bound, Optimal resilience, Reliable broadcast, Signature-free algorithm, Synchrony assumption.

Permission to make digital or hard copies of all or part of this work for personal or classroom use is granted without fee provided that copies are not made or distributed for profit or commercial advantage and that copies bear this notice and the full citation on the first page. Copyrights for components of this work owned by others than ACM must be honored. Abstracting with credit is permitted. To copy otherwise, or republish, to post on servers or to redistribute to lists, requires prior specific permission and/or a fee. Request permissions from permissions@acm.org.
PODC'15, July 21–23, 2015, Donostia-San Sebastián, Spain.
Copyright © 2015 ACM 978-1-4503-3617-8 /15/07 ...$15.00.
DOI: http://dx.doi.org/10.1145/2767386.2767418..

1. INTRODUCTION

Byzantine consensus.

A process has a *Byzantine* behavior when it behaves arbitrarily [26]. This bad functioning can be intentional (malicious behavior, e.g., due to intrusion) or simply the result of a transient fault that altered the local state of a process, thereby modifying its execution in an unpredictable way.

We are interested here in the *consensus* problem in message-passing distributed systems prone to Byzantine process failures whatever their origin. Consensus is an agreement problem in which each process first proposes a value and then decides on a value [26]. In a Byzantine failure context, the consensus problem is defined by the following properties: every non-faulty process decides (termination), no two non-faulty processes decide differently (agreement), and the decided value is not arbitrary, i.e., it is related in one way or another to values proposed by non-faulty processes (validity).

Context of the paper.

A synchronous distributed system is characterized by the fact that both processes and communication channels are synchronous (or timely) [3, 21, 28]. This means that there are known bounds on process speed and message transfer delays. Let t denote the maximum number of processes that can be faulty in a system made up of n processes. In a synchronous system, consensus can be solved (a) for any value of t (i.e., $t < n$) in the crash failure model, (b) for $t < n/2$ in the general omission failure model, and (c) for $t < n/3$ in the Byzantine failure model [20, 26]. Moreover, these bounds are tight.

Differently, when all channels are asynchronous (i.e., when there is no bound on message transfer delays), it is impossible to solve consensus even if we consider the weakest failure model (namely, the process crash failure model) and assume that at most one process may be faulty (i.e., $t = 1$) [15]. It trivially follows that Byzantine consensus is impossible to solve in a failure-prone asynchronous distributed system.

As Byzantine consensus can be solved in a synchronous system and cannot in an asynchronous system, a natural question that comes to mind is the following "*When considering the synchrony-to-asynchrony axis, which is the weakest synchrony assumption that allows Byzantine consensus to be solved in a message-passing system?*" This long-lasting question is the issue addressed in this paper. To that end, the paper considers a synchrony assumption capturing both the structure and the number of eventually synchronous channels among correct processes.

Related work.

Several approaches to solve Byzantine consensus have been proposed. We consider here only deterministic approaches[1]. One consists in enriching the asynchronous system (hence the system is no longer fully asynchronous) with a failure detector, namely, a device that provides processes with (possibly unreliable) hints on failures [10]. Basically, in one way or another, a failure detector encapsulates synchrony assumptions. Failure detectors suited to Byzantine behavior have been proposed and used to solved Byzantine consensus (e.g., [13, 16, 19]).

Another approach proposed to solve Byzantine consensus consists in directly assuming that some channels satisfy a synchrony property ("directly" means that the synchrony property is not hidden inside a higher level abstraction such as a failure detector). This approach, which relies on the notion of an $\diamond\langle x+1\rangle$*bisource* (read "$\diamond$" as "eventual"), was introduced in [1]. Intuitively, this notion states that there is a correct process that has x input channels from correct processes and x output channels to correct processes that are eventually timely [12, 14] (the "+1" comes from the fact that it is assumed that each process has a "virtual" input/output channel from itself to itself, which is always timely).

Considering asynchronous systems with Byzantine processes without message authentication, it is shown in [1] that Byzantine consensus can be solved if the system has an $\diamond\langle n-t\rangle$bisource (all other channels being possibly fully asynchronous). Moreover, the process that is the $\diamond\langle n-t\rangle$bisource can never be explicitly known by the whole set of processes. Considering systems with message authentication, a Byzantine consensus algorithm is presented in [25] that requires an $\diamond\langle t+1\rangle$bisource only. As for Byzantine consensus in synchronous systems, all these algorithms assume $t < n/3$. Finally, it has been shown in [4] that the "$\diamond\langle t+1\rangle$bisource" synchrony assumption is a necessary and sufficient condition to solve Byzantine consensus in asynchronous bi-directionnal message-passing systems, enriched with message authentication.

Content of the paper.

This paper presents a signature-free Byzantine consensus algorithm for asynchronous message-passing systems, which requires only the two assumptions: $t < n/3$ and the existence of an $\diamond\langle t+1\rangle$bisource. As these assumptions are necessary and sufficient to solve Byzantine consensus in the asynchronous model enriched with message authentication [4], it follows that (a) the existence of an $\diamond\langle t+1\rangle$bisource is necessary and sufficient to solve Byzantine consensus in an asynchronous signature-free system, and (b) the proposed algorithm is optimal with respect to underlying synchrony assumptions.

The proposed algorithm, which is round-based, assumes that at most $m \leq \lfloor \frac{n-(t+1)}{t} \rfloor$ different values can be proposed by the correct processes (see also the paragraph "variant" in the conclusion). To attain its goal, it relies on a modular construction involving two communication abstractions and two distributed objects. More precisely, we have the following.

- The communication abstractions are the one-to-all *reliable broadcast* (RB) abstraction introduced in [7], and a very simple new communication abstraction that we call *cooperative broadcast* (CB). As suggested by its name, it is an all-to-all broadcast abstraction. This abstraction, which uses RB as an underlying subroutine, is particularly simple. It actually captures important cooperation properties, which make easier the design of upper layer distributed agreement algorithms.
- The two distributed objects are the following ones (the implementation of each of them use the underlying CB broadcast abstraction).
  - The first object is a message-passing version of the *adopt-commit* (AC) object (introduced in [17]) appropriately modified to cope with up to $t < n/3$ Byzantine processes. Each round of the consensus algorithm uses a specific AC object. The aim of these objects is to prevent the consensus safety property from being violated.
  - The second object is a round-based object called *eventual agreement* (EA) object. Its aim is to ensure the consensus termination property. Hence, its implementation relies on the $\diamond\langle t+1\rangle$bisource assumption.

It is important to emphasize that, when designing the algorithm presented in the paper, modularity and simplicity were considered as first class design criteria. The algorithm presented is only the last step of a long quest: "Simplicity does not precede complexity, but follows it" (Alan Perlis, First Turing Award).

Road map.

The paper is made up of 7 sections. Section 2 presents the basic underlying asynchronous Byzantine computation model, the RB broadcast abstraction and the new CB broadcast abstraction. Section 3 presents an AC object suited to message-passing systems prone to Byzantine failures. Then, Section 4 presents the $\diamond\langle t+1\rangle$bisource behavioral assumption. Section 5 presents the round-based eventual agreement object. Section 6 pieces together the previous abstractions to obtain the synchrony-optimal Byzantine consensus algorithm. Finally, Section 7 concludes the paper. Due to page limitation, the missing proofs can be found in [6].

2. BASIC MODEL, RELIABLE BROADCAST, AND COOPERATIVE BROADCAST

2.1 Processes, communication network, and failure model

Asynchronous processes.

The system is made up of a finite set Π of $n > 1$ sequential processes, namely $\Pi = \{p_1, \ldots, p_n\}$. As local processing times are negligible with respect to message transfer delays, they are considered as being equal to zero. Both notations $i \in Y$ and $p_i \in Y$ are used to say that p_i belongs to the set Y.

Communication network.

The processes communicate by exchanging messages through an asynchronous reliable point-to-point network. "Asynchronous" means that there is no bound on message transfer delays. "Reliable" means that the network does not lose, duplicate, modify, or create messages. "Point-to-point" means that any pair of processes is connected by two uni-directional channels (one in each direction). Hence, when a process receives a message, it can identify its sender. Moreover, as there is no message loss, all message transfer delays are finite.

A process p_i sends a message to a process p_j by invoking the primitive "send TAG(m) to p_j", where TAG is the type of the message and m its content. To simplify the presentation, it is assumed

[1]Enriching the system with random numbers allows for the design of randomized Byzantine consensus algorithms. These algorithms are characterized by a probabilistic termination property (e.g., [5, 9, 22, 27]).

that a process can send messages to itself. A process p_i receives a message by executing the primitive "receive()". Then say that the message is *received* by p_i.

Failure model.

Up to t processes can exhibit a *Byzantine* behavior. A Byzantine process is a process that behaves arbitrarily: it can crash, fail to send or receive messages, send arbitrary messages, start in an arbitrary state, perform arbitrary state transitions, etc. Moreover, Byzantine processes can collude to "pollute" the computation (e.g., by sending messages with the same content, while they should send messages with distinct content if they were non-faulty).

A process that exhibits a Byzantine behavior is called *faulty*. Otherwise, it is *correct* or *non-faulty*. Given an execution, $\mathcal{C}$ denotes the set of processes that are correct in this execution.

Let us notice that, as each pair of processes is connected by a channel, no Byzantine process can impersonate another process. Moreover, it is assumed that the Byzantine processes do not control the network (they can neither corrupt the messages sent by non-faulty processes, nor modify the message reception schedule).

Discarding messages from Byzantine processes.

If, according to its algorithm, a process p_j is assumed to send a single message TAG() to a process p_i, then p_i processes only the first message TAG(v) it receives from p_j. This means that, if p_j is Byzantine and sends several messages TAG(v), TAG(v') where $v' \neq v$, etc., all of them except the first one are discarded.

Unreliable (best effort) broadcast.

This simple broadcast is defined by a pair of operations denoted broadcast() and receive(), where broadcast TAG(m) is used as a shortcut for

for each $j \in \{1, \dots, n\}$ send TAG(m) to p_j **end for**.

This means that a message *broadcast* by a correct process is *received* at least by all the correct processes. Differently, while it is assumed to send the same message to all the processes, a faulty process can actually send different messages to distinct processes and no message to others.

Notation.

The notation $\mathcal{BZ\_AS}_{n,t}[\emptyset]$ is used to denote the previous basic Byzantine asynchronous message-passing computation model.

2.2 Reliable broadcast abstraction

This broadcast abstraction (in short, RB-broadcast) was proposed by G. Bracha [7]. It is a one-shot one-to-all communication abstraction, which provides processes with two operations denoted RB_broadcast() and RB_deliver(). When p_i invokes the operation RB_broadcast() (resp., RB_deliver()), we say that it "RB-broadcasts" a message (resp., "RB-delivers" a message). An RB-broadcast instance where process p_x is the sender is defined by the following properties.

- RB-Validity. If a non-faulty process RB-delivers a message m (from p_x), then, if p_x is correct, it RB-broadcast m.
- RB-Unicity. A correct process RB-delivers at most one message from p_x.
- RB-Termination-1. If p_x is non-faulty and RB-broadcasts a message m, all the non-faulty processes eventually RB-deliver m from p_x.
- RB-Termination-2. If a non-faulty process RB-delivers a message m from p_x (possibly faulty) then all the non-faulty processes eventually RB-deliver the same message m from p_x.

The RB-Validity property relates the output to the input, while RB-Unicity states that there is no message duplication. The termination properties state the cases where processes have to RB-deliver messages. The second of them is what makes the broadcast reliable. It is shown in [8] that $t < n/3$ is an upper bound on t when one has to implement such an abstraction. An algorithm implementing RB-broadcast is described in [6, 7]).

Notation.

The basic computing model strengthened with the additional constraint $t < n/3$ is denoted $\mathcal{BZ\_AS}_{n,t}[t < n/3]$. RB-broadcast can consequently be implemented in this model.

2.3 Cooperative broadcast abstraction

Definition.

This new communication abstraction (in short CB-broadcast) is a one-shot all-to-all broadcast defined by an operation, denoted CB_broadcast(), plus a read-only set at every process p_i, denoted cb_valid_i. "All-to-all" means that it is assumed that all correct processes invoke CB_broadcast(). When a process p_i invokes CB_broadcast(v), we say that "it cb-broadcasts v".

An invocation of CB_broadcast() by a process p_i has an input parameter, namely the value that p_i wants to broadcast, and returns a value, which is a value CB-broadcast by a correct process. The CB-broadcast abstraction is formally defined by the following properties.

- CB-Operation Termination. The invocation of the operation CB_broadcast() by a correct process terminates.
- CB-Operation Validity. If the invocation of CB_broadcast() returns v to a correct process p_i, $v \in cb\_valid_i$.
- CB-Set Termination. The set cb_valid_i of a correct process p_i is eventually non-empty.
- CB-Set Validity. The set cb_valid_i of any correct process p_i contains only values cb-broadcast by correct processes.
- CB-Set Agreement. The set cb_valid_i and cb_valid_j of any two correct processes p_i and p_j are eventually equal.

Feasibility condition in the presence of up to t Byzantine processes.

Let m be the number of different values that can be cb-broadcast by correct processes. It follows from the previous specification that, even when the (at most) t Byzantine processes propose a same value w, not proposed by a correct process, w can neither be returned, nor belong to the set cb_valid_i of a correct process p_i. This can be ensured if and only if there is a value cb-broadcast by at least $(t + 1)$ correct processes. This feasibility condition is captured by the predicate $n - t > mt$. (A proof of this feasibility condition can be found in [18]).

operation CB_broadcast(v_i) **is**
(1) RB_broadcast CB_VAL(v_i);
(2) wait ($cb\_valid_i \neq \emptyset$);
(3) return (any value in cb_valid_i).

when CB_VAL(v) **is RB_delivered from** p_j **do**
(4) **if** (v RB_delivered from $(t + 1)$ diff. processes)
then add v to cb_valid_i **end if**.

Figure 1: An algorithm implementing m-valued CB-broadcast in $\mathcal{BZ\_AS}_{n,t}[t < n/3]$

```
operation AC_propose(v_i) is
(1)  est_i ← CB_broadcast AC_PROP(v_i);
(2)  RB_broadcast AC_EST(est_i);
(3)  wait (AC_EST(est) messages have been RB-delivered from (n − t)
          different processes, and their est values belong to cb_valid_i);
(4)  mfv_i ← most frequent value in the previous (n − t) AC_EST() messages;
(5)  if (each of the previous (n − t) AC_EST() messages carries mfv_i)
(6)    then return (⟨commit, mfv_i⟩)
(7)    else return (⟨adopt, mfv_i⟩)
(8)  end if.
```

Figure 2: An algorithm implementing an m-valued adopt-commit object in $\mathcal{BZ\_AS}_{n,t}[t < n/3]$

Hence, we assume in the following that at most $m \leq \lfloor \frac{n-(t+1)}{t} \rfloor$ different values can be cb-broadcast by the set of correct processes, and the corresponding abstraction is called *m-valued* CB-broadcast.

An algorithm implementing CB-broadcast.

A simple algorithm implementing CB-broadcast is described in Figure 1. When p_i invokes CB_broadcast(v_i), it first invokes the underlying RB_broadcast CB_VAL(v_i) for all correct processes to be eventually aware of v_i (line 1). Then, it waits until its set cb_valid_i becomes non-empty (line 2). When this occurs, p_i takes any value from cb_valid_i and returns it (line 3). Finally, p_i adds to cb_valid_i all the values it RB-delivers from $(t + 1)$ different processes (i.e., v was RB-broadcast by at least one correct process). It is important to notice that, after the predicate $cb\_valid_i \neq \emptyset$ became satisfied, new values can still be added to cb_valid_i.

THEOREM 1. *The algorithm described in Figure* 1 *implements the m-valued CB-broadcast abstraction in* $\mathcal{BZ\_AS}_{n,t}[t < n/3]$.

Proof Proof of the CB-Termination properties.
It follows from the feasibility condition, that there is a value v that is proposed by at least $(t + 1)$ correct processes. Hence, these processes RB-broadcast CB_VAL(v). It then follows from line 4 and the RB-termination property that v will be added to the set cb_valid_i of each correct process p_i. Hence, the CB-Set Termination property is satisfied, and no correct process can be blocked forever at line 2, from which follows the CB-Operation Termination property.
Proof of the CB-Validity properties.
To prove the CB-Set Validity property, let us consider a value v cb-broadcast only by Byzantine processes. It follows that a correct process p_i can RB-deliver v from at most t different processes. Hence, p_i cannot add v to cb_valid_i at line 4, which proves the property. The CB-Operation Validity property is then a trivial consequence of the CB-Set Validity property.
Proof of the CB-Set Agreement property.
Let us consider a value $v \in cb\_valid_i$. This means that p_i RB-delivered the message CB_VAL(v) from $(t+1)$ different processes (line 4). It then follows from the RB-termination property of RB-broadcast that each correct process p_j RB-delivers these $(t + 1)$ messages CB_VAL(v). Consequently, any correct process p_j adds v to its local set cb_valid_j, which concludes the proof. $\Box_{Theorem\ 1}$

3. ADOPT-COMMIT IN THE PRESENCE OF BYZANTINE PROCESSES

This object was introduced in [17] in the context of read/write communication. Here we slightly modify its definition to cope with Byzantine processes (which by definition can decide anything).

Definition.

An adopt-commit (AC) is a one-shot object which encapsulates the safety part of agreement problems. It provides processes with a single operation denoted AC_propose(). This operation takes a value as input parameter (we say that the invoking process proposes this value), and returns a pair $\langle d, v\rangle$ (we say that the invoking process decides $\langle d, v\rangle$), where d is a control tag and v a value. An AC object is defined by the following properties.

- AC-Termination. An invocation of AC_propose() by a correct process terminates.
- AC-Validity. This property is made up of two parts.
  - AC-Output domain. If a correct process decides $\langle d, v\rangle$, $d \in \{$`commit`, `adopt`$\}$, and v is a value that was proposed by a correct process.
  - AC-Obligation. If all the correct processes propose the same value v, only $\langle$`commit`$, v\rangle$, can be decided.
- AC-Quasi-agreement. If a correct process decides $\langle$`commit`$, v\rangle$, no other correct process can decide $\langle -, v'\rangle$ where $v' \neq v$.

Implementations of an AC object in the presence of process crash failures can be found in [17, 23, 29, 30]. The implementations of [17, 30] are for asynchronous systems where any number of processes may crash and communication is by atomic read/write registers. The implementations of [23, 29] are for asynchronous message-passing systems where a minority of processes may crash.

It follows from the AC-Output domain property, that a value proposed only by Byzantine processes cannot be decided by a correct process. This means that an AC object has the same feasibility condition as CB-broadcast (let us also notice that this is independent from the fact that an AC object can be built on top of CB-broadcast). Hence, we assume that at most $m \leq \lfloor \frac{n-(t+1)}{t} \rfloor$ values can be proposed by the correct processes, and the corresponding object is called an *m-valued* adopt-commit object.

Implementation of an m-valued adopt-commit object.

A distributed algorithm implementing an AC object in the presence of up to $t < n/3$ Byzantine processes is described in Figure 2, for a correct process p_i. This algorithm is based on an underlying CB-broadcast, which means that each process has a read-only local set cb_val_i (initially empty).

When a process p_i invokes AC_propose(v_i), it first issues the operation CB_broadcast AC_PROP(v_i) from which it obtains a value that it saves in est_i (line 1). It then RB-broadcasts the message AC_EST(est_i) (line 2), and waits until (a) it has RB-delivered messages AC_EST() from $(n-t)$ different processes, and (b) the values carried by these messages belong to the set cb_valid_i supplied by CB-broadcast (line 3). Let us remember that, after the predicate $cb\_valid_i \neq \emptyset$ became satisfied, new values can still be added to cb_valid_i.

When this predicate becomes satisfied, p_i computes the most frequent value mfv_i carried by the previous $(n-t)$ AC_EST() messages (line 4). If there are several "most frequent" values, p_i takes any of them. Finally, if all the messages who made satisfied the predicate of line 3 carried the same value mfv_i, p_i returns the pair $\langle \texttt{commit}, mfv_i \rangle)$ (line 6); otherwise it returns the pair $\langle \texttt{adopt}, mfv_i \rangle)$ (line 7).

THEOREM 2. *Assuming that each correct process invokes the operation* AC_propose()*, the algorithm of Figure 2 implements an* m-valued adopt-commit *object in* $\mathcal{BZ\_AS}_{n,t}[t < n/3]$.

Proof Proof of the AC-termination property.
Due to the CB-Operation termination property, no correct process blocks forever at line 1. So, we have only to show that no correct process can block forever at line 3. It follows from CB-Set Termination and CB-Set Validity that the sets cb_valid_i of the correct processes are eventually not empty and contain only values proposed by correct processes. As (i) the value RB-broadcast by each correct process at line 2 is a value of its set cb_valid_i, (ii) there are at least $(n-t)$ correct processes, and (iii) the sets cb_valid_i of the correct processes are eventually equal (CB-Set Agreement property), it follows that the predicate of line 3 is eventually satisfied at each correct process, which concludes the proof of AC-termination property.
Proof of the AC-Output domain property.
Let us first observe that a correct process can decide only the pair $\langle \texttt{commit}, v \rangle$ or the pair $\langle \texttt{adopt}, v \rangle$ (lines 6-7). Hence, we have only to show that v is a value proposed by a correct process. A value v decided by a correct process p_i was RB-delivered in a message AC_EST(v). It follows from the predicate of line 3 that $v \in cb\_valid_i$. Finally, if follows from the CB-Set Validity property that v is a value proposed by a correct process.
Proof of the AC-Obligation property.
If all correct processes propose the same value v, it follows from the CB-Set (Termination, Validity, and Agreement) properties that the set cb_valid_i of each correct process p_i is eventually equal to $\{v\}$. Hence, each correct process RB-broadcasts the message AC_EST(v) at line 2. It then follows from the predicate of line 3 that no value different from v can be decided.
Proof of the AC-Quasi-agreement property.
Let p_i and p_j be two correct processes such that p_i decides the pair $\langle \texttt{commit}, v \rangle$ while p_j decides $\langle -, v' \rangle$. As p_i decides $\langle \texttt{commit}, v \rangle$, it follows from line 3 that it RB-delivered the message AC_EST(v) from $(n-t)$ different processes. As, due to the RB-Unicity and RB-Termination-2 properties, no two correct processes RB-deliver different values from the same process, it follows that, among the $(n-t)$ messages AC_EST() RB-delivered by p_j, at most t of them may carry a value different from v, i.e., at least $n-2t \geq t+1$ carry the value v. It follows that v is the most frequent value RB-delivered by p_j, and consequently $v' = v$. $\Box_{Theorem\ 2}$

4. THE $\diamond\langle T+1 \rangle$BISOURCE ASSUMPTION

Eventually timely channel.
Let us consider the channel connecting a process p_i to a process p_j. This channel is *eventually timely* if there is a finite time τ and a bound δ, such that any message sent by p_i to p_j at time τ' is received by p_j by time $\max(\tau, \tau') + \delta$. Let us observe that neither τ, nor δ, is known by the processes.

As already indicated, there is an input/output channel from each process to itself.

$\diamond\langle k \rangle$sink, $\diamond\langle k \rangle$source, and $\diamond\langle k \rangle$bisource.
A correct process p_i is an $\diamond\langle k \rangle$sink if it has eventually timely input channels from k correct processes (including itself). This set of processes is denoted X_i^-. Similarly, a correct process is an $\diamond\langle k \rangle$source if it has k eventually timely output channels to correct processes (including itself). This set of processes is denoted X_i^+.

An $\diamond\langle k \rangle$bisource is a correct process p_i that is both $\diamond\langle k \rangle$sink and $\diamond\langle k \rangle$source. Let us remark that the timely input channels and the timely output channels do not necessarily connect p_i to the same subset of processes.

Notation for system models.
The system model $\mathcal{BZ\_AS}_{n,t}[t < n/3]$ enriched with an $\diamond\langle t+1 \rangle$bisource is denoted $\mathcal{BZ\_AS}_{n,t}[t < n/3, \diamond\langle t+1 \rangle\text{bisource}]$.

Discussion.
The previous notions were introduced in [1, 14]. Our definition of an $\diamond\langle t+1 \rangle$bisource is slightly different from the original definition introduced in [1]. The difference is that it considers only eventually timely channels connecting correct processes, while [1] considers eventually timely channels connecting a correct process to correct or faulty processes. Hence, an $\diamond\langle t+1 \rangle$bisource is an $\diamond\langle 2t+1 \rangle$bisource in the parlance of [1]. We consider only eventually timely channels connecting pair of correct processes for the following reason: an eventually timely channel connecting a correct process and a Byzantine process can always appear to the correct process as being an asynchronous channel.

5. EVENTUAL AGREEMENT OBJECT

5.1 Motivation and definition

This object, which is round-based, will be used to ensure the termination of the consensus algorithm, namely, its aim is to allow the correct processes to eventually converge on a single value. To this end, it provides the processes with a single operation denoted EA_propose(r, v) where r is a round number and v is the value proposed at this round by the invoking process. Each invocation of EA_propose() by a correct process returns a value. It is assumed that each correct process invokes this operation once per round, and its successive invocations are done according to consecutive round numbers. When a process invokes EA_propose(r, v), we say that it "ea-proposes v at round r".

Definition.
An eventual agreement (EA) object is defined by the following properties.

- EA-Termination. For any r, if all correct processes invoke EA_propose($r, -$), each of these invocations terminates.
- EA-Validity. For any r, if all correct processes invoke the operation EA_propose(r, v) no correct process returns a value different from v.
- EA-Eventual agreement. If the correct processes execute an infinite number of rounds, there is an infinite number of rounds r at which all the correct processes return the same value v, where v is such that a correct process invoked the operation EA_propose(r, v).

It is important to notice that the EA-Validity property is particularly weak. More precisely, if, during a round r, two correct processes invoke EA_propose($r, v1$) and EA_propose($r, v2$), with $v1 \neq v2$, the invocation of EA_propose($r, -$) by any correct process is allowed to return an arbitrary value (i.e., even a value proposed neither by a correct nor by a Byzantine process).

As the implementation that follows uses at every round an instance of CB-broadcast, we assume that at most $m \leq \lfloor \frac{n-(t+1)}{t} \rfloor$ different values are ea-proposed by correct processes.

5.2 Implementation of an m-valued eventual agreement object

Definitions.

The algorithm presented below uses the following sets and functions.

- There are $\alpha = \binom{n}{n-t}$ possible combinations of $(n-t)$ processes among the n processes p_1, ..., p_n. Let us call them $F_1 \dots F_\alpha$.
- Given any round number $r \geq 1$:
  - $\mathsf{coord}(r)$ denotes the function $\big((r-1) \bmod \mathsf{n}\big) + 1$. Given a round r, $\mathsf{coord}(r)$ defines its coordinator process. As we can see, if there is an infinite number of rounds, each process is infinitely often round coordinator.
  - $F(r)$ denotes the function $F_{\mathsf{index}(r)}$, where $\mathsf{index}(r) = \big((\lceil \frac{r}{n} \rceil - 1) \bmod \alpha\big) + 1$.
    Hence, each set $F(r)$ returns a set made up of $(n-t)$ processes. During each round, its coordinator strives to decide a value. To this end, it requires the help of the processes in $F(r)$ to broadcast the value it champions. F_1 is used by the coordinators of the rounds 1 to n; F_2 is used by the coordinators of the rounds $(n+1)$ to $2n$; ..., F_α is used by the coordinators of the rounds $((\alpha-1)n+1)$ to αn; F_1 is used by the coordinators of the rounds $((\alpha n+1)$ to $(\alpha+1)n$; etc.

Considering an infinite sequence of rounds, it is important to notice that there is an infinite number of rounds r and r' such that $(\mathsf{coord}(r) = \mathsf{coord}(r')) \wedge F(r) = F(r')$ and an infinite number of rounds r and r' such that $\big(\mathsf{coord}(r) = \mathsf{coord}(r')\big) \wedge \big(F(r) \neq F(r')\big)$.

Local variables.

Each process p_i manages the following local variables.

- $timer_i[1..]$ is an array of timers, such that $timer_i[r]$ is the timer used by p_i for round r.
- $CB[1..]$ is an array of CB-broadcast instances shared by all processes. $CB[r]$ is the instance associated with round r. Hence, $CB[r].cb\_valid_i$ is the set of values supplied to p_i by $CB[r]$.

To distinguish messages which have the same tag but are sent at different rounds, a message XXX() associated with round r is denoted XXX$[r]()$.

Algorithm: first part of EA_propose().

(Lines 1-5) The algorithm executed by a correct process p_i is described in Figure 3. Let us remind that, it is assumed that each correct process invokes EA_propose() at every round.

When a correct process p_i invokes EA_propose(r_i, val_i) (r_i is a round number and val_i the value it ea-proposes at this round), it first invokes $CB[r_i]$.CB_broadcast EA_PROP1(val_i), and saves the value returned in aux_i (line 1).Then, p_i broadcasts the message EA_PROP2$[r_i](aux_i)$ (line 1) and waits until (a) it has received messages EA_PROP2$[r_i]()$ from $(n-t)$ different processes, and (b) the values carried by these messages belong to the set denoted $CB[r_i].cb\_valid_i$, which is locally supplied by the CB-broadcast instance $CB[r_i]$ (line 3). If all these messages carry the same value v, p_i returns v as result of its invocation EA_propose(r_i, val_i) (line 4)[2]. Otherwise, p_i sets the timer associated with the round r_i to the value r_i (line 5)[3].

Algorithm: message processing and role of the round coordinator.

(Lines 11-19) Each round r uses a round coordinator, defined by $\mathsf{coord}(r)$. As we have also seen, the set of $(n-t)$ processes denoted $F(r)$ is associated with round r.

When p_i is the coordinator of round r and receives for the first time a message EA_PROP2$[r]()$ from a process in the set $F(r)$, it champions the value w carried by this message to become the value returned by the invocations of EA_propose$(r, -)$. To that end, it simply broadcasts the message EA_COORD$[r](w)$ (lines 11-14).

When a process p_i receives a message EA_COORD$[r](v)$ from the coordinator of round r, if not yet done, it broadcasts the message EA_RELAY$[r](v)$ to inform the other processes that it has received the value v championed by the coordinator of round r. If the local timer associated with this round ($timer_i[r]$) has already expired, p_i broadcasts the message EA_RELAY$[r](\perp)$, to inform the other processes that it suspects the coordinator of round r not to be an $\diamond\langle t+1\rangle$bisource (this suspicion can be due to the asynchrony of the channel connecting $p_{\mathsf{coord}(r)}$ to p_i, or the fact that –while $p_{\mathsf{coord}(r)}$ is an $\diamond\langle t+1\rangle$bisource– the link from $p_{\mathsf{coord}(r)}$ to p_i is not yet synchronous, or the fact that $p_{\mathsf{coord}(r)}$ has a Byzantine behavior). In all cases, as $timer_i[r]$ will no longer be useful, p_i disables it. This behavior of p_i is captured by the lines 15-19.

Algorithm: second part of EA_propose().

(Lines 6-10) After it has set $timer_i[r_i]$ (line 5), p_i waits until it has received a message EA_RELAY$[r_i]()$ from $(n-t)$ different processes (line 6). When this occurs, the invocation of the operation EA_propose(r_i, val_i) by p_i returns a value. This value is $v \neq \perp$ if p_i received a message EA_RELAY$[r_i](v)$ from a process in the set $F(r_i)$ (lines 7-8). Otherwise, no process of $F(r_i)$ witnesses the value championed by the coordinator of round r. In this case, p_i returns the value val_i, i.e., the value it ea-proposed (line 9).

5.3 Proof

Let us remember that, by assumption, all correct processes invoke EA_propose$(r, -)$, where $r = 1$. Moreover, they ea-propose at most m different values.

LEMMA 1. *Whatever the round r, if all correct processes invoke* EA_propose(r, v) *no correct process returns a value different from v.* (Proof in [6].)

LEMMA 2. *Let $r \geq 1$. If all correct processes invoke the operation* EA_propose$(r, -)$*, then each of these invocation terminates.* (Proof in [6].)

LEMMA 3. *If the correct processes execute an infinite number of rounds, there is an infinite number of rounds r at which all the*

[2]Let us remark that lines 1-3 of Figure 3 and lines 1-3 of Figure 2 differ only in the fact that an RB-broadcast is used at line 2 for the AC object, and a simple broadcast is used at line 2 for the EA object. These lines have not been encapsulated to define a higher level object because the messages EA_PROP2$[r_i]()$ are explicitly used in lines 11-14 of Figure 3, while their counterparts in an AC object –messages AC_EST()– are not used by the upper layer.

[3]The important point here is that the value of the timer increases; as r_i increases at every round, it is used as a timeout value. More generally, it is possible to assign to $timer_i[r_i]$ the value returned by an increasing function $f_i(r_i)$, which can be specific to each process p_i.

```
operation EA_propose(r_i, val_i) is
(1)  aux_i ← CB[r_i].CB_broadcast EA_PROP1(val_i);
(2)  broadcast EA_PROP2[r_i](aux_i);
(3)  wait (EA_PROP2[r_i]() messages have been received from (n − t)
             different processes, and their aux values belong to CB[r_i].cb_valid_i);
(4)  if (the (n − t) previous messages carry the same value v) then return(v) end if;
(5)  set timer_i[r_i] to r_i;
(6)  wait (EA_RELAY[r_i](aux) messages received from (n − t) different processes);
(7)  if (EA_RELAY[r_i](v) where v ≠ ⊥ received from a process in F(r_i))
(8)       then return(v)
(9)       else return(val_i)
(10) end if.

when EA_PROP2[r]() is received from a process in F(r) do
(11) if ((i = coord(r) ∧ (EA_COORD[r]() not already broadcast))
(12)      then let w be the value carried by the message EA_PROP2[r]();
(13)           broadcast EA_COORD[r](w)
(14) end if.

when EA_COORD[r](v) is received from p_coord(r) or (timer_i[r] expires) do
(15) if (EA_RELAY[r]() not already broadcast)
(16)      disable timer_i[r];
(17)      if (timer_i[r] expired) then v_coord_i ← ⊥ else v_coord_i ← v end if;
(18)      broadcast EA_RELAY[r](v_coord_i)
(19) end if.
```

Figure 3: An algorithm implementing an m-valued EA object in $\mathcal{BZ_AS}_{n,t}[t < n/3, \Diamond\langle t+1\rangle$bisource$]$

correct processes return the same value v, where v is such that a correct process invoked EA_propose(r, v).

Proof Let us define the following rounds:

- Let r_1 be the first round that is strictly greater than 2δ.
- Let p_ℓ be an $\Diamond\langle t+1\rangle$bisource. There exists a round r_2 such that in every subsequent round:
  - Each message sent by any $p_x \in X_\ell^-$ to p_ℓ is received within an interval of at most δ time units.
  - Each message sent by p_ℓ to any $p_y \in X_\ell^+$ is received within an interval of at most δ time units.
- Let $r > \max(r_1, r_2)$ be any round coordinated by p_ℓ such that $X_\ell^+ \subseteq F(r)$ and $F(r) \subseteq \mathcal{C}$. Let us notice that, due to the definition of $F(r)$, an infinity of such rounds r exists.

Claim C. For every process $p_i \in X_\ell^+$, we have $v\_coord_i \neq \bot$ in round r (line 18).

Proof of claim C. Let p_i be any process in X_ℓ^+. Let τ be the time at which p_i sets the timer at line 5 of round r. At this moment, since p_i finished executing line 4, there are at least $(n-t)$ processes from which p_i received an EA_PROP2$[r]()$ message. Since $|X_\ell^-| \geq t+1$, it follows that among these $(n-t)$ processes, there is at least one, say p_k, that belongs to X_ℓ^-. Observe that p_k necessarily broadcast the message EA_PROP2$[r]()$ before τ. Since $r > r_2$, this message is received by p_ℓ before time $\tau + \delta$.

Therefore, if p_ℓ did not broadcast a message EA_COORD$[r]()$ before receiving EA_PROP2$[r]()$ from p_k, as $p_k \in X_\ell^- \subseteq F(r)$, the condition of line 11 and the when statement preceding it are both satisfied, and p_ℓ broadcasts EA_COORD$[r]()$ at line 13. Consequently, in all cases, p_ℓ broadcasts a message EA_COORD$[r]()$ by time $\tau + \delta$. Finally, since $p_i \in X_\ell^+$ and $r > r_2$, this message is received by p_i before time $\tau + 2\delta$.

Let us recall that, as $r > r_1$, it holds that $r > 2\delta$, and consequently, since p_i set $timer_i[r]$ to r (line 8) at time τ, the timeout occurs after time $\tau + 2\delta$. Therefore, p_i receives the message EA_COORD$[r]()$ from p_ℓ before the timeout. Consequently, when evaluated by p_i, the predicate of line 17 is necessarily `false`, and $v\_coord_i \neq \bot$. This proves the claim.

We show in the following that all correct processes return the same value in round r. Let us first observe that every correct process broadcasts an EA_PROP2$[r]()$ message that carries a value which was necessarily ea-proposed by a correct process. Therefore, since p_ℓ is correct (and is the coordinator of r), the message EA_COORD$[r]()$ it broadcasts in round r contains a value, say w, that was sent to it by a correct process. Therefore, since (due to the definition of r), the processes of $F(r)$ are correct, the EA_RELAY$[r]()$ messages broadcast by them carry either w or $\bot$. Consequently, every correct process p_i can either returns w or val_i after executing the lines 7-10. To finish the proof, it remains to show that no correct process p_i returns val_i (if $val_i \neq w$).

Let us observe that each correct process waits at line 6 until it receives $(n-t)$ EA_RELAY$[r]()$ messages. Since $|X_\ell^+| > t$, it follows that at least one of these messages was broadcast by a process in X_ℓ^+. Due to Claim C, this message cannot carry $\bot$. It then follows from the predicate of line 7 that any correct process executes line 8 and returns w, which proves the lemma. $\Box_{Lemma\ 3}$

THEOREM 3. *The algorithm of Figure* 3 *implements an* m-valued eventual agreement *object in* $\mathcal{BZ\_AS}_{n,t}[t < n/3, \Diamond\langle t+1\rangle$*bisource*$]$. (The proof follows from Lemma 1, Lemma 2, and Lemma 3.)

5.4 Looking for efficiency: Parameterized eventual agreement

Time complexity of the EA algorithm.

The aim of the previous algorithm was to attain a round r during which all correct processes return the same value (ea-proposed by one of them). Hence its time complexity can be measured by the value of this round number. As the underlying synchrony assumption is *eventual*, we only know that this number r is finite.

Hence, to eliminate the noise created by the "eventual" attribute, and consequently be able to compute a time complexity of the algorithm, let us replace the $\Diamond\langle t+1\rangle$bisource synchrony assumption by the $\langle t+1\rangle$bisource assumption, i.e., we consider that there is a $\langle t+1\rangle$bisource from the very beginning. The corresponding system model is denoted $\mathcal{BZ\_AS}_{n,t}[t < n/3, \langle t+1\rangle\text{bisource}]$.

The uncertainty created by the "eventual" attribute is consequently eliminated, and the only uncertainty is the identity of the bisource and its associated input and output timely channels. As there are n processes and $\alpha = \binom{n}{n-t}$ combinations for the sets $F(r)$, it follows that the algorithm, which works in $\mathcal{BZ\_AS}_{n,t}[t < n/3, \Diamond\langle t+1\rangle\text{bisource}]$, terminates in at most αn rounds when the system behaves as $\mathcal{BZ\_AS}_{n,t}[t < n/3, \langle t+1\rangle\text{bisource}]$.

Improving the time complexity.

One way to improve the time complexity of the algorithm (as measured previously) is to consider a "tuning" parameter k, $0 \leq k \leq t$, and use it in both the synchrony assumption and the size of the sets $F(r)$, as follows.

- The assumption $\langle t+1\rangle$bisource is replaced by the stronger assumption $\langle t+1+k\rangle$bisource.
- Instead of $(n-t)$, the size of the sets $F(r)$ is now $n-t+k$.

An algorithm, parameterized with k, extending the basic algorithm of Figure 3 and based on the previous definition is described in [6]. Designed for the system model $\mathcal{BZ\_AS}_{n,t}[t < n/3, \Diamond\langle t+1+k\rangle\text{bisource}]$, this algorithm has a time complexity of βn where $\beta = \binom{n}{n-t+k}$ when executed in $\mathcal{BZ\_AS}_{n,t}[t < n/3, \langle t+1+k\rangle\text{bisource}]$. As simple instances of this parameterized algorithm, let us consider two particular values of k. For $k = 0$, we obtain the basic algorithm. For $k = t$, the time complexity is n, which is the best that can be obtained with a round coordinator-based algorithm (up to n rounds can be needed to benefit from the $\langle t+1+k\rangle$bisource).

6. BYZANTINE CONSENSUS ALGORITHM

m-Valued Byzantine consensus.

In the m-valued Byzantine consensus, the correct processes propose values from a set of at most m values. The corresponding object is a one-shot object, that provides the processes with a single operation denoted $\mathsf{CONS\_propose}(v)$, where v is the value proposed by the invoking process. This operation returns a value to the invoking process. If p_i obtains the value v, we say that it "decides" v. The consensus object is defined by the following properties.

- CONS-Termination. The invocation of $\mathsf{CONS\_propose}()$ by a correct process terminates.
- CONS-Validity. If a correct process decides v, a correct process invoked $\mathsf{CONS\_propose}(v)$.
- CONS-Agreement. No two correct processes decide different values.

An algorithm solving m-valued Byzantine consensus.

Assuming $m \leq \lfloor \frac{n-(t+1)}{t} \rfloor$, the algorithm described in Figure 4 implements an m-valued consensus object in $\mathcal{BZ\_AS}_{n,t}[t < n/3, \langle t+1\rangle\text{bisource}]$. This algorithm, which –thanks to the previous abstractions– is simple, uses the following underlying objects.

- Each process p_i manages a round number r_i (initialized to 0), and a current estimate denoted est_i.
- EA_OBJECT is a shared m-valued EA object. Its aim is to allow processes to eventually converge to the same estimate value. Hence, the associated line 4 is related to CONS-Termination.
- $AC\_OBJECT[1..]$ is an unbounded array of m-valued adopt-commit objects, shared by all processes. $AC\_OBJECT[r]$ is the adopt-commit object used at round r. The aim of these objects (line 6) is to allow correct processes to decide a value proposed by one of them, and prevent them from deciding different values, i.e., to guarantee consensus safety.
- $CB[0]$ is a CB-broadcast instance, used at the very beginning to obtain a value proposed by a correct process and allow a process p_i to use the associated set $CB[0].cb\_valid_i$ to check the validity of the values returned by the EA_OBJECT object (i.e., check if this value is from a correct process).

When a correct process p_i invokes $\mathsf{CONS\_propose}(v_i)$, it first invokes $CB[0].\mathsf{CB\_broadcast}\text{VALID}(v_i)$ to obtain a value that was proposed by a correct process (line 1)[4]. As already indicated, this invocation also ensures that the sets $CB[0].cb\_valid_i$ of correct processes are eventually equal and contain values proposed only by correct processes.

Then process p_i enters an infinite loop (lines 2-8). After it has entered its current round (line 3), process p_i proposes its current estimate of the decision value est_i to the to the EA object, namely, it invokes $EA\_OBJECT.\mathsf{EA\_propose}(r_i, est_i)$ (line 4). If the value returned by this invocation is a value that it knows as proposed by a correct process, it adopts it as new estimate, otherwise it keeps its previous estimate (line 5).

Process p_i proposes then the current value of est_i to the adopt-commit object associated with the current round, from which it obtains a pair $\langle tag, est_i\rangle$ (line 6). If the value of the tag is `commit` (line 7), p_i RB-broadcasts the message DECIDE(est_i) to inform the other processes that the value of est_i can be decided. Then, whatever the value of the tag, p_i proceeds to the next round with its (possibly new) estimate value est_i.

Finally, as soon as a process, that not yet decided, has RB-delivered the same message DECIDE(v) from $(t+1)$ different processes, it decides v and stops (line 9). Let us notice that at least one of these messages is from a correct process.

THEOREM 4. *The algorithm of Figure* 4 *solves the* m-valued Byzantine consensus *problem in the system model* $\mathcal{BZ\_AS}_{n,t}[t < n/3, \Diamond\langle t+1\rangle\textit{bisource}]$.

Proof We say that a process p_i starts round r when it assigns value r to its local variable r_i (line 3).

Proof of the CONS-Termination property.

If a process decides at line 9, it previously RB-delivered the message DECIDE(v) from $(t+1)$ different processes. Due to the RB-termination property of the corresponding $(t+1)$ RB-broadcasts, each correct process RB-delivers this message from the same set of $(t+1)$ processes, and consequently decides. So, let us assume by contradiction that no correct process decides at line 9.

Let us first observe that, due to the CB-Operation Termination property that no correct process p_i blocks forever at line 1. Moreover, it follows from the CB-Operation Validity property that that the set $CB[0].cb\_valid_i$ is not empty when this invocation terminates.

As no correct process decides, and all correct processes invoke $\mathsf{EA\_propose}(1, -)$, it follows from the EA-Termination and AC-Termination properties that they all terminate the first round, and consequently start the second. Moreover, if the estimate est_i of a correct process p_i is updated at line 5, its new value is a value

[4]Even if, up to now, a process behaved "correctly", it may crash in the future and become then faulty. Hence, no process can a priori consider the value it proposes as a value proposed by a correct process.

operation CONS_propose(v_i) **is**
(1) $est_i \leftarrow CB[0]$.CB_broadcast VALID(v_i); % safety: validity %
(2) **repeat forever**
(3) $r_i \leftarrow r_i + 1$;
(4) $v \leftarrow EA\_OBJECT$.EA_propose(r_i, est_i); % liveness %
(5) **if** ($v \in CB[0].cb\_valid_i$) **then** $est_i \leftarrow v$ **end if**; % safety: validity %
(6) $\langle tag, est_i \rangle \leftarrow AC\_OBJECT[r_i]$.AC_propose($est_i$); % safety: agreement %
(7) **if** ($tag =$ `commit`) **then** RB_broadcast DECIDE(est_i) **end if**
(8) **end repeat**.

when DECIDE(v) **is RB-delivered do**
(9) **if** (DECIDE(v) RB-delivered from $(t+1)$ diff. processes) **then** return(v) **end if**.

Figure 4: An algorithm for m-valued Byzantine consensus in $\mathcal{BZ_AS}_{n,t}[t < n/3, \diamond\langle t+1\rangle$bisource$]$

proposed by a correct process. It follows that the correct processes start the second round with estimate values est_i containing values proposed by correct processes. As no correct process decides, the same reasoning applies to all rounds $r > 1$.

Let us observe that the local variables $CB[0].cb\_valid_i$ of the correct processes eventually converge to the same content (CB-Set Agreement and Termination of $CB[0]$). Hence, there is a round r_0 such that, for every correct process p_i, the set $CB[0].cb\_valid_i$ is never updated after it starts r_0.

It then follows from the EA-Eventual Agreement property of EA_OBJECT, that there is a round $r > r_0$ during which all correct processes obtain the same value v at line 4, where v is a value proposed by a correct process. Hence, since $r > r_0$, they all succeed the test of line 5 and adopt v as their new estimate est_i. Therefore, all correct processes invoke$AC_OBJECT[r]$.AC_propose(v) at line 6. Due to the AC-Obligation property of $AC\_OBJECT[r]$, all correct processes obtain $\langle$`commit`$, v\rangle$ at line 6. Consequently, they all RB-broadcast the same message $\langle$`commit`$, v\rangle$ at line 7. An $n - t \geq t + 1$, the decision predicate of line 9 becomes eventually true at every correct process, which contradicts the initial assumption.

Proof of the CONS-Validity property.
Let us consider the first round. Let p_i be a correct process. It follows from the CB-Operation Validity property of $CB[0]$ that est_i is a value proposed by a correct process. Moreover, it follows from the CB-Set Validity property, that $CB[0].cb\_valid_i$ contains only values proposed by correct processes. It follows from these observations that, be or not est_i modified at line 5, when p_i invokes $AC\_OBJECT[1]$.AC_propose(est_i) at line 6, est_i contains a value proposed by a correct process. It then follows from the AC-Validity property of $AC\_OBJECT[1]$ that the value assigned to est_i at line 6 is a value proposed by a correct process. The same reasoning applies iteratively to all rounds, from which it follows that a value that is RB-broadcast by a correct process at line 7 is a value proposed by a correct process.

If a correct process p_i decides a value v at line 9, it follows from the decision predicate used at this line that v was RB-broadcast at line 7 by at least one correct process p_j. The previous paragraph has shown that such a value v was proposed by a correct process.

Proof of the CONS-Agreement property.
Let us first observe that, if a correct process decides at line 9, it decides a value RB-broadcast by a correct process at line 7. Hence, the proof consists in showing that no two correct processes RB-broadcast different values at line 7.

Let r be the first round at which a correct process p_i RB-broadcast a message DECIDE() at line 7. Let v the value carried by this message. It follows that, at line 6, p_i obtained the pair $\langle$`commit`$, v\rangle$ from the object $AC\_OBJECT[r]$. Let us consider another correct process p_j. There are two cases.

- p_j RB-broadcast DECIDE(w) at line 9 of round r. This means that it obtained $\langle$`commit`$, w\rangle$ from $AC\_OBJECT[r]$. It then follows from the AC-agreement property of $AC\_OBJECT[r]$ that $v = w$. Moreover, p_j proceeds to the next round with $est_j = v$.
- p_j did not RB-broadcast the message DECIDE(w) at line 9 of round r. It then follows from the AC-agreement property of $AC\_OBJECT[r]$ that p_j obtained the pair $\langle$`adopt`$, v\rangle$. Hence, at line 6, p_j assigned the value v to est_j.

It follows that the estimate values of all the correct processes that progress to the next round are equal to v. Let p_x be any correct process executing round $(r+1)$. It follows from the EA-Validity property of EA_OBJECT, that the invocation by p_x of EA_OBJECT.EA_propose($r + 1, est_x$) returns v, and from the AC-Obligation property of $AC\_OBJECT[r+1]$ that this object returns $\langle -, v\rangle$ to p_x. This means that the estimates of all the correct processes remain forever equal to v. Hence, no value different from v can be RB-broadcast at line 7 by a correct process during a round $r' \geq r$. $\Box_{Theorem\ 4}$

7. CONCLUSION

A variant.

To ensure that a value decided by a correct process is always a value that was proposed by a correct process, the paper considered m-valued consensus, i.e., at most $m \leq \lfloor \frac{n-(t+1)}{t} \rfloor$ different values can be proposed by the correct processes (i.e., there is a value that is proposed by at least $(t+1)$ correct processes). To ensure that no value proposed only by Byzantine processes is ever decided, some Byzantine consensus algorithms (e.g., [11, 24]) do not have such an "m-valued" requirement. They instead allow the correct processes to decide a default value $\perp$ when they do not propose the same value. The algorithms proposed in the paper can be modified to satisfy this different validity requirement.

The aim and the content of the paper.

This paper presented a consensus algorithm for asynchronous Byzantine message-passing systems, that is optimal with respect to the underlying synchrony assumption. This assumption is the existence of a process that is an *eventual* $\langle t+1\rangle$*bisource*. Such a process p is a non-faulty process that eventually has (a) timely input channels from t correct processes and (b) timely output channels to t correct processes. Moreover these input and output channels can connect p to different subsets of processes.

In addition to a reliable broadcast abstraction, the design of the algorithm, which is very modular, is based on simple abstractions: a new broadcast abstraction called *cooperative broadcast*, adopt-commit objects that cope with Byzantine processes (as far as we know, the paper presented the first implementation of such objects in the presence of Byzantine processes), and a new round-based object called *eventual agreement*, whose definition involves a pretty weak validity property.

This paper answered a long-lasting problem, namely, solving Byzantine consensus with the weakest underlying synchrony assumptions. Finally, as claimed in the introduction, and in addition to its optimality with respect to synchrony requirements, a very important first class property of the proposed algorithm lies in its *design simplicity*. "Simplicity $\Rightarrow$ easy" is rarely true for non-trivial problems [2].

Acknowledgments

This work has been partially supported by the French ANR project DISPLEXITY, which is devoted to computability and complexity in distributed computing, and the Franco-German ANR project DISCMAT devoted to connections between mathematics and distributed computing.

8. REFERENCES

[1] Aguilera M.K., Delporte-Gallet C., Fauconnier H., and Toueg S., Consensus with Byzantine failures and little system synchrony. *Proc. 45th IEEE/IFIP Int'l Conference on Dependable Systems and Networks (DSN'06)*, IEEE Press, pp. 147-155, 2006.

[2] Aigner M. and Ziegler G., *Proofs from THE BOOK* (4th edition). Springer, 274 pages, 2010.

[3] Attiya H. and Welch J., Distributed computing: fundamentals, simulations and advanced topics, (2d Edition), *Wiley-Interscience*, 414 pages, 2004.

[4] Baldellon O., Mostéfaoui A. and Raynal M., A necessary and sufficient synchrony condition for solving Byzantine consensus in symmetric networks. *Proc. 12th Int'l Conference on Distributed Computing and Networks (ICDCN'11)*, Springer LNCS 6522, pp. 215-226, 2011.

[5] Ben-Or M., Another advantage of free choice: completely asynchronous agreement protocols. *Proc. 2nd Annual ACM Symposium on Principles of Distributed Computing(PODC'83)*, ACM Press, pp. 27-30, 1983.

[6] Bouzid Z., Mostéafoui A., and Raynal M., Minimal synchrony for asynchronous Byzantine consensus. *Tech Report 2025*, 20 pages, IRISA, Univ. Rennes 1 (F), 2015.

[7] Bracha G., Asynchronous Byzantine agreement protocols. *Information & Computation*, 75(2):130-143, 1987.

[8] Bracha G. and Toueg S., Asynchronous consensus and broadcast protocols. *J. of the ACM*, 32(4):824-840, 1985.

[9] Cachin Ch., Kursawe K., and Shoup V., Random oracles in Constantinople: practical asynchronous Byzantine agreement using cryptography. *Proc. 19th Annual ACM Symposium on Principles of Distributed Computing (PODC'00)*, ACM Press, pp. 123-132, 2000.

[10] Chandra T. and Toueg S., Unreliable failure detectors for reliable distributed systems. *Journal of the ACM*, 43(2):225-267, 1996.

[11] Correia M., Ferreira Neves N., and Verissimo P., From consensus to atomic broadcast: time-free Byzantine-resistant protocols without signatures. *The Computer Journal*, 49(1):82-96, 2006.

[12] Delporte-Gallet C., Devismes S., Fauconnier H. and Larrea M., Algorithms for extracting timeliness graphs. *17th Int'l Colloquium on Structural Inf. and Comm. Complexity (SIROCCO'10)*, Springer LNCS 6058, pp. 127-141, 2010.

[13] Doudou A., Garbinato B., Guerraoui R. and Schiper A., Muteness failure detectors: specification and implementation. *3rd European Dependable Computing Conf. (EDCC'99)*, Springer LNCS 1667, pp. 71-87, 1999.

[14] Dwork C., Lynch N., and Stockmeyer L., Consensus in the presence of partial synchrony. *Journal of the ACM*, 35(2), 288-323, 1988.

[15] Fischer M.J., Lynch N.A., and Paterson M.S., Impossibility of distributed consensus with one faulty process. *Journal of the ACM*, 32(2):374-382, 1985.

[16] Friedman R., Mostéfaoui A., and Raynal M., Simple and efficient oracle-based consensus protocols for asynchronous Byzantine systems. *IEEE Transactions on Dependable and Secure Computing*, 2(1):46-56, 2005.

[17] Gafni E., Round-by-round fault detectors: unifying synchrony and asynchrony. *Proc. 17th ACM Symposium on Principles of Distributed Computing (PODC)*, ACM Press, pp. 143-152, 1998.

[18] Herlihy M.P., Kozlov D., and Rajsbaum S., *Distributed computing through combinatorial topology*, Morgan Kaufmann/Elsevier, 336 pages, 2014.

[19] Kihlstrom K.P., Moser L.E. and Melliar-Smith P.M., Byzantine fault detectors for solving consensus. *The Computer Journal*, 46(1):16-35, 2003.

[20] Lamport L., Shostack R., and Pease M., The Byzantine generals problem. *ACM Transactions on Programming Languages and Systems*, 4(3)-382-401, 1982.

[21] Lynch N.A., *Distributed algorithms*. Morgan Kaufmann Pub., San Francisco (CA), 872 pages, 1996 (ISBN 1-55860-384-4).

[22] Mostéfaoui A., Moumen H., and Raynal M., Signature-free asynchronous Byzantine consensus with $t < n/3$ and $O(n^2)$ messages. *Proc. 33th ACM Symp. on Principles of Distr. Computing (PODC'14)*, ACM Press, pp. 2-9, 2014.

[23] Mostéfaoui A. and Raynal M., Solving consensus using Chandra-Toueg's unreliable failure detectors: a general quorum-based approach. *Proc. 13th Int'l Symposium on Dist. Comp. (DISC'99)*, Springer LNCS 1693, pp. 49-63, 1999.

[24] Mostéfaoui A. and Raynal M., Signature-free broadcast based intrusion tolerance: never decide a Byzantine value. *Proc. 14th Int'l Conf. On Princ. Of Distr. Systems (OPODIS'10)*, Springer LNCS 6490, pp. 144-159, 2010.

[25] Moumen H., Mostéfaoui A., and Trédan G., Byzantine consensus with few synchronous links. *Proc. 11th Int'l Conference On Principles Of Distributed Systems (OPODIS'07)*, Springer LNCS 4878, pp. 76-89, 2007.

[26] Pease M., R. Shostak R., and Lamport L., Reaching agreement in the presence of faults. *Journal of the ACM*, 27:228-234, 1980.

[27] Rabin M., Randomized Byzantine generals. *Proc. 24th IEEE Symposium on Foundations of Computer Science (FOCS'83)*, IEEE Computer Society Press, pp. 116-124, 1983.

[28] Raynal M., *Fault-tolerant agreement in synchronous message-passing systems*. Morgan & Claypool, 165 pages, 2010.

[29] Raynal M., *Communication and agreement abstractions for fault-tolerant asynchronous distributed systems.* Morgan & Claypool Publishers, 251 pages, 2010.

[30] Raynal M., *Concurrent programming: algorithms, principles, and foundations.* Springer, 530 pages, 2013.

Stabilizing Server-Based Storage in Byzantine Asynchronous Message-Passing Systems

[Extended Abstract]

Silvia Bonomi
DIAG
Università La Sapienza
Roma, Italia
bonomi@dis.uniroma1.it

Shlomi Dolev
Dept. of Computer Science
Ben-Gurion Univ. of the Negev
Beer-Sheva, Israel
dolev@cs.bgu.ac.il

Maria Potop-Butucaru
LIP6, Univ. P. & M. Curie
Paris, France
maria.potop-butucaru@lip6.fr

Michel Raynal
Institut Universitaire de France
IRISA, Université de Rennes
Rennes, France
raynal@irisa.fr

ABSTRACT

A stabilizing Byzantine single-writer single-reader (SWSR) regular register, which stabilizes after the first invoked write operation, is first presented. Then, new/old ordering inversions are eliminated by the use of a (bounded) sequence number for writes, obtaining a practically stabilizing SWSR atomic register. A practically stabilizing Byzantine single-writer multi-reader (SWMR) atomic register is then obtained by using several copies of SWSR atomic registers. Finally, bounded time-stamps, with a time-stamp per writer, together with SWMR atomic registers, are used to construct a practically stabilizing Byzantine multi-writer multi-reader (MWMR) atomic register. In a system of n servers implementing an atomic register, and in addition to transient failures, the constructions tolerate $t < n/8$ Byzantine servers if communication is asynchronous, and $t < n/3$ Byzantine servers if it is synchronous. The noteworthy feature of the proposed algorithms is that (to our knowledge) these are the first that build an atomic read/write storage on top of asynchronous servers prone to transient failures, and where up to t of them can be Byzantine.

Categories and Subject Descriptors

C.2.4 [**Computer-Communication Network**]: Distributed Systems -*distributed applications, network operating systems*; D.4.5 [**Operating Systems**] Reliability -*fault-tolerance*; F.1.1 [**Computation by Abstract Devices**]: Models of Computation -*Computability theory*

General Terms: Algorithms, Reliability, Theory

Permission to make digital or hard copies of all or part of this work for personal or classroom use is granted without fee provided that copies are not made or distributed for profit or commercial advantage and that copies bear this notice and the full citation on the first page. Copyrights for components of this work owned by others than ACM must be honored. Abstracting with credit is permitted. To copy otherwise, or republish, to post on servers or to redistribute to lists, requires prior specific permission and/or a fee. Request permissions from Permissions@acm.org.
PODC'15, July 21–23, 2015, Donostia-San Sebastián, Spain.
Copyright © 2015 ACM 978-1-4503-3617-8 /15/07 ...$15.00.
DOI: http://dx.doi.org/10.1145/2767386.2767441 .

Keywords: Asynchronous message-passing system, Atomic read/write register, Byzantine server, Clients/servers architecture, Distributed algorithm, Fault-tolerance, Read/write register, Regular register, Self-stabilization, Transient failures.

1. INTRODUCTION

Byzantine processes and self-stabilization. Algorithms that tolerate Byzantine faults are of extreme interest, as they can tolerate malicious takeovers of portions of the system, and still achieve the desired goal. Moreover, as the program executed by several of the participants may include programming mistakes, it is possible that these participants will (unintentionally) behave in a malicious way. Obviously, when all participants exhibit Byzantine arbitrary behavior, the system output will be arbitrary too.

Usually, upper bounds on the number of Byzantine participants are used as part of the algorithm design assumptions. The cases in which the lower bound is not respected are not considered, as the system can reach an arbitrary configuration due to the possibly overwhelming malicious actions. Assume that some of the Byzantine participants regain consistency (possibly by rebooting, running anti-virus software, environment change) so that the assumed threshold on the number of Byzantine participants is now respected. Will the system regain consistency, from this arbitrary configuration? Or in other words will the system stabilize to a correct behavior?

Related work and aim of the paper. An active research area concerns the construction of a Byzantine-tolerant disk storage (e.g.,[2, 5, 15] to cite a few). Many of these papers consider registers built on top of duplicated disks (servers), which are accessed by clients, and where disks and clients may exhibit different type of failures. The construction of a reliable shared memory on top of a Byzantine message-passing system is addressed in [11].

Recently, several works investigated stabilizing Byzantine algorithms e.g., [4, 9, 10]. The first of these papers is the most related to our research, as it constructs a stabilizing

Byzantine multi-writer multi-reader regular register, where t out of n servers (with $n \geq 5t+1$) can be Byzantine. Such a construction relies on the *write operation quiescence* assumption, i.e., it is assumed that, after a burst of write operations executed by the writer, there exists a sufficiently long period during which the writer does not invoke the write operation. Differently, we construct a *practically stabilizing Byzantine multi-writer multi-reader atomic* register in a client/server system which is able to tolerate transient failures and up to t Byzantine servers. Given t, our solutions require $n \geq 8t+1$ servers when client/server communication is asynchronous, and only $n \geq 3t+1$ servers when it is synchronous. This gap comes from the fact that, as they provide bounds on message transfer delays, synchronous settings allows readers and writers to use timers. As far as we know, our construction is the first that builds a distributed atomic read/write memory on top of asynchronous servers, which communicate by message-passing, can suffer transient failures, and where some of them can exhibit a Byzantine behavior.

Roadmap. The paper is made up of 6 sections. The computing model and the problem which is addressed are presented in Section 2. Then, Section 3 presents and proves correctness of an algorithm that builds a stabilizing single-writer single-reader (SWSR) regular register. This algorithm is extended in Section 4 to obtain an SWSR atomic register, and Section 5 shows how to go from "single-reader" to "multi-reader" and from "single-writer" to "multi-writer". Finally Section 6 concludes the paper. Due to page limitation, the synchronous communication case and proofs can be found in [3].

2. COMPUTING MODEL AND THE PROBLEM WE WANT TO SOLVE

2.1 Computing model

Basic system model. The basic system model we consider consists of $(n+2)$ asynchronous sequential processes. One of them is called "writer" (denoted p_w), another is called "reader" (denoted p_r), while the n others are called "servers" (denoted s_1, ..., s_n).

From a communication point of view, there are $4n$ directed asynchronous communication links, connecting each server to p_w and p_r (one in each direction). Each link is FIFO and reliable (neither loss, corruption, duplication, nor creation of messages).

It is assumed that processing times are negligible, and are consequently assumed to take zero time. Only message transfers take time.

This basic model will be later enriched in two directions: one concerning the number of writers and readers, and a second concerning the synchrony of the communication links.

Failure model. At most $t < n/8$ servers can commit Byzantine failures[1]. Let us remember that a server commits a Byzantine failure when it behaves arbitrarily [12]. Classical examples of a Byzantine behavior consists in sending erroneous values, not sending a message when this should be done, stopping its execution, etc.

In addition to the possibility of Byzantine servers, the local variables of any process (writer, reader, servers) can suffer transient failures. This means that their values can be arbitrarily modified [6]. It is nevertheless assumed that there is a finite time τ_{no_tr} (which remains always unknown to the processes) after which there are no more transient failures[2].

From a terminology point of view, a server is *correct* if it does not commit Byzantine failures. Hence, as the reader and the writer, any correct server can suffer transient failures.

Configurations and executions. Each process (writer, reader, or server) is a state machine, enriched with the operations send and receive. Its state (called "local state") is defined by the current values of its local variables. The state of a directed link consists of the messages that have been sent on this link, and are not yet received.

A configuration (or global state) is composed of the local state of each process and the state of each link. Due to the "transient failures" behavioral assumption, the initial configuration can be arbitrary.

Underlying ss-broadcast abstraction. It is assumed that the system has a built-in communication abstraction, denoted ss-broadcast, that provides the reader and the writer with an operation denoted ss_broadcast(), and each server with a matching operation denoted ss_deliver(). When the reader or the writer (resp., server) uses this broadcast abstraction, we consequently say that it "ss-broadcasts" (resp., "ss-delivers") a message. This communication abstraction is defined by the following properties.

- *Termination.* If the reader or the writer invoke the operation ss_broadcast(m) then such invocation terminates.
- *Eventual delivery.* If the reader or the writer invokes ss_broadcast(m) then every correct server eventually ss-delivers m.
- *Synchronized delivery.* If a process p_x (reader or writer) invokes ss_broadcast(m) at time τ_1^x and returns from this invocation at time τ_2^x, then there exists a set S of $(n-2t)$ correct servers, such that, for each $s_i \in S$, there exists a time $\tau(i)$ such that $\tau_1^x < \tau(i) < \tau_2^x$ at which s_i executed ss_deliver(m).
- *No duplication.* An invocation of ss_broadcast(m) by a process p (reader or writer) results in at most one ss_deliver(m) at any correct server s_i.
- *Validity.* If a correct server s_i ss-delivers a message m from p (reader or writer), then either p ss-broadcasts m, or m belongs to the initial state of the corresponding link.

[1]Actually, Byzantine failures can be "mobile" [17, 18].This means that, if, after some time, a server that committed Byzantine failures, starts behaving correctly, a server that was previously behaving correctly can become Byzantine. This "failure mobility" can occur at any time during the periods where there is no pending read or write operation, issued by p_w or p_r. In fact, in any case, the system is guaranteed to converge to exhibiting the desired behavior once the assumptions concerning the system hold again for a "long enough" period of time.

[2]This assumption is required to ensure that, despite asynchrony and Byzantine behaviors, the problem we are interested in can be solved. In fact, if the time between two successive transient faults is long enough, the system converges and produces useful outputs between transient failures.

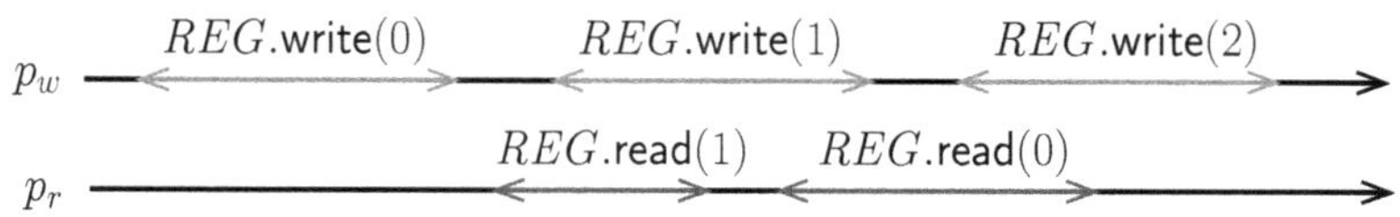

Figure 1: Regular register: new/old inversion

- *Order delivery.* Any correct server ss-delivers the messages ss-broadcast by a process p_x (reader or writer) in the order in which they have been ss-broadcast.

Implementations of such a broadcast abstraction are presented in Section 4.2 of [6], (see also [7, 8]). They rely on bounded capacity communication links[3].

2.2 Problem Statement

Construction of a read/write register and assumptions. The problem in which we are interested is the construction of a stabilizing server-based atomic register REG, that can be written by the writer p_w, and read by the reader p_r. From an abstraction point of view, the register provides the writer with an operation write(v), where the input parameter v is the new value of the register, and the reader with an operation read(), which returns the value of the register.

The construction is done incrementally. A regular register is first built. Then this construction is enriched to obtain an atomic register. Both constructions assume that (a) there is a time after which there is no more transient failures (instant τ_{no_tr}), and (b) the writer invokes at least once the write() operation after τ_{no_tr}. According to case (b), let $\tau_{1w} > \tau_{no\_tr}$ be the time at which the first write invoked after τ_{no_tr} terminates.

Concurrent operations, read and write sequences. Let W and R be the executions of a REG.write() operation by the writer and REG.read() operation by the reader, respectively. If W and R overlap in time, they are said to be *concurrent*. If they do not overlap, they are said to be *sequential.*

Let us observe that, as the writer p_w (resp., reader p_r) is sequential, the set of invocations of the operation write() (resp., read()) defines a sequence S_W (resp., S_R).

Stabilizing regular register. A *regular* read/write register is defined by the following properties[4].

- *Liveness.* Any invocation of REG.write() or REG.read() terminates.

- *Eventual regularity.* There is a finite time $\tau_{stab} > \tau_{1w}$ after which each REG.read() R returns a value v that was written by a REG.write() operation W that is (a) the last write operation executed before R, or (b) a write operation concurrent with R.

Let us observe that, as there is at least one invocation of REG.write() (assumption), and any invocation of REG.write() terminates (liveness), τ_{1w} exists. Let us also observe that, before τ_{stab}, read operations can return arbitrary values. If a read/write register is regular, we say that the value returned by each of its read operations is regular.

The duration $\tau_{stab} - \tau_{no\_tr}$ is the time needed for the system to stabilize. After τ_{stab}, no invocation of REG.read() returns an arbitrary value. But, while after τ_{stab} regularity prevents REG from returning too "old" values, it still allows REG to return values in an order different from their writing order, as described in Figure 1. The first read returns the value 1 (whose write is concurrent with it), while the second read returns the value 0 (which was the last value written before it starts). This phenomenon is known under the name "new/old inversion".

Stabilizing atomic register. Such a register is a stabilizing regular register that, after some time, does not allow new/old inversion. It is defined by the following properties.

- *Liveness.* Any invocation of REG.write() or REG.read() terminates.

- *Eventual atomicity.* There is a finite time $\tau_{stab} > \tau_{1w}$ after which any invocation of REG.read() returns a regular value, and there are no two invocations of REG.read() that return new/old inverted values.

Informally, this means that it is possible to merge sequences S_W and S_R to obtain a sequence S where, after time τ_{stab}, each read operation returns the last value written by the closest write operation that precedes it.

Notation and other read/write registers. The previous registers are called stabilizing regular (or atomic) single-writer single-reader (SWSR) registers. The SWSR atomic register will be used in Section 5 as a building block to construct stabilizing atomic single-writer multi-reader (SWMR) registers, and stabilizing atomic multi-writer multi-reader (MWMR) registers.

3. CONSTRUCTION OF A STABILIZING SWSR REGULAR REGISTER

This section presents a stabilizing algorithm that implements a single-writer single-reader regular register in the system model introduced in Section 2.1.

3.1 Algorithm

The algorithms implementing the operations REG.write(), REG.read(), and the behavior of the servers s_i, are described in Figure 2. The writer and the reader terminate their operations when they execute the statement return() (line 06 for the writer, and lines 13 or 15 for the reader).

[3]Roughly speaking, in a simple implementation, when a message m send operation is invoked by a correct process p_i to a correct process p_j, p_i repeatedly sends the packet $(0, m)$ to p_j until it receives $(cap + 1)$ packets from p_j (where cap is the maximal number of packets in transit from p_i to p_j and back). Then p_i repeatedly sends the packets $(1, m)$ to p_j until it receives $(cap + 1)$ packets from p_j. Process p_j sends (bit, ack) only when receiving (bit, m), and executes ss_deliver(m) when receiving the packet $(1, m)$ immediately after receiving the packet $(0, m)$.

[4]These definitions of a stabilizing regular register, and a stabilizing atomic register, are straightforward extensions of the basic definitions given in [13].

```
operation write (v) is      % issued by the writer p_w %
(01) ss_broadcast WRITE (v) to all servers;
(02) wait (messages ACK_WRITE (helping_val) received from (n − t) different servers);
(03) if ¬(∃ w ≠ ⊥ such that helping_val = w for (4t + 1) of the previous messages)
(04)      then ss_broadcast NEW_HELP_VAL(v) to all servers
(05) end if;
(06) return().

operation read () is      % issued by the reader p_r %
(07) new_read_r ← true;
(08) while (true) do
(09)      ss_broadcast READ (new_read_r) to all servers;
(10)      new_read_r ← false;
(11)      wait (messages ACK_READ (last_val, helping_val)
                              received from (n − t) different servers);
(12)      if ((2t + 1) of the previous messages have the same last_val)
(13)        then let v be this value; return(v)      % the value returned is regular or atomic %
(14)        else if ((2t + 1) of the previous messages have the same helping_val ≠ ⊥)
(15)              then let w be this value; return(w)   % the value returned is atomic %
(16)             end if
(17)      end if
(18) end while.
--------------------------------------------------------------------------------
when WRITE (v) is ss_delivered from p_w do
(19) last_val_i ← v;
(20) send ACK_WRITE (helping_val_i) to p_w.

when NEW_HELP_VAL (v) is ss_delivered from p_w do
(21) helping_val_i ← v.

when READ (new_read) is ss_delivered from p_r do
(22) if (new_read) then helping_val_i ← ⊥ end if;
(23) send ACK_READ (last_val_i, helping_val_i) to p_r.
```

Figure 2: Byzantine-tolerant stabilizing SWSR regular register

Local variables and update messages. Each server s_i, $1 \leq i \leq n$, manages two local variables, which locally define its internal representation of the constructed regular register REG.

- The aim of the variable $last\_val_i$ is to store the last value written by the writer, as known by s_i.
  To that end, when it invokes REG.write(v), the writer ss-broadcasts the message WRITE (v) to inform the servers of the new value v.

- The aim of the variable $helping\_val_i$ is to contain the last value ss-broadcast by the writer to each server s_i, when identifying that the reader requests assistance as write operations are too frequent. This variable is reset to $\perp$ at the beginning of every new read.

There is no specific local variable managed by the writer. As far as the reader is concerned, it has to manage a single local variable.

- new_read_r is a Boolean flag, that, when true, demands each server to reset to $\perp$ its helping local variable $helping\_val_i$. To this end, the reader ss-broadcasts the message READ(new_read_r), where new_read_r = `true`, each time it starts a new read operation.

Algorithm implementing REG.write(). As already said, when the writer invokes REG.write(v), it first ss-broadcasts the message WRITE(v) (line 01), and waits until it receives an acknowledgment message ACK _WRITE($helping\_val$) from $(n-t)$ servers, (i.e., from at least $(n-2t)$ correct servers) (line 02).

When a server s_i ss-delivers the message WRITE(v), it updates $last\_val_i$ (line 19), and sends by **return** (line 20) the acknowledgment ACK _WRITE($helping\_val_i$) to give the writer information on the state of the reader (namely, the equality $helping\_val_i = \perp$ means that the reader started a new read operation, and accordingly $helping\_val_i$ needs to be refreshed).

When the writer stops waiting, it checks if it has received the same value $helping\_val \neq \perp$ from at least $(4t+1)$ different servers (line 03). If this predicate is false, the local variables $helping\_val_i$ of the servers s_i needs to be refreshed. To this end, the writer ss-broadcasts the message NEW_HELP_VAL(v) to inform them that, from now on, they must consider v as the new helping value (lines 04 and 21).

Algorithm implementing REG.read(). When the reader invokes REG.read(), it sets new_read_r to `true` (line 07) and enters a while loop (lines 08 and 18), that it exits at line 13 or 15. Once in the loop body, the reader starts a new inquiry by ss-broadcasting the message READ(new_read_r) to the servers. If $new\_read_r = \texttt{true}$, the message is related to a new read operation (line 07); if $new\_read_r = \texttt{false}$, it is from the same read operation as before (line 10). Then, the reader waits until it has received an acknowledgment message ACK _READ($last\_val, helping\_val$) from $(n - t)$ servers (line 11).

When a server s_i receives the message READ(new_read_r), it resets $helping\_val_i$ to $\perp$ if this message indicates a new read operation started (line 22). In all cases (i.e., whatever the value of new_read_r), it sends by return its current local state in the message ACK _READ($last\_val_i, helping\_val_i$) (line 23).

When the reader stops waiting, it returns the value v if the field $last\_val$ of $(2t + 1)$ messages ACK _READ() is equal to v (lines 12-13). Otherwise it returns the value w if the field $helping\_val$ of $(2t+1)$ messages ACK _READ() is equal to $w \neq \perp$ (lines 14-15). If none of these predicates is satisfied, the reader re-enters the loop body.

Remark on the reception order of the acknowledgment messages ACK_WRITE() **and** ACK_READ()**.** It is important to notice that, thanks to the properties of the ss-broadcast abstraction, and the fact that the links are FIFO, we have the following. When the writer invokes ss_broadcast(), and later waits for associated acknowledgments ACK_WRITE() from $(n-t)$ servers (lines 01-02), the sequence of acknowledgments received from each correct server matches the sequence of ss_broadcast() it issued (the same holds for the reader and the acknowledgments ACK_READ(), lines 09-11). This means that ss_broadcast() and the associated acknowledgments do not need to carry sequence numbers.

3.2 Proof of the construction

All the poofs assume $n \geq 8t + 1$.

LEMMA 1. *Any invocation of* write () *terminates.*

Proof Due to the ss-broadcast termination property, the writer cannot block forever when it invokes ss_broadcast() at line 01 or line 04. As far the wait statement of line 02 is concerned, we have the following: due to the ss-broadcast eventual delivery property, eventually at least $(n - t)$ non-Byzantine servers ss-deliver the message WRITE() ss-broadcast by the writer, and then they will eventually answer by returning the acknowledgment message ACK_WRITE(), which concludes the proof of the lemma. $\square_{Lemma\ 1}$

LEMMA 2. *Any invocation of* read () *terminates.*

Proof Using the same reasoning as in Lemma 1, it follows that the reader cannot block forever in the wait statement of line 11. So, the proof consists in showing that the predicate of line 12, or the one of 14, becomes eventually true. The rest of the proof is by contradiction. Let R be the first invocation of read () that does not terminate and let us consider an execution of the loop body after time τ_{stab}.

Claim C. At the time at which a write that started after τ_{no_tr} terminates, there are (a) at least $(n - 2t)$ correct servers s_i such that $last\_val_i = v$, and (b) at least $(3t + 1)$ correct servers s_j such that $helping\_val_j = w \neq \perp$.

Proof of the claim. Let us consider a write started after τ_{no_tr} and let τ_w be the time at which such write terminates. Considering that after τ_{no_tr} there are no more transient failures and due to the synchronized delivery property of the ss-broadcast we have that at time τ_w there are at least $(n - 2t)$ correct servers s_i such that $last\_val_i = v$. Moreover, if the predicate of line 03 is true, it follows from (a) the synchronized delivery property of the ss-broadcast of the message NEW_HELP_VAL() (line 04), and (b) the fact that $n-2t > 3t+1$, that at least $(3t+1)$ correct servers s_j are such that $helping\_val_j = w \neq \perp$. If predicate of line 03 is false, there are $(4t + 1)$ servers that sent ACK_WRITE(w) where $w \neq \perp$ (line 20), from which we conclude that at least $(3t+1)$ of them are correct and are such that $helping\_val_j = w \neq \perp$. *End of the proof of the claim* C.

Let us consider the last write that terminated before R started, and let us assume it wrote x. Due to part (a) of Claim C, just after this write terminated, at least $(n - 2t)$ correct servers s_i are such that $last\_val_i = x$. If no write is concurrent with R, as R receives from $(n - t)$ servers at line 11 messages ACK_READ($last\_val, -$) (i.e., from at least $(n - 2t)$ correct servers), it follows from the fact that the intersection of any two sets $Q1$ and $Q2$ of $(n - 2t)$ correct servers (the set $Q1$ of correct servers s_i such that $last\_val_i = x$, and the set $Q2$ of correct servers from which R receives ACK_READ ($last\_val, -$)) contains at least $(2t + 1)$ correct servers, that R terminates at lines 12-13.

Let us now assume that there is exactly one write that is concurrent with R, and let y be the value it writes. Due to the synchronized delivery property of ss-broadcast, R first resets to $\perp$ the variables $helping\_val_i$ of at least $n-2t \geq 6t+1$ correct servers s_i (lines 07, 09, and 22), and then receives (line 11) messages ACK_READ($last\_val, -$) from at least $n - 2t \geq 6t+1$ correct servers. We show that at least $(2t+1)$ of these messages carry either x or y, from which R terminates at lines 12-13. Due to part (a) of Claim C, there were at least $n-2t \geq 6t+1$ correct servers s_i such that $last\_val_i = x$ when the write of x finished. Let Q be this set of servers. R receives messages ACK_READ($last\_val, -$) from at least $(4t+1)$ servers in Q. Due to the operation write(y) (concurrent with R), variables $last\_val_i$ of some of these servers may have been updated to the value y. Hence, some of the previous $(4t+1)$ messages ACK_READ($last\_val, -$) received by R carry x, while others carry y. Hence, at least $(2t+1)$ of them carry either x or y, and R terminates at lines 12-13.

Let us finally consider the case where there are more than one write concurrent with R. When R terminates its invocation of ss_broadcast READ(true) (there is only one such invocation per read operation, line 09), the local variables $helping\_val_i$ of $(n - 2t)$ correct servers are equal to $\perp$. Let Q' be this set of servers. (The proof of this statement is the same as the proof appearing in the first part of claim C.) Hence, when this ss-broadcast terminated, the messages ACK_READ($-, helping\_val_i$) sent by each server $s_i \in Q'$ (at line 23), is such that $helping\_val_i = \perp$. Let us consider the first write (e.g., write(z)) that occurs after the servers $s_i \in Q'$ have set $helping\_val_i$ to $\perp$. This write receives $(n-t)$ messages ACK_WRITE ($helping\_val$), and at least $(4t + 1)$ of them are from servers in Q' and carry $helping\_val = \perp$. Hence the predicate of line 03 is satisfied, and the writer issues ss_broadcast NEW_HELP_VAL(z). If later (i.e., after the invocation of write(z) terminated), there are other invocations of write() concurrent with R, none of them will execute line 04. This is due to the fact that R does not reset the variables $helping\_val_i$ to $\perp$, and the $(n - t)$ messages ACK_WRITE ($helping\_val$) sent by the servers at line 20 are such that at most t are from Byzantine servers, and at least $(4t+1)$ carry z, from which follows that there is a finite time τ_R after which the variables $helping\_val_i$ of the correct servers are no longer modified. Let us finally consider the first invocation of ss_broadcast (new_read_r) issued by R after τ_R, such that new_read_r = **false**. It follows from the previous discussion that, among the $(n-t)$ messages ACK_READ$(-, helping_val)$ received by R, at most t (the ones from Byzantine servers) carry arbitrary values, and at least $(n-t)-3t \geq 4t+1$ carry the value z. When this occurs, R terminates at lines 14-15. $\square_{Lemma\ 2}$

LEMMA 3. *Let $t < n/8$. There is a finite time $\tau_{stab} > \tau_{1w}$ after which each read invocation R returns a value v that was written by a write operation W, which is (a) the last write operation executed before R, or (b) a write operation concurrent with R.*

Proof Let us assume that a read operation R returns z, a value different from the value v of the last completed write prior to R, and from any value u of a concurrent write. Let us consider the first write concurrent with R. For R to return z, the reader must receive $(2t+1)$ messages ACK_READ$(z, -)$ or $(2t+1)$ messages ACK_READ$(-, z)$. However, immediately following the termination of the write of v there were $(n-2t)$ correct servers s_i with $last\_val_i = v$. Thus, following the termination of the write of v, and until the termination of the next write of some value u, the reader cannot receive $(2t+1)$ values for a value z different from v and u. The above argument holds for the second concurrent write, where we start with $(n-2t)$ values of u, and so on and so forth. $\square_{Lemma\ 3}$

THEOREM 1. *Let $t < n/8$. The algorithm described in Figure 2 implements a stabilizing regular register in the presence of at most t Byzantine servers.* (The proof follows from Lemmas 1, 2, and 3.)

3.3 The case of synchronous links

Let us consider a communication model where the links are synchronous. *Synchronous* means here that each link, connecting the reader or the writer and a correct server, is timely i.e., there is an upper bound on message transfer delays and this bound is known by the processes. When considering the construction of an SWSR regular register, this allows the reader or the writer to know how long it has to wait for a round trip delay with respect to the correct servers, and consequently use a timer with an appropriate timeout value.

It appears that the previous algorithm can be adapted, with very a simple modification, to this synchronous communication model to build a stabilizing SWSR regular register. Due to page limitation, this algorithm is described and proved correct in [3]. Hence, this algorithm implements a stabilizing regular register in the presence of at most t Byzantine servers.

4. CONSTRUCTION OF A STABILIZING SWSR PRACTICALLY ATOMIC REGISTER

Practically stabilizing SWSR atomic register. A stabilizing SWSR *practically* atomic register is a stabilizing SWSR regular register with no new/old inversions as long as the number of writes between two successive reads (that are not executed concurrently with any write) is less than a given constant called *system-life-span* (e.g., 2^{64}) [1].

This section presents a practically stabilizing SWSR atomic register that stabilizes after the first read that (a) is not concurrent with a write, and (b) follows the first write that follows the last transient failure. Its operations are denoted prac_at_write() and prac_at_read().

Algorithm. The stabilizing SWSR *practically* atomic register algorithm is described in Figure 3. It is an extension of the algorithm implementing a stabilizing regular register presented Figure 2. The lines with the same number xy are exactly the same in both algorithms. A line numbered Nx is a new line, while a line numbered xyMz corresponds to a modification of the line xy of Figure 2.

Underlying principle. To obtain an algorithm implementing such a register, the main idea is to count the invocations of prac_at_write() so that no new/old inversion can occur if the reader traces the sequence number attached to each written value, and exchange an older value with a newer that is already known. This is the role of the write sequence number denoted $\underline{wsn}$. Hence, the data value v appearing in Figure 2 in now replaced by the pair $(\underline{wsn}, v)$ in Figure 3. Therefore, $last\_val_i$ contains now such a pair, and $helping\_val_i$ contains now either such a pair, or the default value $\perp$.

Special care must be taken to bound $\underline{wsn}$ so that there is no ambiguity on its current value. Hence, a relation $\succeq$ on sequence numbers has to be defined, such that it always reflects the write order of the values they are associated with. This relation is defined as follows: given two integer x and y (e.g., in range $[0, 2^{128}+1]$), $x \geq_{cd} y$ iff the clockwise distance (hence the subscript cd) from y to x is smaller than their anti-clock distance; moreover, $x >_{cd} y$ if $x \geq_{cd} y$ and $x \neq y$. Such precedence relation is used at lines N6 and 13M2 to compare the highest previously received sequence number $pwsn$ with the current one and to update it (lines N6, 13M2, and 15M). As transient failures may corrupt counter values, those must be automatically corrected. This is done as follows. After the first read, which follows a write invocation and does not overlap a write, it holds that the local pair $(pwsn, pv)$ stored by the reader reflects the last read correct value. Thus, the bookkeeping of $pwsn$, pv, and the values of $\underline{wsn}$ and v, which are read, reflects the right value ordering which allow their correct reordering, thereby providing the writer and the reader with an atomic register.

The aim of the lines N2-N7 is to do a sanity check for the the local pair $(pwsn, pv)$ managed by the reader. To that end, the reader ss-broadcasts the message READ (**false**), and wait for $(n-t)$ associated acknowledgments ACK_READ $(-, helping\_val)$ (lines N2-N3). If $(2t+1)$ of these messages carry the same pair $helping\_val = (\underline{wsn}, v)$, and $\underline{wsn}$ is smaller than $pvsn$, then the reader adopts this pair as current value of $(pvsn, pv)$. This is because, if $(2t+1)$ of these messages carry the same pair, they reflect the last value written, and therefore carry the correct wsn. Hence, the "if" statement in line N6, whose aim is to refresh the pair $(pvsn, pv)$. This preliminary sanity check, which relies on values provided by the servers, helps the rest of the read algorithm (lines 07-18 which are nearly the same as the ones of Figure 2) prevent new/old inversions from occurring.

operation prac_at_write (v) **is** % issued by the writer p_w %
(N1) $\underline{wsn} \leftarrow (\underline{wsn}+1) \bmod (2^{64}+1)$;
(01M) ss_broadcast WRITE ($\underline{wsn}, v$) to all servers;
(02) wait (messages ACK_WRITE ($helping\_val$) received from $(n-t)$ different servers);
(03) **if** $\neg(\exists\, w \neq \perp$ such that $helping\_val = w$ for $(4t+1)$ of the previous messages$)$
(04M) **then** ss_broadcast NEW_HELP_VAL($\underline{wsn}, v$) to all servers
(05) **end if**
(06) return().

operation prac_at_read () **is** % issued by the reader r_i where $1 \leq i \leq r$ %
(N2) ss_broadcast READ (false) to all servers;
(N3) wait (messages ACK_READ ($last\_val, helping\_val$) received from $(n-t)$ different servers);
(N4) **if** ($(2t+1)$ of the previous messages have the same $helping\_val \neq \perp$)
(N5) **then let** ($\underline{wsn}, v$) be this value;
(N6) **if** ($pwsn >_{cd} \underline{wsn}$) **then** $pwsn \leftarrow \underline{wsn}$; $pv \leftarrow v$ **end if** % sanity check for $pwsn$ and pv %
(N7) **end if**;
(07) $new\_read_r \leftarrow$ true;
(08) **while** (true) **do**
(09) ss_broadcast READ (new_read_r) to all servers;
(10) $new\_read_r \leftarrow$ false;
(11) wait (messages ACK_READ ($last\_val, helping\_val$) received from $(n-t)$ different servers);
(12) **if** ($(2t+1)$ of the previous messages have the same $last\_val$)
(13M1) **then let** ($\underline{wsn}, v$) be this value;
(13M2) **if** ($\underline{wsn} >_{cd} pwsn$) **then** $pwsn \leftarrow \underline{wsn}$; $pv \leftarrow v$; return(v)
(13M3) **else** return(pv) % prevention of new/old inversion %
(13M4) **end if**
(14) **else if** ($(2t+1)$ of the previous messages have the same $helping\_val \neq \perp$)
(15M) **then let** ($\underline{wsn}, w$) be this value; $pwsn \leftarrow \underline{wsn}$; $pv \leftarrow w$; return(w) % already atomic %
(16) **end if**
(17) **end if**
(18) **end while**.

---

when WRITE (sn, v) **is** ss_delivered **from** p_w **do** % v is now a pair ($seq.\ nb, value$) %
(19) $last\_val_i \leftarrow v$;
(20) send ACK_WRITE ($helping\_val_i$) to p_w.

when NEW_HELP_VAL (v) **is** ss_delivered **from** p_w **do** % v is now a pair ($seq.\ nb, value$) %
(21) $helping\_val_i \leftarrow v$.

when READ (new_read) **is** ss_delivered **from** p_r **do**
(22) **if** (new_read) **then** $helping\_val_i \leftarrow \perp$ **end if**;
(23) send ACK_READ ($last\_val_i, helping\_val_i$) to p_r.

Figure 3: Byzantine-tolerant practically stabilizing SWSR atomic register

5. CONSTRUCTION OF STABILIZING SWMR AND MWMR ATOMIC REGISTERS

5.1 Construction of a Practically Stabilizing SWMR Atomic Register

The technique to obtain a SWMR atomic register from SWSR atomic registers is a classical one [14, 16]. The writer interacts with each reader, writing the same value to all readers, the servers maintaining variables for each reader. Since the result is atomic register for each reader, and any write is executed to all, then the result is a single-writer multi-reader register. Let swmr_write() and swmr_read() denote the operations associated with such a SWMR atomic register.

5.2 Construction of a Practically Stabilizing MWMR Atomic Register

This section presents a stabilizing algorithm that implements a multi-writer multi-reader atomic register in the system model introduced in Section 2.1.

Underlying SWMR atomic registers. It is assumed that each process is both a reader and a writer. Hence, in the following we use the term "process". Let m be the number of processes. A process is denoted p_i, $1 \leq i \leq m$. The construction uses one stabilizing SWMR register per process. Let $REG[i]$ be the SWMR register associated with p_i, which means that any process can read it but only p_i can write it.

When p_i wants to write $REG[i]$, it invokes the operation $REG[i]$.swmr_write($v, epoch, seq$), where $epoch$ is a bounded

```
operation mwmr_write (v) is    % issued by process p_i %
(01) for j ∈ {1,...,m} do reg_i[j] ← REG[j].swmr_read() end for; % obtains m triples (val, epoch, seq) %
(02) if ((∄ max_epoch(reg_i[1..m])) ∨ (∃j : [(reg_i[j].epoch = max_epoch(reg_i[1..m])) ∧ (reg_i[j].seq ≥ 2^64)]))
(03)    then reg_i[i] ← (v, next_epoch(reg_i[1..m]), 0)
(04) end if;
(05) let M be the set of indexes j such that max_epoch(reg_i[1..m]) = reg_i[j].epoch;
(06) seq_max ← max(reg_i[j].seq, j ∈ M);
(07) REG[i].swmr_write(v, max_epoch(reg_i[1..m]), seq_max + 1);
(08) return().

operation mwmr_read () is    % issued by process p_i %
(09) for j ∈ {1,...,m} do reg_i[j] ← REG[j].swmr_read() end for; % obtains m triples (val, epoch, seq) %
(10) if ((∄ max_epoch(reg_i[1..m])) ∨ (∃j : [(reg_i[j].epoch = max_epoch(reg_i[1..m])) ∧ (reg_i[j].seq ≥ 2^64)]))
(11)    then reg_i[i] ← (reg_i[i].v, next_epoch(reg_i[1..m]), 0); REG[i].swmr_write(reg_i[i].v, reg_i[i].epoch, 0)
(12) end if;
(13) let M be the set of indexes j such that max_epoch(reg_i[1..m]) = reg_i[j].epoch;
(14) seq_max ← max(reg_i[j].seq, j ∈ M);
(15) let min ∈ M be the minimal index such that reg_i[min].seq = seq_max;
(16) return(reg_i[min].v).
```

Figure 4: Byzantine-tolerant stabilizing MWMR atomic register from SWMR registers

label (see below), and seq is a sequence number bounded by some large constant 2^{64}. Any process p_j reads $REG[i]$ by invoking $REG[i]$.swmr_read(). Such an invocation returns a triple $(v, epoch, seq)$, where v is a data value, whose associated timestamp is the pair $(epoch, seq)$.

The notion of an epoch. This notion was introduced in [1] where a bounded labeling scheme is proposed with uninitialized values. Let $k > 1$ be an integer, and let $K = k^2 + 1$. We consider the set $X = \{1, 2, .., K\}$ and let $\mathcal{L}$ (the set of epochs) be the set of all ordered pairs (s, A) where $s \in X$ and $A \subseteq X$ has size k.

The comparison operator $\succ$ among two epochs is defined as follows:

$$(s_i, A_i) \succ (s_j, A_j) \stackrel{def}{=} (s_j \in A_i) \wedge (s_i \notin A_j).$$

Note that this operator is antisymmetric by definition, yet may not be defined for every pair (s_i, A_i) and (s_j, A_j) in $\mathcal{L}$ (e.g., $s_j \in A_i$ and $s_i \in A_j$).

Given a subset S of epochs of $\mathcal{L}$, a function is defined in [1] which compute a new epoch which is greater (with respect to $\succ$) than every label in S. This function, called next_epoch(), is as follows. Given a subset of k epochs $(s_1, A_1), (s_2, A_2), \ldots, (s_k, A_k)$, next_epoch$((s_1, A_1), (s_2, A_2), \ldots, (s_k, A_k))$ is the epoch (s, A) that satisfies:

- s is an element of X that is not in the union $A_1 \cup A_2 \cup \ldots \cup A_k$ (as the size of each A_s is k, the size of the union is at most k^2, and since X is of size $k^2 + 1$ such an s always exists).
- A is a subset of X. Its isz k and it contains all values $(s_1, s_2, \ldots, s_k)$ (if they are not pairwise distinct, add arbitrary elements of X to get a set of size exactly k).

The relation $\succ$ is extended to $\succeq$ as follows:

$$(s_i, A_i) \succeq (s_j, A_j) \stackrel{def}{=} ((s_i, A_i) \succ (s_j, A_j)) \vee ((s_i = s_j) \wedge (A_i = A_j)).$$

The predicate max_epoch() applied to a set of epochs returns true if there is an epoch in the set such that is equal to or greater (in the sense of the relation $\succeq$) than any other epoch in the set.

Algorithm implementing mwmr_write(). When a process p_i invokes mwmr_write (v), it first checks if it has to start a new epoch (lines 01-04), in which it first reads all the underlying SWMR registers $REG[1..m]$, and saves their values in its local array $reg_i[1..m]$ (line 01). This constitutes its view of the global state. Hence, for any $j \in \{1, ..., m\}$, $reg_i[j]$ contains a triple $(v, epoch, seq)$, namely, $reg_i[j].v$ is the data value of REG_j, $reg_i[j].epoch$ is the epoch of the timestamp of v, and $reg_i[j].seq$ is the sequence number of the timestamp of v.

Then, if there is no greatest epoch in $reg_i[1..m]$, or there is one $(reg_i[j].epoch)$, but the associated sequence number $(reg_i[j].seq)$ is equal to or greater than the bound 2^{64}, p_i must start the next epoch ($ne =$ next_epoch$(reg_i[1..m])$ with starts with the sequence number 0, and informs the other processes. To this end p_i writes the value v and its timestamp $(ne, 0)$ in $REG_i[i]$.

Then p_i writes the value v with its epoch and sequence number (line 07). The pair (epoch, sequence number) is computed at lines 05-07 so that it is greater than all the previous pairs known by p_i.

Algorithm implementing mwmr_read(). The algorithm implementing the operation mwmr_read () is nearly the same as the one implementing the operation mwmr_write (). The lines 09-12 are the same as the lines 01-04, except line 11 where p_i writes into the timestamp of $reg_i[i]$ a new epoch.

The second difference is at lines 14-16, where the value returned by the read operation is computed. This value is the one associated with the greatest epoch known by p_i and the greatest sequence number, and where process identities are used to do tie-breaking (if needed).

6. CONCLUSION

This paper was on the implementation of stabilizing server-based storage on top of an asynchronous message-passing system where up to t servers can exhibit a Byzantine behavior. A first basic algorithm was represented, which implements a single-writer single-reader *regular* register stabilizing after the first write invocation. This algorithm tolerates $t < n/8$ if communication is asynchronous, and $t < n/3$ if it is synchronous. This algorithm was then extended to obtain a *practically stabilizing atomic* single-writer single-reader register. Finally, the paper presented a generalization allowing any number of processes to read and write the practically stabilizing atomic register.

This paper, together with [4], is one of the very first to address the construction of a read/write register in an asynchronous system where all servers can experience transient failures, and some of them can behave arbitrarily. While the algorithms presented in [4], require the "operation quiescence" assumption, and build only regular registers, (as already noticed in the introduction) our constructions are the first that build a distributed atomic read/write memory on top of asynchronous servers, which communicate by message-passing with the readers and writers processes, can suffer transient failures, and where some of them can exhibit a Byzantine behavior.

Acknowledgments

Shlomi Dolev wants to acknowledge the support of the following institutions: Rita Altura Trust Chair in Computer Sciences; Israel Science Foundation (grant 428/11); Israeli Internet Association; Israeli Ministry of Science and Technology; Infrastructure Research in the Field of Advanced Computing and Cyber Security. Michel Raynal wants to acknowledge the support of the French ANR project DISPLEXITY (devoted to distributed computability and complexity) and the Franco-German ANR project DISCMAT (devoted to the mathematics of distributed computing). Silvia Bonomi wants to acknowledge the support of the Italian PRIN project TENACE (MIUR-PRIN 20103P34XC) and the EU FP7 project PANOPTESEC.

7. REFERENCES

[1] Alon N., Attiya H., Dolev S., Dubois S., Potop-Butucaru M., and Tixeuil S., Pragmatic self-stabilization of atomic memory in message-passing systems. *Proc. 13th Int'l Symposium on Stabilization, Safety, and Security of Distr. Systems (SSS'11)*, Springer LNCS 6976, pp. 19-31, 2011. Journal version in *Journal of Computer and System Sciences* 81(4): 692-701 (2015).

[2] Attiya H. and Bar-Or A., Sharing memory with semi-Byzantine clients and faulty storage servers. *Parallel Processing Letters*, 16(4):419-428, 2006.

[3] Bonomi S., Dolev S., Potop-Butucaru M., and Raynal M., Stabilizing server-based storage in Byzantine asynchronous message-passing systems. *CoRR abs/1503.00140*, 2015.

[4] Bonomi S., Potop-Butucaru M., and Tixeuil S., Stabilizing Byzantine fault-tolerant storage. To appear in *Proc. 29th IEEE Int'l Parallel & Distributed Processing Symposium*, IEEE Press, 2015.

[5] Chockler G. and Malkhi D., Active disk Paxos with infinitely many processes. *Distributed Computing*, 18(1):73-84, 2005.

[6] Dolev S., *Self-stabilization*, MIT Press, 197 pages, ISBN 0-262-04178-2, 2000.

[7] Dolev S., Dubois S., Potop-Butucaru M., and Tixeuil S., Stabilizing data-link over non-FIFO channels with optimal fault-resilience. *Information Processing Letters*, 111(18): 912-920, 2011.

[8] Dolev S., Hanemann A., Schiller E., and Sharma S., Stabilizing end-to-end communication in (bounded capacity, omitting, duplicating and non-FIFO) dynamic networks. *Proc. 14th Int'l Symposium on Stabilization, Safety, and Security of Distributed Systems (SSS'12)*, Springer LNCS 7596, pp. 133-147, 2012.

[9] Dolev S., Liba O., and Schiller E., Stabilizing Byzantine resilient topology discovery and message delivery. *Proc. of the First International Conference Networked Systems (NETYS'13)*, pp. 42-57, 2013.

[10] Dolev S.. Welch J., Stabilizing clock synchronization in the presence of Byzantine faults. *Journal of the ACM*, 51(5):780–799, 2004.

[11] Imbs D., Rajsbaum R., Raynal M., and Stainer, J., Reliable shared memory abstractions on top of asynchronous t-resilient Byzantine message-passing systems. *Proc. 21st International Colloquium Structural Information and Communication Complexity (SIROCCO 2014)*, Springer LNCS 8576, pp. 37–53, 2014.

[12] Lamport L., Shostack R. and Pease M., The Byzantine generals problem. *ACM Transactions on Programming Languages and Systems*, 4(3)-382-401, 1982.

[13] Lamport L., On inter-process communications, Part I: basic formalism. *Distributed Computing*, 1(2): 77–85, 1986.

[14] Lamport L., On interprocess communication, Part II: algorithms. *Distributed Computing*, 1(2):77-101, 1986.

[15] Martin J.-Ph. and Alvisi L., A framework for dynamic Byzantine storage. *Proc. Int'l Conference on Dependable Systems and Networks (DSN'04)*, IEEE Press, pp. 325-334, 2004.

[16] Raynal M., *Concurrent programming: algorithms, principles, and foundations.* Springer, 516 pages, ISBN 978-3-642-32027-9, 2013.

[17] Santoro N. and Widmayer P., Time is not a healer. *Proc. 6th Annual Symposium on Theoretical Aspects of Computer Science (STACS'89)*, Springer LNCS 349, pp. 304-313 (1989)

[18] Santoro N. and Widmayer P., Agreement in synchronous networks with ubiquitous faults. *Theoretical Computer Science*, 384(2-3): 232-249, 2007.

Dual Failure Resilient BFS Structure

Merav Parter *
Dept. of Computer Science and Applied Math
The Weizmann Institute
Rehovot, Israel
merav.parter@weizmann.ac.il

ABSTRACT

We study *breadth-first search (BFS)* spanning trees, and address the problem of designing a sparse *fault-tolerant* BFS structure, or *FT-BFS* for short, resilient to the failure of up to two edges in the given unweighted undirected graph G, i.e., a sparse subgraph H of G such that subsequent to the failure of up to two edges, the surviving part H' of H still contains a BFS spanning tree for (the surviving part of) G. FT-BFS structures, as well as the related notion of replacement paths, have been studied so far for the restricted case of a single failure. It has been noted widely that when concerning shortest-paths in a variety of contexts, there is a sharp qualitative difference between a single failure and two or more failures [7]. Our main results are as follows. We present an algorithm that for every n-vertex unweighted undirected graph G and source node s constructs a (two edge failure) FT-BFS structure rooted at s with $O(n^{5/3})$ edges. To provide a useful theory of shortest paths avoiding 2 edges failures, we take a principled approach to classifying the arrangement these paths. We believe that the structural analysis provided in this paper may decrease the barrier for understanding the general case of $f \geq 2$ faults and pave the way to the future design of f-fault resilient structures for $f \geq 2$. We also provide a matching lower bound, which in fact holds for the general case of $f \geq 1$ and multiple sources $S \subseteq V$. It shows that for every $f \geq 1$, and integer $1 \leq \sigma \leq n$, there exist n-vertex graphs with a source set $S \subseteq V$ of cardinality σ for which any FT-BFS structure rooted at each $s \in S$, resilient to up to f-edge faults has $\Omega(\sigma^{1/(f+1)} \cdot n^{2-1/(f+1)})$ edges. In particular, for $f = 2$ and $\sigma = 1$, a dual failure FT-BFS structure rooted at s must have $\Omega(n^{5/3})$ edges in the worst case. Finally, we also consider the optimization variant for this problem, and propose an $O(\log n)$ approximation algorithm for constructing FT-BFS structures resilient to up to f-faults for any constant $f \geq 1$ and any source set $S \subseteq V$.

*Supported in part by the Israel Science Foundation (grant 894/09), and the I-CORE program of the Israel PBC and ISF (grant 1549/13). Recipient of the Google European Fellowship in distributed computing; research is supported in part by this Fellowship.

Permission to make digital or hard copies of all or part of this work for personal or classroom use is granted without fee provided that copies are not made or distributed for profit or commercial advantage and that copies bear this notice and the full citation on the first page. Copyrights for components of this work owned by others than ACM must be honored. Abstracting with credit is permitted. To copy otherwise, or republish, to post on servers or to redistribute to lists, requires prior specific permission and/or a fee. Request permissions from permissions@acm.org.
PODC'15, July 21–23, 2015, Donostia-San Sebastián, Spain.
Copyright is held by the owner/author(s). Publication rights licensed to ACM.
ACM 978-1-4503-3617-8 /15/07 ...$15.00.
http://http://dx.doi.org/10.1145/2767386.2767408.

Categories and Subject Descriptors

F.2.3 [**Theory of Computation**]: Analysis of Algorithms and Problem Complexity—*Tradeoffs among Complexity Measures*

General Terms

Algorithms, Reliability, Theory

Keywords

Fault-tolerance, replacement-paths, lower bounds

1. INTRODUCTION

Background and motivation. Large network systems of electricity, telephony or communication are traditionally designed to withstand the possibility of a *single* failure in one of their components. This is partially justified by the optimistic view that a failure is a rare event. Yet, since in modern day huge communication networks several components may fail or malfunction at any given time, the restriction to single failure events mainly stems from the unfortunate fact that supporting the capability of coping two failures or more is, in many cases, considerably more complex than having to overcome just a single failure. For example, when considering the setting of shortest path in some underlying graph, it has been widely noted that there is a sharp qualitative and quantitative difference between shortest paths avoiding just one failure and paths avoiding two or more failures. We consider the structure of *breadth-first search (BFS)* spanning trees, and address the problem of designing dual failure *fault-tolerant* BFS structure, or FT-BFS for short. By this we mean a subgraph H of the given network G, such that subsequent to the failure up to two of the edges, the surviving part H' of H still contains a BFS spanning tree for the surviving part of G.

Typical network design problems involve three types of objectives: (1) construction time (i.e., cost of the preprocessing phase) (2) quality of usage, i.e., efficiency of operations preformed in the constructed structure, and (3) the size of the constructed structure. The current work is motivated by settings in which objectives (2) and (3) play a dominant role. In particular, objective (2) is important in cases where using approximate shortest paths instead of exact ones (e.g., for routing), entails a high cost on the system and it is preferable to purchase a larger structure that will allow optimal operation (e.g., routing on shortest paths). Subject to objective (2), it is still desirable to construct (or purchase) the minimum cost structure satisfying the usability requirements (e.g., optimum routing). A typical motivation for this is a setting where the graph edges represent the channels of a communication network, and the system designer would like to purchase or lease a minimal collection of channels (i.e., a subgraph $G' \subseteq G$) that maintains its functionality as a BFS tree with respect to the source s upon failures in G. In such a context, the cost of computation at the preprocessing stage (i.e., objective (1)) may be negligible compared to the purchasing/leasing cost of the resulting structure. Hence, our key cost measure in this paper is the *size* of the fault tolerant structure that provides the exact shortest paths distance from a given source vertex s, and our main goal is to achieve *sparse* (or *compact*) such structures (our construction time is still polynomial in n). The notion of FT-BFS structure is closely related to the problem of constructing *replacement paths* and in particular to its *single source* variant, studied in [8] only for the single failure case. For a source node s, a target node v and an edge $e \in G$, the shortest $s - v$ path $P_{s,v,e}$ that does not go through e is known as a *replacement path*. The replacement path problem requires to compute the collection $\mathcal{P}_{s,v}$ of all $s - v$ replacement paths $P_{s,v,e}$ for every failed edge e that appears on the $s - v$ shortest-path $\pi(s, v)$ in G. Note that a replacement path is, by definition restricted to a single failure event. Under this restricted setting, the replacement path $P_{s,v,e}$ admits a rather convenient form[1], consisting of three segments: a prefix of the shortest-path $\pi(s, v)$ up to some vertex $b \in \pi(s, v)$ occurring before the failing edge e, followed by a "detour" avoiding the path $\pi(s, v)$ (and in particular the failing edge e), and terminating with a suffix of $\pi(s, v)$. This clean decomposition has led to the development of algorithms that compute the collection $\mathcal{P}_{s,v}$ efficiently (cf. [9, 15, 2, 18, 8]). A replacement path $P_{s,v,e}$ is called *new-ending* if its last edge is different from the last edge of the shortest path $\pi(s, v)$. Put another way, a new-ending replacement path $P_{s,v,e}$ has the property that once it diverges from the shortest-path $\pi(s, v)$ at the vertex b, it joins $\pi(s, v)$ again only at the final vertex v. It is shown in [10] that for a given graph G and source vertex s, a structure $H \subseteq G$ containing a BFS tree rooted at s plus the last edge of each new-ending replacement path $P_{s,v,e}$ for every $e \in G$ and $v \in V$, is a single-failure FT-BFS structure. This means that it suffices to focus on the new-ending replacement paths and pick a single edge from each of them (specifically, the last). Furthermore, by analyzing the special structure of the new-ending paths, it is shown therein that such a structure consists of $O(n^{3/2})$ edges where n is the number of vertices in the graph. This result is complemented by a matching lower bound showing that for every sufficiently large integer n, there exist an n-vertex graph G and a source $s \in V$, for which every single failure FT-BFS structure is of size $\Omega(n^{3/2})$. Since *exact* FT-BFS structures may be rather expensive, [12, 3] exploit the structure of replacement-paths to construct *approximate* FT-BFS structures with $O(n)$ edges for unweighted undirected graphs.

Indeed, the convenient structure of the replacement paths has facilitated the development of solutions to many other related problems, such as dynamic algorithms for shortest paths and *f-sensitivity distance oracles*, capable of efficiently answering proximity queries following a f-failures event [5, 2]. Recently, distance sensitivity oracles have been considered for weighted and directed graphs in the *single source* setting [8]. An efficient construction of single source distance oracles for planar graphs is provided in [1].

Yet, this long line of results, heavily exploits the structure of the single failure replacement path, and is consequently limited to handling no more than one fault in the network. A natural goal is to generalize some of these results to settings with two or more failures. It appears that the main barrier for such an extension is rooted in the fact that the structure of a replacement path $P_{s,v,F}$ avoiding an edge pair F is rather involved and no longer admits a nice decomposition as its single failure counterparts. Since understanding the structure of replacement paths and their interactions proved to be fundamental when designing fault resilient structures, understanding the structure $P_{s,v,F}$ is key essential step for making the desired jump from a single failure to at least two, for many network design tasks. A remarkable breakthrough in this direction is obtained in [7], presenting the first 2-sensitivity distance oracle of size $O(n^2 \log^3 n)$, capable of answering 2-sensitivity queries in $O(\log n)$ time. Indeed, both the data structure and the query algorithm of [7] are considerably more complex than the single failure case studied in [5, 2]. An f-sensitivity distance oracle overcoming $f \geq 1$ failures is given in [18]. By using fast matrix multiplication, [18] yields the first sub-cubic time (randomized) algorithm for the replacement paths problem when the edge-lengths are small integers. Yet, despite the time efficient algorithm of [18] the understanding of the underlying structural properties of these paths is still lacking.

We note that in certain cases the jump from one fault to multiple faults is quite natural and tractable. For example, in the setting of *fault tolerant spanners* for an arbitrary undirected weighted graph, it is shown in [4] that there exists a (polynomially constructible) f-vertex fault tolerant $(2k-1)$-spanner of size $O(f^2 k^{f+1} \cdot n^{1+1/k} \log^{1-1/k} n)$ and an f-edge fault tolerant $(2k-1)$-spanner of size $O(f \cdot n^{1+1/k})$ for a graph of size n. A randomized construction attaining an improved tradeoff for vertex fault-tolerant spanners was shortly afterwards presented in [6].

Finally, observe that the dual-failure FT-BFS structure studied in this paper is limited in three senses: (1) it is rather dense, although it matches the lower bound, (2) it deals with a single source, and (3) it supports up to two edge faults. Given the density of the structure (i.e., (1)), one may claim that it may be better to use approximate structures as provided in [12, 13] for example, instead of exact ones. While this is true, we believe that it is still very important to understand the more fundamental exact problem first. The "theory" of paths avoiding two faults provided in this paper would surely be a key building block for designing *approximate* structures that avoid two faults (e.g., in the same manner that the theory of single fault replacement paths of [10] laid the basis for approximate structures avoiding single fault in [12, 13]). In particular, we believe that understanding the single source case, beyond the single edge failure event, is an important milestone for designing fault tolerant structures under more generalized settings: One axis of generalization is increasing the number of supported sources, i.e., considering a setting where

[1]upon a proper construction, e.g., breaking shortest-path ties in a consistent manner

one is given a subset of sources $S \subseteq V$, and it is desired to provide a dual failure FT-BFS tree rooted at each source $s \in S$. Multi-source FT-BFS structures, referred to hereafter as FT-MBFS have been studied in [10] for the case of a single edge (or vertex) failure and have been later shown to provide an important building block in designing sparse *fault tolerant additive spanners*, that provide a bounded additive stretch for *all* pairs in the graph under the failing of a single edge (or vertex) [13]. An additional axis of generalization is increasing the number of supported faults. A natural generalized structure is an f-FT-BFS which contains the collection of all single source replacement paths avoiding up to f edges in the graph. Combining these two axes results in f-FT-MBFS structure, that for a given source set $S \subseteq V$ provides an f-FT-BFS structure with respect to each source $s \in S$. We believe that the structural theory of dual failure replacement paths developed in this paper paves the way to understanding these generalized structures. Towards this end, we provide two results for the generalized setting, namely, lower bound constructions and approximability results, as elaborated in next paragraph.

Contributions. We present an algorithm that for every n-vertex unweighted undirected graph G and source node s, constructs a dual failure FT-BFS structure rooted at s with $O(n^{5/3})$ edges. The size analysis of the output subgraph requires a deep understanding of the various configurations that may be assumed by replacement paths avoiding two faults. An essential component in our analysis deals with the detour segment of the single failure replacement paths. While a tight universal upper bound on the size of f-fault FT-BFS structures for general $f \geq 1$ is currently beyond our reach, we do have several results for the case of f failures for any constant $f \geq 1$. We also present a lower bound stating that for every cardinality of sources $1 \leq \sigma \leq n$, there exists an n-vertex graph and a source set $S \subseteq V$ where $|S| = \sigma$, for which any f-fault FT-MBFS structure for each $s \in S$ requires $\Omega(\sigma^{1/(f+1)} \cdot n^{2-1/(f+1)})$ edges. Hence, for $f = 2$ and $\sigma = 1$ the lower bound translates into $\Omega(n^{5/3})$ edges, which matches our upper bound construction. Finally, note that while our upper bound algorithm matches the worst-case lower bounds, they might still be far from optimal for certain instances, see [11]. Consequently, in Sec. 5 of the full paper [14], we complete the upper bound analysis by presenting an $O(\log n)$ approximation algorithm for the Minimum FT-MBFS problem in which one is given a graph $G = (V, E)$, constant integer $f \geq 1$, a source set $S \subseteq V$, and it is required to construct an f-failure FT-MBFS subgraph H of minimum size (i.e., number of edges). This approximation algorithm is superior in instances where the graph enjoys a sparse f-failure FT-MBFS tree (even linear in $O(n)$), hence paying $O(\sigma^{1/(f+1)} \cdot n^{2-1/(f+1)})$ edges is wasteful. Missing proofs are deferred to the full version [14].

THEOREM 1.1 (UPPER BOUND, SINGLE SOURCE). *For every unweighted undirected graph $G = (V, E)$ and source vertex $s \in V$, there is a (polynomially time constructible) dual failure FT-BFS structure $H \subseteq G$ with respect to s, with $O(n^{5/3})$ edges.*

THEOREM 1.2 (LOWER BOUND FOR MULTIPLE SOURCES). *For every constant $f \geq 1$, $n \geq o(1)$ and $1 \leq \sigma \leq n$, there exist an n-vertex graph $G(V, E)$ and a source set $S \subseteq V$ of cardinality σ such that any f-FT-MBFS structure for the source set S has $\Omega(\sigma^{1-1/(f+1)} \cdot n^{2-1/(f+1)})$ edges. In particular, dual failure FT-BFS structures requires $\Omega(n^{5/3})$ edges.*

THEOREM 1.3 (APPROXIMATION FOR f-FAILURES). *There exists a polynomial time algorithm that for every constant $f \geq 1$ and n-vertex graph G and source set $S \subseteq V$ constructs an f-failure FT-MBFS structure H with respect to S whose size (i.e., number of edges) is larger by a factor of at most $\Theta(\log n)$ than the optimal structure H^* (by Thm. 1 of [10], this is tight up to constants, assuming $P \neq NP$).*

Preliminaries and notation. Given an unweighted undirected graph $G = (V, E)$ and a source node s, let $T_0(s) \subseteq G$ be a shortest paths (or BFS) tree rooted at s. Throughout, the edges of these paths are considered to be directed away from the source node s. For a path $P = [v_1, \ldots, v_k]$, let LastE(P) be the last edge of path P. Let $|P|$ denote the length of the path and $P[v_i, v_j]$ be the subpath of P from v_i to v_j. For paths P_1 and P_2, $P_1 \circ P_2$ denote the path obtained by concatenating P_2 to P_1. A vertex w is a *divergence point* of the $s - v$ paths P_1 and P_2 if $w \in P_1 \cap P_2$ but the next vertex u after w (i.e., such that u is closer to v) in the path P_1 is not in P_2. Given an $s - v$ path P and an edge $e = (x, y) \in P$, let dist(s, e, P) be the distance (in edges) between s and e on P.

Assuming an edge weight function $W : E(G) \rightarrow \mathbb{R}^+$, let $SP(s, v_i, G, W)$ be the set of $s - v_i$ shortest-paths in G according to the edge weights of W. If W is a weight assignment that guarantees the uniqueness of the shortest paths, then we override the definition and let $P = SP(u, v, G, W)$ be the unique $u - v$ shortest path in G according to W. Throughout, the edges of these paths are considered to be directed away from the source node s.

Techniques and proof outline. For a source node s, a target node v and a pair $F = \{e_i, t_j\} \subseteq G$ of failed edges, the shortest $s - v$ path $P_{s,v,F}$ that does not go through the edge pair F is the natural extension of the well studied single failure *replacement path*. Thus, our dual failure FT-BFS structure must contain some replacement path $P_{s,v,F}$ for every $v \in V(G)$ and every edge pair $F \subseteq E(G)$. It is convenient to view the failing edges $F = \{e_i, t_j\}$ as corresponding to two subsequent independent failing events where first the edge e_i fails and later on, the second edge t_j fails. If the first failing edge e_i does not lie on the $s - v$ shortest-path $\pi(s, v)$, then the replacement path $P_{s,v,\{e_i\}}$ is simply $\pi(s, v)$. Otherwise, when $e_i \in \pi(s, v)$, the replacement path $P_{s,v,\{e_i\}}$ consists of a prefix of $\pi(s, v)$ followed by a detour D_i avoiding $\pi(s, v)$ (and e_i), followed by a suffix of $\pi(s, v)$. Consider now the second failing edge t_j. Clearly, if t_j is not on $P_{s,v,\{e_i\}}$ then the dual failure replacement path $P_{s,v,F}$ remains as is, i.e.,$P_{s,v,F} = P_{s,v,\{e_i\}}$. The interesting case is where $t_j \in P_{s,v,\{e_i\}}$. This case is further divided into two subcases. In the first subcase, t_j appears on either the prefix or the suffix segments of $P_{s,v,\{e_i\}}$, i.e., t_j appears on $\pi(s, v)$. A replacement path $P_{s,v,F}$ protecting against two faults on $\pi(s, v)$ is called hereafter a (π, π)-*replacement path*, see Fig. 1(a). In the complementary subcase, the second failing edge t_j appears on the detour segment D_i, i.e., $t_j \in P_{s,v,\{e_i\}} \setminus \pi(s, v)$. A replacement path $P_{s,v,F}$ for $F = \{e_i, t_j\}$ where e_i lies on $\pi(s, v)$ and the t_j lies on the detour D_i is called hereafter a (π, D)-*replacement path*. See Fig. 1(b). Our algorithm for constructing the dual failure FT-BFS structure, Alg. Cons2FTBFS, carefully selects a replacement path

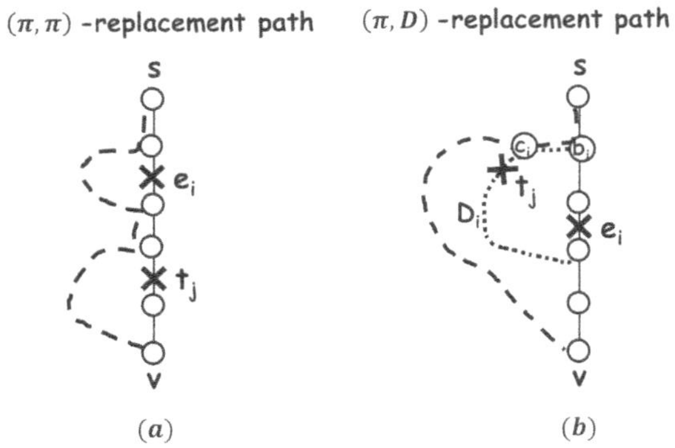

Figure 1: Illustration of dual failure replacement paths $P_{s,v,F}$ for $F = \{e_i, t_j\}$. (a) (π, π)-replacement path $P_{s,v,F}$ where $F \subseteq \pi(s, v)$. (b) (π, D)-replacement path where $e_i \in \pi(s, v)$ and t_j occurs on the detour D_i protecting the failing of e_i.

$P_{s,v,F}$ for every $v \in V$ and for every edge pair $F \subset E$. Essentially, for each vertex v, the algorithm constructs a subgraph $H(v)$ consisting of the *last edges* of the replacement paths $P_{s,v,F}$, i.e., $H(v) = \bigcup_{F \subseteq E, |F| \leq 2} \texttt{LastE}(P_{s,v,F})$ where $\texttt{LastE}(P_{s,v,F})$ is the last edge of the replacement path $P_{s,v,F}$. The final structure H is then given by taking the union, i.e., $H = \bigcup_{v \in V} H(v)$. In the analysis section, we show that (a) taking the last edge of each replacement path is *sufficient* and (b) the size (number of edges) of each $H(v)$ is bounded by $O(n^{2/3})$. A replacement path $P_{s,v,F}$ is called a *new-ending* path if its last edge was not present in the structure at the time that the path was selected by the algorithm. [2] Since only the last edges of the replacement paths are taken into the structure, it is required to bound the number of new-ending paths $P_{s,v,F}$. Indeed, the lion share of this paper is dedicated to bounding the size of $H(v)$, which turns out to be significantly more involved compared to the single failure case of [10]. We first consider the simplified case where the two failing edges lie on $\pi(s, v)$ and bound the number of new-ending (π, π)-replacement paths by $O(\sqrt{n})$. This is shown by using a very similar argument to that of the single failure case. The most technically involved task is bounding the number of new-ending (π, D)-replacement paths $P_{s,v,F}$. We classify these paths into two main classes. The first class consists of the paths $P_{s,v,F}$ that do not intersect the edges of the detour of the replacement path protecting their *first* failing edge. A new-ending path in this class has the following structure: it diverges from the shortest-path $\pi(s, v)$ at some vertex b (above the failing edge e_i) and joins $\pi(s, v)$ again only at the final vertex v, without intersecting the detour D_i at all (see Fig. 2(d)). The second class consists of new-ending paths $P_{s,v,F}$ that intersect their detour D_i in at least one edge. Any path in this class has the following structure: it diverges from the shortest-path $\pi(s, v)$ at the first vertex of the detour D_i, it then follows the detour D_i up to some vertex c above the failing edge t_j, and joins $\pi(s, v)$ and D_i again only at the final vertex v. In other words, such a path has two divergence points: a unique π-divergence point b_i where it departs from $\pi(s, v)$ and a D-divergence point c_i where it departs from D_i (see Fig. 2(c)). We proceed by briefly outlining the proof for the single failure case, i.e., bounding the number of $s - v$ new-ending $P_{s,v,\{e_i\}}$ paths by $O(\sqrt{n})$. We then consider the simplifying case where all shortest paths in $G \setminus F$ are unique (there are no two equally shortest replacement-paths) for every $F \subseteq E$, $|F| \leq 2$. Finally, we highlight the technicalities that arise in the general case (whose detailed treatment is deferred to the full paper, [14]).

[2]Note that in [10], a path is new-ending if its last edge is not in the initial BFS tree $T_0(s)$. Here the definition is more strict and depends on the time step in which the path was considered by the algorithm. Yet, since the initial graph H_0 used by the algorithm at step 0 contains the BFS tree $T_0(s)$, a new-ending path in the current definition, is also new-ending according to the definition of [10] (but not vice-versa).

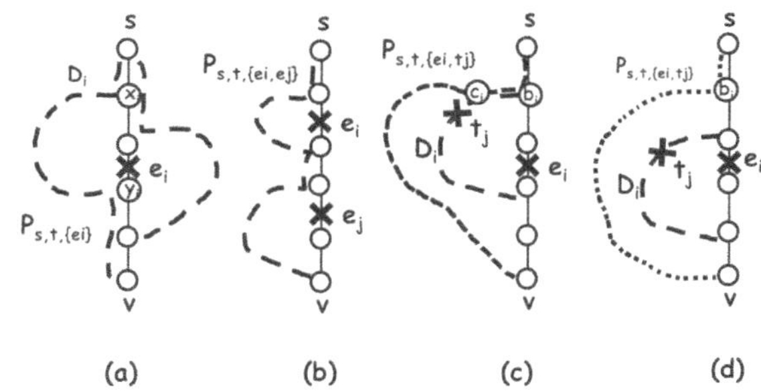

Figure 2: Three types of replacement paths each constructed by a distinct steps of Alg. Cons2FTBFS. (a) Single edge failure $e_i \in \pi(s, v)$. The algorithm selects the replacement path $P_{s,v,\{e_i\}}$ whose divergence point from $\pi(s, v)$ is as close to s as possible. (Shown on the right hand side is another candidate path of the same length with a lower distinct divergence point, the was not chosen.) (b) Two edge faults both occurring on $\pi(s, v)$. The corresponding replacement path $P_{s,v,\{e_i,e_j\}}$ may have two divergence points from $\pi(s, v)$. (c) One edge fault e_i is on $\pi(s, v)$ and one t_j is on of the detour segment D_i. The algorithm selects the replacement path $P_{s,v,\{e_i,t_j\}}$ with the "highest" (closest to s) divergence points b_i from $\pi(s, v)$ and c_i from the detour segment D_i. (d) As in (c), only that the replacement path $P_{s,v,\{e_i,t_j\}}$ does not intersect with its detour D_i.

Recap for the single failure case and first attempt. Assume that all shortest-paths are computed according to a weight assignment W that guarantees the uniqueness of the shortest-paths (i.e, breaking ties in a consistent manner). Consider the collection $P_1, \ldots, P_t$ of $s - v$ new-ending replacement paths where $P_i = P_{s,v,\{e_i\}}$ for $e_i \in \pi(s, v)$ and every path P_i ends with a distinct edge of v, i.e., $\texttt{LastE}(P_i) \neq \texttt{LastE}(P_j) \neq \texttt{LastE}(\pi(s, v))$ for every $i, j \in \{1, \ldots, t\}$.[3] We

[3]The replacement-paths are computed according to the weight assignment W that breaks the shortest-path ties.

now bound t by $O(\sqrt{n})$ and as there are n vertices, overall there are total of $O(n^{3/2})$ edges in a FT-BFS structure that contains the last edges of all replacement paths. For every path P_i, let b_i be the unique divergence point from $\pi(s,v)$. The following observation is crucial in this context.

OBSERVATION 1.4. *The suffixes* $\widetilde{P}_i = P_i[b_i, v] \setminus \{v\}$ *are vertex-disjoint, i.e.,* $\widetilde{P}_i \cap \widetilde{P}_j = \emptyset$ *for every* $i, j \in \{1, \ldots, t\}$.

Proof: Since b_i is the unique divergence point of P_i from $\pi(s,v)$, it holds that $\widetilde{P}_i \cap E(\pi(s,v)) = \emptyset$, for every $i \in \{1, \ldots, t\}$. Assume towards contradiction that there exists a common vertex $w \in \widetilde{P}_i \cap \widetilde{P}_j$ in the intersection. For an illustration see Fig. 3(a). This implies that there two distinct $w-v$ paths, namely, $P_i[w,v]$ and $P_j[w,v]$ in $G \setminus E(\pi(s,v))$, leading to contradiction by the uniqueness of W. (Informally, since in this case the failing edge e_i protected by P_i is not on $P_j[w,v]$ and vice-versa, it implies that one of the last edges, namely, LastE(P_i) or LastE(P_j) can be avoided in the structure.) The observation follows. ▮

In particular, by Obs. 1.4, we have that the collection of divergence points $b_1, \ldots, b_t$ are *distinct*. For an illustration see Fig. 3(b). This allows us to order the paths $P_1, \ldots, P_t$ in increasing distance between b_j and v where $\text{dist}(b_1, v, G) < \ldots < \text{dist}(b_t, v, G)$. For every $j \in \{1, \ldots, t\}$, we then have that $|\widetilde{P}_j| \geq \text{dist}(b_j, v, G) \geq j - 2$. Finally, by exploiting the disjointness of the suffixes, we can bound the total number of vertices occupied by these suffixes, by $n \geq |\bigcup_{j=1}^{t} \widetilde{P}_j| = \sum_{j=1}^{t} |\widetilde{P}_j| \geq \sum_{j=1}^{t} j - 2 = \Omega(t^2)$, hence $t = O(\sqrt{n})$. In addition, by Obs. 1.4, it also holds that $t \leq \text{dist}(s, v, G)$ and hence the FT-BFS structure contains $O(\min\{\sqrt{n}, \texttt{depth}\} \cdot n)$ edges where depth is the depth of the BFS tree.

Unfortunately, when considering the dual failure case, the key observation, Obs. 1.4, fails to hold. Consider two dual failure new-ending replacement paths $P_i = P_{s,v,\{e_i,t_i\}}$ and $P_j = P_{s,v,\{e_j,t_j\}}$ where t_k is on the detour segment D_k of $P_{s,v,\{e_k\}}$ for $k \in \{i,j\}$. In addition, since we only care for bounding the number of edges incident to v, these paths are selected so that each ends with a new and distinct edge, i.e., LastE$(P_i) \neq$ LastE$(P_j) \neq$ LastE$(\pi(s,v))$. Let b_i (resp., b_j) be the unique divergence point of P_i (resp., P_j) from $\pi(s,v)$. By definition it holds that the suffix $\widetilde{P}_k = P_k[b_k, v] \setminus \{v\}$ is disjoint with $\pi(s,v)$ for both $k \in \{i,j\}$. Yet, in contrast to the single failure case, we can no longer show that these suffixes are disjoint. To see this, assume there exists a common vertex w in the intersection where $w \in \widetilde{P}_i \cap \widetilde{P}_j$. In the single failure case, since both failing edges e_i and e_j lie on $\pi(s,v)$, we had the guarantee that they do not appear on either of the segments $P_i[w,v]$ and $P_j[w,v]$. Hence, in such a case, the two $w-v$ subpaths $P_i[w,v]$ and $P_j[w,v]$ are interchangeable and safe to be used by both of the paths P_i and P_j (i.e., safe in the sense that they do not contain the failing edges of these paths). Unfortunately, in our case, since the second failing edge of P_j, namely, t_j, is not on $\pi(s,v)$ (but rather on the detour D_j), we no longer have such guarantee. Specifically, it might be the case that t_j appears on the suffix $P_i[w,v]$ and hence the subpath $P_i[w,v]$ is no longer *safe* for P_j, which justifies the introduction of the two new edges, LastE(P_i) and LastE(P_j). For an illustration see Fig. 3(c).

Since only the last edges of each replacement-path are taken into the structure, in our analysis, we consider one representative replacement-path for each new edge incident to v.

This toy example illustrates that dual failure replacement paths may share many vertices, which makes the mission of bounding their number much less tractable.

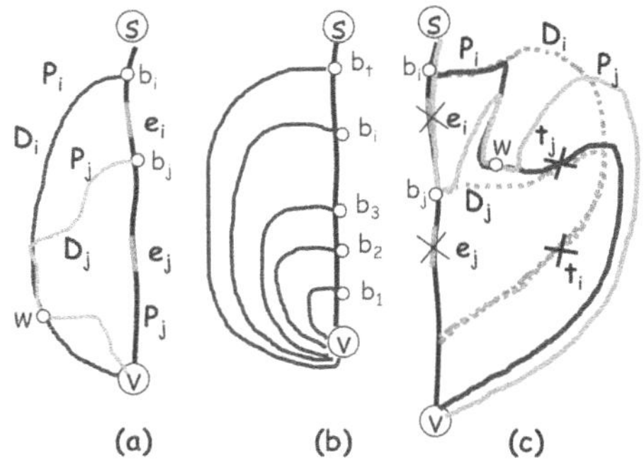

Figure 3: (a) The single failure case. The suffixes $\widetilde{P}_i = P_i[b_i, v]$ are disjoint. The existence of a vertex w in the intersection implies that there are two safe routes from w to v (of the same lengths). Note that these routes are safe since they do not intersect with the edges of $\pi(s,v)$. (b) The disjointness of the suffixes implies that the divergence points are distinct and hence can be ordered on the $\pi(s,v)$ path in increasing distance from v. (c) The dual failure case. Shown are two (π, D)-replacement paths $P_i = P_{s,v,\{e_i,t_i\}}$ and $P_j = P_{s,v,\{e_j,t_j\}}$ where $t_i \in D_i$ and $t_j \in D_j$. The suffixes $\widetilde{P}_i$ and $\widetilde{P}_j$ intersect at the common vertex w, however the subpath $P_i[w,v]$ contains the failing edge t_j and hence cannot be used by the path P_j.

Easy case (1) : f-faults on $\pi(s,v)$. To warm up, we proceed by claiming that the collection of last edges of the $s-v$ replacement-paths protecting against at most f faults on the shortest path $\pi(s,v)$ is bounded by $O(\sqrt{n})$. Consider the collection of $s-v$ replacement paths $\mathcal{P}_v = \{P_{s,v,F} \mid F \subseteq \pi(s,v), |F| \leq f\}$ and let $\widehat{E}_v = \{\text{LastE}(P) \mid P \in \mathcal{P}_v\}$.

LEMMA 1.5. $|\widehat{E}_v| = O(\sqrt{n})$ *for every* $v \in V$.

Proof: Fix v and consider $\mathcal{P}'_v$, the collection of representative paths from $\mathcal{P}_v$, each ending with a distinct last edge, i.e., LastE$(P) \neq$ LastE(P') for every $P, P' \in \mathcal{P}'_v$. For every $P \in \mathcal{P}'_v$, let $d(P)$ be the last divergence point from $\pi(s,v)$. We first claim that the suffix segments $P[d(P), v]$ are vertex disjoint besides the common endpoint v. To see this, assume towards contradiction that there exists a mutual vertex w in the intersection of $P[d(P), v]$ and $P'[d(P'), v]$ for two distinct paths $P, P' \in \mathcal{P}'_v$. Since P and P' ends with a distinct last edge, and as $d(P), d(P')$ are the last divergence points from $\pi(s,v)$, we get that there are two distinct $w-v$ paths in $G \setminus E(\pi(s,v))$, namely, $P_1 = P[w,v]$ and $P_2 = P'[w,v]$, contradiction to the uniqueness of the shortest-paths.

We can then sort the paths P in $\mathcal{P}'_v$ in increasing distance of $d(P)$ and v, and the argumentation follows the exact same line as for the single edge fault case (i.e., the i'th segment $P_i[d(P_i), v]$ is of length at least i for every $i \in \{1, \ldots, |\widehat{E}_v|\}$ and these segments are vertex disjoint). ▮

Easy case (2) : small FT-diameter graphs. Let $\texttt{depth}_f(G) = \max\{\text{dist}(s, v, G \setminus F) \mid F \subseteq E, |F| \leq f-1\}$ be the *f-FT-diameter* of the graph G. We proceed by claiming that graphs of small f-FT-diameter have relatively sparse f-**FT-BFS** structures (i.e., BFS structures that are resilient against the failing of at most f edges.) Since it is sufficient to collect the last edge from each replacement-path (by the same argument as for the single fault case), we have the following.

OBSERVATION 1.6. *For every n-vertex graph G and source vertex $s \in V$, there exists an f-FT-BFS structure $H \subseteq G$ with $O((\texttt{depth}_f(G))^f \cdot n)$ edges.*

A bit harder: the dual failure case with simplifying assumptions. We next sketch the size analysis for dual failure FT-structures, for a very degenerate case. We focus on vertex $v \in V$ and show that it has at most $O(n^{2/3})$ edges in the final structure H. The following notation is useful in our analysis. For every (π, D)-replacement path $P = P_{s,v,\{e_i,t_i\}}$, let $D(P) = P_{s,v,\{e_i\}} \setminus \pi(s,v)$ be the detour segment of $P_{s,v,\{e_i\}}$ such that $t_i \in D(P)$ (including the endpoints on $\pi(s,v)$), let $F(P) = \{e_i, t_i\}$ be the failing edges protected by P, $F_1(P) = e_i \in \pi(s,v)$ and $F_2(P) = t_i \in D(P)$. For two $s-v$ (π, D)-replacement paths P_i, P_j, we say that P_i *interferes* with P_j, if $F_2(P_j) \in P_i \setminus D(P_i)$. The (π, D)-paths P_i, P_j are *independent* if P_i does not interfere with P_j and vice-versa. For a fixed $v \in V$, define $H(v) = \{\texttt{LastE}(P_{s,v,F}) \mid F \subset E, |F| \leq 2\}$ as the collection of last edges of all $s-v$ replacement-paths where $P_{s,v,F}$ is the (unique) $s-v$ shortest-path in $G \setminus F$. It is sufficient to consider one representative replacement-path for each new edge of v in $H(v)$. Hence, assume throughout, that the last edge of each path in the collection of new-ending $s-v$ replacement paths is *distinct*. Since bounding the collection of (π, π)-replacement paths (protecting against two edges faults on $\pi(s,v)$) is very similar to the single fault case, we restrict attention to the more technically challenging part of bounding (π, D)-paths. We now bound $H(v)$ in the special case obtained by making the following simplifying assumptions: (S1) all $s-v$ replacement paths in $G \setminus F$ are *unique* for every $F \subseteq E$, $|F| \leq 2$, (S2) the detour segments D_i of the $s-v$ single edge replacement paths $P_{s,v,\{e_i\}}$, $e_i \in \pi(s,v)$, are edge disjoint, and (S3) all replacement-paths are *independent*. We then classify the (π, D)-replacement paths into two classes depending on whether or not they intersect their detour (i.e, the detour that protects their first failing edge and contains their second failing edge). Let $\mathcal{P}_{nodet}$ be the subset of replacement paths P that do not intersect the edges of their detours and let $\mathcal{P}_{inter}$ be the remaining paths.

(π, D)-paths that do not intersect their detour. To bound this class, it is sufficient to use assumptions (S1) and (S2). We begin by noting that each path $P_i \in \mathcal{P}_{nodet}$ protects a distinct edge on $\pi(s,v)$. Order these paths $\mathcal{P}_{nodet} = \{P_1, \ldots, P_N\}$ in increasing distance between s and $F_1(P_j)$, i.e., $\text{dist}(s, F_1(P_1)) < \ldots < \text{dist}(s, F_1(P_N))$. Let $e_i = F_1(P_i)$ and $M = \lfloor N/2 \rfloor$. We now restrict attention to the set of first M paths $\mathcal{P}_M = \{P_j \mid 1 \leq j \leq M\}$. Let $\mathcal{D}_M = \{D(P) \mid P \in \mathcal{P}_M\}$ be the collection of their corresponding detours and let $V(\mathcal{D}_M) = \bigcup_{D \in \mathcal{D}_M} V(D)$. The paths of $\mathcal{P}_{nodet}$ are classified into two classes depending on whether or not they intersect the edges of $\mathcal{D}_M$. In a way similar to the proof of the single failure case, one can show that there are $O(\sqrt{n})$ paths in $\mathcal{P}_M$ that do *not* intersect the edges of $\mathcal{D}_M$. Hence, it remains to bound the remaining paths in $\mathcal{P}_M$. For every such path P_i, let a_i be their last mutual vertex in $V(\mathcal{D}_M) \setminus \{v\}$. Again, by the uniqueness of the shortest-path, we can show the following.

LEMMA 1.7. *(a) $F_1(P_i) \neq F_1(P_j)$ for every $P_i, P_j \in \mathcal{P}_{nodet}$ and hence by assumption (S2) $D(P_i)$ and $D(P_j)$ are edge disjoint; (b) $V(P_i[a_i, v]) \cap V(P_j[a_j, v]) = \emptyset$.*

We next classify the detours $D_i \in \mathcal{D}_M$ according to their lengths. A detour D_i is *expensive* if $|D_i| \geq M/2$, otherwise it is *cheap*. Next, the new-ending paths $P_i \in \mathcal{P}_M$ that intersect $\mathcal{D}_M$ are classified according to the detour $D(a_i)$ on which a_i (the last common vertex of $P_i \setminus \{v\}$ and $V(\mathcal{D}_M)$) appears. Then P_i is expensive (resp., cheap) if $D(a_i)$ is expensive (resp., cheap). Let $\mathcal{P}_{cheap} = \{P_i \in \mathcal{P}_M \mid D(a_i) \text{ is cheap}\}$ and $\mathcal{P}_{expen} = \{P_i \in \mathcal{P}_M \mid D(a_i) \text{ is expensive}\}$. We next separately bound $|\mathcal{P}_{cheap}|$ and $|\mathcal{P}_{expen}|$.

CLAIM 1.8. $|\mathcal{P}_{cheap}| = O(\sqrt{n})$.

Proof: Let $V_{cheap} = \bigcup_{P_i \in \mathcal{P}_{cheap}} V(P_i[a_i, v]) \setminus \{v\}$. By Obs. 1.7, $|V_{cheap}| = \sum_{P_i \in \mathcal{P}_{cheap}} (|P_i[a_i, v]| - 1)$. We now focus on some P_i and show that $|P_i[a_i, v]| \geq M/2$. First note that $P_i[a_i, v]$ and $\pi(s,v)$ are vertex disjoint (except for the common endpoint v), as a_i occurs after the unique π-divergence point of P_i from $\pi(s,v)$. Hence,

$$|P_i[a_i, v]| \geq \text{dist}(a_i, v, (G \setminus V(\pi(s,v))) \cup \{v\}) \ . \quad (1)$$

Let $D_j = D(a_i) \in \mathcal{D}_M$ be the detour protecting against the failing of the edge e_j. Then,

$$\text{dist}(x_j, v, G \setminus \{e_j\}) \geq \text{dist}(x_j, v, G) \geq \text{dist}(e_j, v) \geq M/2 \quad (2)$$

where the penultimate inequality follows as x_j appears above the failing edge on $\pi(s,v)$ and last inequality follows by the fact that $D_j \in \mathcal{D}_M$. Since a_i appears on a cheap detour D_j, we get that $\text{dist}(x_j, a_i, G \setminus \{e_j\}) \leq |D_j| < M/2$, and combining this with Eq. (2), we get that $\text{dist}(a_i, v, G \setminus \{e_j\}) \geq M/2$. By combining with Eq. (1), we get that overall $|P_i[a_i, v]| \geq M/2$. We therefore have that $M/2 \cdot |\mathcal{P}_{cheap}| \leq |V_{cheap}| \leq n$. It follows that $|\mathcal{P}_{cheap}| \leq 2n/M$. Since clearly also $|\mathcal{P}_{cheap}| \leq M$, we have $|\mathcal{P}_{cheap}| \leq \min\{M, 2n/M\} \leq \sqrt{2n}$. The claim follows. ∎

CLAIM 1.9. $|\mathcal{P}_{expen}| = O(n^{2/3})$.

Proof: Let $\mathcal{D}_{expen} = \{D_j \in \mathcal{D}_M \mid |D_j| \geq M/2\}$ be the collection of expensive detours, $z = |\mathcal{D}_{expen}|$. We now classify the expensive paths of $\mathcal{P}_{expen}$ into z classes where each path P_i is mapped to the class of the detour $D_j \in \mathcal{D}_{expen}$ on which a_i appears. For every $D_j \in \mathcal{D}_{expen}$, let $\mathcal{P}_j = \{P_i \in \mathcal{P}_{expen} \mid D(a_i) = D_j\}$, and let $N_j = |\mathcal{P}_j|$ be the cardinality of this set. We begin by bounding the number of vertices appearing in the expensive detours, let $V_{\mathsf{D}} = \bigcup_{D_j \in \mathcal{D}_M \mid |D_j| \geq M/2} V(D_j)$ be the vertices appearing on the expensive detours. By edge-disjointness of the detours (assumption (S2)), we get that $|V_{\mathsf{D}}| \geq z \cdot (M/2 - 2)$. We now proceed by bounding the number of vertices appearing on the expensive replacement paths, $V_P = \bigcup_{P_i \in \mathcal{P}_{expen}} V(P_i[a_i, v]) \setminus \{a_i, v\}$. Note that for every expensive path P_i, its segment $P_i[a_i, v]$ is vertex disjoint (expect for its endpoints a_i and v) with the vertex set V_{D}. Fix some $j \in \{1, \ldots, z\}$, with N_j expensive paths $\mathcal{P}_j$. We now claim that $V_j = \bigcup_{P_i \in \mathcal{P}_j} P_i[a_i, v]$

contains $\Omega(N_j^2)$ vertices. By Cl. 1.7, the $P_i[a_i, v]$ segments are disjoint. Order the paths of $\mathcal{P}_j$ in increasing distance of a_i from v. Since $a_i \in D_j$ for every $P_i \in \mathcal{P}_j$ and the a_i's are distinct it holds that $|V_j| \geq (N_j - 1)^2/2$ and summing over all j (as the suffixes $P_i[a_i, v] \setminus \{v\}$ are disjoint) and using the Cauchy-Schwarz inequality, we get that $|V_P| \geq \sum_{j=1}^{z}(N_j - 1)^2/2$. Recall that the sets V_P and V_{D} are disjoint, and thus, we get that $n \geq |V_P \cup V_{\mathsf{D}}| = |V_P| + |V_{\mathsf{D}}| \geq \sum_{j=1}^{z}(N_j - 1)^2/2 + z \cdot M/2 = \Omega(M^{3/2})$. We get $M = O(n^{2/3})$, as required. ∎

(π, D)-paths that intersect their detour. We next consider the replacement-paths in $\mathcal{P}_{inter}$ that intersect the edges of their detour, under assumptions (S1-S3). For every $P_i \in \mathcal{P}_{inter}$, let $D_i = D(P_i)$, and $x_i, y_i \in \pi(s, v)$ be the first (resp., last) vertices of the detour D_i. Let b_i (resp., c_i) be the first divergence point of P_i and $\pi(s, v)$ (resp., $D(P_i)$). Let $e_i = F_1(P_i)$ be the first failing edge protected by P_i. It is easy to see that by the uniqueness of the shortest-paths, $x_i = b_i$ and $P_i = \pi(s, x_i) \circ D_i(x_i, c_i) \circ P_i[c_i, v]$. That is, b_i and c_i are unique divergence points from $\pi(s, v)$ and $D(P_i)$ respectively and thus the suffix $P_i[c_i, v]$ is edge disjoint with $\pi(s, v)$ and D_i, see Fig. 1(b). In addition, since the detour segments are disjoint (by assumption (S2)), we have the following.

OBSERVATION 1.10. *For every two paths $P_i, P_j \in \mathcal{P}_{inter}$, (1) $P_i' = P_i[c_i, v] \setminus \{v\}$ and $P_j' = P_j[c_j, v] \setminus \{v\}$ are vertex disjoint. (2) If $e_i = e_j$ then $D(P_i) = D(P_j)$ and $c_i \neq c_j$.*

We now induce an (e, c)-ordering on the paths of $\mathcal{P}_{inter}$, which can be viewed as based on treating e_i and c_i lexicographically: For $e_i \neq e_j$, we say that $(e_i, c_i) < (e_j, c_j)$ if $\text{dist}(s, e_i, \pi(s, v)) < \text{dist}(s, e_j, \pi(s, v))$. For $e_i = e_j$, let $(e_i, c_i) < (e_j, c_j)$ if $\text{dist}(x_i, c_i, D(P_i)) < \text{dist}(x_i, c_j, D(P_i))$. By Obs. 1.10, this is well defined. We then order the paths of $\mathcal{P}_{inter}$ in increasing (e, c) order. Let $\overrightarrow{\mathcal{P}}_{inter} = \{P_1, \ldots, P_\ell\}$ where $(e_1, c_1) < \ldots < (e_\ell, c_\ell)$. By showing that $F(P_j) \notin E(P_i)$ for every $i < j$, we have that the lengths of the paths in the ordered set $\overrightarrow{\mathcal{P}}_{inter}$ are strictly monotone decreasing.

LEMMA 1.11. $|P_1| > \ldots > |P_\ell|$.

We now group the ordered paths P_i of $\mathcal{P}_{inter}$ into classes depending on their e_i-value (i.e., the first failing edge they protect in $\pi(s, v)$). For every vertex $e_k \in \pi(s, v)$, let N_k be the number of replacement paths in $\mathcal{P}_{inter}$ whose first failing edge is e_k. Let $z = |\text{dist}(s, v)|$. By assumptions (S1-S3) and the ordering of Lemma 1.11, we get:

LEMMA 1.12. *For every $P_i \neq P_j \in \mathcal{P}_{inter}$: (a) $V(P_i[c_i, v]) \cap V(P_j[c_j, v]) = \{v\}$. (b) If $F_1(P_i) \neq F_1(P_j)$, then $P_i[b_i, v] \setminus \{b_i, v\}$ and $P_j[b_j, v] \setminus \{b_j, v\}$ are vertex disjoint. (c) The total number of vertices occupied by these paths is*

$$\Omega(\sum_{i=1}^{z}\sum_{k=1}^{i} N_k + \sum_{i=1}^{z} N_i^2).$$

Note that $|\mathcal{P}_{inter}| = \sum_{i=1}^{z} N_i$. Hence, by combining this with Lemma 1.12(c), we get that there are $O(n^{2/3})$ such paths. This completes the analysis for the simplified case.

Road map.

We now provide a high level road map of the general proof of the upper bound *without* assuming (S1-S3). First, the algorithm needs to support the case where the replacement-paths are not unique and hence have to be carefully chosen. The guiding principle for selecting the desired replacement paths is to favor replacement-paths that diverge from $\pi(s, v)$ as close to s as possible. Among these, the algorithm favors replacement-paths that diverge from their detour segment as early as possible. Second, when removing assumption (S2), one has to incorporate into the analysis the optional *complex interactions* between detour segments. The main structural theory developed in this paper is meant to deal this complication. Hence, a crucial step for understanding the structure of dual failure replacement paths is the understanding of the structure of the detours. To do that, we focus on pairs of detours D_i and D_j and classify their structural dependency into six classes. We then provide some simplifying rules for each class that are frequently used in our argumentation. Quite interestingly, understanding the pairwise relation between the detours was sufficient in order to obtain an understanding of the *global* picture (i.e., which might contain complex interaction between many detours). Finally, removing assumption (S3) entails another major complication in our analysis. In particular, when two paths P_i and P_j interfere, Lemma 1.12(a) is no-longer guaranteed to hold. In our analysis, the set of interfering paths is further classified into two subsets by distinguishing between two types of interference, namely, *π-interference* and *D-interference* (see Sec. 3.2.2 in the full paper [14] for more details). We show that each of these two classes imposes different structural constraints which allow us to bound their cardinality. Our tool kit consists of two main components: (a) complete mapping of the pairwise interactions between detours and (b) a subgraph $\mathcal{K}$ denoted hereafter as a *kernel subgraph* that contains the entire required information from G but has some convenient properties that facilitate the analysis. This structure is heavily based on the detour configuration machinery established in (a). For every vertex v, the kernel subgraph $\mathcal{K}_v(\mathcal{D})$ is imposed on a given collection of detours $\mathcal{D} = \{D_1, \ldots, D_t\}$. Clearly the set of relevant faulty edges of the (π, D)-replacement paths is given by the subgraph $G_v(\mathcal{D}) = \pi(s, v) \cup \{D_i \mid D_i \in \mathcal{D}\}$. Quite surprisingly, we show that in order to analyze the structure of the new-ending (π, D)-replacement paths, it is sufficient to consider the subgraph $\mathcal{K}_v(\mathcal{D})$ which contains all the relevant faulty edges. The kernel graph is used, for example, to bound the number of replacement-paths that do not intersect their detours. For example, it is essential for establishing Lemma 1.8 and 1.9 without assuming (S2). We note that these tools might be used in further contexts to pave the way to the future design of f-fault resilient structures for $f \geq 2$. Equipped with these tools, to bound the number of new-ending (π, D) paths, we employ the same high level strategy as taken for the single failure case: new-ending paths consume many vertices, and since the number of vertices is limited by n, the number of new-ending paths is bounded as well (as a function of n). To do that, we would like to show that every new-ending path has an nonnegligible number of distinct vertices, not appearing on any other path. The main technical question is to identify a subpath of the new-ending path that is guaranteed to be sufficiently long and disjoint from all others. Since our replacement paths may overlap and share many common vertices, towards achieving this goal we classify the new-ending paths into five classes and bound that size of each class separately.

The size analysis of each class exploits the tools described above and provides a deeper understanding of the complex behavior of dual failure replacement paths.

We now present Alg. Cons2FTBFS, that given an unweighted undirected n-vertex graph $G = (V, E)$ and a source $s \in V$, constructs a dual failure FT-BFS subgraph $H \subseteq G$. We then analyze the correctness of the algorithm and bound the size of the output structure. The size analysis of the subgraph H constitutes the main technical contribution of this paper, see [14].

Algorithm Cons2FTBFS.

Let W be a weight assignment that guarantees the uniqueness of the shortest-paths.[4] Let $T_0 = \bigcup_{v \in V} \pi(s, v)$ be the BFS tree rooted at s where $\pi(s, v)$ is the shortest path from s to v in G, namely, $\pi(s, v) = [s = u_0, u_1, \ldots, u_\ell = v] = SP(s, v, G, W)$. We fix one vertex v and concentrate on constructing $s - v$ replacement paths $P_{s,v,F}$ protecting against at most two failures in $E(G)$. Algorithm Cons2FTBFS consists of three steps depending on the type of the failing edges. See Fig. 2 for a schematic illustration. First, it constructs a collection of paths $P_{s,v,F} \in SP(s, v, G \setminus F)$ where only one edge failure occurs, i.e., $F = \{e_i\}$ for every $e_i \in \pi(s, v)$. The selection prefers the replacement path that diverges from $\pi(s, v)$ as early as possible. Then, the algorithm considers the case where the two failing edges occur on $\pi(s, v)$. Finally, letting $D_i = P_i \setminus \pi(s, v)$ be the detour segment of $P_i = P_{s,v,\{e_i\}}$ from $\pi(s, v)$, the last step considers the case where the second failing edge occurs on D_i. In this case, the procedure would attempt to construct a replacement path whose divergence point from $\pi(s, v)$ is as close to s as possible and under certain conditions it imposes also the requirement that the divergence point from D_i is as closest to s as well. Eventually, only the *last* edge of each replacement path is added to the construction. The following definition is useful. For every $e_i = (u_i, u_{i+1}) \in \pi(s, v)$, and $k \in \{0, \ldots, i\}$, we would like to consider the possibility that u_k is the point where the replacement path protecting against a failure in e_i diverges from $\pi(s, v)$. To enforce that possibility, for every two vertices, $u_k, u_\ell \in \pi(s, v)$, we define the graph

$$G(u_k, u_\ell) = (G \setminus V(\pi(u_k, u_\ell)) \cup \{u_k, v\} \ . \qquad (3)$$

that contains u_k and v but does not contain the other vertices on the segment $\pi(u_k, u_\ell)$. Intuitively, for an edge $e_i = (u_i, u_{i+1}) \in \pi(s, v)$ and a vertex $u_k \in \pi(s, u_i)$, the first divergence point of the $s - v$ replacement path $P \in G(u_k, u_i) \setminus \{e_i, e_j\}$ from $\pi(s, v)$ is u_k. Since the divergence point from $\pi(s, v)$ of any replacement path protecting against the failing of e_i must occur above the failing edge e_i, it holds that $u_k \in \pi(s, u_i)$. Analogously, an $s - v$ replacement path P in $G(u_k, v) \setminus \{e_i, e_j\}$ diverges from $\pi(s, v)$ at the point u_k and its last edge is not in $\pi(s, v)$. In such a case, $P[u_k, v]$ and $\pi(s, v)$ are edge disjoint. The algorithm would attempt to find the upmost divergence point $u_k \in \pi(s, u_i)$ such that $G(u_k, u_i)$ contains a replacement path for the failures e_i, e_j.

(1) Single edge fault replacement paths. The first step considers single edge failure scenarios. Denote the collection of possible edge failures by $\mathcal{F}_v^1(\pi) = \{\{e_i\} \mid e_i \in \pi(s, v)\}$. Let $k_0 \in \{0, \ldots, i\}$ be the minimal index k satisfying that $\text{dist}(s, v, G(u_k, u_i) \setminus \{e_i\}) = \text{dist}(s, v, G \setminus \{e_i\})$. Let $P_{s,v,\{e_i\}} \in SP(s, v, G(u_{k_0}, u_i) \setminus \{e_i\}, W)$. For each $e_i \in \mathcal{F}_v^1(\pi)$, let $D_i = P_{s,v,\{e_i\}} \setminus \pi(s, v)$ be the detour segment of the replacement path chosen for e_i. In Cl. 3.4 of [14], we show that $P_{s,v,\{e_i\}} = \pi(s, x_i) \circ D_i \circ \pi(y_i, v)$ where x_i (resp., y_i) is the first (resp., last) vertex of D_i and $e_i \in \pi(x_i, y_i)$. As mentioned earlier, we do not have to add the entire replacement paths to the constructed structure; we later prove that it suffices to add the last edge of each replacement paths. Let $E_1(\pi) = \{\texttt{LastE}(P_{s,v,\{e_i\}}), e_i \in \pi(s, v)\}$ be the last edges of replacement paths protecting against faults in $E(\pi(s, v))$. These edges will be added to the constructed structure. For every edge $e_i \in \pi(s, v)$, let $D_i = \in E(P_{s,v,\{e_i\}}) \setminus E(\pi(s, v))$ be the detour segment of $P_{s,v,\{e_i\}}$. In Cl. 3.4 of [14], we show that $P_{s,v,\{e_i\}}$ can be decomposed into three segments such that $P_{s,v,\{e_i\}} = \pi(s, x_i) \circ D_i \circ \pi(y_i, v)$ where $D_i = P_{s,v,\{e_i\}}[x_i, y_i]$ is the detour segment.

(2) Two faults on $\pi(s, v)$. The second step considers pairs of failures occurring both on $\pi(s, v)$. The collection of failure events considered is thus $\mathcal{F}_v^2(\pi) = \{F = \{e_i, e_j\} \mid F \subseteq \pi(s, v)\}$. Without loss of generality, assume throughout that e_i appears above e_j on the path $\pi(s, v)$. Recall that D_i (respectively, D_j) is the detour segment of $P_{s,v,\{e_i\}}$ (resp., $P_{s,v,\{e_j\}}$). The procedure constructs the shortest path $P_{s,v,F}$ in the following manner. First the algorithm prefers a replacement path that is composed of the detours D_i and D_j constructed at step (1). Specifically, if the intersection $D_i \cap D_j \neq \emptyset$, then let $w \in D_i \cap D_j$ be the last point on D_j that is common to D_i. Define the path $P = \pi(s, x_i) \circ D_i[x_i, w] \circ D_j[w, y_j] \circ \pi(y_j, v)$. If $|P| = \text{dist}(s, v, G \setminus F)$, then let $P_{s,v,F} = P$. Otherwise, define $P_{s,v,\{e_i,e_j\}} = SP(s, v, G \setminus \{e_i, e_j\}, W)$. The set of edges to be added in this step is $E_2(\pi) = \{\texttt{LastE}(P_{s,v,F}), F \in \mathcal{F}_v^2(\pi)\}$, the collection of last edges of replacement paths protecting against two edges faults on $\pi(s, v)$.

(3) One fault on $\pi(s, v)$ and one on the detour. The third step considers the remaining (relevant) case where one of the failing edge e_i occurs on the path $\pi(s, v)$ and the second failing edge occurs on the detour segment D_i. Hence, the collection of failure scenarios considered in this step is $\mathcal{F}_v(\mathsf{D}) = \{\{\mathsf{e_i}, \mathsf{t_j}\} \mid \mathsf{e_i} \in \pi(\mathsf{s}, \mathsf{v}), \mathsf{t_j} \in \mathsf{D_i}\}$. We now order the pairs $F = \{e_i, t_j\} \in \mathcal{F}_v(\mathsf{D})$ in the following manner. Let $F_{i_1} = \{e_{i_1}, t_{j_1}\}$ and $F_{i_2} = \{e_{i_2}, t_{j_2}\}$. If $e_{i_1} \neq e_{i_2}$, then let $F_{i_1} > F_{i_2}$ iff $\text{dist}(s, e_{i_1}, G) > \text{dist}(s, e_{i_2}, G)$. Else, if $e_{i_1} = e_{i_2}$, then we use the second coordinate t_i to break the tie where $F_{i_1} > F_{i_2}$ iff $\text{dist}(x_{i_1}, t_{j_1}, D_{i_1}) > \text{dist}(x_{i_1}, t_{j_2}, D_{i_1})$ where $D_{i_1} = P_{s,v,\{e_{i_1}\}}[x_{i_1}, y_{i_1}]$ is the detour segment of $P_{s,v,\{e_{i_1}\}}$. Let $\overrightarrow{\mathcal{F}}_v(D) = \{F_1, F_2, \ldots, F_k\}$ be the ordering of the faulty pairs $\mathcal{F}_v(\mathsf{D})$ in decreasing order where $F_1 > F_2 > \ldots > F_k$. Let $E_0(v) = E(v, T_0) \cup E_1(\pi) \cup E_2(\pi)$ be an initial collection of edges incident to v be added to the structure by steps (1) and (2). The algorithm considers the faulty pairs F according to the ordering of $\overrightarrow{\mathcal{F}}_v(D)$, where at step $\tau \geq 1$, given $E_{\tau-1}(v)$, it considers the pair $F_\tau = (e_\tau, t_\tau) \in \overrightarrow{\mathcal{F}}_v(D)$ and computes the replacement path $P_{s,v,F_\tau} \in SP(s, v, G \setminus F_\tau)$ in the following manner. Let $G_{\tau-1}(v) = (G \setminus E(v, G)) \cup E_{\tau-1}(v)$ be a subgraph of G in which the edges incident to v are only the edges of $E_{\tau-1}(v)$. First, if there exists a shortest replacement path for F_τ in $G_{\tau-1}(v)$, namely, one that uses the edges of $E_{\tau-1}(v)$, then no new edge of v should be introduced. I.e., If $\text{dist}(s, v, G_{\tau-1}(v) \setminus F_\tau) = \text{dist}(s, v, G \setminus F_\tau)$, then let $P_{s,v,F_\tau} = SP(s, v, G_{\tau-1}(v) \setminus F_\tau, W)$. Otherwise, a new edge

[4] Note that the given graph is unweighted and the fractional weights of W only break the unweighted shortest-path ties in a consistent manner.

of v that is not in $E_{\tau-1}(v)$ is essential for satisfying the pair F_τ. The algorithm then aims to select a new-ending replacement path whose first divergence point b_τ from $\pi(s,v)$ is as close to s as possible. Let x_τ be the first vertex of the detour D_τ. The point b_τ is found as follows. Let $e_\tau = (u_{i_\tau}, u_{i_\tau+1})$, define $u_k \in \pi(s, u_{i_\tau})$ as the closest vertex to s satisfying that $\text{dist}(s,v,G(u_k,v)\setminus F_\tau) = \text{dist}(s,v,G\setminus F_\tau)$. Then $b_\tau = u_k$ and let $P = SP(s,v,G(u_k,v)\setminus F_\tau, W)$. If the first divergence point b_τ of P from $\pi(s,v)$ is not x_τ (i.e., the divergence point is not as that of $P_{s,v,\{e_\tau\}}$ and $\pi(s,v)$) then let $P_{s,v,F_\tau} = P$. Else, if $b_\tau = x_\tau$, the replacement path P_{s,v,F_τ} is selected so that its unique divergence point from the detour D_τ is as close to x_τ as possible. To enforce that, let $D_\tau = [x_\tau = w_0, \ldots, w_q = y_\tau]$ where the second failing edge is $t_\tau = (w_j, w_{j+1})$, then for every $j \geq 1$ and every $\ell \in \{0,\ldots,j\}$, define $G_{\mathsf{D}}(w_\ell) = (G(x_\tau, v)\setminus V(D_\tau[w_\ell, y_\tau])) \cup \{w_\ell\}$. That is, an $s-v$ replacement path in the subgraph $G_{\mathsf{D}}(w_\ell)\setminus F_\tau$ diverges from $\pi(s,v)$ at the unique point b_τ and diverges from D_τ at the point w_ℓ. Since the divergence point from D_τ must occur above the second failing edge t_τ it holds that $w_\ell \in D[w_0, w_j]$. The algorithm computes a P_{s,v,F_τ} path whose divergence point from D_τ is as close to w_0 on the detour D_τ as possible: let $\ell \in \{0,\ldots,j\}$ be the minimum index satisfying that $\text{dist}(s,v,G_{\mathsf{D}}(w_\ell)\setminus F_\tau) = \text{dist}(s,v,G\setminus F_\tau)$. Let $P_{s,v,F_\tau} = \pi(s,x_\tau)\circ D_\tau[x_\tau, w_\ell]\circ SP(w_\ell, v, G_{\mathsf{D}}(w_\ell)\setminus F_\tau, W)$. Finally, let $E_\tau(v) = E_{\tau-1}(v)\cup\{\texttt{LastE}(P_{s,v,F_\tau})\}$. This completes the description of the algorithm.

Let $\mathcal{F}_v = \mathcal{F}^1_v(\pi)\cup\mathcal{F}^2_v(\pi)\cup\mathcal{F}_v(\mathsf{D})$ be the collection of single edge and edge pair failure events for which an $s-v$ replacement path $P_{s,v,F}$ was constructed. Let $H(v) = \bigcup_{F\in\mathcal{F}_v}\{\texttt{LastE}(P_{s,v,F})\}$ be the collection of last edges of all replacement paths in $P_{s,v,F}$. Finally, the algorithm outputs $H = \bigcup_{v\in V} H(v)\cup T_0$ as the resulting dual failure FT-BFS structure.

2. LOWER BOUND FOR f-FAILURE FT-BFS STRUCTURE

In this section, we consider a lower bound constructions for FT-MBFS structures resilient to up to f-faults for general $f\geq 2$ and for every number of sources σ. These construction extends the construction of [10] for the single failure case.

THEOREM 2.1. *For every $n \geq o(1)$ and $1 \geq f$, there exists an n-vertex graph $G^*_f(V,E)$ and a source set $S\subseteq V$ such that any f-failure FT-MBFS structure with respect to S has $\Omega(|S|^{1-1/(f+1)}\cdot n^{2-1/(f+1)})$ edges.*

Note that for $f=\Omega(\log n)$ the claimed bound becomes trivial. Hence we will assume that $f = o(\log n)$. We begin by showing the construction for the single source case and then extend it to the case multiple sources. Our construction is based on the graph $G_f(d) = (V_f, E_f)$, defined inductively. For $f=1$, $G_1(d) = (V_1,E_1)$ consists of three components: (1) a set of vertices $U=\{u^1_1,\ldots,u^1_d\}$ connected by a path $P_1 = [u^1_1,\ldots,u^1_d]$, (2) a set of terminal vertices $Z=\{z_1,\ldots,z_d\}$ (viewed by convention as ordered from left to right), and (3) a collection of d vertex disjoint paths Q^1_i of length $|Q^1_i| = 6+2\cdot(d-i)$ connecting u^1_i and z_i for every $i\in\{1,\ldots,d\}$. The vertex $\mathtt{r}(G_1(d)) = u^1_d$ is fixed as the root of $G_1(d)$, hence the edges of the paths Q^1_i are viewed as directed away from u^1_i, and the terminal vertices of Z are viewed as the *leaves* of the graph, denoted $\texttt{Leaf}(G_1(d)) = Z$. See Fig. 4 for illustration. Overall, the vertex and edge sets of $G_1(d)$ are $V_1 = U\cup Z\cup\bigcup_{i=1}^d V(Q^1_i)$ and $E_1 = E(P_1)\cup\bigcup_{i=1}^d E(Q^1_i)$.

For ease of future analysis, we assign labels to the leaves $z_i\in\texttt{Leaf}(G_1(d))$. Let $\texttt{Label}_f : \texttt{Leaf}(G_f(d))\to E(G_1(d))^f$. The label of each leaf corresponds to a set of edge faults under which the path from root to leaf is still maintained (this will be proved later on). Specifically, $\texttt{Label}_1(z_i, G_1(d)) = (u^1_i, u^1_{i+1})$ for $i\leq d-1$ and $\texttt{Label}_e(z_i, G_1(d)) = \emptyset$. In addition, define $P(z_i, G_1(d)) = P_1[\mathtt{r}(G_1(d)), u^1_i]\circ Q^1_i$ to be the path from the root u^1_1 to the leaf z_i.

To complete the inductive construction, let us describe the construction of the graph $G_f(d) = (V_f, E_f)$, for $f\geq 2$, given the graph $G_{f-1}(d) = (V_{f-1}, E_{f-1})$. The graph $G_f(d) = (V_f,E_f)$ consists of the following components. First, it contains a path $P=[u^f_1,\ldots,u^f_d]$, where the node $\mathtt{r}(G_f(d)) = u^f_1$ is fixed to be the root. In addition, it contains d disjoint copies of the graph $G' = G_{f-1}(d)$, denoted by $G'_1,\ldots,G'_d$ (viewed by convention as ordered from left to right), where each G'_i is connected to u^f_i by a collection of d vertex disjoint paths Q^f_i, for $i\in\{1,\ldots,d\}$, connecting the vertices u^f_i with $\mathtt{r}(G'_i)$. The length of Q^f_i is $|Q^f_i| = (d-i)\cdot\texttt{depth}(G_{f-1}(d))$. The leaf set of the graph $G_f(d)$ is the union of the leaf sets of G'_j's, $\texttt{Leaf}(G_f(d)) = \bigcup_{j=1}^d\texttt{Leaf}(G'_j)$.

Next, define the labels $\texttt{Label}_f(z_i)$ for each $z_i\in\texttt{Leaf}(G_f(d))$. For every $j\in\{1,\ldots,d-1\}$ and any leaf $z_j\in\texttt{Leaf}(G'_j)$, let $\texttt{Label}_f(z_j, G_f(d)) = (u^f_j, u^f_{j+1})\circ\texttt{Label}_{f-1}(z_j, G'_j)$.

Denote the size (number of nodes) of $G_f(d)$ by $\mathtt{N}(f,d)$, its depth (maximal distance between two nodes) by $\texttt{depth}(f,d)$, and its number of leaves by $\texttt{nLeaf}(f,d) = |\texttt{Leaf}(G_f(d))|$. Note that for $f=1$, $\mathtt{N}(1,d) = 2d+\sum_{i=1}^d 4+2\cdot(d-i)\leq 7d^2$, $\texttt{depth}(1,d) = 6+2(d-1)$ (corresponding to the length of the path Q^1_1), and $\texttt{nLeaf}(1,d) = d$. We now observe that the following inductive relations hold.

OBSERVATION 2.2. *(a)* $\texttt{depth}(f,d) = O(d^f)$; *(b)* $\texttt{nLeaf}(f,d) = d^f$; *and (c)* $\mathtt{N}(f,d) = c\cdot d^{f+1}$ *for some constant c.*

Consider the set of $\lambda = \texttt{nLeaf}(f,d)$ leaves in $G(f,d)$, $\texttt{Leaf}(G(f,d)) = \bigcup_{i=1}^d\texttt{Leaf}(G'_i) = \{z_1,\ldots,z_\lambda\}$, ordered from left to right according to their appearance in $G(f,d)$. one can show the following via induction on f.

LEMMA 2.3. *For every z_j it holds that:*
(1) The path $P(z_j, G(f,d))$ is the only $u^f_1 - z_j$ path in $G(f,d)$.
(2) $P(z_j, G(f,d))\subseteq G\setminus\texttt{Label}_f(z_j, G(f,d))$.
(3) $P(z_i, G(f,d))\not\subseteq G\setminus\texttt{Label}_f(z_j, G(f,d))$ for every $i>j$.
(4) $|P(z_i, G(f,d))| > |P(z_j, G(f,d))|$ for every $i<j$.

Finally, we turn to describe the graph $G^*_f(V,E)$ which establishes our lower bound. The graph $G^*_f(V,E)$ consists of three components. The first is the graph $G_f(d)$ for $d = \lceil (n/2c)^{1/(f+1)}\rceil$, where c is some constant to be determined later. By Obs. 2.2, $n/2\leq |V(G_f(d))|$. Note that $d\leq (5/4)^{1/(f+1)}\cdot(n/2c)^{1/(f+1)} = (5n/8c)^{1/(f+1)}$ for sufficiently large n, hence $\mathtt{N}(f,d) = c\cdot d^{f+1}\leq 5n/8$. The second component of $G^*_f(V,E)$ is a set of nodes $X=\{x_1,\ldots,x_\chi\}$ and an additional vertex v^* that is connected to u^f_d and to all the vertices of X. The cardinality of X is $\chi = n-\mathtt{N}(f,d)-1$. The third component of $G^*_f(V,E)$ is a complete bipartite graph B connecting the nodes of X with the leaf set $\texttt{Leaf}(G_f(d))$, i.e., the disjoint leaf sets $\texttt{Leaf}(G'_1),\ldots,\texttt{Leaf}(G'_d)$. The vertex set of the resulting graph is thus $V = V(G_f(d))\cup\{v^*\}\cup X$

and hence $|V| = n$. See Figures 5 and 6 for illustration of G_2^* and G_f^*. By Prop. (b) of Obs. 2.2,

$$\texttt{nLeaf}(G_i') = d^f = \lceil (n/2c)^{1/(f+1)} \rceil^f \geq (n/2c)^{f/(f+1)},$$

hence $|E(B)| \geq (3n/8 - 1) \cdot (n/2c)^{f/(f+1)} = O(n^{2-1/(f+1)})$. In the full paper [14], we complete the proof of Thm. 2.1 for the single source case.

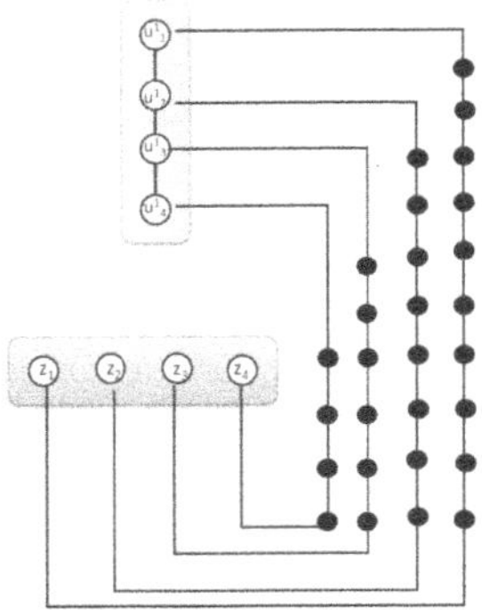

Figure 4: The graph $G_1(d)$.

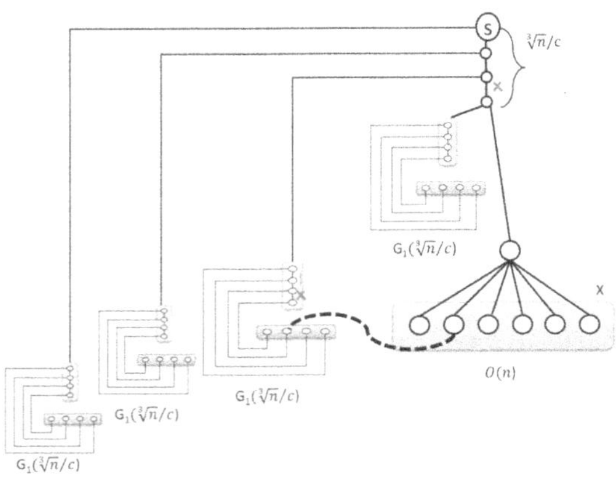

Figure 5: Lower bound construction for dual failure FT-BFS structure. The set of X vertices is fully connected to the leaf set of each of the d copies of $G_1(d)$. Overall $|E(G_2^*)| = O(n^{5/3})$. The dashed wide edge is required in any dual failure FT-BFS structure upon the faults of the edges marked in figure.

In the full paper [14], this construction is extended to the multi-source case.

Acknowledgment. I am very grateful to my advisor, Prof. David Peleg, for many helpful discussions and for reviewing this paper.

3. REFERENCES

[1] S. Baswana, L. Utkarsh, and S.M. Anuradha. Single source distance oracle for planar digraphs avoiding a failed node or link. In Proc. *SODA*, 223–232, 2012.

[2] A. Bernstein and D. Karger. A nearly optimal oracle for avoiding failed vertices and edges. In Proc. *STOC*, 101–110, 2009.

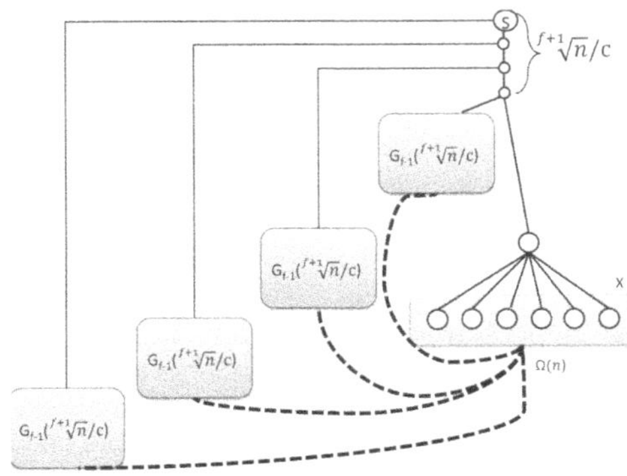

Figure 6: Schematic illustration of the graph G_f^*. The set of X nodes are fully connected to the leaf set of $G_{f-1}(d)$ graphs. Each such edge is necessary for a certain fault set.

[3] D. Bilò and L. Gualà and S. Leucci and G. Proietti. Fault-Tolerant Approximate Shortest-Path Trees. In Proc. *ESA*, 137–148, 2014.

[4] S. Chechik, M. Langberg, D. Peleg, and L. Roditty. Fault-tolerant spanners for general graphs. In Proc. *STOC*, 435–444, 2009.

[5] C. Demetrescu, M. Thorup, R. Chowdhury, and V. Ramachandran. Oracles for distances avoiding a failed vertex or link. *SIAM J. Computing*, 37:1299–1318, 2008.

[6] M. Dinitz and R. Krauthgamer. Fault-tolerant spanners: better and simpler. In Proc. *PODC*, 169–178, 2011.

[7] R. Duan and S. Pettie. Dual-failure distance and connectivity oracles. In Proc. *SODA*, 506–515, 2009.

[8] F. Grandoni and V.V Williams. Improved Distance Sensitivity Oracles via Fast Single-Source Replacementg Paths. In Proc. *FOCS*, 748–757, 2012.

[9] J. Hershberger and S. Subhash. Vickrey prices and shortest paths: What is an edge worth? In Proc. *FOCS*, 252–259, 2001.

[10] M. Parter and D. Peleg. Sparse Fault-tolerant BFS trees. In Proc. *ESA*, 779–790, 2013.

[11] M. Parter and D. Peleg. Sparse Fault-Tolerant BFS Trees. http://arxiv.org/abs/1302.5401, 2013.

[12] M. Parter and D. Peleg. Fault Tolerant Approximate BFS Structures. In Proc. *SODA*, 1073–1092, 2014.

[13] M. Parter. Vertex Fault Tolerant Additive Spanners. In Proc. *DISC*, 167–181, 2014.

[14] M. Parter. Dual Failure Resilient BFS Structure. http://arxiv.org/abs/1505.00692.

[15] L. Roditty and U. Zwick. Replacement paths and k simple shortest paths in unweighted directed graphs. *ACM Trans. Algorithms*, 8(4): 33, 2012.

[16] M. Thorup and U. Zwick. Approximate distance oracles. *J. ACM*, 52:1–24, 2005.

[17] V. Vazirani. Approximation Algorithms. *Georgia Inst. Tech.*, 1997.

[18] O. Weimann and R. Yuster. Replacement paths via fast matrix multiplication. In Proc. *FOCS*, 655–662, 2010.

Author Index

www.ingramcontent.com/pod-product-compliance
Ingram Content Group UK Ltd.
Pitfield, Milton Keynes, MK11 3LW, UK
UKHW051414290926
15471UKWH00009B/1605